Mastering Skype® for Business 2015

Mastering Skype® for Business 2015

Keith Hanna

Senior Acquisitions Editor: Kenyon Brown
Development Editor: Alexa Murphy
Technical Editor: Martin Rinas
Production Editor: Christine O'Connor
Copy Editor: Kim Wimpsett
Editorial Manager: Mary Beth Wakefield
Production Manager: Kathleen Wisor
Associate Publisher: Jim Minatel
Book Designers: Maureen Forys, Happenstance Type-O-Rama and Judy Fung
Proofreader: Josh Chase, Word One New York
Indexer: Johnna VanHoose Dinse
Project Coordinator, Cover: Brent Savage
Cover Designer: Wiley
Cover Image: Kriang Kan/Shutterstock

ISBN: 978-1-119-22535-5
ISBN: 978-1-119-22537-9 (ebk.)
ISBN: 978-1-119-22536-2 (ebk.)

Library of Congress Control Number: 2016933972

10 9 8 7 6 5 4 3 2 1

I'd like to dedicate this book to my wonderful family. To my wife, Sharon, for giving me the time (and space) to finish it. She has the patience of a saint (not just on this book but always). I promise you don't have to remind me anymore. To my daughter, Rosie, for always being right, and to my son, Jamie, who also teaches patience. We still make a great team!

Acknowledgments

Wow, what a journey from the days of Lync Server 2010, when Nathan Winters asked me to co-author our *Mastering Lync Server 2010*, through the next release and now to *Mastering Skype for Business 2015* on my own. Nathan's role has changed to focus more on the cloud, so, sadly, he wasn't able to contribute as much to this one as with the previous books.

Thank you to the many readers of the Lync books who have gotten in touch either via email or direct meetings at conferences and user groups and to the other customers—without your feedback and ongoing support, I wouldn't have gotten to book 3! Keep the feedback coming (even the ~~bad~~ constructive stuff!).

Throughout the process, I have been supported, guided, and mostly cajoled by the great team at Sybex. Several of the original editors have moved on in the five-year journey to this edition but have been ably replaced by Ken Brown, Grace Davis, Alexa Murphy, and Christine O'Connor. All have been responsible in some way to take the scrawls that I have pulled together and turn them into something readable. Any errors are certainly not their fault. There are many more nameless (to me at least) people at Sybex working behind the scenes, who also deserve thanking.

Speaking of which, no technical book can be released without thorough cross-checking, and for that I am extremely thankful to Martin Rinas, our technical editor, who spent many hours going through the material and replicating the examples to ensure technical accuracy. In the past I've been the one correcting him, but things have certainly swapped around now.

Some vendors have provided test devices and support and in some cases have contributed directly to chapters with content. Thanks to the following:

Actiance: Robin Smith

Kemp: Barghav Shukla

MindLink: Howard Travers, Annekathrin Hase, Dalia Valkiunaite

Sennheiser: Charlotte Gaskin, Steve Bailey

Snom: Lesley Hansen, Alison Tetlow, Hoang-Hoa Nguyen

My thanks go to all involved in helping to create this book.

My advice to others: For anyone interested in learning more about or swapping UC war stories (or even those who just fancy a beer), join your local UC user group. These groups are invaluable resources both for learning and for networking. Catch up with these people; they don't bite!

About the Author

Keith Hanna started university life at Sheffield University studying software engineering but finished by graduating from Queen's University, Belfast, in computer science. His first "real" job was with Lucas Aerospace as a software developer working on aircraft engine control systems—it wasn't rocket science, but it was close! Moving to England from Ireland, Keith helped to design and deploy a communications system for the emergency services, but found his calling in Windows-based application design and support, eventually making his way to Microsoft, where he stayed for eight years, working in a number of roles from engineer to consultant to architect. He left in November 2014 to start a two-year study period for an MBA, while picking up small pieces of Skype for Business consultancy and training work.

Keith has contributed several articles to TechNet as well as several chapters in the *Lync 2010 Resource Kit*. He has written training courses for OCS R2 and Lync, as well as exam questions. He is a Microsoft Certified Master. He's not aware of any life outside work, and he will be keen to discover if such a thing exists now that the book is finished, although it didn't really happen after the previous one.

Contents at a Glance

Contents

Introduction

This book is the third in the Sybex Mastering series on the subject of Microsoft's Unified Communications (UC) platform. With the release of Skype for Business, we are into the fifth generation of a platform that provides a comprehensive set of functionality, which has continually placed it in the top right of the Gartner Magic Quadrant for UC.

Skype for Business is a new name for the platform, which while clearing things up causes an equal amount of confusion. For the last several years, I have been trying to explain to people what I do, and in speaking with others working with these products, the conversation is familiar, along the lines of this:

Me: "Hi, how are you?"

Other: "Good, thanks. So, what is it you do?"

Me: "I work in IT." (Often this will end the conversation!)

Other: "Oh, really what specifically?"

Me: "Lync."

Other: <blank stare> "Oh, never heard of it."

Me: "Have you heard of Skype?"

Other: "Yes."

Me: "Well, think of it as Skype, but for businesses."

Other: "Ah."

Now Microsoft has made our lives slightly easier with the name change, but of course there is always the risk that businesses think they don't need any help to implement it. Skype just works, right?

While Skype for Business brings a new name and interface to Lync, you'll see a lot of the functionality remains similar if not identical. Under its new leadership, Microsoft is changing the way products are developed, released, and paid for. This has an impact in that the products evolve quickly over short periods of time—even in the time taken to write this book (around seven months from beginning to end) there have been updates. Traditionally these would have been patches to fix bugs; however, now they are being used to deploy new functionality.

With this in mind, I set out to reinforce any prior knowledge you might have of the server platform but not to assume any and thereby take you on a journey from the key fundamentals of Skype for Business all the way through deployment and how best to integrate with third-party systems. All of this is based on the release-to-manufacture (RTM) code.

I have attempted to ensure that you can gain insight into real-world environments both through the use of lab systems that represent those that might be found in an enterprise network and through the use of real-world case studies that highlight examples of day-to-day experience as a consultant to some of the world's largest organizations.

What You Need to Run Skype for Business Server 2015

As you read this book, you will find that there are a range of components that all come together to make Skype for Business function. These include the Skype for Business Server software, the Skype for Business client, and the supporting technology from Microsoft Windows Server 2012 R2 and Microsoft SQL Server 2014. Of course, there are additional pieces that can be integrated, such as gateway devices, telephone devices, and software components such as Exchange and SharePoint.

With this much complexity, you may be wondering how on Earth you are going to be able to get started with learning. In addition to all the components, you will find when looking at the published minimum system requirements for Skype for Business that the main Front End (or Standard Edition) servers require a minimum of 16GB of RAM and eight CPU cores alone. I cover all this in depth in Chapter 7, but no doubt you will think that is rather a challenge for a lab. Well, don't worry! It is perfectly possible to set up a capable lab system on a single machine. In fact, while writing this book, I ran the numerous lab systems on a variety of hardware, ranging from laptops with 16GB of RAM and a pair of fast hard drives for the virtual machines to large workstation hardware with 64GB and six hard drives. All in all, this is equipment that is well within the reach of any enterprise looking to get up to speed with Skype for Business and something that anyone studying IT as they learn for their career can get hold of for not ridiculous sums.

Within the constraints of the hardware mentioned, I created the labs using Microsoft Hyper-V technology to virtualize many machines. The labs ranged from two machines covering a domain controller and a single Skype for Business server all the way up to the migration lab, which had both Lync and Skype for Business installed with full external communication and mediation servers for connectivity to the PSTN, where I was running 20 servers on a single piece of hardware. So while for production use you must take care to size things according to best practice, in the lab you can learn a great deal with a single server, Hyper-V, some public IP addresses, public certificates, and a SIP trunk—which are all readily available for affordable amounts of money.

What's Inside

This book is arranged in five main sections, which focus on key elements that help build your knowledge of Skype for Business, starting with fundamentals that get you up to speed. You will then move on to getting your first Skype for Business system up and running through to administrating your system. At that point, the book takes a deep look into using Skype for Business as your telephony platform, before moving on to cover how to integrate Skype for Business into other systems.

When first picking up a new book, people frequently jump straight to a chapter that answers some immediate need or interest. I have attempted to build concepts throughout this book, with most of the later chapters assuming you are familiar with the previous material. I have, of course, referenced that earlier material wherever possible in case you need to brush up, but as a general recommendation, if you're new to Skype for Business, you will have the most success by reading through the chapters in order.

Part I: Fundamentals

This section covers the background information that will help you understand what makes Skype for Business tick.

Chapter 1: What's in Skype for Business 2015? This chapter runs through Skype for Business from top to bottom, covering key concepts, features, and where Skype for Business sits in the history of real-time communication products from Microsoft.

Chapter 2: Standards and Protocols Like any technical product, Skype for Business is underpinned by numerous protocols and standards that enable it to operate and interoperate with other platforms. This chapter focuses in particular on SIP, which enables the majority of Skype for Business communications.

Chapter 3: Security Security is front of mind for all administrators these days. This chapter outlines the threats to Skype for Business and explains its architecture in a security-focused manner that will enable you to discuss requirements with your security team. Also covered are some of the administrative practices needed to help you administrate Skype for Business securely.

Chapter 4: Desktop Clients Without clients, any server product would be pretty useless! In this chapter, you'll look at the clients available on a PC, Mac, and browser, and then you'll do a dive deep into how the clients connect to Skype for Business infrastructure.

Chapter 5: Mobile Clients Mobility has become a much more significant usage case in recent years, and in this chapter, you will look at the clients available on a Windows Phone and iOS devices (Android clients will be available by the time you read this) and dive deeper into how the mobile clients connect to Skype for Business infrastructure.

Chapter 6: Devices This chapter wraps up the client connectivity methods by looking at specifically manufactured devices for connectivity for telephony and/or conferencing, covering the clients that run Skype for Business directly as well as non-Skype for Business clients that can integrate.

Part II: Getting Skype for Business Up and Running

This part is where you actually get hands-on. It covers planning and sizing and then both the installation and upgrade processes.

Chapter 7: Planning Your Deployment While you're probably all keen to dive in and start playing with the nuts and bolts, planning is essential to ensure you achieve what is required. This chapter shows you how to plan utilizing the available tools, and it helps you understand the Skype for Business prerequisites, enabling you to choose which hardware to use and whether virtualization will work for you.

Chapter 8: Installation By the end of this chapter, you should have installed your first system. This chapter covers preparing your underlying server OS through publishing Skype for Business to the Internet, with all the steps in between!

Chapter 9: Migration and Upgrades Skype for Business is the latest in a line of real-time communications products from Microsoft. This chapter shows you how to get from the earlier Lync Server products to Skype for Business.

Chapter 10: Online and Hybrid The "cloud" is becoming more dominant in everyday computing, and Microsoft is driving cloud adoption specifically through Office 365. Skype for Business is included in the Office 365 product suite, and through this offering you can join an on-premises solution to the cloud solution, creating a hybrid. This chapter walks through the requirements to do so, as well as discusses the features. There will be more available by the time you read this!

Part III: Administration

Having planned and installed Skype for Business in the previous section, this part moves on to cover administration. These chapters cover role-based access, explain admin roles and policies, and even cover troubleshooting.

Chapter 11: Role-Based Access Control Role-Based Access Control (RBAC) changes the granularity and ease with which an administrator can be granted permissions required for their job and only their job, allowing specific delegation of functionality to groups of people. This chapter shows you how Skype for Business implements RBAC and how to use it to implement secure administration of Skype for Business.

Chapter 12: User Administration This chapter shows how to manage users, enabling, disabling, and configuring them both individually and through policies and to use the Skype for Business features they require.

Chapter 13: Archiving and Monitoring Skype for Business enables communication, and in many organizations communications must be archived. This chapter covers how this is achieved with the Archiving role, as well as options to allow Exchange to archive the data. It also covers the way in which you can inspect the communication passing through Skype for Business, not only for quality but also more traditionally, showing who spoke with whom. Finally, the chapter also covers how to monitor the Skype for Business service as a whole using System Center Operations Manager (SCOM).

Chapter 14: Planning for Adoption While this book has focused on the technology that is Skype for Business, there is another major aspect to utilizing Skype for Business: how do you get Skype for Business adopted in your organization? Without a proper plan and a great team that includes people ranging from senior personnel to those using the technology every day, you may not have great success deploying Skype for Business. This chapter discusses some of the key elements that come together to enable a business to successfully adopt Skype for Business.

Chapter 15: Troubleshooting As with any system, there will be times where things don't work as they should. This chapter works through key troubleshooting concepts and then looks at the tools available in Skype for Business, or available separately as downloads, and how to use them when trouble strikes.

Part IV: Voice

Skype for Business builds on the vision of Lync Server toward becoming a full-fledged telephony system (PBX). This section focuses on using Skype for Business as your PBX, taking you from basic phone calls through to complex automated call distribution systems.

Chapter 16: Getting Started with Voice Skype for Business provides all the capability needed to be a large enterprise telephony platform. This chapter introduces you to the world of the PBX. It covers the features available in Skype for Business and the architecture that supports them.

Chapter 17: Call Admission Control One of the biggest considerations when utilizing data networks for audio and video communication is bandwidth usage. Call Admission Control enables you to map out your network and protect it from overuse. This chapter shows you how to do this with Skype for Business.

Chapter 18: E9-1-1 and Location Information Services Especially in North America, the ability to locate where a phone call is being made from and to provide that information to the emergency services is mandatory. This chapter discusses how to provide this functionality with Skype for Business; it also shows how those outside of North America can use this innovative technology.

Part V: Other Dependent Infrastructure

One of the huge benefits of Skype for Business being a software platform is that it is easy to extend and integrate with other systems. This part covers that extensibility, looking at the way Skype for Business integrates with both other Microsoft and non-Microsoft products.

Chapter 19: Extended Voice Functionality Skype for Business can do far more than just basic phone calls. This chapter looks at how to implement your own audio-conferencing bridge, how to set up your own mini call center or help desk, and how to deal with other voice scenarios, such as the need to park calls for others to pick up and to deal with calls to people who have left your company.

Chapter 20: SQL SQL is the engine room that drives Skype for Business. Every server has at least one SQL Express installation locally, and it is critical to the ongoing operations. In this chapter, you will see how to deploy and configure SQL to cater for high availability, as well as moving from SQL mirroring to SQL AlwaysOn Availability Groups.

Chapter 21: Reverse Proxies, Load Balancers, and Gateways These devices (or services) are the gateway to the outside world; reverse proxies are used for external client connectivity via the Internet, and gateways are used via the PSTN. Load balancers are there to help with the high availability of the services. This chapter looks at the features enabled and configuration requirements of these devices.

Chapter 22: Exchange, SharePoint, and Office Web Application Server While Skype for Business contains a huge amount of technology, it is enhanced even further through tight integration with other Microsoft products. This chapter covers the provision of voice mail and presence integration with Exchange, as well as presence integration and workflow with SharePoint. It also covers how client PowerPoint content is presented via the Office Web Application Server.

Chapter 23: Skype for Business 2015 Development This chapter provides an overview of the development capabilities of Skype for Business, such as how you can leverage the infrastructure to integrate into existing line-of-business applications or create your own.

Appendixes

There are three appendixes. The first covers all the learning points from throughout the book, the second covers some basic PowerShell capability for those new to PowerShell, and the third discusses Persistent Chat use cases.

Appendix A: The Bottom Line Throughout the book, "The Bottom Line" section appears at the end of each chapter. It asks relevant questions to help test your understanding of the material in that chapter. This appendix covers all those questions and includes the answers so you can verify yours.

Appendix B: Introduction to PowerShell, the Skype for Business Management Shell, and Regular Expressions PowerShell is what underpins the whole management interface of Skype for Business. While most people are likely to be familiar with PowerShell (it's been released for more than eight years now), it may be new to some. In this chapter, you learn what PowerShell is, how to use it, and more importantly how to work with Skype for Business using PowerShell.

Appendix C: Using Persistent Chat Effectively Persistent Chat is a difficult aspect of Skype for Business to understand and use well in organizations. This chapter will showcase a number of scenarios where it is used well and can bring value.

The Mastering Series

The Mastering series from Sybex provides outstanding instruction for readers with intermediate and advanced skills in the form of top-notch training and development for those already working in their field and clear, serious education for those aspiring to become pros. Every Mastering book includes the following:

- Real-World Scenarios, ranging from case studies to interviews that show how the tool, technique, or knowledge presented is applied in actual practice
- Skill-based instruction, with chapters organized around real tasks rather than abstract concepts or subjects
- Self-review test questions, so you can be certain you're equipped to do the job right

Conventions Used in This Book

Before you set off into the world of Skype for Business described in this book, there is one final piece of information you should know. Throughout the book, we have used various methods to describe things. In particular, we have had many discussions about how best to refer to Skype for Business. After all, it's much more of a mouthful than Lync.

Aside from trying to shorten the name, Microsoft isn't happy about using variations of S4B or SfB. Skype was an option, but this refers to the "consumer" brand of Skype. The best I've come up with is to use the following variations when referring to different aspects of Skype for Business:

- Skype for Business Server 2015: This is the server product, in other words, the infrastructure where you do the configuration.

- Skype for Business 2016: This is the client, which users will use. (Note the different numbering also.)
- Skype for Business 2015: This is also the client, but with the Lync 2013 client upgraded (see Chapter 9, "Migrations and Upgrades," for details).
- Skype for Business client: This primarily would be the Skype for Business 2016 client, but it can also be more generic to include older clients such as the Lync clients that continue to work.
- Skype for Business Online: This is the Office 365 version of the Skype for Business product, which is hosted and operated by Microsoft directly.
- Skype for Business: This generically refers to all of the above, in other words, this generation of the product (previously called Lync).

In addition, when it comes to the management tools, there are two main interfaces: a web-based control panel called Skype for Business Server Control Panel and a command-line shell called the Skype for Business Server Management Shell, which is PowerShell based. In the book, I used the term *PowerShell* to describe the Skype for Business Server Management Shell.

Later versions of Windows Server (2012 +) are able to dynamically load the cmdlets from other modules as needed, so there is no direct need to import the Skype for Business cmdlets; simply start any PowerShell prompt and go. However, on older versions of Windows, when working with Skype for Business, unless explicitly stated otherwise, you should be using the Skype for Business Server Management Shell.

How to Contact the Author

I welcome feedback from you about this book. Obviously, it's always nice to get messages about what you liked about the book, but I also welcome suggestions for improvements I could make in future editions. You can reach me at `hannakeith@hotmail.com`.

Sybex strives to keep you supplied with the latest tools and information you need for your work. Please check its website at `www.sybex.com/go/masteringskypeforbusiness`, where I'll post additional content and updates that supplement this book should the need arise.

Part 1

Fundamentals

Chapter 1

What's in Skype for Business?

Skype for Business 2015 is the latest in the line of the Communications Server platforms from Microsoft. The platform originally started with Live Communications Server 2003 (some would say with Exchange Conference Server 2000!) and continued through Live Communications Server 2005, Office Communications Server (OCS) 2007, Office Communications Server 2007 R2, and the two incarnations of Lync: Lync Server 2010 and Lync Server 2013.

For those of you experienced with either version Lync Server (or indeed previous versions of OCS/LCS), this chapter will call out some of the core capabilities introduced in previous versions as well as the new capabilities specific to Skype for Business, so some of this content may be a refresher to knowledge you already have.

In this chapter, you will learn to

- Describe the features of the client
- Describe the features of the server
- Describe the voice features

Understanding the Skype for Business Client

As an administrator, the first thing you'll see is the Setup tool; however, the users will see the client. Therefore, understanding what the client can and will provide is important for administrators trying to sell the business justification. It is also important in terms of what policies will need to be configured to enable (or disable) features. The Microsoft Unified Communications family is so much more than a simple instant messaging (IM) tool or a phone, and treating it as either end of the messaging scale will impact the way you deploy it to users. At one end, the IM capabilities can be deployed quite simply, whereas the phone integration will take significant planning and should not be underestimated. Some of the additional training capabilities freely provided by Microsoft are covered in Chapter 14, "Planning for Adoption."

With OCS (and to some extent LCS), the user experience was made up of a number of clients.

- Communicator
- Live Meeting
- Group Chat

Lync 2010 consolidated the Communicator and Live Meeting clients into one; however, that still left the Group Chat client as a separate installation requirement. A number of large financial institutions that have a heavy reliance upon the Group Chat functionality have been asking for some time for the consolidation of this client. Group Chat (now known as Persistent Chat) was incorporated into the Communicator client in Lync 2013, so there's only a single installation required. In addition, Persistent Chat is now a "full" function of Lync 2013 rather than a download add-on as it was previously—more on this later.

Chapter 5, "Mobile Clients," covers in detail the mobility capability; this was first introduced with Cumulative Update 4 in Lync Server 2010 and has been expanded with each new iteration of the product.

With the Skype for Business branding, the client has had a facelift; new features introduced with Lync 2013, such as user photos, have been further improved, and other features have been moved around to make them easier to find for users.

In addition, device selection has been considered, with the clients being adapted to tablet devices as well as the expected mobile and desktop/laptop-style devices.

The Communicator client is also now part of the Office suite and is no longer available separately. Figure 1.1 shows the client when a user is first logged in.

FIGURE 1.1
The client startup screen

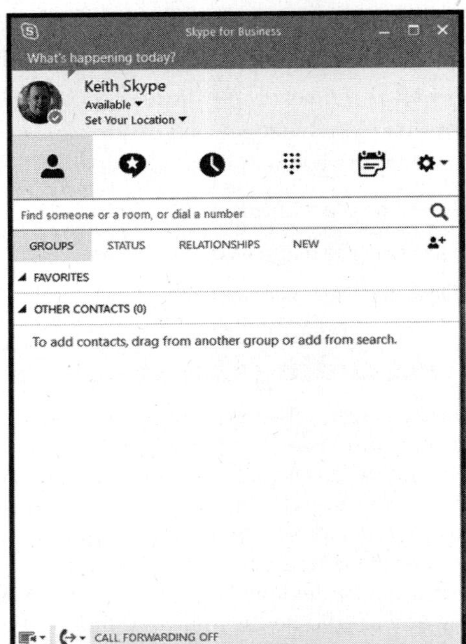

Connecting via the Skype for Business 2016 Client

To communicate and collaborate, Skype for Business client users need to be able to locate and connect to each other on the network. Over time, users will build their own contacts list (sometimes called a *buddy list*); however, they need to find other users to be able to create and add to the list. The basic search functionality from previous versions has been retained and has been expanded to include integration and key-skills searching within SharePoint as well as the expected Address Book search. Also available (introduced in Lync 2010) is the ability to remove the Address Book download capability and provide only an online web-based search function. Figure 1.2 shows the client search bar and results window when data has been entered into the search bar.

FIGURE 1.2
The client search bar and results window

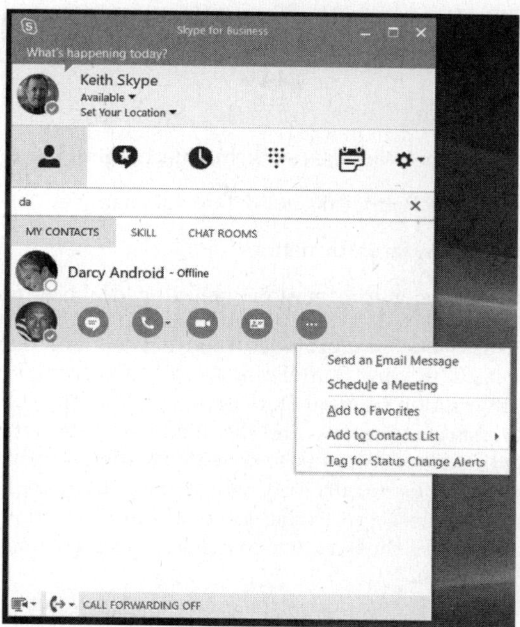

From these results, you can initiate any type of communications modality. The submenu is opened by selecting the ellipsis (…).

To find more information from the user (the contact card), you have to at least appear to begin a conversation with them. Starting an IM conversation has the least impact in that until you actually send a message, there is no prompt to the recipient. Figure 1.3 shows the new-style contact card, which you can see once you initiate communications and expand the user data. This information is captured from a combination of Skype for Business, Outlook, and Active Directory attributes; if you don't see information you'd expect to see, make sure the data is available in the source first!

FIGURE 1.3
The user contact card

The User Properties box is extended to provide a lot more contextual information.

- Department
- Office
- Phone numbers (work, mobile, home, if permitted)
- SharePoint links (to MySite, for example)
- Calendar information
- Location information (including local time and time zone)

This *contact card* provides a consistent client interface across all the integrated applications, such as Office and SharePoint. Connecting from other applications preserves context; if you start a conversation from an Outlook email, both the subject and the priority are carried across to the conversation windows and the document title is transferred from SharePoint. The contact card now includes the ability to provide location information, giving users a way to quickly establish where people are currently, which can help them determine whether personal contact or a video call is the more appropriate type of communication. The location information also provides the local time for the user, which can be extremely useful when people are spread across multiple geographies.

You can search across the following locations:

- Skype for Business contacts
- Active Directory
- Outlook contacts (including suggested contacts)
- The public Skype directory (optional, requires configuration)

Introduced with Lync 2013, in conjunction with Exchange 2013, is the Unified Contact Store, where all contacts are merged and stored within the user mailbox (specifically within the contacts folder). An additional capability introduced by the Unified Contact Store is the ability to store high-definition (HD) photographs of the users. In the past, photographs were stored in SharePoint or Active Directory; now they are stored within the user mailbox in Exchange 2013.

Searching allows you to easily establish availability and identity (the extended contact card provides more information to help identify the correct recipient) and quickly establish contact using any modality. In addition to searching by name, the SharePoint integration allows you to search by skills (or keywords) to help identify the correct person.

As mentioned, the ability to add contacts (or *buddies*) and group them is retained; in fact, it is expanded to include an auto-populated Frequent Contacts group. This group is automatically populated with your 10 most-frequent contacts, which are weighted based on modality. For example, someone you regularly call is going to be placed higher in the list than someone you IM. You'll learn about other automatically created groups later in this chapter.

The Contacts tab, which is the default, contains a number of subtabs that provide different views (shown in Figure 1.4).

FIGURE 1.4
The Groups subtab on the Contacts tab

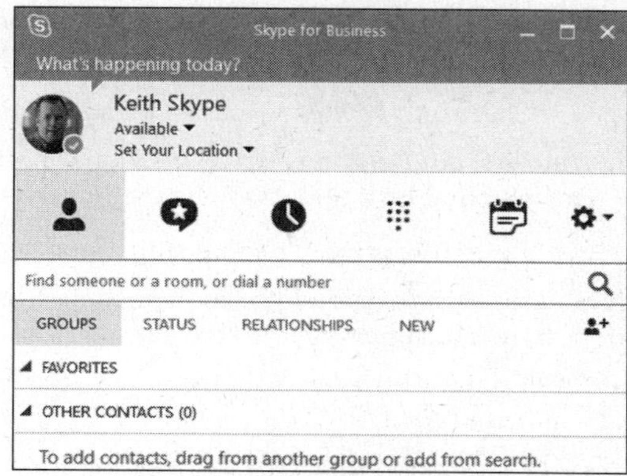

Groups This is probably the most frequently used subtab; it is where you can find all the contacts sorted alphabetically but also grouped together in user-defined groups.

Status Under this subtab, all the contacts are sorted by availability, under the following groups:

- Away (includes Off Work)
- Unknown
- Unavailable
- Online (includes Busy, In a Meeting, and Do Not Disturb)

Relationships Here, you can manage the permissions assigned to each contact. The default categories are as follows:

Friends and Family This relationship must be assigned manually. It provides the following setting:

"Share all my contact information except meeting details."

Workgroup This relationship must be assigned manually. It provides the following setting:

"Share all my contact information except Home and Other phone; contact can interrupt Do Not Disturb status."

Colleagues Any users from within the same Skype for Business organization (or Lync if in coexistence) are automatically placed within this group and receive the following setting:

"Share all my contact information except Home, Other, and Mobile phone, and meeting details."

External Contacts Any external (federated) users are placed within this group by default and receive the following setting:

"Share only my name, title, email address, company, and picture."

Blocked Contacts This relationship must be manually assigned and provides the following setting:

"Share only my name and email address; blocked contacts can't reach me via Lync."

Auto-Assign Relationship This item is not found in the Relationships tab; however, it can be found on a contact and is used to reset the privacy level.

"Reset this privacy relationship to the default."

New If users have added you to their contact list but you have not (yet) added them to yours, they will appear on the New tab.

Add A Contact Provides a submenu with the following list of options for finding and adding a new contact:

- Add A Contact In My Organization
- Add A Contact Not In My Organization
- Create A New Group
- Display Options

Voicemail Display

The voicemail display within the Skype for Business 2016 client is not as fully featured as the voicemail integration from within Outlook. Skype for Business allows only basic integration, providing the name of the user (or phone number display, if caller ID could not be matched to a contact), a Play button, and the Skype for Business interaction options allowing the call to be responded to from the client (using any modality).

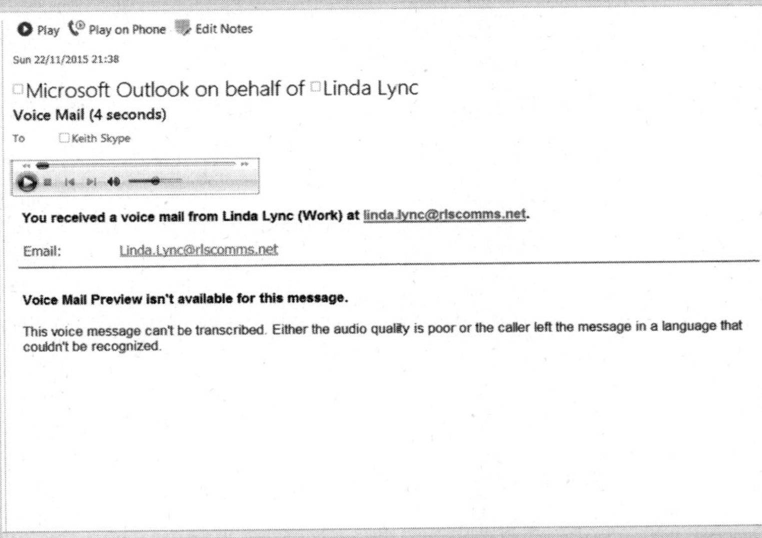

Outlook (2007 or higher) provides additional capability such as Notes, Play-on-Phone, and fully integrated media controls for playback. Exchange 2010 and Exchange 2013 also provide speech-to-text translation for certain language packs, the output of which will be displayed in Outlook only.

Communicating via the Client

As mentioned in the previous section, the Skype for Business 2016 contact card lets users quickly and easily establish any modality from any integrated application. In particular, Skype for Business allows users to receive phone calls on any device (including non-Skype for Business devices) as well as manage their own (and potentially other users') communications easily and more effectively than before.

The final button (telephone icon) provides a single page for telecom interaction (see Figure 1.5), so users can make calls (from a dial-pad) and display and listen to voicemails. The dial-pad operates exactly as you would expect; for example, press and hold 1 to call your voicemail. If you need to access your voicemail box when it is empty (for example, to set your greeting), this is the only method to do so other than dialing the voicemail access number. The voicemail section allows quick and easy access to voicemails stored in your inbox. When there are voicemails in your inbox, a drop-down menu is available for direct access to set your greeting. If you are not enabled for Enterprise Voice, this button will not be visible.

FIGURE 1.5
The dial-pad

Video Calling

Since Office Communications Server 2007 R2, high definition has been supported for peer-to-peer video only; Skype for Business now provides the capability for HD (using H.264 SVC codec support) conference calls (VGA was the default with Lync 2010). In addition to the higher resolution provided by this default codec, the Lync 2013 client supports direct integration with the Microsoft RoundTable devices, providing a panoramic video strip when used in calls.

The video screen can be detached from the client and viewed in a separate window, which can be extremely useful for users who have multiple monitors because the video channel can be displayed on a separate display from the main conference window, allowing a more true-life experience.

H263 codecs are no longer supported since Lync 2013, so organizations may need to upgrade legacy non-Skype for Business (or Lync) video hardware or look to additional gateway capability to continue operating.

Device Management

New device management functionality allows the client to intelligently select the appropriate device for your calls. Even changing devices within a call is much easier. The Audio And Video Tuning Wizard is no longer required; you simply use a drop-down menu with all the devices listed and select a new one to transfer the call to the selected device immediately with no further interaction. Devices can even be added mid-call, and the audio (or video) can be directed to the newly added device.

Audio and video device management and tuning is still possible from within the Options page from the Tools menu; however, doing so is now an optional task, whereas previously it was required every time a device was inserted.

The call-forwarding and team-call settings can now be managed with a single click in the main client window, shown in Figure 1.6.

Figure 1.6
Making a call forwarding selection

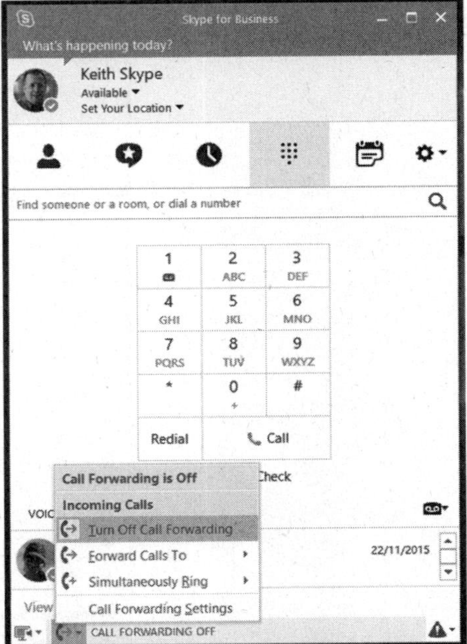

Managing Communications

Tabbed conversation view allows all conversations to be viewed in a single window. With previous versions, a new conversation window would open for each person. Indeed, the client can be configured to allow this mode of operation if preferred. Figure 1.7 shows the tabbed conversation view.

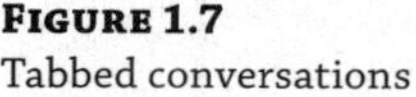

Figure 1.7
Tabbed conversations

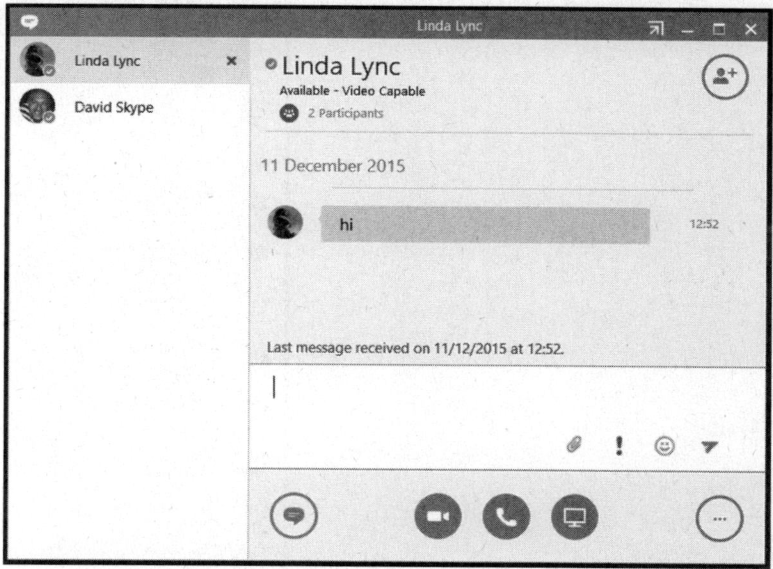

The tabbed conversation view can be confusing at times. If you move from IM to audio modalities, the new audio window does indeed detach to form a separate "floating" window (containing the previous IM conversation), and when the audio portion is finished and the call ends, the window "pops" back into the tabbed view.

The Conversations tab provides a single location where you can keep track of ongoing communications. From this tab, it is easy to bring up previous conversations, assuming this information has been stored in Outlook (or more accurately, Exchange). Figure 1.8 shows this tab with content.

Each entry contains the history of the interaction, including all attendees and the modalities in use. Conversations can be resumed from this tab, and they will include the information from the previous conversation if it is still available. From the user's perspective, this will look like a continuation of the previous conversation.

A private line can be enabled for a user, in addition to their primary line, and is the equivalent of an incoming-only line. A user can have only a single private line, and when enabled, it is associated with the same Session Initiation Protocol (SIP) address (that is, the user does not get a second SIP address). It is an unlisted number and does not appear within any address books or Active Directory. The Private Line function provides a user with the ability to give out a number that will always get through; any Do Not Disturb or delegated-call scenarios are ignored by an incoming private line, and a different style of *toast* (the name given to the pop-up notification for any incoming communications) will appear, indicating an incoming call on the private line. In addition, a different ringtone is sounded for private.

FIGURE 1.8
The Conversations tab

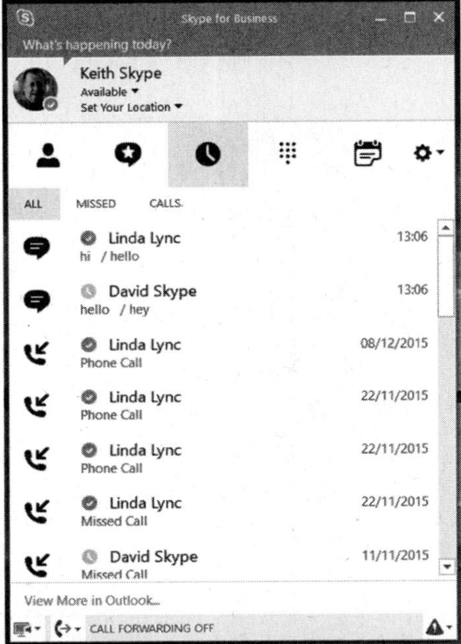

Skype for Business provides an easy method to initiate calls on behalf of others. Once you are configured as a *delegate* for someone (as an assistant might be for a boss), additional options are provided for making calls.

In the delegated-call scenario, incoming calls are displayed on the client for both the delegate and the boss, enabling the delegate to handle any call on the boss's behalf. On the incoming toast, the availability of the boss is also displayed, allowing the delegate to quickly evaluate whether to pick up the call.

When added as a delegate, the user receives a notification indicating who added them. As shown in Figure 1.9, additional groups are also created, showing who the user's delegates are as well as those for whom they act as a delegate.

When a user is designated as a delegate of someone, they can also place calls on their behalf, as shown in Figure 1.9.

Figure 1.10 shows the additional information added to the toast when a call is for someone who has delegates. If the delegate picks up the call, the toast will change to briefly show who picked up the call and an email message will be sent.

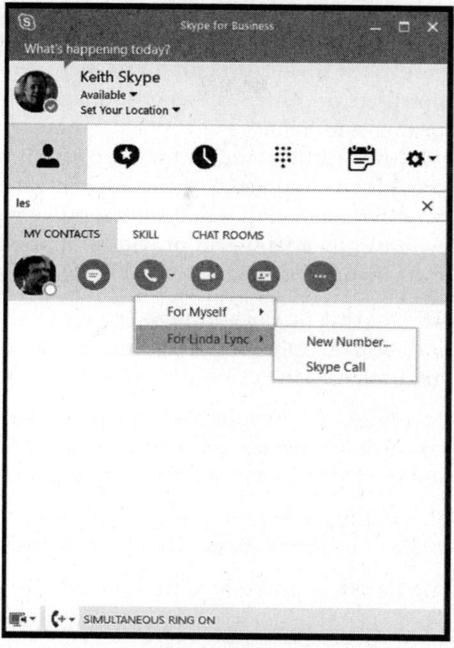

FIGURE 1.9
Delegation groups

FIGURE 1.10
The toast received for an incoming call

Collaborating via the Client

As mentioned earlier, previous versions of the Microsoft communications platform provided a separate client targeted for group collaboration: Live Meeting. This provided an interface whereby large groups could "meet" and collaborate on shared content (desktop or documents). Also, an additional add-in client, the Conferencing Add-In for Microsoft Office Outlook, was required to provide integration with Outlook, allowing meetings to be scheduled from the Outlook client.

Since Lync 2010, both the additional Live Meeting client and the Conferencing Add-In for Outlook have been removed, simplifying not only the installation process but also the user interaction. In addition, Lync 2013 removed the need for a separate Group Chat (now called Persistent Chat) client. All functionality from within the Live Meeting client is included in the client. The single installation package includes the Online Meeting Add-In for Skype for

Business, which provides the online meeting capability previously provided via the separate installation of the Conferencing Add-In for Outlook.

In some cases, it was difficult for users to understand which client was the correct one to use to join meetings or conferences; consolidating the features into the single client removes any scope for this confusion.

The Online Meeting Add-In for Skype for Business (automatically installed as part of the client) provides a single-click approach to creating a meeting. The user no longer needs to decide whether a meeting will be audio only or whether it will require desktop sharing; the client dynamically adapts and provides the needed resources from the server.

Here are some other collaboration highlights:

- The sharing model within Skype for Business provides a flexible approach to sharing individual applications, screens, or the full desktop as well as enabling the coediting of a document opened from SharePoint.
- Meetings now include a *lobby*, where users can wait to join a meeting. Previously users could only enter the conference directly or have their call dropped if the conference had not started or they were not permitted to join.
- Presenting PowerPoint sessions enables an Asynchronous Viewing mode, allowing other presenters to navigate through the content and review it.
- Media can be embedded into PowerPoint presentations and played back to participants.
- Dial-in conferencing supports the use of DTMF (touch-tone) commands for control of the conference as well as providing voice announcements of attendees.
- Users can share notes from OneNote during a meeting rather than sharing the app itself.
- Web-based access to conferences is provided on the platforms shown in Table 1.1.

TABLE 1.1: Web-based access supported

OS	IE 11	IE 10	IE 9	Firefox 12.x	Safari 5.x, 6.x, 7.x	Chrome 18.x
Windows 10**	Yes			Yes		Yes
Windows 8.1	Yes			Yes		Yes
Windows 8 (Intel based)		Yes		Yes*		Yes*
Windows 7 SP1	Yes	Yes	Yes	Yes*		Yes*
Windows Server 2008 R2 SP1	Yes	Yes	Yes	Yes*		Yes*
Windows Server 2008 SP2	Yes*	Yes*	Yes*	Yes*		Yes*
Mac OS X 10.8				Yes	Yes	Yes

** 32-bit-only versions of the browser.*

*** Edge is supported on Windows 10.*

Conference call video management has been further improved with the ability to view multiple live video streams (maximum of five) simultaneously. Previously, you could view only active speaker and previous active speaker video streams (and potentially active panorama and previous active panorama if multiple RoundTable devices were present). While this function is limited to five concurrent active streams, any additional users are moved to the "sitting" row in the video view, and these sitting users, rather than display a video stream, provide their photo view. This is also known as the Gallery View; see Figure 1.11 for standing and sitting row views.

A specific video stream can be locked as the meeting focus for everyone in the conference call if required. This stops the video stream from bouncing from person to person in the event of strong background noise (this was often distracting with older client conference calls).

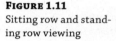

FIGURE 1.11
Sitting row and standing row viewing

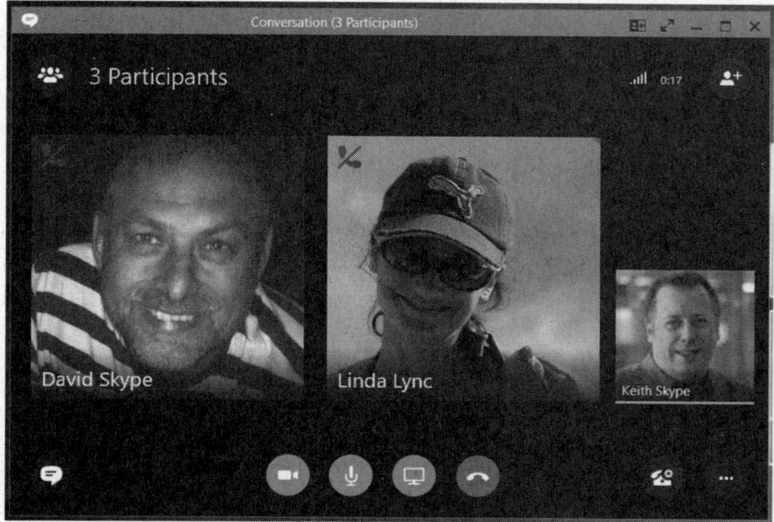

Understanding Skype for Business Server 2015

Customer feedback always plays a large role in driving the changes implemented by Microsoft. Some of this is purely reacting to the types and volume of support cases received, and some of it is the direct feedback from customers. Some of the issues admins brought to Microsoft's attention in previous versions are listed here:

- There was no common store for configuration items, which could be found in Active Directory and SQL Server as well as in individual server metabases or WMI.
- There were no methods to validate configuration changes prior to deployment.
- Microsoft Management Console (MMC) was becoming complex.
- Automation was difficult.
- Deploying certificates correctly the first time was complicated.

- There was no "proper" support for virtualization.
- Multiple-site deployments required too many servers.
- Complicated sign-in processes for hybrid scenarios.
- Windows Fabric was too much of a "black box."

These issues were addressed within the Lync Server 2010 and 2013 releases, and further updates were made within Skype for Business Server 2015 to address the following issues:

- High-availability options that were unrealistic and unnecessarily complex for multiple datacenters
- Failover from pool to pool, providing only basic voice capability
- Archiving capability not compliant with many industry requirements
- Client-side virtualization
- Video gateway integration
- Cloud-capable/hybrid scenario support

Managing Skype for Business Server 2015

Lync Server 2010 introduced a completely new interface compared to any of the previous communications platforms, and this is continued with Skype for Business Server 2015, with another update, albeit mostly branding. Gone is the MMC interface used to navigate and manage the configuration of Live Communications Server and Office Communications Server. (Well, the MMC interface is almost gone. The Topology Builder application is the only application to continue to use it.) Replacing it is a combination of PowerShell and a Silverlight-based Control Panel application.

Following the lead of Exchange Server and other applications, Microsoft built Lync Server 2010 on a base of PowerShell, which you can learn more about in Appendix B, "Introduction to PowerShell, the Skype for Business Management Shell, and Regular Expressions." When carrying out configuration requests, Skype for Business Server's Silverlight-based Control Panel interfaces directly to PowerShell.

Lync Server 2013 also built on the initial Lync Server 2010 introduction of role-based access control (RBAC), allowing separate disparate groups to manage separate areas of the application, such as users or telephony. Skype for Business has not changed the RBAC capability and is covered in detail in Chapter 11, "Role-Based Access Control."

Topology Builder

You'll learn how to use Topology Builder in Chapter 7, "Planning Your Deployment," where we'll define the architecture and overall topology of the environment. The actual configuration of policies and implementation, however, is carried out using either PowerShell or the Control Panel application (in some cases, configuration items are available only in PowerShell). As you'll see, Topology Builder provides the first checkpoint for the topology and ensures configuration consistency; it will not allow configuration items to be removed if they are still in use.

The Topology Builder also consolidates all the information required for generating a certificate. It ensures that any additional subject alternative name (SAN) entries are included as required, ensuring that when the Setup program for a server gets to the Certificate Wizard, all the information is already in place. Additional user input and control over the certificate template used are provided using this wizard. The Edge server consolidates the external-facing requirements from three separate certificates in previous versions to a single external certificate.

Central Management Store

The multiple configuration stores from previous versions have been replaced with the *Central Management Store*. It is the sole location for all the configuration data for the deployment and operation of Skype for Business. Combining all the various configuration stores into a single Central Management Store means there is only a single point of failure, which is this database. Replicating this database to all servers in the environment results in the following benefits:

- Mitigates the single point of failure
- Allows servers to continue operating without access to Active Directory
- Removes reliance on Active Directory schema changes
- Provides consistency in server configuration (especially the Edge server)

The Central Management Store is stored within SQL Server (in a Standard Edition deployment, this is SQL Express) and can be made highly available by the use of a supported SQL high-availability mechanism (such as clustering, mirroring, or AlwaysOn).

The Central Management Store operates in a master-replica state. In the event of a catastrophic loss of the Central Management Store, a replica can be promoted to be the master database. During an outage of the master database, no changes can be made to the environment; however, Skype for Business will continue to operate based on the configuration at the time of loss (this also includes server restarts).

Central Management Store Replicas

During a server-role installation, local instances of SQL Express are installed, and the Central Management Store is replicated to this database. The instances are called `RTCLOCAL` and `LYNCLOCAL`. This occurs on all server roles installed, including the Edge server.

Some companies are wary about proliferating SQL Express throughout the environment, mostly in the wake of the SQL Slammer virus and similar attacks. (In January 2003, the SQL Slammer virus impacted more than 75,000 systems within 10 minutes, causing a large denial of service and Internet slowdown.)

By introducing these additional databases—`RTCLOCAL` was introduced with Lync Server 2010 and `LYNCLOCAL` was introduced with Lync Server 2013—Skype for Business gives the admin more to manage and patch (if required). In addition, because the configuration information is replicated to the perimeter network on the Edge servers, availability of the configuration is at greater risk if the Edge servers are compromised.

The advantages provided by the local database replication, as well as the measures taken to protect them (e.g., encryption), outweigh the risks involved in most cases.

Many large financial service companies have already deployed Skype for Business and/or Lync Server Edge servers. If there were significant risk of compromise, they'd be the first to provide feedback!

Lync Storage Service

The Lync Storage Service (LYSS) provides an abstract storage framework allowing Skype for Business to access storage systems within other applications. Currently the other applications are limited to Microsoft SQL Server and Microsoft Exchange 2013 (via Exchange Web Services). Aside from the Skype for Business databases, it is used for Exchange 2013 archiving integration and the Unified Contact Store.

Windows Fabric

Another underlying infrastructure change is the implementation of the Windows Fabric system. This provides a background enablement function that places users within a pool. This feature was introduced with Lync Server 2013 and is responsible for defining the user accounts' primary, secondary, and tertiary home server locations.

LYSS uses Windows Fabric for replication.

As a result of the Windows Fabric replication, additional requirements are needed to ensure full capability within a Front End pool. Table 1.2 shows the number of servers required to be functional in a pool for the pool to be functional.

Table 1.2: Servers required in a pool for pool quorum

Total Servers in the Pool	Minimum Required for Full Functionality
1 or 2	1
3 or 4	2
5 or 6	3
7 or 8	4
9 or 10	5
11 or 12	6

What happens if the number of available servers drops below the minimum listed here? Well, the pool goes into survivability mode, and if after five minutes the pool is still in survivability mode, it will shut down all Skype for Business services. See `http://technet.microsoft.com/en-us/library/gg412996.aspx` for more information.

DNS Load Balancing

Lync Server 2010 introduced DNS load balancing as a method to provide connection-based resilience to both client and server interactions. DNS load balancing provides functionality only for SIP-based traffic.

Using DNS load balancing reduces the configuration requirements of a hardware load balancer (at the cost of creating a few additional DNS entries), allowing the hardware load balancer to focus on load balancing HTTP traffic (a job for which it is much better suited).

For example, Table 1.3 shows the configuration required when using hardware to load balance a pool of three Front End servers.

TABLE 1.3: DNS records required when using hardware load balancing

ITEM	DNS FQDN	DNS A RECORD
Pool VIP	Pool.company.com	192.168.0.1
Front End	FE1.company.com	192.168.0.2
Front End	FE2.company.com	192.168.0.3
Front End	FE3.company.com	192.168.0.4

Table 1.4 shows the configuration required when using DNS load balancing on the same pool of three Front End servers.

TABLE 1.4: DNS records required when using DNS load balancing

ITEM	DNS FQDN	DNS A RECORD
Web VIP	Poolweb.company.com	192.168.0.1
Pool	Pool.company.com	192.168.0.2
Pool	Pool.company.com	192.168.0.3
Pool	Pool.company.com	192.168.0.4
Front End	FE1.company.com	192.168.0.2
Front End	FE2.company.com	192.168.0.3
Front End	FE3.company.com	192.168.0.4

Figure 1.12 diagrams the process through which a client will connect when using DNS load balancing. It is important to note that this is only for the first connection; once connected, the client will cache the server name and IP address for subsequent connections.

The following steps correspond to the numbered links in Figure 1.12 and describe the actions within each communications step:

FIGURE 1.12
The client connection process

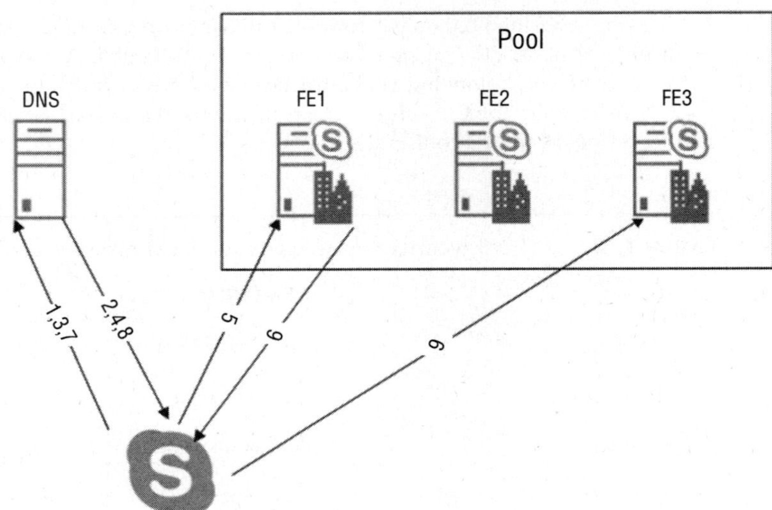

1. The client queries DNS for the service record (SRV). (A service that was published using the Domain Name System [DNS] can be discovered through its SRV record. Its SRV record includes information such as protocol, port, priority, and weight in the single record entry.)
2. The DNS server returns the SRV record pointing to the pool fully qualified domain name (FQDN).
3. The client queries DNS for the pool FQDN.
4. The DNS server returns the IP addresses of pool members.
5. The client connects to a randomly selected IP address from the list returned by the DNS server.
6. If this server is not the home server for the client, the server returns the home server name.
7. The client queries DNS for the address of the home server.
8. DNS returns the IP address of the home server.
9. The client connects to the server and registers the user.

Installable Server Roles

Skype for Business Server introduces the new Video Interoperability server role, but more importantly it restructures and consolidates the existing roles (compared to OCS or Lync Server 2010), allowing organizations to consolidate resources by combining various roles onto a single server deployment. Chapter 8, "Installation," covers the steps required to define and install each role.

Office Communications Server 2007 introduced the concept of an *expanded topology*, whereby a single pool could be separated into its constituent parts: web services, conferencing, and Front Ends. The move to a 64-bit deployment with Office Communications Server 2007 R2 allowed this topology to disappear (it was still supported, although not recommended) because of the capability of the 64-bit hardware to address more memory resources and make them available to the application.

Lync Server 2010 provided the capability to do either, depending on the deployment needs. When the user count was greater than 10,000 in a pool, Microsoft recommended separation of the Audio/Video Conferencing Multipoint Control Unit (MCU) to a separate server/pool.

Lync Server 2013 removed this expansion option, and Skype for Business has continued this separation of resources and supports only the consolidated model.

Virtualization is now fully supported for all server roles (except the Survivable Branch Appliance), and more detail is provided in Chapter 5.

The following server roles are provided in Skype for Business Server 2015:

- Front End
- Back End
- Edge
- Director
- Mediation
- Persistent Chat
- Video Interoperability Server
- Survivable Branch Appliance
- Survivable Branch Server

The next sections describe these roles in detail.

Front End

The Front End server provides the connection point for the client. It is responsible for all registration, via the Registrar service, and routing requests for clients. Because of this routing responsibility, all clients belonging to the same user must register on the same Front End server. In addition, the Front End server holds all the conference MCUs.

- Web
- App sharing
- IM
- Audio/video

The Front End server is also home to the web component services, such as Address Book, Group Expansion, Control Panel, and Reach, which the Silverlight application that provides web-based access to conferences.

High availability is achieved by the deployment of multiple (up to 12) Front End servers into a single pool and the utilization of hardware (with or without DNS) load balancing.

Back End

The Back End role is the SQL Server database, which provides both conference capability and contact/buddy lists. In deployments that also configure the built-in voice applications (Response Group Service, Call Park, and Dial-In Conferencing), their data is also stored within this SQL Server database. The Central Management Store is also stored in the Back End role.

High availability is achieved by deploying SQL Server in a log shipping configuration, with an optional Witness server. The advantage of the Witness server is that it will allow for automatic failover, whereas it's a manual process without the Witness server.

> **STANDARD EDITION SERVER**
>
> The Standard Edition server combines both the Front End and Back End roles into a single package. In this scenario only, the Back End role is stored within a SQL Express database. High availability is not possible with Standard Edition. However, two Standard Edition pools can act as backups for each other.

Edge

The Edge role is deployed within the perimeter network and provides remote capability to Skype for Business. Remote capability is defined as follows:

- Remote access
- Federation with other organizations
- Public Internet Connectivity (PIC) federation with Skype and XMPP gateways (such as Google's gTalk). In addition, the Edge server provides a method to reroute calls via the Internet if insufficient internal bandwidth is available. In this case, an Edge server (or pool) is required at each location.

Multiple Edge servers may also be deployed to localize Internet conference traffic. For this purpose, each Edge server (or pool) is associated with an internal Front End pool, and users homed on the Front End pool use their locally defined Edge server for all traffic except SIP. SIP traffic (including federation) will travel only via a single Edge location.

High availability of the Edge environment is achieved with the deployment of multiple Edge servers in a single location. High availability of the federation functionality (including PIC) requires the use of a hardware load balancer and is available in only a single location.

Skype for Business includes the ability to communicate with Extensible Messaging and Presence Protocol (XMPP) gateways natively. Previously this was enabled via a separate download and separate server instance. XMPP is used by systems such as Google Talk.

Director

The Director role performs authentication and previously was recommended when you are also deploying an Edge server; it is now optional. You should consider using the Director role to perform authentication when you are deploying an Edge server. The Director role provides a stop-off point for all external traffic. By placing this function at the first point of authentication, you ensure that all (any) malicious traffic is intercepted here rather than at a Front End (where internal clients may be impacted). When an Edge server is used, the Director server is configured as the next hop and proxies the external traffic to its final destination. Figure 1.13 shows a typical Director placement.

FIGURE 1.13 Typical Director architecture

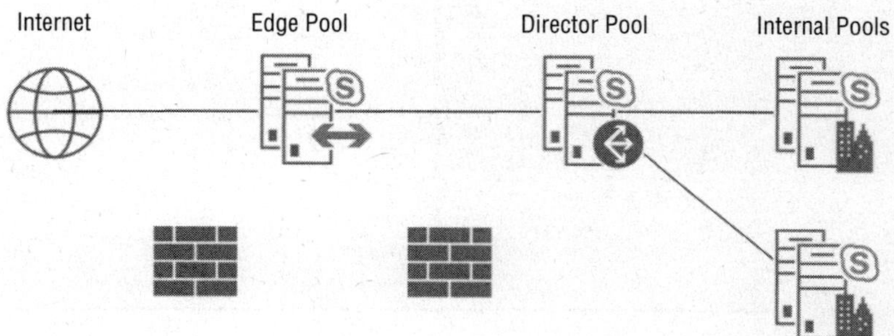

Real World Scenario

AUTHENTICATION MODES

Like previous versions of the platform, Skype for Business supports both NT LAN Manager (NTLM) and Kerberos authentication modes. Traditionally, Kerberos was the preferred authentication method for internal client connections, and NTLM was used for external (remote user) access because the client could not receive a Kerberos ticket when it wasn't connected to the domain.

Skype for Business allows clients to log in without access to Active Directory, so NTLM or Kerberos authentication is not required. Instead, a certificate is downloaded to the client upon first successful login (via either NTLM or Kerberos, so those tools are still required).

This certificate is provided by the web services component of the Front End server. By default, it is valid for 180 days, but the time is configurable. The certificate is valid only for sign-in to Skype for Business.

A copy of the certificate is shown here. As you can see, the certificate is issued by Communications Server, and further investigation will show it can be used only for client authentication.

continues

continued

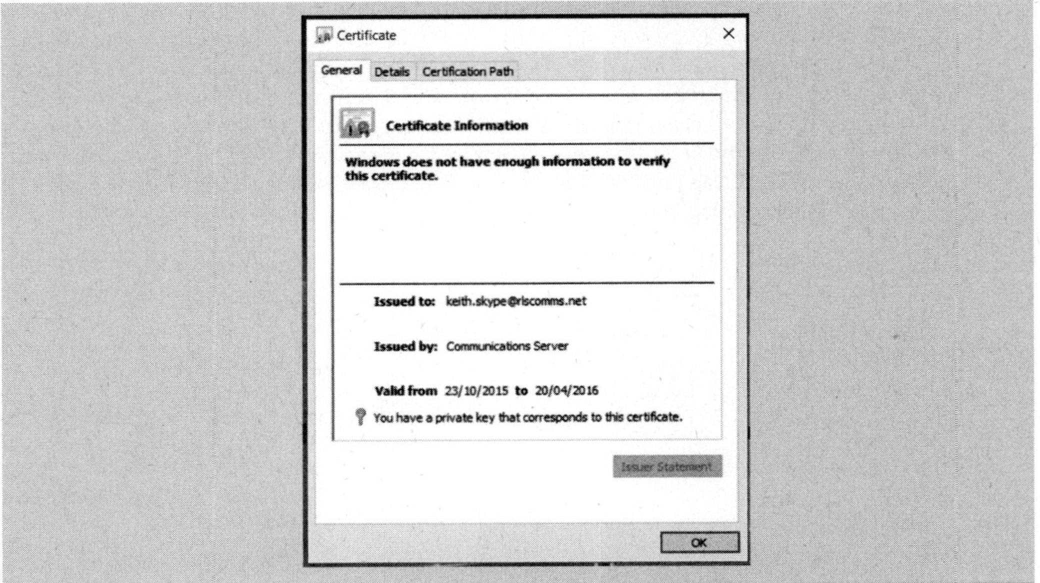

When used for internal traffic, the Director is defined as the result of the DNS SRV query for automatic login and, in this scenario, will redirect traffic to the correct home pool. With the additional support for multiple DNS SRV records, this requirement is redundant within the internal infrastructure.

Unlike the Office Communications Server versions, Skype for Business Server 2015 makes the Director a defined role, not a normal pool with its features disabled.

High availability of the Director role is provided by deploying multiple servers and using DNS (or hardware) load balancing.

Mediation

The Mediation role is the interface into the public switched telephone network (PSTN). Typically, it is used in conjunction with a media gateway device, allowing an interface either into an existing PBX (private branch exchange) or directly to the PSTN. The latter configuration, known as *SIP trunking*, is now becoming more prevalent; it allows the Mediation server to connect directly to the PBX or PSTN without the need for an additional hardware media gateway device.

With previous versions of the Communications Server platform, the Mediation server was used to transcode the codec used internally (typically, RTAudio) into the codec used by the media gateway, whether it was PBX or PSTN (typically, G711). Lync 2010 introduced the concept of *media bypass*, whereby the client can communicate using G711 directly to the media gateway or PBX, alleviating the need for the transcoding to occur and thus removing the need for transcoding by the Mediation role. Media bypass direct to the PSTN is not possible because there is no termination point to which the client can connect.

By removing (or at worst reducing) the need for transcoding on the Mediation role, media bypass reduces the tasks carried out by this role, which means that less-powerful hardware can be used to run this role. This, in turn, allows for colocation of the Mediation role with a Front End role, reducing the server footprint required.

Office Communications Server 2007 (both versions) had a one-to-one ratio of Mediation servers to media gateways; Lync Server 2010 removed this requirement, introducing a one-to-many ratio, and Lync Server 2013 supported a many-to-many ratio. Also, introduced with Lync Server 2013 was the concept of *trunks*. These allow for additional configuration to be applied to calls traversing the trunk.

High availability of the Mediation role is provided by deployment of multiple servers. Certain configuration options may perform better with or even require the hardware load balancing.

Persistent Chat

Persistent Chat functionality previously was available via a separate download and was called Group Chat.

Skype for Business Server 2015 incorporates this functionality directly into the client as well as providing a fully fledged role deployed via Topology Builder.

Persistent Chat provides chat room, or channel, capability where the content is not lost after a user has logged out and is retained indefinitely. It also provides a searchable resource to users.

A maximum of four active Persistent Chat servers can be deployed for high availability and load sharing. Channels will be instantiated on a single server initially, and when the load of users trying to connect becomes large enough, the channel will then be created on another server. New clients will be directed to the channel on the new server by the lookup service. This process will continue until the channel is created on all available servers.

Data submitted to a channel is broadcast to all other subscribing servers and then broadcast back to listening clients while at the same time the data is written back to the SQL database for future queries.

Survivable Branch Appliance

The Survivable Branch Appliance (SBA) is a hardware device provided by one of three hardware vendors (all support for these devices is provided by the hardware vendor directly).

- Audiocodes
- Sonus
- Ferrari Electronics

The SBA is an all-in-one device that provides some of the functionality of a pool (specifically, registrar and routing) as well as having a colocated Mediation role and media gateway. The function of this device is to continue to provide local service to users in the event of a wide area network (WAN) or pool outage in the central location.

Users are provided local calling functionality via the device, but they rely on a central pool for conference and contact/buddy list information. In the event of a WAN or pool outage, the local PSTN breakout will continue to operate, allowing both incoming and outgoing calls. However, contact/buddy list information and access to conferencing will be unavailable, and the client will go into *Survivable mode*. Figure 1.14 shows the client feedback when in Survivable mode, and as with OCS 2007 R2, any calls currently in progress will continue. Upon restoration of the failed service (network or server), the client will return to normal operations automatically.

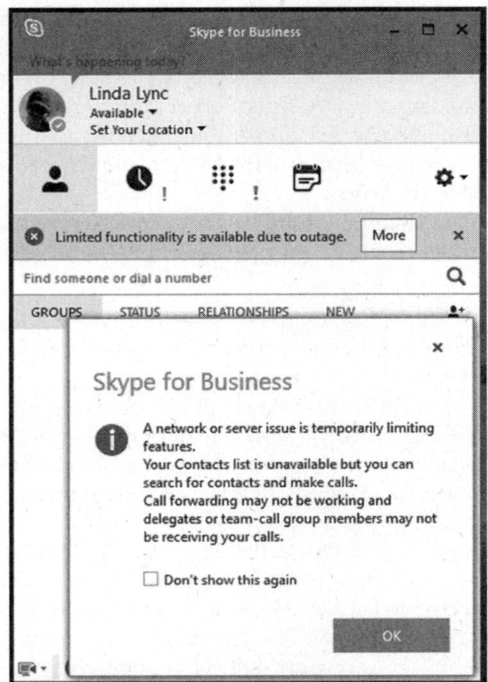

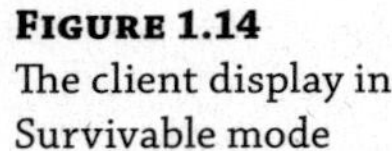
FIGURE 1.14
The client display in Survivable mode

A Survivable Branch Appliance may only be a primary registrar and must be configured with a backup central pool.

High availability is provided by the backup central pool.

Survivable Branch Server

The Survivable Branch Server provides similar functionality to a Survivable Branch Appliance, except that it includes no media gateway. This option is typically used in locations that already have a media gateway deployed, such as, for example, where OCS 2007 was previously deployed, and the cost of replacement cannot be justified.

The Survivable Branch Server is simply defined in Topology Builder and deployed as a server directly by an organization's IT department, like any other server would be. It's not a directly purchased device (appliance) and could even be virtualized if required (assuming, of course, the virtualization requirements are met).

Like a Survivable Branch Appliance, the Survivable Branch Server may only be a primary registrar and must be configured with a backup central pool.

High availability is provided by the backup central pool.

Monitoring and Archiving

Monitoring and Archiving are no longer separate roles; rather, they are incorporated into the Front End role. In essence, they have been reduced to a feature. The Monitoring feature provides the capability to capture both Quality of Experience and Call Detail Record information objects about all the calls in the environment.

This information is stored in a SQL Server database and evaluated using the provided SQL Reporting Services report pack, which contains almost 50 built-in reports. Additional reports can be created using SQL Reporting Services Report Builder.

The Archiving role provides a capture of all IM traffic and records any file transfers (filename and location, not content) occurring in the environment.

This information, like that captured by the Monitoring role, is stored within a SQL Server database. However, it should be noted that there are no additional compliance checks on this database; it is a store only.

High availability is provided through the use of an Enterprise pool, with multiple Front End servers, and through a SQL database configured for high availability using SQL mirroring.

For those organizations with stricter compliance needs or those that want archiving of all products to be centralized in one location, the Archiving feature can be enabled to use the archiving capabilities built into Exchange 2013, such as Legal Hold and Compliance Search.

Video Interoperabilty Server

The Video Interoperability Server (VIS) provides an integration point between Skype for Business and other third-party video conferencing solutions. The best way to think of it is as a mediation server for video. You need to create and configure "video trunks" to enable and apply the configuration.

At the time of writing, integration with the following video conferencing solutions is supported:

- Cisco C40
- Cisco C60
- Cisco C90
- Cisco MX200
- Cisco MX300
- Cisco DX80
- Cisco EX60
- Cisco EX90
- Cisco SX20

All are required to be running TC7.0.0 or higher for interoperability.

Office Web Applications Server

The Office Web Applications (OWA) server (not to be confused with Outlook Web Access) is used to enhance presentation capability with Skype for Business. It is not part of the Skype for Business Server installation media and is not a required role. However, some functionality is available only if it is present (such as video streaming in PowerPoint).

It has separate installation (as well as licensing) requirements, and the detailed installation is out of scope of this book; we do cover how to configure Skype for Business Server 2015 to leverage it, though, in Chapter 8!

Colocation

With previous versions of the Microsoft Unified Communications platform, there were significant limitations on what can be colocated. Table 1.5 calls out the permitted colocation options for Skype for Business.

TABLE 1.5: Supported Skype for Business Server 2015 colocation deployments

SERVER ROLE	COLOCATED ROLES	NOTES
Enterprise Edition Front End	Mediation	
Back End database of Front End pool	Database for Persistent Chat Database instance for Archiving Database instance for Monitoring	
Mediation	None	The Mediation server may be colocated with the Front End pool.
Director	None	
Edge	None	
Video Interoperability Server	None	
Survivable Branch Appliance	Mediation Media Gateway	
Survivable Branch Server	Mediation	No gateway is included in a Survivable Branch Server.
Persistent Chat Server	Standard Edition server	The Persistent Chat server still requires a separate SQL server installation. This is not a recommended configuration for production environments but is suitable for testing.
Trusted Application servers	None	

Table 1.5: Supported Skype for Business Server 2015 colocation deployments *(continued)*

Server Role	Colocated Roles	Notes
Exchange Unified Messaging (no longer a stand-alone Exchange role, but combined with CAS and Mailbox roles)	None	Exchange Server roles may be colocated with each other but not with Skype for Business Server 2015 roles.
Reverse proxy	None	Reverse proxy may be colocated with other server applications as detailed in the reverse proxy support guidelines; however, no Skype for Business roles may be colocated.

Archiving and Monitoring have not been specifically called out here because, unlike with previous versions, they can no longer be installed as stand-alone servers; their database instances can, of course.

Automation Capabilities

Skype for Business is built from the ground up on PowerShell. This architecture provides significantly easier scripting and automation capability than Office Communications Server and Live Communications Server, which relied on Windows Management Instrumentation (WMI) for most (but not all) configuration options. You can find more information about the use of PowerShell in Skype for Business in Appendix B.

Hybrid and Cloud Scenarios

Skype for Business enables hybrid scenarios where some infrastructure is located in the cloud and some infrastructure is located on the customer premises. This is enabled by supporting a split-domain model, whereby the same domain can be shared between two Skype for Business organizations—one being on premises and the other being in the Office 365 cloud.

As this book goes to press, this functionality is still developing with additional functionality, currently known as Broadcast Meetings and Cloud PBX in beta. Hybrid is covered in more depth in Chapter 10, "Online and Hybrid," which covers the configuration aspects directly and touches on some of the (currently) beta functionality. Lync 2013 provided capability for "private cloud" scenarios with a separate version known as Lync Server 2013 Hosting Pack, and while support continues on that version, it is no longer available and no equivalent is planned for Skype for Business.

Understanding the Voice Capabilities

Since the release of Office Communications Server 2007 in October 2007, Microsoft has been relentlessly developing and pushing the voice capabilities of OCS. Skype for Business continues to develop this functionality, and most of the changes expected in this version will be focused on Office 365 capability.

There are still areas in which Skype for Business Server 2015 does not completely address the functionality provided by a traditional PBX. Many of these functions, however, are being made redundant as people move to new ways of communication. One example is ringback. On a PBX, if you call a number and it is busy, you can enter a DTMF code to tell the PBX to call you back when the line becomes free. It can be argued that the use of presence information removes this requirement (if the *callee* is busy initially, the call will not be placed) and provides the capability to notify of presence changes.

The focus points for voice capabilities are as follows:

Resiliency Lync Server 2010 introduced the concept of a backup registrar and also increased the scope of the multidatacenter (Metropolitan) pool scenario supported to include all modalities. Lync Server 2013 expanded the resiliency options further by increasing the backup registrar functionality to be more than simply registrar backup but is capable of providing significantly more redundancy. Skype for Business continues to develop and build on this model, mostly by minor improvements in this version rather than a step change.

The Metropolitan pool scenario—a single pool stretched between two data centers—was no longer a supported model under Lync Server 2013, and Skype for Business continues with this nonsupported approach.

The backup registrar continues to provide telephony functionality in the event of a failure to the primary registrar. The client will register to the primary registrar when available; however, in the event that either the network connection to the primary registrar or the registrar itself fails, the client (following a configurable timeout) will register to the backup registrar and enter Survivable mode. As mentioned previously, this mode provides only telephony functionality and limited search capability for other users; all centralized services are lost, including conferencing, contact/buddy lists, and voice applications.

Any pool type (Enterprise or Standard) can act as a backup registrar to only a pool of the same type (Enterprise or Standard) as well as to a Survivable Branch Appliance (or Server). The Survivable Branch Appliance (or Server) can be designated only as a primary registrar. When you are configuring backup registrars, you need to consider the server specification and overall capacity of the backup registrar, taking into account a potential failure of the primary registrar and the total number of users who could then be homed in on the backup registrar.

In addition to the backup registrar, Skype for Business includes the capability to pair pools. This provides increased functionality in the case of a failure. With the backup registrar, only telephony voice capability was provided; however, with paired pools, significantly more functionality is available, such as conferencing, presence, and buddy lists.

Call Admission Control Call Admission Control (CAC) is the capability to manage the number of Skype for Business calls being placed on the network at any time. It is covered in detail in Chapter 17, "Call Admission Control."

Call Park Call Park is the capability to place a call into a parked location for pickup (typically by another person) on another device or even location. Call Park is frequently used in conjunction with paging systems. A call will be received by an operator and put into an *orbit*. Then a notification will go out on the paging system/intercom; the callee can then retrieve the call from orbit simply by dialing the orbit number. Hospitals and manufacturing plants typically use this feature; everyone has heard something like "Call for Dr. Smith on 1234."

Media Bypass The introduction of media bypass in Lync Server 2010 (and client) reduces the role of the Mediation server, which is no longer involved in the transcoding of the codecs, because both the client and the gateway are talking to each other with a common codec (typically, G711). As mentioned, removing this transcoding requirement from the mediation role also means there no longer needs to be one Mediation server per media gateway, allowing a single mediation role to support and control multiple media gateways.

Removing the extra hop of a Mediation server has the side benefit of improving voice quality (because the media traffic has a shorter path to travel) and also removes another potential point of failure.

Enhanced 9-1-1 Enhanced 9-1-1 is the provision of location-based information when calling emergency services within North America. E9-1-1 is covered in detail in Chapter 18, "E9-1-1 and Location Information Services (LIS)."

Analog Device Management Although Skype for Business does not directly support and manage analog devices, it does control the signaling information and, as such, can provide controls to restrict the class of service to which the devices have access (for example, you can choose not to permit international dialing, and you can place similar restrictions). The device is connected to the environment via a media gateway using an analog terminal adapter (ATA), and Skype for Business does not interfere in the media stream, only the signaling. Not being involved in the media stream allows fax machines to also benefit from this management.

Call detail records can be captured for all these analog devices because the signaling is controlled from the Skype for Business servers.

Private Line As mentioned previously, the Private Line functionality is a means to assign a second number to a user. Incoming calls to this Private Line number do not follow any delegation rules (or other routing options, such as Do Not Disturb or Call Forward) and will always go through to the recipient. This function is for incoming calls only. Figure 1.15 shows the incoming toast, which has a different ringtone associated with it.

FIGURE 1.15
Private line toast

Routing Changes For anyone familiar with the routing within OCS 2007, you will see significant improvements with Skype for Business Server, such as changes to the number normalization and outgoing caller ID capability. Outbound normalization is now possible and can be defined centrally on a per-route (or per-gateway) basis; this allows simplified administration of the media gateways, especially in a global deployment where, perhaps, the same media gateway model (or indeed manufacturer) cannot be used in every country.

Caller ID can be managed on a per-user or per-group basis to suppress or alter the calling party number data presented. This feature is automatically overridden for the simultaneous-ringing scenario, where when the call is forwarded to a mobile device, you want to present the originator number.

Common Area Phones *Common area phones* are Phone Edition devices that are deployed in a communal area such as a lobby. Figure 1.16 shows a Polycom common area phone.

Skype for Business provides the capability to manage these devices, even though they are not associated with a user and no one is logged onto them.

FIGURE 1.16
Polycom CX500 common area phone

The ability to control the functions of these common devices ensures that they cannot be misused (e.g., by placing international calls).

In addition to these functionality changes, the portfolio of devices has been significantly increased, with additional device partners on both the end user and media gateway sides.

A number of additional certification programs are in place for each of these areas, and all can be found here:

`http://technet.microsoft.com/en-us/lync/gg236602`

Open Interoperability Program The Open Interoperability Program is an interoperability testing and certification program not managed by Microsoft. Any devices (not limited to user devices, but also gateways and services such as SIP trunks) qualified through this program are fully supported for interoperability with Skype for Business Server 2015.

As this book is going to press, Skype for Business is transitioning from the Open Interoperability Program to the Partner Solutions Program; you can find details here:

`http://partnersolutions.skypeforbusiness.com/solutionscatalog/all`

The principal of both is the same; they will provide a catalog for supported products in different categories for Lync Server or Skype for Business Server as necessary.

Optimized for Skype for Business The Optimized For program ensures that devices "just work" on installation—meaning there is no user configuration required; they simply need to be plugged in—and provide high-quality audio/video user experience. These devices are built and tested following the Skype for Business specifications, and they are created by global partners at the Certified or Gold Certified level.

Other Compatible IP Phones This program is designed for IP phones based on the publicly available Windows protocols and the Microsoft Office protocols documentation. As with the Optimized For program, they are created by global Certified or Gold Certified partners.

Software and Hardware Load Balancers These applications and appliances are tested by the vendor and reviewed by Microsoft to meet Skype for Business requirements.

Understanding the Unified Communications Managed API Capabilities

The Microsoft approach to unified communications is to remove the islands of legacy technology—the voicemail solution that doesn't integrate with the switchboard solution, and so on—to provide one identity and one mailbox from which all capabilities can be taken.

Microsoft provides the familiarity of both the platform and the infrastructure to build new applications, ensuring that they can fully integrate across the environment.

Skype for Business includes a RESTful API and provides extensibility and interoperability by building on the two pillars of development.

- .NET
- Web services

By building on the Skype for Business infrastructure, developers know they already have an enterprise-class platform; by using the .NET framework and the web services layer, they have an easily extensible foundation, which can be developed using skills they already have.

Skype for Business allows the creation of presence-aware (known as Communications-Enabled Business Process [CEBP]) applications; this allows the applications to react and make decisions based on the presence of users in the environment, providing notifications or alerts as needed and in the modality required.

Presence can be embedded in already developed applications, or the Skype for Business 2016 client can be expanded to include the conversation window to show rich context on both sides of the conversation.

Unwrapping the SDK

The Skype for Business software development kit (SDK) allows four scenarios for which developers might need to customize a deployment.

- To integrate with existing line-of-business applications
- To provide contextual conversations
- To add custom applications to the client
- To completely customize the client UI

Developers can utilize the Visual Studio Windows Presentation Foundation and Silverlight controls to quickly add Skype for Business functionality (drag-and-drop controls) into internal applications; this can include functionality such as docking the conversation windows within the application itself.

Deploying the Skype for Business client and (ideally) using it as the main collaboration toolset doesn't mean you're stuck with the feature set provided. *Application launch links* can be sent within conversations, allowing data to be shared in third-party applications; you can see this in the continuation of subject and priority messages started from Outlook. These links also enable developers to extend the menu functionality of both contact cards and the client itself.

An important point with application launch links is that no code is registered on the receiver side; the client simply calls out to existing installed applications. A current example of this functionality is sending of hyperlinks, where clicking the link does nothing other than open the web browser with the address listed in the link; no additional code is executed.

Even scenarios where the client is completely customized are supported; the Skype for Business controls can be retemplated in Expression Blend.

It should be noted that the Skype for Business client is still required to be installed in all of these scenarios (with the exception of the web services development); however, it is possible to run the client in UISuppressionMode, whereby only the features from the customized user interface (UI) are presented to a user and all the interaction is behind the scenes.

Further investigation into the customization and development of applications is beyond the scope of this book. See *Professional Unified Communications Development with Microsoft Lync Server 2010* by George Durzi and Michael Greenlee (Wiley, 2011) for more information about developing custom applications; although the book is focused on Lync Server 2010, a large number of the technologies continue within Skype for Business, and the approach is equally valid across product versions.

The Bottom Line

Describe the features of the client. The Skype for Business client is designed to achieve three core goals: connect, communicate, and collaborate. This new client makes it much easier to find people and verify identity, initiate communications (typically, with a single click), and collaborate with full-blown information sharing. Device integration and call management have been greatly simplified, removing the need to run through wizards constantly.

Master It You are assembling a new product development team. The new product will be similar to a previously released product, and you want to ask members of the previous team for guidance. How can you find people associated with the previous product team?

Describe the features of the server. Skype for Business Server 2015 provides most of the server roles included in Office Communications Server and introduces the Survivable Branch Appliance (or Server) to help in the high-availability scenarios. The management approach has changed through the introduction of the Topology Builder application and role-based access control to limit administrative access to defined users and scopes as required. PowerShell and Silverlight combine to provide the day-to-day administration of the environment.

Master It When deploying high availability, which of the following roles can be a primary registrar?

- Director
- Enterprise Edition Front End
- Standard Edition Front End
- Survivable Branch Appliance
- Survivable Branch Server

Describe the voice features. Significant investment and development have gone into Skype for Business Server 2015's voice feature set. The new set has allowed it to become a match for a large portion of the PBX workload and, in many cases, a viable replacement for a PBX.

New functions (such as Private Line, Call Admission Control, Call Park, E9-1-1, and Common Area Phones) provide welcome additions to the user experience. By contrast, behind-the-scenes features (such as Media Bypass, routing improvements, resiliency improvements, and analog device management) provide a more integrated and available solution for the administrator while they help reduce the number of servers required.

> **Master It** As the network and telephony administrator for your company, you want to invest in SIP trunks rather than legacy PBX-style PSTN connectivity using media gateways.
>
> How should you configure media bypass and deploy mediation servers?

Chapter 2

Standards and Protocols

Any platform that needs to interoperate with other platforms will rely on standards, and a communications platform is no different in that respect. As with previous versions of the platform, Skype for Business Server 2015 uses the Session Initiation Protocol (SIP) standard to provide its backbone, and it builds on that backbone by extending SIP to accommodate additional functionality.

Regardless of whether communication is conducted via the public telephone network using voice or via the Internet with other instant messaging products, you need to know the limitations of the protocols used and understand where interface gateways will be needed to extend beyond the edges of the Skype for Business Server 2015 infrastructure. (Communication may include other organizations running any versions of the Microsoft Unified Communications platform and using federation.)

This chapter introduces the history behind the signaling that led to the introduction of SIP. While the protocol itself is interesting, understanding the background network infrastructure will improve your understanding to better design and troubleshoot Skype for Business Server 2015.

In this chapter, you will learn to

- Understand the basics of SIP for signaling
- Understand how SIP has been extended to provide additional functionality for Skype for Business Server 2015
- Identify additional protocols used by Skype for Business Server 2015

Understanding SIP's Origins

Before the Internet (yes, there was a time when there was no Internet), the only real-time communication was via the public telephone network. This network was extremely easy to use (pick up the phone and dial) and highly reliable, and communications were understandable at both ends (it was just talk). The system was based on a circuit-switched network.

Circuit-Switched Networks

At some time in their youth, most people have played with a tin-cans-on-a-string communications system (see Figure 2.1). The tin-can system essentially is a basic, circuit-switched network. It's extremely basic because there is only a single circuit—and even adding one more user requires significant investment because two additional lines are needed so that everyone can talk to each other. With this type of system, complex signaling isn't needed. Each endpoint is connected to only one other endpoint; therefore, when one endpoint is picked up, the users immediately know where the communication is going.

FIGURE 2.1
A primitive communication system

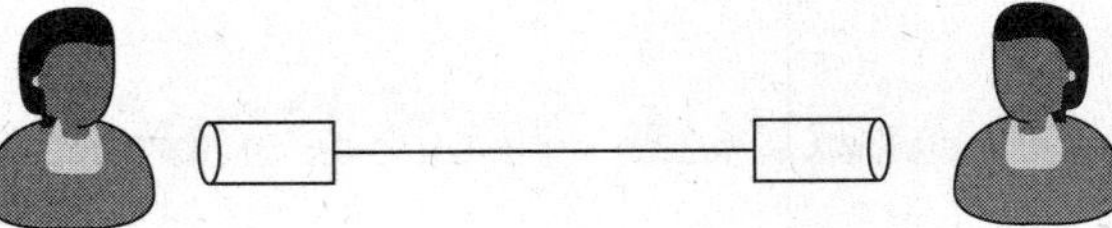

Adding a third person would require two more lines (one for each existing endpoint); adding a fourth person would require three additional lines; a fifth, four more lines; and so on. With this system, any individual must have an equivalent number of lines coming to them to the total number of people in the system minus one. This type of basic system can quickly become unmanageable.

The solution to this management nightmare was the *switch*. All endpoints terminated at the switch (in a star or hub-and-spoke topology), and it is the responsibility of the switch to determine (or *route*) the call from one endpoint to another. In the early telephony days, the routing was performed by a human switchboard operator who physically connected the two endpoints with a patch cable. Figure 2.2 depicts a manual switchboard.

FIGURE 2.2
A manual switchboard

As technology improved and automation became more prevalent, the endpoints acquired dialing capability and were allocated unique identifiers (extension numbers). A termination endpoint could be signaled simply by dialing the extension number.

Building up to today's larger, modern telephony infrastructure, these switches were connected to each other (they were beginning to be known as *exchanges*), and this allowed for a wider distribution of calls.

Each exchange was allocated a routing number. When the routing number of the exchange was dialed, followed by the extension of the endpoint, a call could be routed from one location to another. Of course, in the early days, this was achieved by calling and asking the operator to perform the routing manually.

In the rudimentary example shown in Figure 2.3, if you are using Extn 100, connected to Switch 1, you dial only the extension number to reach another internal (connected to the same switch) extension number. However, simply dialing the extension number will not work when you need to reach an extension at another location (switch)—especially when the extensions are duplicates of local extensions—because you will be connected to the local extension on the same switch.

FIGURE 2.3
Endpoint and switches

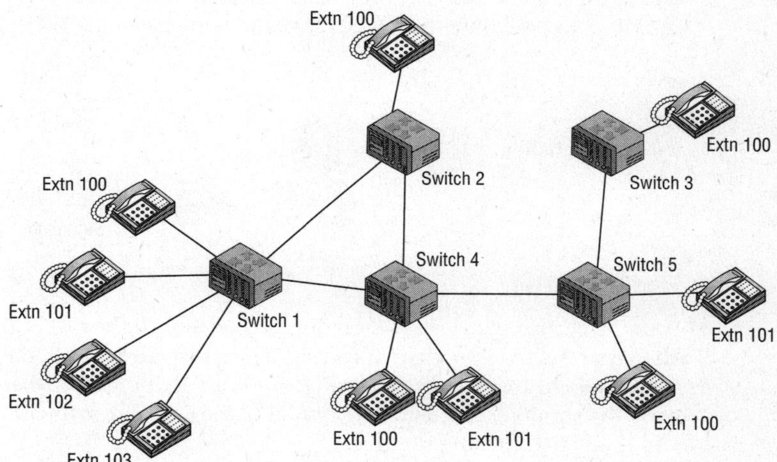

This is where the routing number comes into play. To connect to Switch 5, Extn 101, for example, you could dial 5101. You need to ensure that there is no numerical overlap like there could be when you are dialing to Switch 1. This is when the concept of dialing a specific number (typically, 9 or 0) for an "outside line" comes into play. When the switch sees this outside line number first, it knows to route the following digits away from the internal extensions.

This concept of endpoint/exchange numbering and routing has expanded to include national and international routing, and it has led to the national and international numbering plans that are so familiar to everyone making telephone calls today.

Pros and Cons of Circuit Switching

Circuit switching is so called because to establish a connection from one point to the other, a *circuit* is created, which is in effect a dedicated connection between endpoints—think back to our piece of string between the two cans.

Once this *circuit* has been established, the system is fast. There are no more decisions to be made or content to be inspected; the call is simply forwarded to the destination (or, on a switch basis, to the next interface).

This dedicated path is perfect for analog transmissions because there is no (or, more accurately, an extremely small) delay between the sending and receiving of the signal. However, there is a delay with the establishment of the path before any transmission can occur.

Once the path is in place, it will stay in use until closed down, even if transmission has stopped. This results in wasted capacity, and although it has not had a big impact in voice transmissions, it has much bigger implications when the move is made to digital transmissions where speed of transmission is much greater than the speed of interpretation, resulting in idle time on the transmission path.

Circuit-Switched Signaling

Outside of the tin-cans-on-a-string scenario, signaling information needs to be provided along with a call. As you can see from Figure 2.4, any transmission type is built of at least two parts, signaling and data (there may be more than one data channel).

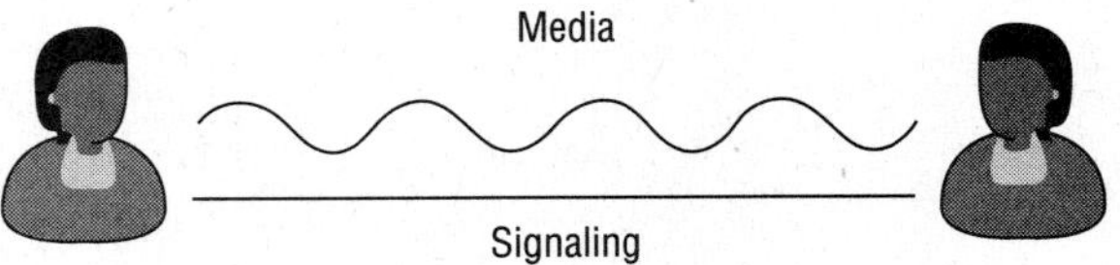

Figure 2.4
Separation of signaling and media

In the basic scenario, this signaling will establish the call in the first place and then stop it when it's finished. More advanced signaling provides additional features, such as placing the call on hold or transferring the call to another endpoint. For these more advanced features to work, the signaling needs to be parallel to the actual transmission—you couldn't put a call on hold if you had to hang up first!

Early signaling simply completed an electrical current when the receiver was picked up. The operator saw a light being lit on the switchboard and connected to that endpoint; once the operator understood the target, they used a patch cable to connect the caller to the called party. Although manual switchboards were still around into the eighties, they obviously made way for automated switching systems.

Frequency Division Multiplexing (FDM) allowed multiple calls to be provisioned across a single wire connection, but it also required a new method of signaling. The solution to this was *in-band* signaling, using the same connection for both the signaling and the data transmission.

FDM is extremely expensive to operate, requiring the use of analog filters tuned to specific frequencies to allow continued operations.

Digital Transmission

With the advent of digital transmission in the early 1960s, signaling needed to evolve even more. Digital signals comprise discrete 0s and 1s (represented in the system as changes of voltage), whereas analog signals are acoustic and must be translated to digital for transmission and then translated back to analog—sound—at the receiving end to be heard. Many different *codecs* (coder-decoders) are available to do this. Modems (modulator-demodulators) were used to connect to the early Internet; they provided a service similar to codecs except in reverse, converting the digital computer signal to an analog signal suitable for transmission on the telephone network. In actual effect, the telephone network was converting the message back to digital for transmission.

Pros and Cons of Digital Transmissions

The first advantage to digital transmission is that digital equipment is extremely cheap (relatively speaking) because it uses computers rather than the electromechanical valves in analog switching, resulting in less required maintenance.

Second, quality is much higher with digital transmission. The data is either a 1 or a 0; there are no "in-between" values, and any corrective measure required in a digital signal results in retransmission (newer digital protocols include built-in error correction mechanisms). To have digital data travel farther, it is repeated; conversely, to have analog data transmitted farther, it is amplified. Amplification will increase the signal strength, which will also include any interference (or noise). Repetition will simply repeat the clean signal, meaning it is effectively a new signal.

Of course, there are also downsides to digital. The signal must be processed, resulting in a delay while the transformation takes place. Naturally, this occurs twice—once at each end. Additionally, delays are introduced through the switching and signaling mechanisms. Typically, for voice transmissions, a delay higher than 250 milliseconds (ms) round-trip will make it difficult to follow a conversation. Individually, delays are likely to be negligible, but in a badly designed network with multiple congested hops, they will be a major factor.

Digital Signaling

Digital transmissions are typically *bursty*; the transmission and idle times have peaks (and consequently an average data rate). Because the data did not flow at a steady stream, a new signaling method, known as Time Division Multiplexing (TDM), was introduced to address the associated issues. TDM, like FDM, allows multiple signals to be transmitted across a single line, but each connection is given a specific time slot during which it is allowed to transmit. Compared with FDM, TDM allows significantly higher bandwidth (number of connections) on the same cable.

TDM requires the use of buffers in the switches, ensuring that the data is stored ready for transmission when the relevant time slot becomes available (time slots always transmit in the same order: 1, 2, 3, 4, and so on; once finished, they restart).

Early transmissions were 64Kbps channels, which exactly matched the output rate of the telephony codecs. Increases to the amount of data that could be sent meant that more options were made available for sending that data. Bits could discretely define letters, words, and sentences, allowing rules to be easily built around a signal—for example, the signaling command to place a call on hold could now be defined as *HOLD*, making it easily understood by people troubleshooting.

Signaling between switches (exchanges) is known as *trunk* signaling, and signaling between an endpoint and the switch is known as *access* signaling, as illustrated in Figure 2.5.

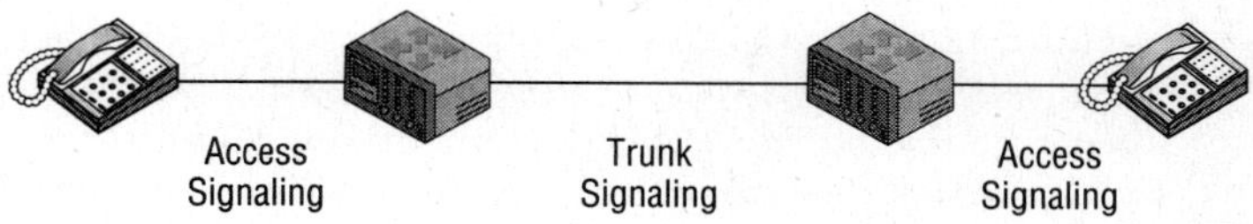

Figure 2.5 Switch signaling types

Access Signaling

Initially, access signaling consisted simply of on-hook/off-hook requesting a dial tone (or hanging up). It has progressed to include pulse signaling, or commonly now Dual-Tone Multi-Frequency (DTMF) tones used for signaling. Standard tones have been defined (typically, per country or region) to indicate busy, call waiting, and other common states to the user.

Digital Subscriber Signaling System No. 1 (DSS1), which is used in Europe and elsewhere, is an example of an access signaling protocol.

Trunk Signaling

The trunk signaling used between switches is either Channel Associated Signaling (CAS) or Common Channel Signaling (CCS). The difference between these two methods is that in CAS the signaling travels the same path as the data and in CCS there may be a completely separate signaling path. The CAS data path takes up a single channel; in European systems this is typically channel 16 in a 32-channel link. The CCS separate signaling path allows a signaling network to be completely separate from the data network.

CCS allows advanced network features, such as toll-free calling, to be implemented. For example, a toll-free number on the network translates into the actual number required (seamlessly to a user); this is achieved by the separation of the signaling to allow this number translation/lookup functionality.

SS6 and SS7 are the two main CCS methods in use, and they provide access to supplementary services such as call forwarding; typically, these supplementary services are implemented differently from one telecom provider to another, so the signaling boundary tends to be at the provider level—that is, the specific code used to enable call forwarding is different on Verizon than on AT&T. Typically, these codes are difficult to remember unless frequently used. This is an area where the user interface within the Skype for Business client excels, by removing this complexity from the user; you simply point and click.

Circuit-switched networks work on the principle that the intelligence is in the network rather than the endpoint, meaning that the availability of the network nodes is critical, which implies that added expenses will be accrued to ensure that the network nodes are always available.

Packet-Switched Networks

Packet-switched networks work on the assumption that the intelligence is in the endpoint and the network is purely a routing mechanism. The Internet is the largest public packet-switched network in the world. As mentioned, data networks are bursty, going from busy to idle to busy. Using dedicated circuits to handle this type of traffic wastes resources. By separating the data into sections (packets) and transmitting them separately, you can better utilize resources by mixing packets from multiple sources being sent to multiple destinations through the same resources. The result is a smoother distribution of data. Each packet is tagged with the destination address in the header and sent to the first network node (router). The router analyzes the packet header to determine the route (the next network node) and forwards the packet to this intermediate point. This process is repeated until the packet arrives at its destination, where the packet header is removed and the data remains. (This description is somewhat simplified, but the outlines should be clear.)

Some of the routers may be visible to route analysis, but with *virtual circuits* many more routers may be hidden behind the physical route. *Virtual circuits* can appear similar to a circuit-switched network because they seem to provide a point-to-point link (remember the string from the tin cans?) between two networks. Virtual circuits can be permanent connections or temporary, where the first packet will establish the link and the final one will disconnect it.

Pros and Cons of Virtual Circuits

Virtual circuits can be beneficial because they ensure that all packets travel the same path. This means that all traffic is likely to suffer the same delays because of the underlying network conditions, resulting in all traffic being treated equally. However, this consistency comes at a cost: The network will need more resources to ensure that the state is kept.

Like circuit-switched networks, virtual circuits must be established, a task that has an associated delay, and interruptions to the network nodes in the underlying infrastructure will result in interruption to the virtual circuit, requiring the establishment of a new one. Additionally, if a virtual circuit cannot be established end to end, the connection will not be established.

Without the virtual circuit overhead, packets are dynamically rerouted in the event of infrastructure problems, possibly introducing delays or even packet loss.

Pros and Cons of Packet Switching

The use of packet switching provides efficiency to the network, allowing better utilization of the available bandwidth by sharing resources. It also allows differing rates of bandwidth between networks. Routers naturally buffer incoming data, so the outgoing data rate may differ from the incoming; this allows multiple networks of differing speeds to be joined and still communicate with each other.

Packet-switching infrastructure is much cheaper than circuit-switching infrastructure; simply put, the packet-switched infrastructure reads the packet header and forwards it as appropriate, whereas a circuit-switched infrastructure must keep the state of all packets (resulting in more resource overhead, which results in more expense).

However, the delay introduced by analyzing every packet is a weakness compared to circuit switching; with circuit switching, once a connection is established, the data is simply switched from one circuit to another. Compounded with this delay is the queue delay introduced while the packet is being received and waiting to be transmitted. Later, you'll see that this can be mitigated by assigning priorities to packets, but in busy networks, queues can still introduce significant delay.

Finally, every packet has a header attached, adding to the data to be transmitted. The actual impact here depends on the overall packet size because the headers will typically be the same size, resulting in greater overhead if smaller packet sizes are used.

Early packet-switched networks were based on X.25 (for the access signaling) and X.75 (for the trunk signaling). The Internet is based on Internet Protocol (IP), defined in Request for Comments (RFC) 791.

Requests for Comments

Requests for Comments are memos published by the Internet Engineering Task Force (IETF) that describe methods and innovations applicable to the working of the Internet and Internet-type systems.

continues

continued

RFCs started as a document circulated among the early pioneers of the Internet (ARPANET) in 1969. As each document was circulated and feedback generated, it eventually became a standard ensuring the interoperability and communications on the Internet as we know it today. Indeed, the RFC process continues to develop new standards. Although not all RFCs become standards, they will be designated as one of the following:

- Informational
- Experimental
- Best Current Practice
- Standards Track
- Historic

The *Standards Track* can be further broken down into these categories:

- Proposed Standard
- Draft Standard
- Internet Standard

Each RFC is uniquely identified by its number, and each RFC may refer to previous RFCs to expand or even deprecate that piece of work.

Later in this chapter, you'll see that SIP is a combination of multiple RFCs, some of which are still in the draft stage.

Not all RFCs are serious documents; almost every year since 1989 (and first appearing in 1978), April 1 has seen at least one humorous RFC released. (Indeed, we suspect that some tangled networks are genuine implementations of A Standard for the Transmission of IP Datagrams on Avian Carriers, RFC 1149—or, Internet by homing pigeon.)

You can find RFCs here:

`www.rfc-editor.org/rfc.html`

As described there, the IP layer traffic travels on top of many different types of underlying infrastructure, and when IP is leveraged as the common infrastructure platform, endpoints can easily communicate with various applications and services. Chapter 7, "Planning Your Deployment," discusses the additional network services that Skype for Business Server 2015 relies on; the use of the common IP networking stack allows these services to interoperate easily.

The main IP network relies on the assumptions that intelligent endpoints run the applications and a dumb network is simply routing the packets to their destination. Current-generation IP routers can obviously provide much more functionality than simple routing, such as packet inspection and firewalls; however, the principle of the dumb network remains!

Internet Protocol makes the network almost stateless; that is, the state of each packet is not stored, only the state of routes. By doing so, it allows high availability to be achieved because there are multiple routes to a destination. In the event of a failure on one circuit, traffic is simply rerouted to another. For example, what would you do if you encountered road maintenance on your commute to work? You would take a different route to the same destination, of course. However, taking a different route would be much more difficult by train than by car. Provision of multiple paths is much easier (and cheaper) than trying to ensure that equipment is always available. IP is considered to be layer 3 in the standard seven-layer Open Systems Interconnection (OSI) network model, illustrated in Figure 2.6. Each layer in the OSI model can request services only from the layer below it. The contents of the layer above become the *payload* of the lower layer and are encapsulated with headers (and/or footers), enabling onward routing to the final destination.

FIGURE 2.6
OSI Network layer model

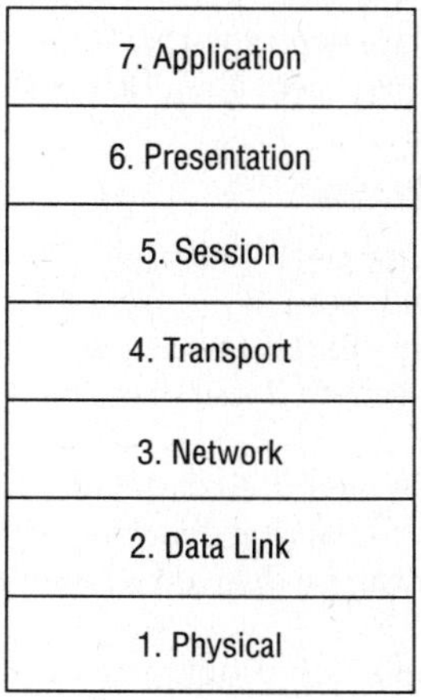

7. Application
6. Presentation
5. Session
4. Transport
3. Network
2. Data Link
1. Physical

At the destination, the reverse occurs, where each layer will inspect and remove the headers/footers and pass the data up to the layer above it.

Some named protocol definitions comprise more than one layer; for example, Ethernet is both layer 1 and layer 2.

Here are examples of what you would find at each layer:

- Physical cable layout, pins, voltages, and so on
- Physical addressing, such as MAC address
- Routing protocols; logical addressing, such as X.25
- Flow control and reliability functionality, such as TCP and UDP
- Full-duplex or half-duplex
- Establishment of context, such as XML
- Synchronization of communications and establishment of resources, such as SIP

Transport Layer Protocols

The two Transport layer protocols you are interested in are Transport Control Protocol (TCP), RFC 793, and User Datagram Protocol (UDP), RFC 768. The difference between them is that TCP provides a reliable (or connection-oriented) connection. The traffic is acknowledged, and if any packets are not received or errors encountered, they will be retransmitted. The delay introduces an additional overhead to be considered. UDP is considered to use a *fire-and-forget* (or connectionless) approach, meaning that it cares only about transmitting the data. If it gets there, great; if it doesn't, the data is not retransmitted. There is no guarantee of delivery. Both TCP and UDP require the use of *port numbers* in addition to the IP address to route traffic correctly.

Consider the postal service analogy: You want to send a birthday card (packet) to a friend. For the birthday card to be correctly delivered, it would need a postal/ZIP code (consider this the IP address) and a house number (the port). Now, suppose you want to send some cash in the birthday card. You would then want to make sure the card was delivered, so you would require proof of delivery, such as with a registered letter. This is equivalent to TCP. On the other hand, if you aren't sending cash, you don't really care as much to confirm delivery; this is UDP.

Real-Time Data

Real-time (or very near real-time) transmission is required for two-way audio and video communications and as such imposes different engineering considerations than non-real-time communications. For example, a delay of minutes when sending an email is typically not significant, whereas a delay of even a second or two can make a conversation (audio or video) unbearable.

As previously mentioned, delay can occur at many points throughout the transmission of audio (or video) data; this delay is normally measured in milliseconds. At a certain point, traffic received can be delayed so much that it is no longer useful and the delay can no longer be ignored.

Both UDP and TCP provide mechanisms to ensure that packets arrive in the correct order when they are received. These ordering mechanisms guarantee only that the packets are replayed in the correct order, not that they appear on time. Packets that arrive late are ignored; however, there are mechanisms within Skype for Business that attempt to cover up these missing packets, as discussed in the section "Understanding Skype for Business Codecs and Standards" later in this chapter.

When packets are not received in a regular pattern (they may be out of order, or there may be variations in the time to transmit and receive), this variation in the time to receive is called *jitter*, and the amount of jitter can differ based on many factors, such as the devices used for encoding as well as the routers and switches in the network path. The amount of jitter is not necessarily the same for both endpoints involved in a call.

The Jitter Buffer

With the Real-Time Transport Protocol (RTP), RFC 1889, a jitter buffer is used to attempt to reduce the delay introduced by the different processing required in transmission (if the delay time exceeds the size of the jitter buffer, packets will be lost). The receiving system buffers the incoming data to allow some delay, resulting in the appearance of no delay to the user listening (or watching) because the stream will appear to have a continuous playback. Figure 2.7 shows the impact of the jitter buffer as traffic is sent, received, and played back.

From this example, you can see that the packets are sent in an orderly fashion; however, some delays are incurred through the transmission. Packets 2, 4, and 6 are beginning to be received before the previous packet has finished, and packet 7 actually arrives after packet 8.

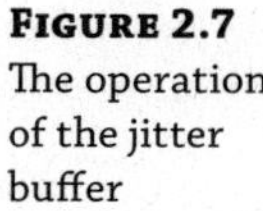

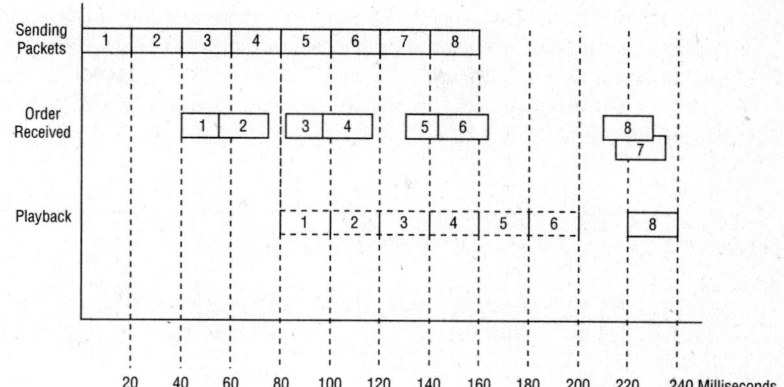

FIGURE 2.7
The operation of the jitter buffer

The jitter buffer allows a way to store these packets until the correct time for them to be played back. Unfortunately, packet 7 arrives after it is due to be played, so it is useless. Dealing with this is where the codecs may differ in approach—some may replay the previous packet, while others may attempt to "guess" what the packet contained. Remember that individually these packets are only 20ms in duration, so they are extremely difficult to detect by the human ear.

The jitter buffer size may change throughout the course of a call (this is automatic) but is likely to be around 40ms in most cases for Skype for Business Server 2015.

Synchronization of Traffic

Until now we've mentioned audio and video separately but have not covered that each is actually a separate media stream in its own right. This provides an additional level of complexity because you have to ensure that the audio and video are synchronized—after all, they were when they were captured at the sender endpoint. However, because they are two separate streams, there is no guarantee that the traffic has followed the same route from source to destination, and indeed Skype for Business Server 2015 provides the capability to prioritize each traffic stream (modality) separately.

Real-Time Transport Control Protocol (RTCP), RFC 1889, is used to associate the time stamps of the data packets with the actual time points in the session. RTCP is also used to track the quality of the RTP transmission, measuring the number of lost packets, total delays, and jitter.

Quality of Service

Being able to prioritize traffic on a network allows you to guarantee a level of traffic delivery. In a busy network, it's a good idea to prioritize voice traffic over file copy traffic, thereby ensuring that the network routers keep any delays to the voice traffic to an absolute minimum. This will result in a longer time to copy a file, but it will at least allow an understandable conversation.

There are two methods to enable Quality of Service (QoS) on a network.

- Integrated Services, RFC 1633
- Differentiated Services, RFC 2475

Skype for Business Server 2015 supports only the use of Differentiated Services, by marking packets using a Differentiated Services Code Point (DSCP)—effectively, an additional flag in the packet header.

Skype for Business Server 2015 allows you to apply a different packet marker to each modality, as shown in Table 2.1.

TABLE 2.1: Default DSCP marking per modality

MEDIA TYPE	DEFAULT PER-HOP BEHAVIOR	QUEUING AND DROPPING	NOTES
Audio	EF	Priority Queue	Low loss, low latency, low jitter, assured bandwidth. Pair with wide area network (WAN) bandwidth policies on constrained links.
Video	AF41	BW Queue + DSCP WRED	Class 4. Low drop priority. Pair with WAN bandwidth policies on constrained links.
SIP signaling	CS3	BW Queue	Class 3. Bandwidth allocation should be sufficient to avoid drops.
App sharing	AF21	BW Queue + DSCP WRED	Class 2. Low drop priority. Pair with end-user policy caps.
File transfer	AF11	BW Queue + DSCP WRED	Class 1. Low drop priority. Pair with end-user policy caps.

The Default Per-Hop Behavior column indicates the DSCP tag applied to the packet (a numeric value provides further differentiation where listed):

- *EF*: Expedited Forwarding, RFC 2598.
- *AF*: Assured Forwarding, RFC 2597.
- *CS*: Class.
- *Numeric value*: When associated with the same DSCP text, a higher value indicates a higher priority.

It is important to understand that when QoS is used on a network, the same configuration must be on all routers and switches in the path of the traffic; otherwise, the correct priority will fail to be applied at one (or more) hops, thereby introducing unwanted delay.

Session Description Protocol

Session Description Protocol (SDP, RFC 2327) provides the information required to enable a media session to be encoded for transmission; it also provides the receiving endpoint with the information required to decode. In many cases, SDP is used to notify users of upcoming Internet broadcasts (webcasts).

It provides the ability to negotiate information such as IP and port addresses, media codecs used, and authentication, and it can be extended further to future needs through the a= information lines.

The SDP syntax is text-based and consists of lines of human-readable text, providing an easy-to-understand view for troubleshooting. A sample session (taken from the RFC document) is shown here:

```
v=0
o=mhandley 2890844526 2890842807 IN IP4 126.16.64.4
s=SDP Seminar
i=A Seminar on the session description protocol
u=http://www.cs.ucl.ac.uk/staff/M.Handley/sdp.03.ps
e=mjh@isi.edu (Mark Handley)
c=IN IP4 224.2.17.12/127
t=2873397496 2873404696
a=recvonly
m=audio 49170 RTP/AVP 0
m=video 51372 RTP/AVP 31
m=application 32416
```

From this sample, you can immediately discern (or at least make an educated guess at) some of the values of this media stream before even knowing what the field identifiers are. Here is a list of some of these values:

- *Subject*: `s=SDP Seminar`
- *Information*: `I = A Seminar on the session description protocol`
- *Email*: `e=mjh@isi.edu (Mark Handley)`
- *Media*: `m=audio/m=video/m=application`

The following values taken from the RFC show the valid session description identifiers for SDP; for further descriptions of the fields, see the RFC document (any value marked * is optional):

```
v= (protocol version)
o= (owner/creator and session identifier)
s= (session name)
i=* (session information)
u=* (URI of description)
e=* (email address)
p=* (phone number)
c=* (connection information - not required if included in all media)
b=* (bandwidth information)
```

```
z=* (time zone adjustments)
k=* (encryption key)
a=* (zero or more session attribute lines)
t= (time the session is active)
r=* (zero or more repeat times)
m= (media name and transport address)
i=* (media title)
c=* (connection information - optional if included at session-level)
b=* (bandwidth information)
k=* (encryption key)
a=* (zero or more media attribute lines)
```

The Session Initiation Protocol in Depth

What is commonly referred to as Session Initiation Protocol is more accurately known as SIPv2. The first version (SIPv1) was submitted to the Internet Engineering Task Force as a draft standard for session establishment and was called Session Invitation Protocol. Its job was done once the users joined the session, relying on something like SDP to continue control of the established session. SIPv1, which was created by Mark Handley and Eve Schooler, was UDP-based.

At the same time, another draft standard, Simple Conference Invitation Protocol (SCIP), was also submitted to the IETF by Henning Schulzrinne. SCIP used an approach similar to Hypertext Transfer Protocol (HTTP) for communication and defined a new method to continue the session controls. SCIP was based on TCP.

The outcome of these two proposals was SIPv2, which is based on HTTP but able to use both UDP and TCP. For the remainder of this book, we'll use *SIP* to refer to SIPv2.

RFC 2543 describes the basics of SIP; however, a number of extensions have been defined in other RFCs. In the following list, the values in parentheses indicate the SIP message defined in the RFC:

- RFC 2976 (`INFO`)
- RFC 3261 (`ACK`, `BYE`, `CANCEL`, `INVITE`, `OPTIONS`, `REGISTER`)
- RFC 3262 (`PRACK`)
- RFC 3265 (`SUBSCRIBE`, `NOTIFY`)
- RFC 3311 (`UPDATE`)
- RFC 3428 (`MESSAGE`)
- RFC 3515 (`REFER`)
- RFC 3903 (`PUBLISH`)

Each of these extensions shows how flexible SIP is with its ability to operate with early implementations while bringing new functionality to bear where possible. The flip side of this extensibility is that it can be difficult to fully define which version of SIP is actually implemented by an application. Later, you'll learn how you can query an application (or endpoint) to see what is supported.

In addition, Microsoft has provided extensions to the Lync Server 2010 (and subsequently both Lync Server 2013 and Skype for Business Server 2015) implementation of SIP in the form of message headers, which are all prefixed with `ms-`. These extensions, which we'll discuss shortly, are supported only within Skype for Business and Lync Server (both 2010 and 2013). Although some of them may become standard in a future version, they do not provide any interoperability with other systems at this point.

From this point on, we will focus on the Microsoft implementation of SIPv2 and the architecture within Skype for Business Server 2015 (although in most cases this is also relevant to both previous versions of Lync Server); if you want a wider understanding, please refer to the RFC documentation.

Using SIP

In its basic form, SIP is used to create, modify, and end individual sessions between users (or a user and a server). Let's say Linda wants to call Keith. At a high level, SIP would begin this process with an `INVITE` message and finish with a `BYE` message. However, prior to the `INVITE`, both Linda and Keith would have to issue `REGISTER` messages to the server, providing the address information for the client on which they are logged in. During the message exchange, there are likely to be several `ACK` messages and possibly more `INVITE` messages if the call were to change from one device to another or additional functionality were added (such as video or desktop sharing).

SIP is a request-and-response protocol similar to HTTP (on which it is based), meaning that for every request sent out, a response is expected, and within these responses are human-readable *reason phrases*. As you might expect, the response codes are similar to HTTP codes, and many will be familiar—for example, `404 Not found`.

Table 2.2 shows the response classes and some common examples.

TABLE 2.2: SIP responses

RANGE	RESPONSE CLASS	EXAMPLES
100–199	Informational	`100 Trying` `180 Ringing`
200–299	Success	`200 OK`
300–399	Redirection	`301 Moved permanently` `302 Moved temporarily`
400–499	Client error	`401 Unauthorized` `404 Not found`
500–599	Server error	`500 Internal server error` `502 Bad gateway`
600–699	Global error	`600 Busy everywhere`

The SIP requests each have a different purpose (some are paired) and, as mentioned previously, have been implemented through many additional extensions and new RFCs. We'll cover each of them in turn now.

INVITE The INVITE message is the initiation of a SIP session, an invitation from one user to another (or more) to begin a communications method. This will precede any modality, and indeed changing modalities will require additional INVITEs to be sent for each modality. The SDP carried in the INVITE will detail the actual session modality information, and further communications will establish the connection points for the session.

Figure 2.8 shows the INVITE message in the ladder diagram format commonly used to illustrate SIP flows; the latest version of the Skype for Business log analysis tool (snooper.exe) includes the capability to generate a ladder diagram from the log files. You'll see more of this in Chapter 15, "Troubleshooting."

FIGURE 2.8 An INVITE ladder diagram

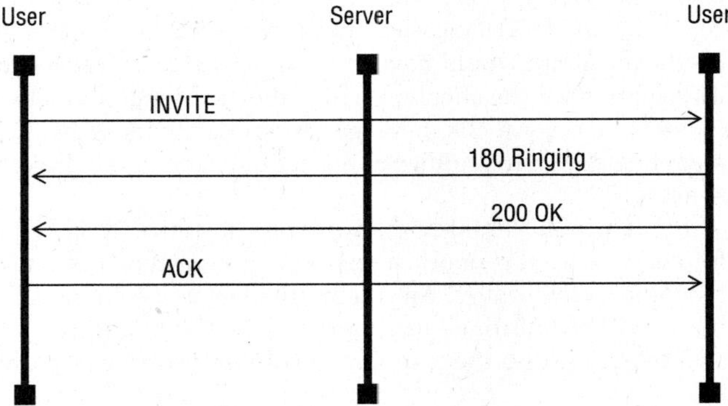

The 180 Ringing response shown here is an informational response, and there is no expectation or guarantee of informational responses being received. When the remote user accepts the request, a 200 OK response is sent.

INFORMATIONAL RESPONSES

The SIP protocol defines that there is no guarantee of informational responses being received and that connections using it should not rely on such data. However, when TCP is used as the transport, as with the Microsoft implementation, there is a guaranteed response, and Microsoft has included additional useful troubleshooting information in these responses. These additional headers are prefixed with ms- (for example, ms-received-port and ms-received-cid).

ACK The ACK shown in Figure 2.8 is the acknowledgement of the INVITE from the *initiating* user. It is required because the INVITE message may take longer than expected to receive a response. INVITE is the initiation of a session; at this point the location of the recipient endpoints is not known, and the user may not be nearby, resulting in a delay in the acceptance of the call.

In a scenario with multiple receiving endpoints (forking), multiple responses will be received, and each response needs to be acknowledged. This is partly a remainder from the initial SIPv1 implementation, in which the expectation was to use UDP, an unreliable transport protocol.

An ACK message also allows additional information to be sent within its SDP.

CANCEL The CANCEL message is used to cancel any pending INVITEs. As you can see in Figure 2.9, a CANCEL message is acknowledged through the separate cancellation message (487 Transaction cancelled); this is to accommodate the case where the 200 OK response and the CANCEL happen to cross paths on the network. Finally, even though the INVITE is cancelled, an ACK message is sent to acknowledge the 200 OK response.

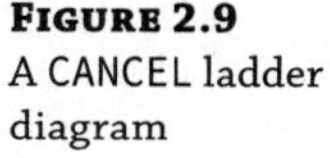

FIGURE 2.9 A CANCEL ladder diagram

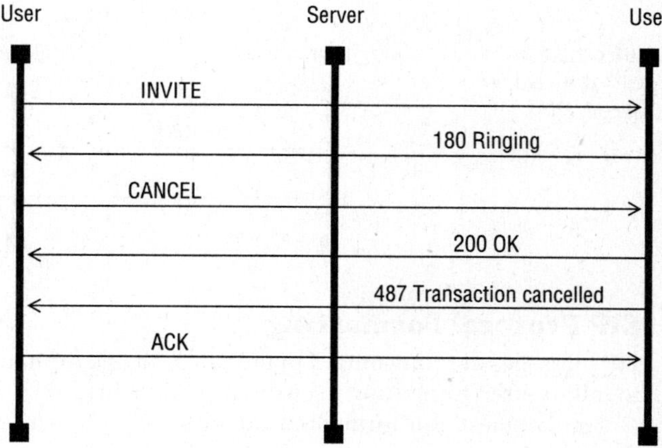

BYE A BYE message is used to disconnect an established session. Figure 2.10 shows the SIP ladder diagram including the BYE.

FIGURE 2.10 A BYE ladder diagram

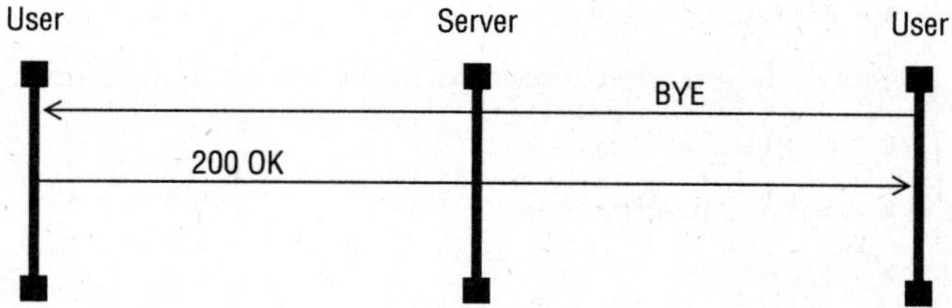

REGISTER A REGISTER is used to inform the server of the location of a user endpoint. Skype for Business Server 2015 supports Multiple Points of Presence (MPOP), and this requires each endpoint to uniquely provide its location (IP address) so that follow-up messages (INVITE, SUBSCRIBE, or OPTION) can be directed to each endpoint on which the user is logged in. Figure 2.11 shows a ladder diagram for REGISTER.

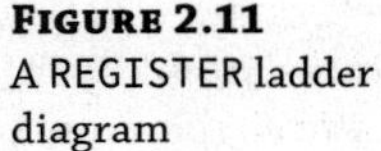

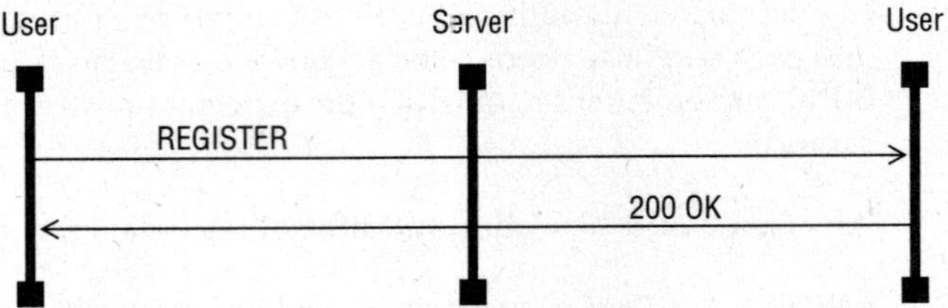

FIGURE 2.11
A REGISTER ladder diagram

OPTIONS OPTIONS messages provide the capability to query an endpoint (including a server) for the functionality it supports. This is how different SIP applications can still function with differing implementations of the SIP standard. Figure 2.12 shows the ladder diagram, and in this case the `200 - OK` response will include the data of the capabilities provided.

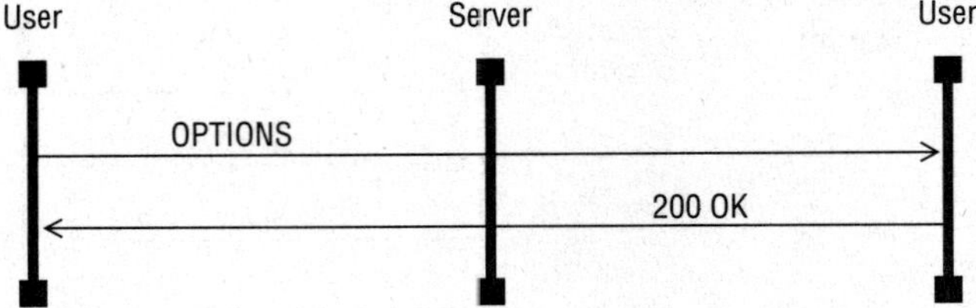

FIGURE 2.12
An OPTIONS ladder diagram

SIP Protocol Formatting

SIP messages are transmitted in human-readable format; however, this means they are required to follow strict formatting to ensure functionality.

For a request, this format is as follows:

- Request line
- Several header lines
- Empty line
- Message body

Similarly, a response consists of the following elements:

- Status line
- Several header lines
- Empty line
- Message body

The request line comprises the request, request URI, and finally the version, as shown here:

```
INVITE sip:Linda.lync@rlscomms.info SIP/2.0
```

The response line consists of simply the version, response code, and reason phrase:

```
SIP/2.0 180 Ringing
```

There are many available header lines, and some of the more interesting standard ones are listed here:

- `Accept`
- `Alert-info`
- `Authorization`
- `Call-ID`
- `Contact`
- `Content-length`
- `Content-type`
- `Cseq`
- `Date`
- `Encryption`
- `Error-Info`
- `From`
- `In-reply-to`
- `Max-forwards`
- `Record-Route`
- `Route`
- `Server`
- `Subject`
- `Supported`
- `Timestamp`
- `To`
- `User-agent`
- `Via`

However, headers can be extended, and as mentioned, Microsoft has added many customized headers, all beginning with `ms-`. It's worth looking at some of the more useful headers in more detail. Understanding them will dramatically help you when troubleshooting (see Chapter 15 for more information). Here are a few of the standard headers explained:

`Call-ID` The `Call-ID` header is unique for each SIP session; it allows the flow of a single session to be monitored across several servers and indeed different systems, ensuring consistency and ease of troubleshooting.

If an original call is transferred, the `Call-ID` header is changed, and if multiple calls are merged, a new `Call-ID` header is also generated.

`Contact` The `Contact` header is similar to the `From` header except that it contains the specific IP address and port information for which the user/endpoint can be contacted. This becomes extremely useful when you're dealing with a forked session, which will be delivered to multiple endpoints; you can uniquely identify each one.

`Cseq` The Command Sequence (`Cseq`) header is used to keep track of individual requests within a session. For example, the first `INVITE` will be

```
Cseq: 1 INVITE
```

The corresponding `200 OK` response will include this `Cseq` value also. If the session is modified to include additional modalities, the next `INVITE` will be

```
Cseq: 2 INVITE
```

(and it will have a corresponding `200 OK` response). If there are any delays in the first `200 OK` response, the `Cseq` value will indicate which `INVITE` is being referenced.

The `ACK` message will always have the same `Cseq` value as the `INVITE` to which it corresponds, as will any `CANCEL` request. Other request messages will have an incremented `Cseq` value.

`From` This header is the SIP URI for the user sending the message, similar to the From field in an email.

```
From: "Linda Lync"<sip:linda@rlscomms.info>;tag=0769872b19;epid=2b663e94f4
```

`Record-Route/Route/Via` These three headers indicate the routing through which the SIP message has traversed in terms of SIP proxy servers. The `Record-Route` header indicates a proxy server that must remain in the return route. This may be for security reasons, where a specific path is required.

The `Route` header provides the return path, without forcing a specific route hop by hop.

The `Via` header is used to detect routing loops; it stores each proxy that has handled the request, as shown in this example:

```
Record-Route: <sip:SE01.rlscomms.info:5061;transport=tls;opaque=state:T:F:Ci.
R1364600;lr;ms-route-sig=fbsuOh4pZ0b5QPLATntawrW1TbzxFmaEBIc0Qsh89ClfyeUtcgv8L
q1QAA>;tag=2EC6A1159F9FC738075EDD59C27F45C0

Via: SIP/2.0/TLS
192.168.2.4:5061;branch=z9hG4bK1AEEEECC.20D7529ED18C1AF6;branched=FALSE;
ms-internal-info="baRiub04VXxb6vw502CuXS9lPngcMAbhMUPLl9C6gLAzieUtcgkpDG4wAA"
```

`To` This header is the SIP URI for the recipient of the message, similar to the To field in an email.

```
To: <sip:keith@rlscomms.info>;epid=7f3d62f538
```

Providing Presence

So far you've seen how to register (REGISTER) your endpoints and invite (INVITE) sessions. However, you haven't looked at one of the key features of Skype for Business Server 2015 (and previous versions, including Lync, LCS, and OCS), which is also implemented via SIP: presence.

Presence in the user sense is the availability and willingness of a user to communicate. Technically, it is the functionality behind knowing how available or how busy a user is. When a user is logged in with multiple sessions, a level of aggregation is provided so that other users will see only the result of this presence, not each individual state. The two SIP messages SUBSCRIBE and NOTIFY are used to indicate this functionality.

NOTIFY is used to update the presence state of an endpoint to the server, and within Skype for Business Server 2015 an aggregation script runs to provide a final updated result of the user's presence based on this change.

For example, assume a user is logged in on both a laptop and a Phone Edition device. If the user picks up the phone and dials a number, the status of the phone device becomes *busy* (or more accurately *in a call*); at the same time, the user is no longer using the laptop client, so this client changes to *away*. Any other users who have this user in their own buddy list will simply see the status to be *in a call*; there is no indication of the second client (on the laptop) and certainly no indication of the user being *away*. The Skype for Business Server 2015 server is responsible for this aggregation of presence from all the endpoints and provision of the data out to other users. In fact, the client (on the laptop) will show *in a call* as the aggregated presence update and will also feed back to the user on all logged-in clients.

For a user to receive presence updates of contacts (buddies), the contacts must be added to the *contacts list* on the client (see Chapter 4, "Desktop Clients," for further information). The background SIP message used by the client is SUBSCRIBE. This message contains the SIP URI of the user whose presence is to be added to the contacts list.

For presence information outside the client, an ad hoc request is created for a single view of presence; this is typically the case for email messages or SharePoint sites where the users involved are not necessarily on the contacts list.

After logging in to the Skype for Business Server 2015 client and downloading the contacts list from the server, a *batch subscription* is requested for all the users listed in the contacts list. A batch subscription also sets up a request for permanent updates to any of the presence states of the contacts on the contacts list.

Figure 2.13 shows the ladder view when multiple users log in, change state, and subscribe to presence. Notice that the users also subscribe to their own presence state.

Sending an Instant Message

After presence updates, sending instant messages (IMs) is probably the second most popular SIP feature.

Once you have identified the user you want to send a message to, the new IM window will open so that you can type the message. At this point, in the background you will have already logged in (REGISTER) and received the presence status of the user (SUBSCRIBE, NOTIFY). Not surprisingly, the MESSAGE request is used to process the sending and receiving of IMs.

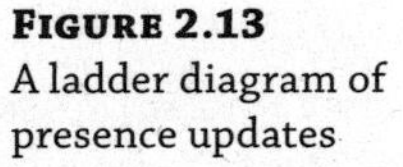

FIGURE 2.13
A ladder diagram of presence updates

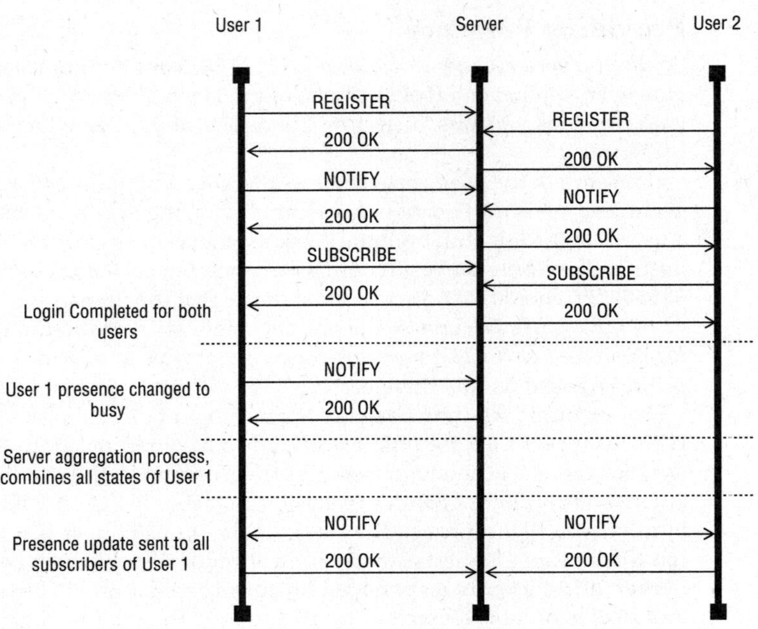

The content (SDP) of the `MESSAGE` is not visible within the logs of the client (or server) for privacy reasons. Figure 2.14 shows the SIP message exchange process in ladder format.

FIGURE 2.14
A ladder diagram for sending an IM

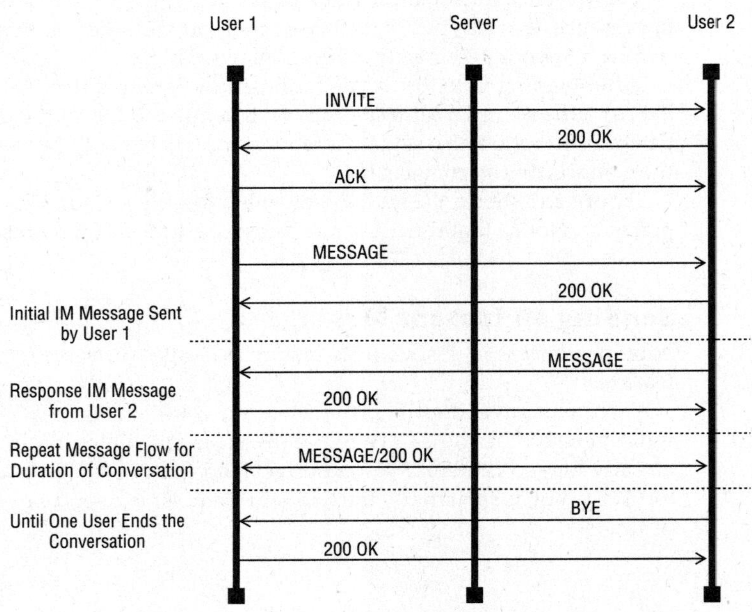

Understanding Skype for Business Codecs and Standards

So far you've looked at SIP's background and how SIP is used to provide the IM and presence functionality in Skype for Business Server 2015. Obviously, Skype for Business Server 2015 (like its predecessors of both versions of Lync and OCS) extends the client functionality beyond IM and presence to include peer-to-peer desktop sharing, voice, and video as well as conferencing versions of all of these. These features are not just for internal communication; the Edge server provides the same client functionality to remote users in a secure way. All of these extensions to SIP are implemented in Lync using the codecs we'll discuss next.

Call Admission Control (CAC) can be used to control which codecs are available for communications between endpoints; for more information, see Chapter 17, "Call Admission Control."

Using the Voice Codecs

Prior to Lync Server 2010, with all other factors being ignored (network capacity, jitter, and so on), the default codec for peer-to-peer calling was Real-Time Audio (RTAudio); with Lync Server 2010 onward, the preferred codec was G711. With Skype for Business Server 2015 this changes again to SILK. From the session setup perspective, the codec used is irrelevant because it is negotiated (via the SDP content) in the initial `INVITE`, as shown in the following example log:

```
From: <sip:linda@rlscomms.info>;tag=da0cb8559f;epid=2b663e94f4
To: <sip:keith@rlscomms.info>
Call-ID: ed775704eb7e4c2ba2669bd829f22f87
CSeq: 1 INVITE
Contact: <sip:linda@rlscomms.info;opaque=user:epid:
 0gl4pEfyilmmUkY7R1Tx3wAA;gruu>
User-Agent: UCCAPI/15.0.4745.1000 OC/15.0.4745.1000
(Skype for Business)
Supported: ms-dialog-route-set-update
Ms-Conversation-ID: AdDY6gKCF/1OjtDGQNGW34h895fM6QAAMR8gAAEONlA=
Supported: timer
Supported: histinfo
Supported: ms-safe-transfer
Supported: ms-sender
Supported: ms-early-media
Supported: 100rel
ms-keep-alive: UAC;hop-hop=yes
Allow: INVITE, BYE, ACK, CANCEL, INFO, UPDATE, REFER, NOTIFY,
BENOTIFY, OPTIONS
ms-subnet: 192.168.2.0
Accept-Language: en-US
ms-endpoint-location-data: NetworkScope;
ms-media-location-type=Intranet
P-Preferred-Identity: <sip:linda@rlscomms.info>
Supported: replaces
Supported: ms-conf-invite
Proxy-Authorization: TLS-DSK qop="auth",
realm="SIP Communications Service", opaque="FCED8216",
targetname="SE01.rlscomms.info", crand="082c2a64", cnum="37",
response="e26776a9b787683d59144576aa44f53d29be122b"
Content-Type: multipart/alternative;boundary="----=_NextPart_000_0003_01D0D8F7.63
072A00"
```

```
Content-Length: 3373

------=_NextPart_000_0003_01D0D8F7.63072A00
Content-Type: application/sdp
Content-Transfer-Encoding: 7bit
Content-ID: <c093d767316aeb5e274e1d4ed325f3f4@rlscomms.info>
Content-Disposition: session; handling=optional;
ms-proxy-2007fallback
v=0
o=- 0 0 IN IP4 192.168.2.100
s=session
c=IN IP4 192.168.2.100
b=CT:99980
t=0 0
m=audio 1428 RTP/SAVP 104 114 9 112 111 0 103 8 116 115 97 13 118 101
a=candidate:tY4RlVeEewWZvG55t3EjhqhpefVE0AtSSqVy3dHrxL8 1
 AfThflFD58OIwk5yPc/jNg UDP 0.830 192.168.2.100 1428
a=candidate:tY4RlVeEewWZvG55t3EjhqhpefVE0AtSSqVy3dHrxL8 2
 AfThflFD58OIwk5yPc/jNg UDP 0.830 192.168.2.100 1429
a=cryptoscale:1 client AES_CM_128_HMAC_SHA1_80 inline:
 LkKRJ+CERcnKhuc69bJ7cu8KJS7bCfXNB916gAbX|2^31|1:1
a=crypto:2 AES_CM_128_HMAC_SHA1_80 inline:
 x3ov05YkeSpo6WyXGaFcBofHzhqHS83z88Ga+FOV|2^31|1:1
a=crypto:3 AES_CM_128_HMAC_SHA1_80 inline:
 ILDqxpOMP+++qVqK/JNd0x3gzaDBBOLXBvNpnlA6|2^31
a=maxptime:200
a=rtpmap:104 SILK/16000
a=fmtp:104 useinbandfec=1; usedtx=0
a=rtpmap:114 x-msrta/16000
a=fmtp:114 bitrate=29000
a=rtpmap:9 G722/8000
a=rtpmap:112 G7221/16000
a=fmtp:112 bitrate=24000
a=rtpmap:111 SIREN/16000
a=fmtp:111 bitrate=16000
a=rtpmap:0 PCMU/8000
a=rtpmap:103 SILK/8000
a=fmtp:103 useinbandfec=1; usedtx=0
a=rtpmap:8 PCMA/8000
a=rtpmap:116 AAL2-G726-32/8000
a=rtpmap:115 x-msrta/8000
a=fmtp:115 bitrate=11800
a=rtpmap:97 RED/8000
a=rtpmap:13 CN/8000
a=rtpmap:118 CN/16000
a=rtpmap:101 telephone-event/8000
a=fmtp:101 0-16
a=ptime:20
```

```
--=_NextPart_000_0003_01D0D8F7.63072A00
Content-Type: application/sdp
Content-Transfer-Encoding: 7bit
Content-ID: <a56e0679947ecb81ab15c7059a7c2921@rlscomms.info>
Content-Disposition: session; handling=optional
v=0
o=- 0 1 IN IP4 192.168.2.100
s=session
c=IN IP4 192.168.2.100
b=CT:99980
t=0 0
a=x-devicecaps:audio:recv;video:recv
m=audio 10356 RTP/SAVP 104 114 9 112 111 0 103 8 116 115 97 13 118 101
a=x-ssrc-range:1477293568-1477293568
a=rtcp-fb:* x-message app send:dsh recv:dsh
a=rtcp-rsize
a=label:main-audio
a=x-source:main-audio
a=ice-ufrag:sNmC
a=ice-pwd:60AopH/NgeBvfqJicVoQkPD2
a=candidate:1 1 UDP 2130706431 192.168.2.100 10356 typ host
a=candidate:1 2 UDP 2130705918 192.168.2.100 10357 typ host
a=candidate:2 1 TCP-ACT 1684798975 192.168.2.100 10356 typ srflx
 raddr 192.168.2.100 rport 10356
a=candidate:2 2 TCP-ACT 1684798462 192.168.2.100 10356 typ srflx
 raddr 192.168.2.100 rport 10356
a=cryptoscale:1 client AES_CM_128_HMAC_SHA1_80 inline:
 LkKRJ+CERcnKhuc69bJ7cu8KJS7bCfXNB916gAbX|2^31|1:1
a=crypto:2 AES_CM_128_HMAC_SHA1_80 inline:
 x3ov05YkeSpo6WyXGaFcBofHzhqHS83z88Ga+FOV|2^31|1:1
a=crypto:3 AES_CM_128_HMAC_SHA1_80 inline:
 ILDqxpOMP+++qVqK/JNd0x3gzaDBBOLXBvNpnlA6|2^31
a=maxptime:200
a=rtcp:10357
a=rtpmap:104 SILK/16000
a=fmtp:104 useinbandfec=1; usedtx=0
a=rtpmap:114 x-msrta/16000
a=fmtp:114 bitrate=29000
a=rtpmap:9 G722/8000
a=rtpmap:112 G7221/16000
a=fmtp:112 bitrate=24000
a=rtpmap:111 SIREN/16000
a=fmtp:111 bitrate=16000
a=rtpmap:0 PCMU/8000
a=rtpmap:103 SILK/8000
a=fmtp:103 useinbandfec=1; usedtx=0
a=rtpmap:8 PCMA/8000
a=rtpmap:116 AAL2-G726-32/8000
```

```
a=rtpmap:115 x-msrta/8000
a=fmtp:115 bitrate=11800
a=rtpmap:97 RED/8000
a=rtpmap:13 CN/8000
a=rtpmap:118 CN/16000
a=rtpmap:101 telephone-event/8000
a=fmtp:101 0-16
a=rtcp-mux
a=ptime:20
```

Here, you can see the `a=rtpmap` entries, listing each of the different codecs available; the value after the codec name is the sample rate used, so there may be multiple entries for the same codec but different sample rates (for example, `a=rtpmap:114 x-msrta/16000` and `a=rtpmap:115 x-msrta/8000`).

The line

```
m=audio 1428 RTP/SAVP 104 114 9 112 111 0 103 8 116 115 97 13 118 101
```

shows the order in which the codecs are negotiated, with each number corresponding directly to the number immediately after the `a=rtpmap` designator. This is not a codec selection preference order. You may notice that the first codec in the list is SILK.

The actual workings of the codec are the interesting parts, and you'll look at how generic codecs operate in the Skype for Business Server 2015 environment.

We've already discussed how the media stream is negotiated via SDP and is separate from the signaling. Skype for Business Server 2015 includes healing capability to allow recovery from the loss of packets, using Forward Error Correction (FEC). FEC is dynamic, so it will be in effect only when problems are detected on the network.

For example, consider the sound wave shown in Figure 2.15.

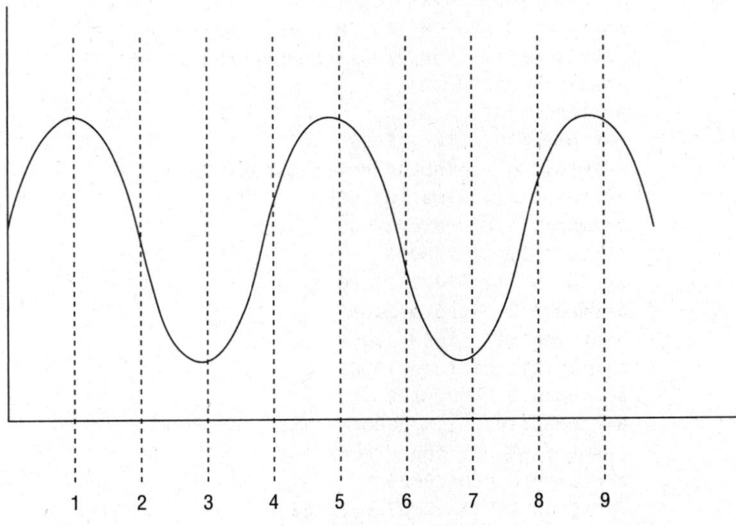

FIGURE 2.15
Input audio wave

The client will sample the input, in this example at a rate assumed to be 20ms per packet (shown in the previous trace with the `a=ptime:20` value), and it will output the data in a number of packets to be sent across the network (Figure 2.16).

FIGURE 2.16 Sampled data for packetization

1	2	3	4	5	6	7	8	9

Now suppose that a problem occurs on the network, resulting in packet loss, and some of the data is lost. At this point, the endpoints will be aware of the packet loss and implement FEC on the audio stream. This means that another copy of the previous packet will be sent with each actual packet (Figure 2.17).

FIGURE 2.17 Sampled data for packetization with FEC

2|1	3|2	4|3	5|4	6|5	7|6	8|7

This will result in additional data on the network; however, it compensates well for packet loss and allows the codec to "heal" the data into a more usable form. Figure 2.18 shows a comparison with and without FEC, assuming packet loss of packets 4 and 5.

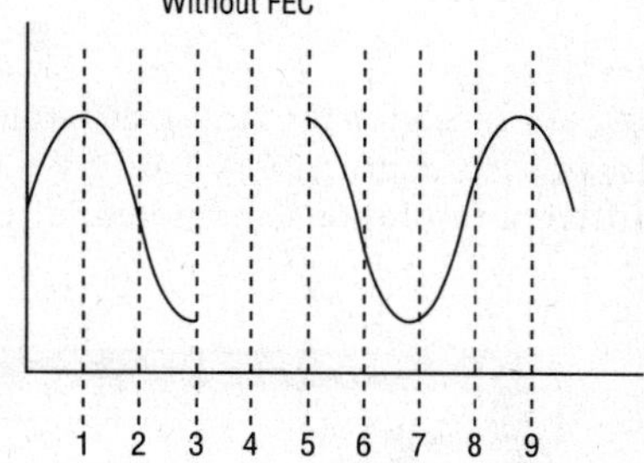

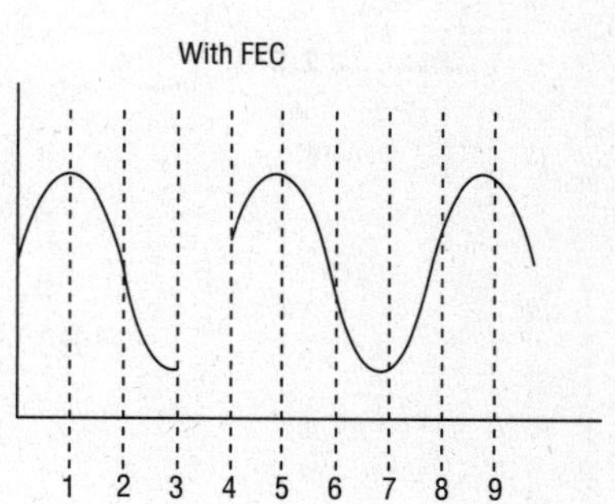

FIGURE 2.18 Received audio wave after packet loss (top); after packet loss using FEC (bottom)

Losing two consecutive packets with FEC means that the healing capability has to try to recover 40ms worth of data; on the other hand, using FEC means that you actually have the information for the second packet, thereby reducing the amount of data the healing algorithm needs to repair.

USING THE VIDEO CODECS

With Lync Server 2010 and video, there was a change only in the default supported resolution for conferencing, changing from Common Interchange Format (CIF) to Video Graphics Array (VGA). However, Lync Server 2013 introduced a new video codec that could dramatically expand the interoperability capabilities.

The announcement of H264 Advanced Video Coding/Scalable Video Coding (AVC/SVC) support in Lync 2013 was well received in the user communities but should equally be read with caution—there are many different variations of the H264 standard (of course!).

H264 in Skype for Business Server 2015 uses a layered approach to provide video streams to clients. Each layer builds on top of the previous layer with additional details. This allows multiple resolutions to be delivered without each having to be transcoded separately.

For example, layer 1 will be 15 frames per second (fps), and to provide 30fps at layer 2, layer 2 will include the additional 15fps (see Figure 2.19).

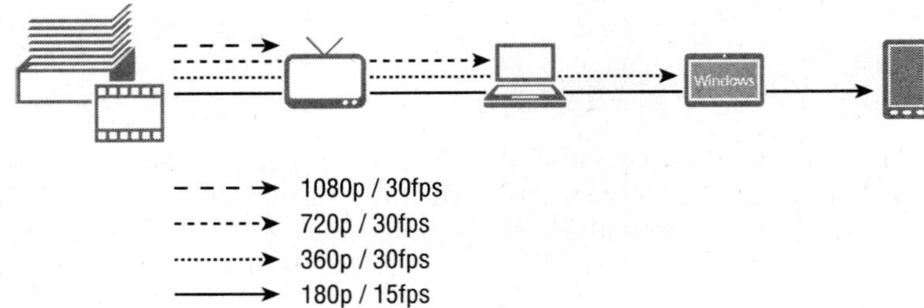

FIGURE 2.19 Video codec layering

In addition to the layering approach for providing different frame rates, different resolutions are provided in separate streams (see Figure 2.20). This gives the ability for a client to request multiple streams, each at different resolutions and potentially different layering as well.

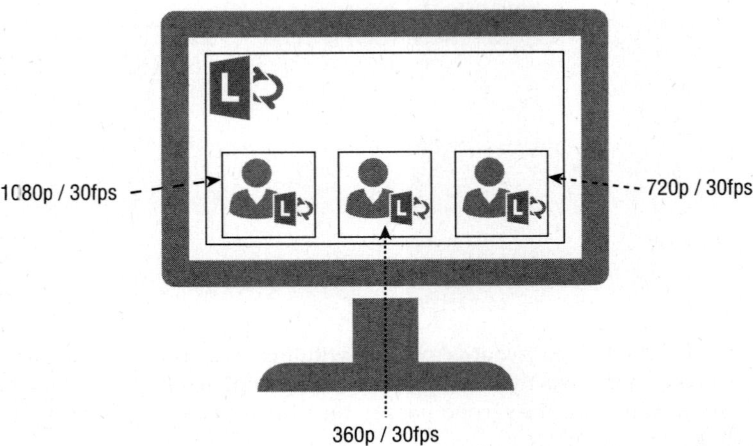

FIGURE 2.20 Video codec streaming

The Gallery View allows multiple separate video streams to been seen simultaneously, each of which could potentially be a different resolution (as mentioned in Chapter 1, "What's in Skype for Business 2015?"). Taking the approach of layering and streaming in the codec reduces the Media Conferencing Unit (MCU) to more of a relay role rather than a transcoding role as with previous versions of Lync and OCS. This allows for high resolution and potentially more users to be able to connect to a conference.

Skype for Business Server 2015 uses compressed video to reduce the amount of data required to be transferred over the network. The video codec is negotiated in the same way as the audio, via the SDP associated with the `INVITE`. Here's a sample log:

```
CSeq: 1 INVITE
<shortened for brevity, but would include the same audio details as the
previous example>
m=video 24628 RTP/SAVP 122 121 123
a=x-ssrc-range:1477293570-1477293669
a=rtcp-fb:* x-message app send:src,x-pli recv:src,x-pli
a=rtcp-rsize
a=label:main-video
a=x-source:main-video
a=ice-ufrag:AIUz
a=ice-pwd:UXteI+FbvuLUuZMU0Ef6snN0
a=x-caps:121 263:1920:1080:30.0:2000000:1;
4359:1280:720:30.0:1500000:1;
8455:640:480:30.0:600000:1;
12551:640:360:30.0:600000:1;
16647:352:288:15.0:250000:1;
20743:424:240:15.0:250000:1;
24839:176:144:15.0:180000:1
a=candidate:1 1 UDP 2130706431 192.168.2.100 24628 typ host
a=candidate:1 2 UDP 2130705918 192.168.2.100 24629 typ host
a=candidate:2 1 TCP-ACT 1684798975 192.168.2.100 24628 typ srflx
 raddr 192.168.2.100 rport 24628
a=candidate:2 2 TCP-ACT 1684798462 192.168.2.100 24628 typ srflx
 raddr 192.168.2.100 rport 24628
a=cryptoscale:1 client AES_CM_128_HMAC_SHA1_80 inline:
 HmTnPk00sM9MOu8Eloay95MuGnGudN/uE8d4J2i/|2^31|1:1
a=crypto:2 AES_CM_128_HMAC_SHA1_80 inline:
/j7g56QtpQqAvo4BnklwU4xmJjsuRhR3oEfWn80C|2^31|1:1
a=crypto:3 AES_CM_128_HMAC_SHA1_80 inline:
03vcKkTkEOB6+8B7QsLOnNX8q5uPVll7MM/l1FXh|2^31
a=rtcp:24629
a=rtpmap:122 X-H264UC/90000
a=fmtp:122 packetization-mode=1;mst-mode=NI-TC
a=rtpmap:121 x-rtvc1/90000
a=rtpmap:123 x-ulpfecuc/90000
a=rtcp-mux
```

In this case, you can see that the `m=video 24628 RTP/SAVP 122 121 123` line, listing three codecs and translating via their relevant `rtpmap` entries, results in the codecs being RTVideo (`x-rtcv1`) and H264, with `x-ulpfecuc` actually being an audio codec.

The additional `a=x-caps` line provides the encapsulation details for each codec (as with audio, the number is the identifier). This `x-caps` line definition has the following format for each video quality contained within the protocol:

```
port:width:height:framerate:bitrate;
```

Therefore, the entry

```
a=x-caps:121 263:1920:1080:30.0:2000000:1;
4359:1280:720:30.0:1500000:1;
8455:640:480:30.0:600000:1;
12551:640:360:30.0:600000:1;
16647:352:288:15.0:250000:1;
20743:424:240:15.0:250000:1;
24839:176:144:15.0:180000:1
```

corresponds to the following quality definitions:

1920 × 1080 (1080p)

1280 × 720 (720p)

640 × 480 (VGA; screen 4:3 ratio)

640 × 360 (VGA; widescreen 16:9 ratio)

352 × 288 (CIF; screen 4:3 ratio)

424 × 240 (CIF; widescreen 16:9 ratio)

176 × 144 QCIF

Figure 2.21 shows a typical sample for a conference video codec using a frame rate of 30 frames per second.

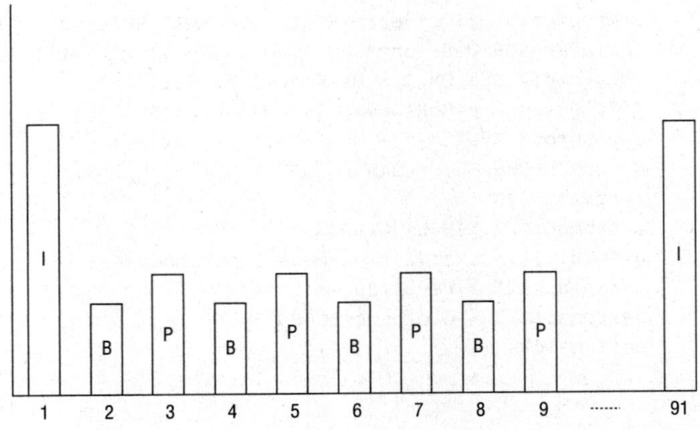

FIGURE 2.21 Video codec frame breakdown

Each full sample will begin and end with an *I-frame* (Intra-coded picture), which appears every four seconds for peer-to-peer video and every three seconds for conferences; the period between I-frames is known as the Group of Pictures (GoP). No compression is available with this frame.

Within the full sample period is a combination of *P-frames* (predicted picture) and *B-frames* (bi-predictive picture). Each of these P-frames and B-frames contains only changes from the previous frame, with the B-frame also containing changes from the *next* frame.

Figure 2.22 shows the content within an I-frame and a P-frame (the dotted line represents the removal of content). Here, the P-frame predicts that the character will next raise her arms. It describes only their new position and the deletion of the old.

FIGURE 2.22
I-frame vs. P-frame

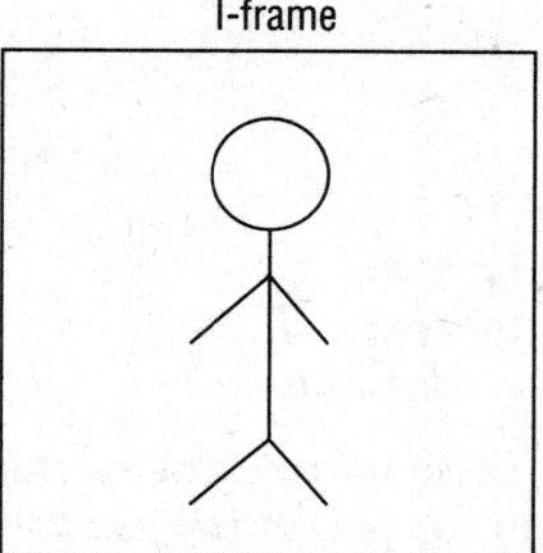

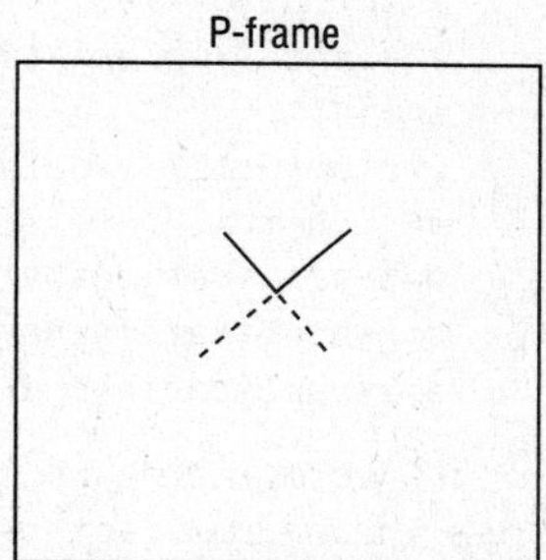

Lost frames are simply ignored because the next frame will provide more information, and frames appearing out of order are useless to the picture. But because some frames are dependent upon others, this approach can lead to a "stuttering" or "artifact" effect in the playback.

An individual frame loss will not have a massive impact; however, depending on the specific type of frame lost, it may lead to a pause or some ghosting of images, in which a frame has been dropped and some updated information has been missed (such as an artifact not being removed).

A packet loss will cause an artifact to appear until the next same type or larger frame. For example, an I-frame is the largest frame, and losing it will cause a problem until the next I-frame. On the other hand, losing a P-frame will result in a problem until the next P-frame or I-frame (whichever occurs first).

Each P-frame is tagged to allow the SVC profile to either decode or discard as needed.

Using Desktop Sharing

Desktop sharing uses Remote Desktop Protocol (RDP) as its media stream. The Desktop Sharing function has improved, providing users with more control; they can now specify individual applications for sharing, individual screens, or the full desktop.

From the communications perspective, Skype for Business Server 2015 leverages only the RDP protocol and uses SIP as the signaling method, as it does with all other communication functions. Apart from permissions and workstation configuration, there is nothing specifically different between an RDP session within the Skype for Business Server 2015 client and a direct RDP session.

The relevant trace data is shown here:

```
CSeq: 1 INVITE
<shortened for brevity, but would include the same audio details as the
previous example>
m=applicationsharing 21653 TCP/RTP/SAVP 127
a=ice-ufrag:h9FW
a=ice-pwd:yLM1Cg8n/On6GIQMmztGON8J
a=candidate:2 1 TCP-ACT 2121006591 192.168.2.100 21653 typ host
a=crypto:2 AES_CM_128_HMAC_SHA1_80 inline:
 ERXyIVn9H+GtDY0jkdoUOoP5WZRq0RkzUmsV8Vop|2^31|1:1
a=remote-candidates:1 192.168.2.254 22919 2 192.168.2.254 22919
a=setup:active
a=connection:existing
a=mid:1
a=rtpmap:127 x-data/90000
a=rtcp-mux
a=x-applicationsharing-session-id:1
a=x-applicationsharing-role:sharer
a=x-applicationsharing-media-type:rdp
```

It's worth noting a screen share session cannot be started without a previous session in progress (the `a=setup:activea=connection:existing` lines show you this call was "escalated" to a desktop share).

With the upgrade to Microsoft Office 2016, RDP has been replaced by video-based screen sharing, which gives dramatic bandwidth improvements over RDP. However, it is for sharing screens only; any attempt (even a request) for changing who is in control will revert to RDP for the traffic. You will see setup information similar to the following in the trace:

```
a=sendonly
a=rtpmap:122 X-H264UC/90000
a=fmtp:122 packetization-mode=1;mst-mode=NI-TC
a=rtpmap:123 x-ulpfecuc/90000
a=rtcp-mux
```

The "Odd" Protocol: XCCOS

SIP is a great and simple protocol for basic messaging, and you've seen how it can "carry" a payload in SDP, which in turn allows you to enable voice, video, and desktop sharing.

One additional capability provided by Skype for Business Server 2015 is persistent chat, which uses Extensible Chat Control Over SIP (XCCOS).

Leveraging the SDP in a similar way to the audio/video/desktop sharing functionality, the "chat" protocol information is carried within the SIP messages as type `text/plain` but formatted in a similar way to XML.

```
CSEQ: 9 INFO
CALL-ID: d85a0a91c0254216b9b7c4dccce085df
CONTACT: <sip:pc01.rlscomms.net@rlscomms.net;gruu;opaque=srvr:PersistentChat:6SIA
qzKS1FK01KBPNR05FAAA>
```

```
CONTENT-LENGTH: 1425
SUPPORTED: gruu-10
USER-AGENT: RTCC/6.0.0.0 PCS/6.0.9319.0
CONTENT-TYPE: text/plain
<xccos xmlns:xsd="http://www.w3.org/2001/XMLSchema"
xmlns:xsi="http://www.w3.org/2001/XMLSchema-instance" ver="1"
envid="FileName_4020351744089767336" xmlns="urn:parlano:xml:ns:xccos">
  <rpl id="rpl:bjoin" seqid="FileName_1">
    <commandid seqid="1" envid="1474513131" />
    <resp code="200">SUCCESS_OK</resp>
    <data>
      <chanib name="Chat room 1" description="" parent="ma-cat://rlscomms.
      net/76bc6096-0b14-4e01-bea0-2b7becd8af4b" uri="ma-chan://rlscomms.
      net/4f66eb6f-5ba0-4b5b-b9e0-41bda16117b0" behavior="NORMAL" topic=""
      disabled="false">
        <aib key="11652" value="0" />
        <audit updatedby="David Skype" updatedon="2015-11-11T10:12:06.5816131Z"
createdby="David Skype" createdon="2015-11-11T10:12:06.2151214Z" />
        <info id="urn:parlano:ma:info:visibility">OPEN</info>
        <info id="urn:parlano:ma:info:ucnt">1</info>
        <info id="urn:parlano:ma:info:filestoreuri">https://se01.rlscomms.net/
        PersistentChat/MGCWebService.asmx</info>
        <prop id="urn:parlano:ma:prop:filepost">True</prop>
        <prop id="urn:parlano:ma:prop:logged">True</prop>
        <prop id="urn:parlano:ma:prop:invite">True</prop>
      </chanib>
      <uib uri="sip:David.Skype@rlscomms.net" guid="8E964AB5-F988-4A42-BE4F-
      40481D72E63D" type="5" uname="David Skype" disabled="false" dispname="David
      Skype" id="FileName_0">
        <perms inherited="1" inheriting="true" />
      </uib>
    </data>
  </rpl>
</xccos>
```

Connecting Remotely

During the session establishment process of the INVITE, SDP will carry information of the IP address on which the client can be reached. This will always be the direct interface address from the client because the clients will always try to connect peer to peer.

This scenario fits perfectly into an enterprise environment, where all clients share a network (likely via a WAN connection) and can be directly reached. However, it doesn't work as well when firewalls have been implemented and even less so when clients are connecting via the Internet.

The solution to this is the Edge server, which will act as a SIP proxy server but also as a media relay. Where clients previously connected directly to each other, they can now use the Edge server to provide a common connection point to exchange media.

The establishment of this relay point is a multistep process.

1. Log in to the front-end server using SIP via the Edge server (as a proxy).
2. Request the Media Relay Authentication Service (MRAS) credentials via the front-end server.
3. Request the Edge endpoint details.
4. Send the `INVITE` to another user, populating the SDP with Edge endpoint details.
5. Negotiate which endpoint to use for media communications.
6. Begin the session.

When an endpoint is located remotely, it can be directly connected to the Internet or connected behind a Network Address Translation (NAT) device, effectively hiding its direct IP address (Figure 2.23).

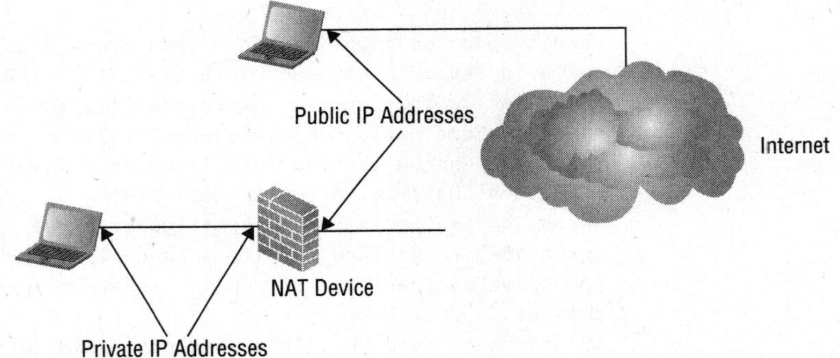

FIGURE 2.23 Remotely connected devices

Even though the endpoint may be behind a NAT device, it will not automatically be aware of that and will continue to include its local IP address in the SDP exchange. If it is behind a NAT device, it needs to have a method to determine that and also to determine the actual IP address (and port) to use on the Edge server.

This is where Internet Connectivity Establishment (ICE), RFC 4091; 5245/Session Traversal Utilities for NAT (STUN), RFC 3489; and 5389/Traversal Using Relay NAT (TURN), RFC 5766, come into play. All of them provide methods to overcome the problem of hidden IP addresses with NAT when using media connectivity.

Simply put, using STUN and TURN methods allows the endpoint to identify addresses via the Edge server; STUN provides a reflexive address (on the NAT device), and TURN provides a relay (on the Edge server). Figure 2.24 shows this in detail.

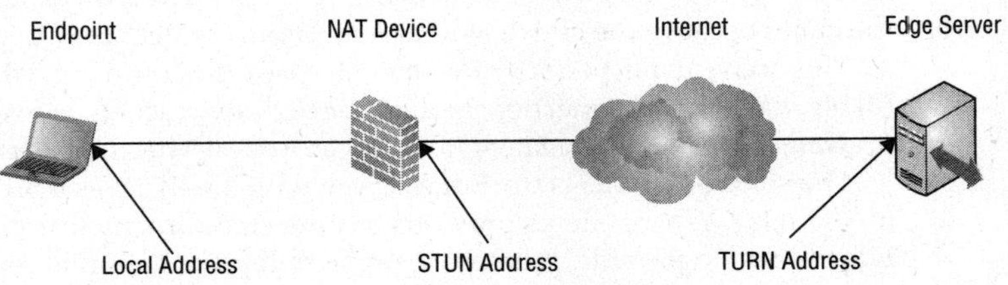

FIGURE 2.24 STUN and TURN addressing

Once the endpoint has identified its own available addresses, it can populate the SDP and begin negotiating which address to communicate.

Once the SDPs have been exchanged, the negotiation of connection addresses will begin and follow this order:

1. UDP direct
2. TCP direct
3. UDP NAT (STUN)
4. UDP Relay (TURN)
5. TCP Relay (TURN)

Once bidirectional connectivity is established, the `INVITE` is stopped and reissued, this time including only the valid address information. From here the session will begin as normal.

The SDP is the best place to find information for troubleshooting because it contains the complete call flow as well as all the negotiation steps. You can find more detailed information on troubleshooting in Chapter 15.

The Bottom Line

Understand the basics of SIP for signaling. SIP originates from an extensive background of telephony signaling. Although knowing that background is not strictly required for Skype for Business Server 2015 administration, understanding how we have gotten to where we are today will help you overcome some of the challenges you'll face when integrating with legacy telephony environments.

Master It For what is a jitter buffer used?

Understand how SIP has been extended to provide additional functionality for Skype for Business Server 2015. In its plainest form, SIP provides session-based signaling; however, with some of the extensions for SIP, you can extend this session-based signaling approach to incorporate additional functionality within the SIP request itself, such as IM and presence information.

Master It Assuming a user is not yet logged in, describe the SIP requests required to log in and establish an IM session with another user.

Identify additional protocols used by Skype for Business Server 2015. Skype for Business Server 2015 uses many different protocols for its various modalities as needed by the user. It can also tie many of these modalities together, providing an integrated solution running on top of SIP. Microsoft has also been able to successfully (and securely) extend this functionality to the Internet.

Master It What is the default codec used in peer-to-peer audio calls?

Chapter 3

Security

In today's world, where security breaches are all too common, the ability to secure your Skype for Business Server 2015 deployment is critical. In particular, your key focus should be protecting external access, especially as federation capability has been further extended, allowing interaction with a wider range of systems. The Edge role and its supporting components deliver the ability to communicate with billions of people worldwide. However, the possibility of communicating with that many people entails risk. When correctly configured, Skype for Business Server's design will help you mitigate that risk.

Of course, its various core capabilities provide security. For example, Skype for Business encrypts all its communications, both the signaling and the media, which means that as a platform it can be used in highly secure environments where systems that leave the media unencrypted on the wire would be less useful. With Skype for Business, there is no need to implement another security system, such as IP Security (IPsec), just to secure media traffic. Indeed, adding an additional security layer on top of the encryption used typically results in a deterioration of audio and video quality. The authentication mechanisms available constitute another key element to securing Skype for Business. While the standard username and password (NTLM and Kerberos) options, as well as a self-signed certificate authentication, are used for several clients (the PC-based ones), PIN and extension authentication (in conjunction with certificate authentication) are used on some of the Phone Edition devices. Non–Phone Edition devices (such as the SNOM range) can use NTLM or PIN and extension authentication; certificate-based authentication is not available on these devices. Tighter integration with Office 365 and developments originating with Lync Server 2013 allow for two-factor authentication methods.

Finally, many policies enable you as an administrator to run a secure platform. Chapter 12, "User Administration," covers policies in depth; this chapter covers security-based policy topics. For example, you'll learn how to determine PIN policies, you'll learn about the length and complexity of the PIN, and you'll learn how to define who can federate with external parties.

In this chapter, you will learn to

- Secure external access
- Understand core security
- Provide security administratively

Securing External Access

One of the most exciting features of Skype for Business is its ability to provide communication functionality not only to users within your network but to those outside it, whether they are employees working from home or on the go, partners, or even the general public. It is possible to communicate with millions of people worldwide through a variety of networks, including Google, AOL, and now Skype. Table 3.1 summarizes the available types of communication based on the different types of external users.

TABLE 3.1: Communication types available to different types of external users

SCENARIO	REMOTE USER	FEDERATED USER	PUBLIC IM CONNECTIVITY/ INTEROP	ANONYMOUS USER
Presence	Yes	Yes	Yes	No
Instant messaging (IM) peer-to-peer	Yes	Yes	Yes	No
IM conferencing	Yes	Yes	No	Yes
Collaboration	Yes	Yes	No	Yes
A/V peer-to-peer	Yes	Yes	Yes, if using the latest version of Skype Messenger	No
A/V conferencing	Yes	Yes	No	Yes
File transfer	Yes	Yes	No	No

All of this communication potential can send security professionals running scared! Think about opening up all that traffic through firewalls…and what about information leakage?

If you look closely, you will see that the way Skype for Business has been designed combined with the best practices for its deployment will go a long way toward mitigating the risks of broad communication. Clearly, though, you need to get your security folks to understand that. The next few sections will help you do so.

Edge Security Components

Like other elements of architecture, the way you provide external access offers choices—but not as many as back in the Office Communications Server (OCS) 2007 days, when it was possible to have a whole range of different roles split onto different servers. Now with Skype for Business, all the Edge roles are consolidated onto a single Edge server, and your main choice is whether to have one or many of these servers and, if there will be many, how to load balance them to provide high availability. The deployment options for an edge topology are as follows:

- Single consolidated Edge with private IP addresses and NAT
- Single consolidated Edge with public IP addresses
- Scaled consolidated Edge and DNS load balancing with private IP addresses using NAT
- Scaled consolidated Edge and DNS load balancing with public IP addresses
- Scaled consolidated Edge with public IP addresses, with load balancers

Each of these options has been developed to cater for different needs of deployments, notably high availability and the use of Network Address Translation (NAT). The first two listed are solitary server deployments, whereas the final three consider multiple servers in a "load balanced" form. Only the final option (using the load balancers) is truly load balanced, as external devices (hardware or software) are used to balance some of the load among available Edge servers. And even that "load balancing" is only for the first connectivity traffic.

Of course, the Edge server is not the only element that comes into play in enabling external access to Lync functionality; there are also many supporting components, which are detailed throughout the chapter.

The Edge Server

The single consolidated Edge model takes all the Edge roles—Access Edge, XMPP Federation, AV Edge, and Web Conferencing Edge—and runs them on a server. This provides all the external access capabilities of Skype for Business in a single box. Each of these roles provides specific security capabilities and has specific requirements. In particular, each requires certificates that have the correct name entries to be provided and firewalls to be configured with the relevant ports open.

The Access Edge role is a specially designed proxy concerned with passing Session Initiation Protocol (SIP) signaling traffic. It is a routing solution in that two network interface cards (NICs) are used and traffic is terminated on the way into the external NIC and then reestablished through the internal NIC on the way out. This creates a barrier between external and internal components. The Access Edge role doesn't carry out authentication, so it is not required to be a member of the Active Directory (AD). Remote user authentication traffic is passed through to the next internal hop, either the Director pool or the Front End pool, which, being a member of AD, carries out the authentication. The Access Edge role is responsible for all kinds of federation traffic: SIP, PIC, eXtensible Messaging and Presence Protocol (XMPP), and Skype.

The Web Conferencing Edge is a proxy for Persistent Shared Object Model (PSOM) traffic. This protocol is used to provide access to conferencing content, such as whiteboards, and poll pages shared between internal and external users. It works in conjunction with the Access Edge for SIP session setup and the reverse proxy for slide/attachment content downloads.

The AV Edge role is where Skype for Business implements the Interactive Connectivity Establishment (ICE) protocol, which provides the ability to enable media traffic to traverse a NAT environment, using STUN or TURN. Since Lync Server 2010, the AV Edge role also introduced the ability to allow file transfers through NAT via the Edge server, whereas in previous OCS versions, clients had to be on a directly routable network between them for transfers to work.

The key benefits of combining these three roles into a consolidated Edge server are simplicity and fewer hardware requirements. As mentioned, each Edge server will have at least two NICs, one of which is on the external side of the demilitarized zone (DMZ) and the other on the internal side; additional NICs can be used for the other external-facing roles, AV and Web Conferencing, for additional capacity. The external NICs will require three IP addresses assigned, one for each of the Edge roles. This will equate to three separate URLs, one for each role. The internal interface requires a single IP on a different subnet that is routable from the internal LAN; this internal interface may not be configured with NAT.

Using a Single External IP Address

Although it is possible to use a single IP address on the external Edge interface, doing so is not recommended because it would require the ports on which each Edge role listens to be reconfigured. By default, Lync was designed (where possible) to require only well-known ports, such as TCP/443, to be opened. This port is required by all the Edge roles, and so having a single IP only would cause clashes as these ports overlapped. You would, therefore, have to change to other ports, thereby complicating deployment (by moving away from the defaults) and making the system harder to understand for other administrators who might not be aware of the changes.

Another advantage of using the well-known ports is the likelihood that corporate proxy servers already allow client requests on these ports. For example, most corporate proxy servers will allow traffic to leave the organization with a target port of 443—after all, this is what secure websites will use.

As mentioned, four IP addresses and, therefore, four FQDNs will be required on each Edge server (except in a load-balanced environment, where some of the URLs will be shared between Edge servers, and they will be directed to the load balancer). When you're setting up Edge servers, choose these FQDNs carefully. For example, if Lync Server is already deployed and you are migrating, you must consider the FQDNs already in use. To enable the Skype for Business Server 2015 Edge role to be deployed side by side with existing Edge servers, you should use new FQDNs. For more information about these options, see Chapter 9, "Migration and Upgrades." The specifics of topology are discussed later in this chapter.

When you are deploying Edge servers, another key consideration is where they will be deployed. If you have a single central site, the choice is simple because the Edge server will be there; however, once you scale out to several central sites, perhaps in a global deployment, you need to consider how best to route external traffic. Keep in mind that there is only one path to the external world for all federation traffic for a particular SIP domain. As discussed in the "DNS Entries" section later, a specific DNS Service (SRV) record is needed for federation, and it can point to only one fully qualified domain name—namely that of the Access Edge, which provides the route for federation traffic. Either this would be a virtual IP (VIP) on a load balancer device or load balancing would be provided through DNS load balancing, as discussed later in the chapter. Other Edge traffic (based on the nature of its content, such as real-time audio) is typically better being localized to where the Front End pool is, reducing network hops and therefore improving audio and video quality. In such cases, you can have multiple Edge pools, each paired with their respective Front End pools.

The Director

The Director role is a fully fledged role in its own right. Prior to Lync Server 2010, the Director was a modified Front End server that had to be manually customized by turning off certain services; it was, however, still possible to accidentally end up with users homed to the Director. Since Lync Server 2010, this is no longer possible. The Director role provides user authentication and redirects users to their home pool. The ability to provide authentication and redirection means that the Director is essentially an additional layer sitting between the Edge servers and the Front End servers and is, therefore, in the path of external users coming through the Edge servers to the internal Front End servers. This functionality provides a range of benefits.

First, in organizations with multiple pools deployed, the Director is configured as the first point of contact for users who are signing in. This means that all user registration/authentication requests first arrive at the Director, which can then authenticate and route the traffic to the relevant Front End server pool rather than having the Front End servers burdened with all this redirection traffic when they could be providing resources for all the other functions they support. For clarity, the traffic is then re-authenticated on the Front End pool.

The second area where the Director role comes into play is in providing a stopgap between external users and the Front End servers. As traffic is passed on from the Edge to the Director, it is the Director that does the first authentication. Therefore, if your system were to be subjected to an externally sourced denial of service (DoS) attack, where large quantities of malformed authentication traffic were blasted at your Edge, the Director would take the brunt of the attack rather than the Front End servers that serve the internal users. Admittedly, external users would no longer be able to gain access, but internal users who were already logged onto the system would be able to continue working.

Like many of the other roles, the Director can be installed either as a stand-alone server or as a pool of Directors that have some form of load balancing. As with the Edge and Front End servers, this load balancing can be either DNS load balancing or hardware load balancing, about which you'll learn more shortly.

The Director is an optional role, and with the ability of the Skype for business client (Lync 2010 onward) to support multiple DNS SRV responses, the first scenario highlighted earlier becomes less necessary, and the Director becomes useful only in a scenario with external user connectivity (either remote or federated users).

The Reverse Proxy

While the Edge server and the Director provide access to the SIP and media facilities within Skype for Business, another type of remote access is required by clients. This is the requirement for access to the various web-based elements provided through IIS websites. The role of the reverse proxy is to publish the required URLs on the Front End and Director pools. The process by which it does so is discussed in depth in Chapter 8, "Installation."

It is important to note that mobile clients use a web-based connection for their login process.

The external access to web services allows remote users to connect to meetings or dial-in conferences using simple URLs, to download meeting content when in a conference, to expand distribution groups, to obtain a user-based certificate for client certificate–based authentication, to download files from the Address Book server, to submit queries to the Address Book Web Query service, and to obtain updates to client and device software.

Table 3.2 shows the URLs that are published through the reverse proxy and describes the certificates that are needed.

TABLE 3.2: URLs that must be published through the reverse proxy

ROLE/SUBJECT NAME	USED TO PUBLISH	SUBJECT NAME SYNTAX EXAMPLE
Lyncdiscover	Login process for clients	`Lyncdiscover.rlscomms.net`
External Web Services/FQDN of the Front End pool	Address Book files Distribution group expansion Conference content Device update files	`Se01webext.rlscomms.net`
External WebServices/FQDN of the Director pool	Address Book files Distribution group expansion Conference content Device update files	`Directorwebext.rlscomms.net`
Simple URL/AdminFQDN	AdminFQDN is not published externally; used only internally	N/A
Simple URL/DialinFQDN	Dial-in conferencing information	`dialin.rlscomms.net`
Simple URL/MeetFQDN	Meeting URL	`meet.rlscomms.net`
Office Web Apps Server	Enhanced meeting content, such as PowerPoint streaming capability	`Owafarm01.rlscomms.net`

Multiple areas of functionality are listed in the "Used to Publish" column of Table 3.2; however, best practice is to publish them all using a single rule that uses `FQDN/*` in the paths field.

PUBLISHING HTTP EXTERNALLY

You may notice that the bulk of external connections come over HTTPS. However, HTTP is still required for device updates to work.

One of the elements published is the *simple URL*. Simple URLs are a method of making the URL used in conferencing a lot easier for end users to understand. Where there is a Director pool in place, the URLs are published on the Director because this gives a single point of ingress to the network. You can configure the simple URLs in a variety of ways. You should consider this configuration carefully during your planning phase; once the URLs are set, changing them will require rerunning Setup on the Front End server and can also require certificate changes. You will need three simple URLs: the Meet URL, the Dial-in URL, and the Admin URL. The Admin URL is optional, but it simplifies internal access to the Skype for Business Control Panel. It is never published externally. One thing to be aware of is that the Meet URL is set per supported SIP domain, while only one Admin URL and Dial-in URL are needed per organization. The following three examples demonstrate different ways you can configure your simple URLs.

The simplest option is to have a dedicated simple URL for each site.

```
https://meet.rlscomms.net
https://dialin.rlscomms.net
https://admin.rlscomms.net
```

You will need additional Meet URLs for any additional SIP domains.

```
https://meet.anotherdomain.com
```

This method requires a significant number of certificates or subject alternative names to support each URL and many different DNS entries.

In the next option, the simple URL is essentially presented as a virtual directory under the external web services URL. This is called the *shared simple URL* syntax.

```
https://directorwebext.rlscomms.net/meet/
```

Additional domains would be as follows:

```
https://directorwebext.anotherdomain.com
https://directorwebext.rlscomms.net/dialin/
https://directorwebext.rlscomms.net/admin/
```

Here you benefit from using the same base URL as the external web services and, therefore, the same DNS records and certificate.

Finally, to make the most efficient use of URLs, you can tweak the shared format, as shown here:

```
https://directorwebext.rlscomms.net/abc/meet/
https://directorwebext.rlscomms.net/anotherdomain/meet/
https://directorwebext.rlscomms.net/dialin/
https://directorwebext.rlscomms.net/admin/
```

This technique uses the least number of certificates or subject alternative names and DNS entries and is, therefore, the simplest to configure and most cost effective.

Now that you've seen the various types of simple URLs, here's a summary of when you would use each one:

Format	Used For
Shared	Single-pool deployments
	Multiple-pool deployments where each pool shares global simple URLs
	Multiple-pool deployments where each pool has dedicated simple URLs and public certificate cost is an issue (you can save one certificate per pool by using shared simple URLs)
Dedicated	Multiple-pool deployments where each pool has dedicated simple URLs
	Deployments where you do not want to potentially display internal server names externally

When a reverse proxy publishes sites, it actually intercepts the traffic from the external source, inspects it, and then sends it to the internal server. This process has two elements with specific requirements. First, one important step during this process is for the reverse proxy to translate incoming requests on the public ports 80 and 443 to internal requests for the external websites on ports 8080 and 4443. Second, certificates are used to terminate the encrypted traffic and then send it on again also encrypted. Externally, these should be trusted certificates from a public certificate authority (CA). The reverse proxy uses them to identify itself externally. When re-encrypting the traffic to pass on to the internal server, it uses the certificates on the Front End or the Directors, which come from the internal CA. If this is not possible because the reverse proxy cannot trust additional internal CAs, then you need to set up the external web services site on the pool servers with trusted public certificates.

In Table 3.2, you can see that both the Director and the Front End pools have external web URLs that must be published. The Director must be published because it plays a role in web ticket authentication, which you'll learn more about later. The Front End must be published because the URLs of the Front End are sent in-band to the client for operations such as distribution group expansion.

High Availability

Because all the Edge roles are provided on a single server, making them highly available is a relatively simple case of adding more Edge servers. Of course, when you do this, you need some way to balance and route the traffic between the different Edge servers accordingly so that they can present a single identity. In Skype for Business, you have two ways of doing this: DNS load balancing and load balancing using either a hardware device (HLB) or a software implementation (SLB). Both have advantages and disadvantages.

Back in the day with OCS, it was a challenge to set up HLB devices correctly to support both the web and SIP traffic that needed to be load balanced (OCS did not support the use of SLBs). To simplify the load balancing requirements, DNS load balancing was introduced in Lync Server 2010 to deal with non-web-based traffic (HTTP/HTTPS). Another benefit is that DNS load balancing supports the *server draining* feature, which allows a server to be prepared for shutdown by not accepting any new connections but still allowing existing ones to come to a natural conclusion.

Because of the way in which Skype for Business is implemented, HLB and SLB do not provide the application layer mechanisms required to support the server draining feature correctly.

The simplicity of DNS load balancing comes from the fact that it is application based and uses client intelligence to determine which traffic can and can't be load balanced. Each Front End server in a pool registers its FQDN as an A record in DNS, and then the pool FQDN is configured in DNS with an entry of each of the Front End IP addresses.

The client will then try each record as required (in a random order) until it receives a response from the server. This response will be either a successful login or a redirect to the client's home pool.

If a Director pool is in place, this will work in the same way: The client will receive a redirect to the home pool.

Once directed to the home pool, the client will follow the same process using DNS load balancing as before, only this time it will be directed (if needed) to the home server within the pool.

For Edge servers using DNS load balancing, the client will continue until it gets a response. This response will be the proxied login attempt, which is further directed internally by the Edge server next-hop configuration (either a Front End pool or a Director pool).

When you're using an HLB/SLB device to load balance the internal NIC of the Edge server, you must ensure that traffic to the Web Conferencing Edge role is not load balanced, even though the rest of the traffic to the other two Edge roles should be load balanced.

When using DNS load balancing, another benefit of the client intelligence is that the client knows how to handle the traffic flow and setup is simpler.

Another key consideration is compatibility. Although DNS load balancing is simpler to set up, you must ensure that the clients and third parties to which you will be connecting can use the new method. As mentioned, DNS load balancing requires intelligence in the client. For example, the RTM version of Exchange 2010 Unified Messaging (UM) doesn't understand DNS load balancing; therefore, if you provide remote access to UM, you could end up with remote users always hitting a single server. If that single server were down, no redundancy would kick in. When referring to things specifically related to the Edge role, some Public Internet Connectivity (PIC) providers, eXtensible Messaging and Presence Protocol (XMPP) clouds, and older OCS/LCS networks as federated partners all have issues with DNS load balancing. All in all, you may find DNS load balancing useful inside the network; however, for external communication, you may still need to use an HLB/SLB, although the reasons are reducing.

If HLB/SLB is chosen, the configuration must still allow a direct connection to each server in the pool—the servers cannot be "hidden" behind the load balancer. In some cases, the clients will still need a direct SIP connection; however, in *all* cases the client needs a direct connection to the server for conferencing and media traffic.

DNS Load Balancing Does Not Load Balance

When configuring Skype for Business Server 2015 and clients using DNS load balancing, it would not be unreasonable to expect the connections to be load balanced across the Edge server (or Front End pool) to which the clients are connecting. However, if you look at the performance counter showing the number of connections on each server, you will see they are not balanced. And indeed, in some cases they are extremely unbalanced!

This has created cause for concern since the Lync Server 2010 time frame and, for unsuspecting administrators, could do so again with Skype for Business Server 2015.

Basically, because the "load balancing" is carried out by the DNS server (in the order in which the IP addresses relating to the Edge/Front End pool are returned) and the client (in the order in which it attempts each connection), there is no correlation of load on the servers, and therefore there is no load balancing carried out.

Based on the "randomness" of the DNS server and the client decisions, there "should" be an even spread of initial connections to the servers, but in the case of Front End pools, these may be redirected after that initial connection, and this is where the "load balancing" falls down.

Of course, you may not realize that whatever you do, HLB/SLB devices are still required to implement high availability. They are, as mentioned, required only for the HTTP and HTTPS traffic unless you need some of the elements listed earlier, which are not possible with DNS load balancing. This is because the web traffic is stateful and, therefore, the session must be maintained between a single client and server. Currently, there is no way to build this technology into the client (essentially the browser), unlike the way it is built into the Lync client for the other traffic streams.

Mixing LB Types

You cannot mix and match load-balancing methods on the internal and external interfaces of the Edge server.

The traditional option for making the web service and reverse proxy components highly available requires an HLB/SLB device in front of an array of reverse proxies.

Getting the Right Load Balancer

Given that so many load balancer devices are available, it is important to make sure you follow proper procedures and use one that is qualified for use with Skype for Business. To find out which models are certified, see this TechNet article:

`http://partnersolutions.skypeforbusiness.com/solutionscatalog/networking-hardware-infrastructure`

Certificates

There are two types of certificates used by Skype for Business Server 2015.

- Client-based certificates
- Server-based certificates

Client-based certificates are used in conjunction with/instead of username and password login for authentication; they will be discussed later in this chapter.

Server-based certificates are what we are discussing now.

As well as being required on all internal servers, certificates play an important role in publishing Skype for Business externally. They establish trust between the client and server so that the client knows it is talking to the correct server and not one that is spoofing its identity. Certificates are used on both interfaces of the Edge server. On the external interface, a public CA trusted certificate should be used to identify all three roles. A public CA is suggested because, in most cases, the root CA will already be trusted by the underlying operating system, ensuring a seamless connection experience.

Another change since OCS is that a single, public trusted certificate can now be used for all these roles, as long as it has the right names. Getting the names on the certificate correct is critical. Thankfully, the Certificate Wizard within the Setup application helps you do this, as shown in Chapter 8.

The subject of the external certificate is the Access Edge name. The subject name should also be the first subject alternative name (SAN), and then further SANs should be used to include the other required URLs, such as the FQDN of the Web Conferencing Edge. When running the wizard, you may notice that the AV Edge FQDN is not included on the certificate. This is because it doesn't need the name to use the certificate for encryption. This saves you the cost of an additional SAN.

For client autoconfiguration to work, the SANs should contain the `sip.`*domainname*`.com` URL for each SIP domain supported because this is one of the failback URLs used by the clients. See Chapter 4, "Desktop Clients," to learn more.

As a rule, you should create the external certificate with an exportable private key. This is a requirement if you are running a pool of servers because the certificate used for the AV Edge authentication on the external interface must be the same on each server in the pool. It is also needed if you create the certificate request on a server other than where it will be used.

You must also take into account that certificates are required on the reverse proxy. This is covered in depth in Chapter 6, where you will configure these components. Briefly, the reverse proxy needs a certificate to identify all the websites it must publish. The certificate should come from a trusted CA. This certificate should cover the simple URLs and the external web services URLs, which are published as described in the section "The Reverse Proxy" earlier. The certificates you require will vary depending on your defined topology. If you split out simple URLs, each will need to be published with a certificate. If not, and the simple URLs all point to a single central location, then the URLs can be published via the standard URL used for external web services for that location. For example, you would publish `meet.rlscomms.net` with a certificate that has the same subject name rather than using the `se01webext.rlscomms.net/meet` version, which could be published using the same external certificate at the reverse proxy.

DNS Entries

Of course, all the components just described are useless unless you can locate them, which is where DNS comes in. Skype for Business uses two types of DNS entries, the A record and the SRV record, and is generally deployed in a *split-brain* DNS implementation where the same zones are configured internally as well as externally but have different entries to give different results based on where the query originates.

Split-brain ensures that externally, the client will receive information only for the external servers (Edge), whereas, internally, the same DNS entry will point to a Front End pool. For example, for autoconfiguration of clients to work, you would configure the SRV records `_sipinternaltls._tcp.rlscomms.net` to point to `se01.rlscomms.net` internally, whereas externally you would configure `_sip._tls.rlscomms.net` to point to `accessedge.rlscomms.net`. As well as the SRV records, you can utilize the `lyncdiscover.rlscomms.net` and `lyncdiscoverinternal.rlscomms.net` records.

With this configuration, you need to make sure that the machines in your network resolve the correct addresses. In particular, it is important to consider where Edge servers resolve their DNS queries.

Essentially, they can point either internally or to external-facing DNS servers. Either way, what is really important is that they can resolve the correct addresses for queries. You may, therefore, find that a combination of DNS and HOSTS file entries are needed. It is important to note that internal clients and servers must resolve the external address for the AV Edge service.

The Edge server should resolve as follows:

FQDN	Expected Behavior
`Accessedge.rlscomms.net`	Public IP of Access Edge (or VIP)
`sip.rlscomms.net`	Public IP of Access Edge (or VIP)
`webconf.rlscomms.net`	Public IP of Web Conferencing Edge (or VIP)
`avedge.rlscomms.net`	Public IP of AV Edge server (or VIP)
`se01.rlscomms.net`	Private IP of Front End server (or VIP)

A computer on the internal network should resolve as follows:

FQDN	Expected Behavior
`avedge.rlscomms.net`	Public IP of AV Edge server (or VIP)
`edge01.rlscomms.net`	Internal IP of Edge server

The Front End server should resolve as follows:

FQDN	Expected Behavior
`avedge.rlscomms.net`	Public IP of AV Edge server (or VIP)
`edge01.rlscomms.net`	Internal IP of Edge server

A computer outside your network should resolve from external DNS as follows:

FQDN	Expected Behavior
`Accessedge.rlscomms.net`	Public IP of Access Edge (or VIP)
`sip.rlscomms.net`	Public IP of Access Edge (or VIP)
`webconf.rlscomms.net`	Public IP of Web Conferencing Edge (or VIP)
`avedge.rlscomms.net`	Public IP of AV Edge server (or VIP)
`se01.rlscomms.net`	Not resolved (internal only record)

As long as the name resolution laid out here is possible, Skype for Business will work correctly.

Of course, there are scenarios where split-brain DNS simply isn't possible. For example, suppose your internal AD domain is not the same as your external presence, such as `corp.rlscomms.net` rather than `.rlscomms.net`; in this case, you would need to either create a zone internally for `rlscomms.net` and populate it with entries for your external resources or use another type of client autoconfiguration, as described in Chapter 4.

The problem here is that you might not be able to create an internal zone matching your external zone because you might have hundreds of entries in the external `rlscomms.net` zone that you don't want to have to transpose to the internal zone and continue to keep up-to-date.

In that case, what can be done? Well, you can create something called a *pin-point zone.* This internally created zone is essentially the specific SRV record you wanted to create in the `rlscomms.net` zone you were not allowed or were unable to create. To create it, you must use the command line because the Windows DNS server GUI doesn't allow you to create pin-point zones. Therefore, open `cmd.exe` as an administrator on your DNS server and run the following commands:

```
dnscmd . /zoneadd _sipinternaltls._tcp.rlscomms.net. /dsprimary
dnscmd . /recordadd _sipinternaltls._tcp.rlscomms.net g. @ SRV 0 0 5061 se01.
rlscomms.net
dnscmd . /zoneadd .rlscomms.net. /dsprimary
dnscmd . /recordadd .rlscomms.net. @ A 192.168.2.1
```

Note that if you were performing DNS load balancing, you would need to add the additional A records for each Front End. Here's an example:

```
dnscmd . /zoneadd _sipinternaltls._tcp.rlscomms.net. /dsprimary
dnscmd . /recordadd _sipinternaltls._tcp.rlscomms.net. @ SRV 0 0 5061 eepool01.
rlscomms.net.
dnscmd . /zoneadd eepool01.rlscomms.net. /dsprimary
dnscmd . /recordadd fe01.rlscomms.net. @ A 192.168.1.23
dnscmd . /recordadd fe02.rlscomms.net. @ A 192.168.1.24
dnscmd . /recordadd fe03.rlscomms.net. @ A 192.168.1.25
```

Although these commands are shown for a Windows-based DNS solution, the concepts apply equally to other DNS server products; simply the implementation will differ.

FIREWALLS

Given the extent of external communication that Skype for Business allows through use of machines in the DMZ, it is not surprising that firewalls come into play. In a deployment, the recommended route is to have two firewalls as part of the topology. There should be a front firewall that sits between the Internet connection router and the external DMZ subnet. There should then also be a back firewall, which sits between the internal DMZ subnet and the LAN. This means that there are routed connections between the LAN and the DMZ and between the DMZ and the Internet, and it ensures that all external traffic passes through two firewalls before entering the LAN. Figure 3.1 shows this configuration.

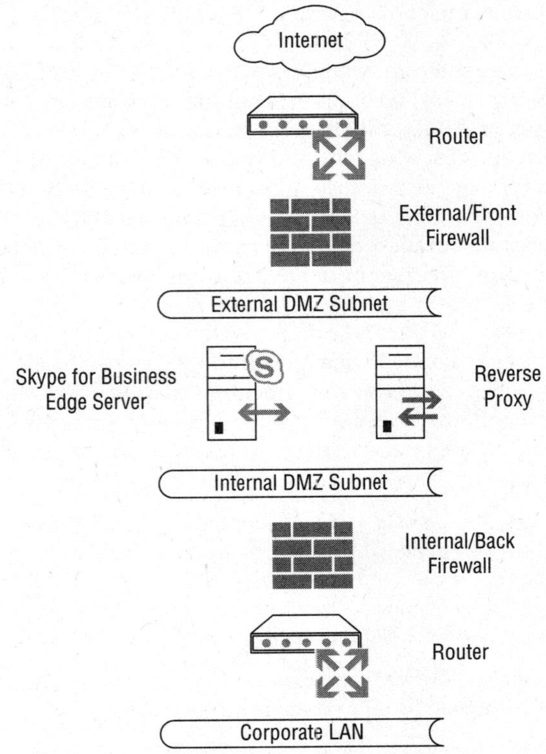

Figure 3.1
The Skype Edge Network layout

After you establish the location of firewalls, you must look at what holes need to be poked in them. As with any product that communicates using TCP/IP or UDP/IP, there is a requirement for specific firewall ports to be open.

Dealing with Three-Tiered Networks

In Figure 3.1, you can see that Skype for Business is essentially a two-tiered system. The Edge server sits in the first tier in a DMZ and is exposed to the Internet, while the LAN containing the Front End servers is on the second tier. Throughout our consulting experience, we sometimes come across organizations that operate systems where there is a middle tier between the DMZ and LAN. These organizations are commonly in highly secure or regulated industries such as financial services.

This causes problems because Skype for Business has no out-of-the box way of working in these networks. The Edge would have to be in the middle tier, and therefore, the Internet would have to be opened into that tier (not supported by the organization in question) or the Front End would have to be moved to the middle tier with the Edge in the first tier (DMZ). Again, having LAN-based servers with all their AD requirements in the middle tier was not supported in such cases.

> Fortunately for these installations, a company called Sipera previously has come up with a range of gateway devices that can act as a super proxy for all traffic destined for an Edge server. The gateway device sits in the first tier (DMZ), allowing the Edge to sit in the middle tier and the Front End to sit securely in the third tier (LAN). These devices were released for Lync Server and at the time of writing were not available for Skype for Business Server. In addition, since the release of Lync Server, Sipera has been purchased by Avaya, a Microsoft competitor, so whether a product for Skype for Business will be released is unknown. For more information, check out `www.sipera.com/company/`.

As an example, the following series of figures illustrates an enterprise perimeter network configuration in which Skype for Business is deployed with a single consolidated Edge server and the ports that need to be opened for Skype for Business to work externally. Figure 3.2 shows the reverse proxy server and its external and internal connections.

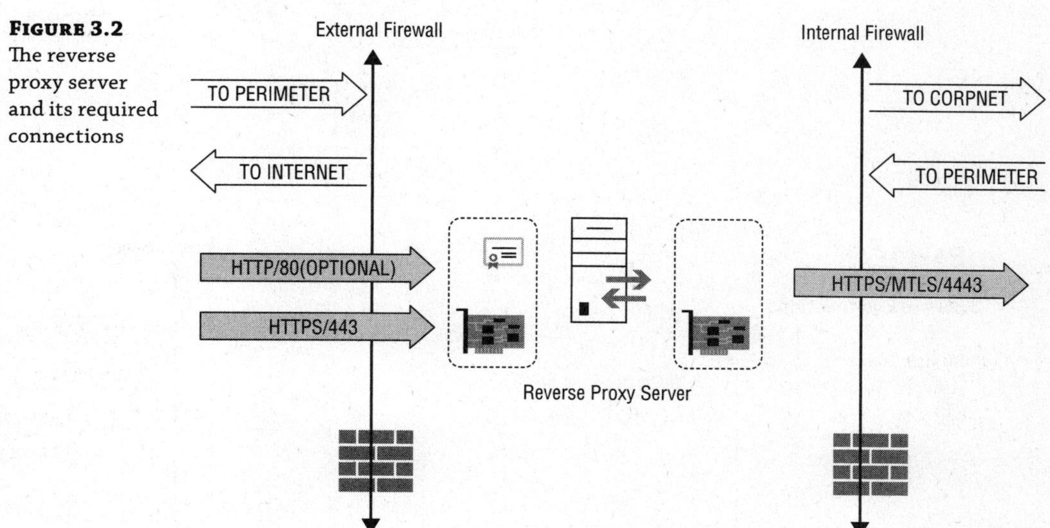

FIGURE 3.2 The reverse proxy server and its required connections

Figure 3.3 shows the external Internet port connections to the consolidated Edge server, and Figure 3.4 shows the internal network connections. This configuration forms the basis of the ports needed even when load balancing is introduced.

Note that a range of ports is required for the AV Edge server role. If you look closely, you may also notice that the Access Edge role is enabled for port 53 outbound to resolve DNS. If instead you allow DNS resolution to the internal DNS servers, port TCP 53 and UDP 53 access for DNS queries would be needed through the other side of the DMZ network via the back firewall.

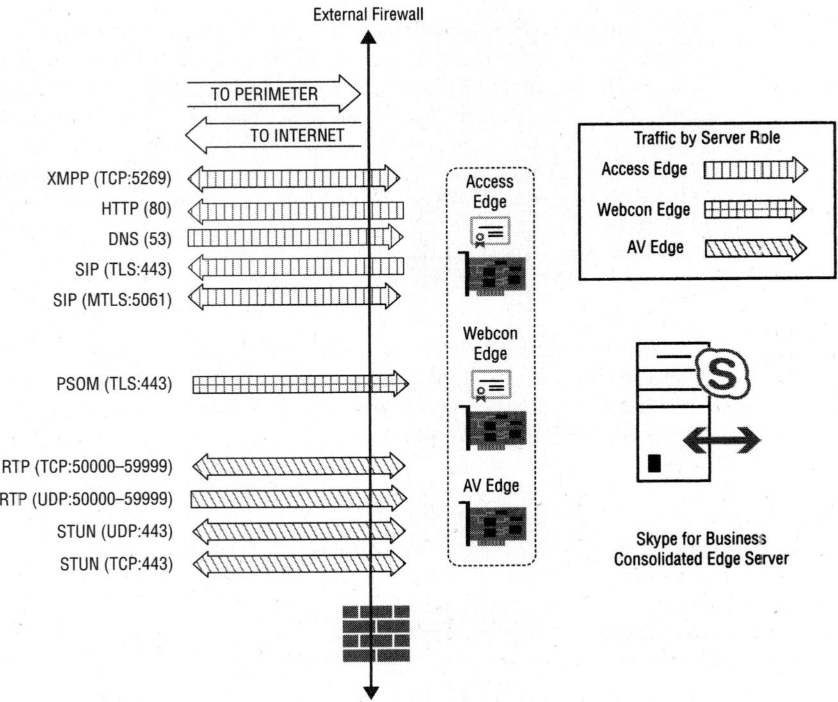

FIGURE 3.3 Internet connections with the Skype for Business Server 2015 consolidated Edge server

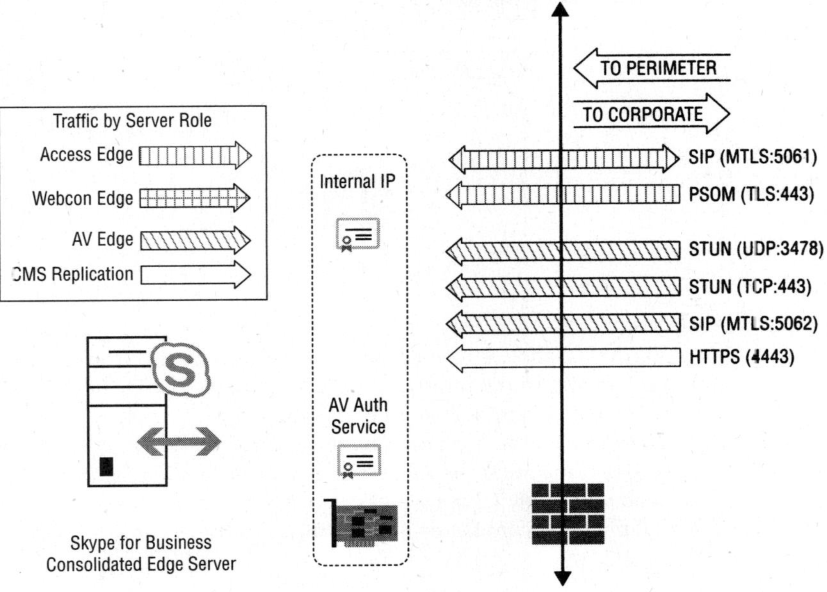

FIGURE 3.4 Internal corporate network connections with the Skype for Business Server 2015 consolidated Edge server

Because the AV Edge role has the most complex port requirements (and possibly the most concerning security), it is worth exploring those requirements in more detail. Another reason this is worth doing is that while the external ports required by the other external services stay the same no matter who you are communicating with or how, the AV Edge requirements can change—for example, if you talk with an OCS 2007 (down-level federation is still supported) system rather than a Lync system. Table 3.3 details these requirements.

TABLE 3.3: Ports required under different circumstances by the AV Edge role

FEDERATION WITH	FEATURE	TCP/443	UDP/3478	RTP/UDP 50000–59999	RTP/TCP 50000–59999
Skype for Business/ Lync	Skype for Business/ Lync	Open in	Open in and out	Not open	Open in
Skype for Business/ Lync	Application sharing/desktop sharing	Open in	Open in and out	Not open	Open in
Skype for Business/ Lync	File transfer	Open in	Open in and out	Not open	Open in
Office Communications Server 2007 R2	A/V	Open in	Open in and out	Not open	Open in
Office Communications Server 2007 R2	Desktop sharing	Open in	Open in and out	Open in and out	Open in and out
Office Communications Server 2007 R2	File transfer	N/A	N/A	N/A	N/A
Office Communications Server 2007	A/V	Open in	Open in	Open in and out	Open in and out
Office Communications Server 2007	Desktop sharing	N/A	N/A	N/A	N/A
Office Communications Server 2007	File transfer	N/A	N/A	N/A	N/A

As you can see, generally it is best practice to open the range TCP 50000–59999 from the AV Edge interface outbound to any remote hosts because this allows the widest level of communication. Strictly speaking, UDP 50000–59999 is required only if you need to communicate with those on OCS 2007. It is required both inbound and outbound. The requirements for opening large port ranges have significantly improved since the early days of OCS. If you don't need the ability to talk to partners running OCS 2007, only three ports require opening inbound: TCP 5061 for SIP traffic, TCP 443 for a variety of traffic (this port is usually open for other services anyway), and UDP 3478, which is for STUN traffic, which provides external access to AV traffic.

Support for NAT on the Edge interfaces has been a long-running topic for OCS administrators. When OCS 2007 first shipped, administrators were faced with the need for large numbers of externally routable IP addresses. NAT was not supported for all interfaces (in particular the AV Edge interface/IP address). OCS 2007 R2 improved matters by allowing all the Edge interfaces to sit behind a NAT device (whether a router or firewall), but only in the single consolidated Edge server mode. Since Lync Server 2010, NAT can be used for all external Edge server interfaces, including Scaled Consolidated mode. NAT is still not supported on the internal Edge interface. This must be routable from the internal LAN.

To implement NAT on the Edge interfaces, some specific requirements must be met, in particular for the AV Edge address. These requirements cover how the destination and source addresses of the IP packets are modified when passing through the NAT device. Essentially, the principle is that traffic coming from the outside (that is, the Internet) should have its destination address in the packet header changed and traffic coming from the inside should have its source address in the IP header changed. This means that both types of traffic maintain a return path; the outside traffic maintains its source, and the internal traffic changes its source. If the internal traffic did not change its source, then return traffic would try to reach the internal NAT address, which would not be routable from the Internet.

Running Skype for Business with Firewalls on Your Internal Network

It is not uncommon to find networks on which Skype for Business is to be installed and that have firewalls separating the various internal elements of the LAN. For example, a company may have a LAN/WAN system with elements in which certain sites are less trusted than other sites. Frequently, there is a firewall between a branch site and the central site. In such cases, it is important to fully understand which ports need to be opened. Although written for Lync Server 2010, this useful blog goes into some depth on this subject and is also relevant for Lync Server 2013 and Skype for Business Server 2015:

`http://ucmadeeasy.wordpress.com/2011/04/26/deploying-a-lync-sba-watch-out-for-port-444/`

One final element worth noting is that although it is not a firewall as such, the use of IPsec on a network affects traffic—particularly the media components, which carry real-time communications. IPsec creates a delay as security is negotiated. Therefore, you should turn off IPsec for all media traffic, as outlined in Table 3.4.

Table 3.4: Media traffic for which IPsec needs to be disabled

Rule Name	Source IP	Destination IP	Protocol	Source Port	Destination Port	Filter Action
A/V Edge Server Internal Inbound	Any	A/V Edge Server Internal	UDP and TCP	Any	Any	Permit

TABLE 3.4: Media traffic for which IPsec needs to be disabled *(CONTINUED)*

RULE NAME	SOURCE IP	DESTINATION IP	PROTOCOL	SOURCE PORT	DESTINATION PORT	FILTER ACTION
A/V Edge Server External Inbound	Any	A/V Edge Server External	UDP and TCP	Any	Any	Permit
A/V Edge Server Internal Outbound	A/V Edge Server Internal	Any	UDP and TCP	Any	Any	Permit
A/V Edge Server External Outbound	A/V Edge Server External	Any	UDP and TCP	Any	Any	Permit
Mediation Server Inbound	Any	Mediation Server(s)	UDP and TCP	Any	Any	Permit
Mediation Server Outbound	Mediation Server(s)	Any	UDP and TCP	Any	Any	Permit
Conferencing Attendant Inbound	Any	Any	UDP and TCP	Any	Any	Permit
Conferencing Attendant Outbound	Any	Any	UDP and TCP	Any	Any	Permit
A/V Conferencing Inbound	Any	A/V Conferencing Servers	UDP and TCP	Any	Any	Permit
A/V Conferencing Server Outbound	A/V Conferencing Servers	Any	UDP and TCP	Any	Any	Permit
Exchange Inbound	Any	Exchange Unified Messaging	UDP and TCP	Any	Any	Permit
Application Sharing Servers Inbound	Any	Application Sharing Servers	TCP	Any	Any	Permit
Application Sharing Server Outbound	Application Sharing Servers	Any	TCP	Any	Any	Permit
Exchange Outbound	Exchange Unified Messaging	Any	UDP and TCP	Any	Any	Permit
Clients	Any	Any	UDP	Specified media port range	Any	Permit

Understanding Core Security

By its very nature, Skype for Business was designed to fulfill Microsoft security standards. That is, it is secure by default both in the way it is designed and in the way a deployment using default settings will work. When designing any feature in a product, Microsoft product groups conduct threat assessments to determine how the feature could be subverted to create problems. With this in mind, we will cover some of the key elements that make Skype for Business secure, starting with media security and moving on to authentication and certificates.

Media and Signaling Security

Because it is a wide-ranging communication platform, Skype for Business Server 2015 is subject to a lot of threats. Many of them involve someone trying to hijack traffic and manipulate it to gain access to the system. For example, common threats include *spoofing* (where someone pretends to be someone they are not), *eavesdropping* (where an attacker tries to look at traffic to ascertain its contents), and *replay* (where an attacker takes the traffic and changes it to gain access or alter content). All of these threats can be mitigated through the use of Mutual Transport Layer Security (MTLS) between trusted servers and Transport Layer Security (TLS) between client and server.

TLS and MTLS allow both encryption of traffic and authentication of endpoints. Lync clients must validate a certificate on the server; the certificate is issued by a CA that the client trusts and identifies that the server is indeed who it says it is. When MTLS is used between servers, both servers exchange certificates from a trusted CA so they can verify (trust) each other's identity. This security is in place between internal servers, and it is used when talking to gateway devices and Edge servers.

So far we have described *signaling traffic*—that is, SIP between servers or clients. There are other types of traffic, including AV media, traffic from gateways to a Mediation server, traffic from the reverse proxy to Skype for Business servers and clients downloading content from meetings. All of this traffic is also encrypted. The reverse proxy traffic is encrypted using SSL or TLS as normal, secure web traffic. The traffic from the Mediation server to the gateway can be encrypted, assuming the gateway is capable of supporting a certificate to use for MTLS. The client content download uses standard HTTPS.

One use case warrants a further comment—media traffic uses a different protocol, known as Secure Real-Time Transport Protocol (SRPT), a specialized media transfer protocol that supports encryption and traffic authentication.

FIPS SUPPORT

Readers in the United States may be pleased to know that while no specific announcements have (yet!) been made regarding Skype for Business, Lync supports the Federal Information Processing Standard (FIPS) 140-2 algorithms, and as Lync can be upgraded to Skype for Business, we expect an announcement confirming this soon. Each server would need to be configured to use the correct FIPS algorithms, a process that is described in the following KB article:

`http://go.microsoft.com/fwlink/?linkid=3052&kbid=811833`

In summary, all media/traffic is encrypted. This has enabled companies that were concerned with the use of traditional Voice over IP (VoIP) systems, which didn't encrypt traffic, to use Skype for Business in secure environments, such as trading floors. Table 3.5 details the security methods for the different types of traffic.

TABLE 3.5: The protection methods used to secure traffic

COMMUNICATION TYPE	SECURITY METHOD
Server to server	MTLS
Client to server	TLS
Instant messaging and presence	TLS
Audio and video and desktop sharing of media	SRTP
Desktop sharing (signaling)	TLS/SRTP (VBSS)
Web conferencing	TLS
Meeting content download, address book download, distribution group expansion	HTTPS

Authentication

One of the most fundamental aspects of security is authenticating those who try to access a system. In Skype for Business, there are many ways in which a user can attempt to access the system:

- Through an internal client
- Through an external client
- Via a web application
- Anonymously (conferencing or via a web application)
- Through an IP phone device
- Through a mobile device

The most obvious is through the standard desktop client, which operates based on authentication against credentials stored in Active Directory whether the client is internal or external to the network. Earlier in the chapter, we laid out the external authentication path via the Director, so let's look at how the authentication itself occurs. If the client is on the internal LAN, Kerberos V5 is used. For details of Kerberos and the way it operates, see the following URL:

`http://msdn.microsoft.com/en-us/library/aa378747(VS.85).aspx`

If the client is outside the network, NT LAN Manager (NTLM) is used because Kerberos requires direct access to the AD. NTLM is not as secure as Kerberos for many reasons. It doesn't allow mutual authentication; also, with Kerberos, passwords are never sent across the wire, thereby protecting them from man-in-the-middle attacks. Another benefit of Kerberos is that it is an open standard, whereas NTLM is not. Finally, in most recent operating systems (since Vista and Windows Server 2008), Kerberos supports AES encryption but NTLM doesn't. You can find more information about NTLM here:

`http://msdn.microsoft.com/en-us/library/aa378749(VS.85).aspx`

Because NTLM is less secure, some companies no longer allow it to be used as a method of authentication. This restriction may mean you need to prevent remote access to Skype for Business or you may need to use an alternative, such as Direct Access, to provide connectivity to AD.

That covers the initial default authentication of the main client both inside and outside the network. However, by default, once authenticated, the client will download a Skype for Business certificate, signed by the Front End server (this is not associated with any internal or external CAs) that can be used only to authenticate from this single client. Each client will have a different certificate associated with it (see Figure 3.5 for a sample certificate).

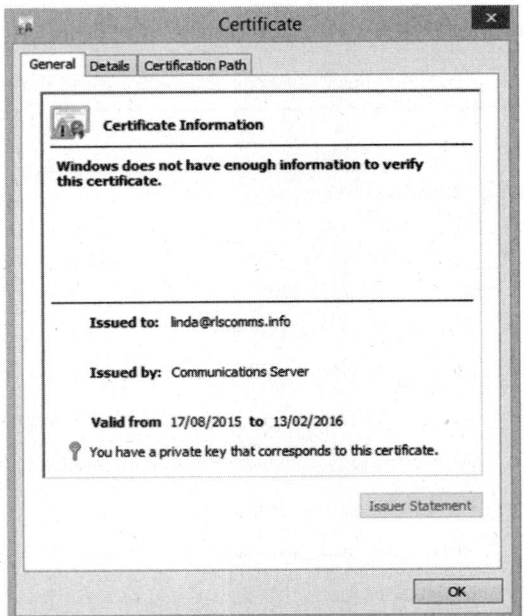

FIGURE 3.5
Client login certificate

Note that a certificate is generated for each individual client, not each user. A user using multiple clients will have multiple certificates generated. Even using the same client version on different computers (or same phone software version on different devices) will result in additional certificates being generated.

This certificate is valid for 180 days by default and can allow a user to continue to log in even if the user account in AD has been disabled. This method of login can be used on all clients (PC or phone) and was developed to cater to the branch disaster scenarios in which access to AD was unavailable because of a network outage (or similar).

However, other types of clients with their own types of authentication are used in Skype for Business.

The Skype for Business Web App provides remote access to conferences. It allows you to authenticate using your corporate credentials using either NTLM or Kerberos, depending on where your client is located. Anonymous authentication can also be made available. This works using the Digest authentication protocol and requires the client/user to have a meeting ID, which can be passed as part of the authentication process. For more information about Digest authentication, go to the following location:

```
http://technet.microsoft.com/en-us/library/cc778868(WS.10).aspx
```

For anonymous authentication to be allowed, you must enable it in a couple of places, first on the default Access Edge configuration as follows:

```
Set-CsAccessEdgeConfiguration -AllowAnonymousUsers $True
```

This allows anonymous connections to the Access Edge. However, you must also enable it on one or more of your conferencing policies, as follows:

```
Set-CsConferencingPolicy -Identity Global
-AllowAnonymousParticipantsInMeetings $True
```

This would allow anonymous participants in meetings governed by the global conferencing policy. Both of these steps can also be carried out through the Control Panel under the Federation and External Access and Conferencing sections, respectively.

The final type of authentication available is PIN authentication. This is part of what allows users to authenticate using just a PIN and extension combination (instead of a full username and password) on IP phone handsets and when signing into conferences. Once authenticated via PIN, a certificate is downloaded to the device and is retained on the device until the user logs out.

Disabling a User

Using certificate authentication has many advantages. However, one disadvantage is that users can continue to log in even when their Active Directory account has been disabled. This requires an additional step to be considered for any “user leaving” process.

From PowerShell, the command to view the certificates is as follows:

```
Get-CsClientCertificate -Identity <userID>
```

This results in the following (one entry for each certificate):

```
Identity        : sip:keith.skype@rlscomms.net
CertificateType : OcsSigned
DeviceId        : {42defd52-e069-5a0c-981d-3284caea21a0}
PublicationTime : 15/08/2015 07:59:52
```

continues

continued

```
ExpirationTime  : 11/02/2016 07:44:49
```

Removing the certificates from a user requires this command:

```
Revoke-CsClientCertificate -Identity <userID>
```

This action can also be carried out from the GUI, as shown in the following image.

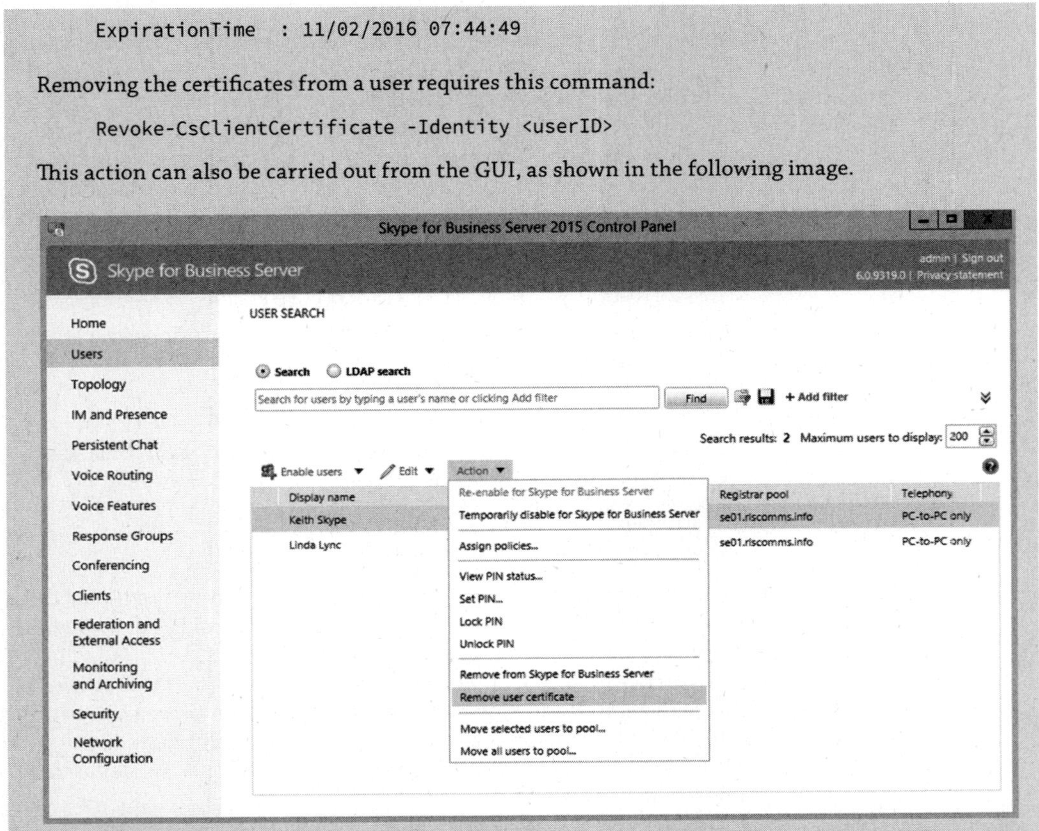

How do these certificates get to the phone devices, and how are they associated with the user? The devices are configured to look at AD for an object with the category of `certificationAuthority`. If one is found, the `caCertificate` attribute is checked, and the root CA certificate is installed on the device.

To load the relevant certificate into the `caCertificate` attribute, you must use the following command from an administrative CMD prompt:

```
certutil -f -dspublish "c:\skypebookCA.cer" cn=DC01-CA,
cn=Certificate Authorities, cn=Public Key Services,
CN=Services, cn=Configuration, dc=rlscomms, dc=info
```

This command will insert the `skypebookCA.cer` certificate, which is the `DC01-CA` root certificate, into the directory.

As long as the device is able to locate and install the relevant root CA certificate, authentication progresses as follows:

1. Obtain the root CA.
2. Verify the web services certificate using the root CA trust.
3. Store the certificate chain.
4. Take the credentials from the user, consisting of conferencing PIN and phone number.
5. Check the credentials.
6. Request a certificate for the user.
7. Receive the certificate on the device and publish it in the user store.
8. Use the certificate for all further authentications for the user.

Because the certificate needs to be obtained from AD, this procedure must be performed on the LAN the first time a user sets up the phone device. After it is set up, the device can be used remotely.

For devices that are "tethered"—that is, connected to a PC via USB—a username/password prompt will appear on the PC screen, allowing for authentication via Kerberos and onward access to information stored in Exchange. For more information, see Chapter 6, "Devices."

TWO-FACTOR AUTHENTICATION

In some environments, *two-factor authentication* is a must for any externally accessible system. Two-factor authentication is a system whereby the user has to authenticate with both something they have and something they know (for example, a PIN provided through a token device as well as a username and password). Of course, Skype for Business is often available externally. However, providing two-factor authentication is not all that simple. In cases where extreme security is a must, various steps can be taken. You could remove external anonymous access so that all conferences require users to know both the conference ID and the PIN. Second, you could ensure that only business-owned laptops are used to connect to the system externally. This could be done by using an internally signed certificate on the Edge server, which would require you to install the root CA as a trusted certificate on any remote machines. This would sacrifice the availability of PIC federation, but it would provide a loose level of security. Finally, you could provide two-factor authentication on the remote laptops by using BitLocker and requiring a smart card to boot the machines.

Certificates

We have examined certificates in various contexts in this chapter already, but there are still a couple of areas that need to be addressed to ensure that Skype for Business can use certificates.

First, public certificates should be obtained from a suitable CA. Table 3.6 lists a few of the more familiar CAs that have been validated by Microsoft as properly supporting Unified Communications.

Table 3.6: Familiar CAs supported by Skype for Business

Certification Authority	URL
Entrust	`www.entrust.net/microsoft/`
Comodo	`www.comodo.com/msexchange`
DigiCert	`www.digicert.com/unified-communications-ssl-tls.htm`
GlobalSign	`www.globalsign.com/en/ssl/multi-domain-ssl/`

Second, it is important that you set up the required certificate revocation list (CRL) distribution points for internal CAs. A CRL distribution point allows systems to validate whether a certificate has been revoked and, therefore, is no longer valid. You can find more information about this process here:

`http://technet.microsoft.com/en-us/library/cc753296.aspx`

Third, it is important to configure the relevant Enhanced Key Usage (EKU) settings for certificates. All certificates must support the Server Authentication EKU, which is essential for MTLS to function. Also, while previous versions of Microsoft OCS required the Client Authentication EKU, now it is required only on Edge servers that connect to the AOL cloud.

Finally, as discussed earlier in the section on authentication, it is possible to allow certificate-based authentication. This can be enabled or disabled externally using the following PowerShell cmdlet:

```
Set-CsProxyConfiguration -UseCertificateForClientToProxyAuth
```

It can be enabled or disabled entirely using this cmdlet:

```
Set-CsWebServiceConfiguration -UseCertificateAuth
```

See Appendix B for more information about working with PowerShell.

Providing Security Administratively

No matter how secure a system is "out of the box," without correct administration, holes can easily be created through which attackers can penetrate. In the following sections, you will see how policies can be used to prevent attacks, how a company can meet regulatory requirements through the use of disclaimers, how users can protect their presence information, and how to use antivirus software with Skype for Business.

Client-Version Filtering

To create a secure environment, narrowing down the variables in that environment can be useful. One way of doing this in Skype for Business is to restrict access to a known set of clients. Skype for Business allows you to do this by using `CsClientVersionPolicy`. This policy is composed of a collection of rules that specify which particular clients, based on their identity in SIP headers, are allowed to connect. By default, a global policy is in place. You can also set policies in a more granular way—for example, at the site or registrar level. This would allow you to have a group of users who must continue to use a Lync client, perhaps because of desktop OS compatibility issues, while most of your other users are mandated to use the latest Skype for Business client. For more information about how policies work, see Chapter 12, "User Administration." For more information about PowerShell, see Appendix B.

To investigate the global policy, you must first `Get` the policy using the PowerShell.

```
Get-CsClientVersionPolicy -Identity global
```

This will return the policy, and you will see a blob of text showing the rules. To see each rule individually, you must use the following command:

```
Get-CsClientVersionPolicy -Identity global | Select-Object -ExpandProperty Rules
```

This first gets the policy and then pipes the output to `Select-Object`, which then extracts all the information from the `Rules` attribute and lists them separately. The following is an example of one of the rules:

```
RuleId            : d957a4a4-6053-4f70-b28b-335145a4c53f
Description       :
Action            : Allow
ActionUrl         :
MajorVersion      : 4
MinorVersion      : 9999
BuildNumber       : 9999
QfeNumber         : 9999
UserAgent         : OC
UserAgentFullName :
Enabled           : True
CompareOp         : LEQ
```

From this output, you can see the elements that go into a rule.

To create a new policy, enter the following command:

```
New-CsClientVersionPolicy -Identity site:EMEA
```

This simple command creates a new policy with the default settings and links it to the EMEA site. However, if you wanted to amend the default rules while creating the policy, you could. To do so, you may use either the `CsClientVersionPolicyRule` cmdlet or the Control Panel, as shown in Figure 3.6.

Whether you use the cmdlet or the GUI, the requirements are relatively complex, so it is important to understand them.

First, each rule must have a *unique identifier*. This means it must have a reference to where it will be attached—that is, the scope of the policy to which it will be applied. It must also have a globally unique identifier (GUID).

Next, you must specify the client type from those shown in Figure 3.6 and Table 3.7, along with the version that will be referenced in the policy and whether the client will be allowed or blocked or one of the other actions will be chosen. For example, you could allow the client to be blocked and show the user a URL where they can get more information about why the client has been blocked or even download a newer version. Equally, you could have the client blocked and then automatically upgraded based on software available through Windows Update or Windows Software Update Services. Whether it is enabled or not, you can also configure how the rule is matched (that is, versions equal to that specified, or less than or equal to, and so on). For the full list, see Table 3.7.

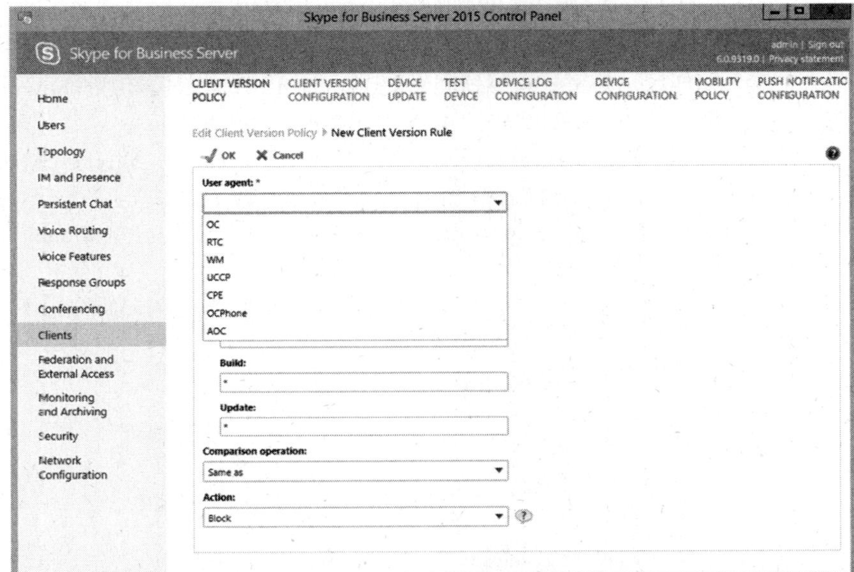

FIGURE 3.6 The client types available in Rules

TABLE 3.7: Client codes and associated clients

CLIENT CODE	CLIENT DETAIL
OC	Office/Lync/Skype for Business client
RTC	LCS clients
WM	Live Messenger
UCCP	Applications such as response groups
CPE	IP Phone
OCPhone	IP Phone
AOC	Attendee-only client
iPadLync*	iPad client
iPhoneLync*	iPhone client
WPLync*	Windows Phone client

TABLE 3.7: Client codes and associated clients *(CONTINUED)*

CLIENT CODE	CLIENT DETAIL
NokiaLync*	Nokia client
AndroidLync*	Android client
McxService*	Mobility service

**Items are available for configuration only in the Lync Management Shell.*

Finally, it is important to note that the rules in a policy are listed in order of precedence. This is why you have the option to specify the priority of the rule. If you specify a priority that is already in use, the new rule will take the priority number given and all the other rules will move down one.

Now that you've seen the possibilities, let's create a couple of rules for different scenarios. You will do the first one in the Control Panel.

1. Log into the Control Panel with an account that is a member of the `CsAdministrator` RBAC group (for more information, see Chapter 11, "Role-Based Access Control").
2. Locate the Clients tab and then double-click the Global policy in the right pane. This will open it for editing.
3. Click New. On the page that opens, specify the client type in the User Agent drop-down shown earlier in Figure 3.7. Select OC, which is the client type for Skype for Business, Lync, and Office Communicator clients. This becomes the identifier of the rule. Figure 3.8 shows the completed rule.

FIGURE 3.7
The match types available in Rules

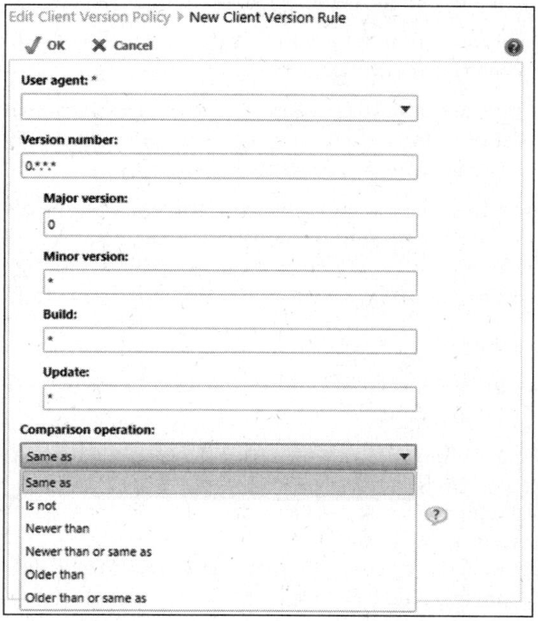

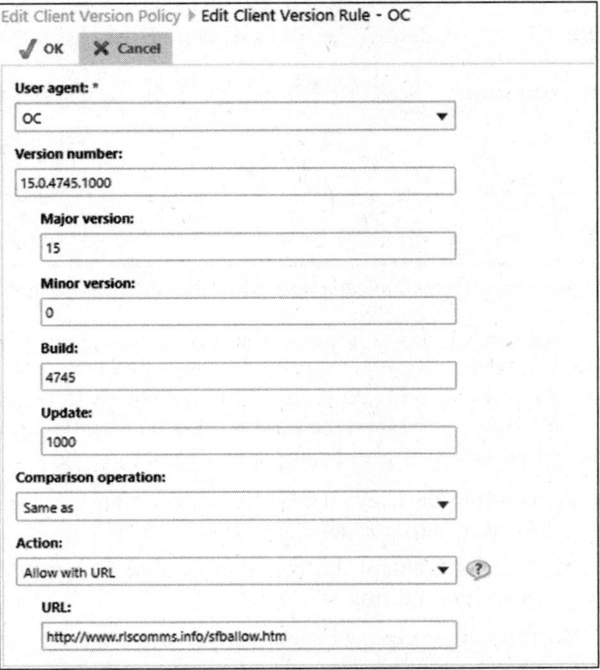

FIGURE 3.8
The finished rule

4. Enter the relevant version information to match the client—for example, Skype for Business client version 15.0.4745.1000. Newer versions are typically released each quarter.
5. Set the action, which in this case is to allow and launch a URL. Enter the URL that hosts your redirection page and then click OK.
6. On the main policy page, locate the rule, which by default will be at the bottom of the list of rules in the policy. Use the green up and down arrows to position it where needed. Once you are satisfied, click Commit.

Now when users log in using the specified Skype for Business client version, they will be presented with a pop-up in the Windows taskbar, which suggests that a new version of the client is available. If they click the pop-up, they will be taken to the appropriate website.

To create a similar rule from PowerShell, do the following. First, create a GUID for the rule:

```
$g = [guid]::NewGuid()
```

This generates a GUID and stores it in the `$g` variable. Next, create the rule using the following command:

```
New-CsClientVersionPolicyRule -Parent "Global" -RuleId $g
-MajorVersion 15 -Minor Version 0
-BuildNumber 4745 -QfeNumber 1000 -UserAgent OC
-Action AllowWithUrl
-ActionUrl "http://www.rlscomms.com/SfbRuleAllow.htm"
-CompareOp EQL -Priority 0
```

This will create the same rule as the one created through the GUI. Do *not* do this if you've already created the rule in the GUI; you will get an error if you do. You will need to change the version details to prevent a duplicate entry to get it to run.

Now you can create new rules and add them to existing policies. You need to understand that the way all Client Version policies are applied is governed by the cmdlet `CsClientVersionConfiguration`. Among other things, `CsClientVersionConfiguration` allows you to modify the default action for clients not specifically mentioned in the active policy, to enable or disable Client Version checks entirely, and to specify the default URL to which clients are pointed if the action of a rule is set to point users to a URL but no URL is specified. The following is an example:

```
New-CsClientVersionConfiguration -Identity site:EMEA -Enabled $True
-DefaultAction Block
-DefaultURL "http://www.rlscomms.com/SfbRuleBlock.htm"
```

This command creates a new Client Version Configuration policy for the Europe Middle East and Africa (EMEA) site; it enables version checking, blocks any clients not specifically listed on Client Version policies, and points any users that match rules with an action pointing to a URL, if they do not have their own URL defined, to the `www.rlscomms.com/SfbRuleBlock.htm` site.

Note that both the new Client Version policy rule and the new Client Version configuration can be configured from the Clients tab in the Control Panel.

Message Hygiene

The Skype for Business IM functionality has many uses, and it frequently cuts down on email usage by implementing a quick efficient method of communicating. One element of an IM conversation is the ability to send files and links. Of course, this ability has the potential to open users up to malicious or inadvertent threats because files can contain viruses and links can point to unsafe files or sites. Skype for Business, therefore, allows administrators to control what can and can't be sent in an IM conversation.

The `CsImFilterConfiguration` cmdlet allows you to control what happens when a user attempts to send a link through IM. By default, links are allowed in IM messages. To control this, you can enable the `CsImFilterConfiguration` policy. These settings can be manipulated either as shown (through PowerShell) or in the Control Panel within the IM & Presence section.

Once set, all messages sent by those users within the scope of the policy (for more information about scope, see Chapter 12) will be checked for links. The options are to block the link so that the message will not be sent, allow it but disable the link by inserting an underscore (_) character at the beginning of the link, or warn the user with a specific message but still allow the link to operate. By default, the `CsImFilterConfiguration` settings pick up the following link types:

- `callto:`
- `file:`
- `ftp.`
- `ftp:`
- `gopher:`
- `href:`

- `http:`
- `https:`
- `ldap:`
- `mailto:`
- `news:`
- `nntp:`
- `sip:`
- `sips:`
- `tel:`
- `telnet:`
- `www*`

For example, to create a new policy for the EMEA site, use this command:

```
New-CsImFilterConfiguration -Identity site:EMEA -Action Warn
-WarnMessage "This link could be dangerous,
make sure you know where it is taking you!"
-Prefixes http: -Enabled $true
```

This will create a new policy for the EMEA site. When it sees a link starting with the `http:` prefix, it will warn users with the text shown next to the `WarnMessage` parameter. Note that if you wanted to have all the prefixes listed as defaults here, you would not specify the `Prefixes` parameter. Figure 3.9 shows the client result with this rule in place.

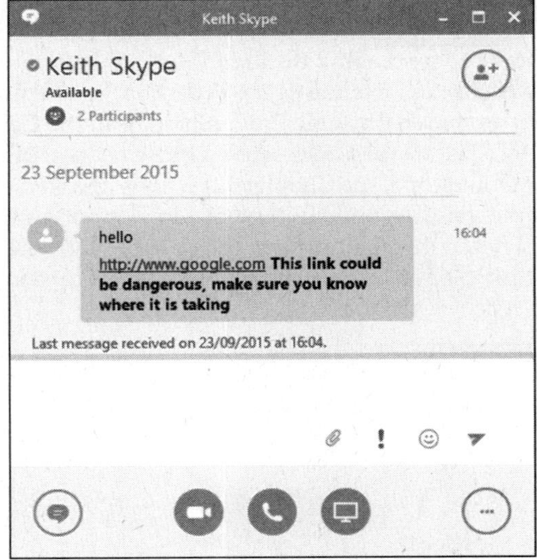

FIGURE 3.9 Warning message on Skype for Business client after sending an IM containing a URL

One issue with this process is that if the link is sent as the first message in a conversation and appears in the "toast," then no warning message is attached; simply the link itself is.

To remove the newly created policy, use the following command:

```
Remove-CsImFilterConfiguration -Identity site:EMEA
```

This command removes the `CsImFilterConfiguration` policy assigned to the EMEA site. Basic enabling and disabling of hyperlinks, which you can do through `CsClientPolicy` using the `EnableURL` setting, is another way to block URLs in IM.

Now that you've seen how to mitigate one threat, let's look at the threat associated with file transfer via IM. Just as with email attachments, normal antivirus scanning on client machines will provide a lot of protection. However, you can also control whether all or no attachments are allowed and whether specific file types are allowed. This is done using the `CsFileTransferFilterConfiguration` cmdlets.

The `New-CsFileTransferFilterConfiguration` cmdlet is relatively simple. It enables you to create a policy that affects a certain scope of users, defined using the `Identity` parameter as discussed in Chapter 12. The key parameters that make up the policy settings are `Action`, `Enabled`, and `Extensions`. The `Extensions` parameter is simply a list of the allowed (or disallowed) file types. By default, the following file types are part of a policy:

```
.ade, .adp, .app, .asp, .bas, .bat, .cer, .chm, .cmd, .com, .cpl, .crt, .csh, .exe, .fxp,
.grp, .hlp, .hta, .inf, .ins, .isp, .its, .js, .jse, .ksh, .lnk, .mad, .maf, .mag, .mam, .maq,
.mar, .mas, .mat, .mau, .mav, .maw, .mda, .mdb, .mde, .mdt, .mdw, .mdz, .msc, .msi, .msp,
.mst, .ocx, .ops, .pcd, .pif, .pl, .pnp, .prf, .prg, .pst, .reg, .scf, .scr, .sct, .shb, .shs,
.tmp, .url, .vb, .vbe, .vbs, .vsd, .vsmacros, .vss, .vst, .vsw, .ws, .wsc, .wsf, .wsh
```

The `Enabled` parameter lets you turn filtering on or off entirely. By default, file transfers of the types just listed are blocked. The `Action` parameter controls what happens when a file type listed in the `Extensions` parameter is detected. It has two possible settings, `BlockAll` and `Block`. The default is `Block`, which blocks file types listed in the `Extensions` parameter; by contrast, `BlockAll` simply prevents any file transfers.

To create a new file transfer configuration policy for the EMEA site, use the following command:

```
New-CsFileTransferFilterConfiguration -Identity site:EMEA
```

This command creates a new policy for the EMEA site with default extension values. Alternatively, you could specify different file types as shown here:

```
New-CsFileTransferFilterConfiguration -Identity site:EMEA
-Extensions .moo, .too
```

If you only want to add to the default types, enter the following:

```
New-CsFileTransferFilterConfiguration -Identity site:EMEA
-Extensions @{Add=".moo",".too"}
```

Finally, you can also add to an existing `CsFileTransferFilterConfiguration` policy, using this command:

```
Set-CsFileTransferFilterConfiguration -Identity site:EMEA
-Extensions @{Add=".doo",".foo"}
```

Configuring Antivirus Scanning

As with other Microsoft server–based systems, having an antivirus product in place on both the servers and the clients is sensible. On the client, antivirus scanning will be most relevant to Skype for Business when using the file transfer and content download features because these elements will be scanned and protected by the antivirus software. On the server side, there are no such features; however, as a best practice, AV software should still be deployed. It is important to configure that software correctly so that scanning does not compromise performance. To do so, you must configure the following exclusions.

Skype for Business Server 2015 processes:

- `ABServer.exe`
- `ASMCUSvc.exe`
- `AVMCUSvc.exe`
- `ClsAgent.exe`
- `DataMCUSvc.exe`
- `DataProxy.exe`
- `Fabric.exe`
- `FabricDCA.exe`
- `FabricHost.exe`
- `FileTransferAgent.exe`
- `HealthAgent.exe`
- `IMMCUSvc.exe`
- `LysSvc.exe`
- `MasterReplicatorAgent.exe`
- `MediaRelaySvc.exe`
- `MediationServerSvc.exe`
- `MeetingMCUSvc.exe`
- `MRASSvc.exe`
- `OcsAppServerHost.exe`
- `QmsSvc.exe`
- `ReplicaReplicatorAgent.exe`
- `RTCArch.exe`
- `RtcCdr.exe`
- `RtcHost.exe`
- `RTCSrv.exe`
- `XmppTGW.exe`

IIS processes:

- `%systemroot%\system32\inetsrv\w3wp.exe`
- `%systemroot%\SysWOW64\inetsrv\w3wp.exe`

SQL Server processes:

- `%ProgramFiles%\Microsoft SQL Server\MSSQL14.LYNCLOCAL\MSSQL\Binn\SQLServr.exe`
- `%ProgramFiles%\Microsoft SQL Server\MSSQL14.RTCLOCAL\MSSQL\Binn\SQLServr.exe`
- `%ProgramFiles%\Microsoft SQL Server\MSSQL14.LYNCLOCAL\Reporting Services\ReportServer\Bin\ReportingServicesService.exe`
- `%ProgramFiles%\Microsoft SQL Server\MSSQL14.LYNCLOCAL\OLAP\Bin\MSMDSrv.exe`

Directories:

- `%systemroot%\System32\LogFiles`
- `%systemroot%\SysWow64\LogFiles`

Disclaimers

In many countries, regulations specify how a company should identify itself in business communications. IM is just another form of business communication, and, like email, it can be used to communicate with other companies. Therefore, applying disclaimers or footnotes to messages is often required. In the United Kingdom, this footnote typically contains the company's registration details.

Skype for Business has a couple of places where you can add disclaimers. One is applicable to those who join conferences and is configured using `Set-CsConferenceDisclaimer`. You could, for example, use the following command to set up a disclaimer that will be shown to anyone joining the conference using a web link, such as the Join URL:

```
Set-CsConferenceDisclaimer -Header "RLS Comms Limited Conference Service"
-Body "Please Note: Conferences can be recorded. You will be notified if a
conference is recorded in the client and can choose to leave."
```

This displays the text in the `Body` parameter to users joining conferences.

The more common disclaimer used in Skype for Business is the one added to IM messages. To apply disclaimers to IMs, you need to use the `CsClientPolicy` cmdlets. In particular, the `IMWarning` parameter must be set as follows:

```
Set-CsClientPolicy -Identity Global
-IMWarning "IM message from Company RLS Comms Limited"
```

This command simply applies the warning text to all users. However, it is possible to target different IMWarning text at different users using the standard method of creating new policies with specific User scopes, as described in Chapter 12.

PIN Policy

As discussed in the section "Authentication" earlier in this chapter, you can log into Skype for Business using a PIN in conjunction with your extension or phone number. This is used when connecting to conferences via a phone line rather than using the Skype for Business client and also when using a Lync IP phone device. As with any other authentication method, controlling the form of credentials that can be used is important. PIN policies allow you to define the minimum length for a PIN and also to configure whether to allow common patterns, such as consecutive digits (for example, a PIN such as 123456 or 111111). You can also define the length of validity for a specific PIN and the number of PINs the system remembers so a user can't continually use the same one.

To create a new PIN policy, use the New-CsPinPolicy cmdlet. The next command shows how to create one for the EMEA site:

```
New-CsPinPolicy -Identity "site:EMEA" -MinPasswordLength 7
-PINHistoryCount 5 -PINLifetime 60
```

This command will create a new PIN policy and assign it to the EMEA site. The minimum length will be seven digits, five previous PINs will be remembered, and the PIN will expire in 60 days. As described in Chapter 12, these policies could be assigned to either the site or the per-user scope. This feature can also be configured in the Control Panel in the Security section.

Federation and How to Control It

We'll end with a discussion of *federation*. This feature enables you to communicate using Skype for Business not only internally but also externally with those who also have Skype for Business (or previous versions of Lync or Office Communications Server) and even those on public IM services such as Yahoo! and Skype. Skype for Business Server 2015 also has built-in XMPP federation capability—some previous versions required a separate download and also a separate server installation for XMPP.

Being able to talk not only within your company but with others over voice, video, and of course IM is a great benefit; however, some companies have concerns about the level of flexibility this brings. For example, while it is usually possible to email companies outside your own, your organization may have detailed controls in place to monitor such traffic. These restrictions may not be in place for Skype for Business; therefore, your company may want to restrict your ability to federate entirely or limit it to specific external parties.

By default, federation is disabled. You can enable it during the setup of the Edge server or afterward using this command:

```
Set-CsAccessEdgeConfiguration -AllowFederatedUsers:$True
```

This command configures the Access Edge role to allow federation. There is one more step to enable federation. You need to ensure that the users you want to be able to communicate with federated contacts are covered by a CsExternalAccessPolicy that enables federation for those users.

To edit the default global policy, use a command like this:

```
Set-CsExternalAccessPolicy -Identity Global
-EnableFederationAccess:$True
-EnablePublicCloudAccess:$True
```

This command enables standard external federation with other companies and also access to public clouds such as Messenger, assuming they have been allowed globally using the `Enable-CsPublicProvider` cmdlet as shown here:

```
Enable-CsPublicProvider -Identity "Messenger"
```

This would enable global access to Skype (the consumer version); other options would be Yahoo!, AIM, and Skype for Business Online.

Of course, you may not want to simply enable all federation. This can be controlled using the `Set-CsAccessEdgeConfiguration` cmdlet. Here's an example:

```
Set-CsAccessEdgeConfiguration - EnablePartnerDiscovery:$True
```

This command enables essentially open federation where companies looking to federate will locate each other through DNS SRV records and connect automatically, while setting `EnablePartnerDiscovery` to `$False` would restrict federation to those domains specified manually. This leaves us with how to manipulate the list of allowed or blocked federation domains, which is done using the `CsAllowedDomain` and `CsBlockedDomain` cmdlets. Here's an example:

```
New-CsAllowedDomain -Identity "rlscomms.net"
-ProxyFqdn "edgeserver.rlscomms.net"
-MarkForMonitoring $True -Comment "Contact: Keith Hanna (keith@rlscomms.net)"
```

Here we created a new entry to allow the domain `rlscomms.net` to participate in a federated relationship. We also specified the URL for the Edge server in the federated domain and that we want to monitor the traffic. Finally, we added a comment labeling the domain with a contact person.

The method of blocking domains is similar.

```
New-CsBlockedDomain -Identity "rlscomms.net" -Comment "Blocked by Keith."
```

This simple command blocks the `rlscomms.com` domain from federating with our system and lists Keith as the person who carried out the configuration. Again, note that although PowerShell is used in this section to perform the configuration, these settings could have been set from the Control Panel in the External Access section.

The Bottom Line

Secure external access. Skype for Business utilizes the Edge server and supporting components to provide external access to communications modalities. The Edge server sits in the DMZ and is a proxy between internal and external users. Many layers of security are in place to ensure that communicating externally won't cause security breaches.

Master It Describe the role the Director plays in external access. Why would you use one?

Understand core security. Skype for Business is designed to be secure by default. It does this in many ways, not least of which is by encrypting all traffic and using certificates as part of mutual authentication of connections.

Master It In different circumstances, Skype for Business can use five different authentication mechanisms. What are they, and where are they used?

Provide security administratively. No matter how secure a product is by design, an administrator can easily open up holes in its defenses. Skype for Business provides many ways in which administrators can participate in tightening or relaxing security. Numerous policies are available to control users, including the clients they are allowed to use and the length and complexity of PINs. Equally, you can configure Skype for Business to block links in IMs and prevent the transfer of files. Finally, Skype for Business can be set up to add disclaimers to messages so that regulatory issues can be managed.

Master It You have been asked to ensure that users in the EMEA site can send only files with extension `.txt` in IM messages and that any links in the messages will be prefixed with an underscore character so they must be copied into a browser manually. How would you do this?

Chapter 4

Desktop Clients

Client applications tend to be one of the most important aspects of a deployment, and they can cause the most pain if they are not fully understood. Skype for Business includes several significant changes from the previous release, updating the main desktop client with a new look and feel and branding similar to the Skype consumer client.

Understanding the features the various clients have to offer, how they should be configured, and how they interoperate with each other and previous versions ensures that the correct clients are deployed to the correct people at the correct phase of the Lync deployment project.

In this chapter, you will learn to

- Understand usage scenarios for each client
- Understand changes in Group Chat
- Understand how clients discover and communicate with various server roles, such as the Director, Front End, Persistent Chat, and the various Media Conferencing Units (MCUs) for conferencing

User Clients

With Skype for Business, this chapter will focus on two main clients.

- Skype for Business, which is the Windows desktop client
- Skype for Business Web App, which is the significantly redesigned Web App found first in Lync Server 2010; it now supports IP audio and video

Skype for Business on mobile devices (including iPad) is covered in Chapter 5, "Mobile Devices," and the Lync Attendee and Attendant clients have not been updated since Lync Server 2010. Furthermore, use of the Lync Attendee 2010 client is no longer recommended because Skype for Business Web App is now the preferred meeting experience client.

Skype for Business

Skype for Business 2016 is the updated version of the Lync 2013 client and provides access to all the functionality of Lync Server 2013; indeed, the first iteration is simply an upgrade patch. Like Lync 2013, the latest client can be used against a legacy infrastructure, meaning Skype for Business can also be used against a Lync Server 2010 (or 2013) pool, allowing you to deploy the latest client (which is included as part of Microsoft Office 2016) without having to migrate everybody to Skype for Business Server 2015 first.

Feature Overview

The client is a full-featured client for Skype for Business Server 2015. The user interface has been redesigned with a new look and feel, and it retains features such as Persistent Chat (previously a separate client with Lync Server 2010), tabbed conversations, video preview, and multiparty video. At a high level, the client provides the following features:

Contacts Similar to Lync, the contact list displays the name, presence, photo, and communication modalities available for users.

Contact Photos Lync 2010 allowed you to set your photo using a specific URL, which requires unauthenticated access to the URL (in other words, no proxy prompts). Skype for Business continues to honor this URL but does not allow you to set it—only linking to Active Directory—or Exchange/SharePoint-hosted photos. It has continued support for HD photos (introduced in Lync 2013), although this feature requires Exchange Server 2013 (more about this in the section "High-Resolution Photos" later in this chapter). This is particularly useful when you're in a conference and are not sharing video because instead of showing an up-scaled version of the low-resolution photo in Lync 2010, you can now display an HD-quality photo. Photos are capped at about 300Kb and are shared across Office (for example, Outlook, Outlook Web App, Lync, and so on). A small version of the photo is also written to the `thumbnailPhoto` attribute in Active Directory for backward compatibility with Lync 2010.

New Contacts View Skype for Business includes a New Contacts view to allow you to easily see who has added you to their contacts list recently.

Presence Skype for Business supports many presence states, some of which can be manually defined and others of which are automatically set based on the current state, such as Off Work and Presenting, which are triggered automatically when setting up an out-of-office notification or sharing PowerPoint slides.

Instant Messaging Instant messaging is supported between users in the same organization as well as in other organizations running Skype for Business Server, Lync Server, or Office Communications Server via federation.

XMPP While not different to the end user, Extensible Messaging and Presence Protocol (XMPP) is natively supported. You can add an XMPP user to your contacts list and engage in IM/presence conversations with them the same way you could before, but this no longer requires the separate Office Communications Server 2007 R2 XMPP Gateway role. This functionality is built into the Edge and Front End server roles.

Tabbed Conversations One change from previous clients is the support for tabbed conversations. This allows the user to have all IM conversations appear in a single window, with tabs representing each conversation for easy switching. This feature also extends to Persistent Chat, which is now natively supported in the client (see the section "Persistent Chat" later in this chapter for more information).

Voice The preferred voice codec has changed to SILK, which is a "native" Skype codec allowing for better-quality voice.

Video Lync 2013 represented a major investment in video, which Skype for Business continues. At a technical level, the video codec used is the standard-based H.264 AVC/SVC codec rather than RTVideo. Additionally, a number of user interface changes are apparent in the client.

Multiview Video Instead of being based on the *active* and *last active* speaker, multiview video is preferred for more natural integrations, showing you the video stream of the five most active users in the conference, with support for up to 75 users being promoted from the 'seated' row to the 'standing' row.

HD in Conference HD video of up to 720p for conferences as well as 1080p for room-based systems is used.

Collaboration Skype for Business has been significantly redesigned to improve feature use and incorporate new features related to collaboration.

PowerPoint Viewing Lync 2010 relied on the Microsoft Office PowerPoint viewer, embedded in the Lync client, to render PPT slides with animations and transitions. This limited PowerPoint sharing to platforms where the PowerPoint viewer was available. In Lync 2013, the Office Web Apps companion server role was introduced to render PowerPoint slides. For more details, see the section "Conferencing Clients" later in this chapter.

Application and Desktop Sharing Although the client provides the option to "share a program" vs. "share the desktop," both are treated in the same way. The only difference is partial-screen vs. full-screen sharing.

Desktop Sharing For sharing-only sessions, the video stream is encoded using video codecs rather than using RDP (assuming both endpoints are running the latest Skype for Business client), resulting in a significant drop in the bandwidth used. For sharing sessions that transfer control, RDP is used.

DRM Following customer feedback, Lync 2013 introduced support for digital rights management (DRM) in a desktop sharing session. If a user opens a DRM-protected document, it will appear blacked out in a desktop sharing session.

Web App Application and desktop sharing are supported in Web App. This requires a browser plug-in, which can be installed in user mode. See the later "Web App" section.

Whiteboard Skype for Business supports sending whiteboard images directly to OneNote. Additionally, touch is supported for whiteboards when viewed on Windows 7 or higher as well as Smart Board devices.

Recording Lync 2013 removed the intermediate file format used for recording in Lync 2010 and instead records natively into MP4 format. Additionally, Skype for Business supports active speaker recording, which will record the video or photo of the active speaker, unlike Lync 2010, which would record one person for the whole meeting if they were the only person sharing video. Recordings are also in HD format.

File Transfer File transfer is unchanged.

Persistent Chat Another large area of investment in Lync 2013 is the integration of Persistent Chat, formerly Group Chat, into both the server architecture (although it is still a separate pool, it is defined and managed through standard tools now, such as Topology Builder and Lync Server Management Shell) and the client user interface.

Built-in Persistent Chat Since Lync 2013, there is no longer a separate Persistent Chat client, as was the case in Lync 2010. The Skype for Business desktop client is a truly unified client, providing IM and presence, audio, video, conferencing and collaboration, desktop and application sharing, and Persistent Chat in a single user interface. See the section "Persistent Chat" later in this chapter for more details.

Notable Changes Since Lync 2010

As Skype for Business is mainly an update (patch!) to Lync 2013, there are significant similarities; however, there are still some changes from Lync 2010 that should be highlighted for those migrating from this older environment.

Integration with Office Setup Skype for Business and the Online Meeting add-in for Skype for Business, which supports meeting management from within Microsoft Outlook, are both included with Office 2016. In addition to including the client as part of Office 2016, this change allows administrators to customize and control the installation using the Office Customization Tool (OCT), `Config.xml`, and set up command-line options.

Group Policy Deployment Lync 2013 introduced the Lync ADMX and ADML administrative templates that are provided with Office Group Policy administrative templates.

Outlook Scheduling Add-in Updates Administrators can now customize the organization's meeting invitations by adding a custom logo, a support URL, a legal disclaimer URL, and custom footer text. These can be enabled and customized using Skype for Business Server Control Panel or Skype for Business Server Management Shell, specifically the `CsMeetingConfiguration` cmdlets. Additionally, new controls allow the meeting organizer to schedule conferences that have attendee audio and video muted by default.

Virtual Desktop Infrastructure (VDI) Plug-in Skype for Business supports all modalities, including audio and video, when deployed in a Virtual Desktop Infrastructure (VDI) environment, with some caveats. Users can connect an audio or video device (for example, a USB headset) to the local computer (for example, a thin client). The user can connect to the virtual machine, sign in to Skype for Business running inside the virtual machine, and participate in real-time audio and video as though the client is running locally. This is achieved by using the Lync VDI plug-in (yes, it's still the Lync VDI plug-in!), a stand-alone application that installs on the local computer and allows the use of local audio and video devices. The plug-in does not require Skype for Business to be installed on the local computer. Skype for Business, running inside the virtual machine, will prompt the user to enter their credentials to establish a connection to the VDI plug-in. The caveats are as follows:

- The virtual machine must be running Windows 7 or Windows Server 2008 R2 with the latest service pack, or higher.
- The user's local computer (for example, thin client) must be running Windows Embedded Standard 7 with SP1, Windows 7 with SP1, or higher.
- If Remote Desktop Services is used, the Lync VDI plug-in platform architecture (32-bit or 64-bit) must match the local computer's operating system platform architecture.
- On the local computer (for example, thin client), the remote desktop client settings must be configured so that audio plays on the local computer. Remote recording must be disabled.

In addition to the caveats listed here, there are a number of limitations of the Lync 2013 VDI plug-in. There is limited support for call delegation and Response Group Agent anonymization, and there is no support for integrated audio and video device tuning, multiview video, recording of conversations, joining meetings anonymously (for example, joining a meeting hosted by an organization that does not federate with your company), pairing a Phone Edition device, call continuity in the event of a network outage, or customized ringtones and music on hold (MOH).

Sign-in Changes

Lync 2010 introduced certificate-based authentication using TLS-DSK. Clicking Save Password when signing in results in the Lync Server issuing you a certificate, which is then saved in the Personal certificate store on the individual computer, as shown in Figure 4.1. This certificate is then used to authenticate future sign-in requests, allowing Lync to sign in without communicating with an Active Directory domain controller, which is useful in branch-office scenarios during a WAN outage. Certificate authentication is also faster than Kerberos or NTLM authentication.

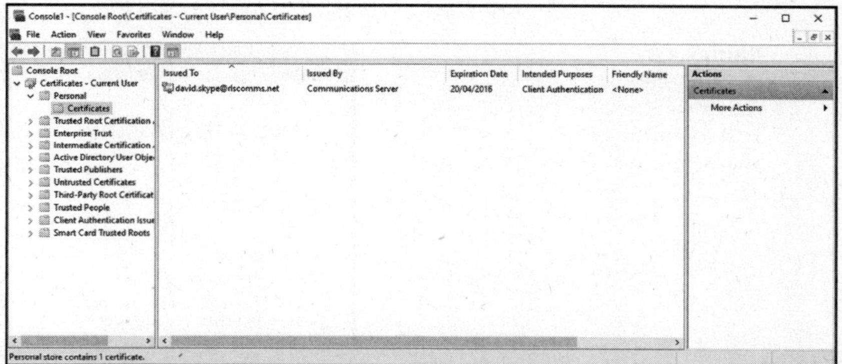

Figure 4.1 The user certificate in the Personal certificate store

Skype for Business continues the support for TLS-DSK authentication but with a couple of changes in the client. First, when you check the Save Password check box when signing in for the first time, you are now clearly prompted to indicate whether you want to save your sign-in information for use in the future, as shown in Figure 4.2.

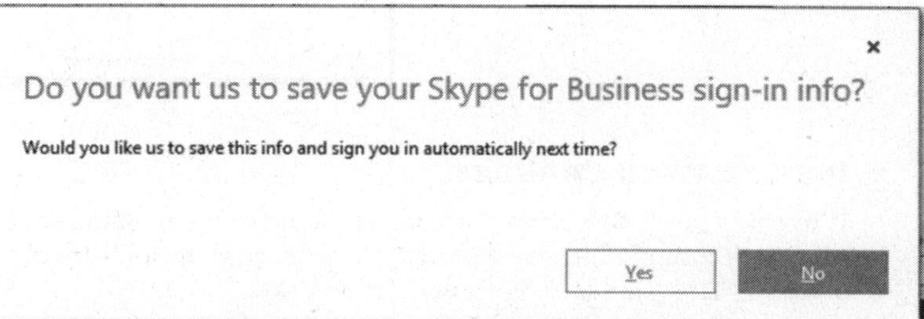

Figure 4.2 User being prompted about saving sign-in credentials

Second, the option to delete sign-in information, effectively asking Skype for Business to forget you, is now displayed at the sign-in screen, as shown in Figure 4.3. Clicking this will provide a prompt asking you to confirm. Clicking Yes will remove the Skype for Business certificate from the user's certificate store. It will also remove a number of files (listed here) from the AppData folder, located in %userprofile%\appdata\local\microsoft\office\<office version>\lync\<sipuri>:

- ABS.cache
- CoreContact.cache
- EndpointConfiguration.cache
- EwsFolder.cache
- MfuGroup.cache

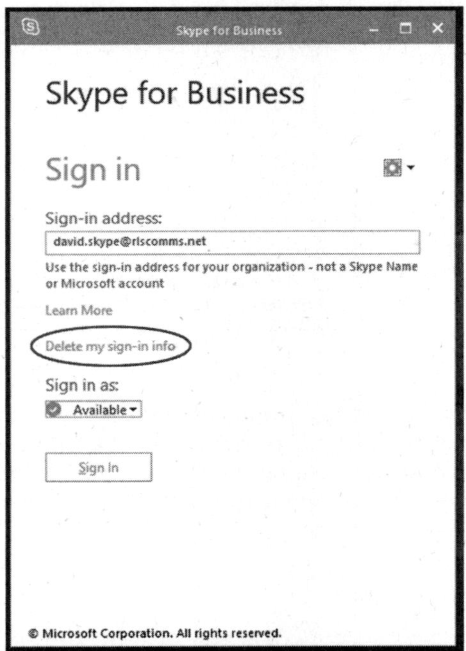

FIGURE 4.3
The link allowing you to ask Skype for Business to forget your sign-in details

INSTALLATION CHANGES

While it is possible to obtain a separate stand-alone installer for Skype for Business (from the Microsoft Volume License website), the preferred option is to deploy Skype for Business as part of Office. There are two methods of doing this.

Office 2016 Windows Installer This is the traditional Windows Installer package that contains multiple MSI files.

Office 2016 Click-to-Run Primarily intended for Office 365 customers, this is an installation method that streams Office 2016 setup files from the Office 365 portal or another installation source. Administrators can download the Office 2016 Click-to-Run application and language source files to an on-premises location. You can find more details about Click-to-Run in the Office 2016 Resource Kit.

Note: Click-to-Run is the Microsoft preferred installation method because it includes a level of self-notification and updating (where permitted), allowing for better control of patch levels. This applies across all products, not just Skype for Business.

Dependency on Exchange Server 2013

A number of features in Skype for Business rely on the user's mailbox being hosted on Exchange Server 2013. These features are Unified Contact Store, high-resolution photos, and Exchange archiving, and each is introduced here and covered in more detail in Chapter 22, "Exchange, SharePoint, and Office Web Applications Server."

Unified Contact Store

Unlike in previous versions, in Skype for Business, Exchange Server is the Unified Contact Store across Office. This is enabled by policy when Exchange Server 2013 is deployed in the environment. Unified Contact Store can be enabled only when both Skype for Business Server 2015 and Exchange Server 2013 are deployed in the environment. Communication between Skype for Business and Exchange is handled by Exchange Web Services (EWS). Lync 2010 can leverage the Unified Contact Store in read-only mode, but only Skype for Business 2016 and Lync 2013 clients can modify the contact list once Unified Contact Store is enabled by policy for a given user. The benefits of this are that it provides a single repository of contact data—Exchange, which is utilized across Office as well as Windows Phone.

High-Resolution Photos

Lync 2010 supported contact photos that could be stored either in Active Directory or as a user-specified URL, referencing a public website. Whether the photo was stored or not depended on the photo's source. If the photo was from Active Directory, it would be stored in the `thumbnailPhoto` attribute and replicated to other domain controllers in the environment. If the photo was from a user-specified URL, the photo was not stored in the environment. Instead, the URL was stored and communicated to other presence watchers via the user's presence document.

The size of photos stored in Active Directory was limited by the size of the `thumbnailPhoto` attribute in Active Directory, which needed to remain relatively small so as not to negatively impact replication traffic.

Skype for Business supports the ability to use photos with resolutions ranging from 48×48 up to 648×648 pixels, provided your mailbox is hosted on Exchange Server 2013. This is because the photos are now stored in Exchange as one of three typical resolutions.

- 48×48, which is also used for the `thumbnailPhoto` attribute in Active Directory
- 96×96, which is the format Outlook 2013, Outlook Web App, Skype for Business, and Skype for Business Web App will use in various places
- 648×648, which is the format used by Skype for Business and Skype for Business Web App in specific scenarios, such as when you're the active speaker in a conference and you're not sharing your video

As mentioned, a change in Lync 2013 is that the ability to specify a photo from a URL has been removed from the client. If a user still has a photo from a user-specified URL stored in their presence document, Skype for Business will honor it. However, as soon as a high-resolution photo is stored in the user's Exchange Server 2013 mailbox, this replaces the URL and also triggers the 48×48 version of the photo being stored in Active Directory for backward compatibility. Additionally, because the photos are now stored in the Exchange mailbox rather than being a URL referenced in the presence document, photos will no longer be displayed to federated users. This was always the case in Lync 2010 for photos stored in the `thumbnailPhoto` attribute in Active Directory. Users can change their photos via Outlook Web App. One thing to keep in mind is that changing the photo in Active Directory does not trigger an upscaled version of that photo to replace the one stored in the Exchange Server 2013 mailbox. Because of Skype for Business's use of photos in places such as multiparty conversations, it is recommended that users have a photo to replace the default icon and display name that Skype for Business will use instead.

Archiving

The final feature where Skype for Business has a reliance on Exchange Server 2013 is archiving. When this is enabled, archive data is written to the Exchange Server 2013 mailbox instead of the Skype for Business archiving database (in SQL). This does not mean you can enable archiving in Skype for Business only once everybody is on Exchange Server 2013; users who do not have an Exchange Server 2013 mailbox can continue to use the archiving database store (SQL) instead. However, the benefit of using the Exchange integrated archiving feature is that it results in a single archive repository—the Exchange Server mailbox—and makes legal hold and compliance easier to administer.

Multiparty Video

In Lync 2010, active speaker switching was used to switch the video stream between whoever was speaking. It was not possible to see the video streams of other participants in the meeting, with the exception of using a room-based system or a RoundTable device for video panorama, but that relied on all participants being in the same physical location.

Skype for Business 2015 supports multiparty video, allowing the video stream (or high-resolution picture if no video is shared) to be displayed for five speakers, plus yourself, in the standing row, with support for up to 75 participants in total, with the others making up the seated row.

In Figure 4.4, you can see three users who are taking part in a meeting. The screenshot shows Keith's view of the conversation, indicated by the fact that his is the smallest of the three tiles in the window.

Video Preview

Another feature in Skype for Business is the video preview. This allows you to hover your cursor over the video icon in the client and display a "peek," showing you what your video looks like to others, before you actually start sharing it. If you're happy with what you see (within reason), you can click Start My Video to start sharing your video. In Figure 4.5 and then Figure 4.6, you can see Keith's video replacing the photo currently displayed on Keith's tile in the conversation window.

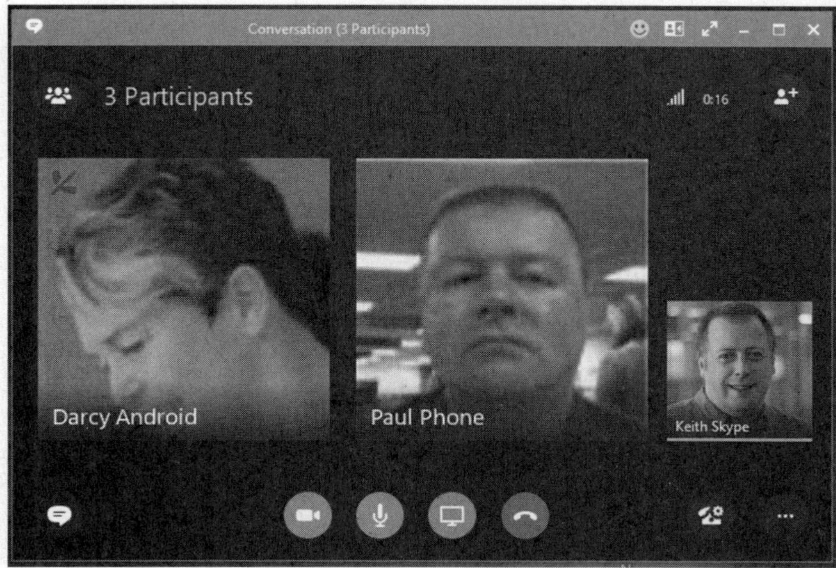

FIGURE 4.4 A multiparty call showing the user experience

FIGURE 4.5 Viewing a video preview

Figure 4.6 actually shows this conversation window from another participant—Linda in this case. She sees the video of Keith as one of the (up to) five people in his standing row. Rob is represented by a high-resolution photo, if available, or, as in Figure 4.7, the default tile if no photo is uploaded for Darcy.

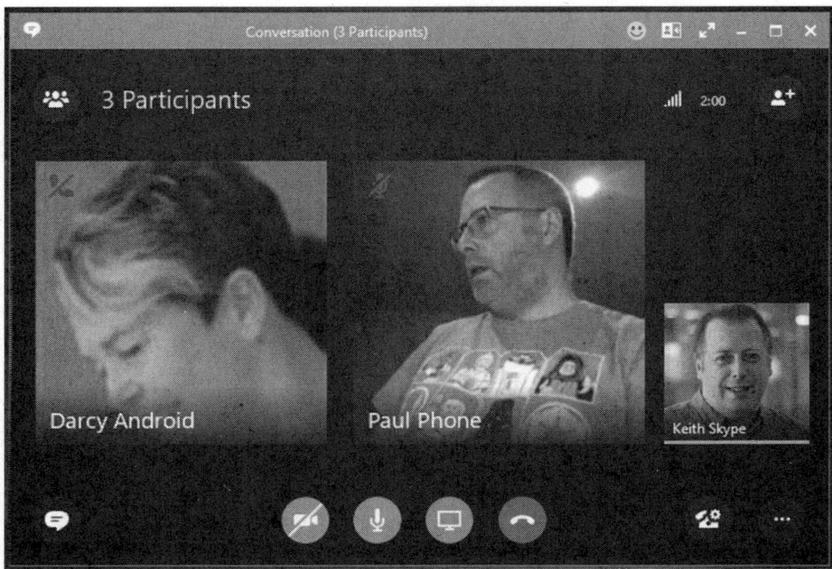

FIGURE 4.6
Video now shown in the call

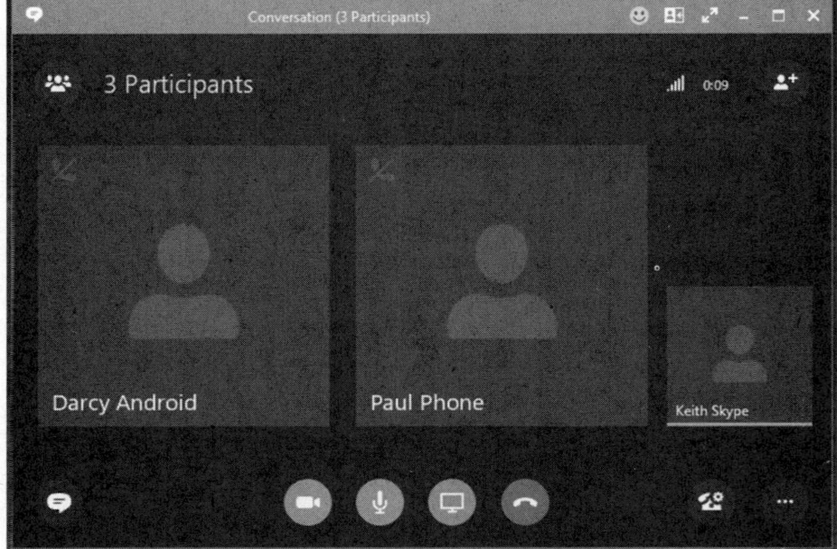

FIGURE 4.7
Default tile view

Smart Framing

Video framing and smart sizing ensure that the video feed automatically centers the participant in the frame. When in a Skype for Business Meeting, the client will expand the video tile for a particular user if two people are in the frame. It will expand to include the second person so both are centered properly. It automatically shrinks if the second person leaves.

Web App

Skype for Business Web App is a browser-based meeting client that allows users to join meetings. Clicking the Join Skype Meeting link in a meeting invite will cause Skype for Business Web App to start, assuming either one of the following is true:

- The computer you are using does not have Skype for Business (or Lync 2013) client installed.
- You're using an Apple Mac.

The Skype for Business Web App provides a rich meeting experience across different platforms. It does not provide IM and presence or contacts lists outside a Skype for Business Meeting, however.

In Lync 2010, if you did not have the full Lync client installed and wanted to join a meeting with computer audio and video, you needed to download and install the Lync 2010 Attendee client. In Skype for Business 2015, the Web App supports computer audio and video, meaning the Attendee client is no longer required. Furthermore, Lync 2010 Attendee is not supported against a Skype for Business 2015 pool.

Skype for Business Web App is also preferred over Lync 2010 when joining a meeting hosted on a Skype for Business pool because the Web App will support features in Skype for Business, such as multiparty video and additional conference controls that are not supported when joining from Lync 2010. This is an important change in people's perception that web-based clients are second-class citizens to the full Windows application client. This may have been the case in Lync 2010, where Lync Web App was restricted to Windows because of its use of Silverlight and did not support computer audio and video, but this is no longer true.

Audio and Video in the Browser

The major change required to help achieve voice and video in the browser is that Skype for Business Web App is based on HTML5 and JavaScript instead of Silverlight, meaning it can be used on Windows, Mac, and other platforms that support these web standards.

It should be noted that audio, video, and desktop sharing require a client plug-in. The good news is that this plug-in can be installed in user mode rather than requiring administrative permissions. You can still join a meeting without the plug-in and will still be able to participate in IM and PowerPoint viewing.

Prior to joining the meeting from Skype for Business Web App, the user will be prompted to install the plug-in. This is the default option, and the user must clear the check box if they do not want to install the browser plug-in. In Figure 4.8, we are joining the meeting from Skype for Business Web App on Windows 10, using the Google Chrome Browser. Notice that Skype for Business Web App will open in a new window.

You will see the same behavior when using Skype for Business Web App with Internet Explorer or on a Mac. The user will be prompted to provide a name or to authenticate with their username and password.

When using Google Chrome and launching using the Join the Meeting button, you will get a prompt asking how to handle a new type of link, `sfb-16.0:` (shown in Figure 4.9). You should think of this as the Skype for Business equivalent of `http:`.

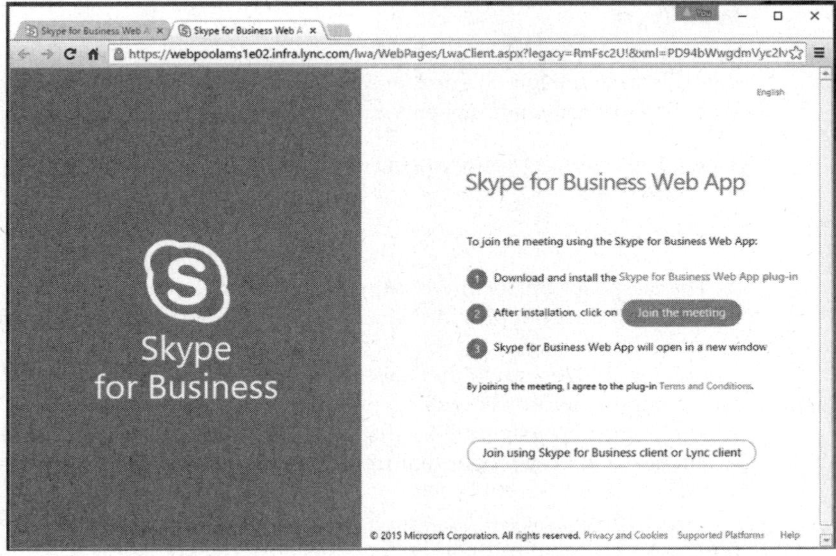

FIGURE 4.8 Joining a meeting with Skype for Business Web App on Google Chrome Browser

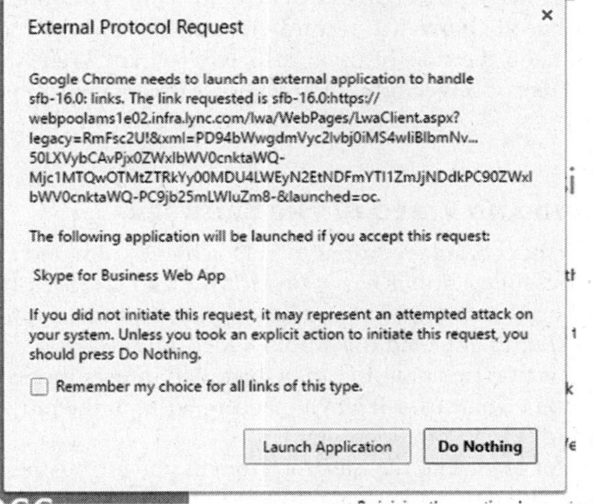

FIGURE 4.9 Launching the new protocol link

When Skype for Business Web App has launched, the web page will reflect this, as shown in Figure 4.10.

OTHER AUDIO OPTIONS WHEN JOINING WITH A BROWSER

Of course, like with the desktop client, it is possible to have other options for audio. When joining via the web browser, the user has three options to choose from and can be prompted upon joining a conference, as shown in Figure 4.11.

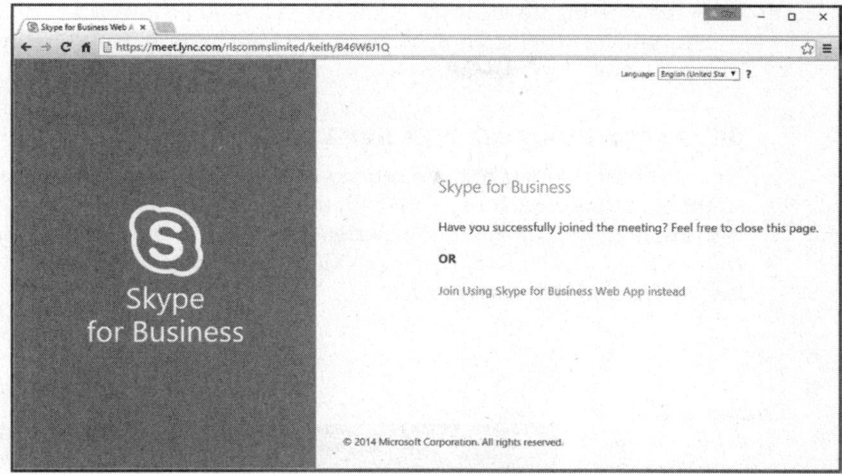

Figure 4.10 Skype for Business Wep App launched notification

Figure 4.11 The meeting join options without a plug-in

The options are as follows:

Using My Computer This will use the default audio settings. In testing, this is the actual computer audio settings, which may be different from the default communications settings.

Have The Meeting Call Me This will initiate a call to the number you specify in the box. In Lync Server 2010, this required the organizer to be Enterprise Voice enabled (or it required a potentially unsafe and definitely unsupported workaround by adding a static route to the Mediation server, allowing Lync Server 2010 to place calls to any number). In Skype for Business Server, it is possible for the administrator to assign a voice policy to users not enabled for Enterprise Voice, so dial-out conferencing is still possible without introducing the risk of toll fraud.

I Will Dial In To The Meeting This will close the prompt. The user will manually dial in using another phone (mobile, PSTN) using the dial-in conferencing numbers provided in the meeting invite. If the organizer is hosted on Office 365, dial-in conferencing numbers will be provided only if the tenant has configured audio conferencing provider (ACP) integration.

Skype for Business Web App Experience

Once the user is joined to the meeting via Skype for Business Web App, the experience is so similar in terms of feature parity with the desktop client that it's difficult to tell the two apart. It is worth highlighting that this experience is not just restricted to Windows, however. Figure 4.12 shows Paul, Les, and Rob in a Skype Meeting, with Paul using a Windows Phone device, Les on iOS, and Rob via a browser.

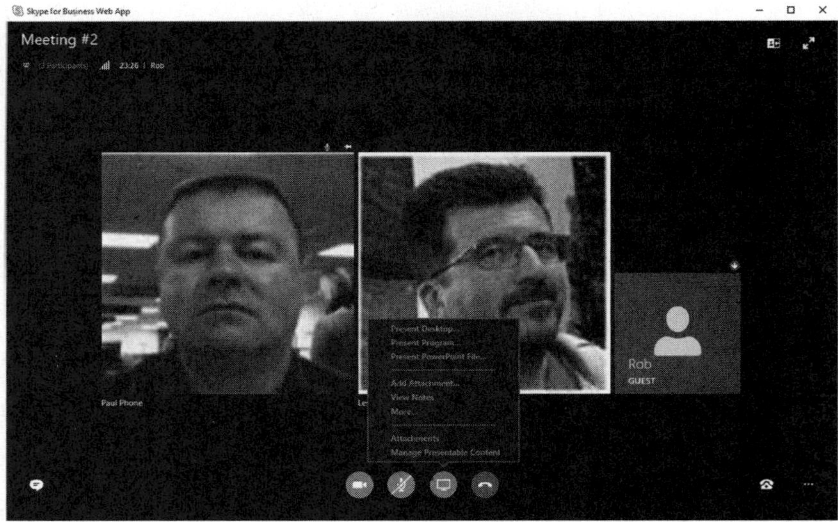

Figure 4.12 Paul, Les, and Rob in a Skype Meeting with Rob on the Google Chrome browser

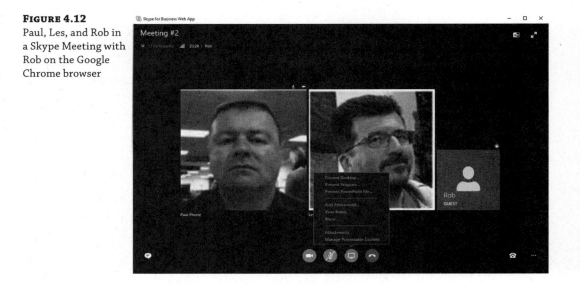

Rob, connected via Google Chrome, is showing the presenting capability provided via the browser interface. In Figure 4.13, you can see the video preview capability; it's on par with the desktop client.

Signaling

For all signaling, Skype for Business Web App communicates via HTTPS to the Unified Communications Web API (UCWA), which acts as a web relay and in turn communicates with the Focus (the component responsible for managing the conferences) and all MCUs using C3P/HTTP.

Skype for Business Web App does not support connecting to a RoundTable (for example, Polycom CX5000) device, although it does support viewing the video panorama stream.

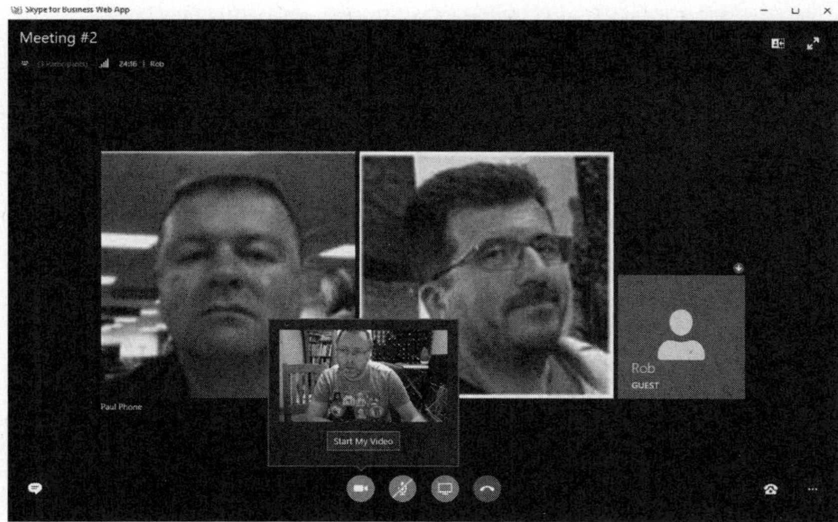

Figure 4.13 Rob previewing his video

Windows Store App

With Lync 2013, Microsoft provided a Windows Store app client designed specifically for Windows 8 and Windows RT and is optimized for touchscreen devices. However, unlike other clients (such as mobile), this has not been updated for Skype for Business, and while it will continue to work in the same way a Lync 2013 client would against a Skype for Business Server pool, further development of this particular client is unlikely to occur.

As a result, it's not being covered in this book. Connectivity-wise, please see Chapter 5 for details on how it will connect to a pool, as the call flows are identical to mobile clients.

Skype for Business 2016 Basic

Skype for Business 2016 Basic provides IM, audio, and video plus the ability to join a Skype Meeting. It is a cut-down version of the Skype for Business 2016 client; however, it provides the same core functionality. It is primarily intended as a downloadable client for customers with an Office 365 subscription that does not include the full client, although it can also be used against an on-premises deployment of Skype for Business Server 2015. It is provided as a free download to customers with Office 365 Plan P1, E1, or E2 as well as customers with Lync/Skype Online Plan 1, 2, or 3.

As the name implies, not all the features available in Skype for Business are available in the Skype for Business 2015 Basic client. The following advanced features require the full desktop client or Skype for Business Web App:

- Advanced call features, specifically call forwarding, team calls, and delegates. You cannot initiate a call to a response group, and Enhanced 911 is not supported. Additionally, you cannot connect to voicemail or make calls on behalf of another user (for example, a Manager/Delegate scenario). You also cannot handle calls on behalf of another user. PC-to-PC calling is supported, however.

- Gallery View in Skype Meetings is not available.
- OneNote and SharePoint integration (for example, Skill Search) is not available.
- You cannot use the VDI plug-in with Skype for Business 2016 Basic. This feature is not supported in Office 365.

Here are some other things to note about Skype for Business 2016 Basic when used with Office 365:

- Conversation history is available only if you're also using Exchange Server and Outlook.
- At the time of writing, you can't interact with customers who are using an IM service other than Skype for Business/Lync/OCS Server.
- Setting up meetings without Outlook requires the Skype for Business Web Scheduler.
- Dial-in conferencing requires that your Office 365 subscription be configured to integrate with an audio conferencing provider (ACP). If, when you send a meeting invite, the invitation does not include a dial-in number, then ACP integration is not deployed.
- Persistent Chat is not available in Office 365, so the chat room functionality will not be displayed in the Skype for Business 2016 Basic client.
- Telephony integration (for example, Remote Call Control) is not supported in Office 365, so these features are disabled in the Skype for Business 2016 Basic client.
- Finally, the ability to make and receive calls to and from standard PSTN phone numbers (instead of using PC-to-PC computer audio) is available only with Lync/Skype Online Plan 3 when configured with a PC-to-phone service provider.

Client Configuration

As introduced with Lync 2010, in Skype for Business the majority of client configuration takes place in server-side policies, applied via in-band provisioning, instead of Group Policy. Some client bootstrapping policies are still available in Group Policy, however. These are typically settings that need to apply before a user signs in to the client, and as they are usually generic and apply to the whole environment, they can be set at a higher level using Group Policy in Active Directory. Details are covered in this section.

Server policies provide administrators with greater control and more flexibility over the settings they need to configure. Additionally, the settings can be applied more granularly because they can be scoped to global, site, and user levels in the server environment.

Group Policy Settings: Client Bootstrapping

In previous versions of Lync and Office Communicator, a stand-alone `Communicator.adm` administrative template was available for configuring client Group Policy settings. As Skype for Business is included as part of Office 2016, new administrative templates (`*.admx` and `*.adml`) are included with the Office Group Policy Administrative template, which is available here:

```
www.microsoft.com/en-us/download/details.aspx?id=49030
```

You can find details of the client bootstrapping policies in the Skype for Business Help file. Of interest in Skype for Business 2016 is the Disable Automatic Upload Of Sign-In Failure Logs setting.

This setting automatically uploads sign-in failure logs to Skype for Business Server for analysis. No logs are uploaded if sign-in is successful, however. This setting is applied differently depending on whether you are trying to connect to an on-premises or online version of Skype for Business. For Skype Online, sign-in failure logs are automatically uploaded. For Skype for Business on-premises, a confirmation window is displayed that prompts the user to upload the logs, as shown in Figure 4.14.

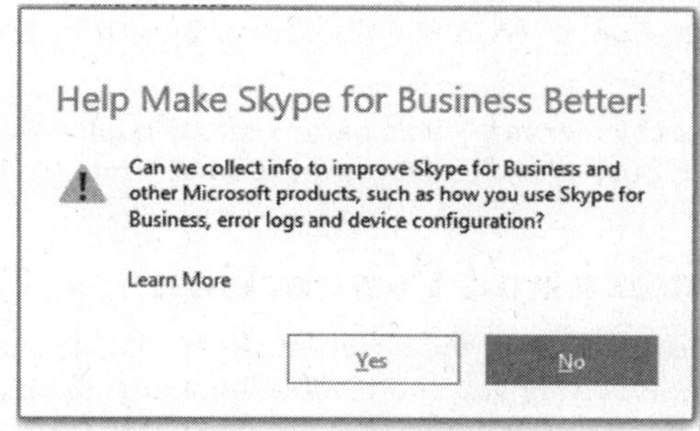

Help Make Skype for Business Better!
Can we collect info to improve Skype for Business and other Microsoft products, such as how you use Skype for Business, error logs and device configuration?
Learn More
Yes
No

FIGURE 4.14 The user being prompted to upload logs

CLIENT POLICIES: IN-BAND PROVISIONING

Client policies can be created, modified, and deleted by the administrator using Skype for Business Server Management Shell. They are passed to the client during sign-in. The Skype for Business client will request in-band provisioning settings in a SIP SERVICE message. The settings are returned in a SIP 200 OK message. Using a tool such as Snooper from the Skype for Business Server Debugging Tools, it is possible to read the XML body of the SIP conversation and observe the settings that were actually passed to the client.

Skype for Business provides a number of new client management parameters that can be used by the client. You can find a full list in the help file, but the following four configured via `CsClientPolicy`, are explained here:

`EnableMediaRedirection` When set to `true`, this setting allows audio and video streams to be separated from other network traffic. This allows client devices to do the encoding and decoding of audio and video locally, resulting in lower bandwidth usage. This setting is required for the Lync 2013 VDI plug-in to work.

`TracingLevel` When set to `true`, this setting allows the tracing level in Skype for Business to be configured by the administrator. Tracing can be off, light, or on.

Off Tracing is disabled, and the user cannot change the setting.

Light Tracing is enabled, and minimal tracing is performed. The user cannot change this setting.

On Verbose tracing is performed. The user cannot change this setting.

Additionally, some of the policies available in Lync Server 2010 have been deprecated.

`EnableSQMData` This parameter has been removed from `CsClientPolicy` and is instead controlled by the shared Group Policy setting for Software Quality Management, which is part of the Office Group Policy template. It relates to the following key in the Windows registry and can be either enabled (1) so the user can clear the check box or disabled (0), which prevents the user from modifying the check box:

```
HKEY_CURRENT_USER\Software\Policies\Microsoft\Office\Common\QMEnable
```

`AllowExchangeContactStore` This parameter has been removed. Instead, when you deploy and publish the topology, Unified Contact Store is enabled for all users by default. This means users' contacts are stored in their Exchange Server 2013 mailboxes. You can change this functionality using `Set-CsUserServicesPolicy` if you want to enable/disable Unified Contact Store for all users or by site, by tenant (Office 365), or by individual users or groups.

`MAPIPollInterval` This parameter is no longer used. In Lync 2010, this parameter specified how frequently the client retrieved MAPI data from Exchange public folders.

Discovery and Connection

Having learned about the different clients, it is important to know how they connect to Skype for Business so that you can troubleshoot any issues in this area. The following sections cover not only how the client discovers the server to connect to but also how it connects.

Discovery

Cumulative Update for Lync Server 2010: November 2011 (CU4) added support for Lync Mobility. One of the features this cumulative update included is the Autodiscover Service, which is used by mobile clients to locate the server.

Skype for Business desktop clients now also use this service for connectivity.

Since Lync 2013, the Autodiscover service is favored over DNS SRV records as a method of resolving the SIP registrar—the Front End, Director, or Edge—for all clients. The desktop client will fail back to using DNS SRV if the Autodiscover method fails; however, the Lync Windows Store app and mobile clients will not.

All clients will attempt to use the Autodiscover service as their preferred method of discovering their SIP registrar. The discovery and connection process is outlined here:

1. The client will attempt to resolve `lyncdiscoverinternal.`*`<sipdomain>`*. This DNS (A) Host record would typically be available only on the internal DNS server(s), so the inability to resolve it suggests that the client is external (or LyncDiscover has not been configured!).
2. If the previous attempt is unsuccessful, the client will attempt to resolve `lyncdiscover.`*`<sipdomain>`* instead.

If neither of the LyncDiscover records works, then the client will fail back to using DNS (SRV) and (A) records, which will be resolved in parallel and tried in the following order, in the same way as in Lync 2010:

1. Internal DNS SRV using TLS, specifically `_sipinternaltls._tcp.<sipdomain>`
2. Internal DNS SRV using TCP, specifically `_sipinternal._tcp.<sipdomain>`
3. External DNS SRV using TLS, specifically `_sip._tls.<sipdomain>`

Lync Windows Store app and mobile clients will not fail back, and the sign-in will be unsuccessful.

Connection

Once the client has successfully resolved one of the preceding DNS SRV records, it will attempt to connect. The DNS SRV record informs the client of the fully qualified domain name (FQDN) and the port number the SIP registrar is listening on. This will be TCP/5061 for internal connections and TCP/443 for external connections. The client will issue a SIP REGISTER message to begin the sign-in process.

The DNS (A) records returned to the client depend on whether DNS load balancing or hardware load balancing is being used in the environment. If hardware load balancing is being used, the client will be returned a single IP address—this is the virtual IP (VIP) of the hardware load balancer. If DNS load balancing is being used, which is the preference, then the client will be returned the IP address of each server in the pool. The ordering of the IP addresses changes in a round-robin fashion and is not important because the chances are that the client will still require redirecting, which happens via a SIP 301 Redirect once it successfully registers. This is because all endpoints for a single user must be registered on the same SIP registrar.

Once the client has successfully registered, it will receive a SIP 200 OK message, which will trigger the creation of the `EndpointConfiguration.cache` file. The client will use this local file to avoid having to do the autodiscover or DNS lookup again.

Persistent Chat Client

Persistent Chat, formerly Group Chat, is an optional role in Skype for Business Server. If your topology includes Persistent Chat, you can use the desktop client to access chat rooms, without the need for a separate client.

Skype for Business communicates with the Persistent Chat service using a combination of Session Initiation Protocol (SIP) for registration and the Extensible Chat Communication Over SIP (XCCOS) protocol for chat.

Sign-in

The following sequence describes the sign-in process in detail:

1. Skype for Business sends a SIP SUBSCRIBE message to retrieve in-band provisioning from the server. This document includes a number of client settings in XML format, one of which indicates if Persistent Chat is enabled or disabled for the user, as shown in Figure 4.15. If it is enabled, in-band provisioning also provides the list of SIP URIs for the Persistent Chat pool.

FIGURE 4.15
The SIP messages showing whether Persistent Chat is enabled for the user and the Persistent Chat SIP URIs

```
- <provisionGroupList xmlns="http://schemas.microsoft.com/2006/09/sip/provisiongrouplist-notification">
    <provisionGroup name="publicProviders"/>
  + <provisionGroup name="userSetting">
  + <provisionGroup name="ServerConfiguration">
  + <provisionGroup name="locationPolicy">
  - <provisionGroup name="persistentChatConfiguration">
    - <propertyEntryList>
        <property name="EnablePersistentChat">true</property>
        <property name="DefaultPersistentChatPoolUri">sip:GC-1-PersistentChatService-11@rlscomms.net</property>
        <property name="PersistentChatPoolUris">sip:GC-1-PersistentChatService-11@rlscomms.net </property>
        <property name="PersistentChatWebManagerUriInt">https://se01.rlscomms.net:443/PersistentChat/RM</property>
        <property name="PersistentChatWebManagerUriExt">https://se01.rlscomms.net:443/PersistentChat/RM</property>
      </propertyEntryList>
    </provisionGroup>
  + <provisionGroup name="mediaConfiguration">
  + <provisionGroup name="meetingPolicy">
  + <provisionGroup name="privacyPublicationGrammar">
  + <provisionGroup name="presencePolicyV2">
  + <provisionGroup name="ucPolicy">
  + <provisionGroup name="publicationGrammar">
  + <provisionGroup name="endpointConfiguration">
```

2. The settings requested in the SIP SUBSCRIBE message are provided in the accompanying SIP 200 OK message.
3. Skype for Business will then send a SIP INVITE message to the SIP URI of the Persistent Chat server that was obtained in step 1, as shown in Figure 4.16. The INVITE should be followed by a 200 OK and associated ACK, which means that Skype for Business has established a SIP session with the Persistent Chat server.

FIGURE 4.16
Sending the SIP INVITE message to the Persistent Chat server

```
11/21/2015|20:26:37.824 DC8:1084 INFO :: Sending Packet - 192.168.3.2:5061 (From Local Address: 192.168.3.100:62060) 1353 bytes:
11/21/2015|20:26:37.824 DC8:1084 INFO ::
INVITE sip:GC-1-PersistentChatService-11@rlscomms.net SIP/2.0
Via: SIP/2.0/TLS 192.168.3.100:62060
Max-Forwards: 70
From: <sip:david.skype@rlscomms.net>;tag=00944279be;epid=10040d6012
To: <sip:GC-1-PersistentChatService-11@rlscomms.net>
Call-ID: 8ba78413ed604a318f02d9cf37c6a626
CSeq: 1 INVITE
Contact: <sip:david.skype@rlscomms.net;opaque=user:epid:I0bmUKM41q4aiAipFVh5gAA;gruu>
User-Agent: UCCAPI/16.0.4266.1003 OC/16.0.4266.1003 (Skype for Business)
Supported: ms-dialog-route-set-update
Supported: timer
Supported: histinfo
Supported: ms-safe-transfer
Supported: ms-sender
Supported: ms-early-media
Supported: com.microsoft.rtc-multiparty
Roster-Manager: sip:david.skype@rlscomms.net
EndPoints: <sip:david.skype@rlscomms.net>, <sip:GC-1-PersistentChatService-11@rlscomms.net>
ms-keep-alive: UAC;hop-hop=yes
Allow: INVITE, BYE, ACK, CANCEL, INFO, MESSAGE, UPDATE, REFER, NOTIFY, BENOTIFY
ms-subnet: 192.168.3.0
Proxy-Authorization: TLS-DSK qop="auth", realm="SIP Communications Service", opaque="6FE38235", targetname="SE01.rlscomms.net",
crand="f99c5631", cnum="10", response="5f9d8ccb59611846c177fbadf03d5b1ae22a8b88"
Content-Type: application/sdp
Content-Length: 153

v=0
o=- 0 0 IN IP4 192.168.3.100
s=session
c=IN IP4 192.168.3.100
t=0 0
m=message 5060 sip null
a=accept-types:text/plain application/ms-imdn+xml


11/21/2015|20:26:37.824 DC8:1084 INFO :: End of Sending Packet - 192.168.3.2:5061 (From Local Address: 192.168.3.100:62060) 1353 bytes
```

For the remainder of this SIP dialogue, the client and the Persistent Chat server will communicate via SIP INFO messages, which contain either chat messages or commands requesting that the server take action.

For comparison, this is similar to how conferencing works in Skype for Business. Conferencing uses the Centralized Conference Control Protocol (C3P) for signaling between the client and server. The C3P messages are embedded in the body of SIP messages. Persistent Chat works in the same way, utilizing the XCCOS protocol to send signaling commands to, and receive responses from, the Persistent Chat server. These XCCOS messages are embedded inside SIP INFO messages.

4. Once a SIP session has been established between Skype for Business and the Persistent Chat server, the client will send a SIP INFO message that contains the XCCOS `getserverinfo` command, as shown in Figure 4.17.

FIGURE 4.17 The SIP INFO message that contains the XCCOS `getserverinfo` command

```
crand="bac394af", cnum="12",
response="91b8acde3e56e0265e160d298e1dfccb256e76a0"
Content-Type: text/plain
Content-Length: 221

- <xccos xmlns="urn:parlano:xml:ns:xccos"
         ver="1"
         envid="2376181547">
  - <cmd id="cmd:getserverinfo"
         seqid="1">
    - <data>
        <sib domain="rlscomms.net"
             infoType="2047"
             clientVersion="16.0.4266.1003"/>
      </data>
    </cmd>
```

5. The Persistent Chat server replies with a new SIP INFO message containing information about the Persistent Chat service configuration, as shown in Figure 4.18.

FIGURE 4.18 The SIP INFO messaging containing configuration info about Persistent Chat

```
- <xccos xsd="http://www.w3.org/2001/XMLSchema"
         xsi="http://www.w3.org/2001/XMLSchema-instance"
         ver="1"
         envid="4020351744089767417" xmlns="urn:parlano:xml:ns:xccos">
  - <rpl id="rpl:getserverinfo"
         seqid="1">
      <commandid seqid="1"
           envid="2376181547"/>
      <resp code="200">SUCCESS_OK</resp>
    - <data>
        <sib infoType="1787"
             serverTime="2015-11-21T20:26:38.0391317Z"
             searchLimit="999"
             messageSizeLimit="8000"
             storySizeLimit="8000"
             rootUri="ma-cat://rlscomms.net/ca350da9-8262-458a-9d6f-3e72e24d87a9"
             dbVersion="14f5f4c7-dbc4-4ace-871f-1f543a190b8a"
             serverVersion="6.0.9319.0"
             displayName="PChat"/>
      </data>
    </rpl>
```

In Figure 4.18, you see that the server response code was `"200"`, which is SUCCESS_OK, and you see the requested information from the Persistent Chat server. For example, you can see that Search Limit is `"999"` and Message Size Limit and Story Size Limit are both `"8000"`. You also see the database and server version numbers and the display name of the Persistent Chat server, which in this example is Persistent Chat.

6. The client sends a SIP INFO message containing a single XCCOS `bjoin` command, containing only the domain name, as shown in Figure 4.19.

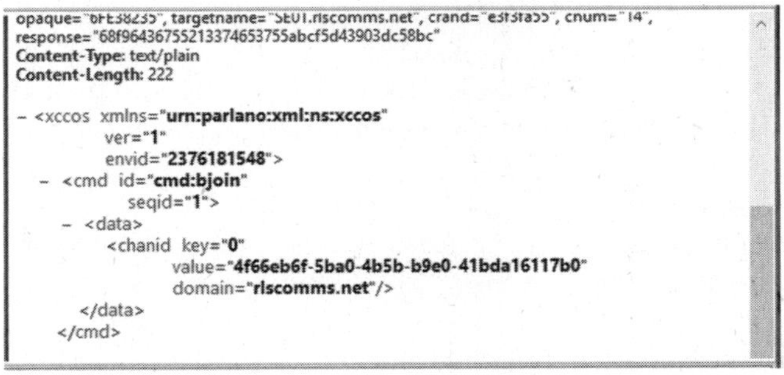

FIGURE 4.19
The SIP INFO message containing the single domain `bjoin` command

```
opaque="6FE38235", targetname="SE01.rlscomms.net", crand="e3f3fa55", cnum="14",
response="68f96436755213374653755abcf5d43903dc58bc"
Content-Type: text/plain
Content-Length: 222

- <xccos xmlns="urn:parlano:xml:ns:xccos"
         ver="1"
         envid="2376181548">
  - <cmd id="cmd:bjoin"
         seqid="1">
    - <data>
        <chanid key="0"
                value="4f66eb6f-5ba0-4b5b-b9e0-41bda16117b0"
                domain="rlscomms.net"/>
      </data>
    </cmd>
```

7. The client sends a SIP INFO message containing the XCCOS `getassociations` command, as shown in Figure 4.20.

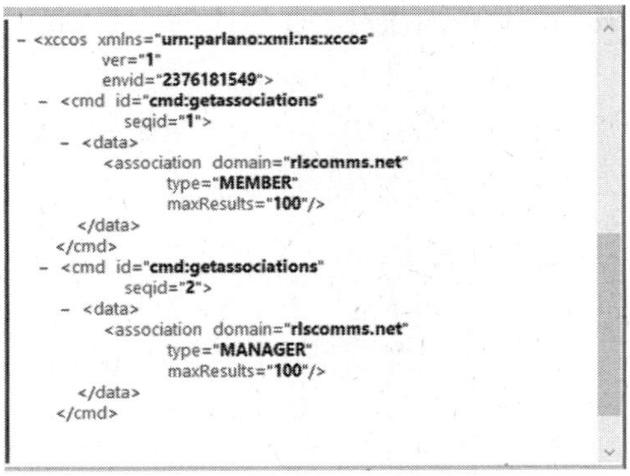

FIGURE 4.20
Sending the SIP INFO message containing the XCCOS `getassociations` command

```
- <xccos xmlns="urn:parlano:xml:ns:xccos"
         ver="1"
         envid="2376181549">
  - <cmd id="cmd:getassociations"
         seqid="1">
    - <data>
        <association domain="rlscomms.net"
                     type="MEMBER"
                     maxResults="100"/>
      </data>
    </cmd>
  - <cmd id="cmd:getassociations"
         seqid="2">
    - <data>
        <association domain="rlscomms.net"
                     type="MANAGER"
                     maxResults="100"/>
      </data>
    </cmd>
```

8. This causes the Persistent Chat server to respond with a new SIP INFO message providing a list of rooms of which the user is a member, as shown in Figure 4.21. Skype for Business repeats this process to obtain a list of rooms for which the user is a manager.

FIGURE 4.21
Skype for Business responding with the rooms of which the user is a member

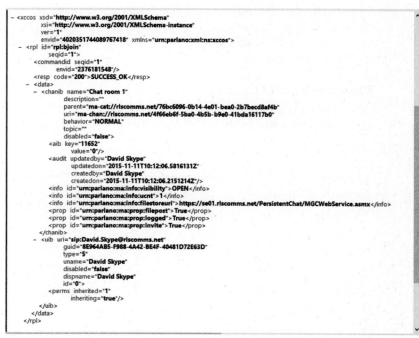

```
- <xccos xsd="http://www.w3.org/2001/XMLSchema"
        xsi="http://www.w3.org/2001/XMLSchema-instance"
        ver="1"
        envid="402035174408976741" xmlns="urn:parlano:xml:ns:xccos">
  - <rpl id="rpl:bjoin"
        seqid="1">
      <commandid seqid="1"
          envid="2376181548"/>
      <resp code="200">SUCCESS_OK</resp>
    - <data>
      - <chanib name="Chat room 1"
              description=""
              parent="ma-cat://rlscomms.net/76bc6096-0b14-4e01-bea0-2b7becd8af4b"
              uri="ma-chan://rlscomms.net/4f66eb6f-5ba0-4b5b-b9e0-41bda16117b0"
              behavior="NORMAL"
              topic=""
              disabled="false">
          <aib key="11652"
              value="0"/>
          <audit updatedby="David Skype"
              updatedon="2015-11-11T10:12:06.5816131Z"
              createdby="David Skype"
              createdon="2015-11-11T10:12:06.2151214Z"/>
          <info id="urn:parlano:ma:info:visibility">OPEN</info>
          <info id="urn:parlano:ma:info:ucnt">1</info>
          <info id="urn:parlano:ma:info:filestoreuri">https://se01.rlscomms.net/PersistentChat/MGCWebService.asmx</info>
          <prop id="urn:parlano:ma:prop:filepost">True</prop>
          <prop id="urn:parlano:ma:prop:logged">True</prop>
          <prop id="urn:parlano:ma:prop:invite">True</prop>
        </chanib>
      - <uib uri="sip:David.Skype@rlscomms.net"
              guid="8E964AB5-F988-4A42-BE4F-40481D72E63D"
              type="5"
              uname="David Skype"
              disabled="false"
              dispname="David Skype"
              id="0">
          <perms inherited="1"
              inheriting="true"/>
        </uib>
      </data>
    </rpl>
```


In Figure 4.21, you can see that David Skype is a member of the Persistent Chat room called Chat room 1, with a description of "This is a test room." An additional SIP INFO message, not shown for brevity, provides the same information because David Skype is both a member and a manager of Chat room 1.

9. The client obtains the list of followed rooms from the presence document, whereby each followed room is represented by a `roomSetting` category. All followed rooms are joined by a single SIP INFO message that contains the XCCOS `bjoin` command, which contains the list of room URIs. The list of followed rooms is stored on the server, meaning any client on any computer has the same list of rooms for the specified URI. Additionally, the client will cache a list of open rooms (if this option is enabled by the user) in the local computer registry. The Skype for Business client will join each of these rooms at sign-in by sending a SIP INFO message containing the XCCOS `bjoin` command for each opened room. This will differ between the computers the user may use because the information is stored in the local registry.

10. For each room joined, a SIP INFO message containing the XCCOS `bcontext` command is sent. The Persistent Chat server replies with a new SIP INFO message containing the most recent chat message in the room.

11. Finally, a SIP INFO message containing the XCCOS `getinv` command (short for "get invitation") is sent to request any new room invitations that the client has not yet seen. The Persistent Chat server responds with a list of rooms in a separate SIP INFO message.

Persistent Chat Client Experience

When configured in the topology and enabled via policy, clients will show an additional icon in the row of tabs in the desktop client, as shown in Figure 4.22.

Figure 4.22
The Persistent Chat tab

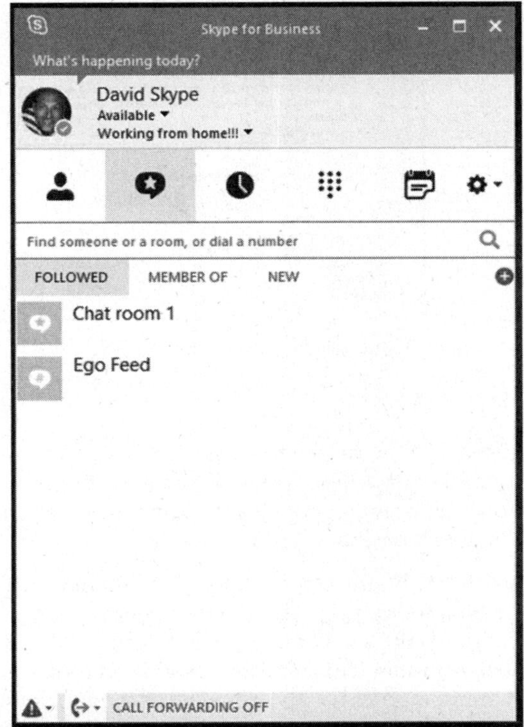

The Persistent Chat tab includes the following additional views:

Followed This displays all the rooms that the user is following. It is also where the *ego* feed and *topic* feeds will be displayed—in bold—when there is new content requiring attention.

Member Of This displays all the rooms that the current user is configured as a member of. Following a room is optional and results in notifications being displayed for the room in the client. Membership of a room is not optional; if you're configured as a member of a Persistent Chat room, that membership will be reflected in the client here.

New This displays a menu with the options shown in Figure 4.23.

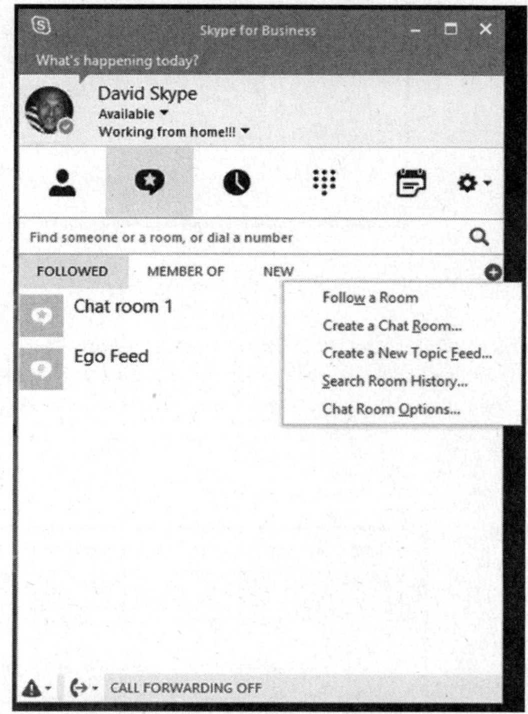

FIGURE 4.23
Options for creating a new room

One of the New menu items that you will see is Chat Room Options. This displays global options for chat rooms. These can be changed here to affect all chat rooms or can be changed on a per-room basis as rooms are created or as you choose to follow a room or receive topic feeds about the room.

Creating a Chat Room

Another option on the New menu shown in Figure 4.23 is Create A Chat Room. End users (rather than administrators) will typically create chat rooms, and the user will see this menu option regardless of whether they have permission to create a chat room. Clicking Create A Chat Room will open Internet Explorer and, if necessary, after you provide credentials, will display the Persistent Chat Management website, shown in Figure 4.24.

FIGURE 4.24 The Persistent Chat Management website

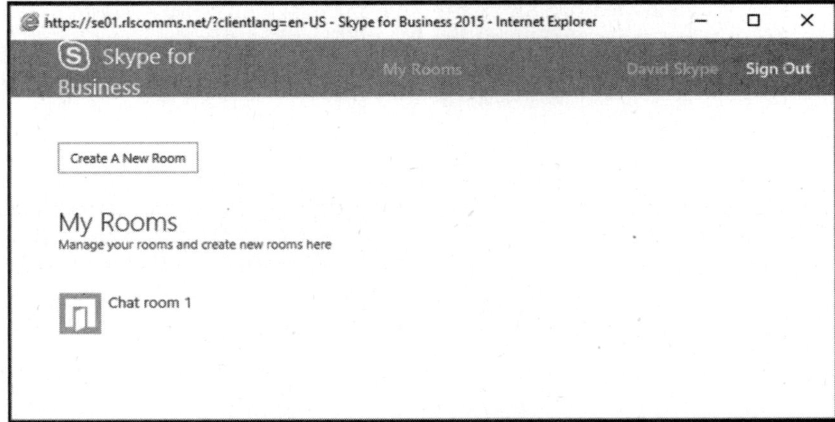

Users create rooms by clicking Create A New Room. They can also modify rooms they have already created here. In this example, Linda Lync does not have permission to create rooms, so when she clicks Create A New Room, she'll receive the error shown in Figure 4.25.

FIGURE 4.25 The error shown when you don't have permissions to create a room

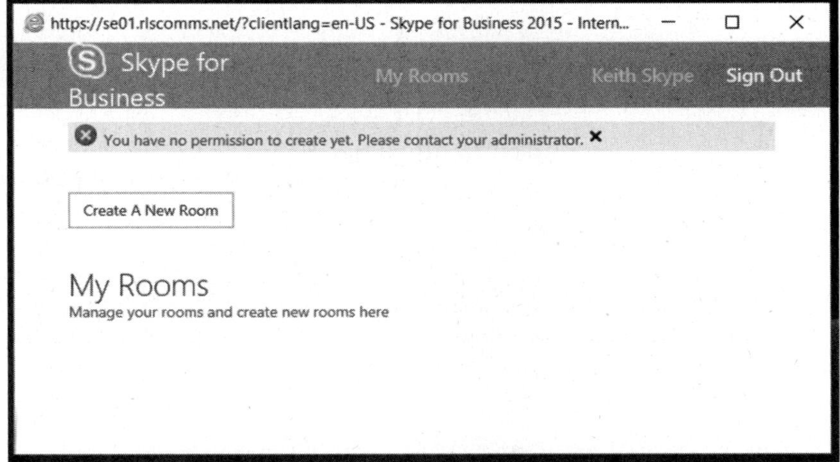

When David Skype, who does have permission, is logged in, clicking Create A New Room will display the page shown in Figure 4.26.

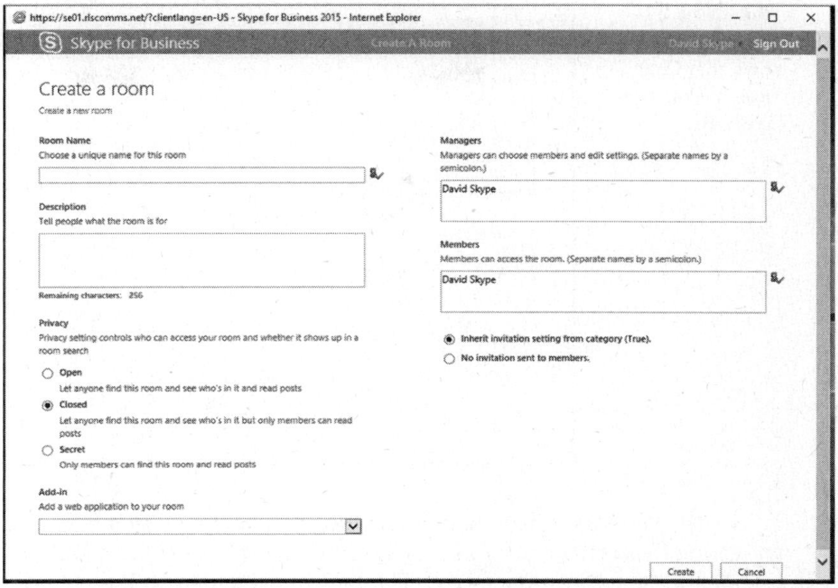

FIGURE 4.26
The Create A Room page

From here, David Skype can specify the following details:

Room Name This uniquely identifies the room.

Description This is an optional description to tell people what the room is for.

Privacy This can be one of three settings:

> **Open** Anybody can find the room and read the contents.
>
> **Closed** Anybody can find the room and see the room's membership, but only members can read posts in the room. This is the default.
>
> **Secret** Only members can find the room, view membership, and read posts.

Add-In This allows a web application add-in to be configured for your room.

Managers This is automatically populated with David Skype as the creator of this room. He can add other users by typing their names or SIP URIs. Users entered here have management capability of the room.

Members This is automatically populated with David Skype as the creator of this room. He can add other users by typing their names or SIP URIs. Users added here can access the room to read or post but not manage it.

Invitations By default, the invitation setting is inherited from the category that applies to this room on the Persistent Chat server. The other option is to not send invitations to members.

At this point, David Skype will see the newly created room on his My Rooms page, as shown in Figure 4.27.

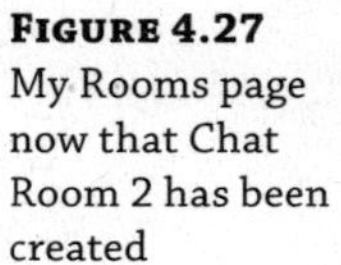

FIGURE 4.27 My Rooms page now that Chat Room 2 has been created

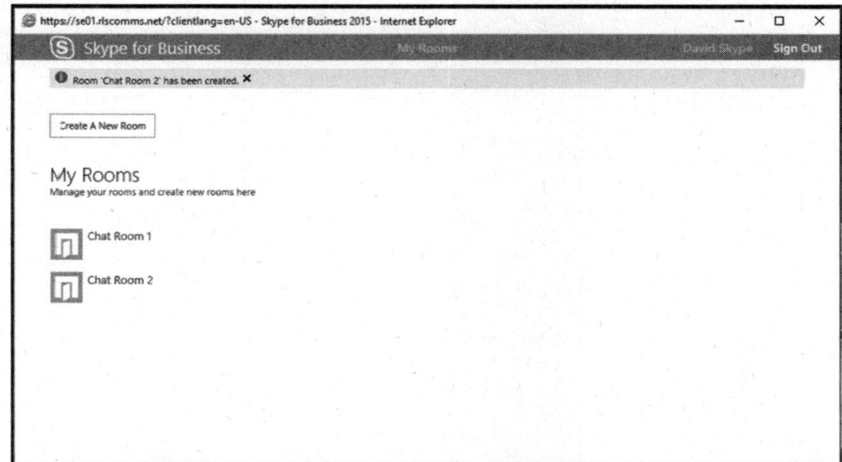

The Persistent Chat tab in David Skype's client now shows a number next to the icon, indicating there is unread content. Clicking the Persistent Chat tab shows Chat Room 2 in bold to identify that this room is new. The same will happen on Linda Lync's and Keith Skype's clients because they were added as members and invitations were enabled for the category of room that was just created.

Conferencing Clients

Chapter 6, "Devices," will cover conference room–style clients in more detail. Here you'll look at the desktop aspects of conferencing.

The following clients can be used as conferencing clients in Skype for Business:

Skype for Business 2016 The full, unified Windows desktop client is preferred for meetings.

Skype for Business Web App The web-based browser version of the client can be used in meetings.

Lync Windows 8 Store App The Windows 8 store app can be used to join audio and video and view PowerPoint slides being presented in a meeting.

As mentioned earlier in this chapter, Skype for Business Web App now supports audio and video natively in the browser through the use of a browser plug-in, which can be installed in user mode rather than in administrator mode. Because of this change, Skype for Business Web App is now considered a first-class meeting client and is actually preferred rather than continuing to use the Lync 2010 desktop application in a coexistence scenario because it supports new features such as multiparty video and conference controls, as described in the following sections.

Join Launcher

The Join Launcher—the component responsible for accepting requests to the Meet simple URL and processing theme—has been updated in Skype for Business to provide support for additional conferencing on operating systems, including Windows Phone, Android devices, Apple iOS devices, Windows 10, and Internet Explorer 11.

Chapter 5 covers Skype for Business Web App in more detail.

One notable point worth highlighting here is the in-page web feedback for errors (shown in Figure 4.28). The page will include details of the error message to allow for feedback to your organization's support team.

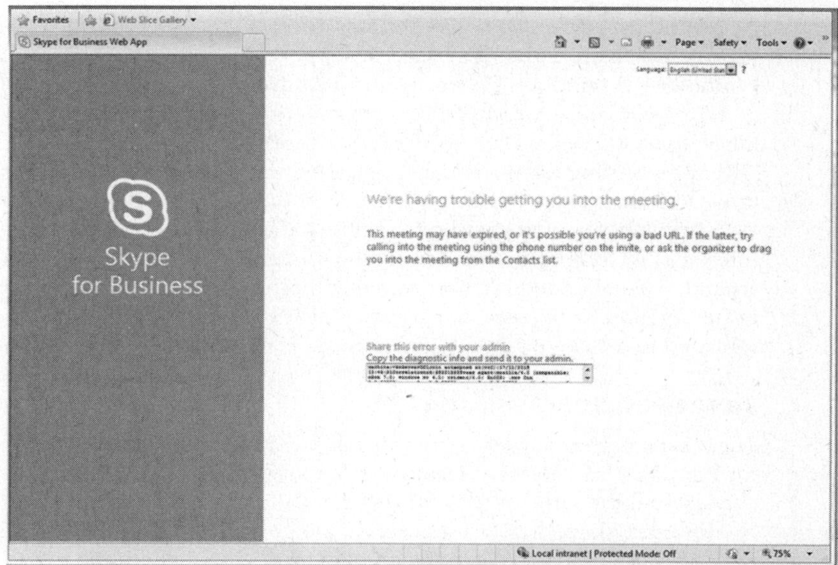

FIGURE 4.28 Error feedback on the Join Launcher page

VIDEO SPOTLIGHT

Presenters can configure a conference, using either the desktop client or Web App, so that only the video stream from a selected participant is seen by others in the meeting. When configured, this also applies to video captured and provided by conferencing devices for panoramic video (for example, RoundTable). This is useful in a classroom-like scenario, where a single speaker should be the focus of the participants' attention.

LIVE MEETING MCU

For anyone migrating from a Lync Server 2010 environment, one change on the server side that affects the client application used for meetings is the removal of the Web Conferencing Compatibility Service MCU from the Front End server. This MCU simulated the Live Meeting MCU from the Office Communications Server time frame and made it possible for a user migrated from OCS 2007 R2 to Lync Server 2010 to continue to participate in meetings using the Live Meeting client.

Live Meeting would connect to the Web Conferencing Compatibility Service MCU on the Front End, which would simulate being a Live Meeting server, tricking the client into thinking it was connected to Live Meeting instead of Lync Server 2010.

Lync Server 2013 removed this MCU, meaning Live Meeting is no longer a supported meeting client when running against a user who is hosted on Skype for Business Server (or Lync Server 2013). If users will not have the Skype for Business desktop client installed immediately following migration, they can use Lync Web App to join the meeting instead.

Office Web Apps and PowerPoint Slides

As mentioned earlier, PowerPoint slides are rendered via the Office Web Applications server, making this more standards based to support a wider number of platforms, including Windows, Windows RT, Windows Phone, iOS, and Android.

When you upload a PowerPoint presentation to a meeting using Skype for Business, the file is uploaded to the Data MCU on the Front End server. The Data MCU returns a broadcast URL representing the file you just uploaded, causing Skype for Business to start an embedded browser frame inside the client. The URL returned to the client is actually the URL of the Office Web Apps server, which will retrieve the file from the Data MCU using the Web Open Platform Interface (WOPI) protocol and will then render the slides into web-based presentable data. Every second, the embedded browser frame will ping the Office Web App server using Asynchronous JavaScript and XML (Ajax) to confirm which slide it should be viewing. This information is then returned to the client's embedded browser frame, moving the presentation along.

Skype for Business for Mac

There is no new Mac client with this release, and Skype for Business is currently available only for Windows (Microsoft has stated Skype for Business for Mac will be released in 2016—probably around the same time as this book!).

However, Skype for Business Server supports the following legacy Mac clients (when running on Mac OS 10.5.8 or later on an Intel processor), in addition to Skype for Business Web App:

- Microsoft Lync for Mac 2011
- Microsoft Communicator for Mac 2011

Virtualized Clients

Skype for Business supports the use of virtualized clients, also known as *thin clients*. This is the scenario whereby a local device is running a very cut-down version of Windows, or also possibly an older version with fewer resources, and is "streaming" applications, either directly or as a complete desktop stream from a server (or, more typically, a server farm).

From a pure physics perspective, in this scenario the Skype for Business client is actually running on the server in the datacenter. This means that audio from the local machine (caller) must traverse a network connection before being encoded and sent to the callee, who might also be using a virtualized client.

In a worst-case scenario, both the caller and callee may be in the same location, and the datacenter could be hundreds of miles away, meaning the audio (and/or video) would have made a wasted journey to and from the datacenter!

One step to help this would be to deploy IP Phone devices and make the call from them, which is not always practical (or cost effective), because the audio would then be local from the device to the other device.

A solution to this is the Lync VDI plug-in (yep, still called Lync). Figure 4.29 shows the conceptual working of the Lync VDI plug-in.

FIGURE 4.29
Lync VDI plug-in architecture

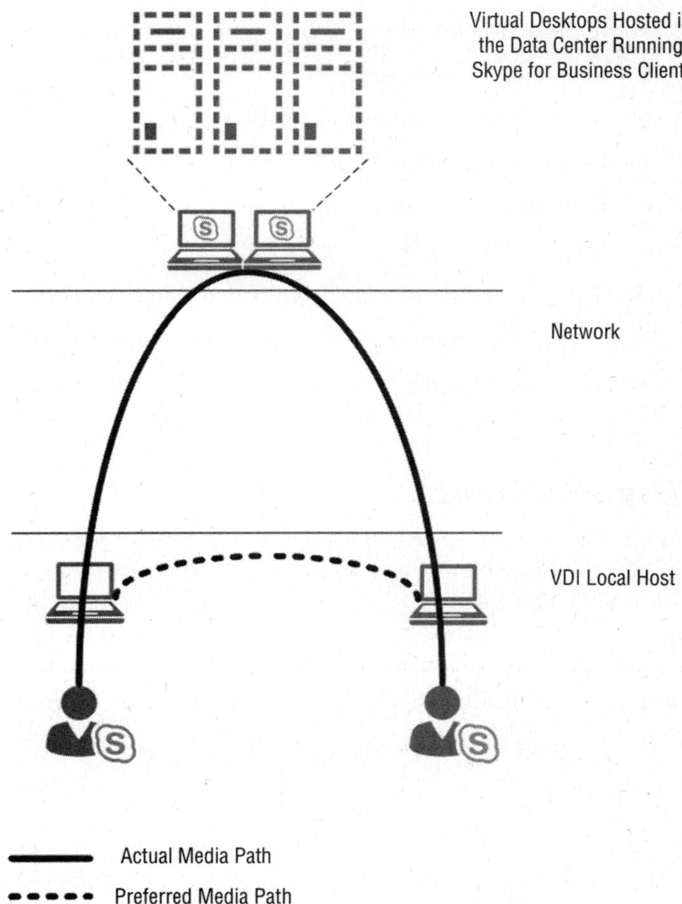

By using the Lync VDI plug-in as a media endpoint, the media can remain local to the device, therefore reducing the delays via the data center and resulting in a better quality call experience.

There are some specific requirements to deploying the Lync VDI plug-in.

- The user must be home on Lync 2013 or higher.
- The local device must be Windows 7 SP1 or higher (including Windows Embedded versions).

- The Lync VDI plug-in "bitness" must match the operating system. If a 32-bit operating system is in use, the plug-in must be the 32-bit plug-in.
- The `CsClientPolicy` must have `EnableMediaRedirection` set to *$True*.

Certain features are not available when configured with the Lync VDI plug-in.

- Audio/video device tuning
- Multiview video
- Recording of conversations
- Anonymous join to remote meetings
- Integration of VDI and Phone Edition device
- Call continuity in event of network issues
- Use with Office 365

The Lync VDI plug-in can be downloaded from the Microsoft Download Center.

32-bit: `www.microsoft.com/en-us/download/details.aspx?id=35457`

64-bit: `www.microsoft.com/en-us/download/details.aspx?id=35454`

Legacy Clients

Skype for Business Server 2015 supports a number of previous versions signing in against a pool. Table 4.1 shows which legacy clients are supported against which type of Skype for Business Server pool.

TABLE 4.1: Which Clients Can Connect to Which Server Versions

CLIENT	SKYPE FOR BUSINESS SERVER 2015	LYNC SERVER 2013	LYNC SERVER 2010
Skype for Business 2016	Supported	Supported	Supported
Skype for Business Web App	Supported	Not Supported	Not Supported
Lync 2013	Supported	Supported	Supported
Lync Web App (2013)	Not Supported	Supported	Not Supported
Lync 2010	Supported	Supported	Supported
Lync 2010 Attendant	Supported	Supported	Supported

TABLE 4.1: Which Clients Can Connect to Which Server Versions *(CONTINUED)*

CLIENT	SKYPE FOR BUSINESS SERVER 2015	LYNC SERVER 2013	LYNC SERVER 2010
Lync 2010 Group Chat	Supported	Supported	Supported
Lync Web App (2010)	Not Supported	Not Supported	Supported
Lync 2010 Attendee	Not Supported	Not Supported	Supported

It is worth highlighting that the Lync 2010 Attendee client is not supported against a Skype for Business 2015 or Lync Server 2013 pool. This is because the new Skype for Business Web App supports IP audio and video, making it a fully featured client.

Finally, the minimum supported operating system for the Skype for Business clients is Windows 7; none of the clients are supported on Windows XP.

The Bottom Line

Understand usage scenarios for each client. Each of the clients discussed in this chapter is designed for a specific usage scenario. For example, Skype for Business 2016 allows IM and presence (among other things) with other users.

Master It You have been engaged by a graphic design company to design and deploy Skype for Business. The company already has Lync Server 2010 and will be migrating to Skype for Business Server 2015 over the next six months. The company has 300 employees who are split almost 50/50 between Apple Mac computers and Windows PCs running Lync 2010. All users need to be able to participate in meetings with partners and customers during this coexistence phase.

Understand changes in Group Chat. In Skype for Business, Group Chat has been built into the main product and is now called Persistent Chat.

Master It You are working with a large financial services company that is in the process of migrating from Lync Server 2010 to Skype for Business. The company's employees are heavy users of Group Chat in Lync Server 2010. What benefit does Skype for Business Server and Skype for Business client introduce in this area?

Understand how clients discover and communicate with various server roles, such as the Director, Front End, Persistent Chat, and the various Media Control Units (MCUs) for conferencing. Manually configuring clients for connecting to the infrastructure can be a massive overhead, so the clients each have a method to automatically determine where and how to connect.

Master It You are planning the migration from Lync Server 2010 to Skype for Business Server 2015. What additional DNS records are required to be created to address the preferred connectivity methods from the Skype for Business client?

Chapter 5

Mobile Devices

Mobility has been a buzzword for the past few years, especially since the launch of the iPhone and the various app stores that have the ability to turn your mobile phone into so much more than just a phone.

The early days had texting; the next big development was the BlackBerry, providing usable email on the go. Then came the iPhone, and finally we're seeing tablets. With tablets, the first to have mass uptake in the consumer market was Apple with the iPad. The iPad was then joined by the Android versions, and along came the attempts by Windows 8 and more recently Windows 10 (and the Microsoft Surface device line). In between, we had variations and attempts to add additional functionality to each device with varying degrees of success.

The past few iterations of Lync (and OCS) have seen a similar development cycle, with more capabilities being added across more platforms.

The focus was obviously on the Microsoft platforms initially, with wider development on later releases of Lync on the more popular platforms (Android and iOS). BlackBerry has a history of developing its own Lync (and OCS) clients, typically leveraging the BlackBerry Enterprise Server (BES). BlackBerry support for Skype for Business was introduced in BlackBerry Enterprise Server (BES) 12.3, and at the same time support for OCS was dropped.

This chapter will focus on the mobile phone clients and highlight any differences between tablet clients. They're all similar, and the aim is to have a consistent experience no matter the device or client; therefore, we don't want to duplicate content if there's no fundamental difference between the clients on each device.

The Windows 8 Store app client (for use while using the Windows 8 Modern UI) was mentioned in Chapter 4, "Desktop Clients," and, as it's been deprecated, will not be covered.

In this chapter, you will learn to

- Understand the different capabilities of each mobile client (including tablets)
- Understand the policies available to manage mobile clients
- Understand the infrastructure configuration required for enabling mobile devices

Mobile Client Capability

Skype for Business Server 2015 has the ability to connect mobile clients across the following mobile platforms:

- iOS (iPhone and iPad)
- Android
- Windows Phone

When the Skype for Business patches were rolling out on the desktop clients (for more details, see Chapter 1, "What's in Skype for Business 2015?"), the mobile clients lagged slightly behind, and the Lync 2013 app was still available in the app store for download. By the time this book is published, only the Skype for Business app will be available, and it will not be possible to "downgrade."

A pre-update was released to the app store, notifying users of the upcoming brand change, as shown in Figure 5.1.

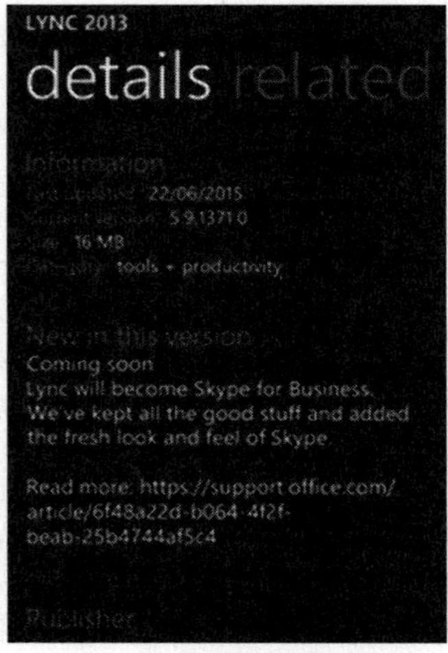

FIGURE 5.1
The Windows Phone app "update"

Table 5.1 summarizes the feature comparison between the desktop, Windows Phone, and iOS clients. (Android information was not available at the time of writing.)

TABLE 5.1: Feature summary per clients

FEATURE	DESKTOP	WINDOWS PHONE	IOS
Session remains signed in	Yes	Yes (if push notification is enabled, for 10 days)	Yes (if push notification is enabled, for 10 days)
Automatic country code population	No	No	Yes
Screen reader	Yes	Yes (English only)	Yes
Passive authentication support	No	Yes	Yes

Table 5.1: Feature summary per clients *(continued)*

Feature	Desktop	Windows Phone	iOS
Publish and view status	Yes	Yes	Yes
Status updates based on calendar or out-of-office messages	Yes	Yes	Yes
Custom locations	Yes	No	No
Manual presence controls	Yes	Yes	Yes
View contacts list/groups	Yes	Yes	Yes
Contact management	Yes	Yes	No
Tag contacts for status change	Yes	No	No
Search corporate address book	Yes	Yes	Yes
Expand distribution groups	Yes	Yes	No
Search for Response groups	Yes	Yes	No
Display or hide photos	Yes	Yes	No
Pin contacts to home screen	No	Yes	No
Initiate IM conversation	Yes	Yes	Yes
Participate and invite users to multiparty conversation	Yes	Yes	Yes
Archive conversation in Exchange	Yes	No	No
Audio calling	Yes	Yes	Yes
Video calling	Yes	Yes	Yes
Click-to-join conferencing	Yes	Yes	Yes
Dial-out conferencing (trigger server to call device)	Yes	Yes	Yes

TABLE 5.1: Feature summary per clients *(CONTINUED)*

FEATURE	DESKTOP	WINDOWS PHONE	IOS
Dial-in conferencing	Yes	Yes	Yes
Multiparty video (gallery view)	Yes	No	No
Wait in lobby	Yes	Yes	Yes
Use presenter controls	Yes	No	No
Access conference roster	Yes	Yes	Yes
Share desktop or app	Yes	No	No
View desktop share	Yes	Yes	Yes
View PowerPoint	Yes	Yes	No
Use meeting tools (whiteboard, and so on)	Yes	No	No
Click to call contact	Yes	Yes	Yes
Transfer a call	Yes	Yes	No
Manage call forwarding	Yes	Yes	No
Manage delegates	Yes	No	No
Call a response group	Yes	No	No
Participate as a response group agent	Yes	No	No
Handle another contact's calls (as a delegate)	Yes	Yes	Yes
Use Call via Work	No (yes for integrated telephony environments; previously Remote Call Control)	Yes	Yes
IM with public or federated contact	Yes	Yes	Yes
Voice with public or federated contacts	Yes	No	No
Client-side archiving	Yes	No	No

The Lync 2013 mobile client was the first client to allow the use of Voice over IP and Video over IP (3g/4g/Wi-Fi). Skype for Business continues with this support.

This can cause confusion because on first read it may lead you to believe that the client can hand off calls from a Wi-Fi network to a mobile operator network (for example, if you walk from your office, connected to Wi-Fi, and go outside where there is no Wi-Fi signal); however, this is *not* a capability provided by the client today.

The client will provide voice and/or video over the network on which the call is initiated. If the call begins on Wi-Fi and the Wi-Fi signal is lost, then the call is dropped. Equally, if the call begins on a mobile operator network and a Wi-Fi signal is received, the call will continue on the mobile network. We hope this "handover" functionality will come in a future release!

As mentioned previously, Skype for Business has significantly improved the high-availability capabilities across the majority of features. Mobile clients are now included in that list. Previous versions of the mobile Lync (and OCS) client were unable to reconnect to other servers if the server to which they had logged in with was unavailable. Now it's seamless to the user. If the expected server is unavailable, the mobile client will try another and then another until the client can connect.

The clients now also include support for the high-resolution (HD) photo that is stored in the Exchange mailbox of the user. As with the traditional clients, if this is unavailable, the photo will be taken from SharePoint or Active Directory, but these will be lower-definition photos.

Table 5.2 shows the minimum OS version support for each device.

TABLE 5.2: Mobile device OS version requirements for running Skype for Business

CLIENT	MINIMUM OS VERSION
Windows Phone	Windows Phone 8.1 or later
iPad	iOS 8.0 or later
iPhone	iOS 8.0 or later
Microsoft Lync 2013 for Android	Android 4.0 or later

That's enough talk about what the client can do; we'll now show what the mobile client looks like on Windows Phone and Apple iOS (unfortunately, Android screenshots were unavailable at press time).

Figure 5.2 shows the account setup screen, Figure 5.3 shows the contacts screen, Figure 5.4 shows the incoming call screen, Figure 5.5 shows the IM conversation screen, and Figure 5.6 shows the call-in-progress screen.

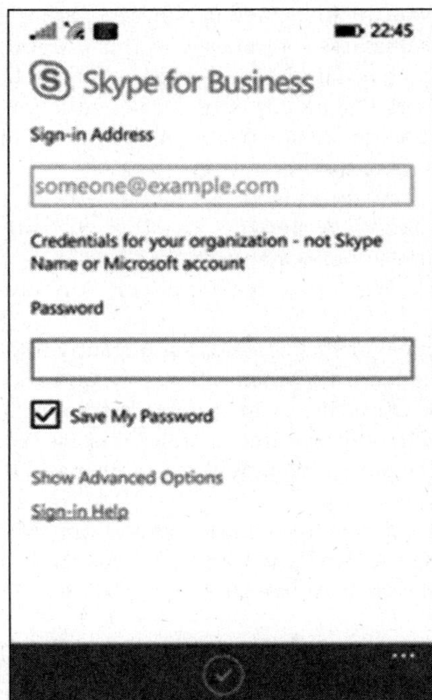

FIGURE 5.2 Account setup screen

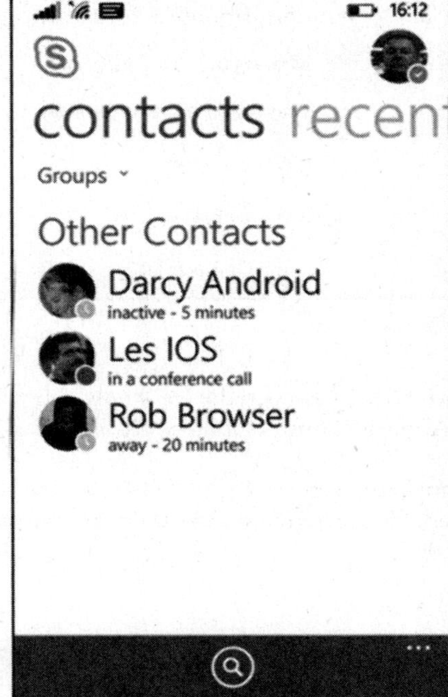

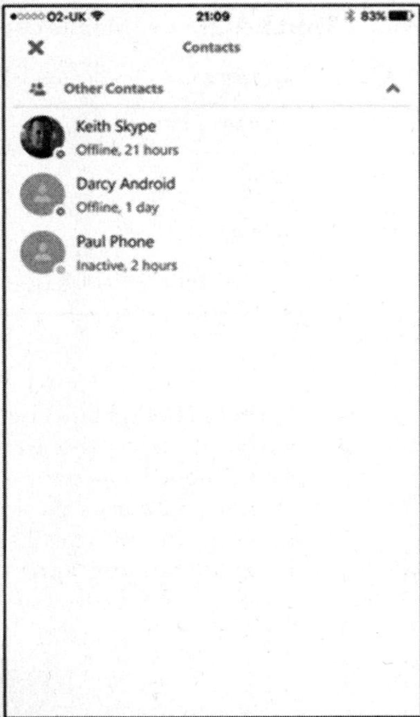

FIGURE 5.3 Contacts screen

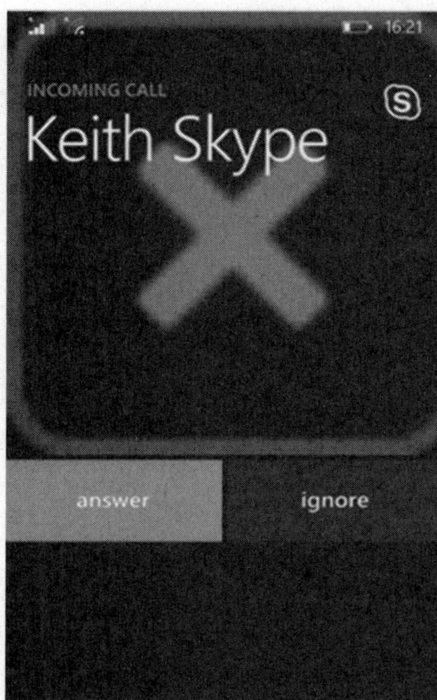

FIGURE 5.4
Incoming call screen

FIGURE 5.5
IM conversation screen

FIGURE 5.6 Call-in-progress screen

As you can see from the screenshots, the user experience on each device is similar, which ensures a consistent look and feel from one device to the next. Users do not need to be retrained if they change their device.

Interestingly, in all our testing, the Windows Phone device would not display the picture of the person calling unless the picture was stored as a local device contact (as well as a Skype for Business contact).

The only obvious difference between the iOS phone and tablet clients is the size of the screen. Figure 5.7 shows the meetings page on the iPad, and you can see the two screens that the iPhone would display.

The mobile clients continue to provide feedback based on actions in the meeting, such as being muted by the presenter (shown in Figure 5.8); these can be "swiped" away.

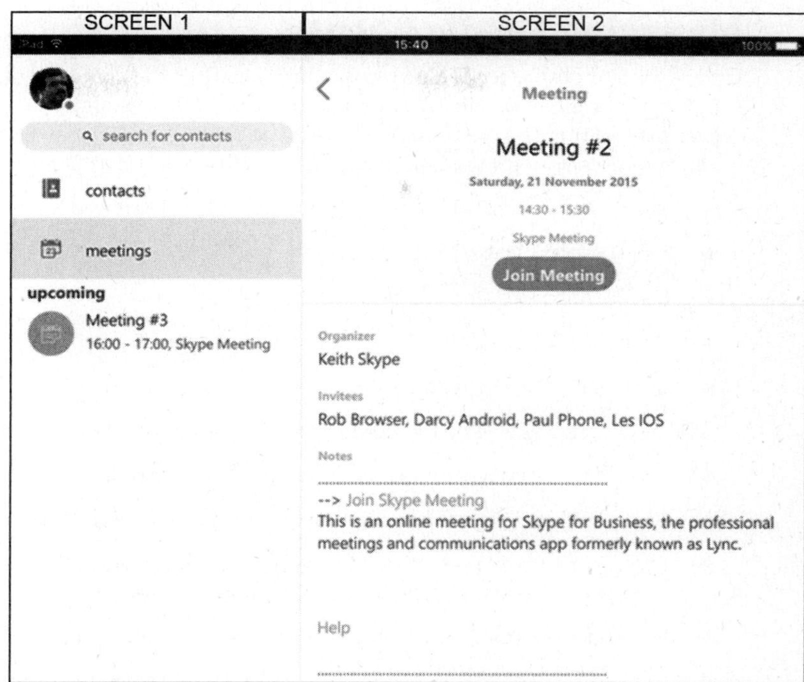

FIGURE 5.7
iPhone vs. iPad meeting screen

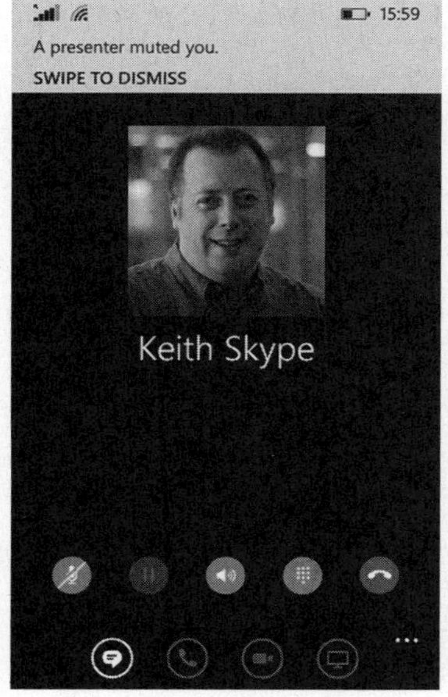

FIGURE 5.8
In-meeting feedback

Managing Mobile Clients

Configuring mobility for Skype for Business requires the configuration of the back-end server capability as well as the mobility policy for users. You'll see how to deploy and configure the server later in this chapter; here we'll focus on the user policy capability.

The cmdlets to define and manage the mobility policy are as follows:

- `New-CsMobilityPolicy`
- `Set-CsMobilityPolicy`
- `Get-CsMobilityPolicy`
- `Grant-CsMobilityPolicy`
- `Remove-CsMobilityPolicy`

The `New-CsMobilityPolicy` cmdlet has the following parameters:

- `Identity`: Used to provide a unique name for the policy
- `Description`: Allows provision of administrative text describing the policy
- `EnableIPAudioVideo`: When `False`, prevents any use of IP for voice and video calling; any calls will be forced through the mobile network operator
- `EnableMobility`: Must be set to `True` to allow users to connect using mobile devices
- `EnableOutSideVoice`: When set to `True`, allows users to use the Call via Work functionality
- `RequireWIFIForIPAudio`: When set to `True`, allows users to place audio calls via the Wi-Fi network rather than via the mobile operator network
- `RequireWIFIForIPVideo`: When set to `True`, allows users to place video calls via the Wi-Fi network when available rather than via the mobile operator network
- `AllowCustomerExperienceImprovemntProgram*`: Enables feedback of the mobile apps to be sent to Microsoft
- `RequireWiFiForSharing*`: When set to `True`, allows users to share screen content via Wi-Fi network when available rather than via the mobile operator network
- `AllowSaveCallLogs*`: When set to `True`, allows users to save a call log of calls made to or from the mobile client on their device
- `AllowExchangeConnectivity*`: When set to `True`, allows users to Exchange services on the mobile device for items such as photos
- `AllowSaveIMHistory*`: When set to `True`, allows users to save the contents of IM conversations on the mobile device
- `AllowSaveCredentials*`: When set to `True`, enables the login credentials to be stored on the mobile device

Those parameters labeled * are new with the update to Skype for Business Server.

Here's an example command that defines a mobility policy:

```
New-CsMobilityPolicy -Identity "WiFi Voice Enabled" -EnableMobility $True
-EnableIPAudioVideo $True -RequireWIFIForIPAudio $True
-RequireWIFIForIPVideo $False
```

This will define a policy named WiFi Voice Enabled, which will allow users to use the Wi-Fi network for voice calls but not for video calling.

Once the policy is created, it must be granted, using the `Grant-CsMobilityPolicy` cmdlet.

```
Grant-CsMobilityPolicy -Identity "sip:keith.skype@rlscomms.net"
-PolicyName "WiFi Voice Enabled"
```

Now, the user will be able to log in and will have the policy applied, be unable to place video calls, but be able to place audio calls when connected via Wi-Fi.

Figure 5.9 shows the Mobility Policy tab in the Control Panel.

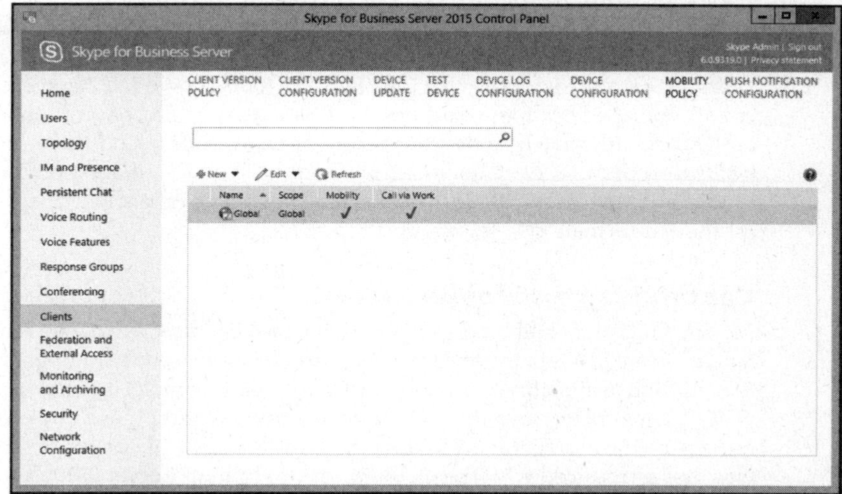

FIGURE 5.9
Configuring a mobility policy in Control Panel

Users can configure the following properties on their own devices:

- Require Wi-Fi for Voice
- Require Wi-Fi for Video
- Require Wi-Fi for sharing
- Mobile Number
- Push notifications on/off
- Phonebook access on/off

- Photos on/off
- Exchange
- HTTP Proxy
- Accessibility – TTY on/off
- Logging
- Customer Feedback
- Upload Sign-in Logs

Deploying and Configuring Mobility on Skype for Business Server 2015

The tools used in Chapter 7, "Planning Your Deployment," include consideration for mobility clients, so assuming that you complete the questionnaire sections correctly when planning, your server specifications and numbers will be able to cope with the additional load incurred by hosting mobile clients.

If not, we advise you to visit the planning tools shown in Chapter 7 and adjust the server counts and specifications as advised. Incorrectly specified environments are likely to introduce bottlenecks, ultimately appearing as a poor experience to end users. In a lot of cases, the bottlenecks introduced will be felt by all users, not just on the underspecified client types. It's always worth bearing this in mind if you start to experience issues; see Chapter 15, "Troubleshooting," for more information.

Configuring for Mobile Access

For any Enterprise Edition deployments, the load balancer (hardware or software) should be configured to *not* use cookie persistence because this was used for the legacy mobile clients (Lync 2010), and for high availability to work correctly, this feature must be disabled on the load balancers.

Chapter 4 introduced the Autodiscover service concept, used by clients to automatically determine the correct connectivity points to access the Skype for Business Server instances. This was first introduced with the mobility service in Lync Server 2010. It should not be confused with the Exchange Autodiscover capability used by Outlook.

Skype for Business clients will look for one of two DNS records:

```
LyncDiscover.<sipdomain>
LyncDiscoverInternal.<sipdomain>
```

These records can be either A records (pointing to IP addresses) or CNAME records (pointing to other FQDNs).

When a client connects to one of these records (they ultimately resolve to web locations on a Front End pool), the data returned will provide all the web service URLs required for the user's home pool.

Once the data is received, the mobile client parses it to determine the mobility server URL and will then connect via that location.

Configuring the Autodiscover service DNS entries and the reverse proxy to ensure that the traffic is forwarded to the pools (and Directors if deployed) allows your mobile clients to connect, log in, and initiate communications. What about for communications initiated by someone else and terminating on your mobile device? Well, the answer to this is the push notification service or, for Android devices, the P-Get event channel (no configuration required!).

Internal vs. External Mobility Connections

The mobile client will use `LyncDiscover` for external connectivity and `LyncDiscoverInternal` for internal (on the corporate network) connectivity; however, both of these will resolve to the external web service's FQDN, ultimately through the external reverse proxy.

The point of this is to ensure that clients are not disconnected when moving from the Wi-Fi network to the external mobile operator network. If a client were to switch between the internal and external web services, they would be forced to disconnect and log in again, losing the cached data connection.

Configuring the push notification service requires a command run with a parameter for the Apple Push Notification Service as well as one for the Microsoft Push Notification Service. Enabling this capability allows users to receive incoming content such as IMs or invitations to conferences.

This is simply the following:

```
New-CsPushNotificationConfiguration
```

And the parameters are as follows:

```
-EnableApplePushNotificationService
```

```
-EnableMicrosoftPushNotificationService
```

Each of these can be set to `True` to enable or `False` to disable. This cmdlet can be scoped to sites, allowing for different policies to apply to users in different locations if required. Configuration is required to allow push notifications to work. First, you configure a new hosting provider (the target for the notification).

```
New-CsHostingProvider -Identity "LyncOnline" -Enabled $True
-ProxyFqdn "sipfed.online.lync.com"
-VerificationLevel UseSourceVerification
```

Next, allow federation to the push service.

```
New-CsAllowedDomain -Identity "push.lync.com"
```

Now notifications will leave the environment to the hosted service, which will in turn forward them to the mobile devices as required. The Lync Online service is responsible for forwarding notifications to the Apple Push Notification Service.

Apple Push Notifications

The iOS devices (iPad and iPhone) do not require the Apple Push Notification Service parameters to be configured in a pure Lync 2013 (or higher) mobile client infrastructure. The push notification cmdlets and configuration are used for backward compatibility with the Lync 2010 mobile clients.

Windows Phone 8 devices do require the Microsoft Push Notification Service to be configured for both Skype for Business and Lync mobile clients.

Confirming the Mobility Service

Once you've followed all the steps to this point, you can use the following test cmdlets to test and confirm the installation and configuration:

- `Test-CsMcxConference`
- `Test-CsMcxIM`
- `Test-CsMcxPushNotification`
- `Test-CsUCWAConference`

Chapter 15 covers the use of the `Test-Cs` cmdlets in detail; however, these three are specifically used to test the mobility feature set, as their names suggest: conference capability, IM, and the Push Notification Service.

How Does Mobility Work?

The mobility clients have a set of unique call flow scenarios, not only through the push notification service but also in terms of discovery. Here we'll cover each of the flows in detail.

Let's start with connectivity; Figure 5.10 shows the process for discovery and then connectivity. We've included both internal and external clients because only the initial steps have a different approach.

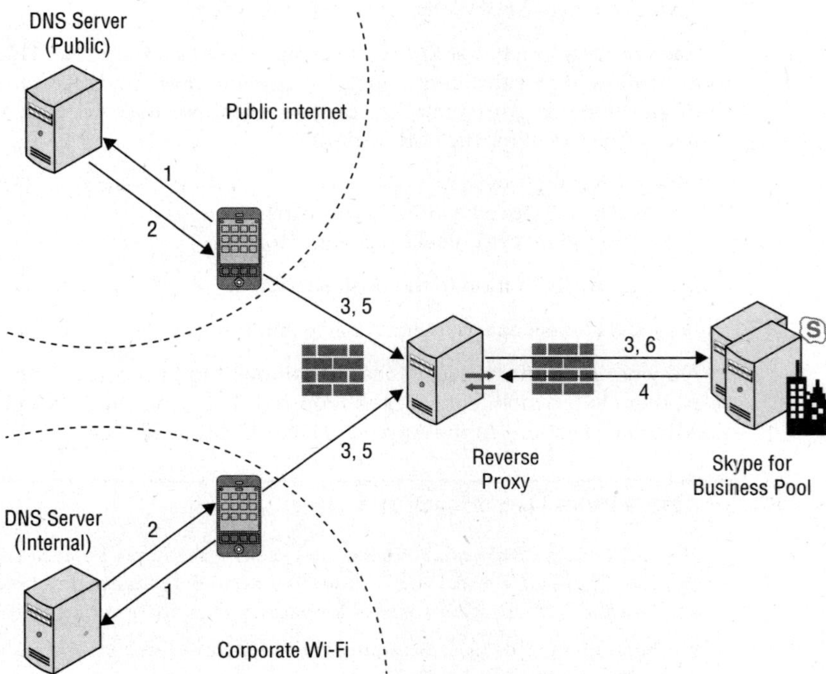

FIGURE 5.10 Mobile client connectivity call flow

Here are the steps:

1. The client carries out a DNS query for `LyncDiscover.<sipdomain>` as well as `LyncDiscoverInternal.<sipdomain>`.
2. The IP address of the mobility web services is returned. This is resolved to the external address of the reverse proxy.
3. The reverse proxy translates the request to the mobility web service on a pool (or Director). This is the Unified Communications Web Application (UCWA) service running on the "external" website.
4. The response to this initial request will include all the web service URLs for the user; these will be specific to their home pool.
5. The client will make another request to the specific mobility service URL provided.
6. The reverse proxy translates the request to the specific mobility web service on the user home pool. This is the Unified Communications Web Application (UCWA) service running on the "external" website.

In a hybrid scenario (both on-premises and in-cloud deployment), the addresses returned in step 4 will be for the online service.

Now, let's take a look at how push notifications work (see Figure 5.11).

FIGURE 5.11
Push notifications

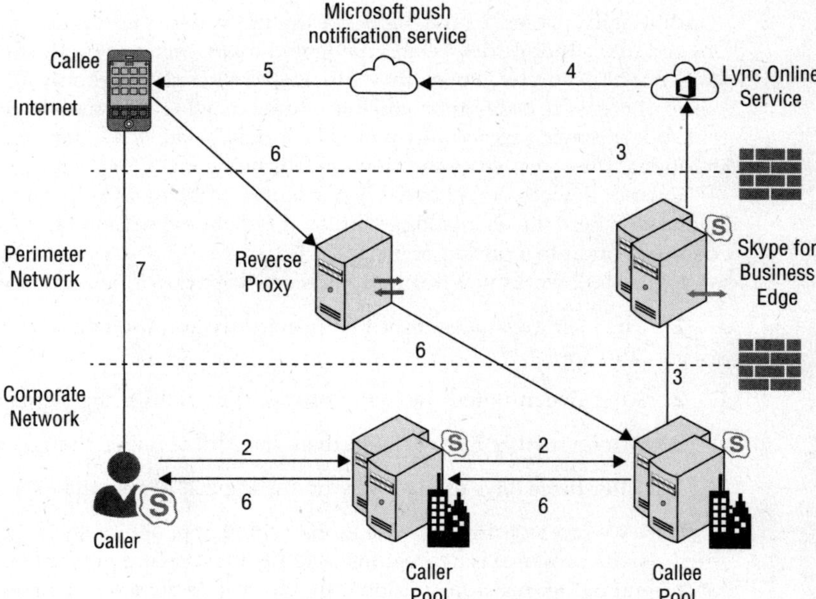

1. The user (the callee) is logged in using the process listed earlier (not shown).
2. The caller places a call, which is sent to the registered endpoints for the recipient.
3. The recipient's home pool will forward the request to the push notification service, via the Edge (using federation).
4. The Lync Online push notification service will send a push message to the device, using the Microsoft Push Notification Service.
5. The Microsoft Push Notification Service will forward the message to the device, the device will display the incoming call details, and the user will accept the call.
6. Signaling information is relayed via the reverse proxy to the user's home pool, as determined during the discovery process, and on to the caller.
7. The call is connected; details of how will come down to the specific policy and device capability at the moment (Wi-Fi enabled/allowed/preferred, and so on).

Step 7 raises an interesting point. What if the user has configured a preference to require Wi-Fi for VoIP calls?

Well, in this case, the call routing information is actually contained within the message via step 6. The pool will determine that a "failback to PSTN" is required, and the call will proceed as if it were a PSTN call. This assumes the caller is permitted to make PSTN calls to mobile devices, of course.

How Does Presence Work?

Traditionally, presence on devices was an up-to-date view of the status of a user. If the user logged into a mobile device and navigated to another app on the device, then presence may or may not be accurate. Especially with older phones that had only a single channel for data and voice, there were easily reproducible situations where the mobile client was showing as available but the user was actually on a call, simply because the device could not send a data packet to update the status since the channel was being used for voice.

Current devices don't have this particular problem. Multiple apps are common and so is the scenario where the user is logged in on the mobile device but then stays logged in when the device is put into a pocket or bag.

Figure 5.12 walks you through the scenario of how this is dealt with in the Lync 2010 app.

1. The user logs in as described previously and then navigates away from the Lync 2010 app.
2. After five minutes, the Lync 2010 app will change the presence state to Inactive.
3. After a further five minutes, the Lync 2010 app will change the status to Away.
4. After three days of inactivity on the Lync 2010 app, the user is logged out.

Here we are covering only the mobile client app; obviously if the user is signed in on other devices, the presence is aggregated, and the most recent presence is provided to other users. If at the end of the three-day period only the mobile device is registering presence, then when the user is logged out, the presence will show as Offline.

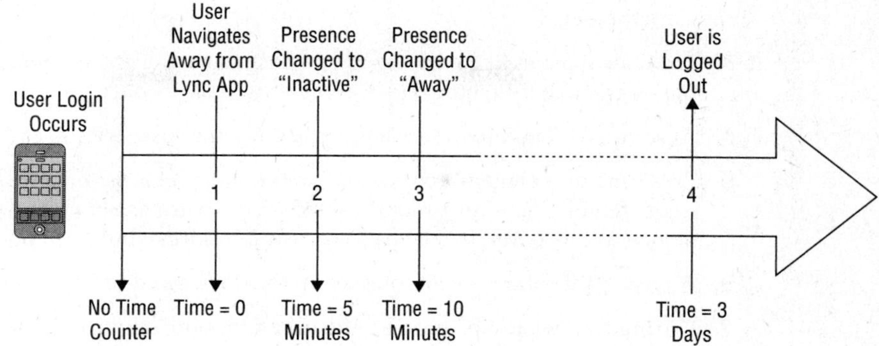

FIGURE 5.12 Mobile presence with Lync 2010

At this point, if you get another user trying to place a call to your mobile user, they will receive a User Unavailable message and not be able to place the call. So, what changed with Lync 2013, and why do you have a better experience with the Skype for Business mobile client? Figure 5.13 walks you through this scenario. Steps 1 through 3 are the same, with one subtle difference; when you sign in, a static registration is created.

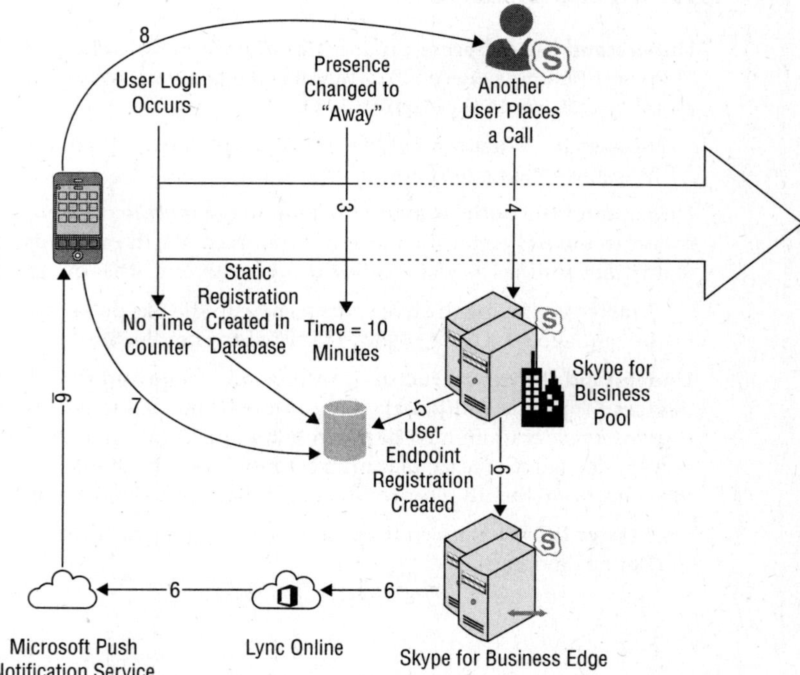

FIGURE 5.13 Mobile presence with Skype for Business

1 2 3

Here are the steps:

1-3. The user signs in like with the Skype for Business client, except this time a static registration is created; this static registration is valid for 15 days.

4. At some point before the 15 days expiry, another user tries to call.

5. This time the call gets "forwarded" to the static registration. The Skype for Business pool understands this is for a mobile device and creates a user endpoint registration for the device; at this point, you won't know the IP address, but push notifications will work.

6. A push notification is sent to wake up the device and notify it of the incoming call.

7. During the "wake-up" process, the user endpoint is updated with the connectivity information.

8. The call will connect as expected.

With Skype for Business, you can see immediately that the experience is a lot better, both for the caller and for the callee, because presence is available for longer as well as because of the ability to wake up the device and get the call notification received for the caller to accept (or not).

The Bottom Line

Understand the different capabilities of each mobile client (including tablets). With Skype for Business Server 2015, mobile clients are natively available and are able to bring new mobility features to the environment.

Master It What capabilities are not available on desktop clients but are available on the Windows Phone or iPhone?

Understand the policies available to manage mobile clients. With another client available to connect to Skype for Business, it's important for the administrator to be able to manage the feature capabilities as well as they would with any other device client.

Master It Name the five settings new to the Skype for Business mobile client, which can be managed via the `*-CsMobilityPolicy` cmdlets.

Understand the infrastructure configuration required for enabling mobile devices. Specific additional configuration is needed to enable the mobility clients, and of course, consideration must be given to the specification of the hardware (and a number of) servers needed. Capacity planning for mobility is built into the capacity planning tools, but the configuration still requires the administrator to lend a hand!

Master It What is required to configure push notifications for Microsoft Windows Phone devices?

Chapter 6

Devices

Skype for Business is a software platform, and without hardware devices to bring it alive, communications wouldn't be the same. Voice would be limited to tiny devices built in to desktop and laptop PCs, and video would be restricted to those webcams that are now standard parts of any laptop.

However, there is a massive devices business from which Skype for Business reaps huge rewards. The list of devices includes USB-connected devices (such as headsets and handsets), stand-alone IP phone devices, and devices that provide full-room immersive video experiences.

Many devices are capable of providing audio (and also video); however, for this chapter we will be covering only devices that are certified for use with Skype for Business. These devices are tested and proven to give a high level of audio (and video) quality of experience when used with Skype for Business. See `https://technet.microsoft.com/en-us/office/dn788951` for information on the Open Interoperability Program (OIP) certification of devices or the newer Partner Solutions Program at `http://partnersolutions.skypeforbusiness.com/solutionscatalog/all`. This program is an ongoing program and will be updated with Skype for Business content as devices get certified.

There are multiple usage scenarios in which these devices can be used, and we'll take a look at them here.

In this chapter, you will learn to

- Integrate with hardware video conferencing platforms
- Configure prerequisites for IP phones

USB Devices

There are so many types of device and connectivity methods it's hard to truly categorize them, but we've tried! First up are USB devices, which are typically headset or handset-style devices. They are "dumb" in the sense they simply plug into a PC (or Mac) and are recognized by the operating system (OS), which in turn presents them to Lync as a "communications device." Figure 6.1 shows a number of connected devices. Note that the second-to-last device is shown as a "default communications device," which means that any Lync sounds will be directed though it.

It's also worth highlighting here that the default device (in this case Realtek High Definition Audio speakers) will play normal OS sounds such as music, audio from applications or websites, operating system (OS) alerts, and so on, and Skype for Business is smart enough to reduce these sounds when a call is in progress. Figure 6.2 shows the configuration settings available to control audio devices in Skype for Business. The Secondary Ringer option is extremely useful because users aren't always wearing their headset when a call comes in. This allows another device to play the ringing alert.

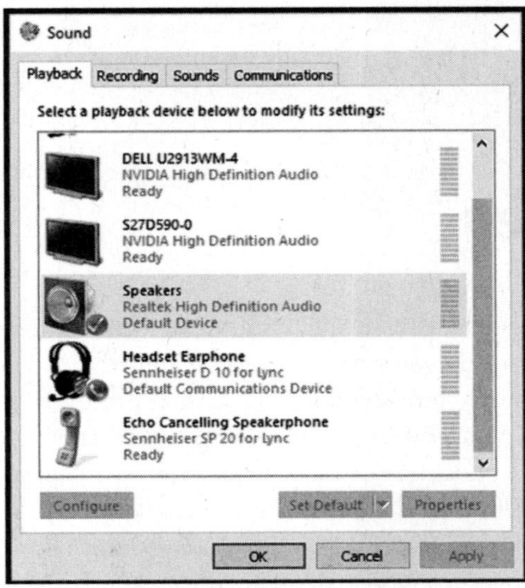

FIGURE 6.1 Sound devices in the operating system

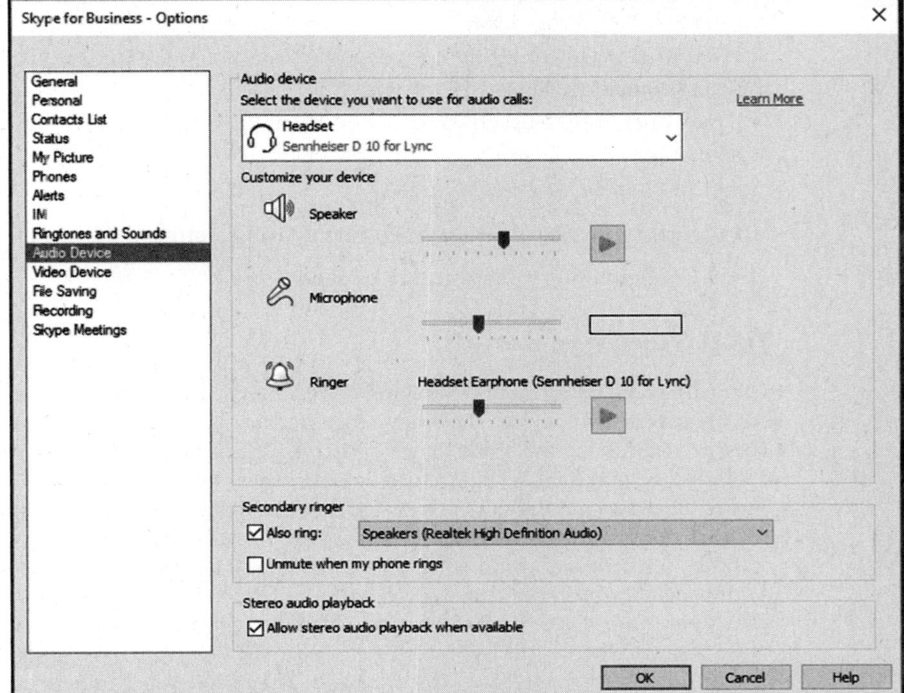

FIGURE 6.2 Skype for Business audio device options

You might ask yourself, "Why don't I just use the built-in 3.5-mm jacks for headphones and microphones rather than a USB device?" Well, aside from the USB devices being tested and qualified for Skype for Business, the built-in jacks are classed as system devices (or "default devices"), so they will play the default operating system alerts, prompts, and so on, potentially disrupting your conversations. USB devices will be classed as communications devices, and the OS allows for a default device setting as well as a default communications device setting.

Headsets

Probably the most obvious device type with a USB connection is a headset. These typically fall into one of the following categories:

- Wired
- Bluetooth
- Digital Enhanced Cordless Technology (DECT)

Each of these types will have USB connectivity of some sort; even the "wireless" ones will have a USB dongle. The reason for this is primarily that the Bluetooth stack within the OS is not certified as part of the OIP; therefore, a device using this connectivity method would not itself be certified, ultimately meaning that vendors have to provide their own (certified) implementation of Bluetooth for their devices.

Headsets will typically offer a range of sound enhancement features.

- Automatic gain control
- Echo cancellation
- Noise canceling

A point often forgotten when specifying devices is that wireless devices need charging. This is the main reason one of the authors continues to carry a wired device in his laptop bag; he is rather forgetful when it comes to charging devices!

Wired

Wired headsets are typically going to be used by users who are at a fixed desk type of location. They are not going to be moving much, and the USB connection can simply be flexible in their localized environment. Wired headsets are the cheapest of the three types available; there's no additional technology required to make them work.

Multiple variations and styles of headsets are available (indeed, some headsets are flexible enough to offer all three in the same package!).

- Over the head
- In, on, or behind ear
- Around the neck

In addition to these form factors, they will have variations on the number of "ears" covered: monaural (one ear) or binaural (two ear).

Figure 6.3 shows the Sennheiser SC40 USB ML, also available as a binaural device (SC70). On the cable itself is a control unit allowing for some noncomputer controls such as the following:

- Answer/end call
- Volume up/down
- Mute
- Redial last call

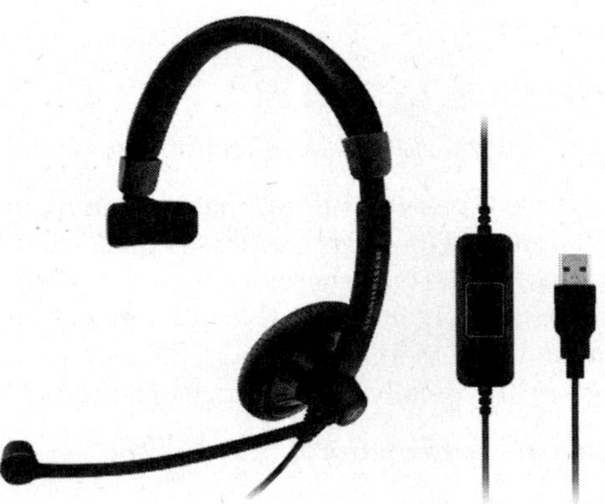

FIGURE 6.3
Sennheiser SC40 USB ML

BLUETOOTH

Bluetooth headsets have the same styles as their wired counterparts but have more flexibility in terms of their location usage because they're not tied to the USB cable.

One massive advantage Bluetooth devices have over both wired and DECT is the ability to connect also to a cell phone device, enabling a user to answer calls on either Skype for Business or their cell phone without having to make any configuration changes. Indeed, some of the newer devices allow for signaling capability from the device itself into Skype for Business, changing the user status to "in a call" even if the call is on their cell phone. These devices have built-in intelligence capability allowing them to "know" their state, to the extent that picking up the device itself will answer the call and moving the device away from your ear will hang up a call in progress. Figure 6.4 shows the PRESENCE UC ML, which has the following key features:

- SpeakFocus technology to focus your voice even in noisy environments
- WindSafe to ensure clearest possible sound
- HD sound quality
- Multiconnectivity to softphone and mobile device

FIGURE 6.4
Sennheiser
PRESENCE UC ML

The more "office-based" devices have a docking station, which will typically also allow for connection of a traditional telephony device.

DECT

DECT devices provide even more range than their Bluetooth brothers, up to 400 feet in some cases, although can be impacted by metal or glass partitions. This can be countered with DECT repeaters. One of the authors of this book has the Sennheiser D 10 ML (see Figure 6.5), which provides the same clarity of audio whether he is sitting at his desk in the basement, in the garden, or in the loft. This particular device has headset controls to allow for answering (or hanging up) a call as well as volume (and mute).

FIGURE 6.5
Sennheiser D 10 ML

The built-in battery allows for easily a full day's talk time or almost a week on standby, and a fantastic improvement over previous models is the ability to charge via USB—no more power adapters required!

A more advanced model, the Sennheiser Office DW, also allows for connection to both Skype for Business and a desk phone, allowing for receipt of calls from either device to the headset and easy selection from the base station as to which device is connected by pressing a switch for either the computer (Skype for Business) or the phone.

DECT devices are likely to be more office based because of the inability to natively connect to cell phone devices. They can connect to the traditional telephony devices, enabling ease of transition from a PBX environment to Skype for Business.

Handsets

Next on the list of USB devices are handsets. In the early days of OCS 2007, we had a device (Polycom CX200) that was simply a phone-shaped microphone and speaker system connected via USB (see Figure 6.6). Yes, it had a few buttons, but these were volume, answer, and speakerphone mode buttons. (It also had the OCS icon that changed color based on your presence state.)

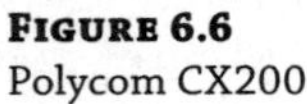

FIGURE 6.6
Polycom CX200

These devices turned out to be quite popular, simply because people are used to having a phone device on their desk. They didn't appreciate fully changing to a softphone client with a headset; they still were looking for the familiarity of the handset, and the Polycom device (along with a few others) allowed organizations to meet this need. (There were devices that were slightly more developed in that they had a number pad!)

At the same time, we also had devices that were shaped and sized more like a cell phone yet still connected via a cable.

In this range, not a lot has truly changed with the ongoing development of OCS R2, Lync, and now Skype for Business.

Where you see the most developments are with IP handsets, covered later in this chapter.

Personal Speakerphones

One device range that sits in among the "great idea implementations" in our minds is the personal speakerphone. This is a device, typically no larger than an ice-hockey puck, that acts as a personal speakerphone when connected via its USB cable. A wide range of devices are available from a number of different manufacturers. Some of the newer ones use Bluetooth (via the dongle) to connect, so they have another level of portability. Figure 6.7 shows the latest device from Sennheiser in this category, the SP 20 ML.

Figure 6.7
Sennheiser SP 20 ML

This device has the following features:

- Dual connectivity 3.5mm jack and USB
- Echo noise cancellation
- Built-in cable management

It's a great comfort to be able to quickly have a Skype for Business call between a number of people via the speakerphone in any environment. Gone are the days when you had to book a conference room that had the speakerphone already in place. These are small enough that you can keep one in your laptop bag and simply whip it out when needed.

IP Desk Phones

IP desk phones for Skype for Business come in two flavors.

- Phone Edition
- Third-Party IP Phone (3PIP)

Phone Edition devices run a version of Windows CE and have a native client installed and configured on them. At the time of this writing, the client remains branded Lync; however, it is expected that an update will rebrand the device to be Skype for Business but not introduce any significant features. While these devices are still supported running against Skype for Business, they are slowly being phased out in favor for the more generic 3PIP devices.

In the following sections, we'll cover both of these types of devices and the configuration required to enable them to integrate into a Skype for Business environment.

Phone Edition

The Lync Phone Edition client hasn't significantly changed since Lync Server 2010. An update removed the 2010 branding, and as mentioned, a similar update is expected to remove the Lync branding.

A number of Phone Edition devices are available from a small number of vendors, including Polycom, Aastra, and HP. You can download a complete list of certified devices from the following URL (at the time of writing, no new devices have been certified against Skype for Business):

`http://partnersolutions.skypeforbusiness.com/solutionscatalog/ip-phones`

Each of these phones has its own look and feel, but the phones run the same software, which is Lync Phone Edition. This software is provided by Microsoft and has the same user interface and functionality regardless of who makes the device.

The IP phones are split into three categories: common area phones, information worker phones, and conference phones. Table 6.1 shows the relevant model numbers for Aastra, Polycom, and HP.

TABLE 6.1: Phone Edition IP phone models

PHONE TYPE	AASTRA	POLYCOM	HP
Common area phone	6720ip	CX500	4110
Information worker phone	6725ip	CX600	4120
Conference phone	N\A	CX3000	N\A

In addition to these phone models, the Polycom CX700 and LG-Nortel 8540 are supported and can be updated to Lync 2010 Phone Edition, but they operate with a reduced feature set. Figure 6.8 shows the Polycom CX500 common area phone, and Figure 6.9 shows the HP 4120 information worker phone.

Figure 6.8
Polycom CX500 common area phone

Figure 6.9
HP 4120 information worker phone

Common Area Phones

Common area phones are designed to be deployed in areas where there is no single user, such as reception areas, warehouses, and so on. Compared to the information worker phones, these phones have a reduced feature set, which is referred to as *basic mode*, and also a reduced hardware configuration. Basic mode offers the following functionality:

- Contacts
- Photos
- Message waiting indicator

- Local call logs
- Remote usage (after intranet provisioning)
- Conference call control

Although referred to as common area phones, they can be used by standard users—for example, in a hot-desking configuration where they are configured as common area phones and also enabled to allow users to log into them. The phones can also be used without common area configuration by a single user.

Information Worker and Conference Phones

From a Phone Edition standpoint, the information worker and conference phone types provide the same functionality, which builds on that of the common area phone and implements what is commonly referred to as *Enhanced mode*.

This Enhanced mode is made possible by connecting the phone to a PC using a USB cable, a technique referred to as *USB tethering*, which is possible to do with these phones. If a user decides to log in using their extension and PIN instead, they will be restricted to Basic mode. Enhanced mode adds the following functionality: Exchange Calendar including Join Conference, Exchange integrated call logs, and visual voice mail. When a user decides to use USB tethering, they will be prompted to reenter their password when they connect their PC and phone together, as shown in Figure 6.10.

Figure 6.10
Login for USB tethering

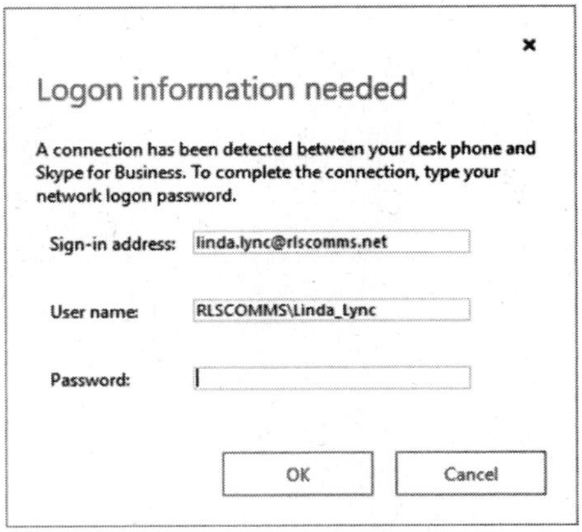

Logon information needed
A connection has been detected between your desk phone and Skype for Business. To complete the connection, type your network logon password.
Sign-in address: linda.lync@rlscomms.net
User name: RLSCOMMS\Linda_Lync
Password:
OK
Cancel

These devices, unlike the common area phones, can also be set up from remote locations without needing to be on the corporate network. This allows organizations to drop-ship the devices without needing to preconfigure anything. Users will be required to log in using USB tethering rather than log in with their extension and PIN.

CX700 and 8540 Phones

The CX700 and 8540 phones are upgradable to Lync 2010 Phone Edition (they're originally OCS phones!), but they operate with a reduced feature set. The features that are supported are in line with those offered in OCS 2007 R2. The features that are not supported are the ability to operate as a common area phone, PIN authentication, and contact photos. For users, the most noticeable change is that they can view their calendar and join Skype Online meetings from the phone.

Configuring IP Phone Prerequisites

A number of elements need to be configured to allow Phone Edition IP phones to operate within your organization so people can use them. The requirements vary depending on how the phone is going to be initially configured. Phones can be configured either through USB tethering or directly on the phone using PIN authentication. USB tethering doesn't depend on the network as much as the method because the required certificates, SIP URI, and authentication information are synced through the USB cable. The main thing you need is Network Time Protocol (NTP); however, depending on your requirements, you may also need Link Layer Discovery Protocol (LLDP) and Power over Ethernet (PoE). For PIN authentication, the phone needs to locate information about the Skype for Business setup; it needs information in DHCP to provide this.

Irrespective of the method used for the initial configuration, DHCP is needed to provide basic information to the phone, such as the IP address, subnet, and default gateway along with the DNS domain name and server.

Dynamic Host Configuration Protocol

Dynamic Host Configuration Protocol (DHCP) is used to provide the information you need for Phone Edition to connect to the Skype for Business server; this information cannot be manually entered into the phone, making the DHCP configuration a requirement for deployment. DHCP provides the following information as part of the in-band provisioning process.

- Skype for Business registrar address, which could be a Director pool or a pool
- URL of the web services
- Relative URL of the certificate provider on the Skype for Business server
- Protocol for the certificate provider (HTTPS by default)
- Port for the certificate provider (443 by default)

The Skype for Business registrar address is provided in Option 120; the other settings are provided under Option 43, using a vendor-specific MS-UC-Client setting. Both of them are provided as hexadecimal strings.

Two methods are available to provide the required DHCP settings. The first is to use the DHCP server that is provided as part of the Skype for Business registrar. This DHCP server is limited in functionality and is used to provide the required information. It will respond only to a DHCP request that contains a Vendor Class ID of MS-UC-Client and asks for Option 120 or 43. A fully functional DHCP server is still required to provide an IP address, subnet, and default gateway along with the DNS domain name and server for the phone. This DHCP server can be useful for labs or for small installations, but once a network becomes segregated by VLANs or WAN connections are used, this method is not usually feasible. To enable the DHCP server, use the following PowerShell command:

```
Set-CsRegistrarConfiguration -EnableDHCPServer $true
```

The second method is to use existing DHCP servers to provide the required configuration settings. This way, you do not have to configure the network to route DHCP requests to the Skype for Business registrar, and you can also use it to deliver additional configuration information to the device.

To help you configure DHCP servers, Microsoft provides a configuration tool that will generate the required DHCP entries. While this tool is mainly aimed at Windows DHCP, the information it generates can be used to configure third-party DHCP servers. The utility, called DHCPUtil, is provided as part of the Lync installation and is located in the `C:\Program Files\Common Files\Skype for Business Server 2015` directory, assuming the default installation path. This tool works in conjunction with a batch file called `DHCPConfigScript.bat`, which configures the DHCP server. The DHCPUtil application generates the DHCP configuration, emulates the client to check the DHCP configuration, and, finally, removes the DHCP configuration.

To create the DHCP configuration, at a minimum the batch file needs to be run on the DHCP server with the required settings passed into it as command-line arguments. These settings are generated by the DHCPUtil application and are created from three parameters.

`-SipServer`, which is the FQDN of the Director or Skype for Business pool

`-WebServer`, which is the FQDN of the web services

`-CertProvUrl`, which is the URL of the certificate provider

For a Standard Edition installation, only the FQDN of the SIP server needs to be specified because it is the same as the web server FQDN. This is also the case for an Enterprise Edition installation in which the SIP server and the web server share the same FQDN, and it's usually the case when a hardware load balancer is used. It is usually not necessary to specify the certificate provider URL.

For example, to configure DHCP for a Standard Edition installation with an FQDN of `se01.rlscomms.net`, use the following syntax:

```
DHCPUtil.exe -SipServer se01.rlscomms.net
```

This will produce an output detailing the configuration (shown in Figure 6.11), along with the syntax required for the `DHCPConfigScript` batch file.

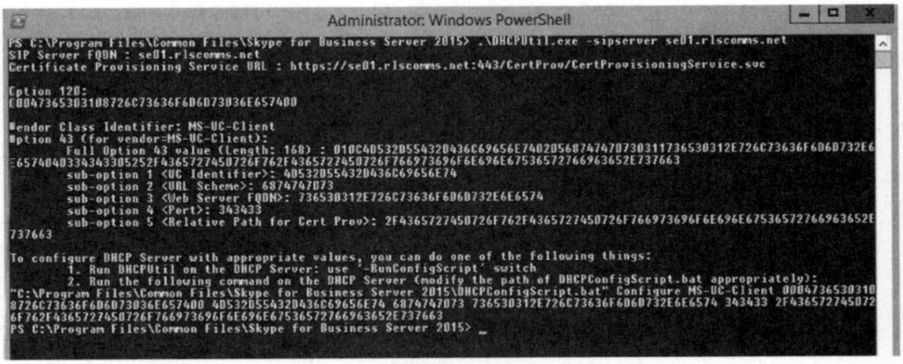

```
Administrator: Windows PowerShell
PS C:\Program Files\Common Files\Skype for Business Server 2015> .\DHCPUtil.exe -sipserver se01.rlscomms.net
SIP Server FQDN : se01.rlscomms.net
Certificate Provisioning Service URL : https://se01.rlscomms.net:443/CertProv/CertProvisioningService.svc

Option 120:
00047365303108726C73636F6D6D73036E657400

Vendor Class Identifier: MS-UC-Client
Option 43 (for vendor=MS-UC-Client):
        Full Option 43 value (Length: 168) : 010C4D532D55432D436C69656E7402056874747073031173653031 2E726C73636F6D6D732E6
E6574040334343305252F4365727450726F762F4365727450726F766973696F6E696E67536572766963652E737663
        sub-option 1 <UC Identifier>: 4D532D55432D436C69656E74
        sub-option 2 <URL Scheme>: 6874747073
        sub-option 3 <Web Server FQDN>: 7365303 12E726C73636F6D6D732E6E6574
        sub-option 4 <Port>: 343433
        sub-option 5 <Relative Path for Cert Prov>: 2F4365727450726F762F4365727450726F766973696F6E696E67536572766963652E
737663

To configure DHCP Server with appropriate values, you can do one of the following things:
        1. Run DHCPUtil on the DHCP Server: use '-RunConfigScript' switch
        2. Run the following command on the DHCP Server (modify the path of DHCPConfigScript.bat appropriately):
"C:\Program Files\Common Files\Skype for Business Server 2015\DHCPConfigScript.bat" Configure MS-UC-Client 0004736530310
8726C73636F6D6D73036E657400 4D532D55432D436C69656E74 6874747073 73653031 2E726C73636F6D6D732E6E6574 343433 2F436572745072
6F762F4365727450726F766973696F6E696E67536572766963652E737663
PS C:\Program Files\Common Files\Skype for Business Server 2015> _
```

FIGURE 6.11 Output for `DHCPUtil.exe`

Copy the `DHCPConfigScript` file to the DHCP server and run the previous command to create the DHCP configuration. These configurations are created as server options, and they will be applied to every DHCP scope on the DHCP server. If scope-specific options are required rather than server options, you will need to write your own configuration script. You can use the batch file as a basis for this. If you need to remove the DHCP configuration, run the following command from the DHCP server:

```
DHCPConfigScript.bat -Cleanup
```

The `DHCPUtil` command can be used to test the DHCP configuration; it sends a DHCP INFORM packet, displaying its contents, and also displays the contents of the DHCP ACK packet it receives along with the decoded settings. If the ACK is not received or the decoded settings appear to be wrong, this indicates a configuration issue. You can run the test using the following command, and you should receive the output shown in Figure 6.12:

```
DHCPUtil.exe -EmulateClient
```

```
Administrator: Windows PowerShell
    DHCP: Server Identifier(  54) = (Length: 0) 0.0.0.0
    DHCP: Client Identifier(  61) = (Length: 7) ☺ (0100155D01E71B)
    DHCP: SIP Server( 120)        = (Length: 0) enc:0  ()
    DHCP: Host Name(  12)         = (Length: 4) SE01
    DHCP: Vendor Identifier(  60) = (Length: 12) MS-UC-Client
    DHCP: Param Req List(  55)    = (Length: 2) 120 43
    DHCP: Vendor Info(  43)       = (Length: 0)  ()
    DHCP: End of this option field
--End Packet--


Received Packet
Sender:192.168.3.4:67, Size:369
--Begin Packet--
DHCP: ACK                 (xid=80337252)
DHCP: Op Code             (op)       = 1
DHCP: Hardware Type       (htype)    = 6
DHCP: Hops                (hops)     = 0
DHCP: Transaction ID      (xid)      = 2150855250
DHCP: Seconds             (secs)     = 0
DHCP: Flags               (flags)    = 0000
DHCP: Client IP Address (ciaddr)     = 192.168.3.2
DHCP: Your IP Address   (yiaddr)     = 0.0.0.0
DHCP: Server IP Address (siaddr)     = 0.0.0.0
DHCP: Relay IP Address  (giaddr)     = 0.0.0.0
DHCP: Client HW Address (chaddr)     = 00155D01E71B
DHCP: Server Host Name  (sname)      =
DHCP: Boot File Name    (file)       =
DHCP: Magic Cookie                   = 99.130.83.99
DHCP: Option Field
    DHCP: DHCP MESSAGE TYPE(  53) = (Length: 1) DHCP ACK
    DHCP: Server Identifier(  54) = (Length: 4) 192.168.3.4
    DHCP: Client Identifier(  61) = (Length: 0)  ()
    DHCP: SIP Server( 120)        = (Length: 20) enc:0 se01.rlscomms.net (0004736530310872 6C73636F6D6D73036E657400)
    DHCP: Host Name(  12)         = (Length: 0)
    DHCP: Vendor Identifier(  60) = (Length: 0)
    DHCP: Param Req List(  55)    = (Length: 0) 0 0
    DHCP: Vendor Info(  43)       = (Length: 89) ☺♀MS-UC-Client☻♣https♥‹se01.rlscomms.net♦♥443♣X/CertProv/CertProvisioni
ngService.svc☺♥NAP (010C4D532D55432D436C69656E74020568747470730311736530312E726C73636F6D6D732E6E657404033434330552F4365
727450726F762F43657274507 26F766973696F6E696E67536572766963652E737663 0C034E4150)
    DHCP: End of this option field
--End Packet--


Result: Success
DHCP Server : 192.168.3.4
SIP Server FQDN : se01.rlscomms.net
Certificate Provisioning Service URL : https://se01.rlscomms.net:443/CertProv/CertProvisioningService.svc
PS C:\Program Files\Common Files\Skype for Business Server 2015>
```

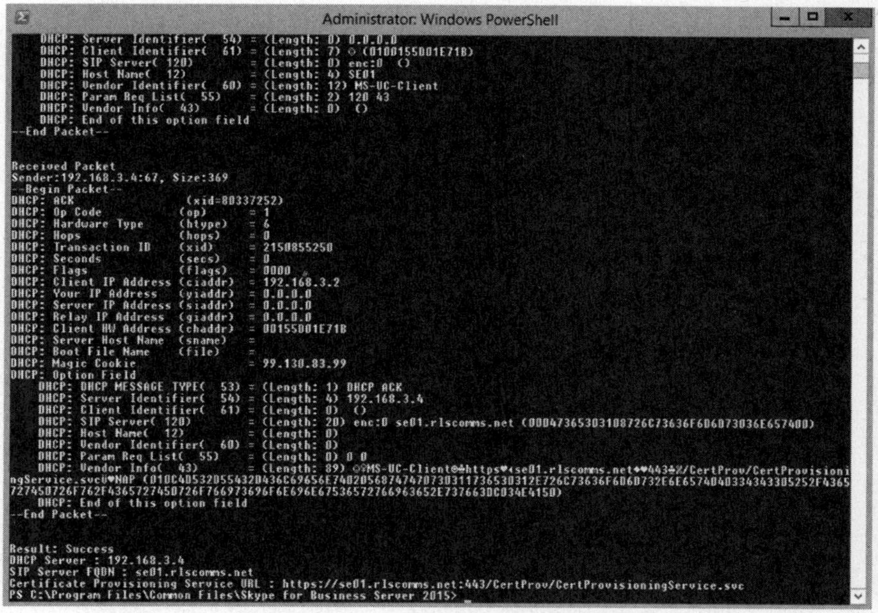

FIGURE 6.12 Output for `DHCPUtil.exe -EmulateClient`

Remember, the output from `DHCPUtil.exe` will depend upon the network location from which it is run; it is advisable to run this from each network location (and possibly even each VLAN) to ensure full coverage!

The final DHCP-related item you need to look at is how to get the IP phone to switch to a specific VLAN. This is often required in scenarios where a PC is connected via a phone and the two devices need to be on separate VLANs. Using DHCP to do this should always be seen as a fallback option; the preferred method is to use Link Layer Discovery Protocol.

The VLAN configuration is provided through Option 43 in a similar way to the configuration of the actual phone, but it is provided under a different vendor-specific class, CPE-OCPHONE. During the boot stage, the phone will try to retrieve a VLAN ID from LLDP; if this fails, it will perform a DHCP request, looking for a VLAN ID. If it receives one, it will release the IP address it was issued and perform another DHCP request; this is tagged with the VLAN ID it just received. If a VLAN ID is not retrieved, the second DHCP request is still performed to retrieve the server details because two different vendor class IDs are being used.

Although you could populate DHCP with the server details, there is no utility to populate the VLAN information, so it must be manually created or scripted. The following method is an example of how it can be scripted:

```
netsh dhcp server add class CPEOCPHONE "Phone Edition VLAN Tagging"
"CPE-OCPHONE" 1
netsh dhcp server add optiondef 10 VLANID Word 0 vendor=CPEOCPhone
comment="Phone Edition VLAN"
netsh dhcp server set optionvalue 10 Word vendor=CPEOCPhone "250"
```

This script creates the vendor class, assigns it the VLAN suboption 10 under Option 43, and adds it as a DHCP server option, applicable to all scopes. To use these commands, replace 250 with the voice VLAN you need.

Once DHCP has been updated, the phones will discover the VLAN the next time they are restarted and begin using it. If you ever need to change the VLAN once the phones have been configured, each phone will need to be hard-reset because the VLAN information is cached.

Caching the VLANs does potentially create an issue for one scenario: If an organization requires IP phones to be used remotely via the Edge servers, a cached VLAN can potentially cause problems. If the IP phone is attached to a switch that honors and routes based on the VLAN tag applied by the phone, there is the possibility that the packets will be placed into a VLAN that may not have a DHCP server configured or Internet access, or they may be dropped by the switch completely if the VLAN does not exist. Therefore, if phones need to be configured onsite before being used off-site, scope-specific options should be used for the VLAN configuration rather than server-wide options, and the phone should be connected to switch ports on the correct voice VLAN.

The final item to consider is the actual switch configuration. Because two VLANs are used on a single port, the primary VLAN needs to be set to the VLAN that the computer will use, while the voice VLAN should be set to a supported VLAN for the port.

Link Layer Discovery Protocol

Link Layer Discovery Protocol allows Phone Edition to discover which VLAN it should use. This is the preferred VLAN Discovery method, but it requires network switches that support LLDP-MED, the protocol's Media Endpoint Discovery extension. The configuration varies depending on the switch make and model. The following is a sample Cisco configuration:

```
!- Enter configuration mode
configure terminal
!- Enable LLDP
```

```
lldp run
!- Configure Ethernet port 1
interface FastEthernet 1/1
!- Set Data VLAN to 100
switchport access vlan 100
!- Set Voice VLAN to 101
switchport voice vlan 101
!- Configure as Access Port
switchport mode access
```

This configuration instructs Phone Edition to use VLAN 101, and all network traffic will be tagged with this VLAN, ensuring that the correct DHCP scope is used and the traffic is prioritized correctly.

Power over Ethernet

Power over Ethernet (PoE) allows a phone device to be powered by the network switch rather than requiring a local power supply for the phone. This often simplifies the deployment because it does not require power sockets local to the phone or additional cables.

The available phones support both 802.3AF and 802.3AT standards for Power over Ethernet; it is important to check that any existing switches support these IEEE standards. If you are upgrading from an existing IP telephony system, the current switches may not support these standards. For example, older Cisco switches use a proprietary PoE implementation that is not compatible with these phones.

Network Time Protocol

Because Phone Edition does not allow any configuration on the device, Network Time Protocol is used to retrieve the current date and time. This lets you check items, such as the certificates, for validity. Phone Edition discovers the NTP server using DNS; the following two DNS records will be tried in order:

- The SRV record, `_ntp._udp.`*`<SIP domain>`* (port 123)
- `time.windows.com`

If there is no SRV record, Phone Edition will fall back to `time.windows.com`. If this is used, the phone will need to be able to access the Internet using UDP on port 123.

If you do not have an internal NTP server and do not want to use `time.windows.com`, then the Windows Time Service, which runs on every Windows server, can be configured to act as an NTP server. You can enable this through a Group Policy change. The Group Policy can be applied to any existing server, and a new policy can be used or an existing one can be changed. The settings that need to be changed are at Computer Configuration ➢ Policies ➢ Administrative Templates ➢ System ➢ Windows Time Service ➢ Time Providers.

To enable the Time server on the server to which the Group Policy applies, set Enable Windows NTP Server to Enabled in the Group Policy Management Editor, as shown in Figure 6.13. This will allow the server to respond to NTP requests.

Once this has been enabled, the SRV record should be created in DNS Manager with the server FQDN specified as the server configured to offer this capability.

Figure 6.13 NTP Group Policy change

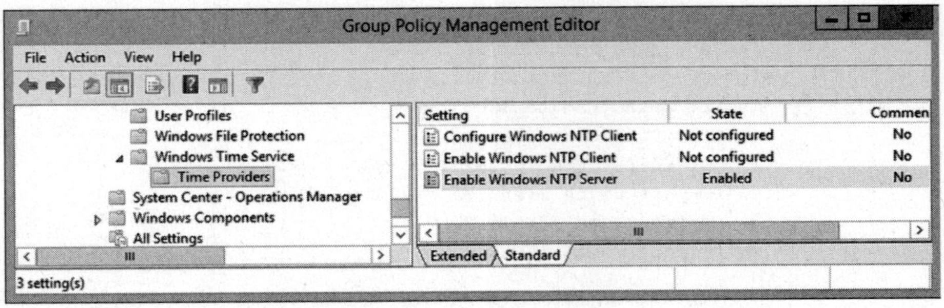

Device Configuration

Device configuration is performed in two parts; the first part is performed through in-band configuration and is configured through the Skype for Business Control Panel (Clients ➤ Device Configuration) and PowerShell using the `CsUCPhoneConfiguration` cmdlets (`New`, `Set`, `Get`, and `Remove`).

These settings are available on either a global basis or a site basis. The following settings are available:

- `Identity`, which is set to global for the global configuration or the site name prefixed with `Site:`
- `SIPSecurityMode`, which is the SIP Signaling Security level for devices
- `LoggingLevel`, which indicates the depth of logging on the device
- `VoiceDiffServTag`, which is the DSCP value for marking voice packets
- `EnforcePhoneLock`, which locks the phone when the timeout occurs
- `PhoneLockTimeout`, which is the length of time until the phone is locked
- `MinPhonePinLength`, which is the minimum length of the device PIN
- `CalendarPollInterval`, which is the interval at which EWS will be polled for changes
- `Voice8021p`, which is the 802.1p value for marking voice packets

The last two settings are exposed only via PowerShell.

Of these settings, the ones most commonly modified are DSCP and Device Lock. The other settings can be left at the factory defaults for most deployments, unless you need to troubleshoot, which requires logging to be turned on. If, for example, you needed to modify the global policy to change the device timeout to five minutes, you would use the following PowerShell command:

```
Set-CsUCPhoneConfiguration -Identity global -PhoneLockTimeout "00:05:00"
```

The second part of device configuration is done on the devices themselves; it is performed as part of the user sign-in process and allows the following information to be configured:

- Time zone
- Date and time format

- Ringtone
- Phone lock code

Unfortunately, there is no method to configure these settings centrally, and configuring them on a per-user basis in large deployments can be a time-consuming process.

Client Connection Process

Phone Edition connects to the servers in a different way than a Skype for Business client. Phone Edition at a high level goes through the following steps for internal clients:

1. Tries to locate a VLAN to use
2. Issues a DHCP request looking for an IP address
3. Checks for device updates
4. Downloads certificate chains
5. Authenticates
6. Receives and publishes the client certificate
7. Registers with Skype for Business

The first three steps were covered earlier in this chapter, so we'll focus on the remaining four steps now.

For Phone Edition to trust the certificates used for web services, the root certificate needs to be downloaded and verified. This process happens only if a root certificate has not already been downloaded. The certificate is downloaded using a standard HTTP query, containing the web services details retrieved from DHCP. Once it is downloaded, an HTTPS request to the web services is performed; this check ensures that the root certificate is valid.

In scenarios where the certificates used are not from the same root CA as those used for the Skype for Business servers, or trusted by those default certificates in the Phone Edition OS, then it is possible to use web services on the Skype for Business pool to provide additional trusted root certificate information. See Chapter 15, "Troubleshooting," for an example of how to do this.

Authentication for first-time logins is performed using either the user's extension and PIN or NTLM details to the Skype for Business web service, which checks to see whether they are valid. If the details are valid, a certificate is returned to the client; the certificate is also published into the data store in the user's home pool. If the phone already has a user certificate, it is used to perform the authentication, and the client can then automatically log in after a restart.

Once the authentication is complete, the phone needs to register with the pool to which the client is allocated. To locate the correct pool to connect to, the Phone Edition client uses DNS and DHCP to locate the initial connection pool. It will try to locate the pool address, using the following order:

- DHCP address using Option 120 (Option 43 is used for certificate services discovery)
- Internal DNS SRV using TLS (`_sipinternaltls._tcp.rlscomms.net`)
- Internal DNS SRV using TCP (`_sipinternal._tcp.rlscomms.net`)

- External DNS using TLS (`_sip._tls.rlscomms.net`)
- DNS using an A record (`sip.rlscomms.net`)

This differs from a PC client in that the DHCP option is first. This is an historic configuration to ensure that the Phone Edition client does not connect to an OCS 2007 R2 pool first because it would be unable to sign in. Once it has connected to the initial pool, for single pool deployment or where the user is allocated to this pool, the client will proceed. If this initial pool is a Director or the client is hosted on a different pool, the client will be redirected to the correct home pool.

Once the client has connected to the home pool, it will connect to the registrar. For Standard Edition deployments or single-server Enterprise deployments, there is only one registrar, so it will be used. Where there are multiple registrars in a pool (each Front End server contains a registrar), the client will be redirected to the registrar to which the user has been allocated. This allocation process is defined when the user is created or moved to the pool. It cannot be changed by an administrator.

At this stage, the client is registered to Skype for Business, and the registrar address is cached to be used for future connections. Should the registrar become unavailable, the process is started again.

While this may seem like a complicated process, it is not seen by end users and is exposed to administrators only when they're troubleshooting. The change to using items such as certificates was necessary to support new functionality in Skype for Business, such as the Survivable Branch Appliance.

For external clients, the process is different. The phones must first be logged in internally; once this has occurred and they are taken external, the following process occurs on the phone:

1. Request an IP address from DHCP.
2. Check for device updates.
3. Authenticate.
4. Register with Skype for Business.

These steps are similar to that of an internal client, but at this stage the user certificate already exists. Instead of connecting directly to a pool, all requests are relayed through an Edge server. In addition, only DNS is used to locate the address to connect to the following records:

- DNS SRV using TLS
- DNS SRV using TCP
- SIP A Record from DNS—i.e., `sip.rlscomms.net`

Deploying Phone Edition Updates

Updates for Phone Edition are managed and distributed by Skype for Business Server. This allows you to control update rollouts, with the ability to configure test devices and to roll back to a previous version if necessary.

For the most part, you can manage any updates through either PowerShell or the Skype for Business Control Panel. The only thing you must do through PowerShell is upload the update files.

Update files are published on the Microsoft download site and are released periodically. One update file is released for each hardware vendor, so a separate update file is released for the Polycom CX700 and LG-Nortel 8540 devices.

Organizations do not usually need to download all of them because they commonly standardize on a single vendor; however, for an upgrade from a previous version, you may need to also download the update for CX700 and 8540 devices.

These update packs have the same filename, `UCUpdates.exe`, so if you are downloading files for multiple vendors, you need to be careful not to overwrite another update file. The downloads are executable files and will extract to the same location, which is the *%userprofile%* path. Likewise, they all extract with the same filename, which is `ucupdates.cab`, so make sure you do not overwrite an existing update file.

Once downloaded and extracted, the update files need to be uploaded to the Skype for Business web services. The following PowerShell command can be used to perform this task; it will upload the file to each web services server. This assumes that the `ucupdates.cab` file is located on the root of the `C:` drive.

```
Get-CsService -WebServer | ForEach-Object {Import-CsDeviceUpdate
-Identity $_.Identity -FileName c:\UCUpdates.cab}
```

Once the updates have been uploaded, they will appear as *pending versions*. When updates are pending, they will be deployed only to test devices. They will not be deployed to other devices until they have been approved.

Device testing, update approval, and version restoration can be managed through either PowerShell or the Lync Control Panel. Test devices are identified using either their MAC address or serial number; both of these should be globally unique, so using either should not cause a problem. In addition, the test devices can be created on either a site or global basis.

To create a test device, use the `New-CsTestDevice` cmdlet, which requires four parameters.

`-Name`, which is the name of the test device

`-Parent`, which is defined as global or `site:`*<sitename>*

`-Identifier`, which is the MAC address or serial number of the device

`-IdentifierType`, which is set to either `MACAddress` or `SerialNumber`

To create a test device at the EMEA site using an `Identifier` value of `AB37_679e`, for example, use the following PowerShell command:

```
New-CsTestDevice -Name "EMEA Test Phone 1" -Parent Site:EMEA
-Identifier "AB37_679e" -IdentifierType SerialNumber
```

Once this command has been run, any future uploaded updates will be deployed to this device for testing. You can use the following cmdlets to manage test devices:

`Get-CsTestDevice`

`Set-CsTestDevice`

`Remove-CsTestDevice`

When planning your test devices, choose at least one of each device to test. You should not use mission-critical devices or high-profile users such as C-level executives; they should be users who use the most of their device's functionality.

Once the updates have been tested, they can be approved to be deployed to all the remaining devices. Updates can be approved using either the Control Panel or the `Approve-CsDeviceUpdateRule` cmdlet. This cmdlet takes a single input, which is the unique identity of the update, and it could look like this:

```
Approve-CsDeviceUpdateRule -Identity service:WebServer:se01.rslcomms.net/
d5ce3c10-2588-420a-82ac-dc2d9b1222ff9
```

To retrieve the identities of updates, use the `Get-CsDeviceUpdateRule` cmdlet, which retrieves all available updates and can be filtered as needed. If you want to approve all pending updates after you've tested the update, use the following command:

```
Get-CsDeviceUpdateRule | Approve-CsDeviceUpdateRule
```

If you need to restore to a previous version of Phone Edition, use the `Restore-CsDeviceUpdateRule` cmdlet. If you want to remove a pending update completely, you can use `Reset-CsDeviceUpdateRule`. Both of these cmdlets use the same syntax as `Approve-CsDeviceUpdateRule`.

Now that you've seen how updates are managed, you need to see how the device updates itself. Updates are handled differently, depending on both the state and the location of the phone. Therefore, we'll cover three different update processes: the process for nonprovisioned devices, for internal devices, and for external devices.

Nonprovisioned devices are ones that do not have a user signed into them. These devices can be updated only if they are on the corporate network because access to the updates website is blocked for anonymous users. The update process is as follows:

1. Send a DNS request for `ucupdates-r2.`*`<DHCPIssuedDomainName>`*.
2. Send an HTTPS request asking if an update is available.
3. If `NumOFFiles = 0` is returned, no update is available.
4. If an update is available, the download path will be provided.
5. The phone downloads the updates, installs them, and, after five minutes of inactivity, reboots the device.

The main issue with this process is that because an HTTPS request is used, the phone needs to trust the certificate that is returned. At this stage, the phone will not trust internal certificates because the root certificate isn't installed; therefore, it will reject it. To work around this, you can use an externally issued certificate, or you can have a user sign in because this process will download the root certificate.

The update process for internal and external devices is similar with one difference—for external access, the anonymous request is rejected and the phone retries using credentials. The process is as follows:

1. On startup, user login, or every 24 hours, a check for updates using the in-band provisioned URL is performed.
2. If `NumOFFiles = 0` is returned, no update is available.
3. If an update is available, the download path will be provided.
4. The phone downloads the update, installs it, and, after five minutes of inactivity, reboots the device.

When the updates have been applied and the device rebooted, the phone will automatically be logged in as the same user.

Phone Edition Logs

To troubleshoot Phone Edition, the log level needs to be specified, and the logs need to be uploaded from the phone to the server and converted. Once at this stage, you can begin analyzing the logs to troubleshoot the issue. This may sound like a cumbersome process, but it is relatively straightforward. The logging level is set through the phone in-band provisioning process, either through the Control Panel or through PowerShell.

To enable logging on a global basis, you can use the following PowerShell command:

```
Set-CsUCPhoneConfiguration -Identity Global -LoggingLevel High
```

To disable logging, change `High` to `Off`. The phone will start logging once the settings have been updated. This will be done through the in-band provisioning periodically, but the quickest way is by rebooting the phone.

Since the phone has logging enabled, you can re-create the issue that you are experiencing, and once this is completed, the log files need to be sent to the server. To do this, if the phone is logged in, use the phone's Settings menu and select Set Log Settings ➢ Send Logs. If the phone is not logged in or locked, use System Information.

Once the log files have been uploaded, they can be found in `DeviceUpdateLogs\Client\CELog` on the File Store for the pool. At a minimum, there will be a file with a `.clg` extension. There could also be a *Dr. Watson* log file if one has been created; this file is created in case of a crash and is automatically uploaded. It is the CLG file you want. It needs to be converted to a readable format using Readlog; the following syntax can be used:

```
readlog.exe -v logfile.clg logfile.txt
```

Now that you have a log file in plain text, you can begin the analysis.

How to Get Your Hands on Readlog

Readlog is part of the Windows CE Platform Builder. It is not freely available, but you can use it for a 180-day trial period. Once you have installed the trial, you can find Readlog here: `C:\WinCE810\Public\Common\Oak\Bin\I386`.

Readlog does not depend on any other files, and the executable can be copied to the machine on which you want to convert the files. To install the trial, you will need a trial license key. You can request one at the following location:

`https://www.microsoft.com/windowsembedded/en-us/windows-embedded-8-pro.aspx`

You will need to log in with your Windows Live ID and complete the registration process.

Configuring Common Area Phones

To use common area phones, you need to create accounts for each phone. These accounts exist only within Skype for Business, but they are represented as contacts within Active Directory and allow users to search for them in the Skype for Business Address Book and call them.

You can create a common area phone through PowerShell using the `New-CsCommonAreaPhone` cmdlet, and you can manage it using the equivalent `Set`, `Get`, and `Remove` cmdlets. There is also a `Move` cmdlet, allowing you to move the phone from one pool to another.

Once you've created the common area phone, you can assign client, voice, conferencing, and PIN policies to it in the same way you assign them to a user. You should create specific policies for these phones so they can be locked down more than a standard user would be. For example, if you want to create a common area phone for the headquarters reception area, you can use the following PowerShell command:

```
New-CsCommonAreaPhone -LineUri "tel:+4455577777"
-RegistrarPool "se01.rlscomms.net"
-DisplayName "HQ Main Reception Phone"
-SipAddress sip:hqmainreception@rlscomms.net
-OU "ou=Common Area Phone,DC=rlscomms,DC=net"
```

This will create the common area phone with a phone number of +4455577777 on the `se01.rlscomms.net` pool with a display name of HQ Main Reception Phone. You can also set a SIP address; this is an optional setting, but if you set the phone to an address that is easy to remember, it will make it easier to grant policies. If it is not set, a SIP address based on the default domain name and GUID is used.

Once the phone has been created, the necessary policies can be assigned to it; this is performed in the same way as assigning policies to a normal user using the `Grant` cmdlets.

The voice and conferencing policies should be configured as follows; these settings will suffice for the majority of requirements. The following voice policy is recommended:

- Call forwarding disabled
- Team call disabled
- Delegation disabled
- Call transfer disabled

The following conferencing policy is recommended:

- Audio conference disabled
- File transfer disabled

The following is not a conferencing policy setting but is set within the conference policy:

- Peer-to-peer file transfer disabled

Once the policies have been granted, a PIN needs to be set for the common area phone. Without this, it is not possible to log in to the phone. The PIN is set using the `Set-CsClientPin` cmdlet. To set it on the common area phone you just created, use the following PowerShell command:

```
Set-CsClientPin -Identity "HQ Main Reception Phone" -Pin 165643
```

Note that the PIN specified must comply with the PIN policy that covers the common area phone. This could be a specific policy or a site or global one. Once the PIN has been set, you can log in to the common area phone using the phone number and PIN.

Enabling Hot-Desking

Hot-desking allows a user to sign into a common area phone, and the phone will become theirs until they sign out or their login times out. This is often useful in conference rooms and offices that have hot-desking or touch-down areas. Users sign into the phone using their phone number and PIN or through USB tethering if the phone supports it.

Hot-desking is enabled through the client policy using the `EnableHotdesking` and `HotdeskingTimeout` options. The `EnableHotdesking` option is set to either `True` or `False`, and `HotdeskingTimeout` is set in an `HH:MM:SS` format, such as 00:05:00 for 5 minutes. The timeout can be set to a minimum of 30 seconds, with a default of 5 minutes. For most organizations this is too low because it is common for a user not to use a phone for a period of time but still be using the hot desk; a setting of at least 60 minutes is usually required.

If you want to enable hot-desking for an existing client policy and set a timeout of 90 minutes, use the following PowerShell command:

```
Set-CsClientPolicy -Identity SalesHotDeskPhone -EnableHotdesking $true
-HotdeskingTimeout 01:30:00
```

This change will become active once the settings on the phone have been refreshed, either through rebooting the phone or through the regular configuration updates.

3PIP

In addition to phones running Phone Edition, which are referred to as "Optimized for" devices, there are phones that are designed to work with Skype for Business that do not run Phone Edition. One vendor of these phones is Snom. These devices are tested to work with Skype for Business and are known as Lync-qualified IP Phones. They may not offer the same features as the "Optimized for" devices, providing additional UC features enabled by the handset with easy-to-use dedicated keys for transfer, hold, and voicemail. In addition, they are configured differently; for instance, Snom provides a dual SIP stack to connect to Skype for Business and a failover gateway introducing business continuity and disaster recovery options to the Skype for Business infrastructure.

Lync 2013 opened the door wider to 3PIP devices in that Phone Edition was not further developed specifically for Lync Server 2013, and therefore the focus has shifted more to these third-party devices and their capabilities.

Of course, the downside of using 3PIP devices is they will likely provide support and capability beyond what Skype for Business can enable, such as a message waiting indicator or specific button capability such as transfer or directory lookup.

In the following sections, we will show how to configure the SNOM D725 device (see Figure 6.14) for working with Skype for Business, and we will be using firmware version 8.8.2.26.

This particular firmware version provides a significant number of Skype for Business–capable features.

- Native Skype for Business Software Update
- Sign in with extension and PIN
- Call Park
- Support for Survivable Branch Appliances

- Music on Hold
- Boss/Admin
- Assigning contacts to buttons for quick presence updates
- Additional language support

FIGURE 6.14
SNOM D725 VoIP handset

SETUP AND LOGIN

Upon first boot (assuming DHCP is in place to provide network address information), the device will prompt for the language, time zone information, and sounds (Tone Scheme). Once these have been completed, you'll see the welcome screen (Figure 6.15).

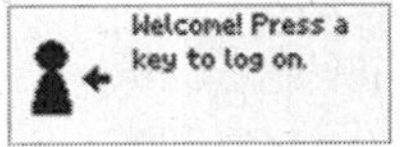
Welcome! Press a key to log on.

FIGURE 6.15
Snom D725 device welcome screen

The Snom D725 device supports up to 12 concurrent identity logins, each one being a separate user, which is ideal for hot-desking scenarios where a single phone is shared on a desk.

(From this point onward the screenshots come from a Snom 821 device. This is an older model but has a larger screen size so you can better see the content. All the functionality is provided by the same firmware version on both the D725 and the 821.)

Figure 6.16 shows the sign-in process.

- SIP-URI
- Domain\User
- Password

FIGURE 6.16
Sign-in process

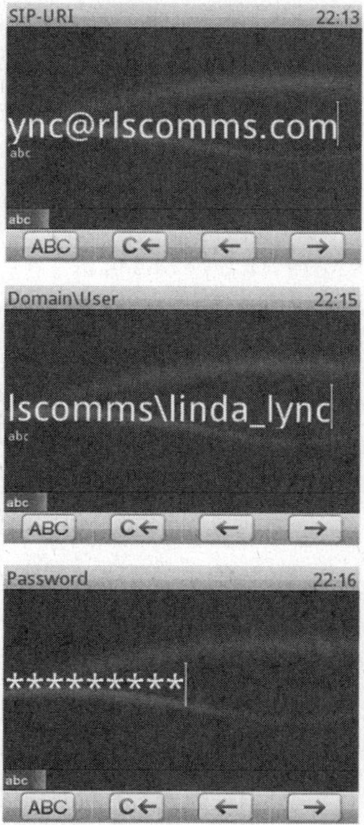

Once you're signed in, the phone will display presence information as you would expect (see Figure 6.17), and the buttons along the bottom of the screen can be used for the following functionality:

- Contacts
- Call History
- Call Forward
- Set Presence

FIGURE 6.17
Logged-in presence state

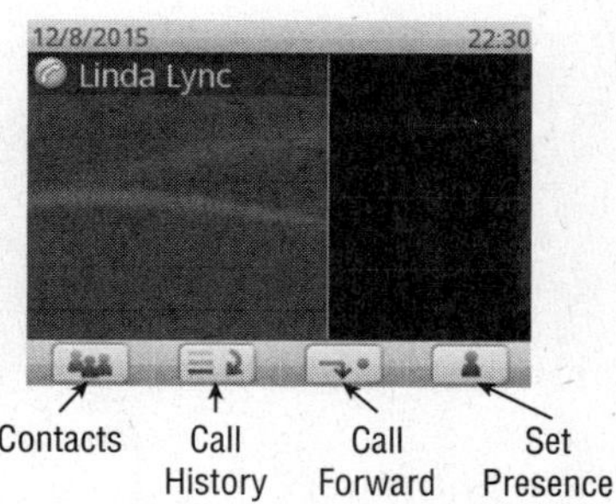

The SNOM D725 device also has a number of feature buttons alongside the numeric keypad.

- DND: Quick setting for Do Not Disturb
- Directory: Access to directory search (see Figure 6.18)
- Menu: Access to the phone menu settings
- Transfer: Quick transfer of calls
- Hold: Quick setting to put calls on hold

FIGURE 6.18
Searching the directory

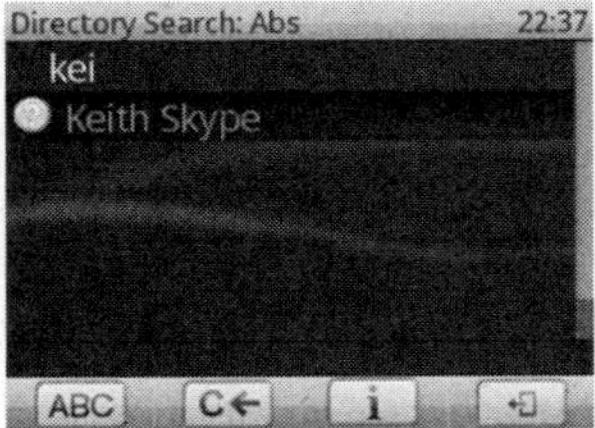

When placing a call, the display shows both the callee and caller identities (or indeed phone numbers), as shown in Figure 6.19.

FIGURE 6.19
Placing a call

When you receive a call, the screen is a similar to the screen you see when placing the call (Figure 6.19), but it has a button enabled on the bottom row to allow forwarding of calls without answering.

Once a call is answered, it can be parked (assuming the user has the ability to park calls as defined in their voice policy) by selecting the P button from the bottom row; see Figure 6.20 for the in-call display.

FIGURE 6.20
In-call display

> **About Snom Technology AG**
>
> Founded in 1996 and headquartered in Berlin, Germany, Snom is a German multinational corporation and the world's first and leading brand of professional and enterprise VoIP telephones. Snom operates wholly owned subsidiaries in the United States, France, the United Kingdom, Italy, and Taiwan.
>
> Snom's German engineering is globally renowned for robust, high-quality, and feature-rich business telephones that are designed exclusively for the trained and certified professional IT and PBX installer. All of Snom's products are universally compatible with leading PBX platforms operating under the SIP standard with more than 4 million endpoint installations globally. Snom products are sold through distributors to more than 25,000 Snom value-added resellers across the world.
>
> For more information, please visit `www.snom.com`.

Device Updating

From version 8.7.3.1 onward, the Snom devices support "native" Skype for Business device firmware management (in other words, the same as with Phone Edition) using the `ucupdates-r2.<domain name>` DNS record or via in-band provisioning (see Figure 6.21). Prior to this version (and potentially with other vendor versions), this would have to be managed directly for each phone or through the vendor-specific update provision.

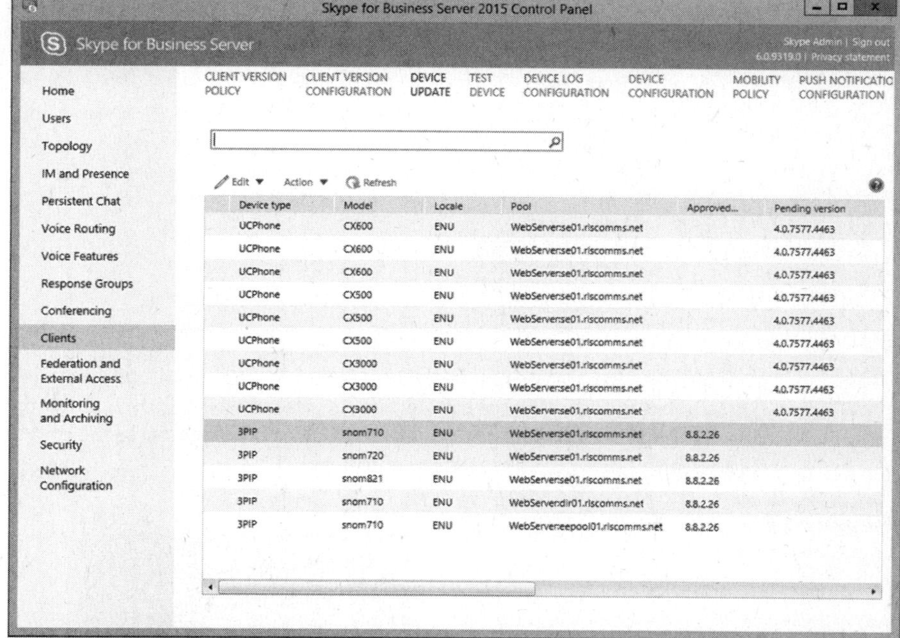

Device type	Model	Locale	Pool	Approved...	Pending version
UCPhone	CX600	ENU	WebServerse01.riscomms.net		4.0.7577.4463
UCPhone	CX600	ENU	WebServerse01.riscomms.net		4.0.7577.4463
UCPhone	CX600	ENU	WebServerse01.riscomms.net		4.0.7577.4463
UCPhone	CX500	ENU	WebServerse01.riscomms.net		4.0.7577.4463
UCPhone	CX500	ENU	WebServerse01.riscomms.net		4.0.7577.4463
UCPhone	CX500	ENU	WebServerse01.riscomms.net		4.0.7577.4463
UCPhone	CX3000	ENU	WebServerse01.riscomms.net		4.0.7577.4463
UCPhone	CX3000	ENU	WebServerse01.riscomms.net		4.0.7577.4463
UCPhone	CX3000	ENU	WebServerse01.riscomms.net		4.0.7577.4463
3PIP	snom710	ENU	WebServerse01.riscomms.net	8.8.2.26	
3PIP	snom720	ENU	WebServerse01.riscomms.net	8.8.2.26	
3PIP	snom821	ENU	WebServerse01.riscomms.net	8.8.2.26	
3PIP	snom710	ENU	WebServerdir01.riscomms.net	8.8.2.26	
3PIP	snom710	ENU	WebServereepool01.riscomms.net	8.8.2.26	

Figure 6.21 Approved 3PIP firmware in Skype for Business Server 2015 Control Panel

Prior to firmware version 8.8.1.1 for this device, the upgrade capability was managed direct via the web interface, either set to poll for updates to a specified URL (by default to the Snom provisioning page at `http://provisioning.snom.com/`) or set to be manually uploaded; see Figure 6.22 for the web interface.

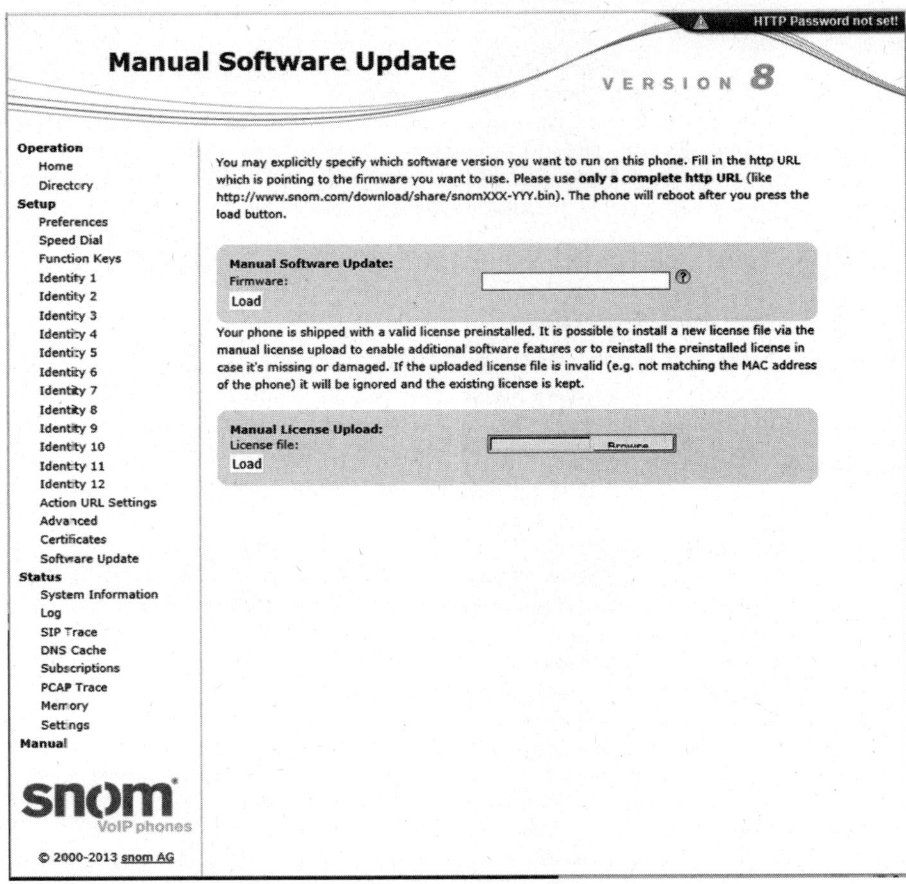

FIGURE 6.22 Configuration of firmware updating on legacy 3PIP devices (or firmware)

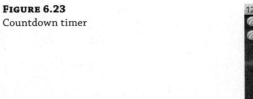

If a firmware update is pending (discovered during in-band provisioning), you'll see a countdown timer in the bottom left of the screen (see Figure 6.23). If the phone device is left untouched for 5 minutes, the update will be applied, causing the phone to reboot. Any interaction with the device will reset the counter.

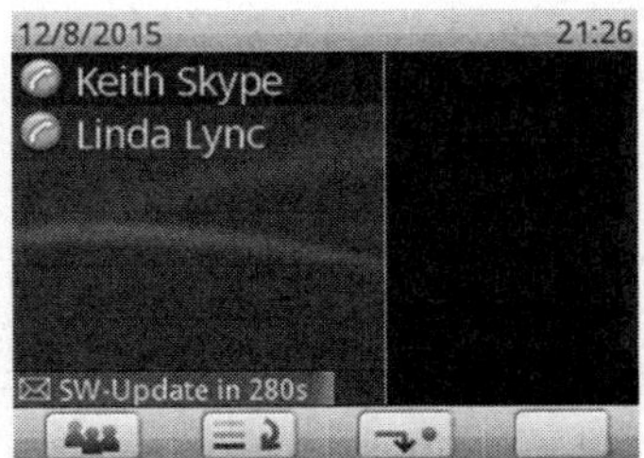

FIGURE 6.23 Countdown timer

Assigning Presence to Keys

One of the features in the Snom devices is the ability to assign users to the "line" buttons. Not only does this give a quick method to contact the user, it also provides an immediate visual as to their presence state because it changes color in line with their presence.

Figure 6.24 shows the screen overlay. When users are assigned to each button (there are four on the handset, and up to an additional 54 programmable keys can be added through adding D7 Expansion Modules), their name and status are displayed in the dark area on the right side, and a button indicating their presence is colored according to their present state.

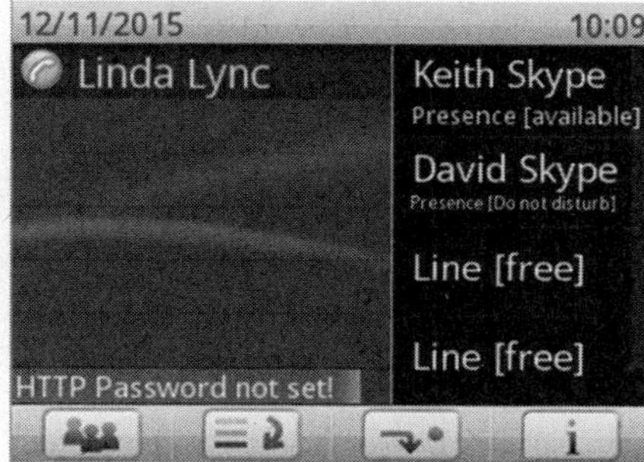

Figure 6.24
Presence buttons

Boss/Admin Scenario

The Snom devices were the first non–Phone Edition devices to support the Boss/Admin scenario. Here, the admin and boss can share line status and call retrieval on a button.

> **Sharing Presence Capability**
>
> With Lync Server 2010, a new presence publication category needed to be defined within the back-end database. This is achieved by running the following command in the `osql` utility:
>
> ```
> osql -E -S <pool fqdn>\RTC -Q
> "use rtc;exec RtcRegisterCategoryDef N'dialogInfo'"
> ```
>
> Lync Server 2013 already has this in place, so it is not required; Skype for Business doesn't need it either.

The supported scenarios are as you would expect on a normal client.

- Monitor line state
- Call pickup
- Call on behalf of
- Safe transfer
- Join conference call

To enable the Boss/Admin scenario, the delegates need to be first configured as normal in the Skype for Business client.

For the boss, you'll see the Delegates group, and for the admin, the group is called People I Manage Calls For. Figure 6.25 shows this configured in the Skype for Business client.

FIGURE 6.25
Delegation setup in the Skype for Business client

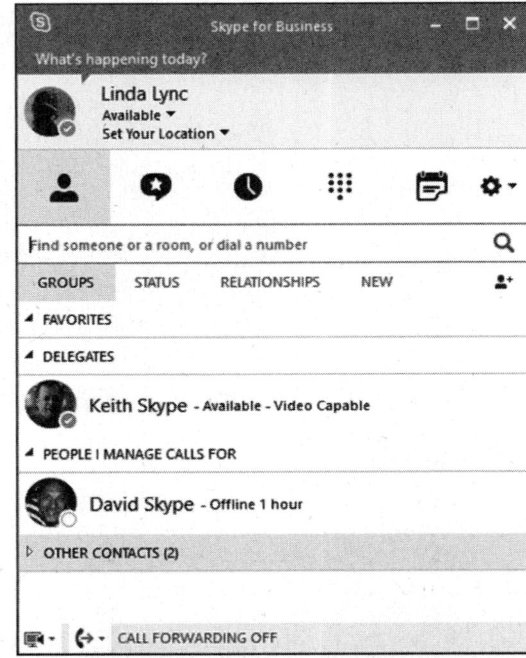

On the device, these contacts need to be assigned to the relevant button. Figure 6.26 shows a number of these having been assigned.

FIGURE 6.26
Boss/Admin

From the top the first item (Keith Skype – Boss/Admin) was configured as a Boss/Admin line item. This shows the Boss/Admin relationship, and when the button is selected, allows calls to be made on behalf of the boss, who in this case is configured as Keith.

The second item down simply shows Boss/Admin. As a boss, you can assign all your administrators to a single button. There is an M:N relationship permitted with the Boss/Admin configuration: Not only can one boss have one or many admins, an admin can be responsible for one or many bosses. Clicking this button will bring up the next display, which will show each of the individual admins and their status.

The third item from the top simply shows the presence status of the delegate, in this case Keith Skype. There is no special relationship flowing from the boss to the admin.

Better Together over Ethernet

As mentioned previously, certain types of phone, classed as information worker phones, provide additional functionality when connected via a USB cable.

As technology has improved over their first releases, manufacturers have been able to remove this need to plug in a physical cable and replace it with a "virtual cable" via the network connection.

This is known as Better Together over Ethernet (BToE).

When connected, the device will function in the same way as if it was directly connected via a USB cable.

Meeting Room Devices

With the introduction of common area phones in Lync 2010, a new type of device was also enabled: the Lync speakerphone. Figure 6.27 shows an example, the Polycom CX3000. This is essentially a common area phone device optimized with microphones and speakers to cover a wider area than the front of the device, as would be seen on a traditional handset-style device.

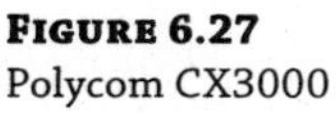

FIGURE 6.27
Polycom CX3000

As well as providing this style of devices for the audio aspects of a call, since OCS 2007 there has also been the RoundTable device (also known as the Polycom CX5000), allowing the display of the "panorama room" view as well as having active microphones to focus on the current speaker.

For Lync Server 2013, the RoundTable device has been upgraded to cater to HD video streams; no further developments were made for Skype for Business.

The observant among you will have noticed a number of cmdlets focused on meeting room capability.

```
Disable-CsMeetingRoom
Enable-CsMeetingRoom
Move-CsMeetingRoom
Set-CsMeetingRoom
```

These cmdlets focus on a new generation of Lync video solutions: the Lync Meeting Room System (LMRS). At the time of writing, an update to these devices is due, again mostly a rebranding update to Skype for Business, although some of the interaction features have been improved to allow for better user experiences.

These systems are similar to common area phones in that they have a dedicated account for each device; however, they are targeted at the full-room videoconference solutions, although not as high end as a "telepresence" room. Because an individual account will exist for each device (or "room"), they can be invited to meetings as a normal user would be, either scheduled or ad hoc.

Announced at the Lync Conference in San Diego in February 2013, LMRS is sold by a number of manufacturers.

- Polycom
- LifeSize
- SMART Technologies
- Cestron

The feature set is expected to remain relatively consistent across manufacturers.

- Single- or dual-touch high-definition displays
- HD camera
- Interactive whiteboard capability
- Ability to email the whiteboard content to participants
- Auto-join to scheduled meetings
- Desk-based control panel

Figure 6.28 shows the design for the SMART Technologies device. SMART Technologies have released devices in multiple variations depending primarily on the size of the room. These will vary based on the number or size of screens as well as the accessories, such as table mics, and so on.

With the release of Windows 10, Microsoft has also released a meeting room device called the Surface Hub. This is due to begin shipping in January 2016; you can find further information at this link:

`www.microsoft.com/microsoft-surface-hub/en-us`

The Surface Hub is a multitouch, single-screen device based on Windows 10, and with the Skype for Business client built in, this enables easy in-room collaboration with the ability to include remote Skype for Business users.

Figure 6.28
SMART Technologies meeting room system

Video Endpoints

At the most basic level, a video endpoint is a webcam either built in to the PC or connected via USB, going up the scale. However, devices from Polycom (such as the HDX 4500 shown in Figure 6.29) and LifeSize are the two main players in this space.

Figure 6.29
Polycom HDX 4500

These devices can register directly with Skype for Business with a username and password, either as a conference room itself or directly as a user. Presence can be provided (typically In a Call or Available), and interactions are as would be expected with any other Skype for Business client device.

Integrating with Hardware Video Conferencing Platforms

Skype for Business provides for videoconferencing natively and can accommodate sessions ranging from a peer-to-peer call to up to 250 participants in a video conference. Although this desktop video capability is useful and gaining traction in organizations, there are already many deployments of room-based and other hardware video platforms. Thankfully, Skype for Business has the capability to integrate with these systems to provide enhanced capability. For example, not only can a hardware video endpoint dial a Skype for Business desktop video user and hold an audio and video call, but equally a Skype for Business user can be dialed into a conference hosted on a hardware video Media Conferencing Unit (MCU), a device to mix and distribute channels of audio and video, to participate in a conference that also includes those on the high-end video system in the board room. It's also possible to use the external access capabilities of Skype for Business to allow remote or federated users to dial into conferences held on hardware systems; such systems can provide connectivity to a wide range of legacy video standards and also different ways of displaying end users so that all video participants can be seen at once.

Before we dive into configuration, it is important to note that Skype for Business can interoperate with a wide variety of video systems, including those from Polycom, LifeSize, and Radvision. In this section, we'll cover some of the points of integration with the Polycom range of devices.

In addition, Skype for Business introduced the Video Interoperability Server, which natively provides support for a number of Cisco video gateway devices.

Polycom devices have two main areas of integration with Skype for Business: endpoints and conference units. They have their HDX systems, which are essentially endpoints of different scales and sizes, ranging from simple desktop video units to room-based systems. They also have telepresence systems that are fitted in an entire room to give the experience of actually sitting around a table with those at the other end of the call. Polycom also has its RMX range; these devices are video MCUs. They provide the ability to host conferences and can tie into a wide range of video systems via various protocols, including ISDN, H.323, and SIP. For more information about the devices available, see the Polycom website at `www.polycom.com`.

Polycom is working closely with Microsoft to ensure that its products integrate closely with Skype for Business, and it is frequently adding new functionality. Two main scenarios are possible. The first is simply enabling one of the endpoint HDX devices to dial into Skype for Business, which is a relatively straightforward process. Assuming that the device has the latest software, it is simply a case of creating an identity for it and letting it register to Skype for Business. This identity could be either that of an end user, if the system is a personal desktop video unit, or one created for a conference room, if the unit is a room-based system. The second scenario we'll cover allows integration between Skype for Business and an RMX unit so that Skype for Business users can internally or externally participate in conferences hosted on the RMX unit.

Given the complex nature of the configuration and the fact that new versions of the Polycom software add features and occasionally change setup steps, we won't cover the step-by-step configuration here. We'll look at the Skype for Business and HDX integration from the Skype for Business perspective. Then you can refer to resources that will provide up-to-date and detailed information about how to configure integration between Skype for Business and the Polycom systems.

Configuring Lync and HDX Integration

As mentioned, having a Polycom HDX system sign on to Skype for Business is relatively straightforward. There are a couple of prerequisites that must be checked before you try, though. First, you must confirm that NTLM authentication is enabled on the registrar, as of course the server itself is configured to permit it. This can be checked in the Skype for Business Server Control Panel on the Security tab under the registrar policy, as shown in Figure 6.30.

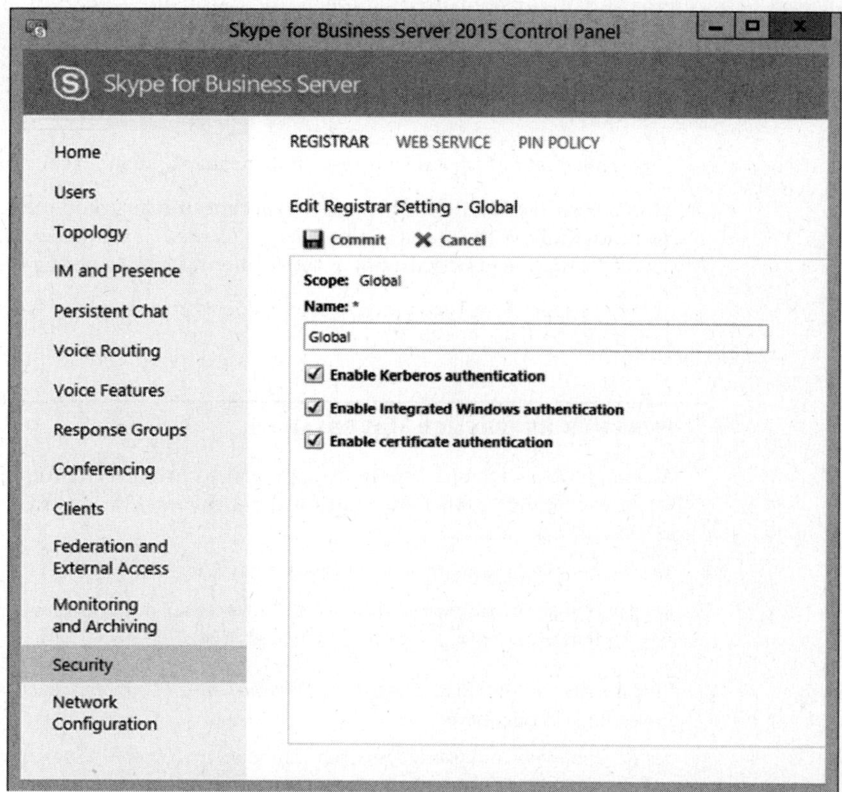

FIGURE 6.30 Checking the authentication types available on the registrar policy

As long as NTLM is enabled, you are ready to create the required users. It is, of course, possible to have any Skype for Business user who has Enterprise Voice enabled (although it doesn't need a number assigned) log on to the HDX, so creating specific users is needed only if this is a room system that you need to specifically identify rather than a personal one.

To refresh your memory, here are the required commands to enable the user for Lync and Enterprise Voice:

```
Enable-CsUser -Identity "Test User1"
-RegistrarPool se01.rlscomms.net
-SipAddressType UserPrincipalName
Set-CsUser -Identity "Test User1" -EnableEnterpriseVoiceEnabled $True
```

This command will enable the user Test User1 for Skype for Business and Enterprise Voice. The user who is now enabled will fall under any relevant Skype for Business policies, so make sure that if you need external access, you have the relevant policies in place as covered in Chapter 12, "User Administration."

The HDX systems have an address book, which should be populated with the entries from the user's buddy list. To populate the list, log on to a PC Skype for Business client with the user and populate the list in the normal way.

Finally, you must ensure that the Skype for Business encryption settings are configured to match those configured on the HDX. The HDX supports the Skype for Business default settings on `RequireEncryption`; however, the HDX can also be configured to not use encryption. In that case, you will need to configure Skype for Business to accept such connections using the following command:

```
Set-CsMediaConfiguration -EncryptionLevel supportencryption
```

This will allow Skype for Business to accept unencrypted media connections.

You must follow the steps in the *Polycom Unified Communications Deployment Guide for Microsoft Environments* document at the following link to configure the HDX:

```
http://support.polycom.com/global/documents/support/setup_maintenance/products/
video/UC_Deploy_Guide_MS.pdf
```

Further Reference Material

Although we have limited space to discuss the connectivity options in this chapter, the following resources provide useful information about the integration of Polycom and Skype for Business (and Lync) systems.

This is a Polycom website with configuration material:

```
http://support.polycom.com/PolycomService/support/us/support/strategic_partner_
solutions/microsoft_software_download.html
```

This is a direct download link for the *Polycom Unified Communications Deployment Guide for Microsoft Environments* document:

```
http://support.polycom.com/global/documents/support/setup_maintenance/products/
video/UC_Deploy_Guide_MS.pdf
```

Here are some other blog sites that are worth viewing:

```
http://blog.schertz.name/category/polycom/

http://mikestacy.typepad.com/mike-stacys-blog/rmx/

http://blogs.technet.com/b/meacoex/archive/2011/05/26/lync-with-polycom-rmx-
integration.aspx
```

The Bottom Line

Integrate with hardware video conferencing platforms. Skype for Business can integrate with several hardware video platforms to provide control and connectivity through Skype for Business to room-based and high-quality video networks.

Master It You are trying to configure Skype for Business integration with a Polycom HDX unit, but it won't connect. What might be causing an issue?

Configure prerequisites for IP phones. IP phones are designed to be as simple as possible to deploy and receive all of their configuration settings automatically. For this to occur, a number of items need to be configured, such as network configuration and DHCP.

Master It You have deployed IP phones, but you are unable to log in to the phones when using extension and PIN authentication; however, logging in using USB tethering works as expected.

What is the likely problem?

Part 2

Getting Skype for Business Up and Running

Chapter 7

Planning Your Deployment

You're probably eager to start implementing Skype for Business in your network and you want to dive in right away.

Stop! Take a step back, breathe deeply, and think about what you want to achieve. Is this a throwaway lab deployment (perhaps virtualized?) utilized just to see what the management interface is like and what changes have been made since Lync or Office Communications Server 2007? Is this a pilot deployment in a production environment that will be removed once the decision to go ahead with full deployment is made? (Of course, everyone knows the pilot is never thrown away; it's just built on, right?) Are you planning to move from an existing Lync Server environment and want to investigate the subtle changes first?

The easiest (and best) way to deploy a solid system is to take the time to plan properly. By all means, jump right into a throwaway system deployment, but for any type of test or production system, proper planning will almost always save time in the long run. Even though many of us want to be "doing stuff" such as installing, troubleshooting, and so on, the best deployments are the ones for which the appropriate amount of time was spent in the planning phase.

Also remember that having a separate test environment will justify its cost in the long term, and it will allow you to catch patches or changes that could inadvertently bring down the system.

In this chapter, you will learn to

- Use the available planning tools
- Determine when virtualization is appropriate
- Understand the prerequisites

Capturing the Requirements

You would never build a house by starting at the builder's yard, buying some bricks and mortar, and taking them back to a field. The same is true for a deployment. To ensure that you are not wasting and repeating work, it is extremely important to plan ahead. For example, if you configure and deploy Skype for Business Server 2015 and later decide to change or add SIP domains, you will have to revisit every pool server and every request certificate (a significant waste of time, especially if you have a manual certificate requisition process).

Experience tells us that most deployments grow organically; they often start with a proof of concept or pilot, and others outside the initial test groups latch onto the excitement of a new product and want to be involved. The next thing you know, your 200-user pilot ends up with 1,000 users, and if proper planning hasn't occurred, issues will start to arise with the exponential growth.

In the same sense, there are two ways to approach any project.

- Define the end goal and then determine how to get there.
- Define the current state and then determine what you want.

Understanding What Is Wanted

The preferred approach is to know the end goal first; then you can work out the best route to get there (considering time, cost, or function) rather than building on what is already in place and trying to "morph" something into something else (the "organic growth" option).

Typically, the result ends up being some sort of migration or coexistence state. The longer that coexistence is in place, the longer (and more complicated) a project will be. By planning toward the end goal, you can reduce the time of coexistence and therefore reduce the risk.

Broadly, high-level needs can be divided into four areas:

- Core (instant messaging and presence, including Persistent Chat, peer-to-peer audio/video, internal conferencing)
- Remote access (and/or federation)
- Telephony integration
- High availability

Once you've established (or confirmed) these four key areas, you can begin to get an idea of the infrastructure required. Here's an example of what you might need:

- You need at least one pool (that's obvious, but it still needs to be stated!).
- Remote access means you'll need at least one Edge server.
- Telephony integration means you'll need Mediation servers (possibly colocated) and possibly gateways or direct SIP support.
- High availability requires Enterprise pool(s) and hardware load balancers.

Now the infrastructure design is taking shape. As you go further into the discovery process, you'll consider things such as the number of users to determine how many servers (and potentially pools) are needed and the location of users to determine how many pools and where they will be located.

Once you have determined the functional requirements, you can build the detailed design. For example, if you have a peak requiring 1,200 concurrent telephony calls through the public switched telephone network (PSTN), this will translate into a requirement of two Mediation servers (plus another for high availability). However, getting to this level of detail requires a lot of investigation and discovery, and it means the organization must already be capturing that type of information from the current telephony system via Call Data Records (CDRs), and it must be able to report the information. Bear in mind that many PBX systems are incompatible with others, resulting in a lot of work to consolidate data across different PBX vendors. Some companies provide consolidation software for reporting purposes on CDRs; however, the software is expensive, so it probably won't be used for a migration unless it is already in place.

Understanding What Is Currently in Place

Once the endgame is established, it's important to take a step back and establish what you have already. In some cases, you may be further along than you expect.

When deploying Skype for Business Server 2015, you will typically be coming from one of the following scenarios:

- Greenfield (a deployment to a company that has never had an instant messaging product in use)
- Lync Server 2010/2013
- OCS 2007 or R2/LCS 2005 (or an earlier Microsoft instant messaging product)
- Other non-Microsoft instant messaging products

The *greenfield* scenario is the easiest and most straightforward of the options because you start with a clean slate and don't need to plan for migration or coexistence.

Migrating from Lync Server 2010 or Lync Server 2013 to Skype for Business Server 2015 is the only migration path supported by Microsoft. For details, see Chapter 9, "Migration and Upgrades."

Migrating from versions prior to Lync Server and non-Microsoft instant messaging products are similar processes. Because no (current) toolsets are available to simplify the process, dealing with these migrations requires extremely detailed planning to handle the user-experience aspects. For example, are buddy lists migrated or are users expected to re-create them? Will meetings be migrated?

A nonsupported migration approach can be successful, but more likely it will involve problems that result in a nonoperative system or a system that appears to work initially but is hiding a more serious problem. These serious problems tend not to be obvious at first and may take some time to manifest. When they finally do arise, Microsoft may refuse to provide support to resolve them because an unsupported approach was used.

Now that you have established where you want to go (the features required) as well as where you are (the current state), you can begin planning the more detailed aspects of the design and deployment.

Understanding the Basics

The next section will walk you through the stages of using the Planning Tool application to get a starting point for your design. However, before you jump in and possibly "get lost in the numbers," it's important to understand the basics in terms of capabilities and requirements. Figure 7.1 shows the functionality that can be achieved with a single server for Skype for Business and an Office Web Application server.

As you can see, there is a significant amount of functionality available from the single Standard Edition server.

Perhaps you have a requirement to enable federation or remote access? Figure 7.2 shows what can be achieved with the addition of a Skype for Business Edge server and a Reverse Proxy server. You may already have a Reverse Proxy server deployed for other functionality or have a device (firewall or load balancer) capable of providing this functionality.

FIGURE 7.1
Standard Edition functionality

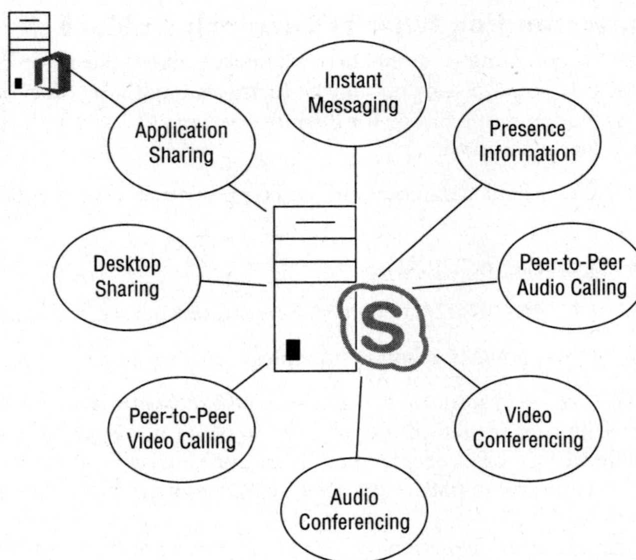

FIGURE 7.2
Enabling Edge functionality

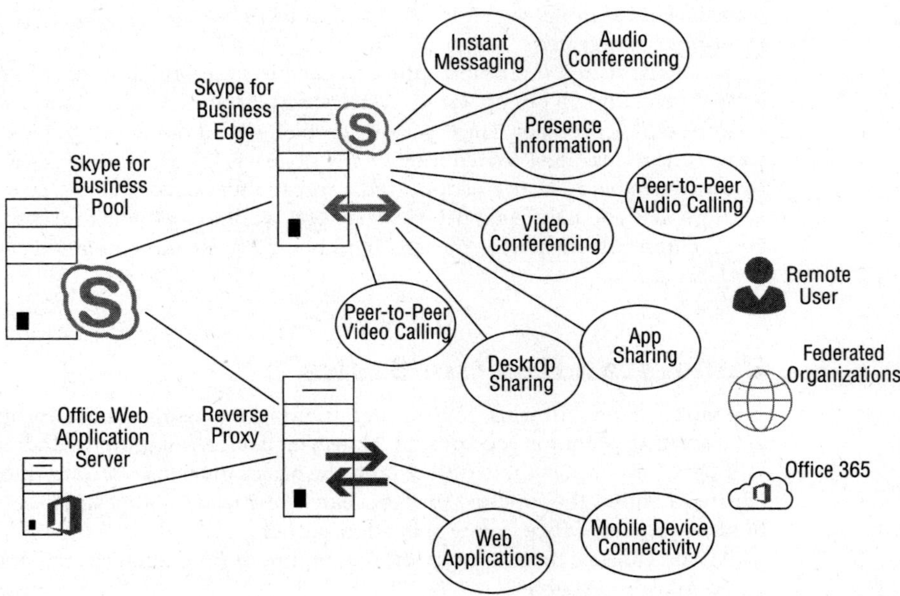

Last on the list is telephony integration, which enables users to call phone numbers on the PSTN. As Figure 7.3 shows, with the addition of the Mediation server, you can start to integrate with PBX systems or Internet Telephony Service Providers to get connected to the PSTN. Microsoft Exchange can be enabled to provide voice mail.

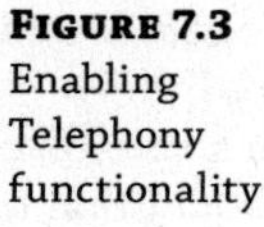

FIGURE 7.3 Enabling Telephony functionality

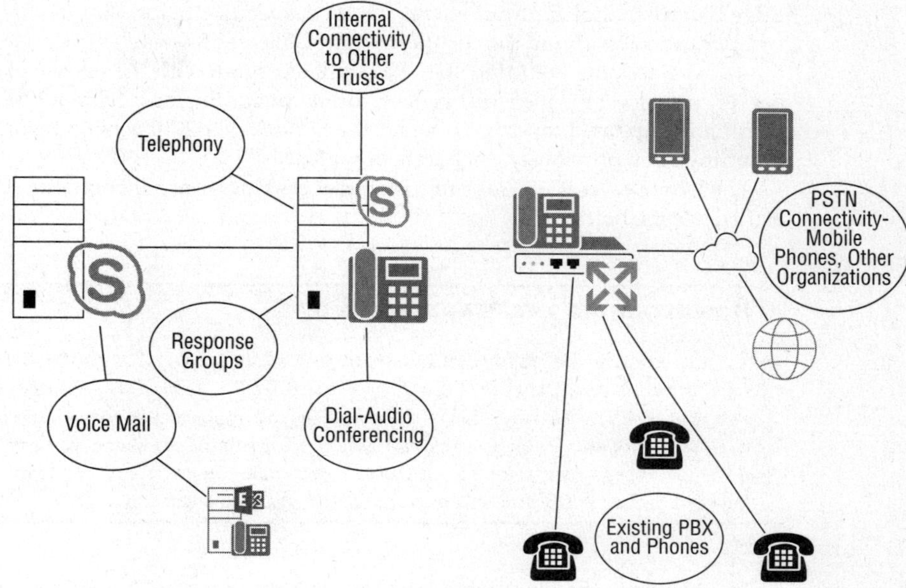

If needed, the Mediation role can be installed colocated on the Standard Edition server to remove the need for additional servers.

Of course, there are additional components within the Skype for Business infrastructure, and this is where the specific requirements will start to drive the exact deployment model. For example, do you require scale of more than 5,000 users? Or high availability protecting against single component failure? Either of these two requirements will drive the need to move from Standard Edition pools to Enterprise Edition.

What about disaster recovery? Well, that means another datacenter, so duplicate server deployment.

Suddenly you can see the server count increase dramatically, but you can always pull it back to the building blocks of internal, external, and telephony functionality.

Using the Capacity Planning Toolset

With the launch of OCS 2007, Microsoft provided a Planning Tool application, which guides the administrator to a suggested topology based on a number of questions. Typically, the questions are feature driven, such as "Do you want to use Enterprise Voice?"

From the resulting answers, the Planning Tool draws a recommended topology for each identified site, suggesting the types and quantities of hardware needed. In addition, it provides links to the specific planning and deployment tasks required to implement the suggested topology.

With the release of OCS 2007 R2, the Planning Tool was updated to take into account the new architecture and features provided in this updated version. In addition, a separate

Edge Planning Tool application was released, specifically focusing on the Edge role and the complications involving the certificates and DNS and firewall entries required.

As expected, the Planning Tool was updated again with the release of each version of Lync Server, and again for the latest version for Skype for Business Server 2015. In addition to supporting the updated topology of Lync, the Lync Server 2010 version incorporated the Edge Planning Tool, previously a separate download.

The Lync Server 2013 Planning Tool now also includes functionality for mobile clients as well as Persistent Chat.

Downloading the Planning Tool

You can find the Skype for Business Planning Tool at `www.microsoft.com/downloads/`, along with versions of the tool for OCS 2007, OCS 2007 R2, OCS 2007 R2 Edge, Lync Server 2010, and Lync Server 2013. Each version of the Planning Tool is specific to the version of the product. Because you have chosen a book on mastering Skype for Business Server, you probably will not need to download previous versions of the tool; however, if you are migrating from Live Communications Server 2003 or 2005, you will need to first migrate to a version of OCS.

In addition to the Planning Tool, Microsoft has provided the following tools to help you plan:

- Edge Server Reference Architecture Diagrams
- Protocol Diagrams for call flow
- Stress and Performance Tool (not yet release for Skype for Business)
- Bandwidth Calculator

With the exception of the Edge Server Reference Architecture Diagrams (simply a package of Visio diagrams), we will cover all of these tools in this chapter.

The Planning Tool will install and run on the following operating system versions:

- Windows 10
- Windows 8.1
- Windows 8
- Windows 7 Service Pack 1
- Windows Server 2012 R2
- Windows Server 2012

Defining a Topology with the Planning Tool

Once downloaded and installed, the Planning Tool will be located in the Skype for Business 2015 folder in the Programs menu. Starting the application will take you to the Welcome screen, where you will have two options for planning, Get Started and Design Sites, as well as the option to open a saved topology.

As you'll see, Design Sites is more efficient when you know what features you need to implement, but Get Started provides you with a little more guidance, so it is more helpful. If you follow the Get Started path, you will be prompted with the following questions:

- Would you like to enable audio and video conferencing for your organization?
- Would you like to deploy dial-in conferencing within your enterprise?
- Do you want to locally host web conferencing?
- Do you want to deploy Enterprise Voice?
- Do you want to deploy Exchange UM?
- Would you like to deploy Call Admission Control?
- Do you want to enable monitoring?
- Do you want to enable archiving?
  - Enable Exchange Archiving Integration and use Exchange data store as archiving storage.
  - Deploy Archiving SQL Database as archiving storage.
- Do you want to deploy Persistent Chat?
- Do you want to deploy Video Interop Server?
- Do you want to deploy mobility?
- Do you want to enable federation with other organizations or with public IM service providers?
  - Yes, I want to enable Skype for Business to OCS cross-enterprise federation through SIP.
  - Yes, I want to enable Skype for Business to other public cloud IM providers' federation through SIP.
  - Yes, I want to enable federation via XMPP.
- Is high availability of communications critical to you? If so, do you want to deploy standby servers for failover support?
- Which IP infrastructure do you want to deploy your Microsoft Lync Server 2013 on?
  - IPv4 only
  - IPv6 only
  - Both IPv4 and IPv6
- Do you want to enable Disaster Recovery?

Once you have answered these questions, you will be taken to the Central Sites page, shown in Figure 7.4. If you choose the Design Sites button on the Welcome page, this is where you will be taken directly.

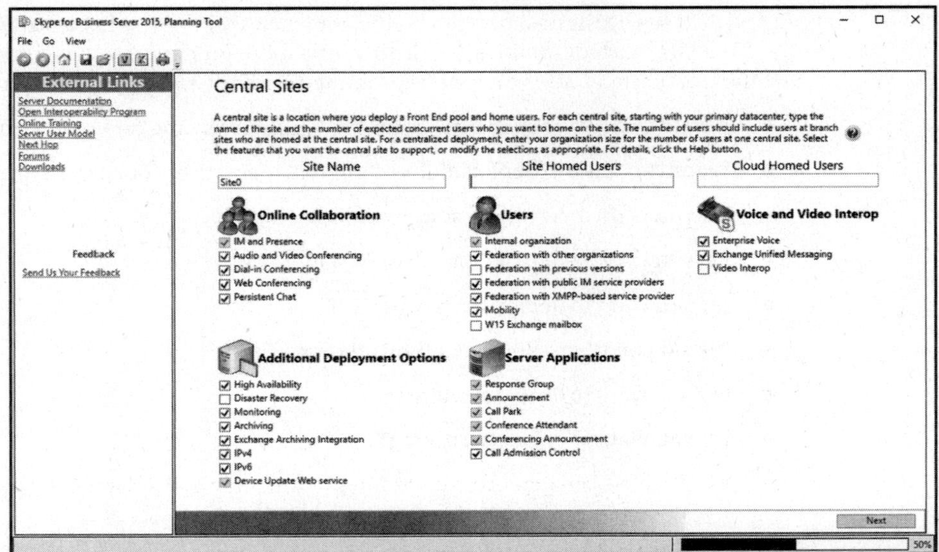

FIGURE 7.4 The Central Sites page

On this page, you can provide the site name along with the number of users located at this site. In addition, you can modify the answers to any of the previous questions simply by checking (or unchecking) the boxes next to each option. If you use the Design Sites button, a default of Yes will be assumed for all questions except "federation with previous versions." Using this quick-start approach will save at least 10 clicks of the mouse to get to the same point.

You also have the opportunity to define users having W15 Exchange mailboxes (which equates to Exchange 2013). Even though integration with Exchange archiving was selected, you still need to select it again for the users here.

If you follow the wizard and answer the prompted questions, the output will provide a great starting point for a design topology; however, it shouldn't be taken as the only option. A lot of the questions are simply "enable/disable this feature" questions; however, some values will already have default suggestions based on the planning profile used to capture the statistics for recommended hardware. Here are some of the topics you'll need to consider in each category:

SIP Domain You'll need to provide a listing of all the SIP domains supported by the deployment. Entering a SIP domain will help generate more accurate output in later sections (such as with the DNS or certificate requirements).

Conference Settings This section will provide the following prompts with their defaults:

Meeting Concurrency: **5%**

Meeting Audio Distribution

What percentage of conferences are dial-in? **15%**

What percentage of conferences have no audio (IM-only)? **10%**

Media Mix for Web Conferences

What percentage of conferences are web conferences with audio plus some other collaboration modalities? **75%**

Video is enabled. **Selected**

Multi-view is enabled. **Selected**

Application Sharing is enabled. **Selected**

Data Collaboration is enabled. **Selected**

Voice Settings You'll be provided with the following prompts:

Enabled users

What percentage of users at this site will be enabled for Enterprise Voice? **60%**

Enable All Users **Not Selected** (This item will force all Enterprise Voice user selection entries to 100%.)

External Phone Traffic

On average, how many calls to the public telephone network do you think that each user at this site will make during the busy hour? **4 calls per hour**

Media Bypass

What percentage of all phone calls will use media bypass? **65%**

Enable All Calls **Not Selected** (If all the locations will have local gateways, this should be selected.)

Types of Calls

What percentage of calls will be UC-PSTN calls? **60%**

Enable All Calls **Not Selected**

Response Group

What percentage of users use Response Group? **0.15%**

Call Park

What percentage of calls will be parked? **0.05%**

Voice Infrastructure You'll be provided with the following prompts:

Infrastructure

I plan to deploy gateway using a direct PSTN connection. **Default**

I plan to use SIP trunking.

I have an existing voice infrastructure with a PBX deployed.

PBX (The default is unavailable unless the previous option includes PBX.)

I have an IP-PBX that is qualified with Skype for Business Server 2015 (Direct SIP).

I plan to deploy an IP-PBX that requires gateways.

I have already deployed a TDM-PBX.

Infrastructure Supportability (The default is unavailable unless the previous option includes PBX.)

My IP-PBX supports DNS local balancing.

My IP-PBX supports media bypass.

Network Line

Are you using a T1 line or an E1 line? **T1**

Type of Gateway

What type of gateway will you deploy? **4 ports**

Exchange Unified Messaging Settings You'll be provided with the following prompts:

Enabled users

What percentage of users at this site will be enabled for Exchange Unified Messaging? **50%**

Enable All Users **Not Selected**

Exchange Unified Messaging Voicemail Traffic

On average, how many times per day do you think users will check their voicemail? **4 times per day**

External User Access You'll be provided with the following prompts:

Do you want to enable external user access?

Yes, and I want to deploy Edge Servers in my perimeter network. **Default**

Yes, but I want to use Edge Servers deployed at another site.

No.

What percentage of users are external? **30%**

Enable high availability for my external users. **Selected**

Which type of load balancer do you want to use?

DNS load balancer using NAT.

DNS load balancer using public IP addresses.

Hardware load balancer using public IP addresses. **Default**

I want to deploy a Director at this site. **Unselected**

What percentage of users who have XMPP contacts? **30%**

Persistent Chat Settings Only a single prompt for the number of users to enable.

What percentage of users will use Persistent Chat? **20%**

Client Settings This section is asking what percentage of clients are using mobility or web access.

What percentage of users will be enabled for mobility? **40%**

Enable all users. **Unselected**

What percentage of users will be almost exclusively use LWA? **50%**

Enable all users. **Unselected**

Colocation Options You'll be asked how you want to deploy your Mediation servers: colocate them on your Front End servers or deploy them as stand-alone Mediation servers. The default value is for Mediation servers to be colocated.

High Availability Options What type of SQL high availability is in place? (Note: SQL clustering is not listed here.)

Database Mirroring. **Selected**

SQL AlwaysOn Availability Group

Branch Sites You'll be asked to define your branch sites, including the number of users, whether there is a resilient WAN connection, and whether Media Bypass is available.

Add Another Central Site? Finally, you'll be asked whether to add another central site. Selecting Yes at this point will repeat the entire question set for the next site; the default is No.

That finishes the Planning Tool data collection; on the next page click Draw to generate the topology.

Global Topology

Once the site definition is completed, the Planning Tool will present the Global Topology page, shown in Figure 7.5.

From this page, the Global Topology view provides the total hardware recommendations for all sites defined based on your answers to the questions on the Central Sites page. The hardware includes not only servers but also the number of hardware load-balanced IP addresses required as well as the concurrent call expectation and required gateways. If a single site is selected, the Actions list changes to show these items:

- Add Site
- Add Branch Site
- View Site
- Edit Site

If more than one site is added, the Actions list adds a Delete Site item.

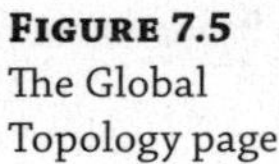

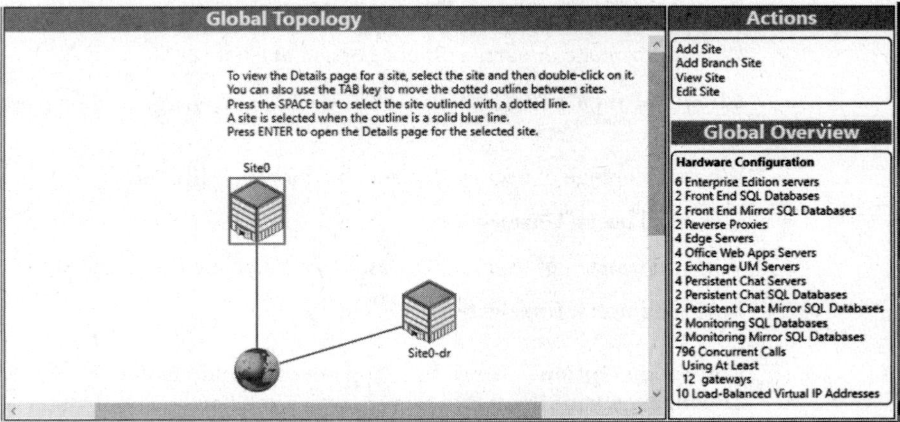

FIGURE 7.5 The Global Topology page

Only additional sites can be deleted; the first site created can never be deleted. If it was designed incorrectly, you will need to start fresh or go back and modify the answers.

- Add Site will take you back through the Planning Wizard questions and provide an additional site configuration once completed. You can define a maximum of eight sites.
- Add Branch Site will provide the opportunity to define additional branch sites associated with this site.
- Edit Site will take you back through the questions you already answered for this site and allow you to make changes.
- Selecting a site and then choosing View Site from the Actions list, or simply double-clicking a site, will open the Site Topology tab, shown in Figure 7.6.

SITE TOPOLOGY

The Site Topology tab displays the servers and devices required to support the site as defined in the Planning Wizard. It also provides a breakdown of the specific configuration required (for non-Skype for Business servers; this will be the generic rules).

On the Site Topology page, the Actions list includes these items:

- View Global Topology
- View Planning Steps
- View Deployment Steps

When you select a specific server on the page, a View Server Information item will be added to the actions list. Clicking this action item (or double-clicking the server) will provide a response similar to Figure 7.7. The specific details provided will vary based on the actual server role selected. As you can see, the recommended hardware is displayed in addition to configuration information.

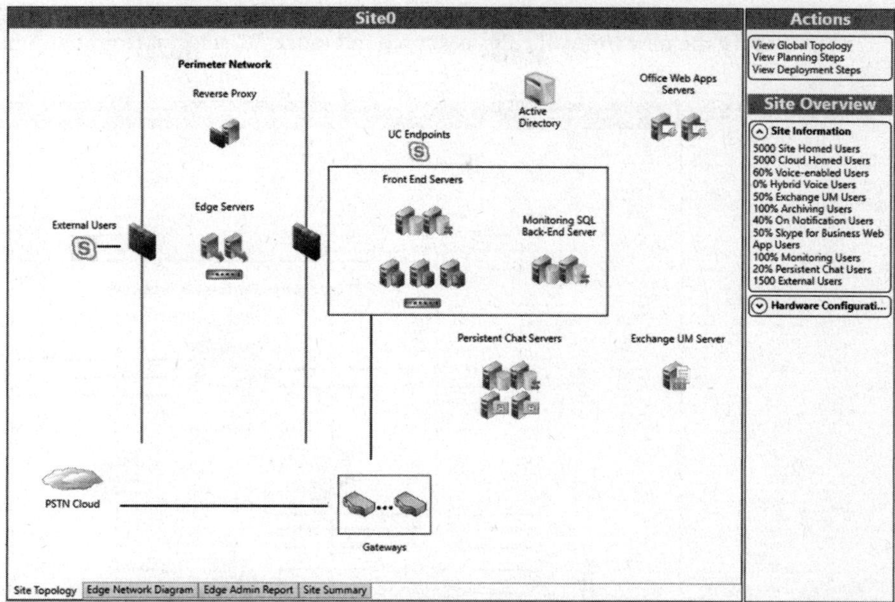

FIGURE 7.6 The Site Topology tab

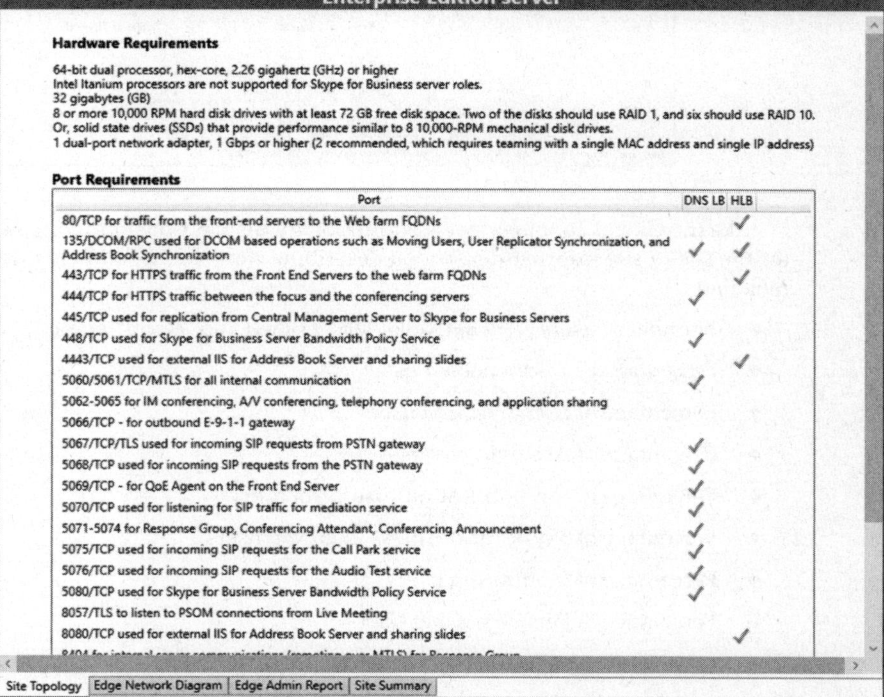

Enterprise Edition server
Hardware Requirements
64-bit dual processor, hex-core, 2.26 gigahertz (GHz) or higher
Intel Itanium processors are not supported for Skype for Business server roles.
32 gigabytes (GB)
8 or more 10,000 RPM hard disk drives with at least 72 GB free disk space. Two of the disks should use RAID 1, and six should use RAID 10.
Or, solid state drives (SSDs) that provide performance similar to 8 10,000-RPM mechanical disk drives.
1 dual-port network adapter, 1 Gbps or higher (2 recommended, which requires teaming with a single MAC address and single IP address)
Port Requirements
Port
DNS LB
HLB
80/TCP for traffic from the front-end servers to the Web farm FQDNs
135/DCOM/RPC used for DCOM based operations such as Moving Users, User Replicator Synchronization, and Address Book Synchronization
443/TCP for HTTPS traffic from the Front End Servers to the web farm FQDNs
444/TCP for HTTPS traffic between the focus and the conferencing servers
445/TCP used for replication from Central Management Server to Skype for Business Servers
448/TCP used for Skype for Business Server Bandwidth Policy Service
4443/TCP used for external IIS for Address Book Server and sharing slides
5060/5061/TCP/MTLS for all internal communication
5062-5065 for IM conferencing, A/V conferencing, telephony conferencing, and application sharing
5066/TCP - for outbound E-9-1-1 gateway
5067/TCP/TLS used for incoming SIP requests from PSTN gateway
5068/TCP used for incoming SIP requests from the PSTN gateway
5069/TCP - for QoE Agent on the Front End Server
5070/TCP used for listening for SIP traffic for mediation service
5071-5074 for Response Group, Conferencing Attendant, Conferencing Announcement
5075/TCP used for incoming SIP requests for the Call Park service
5076/TCP used for incoming SIP requests for the Audio Test service
5080/TCP used for Skype for Business Server Bandwidth Policy Service
8057/TLS to listen to PSOM connections from Live Meeting
8080/TCP used for external IIS for Address Book Server and sharing slides
Site Topology
Edge Network Diagram
Edge Admin Report
Site Summary

FIGURE 7.7 The server information page

To add a View Firewall Diagram item to the list, select a firewall on the Site Topology tab. To display the new firewall rule, as shown in Figure 7.8, select it from the Actions list.

FIGURE 7.8 The firewall diagram

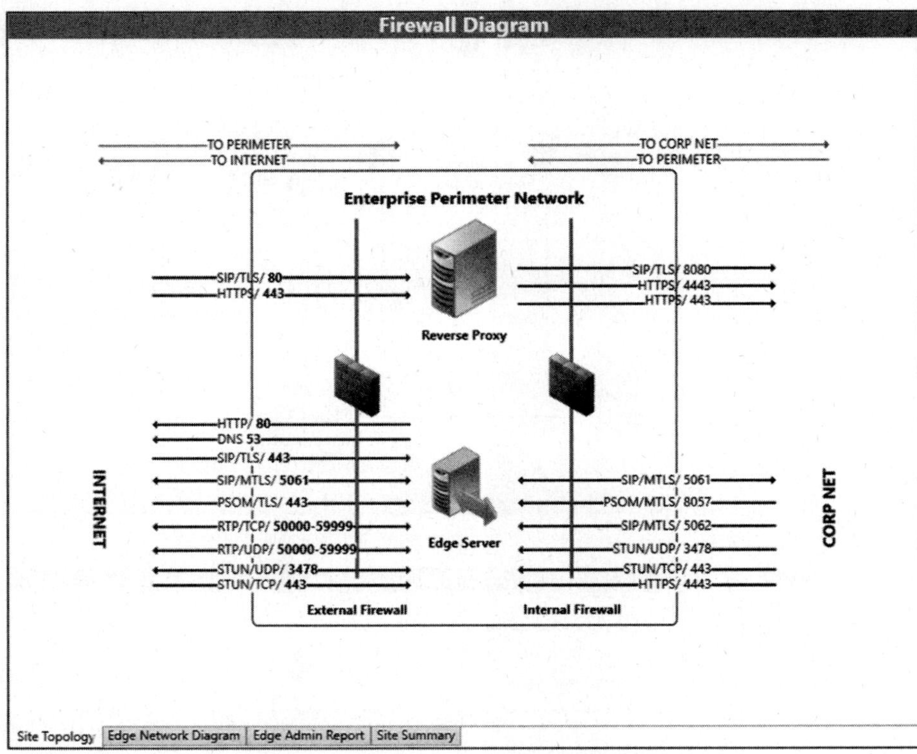

Like the Global Topology page, Site Topology displays the hardware requirements, but only for the site. A site information section describing some of the following definition criteria is also included:

- Number of users (split between "site" homed and "cloud" homed)
- Percentage of voice-enabled users
- Percentage of Exchange UM users
- Percentage of Archiving users
- Percentage of "on-notification" users (mobility)
- Percentage of Skype for Business Web App users
- Percentage of Monitoring users
- Percentage of Persistent Chat Users
- Number of external users

Edge Network Diagram

Selecting the Edge Network Diagram tab on the bottom will display the network diagram view of the Edge infrastructure. This will include IP addresses as well as server names, as shown in Figure 7.9.

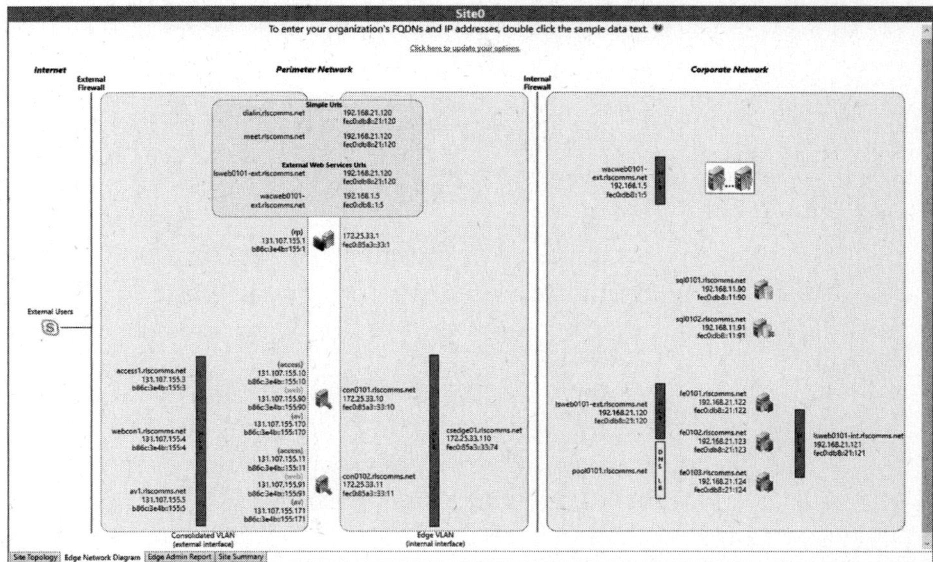

FIGURE 7.9 Viewing the Edge network diagram

At this point, you can populate the details behind the topology. Double-clicking any of the server icons or the data (server names or IP addresses) will provide a pop-up through which you can add the server names and IP address information.

Providing this information now allows the topology from the Planning Tool to be exported to a file and directly imported into any design documentation, which will save time because all the firewall rules are already defined.

Edge Admin Report

The Edge admin report has four sections providing information about the Edge infrastructure. Figure 7.10 shows the beginning of a Summary report.

The four tabs are as follows:

Summary Report This report provides the information such as server role, FQDN, IP address, and specific guidance where required (such as static route requirements).

Certificates Report The Certificates report provides the detailed certificate requirements for each of the roles involved with the Edge infrastructure (Edge and Reverse Proxy as well as the Next Hop pool). This one is useful for the Reverse Proxy certificate because the Installation Wizard will generate the Edge and Next Hop certificates. Also included on this report are whether the certificates are required to be internal or public and which specific Enhanced Key Usage (EKU) settings are required.

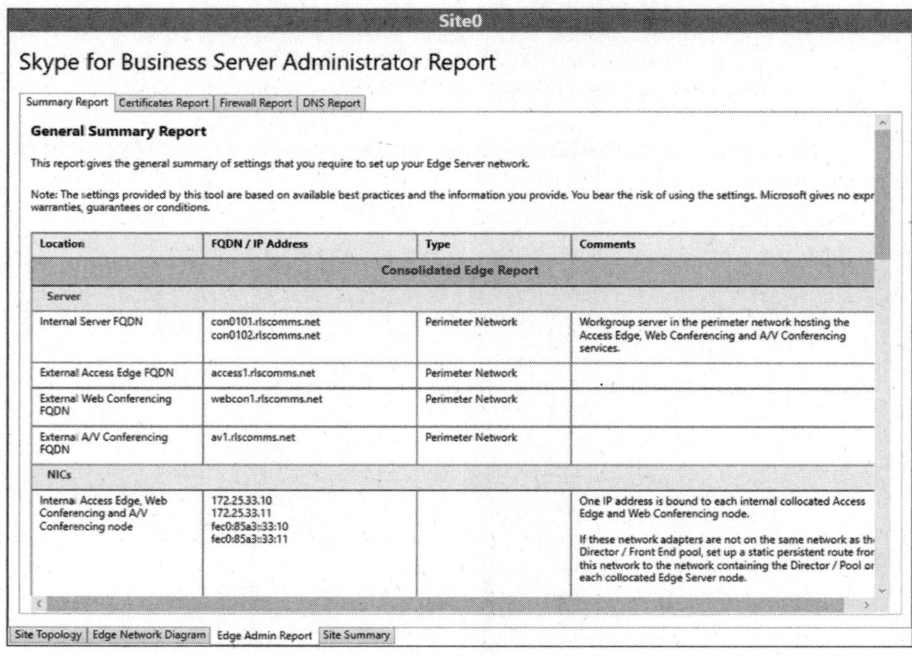

FIGURE 7.10 The Site Summary tab of the Edge admin report

Firewall Report The Firewall report provides all the information required to generate the rules allowing the external configuration. This information is broken down by internal, external, and reverse proxy interfaces.

DNS Report The DNS report provides all the records required, both A and SRV, along with the actual FQDNs to be assigned and the resulting IP address mappings.

In large organizations, the Skype for Business administrator typically is not also the DNS or firewall administrator, so each of these reports can be extremely useful when configuration information needs to be provided to another team.

Site Summary

This page, illustrated in Figure 7.11, lists the enabled features as well as the capacity details. In some cases, it may make more sense to adjust the number of servers based on the information here.

Exporting the Topology

Once the topology has been identified in the Planning Tool, you have several methods to extract that information.

- Exporting to Visio
- Exporting to Excel

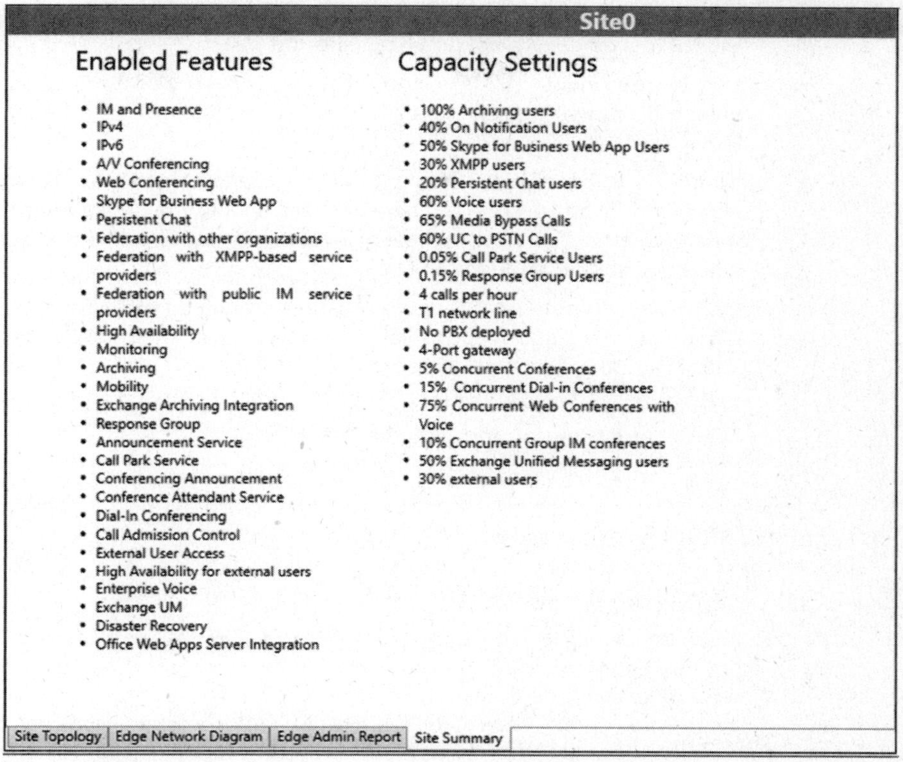

FIGURE 7.11
A site summary

Site0

Enabled Features

- IM and Presence
- IPv4
- IPv6
- A/V Conferencing
- Web Conferencing
- Skype for Business Web App
- Persistent Chat
- Federation with other organizations
- Federation with XMPP-based service providers
- Federation with public IM service providers
- High Availability
- Monitoring
- Archiving
- Mobility
- Exchange Archiving Integration
- Response Group
- Announcement Service
- Call Park Service
- Conferencing Announcement
- Conference Attendant Service
- Dial-In Conferencing
- Call Admission Control
- External User Access
- High Availability for external users
- Enterprise Voice
- Exchange UM
- Disaster Recovery
- Office Web Apps Server Integration

Capacity Settings

- 100% Archiving users
- 40% On Notification Users
- 50% Skype for Business Web App Users
- 30% XMPP users
- 20% Persistent Chat users
- 60% Voice users
- 65% Media Bypass Calls
- 60% UC to PSTN Calls
- 0.05% Call Park Service Users
- 0.15% Response Group Users
- 4 calls per hour
- T1 network line
- No PBX deployed
- 4-Port gateway
- 5% Concurrent Conferences
- 15% Concurrent Dial-in Conferences
- 75% Concurrent Web Conferences with Voice
- 10% Concurrent Group IM conferences
- 50% Exchange Unified Messaging users
- 30% external users

Site Topology | Edge Network Diagram | Edge Admin Report | Site Summary

Exporting to Visio

Selecting the Export To Visio option (via the icon or the File menu) provides a prompt for saving the file as a Visio drawing.

The Visio file opens to show the following worksheets as a minimum:

- Global Topology
- Site0
- Site0 Edge Network Diagram

Each additional site (and, if defined, associated Edge network diagram) will also be represented on individual worksheets.

These aids are great for inclusion in any design documentation being organized and gathered.

Exporting to Excel

Selecting the Export To Excel option (via the icon or the File menu) provides a prompt for saving the file as an XML 2003 spreadsheet.

By default, opening an XML file will launch Internet Explorer to display the content; however, if you launch Excel and then load the file, Excel opens to show the following worksheets as a minimum:

Summary This worksheet provides a summary of the sites and server hardware required as well as a per-site breakdown of the features and capacity provided.

Hardware Profile This worksheet provides a summary hardware count and specifications as well as a detailed breakdown per site and role.

Port Requirements This worksheet summarizes the port requirements per role and provides a list of which ports require hardware load balancing and which can use DNS load balancing.

Summary Report-Site0 This worksheet summarizes the role of each server as well as the FQDN and IP address of each network card. In addition, there are comments associated with each entry detailing the role of each FQDN and IP address as well as information as to whether it should be added to DNS.

Certificates Report-Site0 This worksheet provides a breakdown of each certificate needed, including information such as subject name, subject alternative name, CA (internal or public), and what Enhanced Key Usage settings are required.

Firewall Report-Site0 This worksheet summarizes the firewall rules required, including FQDN, port, protocol, and direction of traffic.

Real World Scenario

Using the Planning Tool Output in Your Design

As you've seen up to this point, the Planning Tool provides an extremely quick way to determine your design requirements. However, there's no such thing as a free lunch. The output should *not* be used as the definitive design. It should instead be used as a starting point. Because the scenarios are rule based, they do not (and cannot) deal with small variations in the requirements. At the time of writing, TechNet has not been specifically updated to reference Skype for Business capacity numbers; however, all guidance indicates the numbers will be the same (or similar) to Lync Server 2013 numbers.

For example, using all the default settings, a single Front End server (without high availability enabled) will support 6,666 users. If you change the number of users to 6,667, the Planning Tool will indicate that two Front End servers are required. A third Front End server is not required until you reach 13,333 users.

According to TechNet, a single Front End server can support up to 6,666 users, and two Front End servers can support up to 13,332 users.

For most of the customers we work with, we round the number of users to the nearest thousand. We typically start with the Planning Tool output and adjust as needed using the information from the help file and planning documentation.

The Planning Tool does have some inconsistencies within it. For example, it is possible to disable high availability for the pool but enable it for the Edge environment. However, doing so would cause the internal environment to become a single point of failure, and it would affect the external environment too.

Note that the help file and planning documentation are updated more frequently than the Planning Tool; therefore, this documentation is more likely to incorporate user feedback than the Planning Tool.

The Stress and Performance Tool

Of course, the only true way to confirm whether your design meets the defined performance requirements is to stress-test it using the Stress and Performance Tool, which you can download from

`http://www.microsoft.com/en-us/download/details.aspx?id=50367`

You can use the Stress and Performance Tool to simulate load for the following modalities:

- Instant messaging and presence
- Audio/video/multiview conferencing
- Application sharing
- Peer-to-peer audio (including PSTN)
- Web Access Client conferencing
- Conferencing Attendant
- Response groups
- Address book download and address book query
- Distribution list expansion
- Emergency calling and location profiles

The Stress and Performance Tool can support multiple pools and federation.

When you deviate from the recommended hardware specifications or usage model, you should carry out performance testing to ensure that the planned design is capable of handling the expected load. This is the only way to validate a deployment prior to deploying in production with live users.

The toolset contains a number of applications to carry out the testing (and, yes, still refers to Lync in most of the naming!).

UserProvisioningTool.exe Used to generate user accounts and contacts information used during the testing; these will be created within Active Directory.

UserProfileGenerator.exe Enables the wizard to build the input criteria for the tests.

LyncPerfTool.exe The Client Simulation Tool, which will consume the data created by the other two tools and carry out the testing.

There are also a number of associated files, such as `Default.tmx` and some example scripts.

Stress and Performance Tool Prerequisites

The `LyncPerfTool.exe` tool is capable of simulating the load of 4,500 users for every machine matching the following hardware:

- 8GB RAM
- Two dual-core CPUs

In addition, LyncPerfTool.exe requires Windows Server 2008 R2 SP1 (64-bit) or Windows Server 2012 (64-bit) with the following software installed:

- Microsoft .NET Framework 4.5
- Desktop Experience (Windows Server 2008 R2 only)
- Microsoft Visual C++ 2008 redistributable package (x64)

The following criteria must also be met:

- The admin running it must be logged on using an account that is a member of the Domain Admins group.
- LyncPerfTool.exe cannot be run on a server with Lync Server installed.
- PowerShell V3 must be installed on the server running UserProvisioningTool.exe.
- UserProvisioningTool.exe must be run on the Front End server where the user accounts will reside (Standard Edition or Enterprise Edition).
- Each test account must have a unique phone number.
- The server page file must be system-managed or at least 1.5 times the size of RAM.
- Windows Server 2008 R2 (or Windows Server 2012) must have Active Directory Remote Admin tools installed.
- The CapacityPlanningTool.msi file must be executed on each server being used to simulate clients.
- The Skype for Business Server environment must be enabled for the scenarios being tested.

RUNNING THE STRESS AND PERFORMANCE TOOL

The Stress and Performance Tool is not supported when run in a production Active Directory environment.

Because of the tool's requirements and the tool's high-risk security requirements needed to access the accounts in Active Directory, it should be run only in test environments.

As a general best practice, any sort of performance testing should be carried out in a separate environment on hardware identical to that which will be used in production.

CREATING USERS

Because you'll be running the stress test in a test environment, you'll need to configure some users before you begin testing. To do that, you'll use the UserProvisioningTool.exe tool. When you run it, the first thing you'll see is the screen shown in Figure 7.9. The information you'll need to provide on each tab is outlined here. Upon first load, the fields will be grayed out, and you'll need to load a configuration file, either the sample or a newly created one.

We have to admit to being slightly disappointed in the latest iteration of the stress testing tools. There's so much more that could've been achieved, even simple things like having a single button to run each section in turn rather than having to manually define and then create each section or the fact that the default entries populated (shown in Figure 7.12) are different from those used in the tools to actually generate the tests!

FIGURE 7.12
UserProvisioningTool.exe

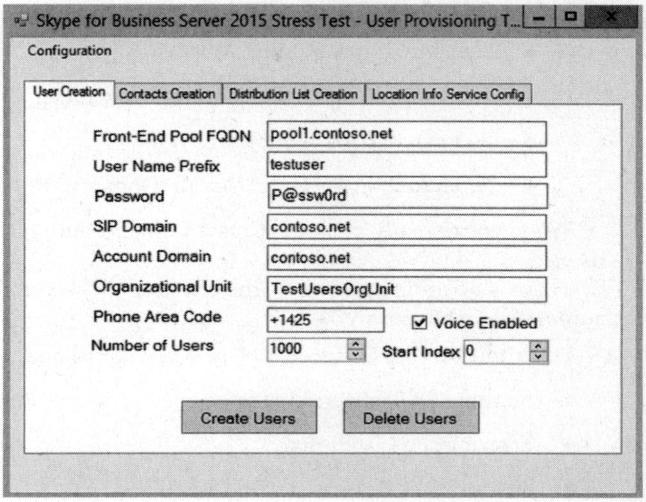

User Creation Here you'll provide the following information to generate the users:

- *Front-End Pool FQDN*: The pool on which the users will be provisioned.
- *User Name Prefix*: All usernames will begin with this prefix.
- *Password*: This must meet the domain password complexity rules.
- *SIP Domain*: This field is for users' URIs.
- *Account Domain*: The user account domain.
- *Organizational Unit*: OU in which to create the objects (both user accounts and distribution lists).
- *Phone Area Code*: This is the starting prefix for users. Please note that when you're assigning phone numbers to new users, the tool does not "pad out" the number to be truly E.164 compliant. It simply joins this phone area code with the user index ID.
- *Voice Enabled*: Check box to indicate whether the users should be enabled for Enterprise Voice.
- *Number Of Users*: Enter the number of users you expect to have.
- *Start Index*: Used to uniquely identify users.

Once all the information has been entered, click the Create Users button to begin the process of creating them; depending on the number of users selected, this will take some time.

When your testing is complete, you can populate the tool with the same information as when you created the users and then select Delete Users to remove the accounts.

Contacts Creation Here you'll define how the user contacts lists are populated.

- Average Contacts Per User
- Fixed (Checking this doesn't allow for variation in number of contacts; the average is given to all.)
- Average Contact Groups Per User
- Federated/Cross Pool Contacts Percentage
- Federated/Cross Pool User Prefix
- Federated/Cross Pool User SIP Domain

When you're ready, click the Create Contacts button to populate the already provisioned users.

There is no option to remove the contacts—when you delete the users, the contacts list will automatically be removed.

Distribution List Creation Here you'll define and populate the distribution lists to be used.

- Number Of Distribution Lists
- Distribution List Prefix
- Minimum Members in a Dist. List
- Maximum Members in a Dist. List

Clicking Create Distribution List will create and populate the distribution lists. Oddly there is no option to delete the distribution lists, so this will have to be manual; deleting an account will remove it from the distribution list, but in the end, you'll be left with a number of empty distribution lists.

Location Info Service Config Here you'll enter the address information to populate the Location Information Services (LIS) database.

- Number Of Addresses
- Offices Per Address
- Number Of WA Ports
- Number Of Subnets
- Number Of Switches
- Number Of Ports

Also, the Civic Address Details section needs to be populated; this has the following fields listed, although not all are needed for each address:

- Company Name
- Street Name
- Street Name Suffix

- Post Directional
- City
- State
- Zip Code
- Country

As you'd expect, the Generate LIS Config Files button will generate the configuration information for importing into LIS.

Correctly defining the LIS content can be quite complicated (especially for locations outside North America where different address definitions are used), so it's best to simply use the sample data given in the documentation and vary the data based on the specific number of addresses and access points you want to define.

Configuring Profiles

After you've created the users, you can configure their user profiles. To do that, you'll run `UserProfileGenerator.exe`, which displays the screen shown in Figure 7.13. (You'll need to display the profile generator on your own screen to see the details.) The information you'll provide on each tab is outlined next.

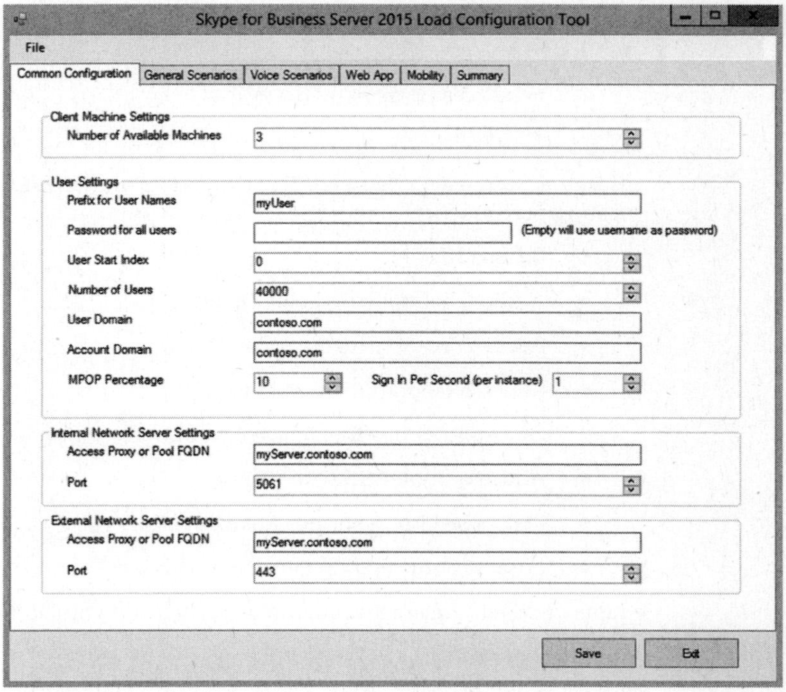

Figure 7.13
The screen displayed by `UserProfileGenerator.exe`

Common Configuration Here you'll provide the following information to enable the stress testing to be performed. (At startup, all the information is defaulted to `contoso.com`, so you will have to reenter it).

- Number Of Available Machines (for running the stress testing)
- Prefix For User Names
- Password For All Users
- User Start Index
- Number Of Users
- User Domain
- Account Domain
- MPOP Percentage (Multiple Points of Presence support—i.e., how many users will log in via multiple clients)
- Sign In Per Second (Per Instance)
- Internal Network Server Settings
  - Access Proxy Or Pool FQDN
  - Port
- External Network Server Settings
  - Access Proxy Or Pool FQDN
  - Port

General Scenarios Here you'll provide the following information to determine the level of testing performed.

- IM Load Level*
- Audio Conferencing Load Level*
- Application Sharing Load Level*
- Data Collaboration Load Level*
- Distribution List Expansion Load Level
- Address Book Web Query Load Level
- Response Group Service Load Level
- Location Information Services Load Level

Items marked * have the ability to be configured with additional settings:

- External
- AdHoc
- Large Conf

Each modality can be configured as follows:

- Disabled
- Low
- Medium
- High
- Custom

The Advanced button allows you to specifically configure each modality as required.

Voice Scenarios Here you'll provide the following information specifically detailing the voice modalities:

- VoIP Load Level
- UC/PSTN Gateway Load level
- Conferencing Attendant Load Level
- Call Parking Service Load Level (requires the phone number to be configured)
- Mediation Server and PSTN

As with the options on the General Scenarios tab, these options can be configured as follows:

- Disabled
- Low
- Medium
- High
- Custom

The Advanced button allows you to specifically configure each modality, such as length of call, which location profile to use, and so on.

Reach Here you'll provide the following information for remote and federated users:

- General Reach Settings
- Application Sharing Load Level
- Data Collaboration Load Level
- IM Load Level
- Voice Conferencing Load Level

Again, as with the options on the General Scenarios tab, these options can be configured as follows:

- Disabled
- Low

- Medium
- High
- Custom

The Advanced button allows you to specifically configure each modality, such as URLs, lobby timeout, and the like.

Mobility Here you can configure the settings available for the mobility modality; this was new with the Lync Server 2013 implementation of these tools.

- General Mobility Settings (This includes definition of the URLs, Autodiscovery enabled, and other mobile specific settings.)
- Presence and P2P Instant Messaging/Audio Load Level

Summary This tab provides an overall summary of the data and allows you to generate custom user ranges.

By default, the system will allocate user ranges for each of the load tests to be performed (see Table 7.1 for an example); tests not being performed will not be listed in the table. To allow the User Range column to be manually edited, check the Enable Custom User Range Generation check box.

TABLE 7.1 User range generation

NAME	LOAD LEVEL	USER RANGE
Distribution List Expansion	Low	0–9
Audio Conferencing	Medium	10–46
Application Sharing Sharer	Low	47–50
Application Sharing Viewer	Low	1–64
Data Collaboration	Medium	65–71
Instant Messaging	High	72–999

When you're ready, click the Generate Files button and indicate where the files should be placed. The test case files will be generated and stored in the specified folder. This folder needs to be copied to each of the client systems that will be executing the stress tests (this folder must be copied to the same folder in which the Stress Tools are installed).

An option is provided to insert an initial sign-in delay when starting up; having a significant number of clients attempt to sign in at the same time can cause unexpected (and potentially unrealistic) delays to the testing.

Now that you've created the users and the profiles and have generated the client test cases, you can execute `runclient x.bat` (where *x* is replaced by the client ID—for example, `runclient0.bat` for the first client) on each of the client computers to begin the execution tests.

Be sure to enable performance counter capturing (using Performance Monitor or `perfmon.exe`) before starting the stress testing.

A number of command prompts will report the testing status, with one prompt for each test.

Interpreting the Results

Now that you've run the performance tests and the servers haven't turned into smoldering lumps of metal and plastic, what's next?

You'll need to analyze the performance during the testing. It's not enough to say the servers didn't crash and therefore it must be fine. You need to determine whether there was any impact, such as dropped connections or busy responses.

Experience indicates that success counters don't really add value in this scenario; the failure rates are where you can establish when the servers start to come under pressure.

The following counters provide the most information to determine whether the pool (or pools) can cope with the load expected:

- Failed Logons
- 5*xx* Responses for SetPresence
- 6*xx* Responses for SetPresence
- 5*xx* Responses for GetPresence
- 6*xx* Responses for GetPresence
- ABS Full/Delta File Downloads Failed
- ABS WS Calls Failed
- Calls Failed
- Calls Declined
- Calls Received 5*xx* (separate counters for IM, VOIP, App Sharing)
- Calls Received 6*xx* (separate counters for IM, VOIP, App Sharing)
- Conference Schedule Failure
- Join Conference Failure

If these failure numbers are significant, then the load is probably beyond the bounds of the environment's capacity and further investigation is needed. Typically, the causes will be due to poor or inadequate disk or memory performance on the SQL Server machine.

On the other hand, if the numbers are minimal, it is a good indication the servers are reaching their peak capacity and any further load would put them over the top.

There are no specific guidelines for what values constitute "significant" or "minimal" numbers; they will vary dramatically based on the number of users and the types of customers. For example, a call center will require better consistency from GetPresence-type responses than from Join Conference Failure because the call-center capability, response groups, relies on the presence states of users to direct calls. Equally, a failure of one call in a 100-user company will have a larger impact than one failure in a 50,000-user company.

In an ideal world, you would run tests to confirm that the servers are capable of supporting the load expected and then go further to establish the maximum the design can support. By doing that, you will determine the design's capability for future expansion.

Bandwidth Calculator

A major piece of feedback that the Lync development team received from OCS deployments was that with the earlier version, admins were unable to determine the bandwidth requirements prior to installation, at which point it was typically too late to do anything. This inability posed a major problem because when there isn't enough bandwidth, users are impacted, and other lines of business applications can be too. Call Admission Control (see Chapter 17, "Call Admission Control") helps provide a level of control on this; however, again it provides it after the fact.

You can use the Bandwidth Calculator to estimate the bandwidth prior to deploying and configuring Skype for Business Server 2015, thereby allowing additional bandwidth to be purchased before rollout if necessary. It is similar to the calculator for Lync Server 2010 and Lync Server 2013, obviously adjusted for the new bandwidth values for the codecs. Some additional calculations are listed here:

- H.264 support
- Multi-View Gallery support
- Both Lync 2010 and Lync 2013 clients
- Internet traffic calculations
- Traffic aggregation per user-definable QoS traffic classes
- Scalability to 300 branches

To calculate those estimates, the Bandwidth Calculator requires the following information:

- Number of sites
- Number of users per site
- Persona of the users (The persona can be thought of as the user profile. A separate worksheet allows the personas to be customized to indicate low/medium/high usage rates for each modality.)
- Usage model
- WAN connectivity and any restrictions placed on traffic
- Thresholds

Figure 7.14 shows a sample of some of the output generated by the Bandwidth Calculator.

At least for the first few times you use it, you should follow the steps in the flowchart guide (located on the Start Here worksheet) to set up the input values (shown reduced to fit the page in Figure 7.15).

FIGURE 7.14 Output from the Bandwidth Calculator

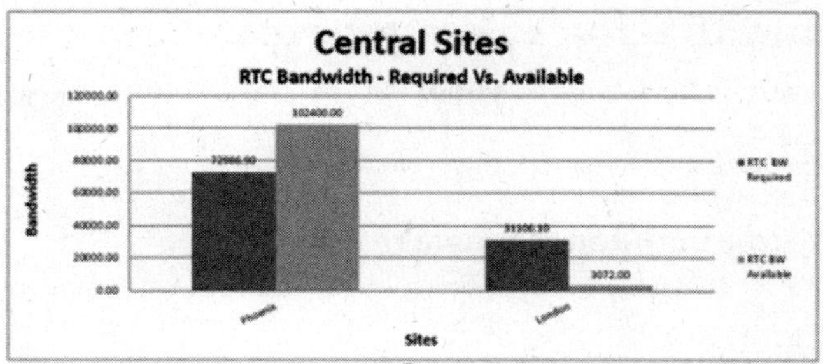

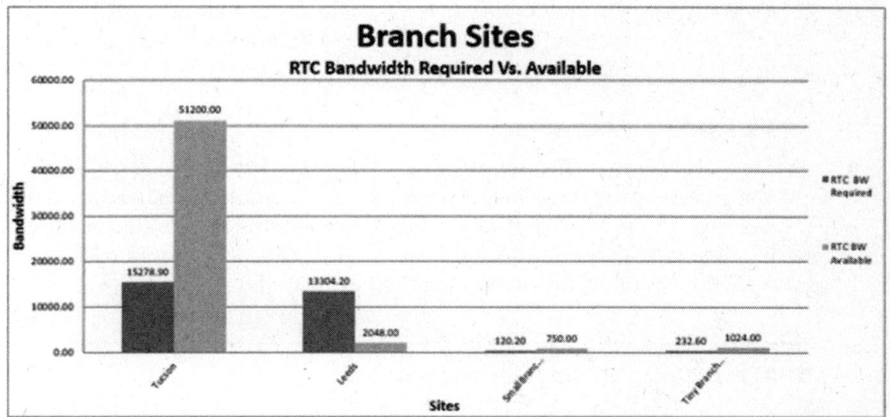

FIGURE 7.15 Bandwidth Calculator flowchart

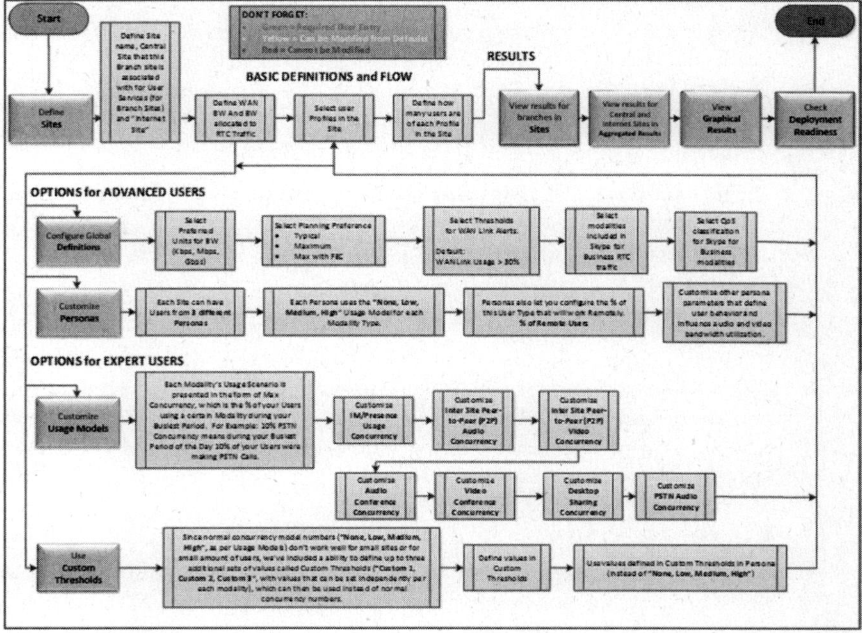

Installation Prerequisites

Once you have completed the planning stage, you are nearly ready to install Skype for Business Server. Before you do, though, you'll need to take care of a few prerequisites for both the infrastructure and the operating system.

Recommended Hardware

The term *recommended hardware* is always a little confusing. Does it mean this is the minimum hardware needed or something else? In the past, it has tended to be a relatively high specification. If you are working for a small company, does this mean Skype for Business is unsuitable for your needs? Can you use lower-spec hardware? Should you virtualize?

The recommended hardware values are based on the tested profiles used by Microsoft and feedback from the beta release programs.

Physical Hardware

The best way to determine your hardware needs is to consider the performance characteristics and profiles provided. The recommended hardware is the hardware that has provided the values used in the Microsoft-provided planning tools and guidance, based on the default user profile. If you deviate significantly from the defaults, you should consider more detailed planning.

Table 7.2 shows the recommended hardware for each role.

Table 7.2 Recommended hardware

Role	CPU	Memory	Disk	Network
Front End, Back End, Standard Edition, and Persistent Chat servers	64-bit dual processor, hex core 2.6GHz	32GB	72GB free disk space 8+ disks, 10,000 RPM Two configured with RAID-1 and remainder RAID-10	Two NICs, 1Gbps
Edge, Standalone Mediation, and Director servers	64-bit quad core, 2.0GHz; or 64-bit dual processor, dual core, 2.0Ghz	16GB	72GB free disk space Four+ disks, 10,000 RPM	Two NICs, 1Gbps

A single pool will support up to 80,000 users with 12 Front End servers (using all modalities). The recommended approach is 6,660 users per Front End server (not catering for high availability); be careful to cater for this number when planning with server failures in mind. At the time of writing, these numbers have been provided only for Lync Server 2013 and may change specifically for Skype for Business Server.

Virtualization

Based on feedback (from the beta program, previous versions of Lync, and general computing trends), Skype for Business supports virtualization of any of the server roles.

At the time of writing, only Windows Server 2012 or Windows Server 2012 R2 is supported for running Skype for Business Server in a virtualized environment. See `http://go.microsoft.com/fwlink/?linkid=200511` for updated details of other hypervisors that may be supported.

Using a mix of virtual and physical servers in the same pool is not supported. For this purpose, Microsoft defines a pool as "two or more servers of the following roles—Front End, Director, Mediation, and Edge." Front End servers are considered separate from Back End servers, so you can virtualize Front End servers and have physical Back End servers, and vice versa—physical Front End servers with virtualized Back End servers.

You can, however, mix virtual and physical pools in the same enterprise deployment (for example, servers in one region could be virtual, while servers in another region could be physical). Within the topology, they would be configured in separate pools (and most likely separate central sites).

There is no requirement to host all types of server roles on the same physical server, such as all virtual Mediation servers on one physical node and all virtual Front End servers on another. However, you should mix the types of roles deployed on physical nodes to reduce the single points of failure introduced by having all of one role on one physical node.

Quick/live migration is not supported and can introduce additional complexity to the client connectivity.

As a rough rule of thumb, 4GB of memory should be assigned to the host OS and the remaining memory allocated as if dealing with physical machines. There are many reasons to virtualize (green computing, cost reduction, etc.); however, there are also reasons not to virtualize. Don't assume that virtualization is the correct answer in every environment.

Software Prerequisites

In addition to the hardware requirements just discussed, a number of software prerequisites must be met before you can begin installation. Some of them are at the operating system or application level; others are at the component level.

Chapter 8, "Installation," will cover the steps required for installation of the prerequisites; however, they are highlighted here to aid in the planning phase.

Active Directory

Of course, before you can install Skype for Business Server 2015, you need to update Active Directory.

The following Active Directory topologies are supported:

- Single forest with single domain
- Single forest with a single tree and multiple domains
- Single forest with multiple trees and disjoint namespaces
- Multiple forests in a central forest topology
- Multiple forests in a resource forest topology

The Active Directory forest version must be Windows Server 2003 Native Mode or higher, and all the domains in which Skype for Business will be deployed must also be Windows Server 2003 Native Mode or higher.

The domain controllers must be Windows Server 2003 (32-bit or 64-bit) or higher, and the Schema, Forest, and Domain prep actions must be performed from a 64-bit machine. There are no tools capable of running the required Skype for Business Active Directory updates from a 32-bit machine.

Don't forget permissions! The account used to install Skype for Business is required to be a member of the CsAdministrator group or, if the installation permissions have been delegated, a member of the delegation group. In addition, when changes are published to the topology, the account used to publish must be a member of the CsAdministrator group as well as the Domain Admins group or, if delegated setup has been configured, only a member of CsAdministrator. Permissions are also required on the SQL database being installed.

Supported Operating System and SQL Server Versions

Skype for Business is supported on the following Windows Server versions:

- Windows Server 2012 R2 Standard
- Windows Server 2012 R2 Enterprise
- Windows Server 2012 Standard
- Windows Server 2012 Datacenter

Only the 64-bit version of the OS is supported, and OSs must not be Server Core versions. Also, covered in Chapter 9, "Migration and Upgrades," Windows Server 2008 R2 is supported when upgrading from Lync Server 2013, but it is not recommended to install a fresh Skype for Business server onto.

A question commonly asked is whether service pack updates are supported. Service packs are supported upon release, but full version updates are not supported until explicitly tested and confirmed. For example, if SP1 for Windows is released, Skype for Business will automatically be supported with this service pack applied to the operating system. However, if instead of SP1 Windows 2012 R3 is released, Skype for Business will *not* be supported until testing has been confirmed on this new operating system.

In addition to the OS, this rule of thumb also applies to the SQL Server version, of which the following are supported (only 64-bit versions are supported):

- SQL Server 2008 R2 Standard
- SQL Server 2008 R2 Enterprise
- SQL Server 2012 Standard
- SQL Server 2012 Enterprise
- SQL Server 2014 Standard
- SQL Server 2014 Enterprise
- SQL Server Express 2014 (for Skype for Business Server 2015 Standard Edition and the local server databases).

The administrative tools may also be installed on the following client OSs (they must also be 64-bit):

- Windows 10
- Windows 8.1
- Windows 8
- Windows 7 with SP1

Remote PowerShell administration does not require installation of the administrative toolset. As discussed in Appendix B, "Introduction to PowerShell, the Skype for Business Management Shell, and Regular Expressions," you can instead remotely connect to a Front End server and access the Skype for Business PowerShell cmdlets as if you were remotely logged into the server and running the cmdlets directly.

Required Operating System Components and Downloads

In addition to the base operating system version, a number of other components are required:

- Windows PowerShell 3.0
- .NET Framework 4.5 (including HTTP Activation)
- Windows Identity Foundation

Depending on your OS, some of these items might be installed already, or they may need to be downloaded. Pay special attention to the .NET Framework. Each version does not replace previous versions, so it is possible (and this is fine!) to have multiple different versions of the .NET Framework installed.

Individual roles have different additional component requirements based on their configuration.

Front End Servers and Directors These require IIS and the following modules to be installed:

- Static content
- Default document
- HTTP errors
- ASP.NET
- .NET extensibility
- Internet Server API (ISAPI) extensions
- ISAPI filters
- HTTP logging
- Logging tools
- Tracing
- Windows authentication
- Request filtering

- Static content compression
- Dynamic content compression
- IIS management console
- IIS management scripts and tools
- Anonymous authentication
- Client certificate mapping authentication

If you attempt an installation without any of these, you will receive an error message.

Unfortunately, this is one of the few generic error messages within Skype for Business 2015. The error states the problem, but it does not mention which modules are not installed. It simply states that all are needed.

In addition to the IIS modules previously listed, the following Windows features are needed:

- Remote System Administration Tools
- Desktop Experience

Mediation Servers No additional components must be installed.

Edge Servers No additional components must be installed.

Persistent Chat Servers No additional components must be installed.

Servers Running Conferencing Components If conferencing is configured on a server, the Windows Media Format Runtime component must be installed, and this requires a reboot.

Archiving and Monitoring Components No additional components must be installed.

Chapter 8 will go into more details of how to install all of these prerequisites via PowerShell to streamline the installation process.

Disaster Recovery

When the resiliency option is configured in Topology Builder and the Skype for Business setup process is run again to update the Front End servers in the pool, a new service is installed: the Skype for Business Backup Service. This service is responsible for ensuring that each database is replicated across to the other pool. Although the service is installed on all the Front End servers in the pool, only a single Front End is running it at any time; this is determined by the pool itself in a random manner.

Figure 7.16 shows the architecture with the backup service dealing with the data replication between pools and also the file share using Distributed File Sharing (DFS) for its replication. While this architecture is shown for SQL mirroring, the concept is similar with SQL AlwaysOn Availability Groups (albeit the underlying SQL process will be different).

It's important to note that changes are first written locally, then replicated to the pool SQL mirror, and then across to the backup pool. Because of the time delays configured in Topology Builder, it is possible that some changes will not be available on the backup pool in the event of a disaster occurring.

It is important to understand that this data loss is likely to be of the following functionalities:

- Change to buddy list
- Meeting creation/modification

- Meeting content (stored in the file share)
- Setting of call forwarding settings

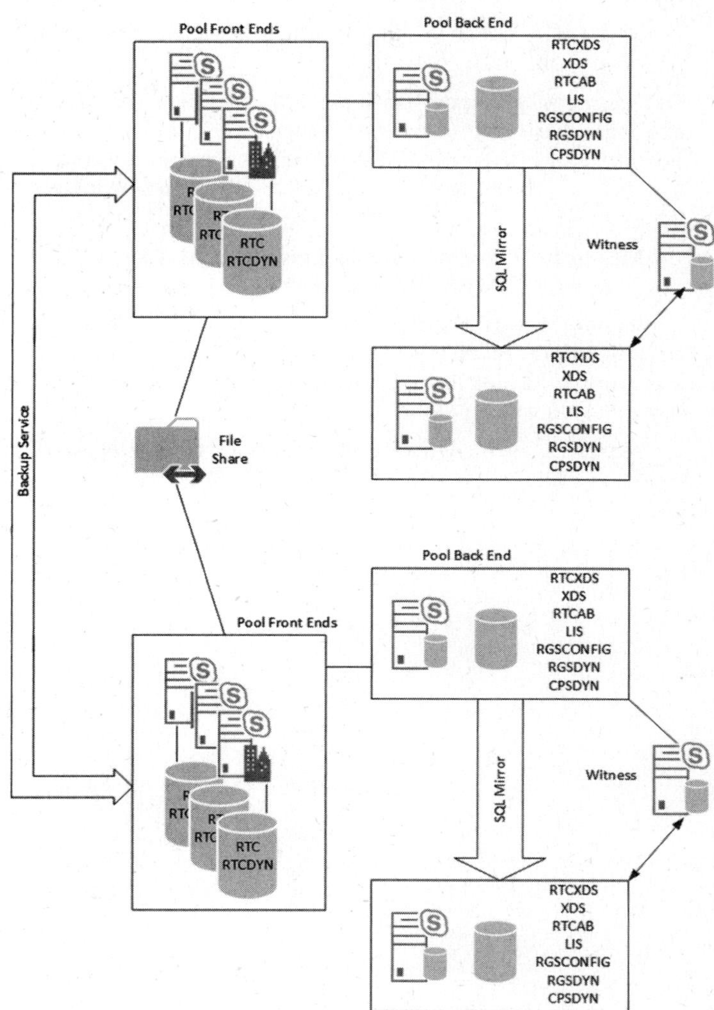

FIGURE 7.16 Skype for Business Backup Service architecture

Settings such as presence are dynamic and as such are not replicated.

Because of this multiple-pool architecture, it's important to scale the pools for the perceived load in a disaster; for this reason, each pool is expected to hold 50 percent of the user base so that in the event of a disaster, 100 percent of the users will be hosted on a single pool and this pool will have the hardware to cope with the scenario.

The Bottom Line

Use the available planning tools. Skype for Business Server 2015 is an extremely complex application, even when only some of the modalities are being used. Being able to plan for capacity, not just the number of servers but also bandwidth, is extremely critical.

Master It Which of the planning toolsets would you use to determine the required bandwidth on the network?

Determine when virtualization is appropriate. Lync Server 2010 introduced support for all modalities when virtualized. Lync Server 2013 has increased the performance capabilities and supported options. Skype for Business builds on this foundation. In certain cases, this enables administrators to reduce the server footprint, giving a better "green computing" deployment.

Master It Describe some of nonsupported features within a virtualization platform when using it with Skype for Business.

Understand the prerequisites. Like most applications, Skype for Business Server 2015 has a number of prerequisites that must be met prior to installation. These range from Active Directory requirements to individual server role requirements, both at the OS level and at the component level.

Master It Which operating systems are supported for deployment of Skype for Business Server 2015?

Chapter 8

Installation

Now you're ready to get up and running with a Skype for Business Server 2015 deployment. If you've already deployed Lync, you'll see that the Skype for Business deployment is extremely similar.

Skype for Business utilizes a central management store (CMS), which holds information about all the roles and settings in the deployment. This is the same approach as used with Lync; Skype for Business also continues to populate Active Directory with configuration information for compatibility with other applications. The benefit of this CMS is that once the topology is defined and published, every installation simply pulls from the defined configuration. This minimizes administrator input and allows for more automated deployment. The CMS has been used since Lync Server 2010 (version ID 5) and continues now with Skype for Business Server 2015 (version ID 7). Once Skype for Business Server 2015 has been introduced to the environment, only the Skype for Business Server 2015 version of the management tools should be used to manage the environment.

Other improvements include the "smart setup" and a wizard by which certificates are requested and deployed.

Like many Microsoft server applications, Skype for Business has a Standard Edition and an Enterprise Edition. The Standard Edition is fully functional but runs on a single server, using a SQL Express back-end database. It is still supported by other roles, such as the Edge, Monitoring, and Archiving roles, some of which would still run on other server installations. The supporting roles don't have a definition of Standard or Enterprise; they simply support the deployed Front End servers.

The Enterprise Edition allows for higher availability and more scalability of the roles to support organizations with hundreds of thousands of users. Both versions of the software can be installed only on a Windows Server 2012 Datacenter or Windows Server 2012 Standard 64-bit operating system (OS) and must be installed on the full GUI version of those OSs rather than the Server Core version.

In this chapter, you will learn to

- Configure Windows Server for a Skype for Business installation.
- Prepare Active Directory for installation.
- Install your first Standard Edition server.
- Implement external access through the Director Edge server.
- Understand the differences in an Enterprise Edition installation.

Getting Up and Running with Skype for Business

In the previous chapters, you explored what Skype for Business is, as well as the client capabilities, so you're familiar with its components and the underlying protocols that enable it to function. Now it's time to get things up and running so you can start to experience Skype for Business hands-on!

As this book goes to print, specific scaling numbers are not yet available for Skype for Business; however, based on that you can upgrade on the same hardware as with Lync Server 2013, we assume these numbers continue to be relevant.

Standard Edition is designed to support up to 2,500 users on its single server, so it is more than capable of supporting an enterprise. However, it doesn't scale beyond those 2,500, and it doesn't provide full high availability (HA). That said, it is perfect for smaller enterprises or branch deployments with significant numbers of users to support. For now, though, Standard Edition provides the best environment to learn the key deployment concepts without needing tons of hardware to support it. This is true in home learning or training class scenarios, although in the more complex scenarios you may need hardware that will enable the progression to enterprise-class deployments.

Be aware that you may read documentation that states 5,000 users on Standard Edition. This is true; however, most companies prefer an Active-Active approach to disaster recovery, and as such the load from one pool fails to the other. Hence, we advise 2,500, allowing for full capacity on a failover.

Preparing Active Directory

Active Directory (AD) is critical to your network. It is the central authentication point, so any changes to it should be carried out with appropriate care and attention. As with other Microsoft server applications, Skype for Business makes significant changes to AD as part of the setup. There are three key elements to these changes. First, the schema is extended with classes and attributes in which to store information about Skype for Business and its users. Second, the forest is prepared; it creates global settings and universal groups that are used in the management of Skype for Business. Finally, each domain where Skype for Business users or servers will be deployed must be prepared. Let's look at each stage in more depth.

THE SCHEMA

Schema preparation is run against the holder of the schema master Flexible Single Master Operation (FSMO). That doesn't actually mean you must be running at the console of the box, but you do need to be a member of the Schema Administrators group and the Enterprise Administrators group in the root domain.

In this simple installation of Standard Edition, you will be running in a single-forest, single-domain model, and the installation will be carried out as the default administrator, so no worries there. Later in the chapter, we will discuss what happens in more complex AD environments, where permissions are heavily locked down or where different teams will be managing AD and Skype for Business.

As you learned in Chapter 7, most of the configuration information is now stored in the CMS; however; there is still some information written into AD. The schema extension adds attributes to user objects to store information such as the SIP Uniform Resource Indicator (URI) of a user (the Skype for Business equivalent of an email address).

There are two ways to extend the schema during installation. One is through the Skype for Business Setup program; the other is through the command line. The cmdlets that handle this are installed as part of the Administrative Tools package during the Topology Builder installation.

At this point, let's prepare the schema. You will use the Deployment Wizard for this and come back to the cmdlets later in the chapter when we talk about automating setup.

Remote Server Administration Tools

When you're running the AD prep steps from a non–domain controller, you will need to ensure that the AD administration tools are installed. These can be installed by using the PowerShell command Add-WindowsFeature RSAT-ADDS or by using the Add Roles and Features Wizard in Server Manager.

1. Run `setup.exe` from within the install media's `\Setup\amd64` directory. See "Installing the Standard Edition Server " later in this chapter for details of the initial setup process; at this stage, follow the prompts to land at the home page of the Deployment Wizard, shown in Figure 8.1.

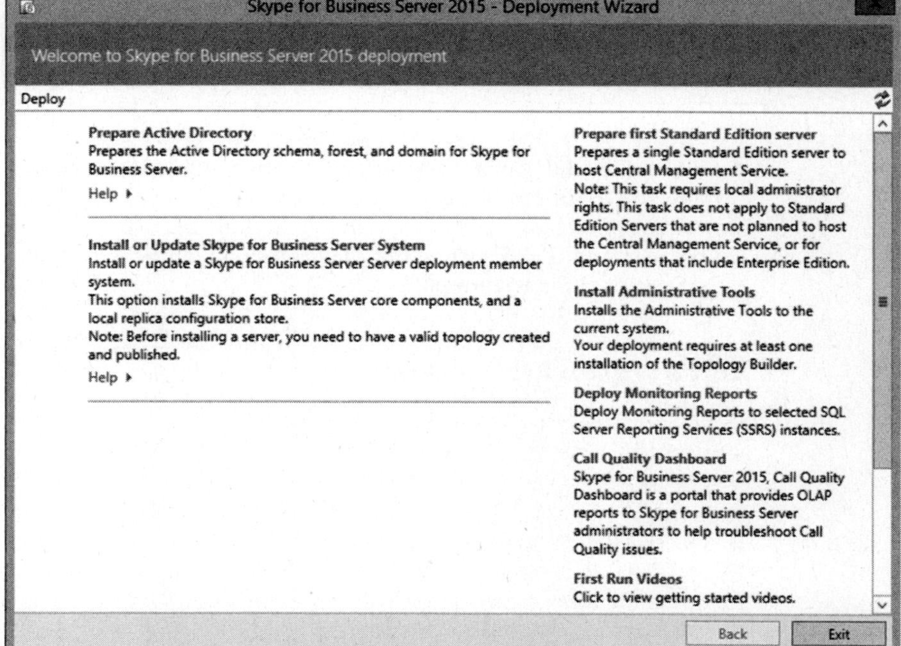

Figure 8.1 The Deployment Wizard home page, from which all setup activities are run

2. On the home page, click Prepare Active Directory, which will take you to the area where all the AD preparation tasks are chosen. In the Prepare Schema section, click Run to kick off the Schema Prep process.
3. Go through the wizard, clicking Next to reach the next page. This will take only a minute at most in this exercise.

On completion, you will see a summary screen of the cmdlet that ran in the background, allowing you to view the log of the process. This Skype for Business Server PowerShell cmdlet is as follows:

```
Install-CSAdServerSchema
```

As long as there are no warnings shown on the summary screen, there is no need to check the log unless you want to know a little more about what happened during the process.

If you do want to check the log, click the View Log button next to the drop-down, which will allow you to select a log based on the activity you want to investigate. The log will open in the web browser. If you are using an older version of Internet Explorer, you may need to click Allow Blocked Content to explore the log. Click Expand All Actions at the top right of the page to see details of the log.

It's All PowerShell

As mentioned, a PowerShell cmdlet ran in the background during the schema-extension process. As you will see in Appendix B, Skype for Business is entirely controlled through PowerShell. The GUI simply calls the relevant cmdlets and indeed does not expose all the PowerShell cmdlets; some capability is available only via PowerShell.

4. If you click the Log button, the log will open in Internet Explorer (IE). You may need to allow IE to run the blocked content, at which point you will be able to click Expand All Actions in the top right of the window to show the entire file. Once satisfied, close the browser and click Finish in the wizard to complete Schema Preparation and return to the AD preparation wizard page.

Check Schema Replication

In our small lab with one domain controller (DC), checking replication is irrelevant because there are no other DCs with which to talk. However, in a larger AD, it is critical to ensure that replication of the schema changes has occurred on all DCs before moving on to the forest preparation.

To do this, log into a server as a member of the Enterprise Admins group and then load `asdiedit.msc`. Note that ADSI Edit is not installed by default and comes either with the Windows Server 2003 resource kit tools or as part of the RSAT-ADDS tools on Windows Server 2008 or newer systems. In the Action menu, click Connect To. In the Connection Settings dialog box under Select A Well Known Naming Context, select Schema, and then click OK.

Under the schema container, search for `CN=ms-RTC-SIP-SchemaVersion`. If this object exists and the value of the `rangeUpper` attribute is 1150 and the value of the `rangeLower` attribute is 3, then the schema was successfully updated and replicated. If not, wait a little longer for replication to occur.

These range values are the same for Lync Server 2013, indicating there are no changes with the schema since Lync Server 2013.

THE FOREST

Now that the schema has been extended, it is time to prepare the forest in which Skype for Business is to be installed. The AD *forest* is a collection of trees (which contain domains) that share a common global catalog and directory schema. The forest represents the security boundary within which users, computers, groups, and other objects reside.

The process of forest preparation is what creates the permission structure by which Skype for Business is managed. It creates a bunch of universal groups, whose names all start with the characters *RTC* and *CS*. These groups are combined to provide administrative rights over Skype for Business objects and are shown in Table 8.1.

TABLE 8.1: RTC and CS groups created by ForestPrep

RTC GROUPS	CS GROUPS
RTCComponentUniversalServices	CSAdministrator
RTCHSUniversalServices	CSArchivingAdministrator
RTCProxyUniversalServices	CSHelpDesk
RTCSBAUniversalServices	CSLocationAdministrator
RTCUniversalConfigReplicator	CSPersistentChatAdministrator
RTCUniversalGlobalReadOnlyGroup	CSResponseGroupAdministrator
RTCUniversalGlobalWriteGroup	CSResponseGroupManager
RTCUniversalReadOnlyAdmins	CSServerAdministrator
RTCUniversalSBATechnicians	CSUserAdministrator
RTCUniversalServerAdmins	CSViewOnlyAdministrator
RTCUniversalServerReadOnlyGroup	CSVoiceAdministrator
RTCUniversalUserAdmins	
RTCUniversalReadOnlyGroup	

The group CSPersistentChatAdministrator was created with a lowercase s in CS by the Lync Server 2013 Forest Prep process. This has now been corrected in the Skype for Business version.

This is covered in much more depth in Chapter 11, "Role-Based Access Control." The forest prep also creates various objects in the configuration partition of AD, which is replicated to all domain controllers in the forest.

> **THE CONFIG PARTITION**
>
> The config partition is used as a store of information, which is readily available to all DCs because it is part of the information set of which all DCs hold a replica. In Office Communications Server (OCS) 2007, this configuration information was by default stored in the System container in the root domain of the forest; however, this often caused issues in large distributed ADs where access to the root forest was slow. Therefore, in OCS 2007 R2, the default was changed to the configuration store, and this is maintained in Lync.

Because you ran the Schema Preparation from the setup GUI, you will run the forest preparation in the same way. Again, you need to be a member of the Enterprise Admins group, but this time not Schema Admins. You will continue running as the default administrator.

1. Either run `setup.exe` again, if you closed it after Schema Prep, or carry on from where you left off. This time click Run in the Prepare Current Forest section of the wizard to start the process. Once the wizard starts, follow through with the defaults. Notice that there is an option to specify a different domain in which to create the universal groups; however, for now there will be only the single domain. We will cover this further in the section "Executing Enterprise Deployments" later in this chapter. You'll notice the Skype for Business Server PowerShell cmdlet used for this stage is as follows:

```
Enable-CSAdForest
```

2. Once the wizard completes, you must recheck replication. This time there is a cmdlet to do this. Open the Skype for Business Server Management Shell by navigating through Start ➢ All Programs ➢ Skype for Business Server 2015 ➢ Skype For Business Server Management Shell. Run the following cmdlet:

```
Get-CsAdForest
```

This will check that your Active Directory forest has been correctly configured to allow installation of Skype for Business Server 2015. As long as the output is as shown here, you are fine to proceed.

```
LC_FORESTSETTINGS_STATE_READY
```

3. If you want more detail about what the `Get-CsAdForest` cmdlet has checked, run the following command to output results to the log file specified:

```
Get-CsAdForest -Report C:\ForestPrep.html
```

This outputs a log file in HTML format that you can open in your browser, and it looks something like Figure 8.2.

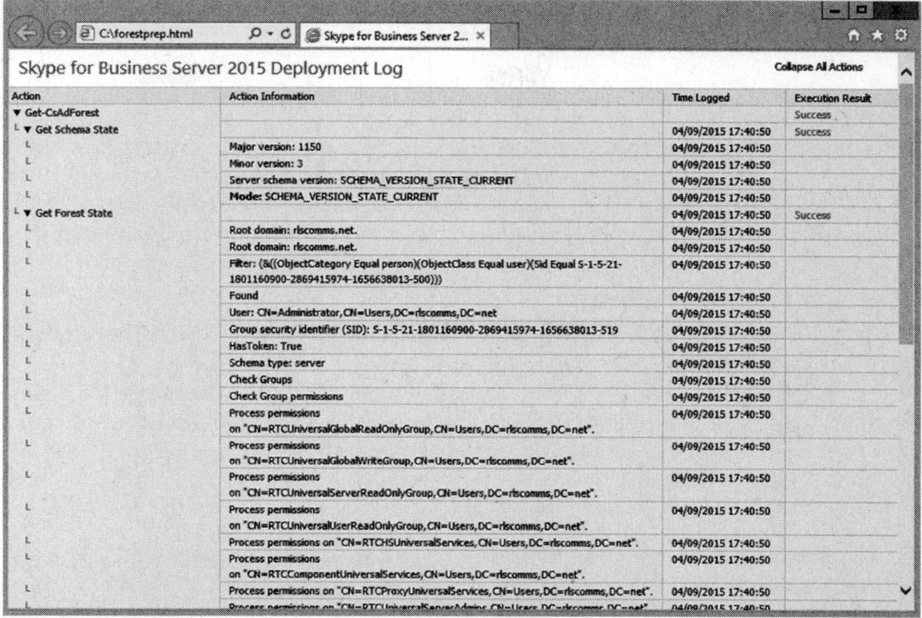

FIGURE 8.2 The deployment log file shows the steps to verify forest prep.

For detailed information about PowerShell and Skype for Business, see Appendix B.

THE DOMAIN

The final step in AD preparation is the domain preparation. This step must be carried out in every domain with Skype for Business users and servers. To run domain prep, you must be either an enterprise admin or a domain admin in the domain being prepared.

The access control entries (ACEs) that allow members of the RTC groups to manage Skype for Business objects and manipulate user objects in the domain are actually created during domain preparation. The permissions are set on the default containers, users, and domain controllers and at the root of the domain.

Again, this step can be run either through the shell or through the setup GUI:

1. Continuing from the completion of forest prep, you should be back in the AD Prep home page section of the Setup application. To start domain prep, click Run in the Prepare Current Domain section of the page. Run through the wizard, selecting the defaults and clicking Next to progress and Finish to end. You'll notice the Skype for Business Server PowerShell cmdlet used for this stage is as follows:

```
Enable-CSAdDomain
```

2. At this point, you once again need to check that things have completed correctly. Run the following command:

```
Get-CsAdDomain -Report "C:\DomainPrepReport.html"
```

This will check the domain prep steps and output a report with the `Get-CsAdForest` cmdlet. The expected output is as follows:

```
LC_DOMAINSETTINGS_STATE_READY
```

Assuming this all checks out, you are ready to move on. If things didn't quite work, your next step will be to leave more time for replication; if that doesn't work, then try rerunning the preparatory steps. If this still isn't successful, then use the logs to localize the area of failure. To identify more ways of fixing common problems, see Chapter 15, "Troubleshooting."

Topology Builder

Once Active Directory is ready, the next stage is defining the Skype for Business topology—the configuration that is stored in the CMS.

Topology Builder is the first deployment tool from the Skype for Business installation media that you will probably use and is part of the Administration Tools installation. We won't detail each step here because it's straightforward; however, see Figure 8.3 for the process to the start the installation.

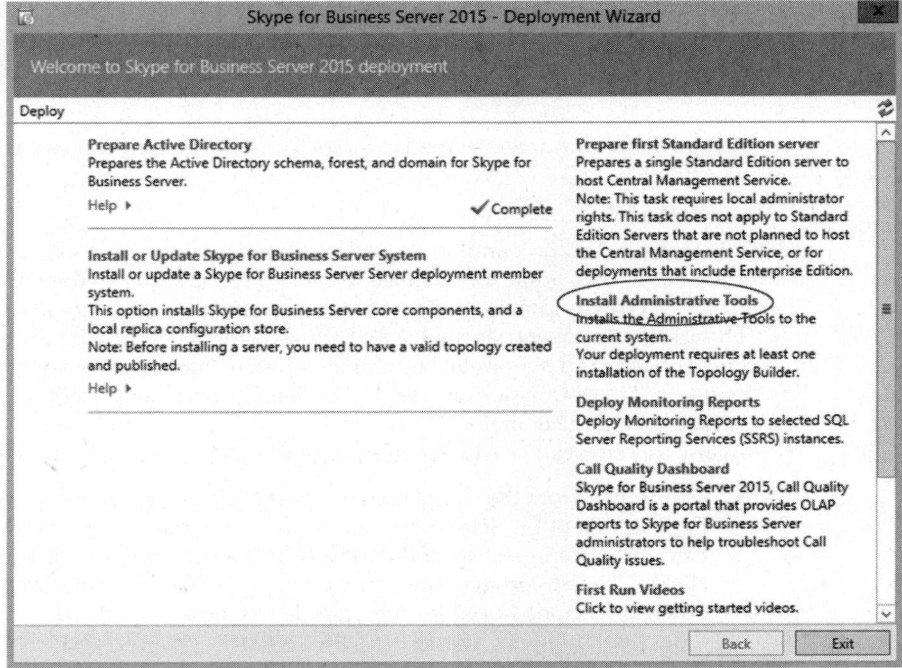

FIGURE 8.3 Installing the Administrative Tools

When you get to this stage, the planning should be complete (unless, of course, this is a test or development environment). This stage is where you define the architecture for your deployment; it is also where the first automated checks are performed.

The Chicken or the Egg?

Once you have planned your topology, you need to run Topology Builder, and once you've input the topology, you need to publish it into the CMS, which is a SQL database. However, the CMS must be in place prior to publishing, and you can't create the CMS until you have defined a SQL database in the topology.

Fortunately, there is a way to get around this chicken-or-egg scenario. Run `setup.exe` to go to the Deployment Wizard screen shown in Figure 8.4. On it you will find an item labeled Prepare First Standard Edition Server, which if selected will install the CMS portion into a SQL Express instance on the server on which it is run.

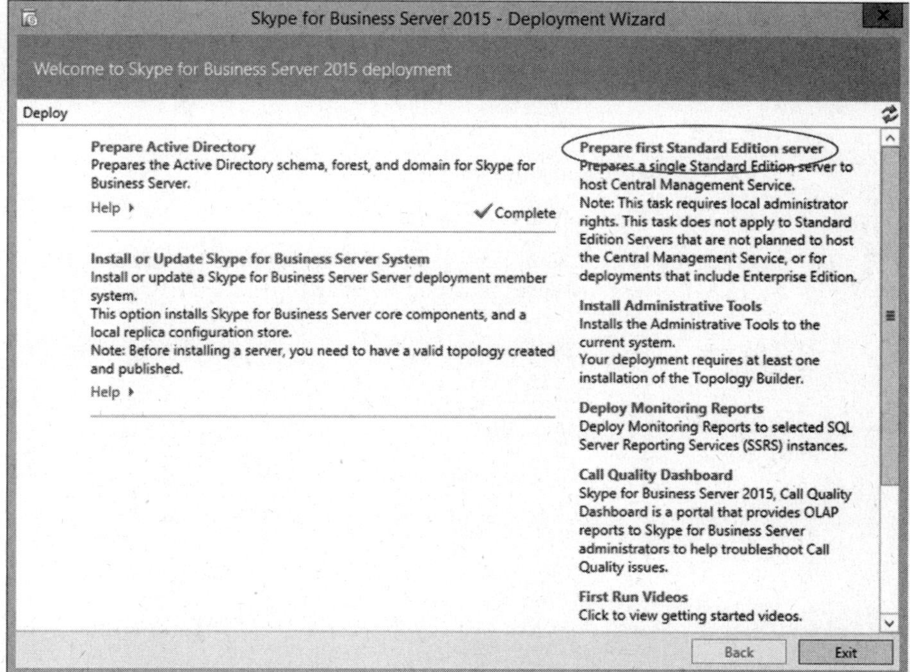

Figure 8.4 The Deployment Wizard includes the option Prepare First Standard Edition Server.

What about high availability in an Enterprise Edition deployment? Here you have two options. If the plan is to start with a pilot where you are deploying a Standard Edition server first, you could choose Prepare First Standard Edition Server. When it's time to move to production, define and publish the SQL Server instance and then move the CMS to it.

Or you could create the Enterprise pool as the initial pool and deploy to that using Topology Builder, although with additional options available for an Enterprise pool, we find it easier to start simple and then move up.

As an alternative, you could use Skype for Business PowerShell to install and create the database, as the following cmdlet shows:

```
Install-CsDatabase -CentralManagementDatabase
-SqlServerFqdn <FQDN of SQL Server> -SqlInstanceName <named instance>
```

```
-DatabasePaths <logfile path>,<database file path>
-Report <path to report file>
```

Then, when you want to define the topology, the location is already defined, and the database has already been created.

Preparing for CMS

Selecting Prepare First Standard Edition Server (shown in Figure 8.4) will take you to the wizard. On the next page, no configuration options are given; just simply clicking Next will begin the installation process of the SQL Express instance, which will store the CMS.

The installation process carries out the following tasks:

- Prerequisites check
- Cache installation files
- Additional prerequisites checks
- SQL Express installation
- Windows firewall rules update

Once the wizard completes, looking at the services installed on the server will show you that the SQL Express instance created and installed is called `RTC` (as shown in Figure 8.5).

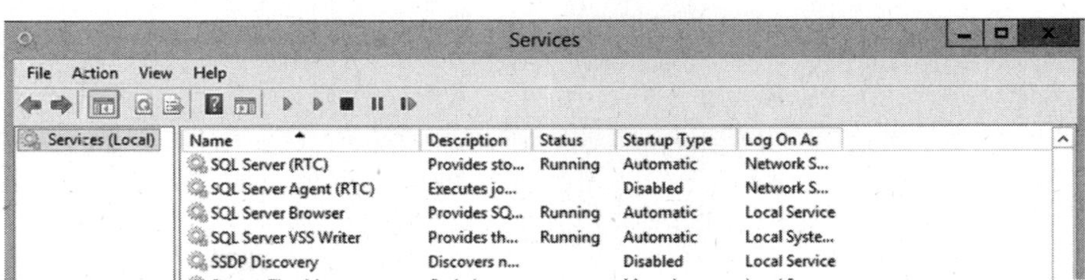

Figure 8.5 The SQL Express service installed and running

When completed, you don't need to run this portion of Setup again on any other servers. If you do, all it will do is leave you with an empty SQL Express installation.

> **Preparing the First Standard Edition Server Might Take a While**
>
> You may well find that the preparatory steps take a while, even as long as 10 to 15 minutes on slower systems, while nothing much seems to be happening on the console. Don't worry at this point! If you are really concerned, fire up Task Manager and take a look at the following processes:
>
> ```
> Deploy.exe
> TrustedInstaller.exe
> Setup.exe
> SQLEXPR_x64.exe
> ```
>
> You will find that these processes require a fluctuating amount of CPU resources and that the memory consumed by the `Setup100.exe` and `SQLsrv.exe` processes grows.
>
> As long as you see these fluctuations, all is well, and you should just keep waiting.

The preparation process not only installs SQL but ensures that remote computers have access to it; that access is provided by creating relevant firewall rules using the following NetSH commands:

```
> Creating firewall exception for SQL instance
netsh advfirewall firewall add rule name=" SQL RTC Access"
dir=in action=allow program="c:\Program Files\Microsoft SQL
 Server\MSSQL14.RTC\MSSQL\Binn\sqlservr.exe"
enable=yes profile=any
> Creating firewall exception for SQL Browser
netsh advfirewall firewall add rule name="SQL Browser" dir=in
action=allow protocol=UDP localport=1434
```

Using Topology Builder

Although Topology Builder is used to configure, the largest part of its job is to define, *check*, and publish the topology. This ability to check the topology offers a significant advantage over what was available with Office Communications Server.

By verifying that the configuration and dependencies are in place *prior* to making any changes, you can achieve an additional, higher level of verification of your changes. For example, Topology Builder will not let you delete a database or share a file that is still being used. (Of course, it can't stop someone from going to the server itself and deleting the database or share. However, even if someone did that, there would still be a record of what it should be.)

In addition to the checks carried out, after publishing, Topology Builder will provide a to-do list of actions to be carried out and the servers on which they need to performed (see Figure 8.6).

Figure 8.6
To-do list

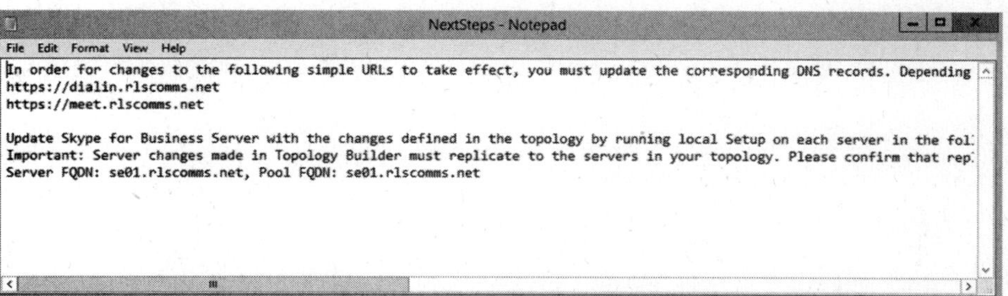

Publishing Multiple Changes with Topology Builder

The to-do list is an extremely useful feature because it provides the next set of steps (rerun setup, request new certificates, and so on) required to complete any configuration changes.

One thing to note is that no records of the completed actions are kept. For example, if you make a change to the SIP addresses supported in the organization, there will be a reminder to request new certificates for each Front End server (and possibly Directors and Edge servers, if they are in the environment). If you remove (or add) the Mediation Server role to a specific Front End server before updating the certificates, the to-do list will report only the last change (the specific Front End server), and the need to request new certificates may be lost.

Therefore, we recommend you make all your changes in a single topology publishing step.

When you start Topology Builder, it opens with the dialog shown in Figure 8.7. Here you are prompted with the following options for dealing with the topology:

Download Topology From Existing Deployment This option will read the topology from Active Directory.

Open Topology From A Local File This option will read a topology from a file.

New Topology This option will create a blank topology to work with.

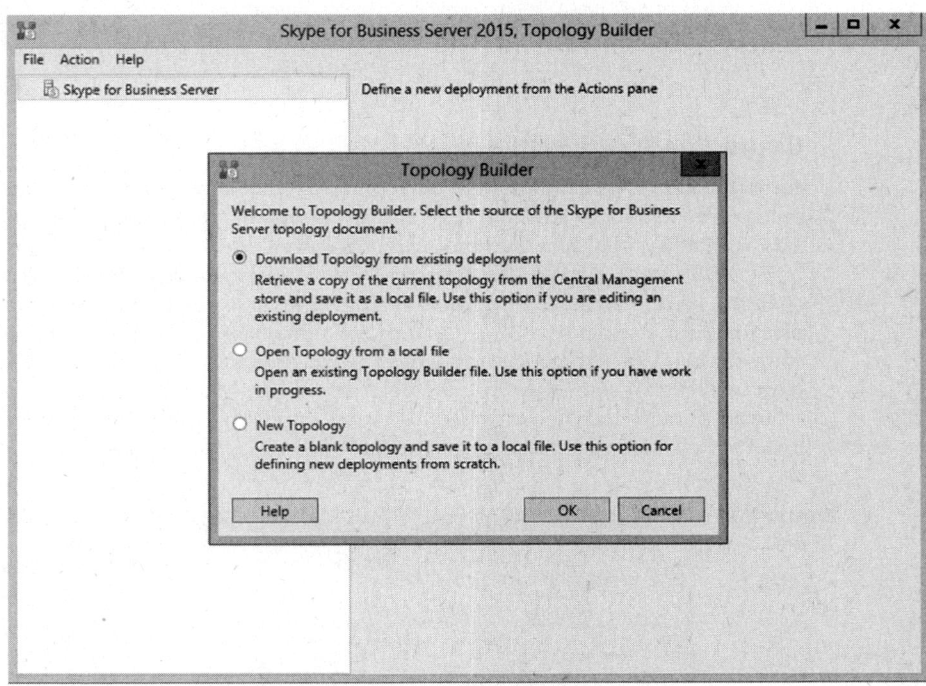

FIGURE 8.7 Starting Topology Builder

Whichever option you choose, the next window prompts for a filename; this is used to save the work in progress and any changes, prior to *publishing* the topology. Publishing the topology commits those changes.

Topology Builder comprises a number of wizards, one for each role. The following lists show the information captured by each wizard. In addition, where a wizard is dependent upon another role (for example, the Enterprise pool requires SQL and a file share), it is possible to launch the New Role Wizard from within the running wizard; there is no need to predefine all the dependencies prior to running a wizard.

When creating a new topology, you're going to be first prompted for generic information such as the following:

- Primary SIP domain (required)
- Additional support SIP domains
- First site definition

- Name (required)
- Description
- City
- State/province
- Country/region code

Once the required fields are defined, Topology Builder will begin to prompt to run the wizard for creating a pool.

We won't go into all the configuration specifics of each role here but will cover them when we talk about the installation of roles later in this chapter.

Until you have the first pool defined, you are not able to *publish* the topology (which means saving it to the CMS and replicating it around the environment). Figure 8.8 shows how to initiate the publishing process.

FIGURE 8.8 Publishing the topology

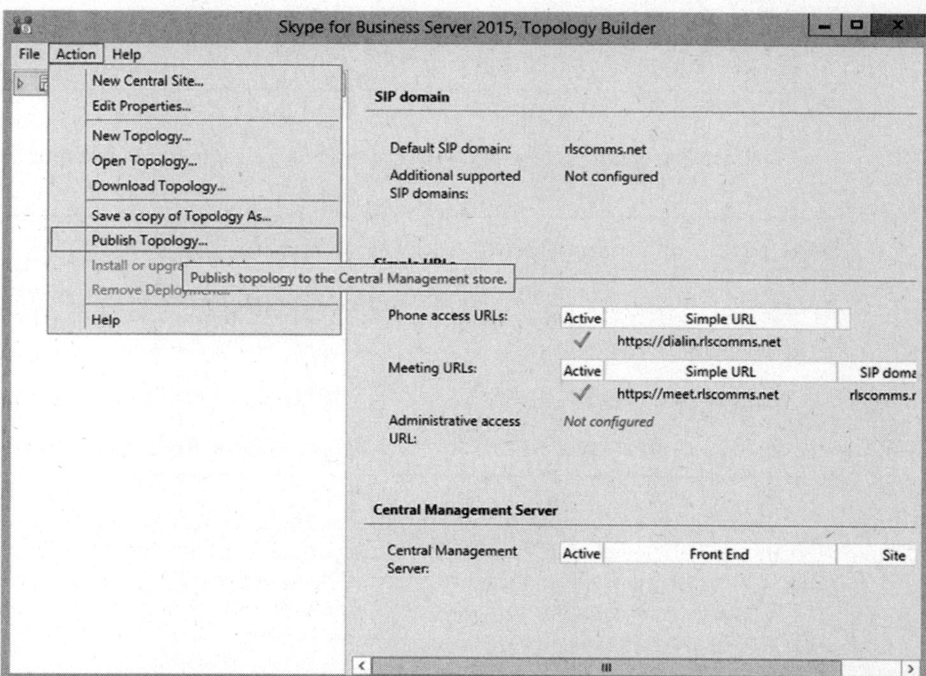

It's at this point the topology checks are carried out and potentially further information is requested. This may be drive locations for SQL databases or a network share to be used for temporary files when enabling the SQL mirroring process (see Chapter 20 for details on this configuration).

Once the checks succeed, then the topology is published and changes replicated are around the existing server environment. Any updates required to servers are highlighted in the to-do list mentioned earlier.

A status report is provided for viewing if necessary to investigate errors or warnings.

Configuring Windows Server 2012

The first step to installing Skype for Business is to prepare the supporting server OS with the prerequisites to support Skype for Business. In Chapter 5, we touched on the major elements required from a planning point of view, such as OS version support and capacity planning. Here we will discuss the specifics required on each server before you can proceed with the installation.

OS Support

At the start of this chapter, we stated that installation is supported only on Windows Server 2012 or 2012 R2. That's not strictly true.

Skype for Business is also supported on Windows Server 2008 R2; however, this version of Windows has come out of mainstream support, and updates to Windows Fabric in Windows Server 2012 (and 2012 R2) provide significant advantages to using a later version of the OS to install on.

For the bulk of this chapter, we will concentrate on installing on Windows Server 2012 R2, which is the latest version of Windows supported at the time of writing.

Table 8.2 lists the prerequisite patches needed for each of the different OS options.

Table 8.2: Prerequisites for each OS

OS	KB article
Windows Server 2008 R2	`http://support.microsoft.com/kb/2533623`
Windows Server 2012	`http://support.microsoft.com/kb/2858668`
Windows Server 2012 R2	`http://support.microsoft.com/kb/2982006`

Depending on the specific configuration at the time of applying the patch, additional prerequisites may be needed. (Typically Windows Update will do most of the patches.)

The software prerequisites differ for the various roles. The prerequisites for the Standard Edition server are similar to those for the Director and Front End server roles used in enterprise deployments. We will discuss the specific requirements of each role as we show how to install it in this and later chapters.

The prerequisites fall into a few different areas. The first requirement is the .NET Framework v4.5; it is required because Skype for Business is written as *managed code*, a program that will run only under Common Language Runtime. For more information, see the wiki page at the following location:

```
http://en.wikipedia.org/wiki/Managed_code
```

Second is the Microsoft Visual C++ 12 x64 Runtime requirement, with a minimum version number of 12.0.21005. Fortunately, the Setup program will install this if it is not already installed.

Third is Windows Identity Foundation, which can be installed using the Add Roles And Features option from within Server Manager.

The next area of software to install is IIS 8 (on Server 2012). Skype for Business has many elements that use IIS, which provides access to the Address Book, client updates, meeting content that is stored in the file store and exposed to users via a virtual directory in IIS on the Front End servers, and of course the Meet, Dial-in, and Admin URLs, which provide access to conferences, the dial-in conferencing settings, and the Skype for Business Control Panel.

Table 8.3 lists the IIS modules required by Standard Edition.

TABLE 8.3 IIS modules required by Standard Edition

MODULE	DESCRIPTION
`Web-Static-Content`	Static content
`Web-Default-Doc`	Default document
`Web-Http-Errors`	HTTP errors
`Web-Asp-Net`	ASP.NET
`Web-Net-Ext`	.NET extensibility version 3.5
`Web-ISAPI-Ext`	Internet Server API (ISAPI) extensions
`Web-ISAPI-Filter`	ISAPI filters
`Web-Http-Logging`	HTTP logging
`Web-Log-Libraries`	Logging tools
`Web-Http-Tracing`	Tracing
`Web-Client-Auth`	Client certificate mapping authentication
`Web-Windows-Auth`	Windows authentication
`Web-Filtering`	Request filtering
`Web-Stat-Compression`	Static content compression
`Web-Dyn-Compression`	Dynamic content compression
`Web-Mgmt-Console`	IIS management console
`Web-Scripting-Tools`	IIS management scripts and tools
`Web-Asp-NET45`	.NET extensibility version 4.5
`NET-WCF-HTTP-Activation45`	Windows Communication Foundation (WCF) web activation

As well as the IIS components, Windows Communication Foundation requires some components to be installed:

- NET-WCF-HTTP-Activation45: Windows Communication Foundation (WCF) web activation
- NET-WCF-TCP-PortSharing: Installed by default

Finally, some elements are required in specific cases. If your Front End (FE) or Standard Edition server is going to run conferences and you intend to provide music on hold, you will also need the Windows Media Foundation Feature or Desktop Experience (as well as deploying an Office Web Apps server; see Chapter 22).

A Lab to Follow

If you want to follow along with this chapter but don't think you will be able to because the specs are so high, don't worry!

Here is what will work (and what we used to write this book): we have a single laptop-class tower machine, with an Intel Core i7 Quad Core CPU and 16GB of RAM, running Windows 10 with Hyper-V.

This formed the platform for deployment and testing. We ran a domain controller, Exchange, Skype for Business, SQL, and clients on this system, with a single virtual CPU allocated to each. The Standard Edition server that we are about to install had 4GB of RAM. Supporting roles had 2GB of RAM, and the DC had a single CPU and 1GB of RAM. SQL had 2GB of RAM. Only servers used for the specific piece of deployment were enabled at that time to ensure that the memory requirements were suitable.

For the federation content, we duplicated this environment.

No, that isn't the supported minimum, and it won't let you run many users, but it works nicely for learning, whether in a training class or at home. To prepare the server on which you plan to install Standard Edition, you will need to log into the server as at least a local administrator. For this exercise, you will perform the steps as the built-in domain administrator account. We will discuss more complex systems where different accounts have different rights later.

The server should already be running Windows Server 2012 R2, and it should be joined to your test domain and have all the latest Microsoft Update patches installed.

Be Safe, Segregate!

Please don't install Skype for Business for the first time in your production network. This has a great chance of becoming a resume-generating event (RGE). A Skype for Business installation will make significant changes to your Active Directory schema that can't be undone. It also creates a bunch of groups and ACLs/ACEs on many objects in your forest, so you should create a safe environment in which to learn by spinning up a test lab.

As you have just seen, preparing the server for installing Skype for Business requires various pieces of software. The Deployment Wizard will actually install some of them automatically if they are not in place; however, many must be manually configured.

NOTE We like to use PowerShell to do these installations because they can be done with a couple of simple commands, and all prerequisites can be installed in a simple script.

For Windows Server 2012 R2, there are a few ways to install .NET Framework 4.5, including through the GUI's Server Manager Features section or through PowerShell. To perform the installation using PowerShell, you must open Windows PowerShell as an administrator. Assuming you are logged on as an administrator, type **PowerShell** in the Start menu search area and click the result, the Windows PowerShell command shell. (You may want to skip to Appendix B if you need an introduction. You'll use PowerShell for numerous installation tasks in this chapter.)

Once in PowerShell, follow these steps:

1. Run the following command:

```
Add-WindowsFeature NET-Framework-Core
```

This installs the core .NET Framework code needed.

Now that the non-OS-specific prerequisites have been installed, you can start with the web components listed earlier. These can be installed in a single PowerShell command.

2. To install all the required web and .NET elements, use the following command:

```
Add-WindowsFeature, Web-Static-Content, Web-Default-Doc,
Web-Http-Errors, Web-Asp-Net, Web-Net-Ext, Web-ISAPI-Ext,
Web-ISAPI-Filter, Web-Http-Logging, Web-Log-Libraries,
Web-Http-Tracing,Web-Windows-Auth, Web-Filtering,
Web-Stat-Compression, Web-Dyn-Compression, Web-Mgmt-Console,
Web-Scripting-Tools, Web-Client-Auth, Web-Asp-Net45,
Net-HTTP-Activation, Net-WCF-HTTP-Activation45
```

Having run the previous command, you should check the output, which should be as shown here:

```
Success Restart Needed Exit Code Feature Result
------- -------------- --------- --------------
True    No             Success   {IIS Management Scripts and Tools,
IIS Man...
```

3. Windows Identity Foundation is installed using the following:

```
Add-WindowsFeature Windows-Identity-Foundation
```

4. At this point, all the required IIS components should be installed on your Lync server. This just leaves RSAT-ADDS, which can be installed with the following command:

```
Add-WindowsFeature RSAT-ADDS
```

Running this command will give you slightly more detailed output than the web component installation because you are warned that a reboot is needed.

```
WARNING: [Installation] Succeeded: [Remote Server Administration Tools] AD DS
Snap-Ins and Command-Line Tools. You must restart this server to finish the
installation process.
WARNING: [Installation] Succeeded: [Remote Server Administration Tools] Server
for NIS Tools. You must restart this server to finish the installation process.
WARNING: [Installation] Succeeded: [Remote Server Administration Tools] Active
Directory module for Windows PowerShell. You must restart this server to finish
the installation process.
WARNING: [Installation] Succeeded: [Remote Server Administration Tools] Active
Directory Administrative Center. You must restart this server to finish the
installation process.
Success Restart Needed Exit Code Feature Result
------- -------------- --------- --------------
True    Yes            Succes... {AD DS Snap-Ins and Command-Line
Tools, Se...
```

Automating the Reboot

You have seen that a reboot is needed. If you don't want to wait and manually reboot, you can add the `-restart` parameter to the command to make the system reboot immediately after completing the RSAT-ADDS install.

5. Now that you have installed .NET, ADDS tools, and the web components, reboot the server.

The last piece of preparation needed is to install the Windows Media Foundation Feature or Desktop Experience.

The Desktop Experience is a Windows feature and can be added in the same way as the IIS components.

```
Add-WindowsFeature Desktop-Experience
```

This will also add the dependency for Ink Support, and a reboot is required.

That is nearly all the prep work that needs to be done manually. All you must do now is run Windows Update again to check for any updates and ensure that the system is fully patched.

You are now ready to start the Skype for Business setup process. Throughout the setup, additional pieces of supporting software will be installed.

Running `setup.exe` will result in the screen shown in Figure 8.9 being displayed, and assuming you click Yes, the Visual C++ Runtime will be installed. Once the Runtime is installed, the Setup application will launch.

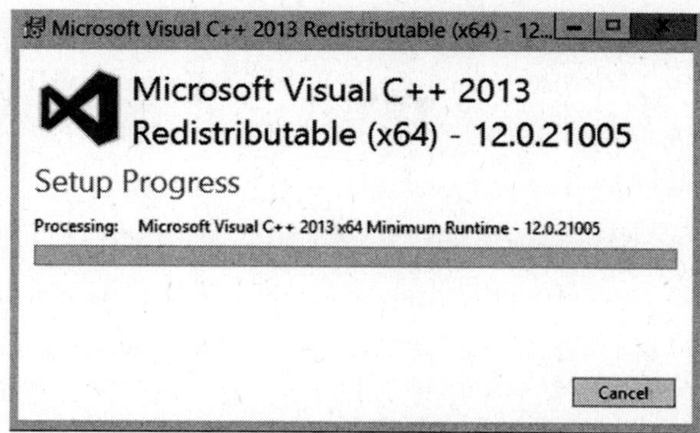

FIGURE 8.9 Automatic installation of Microsoft Visual C++ Runtime by the Setup application

If, for example, you've run Setup to install Topology Builder, this will already be installed. As part of the rest of Skype for Business installation, these other elements will be installed:

- IIS URL Rewrite Module 2
- Microsoft Identity Extensions
- Microsoft ODBC Driver 11 for SQL Server
- Microsoft Server Speech Platform Runtime (x64)
- Microsoft Server Speech Test to Speech Voice (various installations for regional accents/languages)
- Microsoft Server Speech Recognition Language (various installations for regional accents/languages)
- Microsoft SQL Server 2008 Setup Support Files
- Microsoft SQL Server 2012 Native Client
- Microsoft SQL Server 2014 (64-bit)
- Microsoft SQL Server 2014 Management Objects (x64)
- Microsoft SQL Server 2014 Setup (English)
- Microsoft SQL Server 2014 Transact-SQL ScriptDm
- Microsoft System CLR Type for SQL Server 2014
- Microsoft Unified Communications Managed API 5.0, Core Runtime 64-bit
- Microsoft Unified Communications Managed API 5.0, Windows Workflow Activities Runtime 64-bit
- Microsoft Visual C++ 2010 x64 Redistributable – 10.0.40219
- Microsoft Visual C++ 2010 x86 Redistributable – 10.0.40219

- Microsoft Visual C++ 2012 Redistributable (x64) – 11.0.50727
- Microsoft Visual C++ 2013 Redistributable (x64) – 12.0.21005
- Microsoft VSS Writer for SQL Server 2014
- SQL Server Browser for SQL Server 2014
- Windows Fabric
- Skype for Business components (varies based on the role installed)

Most of them are not likely to cause any problems with your server team; for example, Visual C++ is simply a programming interface that allows Skype for Business to operate.

However, you may notice that SQL Server Express and its client pieces are installed, which may cause your SQL team some concern. SQL Express is installed on each Skype for Business server and is part of the replication and data storage mechanism used to ensure that each server has a local copy of the CMS. For more information about the CMS and its replication, see Chapter 7. You may need to discuss the SQL and Skype for Business Server requirements with your database administrators (DBAs).

Installing the Standard Edition Server

As you learned earlier, the installation is driven by the topology you define using Topology Builder and publish to the CMS.

Let's define and publish a topology with a single Standard Edition server. Once that is done, you can begin the actual installation.

PERMISSIONS

In these exercises, we are running all the steps as the default domain administrator account. It has Schema, Enterprise, and Domain admin rights, which give full access to allow the setup to be performed. Later in the process, we will create a specific administrative account, which we will use to administer Skype for Business. Later in the chapter, the section "Executing Enterprise Deployments" covers environments where permissions are locked down more tightly.

At this point, you have one final task to perform before returning to Topology Builder to update and publish the topology. You must set up the file share, which Skype for Business will use, depending on configuration, to store some or all of the following elements:

- Application server files
- Archiving server
- CMS file store
- Web services (including elements such as the Address Book files, meeting content, and device updates)

Multiple pools (in the same site) can share the same file share. You'll learn more about this later in this chapter.

UPDATING THE TOPOLOGY AND CREATING THE CMS

To update the topology, follow these steps:

1. On the Skype for Business server, open Topology Builder (this should have been installed earlier to prepare Active Directory).
2. When you open Topology Builder, you are prompted to load a topology by doing one of the following:
   - Downloading from a CMS
   - Opening from a saved file
   - Creating a new topology

   The first time, select Create A New Topology. Once Topology Builder opens, you can define the pools and other resources as required. At this point, you need to publish the topology to the CMS, but you haven't actually created the CMS yet.

   If you're making changes to an existing topology, select Download Topology.
3. Navigate to the site in which you want to create the pool (or resource), open the Skype For Business Server 2015 item, and then select the relevant component. With a right-click, select New XXXX, where XXXX is the name of the component you are creating. In this case, now it's labeled New Front End Pool.
4. Follow the wizard prompts to complete the configuration.
5. Publish the topology.

On the first publish of topology, the CMS has not yet been populated, so you will be prompted for the location for which to install, as shown in Figure 8.10.

FIGURE 8.10 Selecting the location for the CMS

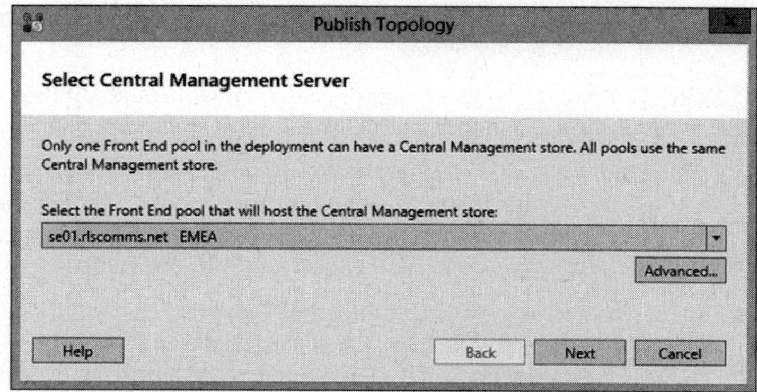

Because you are publishing with only a single pool and it's a Standard Edition pool, there is only the one location it can be stored. Clicking the Advanced button allows you to provide specific configuration information to SQL (which may be needed in an Enterprise pool installation; see Chapter 20 for further information).

DNS Entries

Before publishing the topology, you must make sure all servers are available. One aspect of this is setting up the relevant DNS entries. These entries are detailed in Chapter 7; however, the basics are that you need an A record for the FQDN of the Standard Edition server and SRV records to enable automatic sign-in for each SIP domain.

A = `se01.rlscomms.net` = IP of the Standard Edition server

SRV = `_sipinternaltls._tcp.rlscomms.net` over port 5061 that maps to the FQDN of the Standard Edition server (`se01.rlscomms.net`)

You also need to create the Meet, Dial-in, Admin and Lyncdiscover records.

```
A = meet.rlscomms.net = IP of the Standard Edition server
A = dialin.rlscomms.net = IP of the Standard Edition server
A = admin.rlscomms.net = IP of the Standard Edition server
A = lyncdiscover.rlscomms.net = IP of the Standard Edition server
A = Lyncdiscoverinternal.rlscomms.net = IP of the Standard Edition server
```

Further Preparation

The remaining setup steps are relatively straightforward. First you need to install the local configuration store. This will create a new SQL instance on the server that holds a read-only replica of the CMS.

1. To install the local configuration store, start `setup.exe` from the `\setup\amd64\` folder of the media, and on the Deployment Wizard home page, click Install Or Update Skype For Business Server System.
2. This takes you to a setup page that runs through all the tasks to get the server up and running. Click Run in the Install Local Configuration Store section.
3. This kicks off a wizard where you will first be asked from where you want to pull the config. In this instance, you will pull it from the CMS. The other option would be to pull from a file that you will see later when you configure the Edge server. Click Next to begin installing and creating the local configuration store.

This process of installing another SQL Express instance (RTCLOCAL; see Figure 8.11) will take a few minutes, after which you will get the familiar completion page that allows you to view the steps taken and to launch the log in a browser to delve further into any details. One nice touch to note is that if multiple logs were created for different steps of the process, all of them are available from a drop-down menu.

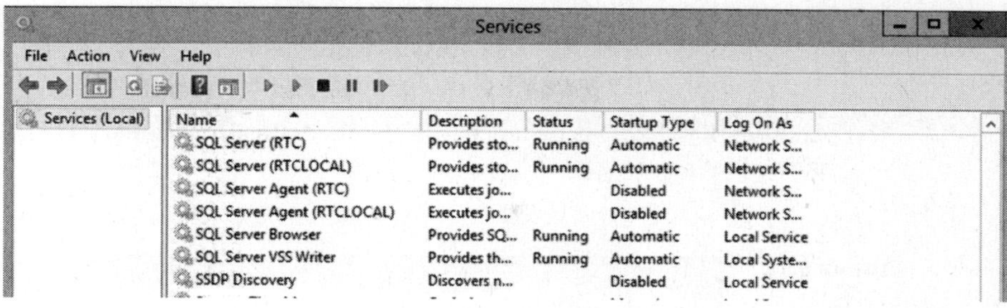

FIGURE 8.11 RTCLOCAL SQL Express instance installed

4. To end the wizard and return to the Install Or Update Member System screen, click Finish.

HOW THE LOCAL CONFIGURATION STORE IS POPULATED

We've discussed that the local configuration store is pulled from the CMS. However, you might be wondering how this is actually done.

What happens is that an `Export-CsConfiguration` command is run against the CMS, which creates a ZIP file. Because this is your first Standard Edition server, this file is stored locally; however, if you were building a server remote from the CMS, this would be sent by SMB over port 445 to the remote server. Once it is received, an `Import-CsConfiguration` is carried out with the `-LocalStore` parameter, which imports the configuration into the local configuration database. At this point, the HTTPS SQL replication process kicks in to maintain consistency between the databases.

INSTALLATION

Let's return to the Install Or Update Skype For Business Server Settings setup page. The next element to complete is the Setup Or Remove Skype for Business Server Components section. This is what actually installs the binaries onto the server.

1. To begin the process, click Run in the Setup Or Remove Skype For Business Server Components section. This kicks off the Setup Skype for Business Server Components Wizard.

In the background, Setup will look in AD to find a service connection point (SCP), which will provide the location where the CMS is held. Setup will review the data in the CMS and then install any required components by checking the local server name against the name of the server listed in the topology. The SCP is of type msRTCSIP-GlobalTopologySetting and can be found in the Configuration Partition of Active Directory here:

CN=Topology Settings, CN=RTC Service, DC=<domain>

2. On the first page of the wizard, click Next to kick off Setup. Like previous notes, the screen will update the progress as it goes as well as provide reports on completion. Assuming all goes well, click Finish to complete the process.

Another SQL Express instance was installed, this time called LYNCLOCAL. Figure 8.12 shows that running.

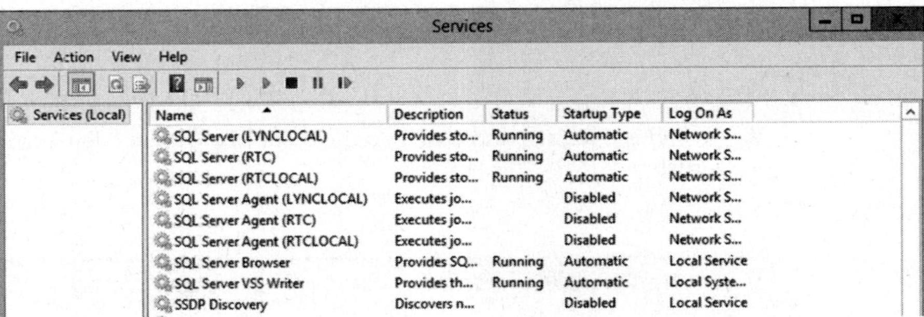

FIGURE 8.12 LYNCLOCAL SQL Express instance installed

Any Skype for Business Server will run both RTCLOCAL and LYNCLOCAL SQL Express instances; only the CMS (and backup CMS) will run the RTC instance.

The next element to configure is certificates. This has been simplified somewhat compared to the OCS installation process.

3. Back at the Install Or Update Skype For Business Server System setup page in the Certificates section, click Run to start the Certificate Wizard. This will open the page shown in Figure 8.13.

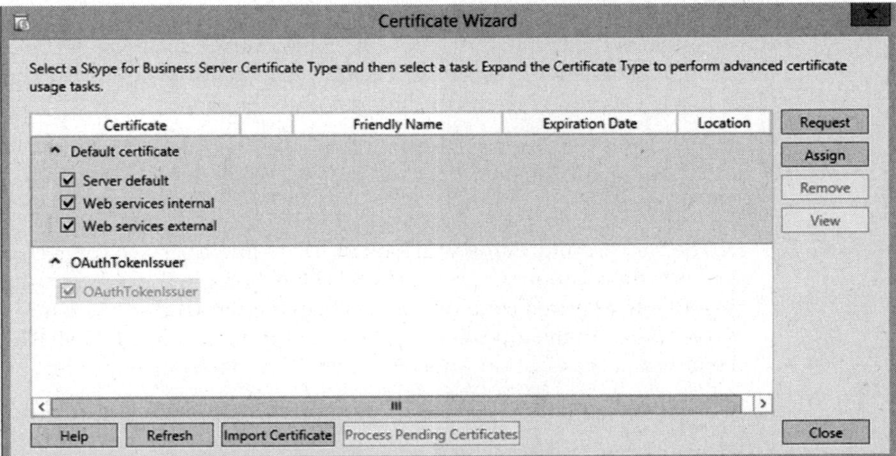

FIGURE 8.13 The Certificate Wizard

You can see that by default the server requires two certificates.

- Default certificate
- OAuthTokenIssuer

  However, if you click the drop-down by the default certificate, you will see that it is possible to install a certificate for each component, including Server Default, Web Services Internal, and Web Services External. This flexibility is particularly useful when providing external access through a reverse proxy that cannot trust an internal certificate authority (CA), which would cause you to need a trusted public certificate on the Web Services External component. In this case, keep the simple, standard installation because you will be using IIS ARR as the proxy, as you will see in Chapter 21, "Reverse Proxies, Load Balancers, and Gateways."

4. To create the required certificate, minimize the drop-down and highlight Default Certificate. Click Request and then follow the wizard that opens.

This certificate request process has been significantly improved over previous versions of Lync; almost all the information is contained in a single page, and only the slightly more exotic information is hidden away in the Advanced button, such as alternative credentials or alternative certificate template names.

Also, by clicking the Advanced button, you can choose whether to use a CA that is internal (private) to your organization and is online to issue certificates automatically (default) or save the request to a file and submit it to a CA manually. This could be the case either if you use trusted public certificates or if your own CA can't provide certificates automatically.

PUBLIC VS. PRIVATE CAS

You will regularly see recommendations to use certificates from either a public CA or a private (internal) CA. Which is best for you?

Well, the recommendation for the use of an internal CA pretty much comes down to cost—once installed, each certificate is free, and the overhead of managing them is relatively minimal (unless you are using certificates on a large scale, at which point you probably already have a solution in place to manage them).

If all (or the vast majority) of your users are internal AD users, with AD-joined machines, then an internal enterprise CA will be a better choice because it will automatically be trusted by all the AD-joined machines.

On the other hand, if you are not running Windows as your main OS or your users are connected to a different forest than the Skype for Business deployment, it may be better to use a public CA because you can select a CA that is in the default trusted root CA list of the OS, ensuring no additional overhead to manage trusted root CAs.

External certificates for the Edge server role are recommended to be from public CAs because (in most cases) they provide the automatic trust from the underlying OS to the certificate provided.

5. In this case, keep it simple and go for the internal CA, which is running as an enterprise root CA on Windows Server 2012 R2. Because this is the only CA in the environment, it is the only one in the drop-down.
6. Change the friendly name if required; it's always a good idea to include the date and purpose of the certificate in the friendly name, allowing for it to be easily found later.
7. Complete the organization information and location.
8. Selecting the All check box ensures that subject alternative names are added for all the SIP domains with the prefix *SIP*. This will ensure proper functionality when using Phone Edition devices. Figure 8.14 shows the certificate request template completed.

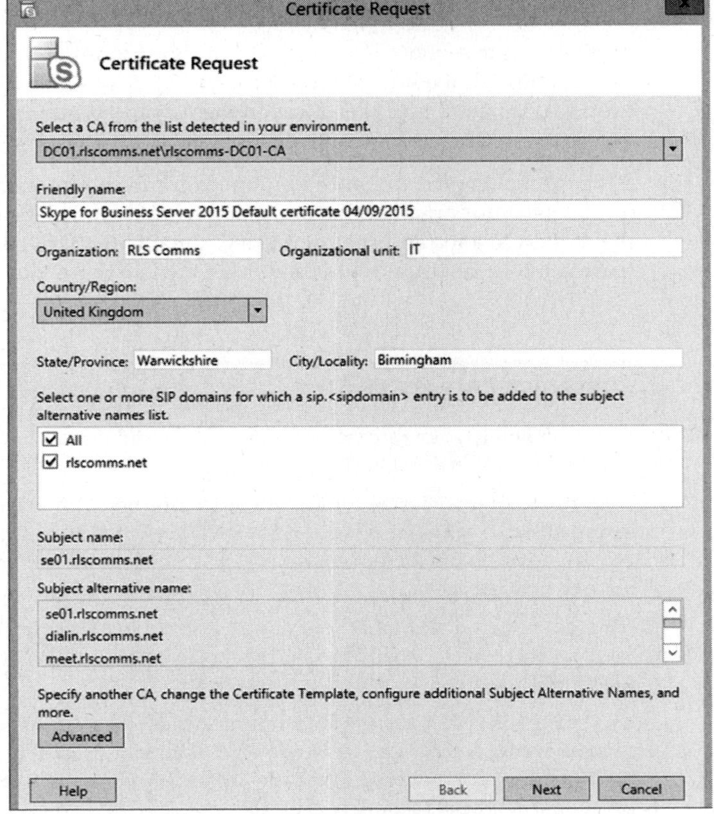

FIGURE 8.14
Setting the certificate friendly name

9. Click Next to show the certificate summary and then Next again to submit the request to the CA.

10. You'll see a response from the CA, and assuming it is successful, you can click Finish to end the request process.

11. By default, the Assign This Certificate To Skype For Business Server Certificate Usages is checked, and the Assign Certificates task will begin.

The Certificate Assignment Wizard opens and gives you a chance to view the certificate. The View Certificate Details button displays the default information about the certificate, such as the expiration date and where it was issued. On the Details tab, shown in Figure 8.15, you can scroll down to view the subject alternative names.

FIGURE 8.15
The certificate shows the details of the SANs (right).

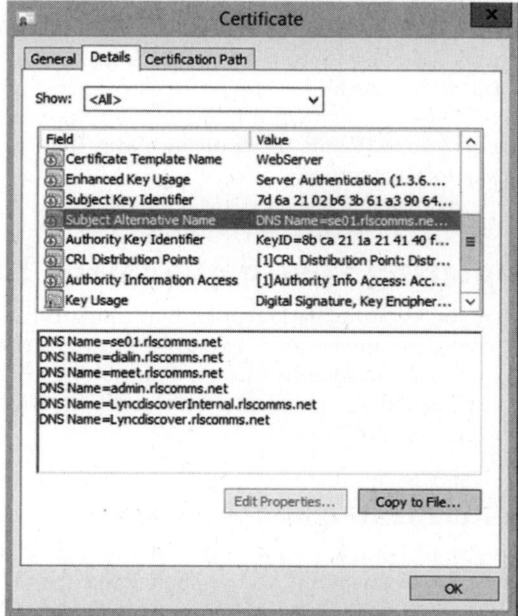

12. In the wizard, click Next to get to the summary page and then Next to assign the certificate. Finally, click Finish to exit the Certificate Assignment Wizard.

Now you return to the main Certificate Wizard, where you can see that you have assigned the certificate you just created.

Follow the previous process to create an OAuth certificate. This is used for interserver communications with other applications, such as Exchange and SharePoint.

Clicking Close takes you back to the Skype for Business Server Deployment Wizard, where you will see that you are now ready to start the services.

13. Unlike previous versions of Lync Server, where there was a Start Services button, the services must now be started manually, through either `Services.mmc` or PowerShell.

Individual servers can have all their services started by using the following cmdlet:

```
Start-CsWindowsService
```

If you want to start a complete pool at once, you can use the following new cmdlet:

```
Start-CsPool
```

As this is a single server pool (in other words, a Standard Edition), either cmdlet is suitable. Progress information is displayed to show how the cmdlet is progressing through each of the steps. When you come to installing an Enterprise Edition pool later in this chapter, you'll see the level of progress is significantly better when using the `Start-CsPool` cmdlet.

At this point, you are done installing the main Skype for Business components for your first Standard Edition server. You can exit from the Deployment Wizard and run one final check to see whether there are any Windows updates. Install anything you find and then reboot the server. Although the process was lengthy to describe, once you have done it a couple of times, you can whip through the setup easily, especially if you have taken a suitable amount of time in the planning phase using Topology Builder. Now you're ready to move on to what to do after setup.

Completing Post-deployment Tasks

Now that you've completed setup of the Standard Edition server, you need to perform several steps before you can get users up and running. You need to create an account with basic administrative permissions before you can do anything else. Then you need to test the installation, install any needed updates, and finally configure Kerberos authentication. The following sections discuss each of those steps.

Basic Administrative Permissions

Once you've finished setup, your first task is to give an account full administrative rights to the server. Up to this point, you've been using the administrator account to perform the setup, but by default Lync includes no accounts in the administration groups created by forest prep. Now you'll create a specific Skype for Business administrator account and use it to manage the system in the future.

First, you need to create a new user in Active Directory.

1. Open Windows PowerShell by typing **PowerShell** into the Start menu search area and running the top result.
2. Import the Active Directory module. This can be done with the following command:

```
Import-Module ActiveDirectory
```

3. This imports all the cmdlets needed to manage AD. Now that you have the cmdlets to manage AD objects, run the following command to create the new administrative user:

```
New-ADUser -SamAccountName "SkypeAdmin" -UserPrincipalName
 "SkypeAdmin@rlscomms.net  -GivenName "Skype" -Surname "Admin"
```

```
-DisplayName "Skype Admin" -Name "Skype Admin" -Enabled $true
-path "CN=Users, DC=rlscomms, DC=net"
-AccountPassword (Read-Host -AsSecureString "AccountPassword")
```

This will create a new user called Skype Admin in the default Users container, and it will prompt you to enter a password. On completion, the account will be enabled. Having done this, you need to add the account to two groups, which will give you all the rights you need to perform basic administration on Skype for Business.

4. The following commands add the Skype Admin account to the required groups:

```
Add-ADGroupMember RTCUniversalServerAdmins skypeadmin
Add-ADGroupMember CsAdministrator skypeadmin
```

This first command will make Skype Admin a member of the RTCUniversalServer Admins group, and then the second will make Skype Admin a member of the CsAdministrator group.

5. The last thing you need to do to ensure that Skype Admin can make any necessary changes to the local server is to add Skype Admin to the Local Administrators group. You can do this by copying the next six lines of code into the Windows PowerShell on the Standard Edition server and running them:

```
$computerName = $env:COMPUTERNAME
$Group = "Administrators"
$LocalGroup = [adsi]"WinNT://$computerName/$Group,group"
$Domain = "rlscomms"
$UserName = "skypeadmin"
$LocalGroup.Add("WinNT://$Domain/$userName")
```

Once these commands are run, the Skype Admin domain user account will also be a member of the Local Administrators group.

POWERSHELL AND PERMISSIONS FOR MANAGEMENT

At this stage, don't worry if the PowerShell commands you've just seen are unfamiliar. Not only is all of Appendix B about PowerShell, but Chapter 10 focuses on setup and delegation of management.

Testing the Installation

Now that you've created the Skype Admin user, you are ready to log into the Standard Edition server as that user and begin testing the installation. The aim is to validate that all server components are installed and communicating correctly and that all services are started before you move on to any complex system configuration.

1. Log into the Standard Edition server as Skype Admin.

2. Once you're logged in, type **`s f b s c p`** (yes, with the spaces) in the Start menu search bar and press Enter.

This will run the Skype for Business Server Control Panel (SFBSCP), which allows you not only to administer the majority of Skype for Business settings but also to validate that Setup has completed properly. In this case, start with validation.

Control Panel Requirements

You thought you'd finished all the installation prerequisites, didn't you? Well, Control Panel requires Silverlight to be installed prior to running. If Silverlight is not installed, you'll still get prompted for credentials, and then the response will be "Silverlight is not installed; please install Silverlight."

This may cause concern for those environments in which servers are highly locked down and the installation of additional software is not permitted. In these cases, the only option is to install the admin tools on a client machine along with Silverlight or to use PowerShell.

3. If prompted, log into the Control Panel with the Skype Admin user credentials and click the Topology tab. This will bring up a view of all the deployed services, as shown in Figure 8.16.

Figure 8.16
The Topology tab in Skype for Business Server Control Panel

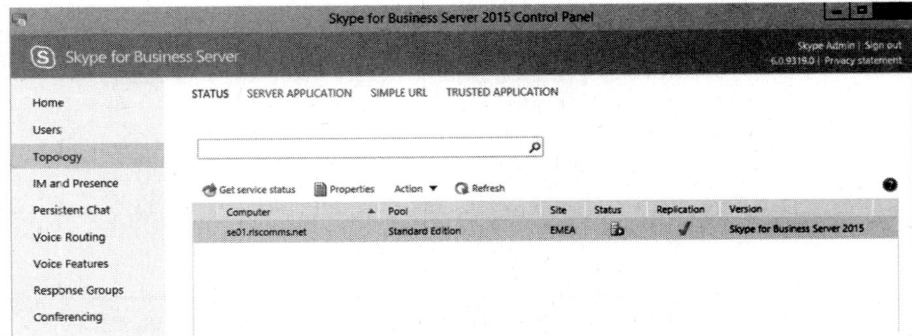

You can see information about the status of the server you installed.

4. Ideally, everything will have a green tick/icon. However, if you can see a warning denoted by the yellow triangle in the Status column, double-click the row to drill into the services to find out what is wrong. You can see in Figure 8.17 that the Conferencing server is stopped.
5. To rectify this, select the impacted row and then click the Action drop-down and select Start Service. The service will start.
6. Once the service is started, click Close to move back to the first page, and you will see all green icons, meaning that the service is healthy.

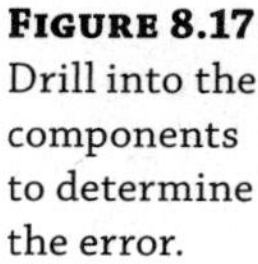

FIGURE 8.17
Drill into the components to determine the error.

Kerberos Authentication Configuration

The last piece of post-setup work to be done on this Standard Edition installation is to set up Kerberos authentication. Skype for Business can use either NT LAN Manager (NTLM) or Kerberos for web services authentication; however, everyone knows that Kerberos is more secure than NTLM because it uses mutual authentication, so it is important to perform this setup.

Skype for Business runs under the Network Service account, which does not allow for service principal names (SPNs) to be assigned; SPNs require actual accounts in Active Directory.

To work around this, Skype for Business creates a dummy computer account on which to place the SPNs needed by IIS. This is used instead of a user account to get around the default password policy, which might require irritating regular changes of password.

It is necessary to have only a single Kerberos computer account, but it is possible to create multiple accounts to provide one for each site. This might be needed if you have a large distributed topology with many sites because the process whereby a password change is communicated to each site happens via Distributed Component Object Model (DCOM), which is a set of Microsoft standards allowing distributed software components to talk to each other. If you have a large network, this password reset may take quite some time to complete; therefore, having local Kerberos accounts may be more sensible.

Just so you get an idea of what SPNs look like, let's check to see what SPNs exist currently for the SE01 computer before you start. Do this by running the following command from an administrative command prompt (`CMD.exe`):

```
SetSPN -L SE01
```

When this is run, you should see output similar to the following, which is a listing of Kerberos SPNs linked to the Standard Edition computer object:

```
Registered ServicePrincipalNames for CN=SE01,CN=Computers,
 DC=rlscomms,DC=net:
        WSMAN/se01
        WSMAN/se01.rlscoms.net
        http/se01.rlscomms.net
        sip/se01.rlscomms.net
        TERMSRV/SE01
        TERMSRV/se01.rlscomms.net
        RestrictedKrbHost/SE01.rlscomms.net
        HOST/SE01.rlscomms.net
        RestrictedKrbHost/SE01
        HOST/SE01
```

Next, create the Kerberos account by following these steps:

1. To create the account, log on to the Skype for Business server as a domain administrator and open the Skype for Business Server Management Shell. Run the following command to create your first Kerberos account:

```
New-CsKerberosAccount -UserAccount "rlscomms\SkypeKerb"
-ContainerDN "CN=Users, DC=rlscomms,DC=net"
```

This command creates an account in the `rlscomms` domain, called `SkypeKerb`, within the default Users container. Obviously, you would use your domain name and create an account name that is meaningful to you. You can also put the account in a different container or OU if you want to keep it separated from the main Users container.

2. Next, you need to assign the account to the site, which you do with the following command:

```
New-CsKerberosAccountAssignment -UserAccount "rlscomms\SkypeKerb" -Identity
"site:EMEA"
```

This will assign the SkypeKerb account to the EMEA site, which is the only one you have at the moment.

3. At this point, you need to update the topology, so use the following cmdlet:

```
Enable-CsTopology
```

This registers all the relevant SPNs against the newly created Kerberos account based on the sites you have assigned to it. The penultimate step is to ensure that all machines in the site have registered the password assigned to the account. The account is assigned a random password on creation, but each machine running IIS needs to know it! This is done using the following command:

```
Set-CsKerberosAccountPassword -UserAccount "rlscomms\SkypeKerb"
```

Once you've run this command, all the IIS instances in the site on Front End servers, Directors, or Standard Edition servers will get the password.

4. Finally, run `SetSPN -L` again, but this time with the computer account you just created as the target.

```
SetSPN -L SkypeKerb
```

Now, you will see output similar to this:

```
Registered ServicePrincipalNames for CN=Skypekerb,
CN=Users,DC=corp,DC=net:
       http/se01.rlscomms.net
```

This is the SPN, which will allow the SkypeKerb account to be used for Kerberos authentication for web services rather than using the local Network Service account.

5. Having created the account and assigned and enabled it, you can run the following command, which will test whether it is operating properly:

```
Test-CsKerberosAccountAssignment -Identity "site:EMEA"
-Report "c:\logs\SkypeKerberosReport.htm" -Verbose
```

This runs through a number of tests and outputs to the familiar HTML format log file in the directory you specify.

Before we move on, there are various considerations worth mentioning about Kerberos accounts. One recommended methodology is that before you configure Kerberos, you complete your deployment, or at least all the elements that are going to use web services, namely, Standard Edition, Director, and Front End servers. Realistically, this may not be possible, which means that when you add a server, like a Director, after setting up Kerberos authentication you need to configure IIS and set the password on the server. This is described later in the chapter, as part of the process of setting up a Director server, but briefly, you use the `Set-CsKerberosAccountPassword` cmdlet to do this.

Similarly, each time you create a new site, you need to decide whether to create a new Kerberos account and link it to the site or reuse an existing one. As mentioned, this depends on the size and scale of your topology. If you choose to use a new Kerberos account, then create it and link it as described earlier.

Configuring External Access

If you've been following along, you now have a full-fledged Skype for Business installation that is perfectly capable of letting people within your organization communicate and collaborate in a wide variety of ways. However, these capabilities are currently limited by the confines of your firewall. It would be so much better if you could access these tools from anywhere and communicate and collaborate in the same way whether you were in your office or in a coffee shop with

Wi-Fi halfway around the world. That is exactly what these next sections are about: configuring the Edge server and supporting components to allow external access.

Three main components are involved in providing external access to Skype for Business.

- The Edge role, which does the majority of the work
- The Director, which is an optional stopgap between the Front End and the Edge server
- The reverse proxy, which allows you to publish externally the various web components, such as the Address Book and the software update service

The process for deploying external access consists of the following major steps:

1. Define/update the topology.
2. Prepare for deployment.
    a. Meet the software prerequisites.
    b. Set up networking, DNS, and firewalls.
    c. Set up/prepare certificates.
    d. Provision public IM connectivity.
3. Set up the reverse proxy (covered in Chapter 21).
4. Set up a Director (optional).
5. Set up the Edge server.
6. Configure users for external access.
7. Test.

The specific prerequisites for each server are outlined in the following sections.

Installing the Director

The Director role is frequently dismissed in designs as more server overhead and so it is left out. However, the Director does have an important role to play, albeit an optional one. Essentially, a Director is a barrier between the Edge and the Front End server. In this role, it is the Director that performs the authentication of users coming in across the Edge server, and thus, it not only takes a load off the Front End server but also helps to isolate the Front End server from any malicious traffic generated as a denial-of-service attack.

If, for example, an attacker were to send large amounts of malformed authentication traffic toward the Edge server, it would be passed on to the Director, which would potentially be overloaded. However, the Front End server would be unaffected, so internal users would be able to continue working with limited disruption.

There are a couple of other roles where the Director server plays a part. One is as part of a large enterprise deployment, as discussed later in the chapter. The other is by way of a method of distributing information to clients about a backup registrar that was covered in Chapter 4 but is worth reviewing briefly now.

When a Skype for Business client registers with the pool it finds through autodiscovery or is pointed to through manual configuration, if that pool is not its home pool, the client is sent a SIP redirect message and is provided the details of the user's primary and backup registrar.

If the client were to connect first to its home server instead of the Director, or indeed, any other pool, then if the home pool was unavailable, it would never get the redirect request telling it about the backup registrar and thus failover wouldn't work. However, if the SRV DNS records are configured correctly, upon timeout and re-query for connection, the client would fail to connect to its home pool because it is unavailable, and then it would try another pool via the DNS load balancing process, resulting in a connection eventually.

Directors, like other components, can be deployed either as a single server or in a pool. If they are deployed in a pool, load balancing must be configured. In this Standard Edition deployment, you will simply deploy a single Director. To do so, you will need another server, and in this example, you will use another Windows Server 2012 R2 machine that is fully patched and joined to the domain.

Since Lync Server 2010 was released, the Director is a role in its own right. It used to be in OCS that it was a Front End pool with various services turned off. The cool thing about having a definite role is that now you no longer have to worry about users getting accidentally homed on the Director server because it simply isn't an available option as it was when it was a cut-down Front End in OCS. Although they are separate roles, the Director and the Front End (or Standard Edition server) have similar prerequisites. In fact, there are only a couple of differences. The first is that the Windows Media Foundation Feature (or the Desktop Experience) is not required. Similarly, neither are the Active Directory tools (RSAT-ADDS).

Configuring the Topology

As you're only building a small environment here (you'll be deploying a single-server Director pool in the example), there is little configuration information you need to provide. Figure 8.18 shows the total information you need.

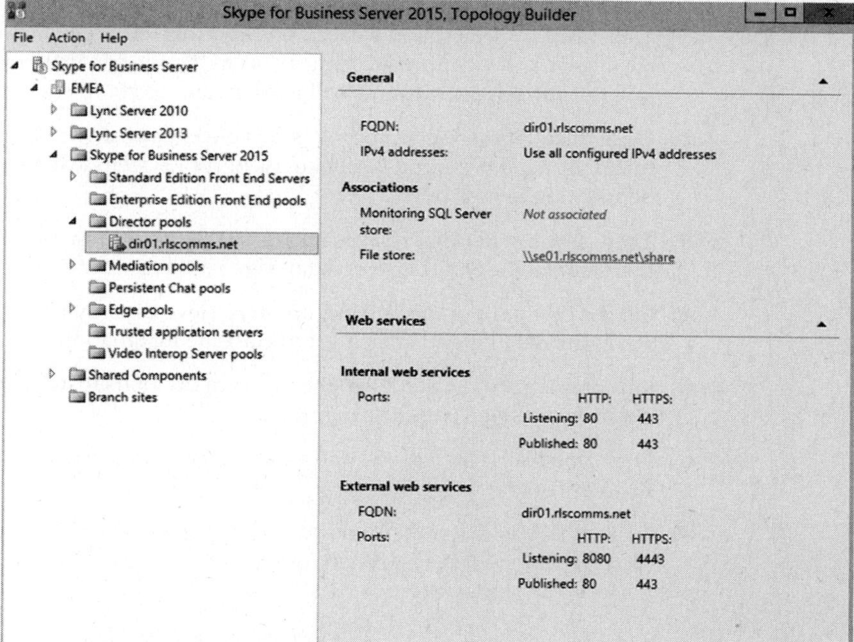

Figure 8.18 Topology information for the Director pool

Once the information is defined in the topology, publish as before, and when successful, you're ready to move to the installation.

Installing the Role Components

Because we spent quite some time detailing the installation prerequisites on the Standard Edition server, at this point, we will simply list the commands that should be run from a PowerShell command prompt with administrator credentials on the local server.

```
Add-WindowsFeature NET-Framework-Core, Web-Static-Content,
 Web-Default-Doc, Web-Http-Errors, Web-Asp-Net, Web-Net-Ext,
 Web-ISAPI-Ext, Web-ISAPI-Filter, Web-Http-Logging,
 Web-Log-Libraries, Web-Http-Tracing, Web-Windows-Auth,
 Web-Filtering, Web-Stat-Compression, Web-Dyn-Compression,
 Web-Mgmt-Console, Web-Scripting-Tools, Web-Client-Auth,
 Web-Asp-Net45, Net-HTTP-Activation, Net-WCF-HTTP-Activation45,
 Windows-Identity-Foundation
```

Running these commands will first import the cmdlets needed to install software and then install the .NET Framework 4.5, PowerShell v3.0, Windows Identity Framework, and the web components. If asked, reboot the server, perform one final check for patches from Windows Update, and install any that are found.

At this stage, you are ready to deploy the Director role.

1. When you insert the media, Setup will autorun, and as with the Standard Edition server, you will be prompted about installing Visual C++ Redistributable. Click Yes and then click Install to agree to the location for install files. Obviously, you can change from the default if you choose to place the installation on another drive. Accept the license agreement by selecting the check box and then click OK to progress with the setup. If any errors are encountered with access to the Internet (such as if you're running from a private lab), select Continue Without Updates to complete the initial install.
2. Once installation bootstrapping is complete, you will be at the Setup home page. Click Install Or Update Skype For Business Server System, which takes you to the steps for deploying the new role.
3. Then, as with all other roles, click Install Local Configuration Store to begin the wizard that installs the SQL Express database to hold the local replica of the CMS.
4. On the first page of the wizard, opt to retrieve directly from the central management store (the default) and click Next to start the installation.
5. On completion, you can view the log as in previous installs or click Finish to return to the deployment steps page and continue.
6. Next, you will install the Skype for Business files by clicking Setup Or Remove Skype For Business Server Components.
7. This takes you to another wizard, where you click Next to kick off a process of installing all the specific services needed for the Director role. On completion, click Finish to return to the setup steps page.

Next, you provision certificates, a procedure similar to that of the Standard Edition install.

1. From the main Deployment Wizard screen, select the Request, Install or Assign Certificates Wizard by clicking the Run button.
2. The main Certificate Wizard will open, and this time, you'll already see a populated certificate—the OAuth TokenIssuer certificate.
3. Once again there is the option to be specific about certificates. However, for this example you will request a single certificate with multiple SANs by clicking the Request button (ensuring the Default Certificate option is highlighted).
4. When the wizard opens, most of the data will already be populated with only a few fields remaining.
5. Enter the location information fields: Organization, Organizational Unit, Country/Region, Sate/Province, and City/Locality.
6. Select the check box next to the SIP domains to ensure that the `rlscomms.net` entry gets populated on the certificate for use later by phone devices.
7. There are no other SANs to add, so click Next, review the summary page, and click Next to make the request. Once it is completed, click Finish to run the Certificate Assignment Wizard. After you click Next twice and then click Finish, you will have assigned the certificate to the relevant services.
8. At this point, click Close on the certificate page and then again on the Install Steps page, which can now be closed. Start the services by using the following PowerShell command:

```
Start-CsPool dir01.rlscomms.net
```

9. You can check that all services have started by launching `Services.msc` using the Run button in the Service Status (Optional) section. This is worth doing especially in a situation where limited RAM may make things start rather slowly. Assuming everything has started as expected, you should have a running Director.

As mentioned earlier, anyone who has configured Kerberos authentication needs to configure it for use on the new Director. Do this from the LMS on a server that has Kerberos already set up (in this case, the Standard Edition SE01), using the following command:

```
Set-CsKerberosAccountPassword -FromComputer SE01.rlscomms.net
-ToComputer dir01.rlscomms.net
```

This command will synchronize the password and account information from the SE01 server to the new Director.

Perform a final check for Windows Update and install the same level of Skype for Business CU as described in the Standard Edition install, and then you'll be nearly ready to move to the next stage, setting up the reverse proxy.

Before you move on, you should check the topology again as you did after installing the Standard Edition server. Open Skype for Business Control Panel as the Skype Admin user created earlier, and on the Topology tab, check that replication has a check mark next to both the Standard Edition server and the Director and that the status is green.

New Prompt When Opening SFBSCP

After installing the Director (and indeed any additional pools), note that there is now a prompt for the URL to use when you open Control Panel from the Start menu. This is because both Director and Standard Edition servers have a set of web URLs to offer to users. You can run the Control Panel from any URL successfully.

Installing the Edge Server

The Edge server role is slightly different from the other roles in that it is the only one not connected to your Active Directory domain; it is installed in the perimeter network.

Edge Best Practices

The Edge server should not be connected to your internal Active Directory. Microsoft supports (but does not recommend) connecting it to an Active Directory forest specifically for use in the perimeter network. The size of your DMZ will determine whether it requires an AD to manage or whether each server can be managed independently.

This difference raises various challenges about how best to manage the installation. Skype for Business does a vastly better job than OCS in this regard, as you will see. As Skype for Business has the CMS, once the first replication of the configuration is complete (done manually as part of setup), secure push replication is carried out so that all management can be performed from the Topology Builder and management tools. This ensures that all Edge servers are consistent with their configurations, a major headache for OCS!

The first step to deploying an Edge server is to set up another server—another Windows Server 2012 R2 server, which you will not join to the domain. The server will be called Edge01. Once the server is built and fully patched, it then needs the relevant prerequisites installed.

First, it is important to configure the primary DNS suffix to match the internal domain suffix of the Lync server pool; in this case it will be `rlscomms.net`. To do this, follow these steps:

1. Open the Properties page of the computer and click Change Settings In The Computer Name, Domain And Workgroup Settings section.
2. On the Computer Name tab, click Change, and then on the Computer Name/Domain Changes tab, click More.
3. Enter the required suffix, and click OK until prompted to reboot, which you should do.

Next, you need to configure the NICs. As discussed in Chapter 7, the Edge server must have at minimum two NICs, each on a different subnet. One is public facing, and the other is closer to the internal LAN. In this exercise, you will use public IP addresses on the external interface instead of using NAT, as discussed in Chapter 3. Ensure that the external NIC has the default gateway defined pointing to the external firewall or router and that this NIC is at the top of the NIC binding order. To do this, take the following steps:

1. Type **`Network and Sharing`** into the Start menu search bar and open the Network And Sharing Center.

2. Click Change Adapter Settings. When the window opens, press the Alt key. This will bring up menu options from which you should select Advanced and then Advanced Settings.

3. The Adapters And Bindings window opens, where you should ensure that the Internet/external NIC is at the top of the bindings, as shown in Figure 8.19.

FIGURE 8.19
The NIC bindings on the Edge server

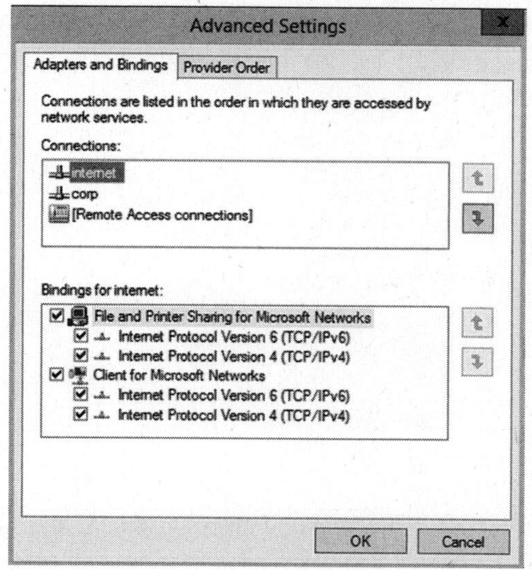

Because you have pointed the default gateway to the external firewall, you may have to create static routes to allow communication with the internal network. This is achieved via the `ROUTE` command, within a command prompt. The syntax is as follows:

```
route ADD <destination subnet> MASK <mask> <gateway> METRIC <metric>
 IF <interface> ****02010;p
```

You can find more information by typing `route /?` within a command prompt window.

The next step is to ensure that the Edge server can resolve the internal servers by name. There are a couple of options here: using DNS servers you control in the perimeter network or using external DNS servers.

If you have DNS servers in the perimeter network, they must contain A records for the internal servers the Edge server needs to talk with—the next-hop server, which will be the Front End, Standard Edition, or Director server. If there is a pool of servers, each should have an individual record under the same FQDN to provide for DNS load balancing.

If you are using external DNS servers, these should be defined purely on the external NIC and should point to public DNS servers. This option will not provide name resolution for the internal server, so you will need to provide entries in the HOSTS file. Figure 8.20 shows how to open the HOSTS file, which should be done from Notepad running as Administrator. Figure 8.21 shows the entries in the HOSTS file in our environment.

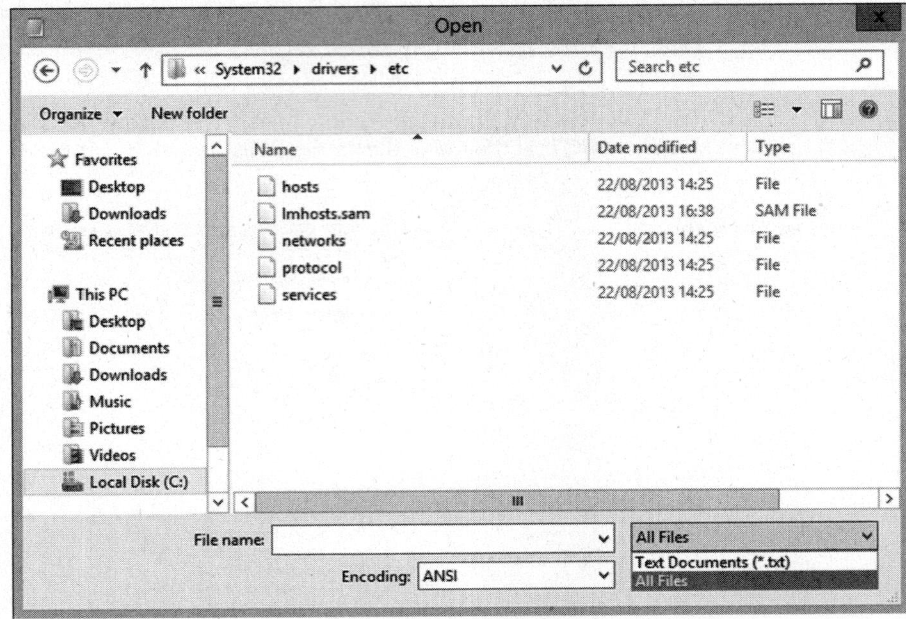

FIGURE 8.20 Opening the HOSTS file using the All Files option

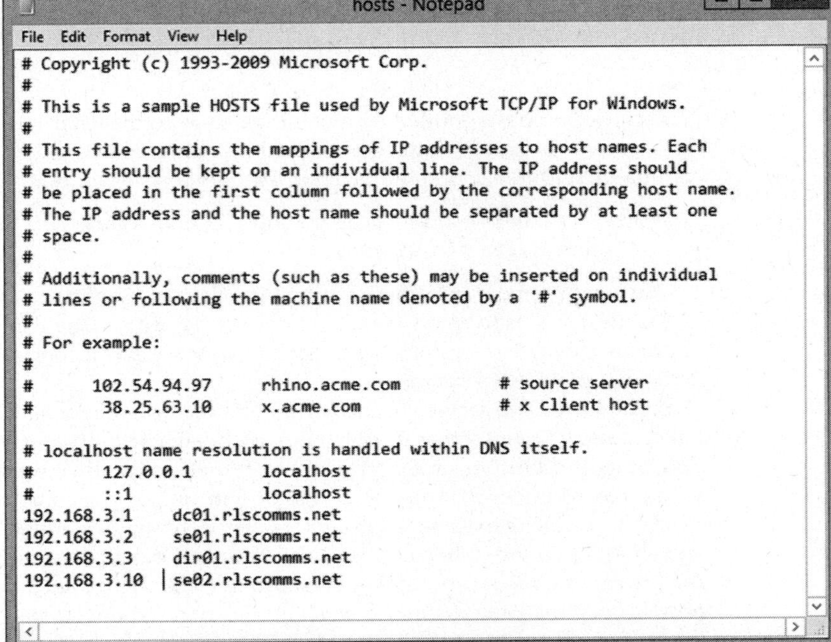

FIGURE 8.21 The HOSTS file entries

At this stage, the basic preparatory steps are done. Now you need to install the prerequisite software, which for the Edge is simply the .NET Framework 3.5.

1. Install this as with the Standard Edition server process.
2. Having installed the .NET Framework, start the Skype for Business Setup program and allow Setup to install Visual C++. As with the previous roles, Setup follows the same format, first installing the local configuration store.

   The difference in the Edge installation is that instead of pulling the first config synchronization from the CMS, you have to pull it from a file. This means you need to create the file, which is done by exporting the CMS on one of the internal servers with the admin tools installed. In this case, go to the Standard Edition server and open PowerShell. Use the following command to export the topology to a file:

   ```
   Export-CsConfiguration -FileName c:\topologyexport.zip
   ```

3. Locate the file and copy it to the Edge server. Next run the local setup, and when prompted, select Import From A File and specify the location of the ZIP file copied from the Standard Edition server, as shown in Figure 8.22.
4. Then, continue with the Setup Or Remove Skype For Business Components setup process.

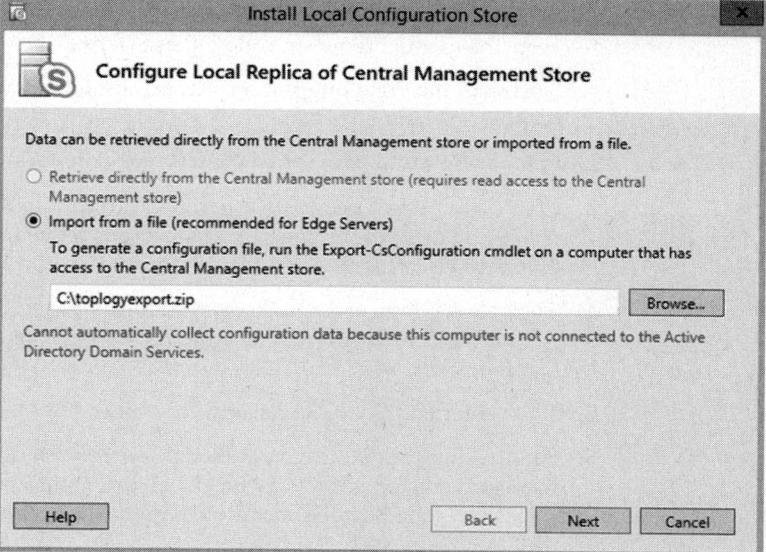

FIGURE 8.22 Importing the topology from a file into the Edge server

Again, as with other roles, you need to install certificates. The specific requirements were discussed in Chapter 7, so for now we will simply list what you need to install on the Edge server.

Cert request for external NIC:

Subject: `Accessedge.rlscomms.net`

SAN: `Accessedge.rlscomms.net`

SAN: `Webconf.rlscomms.net`

SAN: `Sip.rlscomms.net`

SAN: `rlscomms.net`

Note that the first SAN entry must be the same as the subject name of the certificate because TLS encryption is in use and it simply looks at the SANs of the certificate rather than the subject name.

Cert request for internal Edge NIC:

Subject: `Edge01.rlscomms.net`

Another difference in the process of requesting the certificates for the internal servers is that this time, you will not be able to submit the requests to an online CA. The external NIC certificate request should be submitted as an offline request to a public trusted CA such as DigiCert or VeriSign, and although the internal certificate can and should be issued from the internal CA used for the internal servers, that will also need to be completed as an offline request because it is unlikely that relevant ports will be open from the DMZ to the internal network for online enrollment. Sadly, the new improved certificate request wizard is available only for the internal sever roles, so it's back to the "old" wizard!

To create the manual requests, follow these steps:

1. Start with the Edge Internal certificate highlighted and click Request. Elect to prepare the request now and click Next.
2. Enter a name and path for where to save the request file and click Next.
3. Click Next in the Specify Alternative Certificate Template window, and then on the Name And Security Settings page, enter a friendly name for the certificate. Use something in the name that will help you identify the server and interface.
4. Click Next to proceed. On the next couple of pages, enter organizational information. Accept the default subject name on the Subject Name / Subject Alternative Names page and then click Next.
5. Don't enter additional SANs, and click Next.
6. Finally, check the summary and click Next to create the certificate request. As long as the request is created without error, click Next, and then on the Certificate Request File page, click View to look at the certificate request data. This is the text data that must be sent to the CA.
7. Click Finish to return to the first Certificate Wizard page.
8. Once you have received the certificate and installed it into the personal store of the local computer account, return to the first Certificate screen, and with the Edge Internal certificate still highlighted, click Assign.

9. On the first page of the Certificate Assignment Wizard, click Next, and then on the Certificate Store page, locate the certificate to assign by friendly name, as shown in Figure 8.23.

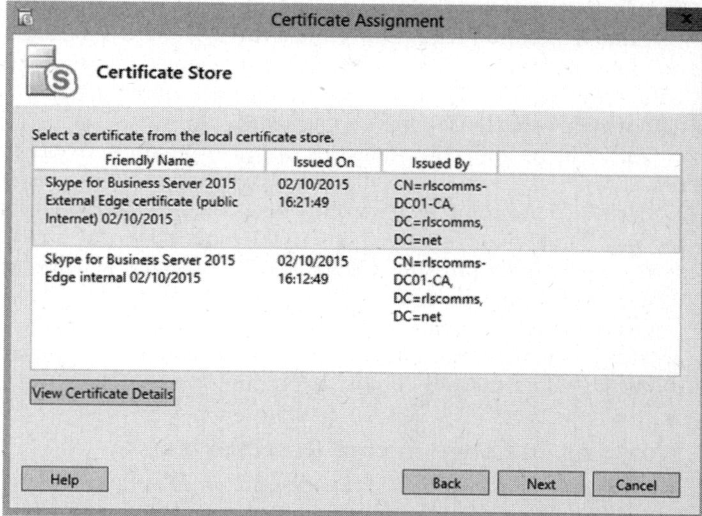

FIGURE 8.23 Choosing the certificate to assign

10. Click Next twice to assign the certificate. On the Executing Commands page, check for any errors and view the log if required; then click Finish to exit.

CA Trust for Internal Certificates

One step to carry out before requesting the certificates is to ensure that the Edge server trusts the internal CA that issues certificates to the internal servers. This is achieved by importing the root CA certificate into the certificate store on the Edge server.

When creating the external certificate, follow the same process. As before, when prompted, select the check box to create the `sip.rlscomms.net` SAN entry for later use by phone devices. This certificate request will be manually sent to an external CA, which will generate and return the certificate. As with the installation of externally trusted certificates on the proxy (see Chapter 21), you must follow the installation instructions carefully. Once the certificate is in the personal store of the local computer, go back to the Certificate Wizard, and with the external interface certificate highlighted, click Assign and follow the wizard to assign the externally trusted certificate.

Now that you've completed the certificate setup, all that remains is to start the services, install any remaining Windows patches, and update Skype for Business to the same CU version as the other servers in the organization (if any CUs have been deployed).

Executing Enterprise Deployments

So far in this chapter, we showed how to install Lync Standard Edition and enabled external access with a single Edge server. In essence, this has been a simple, small-business installation. That is not to say that this system can't support a large number of users; it can.

Standard Edition will, when run on the right hardware, support up to 2,500 users (see the previous explanation in this chapter regarding user numbers); however, there are companies with many more users than that. Other aspects of the installation that were simpler than many deployments are the domain and network.

We set up a single-site and single-forest/-domain Active Directory. Even some small businesses with far fewer than 5,000 users have many sites that need support.

In these more complex environments, there are additional considerations that may change the way deployment is carried out. In the remainder of this chapter, we will look at these issues, starting with installing into a large Active Directory, which potentially has restricted rights for different administrators.

Other topics will include specifying how you want install to work with SQL, working in environments with multiple sites (including both small branch offices and those with tens of thousands of users), and, finally, automating the setup.

Working in Large Active Directories

As discussed in the section "Preparing Active Directory" earlier in this chapter, Skype for Business uses AD less than its predecessors. Lync really used AD only for storing the architecture for backward compatibility with OCS. Now that this is no longer a supported option, there are fewer reasons. That said, there is still a need for schema changes and the creation of a significant number of new objects, which, therefore, requires careful collaboration between all those working with the Active Directory environment.

So, what exactly constitutes a large/complex directory? Anything larger than a single forest, single domain, and single site warrants some discussion. Traditionally, there are various types of structures that form large directories.

- Single forest with a single tree and multiple domains
- Single forest with multiple trees and disjoint namespaces
- Multiple forests in a central forest topology
- Multiple forests in a resource forest topology

The requirements for these directories were discussed in Chapter 7, so this section covers what is needed from an installation perspective. The key rule is to remember the following: Schema Prep needs to be run once in each forest where Skype for Business servers will be deployed.

Coming back to the structure of the forest mentioned earlier, you do not need to run this directly on the schema master (which is likely to reside in the root domain in the forest), as long as the account you run Schema Prep under has rights to the schema master. This is good news because it means that you don't need to gain access to a machine in the root domain, which is likely to be heavily locked down. In a resource forest model, Schema Prep is run in the resource forest where the Skype for Business servers are, not just in the user forest.

The forest prep procedure, which creates the universal group, is run once in a forest that will host Skype for Business servers. It is forest prep that creates the universal groups used to assign permissions to the various components. In a large directory environment, you may want to take advantage of the opportunity to create these groups in a domain other than the forest root. You might particularly want to do this if you operate an empty forest root domain and, therefore, want to keep access as limited as possible to the forest root domain. In a resource forest model, forest prep is run in the resource forest where the Skype for Business servers are, not in the user forest.

Domain prep should be run in each domain where Skype for Business users will be enabled. In a resource forest model, domain prep is run in the resource forest where the Skype for Business servers are not in the user forest. This is because although there will be users in the user forest accessing Skype for Business, they will be linked via the disabled user objects in the resource forest, which are what will hold the properties.

SINGLE-LABEL DOMAINS

It should be noted that unlike Exchange 2010, Skype for Business cannot be installed in a *single-label domain*. That is, for example, a domain called `.rlscomms` rather than `.rlscomms.net`.

When working in an environment that has a complex AD, it is likely that AD will be managed by a dedicated team of directory experts. Before making changes to the AD, you will often need to describe the details behind all the changes Lync will make. One of the biggest and most permanent is the schema update. You can find a great deal of detail in the help file; however, in summary what happens is that Schema Prep imports information from four LDF files in the order shown here:

`ExternalSchema.ldf` This file creates the classes and attributes that allow integration of Skype for Business with Exchange for UM and OWA IM.

`ServerSchema.ldf` This is the primary Skype for Business schema file and contains the majority of classes and attributes associated with Lync.

`BackCompatSchema.ldf` This file provides for interoperability with components from prior releases.

`VersionSchema.ldf` The changes in this file set the version of the schema, making it possible to check which version is installed.

If you want to take a closer look at these files, you can find them in the `\Support\schema` folder on the installation media. It is even possible to import these files manually in AD with the LDIFDE utility. You would no longer need to provide the directory teams with the ability or training needed to run the Setup program, and you'd have a workaround in cases where the only option available is to run the process from a machine that is not 64-bit, which is what Setup needs.

Another difference with a large directory is that once you have run the schema and forest preparation, more care is needed to ensure that the changes have replicated around all domain controllers in the forest. It is also worth noting that making these changes will create replication traffic, so it is worth carrying out these changes over a period of low usage to ensure a smooth replication process.

Delegating Setup Permissions

Closely related to the topic of AD is that of administrative permissions needed to carry out setup in an enterprise deployment.

Delegation of setup permissions is much simpler than before. Running local setup now requires only Local Administrator permissions on the Skype for Business server and the ability to read domain-based information and CMS information. These are granted by the Domain Users and RTCUniversalReadOnlyAdmins groups, respectively. This simplification is possible because so much work has already been carried out in Topology Builder. Of course, a greater level of permissions is needed to publish and enable the changes in a new topology, as discussed in Chapter 7.

The other permissions issue you may come up against when running Setup is that of a locked-down AD. This might occur, for example, if your directory team has turned off inheritance on certain sections of the directory to enable delegated security. When Setup is run, both the domain prep and server activation steps set permissions on objects within the domain. Not having the relevant security entries can prevent Skype for Business from properly understanding the topology of the system and will prevent user administration. Therefore, if inheritance is blocked on a particular OU, you can use the following command to manually set the required security entries after domain prep is run:

```
Grant-CsOuPermission -ObjectType "User" -OU "ou=testusers,
dc=rlscomms,dc=net" -Domain "rlscomms.net"
```

This will set the required permissions on the user objects within the `testusers` OU in the `rlscomms.net` domain.

If instead this were a `Computer` OU, which held Skype for Business computer accounts, you could run the following command:

```
Grant-CsOuPermission -ObjectType "Computer" -OU "ou=Servers,
dc=rlscomms,dc=net" -Domain "rlscomms.net"
```

This would set the permissions on `Computer` objects in the `servers` OU in the `rlscomms.net` domain.

Granting permissions means that members of the RTC groups can access the objects without being members of the Domain Admins group because these groups are used to control access for user accounts as well as machine accounts (now that Skype for Business has moved to a local user approach rather than the service account approach used by OCS).

Installing Enterprise Pools

The Enterprise pool is the infrastructure element that provides the users with high availability and allows for increases in scale. The pool you have already deployed in this chapter, the Standard Edition, provides the same functionality, just to more people and allows for failure of components.

Installation required both the Front End and Back End to be configured separately vs. the single configuration element of the Standard Edition server. Figure 8.24 shows the additional screens allowing for individual servers to be configured and installed.

FIGURE 8.24
Adding Front End servers to the pool

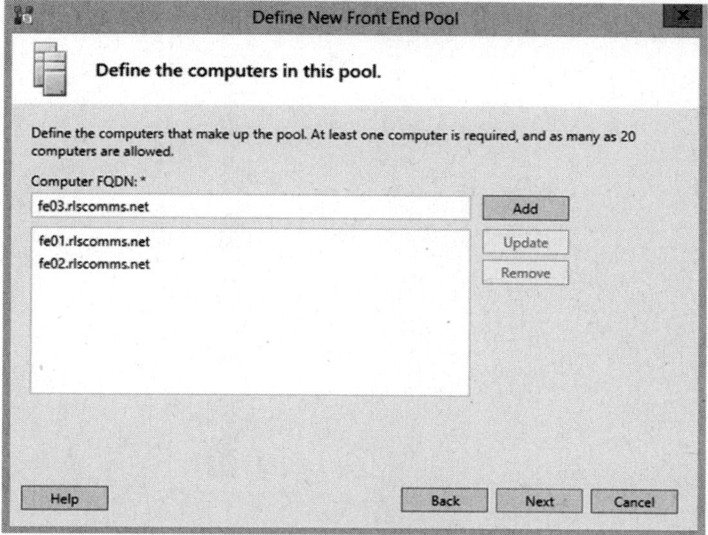

SQL is the additional component needed, providing the back end store capability; you can find details of the SQL options and configuration in Chapter 20.

Once defined and published within Topology Builder, the individual server installation steps are as before:

1. Install the prerequisites.
2. Install the local configuration store.
3. Install the local components.
4. Install the required certificates.

It's these four steps that are common across all the servers when installing the Skype for Business Server application.

One additional piece of infrastructure needed for an Enterprise pool is the load balancer. This can be either a hardware or software load balancer, and its job is to provide high availability to the web services offered by the pool. Figure 8.25 shows the architecture of an Enterprise pool.

FIGURE 8.25
Enterprise pool architecture

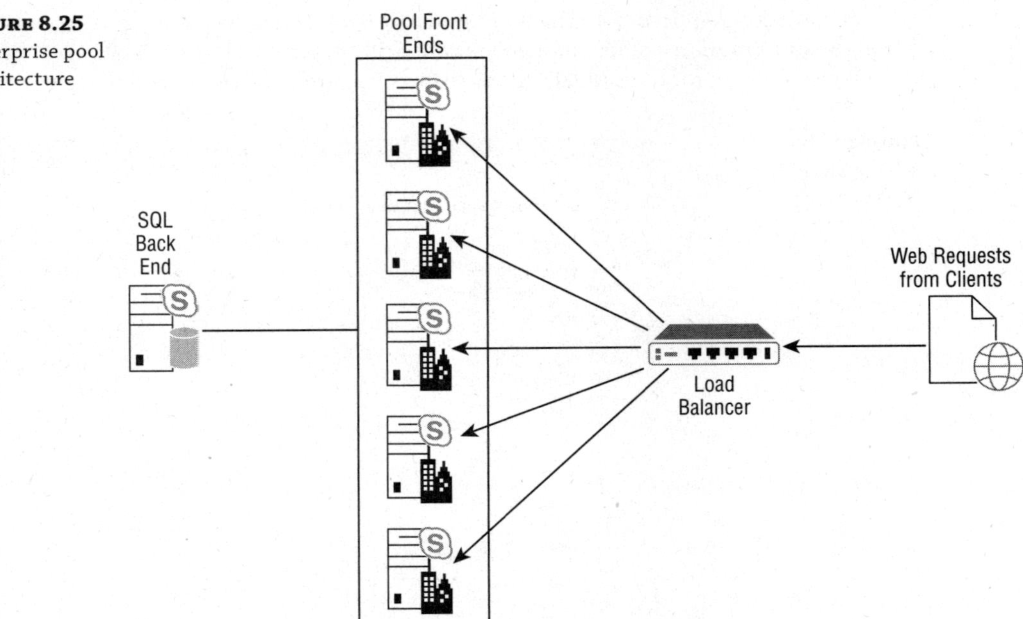

HIGH AVAILABILITY VS. DISASTER RECOVERY

Previously you learned about the disaster recovery capabilities when the Backup pool is defined. Within an Enterprise pool, the steps are the same, and as you'd expect, the user experience is the same.

High availability, on the other hand, is the name given to continuation of service in the event of a single component failure.

Within an Enterprise pool you can allow for a failure of a single server before users may start to become impacted. Depending on the number of servers in the pool, there may be scope to allow for higher numbers of server failure, before impact.

There are two levels of impact:

- User
- Pool

User impact occurs when two servers from a single routing group are disabled. Each user is provided services based on their routing group association. These are set when the user is moved to, or created on, a pool and cannot be changed. A routing group consists of three servers, and while a minimum of two are available, the user will be able to log in and operate. However, if two of the servers in a routing group become unavailable, that whole routing group is unavailable, and the users associated with it are logged out.

Depending upon the state of the pool impact, other users may not be impacted at all and continue to operate. Pool impact occurs when more than 50 percent of the servers in a pool are lost. At this point, the pool is unable to function and host conferences, and so on, so all users will be impacted and be moved into survivable mode.

Figure 8.26 shows the layout of routing groups in a four-server pool, highlighting each user's Primary, Secondary, and Backup servers.

FIGURE 8.26
Routing group layout in a pool

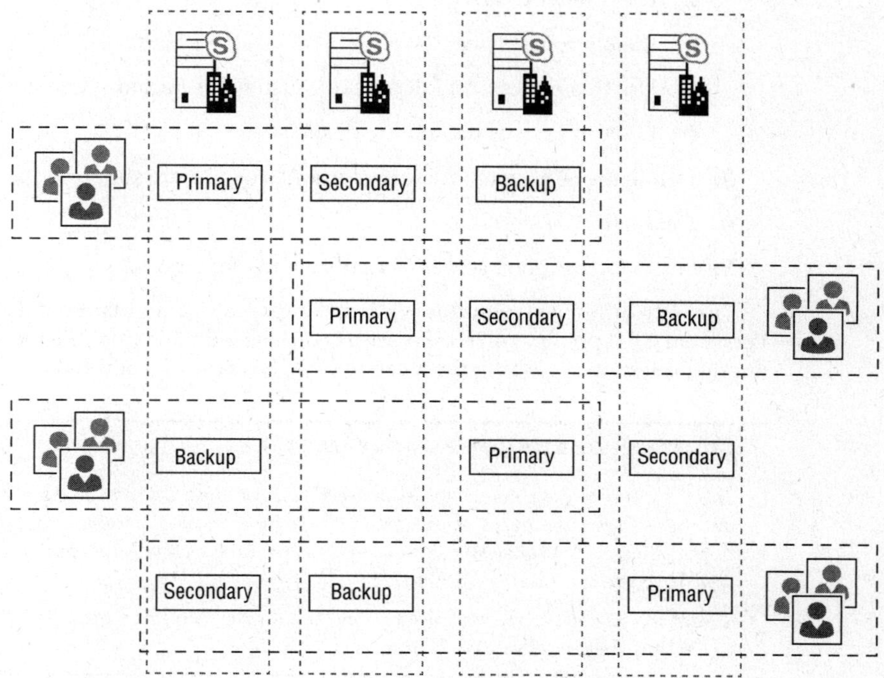

Windows Fabric is responsible for managing this process.

Installing Persistent Chat

Persistent Chat was previously known as Group Chat and has its origins as a product called MindAlign from a company called Parlano (which Microsoft acquired in 2007).

For both OCS R2 and Lync Server 2010, Group Chat was a separate optional download and not seen as core to the product. Lync Server 2013 and Skype for Business have brought the installation into Topology Builder and given the management the same integration and look and feel as the rest of the product.

As with the other roles, installation is carried out using Topology Builder and must be published prior to use.

Opening Topology Builder and selecting New Persistent Chat Pool will open a wizard similar to that for the Standard Edition server you have already installed.

The wizard includes the following steps:

1. Define the FQDN (multiple or single computer pool).
   - If multiple, then define each member.

2. Define the properties of the Persistent Chat pool.
   - Display name
   - Port (default 5041)
   - Enable compliance
   - Use this pool as default for site <currently selected sitename>
   - Use this pool as default for all sites
3. Define the SQL store (mirroring and AlwaysOn are supported).
4. Define the file store.
5. Select the next-hop server (actually asking for a pool).

The only difference with this wizard (compared to a regular pool) is the properties of the Persistent Chat pool page. In this case, if you select Enable Compliance, you will be asked another question regarding the location of SQL server for compliance.

Location of the Compliance Database

The compliance database may be located in the same SQL instance as the main Persistent Chat database. However, permissions are likely to be assigned at the instance level, so this may cause potential issues because the same user DBA permissions will be applied to the original source as well as to the compliance database.

Therefore, to ensure separation, it is better to have a separate instance (and possibly SQL server) to contain the compliance database.

Once the topology has been published, the Setup And Deployment Wizard can be run as with any other servers and will automatically install the required components.

Persistent Chat servers require a certificate, which the Setup and Deployment Wizard can request and assign.

As before, services will need to be started manually.

Considerations for Branches

As discussed in Chapter 7, there are various aspects to consider when deploying in branch offices, including the bandwidth available and the reliability of that bandwidth back to the central site, the number of users in the remote site, and the availability of local IT staff.

Planning might determine that a local server capable of supporting all workloads is needed at the branch office. This would, therefore, not be a survivable branch appliance but would instead be a Standard Edition server.

Deploying a Standard Edition server in a branch site is similar to deploying one in a central site. The main difference is that instead of running the Prepare First Standard Edition Server step, you can progress straight to installing the local configuration store. That is because you will already have a CMS in the topology, which is used to define the updated topology required for deploying the Standard Edition server in the branch office.

Type of Site for Standard Edition Deployment in a Branch

Contrary to common sense, to deploy a Standard Edition server in a branch office, you don't create a branch site, which would be the case for an SBA deployment. Instead, you create another central site.

It is possible to create an additional Standard Edition server in the existing central site and Skype for Business would function perfectly.

The advantage, however, of creating a separate central site is one of management and the ability to define policy specific to that site—for example, emergency calling options.

Automating Installation Using PowerShell

Throughout this chapter, if you looked carefully at the summary pages at the end of the various installation steps, you have seen the PowerShell commands that ran. As stated elsewhere, Skype for Business is underpinned by PowerShell, which means that it is entirely feasible to carry out the installation directly from the command line without using the GUI setup at all. Although it may not be the most user-friendly option, it is great for documentation and repetition.

So, if you are rolling out globally, we highly recommend taking a look at this option and working to build a deployment script that will enable you to deploy servers in a known manner without any administrative errors.

The Bottom Line

Configure Windows Server for a Skype for Business installation. Installing Skype for Business is relatively simple, but many steps are involved. One of the most important is the preparatory work needed. If you get this wrong, it will slow down your installation and you may find that certain features will not work later.

Master It Skype for Business can be installed on several subtly different operating systems. You have been asked to lay out which OS requires the least amount of preparatory work and what the main preparatory stages are before Skype for Business can be deployed.

Prepare Active Directory for installation. Like many Microsoft server applications, Skype for Business has tight ties with AD. Lync Server 2010 was the first version of Microsoft's real-time communications product to start moving away from the reliance on AD, but nevertheless, there are still hard requirements and preparatory steps that must be carried out, which include schema, forest, and domain prep.

Master It You are working in a large corporation with a single forest and multiple domains. You have been instructed to work with your directories team to help them understand the changes that need to be made to the schema as part of setup.

Install your first Standard Edition server. A Standard Edition server is a complex environment requiring careful deployment. It has numerous prerequisites that need to be installed. Once you have completed the installation of prerequisites, setup is relatively straightforward, following a standard process.

Master It You have been tasked with installing the first Standard Edition server in your network. What is one of the unique preparatory steps required for this Standard Edition, and why? Following that, what are the standard steps that the setup takes?

Implement external access through the Director Edge server. There are many elements that come together to provide external access. The Edge server and reverse proxy server sit in the perimeter network and provide access to media and web components, respectively. The Director sits on the LAN and acts as a routing and security buffer between the external users and the Front End pools. The deployment of the Director is similar to the deployment of Standard Edition or Front End servers and requires similar prerequisites.

Master It You are deploying an Edge server as part of providing remote access to your network. What is different about the install compared to the Standard Edition and Director installs?

Understand the differences in an Enterprise Edition installation. There are many differences when working on an Enterprise Edition deployment compared to a Standard Edition install. For example, there is the potential for a complex directory to be present, which requires close cooperation with a directories team. Another change is that SQL is installed separately and does not coexist with the Skype for Business server like it does with Standard Edition. Finally, there is the challenge of scalability and branch offices to overcome.

Master It You have been asked to work with the database team to ensure that everything is in place for the installation. What do you need to explain, and how would you instruct the database team to create the databases?

Chapter 9

Migration and Upgrades

If you've followed along in the book so far, you should have a good understanding of much of Skype for Business, including how to deploy it. However, if you already have a Microsoft real-time communication platform in your environment, things are slightly more complex than if you don't. You will need to consider how to upgrade or migrate from one system to the next and negotiate a period of coexistence. Only migrations or upgrades (yes, upgrades—you'll learn more about this later) from Lync Server are supported. Any other older versions will require a "stepping-stone" approach to migrate to a supported starting point prior to the final move to Skype for Business.

Of course, throughout this period you'll need to work with your users to make sure the transition period is as painless as possible for them as they move from clients they know to the new client.

The main focus in this chapter will be upgrading from Lync Server 2013, although we will briefly cover Lync Server 2010 migrations. The migration is a relatively straightforward process.

In this chapter, you will learn to

- Understand migration considerations
- Consider client pain points

Understanding Migration

Migration to Skype for Business can take a variety of forms. Possibly the simplest would be to install a new system, not have it talk to the old system, and ask users to re-create all their contacts and meetings. Clearly, this isn't possible very often. The disruption would simply be too great.

Therefore, a move to Skype for Business from one of the previous Microsoft real-time communication platforms needs to include a period of coexistence. At the time of writing, this period of coexistence can include only two versions of the product at any one time; Lync Server 2010 and Lync Server 2013 are the only two supported options. Migration from OCS (or earlier versions) directly to Skype for Business is not supported, tested, or documented, and neither is having both OCS 2007 R2 and Lync Server (either version) deployed in the same organization and adding Skype for Business to that. If you have a complex environment with a mix of OCS 2007 and OCS 2007 R2, or even an old Live Communications Server (LCS) system, you have to perform some intermediary steps before you can get to Skype for Business.

To get to a state where Skype for Business can be integrated and coexist with your existing environment, you need to make sure that any LCS or OCS deployments are upgraded to at least Lync Server 2010 and that LCS/OCS is completely decommissioned. Equally, if you have a mixed Lync Server 2010 and Lync Server 2013 deployment, then you'll need to complete the move to Lync Server 2013 and remove all the Lync Server 2010 pools so that you have only Lync

Server 2013 left. Or indeed, reverse and consolidate on Lync Server 2010. This will depend on how far through the migration to Lync Server 2013 you've already gotten—which is quickest?

NOTE We have worked with many customers who, for various reasons, are partway through a Lync to Lync migration. Generally, these are large multinational companies that are phasing in the new version regionally; perhaps they have a legacy application they cannot remove and are stuck with Lync Server 2010 for some time. In either case, we can deploy Skype for Business Server only when there remains a single Lync Server version in place.

Once you've done that, you are ready to move to Skype for Business Server 2015—not as easy as first thought perhaps!

Coexistence

This chapter is called "Migration and Upgrades" because people use both words interchangeably to describe moving to the latest versions of Microsoft software. In general, the term *upgrade* refers to an in-place upgrade, which only really occurs with operating systems or databases these days, and the term *migrate* refers to deploying a parallel system side by side and moving the configuration and users to the new system. You are *upgrading* in the sense that you are moving from one Microsoft real-time communication product to the next version; however, you are *migrating* in the method that you carry out the move.

With all previous versions of the Microsoft Unified Communications platform there was no way to simply put the install media into the existing servers and click Upgrade; however, this has changed with Skype for Business. You can now upgrade from Lync Server 2013 directly to Skype for Business; you'll see how later in this chapter.

The only way to get from Lync Server 2010 is through a side-by-side migration, in which you install Skype for Business Server 2015 on new servers in your existing Active Directory (AD), configure it to coexist with Lync Server 2010, and then simply move users. This is also achievable with Lync Server 2013 if preferred.

A key element of coexistence is the way the Edge and Director roles are handled. The first principle is that the Edge and Director (or next hop) roles should always be deployed together. You should not have a Skype for Business Edge server talking to a Lync Server 2013 Director server, for example. Another similar requirement is not to mix the Skype for Business and Lync Server versions of the Edge and Mediation roles. For example, a Lync Server 2013 Mediation server should have a route out of a Lync Server 2013 Edge, not a Skype for Business one.

In addition to the major issue of version support, you need to be aware of a couple of more detailed points about coexistence. First, when moving Skype for Business, there are a variety of options involving the SQL database. You can either create and use an entirely new SQL Server infrastructure or reuse an existing SQL Server installation. Obviously, you must size the SQL infrastructure correctly in either case so that it can perform adequately for Skype for Business. One thing that is highly discouraged is using an existing SQL Server instance that is supporting another application. Although it is possible to make this work theoretically, you would not be able to control the way CPU and memory resources were assigned even though you could control where the database resided on the disk. Also, if the existing instance is supporting Lync, you would have a clash of default database names, which is definitely something to avoid! You can find more information about SQL Server sizing and configuration in Chapter 20, "SQL."

A final aspect of migration to be aware of is that Skype for Business brings some new roles that didn't exist in Lync Server. It is recommended to complete the deployment of Skype for Business and the removal of Lync Server before deploying new roles.

Considering Client Pain Points

When a move to Skype for Business is being planned, one of the most important considerations is how the migration will affect users. After all, it would be a shame to create a negative feeling about such a great new platform. To ensure that things go smoothly, you need to be aware of common issues and problems that inevitably occur as new functionality is introduced that works differently than its predecessor. This topic is discussed more broadly in Chapter 14, "Planning for Adoption."

The first consideration is the client. Any of the Lync clients (2010 and 2013) can connect to the Skype for Business Server infrastructure, and indeed the Skype for Business client can connect to either of the Lync Server deployments. This gives great flexibility in terms of what your approach should be—client or server first? As you'll see throughout the remainder of this chapter, there are different benefits to either approach, and neither is wrong. It will depend on your environment (both infrastructure as well as users). Also, see Chapter 14 for information on how to manage the user transition.

Of course, new features are not necessarily going to be available with older clients or infrastructure still in the mix.

Indeed, migration from Lync Server to Skype for Business Server is probably one of the least impactful migration processes you'll come across.

Policies

Because of the consistent approach to clients receiving policy configuration via in-band provisioning, there is no impact if the Skype for Business server infrastructure is upgraded ahead of the clients.

In Figure 9.1 you can see the XML text provided at sign-in, containing some of the policy definitions.

FIGURE 9.1
Policy configuration via in-band provisioning


```
- <provisionGroupList xmlns="http://schemas.microsoft.com/2006/09/sip/provisiongrouplist-notification">
  + <provisionGroup name="publicProviders">
  + <provisionGroup name="userSetting">
  + <provisionGroup name="ServerConfiguration">
  + <provisionGroup name="locationPolicy">
  + <provisionGroup name="persistentChatConfiguration">
  + <provisionGroup name="mediaConfiguration">
  + <provisionGroup name="meetingPolicy">
  + <provisionGroup name="privacyPublicationGrammar">
  - <provisionGroup name="presencePolicyV2">
    - <propertyEntryList>
        <property name="EnablePrivacyMode">false</property>
        <property name="AutoInitiateContacts">true</property>
        <property name="PublishLocationDataDefault">true</property>
        <property name="DisplayPublishedPhotoDefault">true</property>
        <property name="PersonalNoteHistoryDepth">3</property>
        <property name="SubscribeToCollapsedDG">true</property>
      </propertyEntryList>
    </provisionGroup>
  - <provisionGroup name="ucPolicy">
    - <instance>
        <property name="name">DefaultPolicy</property>
        <property name="AllowSimultaneousRinging">false</property>
        <property name="AllowCallForwarding">false</property>
        <property name="EnableDelegation">true</property>
        <property name="EnableTeamCall">false</property>
        <property name="EnableCallPark">false</property>
        <property name="EnableCallTransfer">false</property>
        <property name="EnableMaliciousCallTrace">false</property>
        <property name="enableBWPolicyOverride">false</property>
        <property name="VoiceDeploymentMode">OnPrem</property>
        <property name="UcEnabled">false</property>
      </instance>
    </provisionGroup>
  + <provisionGroup name="publicationGrammar">
  + <provisionGroup name="endpointConfiguration">
```

Any Skype for Business or Lync client will receive the XML content and will parse it for the relevant values it is looking for; any additional or unknown values are simply ignored. This is what allows clients to continue and apply the values they expect, without causing any problems.

This approach applies both in terms of unknown policies and in terms of unknown values within a policy.

> **CONFIGURING THE MEETING JOIN PAGE**
>
> Previously with Lync Server 2010, it was possible to configure the Meeting Join page to allow access by legacy clients. However, this option was removed with Lync Server 2013 and continues to be unavailable in Skype for Business Server because the preference now is for connectivity via Skype Web App (now providing audio and video) rather than a legacy client.
>
> Indeed, the only configuration now available is via PowerShell, and it only allows you to download the Lync 2010 Attendee client. You can configure this setting by using the `New-CsWebServiceConfiguration` or `Set-CsWebServiceConfiguration` PowerShell cmdlet with the `ShowDownloadCommunicatorAttendeeLink` parameter.

The Client Experience

As touched on previously, one of the bigger challenges of your move to Skype for Business is making sure things work as expected for users. A big part of this challenge is determining how those users still on the old client can work with those on the new client.

There are (typically) small and subtle differences between the clients from Lync 2010, Lync 2013, Skype for Business 2015, and Skype for Business 2016—too many to list out here. You can find out details about this on TechNet.

`https://technet.microsoft.com/EN-US/library/dn933896.aspx`

Now, those of you paying attention will have noticed we mentioned two Skype for Business clients.

- Skype for Business 2015
- Skype for Business 2016

Where has this other client come from? And what is the difference?

Well, the first stage of the Skype for Business release was mostly a re-branding exercise. Microsoft released a patch (`https://support.microsoft.com/en-us/kb/2889923`), entitled "April 14, 2015 update for Lync 2013 (Skype for Business)(KB2889923)." This update has the result of "re-skinning" the Lync 2013 client to look like the upcoming Skype for Business client. Figure 9.2 shows these two clients side by side.

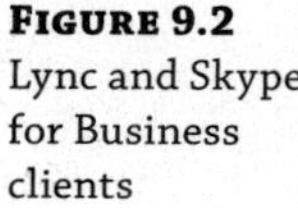

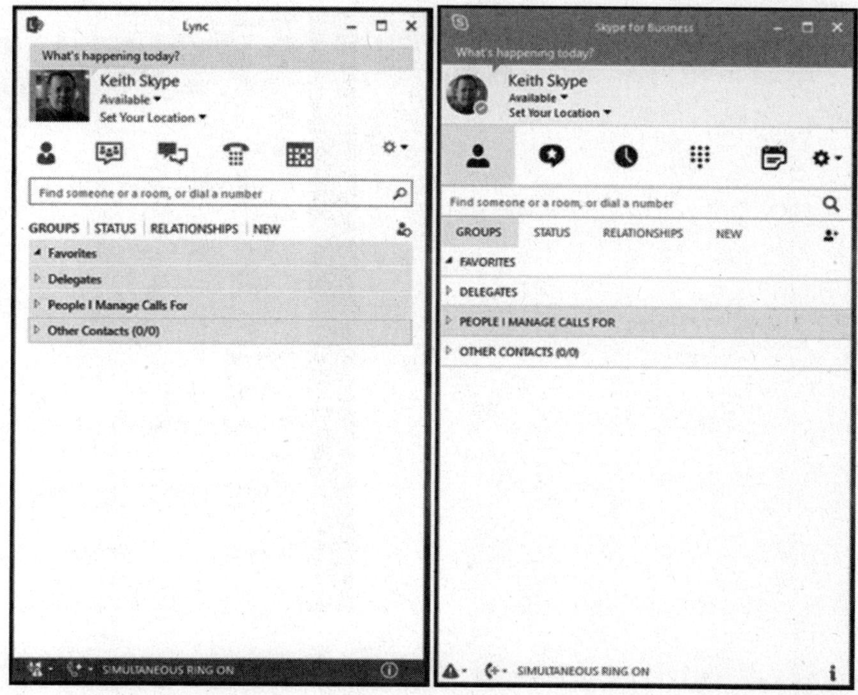

FIGURE 9.2 Lync and Skype for Business clients

By taking this approach, introducing the "new" client is limited to simply patching the existing deployed Lync 2013 client environment, which is much more manageable than deploying a full client to everyone.

However, it can cause a lot of confusion with users, especially if they're not ready and expecting the client to be updated. Microsoft thought about this approach and has enabled a policy setting to force the client to continue to look like the Lync 2013 client. This way users will not know they've been upgraded until the proper communications have gone out.

Sadly, the approach doesn't appear to have been fully thought through, as there are a few issues that don't appear to have been considered.

First, the naming of the application is Skype for Business in the folder structure, which can cause confusion with users. Fortunately, as shown in Figure 9.3, searching for *Lync* will return the application Skype for Business.

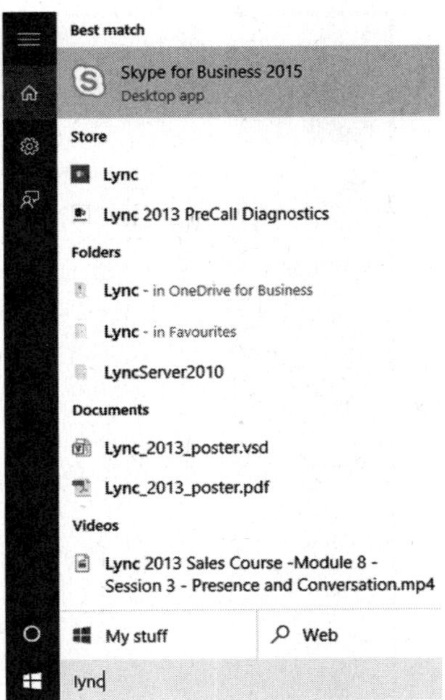

FIGURE 9.3
Searching for Lync

Second, the icon in the task bar has been changed to the Skype for Business icon (see Figure 9.4), which, again, can be confusing to users who are unprepared for the change.

FIGURE 9.4
The Lync icon in the Windows taskbar

Therefore, if you're going to deploy the patch and tell users of these changes, you may as well tell them about the whole client change and forget about the re-skinning.

Anyhow, as for the re-skinning, you can set a registry key on the client machines itself.

```
[HKEY_CURRENT_USER\Software\Microsoft\Office\Lync]
"EnableSkypeUI"=hex:00,00,00,00"
```

A value of 0 enables the Lync UI, and a value of 1 enables the Skype for Business UI.

Obviously, this could be built into a GPO and released within Active Directory, but a much cleaner way of approaching the problem is to define it within a policy on the server, and any client that connects will then receive the policy directly. Indeed, as mentioned earlier in this chapter, clients that are not looking for this particular attribute will simply ignore it.

It is a client policy that needs to be configured, and the value is `EnableSkypeUI`, as shown in the following PowerShell line:

```
New-CsClientPolicy -Identity SkypeUI -EnableSkypeUI $True
```

Figure 9.5 shows the pop-up message presented to a user, which is another potentially confusing message.

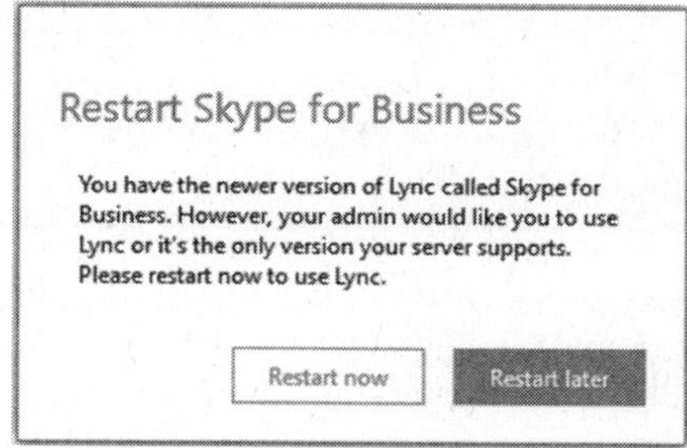

Restart Skype for Business
You have the newer version of Lync called Skype for Business. However, your admin would like you to use Lync or it's the only version your server supports. Please restart now to use Lync.
Restart now
Restart later

FIGURE 9.5 User message to restart for new interface

In summary, Skype for Business 2015 is the upgraded Lync 2013 client, and Skype for Business 2016 is the client deployed with the installation of Microsoft Office 2016.

Migrating to Skype for Business

Now that you're familiar with a broad outline of the migration process and understand how a migration affects users, it's time to dive in and actually migrate a system. This section will discuss moving from a system on Lync Server 2010 to Skype for Business. It is also applicable to move from Lync Server 2013 to Skype for Business; however, there is another approach described in the next section that will achieve that result quicker.

NOTE Although the migration-related aspects of the process will be discussed in depth, this chapter assumes you have read and understand other areas of the book. Given that a migration touches many elements of Skype for Business, if we covered every piece of the process in depth, this chapter would be huge.

There's not a lot of complexity involved in migrating from Lync 2010 to Skype for Business. Granted, there are differences in the client and some of the capability is available if you're using a Lync 2010 client on a Skype for Business server infrastructure (such as multiparty video view or sharing using Office Web Applications server), but fundamentally, the infrastructure is the same.

On the infrastructure, there's the removal of the separate Audio/Video conferencing pool, the addition of the Video Interoperability Server, and further changes "under the covers," but no change is significant enough to justify a major design upheaval.

Monitoring and Archiving During Migration

Although a Monitoring or Archiving server isn't defined in the migration scenario in this chapter, it is something you may need to take into account. This is especially the case when your company relies on archiving for compliance reasons or perhaps monitoring for billing purposes. The main principle is that each version of Skype for Business, Lync or OCS works with only the Monitoring and Archiving server from the same version. Therefore, if you are migrating and

continues

continued

> maintaining these capabilities is critical, you must implement the Monitoring and Archiving roles in your Skype for Business pool before you move any users. The exception to this is Lync Server 2013, which shares the same database schema as the Skype for Business Monitoring and Archiving roles.
>
> For more information on the Monitoring and Archiving roles, see Chapter 13, "Archiving and Monitoring Roles."

Before you get going with the migration, you must pay close attention to a few things throughout the process. First, test at all stages; don't simply plow on after each step without validating that the changes you have made were actually applied correctly.

It is also important to use the correct tools to manage both systems during coexistence. As you might expect, you should (and can only) manage the Topology using the Skype for Business version of Topology Builder. Indeed, the CMS will at least initially remain on the Lync Server 2010 pool, and you can choose when to migrate the role. However, the actual content will be upgraded to Skype for Business with the first pool published.

You should use Skype for Business Server Control Panel (Control Panel) or Skype for Business Server Management Shell (PowerShell) to carry out any migration aspects.

Deploying the First Skype for Business Pool

Now that all the checks have been performed and the rollback plans are in place, it's time to install the new infrastructure. The procedure follows the same steps described in Chapter 8, "Installation." Unless you have deployed a topology with Lync Server 2010, which is no longer supported Skype for Business, it's reasonably likely you will have a design similar to that of your Lync Server 2010 infrastructure.

Begin by installing the first pool in the same location as a Lync Server 2010 pool. How do you choose where to start? Well, assuming the choice hasn't been made for you with only a single pool deployment, it's recommended to start from the inside and work out. So, start with a pool that is not in the federation path, as you'll want to be upgrading edge servers and dependent pools last.

So, you've got a pool that isn't the next federation hop. What next? Deploy the Skype for Business pool, test it, and migrate users. That's relatively straightforward, right? Well, possibly, but at the testing point you may run into some of these common problems/oversights:

- No external traffic
- One-way IM traffic externally
- External meeting joins that don't connect (remote or federated users)

These most common issues are typically resolved with firewall and/or updating host files on the Edge servers and Reverse Proxy servers. As these servers are not connected to the internal LAN, they typically have to be manually updated with the new server's address information.

Once the users are all moved across, use the Skype for Business Control Panel or PowerShell.

```
Move-CsUser -Identity <user> -MoveConferenceData -Target <newpool.fqdn>
```

Then it's time to decommission the legacy servers. Simply remove each server from Topology Builder, publish, and then switch off the older servers. Repeat this process for each of the pools. Next is to take out the mediation servers by following a similar process. This time remember to upgrade the gateway next hop to be the new servers. Finally, when it comes to the Edge server, it can be slightly more complicated, most of which can be overcome with planning and, as may be expected, is network related. (The reverse proxy servers do not need to be replaced; as mentioned, they simply need to be pointed to the new servers.)

- Do you have enough IP addresses to deploy new servers?
- Do you need to reuse IP addresses?
- Do you need to modify firewall rules?

Answers to some of these questions will lead to the next phases. Are you able to deploy a separate Edge server for testing with a few users? Or is it a like-for-like replacement, which will impact availability and be tested live but potentially has less risk, as the network and firewall rules are already in place?

Once the process has been established, it's a case of deploying the servers. Once testing is complete, if required, you update external DNS records to point to the new Edge servers. Remember, of course, that the Edge server version must match the version of the next hop.

It's straightforward indeed!

Continue this approach pool by pool, starting on the inside and working out to the Edge roles, on a site-by-site basis, leaving the federation route to the end.

Upgrading to Skype for Business

Lync Server 2013 can be *upgraded* to Skype for Business—directly. No other considerations needed. Just put in the DVD and select Upgrade. Well, actually, not quite as easy at that. You have to make a topology change and then run the upgrade. Figure 9.6 shows you how to make that change.

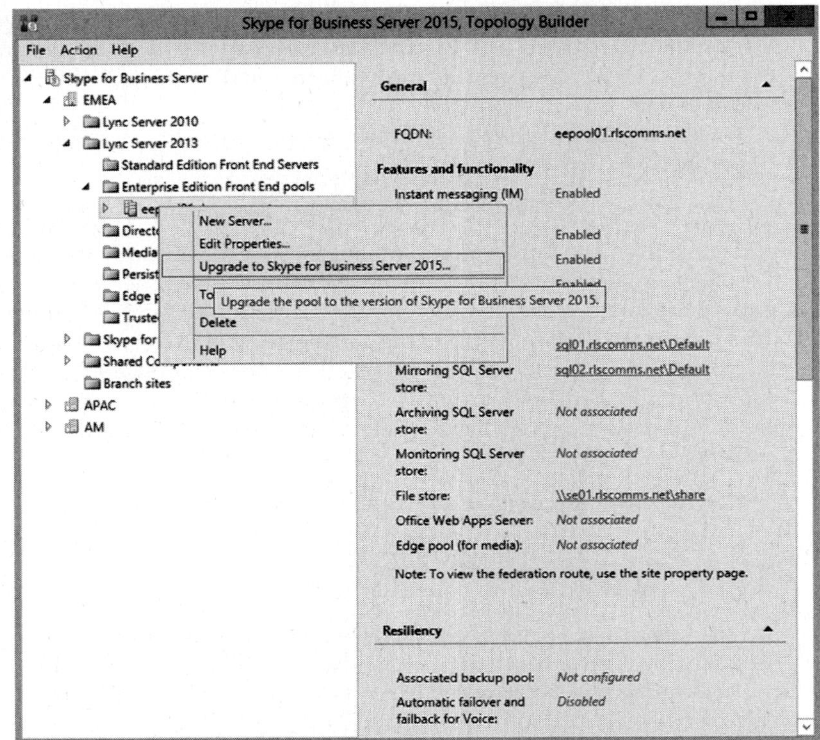

FIGURE 9.6 Upgrading a pool

Any of the infrastructure components will have this capability of being upgraded with a right-click and a topology publish.

Topology Builder will prompt to confirm and then simply move the object from the Lync Server 2013 branch to the Skype for Business branch, as shown in Figure 9.7. Be aware of this move of the pool to the Skype for Business branch. The pool isn't deleted, just moved.

The next stage is to run `Setup.exe` from the Skype for Business Server 2015 media. If the Lync Server 2013 servers are not patched to the correct level of 5.0.8308.815, you will see the error shown in Figure 9.8.

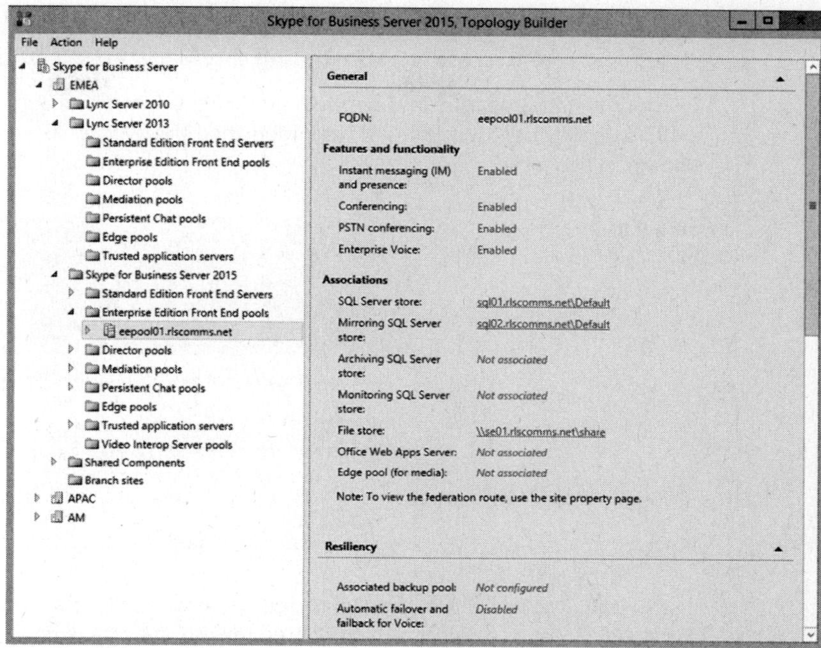

FIGURE 9.7
The Upgraded Lync 2013 pool in Topology Builder

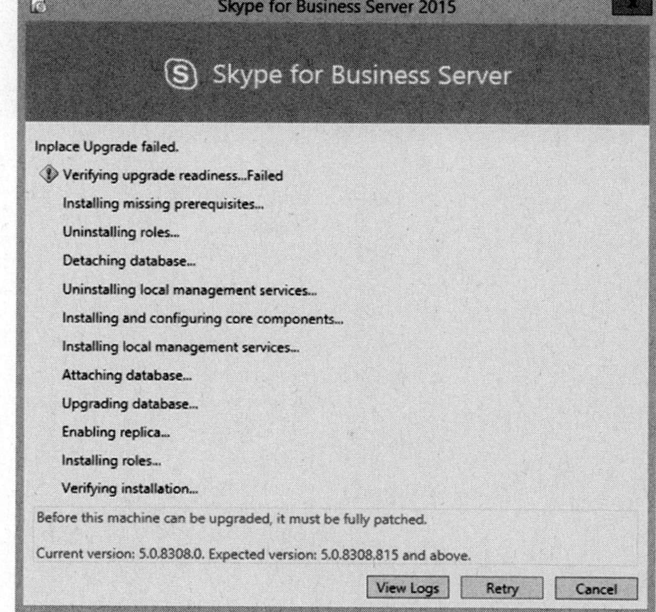

FIGURE 9.8
Lync Server 2013 incorrect patch level

Download the latest Cumulative Update patch for Lync 2013 from here:

`https://www.microsoft.com/en-gb/download/details.aspx?id=36820`

Once it's downloaded and applied, rerun `Setup.exe` and begin the upgrade process.

The deployment wizard will have identified the process as an upgrade and will start, as shown in Figure 9.9.

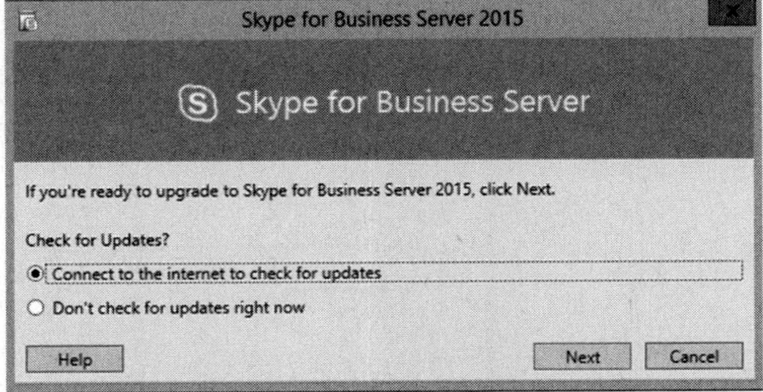

FIGURE 9.9
Starting the upgrade

Next the wizard checks for the correct version of SQL. Skype for Business requires SQL Server 2012 SP1 as a minimum; anything lower than this version will result in the error shown in Figure 9.10.

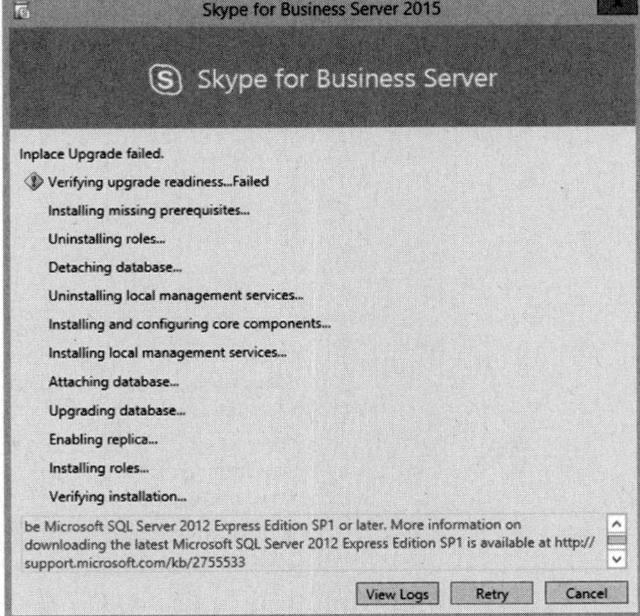

FIGURE 9.10
Incorrect version of SQL in place

You can download the SQL Server 2012 service packs from here:

```
https://support.microsoft.com/en-gb/kb/2755533
```

Once they're downloaded, apply the service pack to the SQL Express instances (remember to apply both).

- RTCLOCAL
- LYNCLOCAL

When the SQL Express instances are upgraded, proceed with the Skype for Business upgrade. The upgrade will go through the following steps automatically:

- Verifying upgrade readiness
- Installing missing prerequisites
- Uninstalling roles
- Detaching database
- Uninstalling local management services
- Installing and configuring core components
- Installing local manager services
- Attaching database
- Upgrading database
- Enabling replica
- Installing roles
- Verifying installation

The pool upgrade can begin only when all services in the pool have been stopped. Obviously this will impact any users currently homed on the pool; however, depending on your configuration, you may be able to move the users to another pool to ensure service during the upgrade. Otherwise, they'll be unable to log in during the process.

At this stage, you might think you should perform a pool failover. *Do not!* It is unsupported to upgrade a pool when in failover state. Moving the users is the only approach to take if you want to manage and limit downtime.

Pool pairing does not have to be removed; however, two pools paired while on a different version of the product should be for as short a time as possible. Microsoft has not defined how long this time period should be.

Stopping the services can be achieved with the following PowerShell cmdlet (run on each Front End server):

```
Stop-CsWindowsService
```

Once the servers and SQL are patched and the services have been stopped, the upgrade process will continue. This will take some time to complete (depending on server spec) and needs to be completed on each server.

Figure 9.11 shows the message displayed when the upgrade is completed.

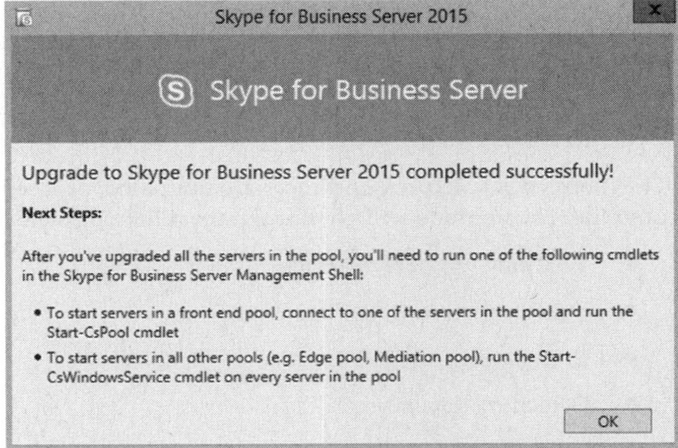

FIGURE 9.11
Upgrade completed

Once all servers in the pool are upgraded, you must restart the services on each of them. Fortunately, Skype for Business has introduced a new cmdlet in PowerShell to save you from doing this on each server. Simply run `Start-CsPool` and all services on all Front Ends will be started. An additional update to PowerShell enables feedback to be received on the state of each of the servers. This is shown in Figure 9.12.

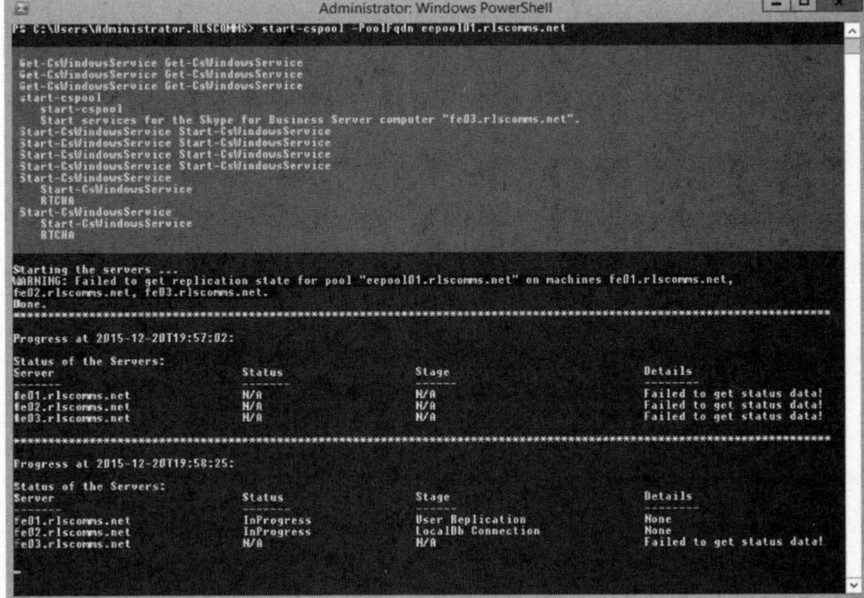

FIGURE 9.12
Starting a pool via PowerShell

As the pool is starting up, you may see errors relating to being unable to get status. These are expected, as the pool will be down initially and nonresponsive. You might even see statements that say "Warning no progress is being made"! However, you should see the status change through the startup process, with the regular updates.

Once all services on all servers are online, it is safe to begin the testing of users prior to moving back the live users to the pool.

Third-Party Applications

The last server-based piece of the migration concerns third-party applications. There are a variety of types; some, such as videoconferencing units, are defined in Lync as trusted application pools. They need to be configured so that they point to the Skype for Business pool as the next hop. This is performed in Topology Builder or can be managed via PowerShell.

Now that everything is migrated, you can move the internal DNS records that currently direct clients to the Lync Server pool so that they point to the Skype for Business pool.

Client Rollout

The final piece of the migration is to complete the rollout of the Skype for Business client along with the same level of cumulative update as is deployed on your Skype for Business servers. These are some considerations for the rollout of the client:

- Use client version filtering rules on the Skype for Business Front End to ensure that only clients with the correct updates installed are able to sign in, as described in Chapter 3, "Security."
- As discussed earlier in this chapter, you may need to configure the Group Policy settings that are required for client bootstrapping.

Decommissioning Legacy Systems

Now that you've migrated everything to the Skype for Business pool, you are ready to remove the legacy Lync pool. This is as simple as updating Topology Builder to remove the pool and then re-publishing; once the topology has replicated, the servers can be safely removed and decommissioned.

Of course, part of removing and re-publishing via Topology Builder is that Topology Builder will check all the pool dependencies and ensure things like Edge or Mediation next hop references do not refer to this particular pool; it's a last-minute sanity check!

Finally, once you've removed all the Lync servers, rerun the `ExchUCUtil.ps1` script on the Exchange UM server to remove the Lync Server IP Gateway entries.

The Bottom Line

Understand migration considerations. The process of migrating to Skype for Business involves many aspects of an organization, not the least of which are the end users who will have new functionality to exploit and skills to learn. It is important to thoroughly evaluate all the phases of a migration and communicate clearly and efficiently to the staff. This is particularly true for any phase of coexistence where some users will be on Lync and others will be on Skype for Business, potentially with different versions of the client in place.

Master It You have been asked to prepare a short presentation covering the key elements of the migration. List the areas you would cover.

Consider client pain points. During Skype for Business migration, your primary concern should be for your users. Throughout the migration users will face a changing environment. How you deal with this and control the changes both through careful process and configuration of policy will have a large impact on the successful completion of the migration.

Master It You have been asked to prepare a short presentation covering the key difficulties faced by users during migration. List the areas you would cover.

Chapter 10

Online and Hybrid

With the advent of Office 365 and the first incarnations for Skype for Business Online (based on Lync Server 2010), customers have been asking for the ability to host voice in the cloud as well as the ability to have some infrastructure on premises and some in the cloud (the *hybrid* model).

Microsoft Office 365 Lync 2010 Online delivered the power of cloud productivity to businesses of all sizes, helping them free up valued resources by not having to maintain an on-premises Lync server infrastructure (in other words, patching, rack space, data center power, high availability, and disaster recovery planning).

Skype for Business Online provides cloud-based instant messaging, presence, and online meeting experiences with PC audio, videoconferencing, and screen sharing, as well as the promise of Cloud PBX. At the time of writing, the Cloud PBX functionality is in beta with a Technology Adoption Program (TAP) underway.

In this chapter, you will learn to

- Understand the hybrid architecture model
- Understand the capabilities of a hybrid deployment
- Understand the call flow for media in different scenarios
- Understand the required steps to configure a hybrid deployment

Putting Skype for Business Online in Context

When Skype for Business Online was first released, it did not offer an Enterprise Voice service, which is essentially the ability to call the public switched telephone network (PSTN); the only voice capability was for calling other Skype for Business Online users. Eventually, for small businesses only, Skype for Business Online was enabled to provide PSTN calling. The service was called Lync-to-Phone, and connectivity provided Skype for Business Online users with the ability to have their Enterprise Voice capability hosted in the cloud. This option was discontinued around the time of the Lync Server 2013 release.

Audio conference providers (ACPs) enabled dial-in conferencing to be hosted in the cloud, which meant organizations could primarily offer instant message/presence to users but supplement the conferencing with the ability to join via PSTN connections.

The speedy evolution of the online environments and demands from customers have led to Enterprise Voice capability coming with Skype for Business. This will be true Enterprise Voice capability, albeit initially it's likely to have a reduced feature set. Still, with the fast deployment of additional cloud features, it will not be long before it is on par with an on-premises deployment. This functionality is expected to be widely available in 2016.

In this chapter, we use the following terminology:

Skype for Business Online An environment where everything is hosted in the cloud.

Skype for Business Online User A user who is hosted in a cloud-based infrastructure. This may be part of a wider hybrid infrastructure configuration.

Skype for Business Hybrid (or Hybrid Voice) An environment that leverages some Skype for Business Online (in the cloud) infrastructure but also has some on-premises infrastructure, both of which share the same SIP domain.

Skype for Business Hybrid Voice User A user whose account is located in the cloud but leverages some on-premises infrastructure for making PSTN calls.

Skype for Business On-Premises A Skype for Business infrastructure wholly deployed on premises for an organization. (This may also be a hosted infrastructure; however, the distinction then becomes that it is a dedicated hosted environment and not shared. In other words, the servers are the same as they would be if the organization deployed them; they are simply in another location.)

Skype for Business On-Premises User A user whose account is located on on-premises infrastructure—whether this infrastructure is part of a wider hybrid deployment or not.

Cloud PBX The in-cloud environment providing PSTN services by Microsoft, including billing and calling plans.

Please be aware these naming conventions are valid only for this chapter. Microsoft may (and often does) change the terminology or the meaning behind the terminology, so some phrases may refer to different configurations/scenarios on final release.

Understanding Hybrid Voice and Cloud PBX

Many organizations are seeking to actively move enterprise services such as Exchange Server, SharePoint Server, and Skype for Business Server to the cloud. With Skype for Business, the move is made much easier with the option to support a Hybrid Voice environment and even easier still with the Cloud PBX offering.

Hybrid Voice

Hybrid Voice allows organizations to take advantage of any investments they have already made with their on-premises Enterprise Voice environment, such as deploying PSTN media gateways or integrating with PBX/IP-PBX deployments, but still move users to the Skype for Business Online environment to take advantage of all the benefits of a cloud-based infrastructure (such as no capital purchase costs, paying only for capacity that has been used, and so on).

This means they can "sweat" their existing assets and not lose any prior investment made but still take advantage of the cloud offering. Skype for Business Hybrid Voice users can use the on-premises voice infrastructure as though they were on-premises Enterprise Voice users. Their inbound and outbound calls are routed through the PSTN infrastructure that forms part of the on-premises Skype for Business Server deployment.

Figure 10.1 shows a typical Hybrid Voice infrastructure.

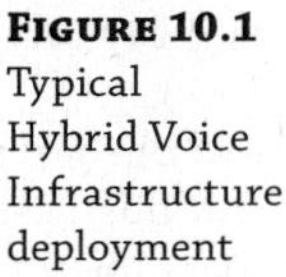

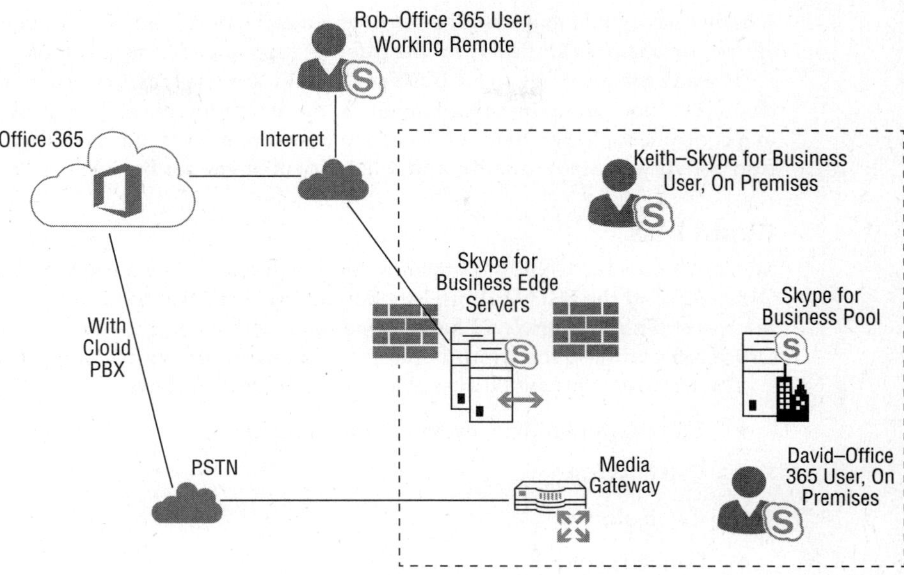

FIGURE 10.1 Typical Hybrid Voice Infrastructure deployment

In Figure 10.1, Keith is a Skype for Business–enabled user who is configured as on premises; in other words, his SIP registrar is a server that is part of the Skype for Business on-premises pool. David and Rob are Skype for Business–enabled users who are configured as Hybrid Voice users; in other words, their SIP registrar server is part of a Skype for Business pool in the Skype for Business Online cloud. David is signed on from within the corporate network, and Rob is working remotely. Both the on-premises and online environments have Skype for Business Edge Servers deployed.

The other exciting developments regarding Hybrid Voice are that on-premises and online users can now share the same SIP domain and that users can be in both infrastructure locations.

Hybrid Voice is configured and kept in sync with the on-premises Active Directory by using Active Directory synchronization. A typical Hybrid Voice deployment will consist of an on-premises Skype for Business pool (Standard or Enterprise Edition) with a colocated Mediation Server role (or, possibly, a stand-alone Mediation Server pool dedicated to call routing), an on-premises Skype for Business Edge Server (or pool), and some on-premises PSTN infrastructure, such as PSTN gateways.

The organization will have an Office 365 tenant with Skype for Business Hybrid users signing in from the corporate network or the Internet. You'll see later in this chapter how to configure hybrid environments.

Features such as call park, response group, and remote call control are not available for Skype for Business Online users enabled for Hybrid Voice. Organizations that require all users to be able to use these features must go with on-premises Enterprise Voice. If an organization requires a contact center solution, this will have to be on premises, and Hybrid Voice users will not be able to act as agents for it if it relies upon deep Skype for Business server integration or indeed the response group functionality.

Voice resiliency refers to the lack of backup SIP registrar capability and survivable branch appliance support for Hybrid Voice users. If the network connection between the organization and the Skype for Business Online service is unavailable, the Skype for Business Online service will be unavailable to users who are enabled as Hybrid Voice users, even if they are accessing Skype for Business Online from the Internet (e.g., outside the corporate network).

The advantage of Skype for Business Hybrid Voice is that it removes many of the barriers to cloud adoption, allowing organizations to more rapidly move users to Skype for Business Online in a controlled, phased manner. Once the users are moved, they can then validate the features, functionality, security, quality, and reliability of Skype for Business Online as Hybrid Voice users.

Cloud PBX

Microsoft uses the Cloud PBX terminology to describe a scenario where the user is hosted in Office 365 and the PSTN calling functionality (via SIP trunking in the cloud) is provided by Microsoft. This scenario will have the advantage that continued administration will be via the Office 365 portal, so the administrators will be working with a familiar interface.

The features that will be available at launch are as follows:

- Call answer/initiate (by name and number)
- Call hold/retrieve
- Call history
- Call delegation and call on behalf
- Call transfer (blind, consult, and mobile)
- Camp-on
- Caller ID
- Call waiting
- Call forwarding and simul-ring
- Device switching
- Distinctive ringing
- Do-not-disturb routing and call blocking
- Enterprise calendar call routing
- Integrated dial-pad
- Music on Hold
- Skype and federated calling
- Team calling
- Video call monitor
- Voice mail
- Clients for PC, Mac, and mobile
- Qualified IP desk phone support

As mentioned, the cloud environment is fast moving, so this feature set is likely to increase quickly.

Voice Mail

Both hybrid and cloud environments support hosting voice mail in Exchange Online. With an on-premises deployment of Skype for Business, you can provide hosted voice mail by having the user's mailbox in Exchange Online. Chapter 22, "Exchange, SharePoint, and Office Web Applications Server," covers the on-premises configuration of Exchange, and later in this chapter you'll see how to configure the Exchange Online aspects.

Configuring for Office 365

The majority of this book is focused on the on-premises deployment; some of this will carry into a hybrid configuration, but for now we'll take a step back to a pure Office 365 environment.

In this case, all infrastructure is managed by Microsoft via the Office 365 data centers. Users and configuration are managed via the Office 365 portal, shown in Figure 10.2.

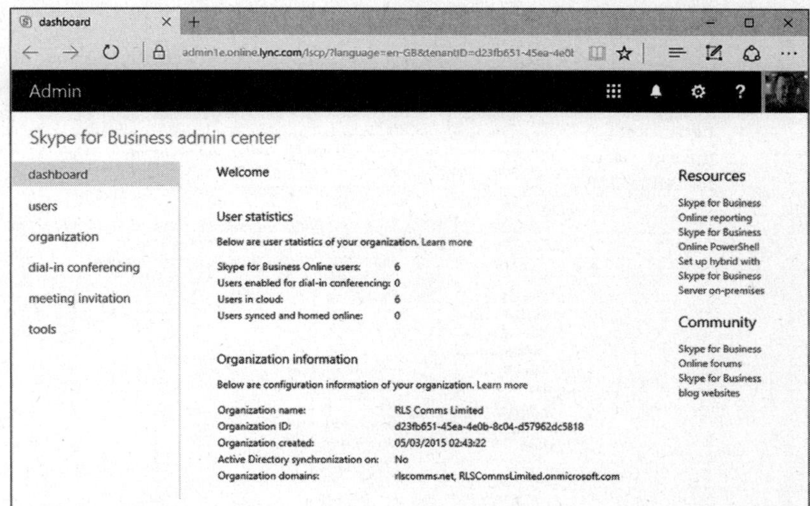

FIGURE 10.2 Office 365 portal showing Skype for Business configuration options

There's not a lot involved. Configuration here consists of the following options:

- Users
- Organization
- Dial-In Conferencing
- Meeting Invitation
- Tools

Please note, while writing this chapter, Microsoft was starting to promote a "new admin experience" with a portal redesign, and with the release of new features, this is likely to change.

With the E3 licensing option, the functionality choices are limited to the following:

- Enable/Disable Users
- Enable/Disable Federation
- Enable/Disable Privacy

- Enable/Disable Push Notifications
- Enable And Configure Audio Conference Providers
- Customize The Meeting Invitation

You can achieve all of this via PowerShell by remoting into the Office 365 environment and importing the Skype for Business Online PowerShell module, as shown here:

```
$credentials = Get-Credential keith_skype@rlscomms.net
$session = New-CsOnlineSession -Credential $credentials
Import-PsSession $session
```

From a user perspective, there is no visible difference. Figure 10.3 shows the configuration information. There's some obvious information (if you know what to look for), such as specific server/pool names, that indicate an Office 365 environment.

FIGURE 10.3 Skype for Business client configuration information for Office 365

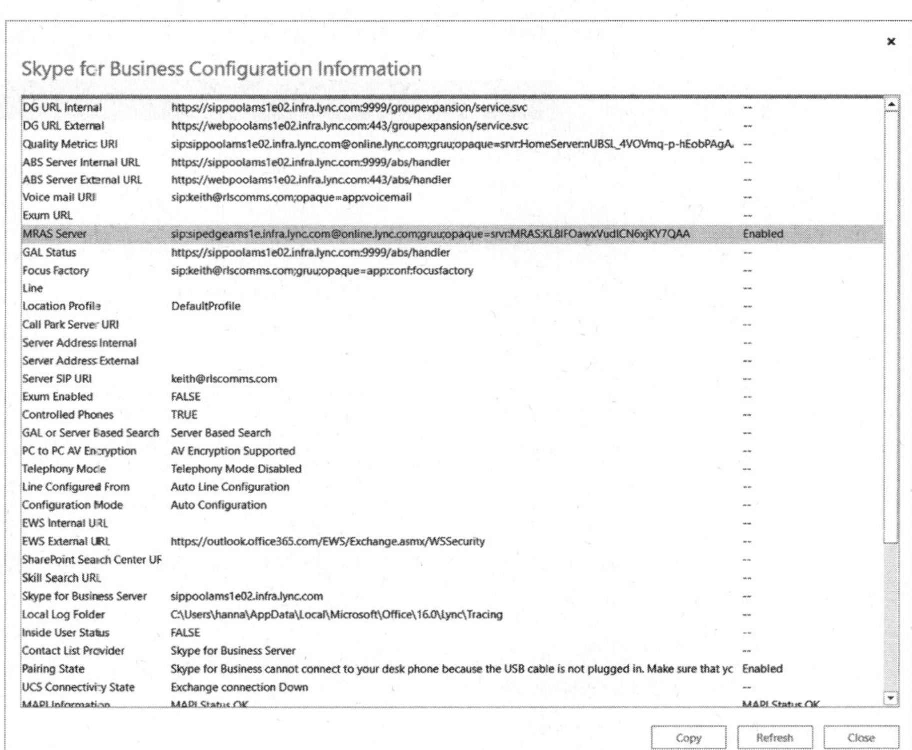

With Skype for Business purely online, all DNS records will point to the online infrastructure—typically `sipfed.online.lync.com` (you'll see this address appear quite regularly).

Configuring Skype for Business Online for Hybrid

One of the steps for setting up Skype for Business Hybrid is to federate the on-premises Edge servers with the Skype for Business Online Edge servers. This important step is explained in the following sections. The Edge federation is used to explain many of the scenarios discussed in the next sections of the chapter.

You will learn how Skype for Business Hybrid works and how it is configured. You'll also look at some call flow examples as well as how advanced features such as Media Bypass and E9-1-1 work when a user is enabled for Hybrid Voice.

First you need to configure both the on-premises and in-cloud environments before you can start to look at clients.

Configuration for Hybrid

With Lync Server, configuration with the cloud was a manual process. Skype for Business has introduced a wizard as part of the Skype for Business Control Panel, so it's now possible to enable the configuration in a few simple clicks.

Of course, there are always a few prerequisites to be checked off prior to starting.

- An on-premises deployment (including Edge servers)
- An Office 365 tenant, with Skype for Business Online enabled
- Single sign-on enabled between on-premises Active Directory and Office 365
- Directory synchronization solution between Office 365 and Active Directory
- Skype for Business Administrative tools installed
- Skype for Business Online, with Windows PowerShell Module installed (download from `http://go.microsoft.com/fwlink/?LinkId=294688`)

Setting Up the Internal Corporate Network for Skype for Business Online

For users to be able to access Skype for Business Online from within the corporate network, specific ports and URLs need to be allowed via firewalls or forward-facing proxies. Table 10.1 shows the required ports on the corporate reverse proxy servers and external firewalls.

Table 10.1: Required firewall ports and protocol configuration

Port	Protocol	Direction	Usage
443	STUN/TCP	Outbound	Audio, video, and application-sharing sessions
443	PSOM/TLS	Outbound	Data-sharing sessions
3478	STUN/UDP	Outbound	Audio and video sessions
5223	TCP	Outbound	Mobile push notifications (if Mobile clients are deployed)
50000–59999	RTP/UDP	Outbound	Audio and video sessions

Configure an exception for Microsoft Online Services URLs and applications from the proxy or firewall. Create these rules/exceptions on the external firewall that apply to all users on the organization's network:

- Allow outgoing connections to the following URLs:
  - `*.microsoftonline.com`.
  - `*.microsoftonline-p.com`.
  - `*.onmicrosoft.com`
  - `*.sharepoint.com`
  - `*.outlook.com`
  - `*.lync.com`
  - `*.verisign.com`
  - `*.verisign.net`
  - `*.public-trust.com`
  - `*.sa.symcb.com`
- Allow TCP and HTTPS.
- Set the HTTPS/SSL timeout to eight hours.

If the firewall being used does not accept URLs such as `*.lync.com`, then exclude the IP address ranges that are used by Skype for Business Online. The following TechNet article lists the IP ranges:

`https://support.office.com/en-us/article/Office-365-URLs-and-IP-address-ranges-8548a211-3fe7-47cb-abb1-355ea5aa88a2?ui=en-US&rs=en-US&ad=US`

Any Internet proxy access needs to be unauthenticated so that the sign-on process is seamless. The preferred approach is to bypass the proxy because a proxy will typically force all traffic to be TCP (potentially impacting call quality).

Skype for Business Online Tenant (Preparing Online Services)

When you create an online tenant, you will be assigned a domain such as, for example, `rlscomms.onmicrosoft.com`; you will then need to add your vanity domain, which is actually your on-premises domain name (such as `rlscomms.net`).

To create an online tenant, you will need to visit the Office 365 online services website.

`www.microsoft.com/office/preview/en/office-365-proplus`

These are the next high-level steps:

1. Enter your email address, physical address, and contact telephone number.
2. Create an administrator account in the online domain; it will be automatically populated—for example `admin@rlscomms.onmicrosoft.com`.
3. Add your vanity domain (e.g., `rlscomms.net`).
4. You will then have to verify your domain.

5. Enable federation for Skype for Business Online.
6. Activate Active Directory synchronization online (this step must be completed before installing the Directory Synchronization Tool).

WHY USE HYBRID DEPLOYMENTS?

There are several reasons for moving to a hybrid deployed model; the most popular is to remove the local server footprint of a highly available Lync deployment. For small organizations, Lync can be expensive to deploy because of the number of servers needed. Although a single Standard Edition server will support up to 2,500 users, voice is typically a business-critical function, so high availability is a requirement. Suddenly two Front End servers (it truly should be three) are needed along with multiple SQL Server machines.

Perhaps this company has only a few hundred users and now the potentially six servers required equates to a massive investment.

Moving to a hybrid deployed model allows all the high-availability aspects—as well as administration, patching, and so on—to be taken care of by someone else. In addition, there is the flexibility to grow the number of users dramatically in a short period of time.

All that is needed from the organization perspective is the minimal local infrastructure to connect to the PSTN and Internet (and, of course, to pay the phone bills)!

WORKING THROUGH THE CONFIGURATION STEPS

You access the wizard via the Skype for Business Control Panel home screen; it requires a login account with Global Admin rights on the Office 365 Tenant, shown in Figure 10.4.

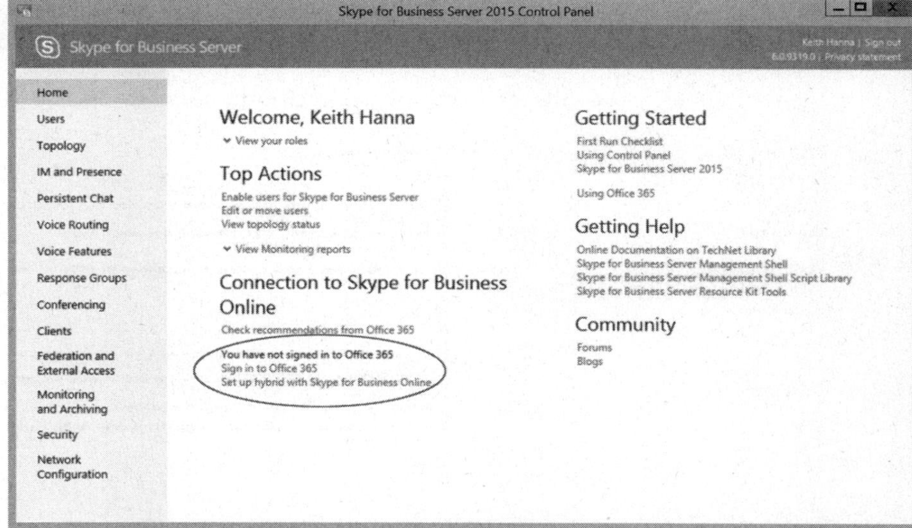

FIGURE 10.4 Launching the hybrid setup wizard

Figure 10.4 shows the screen prior to signing in and shows a link to the sign-in prompt. You can launch the wizard without signing in; it'll simply prompt you to sign in as part of the process. There is a separate sign-in step on this screen simply to allow you to sign in and then go ahead and manage users.

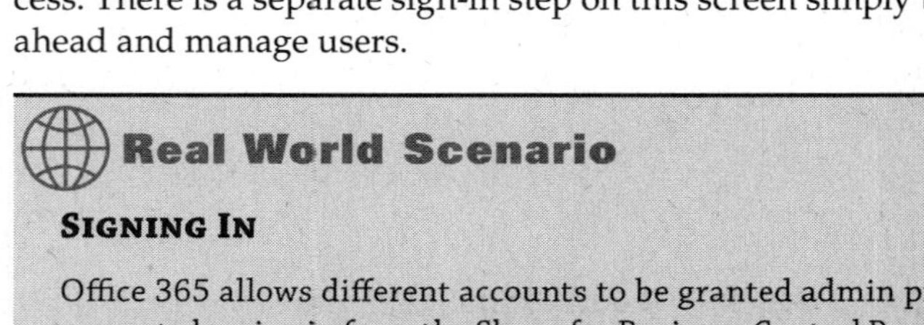

Real World Scenario

SIGNING IN

Office 365 allows different accounts to be granted admin privileges as needed; however, when it comes to logging in from the Skype for Business Control Panel, you must use a *`<user>@<domain>.onmicrosoft.com`* address, as shown here:

By using PowerShell, you can enter **`-OverRideAdminDomain "<domain>.onmicrosoft.com`** when creating the remote session to indicate the account belongs to a specific tenant.

In testing this method, we still receive errors with some of the cmdlets running (such as `Move-CsUser`), but we're able to manage some portions of the tenant. Using the *`<user>@<domain>.onmicrosoft.com`* account gives full control via PowerShell as you'd expect. At the time of writing, we have a support ticket open with Microsoft to clarify this operation; however, no answer has been received.

To enable the sign-in to Office 365 to be successful, the Front End servers need to have Internet access, and the `lyncdiscover.<domain>` record needs to be pointing to the on-premises servers.

Figure 10.5 shows the errors returned in each of these cases.

FIGURE 10.5
Errors when signing in to Office 365 using the wizard

Once you get through the initial connectivity check screens, the wizard will run the configuration checks and provide feedback on the current state. For environments that have been operational with previous versions of Lync Server deployed, you're most likely going to encounter the feedback shown in Figure 10.6.

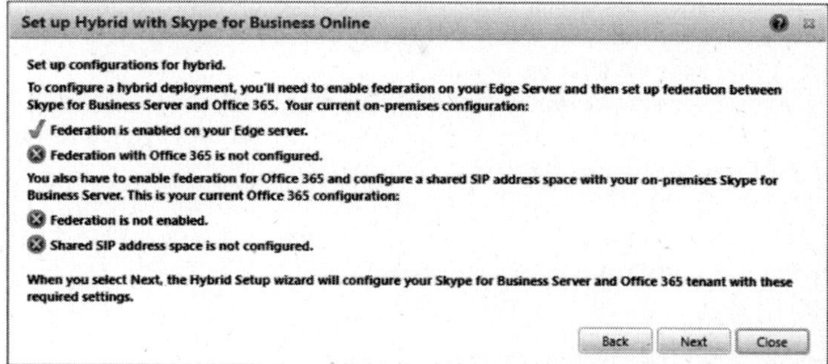

Set up Hybrid with Skype for Business Online
Set up configurations for hybrid.
To configure a hybrid deployment, you'll need to enable federation on your Edge Server and then set up federation between Skype for Business Server and Office 365. Your current on-premises configuration:
Federation is enabled on your Edge server.
Federation with Office 365 is not configured.
You also have to enable federation for Office 365 and configure a shared SIP address space with your on-premises Skype for Business Server. This is your current Office 365 configuration:
Federation is not enabled.
Shared SIP address space is not configured.
When you select Next, the Hybrid Setup wizard will configure your Skype for Business Server and Office 365 tenant with these required settings.
Back
Next
Close

FIGURE 10.6
Initial hybrid configuration status

If you haven't configured federation or are using closed federation (no DNS record exists for `_sipfederationtls._tcp.<domain>`), you will see the first entry marked with a red X. Click Next to have the wizard do all the configurations required in the background. One thing to note is that the wizard will make the required changes only to the Office 365 and local on-premises Skype for Business environments. It is not able to make changes to DNS or firewalls.

Figure 10.7 shows the completed wizard with the check marks all green.

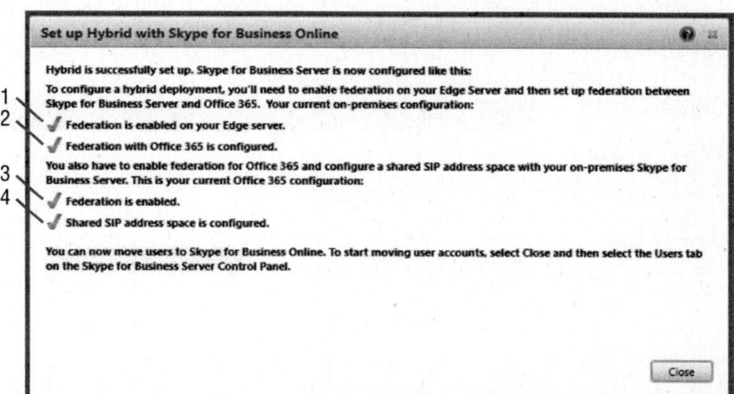

Set up Hybrid with Skype for Business Online
Hybrid is successfully set up. Skype for Business Server is now configured like this:
To configure a hybrid deployment, you'll need to enable federation on your Edge Server and then set up federation between Skype for Business Server and Office 365. Your current on-premises configuration:
1
2
Federation is enabled on your Edge server.
Federation with Office 365 is configured.
You also have to enable federation for Office 365 and configure a shared SIP address space with your on-premises Skype for Business Server. This is your current Office 365 configuration:
3
4
Federation is enabled.
Shared SIP address space is configured.
You can now move users to Skype for Business Online. To start moving user accounts, select Close and then select the Users tab on the Skype for Business Server Control Panel.
Close

FIGURE 10.7
The completed hybrid setup wizard

Each of these steps can be carried out manually using the following configuration steps:

1. Enable federation. You might need to make a topology change to enable federation on the Edge servers, as well as opening port 5061 on the network. You need to make DNS changes to configure the `_sipfederationtls._tcp.<domain>` record and make the following configuration change:

```
Set-CsAccessEdgeConfiguration
-AllowFederatedUsers $true
-EnablePartnerDiscovery $true
```

2. Federate with Office 365. With the local on-premises PowerShell, run the following:

```
New-CsHostingProvider
-Identity SkypeforBusinessOnline
-ProxyFqdn "sipfed.online.lync.com"
-Enabled $true
-EnabledSharedAddressSpace $true
-HostsOCSUsers $true
-VerificationLevel UseSourceVerification -IsLocal $false
-AutodiscoverUrl https://webdir.online.lync.com/Autodiscover/
AutodiscoverService.svc/root
```

3. Set up the Office 365 tenant with federation enabled. Using remote PowerShell to the Office 365 tenant, run the following:

```
Set-CsTenantFederationConfiguration
-AllowedFederatedUsers $true
```

4. Set up the Office 365 tenant with a shared SIP address space. Using remote PowerShell to the Office 365 tenant, run the following:

```
Set-CsTenantFederationConfiguration
-SharedSipaddressSpace $true
```

Although these steps show PowerShell configuration, you can also achieve this via the portal (for Office 365) or via the Skype for Business Control Panel. Figure 10.8 shows step 3 of the configuration via the Office 365 admin portal.

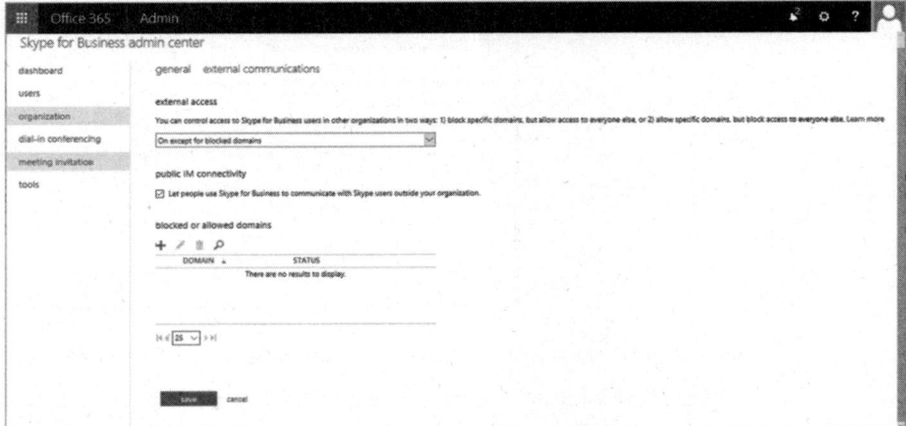

FIGURE 10.8 Enabling tenant federation via the Office 365 portal

Now that you have configured federation, you can move users to the online environment.

Within the Skype for Business Control Panel, the user management options have now changed. Search for and select a user and then select the Action menu. You will see some new options (shown in Figure 10.9).

- Move Selected Users To Skype for Business Online
- Move Selected Users From Skype for Business Online

Depending on the current location of the user, only one option will be highlighted.

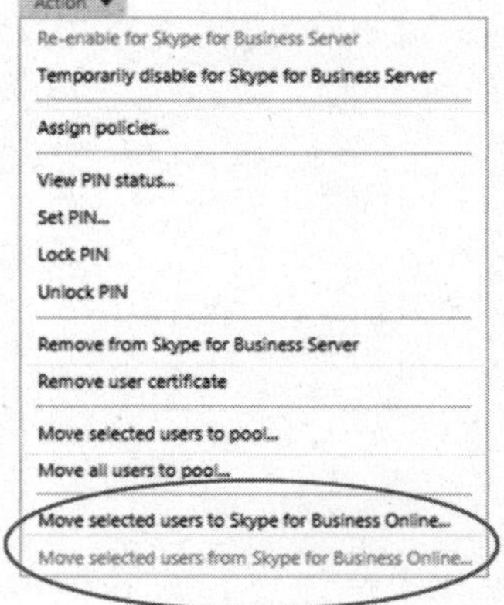

FIGURE 10.9 Moving a user within Skype for Business Control Panel

The Move Selected Users From Skype for Business Online option will provide status updates and feedback on the user move. If the environment still has legacy Edge servers deployed and they are the primary route for federation, you may receive the error shown in Figure 10.10.

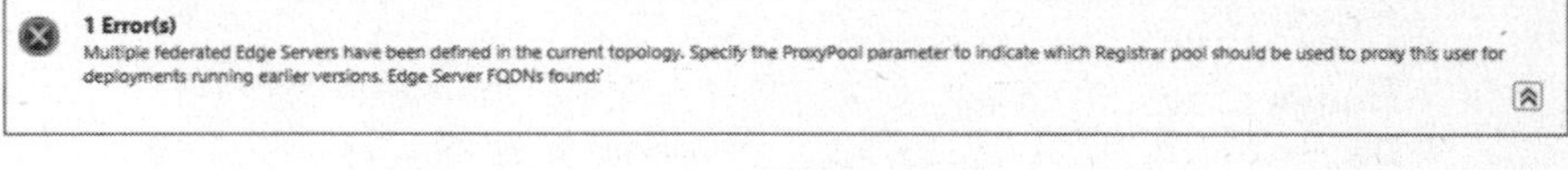

FIGURE 10.10 Error moving users when legacy Edge servers are in use

You can resolve this by using PowerShell with the `-ProxyPool` parameter defined.

```
Move-CsUser -Identity <userid> -Target sipfed.online.lync.com
-HostedMigrationOverrideUrl https:
//<webhost>.online.lync.com/HostedMigration/hostedmigrationservice.svc -ProxyPool
<skypeforbusinesspoolname>
```

The *<webhost>* entry is the URL specified in your online tenant portal. This a shared name across many tenants, used to load balance the management portals across Office 365.

To verify that the user was successfully moved, you can use a `Get-CsUser` command in the on-premises Skype for Business Management Shell and look to make sure the output shows that `HostingProvider` is set to `sipfed.online.lync.com`.

Now that you're set up, how does it work?

Sign-in/Registration Process

The registration process for a Hybrid Voice user is essentially the same as for on-premises Skype for Business Server. When a user is moved from on-premises to Office 365, the Deployment Locator attribute of their Active Directory user account is updated to reflect that they are hosted in the cloud. Figure 10.11 shows this attribute on an Active Directory user.

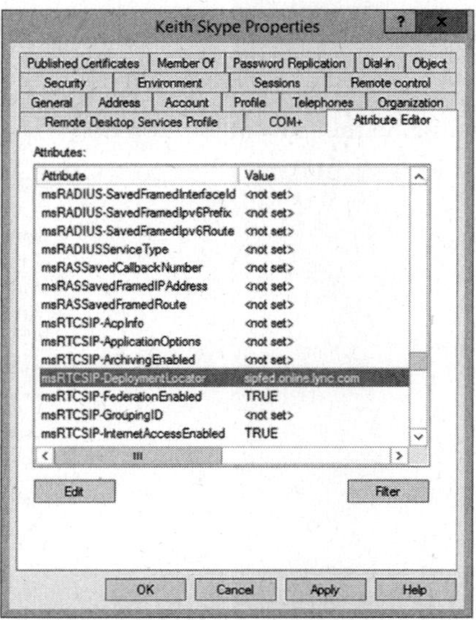

FIGURE 10.11
Deployment Locator attribute

When a user who is a member of the `rlscomms.net` domain signs in to Skype for Business and is using automatic configuration, the Deployment Locator attribute allows the on-premises server to redirect the user to their correct Online pool for registration. Figure 10.12 shows this process.

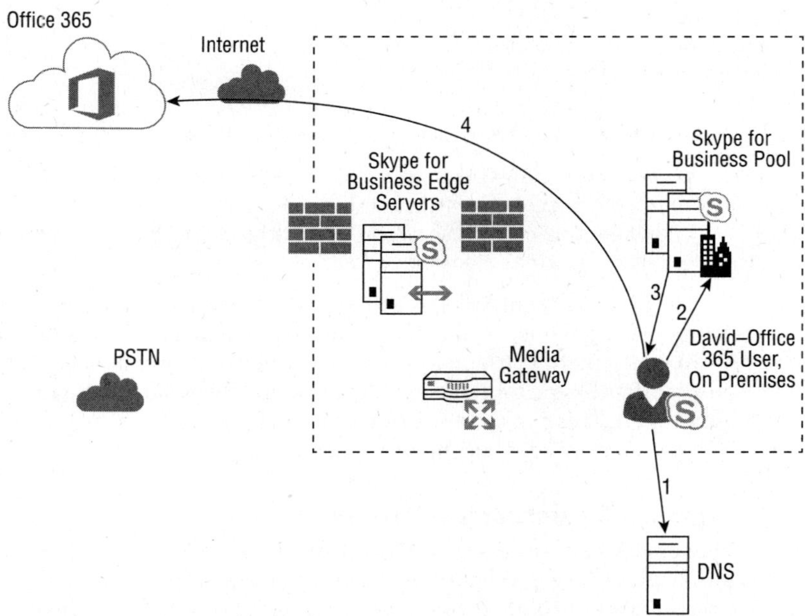

FIGURE 10.12
Skype for Business user sign-in process

In Figure 10.12, Keith logs into his computer, and his Skype for Business client is configured to automatic configuration. For automatic login, there will be an SRV record created on the internal DNS for this purpose, such as `_sipinternaltls._tcp.rlscomms.net` or `lyncdiscover.rlscomms.net`. Then the following occurs:

1. Keith's client performs a DNS SRV record lookup.
2. Because Keith is accessing from inside the corporate network, the internal DNS SRV record will be returned. This resolves to the on-premises Skype for Business deployment. Keith will then authenticate to the on-premises pool.
3. The Skype for Business on-premises pool will redirect Keith with a SIP 301 to the Skype for Business Online service. It knows to do this because Keith's Active Directory user account is stamped with the Deployment Locator attribute.
4. Keith will then register against the Skype for Business Online environment.

For Keith to successfully register with the Skype for Business Online service, he needs to have access to the Internet so that he can reach the service.

If Keith was accessing Skype for Business from outside the corporate network (such as from the Internet because he was working remotely), his client would find the DNS SRV record that had been created in the organization's external DNS, which resolves to the Access Edge service of the on-premises Skype for Business Edge server. His client would then follow the same process and would be redirected to the Skype for Business Online service.

Call Flow Scenarios

To get a good understanding of the various possible call flows, you'll take a step-by-step look at a number of different scenarios.

Scenario 1: Two Hybrid Voice users logged on to the corporate network (peer to peer)

Scenario 2: Two users logged on to the corporate network, one on-premises user and one Hybrid Voice user

Scenario 3: Incoming PSTN call to Hybrid Voice user (peer to peer)

Scenario 4: Incoming PSTN call to Hybrid Voice user who is logging on remotely (from the Internet)

Scenario 5: Hybrid Voice user making an outgoing PSTN call while logged on from the internal corporate network

Scenario 6: Hybrid Voice user making an outgoing PSTN call while logged on remotely (from the Internet)

Remember, in all these cases, registration has already occurred and the users are logged in. We're not covering complex cases where local firewalls restrict direct traffic and media has to flow via an Edge server.

Scenario 1

In this scenario, two Hybrid Voice users are logged on to the corporate network (peer to peer). See Figure 10.13.

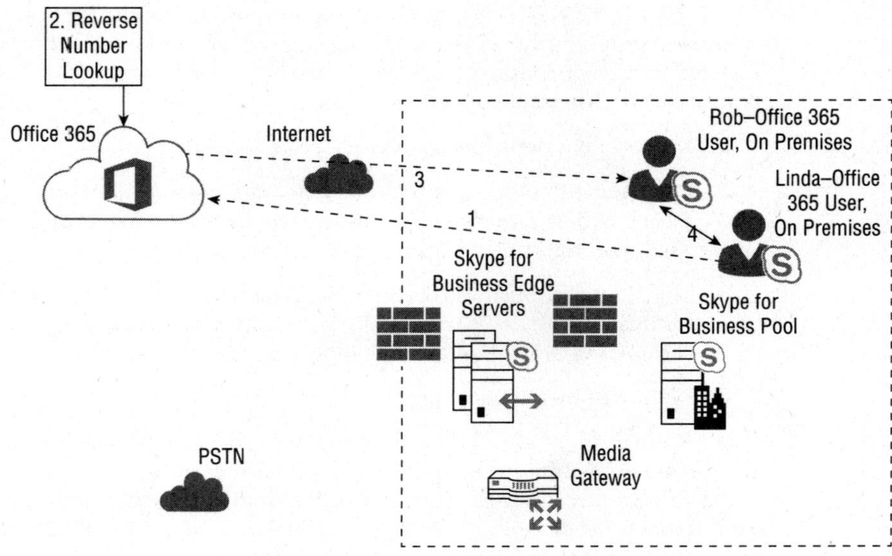

FIGURE 10.13 Two Hybrid Voice users logged on to the corporate network (peer to peer)

Scenario: Linda is a Hybrid Voice user in the office. Rob is a Lync Hybrid Voice user in the same office.

1. Linda initiates a call to Rob by dialing his extension or clicking Work in the client.
2. The Skype for Business Online infrastructure, on which both Linda and Rob are registered, will perform a reverse number lookup that determines that the number Linda dialed resolves to Rob.
3. All the SIP signaling flows through the Skype for Business Online infrastructure. A SIP `INVITE` is sent to Rob's endpoint.
4. When Rob answers the call, the media flows directly between the two clients (peer to peer) because they are both on the corporate network.

SCENARIO 2

In this scenario, two users are logged on to the corporate network, one on-premises user and one Hybrid Voice user (peer to peer). See Figure 10.14.

Scenario: David is an on-premises user in the office. Rob is a Hybrid Voice user in the same office.

1. David, who is an on-premises user, initiates a call to Rob, who is a Hybrid user, by dialing his extension or clicking Work in the client.
2. The Lync on-premises infrastructure knows that Rob has an Active Directory object on-premises. The reverse number lookup can look at Rob's on-premises object and determine that Rob is in the federated Skype for Business Online infrastructure.

3. The SIP signaling (the call) is then routed over the federation route via the Edge server up to the Skype for Business Online infrastructure.
4. The SIP signaling returns from the Skype for Business Online infrastructure to Rob's endpoint.
5. When Rob answers the call, the media flows directly between the two clients (peer to peer) because they are both on the corporate network.

FIGURE 10.14 Two users logged on to the corporate network, one on-premises user and one Hybrid Voice user (peer to peer)

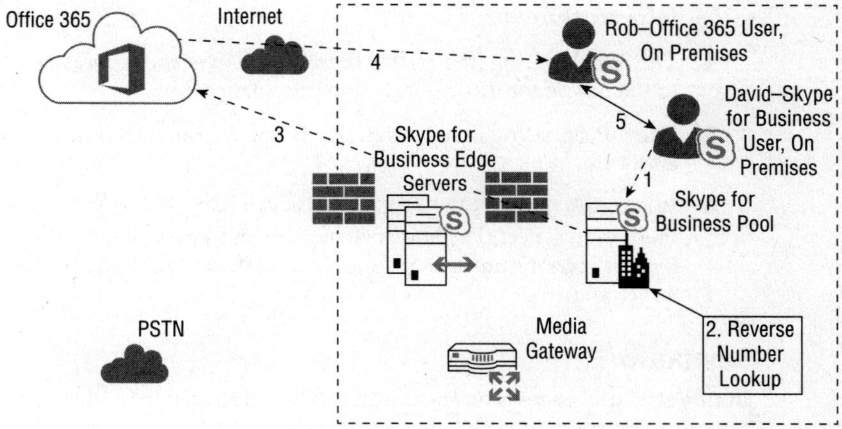

Office 365
Internet
4
3
Rob–Office 365 User, On Premises
5
David–Skype for Business User, On Premises
1
Skype for Business Edge Servers
Skype for Business Pool
PSTN
Media Gateway
2. Reverse Number Lookup

SCENARIO 3

This scenario details an incoming PSTN call to a Hybrid Voice user. See Figure 10.15.

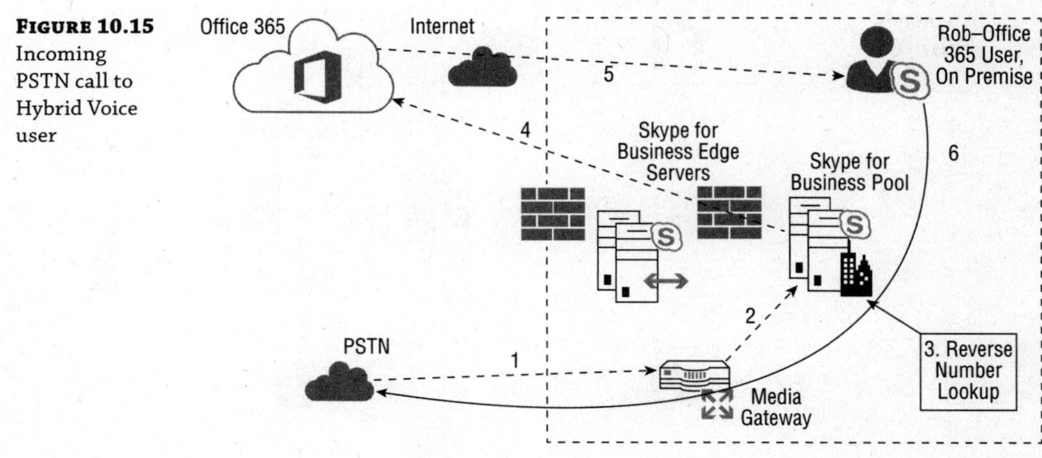

FIGURE 10.15 Incoming PSTN call to Hybrid Voice user

Office 365
Internet
5
Rob–Office 365 User, On Premise
4
6
Skype for Business Edge Servers
Skype for Business Pool
2
PSTN
1
3. Reverse Number Lookup
Media Gateway

Scenario: Rob is a Hybrid Voice user in the office.

1. A PSTN call is placed to Rob's phone number; the call is received on the on-premises PSTN media gateway.
2. The on-premises media gateway directs the call to the Skype for Business Mediation server, which is colocated on the on-premises Lync 2013 pool.
3. The Skype for Business on-premises infrastructure knows that Rob has an Active Directory object on premises. The reverse number lookup can look at Rob's on-premises object and determine that Rob is in the federated Skype for Business Online infrastructure.
4. The SIP signaling (the call) is then routed over the federation route via the Edge server up to the Skype for Business Online infrastructure.
5. The SIP signaling is sent from the Skype for Business Online infrastructure to Rob's endpoint.
6. When Rob answers the call, media is established and flows between the on-premises mediation server/PSTN infrastructure and Rob's client. This could be using Media Bypass if configured, or the media may flow via the Mediation server if Media Bypass is not configured.

SCENARIO 4

In this scenario, there is an incoming PSTN call to a Hybrid Voice user who is logging in remotely (from the Internet). See Figure 10.16.

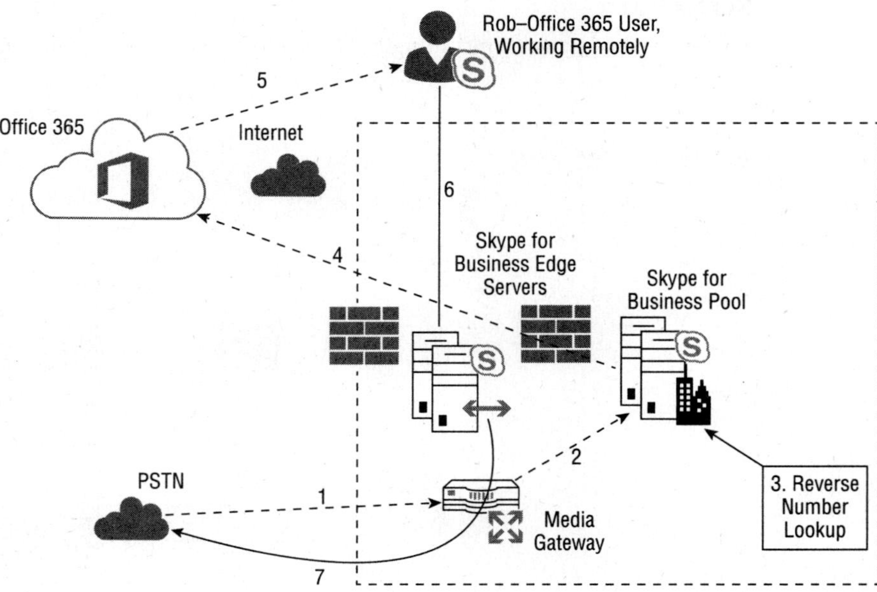

FIGURE 10.16 Incoming PSTN call to Hybrid Voice user who is logging in remotely (Internet)

Scenario: Rob is a Hybrid Voice user working remotely.

1. A PSTN call is placed to Rob's phone number. The call terminates at the on-premises PSTN media gateway.
2. The on-premises media gateway directs the call to the Skype for Business Mediation server, which is colocated on the on-premises pool.
3. The Skype for Business on-premises infrastructure knows that Rob has an Active Directory object on premises. The reverse number lookup can look at Rob's on-premises object and determine that Rob is in the federated Skype for Business Online infrastructure.
4. The SIP signaling to set up the call is then routed over the federation route via the on-premises Edge server to the Skype for Business Online infrastructure.
5. The SIP signaling is sent from the Skype for Business Online infrastructure to Rob's endpoint.
6. When Rob answers the call, media is established and flows through the on-premises Edge server through to the next hop, which is the on-premises pool. Media Bypass cannot happen because the user is working remotely and therefore is not on the same subnet as the media gateway.

Scenario 5

In this scenario, a Hybrid Voice user is making an outgoing PSTN call while logged on from the internal corporate network. See Figure 10.17.

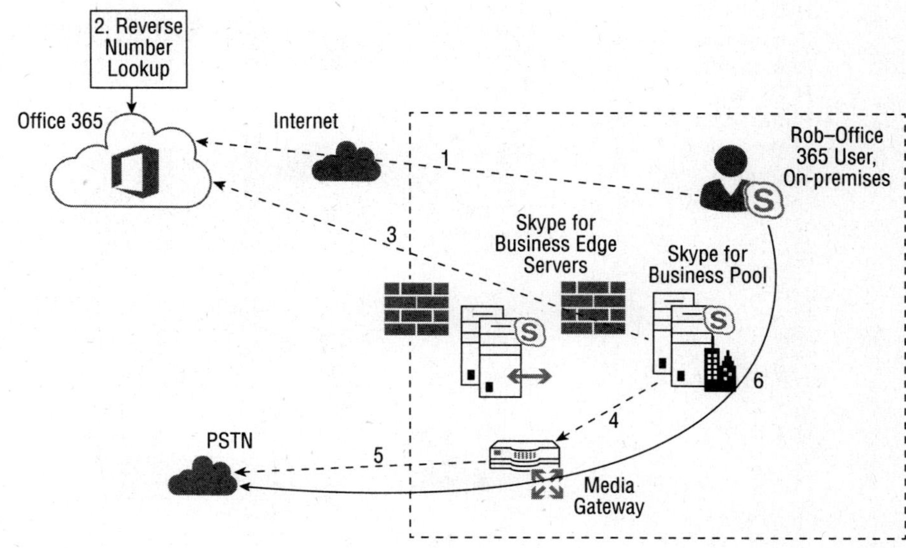

Figure 10.17 Hybrid Voice user making an outgoing PSTN call while logged on from the internal corporate network

Scenario: Rob is a Hybrid Voice user in the office.

1. Rob places a PSTN call. The SIP `INVITE` with the dialed PSTN telephone number is sent to the Skype for Business Online infrastructure. Skype for Business Online is synchronized with user and contact objects from the on-premises AD. This means that reverse number lookup will work for all on-premises and online Enterprise Voice–enabled objects.
2. The reverse number lookup will take place on the online infrastructure and will fail because the telephone number is an external PSTN number and not associated with any objects within the on-premises or online infrastructure.
3. The SIP `INVITE` will be routed to the on-premises Skype for Business infrastructure. The call routing and authorization decisions will be made on premises.
4. Rob's voice routing policy is examined, and based on this, a PSTN media gateway on premises is selected, and the call is allowed to proceed.
5. Media is established and flows using the optimal path between the on-premises Mediation server/PSTN infrastructure and the PSTN device. This could be using Media Bypass if configured, or the media may flow via the Mediation server if Media Bypass is not configured.

Scenario 6

In this scenario, a Hybrid Voice user is making an outgoing PSTN call while logged on remotely (from the Internet). See Figure 10.18.

Scenario: Rob is a Skype for Business Online user working remotely.

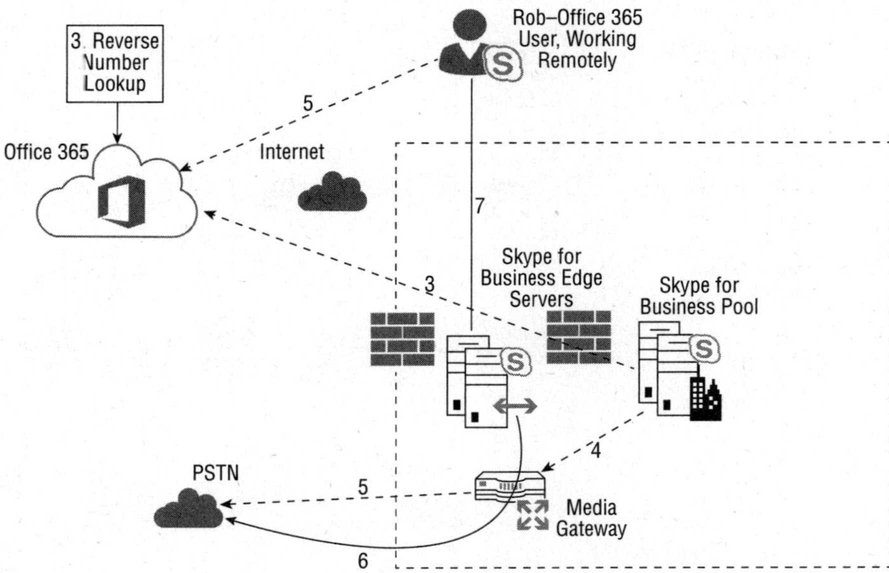

Figure 10.18 Hybrid Voice user making an outgoing PSTN call while logged on remotely (Internet)

1. Rob places a PSTN call. The SIP `INVITE` with the dialed PSTN telephone number is sent to the Skype for Business Online infrastructure. Skype for Business Online is synchronized with user and contact objects from the on-premises AD. This means that reverse number lookup will work for all on-premises and online Enterprise Voice–enabled objects.
2. Reverse number lookup will take place on the online infrastructure and will fail because the telephone number is an external PSTN number and not associated with any objects within the on-premises or online infrastructure.
3. The SIP `INVITE` will be routed to the on-premises Skype for Business infrastructure. The call routing and authorization decisions will be made on premises.
4. Rob's voice routing policy is examined, and based on this, a PSTN media gateway on premises is selected.
5. Media is established and flows through the on-premises Edge server through to the next hop, which is the on-premises pool. Media Bypass will not happen because the user is working remotely and therefore is not on the same subnet as the media gateway.

E9-1-1 and Media Bypass

For a Hybrid Voice user to be able to use advanced features such as Media Bypass and E9-1-1, an on-premises Skype for Business pool must be deployed.

Media Bypass essentially works in the same way for Hybrid Voice users as it does for on-premises users. Media Bypass occurs when the Hybrid Voice user and PSTN media gateway are in the same network location and have matching Bypass IDs. How the client discovers its Bypass ID in a Hybrid Voice scenario is the only difference (shown in Figure 10.19).

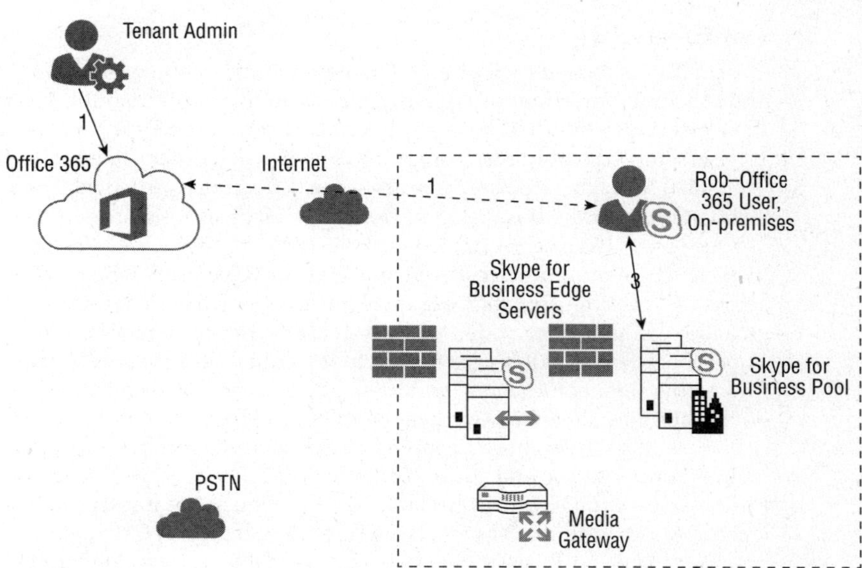

FIGURE 10.19 Skype for Business Online client discovery of Media Bypass ID

Scenario: Rob is a Hybrid Voice user, logging in from the office.

1. The Office 365 tenant administrator is responsible for configuring an internally and externally accessible URL that resolves to the provisioning web service, which is hosted on the on-premises Skype for Business pool.
2. This URL is passed to the Skype for Business client via in-band provisioning during sign-in.
3. The client will perform an HTTP POST to the URL and in return receives its Bypass ID, location policy, and LIS URL.
4. This allows the Skype for Business client, when logged in to by a Hybrid user, to identify which network site it is in because site and subnet definitions are not configurable using Skype for Business Online in Office 365.

Note that the previous steps assume the user is signing in from the organization's corporate network, not the Internet. Media Bypass will not work across the Internet. Although the user client will still follow the process defined and the user will resolve the URL via the reverse proxy, the Media Bypass ID will not match the subnet ID.

E9-1-1 works the same way as for an on-premises Skype for Business user. The location information and policy of Hybrid Voice users is automatically retrieved by the Skype for Business client via the provisioning web service (described earlier) and transmitted during an emergency call. When an E9-1-1 call is placed, the Skype for Business Online infrastructure routes the request through to the on-premises Skype for Business Server infrastructure. The on-premises Skype for Business Server infrastructure then routes the E9-1-1 call to the E9-1-1 provider.

If a Skype for Business Hybrid Voice user is logged on remotely (e.g., from the Internet) and makes an E9-1-1 call, the location cannot be automatically determined; in this case, the user will be prompted to enter an address manually. This address is then passed to the E9-1-1 provider.

Conferencing

Once a user is moved to Skype for Business Online, their conferencing data, meeting content, and scheduled meetings are not migrated with their user account. These users must reschedule their meetings after their accounts have been moved to Skype for Business Online.

Users homed on premises or online can join each other's Skype meetings as before; if a user is enabled for Hybrid Voice, there are some different requirements, and also how the meeting location is determined is different from how it's determined for an on-premises user.

Once users have been enabled for Hybrid Voice, they can no longer use the on-premises infrastructure for dial-in conferencing. Hybrid Voice users who require dial-in and dial-out access for meetings that they organize must be set up with dial-in conferencing accounts with an audio conference provider. ACPs provide dial-in conference capability for the cloud solution. This is because once users are moved to the online service, they will be using the online pools for hosting their conferences, and these pools do not have native on-premises dial-in and dial-out capabilities; they will leverage the ACP configuration numbers.

Figure 10.20 shows how a conference that is hosted online is located.

In Figure 10.20, the first `getConference` SIP/C3P request goes to the on-premises Skype for Business Server pool, which checks Rob's Deployment Locator attribute on his AD user account object. This identifies Rob as a Lync Hybrid user, so the SIP/C3P request gets proxied from the on-premises Skype for Business Server pool, via the Edge, to the cloud to find Rob's conferencing pool.

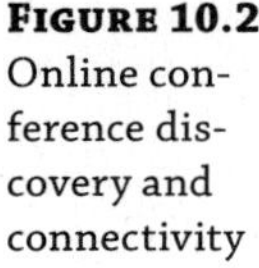
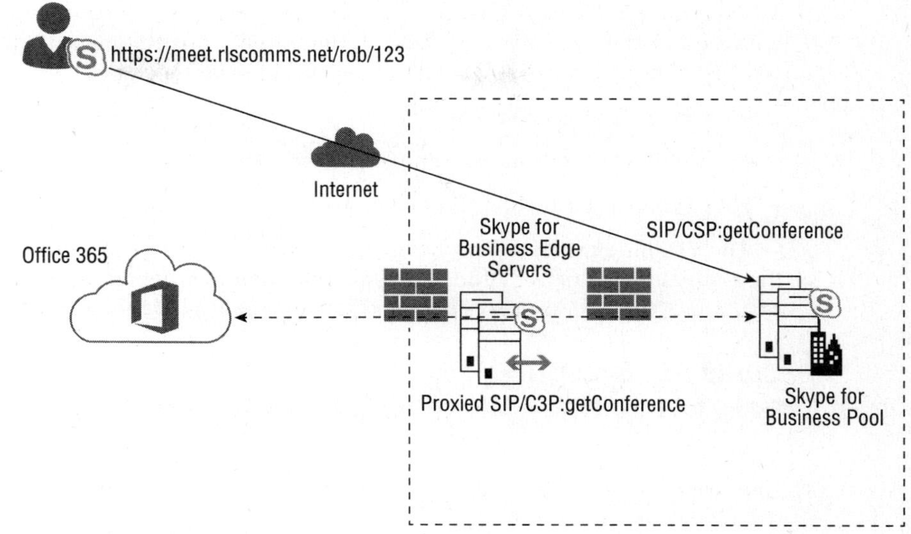

FIGURE 10.20 Online conference discovery and connectivity

> **TROUBLESHOOTING SKYPE FOR BUSINESS HYBRID**
>
> Ensuring that you have prepared your network for Skype for Business Online will enable you to sign in without issues (see the section "Setting Up the Internal Corporate Network for Skype for Business Online" earlier in this chapter). However, you may still experience some.
>
> If your users are unable to sign into Skype for Business Online, there is a guide to what to check here:
>
> `http://support.microsoft.com/kb/2409256`
>
> The following support article also can assist you with troubleshooting sign-in issues to Microsoft Skype for Business Online:
>
> `http://support.microsoft.com/kb/2541980`
>
> Finally, you can install Snooper to troubleshoot sign-in issues (see Chapter 15, "Troubleshooting," for more details on Snooper):

Implementing Cloud PBX

Soon, ideally by the time this book is available, Microsoft will have implemented connectivity from Office 365 to the PSTN for users, not just for the audio conference providers as it is today. As this book is being written, the functionality is in beta testing, and as with any unreleased content, it is subject to change between now and the time of release. The aim of this section is to give you an idea of what functionality will be available without necessarily the detailed configuration steps and options, as these are the items most likely to change.

Simply put, Office 365 users will be able to make and receive calls with no on-premises infrastructure, and Microsoft will provide a regular bill for this feature as well as a usage charge.

The specifics of the usage charge may differ from country to country; it may be a calling plan with a number of minutes included, or you may get charged for each call.

Most currently supported clients are expected to be supported.

- Office clients (both PC and Mac)
- Mobile clients (Windows Phone, iOS, and Android when released)
- IP phones (both Phone Edition and 3PIP)

The VDI plug-in is not expected to be supported at this stage. Conferencing users will have the ability to use a native Office 365 conference dial-in number or continue with existing ACPs if required. At launch, the service is expected to have local dial-in capabilities in 45 countries.

Cloud PSTN Calling

Figure 10.21 shows the relatively simple call flow for a user making a PSTN call.

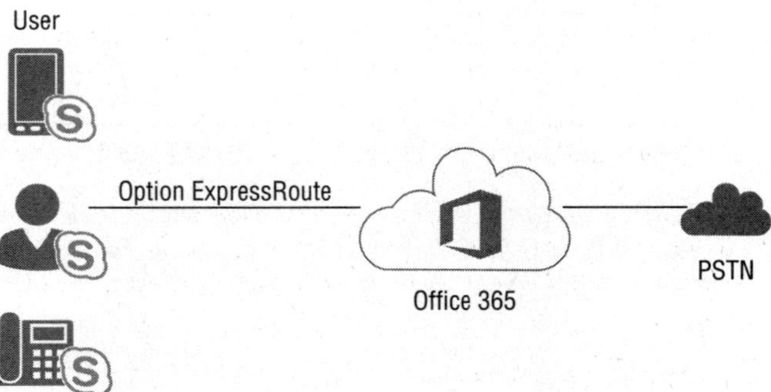

FIGURE 10.21
Call flow for Cloud PBX PSTN calling

Microsoft recommends deploying the ExpressRoute service to ensure call quality is maintained from the customer premises to the Office 365 environment. However, this isn't available in all regions, nor practical for smaller customers. It will give the benefit of being a managed network and being able to have quality of service applied to ensure bandwidth availability.

New numbers can be requested, along with the ability to port your existing numbers into the Office 365 environment, in the same way that it is possible to port numbers from one provider to another today.

On-Premise PSTN Calling

Figure 10.22 shows the call flow for Cloud PBX when using on-premises infrastructures.

The ability to have hosted Office 365 users but continue to leverage local infrastructure enables organizations to continue using existing hardware and potential carrier contracts without having to write off that investment with a replacement approach. More details will be released over the next few months.

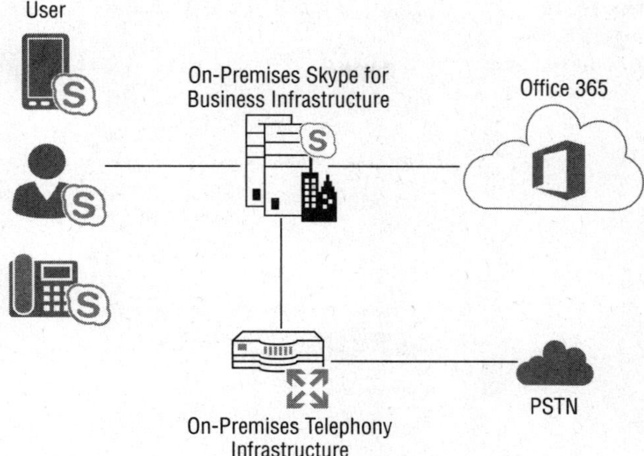

FIGURE 10.22 Call flow for Cloud PBX on-premises PSTN calling

Migrating to Hosted Voicemail

Rather than move all the users' Skype for Business capability into the cloud from the start, many customers are starting with migrations of email to Office 365. This also has the advantage in that email, being non-real-time, is easier to manage remotely, and the Exchange portions of Office 365 are much more mature and feature comparable.

Prior to the Cloud PBX offering, there were significantly more features available with the on-premises deployments of Skype for Business or Lync Server. As a result of this leading by email approach, some customers are continuing with Skype for Business on premises but moving the voicemail aspects (Exchange Unified Messaging) to the cloud.

This is relatively straightforward to configure. You simply need to create the dial plans for Exchange in the cloud, and then rather than run the `OCSUMUtil.exe` application to create contact objects for the dial plans (see Chapter 22), you need to create the contacts manually (using PowerShell).

You also need to set the `HostedVoiceMail` values on the user account to ensure that the on-premises infrastructure knows to direct the traffic to Office 365.

Configuring Office 365 Dial Plans

From within the admin portal of Office 365, you need to create a new dial plan for Unified Messaging. This will be found in the Exchange Admin Center, under the Unified Messaging section.

The dial plan should be a SIP URI dial plan and configured to match your phone extension's digit length. Once created, edit the dial plan and select Configure (see Figure 10.23).

The next window that opens shows a summary of the dial plan configuration and has some additional configuration items on the left side. Select Outlook Voice Access to configure the numbers to be used to access voicemail. This number will be used later when configuring the contact object for Skype for Business.

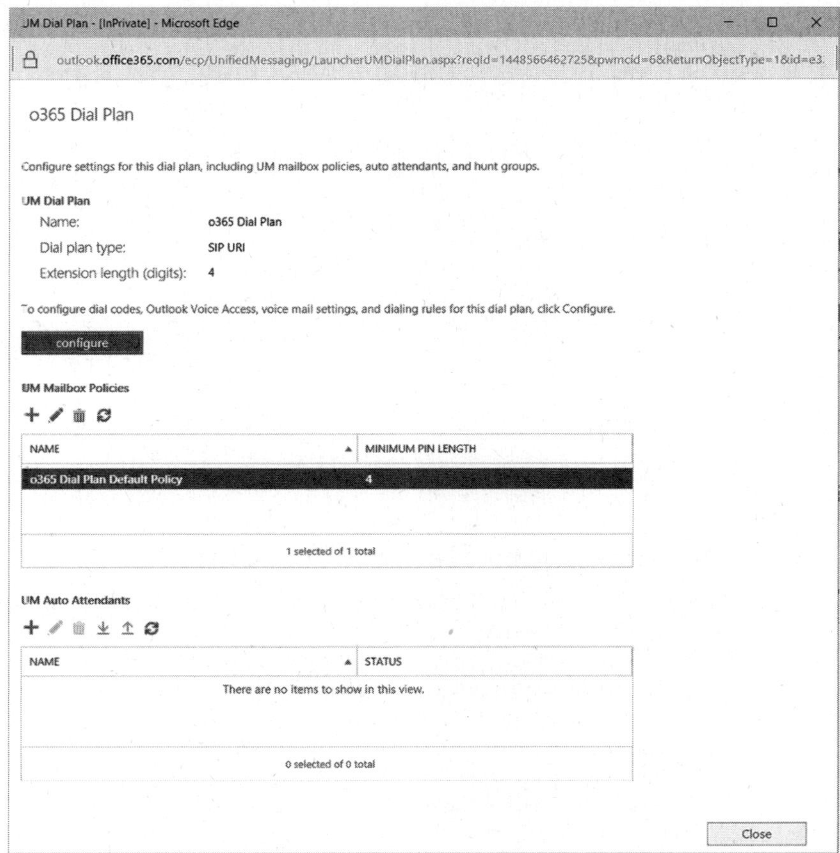

FIGURE 10.23 Editing the Office 365 UM dial plan

Figure 10.24 shows the numbers needed to be configured. The top number must be in E.164 format, and the numbers below are simply text fields so can contain any logical display of numbers, in this case providing the national dialing number of the United Kingdom (0) as well as the E.164 number. These are included in the Unified Messaging welcome email sent to users when they are enabled for Unified Messaging.

Multiple numbers can be entered on this page if required; each will need contact objects created in Skype for Business.

The users can be enabled or disabled for Unified Messaging in the Recipients section of the Exchange Admin Center. Figure 10.25 shows an account as enabled and where to change it.

Now that you've configured Office 365 with a dial plan and enabled users, you need to tell the Skype for Business environment where and how to route calls to voicemail.

FIGURE 10.24
Defining the Outlook Voice Access numbers in Office 365

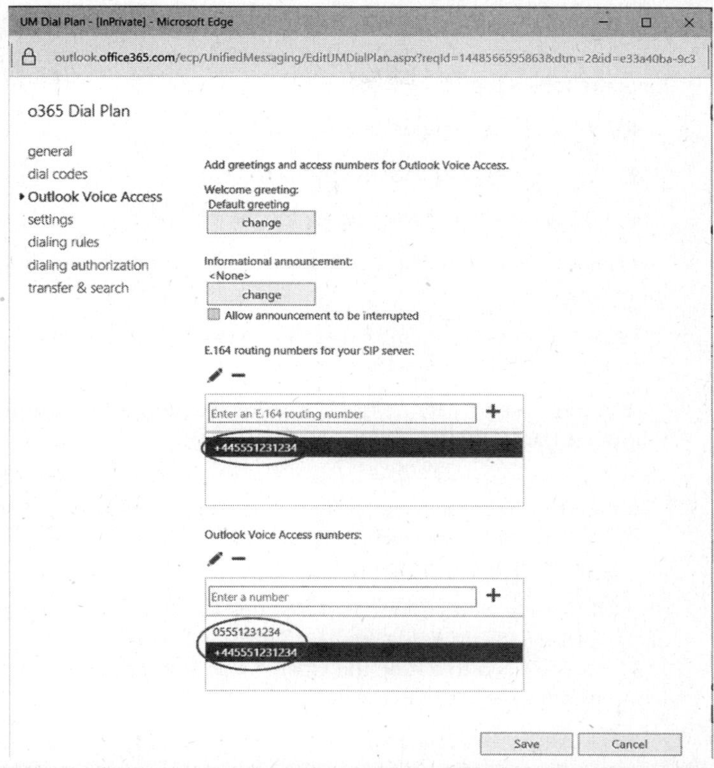

FIGURE 10.25
Enabling or disabling users for Office 365 Unified Messaging

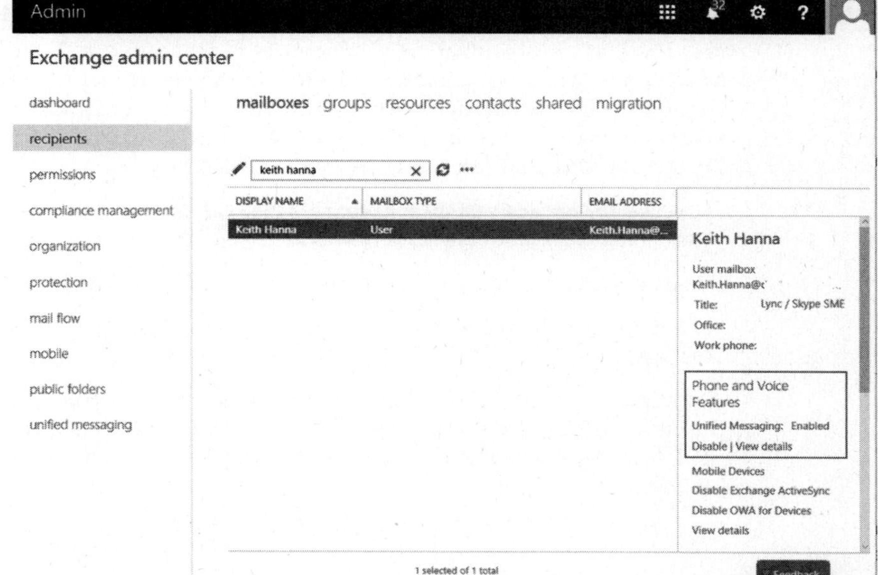

Configuring On-Premises Skype for Business

You first need to ensure federation is enabled with the correct settings. The configuration should have the following:

- `AllowFederatedUsers` set to `True`
- `EnablePartnerDiscovery` set to `True`
- `RoutingMethod` set to `UseDnsSrvRouting`

Use `Get-CsAccessEdgeConfiguration` to confirm and modify as necessary using the following:

```
Set-CsAccessEdgeConfiguration -AllowFederatedUsers $true -EnablePartnerDiscovery
$true -UseDnsSrvRouting
```

You then need to define the Office 365 Exchange environment as a hosting provider using the following PowerShell:

```
New-CsHostingProvider -Identity "Exchange Online" -Enabled $True
-EnabledSharedAddressSpace $True -HostsOCSUsers $False -ProxyFqdn "exap.um.
outlook.com" -IsLocal $False -VerificationLevel
UseSourceVerification
```

At this stage, you've configured Skype for Business for federated access and also the location of the Office 365 UM gateways.

Next, you need to define the Hosted Voicemail policy, which will be applied to the users whose mailboxes are being moved.

```
New-CsHostedVoicemailPolicy -Identity Office365UM -Destination exap.um.outlook.
com -Description "Office 365 Voicemail" -Organization "rlscomms.onmicrosoft.com"
```

Here, you've defined the policy, `Office365UM`, and the destination FQDN, `exap.um.outlook.com`, as well as the organization, `rlscomms.onmicrosoft.com`. The organization must be your `.onmicrosoft.com` domain associated with your Office 365 tenant.

Finally, the last infrastructure configuration step is to configure the contact object associating the Outlook Voice Access number with the online environment. Using the same E.164 number as defined in the Office 365 dial plan, create the contact.

```
New-CsExUmContact -DisplayNumber +445551231234 -SipAddress sip:ex365um@rlscomms
.net -RegistrarPool se01.rlscomms.net -ou "OU=Contacts,DC=rlscomms,DC=net"
```

Then apply the Hosted Voice Mail policy to the contact object.

```
Grant-CsHostedVoicemailPolicy -Identity sip:ex365um@rlscomms.net -PolicyName
Office365UM
```

Once these steps are all completed, the on-premises infrastructure is able to find and route to the Office 365 Unified Messaging infrastructure. The only tasks remaining are to apply the Hosted Voice Mail policy to the user accounts that have been moved and to enable it for hosted voice mail.

```
Grant-CsHostedVoicemailPolicy -Identity sip:keith.skype@rlscomms.net -PolicyName
Office365UM
Set-CsUser -Identity sip:keith.skype@rlscomms.net -HostedVoicemail $true
```

The Bottom Line

Understand the hybrid architecture model. Skype for Business introduces the new capability of a hybrid model that allows hosting some users of an organization on premises in the traditional way of having an on-premises infrastructure deployed but also hosting other members of the organization in a cloud solution.

> **Master It** Lync Server 2013 (and previous versions) provides support for multiple SIP domains in the same deployment within an Active Directory forest. What change to this model does the hybrid deployment in Skype for Business require?

Understand the capabilities of a hybrid deployment. Users can be hosted either online in the cloud or on premises on a local infrastructure. Each location provides a common set of features, but not all are available when users are using Skype for Business Online.

> **Master It** Which features are available only in an on-premises deployment?

Understand the call flow for media in different scenarios. Skype for Business can be a complex product when it comes to understanding signaling flows and media flows. Using Edge servers adds additional complexity, and having an additional pool hosted in the cloud adds a level of complexity beyond simple Edge servers!

> **Master It** Describe the call flow path between two users, Linda and Rob. Linda is calling from a cell phone to Rob's Skype for Business phone number. Rob is a Skype for Business Online user and is located currently on the corporate network.

Understand the required steps to configure a hybrid deployment. Introducing a hybrid scenario to a local Skype for Business environment requires a number of additional configuration items to be carried out. Some are as basic (and expected) as firewall port configuration, while others are significantly more complex, such as ADFS configuration.

> **Master It** You are configuring your organization for a hybrid scenario and need to configure rules for the proxy exceptions list. What do you need to configure?

Part 3

Administration

Chapter 11

Role-Based Access Control

Implemented first in Exchange Server 2010, then in both versions of Lync Server, and continuing in Skype for Business Server 2015, Role-Based Access Control (RBAC) changes the granularity and ease with which an administrator can be granted permissions required for their job and only their job, allowing specific delegation of functionality to groups of people.

In this chapter, you will learn to

- Use PowerShell to list the standard RBAC groups
- Understand the permissions available to each role
- Undertake planning for RBAC roles
- Create custom RBAC roles and assign them to administrators
- Manipulate the cmdlets assigned to a role
- Carry out general administration, including granting and removing RBAC roles
- Report on the use of RBAC roles

Introducing RBAC

In medium to large organizations, the same person does not necessarily administer every system. RBAC was created to address the problems that can arise as a result. In addition, Microsoft and security professionals in general espouse the principle of *least privilege*, whereby each administrator is granted only the minimum permissions needed to carry out their job. Until RBAC was built into the product, companies were forced to work within the constraints of the rather lackluster delegation often provided by Microsoft server applications, or they had to look for a third-party delegation product. This led to the development of rather complex and costly products such as Active Roles, from Quest (now owned by Dell), which enabled more granular delegation based on the need to perform certain tasks, which when grouped together formed roles. If you didn't have the time or budget for such products, you were left with native tools and the myriad possibilities of manually hacking access control lists (ACLs) and, below them, individual access control entries (ACEs) in Active Directory (AD).

Administration of Microsoft server products has long been intertwined with permissions. Administrators need rights to modify, create, and delete objects. Until recently, this required granting complex levels of permissions on Active Directory and file system objects. In OCS 2007 R2, the RTCUniversalReadOnlyAdmins group made a token gesture toward granting permissions based on job role. However, membership in the AD group aligned to the role didn't give all the permissions necessary to do the job, as still other AD group memberships were required to allow basic account access.

Thankfully, in Wave 14 (the 2010 release of Microsoft products), Microsoft answered the call to build in this type of functionality. Starting with Exchange 2010 and then Lync Server 2010 (improved with Lync Server 2013), an implementation of RBAC was provided. It allows delegation of tasks based on role and targeting of objects so the administrator can carry out tasks without the need to manually set ACLs. Skype for Business Server 2015 allows quite granular delegation of administrative commands as well as a couple of specific administrative roles that we will cover shortly.

Roles and Scopes

The concept of RBAC is simple. An administrator is granted the rights to run certain PowerShell cmdlets (a *role*) on a certain group of users or servers (a *scope*).

An RBAC role is built up by defining a set of cmdlets that can be run. Generally, these cmdlets are grouped together to form a set related to a job role. A scope defines the target objects where those cmdlets can be run. For example, a scope could be defined to servers (grouped within a site), to a group of users (in an OU), or to the whole organization using a *global scope*.

Each role has a config and a user scope. This means you can delegate a role both to a set of users and to a site where servers are contained, allowing you great granularity in the way delegation is carried out.

Each role membership is controlled by a linked AD group, which is specified at the creation of the role. The AD groups linked to the standard roles are created in the Users container of the domain specified during AD forest preparation. As discussed in Chapter 8, "Installation," although forest preparation must be run from a machine in the root forest, the domain specified for the groups can be anywhere in the forest and doesn't have to be the root. Given that the membership of these groups governs the roles an administrator holds, if your company heavily locks down the root domain of the forest, you may decide to create these groups in a child domain. Figure 11.1 shows the key elements of role, AD group, and scope in diagram form for the standard role AD group CSAdministrator.

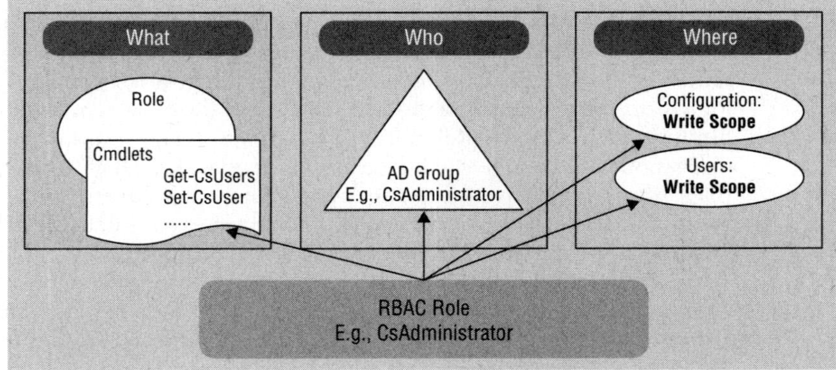

FIGURE 11.1 The key elements of RBAC: role, group, and scope

Cross-Domain Support

One nice improvement that was made in Lync Server 2010 Cumulative Updates 2 (CU2) was the ability to scope to a child domain. When Lync 2010 was first released, its inability to flexibly use scope caused problems; the common name (CN) of the organizational unit (OU) to be delegated under the control of a scope could be only in the root domain. Thankfully, this was fixed, so it is possible to let different groups of administrators, from different child domains, control the users in the domains they administer.

Skype for Business Roles and PowerShell

Appendix B, "Introduction to PowerShell, the Skype for Business Management Shell, and Regular Expressions," covers PowerShell basics and shows how Skype for Business utilizes its cmdlets. As you know, all administration can be undertaken through PowerShell, and indeed, some is possible only from within the shell. In fact, even when you are using the Skype for Business Server 2015 Control Panel (SBSCP), you are actually calling PowerShell commands in the background. This chapter relies primarily on PowerShell because, as in Lync, it provides the only way to manipulate Skype for Business Server roles.

It is this reliance on PowerShell that enables RBAC to work. When you access PowerShell remotely—as described in Appendix B—either through the SBSCP or through remote PowerShell rather than directly on the server via the Skype for Business Server Management Shell (SBSMS), a filter is applied to the commands to which you have access based on the roles you are assigned. In fact, when accessing through remote PowerShell, when you run `Get-Command`, you see only the commands you can run. This is also reflected in the GUI, as shown in Figure 11.2, which shows the SBSCP accessed by a full administrator and an archiving administrator logged on. The difference is clear to see, with far less functionality being made available to the archiving administrator.

So how does this actually work? When an administrator connects to Skype for Business, either through remote PowerShell or via SBSCP, they are authenticated. At this point, the Skype for Business Management Web Service will create a run-space for the user, which contains only the cmdlets the user has access to run as assigned by their role membership. When the administrator then runs a command, authorization is performed to confirm that indeed the administrator does have rights to run that cmdlet and that the cmdlet is targeted at a location (scope) where the administrator has been granted access. At this point, assuming all checks are passed, the CS Management Web Service executes the cmdlet.

Command Filtering in the Control Panel

You can actually see this filtering of commands in action in the Skype for Business Server Control Panel. On a slow system, when you log onto SBSCP as an administrator with limited permissions, you can see the various elements of the graphical user interface (GUI) to which you don't have access disappear as the role is applied.

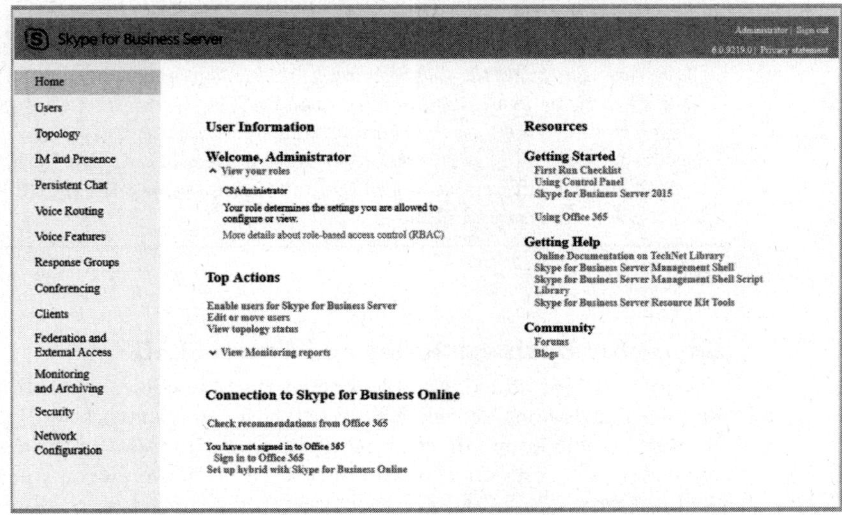

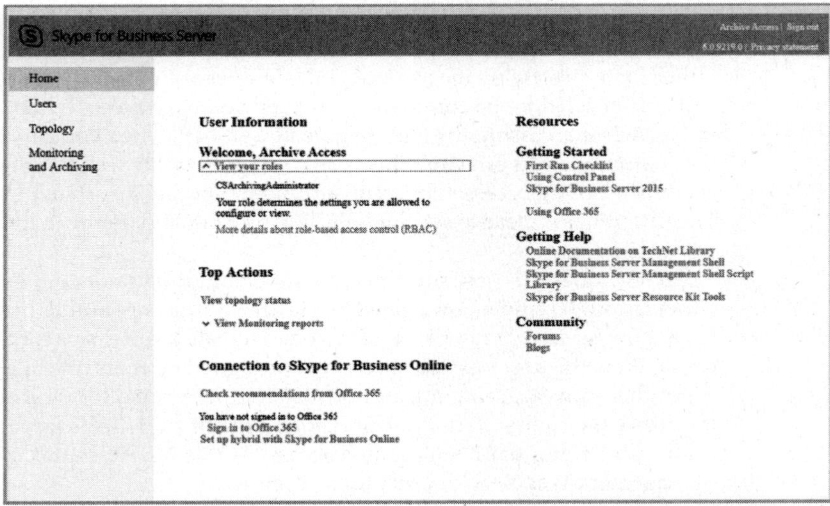

FIGURE 11.2 The Control Panel accessed by an administrator holding the CSAdministrator role, with full administrative rights (top); the CSArchiving Administrator role, with limited admin rights (bottom)

How does this work, given that the administrator doesn't need special permissions in AD? Each RBAC role has an associated Universal security group in Active Directory. Table 11.1 describes the groups for the standard roles.

TABLE 11.1: Details of the standard RBAC role groups

GROUP NAME	GROUP TYPE	DESCRIPTION
CSAdministrator	Security Group - Universal	Members of this group can perform all administrative tasks in Skype for Business Server 2015.
CSArchivingAdministrator	Security Group - Universal	Members of this group can create, configure, and manage archiving-related settings and policies in Skype for Business Server 2015.
CSHelpDesk	Security Group - Universal	Members of this group can view the deployment, including user properties and policies, and can execute specific troubleshooting tasks in Skype for Business Server 2015.
CSLocationAdministrator	Security Group - Universal	Members of this group have the lowest level of rights for E911 management. They can create E911 locations and network identifiers and associate them with each other in Skype for Business Server 2015.
CSPersistentChatAdministrator	Security Group - Universal	Members of this group can run the persistent chat admin cmdlets for Categories/Rooms/Addins.
CSResponseGroupAdministrator	Security Group - Universal	Members of this group can manage the configuration of the Response Group application in Skype for Business Server 2015.
CSResponseGroupManager	Security Group - Universal	Members of this group can manage limited configuration of assigned Response Groups in Skype for Business Server 2015.
CSServerAdministrator	Security Group -Universal	Members of this group can manage, monitor, and troubleshoot Skype for Business Server 2015 and services.
CSUserAdministrator	Security Group - Universal	Members of this group can enable and disable users for Skype for Business Server 2015, move users, and assign existing policies to users.
CSViewOnlyAdministrator	Security Group - Universal	Members of this group can view the Skype for Business Server 2015 deployment, including server information, to monitor deployment health.
CSVoiceAdministrator	Security Group - Universal	Members of this group can create, configure, and manage voice-related settings and policies in Skype for Business Server 2015.

However, the role group in AD doesn't grant any special permission; it is just a placeholder provided so Skype for Business can manage membership of the role. How are the cmdlets run? They are run under the local machine account of the server to which the administrator has the remote connection. This works because that local machine account is itself a member of various AD groups. These groups will be familiar to anyone who has installed any form of Office Communications Server (OCS)—the Real Time Communications (RTC) groups—and they are still the groups that govern what happens when you don't use remote PowerShell. If you access the console of the front-end server and run the Skype for Business Server Management Shell, for example, you will not be authenticated and managed by RBAC. When the admin logs on locally and uses SBSMS on the console of the Skype for Business server, administration rights are governed by membership of the RTC named groups, which are created by Skype for Business forest prep. This system is almost identical to that which was in place with OCS 2007 R2. There is no simple provision for scoping of access.

RBAC ONLY WORKS USING REMOTE CONNECTIONS

If you rely on RBAC to delegate administrative access, you must be careful to protect console access, either via RDP or physically at the server. RBAC only works remotely, so anyone who gains physical access will be governed by membership of the RTC groups, not RBAC roles. It is, therefore, also important to monitor and manage access to the relevant AD group memberships.

So, how are these groups and the RBAC role groups intertwined? The RBAC groups are not granted permissions on anything directly. As mentioned earlier, what actually happens when an RBAC user runs a command is that the CS Management Web Service first confirms that the user is entitled to run the cmdlet, and then runs it under the local Skype for Business Server computer account. These machine accounts get their rights to run cmdlets from membership in the various RTC groups shown in Table 11.2, such as RTCUniversalServerAdmins and RTCUniversalUserAdmins.

TABLE 11.2: RTC groups in the Users container in Active Directory Users and Computers (ADUC)

GROUP NAME	GROUP TYPE	DESCRIPTION
RTCUniversalUserReadOnlyGroup	Security Group - Universal	Members have read access to RTC-related user attributes or property sets.
RTCUniversalUserAdmins	Security Group - Universal	Members can manage RTC users in this forest.

TABLE 11.2: RTC groups in the Users container in Active Directory Users and Computers (ADUC) *(CONTINUED)*

GROUP NAME	GROUP TYPE	DESCRIPTION
RTCUniversalServerReadOnlyGroup	Security Group - Universal	Members have read access to RTC-related server AD objects in the forest.
RTCUniversalServerAdmins	Security Group - Universal	Members can manage all aspects of RTC servers in this forest.
RTCUniversalSBATechnicians	Security Group - Universal	Members have read access to Skype for Business Server 2015 configuration and are placed in the Local Administrators group of survivable branch office appliances during installation.
RTCUniversalReadOnlyAdmins	Security Group - Universal	Members can only read RTC-related server and user properties in this forest.
RTCUniversalGlobalWriteGroup	Security Group - Universal	Members have write access to RTC global settings.
RTCUniversalGlobalReadOnlyGroup	Security Group - Universal	Members have read access to RTC global settings.
RTCUniversalConfigReplicator	Security Group - Universal	Members can participate in configuration replication.
RTCSBAUniversalServices	Security Group - Universal	Members have read access to Skype for Business Server 2015 configuration for survivable branch office installation.
RTCProxyUniversalServices	Security Group - Universal	Members can be used as RTC proxy service logon.
RTCHSUniversalServices	Security Group - Universal	Members can be used as RTC IM service logon.
RTCComponentUniversalServices	Security Group - Universal	Members can be used as RTC MCU and web component services logon.

The RTC groups are then assigned permissions through the setup process on objects in AD. Figure 11.3 shows the Security tab for a user account, which clearly shows the ACE for the RTCUniversalUserAdmins group.

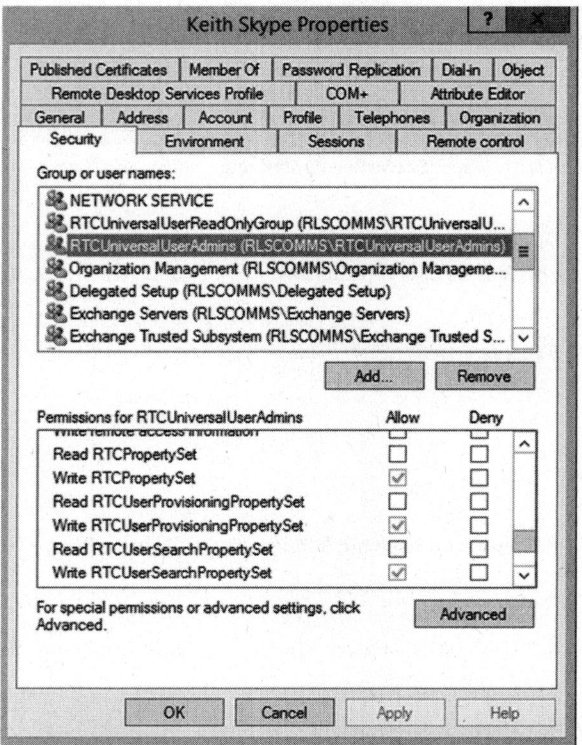

FIGURE 11.3
The Security tab of a standard user showing the ACE for RTCUniversalUserAdmins

Now that you've looked at the building blocks, let's move on and examine the roles available in Skype for Business out of the box.

Understanding the Standard Roles

Out of the box, Skype for Business Server 2015 ships with 11 roles, a range that gives you a fair amount of flexibility in grouping your administrators. However, you may find that you don't want to split things quite as they are out of the box. This is one area where Lync Server 2013 made significant improvements over Lync Server 2010, which have continued into Skype for Business Server 2015. Skype for Business Server 2015 makes it possible not only to give administrators several of the standard roles but also to utilize the ability to create custom roles, as described later in this chapter. It is the ability to create custom roles that changed in Lync 2013 and is continued in Skype for Business Server 2015. Previously, while you could create custom roles, you were limited to making use of the existing groupings of cmdlets. All you could change was the scope and the target group. What you couldn't do was carve up the cmdlets yourself to make custom roles. Thankfully that has now changed. You not only can create custom roles with any cmdlets you choose but also create roles that are only allowed to run specific pre-created scripts. This new approach gives the ability to be extremely granular and controlled about the permissions you give to different groups.

Let's dive into some PowerShell and see how to view the roles. On the Standard Edition server you installed in Chapter 8, make sure you are logged on locally either through RDP to the console or physically at the server console. Ensure that you are logged on as a member of the RTCUniversalServerAdmins group in AD. Open the management shell (SBSMS). This is the simplest command you can use to get Skype for Business to output a list of the roles:

```
Get-CsAdminRole
```

This will bring back any roles, including those you might have created yourself.

You can then be a little more specific and bring back just a single role—for example, the CSAdministrator role as follows:

```
Get-CsAdminRole -Identity CSAdministrator
```

The output, as listed next, shows you the role identity, the security identifier (SID) of the group it is linked to in AD, that it is a standard role, the beginning of the list of cmdlets that are available to those holding the role, and the scopes of the role. At the bottom of the output you will see the template. For the default roles, this is empty; however, as you will see later, when you create custom roles, this is something that you will have to specify.

```
Identity       : CSAdministrator
SID            : S-1-5-21-1801160900-2869415974-1826267308-1118
IsStandardRole : True
Cmdlets        : {Name=Debug-CsInterPoolReplication, Name=Invoke-
                 CsBackupServiceSync,
                 Name=Get-CsBackupServiceStatus, Name=Get-
                 CsPoolBackupRelationship...}
ScriptModules  : {}
ConfigScopes   : {Global}
UserScopes     : {Global}
Template       :
```

To bring back a nicely formatted list of just the standard roles, you need to extend the first PowerShell cmdlets as follows:

```
Get-CsAdminRole | Where-Object {$_.IsStandardRole -eq $True} | fl Identity
```

This pipes the output of the plain `Get-CsAdminRole` cmdlet into `Where-Object`, which checks each role to see whether the attribute `IsStandardRole` is set to `True`. It then pipes those role objects into the `Format-List` cmdlet and shows only the `Identity` attribute.

Having done this, you will have successfully listed all 11 standard roles and will obtain the following output:

```
Identity : CSAdministrator
Identity : CSVoiceAdministrator
Identity : CSUserAdministrator
Identity : CSResponseGroupAdministrator
Identity : CSLocationAdministrator
Identity : CSArchivingAdministrator
Identity : CSViewOnlyAdministrator
Identity : CSServerAdministrator
```

```
Identity : CSHelpDesk
Identity : CSResponseGroupManager
Identity : CSPersistentChatAdministrator
```

As mentioned, a role is a group of cmdlets. From the response to the `Get-CsAdmin` cmdlet shown previously, you can see the list of cmdlets is begun but then tails off in an ellipsis. To see all the cmdlets that make up each role, you need to jump back into PowerShell. For example, to see all the cmdlets assigned to the CSAdministrator role, you would use the following command:

```
Get-CsAdminRole -Identity CSAdministrator | Select-Object -ExpandProperty Cmdlets
  | Out-File c:\csadminrolecmdlets.txt
```

This command first gets the CSAdministrator role, pipes its attributes to `Select-Object`, and then expands the `Cmdlets` attribute. The results are then piped to the `Out-File` cmdlet, which will write them to a text file. Later in this chapter, in the section "Planning Combinations," you'll see a script created by a member of the Skype for Business product group that lists all the cmdlets available to each role.

Now that you've seen how to list the standard roles, let's take a closer look at each one.

CSAdministrator

Of all the RBAC roles, CSAdministrator is the most powerful. It gives the assigned user the full range of functionality, including the ability to carry out user, server, and device administration and to create and assign RBAC roles and other policies. This is the role to which the setup process asks you to add a user, who will become the first Skype for Business administrator. Essentially, this role would be given only to the most senior administrators who require access to deploy and control all aspects of Skype for Business.

One final thing to note about the CSAdministrator role is that although it gives the most functionality available in a role, it doesn't enable you to run all the commands that exist in the Skype for Business PowerShell module.

PowerShell Modules

For more on the use of PowerShell modules and in particular the Skype for Business module, see Appendix B. To output all the commands in the module to a text file called `AllLyncCmds.txt`, you would run this version of `Get-Command`:

```
Get-Command -Module SkypeforBusiness -CommandType All | Out-File c:\AllSfbCmds
.txt
```

If you compare the cmdlets available in the module and those available to the CSAdministrator role, you will see that many are not included in the CSAdministrator role. These are generally system-altering cmdlets like those that allow the preparation of the domain, such as `Prep-Domain`. They, therefore, need greater permissions than granted through Skype for Business groups alone—for example, Domain Administrator permissions. They are also required to be run locally on the Skype for Business server through SBSMS rather than through remote PowerShell.

Related Exchange Role

Given that Exchange also implements RBAC, it is useful to understand the similar roles available. If your administrators run both Exchange and Skype for Business, then you will understand how to assign the standard RBAC groups in Skype for Business to match those in Exchange.

A similar role in Exchange to Skype for Business's CSAdministrator role would be the Organization Administrator role.

CSUserAdministrator

The CSUserAdministrator role enables the holder to manage users. Specifically, it can enable users for Skype for Business, although it cannot create new AD users, and it can move users between pools and disable Skype for Business users. It also allows the holder to assign policies to users but not to create policies. This role also allows the management of devices such as analog and common area phones. Interestingly, the role also allows the creation of the contacts used when integrating Skype for Business with Exchange Unified Messaging (UM) for voicemail provision. For more information about UM, see Chapter 22, "Exchange, SharePoint, and Office Web Application Server."

It is likely that this role would be given to second-level support engineers who were specifically focused on end-user support rather than support of the server infrastructure, which might be left for third-level support and higher.

Related Exchange Role

A similar role in Exchange would be Mail Recipients.

CSServerAdministrator

The CSServerAdministrator role is the most far-ranging role outside of the CSAdministrator role. It allows control of a significant amount of Skype for Business functionality.

In general, the main thing that this policy can't do is interact with users—no granting policy, no enabling, and no disabling. For that, you need the CSAdministrator role or the CSUserAdministrator role. The other key thing it can't do is create new RBAC roles for which the CSAdministrator role is needed.

Other than that, this role does give the ability to manage and monitor the back-end aspects of Skype for Business Server. It allows the management of services, testing of services, and ability to bring servers up and down through the draining process.

This role is likely to be granted to senior or third-level admins who are focused on maintaining and managing Skype for Business on a day-to-day basis.

Related Exchange Role

A similar role in Exchange would be the Server Management role.

CSViewOnlyAdministrator

The CSViewOnlyAdministrator role grants the holder the ability to monitor the Skype for Business implementation. It is made up almost entirely of `Get-` cmdlets that pull back information about a wide variety of Skype for Business elements, such as policies, server configuration, voice configuration, call admission control, and users. The one exception is the `Debug-CsLisConfiguration` cmdlet, which allows you to retrieve detailed configuration information about Location Information Services (LIS).

This role is intended to give reporting powers and would perhaps be granted to architects or compliance officers to enable them to monitor the progress of deployment or see the settings of various policies.

Related Exchange Role

There is a similar role in Exchange: View-Only Organization Management.

CSArchivingAdministrator

The CSArchivingAdministrator role in Skype for Business gives the holder the ability to run a limited set of cmdlets pertaining only to managing the archive and archive policies in Skype for Business. This is the only role other than CSAdministrator that is able to create, grant, and alter archiving policies.

This role is most likely to be delegated to a security/compliance officer who would be specifically tasked with managing archiving by creating and assigning policies to users.

Related Exchange Role

In Exchange, there is the Discovery Management Role Group; however, it is more about performing searches than configuring journaling and retention policy. More similar roles would be the Retention Management Role Group.

CSHelpDesk

In some ways, the CSHelpDesk role is similar to the CSViewOnlyAdmin role in that it is made up of mostly `Get-` cmdlets giving visibility of configuration. However, the CSHelpDesk role also has many `Test-` cmdlets, which can be run to validate end-to-end functionality and thus troubleshoot user issues, and also three PIN-related cmdlets (`Set-CsClientPin`, `Lock-CsClientPin`, and `Unlock-CsClientPin`), which allow control over user access. This role is likely to be given to first-line support to enable them to fix basic issues such as resetting the user PIN and then to provide a useful report to the more senior engineers after running the relevant `Test-` cmdlets.

Related Exchange Role

There is a similar role in Exchange: HelpDesk.

CSVoiceAdministrator

The CSVoiceAdministrator role is a wide-ranging one; it allows configuration and control over the PBX elements of Skype for Business, including phone devices, response groups, location setup, and call routing. In many organizations where unified communication systems haven't been deployed, the teams who manage the PBX and those who manage servers are different. This role allows that type of split to continue.

Related Exchange Role

There is no equivalent role in Exchange. These teams are often separate. The only possible consideration is whether these administrators might take control over aspects of Unified Messaging on Exchange. If there were still a "hard" division between those working on telephony and those on servers, UM would probably be handled by the Exchange team in collaboration with the telephony team, who would be assigned the Exchange UM Management role group.

CSResponseGroupAdministrator

The CSResponseGroupAdministrator role is another role related to the telephony side of Skype for Business. It gives holders the ability to manage response groups to manage call flow and agents who are members of each queue. This role might be given to a suitably trained contact-center administrator so they can change queues and implement working-hour automation as necessary without troubling the wider support team.

Related Exchange Role

As with the CSVoiceAdministrator role, there is no equivalent role in Exchange.

CSResponseGroupManager

The CSResponseGroupManager role was introduced in Lync Server 2013 and is a telephony-related role. It was created to give greater control over delegation of complex response group deployments where instead of central control, individual response group queues are managed by department or group leads. This role doesn't give rights to manage the response group application as a whole.

Related Exchange Role

As with the CSVoiceAdministrator role, there is no equivalent role in Exchange.

CSLocationAdministrator

The CSLocationAdministrator is another limited role, much like the archiving role. It allows the holder to manage location information and, as such, might be used by a facilities or networking administrator who would be tasked with managing and maintaining the mapping of locations to subnets, switches, and buildings.

Related Exchange Role

As with the CSVoiceAdministrator role, there is no equivalent role in Exchange.

CsPersistentChatAdministrator

The CsPersistentChatAdministrator role is another role that was introduced in Lync 2013. As covered in Appendix C, "Using Persistent Chat Effectively," what has evolved from a separate Group Chat in Lync 2010 is now fully integrated into Skype for Business. This role grants the holder rights to manage and maintain the persistent chat components of Skype. This role would be used to provide a specific team of administrators who previously managed Group Chat (or Mind Align, the predecessor to Group Chat) administrative capabilities in the new environment.

Related Exchange Role

There is no equivalent role in Exchange.

> **Differences from Exchange RBAC**
>
> RBAC was new to Lync 2010; however, with updates in Lync 2013 and now with Skype for Business, RBAC is relatively similar in capabilities to Exchange. Both allow you to create custom roles defining specific cmdlets to be delegated. There are, however, still some differences. For example, in Skype for Business, roles are assigned to administrators only. In Exchange, roles are granted not only to administrators but to users, which allows users to undertake basic admin tasks such as updating contact information and carrying out message tracking. No doubt with effort something similar could be achieved in Skype for Business, but there are fewer options (such as message tracking) for which users could be enabled, so this may not be entirely relevant.

Creating New Roles

We have covered what Skype for Business offers out of the box, and you have a lot to consider. It is critical to plan the use of RBAC carefully. Taking the easy road will end up with administrators having too many permissions, which as everyone knows can lead to disaster. Therefore, at this stage you really need to think through how you want administration to work in your organization. The following sections will outline various options and then take you through the steps required to create new roles and perform RBAC management tasks.

Planning Combinations

Now that you've seen the standard roles, you can understand that there is a fair amount of flexibility in the way administrative power can be delegated. One thing to consider is that the structure of the administrative teams in many organizations won't necessarily fit the exact way the standard roles are laid out. It is, therefore, possible to use the standard roles as templates for custom roles that will give more flexibility in what each administrator can do. This is the starting point even if you want to use the new functionality in Skype for Business that allows creation of roles based on a group of cmdlets you define.

Also bear in mind that each of the standard roles has a global scope, so one recommendation is to follow the process of applying least privilege and create custom roles based on the standard roles but with more suitably targeted scope. For example, if there were a group of administrators on a help desk who needed to administer only users in one OU, you would configure a new custom role with a user scope for that specific OU and use the CSUserAdministrator role as the template.

 **Real World Scenario**

SPLIT ADMINISTRATORS FOR A SINGLE SITE: TRADERS AND RESEARCHERS

Throughout my consulting work, I have seen certain organizations in which there were significant regulatory reasons to keep groups of users from communicating, and therefore, there were separate IT teams to manage those groups. In these cases, users could be in the same site, but separation of admin rights was needed.

RBAC can deal with these types of situations through the creation of custom roles. Instead of using the global scope, create two new roles, one for each set of administrators. Each group's config (site) scope will be the same, but by applying different user scopes, specifically focused on the OU containing the users to be administered, the administrators will be able to manage the servers in the site as needed but not to access each other's users.

In addition to the role template and role scope, you must plan the naming conventions of custom roles. First, it is important to realize that the name of the RBAC group must match the SAMAccountName of the group created to hold the members of the role. Therefore, if you have an AD group-naming policy, you must consider how this will affect the name of the RBAC group. Second, to follow best practices, the name of the RBAC role should enable an administrator to easily understand what the role does, identifying, for example, the role template and scope. You could, for example, call your group CsAdministrator-EMEA.

You also need to consider how you might group roles. To help you decide, one of the Skype for Business program managers, Cezar Ungureanasu, put together the following script (originally for Lync, but it still works with Skype for Business). It will run through all the standard RBAC roles and output which cmdlets they contain to a tab-separated values file. This file can be opened in Excel, where it provides an easy reference and comparison method to see which cmdlets are in each role and how they overlap. You can download the script from `www.sybex.com/go/masteringskypeforbusiness`.

```
$roles = Get-CsAdminRole  | where-object { $_.IsStandardRole -eq $true} | Sort
Identity
$d = "Cmdlet"
foreach($role in $roles)
    {
        $d = $d + "'t" + $role.Identity
    }
Out-File -FilePath "C:\cmdlettorole.tsv" -InputObject $d
$x = Get-Command -module SkypeforBusiness -commandType cmdlet | Sort Name
foreach($i in $x)
    {
        $a = $i.Name
        $c = $a +"'t"
        foreach($role in $roles)
            {
                if ($role.cmdlets -match $i.Name)
```

```
                    {
                        $c = $c + "yes" + "'t"
                    }
                else
                    {
                        $c = $c + "no" + "'t"
                    }
            }
        Out-File -FilePath C:\cmdlettorole.tsv -InputObject $c -Append
    }
```

To run the script, you should enter it into your favorite text editor (Notepad will do) and save it as a PowerShell PS1 file (`.ps1`). You can then run it from your front-end server. For more details about saving and running PowerShell scripts, see Appendix B. Table 11.3 shows an extract from the file. Of course, for space reasons, we have cut this down because it is a large sheet encompassing all the roles and cmdlets available. You can find the entire spreadsheet at `www.sybex.com/go/masteringskypeforbusiness`.

TABLE 11.3: An extract from the roles analysis spreadsheet

CMDLET	CSADMINISTRATOR	CSARCHIVINGADMINISTRATOR	CSHELPDESK
`Approve-CsDeviceUpdateRule`	Yes	No	No
`Clear-CsDeviceUpdateFile`	Yes	No	No
`Clear-CsDeviceUpdateLog`	Yes	No	No
`Debug-CsLisConfiguration`	Yes	No	Yes
`Disable-CsAdDomain`	No	No	No
`Disable-CsAdForest`	No	No	No
`Disable-CsComputer`	No	No	No

By looking at the spreadsheet in Excel, you can clearly see that certain roles overlap in functionality, which may mean that if you have a fairly small administrative team where there aren't so many tightly focused roles, you can use the more broadly scoped roles. For example, the CSResponseGroupAdministrator role is entirely a subset of the CSServerAdministrator, CSVoiceAdministrator, and of course CSAdministrator roles. Therefore, this might be one role that you can do without if you have a relatively small administrative team and don't need one person to manage only response groups.

In addition, the CSLocationAdministrator role is a subset of the CSVoiceAdministrator role; so again, where there is not one person or group of people specifically responsible for the management of network locations (for example, network engineers), then granting the CSVoiceAdministrator role would cover all functionality.

On a different note, and as mentioned previously, CSAdministrator and CSArchivingAdministrator are the only roles that can create and grant archiving policy.

Finally, and rather more obviously, CSViewOnlyAdministrator is a subset of the CSAdministrator role.

This type of analysis, in conjunction with your understanding of how administration works in your organization, should help you decide how you will use RBAC roles in your deployment.

The final planning consideration is the functionality first introduced in Lync 2013; it is possible to create custom roles using a set of cmdlets of your choosing and also to add scripts of cmdlets to the allowed tasks of custom roles. Of course, there is the potential to create untold complexity through using the new features, so consider them only after you have worked through the planning stages.

Real World Scenario

Different Organization Types

Organizations come in all shapes and sizes. In general, administration is organized in one of two ways.

Some organizations centralize their administrative efforts. This may be representative of a company in a single site or simply that they have a central team to deal with all users or systems for a particular application. In such cases, a single group controls the entire Skype for Business organization, and there are likely to be tiers of administrators, starting with first-line help-desk personnel who take basic queries and attempt immediate fixes, such as resetting passwords or PINs. More difficult problems are passed up to second-line support, who may visit users at their desks, and this is followed by third- and fourth-level support, who mainly deal with the back-end servers and architecture as a whole. Given this type of organization, a global scope would be assigned to the roles, so the default roles could be used.

Other organizations are highly distributed environments. In this case, companies might have grown from various acquisitions or be global companies where different regions operate as somewhat separate entities; however, they have chosen to merge their IT systems. These companies often have multiple child domains underneath an empty root forest. To work in this environment, roles would be targeted at specific sites and specific end-user OUs. There would likely still be the same type of tiered support, but it would be regional.

Finally, another issue occurs when an organization is simply not structured to manage a unified communications system. Skype for Business is an application that brings together two different worlds: that of Windows servers and that of telephony. In many cases, these are managed by totally separate groups of people, each of whom want to keep control and fear change. In these cases, you have the ability to delegate the telephony administration to the telephony group without requiring the telephony administrators to have full domain-admin rights or other extensive infrastructure permissions.

Creating the Role

Once you have completed planning and understand what custom roles, if any, you will need in your organization, you are ready to create your custom roles. You need to collect various pieces of data to create a role. First, you need a name for the role. As mentioned previously, it is worth sticking to a naming convention that helps identify the role. Having decided on the name, you must create a new Universal security group with the same name as the new role. For example, if your new RBAC role is to be called EMEA-CsAdmin, you can create the group using the following command:

```
New-AdGroup -Name "EMEA CSAdministrator" -GroupScope Universal -SamAccountName
emea-csadmin -GroupCategory Security
```

Notice how this command creates a Universal security group with a display name containing spaces, but SamAccountName, which is what must match the RBAC role name, is without spaces and is shorter than 20 characters.

With this command, the group will be created in the Users container in the domain to which you are connected. Unlike the standard roles, whose related groups are always in the Users container of whichever domain was specified during forest preparation, the groups created for custom roles can be placed in any OU in any domain in the forest. To do this, specify the common name of the parent container as follows:

```
New-AdGroup -Name "EMEA CsAdministrator" -GroupScope Universal -SamAccountName
emea-csadmin -GroupCategory Security -Path "ou=EMEA,ou=GroupsOU,dc=rlscomms,dc=net"
```

That command will create the same group as before, but this time in the Group OU under the EMEA OU.

Once you have created the relevant group in AD, you can create the new custom RBAC role using this command:

```
New-CsAdminRole -Template CSAdministrator -Identity emea-csadmin
```

This will create a role with all the power of the CSAdministrator role and with a global scope and output as follows:

```
Identity       : emea-csadmin
SID            : S-1-5-21-1336847106-355665257-1417932119-1144
IsStandardRole : False
Cmdlets        : {Name=Debug-CsInterPoolReplication, Name=Invoke-
                 CsBackupServiceSync,
                 Name=Get-CsBackupServiceStatus, Name=Get-
                 CsPoolBackupRelationship...}
ScriptModules  : {}
ConfigScopes   : {Global}
UserScopes     : {Global}
Template       : CSAdministrator
```

Of course, the reason for creating custom roles is to be specific about where you want them to apply—in other words, to set the scope. To do this, you need to add one or two more parameters to the command used to create the group. For example, if you want to create a role with a specific site scope to control objects only in an EMEA site, run the command as follows:

```
New-CsAdminRole -Template CSAdministrator -Identity emea-csadmin
-ConfigScopes Site:1
```

This will create the same role as before, but this time those granted the role will only be able to carry out administration in the EMEA (SiteID:1) site. Note that the site is referred to by its numerical site ID, which you can get by running the command `Get-CsSite`. This will give you output similar to the following for each site you have:

```
Identity                   : Site:EMEA
SiteId                     : 1
Services                   : {UserServer:se01.rlscomms.net,
                             Registrar:se01.rlscomms.net,
                             UserDatabase:se01.rlscomms.net,
                             FileStore:se01.rlscomms.net...}
Pools                      : {se01.rlscomms.net,
                             se02.rlscomms.net}
FederationRoute            :
XmppFederationRoute        :
DefaultPersistentChatPool  :
Description                :
DisplayName                : EMEA
SiteType                   : CentralSite
ParentSite                 :
```

Once you have created the new role, the output is different in the ConfigScopes area, as you can see next:

```
Identity       : emea-csadmin
SID            : S-1-5-21-1336847106-355665257-1417932119-1144
IsStandardRole : False
Cmdlets        : {Name=Debug-CsInterPoolReplication, Name=Invoke-
                 CsBackupServiceSync,
                 Name=Get-CsBackupServiceStatus, Name=Get-
                 CsPoolBackupRelationship...}
ScriptModules  : {}
ConfigScopes   : {Site:1}
UserScopes     : {Global}
Template       : CsAdministrator
```

Assuming that you are using a template group that has user-related commands (perhaps CSAdministrator or CSUserAdministrator), you could instead lock down the new role to a specific OU that contains users and would allow those allocated the role to manage only those users in the OU specified. In that case, you would run the following command:

```
New-CsAdminRole -Template CSAdministrator -Identity emea-csadmin
-UserScopes "OU:ou=TestUsersOU,dc=rlscomms,dc=net"
```

This command would create the same new role, but administration would be possible only on users in TestUsersOU. Note that when specifying the OU, you must preface the distinguished name with the `OU:` keyword.

Again, this produces different output, this time in the UserScopes area.

```
Identity        : emea-csadmin
SID             : S-1-5-21-1336847106-355665257-1417932119-1144
IsStandardRole  : False
Cmdlets         : {Name=Debug-CsInterPoolReplication, Name=Invoke-
                  CsBackupServiceSync,
                  Name=Get-CsBackupServiceStatus, Name=Get-
                  CsPoolBackupRelationship...}
ScriptModules   : {}
ConfigScopes    : {Global}
UserScopes      : {OU:ou=TestUsersOU,dc=rlscomms,dc=net}
Template        : CSAdministrator
dc=rlscomms,dc=net
```

Finally, if you want to scope to multiple sites or user OUs to enable one group of administrators to have permissions over a range of objects but not the entire deployment, run a command like the following one:

```
New-CsAdminRole -Template CSAdministrator -Identity emea-csadmin
-UserScopes "CU:ou=TestUsersOU,dc=rlscomms,dc=net",
" OU:ou=AnotherTestUsersOU,dc=rlscomms,dc=net"
-ConfigScopes "Site:1","Site:2"
```

This more complex-looking command will create the same old role but this time scoped for user administration on users in TestUsersOU and AnotherTestUsersOU and for Site 1 and Site 2.

Be Careful with Scopes

One thing that is worth highlighting is that the default scope for a new role is global. Therefore, if you create a new role and scope it for a site using the `ConfigScopes` parameter but do not specify a user scope for that role, the administrative permissions will apply to all users. Don't expect the users to be scoped to the site just because you apply a config scope!

Now that you know how to create new custom roles based solely on the template role provided, you can investigate the creation of custom roles where you define a specific set of cmdlets to use. In this instance, you are still required to specify the template that you want to use as the basis of the role. This gives you the base list of cmdlets and script modules (if you were using an already-existing custom role as the template); however, you can now choose either to add addition cmdlets or to specify only the ones you want as follows.

First create the group SimpleOneCmdletRole. Then run the following command:

```
New-CsAdminRole -Template CSHelpDesk -Identity SimpleOneCmdletRole
-Cmdlets Set-CsUser
```

This command will create a new custom admin role called SimpleOneCmdletRole that will only have permission to use the `Set-CsUser` cmdlet. The scope will be carried over from the template CSHelpDesk role.

You might think this is pretty basic, and it is! It is perhaps more likely that you would want to maintain the general list of cmdlets provided through the template role but with a few modifications. This can be done as follows.

First create the group AddingToHelpDesk. Then run the following command:

```
New-CsAdminRole -Template CSHelpDesk -Identity AddingToHelpDesk
-Cmdlets @{Add="Set-CsUser"}
```

This would create the new custom admin role AddingToHelpDesk, which would have all the cmdlets of the original template role but with the addition of the `Set-CsUser` cmdlet. Of course, you could also remove cmdlets or create a role that has specific access to a certain script. In the next sections, we will cover these scenarios and more of the basic day-to-day administration tasks of either the standard or custom RBAC roles.

Manipulating Roles

Now that we've discussed how RBAC works in Skype for Business and how to create custom roles, let's finish this chapter by reviewing the key ways of manipulating roles: assigning users to and removing them from roles, deleting roles, filtering specific roles, adding and removing cmdlets and scripts from roles, and reporting on them.

Assigning and Removing Roles

You assign a role by adding the user who needs to carry out the role's tasks to the relevant AD group. This is a Universal security group and for the standard roles is named equally to the role; it is found in the Users container of whichever domain was specified during forest prep. Table 11.1 earlier in the chapter shows the groups for the standard RBAC roles.

Because granting a role is as simple as placing the new member's user account in the relevant group, it is important to consider the security of Active Directory as well as that of other systems, such as Skype for Business itself; otherwise, the roles could easily be overridden.

Helpfully, the users who are assigned roles do not necessarily need to be Skype for Business enabled. This is good, because it means that the separate administrative accounts, which should be used to follow the principle of separation of powers, do not need to be Skype for Business enabled and, therefore, will not show up in address books and the like.

In the same way that assigning roles is done through membership of an AD group, removing a role is as simple as removing the member from the relevant administrative group.

Deleting Roles

You may find that over time sites get decommissioned or OUs are removed, and this means that RBAC roles that were scoped to those areas are no longer needed. To remove the role, use the following command:

```
Remove-CsAdminRole -Identity NameOfRoleToRemove
```

This command will prompt you to verify that you really want to remove the RBAC role; if you enter **`Y`**, it will remove the role with the name *`nameofroletoremove`*.

Does Removing a Role Remove the AD Group?

No! So what can you do? You could remove the group manually, but perhaps you want a command-line method.

If you have the Active Directory module loaded as shown in the section "CSAdministrator" earlier, you can do something like the following:

```
$Name = nameofroletoremove
Remove-CsAdminRole -Identity $name; Remove-ADGroup $name
```

This first sets a variable, denoted by the $ sign, with the name of the role to remove. It then runs two PowerShell commands on one line, through the use of the semicolon delimiter (;), and thereby first removes the RBAC role as shown previously and then uses the Active Directory module cmdlet `Remove-ADGroup` to remove the AD group.

Filtering Specific Roles

You've already seen a few examples of how to view the roles; once you have built up a significant group of roles with a suitable naming convention, you might want to pull back all the roles for, say, a certain site. As is often the case in PowerShell, there are a few ways in which you can achieve this. One is to use the `-Filter` parameter.

```
Get-CsAdminRole -Filter "*EMEA*"
```

This will bring back all the roles with `EMEA` in the identity, as shown here:

```
Identity        : emea-csadmin
SID             : S-1-5-21-1336847106-355665257-1417932119-1144
IsStandardRole  : False
Cmdlets         : {Name=Debug-CsInterPoolReplication, Name=Invoke-
                  CsBackupServiceSync,
                  Name=Get-CsBackupServiceStatus, Name=Get-
                  CsPoolBackupRelationship...}
ScriptModules   : {}
ConfigScopes    : {Global}
UserScopes      : {OU:ou=TestUsersOU,dc=rlscomms,dc=net}
Template        : CSAdministrator
dc=rlscomms,dc=net
```

Note the use of the wildcard (*) within the quotes to allow the return of any roles that contain `EMEA`.

Adding and Removing Cmdlets or Scripts from Roles

We showed how to create a new role with only specific cmdlets and touched on the fact that Skype for Business allows the ability to assign the use of specific scripts to a role. We will now cover those capabilities in more depth. You will see that the methods used are the same as those used when creating new groups.

Both the Set-CsAdminRole cmdlet and the New-CsAdminRole cmdlet have two additional parameters than with Lync 2010: -Cmdlets and -ScriptModules.

Manipulating existing roles is done with the Set-CsAdminRole cmdlet in the following ways. If you wanted to wipe out all the cmdlets assigned to the MyRole1 role and create your own list, you could do so using the following command:

```
Set-CsAdminRole -Identity MyRole1 -Cmdlets "Set-CsUser","Set-CsAdminRole"
```

This command would change the cmdlets assigned to the MyRole1 custom admin role to only the two listed: Set-CsUser and Set-CsAdminRole.

If instead of replacing all existing cmdlets assigned to a role you want to add cmdlets, then you would proceed as follows:

```
Set-CsAdminRole -Identity MyRole1 -Cmdlets @{Add="New-CsAllowedDomain",
"New-CsAdminRole"}
```

This would add the New-CsAllowedDomain and New-CsAdminRole cmdlets to the existing cmdlets assigned to the role.

On the other hand, if you wanted to remove some cmdlets, you would need the following:

```
Set-CsAdminRole -Identity MyRole1 -Cmdlets @{Remove="New-CsAllowedDomain",
"New-CsAdminRole"}
```

This command would remove the cmdlets added in the preceding command.

That brings us to assigning scripts to custom roles. This functionality is great if you want to allow a group of administrators to perform a specific task that is defined as a function in a script. The script could even be "hidden" behind a nice custom web console that you create. For more information on functions, see Appendix B.

To add a script to a role, you use steps that are similar to those used to manipulate cmdlets available to a role, as shown in the examples that follow. For example, to add a script, follow this process:

```
Set-CsAdminRole -Identity MyRole1 -ScriptModule MyScript.PS1
```

This command replaces any current scripts assigned to the MyRole1 role with the MyScript.PS1 file.

If you noticed that when specifying scripts you specify only the name of the script, you might ask yourself if these scripts that you are defining have to be placed anywhere special. If you thought the answer is yes, then you would be right! The scripts have to be placed in the %Commonprogramfiles%\Microsoft Skype for Business Server 2015\AdminScripts folder and must have the .ps1 or .psm1 filename extension. This folder may well not exist, so go ahead and create it.

Next, you can add a second script to those that the MyRole1 role can execute using the following command:

```
Set-CsAdminRole -Identity MyRole1 -ScriptModule
@{Add="MyScript.PS1","AnotherScript.PS1"}
```

This command adds both the MyScript1 and AnotherScript scripts in addition to whatever is already defined.

Removing individual scripts is done in the same way as manipulating cmdlets, as described earlier; however, if you want to remove all scripts, you can use this command:

```
Set-CsAdminRole -Identity MyRole1 -ScriptModules $Null
```

This sets the `ScriptModules` parameter to `$Null`.

It is also possible to create admin roles with access to scripts instead of amending existing roles. This would be done by using the parameters shown earlier except with the `New-AdminRole` cmdlet instead of the `Set-AdminRole` cmdlet.

Having added scripts to cmdlets, it may well be useful to check up on which roles have which scripts assigned at a later date. You can gather this information in a couple of places. First, you can run a `Get-AdminRole` cmdlet as follows:

```
Get-AdminRole -Identity MyRole1 | fl
```

This command will output the details of the role, including the scripts assigned, as shown here:

```
Identity        : MyRole1
SID             : S-1-5-21-2281681827-1062710998-2061251255-1145
IsStandardRole  : False
Cmdlets         : {Name=set-csuser, Name=Set-csadminrole}
ScriptModules   : {script1.ps1}
ConfigScopes    : {Global}
UserScopes      : {Global}
Template        : CSHelpdesk
```

Second, the scripts (or more correctly, the functions within the scripts) will be shown to holders of that role when they connect through remote PowerShell.

```
ModuleType Name                                ExportedCommands
---------- ----                                ----------------
Script     tmp_431mkvne.qzg                    RunGetCsPool
```

One thing to bear in mind when adding scripts is that the cmdlets used in the script should be available to the admin role. Adding a script is not a magical way to get around not having certain cmdlets available to a role.

Here are a couple of final things to take into account. You would need to replicate this scripts folder to any Front End server that the user could connect to via the remote PowerShell URL. Also note that you need to make sure this folder is protected. Those delegated roles should not have the ability to edit the scripts; otherwise, clearly they could make changes that may grant them additional permissions.

Reporting on Roles

During the day-to-day management of a Skype for Business system, it is likely that the following questions will arise:

- What roles does a specific user have?
- Which users have a specific role?
- Which roles have access to certain users?
- Which roles have access to certain sites?

Thanks to PowerShell, it is relatively easy to find the answers.

What Roles Does a Specific User Have?

This can be answered with the following command:

```
Get-CsAdminRoleAssignment -Identity "Useralias"
```

This command will return a list of all the roles for the user Useralias.

Which Users Have a Specific Role?

To answer this question, in the PowerShell console you must first import the Active Directory module.

```
Import-Module ActiveDirectory
```

This command will import all the cmdlets related to AD management, such as group creation, deletion, and manipulation.

Once the AD module has loaded, you can use the following command to list the members of the group linked to a specific role, in this case the CSAdministrator:

```
Get-ADGroupMember -Identity CSAdministrator | Select name
```

This command brings back all the members of the group CSAdministrator, as shown here:

```
name
----
Administrator
```

To list members of all the roles, try this:

```
Get-CsAdminRole | ForEach-Object {$_.Identity; (Get-ADGroupMember
-Identity $_.Identity) | fl name}
```

This final command gets all the admin roles and then iterates through them by identity. Within the iteration, another command is run within the parentheses to get the AD group membership of each of the corresponding roles in the AD group. Finally, the output is passed to the `Format-List` format cmdlet, and the name of each member is printed, as shown here:

```
CSAdministrator
name : Administrator
CSVoiceAdministrator
CSUserAdministrator
name : RTCUniversalUserAdmins
CSResponseGroupAdministrator
CSLocationAdministrator
CSArchivingAdministrator
name : ArchiveAdmin
CSViewOnlyAdministrator
CSServerAdministrator
name : RTCUniversalServerAdmins
CSHelpDesk
```

```
CSResponseGroupManager
CsPersistentChatAdministrator
emea-csadmin
name : Test User1
```

Which Roles Have Access to Certain Users?

To list which roles can access a certain OU, run the following command:

```
Get-CsAdminRole | Where-Object {$_.UserScopes
-match "OU:ou=TestUsersOU,dc=rlscomms,dc=net"}
```

This command first gets all the admin roles and then lists each role that has a user scope of the OU common name entered.

Which Roles Have Access to Certain Sites?

In a similar way, you can also find roles that have access to certain servers, based on the site, as follows:

```
Get-CsAdminRole | Where-Object {$_.ConfigScopes -match "site:1"}
```

This command first gets all the admin roles and then lists where any of the roles has a config scope of the site entered.

The Importance of Securing Connection Methods

Now that we've reviewed RBAC, it is worth one final reminder that RBAC does nothing to prevent access on the local machine. It is fundamentally something that protects remote PowerShell connections. Therefore, if an administrator gets access to the local server console, they can run any cmdlets that their AD group membership allows. You need to ensure that delegated administrators can connect only in the way you want so they remain within the scope of RBAC.

The Bottom Line

Use PowerShell to list the standard RBAC groups. RBAC in Skype for Business is administered through the Skype for Business Server Management Shell (SBSMS). There are 11 standard roles that ship with Skype for Business; they provide an organization with the ability to delegate administration with a reasonable degree of granularity.

Master It You are in the middle of planning your enterprise deployment and have been asked by the senior architect to research the available options for administrative delegation. You have been asked to provide a list of standard RBAC roles.

Understand the permissions available to each role. There are 11 RBAC roles in Skype for Business. These roles range from granting high-level administrative access using the CSAdministrator role to granting read-only access with the CSViewOnlyAdministrator.

To use them properly, you need to know what each role does and understand any overlaps where different roles provide the same capability.

Master It As part of an investigation into how to make the best use of RBAC, you have been asked to identify a list of cmdlets each role grants access to so that it can be analyzed to see which RBAC role best fits the way your administrative teams work.

Undertake planning for RBAC roles. Your implementation of RBAC roles should relate to the way your organization is set up for administration. Some organizations are centralized, and others are distributed. You must understand your organizational structures and take them into account when planning RBAC roles. It is also important to follow the principle of least privilege, granting only the rights necessary for an administrator to do the job. This may mean utilizing custom roles and targeted scopes at either user OUs or Skype for Business sites.

Master It You are in the middle of planning your enterprise deployment and have been asked by the senior architect to plan the RBAC deployment in your organization. What should you consider?

Create custom RBAC roles and assign them to administrators. Skype for Business allows the creation of custom RBAC roles. These are not as flexible as in Exchange because you cannot grant access to specified single cmdlets. When creating a custom RBAC role, you must specify a template role from one of the 11 standard roles and then set an appropriate scope.

Master It Having carried out a planning exercise, you have decided that the standard Skype for Business roles are not adequate for your organization. Because you have a separate site supported by a separate team of junior admins who need to manage users in only one site, you need to be more specific about the areas that certain administrators can manage. How would you create an RBAC role to ensure that the junior admins don't have too many permissions?

Manipulate the cmdlets assigned to a role. One of the evolving capabilities of Skype for Business is the ability for RBAC to be far more flexible that it was in its first iteration in Lync 2010. You can now manipulate roles right down to the cmdlet level, enabling far greater granularity of permissioning.

Master It You have an existing RBAC role created called MinimalRole1. Holders of the role need to be allowed to use only the `Get-CsUser` and `Get-CsAdminRole` cmdlets.

Later you decide that the role should be expanded to include the use of the `Get-CsAdminRoleAssignment` cmdlet.

Finally, you realize that allowing the `Get-CsUser` cmdlet was a mistake.

Outline the separate steps you would take to carry out each configuration. You should end up with three commands.

Carry out general administration, including granting and removing RBAC roles. There a few cmdlets that allow management of RBAC roles in Skype for Business, and most use the `CsAdminRole` verb. All PowerShell roles are assigned through the membership of a linked Active Directory Universal security group.

Master It A colleague who administered Skype for Business has moved to a new role, and his replacement starts on Monday. You have been asked to ensure that the new staff member has the appropriate rights to do his job.

Report on the use of RBAC roles. Given that the purpose of RBAC is to provide people with administrative access to a system, there will always be a need to review and provide reports to management on who has what access. Reporting on RBAC takes various forms but can all be done through SBSMS.

Master It You have been asked to provide details on which roles have access to the APAC site and list the membership of those roles. How would you proceed?

Chapter 12

User Administration

"The job would be easy if it weren't for the users!" Or so the saying goes. This chapter is all about how Skype for Business handles users. There are simple elements, such as the ability to use Skype for Business Server Control Panel (SBSCP) and Skype for Business Server Management Shell (SBSMS, commonly known as PowerShell) to find, enable, disable, and generally manipulate users both individually and collectively. Then there are more complex elements, such as understanding how to set the wide variety of policies available. Lync Server 2010 changed this aspect dramatically compared with OCS 2007 R2, and Skype for Business continues this approach. The vast majority of policy is now set using in-band provisioning rather than the mix of Group Policy objects (GPOs), in-band provisioning, and registry settings required in OCS 2007 R2. This means you now have a single place to configure and assign policy, making things far simpler to manage. In addition to the changes in the way you apply policy, many more settings are available to give organizations plenty of control over exactly what users can and can't do with Skype for Business.

In this chapter, you will learn to

- Search for users in the SBSCP and PowerShell
- Perform basic user administration in the SBSCP and in PowerShell
- Understand Skype for Business policies
- Manipulate Skype for Business policies
- Choose the right policy for the job

User Configuration Basics

The starting point for user configuration is the Skype for Business Server Control Panel (SBSCP). As detailed in Chapter 11, "Role-Based Access Control," to carry out the full range of user administration, you must be logged in with an account that has been delegated the CSAdministrator or CSUserAdministrator RBAC role through membership of the CSAdministrator or CSUserAdministrator group or a new role with a superset of these capabilities that you have created yourself using the RBAC features in Skype for Business.

SBSCP can be accessed in various ways. You can do so directly on the Skype for Business server using the SBSCP icon by clicking Start and choosing Skype for Business Server 2013

Control Panel from the app location (of course this changes with each version of Windows, so maybe searching is the best approach).

Skype for Business User Admin

To make the screenshots of the SBSCP in this chapter cleaner, we decided to create a Skype for Business user administrator (SfBUserAdmin) account the same way we created the Admin account in Chapter 8, "Installation." However, this time, instead of granting the Administrator role (CSAdministrator), we added the user to the CSUserAdministrator group to make him a Skype for Business user administrator. This is the account we will be using throughout the chapter.

You can also install the administrative tools on another machine; this approach gets you not only the icon from which to launch the SBSCP but also the Topology Builder and PowerShell. Essentially, the workstation must meet the following prerequisites:

- OS as supported by Skype for Business Server with the addition of Windows 7 SP1 x64, Windows 8 x64, or Windows 10 x64
- Browser with Silverlight plug-in version 5 or later
- .NET Framework 4.5 64-bit version
- Windows Installer version 4.5
- PowerShell v3.0

IE Support

Interestingly, at the time of writing, there is a support message in the SBSCP that states that when running in the latest Chrome browser, "You are using a web browser or operating system that is not supported for use with Skype for Business Server Control Panel. We recommend upgrading to the latest version of Windows Internet Explorer. At a minimum, use Windows Internet Explorer 9." Given that a similar error was shown when using Firefox and Chrome with Lync 2010, it seems unlikely that this will change, and therefore we suggest using Internet Explorer to run the SBSCP.

Finally, you can use the admin simple URL defined in Topology Builder. For the examples used in this chapter, that was `https://admin.rlscomms.net`. To actually access the SBSCP from the admin URL, you must append `/cscp`, which is the required virtual directory. Following these steps allows you to log into the SBSCP from any computer with a supported browser.

Once you have logged in with your SfBUserAdmin account, you will see the SBSCP with only the interface elements related to user administration visible, as shown in Figure 12.1.

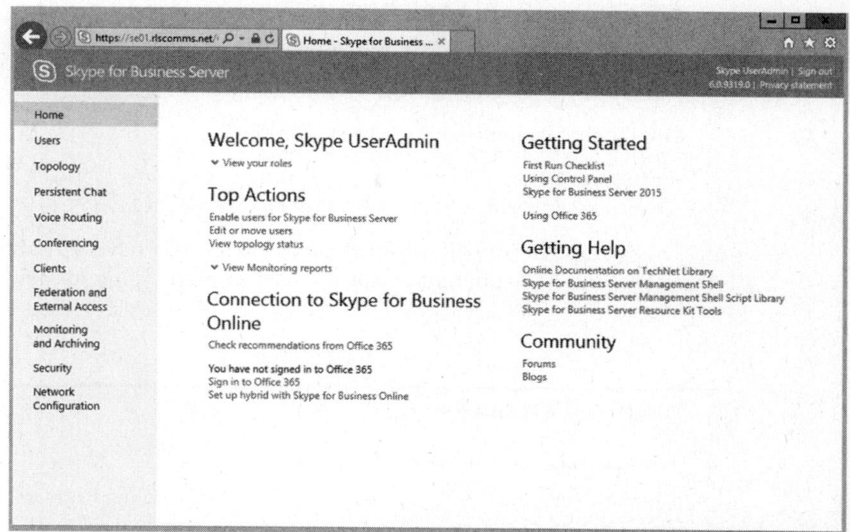

FIGURE 12.1 Logged into the Lync Server Control Panel as SfBUserAdmin

Now that you've gained access to the SBSCP, the first task you need to master is searching; this will allow you to locate users for administration. Each tab of the SBSCP has a search interface, and all of them except the one on the Users tab are very basic. The first thing to note about the searches that can be performed is that they only return objects that are Skype for Business (or Lync!) enabled. Don't get caught out by this if you are looking for users to enable! This is done in a similar way but in a different location, which we will discuss shortly.

To carry out a search, first switch to the Users tab. At this point, if you click Find, you will simply bring back all Skype for Business–enabled users. Thankfully, the search interface on the Users tab allows you to customize certain search parameters. For example, you can perform a standard or LDAP search. The standard search will search for users by display name, first name, last name, Security Accounts Manager (SAM) account name, SIP address, or line Uniform Resource Identifier (URI). Wildcards appear to work only in part. For example, you can search for *2015, which would bring back any user with a name ending in 2015. However, you can't search for *2015* to bring back users with 2015 in the name and neither would 2015* bring back all users starting with 2015. However, you can enter 2015 and have that bring back all users starting with 2015. If you want to search on SIP or line URI fields, you must include the `tel:` or `sip:` preface to the attribute data; otherwise, no results will be returned. The LDAP search allows even greater flexibility. You can use any attribute available through an LDAP query to be very granular about which objects are returned. For example, to start with, you could use the following filter to bring back only user objects:

```
(objectclass=user)
```

Selecting the radio button next to LDAP Search and entering this filter brings back all Skype for Business–enabled users. That's not very exciting, so how about this:

```
(description=Marketing)
```

This brings back all users with a description of Marketing. This next one brings back users with the letter *U* in their common name:

```
(cn=*u*)
```

Finally, this last one is much more complex:

```
(&(objectCategory=person)(objectClass=user)
(userAccountControl:1.2.840.113556.1.4.803:=2))
```

This brings back all Skype for Business users who have a disabled AD account—as might be the case if the AD team had disabled a user in preparation for deletion but not told you yet.

DISABLED AD USERS

Actually, this previous search is extremely useful.

It may be corporate policy to disable user accounts when users actually leave the organization; however, this does not fully disable Skype for Business accounts. User who have certificate authentication enabled (the default setting) will still be able to continue to log in and access resources (including possibly making phone calls!) even with a disabled AD account. By executing the previous search, you can retrieve a list of users that you can then go on and revoke their certificates, ensuring they are unable to log in.

As you can see, there is a huge amount of flexibility with which you can experiment. For more information about the syntax of the search query for LDAP filter, look at the resource here:

`http://msdn2.microsoft.com/en-us/library/aa746475.aspx`

Another feature of the search capability is its ability to create quite complex searches using only the GUI. Clearly a lot is possible through LDAP searches, but if you just want to put together something without needing to research LDAP, you can use the Search Filter feature. Search filters allow you to add various operators to a basic search and operate only in basic search mode rather than LDAP mode. You cannot use wildcards in the search filters, but you can use the operators that PowerShell allows.

- Starts with
- Ends with
- Equal to
- Not equal to
- Contains
- Not contains

To add a filter, click the Add Filter button on the search bar. You can add up to 15 filters to build significantly complex queries. These queries can be saved and reloaded at a later date if this search is regularly used. Saved searches are stored as USF files (filename extension `.usf`). This approach might be useful if, for example, it is needed to regularly check whether a certain group of users have the correct PIN policy. You could set up the relevant saved query, perform the search, and then use the assign policy action to ensure that all the users had the relevant policy.

Figure 12.2 and Figure 12.3 show the filter interface and some of the attributes that can be used in searches built with filters.

Figure 12.2
The Filter interface showing the AND operator, the Add Filter option, and the Save and Import query buttons

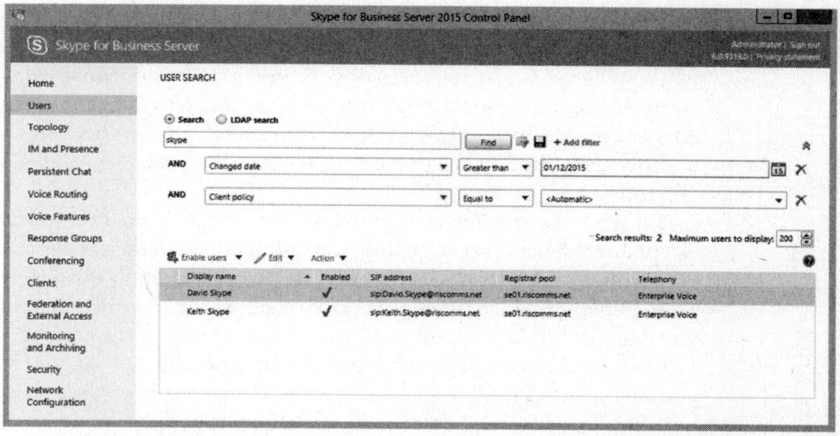

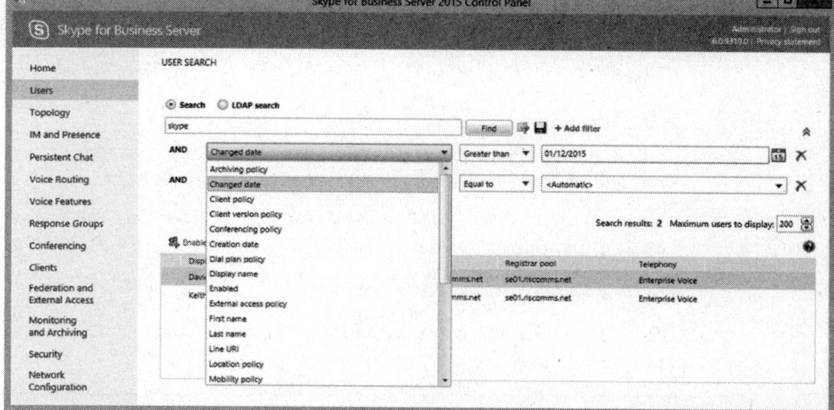

Figure 12.3
Some of the attributes that can be added to searches based on filters

Once the results are returned, you can perform actions on the resulting set of users by selecting one or many of them using either Shift+click or Ctrl+click and using the Actions drop-down; you'll learn more about this shortly.

When you are searching in the SBSCP, you might run into a couple of issues, one of which is that by default the search interface will return only 200 users. However, it is straightforward to change that using the Maximum Users To Display entry box. The other issue is more of a problem: You can't customize the way data results are displayed. For example, you couldn't perform a simple SBSCP search to find and display all the DDI numbers deployed. You could search and return all users with a DDI; however, to see the DDIs you would have to go into the properties of each user because it is not possible to edit the columns of data that are shown. For this level of data manipulation, you would have to dive into PowerShell.

If you want to search using PowerShell, a couple of useful PowerShell cmdlets are available for finding users to manipulate: `Get-CsUser` and `Get-CsAdUser`. `Get-CsAdUser` retrieves all user accounts in Active Directory Domain Services (AD DS), Skype for Business enabled or not, whereas `Get-CsUser` retrieves only Skype for Business enabled users inside AD DS.

In this section, we will discuss `Get-CsUser`, a cmdlet that focuses on Skype for Business–enabled objects and Skype for Business–specific attributes. `Get-CsUser` allows similar searches to those described in the preceding section. We will cover `Get-CsAdUser` in the next section, "Enabling and Disabling."

To run these cmdlets, you need to be connected via a remote PowerShell console to the Skype for Business server using your Skype for Business user admin account. You can do this manually as described in Appendix B, "Introduction to PowerShell, the Skype for Business Management Shell, and Regular Expressions," or if you've installed the administrative tools, you can use SBSMS, which is a little simpler because the connection is made automatically.

Once at the prompt, you have even more flexibility than you had in the SBSCP. For example, you can search for all Skype for Business–enabled users in a specific OU and return up to 2 billion results, which should be enough for most people!

CREDENTIALS

Both the `Get-CsUser` and `Get-CsAdUser` cmdlets have a rather useful parameter that allows you to run them under a user account other than the one with which you are connected to remote PowerShell. To do this, you must first create a PSCredential object using the `Get-Credential` cmdlet, which prompts for credentials and stores them in a variable. Use the following command:

```
$cred = Get-Credential
```

This will bring up a standard credential dialog, which will capture the credentials, including username and password, and store them in the variable `$cred`.

Then, by using the `-Credential` parameter and passing those stored credentials, the `Get-CsUser` or `Get-CsAdUser` cmdlet will run using those credentials. Here is an example:

```
Get-CsUser -Credential $cred
```

This would run the command under the credentials stored in the `$cred` variable and return all Lync-enabled users.

To get started, simply run Get-CsUser, which will return a list of all Skype for Business–enabled users. Next, you can be more specific about which user or users you will return, by using the -Identity parameter as follows:

```
Get-CsUser -Identity "Test User1"
Get-CsUser -Identity "Test User*"
```

The first command brings back only Test User 1, and the second brings back any user starting with Test User.

WILDCARDS

PowerShell accepts wildcards a little more flexibly than SBSCP in that you can use them throughout the search string rather than just in front of a specific ending as in the SBSCP. It does, however, only accept the asterisk (*) wildcard. You cannot use the whole range of wildcards, such as ? and so on. Another thing to bear in mind is that wildcards work only on the Display Name attribute of a user rather than the department and other names.

You could, for example, use the following command, including the wildcard, to find all users starting with *test*:

```
Get-CsUser -Identity test*
```

Of course, you can also be more specific and search within an OU.

```
Get-CsUser -Identity "Test User1" -OU "cn=users,dc=rlscomms,dc=net"
```

Again, as with the SBSCP, you can use filters. They can be of the usual PowerShell filter, as implemented in a Where-Object command, or they can be LDAP filters. You should note that only one of these parameters can be used in any one Get-CsUser command. The next command shows the use of a PowerShell filter via piping to Where-Object:

```
Get-CsUser | Where-Object {[String]$_.Registrarpool ↵
-eq "se01.rlscomms.net"}
```

This command will bring back all users homed on the se01.rlscomms.net pool. As you have seen, the simple Get-User command outputs all the properties on which the user can be filtered. The previous filter was simply performed with only one parameter. You can expand the filter to create complex searches. For more specifics about how to format the filter string, see the article at the following location:

http://technet.microsoft.com/en-us/library/ee177028.aspx

The other type of filter is the LDAP filter. It works in much the same way as through the SBSCP but through PowerShell.

```
Get-CsUser -LDAPFilter Description="Office Based"
```

This command will pull back all users where the description contains the text "Office Based".

Here's another:

```
Get-CsUser -LDAPFilter "!(Department=Marketing)"
```

This will pull back all users who are not in the Marketing department. As you can see, a great deal of flexibility is available to enable you to retrieve only the users you want.

Now that you know how to search and filter users in the SBSCP and in PowerShell, let's move on to what you can do to the users you find.

Enabling and Disabling

Enabling users in the SBSCP is relatively straightforward.

1. Open the SBSCP as a user with CSAdministrator or CSUserAdministrator rights and click the Users tab. In the main pane, click Enable Users, which will open the main page to select and enable users, as shown in Figure 12.4.

FIGURE 12.4 The main configuration page with options for enabling users

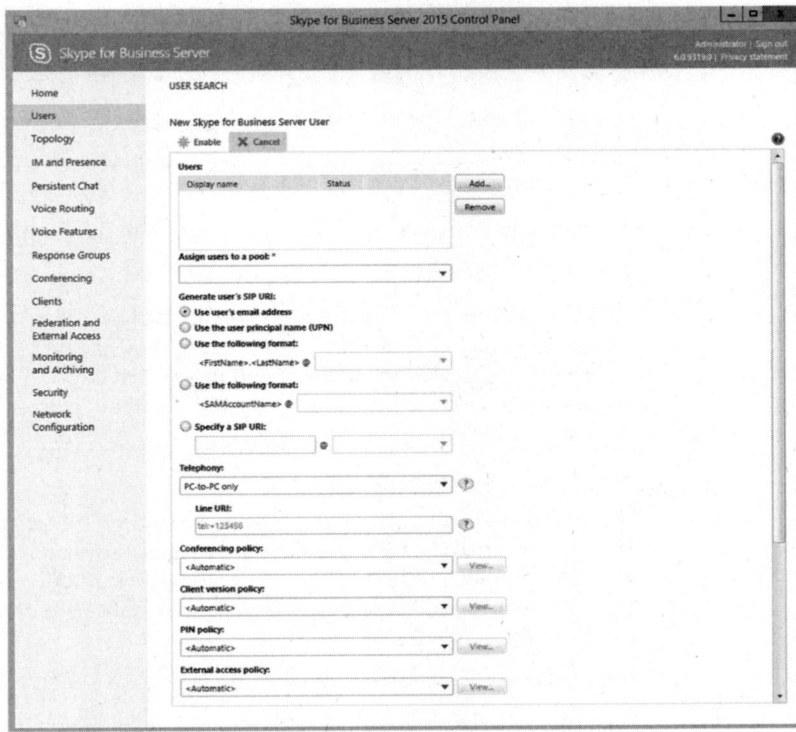

2. Click Add and locate the user or users you want to enable through the searching methods that were described earlier in the chapter. Once you have located and selected the relevant users, click OK.

Note that multiple users can be selected either in one block using the Shift+click method or individually using the Ctrl+click method, which should be familiar from Windows Explorer.

3. You should be back in the main configuration page shown in Figure 12.4, this time with users listed in the Users section. You must assign the users to a Registrar pool. In Figure 12.4, this will be `se01.rlscomms.net`, which is the only pool available in the drop-down; however, your organization may have pools in different locations around the world. You must also select a method to generate a SIP uniform resource identifier (URI). We will cover these choices in more depth later when discussing how to enable the user from PowerShell. At this point, you will simply select Use User's Email Address because you know the email address field is populated with an address that fits the naming scheme of the SIP domain, `@rlscomms.net`.

You could now simply accept the defaults and click Enable to finish setting up the users; however, you should be aware of a few other settings.

4. The Telephony section allows you to configure the way in which the user can use Skype for Business features to make telephone calls. The default is PC-To-PC Only, which is what you should leave set for the user. This setting allows voice and video calls to be made only within the Skype for Business system between machines with the relevant client installed. Other options are to enable coexistence with a third-party PBX, to configure the user to use Skype for Business as a PBX, or to disable audio and video entirely. These settings will be covered in more detail in Chapter 16, "Getting Started with Voice."
5. The rest of the settings you can configure on this page enable you to assign immediately the various policies Skype for Business provides to enable control of the user environment. For now, leave them at the default settings. We will discuss many of the policies in much more depth later in this chapter; at that point, you can come back and change those policies assigned to users if you like.
6. After you've looked through all the settings available, click Enable to make the users selected live on Skype for Business.

Managing Users Who Are Domain Admins

We've used SBSCP throughout this chapter to manage users; however, domain admins can't be managed this way. At this point, we would like to emphasize what a bad idea it is to have domain administrator permissions on users who are enabled for services like Skype for Business and Exchange and who do "regular" work like web browsing. Of course, it does happen in organizations. You may, therefore, come across an SBSCP limitation: Because of the rights it runs under, SBSCP cannot manage domain admins; it can only present information about them in a read-only manner. Therefore, to manage domain admin Skype for Business users, you must use SBSMS and be logged on as a domain admin to do so.

Although the SBSCP is fine for enabling a single user, and even acceptable for doing them in bulk, some people just love to do things from the shell. For those people, here's how you enable a user from PowerShell. As discussed earlier, you need to locate the relevant user or users.

When working in PowerShell, that means using the `Get-CsAdUser` cmdlet, unless you know the display name of the user, in which case you can simply start with the `Enable-CsUser` cmdlet. In this case, you know the display name is `Test User1`, so you can move right on; but if you didn't know the name, you could use the `Get-CsAdUser` cmdlet to bring back the relevant user or users and pipe the output of `Get-CsAdUser` into the `Enable-CsUser` command, discussed next.

As you saw in the SBSCP, certain fields are mandatory. First, of course, you must identify the user or users, using the AD display name, SIP address, user principal name (UPN), or domain\SamAccountName. Again, in this case, you can stick with AD display name. Next, you need to specify the Registrar pool and the SIP address. In this simple example setup, this is pretty straightforward because there is only one Registrar pool (`se01.rlscomms.net`). The choice of SIP address is possibly more complex. As a rule of thumb, the SIP address should match the email address of the user if at all possible. However, unless Exchange is installed, the email address field might not be populated. Make sure it is for the user account you will be creating so you can use it later. In this example, Test User1 is set up with the email address `testuser1@rlscomms.net`.

To enable the user, use the following command:

```
Enable-CsUser -Identity "Test User1" -RegistrarPool ↵
se01.rlscomms.net SipAddressType EmailAddress
```

This command will enable the user Test User1 for Lync on the `se01.rlscomms.net` pool with a SIP address matching the email address `testuser1@rlscomms.net`. The one parameter here that may not be immediately obvious is `SipAddressType`. It could have been very specific, used the `SipAddress` parameter, and manually specified the SIP address `testuser1@rlscomms.net`; however, the `SipAddressType` parameter is potentially more useful because it allows various options to form the SIP address. One thing you will note is that when you use certain `SipAddressType` settings, you will need another parameter, `SipDomain`. In this environment, things are simple with only the one SIP domain. However, large organizations commonly need to support multiple domains, perhaps to represent different brands or company units.

The options for `SipAddressType` are as follows:

`EmailAddress`: As shown previously, this uses the email address from the user in AD and doesn't require the `SipDomain` parameter.

`SamAccountName`: This uses the SamAccountName from AD and does require the `SipDomain` parameter to specify the suffix of the name after the @ sign.

`UserPrincipalName`: This uses the UPN of the user in AD and, because the UPN is in the same form as an email address, doesn't require the use of the `SipDomain` parameter.

`FirstLastName`: This takes the first and last name of the user and puts a period between them—in our example, `test.user1`. It requires the use of the `SipDomain` parameter.

Piping Output from the Enable-CsUser Cmdlet

One thing that you may be used to in PowerShell is the ability to pipe the output from one command into the input of the next. This is one of PowerShell's most useful features. It allows you to do the following:

```
Get-CsAdUser -OU "cn=users,dc=rlscomms,dc=net" | ↵
Enable-CsUser -RegistrarPool se01.rlscomms.net ↵
SipAddressType EmailAddress
```

This would enable all the users in the Users container in AD using their email addresses as the SIP address. However, you may not be aware that piping from the output of the `Enable-CsUser` cmdlet doesn't work by default. This is by design, because `Enable-CsAdUser` enables the given User object for Skype for Business and doesn't pass the User object. Thankfully, if you add the `-PassThru` parameter, it will enable the output to be piped to other cmdlets so that you can set specific settings for the newly enabled user—for example, enabling them for Enterprise Voice.

You now know how to find and enable users for Skype for Business. As you have seen, the SIP address is key. This forms the unique ID and is what makes users show up in searches carried out for Skype for Business–enabled users. On occasion this can cause unintended results, as you might ask yourself what happens if a user already has a SIP address populated in their `msRTCSIP-PrimaryUserAddress` attribute. This could have happened as part of a previous deployment when the user maybe became orphaned. Thankfully, there is a PowerShell command that can help identify these users and get them all set up for Skype for Business.

```
Get-CsUser -UnassignedUser | Select-Object DisplayName
```

When run, this command will identify any users who have a SIP address but are not assigned to a Registrar pool. It will then output their display name. You could, of course, simply pipe the output to the `Enable-CsUser` cmdlet and get them set up directly for Skype for Business.

Making Changes to Users

Now that you've enabled some users for Skype for Business, you no doubt feel suitably pleased. However, it won't be long before the changes start rolling in. For example, someone might move to a different office or even a different country and be served from a different pool. Another typical occurrence is when a name changes because of marriage, and of course, people will leave your organization temporarily or permanently and their accounts will need to be disabled and then deleted. As with all the other user administration tasks, the first requirement is to make sure you target the relevant user or users; that is where the search skills you've learned come in handy.

The SBSCP is well laid out, so by now you should be pretty familiar with it. On the Users tab, search for the user you need to alter. Once you've selected it, you can explore the available options and find the Edit and Action drop-downs.

The Edit drop-down is straightforward. It gives you an easy option to select all the users returned by a search, after which you can move to the options on the Action menu, which we'll discuss shortly. Other than that, the only option is Show Details, which takes you to the configuration page for that particular user. This will look familiar from the steps taken to enable the user in the SBSCP described earlier. The Action drop-down gives many more options, as shown in Figure 12.5.

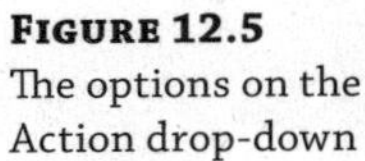

FIGURE 12.5
The options on the Action drop-down

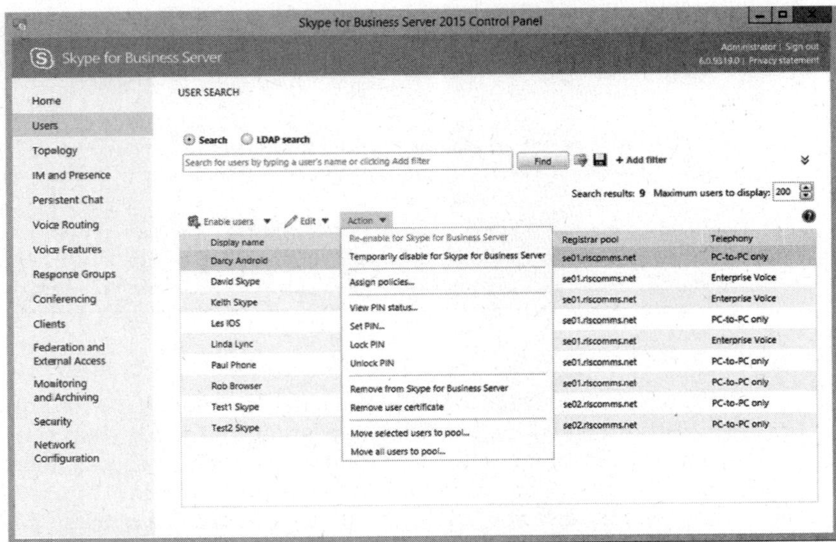

MOVING USERS

As you can see, moving users to another pool is simple. You select the relevant user or users and then, on the Action menu, click the Move Selected Users To Pool entry. This opens a dialog box where you can choose the pool in the drop-down shown in Figure 12.6. There is also a Force check box that should be used if the standard process for moving fails. The standard process of moving users between pools will take across their conferences and buddy lists. If for some reason the source pool is unavailable, you would have to use the Force check box to move the user without this data from the source pool. Be careful, though, because there is a risk of data loss any time the `Force` parameter is used. This is discussed in more detail in Chapter 15, "Troubleshooting."

FIGURE 12.6
The Move Users dialog box allows you to move selected users to a pool.

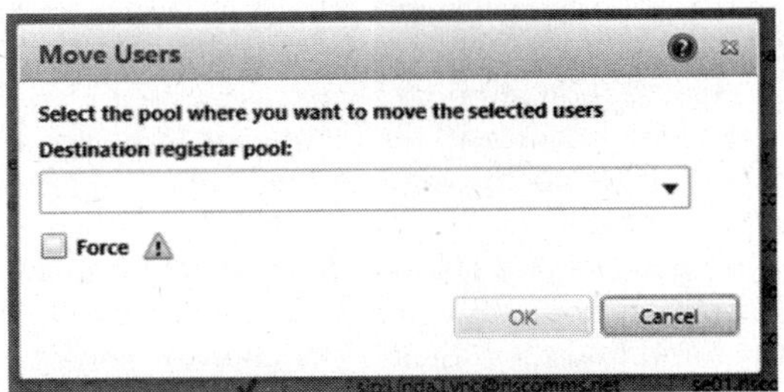

Selecting the Move All Users To Pool option will bring up a dialog that allows you to select both a source pool and a destination pool and enables moving all users from the source to the destination, as shown in Figure 12.7. Again, the Force check box allows scenarios where the source pool isn't available.

FIGURE 12.7
The Move Users dialog box allows you to move all users between pools.

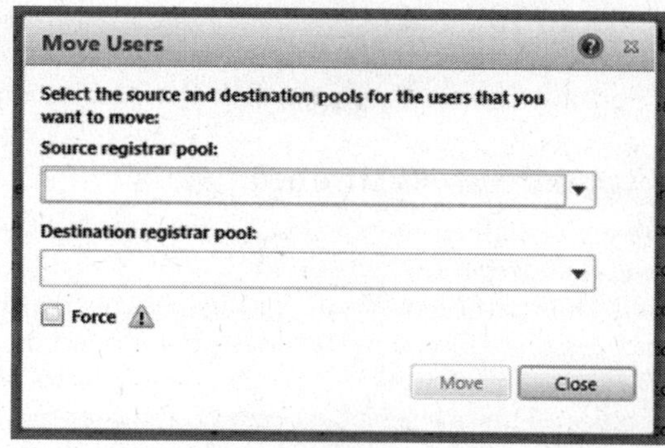

To perform these moves from PowerShell, you would use the `Move-CsUser` cmdlet, a simple cmdlet. The required parameters are `-Identity` to target a specific user and `-Target` to specify the pool to which you want to move the user. There is also the `-Force` parameter, which provides the same functionality to move users in failure scenarios without taking user data across to the new pool. For example, this command moves Test User1 to the SE02 pool:

```
Move-CsUser -Identity "Test User1" -Target "se02.rlscomms.net"
```

Instead of having a separate cmdlet to allow all users to be moved from one pool to another, this time the PowerShell pipe is used for functionality.

```
Get-CsUser | Where-Object {[String]$_.Registrarpool -eq ↵
"se01.rlscomms.net"} | ↵
Move-CsUser -Target "se02.rlscomms.net"
```

This command first runs the `Get-CsUser` command you are familiar with, and using a filter it selects all users on the `Se01.rlscomms.net` pool. These are then piped to the `Move-CsUser` cmdlet, which moves them to the `se02.rlscomms.net` pool.

CHANGING USERNAMES

In addition to moving users between pools, another commonly needed task is to change usernames, for example after a marriage. In this case, most of the work will be done by other teams, namely, the AD and Exchange teams. (Of course that might be you, but that's a topic for a whole other book!) In Skype for Business terms, when the AD team has made its changes, the user will show up in searches with a new display name. However, what won't have changed is the SIP URI, which as we have said should match the primary email address of the user. To ensure that is the case, in the SBSCP locate the user, and on the Edit drop-down, click Show Details. In the configuration pane that opens, edit the SIP Address field as required and then click Commit. To do the same process from PowerShell, use the `Set-CsUser` cmdlet as follows:

```
Set-CsUser -Identity "Test User1" -SipAddress testmarried1@rlscomms.net
```

This command will update the SIP address of Test User 1 to `testmarried1@rlscomms.net`.

This also has the added benefit of updating the contact lists of users who have added the newly married user prior to the name change. Unfortunately, this works only within your organization; any federated users will be required to manually update their contacts.

Disabling and Removing Users

There are actually a couple of ways of disabling users, and they have slightly different effects. On the Edit drop-down, if you click Show Details, one of the options on the user configuration page is an Enabled For Skype for Business Server check box. If this check box is cleared, a user cannot log on to Skype for Business, but it doesn't remove any of the user's settings from Skype for Business and doesn't remove Skype for Business attributes, such as the SIP URI, from the user object. This is a sensible option if the user in question is going to be out of the organization for a period of time but will return. In PowerShell, this is the same as running the following command:

```
Set-CsUser -Identity "Test User1" -Enabled:$False
```

This command will ensure that a user can't log on to Skype for Business but doesn't delete any settings or policy assignments.

To reverse the process, simply run the following command:

```
Set-CsUser -Identity "Test User1" -Enabled:$True
```

This command will bring the user back to life and ensure that they can log on again as before. These steps can be carried out from the Action drop-down using the Temporarily Disable For Skype for Business Server and Re-enable For Skype for Business Server options. If instead you want to be more permanent, then you need to use the Action drop-down in the SBSCP or the `Disable-CsUser` cmdlet in PowerShell. With the relevant user or users selected, move to the Action drop-down and select Remove From Skype for Business Server. You will be prompted to click OK if you are sure. This action will remove the user entirely from the Skype for Business server by removing Skype for Business attributes on the user account and wiping out user data such as buddy lists and policy assignments. It will not remove the Active Directory user object. To carry out the same action in PowerShell, use the following command:

```
Disable-CsUser -Identity "Test User1"
```

This will remove the user from Skype for Business. At this point if you wanted to reenable the user, you would have to go back and use the `Enable-CsUser` cmdlet or the SBSCP process just described.

Bulk Changes

Using the GUI, it is possible to manage more than one user at a time. But unless you really enjoy repetitive tasks, if you need to manage tens or hundreds of Skype for Business users, PowerShell is critical. We've covered some of the basics in this chapter, but take a look at Chapter 8 for more detailed information.

Other User Actions

The other options on the Action menu that we haven't covered are Assign Policies, the various PIN settings, and the Remove User Certificate setting. We will cover the Assign Policies option in the rest of this chapter, and the PIN settings are covered in the chapters in Part 4, "Voice," so the final element to cover is the Remove User Certificate option. As explained in Chapter 3, "Security," Skype for Business allows users to be authenticated not only through traditional username and password combinations but also through the use of a certificate and PIN. This makes authentication from phone devices simpler because users only need to enter the numeric PIN. Of course, as an administrator, you may want a way to prevent a user from logging in this way. That is what the Remove User Certificate option does. Although it doesn't remove the certificates from the devices, it does remove them from the server, which prevents the user from logging on. Through PowerShell, the same thing can be carried out using the `Revoke-CsClientCertificate` cmdlet.

Understanding Skype for Business Policies

The ability to control systems through the use of policies is critical to an enterprise. It is standard to have different groups of people carrying out different functions and to provide them with only the required tools to do the job. In this way, systems can be sized correctly and security can be maintained. In OCS 2007 and OCS 2007 R2 there were, of course, policies to enable control and management of the user experience. However, these policies could not always be applied in a way that provided the same experience for users no matter where they logged on. The policies were also applied in different ways and did not always allow enough granularity of control without significant effort. Thankfully, Lync Server 2010 brought in a completely different methodology for policies that Skype for Business continues to maintain and, indeed, expand. There are numerous policies that can be applied in granular ways to give a single consistent experience to users and to ensure that administrators can control Skype for Business users without constantly needing the approval of other IT teams (as was the case when Group Policy was used). The remainder of this chapter looks in depth at just what you can do—and how—to keep order in your Skype for Business environment.

In-Band Provisioning

In-band provisioning describes the application of policy to the client through information contained in SIP messages and passed to the client during usage so that settings apply immediately. For a really detailed description of how this works, see the following TechNet article. Note that it describes the process in Lync 2010, which is just as valid for Skype for Business Server 2015.

```
https://technet.microsoft.com/en-us/magazine/hh219341.aspx
```

Because of the way policy is applied, different types of clients apply the relevant policy settings to the functionality they offer. Whatever the client, the user will have the same experience because this method of applying policy is as relevant to the browser client as it is to the PC that's not domain joined and even to the domain-joined PC. Another benefit is that administrators are not constrained to fit Skype for Business policies around another policy engine, such as Group Policy in OCS. Almost all Skype for Business policies can be created and applied either through the SBSCP or through PowerShell (see "What About Group Policy?" later in the chapter for the exceptions). Not using group policies provides greater flexibility because policies can be applied at global, site, service, and user levels, and these policies take effect immediately rather than having to wait for a Group Policy refresh cycle.

Understanding Where Policies Apply

One of the principal benefits of moving to the in-band provisioning model is that Skype for Business policy can closely follow Skype for Business architecture and users, allowing a high degree of granularity. As discussed in Chapter 7, "Planning Your Deployment," Skype for Business has added to the architectural concepts of OCS 2007 R2 (the *organization* and the *pool*) and includes the concept of *sites*, which generally map to data centers. It is now possible to apply policy at all these levels. Default policies are applied at the Global level, but administrators can create certain types of policies at other levels, such as the site, service, or tag level. Tag-level policies are what allow policy to be assigned to an individual user or selection of users. (As you will see, the search skills you learned earlier can be used to locate users to apply policy to, thereby giving you the ability to specifically target users.)

Of course, all these different levels mean that you need to understand their precedence. The following rules apply:

- If a per-user policy is assigned to the user, then the per-user policy is used.
- If no per-user policy is assigned to the user, then the service policy is used.
- If there is no per-user or service policy, then the site policy is used.
- If there is no per-user, service, or site policy, then the global policy is used.

Simply summarized, the policy set closest to the user wins! Understanding this is important because it has a material effect on which settings are applied to users. For example, certain settings in a policy could be left blank by the administrator to allow the user discretion over how Lync works for them. For example, you could allow the user to choose whether to display a photo by leaving the DisplayPhoto section of the CsClientPolicy blank. But what would happen if you set the DisplayPhoto section of the CsClientPolicy to force the use of the AD stored photo on the global policy but then left that setting blank on a policy closer to the user (that is, site or user tag)? The user would still be able to choose. The whole policy is applied even if settings are blank, not just the settings that have an explicit value.

To understand the various levels more closely, you need to understand the difference between policy name and scope, which defines how policies are referenced using the `-Identity` parameter in PowerShell. The following are some examples of how different policies are referenced:

`Identity global` pulls back the global policy of whichever cmdlet is used.

`Identity site:PolicyName` reflects a policy that is assigned to a site.

`Identity registrar:server.domain.xyz` reflects a policy that is assigned to a specific service, in this case a registrar.

`Identity Tag:PolicyName` reflects a policy that is assigned to users.

You can see clearly the concept of policy name and policy scope. The element in the identity before the colon (:) is the scope; the element after the colon is the policy name. In the case of either site or service scopes, the policy name matches that of the site or service where the policy is to be assigned. In the case of the tag scope, the policy name should describe where the policy will apply. You will see how this works when you create and assign policies later in this chapter.

What About Group Policy?

We've mentioned that all policies could be created through SBSCP or PowerShell; however, that is not quite true. When the Skype for Business client starts up, it needs certain bootstrapping settings passed to it. For example, if you are not using autoconfiguration through DNS records, the client would need to be provided the Skype for Business server address to log on to. Another such configuration is to enable or disable the welcome screen that pops up when the client is launched for the first time. Clearly in-band provisioning won't work in these instances because the client hasn't logged on or been able to check settings. Therefore, the use of Group Policy is maintained for these client bootstrapping settings only.

To apply these Group Policy settings, you will need to obtain the relevant ADMX (`.admx`) template file. The `Lync16.admx` file is available as part of the pack of Office 2016 ADMX files. At this time of writing, it can be downloaded here:

```
www.microsoft.com/en-us/download/details.aspx?id=49030
```

Interestingly, although part of Office 2016 and called Skype for Business (rather than just an upgrade), the file is still called `Lync16.admx`!

You will see that there are 32-bit and 64-bit versions of the download. Don't worry about this. This is important when you are going to be doing custom installs of Office, but in this case, we will just download the 32-bit version.

The file you download will be called `admintemplates_x86_4286-100_en-us.exe`. On running the application, you will be prompted to extract the contents to a folder. In the folder where you extract the files, you will find that you have two more folders and a spreadsheet. The spreadsheet is called `office2016grouppolicyandoctsettings.xlsx` and contains details of every setting that the GPO can control. Ignore the fact that neither Skype for Business nor Lync is listed on the Introduction tab! To locate the Skype for Business settings that can be manipulated, go to the ADMX tab and filter the first column, File Name, to show `Lync16.admx` only. You will see all the settings that can be set. If you move back to the folder where you extracted the files, you will see the folder called `admx`. Inside is the `Lync16.admx` file. There is also a folder called `en-us`. In here you will find the `Lync16.adml` file, which is a language-specific file for the Lync GPO template file.

Once you have the template file, you will need to load it into a Group Policy object (GPO), which will then be applied at the level in AD where you want to control settings. This is subject to all the usual constraints, such as delays in policy propagation as mentioned earlier.

Since with Skype for Business you are now dealing with ADMX templates rather than the older ADM templates that Lync 2010 used, the method of use has changed. Instead of manually importing the template into a specific GPO, you now have two options to load the new settings template. You can either add them locally on a single machine or load them centrally and have them replicated to any DC for multiple admins to access. Both processes are described in detail here:

```
www.petri.co.il/add-administrative-templates-to-gpo.htm
```

Given that this is Active Directory work, it is out of scope for this book, so we will stick to the simplest method, which allows you to test things by using the local store on one machine. If you are rolling this out in production, then speak with your AD specialist to understand the best method for your network.

1. To load the template into a GPO, on a domain controller (or anywhere else you have the Group Policy Management tools installed), open the `%systemroot%\PolicyDefinitions` folder. Copy the `lync16.admx` file to this folder. Then open the `en-US` folder and copy the `lync16.adml` file in there.
2. Next open the Group Policy Management tool by finding the Group Policy Management app and clicking. On the left pane, drill down into the forest and domain and right-click Group Policy Objects. Select New, as shown in Figure 12.8.

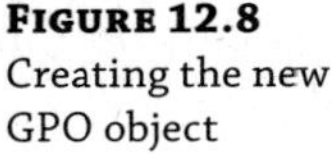

FIGURE 12.8 Creating the new GPO object

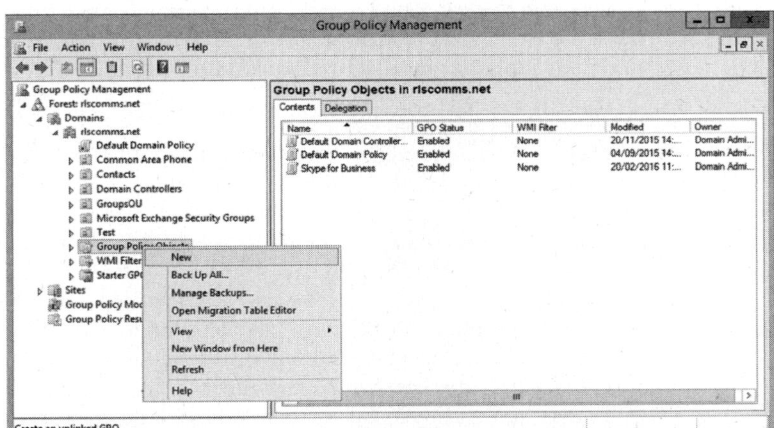

3. Give the policy a name, but don't select a starter GPO, and click OK.
4. Right-click the new GPO and click Edit. In the left pane, drill down to User Configuration ➤ Policies ➤ Administrative Templates: Policy Definitions (ADMX Files) Retrieved from the Local Machine. One of the folders you will find underneath is called `Skype for Business 2016`.
5. If you then drill down to the next level, you will find `Microsoft Lync Feature Policies`, under which all the settings will be visible in the right pane. Each setting is fairly self-explanatory and comes with a useful help article built into the GPO, as shown in Figure 12.9.

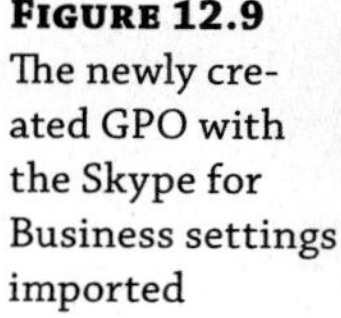

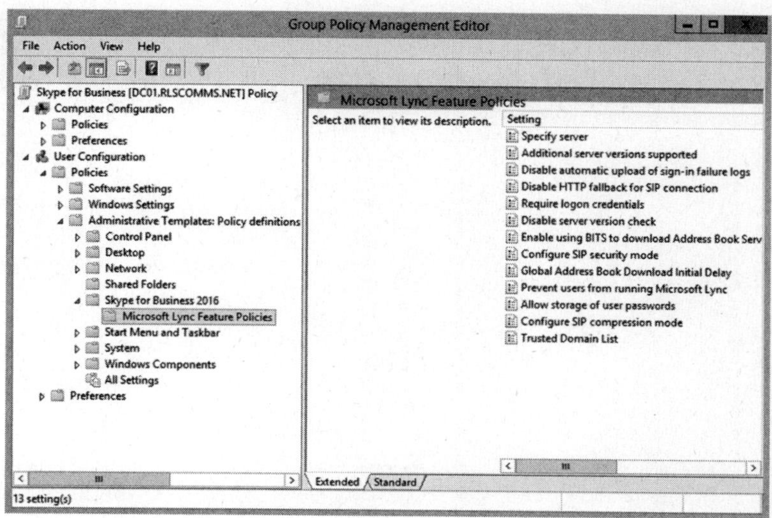

FIGURE 12.9 The newly created GPO with the Skype for Business settings imported

6. After you set up the policy as needed, you can apply it to the relevant group of users by using the standard method.

Manipulating Policies

You are getting close to the process of testing policies. As you will soon come to expect, Skype for Business policies can be manipulated in the usual two ways: either through SBSCP or through PowerShell. In general, though, most manipulation is done through PowerShell because the policies are wide ranging. Because these policies must be manipulated using PowerShell, administrators must take the time to really think through what they are doing as they prepare and research the necessary commands. One final thing to note before you dive right in is that although the SfBUserAdmin account used in this chapter's examples so far can assign policies to users, it can't create them; therefore, to carry out the operations discussed next (except for the assignment of policies), you should be logged on as a member of the CSAdministrator RBAC role.

Viewing Policies

You will undoubtedly want to know what policies already exist before you create new ones. Skype for Business comes with a global policy set up for each policy type available, and the default settings are hard-coded into the software. You will see this in action later in the chapter when we discuss what happens if you try to delete a global policy.

Because we discussed some of the policies earlier in this chapter, you already know several of the policy types. In the SBSCP, they are spread out in the various tabs to which they apply. For example, to see the available ClientVersionPolicies, you would navigate to the Client tab in the SBSCP; in the main pane under Client Version Policy, you would see all available policies. This is shown in Figure 12.10.

Figure 12.10
Viewing the Client Version Policy tab in the SBSCP

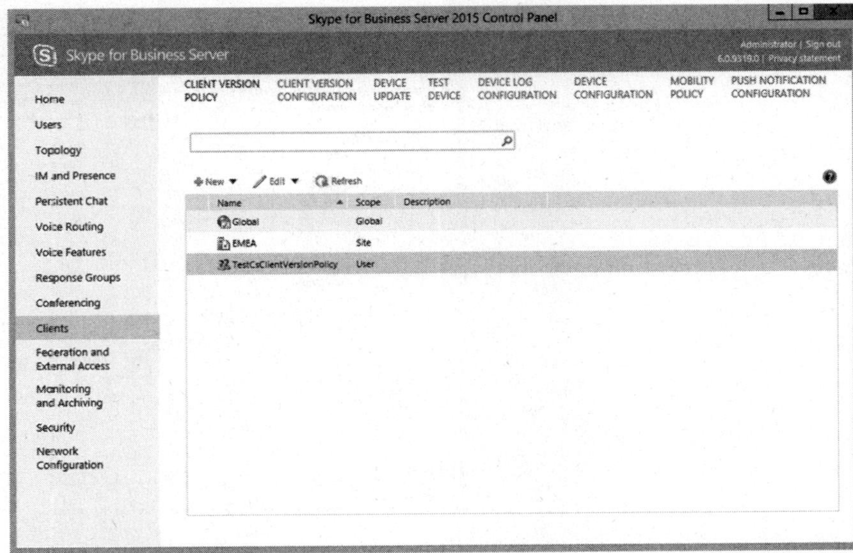

What you can see is not only the default global policy but also some other more focused policies, which you will create shortly. If you view one of the other policy sections, under the Federation and External Access tab, you can see the External Access policy. If you double-click the global policy, you will see the settings in Figure 12.11. Interestingly, this is one of those areas in the GUI that has changed since Lync 2010 (aside from branding) because external access now includes settings to configure XMPP, more of which is covered in Chapter 21, "Reverse Proxies, Load Balancers and Gateways."

Figure 12.11
Viewing the settings of the default global External Access policy

To change any of the settings, simply check the relevant check box and then click Commit. You can see how easy it is to retrieve policy information and change settings in the SBSCP. If you look carefully enough at all the possible options, you will also notice that some of the more wide-ranging policies like the CsClientPolicy are not visible through the SBSCP.

Given that some of the settings are not available through SBSCP and in keeping with the rest of the book, let's take a look at how you would use PowerShell to view policies.

As we have already discussed, there are various default global policies. To retrieve one of them, the CsClientPolicy type, you would use a command such as this:

```
Get-CsExternalAccessPolicy -Identity global
```

Because you want to retrieve the default global policy, notice the naming convention. Also notice the output of this command, which shows the current settings that you saw in Figure 12.11.

```
Identity                           : Global
Description                        :
EnableFederationAccess             : False
EnableXmppAccess                   : False
EnablePublicCloudAccess            : False
EnablePublicCloudAudioVideoAccess  : False
EnableOutsideAccess                : False
```

To get the remaining policies, you simply need to identify the relevant cmdlets. Sadly, this is not as simple as it could be because the developers didn't quite stick to a naming convention. Most of the cmdlets are formatted like the previous one, `Get-CsXxxPolicy`. However, there are a couple that stand out. First, note that although the `Get-CsNetworkIntersitePolicy` and `Get-CsEffectivePolicy` cmdlets follow the relevant naming format, the first actually works with Call Admission Control (CAC) and as such is not related directly to users, and the latter is a new cmdlet enabling administrators to see which set of policies applies to a user. We cover `Get-CsEffectivePolicy` later in this chapter. The other anomaly is the `Get-CsDialPlan` cmdlet; although it doesn't have `Policy` in the name, it retrieves dial plans related to Enterprise Voice that are applied to users, and it is targeted as the other policy cmdlets are, based on global, site, and user. Dial plans are covered in Chapter 13. With this knowledge, you can run the following command to get a list of all the relevant cmdlets:

```
Get-Command -Module SkypeforBusiness | Where-Object {($_.Name -like "Get-
Cs*Policy" ⊠
-or $_.Name -eq "Get-CsDialPlan")} | Where-Object ↵
{$_.Name -notlike "*Effective*"} | Where-Object {$_.Name ↵
-notlike "*Network*"} | Select-Object Name
```

This command will first get all the commands in the Skype for Business module and then sort through them listing only those that fit the criteria of starting with `Get-Cs` and ending with `Policy`. It will omit the `Get-CsNetworkIntersitePolicy` and `Get-CsEffectivePolicy` cmdlets and include the `Get-CsDialPlan` cmdlet. When it is run, you will see the following output:

```
Name
----
Get-CsArchivingPolicy
```

```
Get-CsCallViaWorkPolicy
Get-CsClientPolicy
Get-CsClientVersionPolicy
Get-CsConferencingPolicy
Get-CsDialPlan
Get-CsExternalAccessPolicy
Get-CsHostedVoicemailPolicy
Get-CsLocationPolicy
Get-CsMobilityPolicy
Get-CsPersistentChatPolicy
Get-CsPinPolicy
Get-CsPresencePolicy
Get-CsThirdPartyVideoSystemPolicy
Get-CsUserServicesPolicy
Get-CsVoicePolicy
Get-CsVoiceRoutingPolicy
```

If you are familiar with Lync 2010 or Lync 2013, you will notice that there are a few new policies in Skype for Business Server 2015 (highlighted in **bold** in the previous list). First, `Get-CsCallViaWorkPolicy` is used to define the settings for enabling users to control non-Skype phones, such as legacy PBX devices. Second, `Get-CsThirdPartyVideoSystemPolicy` is similar to `Get-CsVoicePolicy`, except it is focused on the settings and interaction with video systems. Now you have a useful list of all the cmdlets that can be used to retrieve policy settings. They all (even `Get-CsDialPlan`) take the same command structure as shown earlier to get the current global policy settings.

It's useful to see the current settings for each of the global policies, but sometimes you'll want to see the default settings. There are a few ways of doing this.

- Check TechNet.
- Create a new, empty policy and retrieve it to display its settings. This method has a disadvantage that we'll discuss next.
- Create a new policy but use the `-InMemory` parameter. This is rather clever.

As mentioned, creating a new policy with no parameters other than a name will create a policy using the default settings, as shown in this example:

```
New-CsClientPolicy -Identity TestDefaultSettings
```

This command would create a new client policy called `TestDefaultSettings`. However, you don't really want to have to create policies every time you want to see the default settings because it would be too easy to forget one and clutter up the system. Fortunately, another option is available. One of the parameters of the `New-CsXxxPolicy` cmdlets is `-InMemory`. When appended to the command just shown, it creates a policy but holds it in memory and never writes it to the configuration store. To see this parameter in action, run the following command:

```
New-CsClientPolicy -Identity TestDefaultSettings -InMemory
```

This will output the default settings of the client policy but not actually create the policy. Of course, this functionality is not provided just to let you see the default settings of a policy. It will also allow you to create a new policy in memory and assign it to a variable. You can then manipulate the policy settings as you need and put the policy into action, thereby ensuring that the correct settings are applied immediately, as shown in the following example:

```
$newpolvar = New-CsClientPolicy -Identity NewPolicy1 -InMemory
$newpolvar.DisableEmoticons = $True
$newpolvar.DisablePresenceNote = $True
Set-CsClientPolicy -Instance $newpolvar
$newpolvar = $NULL
```

What this does is set the variable `$newpolvar` to the default settings of the `NewCsClientPolicy` cmdlet, creating in memory a policy called NewPolicy1. Next, you edit certain properties of that variable to disable emoticons, for example. Then you write back those setting with the `Set-CsClientPolicy` cmdlet, which actually creates the policy. Finally, you end by resetting the variable `$newpolvar` to `Null` so that it can't accidentally be used.

You've looked at how to retrieve the global policies and the default settings, but what about easily viewing the other policies of a specific type? The next command will list all policies of a certain type:

```
Get-CsClientVersionPolicy | Select-Object Identity
```

This command will list all the CsClientVersionPolicies, as in the output shown here:

```
Identity
--------
Global
Site:EMEA
Service:Registrar:se01.rlscomms.net
Tag:TestDefaultSettings
```

Actually, we've skipped ahead a little; you'll learnt to create policies in the next section, but it's not very interesting to show only one line of output!

This output nicely demonstrates the naming conventions showing scope and assignment. The `Tag:TestDefaultSettings` entry is ready to be assigned to users.

Creating and Assigning Policies

So far we've covered the basics of creating a policy using the `New-CsXxxPolicy` cmdlets. You know that simply using the cmdlet followed by an identity will create a new policy with the default settings. We've also discussed the basics of what the different identities for the policy mean to where they apply, but it will be useful to recap that here. This time you will use the `New-CsClientVersionPolicy` because it can be created against all the various scopes available as follows:

```
New-CsClientVersionPolicy -Identity global
New-CsClientVersionPolicy -Identity Site:EMEA
New-CsClientVersionPolicy -Identity registrar:se01.rlscomms.net
New-CsClientVersionPolicy -Identity TestDefaultSettings
```

These commands will create policies with the default settings. Of course, you can also create new policies through the SBSCP. One of the benefits of this is that you get guidance in creating the policies of different scope, as shown in Figure 12.12.

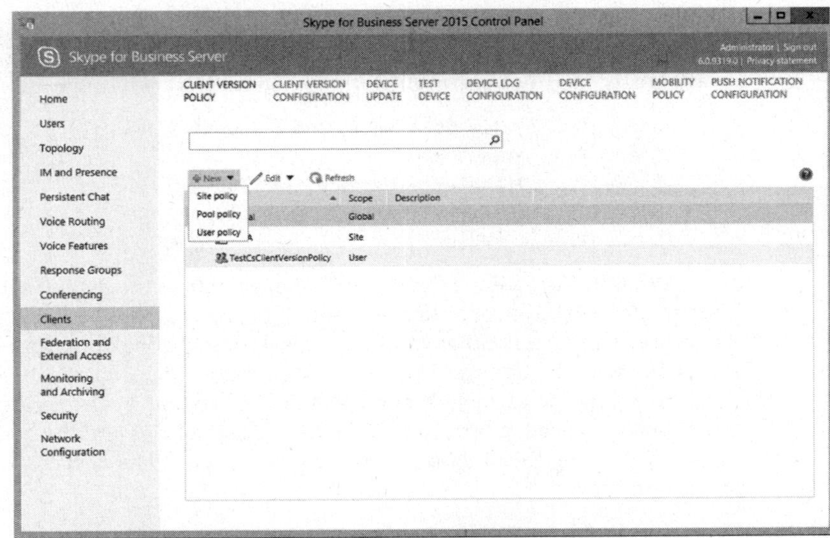

FIGURE 12.12 Creating a new CsClientVersionPolicy through the SBSCP, showing the different policy scopes available

Once you have selected the scope type, you will be presented with a search box to locate the relevant pool (registrar) or site, or you will be taken straight into the policy settings windows with a text box to name the policy if it is to be a user (`Tag:`) policy.

After policies have been created in the SBSCP or PowerShell, the next stage is the assignment of these policies. Global policies, site policies, and service policies don't need to be assigned; they just work immediately on creation because their identity specifically references an element of Skype for Business architecture where they are to be active. That's why the name of a policy can be edited only with user policies. Of course, this means you can't use one site policy on another site; you must create a new one because the naming format is specific to the site, such as Site:EMEA or Site:APAC. If you do need to do this, there is no simple method. It would be worth reviewing the following article, which details a possible workaround:

`http://blogs.technet.com/b/csps/archive/2011/03/21/copypolicies.aspx`

The user policy (sometimes called *tag level*) will need to be assigned. This is where the `Grant-CsXxxPolicy` cmdlets come in. To assign the `TestDefaultSettings` client version policy to the `Keith_Skype` user, you need to do the following:

```
Grant-CsClientVersionPolicy -Identity "rlscomms\keith_skype" ↵
-PolicyName "TestDefaultSettings"
```

This will apply the policy to `Keith_Skype`. But suppose you want to apply this policy to all members of a department or to those with a special custom attribute or specifically to members of an AD group.

Well, this is once again where PowerShell comes in. You can again utilize the searching skills you learned at the beginning of this chapter. You first locate the relevant group of users you need and then pipe the output to the relevant `Grant-CsXxxPolicy` cmdlet. Here is an example:

```
Get-CsUser -LdapFilter "Department=Marketing" | ↵
Grant-CsClientPolicy -PolicyName "TestCsClientPolicy"
```

This will first use an LDAP filter to get all the members of the Marketing department who are Lync enabled and then apply `TestCsClientPolicy` to them. If you are using the SBSCP to assign policy, things follow much the same format. You would use the search skills covered earlier to locate the relevant Skype for Business–enabled users. Then you would select the users and, in the Action drop-down, click Assign Policies. This will open the window you see in Figure 12.13. You can assign the relevant policies to the users by using the relevant drop-down menus and clicking OK to apply.

FIGURE 12.13
Assigning policies in the SBSCP

Applying a policy to members of a specific AD group is unfortunately not quite so simple. Like many things, though, it can be achieved with a line of PowerShell.

You first need to get the members of the group. This can be done as follows:

```
Import-Module ActiveDirectory
Get-AdGroupMember -Identity TestGroup
```

Here, you are first importing the AD module so you can manipulate AD objects and then get the members of the group TestGroup. However, the output looks like this:

```
Get-ADGroupMember -Identity TestGroup

distinguishedName : CN=Keith Skype,Cn=users,dc=rlscomms,dc=net
name              : Keith Skype
objectClass       : user
objectGUID        : 43cea8f9-5d84-4007-bd4b-d2daac38986a
SamAccountName    : Keith_Skype
SID               : S-1-5-21-1801160900-2869415974-1656638013-1144
```

If you try to pipe that directly into the `Grant-CsXxxPolicy` cmdlet, you will get an error because the `Grant-CsXxxPolicy` cmdlet doesn't understand the input. To work around this, you need to understand the type of input that the `Grant-CsXxxPolicy` cmdlet takes. You can get this from the help file, as shown here:

```
String value or Microsoft.Rtc.Management.ADConnect.Schema.ADUser object.
Grant-CsClientPolicy accepts pipelined input of string values
representing the Identity of a user account. The cmdlet also
accepts pipelined input of user objects.
```

This tells you that the cmdlet accepts pipelined user objects, as you proved when passing it output from `Get-CsUser`, and that it also accepts strings that represent user accounts. Therefore, what you need to pass the `Grant-CsXxxPolicy` cmdlet is something in the form of Keith Skype.

As you can see from the output from the `Get-AdGroupMember` cmdlet, this particular format is found under the .name attribute. You can, therefore, use the following PowerShell command to grant policy to the membership of a specific AD group:

```
Get-ADGroupMember -Identity testgroup | ForEach-Object ↵
{Grant-CsClientPolicy -PolicyName testdefaultsettings -identity $_.name}
```

This command first gets the members of the group and then for each member runs the `Grant-CsClientPolicy` cmdlet using the `.name` attribute for the identity.

Real World Scenario

THE NEED TO AUTOMATE POLICY ASSIGNMENT

In many recent discussions with customers, a common scenario has arisen. As you have seen, assigning policy is a process that requires a command to be run. It is perhaps a slight disadvantage to the new way of doing things. With Group Policy, assuming a new user account fell under the scope of a GPO, that new user account would automatically get the new policy applied. In Skype for Business this is not always the case. For example, suppose a new user is created in the Marketing department. Even if you have followed one of the earlier examples to assign a specific policy to all members of the Marketing department using the LDAP filter method, this new member of the Marketing department won't get the same policy as the rest of the department. Instead, they will get the nearest policy to it, following the normal inheritance method. This could be either a service (depending on which pool they register to), a site (depending on which site they are homed in), or the global policy, if none of the others apply.

What is required is a way to ensure that users get the policies they should get. At this point, there is really no good way that we have come up with for doing this. You could of course have scripts that are scheduled, but it would only be reasonable to run those, for example, at the end of each day. This means a user could be live on the system for a day without the correct policies. If this were an archiving policy, that could leave you open to some serious legal consequences!

All we can suggest in this case is to make the assignment of Skype for Business policy part of your provisioning process. This could mean ensuring that assigning policy is added to the checklist of steps taken when creating a user. Or, you may have an automated method, given that PowerShell makes it so simple to assign policy based on user attributes. If so, you can ensure that when the user object is created by Forefront Identity Manager (FIM), which is a Microsoft meta directory and directory synchronization tool used in many provisioning systems, FIM will validate the relevant attributes based on user type (such as Marketing) and then run the relevant PowerShell commands to apply policy.

Finally, as part of operational management of Skype for Business, you could report on policies each month to double-check that people have the correct policies and no one has slipped through the net.

Realistically, you probably don't want to create all your policies with the default settings. After all, there would be little point in that because you could simply use the default global policies. So to create new policies with settings other than the default, you need to specify what settings you want in `New-CsXxxPolicy`. As an example, creating a custom presence policy enables you to manage two important aspects of presence subscriptions: prompted subscribers and category subscriptions.

```
New-CsPresencePolicy -Identity MarketingPresencePolicy ↵
-MaxPromptedSubscriber 600 -MaxCategorySubscription 900
```

This would create a new presence policy using the settings entered. The `MaxCategorySubscription` parameter lets you control the maximum number of category subscriptions allowed at any one time. A category subscription represents a request for a specific category of information—for example, an application that requests calendar data. The `MaxPromptedSubscriber` parameter enables you to control the maximum number of prompted subscribers a user can have at any one time. By default, anytime you are added to another user's contacts list, a notification dialog appears onscreen informing you of this fact and giving you the chance to do such things as add the person to your own contacts list or block the person from viewing your presence. Until you take action and dismiss the dialog box, each notification counts as a prompted subscriber.

Creating a presence policy in this way is easy. However, what about a policy that has many more options you could set, like a client policy? In that case, you need to plow through them and set the ones you want. The options that you don't explicitly set will take on the default settings for that policy.

As you've seen, it is also possible to create policy using the SBSCP. In this case, configuring the relevant settings is simply a case of using the GUI and then clicking Commit.

Editing Existing Policies

We have shown how to create several policies, but what about editing the existing ones? Editing policies is also a simple matter in PowerShell or the SBSCP. With PowerShell, you would use the relevant `Set-CsXxxPolicy` cmdlet and identify the policy using the naming conventions outlined previously (*Scope:Name*) and then use the relevant parameter to change the setting, as in the following example:

```
Set-CsPresencePolicy -Identity Tag:MarketingPresencePolicy ↵
-MaxPromptedSubscriber 200 -MaxCategorySubscription 400
```

There is at least one policy that works slightly differently than the others. That is the client version policy. This policy is made up of rules to allow or disallow certain versions, and it uses the `CsClientVersionPolicyRule` set of cmdlets to amend and create rules.

Having created and assigned all these policies, the last thing we will cover in this section is how to see which user has which policy assigned. After all, it could get rather complex with all those different levels in play.

To see the policies applied to a user, run the following command:

```
Get-CsUser -Identity "Keith Skype"
```

This will output something similar to the following:

```
Identity                  : CN=Keith Skype,CN=Users,DC=rlscomms,DC=net
VoicePolicy               :
VoiceRoutingPolicy        :
ConferencingPolicy        :
PresencePolicy            :
DialPlan                  :
LocationPolicy            :
ClientPolicy              : TestDefaultSettings
ClientVersionPolicy       :
ArchivingPolicy           :
ExchangeArchivingPolicy : Uninitialized
PinPolicy                 :
ExternalAccessPolicy      :
MobilityPolicy            :
PersistentChatPolicy      :
UserServicesPolicy        :
HostedVoiceMail           :
HostedVoicemailPolicy     :
HostingProvider           : SRV:
RegistrarPool             : se01.rlscomms.net
Enabled                   : True
SipAddress                : sip:keith.Skype@rlscomms.net
LineURI                   :
EnterpriseVoiceEnabled    : False
ExUmEnabled               : False
HomeServer                : CN=Lc
Services,CN=Microsoft,CN=1:1,CN=Pools,CN=RTC
Service,CN=Services,CN=Configuration,DC=rlscomms,DC=net
```

```
DisplayName              : Keith Skype
SamAccountName           : Keith_Skype
```

Note that although some of the policies applied are shown, others are not. This is because the only ones shown here are the ones assigned specifically to the user, namely, the `Tag:` policies.

In the past with Lync 2010, seeing all the policies that applied to a user required some fairly serious PowerShell. If you're interested in that, then take a look at the Lync Server PowerShell blog.

```
http://blogs.technet.com/b/csps/archive/2010/06/07/scriptuserpolicyassignments
.aspx
```

However, in Lync 2013 we were given a new built-in cmdlet to do exactly what we need. The `Get-CsEffectivePolicy` cmdlet will return all the policies applied to a user even if they are applied only at a global or site level. For example, if you run the following command, you will see the policies applied to Test User5:

```
Get-CsEffectivePolicy -Identity "Test User5"
```

The output looks like this:

```
Identity                          : Keith Skype
ConferencingPolicy                : Global
PresencePolicy                    : Global
LocationPolicy                    : Global
VoicePolicy                       : Global
LocationProfile                   : Global
ClientVersionPolicy               : Global
ClientPolicy                      : Tag:TestDefaultSettings
ImArchivingPolicy                 : Global
UserPinPolicy                     : Global
ExternalAccessPolicy              : Global
HostedVoicemailPolicy             : Global
MobilityPolicy                    : Global
PersistentChatPolicy              : Global
VoiceRoutingPolicy                : Global
UserServicesPolicy                : Global
ThirdPartyVideoSystem             : Global
CallViaWorkPolicy                 : Global
GraphPolicy                       : Global
AddressBookServerPolicy         : Global
OnlineDialinConferencingPolicy :
```

You can see that all the policies are applied at the global level except for `ClientPolicy`, which is defined at the user level. There is no definition for `OnlineDialinConferencingPolicy` as this environment is not connected to online services.

Removing or Resetting Policies

With all the experimenting with policies you've done in this chapter, you have probably ended up with lots of policies you don't want! You also may well have changed the settings of the default global policies and, for that matter, other policies as well. What can you do about that?

Well, removing a policy at any of the levels other than global is simple. Use the relevant `Remove-CsXxxPolicy` cmdlet with the identity of the policy as follows:

```
Remove-CsClientVersionPolicy -Identity Site:EMEA
Remove-CsClientVersionPolicy -Identity registrar:se01.rlscomms.net
Remove-CsClientVersionPolicy -Identity TestDefaultSettings
```

In the SBSCP, removing policies is just as simple; you simply select the relevant policy and then, from the Edit drop-down, select Delete.

Interestingly, if you remove a policy currently assigned to a user, you will get a warning, and you are given the opportunity to continue. Assuming you select Yes, the policy will be removed, and the user will be reset to a `Global` policy assignment. See Figure 12.14 for the result of rerunning the `Get-CsEffectivePolicy` command.

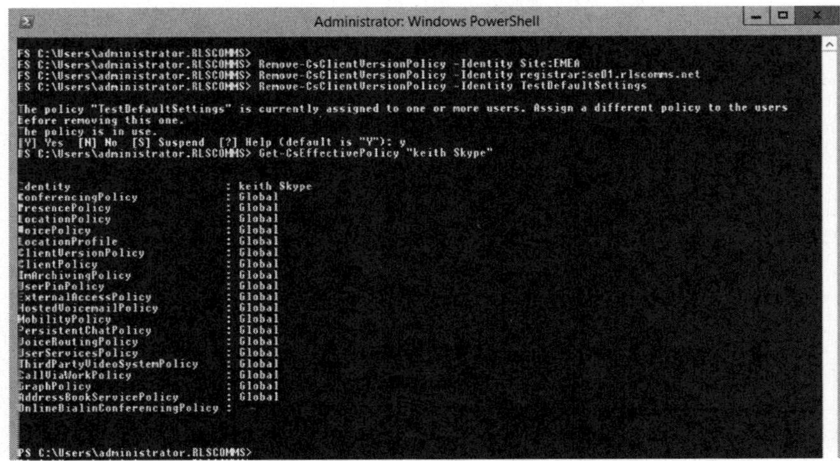

FIGURE 12.14 Results of removing a policy in use

However, if you run the `Get-CsUser` cmdlet, you will receive the following response:

```
WARNING: "ClientVersionPolicy" with identity "2" assigned to "sip:Keith.Skype@
rlscomms.net" has been removed from configuration store.
```

This indicates that the user configuration still believes there to be a policy assigned, and it is identified with the value of 2. This is known as an *anchor*.

WHAT ARE ANCHORS?

When a policy is created, it is given an ID, which is also known as the anchor. The first policy is 1, the second 2, and so on. If you create five policies, they will be anchored 1 through 5. If you delete the policy with anchor 3 and then create a new policy, it will use the anchor 6. Number 3 will never be reused.

In this case, the user will be applied to the next policy defined by the scope, which is why `Get-CsEffectivePolicy` looked OK and, while it may be messy and unclear, there is no specific need to tidy further.

Of course, removing site and service policies automatically removes their assignment because the identity and assignment are intrinsically linked.

> **User Moving to a New Location**
>
> If a user moves from one place to another and therefore needs different policies, you don't need to first remove the policies from the user; you simply apply the new policies in the same way you did before (as discussed previously). The user—and for that matter, the site, service, and global levels—can have only one policy applied at any one time.

Interestingly, if you try to delete the default global policies, Skype for Business won't let you! Essentially, all that happens is that any changes you have made to the global policy revert to the default settings. To try this for yourself, you would use a command like the following one:

```
Remove-CsClientVersionPolicy -Identity global
```

When you run this, you will reset the global `CsClientVersionPolicy` to its default settings. By way of warning, you will see the following output:

```
WARNING: Global configuration for "ClientVersionPolicy" cannot be removed.
Instead of removing it, the Global configuration for ClientVersionPolicy" has
been reset to the default value.
```

Choosing the Right Policy for the Job

You have looked at the policy architecture in Skype for Business and have seen how policies operate, how they are targeted, and also where Group Policy is still needed. You have also looked at the basics of manipulating policies in Skype for Business. Finally, you will dive in and look at the individual policies and the settings they control.

The first element of examining individual policies is knowing where to view and change those settings. Clearly, the SBSCP gives access to many policy elements, including the ability to edit and assign policies as well as create and delete them. However, not all policies can be accessed in this way. Table 12.1 lists the elements of SBSCP that deal with policies (for example, assigning them to various scopes), and it shows how the settings in the SBSCP equate to PowerShell cmdlets; it also indicates which chapter of this book covers the related policies.

TABLE 12.1: A mapping of SBSCP settings to PowerShell cmdlets

SBSCP TAB	SBSCP SETTING	POWERSHELL CMDLET	NOTES	CHAPTER COVERED
IM & Presence	File Filter	`CsFileTransferFilter Configuration`		3
IM & Presence	URL Filter	`CsImFilter Configuration`	Note that the IM Filter Configuration is different from the basic enabling and disabling of hyperlinks that is possible through the CsClientPolicy through the EnableURL setting.	3
Persistent Chat	Persistent Chat Policy	`CsPersistent ChatPolicy`		App C
Persistent Chat	Persistent Chat Configuration	`CsPersistentChat Configuration`		App C
Voice Routing	Dial Plan	`CsDialPlan`		16
Voice Routing	Voice Policy	`CsVoicePolicy`		16
Voice Routing	Trunk Configuration	`CsOutboundTranslation RuleCsTrunk Configuration CsVoiceRegex`		16
Conferencing	Conferencing Policy	`CsConferencing Configuration`		16
Conferencing	Meeting Configuration	`CsMeeting Configuration`		16
Conferencing	PIN Policy	`CsPinPolicy`	Note that this is the same policy defined in the Security tab and controls both Conferencing and Device access.	3, 6
Clients	Client Version Policy	`CsClientVersion Policy`		3, 12

TABLE 12.1: A mapping of SBSCP settings to PowerShell cmdlets *(CONTINUED)*

SBSCP Tab	SBSCP Setting	PowerShell Cmdlet	Notes	Chapter Covered
Clients	Client Version Configuration	`CsClientVersion Configuration`	Allows you to modify the default action for clients not specifically mentioned in the active policy.	3
Clients	Device Log Configuration	`CsUCPhone Configuration`		6
Clients	Device Configuration	`CsDeviceUpdate Configuration`		6
Clients	Mobility Policy	`CsMobilityPolicy`		5
Clients	Push Notification Configuration	`CsPushNotification Configuration`		5
Federation and External Access	External Access Policy	`CsExternalAccessPolicy`		4
Federation and External Access	Access Edge Configuration	`CsAccessEdge Configuration`	Note that this is a global-only setting.	4
Monitoring and Archiving	Call Detail Recording	`CsCdrConfiguration`		13
Monitoring and Archiving	Quality of Experience Data	`CsQoEConfiguration`		13
Monitoring and Archiving	Archiving Policy	`CsArchivingPolicy`		13
Monitoring and Archiving	Archiving Configuration	`CsArchivingConfiguration`		13
Security	Registrar	`CsProxyConfiguration`		3
Security	Web Service	`CsWebServiceConfiguration`		3
Security	PIN Policy	`CsPinPolicy`		3

TABLE 12.1: A mapping of SBSCP settings to PowerShell cmdlets *(CONTINUED)*

SBSCP TAB	SBSCP SETTING	POWERSHELL CMDLET	NOTES	CHAPTER COVERED
Network Configuration	Global Policy	`CsNetworkConfiguration`		17
Network Configuration	Location Policy	`CsLocationPolicy`		18

What you may notice in Table 12.1 is that there is no mention of the CsClientPolicy, CsPresencePolicy, PrivacyConfiguration, CsCallViaWorkPolicy, CsThirdPartyVideoSystemPolicy, or UserServicesConfiguration. Some of the most far-reaching policies can be changed only through PowerShell. In the rest of this chapter, we will drill into the settings of these policies and any particular quirks of operation related to individual policies.

OTHER POLICY TYPES

There are, of course, many other policy types that we are not covering in this chapter. There are settings for conferences, voice, archiving, persistent chat, mobility, and simple URLs, among others. Although these policies can all be applied to users, they are applied in the context of specific areas of functionality that are described in other chapters of this book, so we cover the relevant policies settings there too.

ClientPolicy

The client policy is manipulated using the `CsClientPolicy` cmdlets. It is this policy that replaces the vast majority of settings that would previously have been set using group policies in OCS 2007 R2. Client policies can be applied at the site or user scope.

It is the client policy that allows the configuration of such elements as these: `MaximumNumberOfContacts`, whether to add a disclaimer message to an IM with the `IMWarning` setting, whether to force saving of IMs in Outlook with the `EnableIMAutoArchiving` setting, and whether to display a photo with the `DisplayPhoto` setting.

Of course, there are many more settings available, which are all described in detail in the Skype for Business help file. However, if the setting is not in the default scope, there is a way to make client policies even more flexible. You can use the `New-CsClientPolicyEntry` cmdlet to add additional areas of control to the Skype for Business ClientPolicy. This functionality has to be used in conjunction with Microsoft, which could add the relevant new element to control in a cumulative update, as detailed here:

```
http://technet.microsoft.com/en-us/library/gg399046.aspx
```

In the past, this was used to add a method for providing a link to a feedback URL to capture client requests during the beta periods of Lync.

ClientVersionPolicy

The client version policy is set to ensure control over which different clients can register to a Skype for Business pool. Client version policies are made up of rules that identify specific clients. These rules are defined using the `ClientVersionPolicyRule` cmdlets. Each SIP client sends identifying information in its SIP headers. This identifying information is then matched against the defined rules.

> **SPOOFING HEADERS**
>
> Because clients report their version in a SIP header, it is possible that given a correctly manipulated client, the header could be changed. This would allow a way around the policy. Therefore, you should not think of this as a top security policy—rather, think of it as something that can provide a good consistent service and as a line of defense against casual attackers.

These policies are used to ensure both a consistent user experience and security by making sure that old, unpatched clients cannot connect to the service.

Client version policies can be applied at the global, site, service (registrar), and user scopes.

ClientVersionConfiguration

The `ClientVersionConfiguration` cmdlets allow you to control, at either the global (default) or site (new policy) level, what happens when clients attempt to connect to Skype for Business. This is where you turn on or off the facility in Lync to check client version. If this policy is enabled, the ClientVersionPolicy policies apply. The other side to ClientVersionConfiguration is what happens when Skype for Business denies access to a client. You can use the settings to set the default action if a client version is not specifically noted in a ClientVersionPolicy policy. You can also configure whether to prompt the user with a URL to get an updated client if they have a client that is not compliant with the policy.

PrivacyConfiguration

Presence is a great resource; the ability to see whether someone is available can significantly streamline communication. However, some people are not eager to present this information. Lync 2010 introduced a way of managing this situation, which Skype for Business Server 2015 continues to maintain, by applying Privacy Configuration settings. The fundamental aim of these settings is giving users control. It allows users to show their status to only those people on their contacts list.

Given that only allowing contacts to see your status is very restrictive, you can help users prepopulate their contacts list with their manager and direct reports using the `AutoInitiateContacts` setting. Other settings configure Skype for Business to ensure that the user must specifically opt in to sharing photo and location information with others.

Policies can be configured at the global, site, and service scope. At the service scope, the policy can be applied only to the User Services service.

PresencePolicy

The presence policy controls two settings, the `MaxCategorySubscription` and the `MaxPromptedSubscriber`. Presence as a concept is all about providing information about whether someone or something (a group, for example) is available. However, the simple process of providing that information creates network traffic and database load because all the people who are tracking an object are communicated with and logged. Skype for Business is a fairly efficient system and scales to hundreds of thousands of users; however, if all those users subscribed to a single object, then when it came online or changed status, that would generate hundreds of thousands of messages to let all those users know.

To mitigate this potential flood of network traffic, you can use the settings in the presence policy. The first setting, `MaxCategorySubscription`, controls the individual types of information that each user can subscribe to—for example, calendar information.

The `MaxCategorySubscription` property enables you to limit the number of category subscriptions a user can have.

The second setting is the `MaxPromptedSubscriber` setting. Each time you are added to another user's contacts list, the default client behavior is to prompt you with a pop-up that gives you the chance to reciprocate and add the user to your contacts list. Each of these prompts counts as someone subscribed to the requesting user's presence. It is common practice to limit the number of unacknowledged presence subscriptions; this can be done with the `MaxPromptedSubscriber` property. If a user were to reach the maximum number, they would not receive new contact notifications until some of the outstanding prompts have been acknowledged.

The `CsPresencePolicy` cmdlets can apply at the global, site, or per-user scope.

CsCallViaWorkPolicy

CsCallViaWorkPolicy only has four settings that can be controlled. They are the `Identity` and `Enabled` settings, which every policy has, and then simply `AdminCallBackNumber` (and associated `UseAdminCallBackNumber`).

Of all of these, the only setting of interest is `AdminCallBackNumber`, which allows the use of a generic "administration" number rather than the individual users' number.

CsThirdPartyVideoSystemPolicy

With even less to configure, CsThirdPartyVideoSystemPolicy simply has a flag (`SupportSendingLowResolution`) to indicate whether the particular policy enables lower resolutions.

UserServicesConfiguration

User Services are the services that control the basic settings for maintaining presence for users and also some baseline meeting settings. The meeting settings cover the length of time an anonymous user can remain in a meeting without an authenticated user and the maximum time that any meeting can remain active. On the user side, you can set the maximum number of contacts each user can have and the maximum number of meetings that they can schedule.

The user services configuration policies are applied at site or service scope. You can also edit the global policy.

When the user services configuration settings and the client policy settings are in conflict (for example, when different maximum number of contacts per user has been set), the lower number wins.

The Bottom Line

Search for users in the SBSCP and PowerShell. Skype for Business offers huge flexibility in what can be done to configure and control the user experience. However, to work efficiently, being able to identify and retrieve information about different groups of users based on various criteria is critical. It is this skill that enables you to target specific groups with specific policies. As with most administration, you can search for users in both SBSCP and PowerShell.

Master It

You have been asked to run a report on two groups of users. How would you handle the following requests? Can you use two different types of search?

Locate all users in Marketing.

Locate all users who register to the `se01.rlscomms.net` pool.

Perform basic user administration in the SBSCP and in PowerShell. As would be expected, most basic administration can be performed in the SBSCP and in PowerShell. New users can be created, deleted, enabled, and disabled in both. You can, of course, also change various user properties—in particular, things like the SIP URI of a user and the pool to which they register. User administration is generally carried out by a user who is a member of the CSUserAdministrator RBAC role.

Master It You have been asked to enable all users, except those who are in Sales, for Skype for Business. How would you do this? In addition, one of your colleagues, who is a domain administrator, has asked you to make some changes to his account. What problems might you face?

Understand Skype for Business policies. Skype for Business has significantly improved the policy architecture since OCS 2007 R2. Although AD Group Policy still can have a role to play in getting the client up and running, Skype for Business enforces the majority of policy through in-band provisioning. It uses SIP messages to push policy out to the client instantly and ensures that there is no requirement for domain membership. Users get a consistent experience no matter where they log on. To apply Skype for Business policies properly, it is important to understand the new scope model, in which policies can be applied at the global, site, service, and user levels, and how inheritance works so that the policy closest to the user wins.

Master It You have been asked to explain to a new administrator the different scopes at which a policy can be applied and how different scopes affect the identity of the policy. What would you tell her?

Manipulate Skype for Business policies. Policies are controlled and applied to users either through PowerShell or through the SBSCP. When in the shell, your search skills are critical to ensure that you can closely target relevant user groups. It is here that the piping capabilities of PowerShell are so useful. You can, of course, also apply policy through the SBSCP, which has a helpful Assign Policy page where you can apply applicable policies to one or many users from a single screen.

Master It You have been asked to create a new client policy for the APAC site. You first need to check the default settings for the policy and then customize it to limit the number of users a person can have on their contacts list to 300. How would you proceed?

Choose the right policy for the job. There is a vast range of policy settings available. One of the hardest things an administrator must do is understand where to make certain configurations. SBSCP makes available many policy settings, but it is not always obvious which PowerShell cmdlet sets which setting, compared to what is presented in the SBSCP. Equally, it is not possible to carry out all configuration through the SBSCP, with some of the most wide-ranging policies being configured only through PowerShell.

Master It You have been asked to design a set of policies for your organization. Where would you gather more information about specific settings?

Chapter 13

Archiving and Monitoring

Any company facing the world of compliance will probably need to account not only for who is instant messaging with whom and when but also for the content of those messages. This is where the Archiving role comes into play.

Its partner role is the Monitoring role. Neither Archiving nor Monitoring is a dedicated role in Skype for Business, but both rely on separate databases for storage and are defined within the topology. As such, it's easiest to continue to think of them as roles. Monitoring is often associated with service availability up/down reporting capabilities, but the Skype for Business Server 2015 Monitoring role is responsible for the quality-based call monitoring as well as the call detail recording capability normally associated with PBXs.

Server (and service) availability monitoring is the responsibility of System Center Operations Manager, and Skype for Business Server 2015 has a management pack available to provide specific service alerting and reporting into System Center.

In this chapter, you will learn to

- Understand the architecture of the Archiving and Monitoring roles
- Provide reporting on the data available from the Archiving and Monitoring roles
- Use the capabilities in the System Center Operations Manager management pack to report on the availability of the Skype for Business service

Deploying the Architecture

Live Communications Server (LCS) introduced the archiving and call detail recording (CDR) capability; however, the Monitoring server role was not available until OCS 2007.

In both LCS (2003 and 2005) and OCS 2007, the Archiving database contained the IM logs as well as the CDR data. The Monitoring database introduced with OCS 2007 contained only the quality of experience (QoE) data; however, with the move to OCS 2007 R2, the CDR data was removed from the Archiving database and included with the QoE data. This configuration was similar with both versions of Lync Server; archiving contained only the IM logs, and monitoring included both CDR and QoE data.

Lync Server 2013 changed the way in which archived data is maintained. When Exchange 2013 is also deployed in the environment, archiving can be directed to archive the data within the Exchange 2013 environment and make it subject to the same archiving configuration as Exchange. You can find specific information on this configuration in Chapter 22, "Exchange, SharePoint, and Office Web Applications Server."

Otherwise, Skype for Business can continue to archive data to a SQL Server database.

In this chapter we'll focus on native archiving. You'll look at the prerequisites required, the deployment architecture, and the policies required to enable the archiving and monitoring capability for users.

Prerequisites

Both Archiving and Monitoring roles have been combined into the Front End role, so no additional hardware is required to deploy them; it's just a case of enabling them and publishing the topology. These roles both use SQL Server as a repository for their data. Only Archiving can use Exchange Server 2013 as an alternative.

Unlike in previous versions, neither role requires Microsoft Message Queuing (MSMQ) to be installed.

Installation

Archiving and Monitoring are both defined within Topology Builder; however, since Lync Server 2013, they no longer require separate servers. Rather, they are installed as additional services on top of a Front End server. Either role can be enabled as part of the New Pool Wizard, or they can be added later through editing and publishing the topology. Figure 13.1 shows the associations section of a pool being edited on a previously published pool.

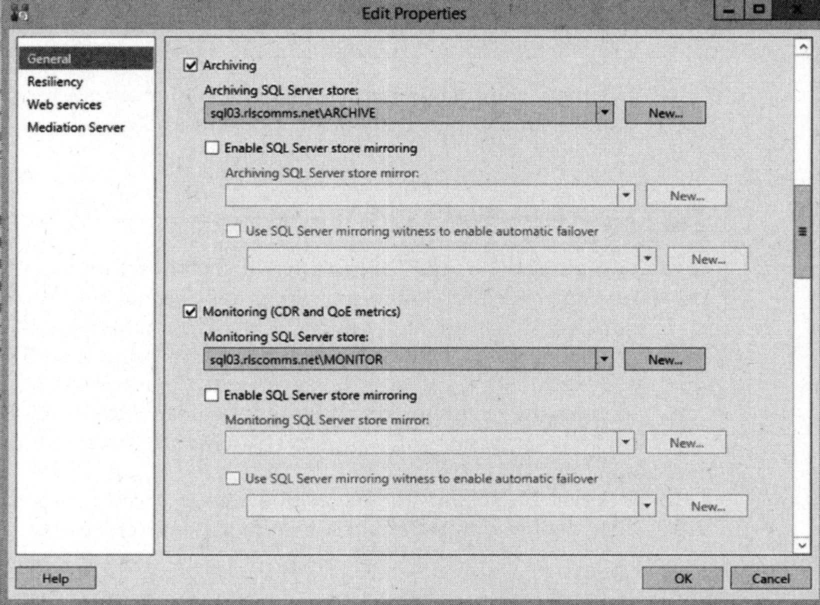

FIGURE 13.1 Defining archiving and monitoring associations on a pool

As with other roles that are reliant upon databases, the act of publishing the topology will also prompt to allow for creation of the databases. You can leave it to Topology Builder to select the locations for the database files, or you can manually control them.

Database Support, Architecture, and Capacity

Microsoft recommends that you deploy separate instances for each of the Archiving and Monitoring installations; however, it does support sharing an instance between Archiving and Monitoring and even sharing within a Back End or Persistent Chat database instance.

While this is a supported configuration, it's not recommended because of the likely capacity of the Archiving database. Larger databases can need more maintenance time, potentially impacting the other databases. Typically, separate instances will be used when the performance of SQL Server is critical.

In the case of a Standard Edition server, a separate SQL Server installation is still required. Archiving and Monitoring cannot use the SQL Express instance used by the Standard Edition server.

The Archiving instance creates a single database called `LCSLog`, whereas the Monitoring instance creates two databases, `LCSCDR`, containing call data record information, and `QoEMetrics`, containing QoE information.

Skype for Business also provides a significant number of reports for accessing and reporting on the QoE data, allowing administrators to help diagnose and troubleshoot call quality problems. You'll see some of these later in this chapter.

Both roles require the 64-bit version of SQL Server to be used; the Monitoring Reporting Pack requires SQL Reporting Services. The following versions of SQL Server are supported (or later service packs):

- SQL Server 2008 R2 Standard
- SQL Server 2008 R2 Enterprise
- SQL Server 2012 Standard
- SQL Server 2012 Enterprise
- SQL Server 2014 Standard
- SQL Server 2014 Enterprise

High Availability

Lync Server 2010 and previous versions did not support high availability for Archiving or Monitoring. There was support for Critical Mode Archiving, meaning that if the solution was unable to archive a message for a given time period (which varied based on version but was configurable), the Front End services would shut down. This resulted in no message transfer possible, and indeed users would be logged out in earlier versions.

With the changes to Lync Server 2013 and how it used SQL Server, coupled with the fact that Archiving and Monitoring are services on the Front End servers, high availability is automatically achieved with an environment that includes the high-availability components in the design and deployment, such as multiple Front Ends and a SQL Server instance in *mirrored* configuration for the Back End.

Skype for Business builds on this with support for SQL Server AlwaysOn Availability Groups.

Configuring Policies

The configurations for both Archiving and Monitoring are defined in the same location within the Control Panel application, as shown in Figure 13.2.

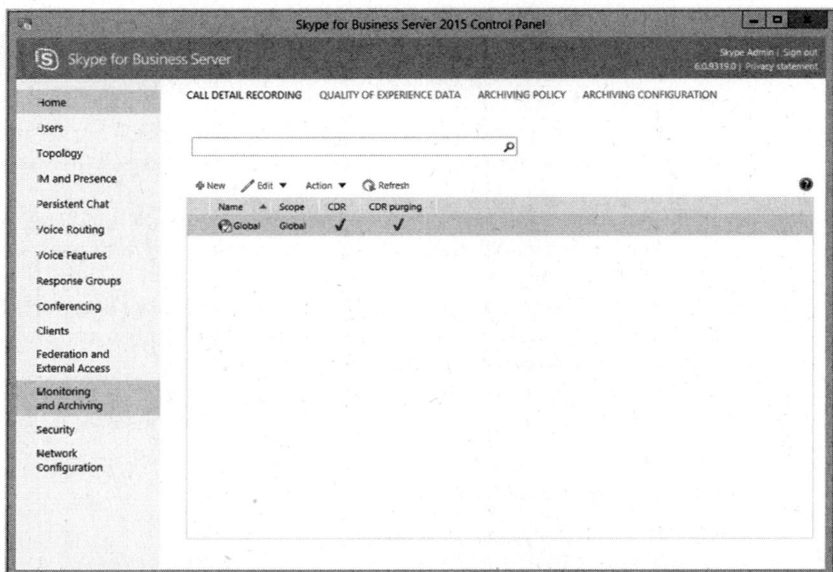

FIGURE 13.2 The Archiving And Monitoring configuration menu

Both policies have the same scope configuration options.

- Global
- Site
- User (Archiving Policy only)

User policies will override both *site* and *global* polices, and *site* policies will override *global* policies. In the case of *archiving*, external and internal communications can be configured separately and can be overridden separately also; for example, if both external and internal archiving are enabled at the *global* level and internal archiving of communications is disabled at the *site* level, then for users at that *site*, only archiving of external communications would occur.

Both call detail recording and quality of experience data have the same options.

- Scope
- Enabled

- Purging
- Number of days for data to be kept (if purging is enabled)

In addition, call detail recording can specify how long error reports are kept.

Archiving policy allows for control over internal and/or external enablement, as shown in Figure 13.3.

FIGURE 13.3 Defining the archiving policy

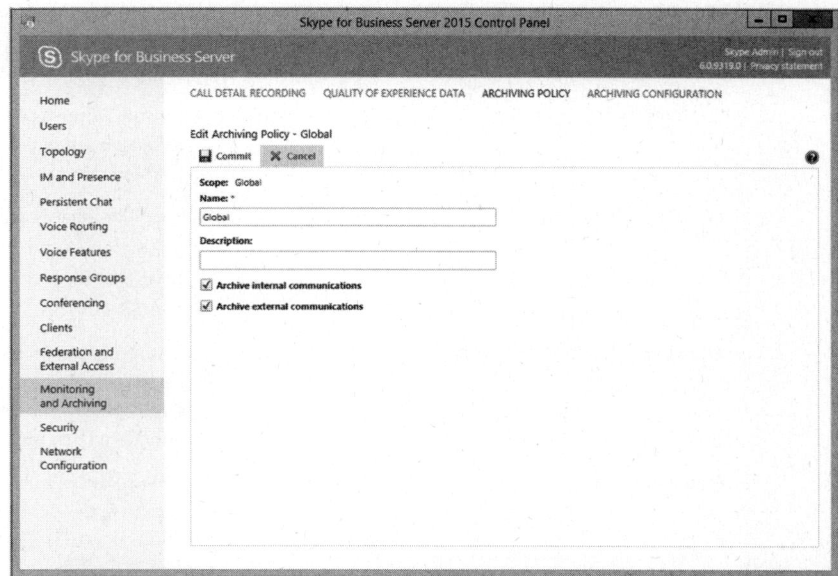

To define the CDR policy using PowerShell, enter this command:

```
New-CsCdrConfiguration -Identity site:EMEA -EnableCDR $true
-EnablePurging $true -KeepCallDetailForDays 30
-KeepErrorReportForDays 30 -PurgeHourOfDay 3
```

To configure the QoE data, use the `New-CsQoeConfiguration` cmdlet.

The `PurgeHourOfDay` parameter allows you to customize when the old data will be purged. Common sense suggests that you define this outside normal office hours; however, other operations (such as backups) may occur at the default time (2 a.m.), and you may find it useful to change this.

Archiving can be enabled for internal or external communications, or both. You can define additional policies to allow this distinction to be made on a per-user or per-site basis if required.

The `New-CsArchivingConfiguation` cmdlet provides the options shown in Table 13.1 to configure the actual policy (using `New-CsArchivingPolicy`).

TABLE 13.1: Archiving configuration cmdlet parameters

PARAMETER	DEFAULT	NOTES
`ArchiveDuplicateMessages`	`True`	Used when dealing with cross-pool messages. If set to `True`, the message will be archived once per pool of users involved. If `False`, it will be archived only once.
`BlockOnArchiveFailure`	`False`	If set to `True`, IMs will be refused if there are any issues with the archiving service. `False` enables message flow to continue in the event of problems.
`CachePurgingInterval`	`24`	Defines how often the system cache is purged of messages when none of the participants is enabled for archiving.

`EnableArchiving`	`None`	Specifies what is archived:
		`None`
		`ImOnly`
		`ImAndWebConf`

`EnableExchangeArchiving`	`False`	If set to `True`, archive data is stored in Exchange Server 2013 rather than SQL Server. If Exchange archiving is enabled, then Exchange archiving policies will be applied, not Lync policies.
`EnablePurging`	`False`	If set to `True`, messages will be removed from the database if older than the value specified in `KeepArchivingDataForDays`. If `False`, messages are not removed.
`KeepArchivingDataForDays`	`14`	Number of days that messages are kept (between 1 and 2,562, approximately 7 years).
`PurgeExportedArchivesOnly`	`False`	If `True`, only messages that have been exported will be purged (overrides the `KeepArchivingDataForDays` value).
`PurgeHourOfDay`	`2`	Time value (hour only) when the data purging will occur.

A common archiving requirement is for compliance purposes, and typically it requires data to be kept for more than the default 14-day period. To create a new policy configuration with a one-year retention period, use the following command:

```
New-CsArchivingConfiguration -Identity site:EMEA
-KeepArchivingDataForDays 365 -EnableArchiving ImAndWebConf
```

If the Archiving role has not yet been deployed, a warning will appear to remind the administrator that enabling archiving requires the Archiving server role to be deployed.

Using `Get-CsArchivingConfiguration` will return the following data for a new policy configuration:

```
Identity                    : Site:EMEA
EnableArchiving             : ImAndWebConf
EnablePurging               : False
PurgeExportedArchivesOnly : False
BlockOnArchiveFailure       : False
KeepArchivingDataForDays  : 365
PurgeHourofDay              : 2
ArchiveDuplicateMessages  : True
CachePurgingInterval        : 24
EnableExchangeArchiving    : False
```

To apply this configuration as a policy, you need to create an associated policy using the `New-CsArchivingPolicy` cmdlet; this will allow you to define whether the configuration applies to internal or external (or both) types of communication.

```
New-CsArchivingPolicy -Identity 1-year-external -ArchiveExternal $True
```

Here, you have created a user policy with only external archiving enabled.

Using `Get-CsArchivingPolicy` will display the following configuration:

```
Identity        : Tag:1-year-external
Description     :
ArchiveInternal : False
ArchiveExternal : True
```

Given that you created a site-based policy configuration and a user-based policy, when you assign the user-based policy to users (with the `Grant-CsArchivingPolicy` cmdlet), this specific site policy will take effect only when users are part of the EMEA site; for locations outside EMEA, the global policy is in effect with the default values.

Deploying the Reporting Pack

The QoE data can be complicated, but Microsoft has provided a pack of built-in reports to help you understand the data captured. They range from simple usage and trending reports to detailed troubleshooting reports. They are deployed into a SQL Reporting Services instance, using the Deployment Wizard setup application (shown in Figure 13.4).

Once you select Deploy Monitoring Reports, the Deployment Wizard prompts you for the following information (although it is already completed with the SQL Server information from Topology Builder, as shown in Figure 13.5):

- Monitoring server
- SQL Server Reporting Services instance
- SQL Server account credentials (for use by the SQL Reporting Services)
- User group (to provide read-only access to the reports)

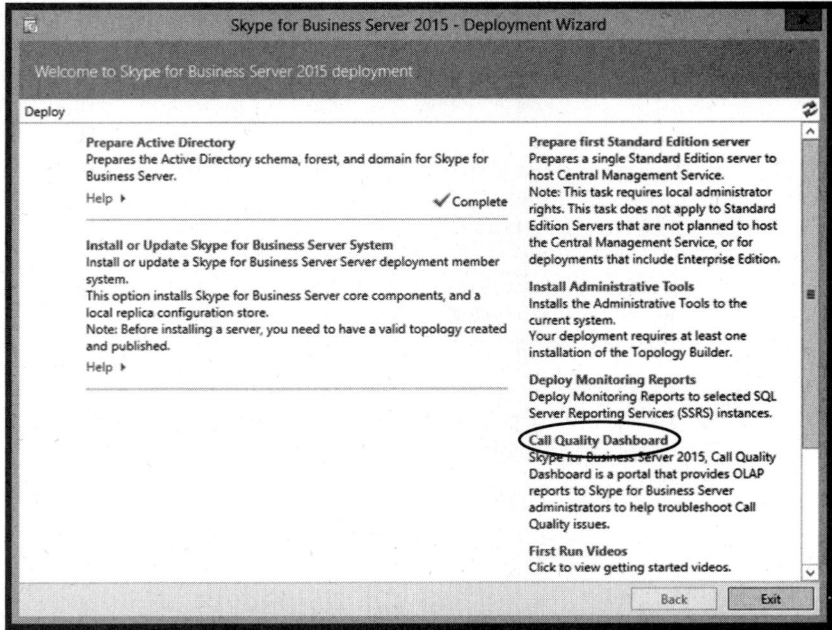

FIGURE 13.4
The Deployment Wizard allows you to deploy Monitoring server reports.

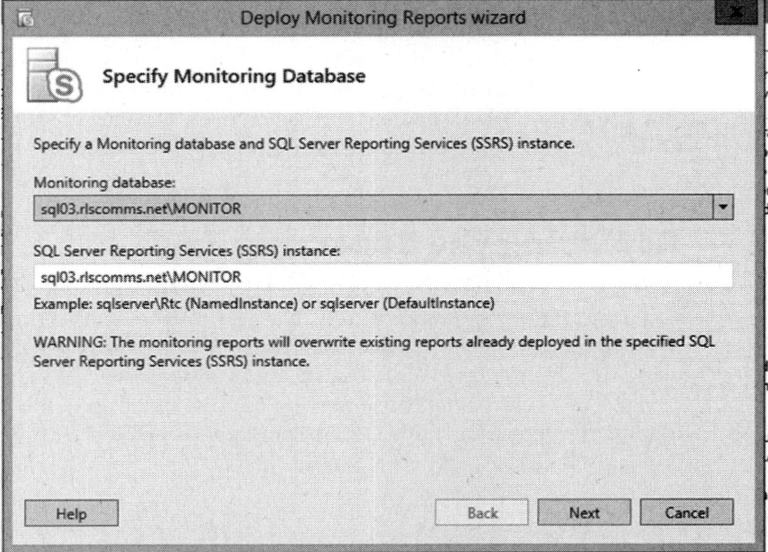

FIGURE 13.5
Deploying the monitoring reports

By default in Lync Server 2010, the wizard attempted to create a secure web page on which to publish the reports (shown in the link on the home page of the Control Panel). However, the installation and configuration of the certificate was a manual process that wasn't really required.

You don't have to install a certificate on this website, and you can access it without deploying a certificate if required.

Skype for Business takes a more realistic approach by configuring the link as a standard HTTP link rather than HTTPS.

Unfortunately, the Reporting Pack covers only the Monitoring server databases (CDR and QOE); from an IM perspective, the best information that can be retrieved from this is that two users had an IM conversation. The contents of that conversation (assuming archiving is enabled) are stored in the Archiving server database (`LCSLog`), which does not have any associated Reporting Pack.

Access to this data is via a SQL query, which, providing the user has the correct permissions, can be achieved using any product that supports Open Database Connectivity (ODBC) to retrieve and then manipulate the data. The actual IM conversation is held in Rich Text Format (RTF) and may require further manipulation before it is readable.

Real World Scenario

Archiving for Compliance

Natively, the Archiving server role is not compliant with many of the regulatory compliance standards found throughout the globe, such as MoReq, UK Companies Act, Sarbanes-Oxley, HIPAA, FSA, and so on.

A copy of the IM data is stored in the SQL database. However, no further controls are in place to protect that data; any user with the appropriate permissions can get to the data and change it, with no record whatsoever of the access or change made. In addition, file transfers are not stored with the conversation transcript for easy recovery, and content from Group Chat channels is put in a separate repository.

Obviously with the updated feature set of Exchange 2013, some levels of "legal hold" capability are available.

To provide additional levels of compliance, you may be required to use a product such as Vantage from Actiance (`http://actiance.com/products/vantage.aspx`).

Vantage installs an agent on each Front End server, captures the data, and sends it to a Vantage server for processing and then onward to a SQL Server repository. This repository is tamperproof, ensuring message and conversation integrity.

As well as providing a compliant repository, Vantage has a built-in capability for IM reporting, both from a system administrator perspective (for policy setting) and from a reviewer perspective (for ediscovery and regulatory compliance reviews).

In addition to the compliance aspect of Vantage, it has other useful features, which either augment existing Skype for Business features or provide new control capabilities.

- Central policy-based logging and analytics.
- Global, group, intergroup, or user-based controls.
- Authentication and authorization. For example, ethical boundaries can be configured to stop users within the same organization from communicating with each other as well as provide granular control over federation.

continues

continued

- Antivirus and antimalware controls. For example, integration with several popular antivirus scanning engines is available.
- Keyword and regular expression triggers to block or alert on content.
- Granular SpIM (spam over IM) and URL blocking controls (including the ability to customize rules).
- Control over legal disclaimers (including the ability to customize disclaimers).
- File transfer capture—that is, it captures complete file data, not just the name.
- Comprehensive analytics engine to show, for example, the volume of Lync usage by users.

The following transcript search is an example of the reporting capabilities from Vantage:

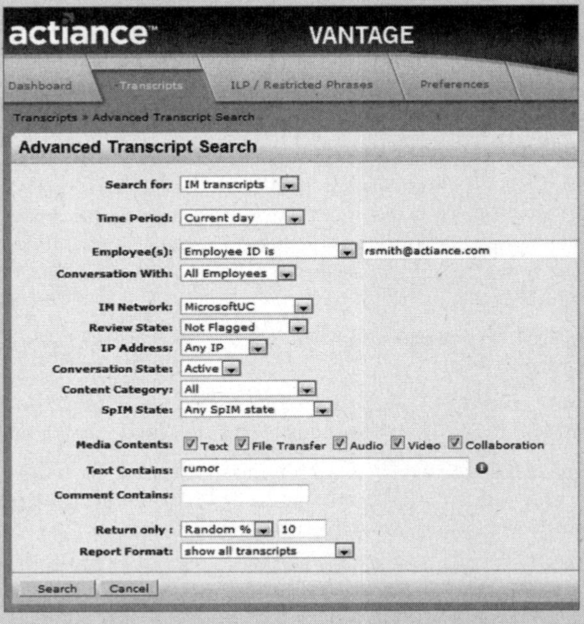

Interpreting the Monitoring Server Reports

Data is useless unless it can be interpreted and understood; the data provided by the Monitoring Reporting Pack is extremely rich and can be used in a number of ways.

- Troubleshooting
- Trend analysis for future capacity planning
- Usage analysis for return on investment (ROI) calculations

The following sections will cover the metrics used and how to interpret them as well as provide details on the reports available.

Understanding Voice Quality

Before delving into the details about the reports and how to interpret them, you really need to understand how voice quality is measured and what steps are taken to ensure that quality is retained throughout a call even when outside events impact that quality.

Some of the key metrics measured per call are listed here:

- Endpoint IP address
- Endpoint subnet
- Internal/external connectivity
- Codec used
- Network connectivity type (wired versus wireless)
- Link speed
- Any bandwidth restrictions applied (due to Call Admission Control)
- Signal level send
- Signal level receive
- Echo
- Device CPU
- Device driver/firmware versions
- Packet loss
- Round-trip time
- Latency
- Jitter
- Burst
- Network MOS
- Listening MOS
- Sending MOS
- Degradation MOS
- Audio healer metrics

Individually, these metrics may report values that would be considered "good." In spite of that, however, the call may still be considered poor quality because often it is the combination of many of the metrics that result in a poor call. For example, latency, jitter, round-trip time, and packet loss may individually be within tolerances, but the combination of packets being dropped along with packets that do arrive but are late will likely create problems on the call from which the healing metrics are unable to recover.

Mean Opinion Score

Traditional telephony provides a subjective assessment of voice quality, based on a scale of 1 to 5, with 5 being perfect and 1 being very poor. A typical PSTN call will rate 2.95 on this scale.

The scoring is carried out by a group of testers listening to an output signal and rating it. This is where the subjective nature of the assessment comes in. It is up to the individual to mark the score, and the average is provided as the final rating.

Because this is a subjective rating, the results can vary from one test to another. Skype for Business Server uses an objective approach, where the output signal is compared to a model to predict the perceived quality, in a way that's similar to the Perceptual Evaluation of Speech Quality (PESQ) standard.

There are four types of Mean Opinion Score (MOS) values.

Listening Quality MOS

This value is commonly used in VoIP deployments, but it does not consider bidirectional effects such as delay or echo. The following three metrics are wideband MOS-LQ scores:

Network MOS The Network MOS value takes into account only network-related factors (packet loss, jitter, and so on) and can be used to identify network conditions that impact audio quality.

Listening MOS The Listening MOS value is a prediction of the wideband quality of an audio stream being played to a user; it considers the output aspects of the device, as well as codec, transcoding, speech level, and background noise. Problems encountered with the sound output will be identified within Listening MOS.

Sending MOS Sending MOS is the counterpart to Listening MOS, and it is a prediction of the wideband quality of an audio stream being sent by a user. It deals with the input levels of the signal, considering the same aspects as Listening MOS. Both Listening and Sending MOS problems typically highlight device issues.

Conversational Quality MOS

This value considers the quality on both ends and includes bidirectional effects such as delay and echo. There is one narrowband MOS-CQ score in Lync Server.

Conversational MOS In addition to the aspects considered by Listening and Sending MOS, Conversational MOS also takes into account bidirectional aspects such as echo and delay.

MOS Values by Codec

Being able to understand the different areas of impact in a call will help you narrow down the problem; if one user reports problems hearing a call but another user reports all is well, it can suggest that you should start investigating Listening MOS and the values associated there. What about comparing calls with each other?

Well, it's extremely difficult to replicate network conditions at any given time; starting with a comparison between the different expectations by codec is useful (shown in Table 13.2).

TABLE 13.2: MOS value by codec

CALL TYPE	CODEC USED	MAX NETWORK MOS
Skype for Business-Skype for Business	SILK	4.42
Media Bypass	G711	4.30
UC-UC	RTAudio (wideband)	4.10
UC-PSTN (non-media bypass scenarios)	RTAudio (narrowband)	2.95
UC-PSTN	SIREN	3.72
Conference Call	G722	4.30
Conference Call	SIREN	3.72

COMPARING CALLS BY CODEC

It is not feasible to compare two calls simply by the codec used to determine which was "better." Because both calls are inherently different, based not only on their own attributes but also the state of the network at the time of the calls, it is impossible to re-create the same conditions to allow any sort of comparison.

A much better approach to comparing calls is to evaluate how much each call has degraded, almost like determining the "least worst" call.

By taking this approach, you can determine which call has been impacted most by the network conditions and establish which has been degraded the most.

Viewing the Reports

Lync Server 2010 reporting offered several improvements to Office Communications Server 2007 R2, including an increase in the number of available reports, tooltips, and color highlighting. (Highlighted text is visible when the mouse is hovered over text, ensuring that potential issues are visible to the reader and easily understood.) Some diagnostic reports are generated only when there is enough data to be worthwhile. For example, problematic-server quality reports are available only on the dashboard when more than 30 data points have been captured.

Reporting in Skype for Business hasn't changed since Lync Server 2013, which was more of an incremental increase in capability. There weren't many new reports (since Lync 2010), but one dramatic change is the increase in the amount of data returned in each report; the number of records has been increased to 1,000.

By default the Reporting Pack is installed at the following location (reachable via a web browser):

```
Http:<SQL server name>:80/ReportServer_<SQL instance name>
```

There are two top-level report types.

Dashboard Provides a weekly or monthly snapshot of the state of the environment, allowing an administrator to quickly see trends in both user usage and hotspots for problems. Each report is a hyperlink to the next level of detail. Figure 13.6 shows the weekly dashboard report.

> ### DASHBOARD SUMMARY ERROR
>
> On occasion when loading the dashboard, you may encounter either of the following errors:
>
> > Report processing stopped because too many rows in summary tables are missing in the CDR database. To resolve this issue, run `dbo.RtcGenerateSummaryTables` on the `LcsCDR` database.
> >
> > Report processing stopped because too many rows in summary tables are missing in the QoE database. To resolve this issue, run `dbo.RtcGenerateSummaryTables` on the `QoEMetrics` database.
>
> To correct this, you must log in to the SQL Server instance and execute the specified procedure.
>
> This will regenerate the summary tables. Only summary tables are affected; no data is lost.

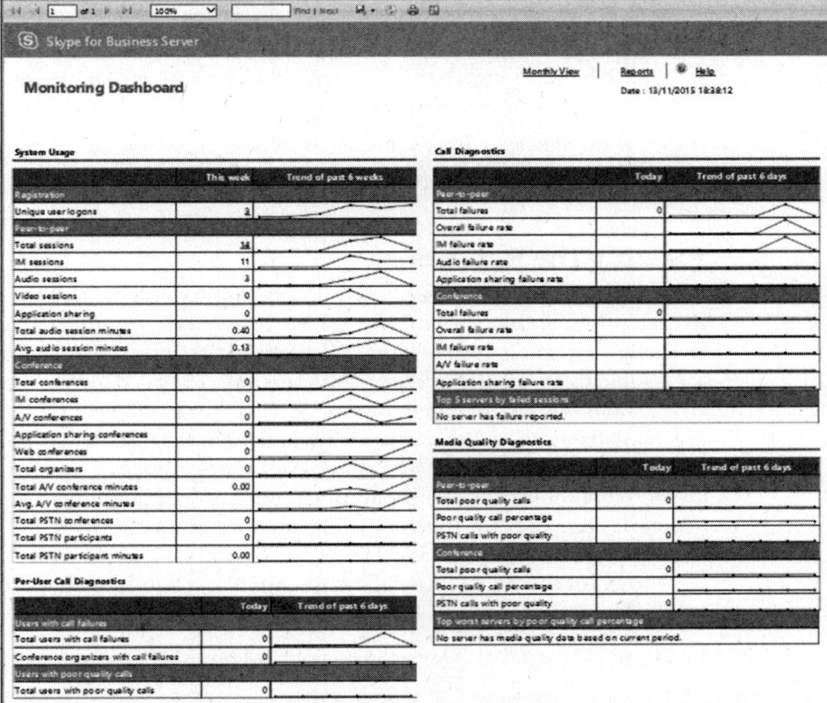

FIGURE 13.6 Weekly dashboard report

Reporting Provides the same types of reports; however, they can be customized based on date ranges or targeted to specific pools or locations.

The reports here can be loosely grouped into four categories.

- System Usage
- Per-User Call Diagnostics
- Call Reliability Diagnostics
- Media Quality Diagnostics

Each of the reports can be further expanded by clicking the built-in hyperlinks in the report to drill further into the details behind the numbers. Figure 13.7 shows the Reporting page.

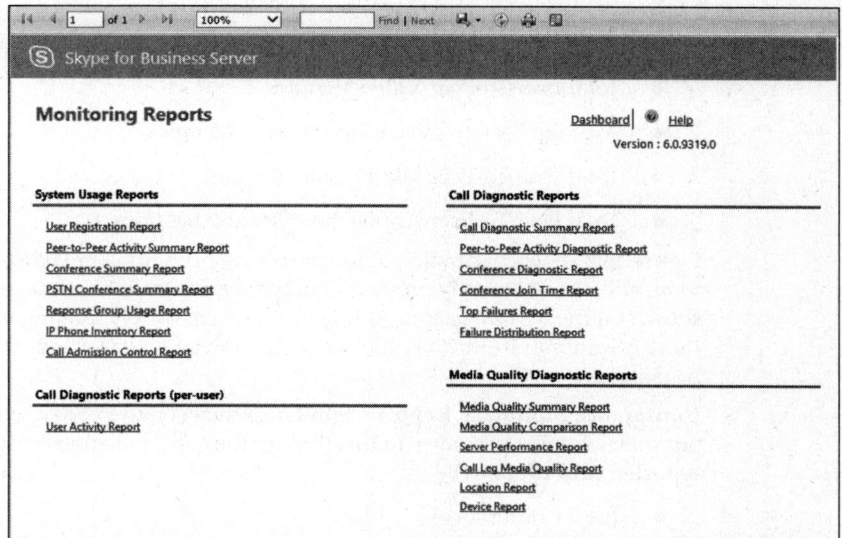

FIGURE 13.7 Reporting home page

System Usage Reports

Within this section, you will find reports used for trend-based analysis, showing the number of connections and typical system usage.

User Registration Report This report provides an at-a-glance view of user login information broken into the following categories:

- Total Logons
- Internal Logons
- External Logons
- Unique Logon Users
- Unique Active Users

By default, this returns both tabular and graphical format broken down on a daily total for all pools; however, this breakdown and pool selection can be modified if required.

Peer-To-Peer Activity Summary Report The Activity Summary Report provides the total breakdown of sessions (the default is daily) for the following communications types:

- Total Peer-To-Peer Sessions
- Total Peer-To-Peer IM Sessions
- Total Peer-To-Peer IM Messages
- Total Peer-To-Peer Audio Sessions
- Total Peer-To-Peer Audio Minutes
- Average Peer-To-Peer Audio Session Minutes
- Total Peer-To-Peer Video Sessions
- Total Peer-To-Peer Video Minutes
- Average Peer-To-Peer Video Session Minutes
- Total Peer-To-Peer File Transfer Sessions
- Total Peer-To-Peer Application Sharing Sessions

Figure 13.8 shows a sample section of this report, with a breakdown of peer-to-peer sessions: total, audio, and IM only on the top graph; with video, file transfer, and application sharing shown on the bottom graph. At this level, you're simply looking at the trend, and as expected, there is minimal traffic over the weekend; however, the various modalities show different peaks.

Conference Summary Report Similar to the Peer-To-Peer Activity Report, the Conference Summary Report provides an insight into the conferencing statistics, with the following data reported (default daily):

- Total Conferences
- Total Participants
- Avg. Participants per Conference
- Total A/V Conferences
- Total A/V Conference Minutes
- Total A/V Conference Participant Minutes
- Avg. A/V Conference Minutes
- Total Unique Conference Organizers
- Total Conference Messages

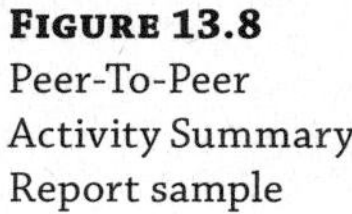

FIGURE 13.8
Peer-To-Peer Activity Summary Report sample

Peer-to-Peer Activity Summary Report

From: 06/11/2015 00:00:00
To: 14/11/2015 00:00:00

Daily	Total peer-to-peer sessions	Total peer-to-peer IM sessions	Total peer-to-peer IM messages	Total peer-to-peer audio sessions	Total peer-to-peer audio session minutes	Avg. peer-to-peer audio session minutes	Total peer-to-peer Video sessions	Total peer-to-peer Video session minutes	Avg. peer-to-peer Video session minutes	Total peer-to-peer file transfer sessions	Total peer-to-peer application sharing sessions
06/11/2015	0	0	0	0	0	0	0	0	0	0	0
07/11/2015	0	0	0	0	0	0	0	0	0	0	0
08/11/2015	0	0	0	0	0	0	0	0	0	0	0
09/11/2015	0	0	0	0	0	0	0	0	0	0	0
10/11/2015	0	0	0	0	0	0	0	0	0	0	0
11/11/2015	14	11	0	3	0	0	0	0	0	0	0
12/11/2015	0	0	0	0	0	0	0	0	0	0	0
13/11/2015	0	0	0	0	0	0	0	0	0	0	0
Total	14	11	0	3	0		0	0		0	0

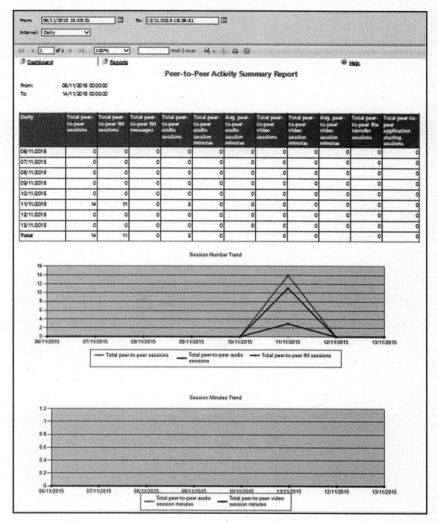

Within these reports, drilling into the detail also shows the conference type, either Audio/Video or Application Sharing.

Figure 13.9 shows a snapshot of the more detailed Conference Activity Report, which is reached via the Conference Summary Report when you select a specific day to view the conference breakdown. This detailed report goes on to break down the different conference types, connection types, and connection locations.

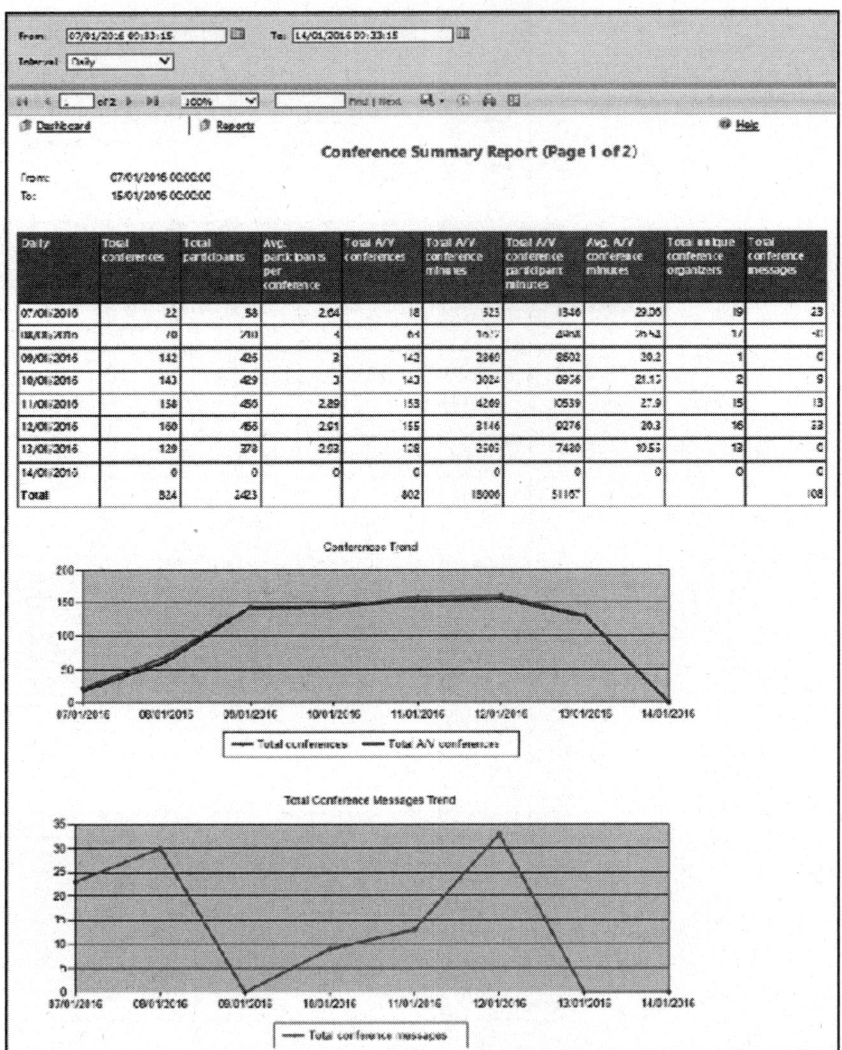

FIGURE 13.9 Conference Summary Report

PSTN Conference Summary Report The PSTN Conference Report provides a view of the conferences that includes PSTN dial-in participants and shows the following:

- Total PSTN Conferences
- Total Participants
- Total A/V Conference Minutes
- Total A/V Conference Participant Minutes
- Total PSTN Participants

- Total PSTN Participant Minutes
- Unique Conference Organizers

Response Group Usage Report This report provides a view of the number of calls being placed to the Response Group service and how they are being answered. The following fields are provided in the initial report:

- Received Calls
- Successful Calls
- Offered Calls
- Answered Calls
- Percentage of Abandoned Calls
- Average Call Minutes by Agent
- Transferred Calls

IP Phone Inventory Report This report provides a view of the deployed phone hardware devices in the environment, specifically these:

- Manufacturer
- Hardware Version
- MAC Address
- User URI
- User Agent
- Last Logon Time
- Last Logoff Time
- Last Activity

Call Admission Control Report This report (shown in Figure 13.10) provides a detailed view of how many calls are being rerouted or rejected based on the policy settings as well as a breakdown of the information per location.

A Diagnostic value of 5 indicates that a call has been rerouted via the PSTN.

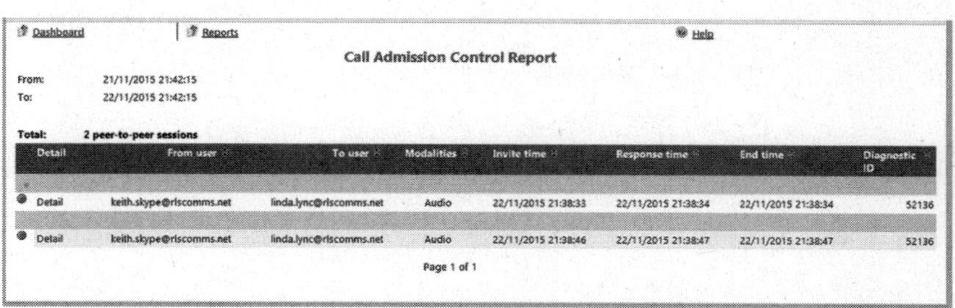

Dashboard | Reports | Help

Call Admission Control Report

From: 21/11/2015 21:42:15
To: 22/11/2015 21:42:15

Total: 2 peer-to-peer sessions

Detail	From user	To user	Modalities	Invite time	Response time	End time	Diagnostic ID
Detail	keith.skype@rlscomms.net	linda.lync@rlscomms.net	Audio	22/11/2015 21:38:33	22/11/2015 21:38:34	22/11/2015 21:38:34	52136
Detail	keith.skype@rlscomms.net	linda.lync@rlscomms.net	Audio	22/11/2015 21:38:46	22/11/2015 21:38:47	22/11/2015 21:38:47	52136

Page 1 of 1

FIGURE 13.10 Call Admission Control Report

Call Admission Control Reporting

Over time, understanding the impact of Call Admission Control is important. If the values are set too high, then potentially the network is overspecified and costs may be reduced by decreasing the capacity. On the other hand, it's more likely that Call Admission Control will reject or reroute calls. If a significant number are reported, this may indicate that Call Admission Control is configured too low. In parallel to this, if the network is nearing capacity, it is an indication that the network is under pressure and bandwidth may need to be increased. See Chapter 17, "Call Admission Control," for more information.

Call Diagnostics Reports (Per-User)

This report is targeted at help-desk staff, and it is used for analysis of activity based on a specific user. The following fields are provided:

- From User
- To User
- Modalities
- Response Time
- End Time
- Diagnostic ID

Call Reliability Diagnostics Reports

The diagnostics reports are most likely to be of interest to network and server administrators; these are the reports that tell you what is going wrong and what needs to be fixed. Within this section, you'll see values such as Expected Failures and Unexpected Failures. Expected failures are items such as a caller hanging up or no answer. Unless there are a significant number of these events, they can typically be ignored. Unexpected failures are the ones that typically need to be investigated and corrected.

This is the section of reporting that has had the biggest change compared to Office Communications Server 2007 R2.

Call Diagnostics Summary Report This diagnostics report covers both peer-to-peer sessions and conferences. A breakdown is provided showing the following data:

- Total Sessions
- Failure Rate
- Session Count by Modality (IM, app share, audio, video, file transfer)
- Failure Rate by Modality

Peer-To-Peer Activity Diagnostic Report The Peer-To-Peer Diagnostics Report focuses only on the peer-to-peer aspect, and it provides a daily breakdown of sessions and failures further broken down by modality. The report shows the following data fields (summary and per modality):

- Date
- Success
- Expected Failures
- Unexpected Failures
- Total Sessions

Conference Diagnostic Report Unsurprisingly, the Conference Diagnostic Report provides the same view as the Peer-To-Peer Diagnostic Report, but for conferences.

Conference Join Time Report This report details how long (in milliseconds) it is taking users to join a conference.

Top Failures Report This report covers the top failures based on reported sessions, also providing the number of users impacted and the weekly trend of a particular failure over the previous eight weeks. Each specific failure item provides the following data in the failure information field:

- Request Type
- Response
- Diagnostic ID
- Category
- Component
- Reason
- Description

This information provides the administrator with a great starting point to begin troubleshooting. Figure 13.11 shows the failure information and trend volume graph for a specific failure item.

Based on this report, the admin would know that the gateway in question is suffering from a relatively steady number of failures before experiencing a sudden peak at the end of the week. This may correlate to a matching increase in call volume, suggesting that the actual failure rate is steady; however, the specific error shown in this case (Unexpected – 504 – Server Internal Error) suggests an issue that needs to be resolved by taking some action. Because it refers to a gateway, this may be faulty hardware or firmware. In this case, further investigation is needed on the gateway itself to determine the cause and resolution.

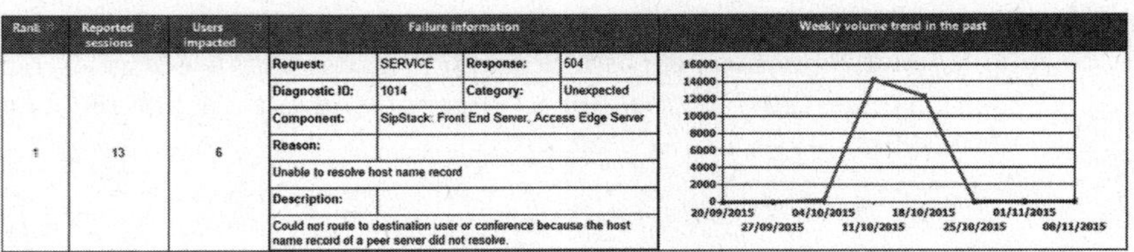

Rank
Reported sessions
Users impacted
Failure information
Weekly volume trend in the past
Request:
SERVICE
Response:
504
Diagnostic ID:
1014
Category:
Unexpected
Component:
SipStack: Front End Server, Access Edge Server
Reason:
Unable to resolve host name record
Description:
Could not route to destination user or conference because the host name record of a peer server did not resolve.
1
13
6
16000
14000
12000
10000
8000
6000
4000
2000
0
20/09/2015
27/09/2015
04/10/2015
11/10/2015
18/10/2015
25/10/2015
01/11/2015
08/11/2015

FIGURE 13.11
Top Failures Report

Failure Distribution Report The Failure Distribution Report provides an overview of the top 10 items on each of the following lists:

- Session Distribution by Top Diagnostic Reasons
- Session Distribution by Top Modalities
- Session Distribution by Top Pools
- Session Distribution by Top Sources
- Session Distribution by Top Components
- Session Distribution by Top From Users
- Session Distribution by Top To Users
- Session Distribution by Top From User Agents

Based on this section, the admin would know that the majority of failures are because of issues with at least one gateway. This is a summary section showing the total of each error type; however, each diagnostic reason is a hyperlink to further break down the issues, allowing specific gateways to be identified.

Media Quality Diagnostics Reports

The final section on the reports home page deals with call quality and diagnostics. These reports provide good information on how the individual components such as servers, devices, and network locations are coping in the environment.

Media Quality Summary Report At a high level, the report is categorized into three sections.

- Audio Call Summary
- Video Call Summary
- Application Sharing Call Summary

Each section provides the quality view of the different endpoints, broken down by the following categories:

- UC Peer to Peer
- UC Conference Sessions
- PSTN Conference Sessions

- PSTN calls (non-bypass): UC Leg
- PSTN calls (non-bypass): Gateway Leg
- Other Call Types

Each of these categories is further broken down by specific software versions of the client or device.

For each combination entry, the following data is displayed:

- Endpoint Type
- Call Volume
- Poor Call Percentage
- Call Volume (Wireless Call)
- Call Volume (VPN Call)
- Call Volume (External Call)
- Round Trip (ms) (Audio Only)
- Degradation (MOS) (Audio Only)
- Packet Loss (Audio Only)
- Jitter (ms) (Audio and App Sharing Only)
- Healer Concealed Ratio (Audio Only)
- Healer Stretched Ratio (Audio Only)
- Healer Compressed Ratio (Audio Only)
- Outbound Packet Loss (Video Only)
- Inbound Packet Loss (Video Only)
- Frozen Frame % (Video Only)
- Outbound Avg. Frame Rate (Video Only)
- Inbound Avg. Frame Rate (Video Only)
- Inbound Low Frame Rate % (Video Only)
- Client Health % (Video Only)
- Avg. Relative One Way (App Sharing Only)
- Avg. RDP Tile Processing Latency (App Sharing Only)
- Total Spoiled Tile % (App Sharing Only)

Media Quality Comparison Report The Media Quality Comparison Report provides a view to the number of calls on a per-day basis over the following items:

- Call Volume
- Degradation (MOS)

- Poor Call Percentage
- Round Trip (ms)
- Packet Loss
- Jitter (ms)
- Healer Concealed Ratio
- Healer Stretched Ratio
- Healer Compressed Ratio

Server Performance Report The Server Performance Report provides insight into the performance of the individual server roles and gateways. It provides data similar to that of the Media Quality Summary Report (and is similarly broken into sections for audio/video/app sharing).

- Server
- Call Volume
- Poor Call Percentage
- Round Trip (ms) (Audio Only)
- Degradation (MOS) (Audio Only)
- Packet Loss (Audio Only)
- Jitter (ms) (Audio And App Sharing Only)
- Healer Concealed Ratio (Audio Only)
- Healer Stretched Ratio (Audio Only)
- Healer Compressed Ratio (Audio Only)
- Outbound Packet Loss (Video Only)
- Inbound Packet Loss (Video Only)
- Frozen Frame % (Video Only)
- Outbound Avg. Frame Rate (Video Only)
- Inbound Avg. Frame Rate (Video Only)
- Inbound Low Frame Rate % (Video Only)
- Client Health % (Video Only)
- Avg. Relative One Way (App Sharing Only)
- Avg. RDP Tile Processing Latency (App Sharing Only)
- Total Spoiled Tile % (App Sharing Only)
- Trend

In addition, an option to view the data trended for the previous week is provided for each server role or gateway.

Codec Healing

The implementation of the media codecs since Lync Server 2010 allowed healing aspects to be contained within them.

These healing capabilities enable the codec to recover from missed or delayed packets, in effect *healing* the media, so that in most cases the user will be unaware of the missing packets because the call will continue and the problems will be undetectable. The impacts of high values in each of these categories are described here:

- High values in *healer concealed ratio* will typically result in distorted or lost audio. This is typically because of packet loss or jitter.
- High values in *healer stretched ratio* will typically result in distorted or robotic-sounding audio. This is typically caused by jitter.
- High values in *healer compressed ratio* will typically result in distorted or accelerated-sounding audio. This is typically caused by jitter.

Location Report Whereas the previous two reports look at the breakdown per endpoint, this report looks at the network viewpoint and shows per subnet (caller and callee).

The following data is provided:

- Caller Subnet
- Callee Subnet
- Call Volume
- Poor Call Percentage
- Round Trip (ms)
- Degradation (MOS)
- Packet Loss
- Jitter (ms)
- Healer Concealed Ratio
- Healer Stretched Ratio
- Healer Compressed Ratio

Device Report The Device Report looks at the specific hardware device model or individual drivers used by the operating system to provide a view on the data. This can provide a useful view of which noncertified devices are being used in the environment, or more likely which calls are being made using built-in devices.

The following view is provided of the data:

- Capture Device
- Render Device
- Call Volume
- Poor Call Percentage
- Unique Users
- Ratio of Voice Switch Time
- Ratio of Microphone Not Functioning
- Ratio of Speaker Not Functioning
- Call With Voice Switch (%)
- Echo in Microphone (%)
- Echo Send (%)
- Calls With Echo (%)

Figure 13.12 shows a sample section from this report.

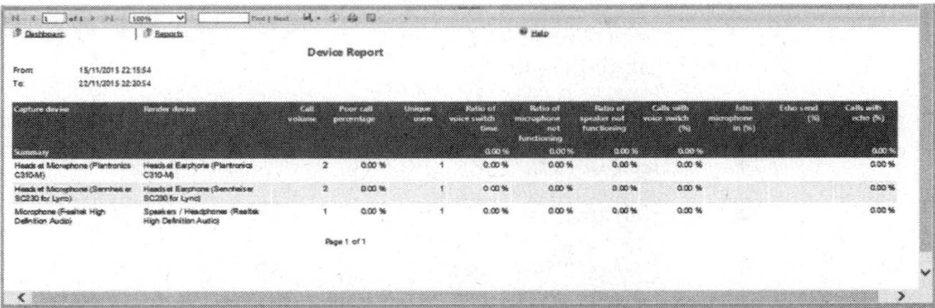

FIGURE 13.12 Device Report

THE CALL DETAIL REPORT

As mentioned, many of these reports link through to other reports, each of which reduces the scope and provides more detailed data resulting in the Call Detail Report, which provides a full breakdown of all the interaction and statistics of the call.

There is no direct method to access this report because it deals with a single call only and, therefore, the data must be filtered in some method first. The quickest route to get call details is to use the User Activity Report to filter on a specific user and then to select the detail of a specific call.

We will discuss the usefulness of this report in Chapter 15, "Troubleshooting." Figure 13.13 shows an example section (note that the "Call Information" section is closed in the screenshot). This report is also known as the Peer-To-Peer Session Detail Report.

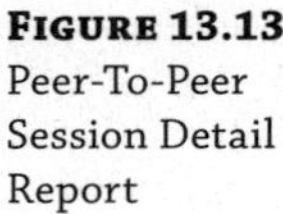

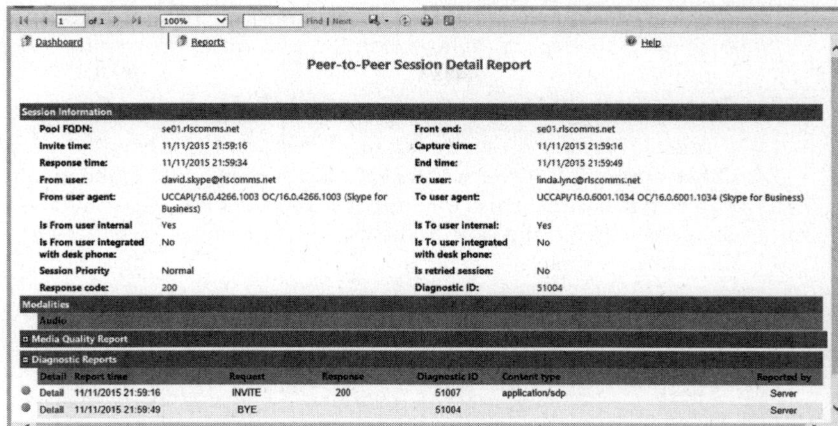

FIGURE 13.13 Peer-To-Peer Session Detail Report

This report contains almost 200 fields of information, broken down into the following sections:

Call Information Here you will see information regarding the users (or PSTN numbers) involved in the call, the start time, and the duration along with client hardware and software version information.

Media Line (Main Audio)—MediaLine Information The Media Line information section deals with the network identifiers such as network address information, internal/external connectivity, connection speeds, and whether any bandwidth controls are in place due to Call Admission Control.

Media Line (Main Audio)—Caller/Callee Device and Signal Metrics Both caller and callee have separate sections here, providing device identifiers (including device driver versions), signal send and receive information, and any hardware (microphone/speaker) issues detected.

Media Line (Main Audio)—Caller/Callee Client Event Again, this is repeated for both caller and callee, and this section provides reporting on the percentage of issues detected around the device hardware and signal.

Media Line (Main Audio)—Audio Stream (Caller ➤ Callee)/(Callee ➤ Caller) This section deals with the specific audio stream in one direction. The following section provides the same data in the other direction. Here you see information regarding the codec used and network impacts (packet loss, jitter, and so on).

Typically, this is the most viewed section because it provides the summary impact due to the underlying network conditions.

Media Line (Main Audio)—Video Stream (Caller ➤ Callee)/(Callee ➤ Caller) The final two sections provide the same information as the preceding except in dealing with the video stream. This is included only for calls that have a video aspect.

A massive amount of information is captured with every call. Some of the fields will be self-explanatory, but you will need more information to understand some of the other fields. In these cases, tooltips are provided, but not all fields have tooltips because they are presumed to be familiar.

Also, to help you understand which values are potentially causing problems, color coding is enabled on the reports. Yellow indicates a warning, and red indicates a high risk of problems.

Customizing Reports

While the number of reports has increased dramatically with each version since the launch of Office Communications Server 2007, they still fall short of the requirements of many customers.

The database schemas for both QoE and CDR databases are detailed in the Skype for Business help file and can also be viewed on TechNet. You can view the QoE schemas at the following location:

```
http://technet.microsoft.com/en-us/library/gg398687.aspx
```

You can view the CDR schemas here:

```
http://technet.microsoft.com/en-us/library/gg398570.aspx
```

Provided the correct permissions are assigned to a user, it is relatively easy to connect to those databases via ODBC and retrieve the data you'll need to provide customized reports. You can also use SQL Server (any version) Report Builder to generate reports that can be added to the web page, enabling easy generation and a single storage/execution location for reports.

Monitoring Service with the Management Pack

The other aspect of monitoring is server or service monitoring, which is needed so that system administrators can alert their users when aspects of the service fail (or begin to fail). Management packs provide a prepackaged set of rules and alert thresholds you can use to quickly set up and monitor the Skype for Business environment. The Skype for Business Monitoring Management Pack is available to download from the following location:

```
https://www.microsoft.com/en-us/download/details.aspx?id=47364
```

Management Pack Improvements

In the feedback that Microsoft received about the previous management packs for Office Communications Server 2007 (specifically the R2 version), one of the most important findings was that the thresholds were set too low, resulting in a deluge of alerts almost upon installation of the management pack. This typically caused administrators to disable the alerts without coming back to tune and enable them at a reasonable level.

Based on this feedback, the management pack was included way back as part of the Lync Server 2010 beta code availability so that customers could provide further feedback, and this has continued with the later beta programs.

The management pack configuration should be tailored to each individual environment (baselined) to ensure that these thresholds do not produce inappropriate alerts. The last thing any administrator wants is to be paged at 1 a.m. for a problem that could wait until morning!

A good example of this scenario is in an Enterprise Edition pool with four Front End servers. If one server fails, the actual Skype for Business services (registrar, routing, Address Book, conferencing, and so on) provided by the pool will continue to operate, and ideally have been scaled to cope with a single server failure, so the impact will be minimal (quite possibly negligible) to the users. The server could wait until morning to be repaired.

Detailed steps on how to configure SCOM are beyond the scope of this book; however, assuming SCOM has been installed and configured with the management pack deployed to discover the Skype for Business servers, the next few steps will show how to change thresholds on alerts from the default. It should be noted that the Lync Server 2010 management pack leveraged the CMS to retrieve the topology, but with Skype for Business (and Lync Server 2013) a slightly different approach is used. The SCOM agents discover themselves and report their existence to the SCOM server. This simplifies the discovery and administration of the environment for SCOM.

From within the System Center Operations Manager (SCOM) 2012 console, select the Authoring tab, and within the management pack objects, select Object Discoveries, change the scope (using the button on the toolbar), and select View All Targets. Enter **Skype** in the Look For box to filter for Skype for Business objects. Figure 13.14 shows the results.

FIGURE 13.14 Changing the scope within SCOM to show Skype for Business objects

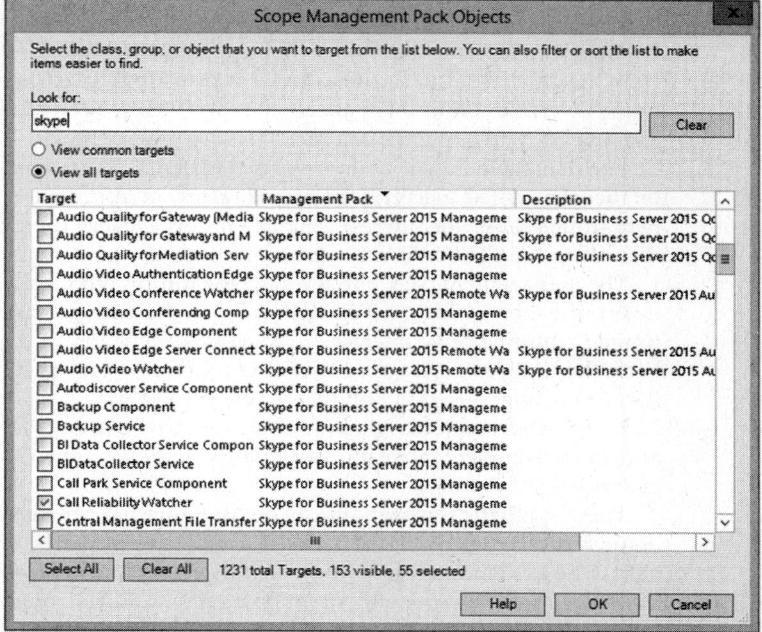

In this example, you will change a scope item, so selecting Audio Quality For Gateway (Mediation Server Bypass) and clicking OK will take you back to the Object Discoveries view, this time including the QoE Discovery entry under the selected type: Audio Quality For Gateway (Mediation Server Bypass).

Right-click QoE Discovery and select Overrides ➢ Override The Object Discovery ➢ For All Objects Of Class: QoE Monitoring. See Figure 13.15.

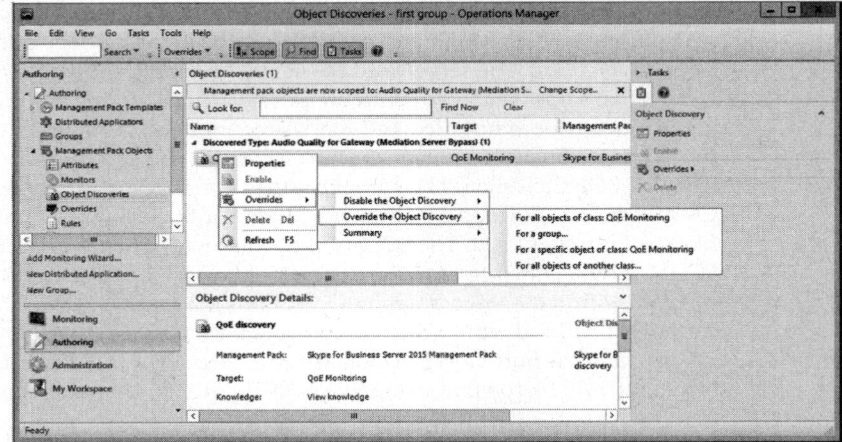

FIGURE 13.15 Enable overrides on Skype for Business–monitored values in SCOM.

The Override Properties page then appears; the Name column indicates the items queried from the database, and the description is provided in the Details window. Selecting an item in the Override column will enable the specific row to be modified at the necessary value, and clicking OK will apply the change.

The management pack raises alerts at different levels, ensuring the correct response based on the impact. The alerts raised provide relevant information to help identify the causes and help troubleshoot, ideally resulting in a faster recovery time. In some cases, there will be links directly to the CDR or QoE record itself.

The management pack will leverage the information from the Central Management Store to determine the topology, which will help you accurately assign the rules to the server roles with limited administrative interaction. So, while Agent Discovery is used for the servers to report back, the CMS is still checked to ensure that the correct capability is assigned on each server—it's just no longer used to find the servers themselves.

End-to-end verification is provided through the use of *synthetic transactions*, which can test almost the complete range of functionality required from a client (including simulation of PSTN calling).

These synthetic transactions can be configured to run periodically (it is recommended to have dedicated accounts configured for this), and a failure can be used to generate a high-priority alert, which is automatically resolved if the command is successful on the next attempt. Synthetic transactions can be run without integration with SCOM; however, for full automated alerting and reporting, SCOM is required. Table 13.3 shows the full list of all synthetic transactions.

TABLE 13.3: Synthetic transactions

SYNTHETIC TRANSACTION CMDLET	DESCRIPTION
`Test-CsAddressBookService*`	Tests the functionality of the Address Book service. This can be used to simulate an individual user.

TABLE 13.3: Synthetic transactions *(CONTINUED)*

SYNTHETIC TRANSACTION CMDLET	DESCRIPTION
`Test-CsAddressBookWebQuery*`	Similar to the `Test-CsAddressBookService`, except it tests the web query functionality.
`Test-CsASConference`	Tests application sharing using a pair of users.
`Test-CsAudioConferencingProvider`	Tests a connection to a third-party audio conference provider.
`Test-CsAVConference*`	Tests audio/video conference functionality using a pair of users.
`Test-CsAVEdgeConnectivity*`	Verifies connectivity using the AV edge component.
`Test-CsCertificateConfiguration`	Returns information on the certificates in use.
`Test-CsClientAuthentication`	Confirms whether a user can log on when using the Skype for Business–provided user certificate.
`Test-CsComputer`	Verifies that services are running, Active Directory groups have been configured correctly, and the firewall ports have been opened.
`Test-CsDatabase`	Tests configuration of the databases.
`Test-CsDataConference*`	Verifies user participation within a data collaboration conference session.
`Test-CsDialPlan`	Tests a phone number against a dial plan, returning the normalization rule, which will be applied, and the results of that normalization.
`Test-CsExStorageConnectivity`	Verifies that the Lync Server Storage Service is working on a Front End server.
`Test-CsExStorageNotification`	Verifies that the Lync Server Storage Service can subscribe to the Exchange Server 2013 notification service.
`Test-CsExUMConnectivity*`	Tests connectivity to Exchange UM.
`Test-CsExUMVoiceMail`	Verifies connectivity and that a voice mail message was left.
`Test-CsFederatedPartner`	Confirms the status of federation with an external domain.
`Test-CsGroupExpansion`	Confirms the functionality of the group expansion capability on the pool.
`Test-CsGroupIM*`	Tests the ability of two users to carry out an IM conference.
`Test-CsIM*`	Tests the ability of two users to carry out a peer-to-peer IM.
`Test-CsInterTrunkRouting`	Verifies routing and PSTN usage via a specific SIP trunk.

TABLE 13.3: Synthetic transactions *(CONTINUED)*

SYNTHETIC TRANSACTION CMDLET	DESCRIPTION
`Test-CsKerberosAccountAssignment`	Verifies that the assigned Kerberos account is working correctly.
`Test-CsLisCivicAddress`	Verifies address information against the Master Street Address Guide held by the E911 provider. This is the only test cmdlet that is not a synthetic test. It is capable of updating the LIS database.
`Test-CsLisConfiguration`	Confirms the address configuration when given a specific subnet (or other location identifier).
`Test-CsLocationPolicy`	Determines which location policy will be used.
`Test-CsMcxConference`	Tests three-user participation in a conference via the Mobility Service.
`Test-CsMcxP2PIM*`	Tests a peer-to-peer IM via the Mobility Service.
`Test-CsMcxPushNotification`	Tests that the push notification (Apple and Microsoft) service is working.
`Test-CsOUPermission`	Verifies that the permissions have been applied correctly within the Active Directory OU.
`Test-CsP2PAV*`	Tests audio/video functionality using a pair of users in peer-to-peer mode (rather than conferencing).
`Test-PersistentChatMessage*`	Verifies that a message between two users using the Persistent Chat service has been sent and received.
`Test-CsPhoneBootstrap`	Verifies that the environment is configured to allow 2010 Phone Edition devices to connect and that a user can log on.
`Test-CsPresence*`	Confirms that a user can log on and publish presence information as well as receive presence updates from another user.
`Test-CsPstnOutboundCall`	Tests the ability of a user to make a PSTN call. A call will actually be placed and must be answered for this test to succeed.
`Test-CsPstnPeerToPeerCall*`	Similar to `Test-CsPstnPeerToPeerCall`, except the cmdlet places a call to another user via the gateway and will answer the call on behalf of the user.
`Test-CsRegistration*`	Confirms whether a user can log on.
`Test-CsReplica`	Verifies the status of replica service on the local computer.

Table 13.3: Synthetic transactions *(continued)*

Synthetic Transaction Cmdlet	Description
`Test-CsSetupPermission`	Confirms that Active Directory has been configured to allow Skype for Business to be installed.
`Test-CsTopology`	Allows testing of the validity of a server or service.
`Test-CsTrunkConfiguration`	Confirms the operation of the trunk configuration when presented with a phone number.
`Test-CsUcwaConference`	Tests connectivity through the web service to a conference for two users.
`Test-CsUnifiedContactStore*`	Verifies whether the Unified Contact Store can access a user's contacts.
`Test-CsVoiceNormalizationRule`	Tests a phone number against a specific normalization rule and returns the resulting number after the rule has been applied.
`Test-CsVoicePolicy`	Tests a phone number against a specific voice policy and returns the determined route.
`Test-CsVoiceRoute`	Tests a phone number against a specific route pattern and returns success or fail based on whether the number is accepted by the route.
`Test-CsVoiceTestConfiguration`	Tests a combination of dial plan and policy to confirm that routing works as expected.
`Test-CsVoiceUser`	Confirms the route for a PSTN call from a specific user based on the voice configuration.
`Test-CsWatcherNodeConfiguration`	Verifies the watcher node configuration.
`Test-CsWebApp`	Verifies that authenticated users can use Web App to join a conference.
`Test-CsWebAppAnonymous`	Verifies that anonymous users can use the Web App to join a conference.
`Test-CsWebScheduler`	Tests whether a user can use the Web Scheduler to schedule an online meeting.
`Test-CsXmppIM*`	Tests sending of a message via an XMPP gateway.

** Indicates items that can be used by SCOM for continuous synthetic transaction testing.*

For component monitoring (via SCOM), the alerts are separated into Key Health Indicators and non–Key Health Indicators. A Key Health Indicator is a service-impacting issue (which is worth being paged about at 1 a.m.), and non–Key Health Indicators are those aspects that do not impact service, such as problems with components that have resiliency. These are automatically resolved if the service returns to health.

Chapter 15 provides more details (and examples) of running synthetic transactions from within PowerShell (without using SCOM integration).

Deploying Synthetic Transactions with SCOM

While running the synthetic transactions from the PowerShell environment is a relatively straightforward task, configuring automatic transaction execution and monitoring within SCOM is a multistep process.

You'll need to define one or more watcher nodes. A *watcher node* is a server responsible for periodically executing synthetic transactions for a pool. If you have deployed multiple pools and want to have automatic synthetic transactions run on each of them, you will need one server per pool.

The server should have the following minimum specifications:

- Four-core processor 2.33GHz or higher
- 8GB RAM
- 1Gbps network adapter
- Windows Server 2008 R2 or Windows Server 2012

The additional software prerequisites for the watcher node are as follows:

- .NET Framework 4.5
- Windows Identity Foundation
- System Center Operations Manager (SCOM) Agent
- Skype for Business core installation files (`OCSCORE.msi`)
- Unified Communications Managed API

In addition to having a SCOM Agent installed, the Skype for Business core and Skype for Business Replica MSI files need to be installed onto the watcher node. The easiest way to do this is to run the Skype for Business Server `setup.exe` file with the `/BootStrapLocalMgmt` switch. Then verify the installation by opening the Skype for Business Management Shell and running the `Get-CsWatcherNodeConfiguration` cmdlet.

If this command is being run for the first time, no response is expected because nothing is yet configured for the watcher node. If a response is received, it typically indicates an error.

Occasionally, we have seen the command-line execution of `setup.exe` fail to enable the Skype for Business services upon completion—be sure to check!

Once the core components are installed, the `Watchernode.msi` executable needs to be run to install the components specific to the watcher node. This executable is available from the same download location as the management pack.

Watcher nodes can be installed both inside and outside the enterprise to verify a large number of aspects of a Skype for Business deployment.

A watcher node can use two types of authentication.

- ◆ Trusted server (using certificates)
- ◆ Credentials (using a username and password)

Because the watcher node is not directly part of the topology, a trusted application pool must be configured with the watcher node as a member server of the application pool. Once the pool is created, a trusted application service is created.

Both of these tasks can be performed using PowerShell or Topology Builder. There are no options to configure trusted applications in the Control Panel.

To create a new Trusted Application pool, first identify the site ID (`SiteId`) for the site to which the application pool will be associated. Figure 13.16 shows the output of `Get-CsSite`.

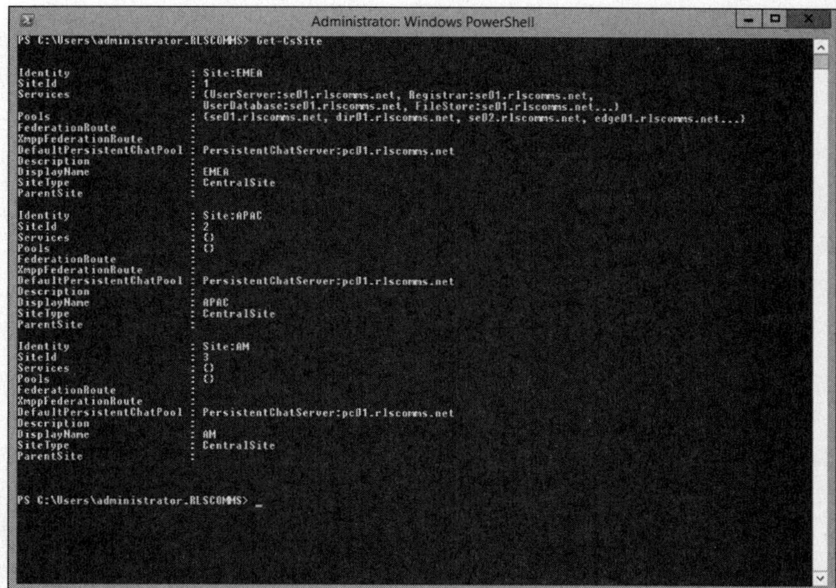

FIGURE 13.16
Output of `Get-CsSite`

With the site ID, run the following command (where the `Identity` parameter is the FQDN of the watcher node):

```
New-CsTrustedApplicationPool -Identity watcher01.rlscomms.net -Site 1
-Registrar se01.rlscomms.net-ThrottleAsServer $True
-TreatAsAuthenticated $True -OutboundOnly $False -RequiresReplication $True
-ComputerFqdn watcher01.rlscomms.net
```

The response will be similar to this:

```
Identity              : 1-ExternalServer-11
Registrar             : Registrar:se01.rlscomms.net
```

```
FileStore             :
ThrottleAsServer      : True
TreatAsAuthenticated : True
OutboundOnly          : False
RequiresReplication  : True
AudioPortStart        :
AudioPortCount        : 0
AppSharingPortStart  :
AppSharingPortCount  : 0
VideoPortStart        :
VideoPortCount        : 0
Applications          : {}
DependantServiceList : {}
ServiceId             : 1-ExternalServer-11
SiteId                : Site:EMEA
PoolFqdn              : watcher01.rlscomms.net
Version               : 7
Role                  : TrustedApplicationPool
```

`Get-CsPool` can also be run to verify that the application pool is configured.

The trusted application service is created using the following command:

```
New-CsTrustedApplication -ApplicationId "STWatcher-01"
-TrustedApplicationPoolFqdn watcher01.rlscomms.net-Port 5061
```

The `ApplicationId` parameter can be any text entry. You can include the site name or ID so that it is easy to identify which application is dealing with which site. The `Port` parameter can be any unused port.

Figure 13.17 shows the result of this command.

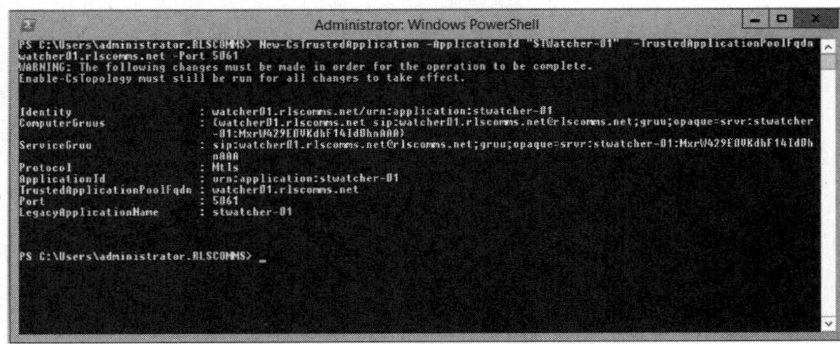

FIGURE 13.17
`New-CsTrustedApplication`

The `Enable-CsTopology` cmdlet needs to be run to apply these topology changes.

There is no output from this cmdlet, although status bars are displayed across the top of the PowerShell window.

To use certificate authentication, you'll need to request a certificate for the watcher node. You can use the same certificate wizard used in the rest of the Skype for Business Server role setup processes, only this time you can start it by using the Skype for Business Server Deployment Wizard from the Start menu. Once it's started, click Install Or Update Skype for Business Server System ➤ Request, Install, Or Assign Certificate and follow the now-familiar certificate wizard to request and assign a default certificate.

Next you'll need to install the actual `Watchernode.msi` file, and because you're using certificate authentication, you must use the following command:

```
Watchernode.msi Authentication=TrustedServer
```

For some reason, Microsoft has made this command case sensitive!

If you wanted to use credential authentication, the watcher node computer network service account should be added to the RTC Local Read-only Administrators group on the local computer. The command for credential authentication is as follows:

```
Watchernode.msi Authentication=Negotiate
```

Once the `WatcherNode.msi` executable has completed, you need to restart the server for it to take effect.

You'll need to create and assign user accounts to the Health Monitoring Configuration entry, using the following command:

```
New-CsHealthMonitoringConfiguration -TargetFqdn se01.rlscomms.net
-FirstTestUserSipUri sip:test1_skype@rlscomms.net
-SecondTestUserSipUri sip:test2_skype@rlscomms.net
```

The output will be as shown here:

```
Identity                  : se01.rlscomms.net
FirstTestUserSipUri       : sip:test1_skype@rlscomms.net
FirstTestSamAccountName   :
SecondTestUserSipUri      : sip:test2_skype@rlscomms.net
SecondTestSamAccountName  :
TargetFqdn                : se01.rlscomms.net
```

The *health monitoring configuration* is the stored configuration that is used for the synthetic transactions. `Test-Cs*` cmdlets that require user accounts will use accounts from this configuration, if available; otherwise, they will prompt for the account information. Obviously, for a noninteractive solution within SCOM, you'll need to use this stored configuration.

`Set-CsTestUserCredential` can also be used to define multiple user credentials for testing. This requires the storing of the user passwords in the Credential Manager Store on the machine in which it is run, so it must be run on the watcher node itself.

For machines outside the corporate network, this method must be used (do not use actual "live" user accounts for this!):

```
Set-CsTestUserCredential -SipAddress "sip:test1_skype@rlscomms.net"
-UserName "rlscomms\test1_skype" -Password "Password1"
Set-CsTestUserCredential -SipAddress "sip:test2_skype@rlscomms.net"
-UserName "rlscomms\test2_skype" -Password "Password1"
```

Up to this point, you have configured the watcher node and the user accounts, but you have yet to define the watcher node configuration; you do this by using the `New-CsWatcherNodeConfiguration` cmdlet as shown here. Figure 13.18 shows the output.

```
New-CsWatcherNodeConfiguration -TargetFqdn se01.rlscomms.net
-PortNumber 5061 -TestUsers
@{Add= "sip:test1_skype@rlscomms.net","sip:test2_skype@rlscomms.net"}
```

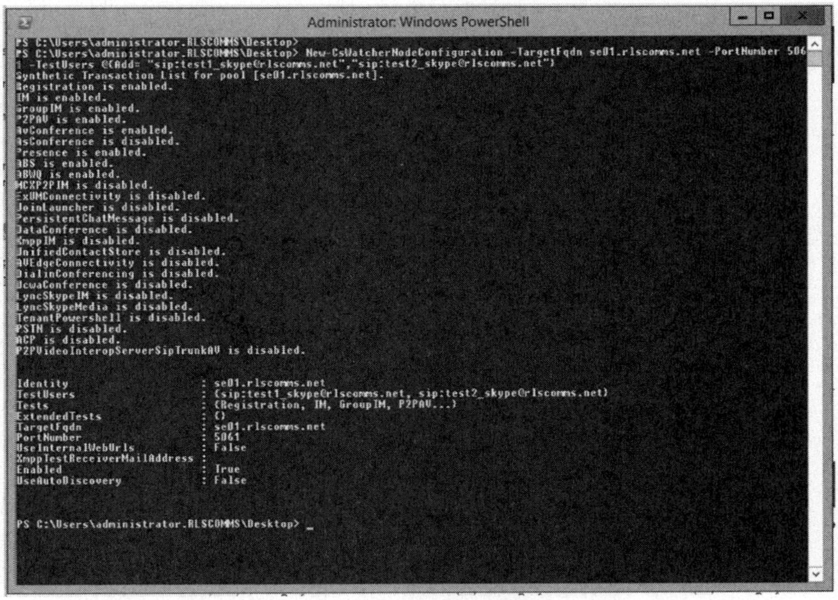

FIGURE 13.18
Defining the watch node configuration

You can see from the output two entries for defined tests.

- `Tests`
- `ExtendedTests`

These entries allow you to configure the tests for each watcher node; you may have certain functionality you want to test on a particular pool, for example. By default, the `ExtendedTests` entry is empty, and the `Tests` entry contains the following tests:

- Registration
- IM
- GroupIM
- P2PAV (peer-to-peer audio/video sessions)
- AvConference (audio/conferencing)
- Presence
- ABS (Address Book service)
- ABWQ (Address Book Web Query)

To create and enable an extended test, you must use the -ExtendedTests parameter, but first you must define the test and assign to a variable, as in the following example:

```
$extest = New-CsExtendedTest -TestUsers "sip:test1_skype@rlscomms.net",
"sip:test2_skype@rlscomms.net" -Name "PSTN Test" -TestType "PSTN"
New-CsWatcherNodeConfiguration -TargetFqdn "se01.rlscomms.net"
-PortNumber 5061 -TestUsers "sip:test1_skype@rlscomms.net",
"sip:test2_skype@rlscomms.net" -ExtendedTests @{Add=$x}
```

Figure 13.19 shows the synthetic transactions in operation. In this case, the Front End server has been shut down, so you can see the synthetic transaction failure alerts. When the servers come back online, they will automatically clear (when the next synthetic transaction is successful).

FIGURE 13.19 Synthetic transaction failure alerts

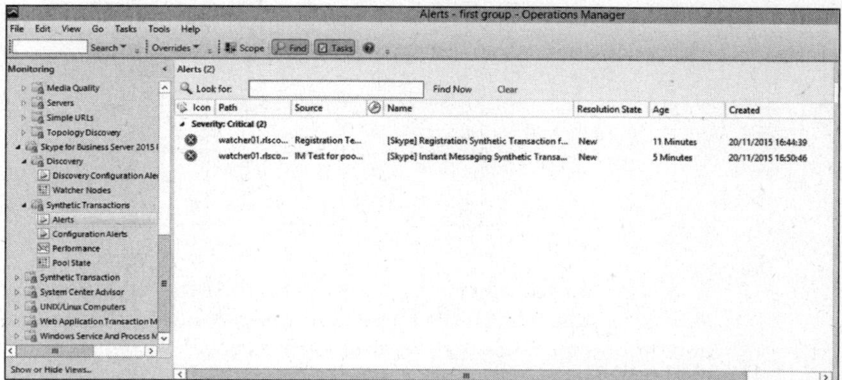

Useful information is contained within the Alert Details section, providing initial suggestions on the problem and where to begin troubleshooting.

Using Statistics Manager

Building on to the SCOM monitoring is a free download from Microsoft called Statistics Manager that enables real-time Key Health Indicator reporting via a web interface.

You can find the download here:

```
https://www.microsoft.com/en-us/download/details.aspx?id=49491
```

Three files are part of the package.

- StatsManPerfAgent.msi
- StatsManPerfAgentListener.msi
- StatsManWebSite.msi

In addition, the installation requires a component called Redis as its prerequisite (version 2.8 or later). You can find it at this location:

`https://github.com/MSOpenTech/redis/releases`

Figure 13.20 shows the architecture of how these tie together.

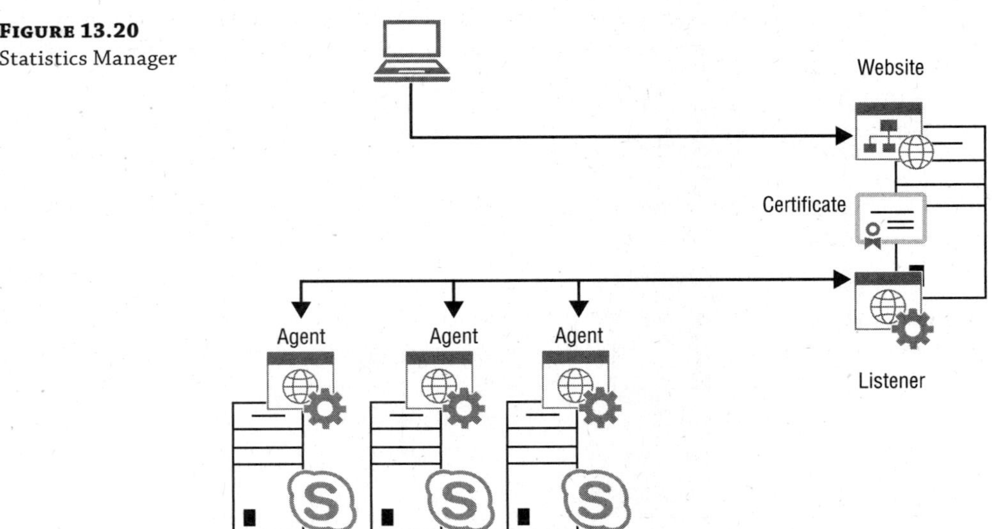

FIGURE 13.20
Statistics Manager

As you can see, you need a server to run this collection and reporting process, and the only prerequisite for this is that it is running Windows Server 2012 R2 or later. The installation process for Redis is straightforward; as usual, accept the EULA and define the installation directory. Figure 13.21 shows only configuration available in the installation, and the recommendation is to leave the default values.

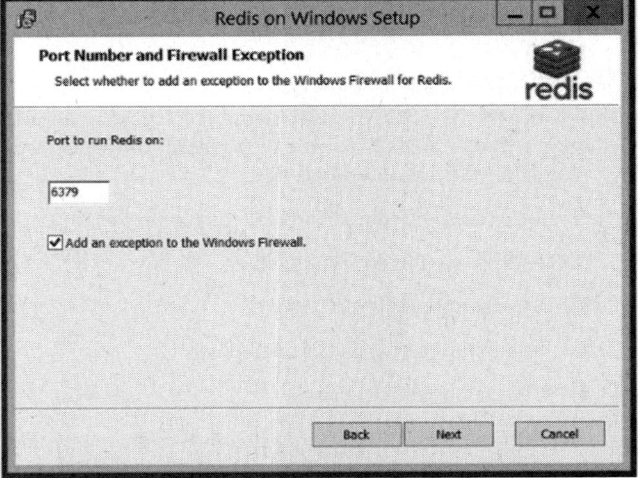

FIGURE 13.21
Redis installation

Once it's installed, you will need to request a certificate. The certificate is used to encrypt the data transfer from the agents to the listener and can be used for the website if required. The agents and listener only use the certificate thumbprint, so there is no need for a "proper" certificate chain to be used; a self-signed one is fine. You can create one using the following PowerShell:

```
New-SelfSignedCertificate -DnsName StatsManListener -CertStoreLocation Cert:
\LocalMachine\My
```

The next step is to install the listener application, `StatsManPerfAgentListener.msi`. As with the Redis app, there's only one configuration page, as shown in Figure 13.22.

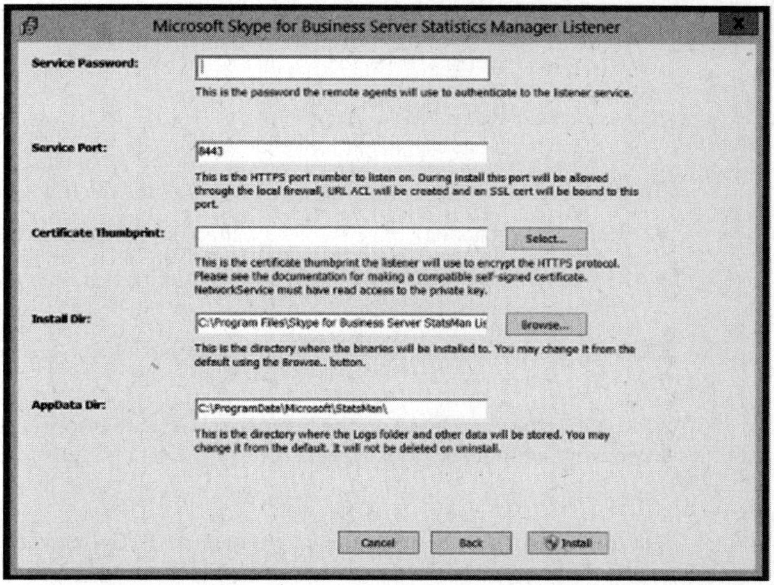

FIGURE 13.22
Configuring the listener

A few items need to be completed here. The service password is used as a preshared key between the agents and the listener. The Select button allows you to define which certificate thumbprint will be used for the encryption.

Once you have it installed, you can check the status by browsing to `https://localhost:8443/healthcheck` on the listener server. A simple text page is returned including some of the text shown here:

```
HealthCheckRequestCount: 1
InvalidCredentialsCount: 0
InvalidHttpRequests: 0
MessageDecodeFailureCount: 0
MessageReceivedCount: 0
ReceivedBytesTotal: 0
```

```
CurrentMessagesReceivedPerSecond: 0
MessagesPerSecondTimeFrameMilliseconds: 79,770
MessagesReceivedPerSecondPeak: 0
ValuesWritten: 0
ValuesWrittenInternal: 0
CurrentValuesWrittenPerSecond: 0
ValuesWrittenPerSecondTimeFrameMilliseconds: 79,770
ValuesWrittenPerSecondPeak: 0
ValuesWrittenSampleStoreFailures: 0
ValuesWrittenPersistentStoreFailures: 0
ValuesWrittenUpdateStoreFailures: 0
ValuesFilteredFromAggregation: 0
CounterStoreWriterCount: 0
KnownServerCount: 1
CounterBucketCount: 0
CounterBucketLostDataCount: 0
BucketAddDataValueFailureCount: 0
TotalCounterBucketAggregationValues: 0
```

To ensure everything is working correctly, look for the following:

- If the `/healthcheck` page shows up, then the listener has been installed successfully.
- If `KnownServerCount` (shown in bold) is 1 or higher, then the connection to the Redis installation was successful.

Once agents have been installed, you can come back and check that the `ValuesWritten` counter is incrementing.

One step to be completed on the listener server is to import the server role configuration; this is taken from a topology pool export.

```
Get-CsPool | Export-CliXml -Path poolinfo.xml
```

On the listener server, navigate to `C:\Program Files\Skype for Business Server StatsMan Listener` and execute the following:

```
.\Updates-StatManServerInfo.ps1 -CsPoolFile poolinfo.xml
```

Next up is to install the Statistics Manager website using `StatsManWebSite.msi`. Another straightforward installation process, Figure 13.23 shows the only configuration options available.

The default web port used is 8080, and if needed, you can change this later using IIS Manager. Security is provided via a local security group called `StatsManWebSiteUsers`, and you can add accounts to this group as needed.

Once that's configured, you'll see a screen similar to Figure 13.24.

Once the website is up and running, it's time to install agents, using the `StatsManPerfAgent.msi` file. Similar to the listener configuration (Figure 13.22), there are prompts for the password and the certificate thumbprint, as well as the usual EULA to accept. Once configured, the agent will run and start to feedback data; it can take up to 15 minutes before data starts to be displayed.

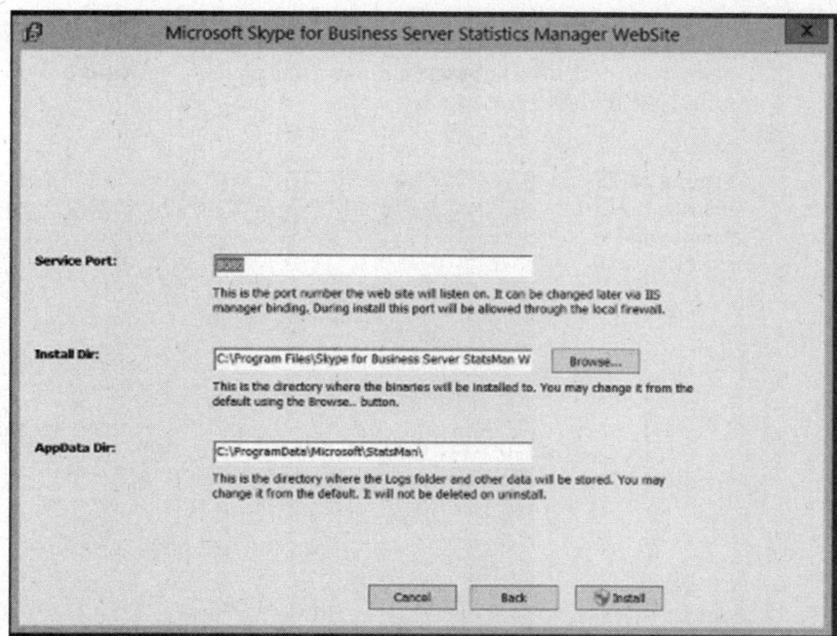

FIGURE 13.23 Configuring the website

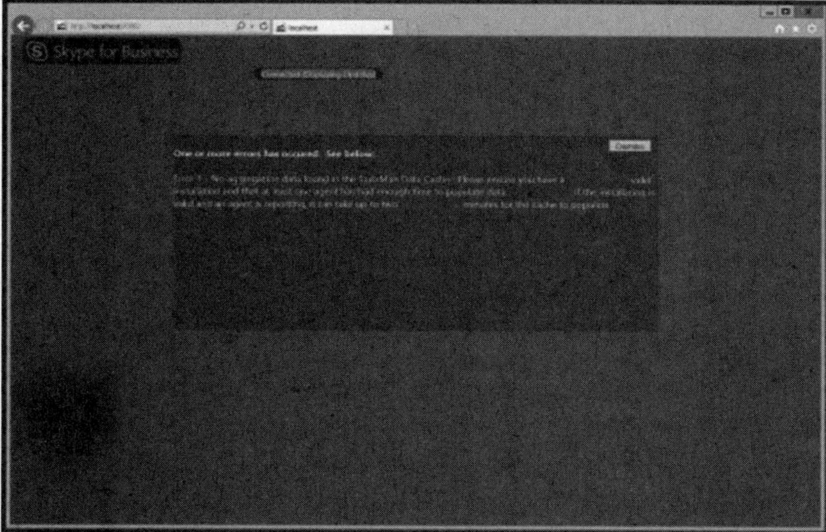

FIGURE 13.24 Viewing the website

Repeat this agent installation on each Skype for Business Server machine.

Once agents are installed, browse to the /heathcheck page to verify, and then once data is being returned, browse to the main website page to view and browse the stats. See Figure 13.25 for a view of the KHI summary.

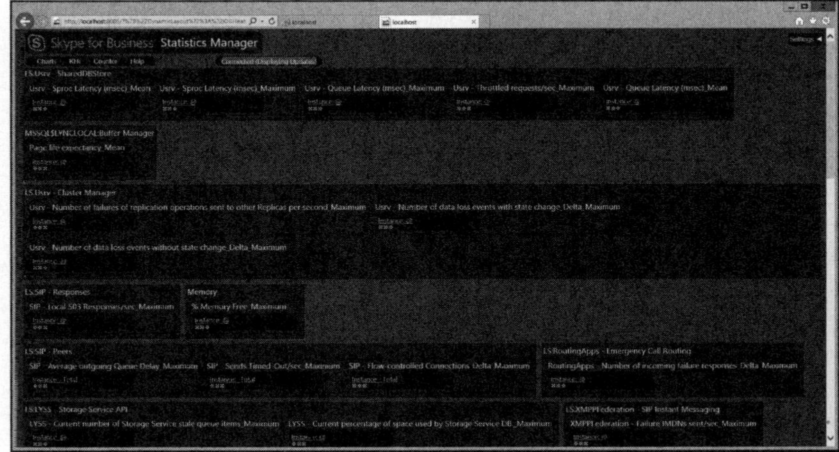

FIGURE 13.25 Viewing the KHI summary website (with data)

The Bottom Line

Understand the architecture for the Archiving and Monitoring roles. Although related to different aspects of the data, the Archiving and Monitoring services are similar in function, and they have similar back-end requirements. This allows them to be easily colocated and share the same database server or instance.

Master It What are the options available for enabling Archiving?

Provide reporting on the data available from the Archiving and Monitoring roles. Skype for Business Server 2015 provides a monitoring reports pack containing more than 50 reports, which focus on the QoE data. Non-Microsoft vendors provide additional report capability for the other databases, and of course, you can always write your own reports.

Master It What options are available for creating customized reports?

Use the capabilities in the System Center Operations Manager management pack to report on the availability of the Skype for Business Server service. With the implementation of the Skype for Business Server 2015 Monitoring Management Pack for System Center Operations Manager, administrators have a consolidated approach and location for collating and monitoring system (and service) uptime.

Master It Which synthetic transactions will confirm the status of the Address Book service?

Chapter 14

Planning for Adoption

Throughout this book, we've discussed a wide range of topics, explored details of the Skype for Business product, and even delved into integration with third-party products. However, all this technical information is not enough to ensure that you have a successful experience with Skype for Business.

Skype for Business is a Unified Communications (UC) platform and, as such, has the potential to radically change a business. In particular, it changes the way people communicate. There are so many potential benefits of Unified Communications that it has become one of the top chief information officer (CIO) priorities in recent years. However, unless this radical change is managed correctly within a business, it can easily cause anxiety and resentment, which hinder the implementation of the technology and slow the pace at which a business sees a return on its investment. After all, a business is simply a bunch of people who know things, and without them all you have is a shell, or perhaps a brand. You need to take these people with you on your journey with Skype for Business. This chapter aims to show you how!

Understanding why the move to Skype for Business is happening will help drive the success criteria. Is it simply an upgrade to stay within supported product boundaries? Or, is it to introduce new functionality?

In this chapter, you will learn to

- Understand the impact of UC on the users
- Understand the importance of choosing the correct users for piloting

Understanding the Power of UC

Unified Communications is one of the big buzz phrases in IT, rivaled only by "the cloud" and "virtualization." It is notoriously hard to define, and people have various understandings of its meaning. For us, *Unified Communications* is all about providing customers—both end users and more widely the companies they work for—with the ability to work efficiently by communicating and collaborating through whatever means necessary, wherever and whenever they need to work. This communication might be either one-to-one or multiparty and either internal or across organizations. Communication should be woven tightly into an organization and integrated with the business process to drive productivity and efficiency. In that sense, UC could be thought of more as ubiquitous communication.

Of course, that utopian vision requires a fair amount of work in the background. There is the technical challenge of integrating and providing communication modalities such as voice, video, instant messaging (IM), email, voice mail, SMS, and fax, which we have covered in depth in this book. However, in many ways, the technical challenge is far simpler than changing the culture of a business, making information about people and process freely available, and changing the way people work and communicate. Any company that embarks on a Unified Communications project needs to clearly identify why they are doing so, what they must achieve, and how they will bring this change to users.

The Promise

As you can see, UC has immense power. It can allow people to communicate more efficiently than ever before, potentially saving companies millions in hard cash in several ways. For example, instead of spending money on a cents-per-minute basis with third-party conferencing services, with Skype for Business you can bring this bridge functionality in house. In large companies, this has regularly shown savings in the order of millions or even tens of millions of dollars per year. Even in small companies of a few hundred people, it can save several thousand dollars a year, which is enough to contribute significantly to the deployment costs. Another significant savings possibility is that of travel reduction. Although we are in no way advocating stopping travel altogether, there might be chance to cut back, by perhaps sending only one person to meet a customer while the other dials in using voice and video to a meeting. Similarly, instead of senior managers all traveling to meet each other on a regular basis, some of these meetings could be held using solely Skype for Business or also in conjunction with a third party like Polycom, thereby saving travel costs and time and reducing the company's carbon footprint, which is so important these days. Other significant reductions in cost can be made through the flexibility Skype for Business brings—for example, enabling people to work from home or from various different locations without necessarily coming into the central office all the time.

Other benefits are harder to quantify. Skype for Business brings people together; as we've said, a business is only a bunch of people who know things working together. In that capacity, if these people cannot communicate quickly and efficiently, then you are simply not allowing them to work to their fullest potential. Enabling efficient communication can speed up business processes—for example, by allowing automated document sign-off through routing to the most suitable person based on availability—and it can make resorting to voice mail a rarity, because presence makes a person's availability known. Finally, all these examples can easily be extended outside a single company to a wide ecosystem of partners and customers, allowing even wider savings and better customer service.

The Pitfalls

Unified Communications products often challenge organizational structure. Skype for Business is no different. In fact, given that it is so successful as a true UC product bringing together IM, voice, video, and conferencing, it is perhaps even more disruptive. Traditionally, companies have had a networking team and a server team. Often there has also been a telephony team, which potentially in recent times has merged or coexisted with the networking team. Skype for Business, of course, doesn't fit nicely into these boundaries. One of the major challenges many organizations will face is how to fit Skype for Business into this structure. For some companies, this can stall the project rollout of Skype for Business; other companies have to take a serious look at why they want Skype for Business and then work out what the future looks like. In many senses, that could be a combined working party or a complete restructuring, as the server team takes on board the new technology and brings in elements of the telephony and networking teams to make this work.

What is important is to be aware of the broader goal of deploying Skype for Business and not to get bogged down in all the politics that inevitably occur as change happens within a business. Clarity of communication is important so that people know what is happening, why it is being done, and what it means to them. Leadership is essential; projects sponsored by a strong CIO have far more chance of success than something led by a team from IT (often the server team), who inevitably end up fighting battles with networks and telecoms.

People react strongly to change, and not usually in a positive way. Of course, there are some who embrace change, but more often than not, people shy away from something different. This is simple human nature. However, in situations where you have placed your reputation on driving a successful rollout of new technology, it is something that needs significant thought to overcome. Much of the reticence can be overcome by explanation and user training. All the elements outlined in "The Promise" earlier, when combined, offer huge potential; it is critically important that these messages are understood not just by the CIO who signs off on the project but by the business as a whole. People need to be shown how this new technology makes their working lives easier.

Introducing Skype for Business to Your Business

Now that you've looked at the power of UC and some of the human-related pitfalls that can befall deployments of this nature, let's move on to how best to address the rollout of Skype for Business in your business. There are two major elements; one is to run a pilot, and the other is to ensure adequate training for users. However, there are also surrounding efforts that can be undertaken to play roles in a successful deployment.

Rolling out a new technology can be seen very much as launching a new product. As such, it is sensible to mount a marketing campaign. Many companies, for example, create posters and ads for display in prominent locations and on intranet portals. They help communicate key messages about the features of the new technology, such as the ability to create conference calls with ease; they also communicate why the business is deploying the technology, such as work flexibility and cost savings.

The most successful examples of this type of campaign that we've been involved with created excitement before deployment, gradually enforced the messaging, added new information about features and functions, and highlighted where users could get support and learn more at their own pace. This type of prelaunch marketing campaign should utilize all the media types available, including items such as posters, websites, email messaging, and videos, perhaps from the CEO or other senior managers.

Skype for Business Is More Than Just a Telephone System

Although Skype for Business can replace a telephony system or conferencing platform, it is really important that you fight the widespread assumption that Skype for Business is simply a replacement for whatever was previously in place. Simply put, it isn't! Yes, Skype for Business takes over many

continues

continued

functions provided by other communication platforms in the past; however, as we've mentioned many times, Skype for Business is much more. It is a unified platform that allows not only communication in its own right, but communication as part of the business process.

It is absolutely essential that this mind-set is positioned correctly at the highest levels of the company. This is not always a problem; sometimes people just "get it." But if your senior personnel think of Skype for Business as "just another phone system," you will be limited, because the messages coming down from them will not be positive and will not have the changing effect that Skype for Business can have. Be aware of this possibility and use all the resources available from Microsoft and the partner community to demonstrate the wider benefits and uses of Skype for Business to ensure that your organization gets the most out of it.

Clearly not all of these and the following ideas will work for everyone, as every company is different; however, these suggestions have been tried and tested in several different scenarios and have been found to be useful.

Piloting Skype for Business

Once you have decided to roll out Skype for Business, running a pilot is essential. This may take a couple of different forms. You may find that running a proof of concept (PoC) is necessary to evaluate specific features and functionality. The PoC would likely have specific success criteria and look at only a handful of features. It would be carried out to prove that Skype for Business can meet the stated requirements. It is important to make sure that the PoC isn't confused with a full pilot. The full pilot program should take place once the production deployment of Skype for Business is completed. That way, people participating in the pilot would be running on the actual systems, which would be taken live if the pilot succeeds.

When starting up the main pilot, the first thing to undertake is to set out the success criteria. Without this, you will never know whether you have succeeded in your aim and can continue with a rollout. Success criteria can be simple, in that you have run with Skype for Business for two weeks across a broad range of users and received notification of issues that have been resolved. It could also be more specific, encompassing the uptime of the service and the number of minutes of voice, video, and conference calls completed. Either way, it is important to lay out these criteria and understand how you will monitor results, either through existing monitoring tools, such as System Center Operations Manager; through Skype for Business–specific tools, such as the Monitoring server reports; or perhaps even through your in-house help-desk tool.

We have found that a pilot is best rolled out in phases, which are outlined here:

Phase 1: Pretesting A good pilot program will begin with testing and evaluation by IT staff. This enables testing of all the main functionality without exposing the program to the wider staff. It also enables IT to make sure they are comfortable monitoring and supporting the service and that they have hit the most common issues users are likely to experience. This is important, because part of the process of rolling out a new technology is to maintain a positive user experience. There is nothing worse than rolling out something to a wide audience too early when IT doesn't know how to support it and when there are still major issues. Doing so causes negativity, and people won't want to use the technology, which is exactly the opposite of what is required for a successful rollout. This IT phase of the pilot is complete once any functionality issues are ironed out and the service has been running for a couple of weeks.

Phase 2: Test on a Selected User Group Of course, tech-savvy IT professionals are unlikely to use the new technology in the same way that the business users will; they can probably work around or fix most issues. Therefore, the next phase of the pilot is to broaden the scope of users. Throughout this phase, communication is key. It is important to prepare pilot users for what they should expect, giving them clear and focused instructions, rather than bombarding them with messages that will not be read! Pilot members should be made aware of the status of the program, the way to get support, and how to give feedback. It is this feedback that will enable the project team to fully evaluate how Skype for Business is performing for users and to tweak systems or policies as necessary to enable a wider rollout to commence.

One element of the pilot is particularly important—the choice of pilot users. The users must be chosen from various areas of the business. It is important to identify areas where different working practices are found and make sure these areas are represented. Given that Skype for Business is a tool for communication, it often makes sense to enable a whole project team. It is, of course, also important to choose users who understand the importance of providing feedback; because without this, it is hard to gauge the status of the deployment.

Don't make the mistake of a partial pilot group, where you have some users enabled for Skype for Business but not their key co-workers. You'll encounter problems reported by these groups of users, mostly in the areas around usability as Skype for Business actually prevents them from doing their job. An example here is enabling the assistants of senior managers but not enabling the managers. If you can't involve the complete interaction group, you're better off not involving anyone.

Choosing the Right Users

It's important to choose users who will test the functionality you are rolling out. One customer we worked with chose their IT department for the pilot phase of the project; with more than 100 IT staff members, this seemed a good choice. However, once the two-week pilot had concluded and no data was captured, it turned out that the pilot users' main phones were their cell phones!

Phase 3: Evaluate the Results Evaluation of the pilot is important. This can take several forms. You can generate reports from systems to evaluate based on your acceptance criteria, and you'll also want human input. As such, it makes sense to invite representative pilot users to a project board meeting to discuss issues and experiences. Although it may not be possible to directly quantify ease of use as a success criteria, the human feedback you get based on ease of use will help you guide the future rollout and will help you tweak the settings and policies. Furthermore, these individuals are likely to be chosen not only because they will give valuable feedback but also because they will become points of contact going forward as the technology is rolled out more widely in their areas of the business. If you like, these people will become the superusers, or champions.

Once you have properly met the criteria set out at the beginning of the pilot, you are ready to deploy more broadly. Be aware that it may take time to reach this stage and that it is far better to spend time understanding issues, getting the support desk up to speed, and reconfiguring systems at this stage than it will be after you have rolled out more broadly. Even if you need to make significant changes, do so now. Then re-evaluate the success criteria and pilot again until you are sure that your Skype for Business deployment is solid, fit for purpose, and meets business requirements.

The Readiness and Adoption Success Kit

The Readiness and Adoption Success Kit (RASK) is a collection of tools and documentation to help organizations ensure the success of the pilot phase. Some if it we have covered earlier; however, the RASK provides all of this in easy-to-use documentation such as project plans as well as task checklists. You can download the RASK from the following location:

`http://technet.microsoft.com/en-us/office/dn788779`

RASK takes the project through five key stages:

1. Project scope
2. Proof of concept
3. Pilot
4. Enterprise rollout
5. Run state

It's important to highlight that RASK does not focus on the technical aspects but rather on the people and process aspects of the design.

Training Your Users

As with any new technology, training users is necessary if you want to ensure that the rollout is smooth and the benefits to the business are maximized. Given the type of technology Skype for Business is, this is all the more important, as otherwise people can be left floundering and significantly slowed down. That is not to say that training needs to be extensive. Skype for Business is an easy-to-use technology; however, many people simply will have no idea of its capabilities. As part of your rollout, you can address this in many ways.

Of course, the flip side to this argument is that the interface is common between Skype for Business and Skype itself, so everyone should know how to use it already!

The client introduces the seven most common tasks when you first run it (see Figure 14.1), making itself easy to use. Be careful when it comes to cutting back on user education; this can have a devastating impact on your project.

The first suggestion would be to carry out "Buzz Days." These events can take varying forms and should be carried out either during or near the Skype for Business rollout. The general premise is that you make Lync available somewhere so people can come and play with it. These sessions can be scheduled, whereby you identify a group of users and let them use it at the same time, or you can just set up timeslots and allow people to sign up. Or you could simply set up machines with access to Skype for Business in a common area with experts on hand so people passing can come and spend a few minutes getting the key points. The important thing with a Buzz Day is to identify the key messages you want to get across. Make sure you show people the functionality that is most important to them and then make sure they know how to back this up when they get stuck.

FIGURE 14.1 The quick tips in the Skype for Business Client

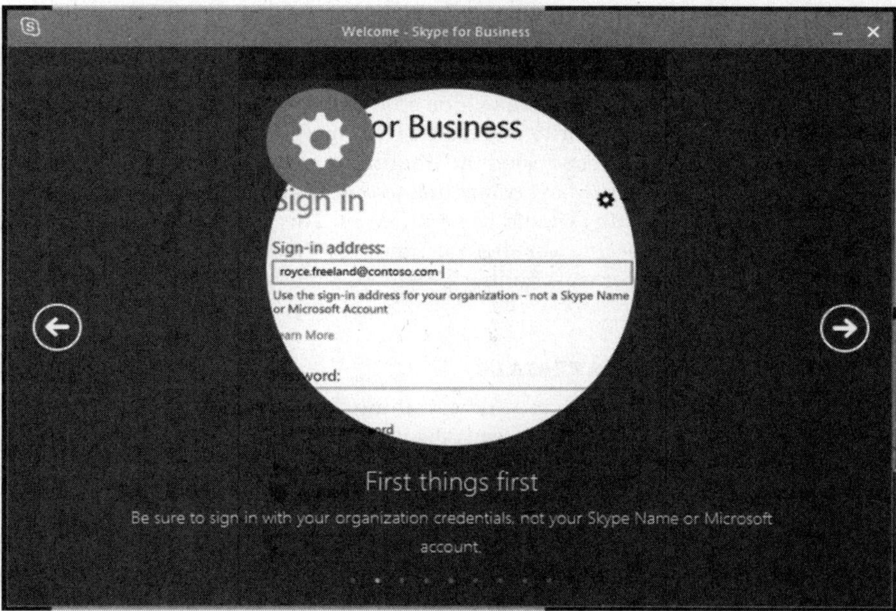

One thing beyond simply tasks that we believe should be covered is etiquette. Over the last 10 to 15 years people have gotten used to how email works and learned the customs associated with it, such as replying to all, using a signature, and setting up out-of-office messages; however, Skype for Business provides entirely new ways to communicate. Central to these is the concept of presence. It is important to discuss how you want people to use presence within your business. For example, frequently someone may be in a meeting and their presence will show as much, but they could take a quick IM. Equally, if someone doesn't want to be contacted, then they should set themselves to Do Not Disturb. A nuance to this is that people should be trained to put contacts into the relevant level of access group so that only those who they want to be able to break through the Do Not Disturb state can do so. With all these subtle differences, it is something worth discussing as part of the pilot and then feeding into your training so that users become accustomed to starting an IM with "Have you got a moment to talk?" rather than barging in with a direct call immediately.

It is likely that a combination of the training types previously outlined will be needed. While it will be fine for some users to come by and play with Skype for Business, others with more specialized needs will need more extensive training. In general, this applies to two particular groups. First, those people identified as local area champions or superusers should be given training. Often this will take an hour or perhaps an hour and a half, where these people are taken through Skype for Business features in detail. They can be taught about common questions and user mistakes, which you will have picked up both from the training materials (discussed next) and also from your experiences in your pilot. Another important group is the executive assistants. This group is critical, because they have the ear of both the senior management and the wider staff in general. They also have a specific role that involves using Skype for Business like few other people, in that they must be able to manage and make communications on behalf of others. The final group that warrants special training is the switchboard operators or receptionists. Again, they have a specific method of using Skype for Business, usually via the Attendee Console, which provides the ability to handle and route multiple calls. Again, any loss in productivity here will be noticed quickly at high levels within the business, so this group must be given priority and have a clear method of escalation should problems occur.

Once you've conducted the training, one element that is perhaps useful is some form of accreditation. Many companies give users credit for completing training, and Skype for Business training should be no different. This could range from online quizzes on a company portal to a specific test after the training. What you choose depends on the culture of your company, but either way, finding a method to measure capability and rewarding new education is valuable.

Training Materials

Now that we've discussed the training that should be conducted, this final section describes some of the materials already available to assist you with putting together your training.

Microsoft has put together a collection of user guides available here:

```
https://support.office.com/en-us/article/Quick-Start-Guides-about-Skype-for-Business-bbb1dd15-3858-4081-9c28-8379020af66d
```

The guides are available for items such as the following:

- Making calls
- Managing contacts
- Meetings
- Video
- Sharing and collaboration

In addition, generic "FastTrack" content across the whole of the Office suite of applications is available here:

```
http://fasttrack.office.com/resources
```

The RASK content also contains a lot of information that allows user feedback to be both captured and reported, which is useful to show users how the project is progressing.

The information located here:

```
www.microsoft.com/en-us/download/details.aspx?id=25051
```

refers to Lync 2010 but can be a valuable resource, albeit one that needs to be rebranded to Skype for Business! There are a number of sets of short videos, which mostly will be out of date because of the client changes. Still, there are some features that can be easily updated and leveraged.

- *QuickStarts*: These show users how to get up to speed quickly; they can be replaced by the content at the start of this section.
- *Training slides*: While needing updating, these are a great starting point to build structured classroom training on topics and functionality used.
- *WorkSmarts*: This is slightly more advanced content, focusing on smarter working practices.

CUSTOMIZING TRAINING MATERIALS

In the QuickStarts and WorkSmarts folders, the material is in HTML format and includes a folder containing style sheets and images related to the page. You have the option to customize these web pages and either publish them on an intranet or make them available to others for local download. Alternatively, they could be cut up and distributed via Word documents or inserted into regular quick-tip emails. In this way, the material can be repurposed for structured training or self-help.

Also at your disposal are a couple of resources for driving adoption. The first set of materials is aimed at helping you promote Skype for Business and communicate with users as you move through the process of pilot and rollout. It is accessible here:

`www.microsoft.com/download/en/details.aspx?id=8737`

There are templates for posters, T-shirts, and perhaps even more usefully a variety of emails, as laid out in Table 14.1. As before, these are branded Lync but can easily be updated to Skype for Business.

TABLE 14.1: The template emails provided by the adoption kit

EMAIL TEMPLATE NUMBER	TIMING	SUBJECT	AUDIENCE	PURPOSE
1	1 month before rollout	Join the Microsoft Skype for Business Rollout	All users	Build awareness and sign up users for the pilot
2a	Several weeks before rollout	Thanks for joining the Skype for Business Pilot Rollout	Users accepted to the pilot	Notify user of acceptance to pilot
2b	Several weeks before rollout	Thanks for your interest in the Skype for Business Rollout	Users rejected from the pilot	Notify user of rejection from pilot

TABLE 14.1: The template emails provided by the adoption kit *(CONTINUED)*

EMAIL TEMPLATE NUMBER	TIMING	SUBJECT	AUDIENCE	PURPOSE
3	1 week before rollout	Migration Warning	Users accepted to the pilot	Awareness of upcoming migration
4a	1 week before rollout	More Information Needed for Delegate Account	Users who will be delegates	Collect necessary information for delegate accounts
4b	Rollout day	Welcome and Installation Instructions	All users	Announcement of account migration/installation instructions
5	Weekly after rollout	Scenario Spotlight—Highlights a common scenario each week and asks for feedback	All users	Provide a timely way to expose users to high-productivity scenarios and offer a way to collect targeted feedback

The second set of adoption materials is a custom intranet site that pulls together much of the information in the various forms previously laid out, including the HTML help pages and videos, into a website ready for deployment on the intranet in your organization. Figure 14.2 shows this custom site (you can see the Lync 2010 branding!), which can be downloaded at the following URL:

`www.microsoft.com/download/en/details.aspx?id=3063`

In the end, these resources are a great starting point. Likely, you will want to customize them for your company's needs. Thankfully, they were designed with that in mind!

In summary, our experience shows that having a controlled process such as the following for the PoC and pilot stages as well as choosing the correct users for the pilot will make the project more successful.

1. Deploy proof of concept to prove functionality.
2. Expand proof of concept to pilot with IT staff.
3. Provide constant communications.
4. Expand the pilot to include business users.
   a. Ensure the users have a realistic opportunity to use the functionality.

   b. Include the users in feedback.
   c. Provide extra training for these users.
5. Provide easily accessible training for the users during the rollout.

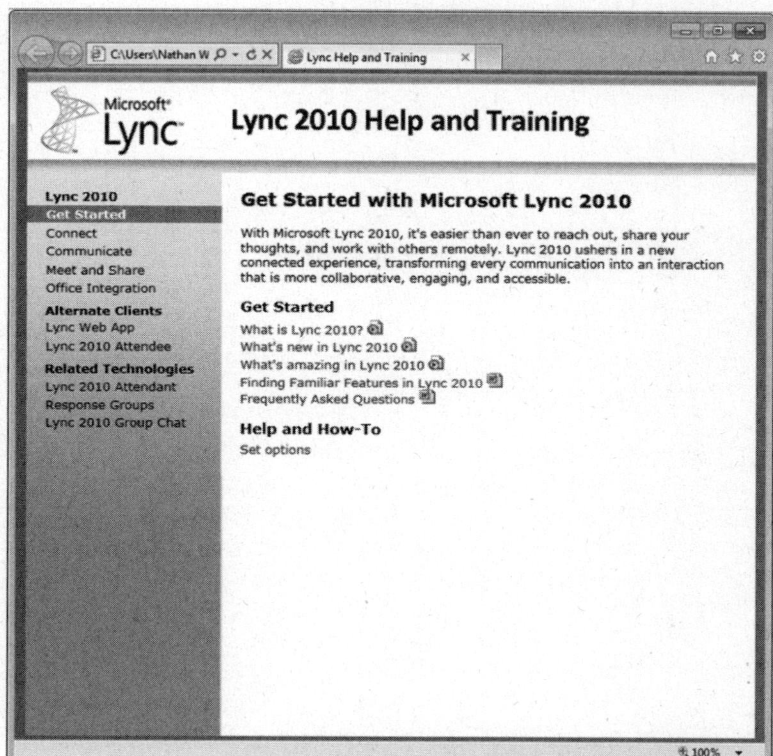

FIGURE 14.2
The custom intranet site for assisting user adoption

The Bottom Line

Understand the impact of UC on the users. Unified Communications has the potential to vastly improve users' productivity. However, depending on where you are starting from (in other words, a greenfield or a previous version), there is going to be a dramatically different impact to the users. Some users may want to have an actual desk phone when the plan is to replace all phones with headsets; how will you deal with these?

> **Master It** You have been asked to prepare a short communications statement covering the key benefits users will receive once using Skype for Business. List the areas you would cover.

Understand the importance of choosing the correct users for piloting. Having a good test plan is one thing, but if you're not targeting the correct users, you can impact the project success levels. The executive assistants are often overlooked when it comes to piloting, but this team often, while having no direct authority, has a direct, and strong, link to the sponsors and decision makers. Getting them on your side early is key; often their role is well placed to have a dramatic improvement with new collaborative technologies.

Master It You have been asked to prepare a migration plan. List the key considerations for user selection.

Chapter 15

Troubleshooting

In an ideal world, every system would work perfectly as soon as it was installed and would continue to work until decommissioned. As we all know, this is never the case, and quite often the simple things (typically, the ones assumed to be correct) are what cause us problems. In this chapter, you will explore the tools available to troubleshoot Skype for Business.

There are some differences between Skype for Business Server 2015 and its predecessor Lync Server, but you still need to make sure the simple things are correct before you can progress to the complex areas. With the many integration points that Skype for Business provides with third-party hardware (gateways, devices, and so on), as well as its strong integration points with the underlying infrastructure, there are many areas to check when it comes to troubleshooting.

In this chapter, you will learn to

- Confirm that the basics are in place from the infrastructure side
- Understand how to troubleshoot the client
- Know how to enable troubleshooting on the server
- Understand and use the troubleshooting tools available

Covering the Basics

Let's say you receive a call from a user saying something is broken (can't log in, can't make calls, or the like). Where do you start?

First, always ask the usual questions.

- Did it ever work?
- What did the user change?
- What has an administrator changed?

NOTE When working in the support department, you'll find that no one ever admits to making a change that breaks something; however, as administrators, we all know it happens! When you're troubleshooting, always check to see whether an administrative change could've caused the break.

Second, you need to establish the scope of the problem. Is it related to a single user, is it related to a single location, or is the whole system down for everybody? The larger-scale impact issues tend to be easiest to troubleshoot, but they also tend to be the ones with the greatest amount of pressure. When 10,000 users are without phone service, the problem can quickly be escalated to the top.

When it comes to networking investigation, the usual suspects typically include the following tools:

- Ping
- Telnet client (not installed by default on Windows since Windows Vista was released)
- `Nslookup.exe` (don't forget to configure to check for SRV records)
- The browser (for checking certificates, and so on)
- A network capture tool such as Message Analyzer or Wireshark

Confirming a Network Connection

Simply put, if a user can't log in, something is wrong with their connection to the server (assuming the account is enabled and not locked or there is a simple typo).

Using automatic login on an internal network, the Skype for Business client will attempt to discover the address of a pool (and therefore registrar) in the following order:

- `Lyncdiscoverinternal.<sip domain>`
- `Lyncdiscover.<sip domain>`
- `_sipinternaltls._tcp.<sip domain>`
- DHCP Option 120
- `sipinternal.<sip domain>`
- `sip.<sip domain>`

The Phone Edition client will use the following methods:

- DHCP Option 120
- `_sipinternaltls._tcp.<sip domain>`
- `sipinternal.<sip domain>`
- `sip.<sip domain>`

The Phone Edition device prefers to use Option 120 (in conjunction with Option 43 for certificate services) to allow the phone to be directed to a Skype for Business (or Lync) server rather than a legacy OCS 2007 or OCS 2007 R2 server, which does not provide certificate (or PIN) authentication.

Using the Skype for Business client, you can modify the connection type to be manual (see Figure 15.1) and enter the FQDN address of the pool to see whether that connection is working. Using this test, you can confirm that the issue is within the DNS resolution of the automatic server discovery or the redirect from another pool.

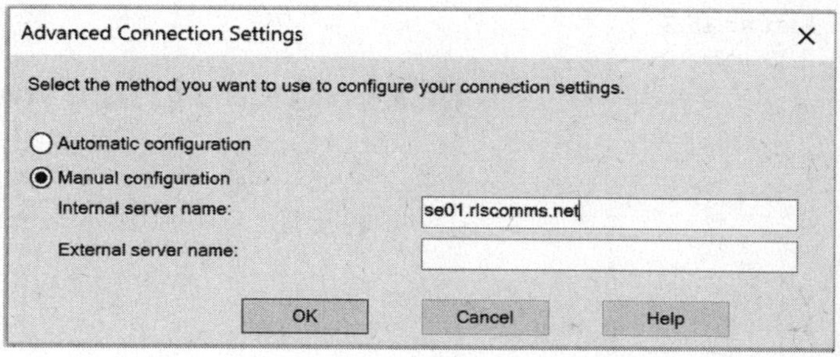

FIGURE 15.1
Configuring a manual server connection

To confirm the connectivity to a server, you can use ping; however, many network administrators will block ping on the firewall, especially when you're trying to communicate with the servers in the DMZ. To confirm communications on a specific port, you must use Telnet and provide the server (or pool) name and the port.

For example, to confirm SIP connectivity via a hardware load balancer, use this command:

```
telnet <pool name> 5061
```

The result, rather confusingly, is a blank window. However, this shows that the Telnet client has successfully connected to the server. If there is a problem, the client will indicate that it cannot connect, and although the error may not be particularly descriptive, you should be able to determine whether it was a DNS issue (if you used the FQDN) or a network connectivity issue (routing or firewall). The potential DNS issue can be determined simply by repeating the test using the IP address in place of the FQDN.

Another useful tool to test this, and that can give a more meaningful output, is PortQry. This tool is available from `www.microsoft.com/en-us/download/details.aspx?id=17148` and is currently in version 2. In Figure 15.2, you will see an example usage and output. PortQry also has the ability to work using UDP, whereas Telnet is limited to TCP only.

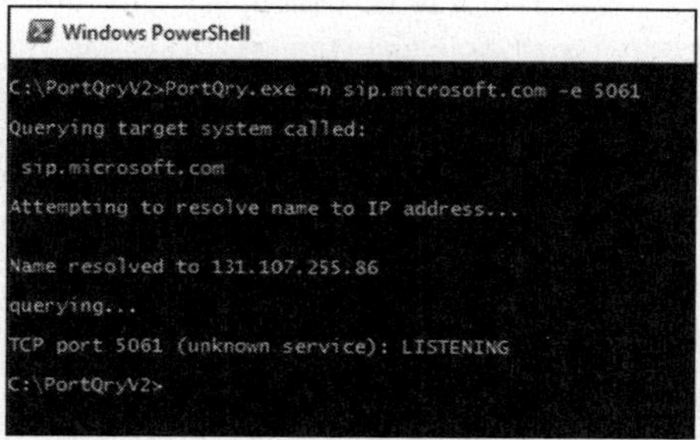

FIGURE 15.2
PortQry output

If the client is not able to find the automatic DNS records, you'll get the error pop-up shown in Figure 15.3.

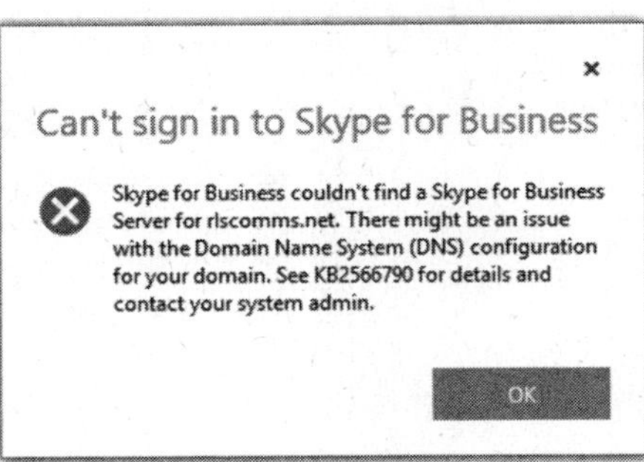

FIGURE 15.3
DNS error

Using the client logs (enabled as shown in Figure 15.4), you can see the following entries, which list the failed DNS resolution for some of the automatic lookup addresses:

```
11/11/2015|10:34:37.182 1088:3F8 ERROR :: ResolveHostNameUsingGetAddrInfo
- getaddrinfo(sip.rlscomms.net) failed hr=0x80072AF9
11/11/2015|10:34:37.182 1088:3F8 WARN  :: ResolveHostName - getaddrinfo
failed for sip.rlscomms.net hr=0x80072AF9
11/11/2015|10:34:37.182 1088:3F8 ERROR :: ResolveHostNameUsingDnsQuery -
DnsQuery(sip.rlscomms.net) failed error=9003
11/11/2015|10:34:37.182 1088:3F8 WARN  :: ResolveHostName - DNS lookup
failed for sip.rlscomms.net hr=0x80004005
11/11/2015|10:34:37.182 1088:3F8 ERROR :: ResolveHostName - Name resolution for
sip.rlscomms.net failed
```

and the following entries:

```
<Lync-autodiscovery>
      <Info><![CDATA[GetBestManagedCredentialByType
return the cred: 00000000, type:specific, userId:LAD]]>
</Info>
      <Info><![CDATA[Discovery request sent to URL
http://lyncdiscoverinternal.rlscomms.net?sipuri=
david.skype@rlscomms.net, txn (13C48918), task(13BF94F0)]]>
</Info>
      <Info><![CDATA[GetBestManagedCredentialByType
return the cred: 00000000, type:specific, userId:LAD]]>
</Info>
    <Info><![CDATA[
 VerifyOnEnableEvent result return 10
     ONENABLE_FAIL_SERVER_NOT_REACHABLE
   status=0x80ee001c
    ACTION: SERVER NOT REACHABLE
        NO MORE SERVER TO TRY
    ACTION : PERMANENT ERROR]]></Info>
```

The client logs provide extremely detailed information in terms of what is going on at the client end. You'll see a lot more of them in this chapter.

FIGURE 15.4
Enabling client logs

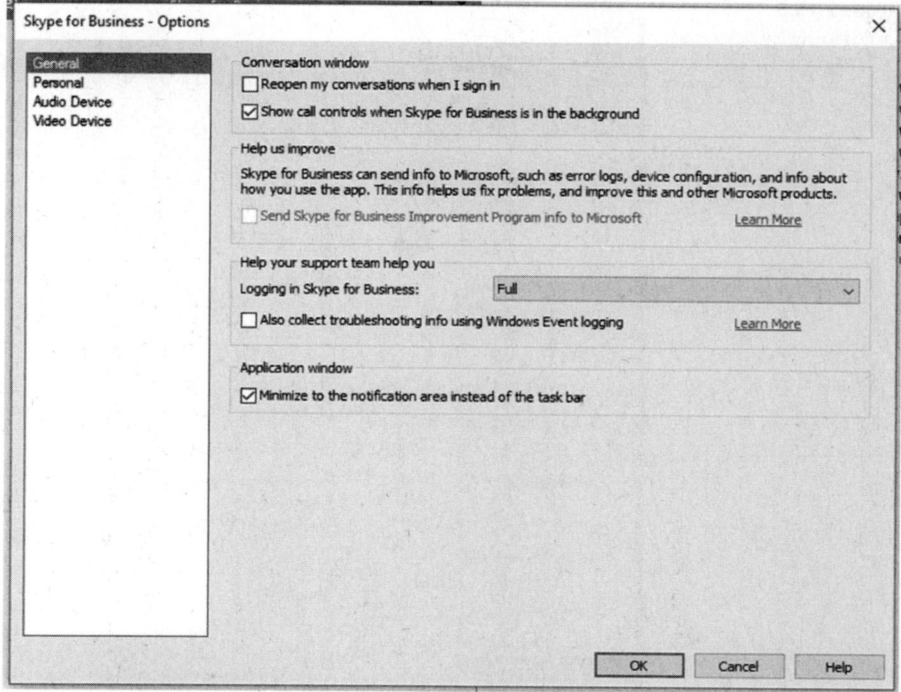

Confirming Secure Connectivity

Once you have the name resolution, routing, and firewall problems out of the way, the next part of the connectivity path is the certificate on the server. With the improvements since the Lync Server 2010 Certificate Wizard (and even more so for the internal pool servers in Skype for Business Server 2015), the task of configuring the certificates became a lot easier; however, changes can still be made and the certificates still might not be updated, which could lead to connectivity issues.

To test for the correct certificate configuration, you can use the following URL (similar to the successful Telnet connection, you can expect a blank screen, but this time white):

```
https://<poolname>/dialin
```

Figure 15.5 shows the result when the certificate is correctly configured (dialog in background) and incorrectly configured (foremost dialog). Also notice the Skype icons on the address bar for the successful connection.

You can repeat this process to confirm each of the expected subject alternative names (SANs) in the certificate simply by replacing the `<poolname>` entry with each of the SAN entries.

Checking for Audio/Video Peer-to-Peer Connectivity

Now that you've established the basics for client connectivity to the servers, the next step is to confirm connectivity between clients when establishing a call. IM connectivity always flows through the server, whereas the clients must negotiate peer-to-peer connectivity between themselves. Where direct connectivity is not available, clients must connect via NAT or the Edge server. Figure 15.6 shows the connectivity options for a client, depending on the path available between them.

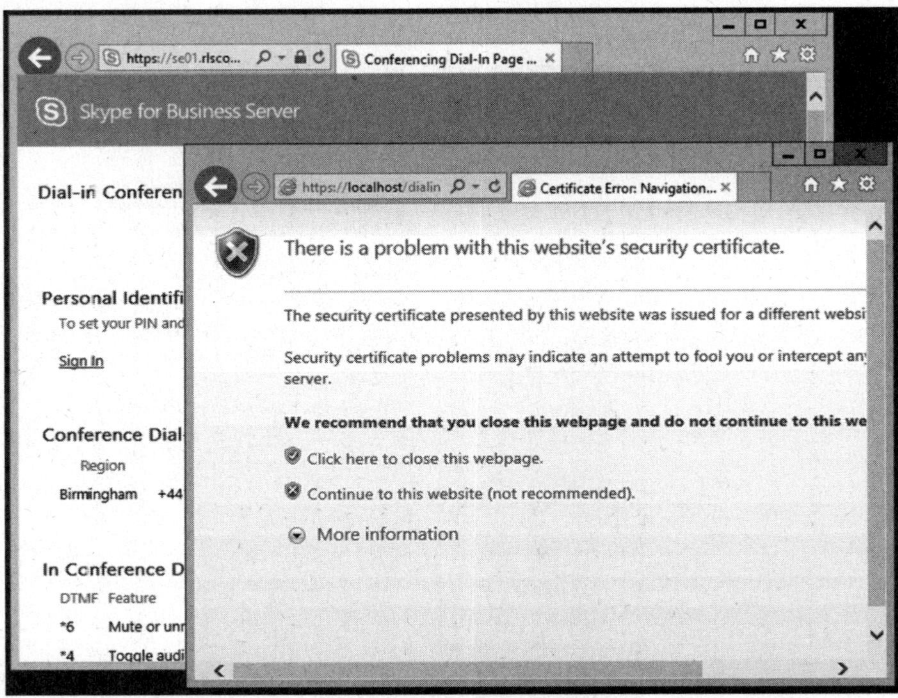

FIGURE 15.5
Confirming the correct certificate

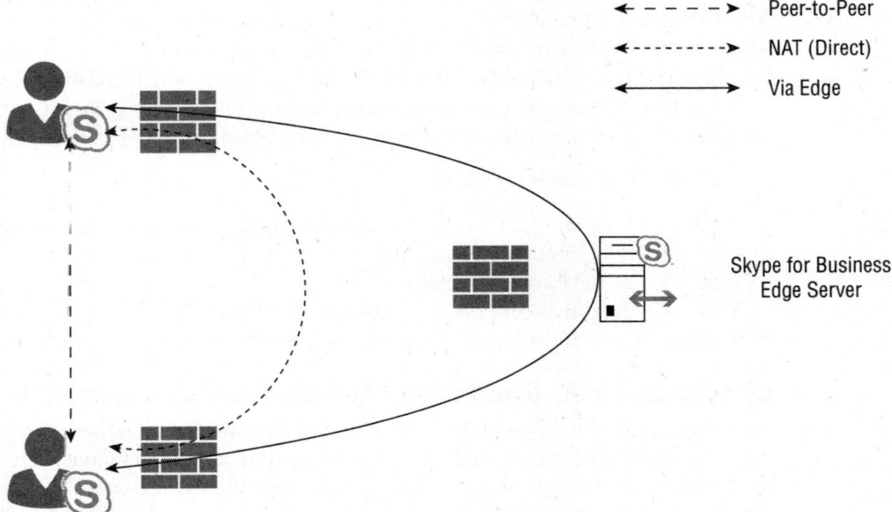

FIGURE 15.6
Client connectivity options

The client logs capture the IP addresses and ports negotiated (known as *candidates*) during the call initiation (audio, video, or desktop sharing). This Internet connectivity exchange (ICE) is shown here:

```
v=0
o=- 0 0 IN IP4 192.168.3.98
s=session
c=IN IP4 192.168.3.98
b=CT:53980
t=0 0
m=audio 56498 RTP/AVP 114 9 112 111 0 8 116 115 4 97 13 118 101
a=candidate:I0j2VRG1VNQG4cWj248JT8iqlOD42gmKoa8xdt4quqo 1 w4WZzoBiHwS3VeihjFFTuw
UDP 0.830 192.168.1.177 71 50028
a=candidate:I0j2VRG1VNQG4cWj248JT8iqlOD42gmKoa8xdt4quqo 2 w4WZzoBiHwS3VeihjFFTuw
UDP 0.830 192.168.1.177 50029
a=candidate:PZWZ6iscBZZ9TjL4kOKnxvcZDP4wODZKIklqiA/YLek 1 fCq9RqLw2pcibQlONAJULQ
TCP 0.190 192.168.1.177 53882
a=candidate:PZWZ6iscBZZ9TjL4kOKnxvcZDP4wODZKIklqiA/YLek 2 fCq9RqLw2pcibQlONAJULQ
TCP 0.190 192.168.1.177 53882
a=candidate:3aT5M3vcWbnE4FzWub2fX5CjNq6oDM61ZlcRKb0u5rQ 1 N9yLzNb17mpUVbCqNC2lAQ
UDP 0.490 192.168.3.98 56498
a=candidate:3aT5M3vcWbnE4FzWub2fX5CjNq6oDM61ZlcRKb0u5rQ 2 N9yLzNb17mpUVbCqNC2lAQ
UDP 0.490 192.168.3.98 55800
a=candidate:H46GRbUExoCxH7kQHprA5E2uVHxBroGV6aTGb56IowU 1 X1veRGhvsDShUEB8ND7GGQ
TCP 0.250 192.168.254.4 50004
a=candidate:H46GRbUExoCxH7kQHprA5E2uVHxBroGV6aTGb56IowU 2 X1veRGhvsDShUEB8ND7GGQ
TCP 0.250 192.168.254.4 50004
a=cryptoscale:1 client AES_CM_128_HMAC_SHA1_80
inline:kDgLmPIv2ufDNctJasF0KIkFq5w/6iXpUDMeWrDW|2^31|1:1
a=crypto:2 AES_CM_128_HMAC_SHA1_80
inline:s40wuCQ33Rw6SysXZs5f7C66IxsF/GdQRqiqcD3M|2^31|1:1
a=crypto:3 AES_CM_128_HMAC_SHA1_80
inline:SljnK0kFx6RtiWHywiCIVavo1SxLE/ztysYrFhZb|2^31
a=maxptime:200
a=rtcp:55800
a=rtpmap:114 x-msrta/16000
a=fmtp:114 bitrate=29000
a=rtpmap:9 G722/8000
a=rtpmap:112 G7221/16000
a=fmtp:112 bitrate=24000
a=rtpmap:111 SIREN/16000
a=fmtp:111 bitrate=16000
a=rtpmap:0 PCMU/8000
a=rtpmap:8 PCMA/8000
a=rtpmap:116 AAL2-G726-32/8000
a=rtpmap:115 x-msrta/8000
a=fmtp:115 bitrate=11800
a=rtpmap:4 G723/8000
```

```
a=rtpmap:97 RED/8000
a=rtpmap:13 CN/8000
a=rtpmap:118 CN/16000
a=rtpmap:101 telephone-event/8000
a=fmtp:101 0-16
```

Each line beginning with `a=candidate` is an IP address/port/protocol combination on which the client can be reached, and the long, seemingly random text is the username/password combination, ensuring that this connection is secured. (This text string is exchanged via the SIP signaling path, which is already secured.)

Let's look at a sample candidate entry:

```
a=candidate:I0j2VRG1VNQG4cWj248JT8iqlOD42gmKoa8xdt4quqo 1 w4WZzoBiHwS3VeihjFFTuw
UDP 0.830 192.168.1.177 50028
```

Broken down, it consists of the following elements:

- `a=candidate:` is the session attribute.
- `I0j2VRG1VNQG4cWj248JT8iqlOD42gmKoa8xdt4quqo` is the username.
- 1 specifies that RTP is to be used (2 = RTCP).
- `w4WZzoBiHwS3VeihjFFTuw` is the password.
- `UDP` is the protocol.
- `0.830` is the weighting (a higher number is preferred).
- `192.168.1.177` is the IP address.
- `50028` is the port number.

The information shown is actually a legacy version of ICE, and you'll find it only in the Skype for Business 2015 client (the Lync 2013 client with the update); it's there to provide legacy compatibility with OCS clients.

With the Skype for Business 2015 client you will also get the newest version of ICE, and in the Skype for Business 2016 client only this new version is provided (therefore there is no OCS compatibility available).

This new version is shown next:

```
v=0
o=- 0 1 IN IP4 192.168.3.98
s=session
c=IN IP4 192.168.3.98
b=CT:99980
t=0 0
a=x-devicecaps:audio:send,recv;video:send,recv
m=audio 28038 RTP/SAVP 114 9 112 111 0 8 116 115 97 13 118 101
a=x-ssrc-range:3287526401-3287526401
a=rtcp-fb:* x-message app send:dsh recv:dsh
a=rtcp-rsize
a=label:main-audio
```

```
a=x-source:main-audio
a=ice-ufrag:lkMR
a=ice-pwd:FNCRfT45UaOKa0iv0Vn6l4Mt
a=candidate:1 1 UDP 2130706431 192.168.3.98 28038 typ host
a=candidate:2 1 UDP 2130705919 192.168.1.177 31230 typ host
a=candidate:3 1 TCP-PASS 174455807 192.168.254.4 58074 typ relay raddr
192.168.3.98 rport 31737
a=candidate:4 1 UDP 184547839 192.168.254.4 53297 typ relay raddr
192.168.3.98 rport 11035
a=candidate:5 1 TCP-ACT 174847999 192.168.254.4 58074 typ relay raddr
192.168.3.98 rport 31737
a=candidate:6 1 TCP-ACT 1684796927 192.168.3.98 31737 typ srflx raddr
192.168.3.98 rport 31737
a=crypto:2 AES_CM_128_HMAC_SHA1_80
inline:wY44XYBqlFxW5w3qbPSLOGkBmdELxK1jx/7FlKZ3|2^31|1:1a=maxptime:200
a=rtpmap:114 x-msrta/16000
a=fmtp:114 bitrate=29000
a=rtpmap:9 G722/8000
a=rtpmap:112 G7221/16000
a=fmtp:112 bitrate=24000
a=rtpmap:111 SIREN/16000
a=fmtp:111 bitrate=16000
a=rtpmap:0 PCMU/8000
a=rtpmap:8 PCMA/8000
a=rtpmap:116 AAL2-G726-32/8000
a=rtpmap:115 x-msrta/8000
a=fmtp:115 bitrate=11800
a=rtpmap:97 RED/8000
a=rtpmap:13 CN/8000
a=rtpmap:118 CN/16000
a=rtpmap:101 telephone-event/8000
a=fmtp:101 0-16
a=rtcp-mux
a=ptime:20
```

Broken down, a sample entry in the latest format looks like this:

```
a=candidate:3 1 TCP-PASS 174455807 192.168.254.4 58074 typ relay raddr
192.168.3.98 rport 31737
```

It breaks down as follows:

- `a=candidate:` is the session attribute.
- 3 is the candidate ID.
- 1 specifies that RTP is to be used (2 = RTCP).
- `TCP-PASS` is the protocol type (`TCP-PASS` = TCP Passive; `TCP-ACT` = TCP Active, UDP).
- `174455807` is the weighting (a higher number is preferred).

- `192.168.254.4` is the IP address.
- `58074` is the port number.
- `typ relay` is the type of relay (`direct` = UDP only; `relay` = TCP-PASS, TCP-ACT, or UDP; `srflx` = self-reflective, TCP-ACT, or UDP).
- `addr 192.168.3.98` is the remote IP address.
- `rport 31737` is the remote port number.

The clients both exchange a candidate (and codec) list and will try each address in order of preference. The logs will also show the address list provided by the remote client. Once you have this information, you can ensure manually that the clients can connect.

Once compatibility is confirmed via the IP address, port, and protocol selection, the remaining task is to establish a common codec. The previous listings include this codec map (`a=rtpmap:`); the clients will negotiate this and will continue to negotiate throughout the duration of the call, ensuring that the codecs adapt to any change in the network conditions. Later in this chapter, you'll see an excerpt from the media quality logs that shows the codec selection.

Device Connectivity

Phone devices don't have the same requirements for connectivity as desktop clients, specifically the need for DHCP configuration.

To enable certificate-based authentication (making sure the phone can connect with no Active Directory available), you must make sure the phone connects to the certificate-provisioning website on a Skype for Business pool. This is provided via DHCP Option 43.

In addition, unless DHCP Option 120 is also configured (you need to provide the SIP registrar information), the phone will display an error to the user while it is performing a DNS query on the SRV records (although once the DNS records are discovered, it will connect as normal).

The `dhcputil.exe` tool (and `DHCPConfigScript.bat` file) provided in the `C:\Program Files\Common Files\Microsoft Skype for Business 2015` folder provides instructions for configuring a Microsoft-based DHCP server.

Device Error from the Field

A colleague recently reported a strange user experience from one of his customers—when the customer logged into the desktop client, everything functioned normally; however, when the customer was logged into a Phone Edition client, the following functionality was missing:

- Voice mail
- Calendar integration
- Call logs

These functions are provided by Exchange Web Services (EWS), so we suggested troubleshooting EWS and verifying that it was operational. However, as our colleague pointed out, this was all functioning from the desktop client.

Next on the list was network routing and address resolution from the device (typically, phone devices are allocated to a separate VLAN). In this case, the device was on the same VLAN as the PC.

The end result was that EWS had been signed by a different certificate chain than the Skype for Business Front End certificates had been. When the phone device connected to the Front End server to download the certificate chain, it had no way of downloading the chain for the Exchange server and, therefore, did not trust it.

There were two possible ways to resolve this certificate issue with the Exchange server:

Ensure that the Exchange server certificates came from the same certificate authority as the certificates' user on the Front End servers

or

Use the `New-CsWebTrustedCACertificate` cmdlet to define the certificates used by the Exchange servers to be loaded onto the Front End servers and, therefore, trusted by the Phone Edition client.

Because the Phone Device will download the Front End server certificates (and root certificate authority certificate chain) anyway, the first option was used. However, both have the same result, and in some cases it may not be possible to easily replace certificates in use by Exchange.

Another area to be aware of, especially when integrating with Exchange, is the use of web proxies. If you publish your web proxy via DHCP, this can affect clients connecting to EWS if the web proxies have not been configured to exclude internal traffic appropriately. You may see multiple attempts at authentication or integration issues because the web proxies are interfering with the traffic.

Sniffing the Network

After you've verified that name resolution, routing, and the firewalls are working and all appears to be fine, the next step is to better understand the actual traffic being sent and received on the network. The following tools are often used for network sniffing:

- Microsoft Message Analyzer (replacing Network Monitor)
- Wireshark

These tools intercept and provide a breakdown of the network traffic, including the protocol and meaning of the packets being transmitted or received. Figure 15.7 shows Microsoft Message Analyzer examining generic network traffic, grouped by process name.

Immediately, from the open section in Figure 15.6, you can see the process (`2760`), and using something like Task Manager you can identify the ID used by the Skype for Business client (`Lync.exe`); so, you know you're looking at the correct network traffic as well as the source and destination IP address information. This means you are connecting to the server (or device) that you should be. You can also see the specific protocol (in this case TCP) and ports in use.

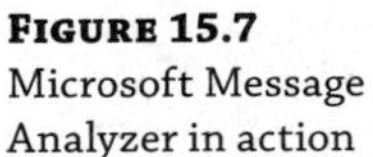

FIGURE 15.7 Microsoft Message Analyzer in action

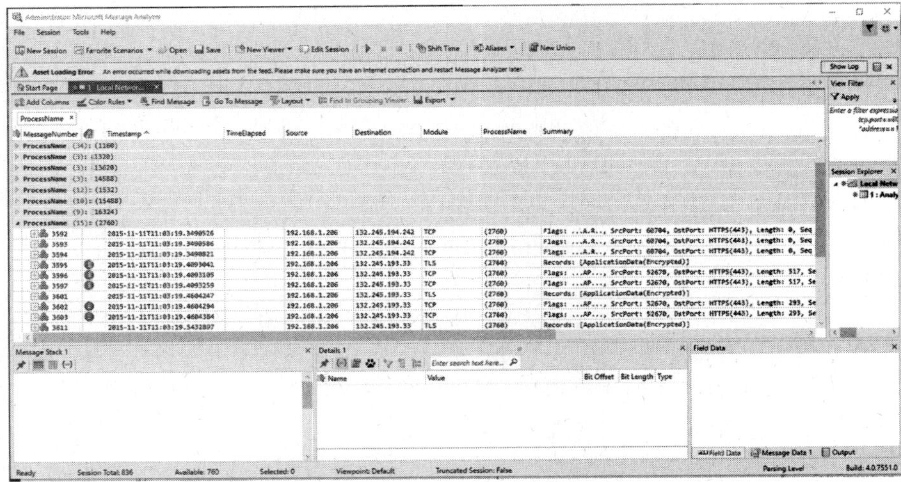

Although Message Analyzer provides protocol parsers for SIP, it is normally much easier to enable logging on the server or client and import the log file into `Snooper.exe` for analysis. Where Message Analyzer comes into its own is in understanding the communications layer. There are two important scenarios.

- Understanding and establishing the certificate exchange (handshake)
- Understanding the hardware load balancer interaction

Certificate traffic analysis will indicate the names being provided by the certificate, ensuring that you can match those names with the ones you expect. It is really important in certificate analysis that you capture the initial handshake for the SSL session you are trying to decrypt. If you don't, all the useful data will be listed as application data in the network trace. By contrast, with the hardware load balancers, a common misconfiguration is the timeout values; here, you can capture a `TCP-RESET` packet showing that the timeout is configured incorrectly. `TCP-RESET` will cause the active session to reset and a new one to establish, which can confuse the troubleshooting process. When searching for `TCP-RESET` sessions, focus and limit your search to the TCP port. Doing this makes it far easier to locate an actual conversation.

Keep in mind these tips from the field when you're using network monitoring tools. Use aliases for naming the IP addresses so you can better track the flow. Use colors to highlight interesting trace information so when it is streaming in real time, you can better track what information you are looking for.

Now that we've covered the methods of troubleshooting connectivity and introduced the snippets of the log files, we'll cover tracing.

Using Logging to Identify Problems

Both the server and the client provide a method to access what is happening "under the covers" by enabling logging. *Logging* enables the server and client to write detailed information to a text file to provide a means for an administrator or support engineer to understand what is occurring at any given time.

The server provides a means to enable subsets of components to log; on a busy server, there is too much information to simply log it all and then parse it. Next, you'll see how to enable and manage individual server components.

The client doesn't have as much information to log because it is dealing with only a single user's interactions, and therefore, everything is either Light, Full, or disabled.

Figure 15.4, earlier in the chapter, shows where you enable logging on the client; it can also be enabled via policy.

The log files are stored at the location

```
%USERPROFILE%\appdata\local\microsoft\office\<office version>\lync\Tracing
```

and are named `Lync-uccapi-0.UCCAPILOG`; the 0 in the filename will increase based on the number of log files available (such as `Lync-uccapi-1.UCCAPILOG`).

These log files use *circular logging*, so there will always be a minimum of two files (occasionally there may be more—normally this would occur only when sustained traffic is being logged and not enough time has passed to close down the first file). Once the second is full, the first will be overwritten, and once the first is full, the second will be overwritten, and so on.

As mentioned, these are text-based log files and can be opened and viewed with any text viewer (such as `notepad.exe`); however, you'll see later in this chapter how a resource kit tool called `Snooper.exe` makes reading and interpreting these log files much easier.

Under this directory you will also notice an Event Trace Log (ETL) file. This is a binary file that cannot be read by `notepad.exe`. These files are generally used by Microsoft support engineers to help provide further information to diagnose issues. To examine these files, you can use `OCSLogger.exe` from a Lync Server 2010 deployment.

Refer to the following location for more information:

`http://blogs.msdn.com/b/leoncon/archive/2012/05/31/getting-amp-reading-the-tracing-logs-for-a-lync-online-client.aspx`

Using Centralized Logging

Lync Server 2013 introduced a new concept called *centralized logging*. It is designed to allow you to trace across multiple servers at one time, making it far easier to locate and troubleshoot a problem to resolve it. Previously, you had to run a trace individually and manually on every node you thought was involved in the communications flow as well as select the right components and flags to trace on.

In Skype for Business, each server runs a new service called Skype for Business Server Centralized Logging Service Agent, as shown in Figure 15.8.

NOTE You can also monitor the Skype for Business Server Centralized Logging Service Agent via Task Manager under `ClsAgent.exe`.

There are global policies configured by default that control the behavior of this agent. These policies can be modified via the PowerShell cmdlet `Get-CsClsConfiguration` (see Figure 15.9). Note that previously this command was `Get-CsCentralizedLoggingConfiguration`.

In Figure 15.9, you will see a list of scenarios that are configured, but more important, you'll see what is enabled. A scenario called AlwaysOn is enabled by default. This in itself is a major leap forward in terms of troubleshooting because now there is the potential to capture the problem with this scenario. Although it does not monitor every component or flag, this scenario should allow you to reduce the time to resolution because you may not have to try to re-create an issue, which can sometimes be a challenge.

FIGURE 15.8
Skype for Business Server Centralized Logging Service Agent

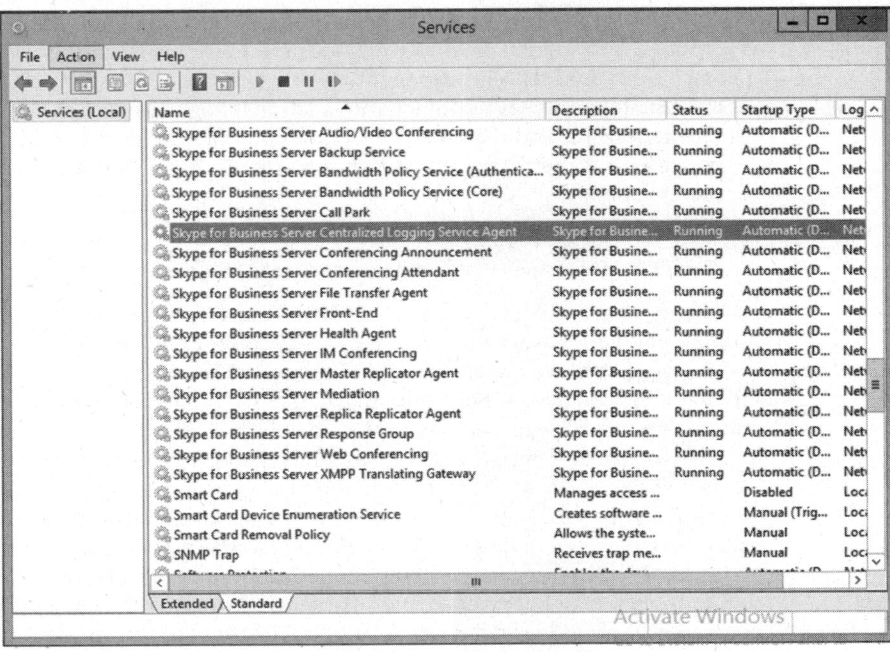

FIGURE 15.9
The Get-CsClsConfiguration cmdlet

```
Administrator: Windows PowerShell
PS C:\Users\administrator.RLSCOMMS> Get-CsClsConfiguration


Identity                        : Global
Scenarios                       : {Name=AlwaysOn, Name=NonTopologyAlwaysOn, Name=MediaConnectivity,
                                  Name=ApplicationSharing...}
SearchTerms                     : {Type=Phone;Inserts=ItemE164,ItemURI,ItemSIP,ItemPII,
                                  Type=URI;Inserts=ItemURI,ItemSIP,ItemPII,
                                  Type=CallId;Inserts=ItemCALLID,ItemURI,ItemSIP,ItemPII,
                                  Type=ConfId;Inserts=ItemCONFID,ItemURI,ItemSIP,ItemPII...}
SecurityGroups                  : {}
Regions                         : {}
EtlFileFolder                   : %TEMP%\Tracing
EtlFileRolloverSizeMB           : 20
EtlFileRolloverMinutes          : 60
TmfFileSearchPath               :
CacheFileLocalFolders           : %TEMP%\Tracing
CacheFileNetworkFolder          :
CacheFileLocalRetentionPeriod   : 14
CacheFileLocalMaxDiskUsage      : 80
ComponentThrottleLimit          : 5000
ComponentThrottleSample         : 3
MinimumClsAgentServiceVersion   : 6
NetworkUsagePacketSize          : 64
NetworkUsageThreshold           : 10
Version                         : 6.0.9319.0


PS C:\Users\administrator.RLSCOMMS>
```

The central logging service can be controlled by the following range of cmdlets:

- `Show-CsClsLogging`
- `Start-CsClsLogging`
- `Stop-CsClsLogging`
- `Sync-CsClsLogging`
- `Update-CsClsLogging`

Here a brief description of each of the cmdlets:

`Show-CsClsLogging` This will query the status of every pool in the environment and report on the state of the Centralized Logging Service (Cls) Logging Agent.

`Start-CsClsLogging` This will prompt for which scenario to apply and try to start the process on all servers in the environment by default, and it can be targeted to specific pools and also for a specific duration if needed.

`Stop-CsClsLogging` This will prompt for which scenario to stop and try to start the process on all servers in the environment by default, and it can be targeted to specific pools if needed.

`Sync-CsClsLogging` This cmdlet will flush the centralized logging cache on the pool specified or all by default.

`Update-CsClsLogging` This cmdlet allows for modification of the duration of scenarios running on pools, as specified by the `Start-CsClsLogging` cmdlet.

Figure 15.10 shows the typical results from running one of these cmdlets.

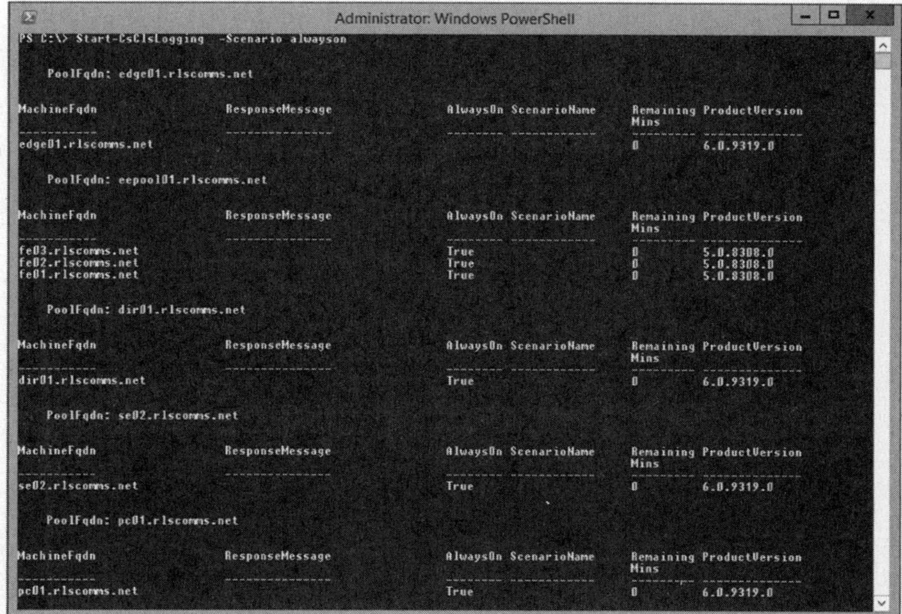

FIGURE 15.10 Output from the `Start-CsClsLogging` cmdlet

Making Logging Easier

Although the PowerShell cmdlets allow for detailed granular control, they can be cumbersome to remember the parameters needed and scenarios to cover. As part of the Skype for Business Server 2015 Debugging Tools download, you can install the GUI for the Centralized Logging Service.

You can find the download here:

`https://www.microsoft.com/en-us/download/details.aspx?id=47263`

Once it's installed on the server, you can run the `ClsLogger.Exe` application to see a screen as in Figure 15.11.

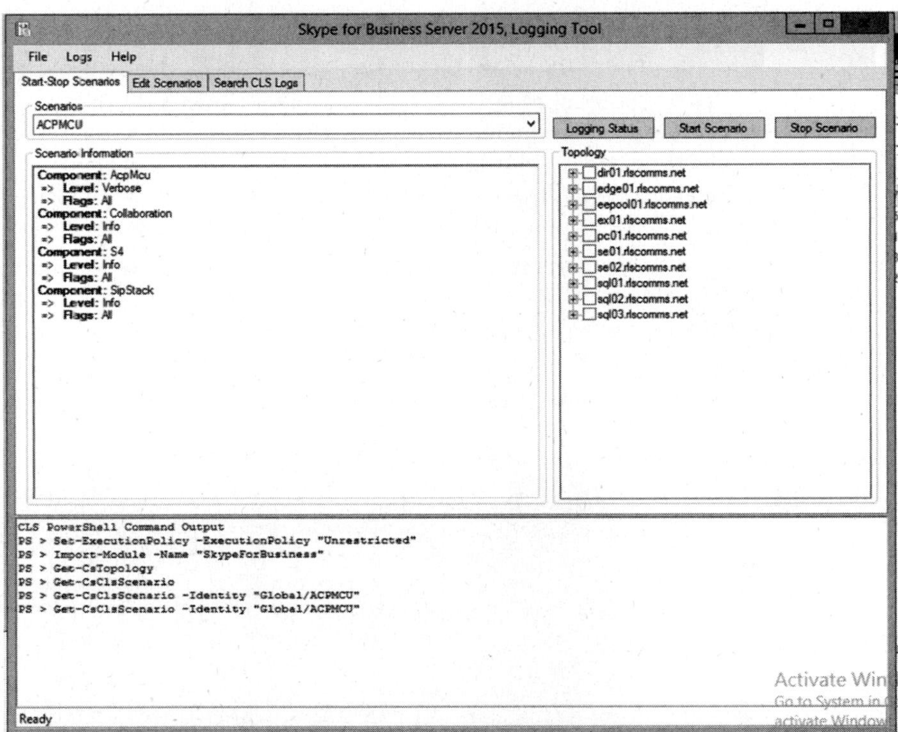

FIGURE 15.11 `ClsLogger.exe` startup screen

Clearly, it is much easier to navigate because all the details are provided and you can simply click to get started. You can define new scenarios and search logs from the other tabs shown.

So, once you've got logs, what next? Well, you need to analyze them, and while this is possible via `Notepad.exe`, it is much easier to use `Snooper.exe`, which is also installed as part of the Debugging Tools download.

Using *Snooper.exe*

In a previous section, you viewed the log file snippets as text. The log file is a text-based file, but it can quickly grow quite large. Snooper is the tool that makes interpreting the logs extremely easy. Figure 15.12 shows Snooper with a file loaded.

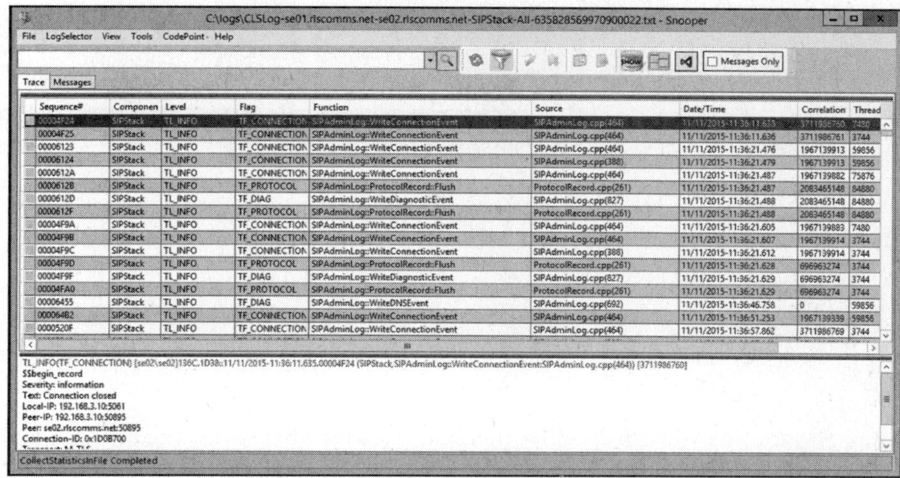

FIGURE 15.12
The Snooper Trace tab

Immediately upon loading a file, Snooper will display the Trace tab (as shown in Figure 15.12) and provide an additional Messages tab (shown in Figure 15.13). If the file is too large (more than 25MB), a prompt will appear asking if you want to load traces, messages, or both.

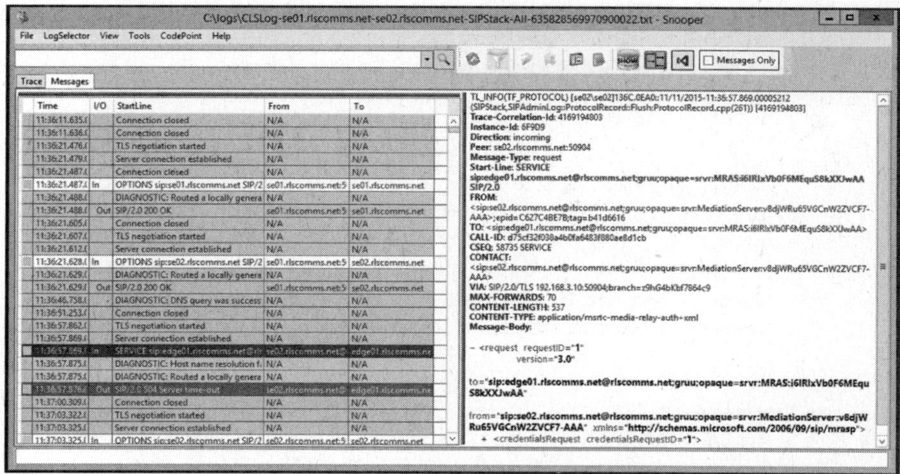

FIGURE 15.13
The Snooper Messages tab

A feature in Snooper provides the ability to switch between multiple logs with relative ease. Selecting LogSelector from the top menu (see Figure 15.13) will provide you with easy access to the logs you have opened, shown in Figure 15.14.

FIGURE 15.14
The Log Selector window

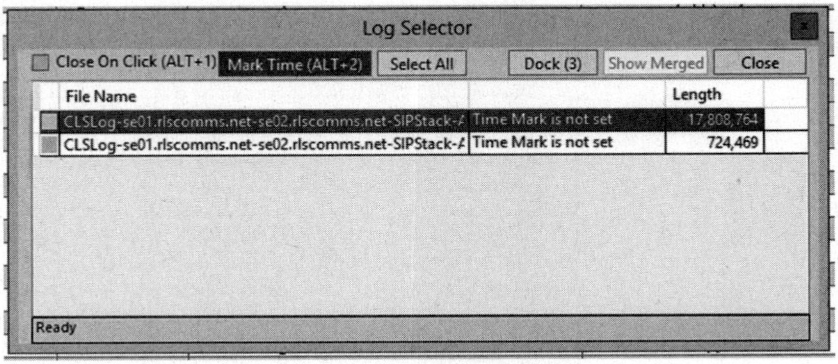

As you can imagine, this can be useful when switching between multiple client logs or even multiple server logs.

As you will see, errors will be highlighted in red, allowing a quick and easy identification process. You may not always be interested in the errors on the Trace tab because they typically show the result of the problem rather than the cause.

On the client, the component view shows Unified Communications Client Platform (UCCP) API; however, server logs provide many different components (288 to be precise). Many of these traces are typically of more use to Microsoft Product Support Services (PSS) than to the administrator.

The Messages tab is more useful to the administrator. Here, you can see the SIP flow of the client. Selecting a single message not only displays the associated content on the right but also highlights all associated messages. For example, selecting a SIP `INVITE` message will display the content directly associated with that particular message, but it will also highlight the relevant message thread, all the way through to the `BYE` message.

However, where Snooper really comes into its own is the search capabilities, quickly allowing you to find the relevant parts of the log file that you are interested in. You can manually add entries into the search bar if you know the criteria to search for (simply type into the search bar)—typically, this starts with an error message or a username (or number) related to the problem.

The simple Search menu (shown in Figure 15.15) allows you to quickly build a search string from the text within the message to narrow down the content in the log file. This becomes more relevant when you are dealing with server-generated log files rather than log files from the client.

FIGURE 15.15
Searching with Snooper

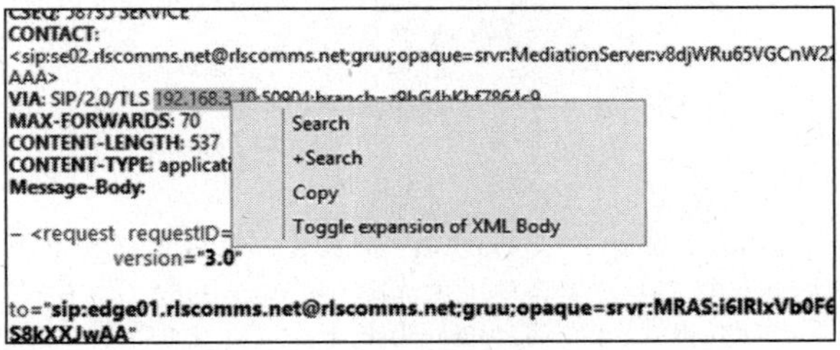

Selecting a text string and then choosing Search will simply replace the current search criteria with the selection. Obviously, being able to understand the expected process (that is, a SIP call flow) makes the troubleshooting easier because you know roughly what to expect and can interpret deviations from this expected flow to troubleshoot. In the latest version of Snooper, there is an option on the menu bar that can provide the call flow sequence (shown in Figure 15.16). This gives you the ability to understand the call flow even if you are a complete novice.

FIGURE 15.16
Location of the Call Flow button

When you click the Call Flow button, the call flow diagram window will appear. As you can see in Figure 15.17, you now receive a graphical representation of the call flow for the particular conversation you have selected.

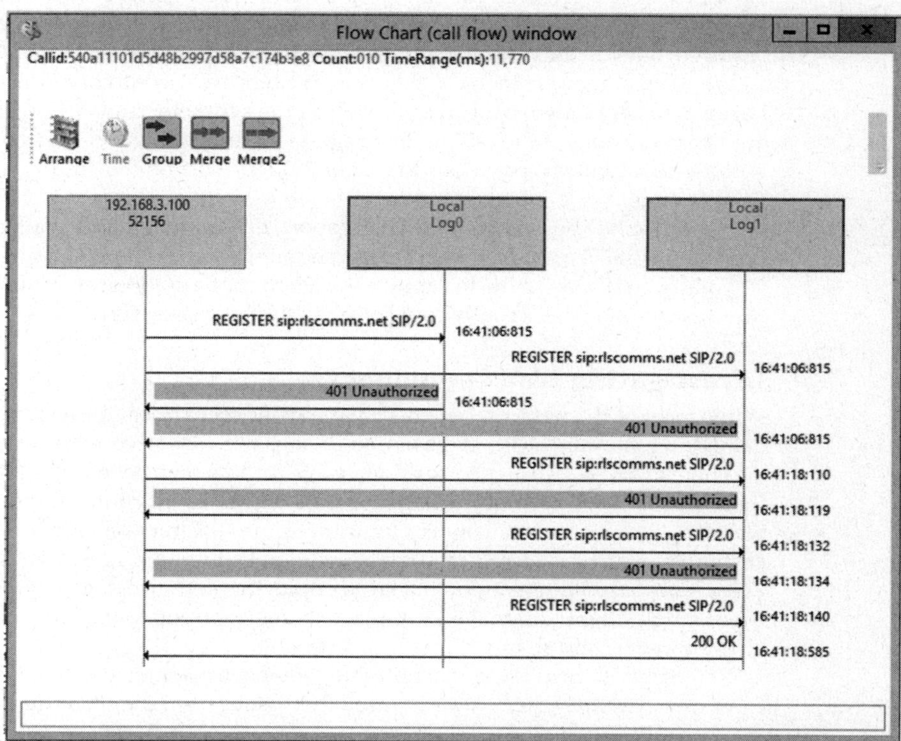

FIGURE 15.17
The call flow diagram window

Pay close attention to the detail it can provide. For example, you will see the host IPs that are involved in the communication. You can also easily see the direction of the response. Figure 15.17 shows the initial signing process.

Chapter 2, "Standards and Protocols," provides an overview of the SIP call flow process.

Diagnostic Message Text

One more feature is worth mentioning in the context of tracing. Besides providing Snooper to help you narrow down a problem, this is something that was introduced as a significant step in Lync Server 2010 and continues with the latest error messages in Skype for Business 2015, by including descriptive diagnostic text with all the messages. Some of these messages are shown here:

```
13004; reason="Request was proxied to one or more registered endpoints"
13014; reason="The routing rules did not result in a final response and callee
  is not enabled for Unified Messaging"
51004; reason="Action initiated by user"
51007; reason="Callee media connectivity diagnosis info"
```

Advanced Troubleshooting Methods

So far, we've covered only the server- and client-side logging of the Skype for Business application. In the following sections, we'll cover some of the other areas where troubleshooting may be required, outside the central logging tool and the client logs.

We'll also touch on the performance counters available to provide a view into how the hardware is actually performing as well as the synthetic transaction capability to provide automated testing of the Skype for Business environment. Ideally, this would be integrated with System Center Operations Manager 2012, providing the administrators with monitoring and alerting.

We'll also talk again about the CDR report, this time in more detail, and you'll see which parts are of particular interest in troubleshooting.

Finally, we'll show how to capture the client configuration information, which will help confirm that the client is actually connecting to the correct servers.

Investigating Web Components

While most of the web components have specific scenarios within the central logging tool for debugging, they are still web based, so IIS logs will also need to be investigated.

There are two websites to consider, each with its own set of log files. (One website is for internal client connectivity, and one is for external client connectivity. There are separate websites because the security configurations are different on each, and indeed some capability—such as administration—is available only internally.) These log files will capture every web-based interaction; in a large deployment, they can grow in size quickly because every single client will make multiple web queries upon login (for Address Book updates, client updates, and so on).

Remember to turn IIS logging off after you have completed troubleshooting. These log files can grow extremely quickly and cause other issues from the space they consume.

Finding the IIS Logs

First, you have to determine whether the user is connecting to the internal website or the external one; then, you need to establish to which server the client is connecting. For a Standard Edition pool, this is straightforward, but you could be connecting to any Front End server in an Enterprise pool, and not only that, different connection types could be going to different servers.

Central logging greatly simplifies this as you can now enable a scenario trace across the entire pool or specific machines if you are sure of the affected nodes.

Control Panel

The Control Panel is a Silverlight application, so any issues involving connectivity and loading this page are going to fall under IIS also. Often we have found that companies using a web proxy forget to configure it to exclude the pool's administration pages/websites.

Device Troubleshooting

In the event of problems with devices (assuming the device has connected), there is a Send Logs option within the device menu, which will force the device to upload its log file to the web server to the following location:

```
\\servername\share\%Pool WebServices Folder%\DeviceUpdateLogs\
```

NOTE Use the PowerShell cmdlet `Get-CsService` to find the server name and file share you created in the topology.

These logs are in Windows CE log file format and require the use of the `ReadLog.exe` tool, which is part of Windows Embedded CE. You can download this tool from the following location:

`https://www.microsoft.com/windowsembedded/en-us/developers.aspx`

Performance Counters

Windows servers come with a tool called `PerfMon.exe`, which can display a detailed view of counters within the server and any applications installed. Figure 15.18 shows `PerfMon.exe` in action.

The following counters are typically used to indicate generic server problems:

- Processor
- Disk (both LogicalDisk and PhysicalDisk)
- Memory
- Network

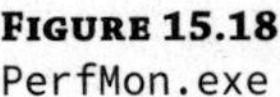

FIGURE 15.18
PerfMon.exe

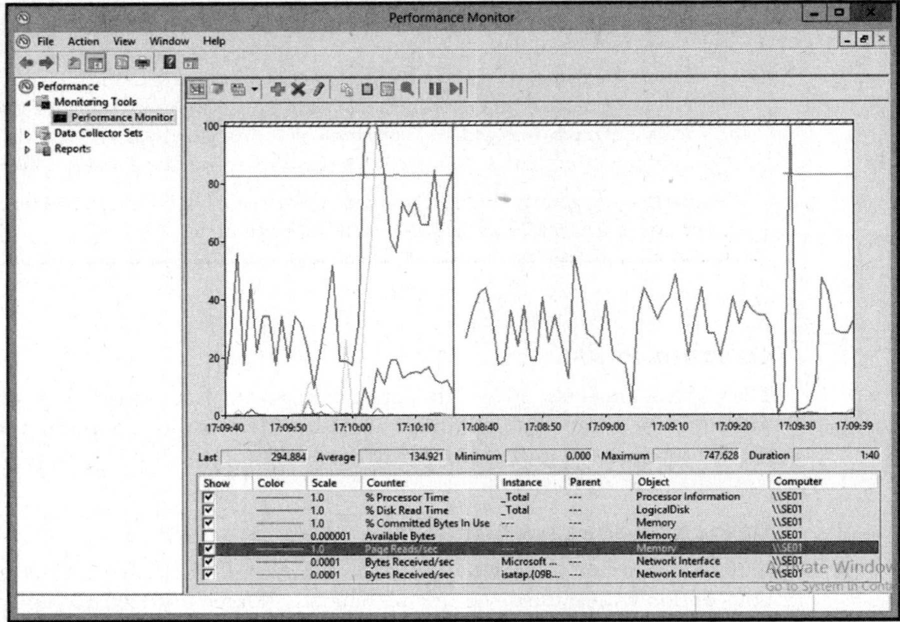

As shown in Figure 15.16, you can view multiple counters at the same time, allowing for correlation of conditions. For example, if both network and disk activity increased simultaneously, it could indicate that a file is being copied across the network to (or from) the server.

Most applications will install application-specific counters; Skype for Business Server 2015 is no different and installs several thousand! (Specific counters will vary based on which actual roles are installed on a server.) Listed here are some of the more common counter categories and specific objects within those categories:

- LS:USrv – DBSTORE\USrv – Queue Latency
- LS:USrv – DBSTORE\USrv – Sproc Latency
- LS:SIP – Load Management\SIP – Average Holding Time for Incoming Messages
- LS:SIP – Peers\SIP – Flow Controlled Connections
- LS:SIP – Responses\SIP – Local 504 Responses/sec
- LS:SIP – Peers\SIP – Sends Outstanding

These were originally detailed in a blog entry regarding server health determination for OCS, at the following location:

`http://blogs.technet.com/b/nexthop/archive/2007/09/20/how-can-i-tell-if-my-server-is-healthy-in-less-than-10-counters.aspx`

The counters and points in the blog are still relevant to Lync.

Each of the counter categories (for example, LS:SIP – Peers or LS:SIP – Responses) has a number of specific counters (for example, Flow Controlled Connections) associated with it. In most cases, they will provide rates of message flow—for example, success per second—and can be used to determine the rate of successful connections, or more likely in the case of troubleshooting, the rates (and count) of failures can be interesting.

SQL Server also installs counters, and because SQL Express is installed on every server role, these allow further in-depth visibility of the databases. (SQL-specific counters are beyond the scope of this book.)

Microsoft has identified a number of performance counters that it classes as Key Health Indicators. They are specific counters that, if the thresholds are crossed, will lead to a significant degradation of service.

You can download this list in spreadsheet format, detailing thresholds for each counter, from here:

`https://www.microsoft.com/en-us/download/details.aspx?id=46895`

Synthetic Transactions

Introduced in Chapter 13, "Archiving and Monitoring," the set of PowerShell cmdlets known as synthetic transactions are most useful when integrated with Microsoft System Center Operations Manager; however, they can be used effectively when troubleshooting because they simulate the activities carried out by the client. You can find the full list of cmdlets in Chapter 13. You'll need only a few of them for troubleshooting in this chapter.

Some of the cmdlets really are for one-time testing—for example, to test permissions prior to installation. The ones you are interested in, though, require a user ID as the parameter; this ensures that when a user reports a problem, an administrator can emulate all the correct policies that the user will be receiving so the test is an accurate reflection of the settings applied to the user.

Before you can use the `Test-Cs` cmdlets that are based on user ID, you need to configure a health configuration. This consists of two test user accounts, typically disabled but enabled for Skype for Business, that the `Test-Cs` cmdlets will use for their accounts to simulate traffic.

```
New-CsHealthMonitoringConfiguration -TargetFqdn se01.rlscomms.net
-FirstTestUserSipUri sip:test1_skype@rlscomms.net
-SecondTestUserSipUri sip:test2_skype@rlscomms.net

Identity                 : se01.rlscomms.net
FirstTestUserSipUri      : sip:test1_lync@rlscomms.net
FirstTestSamAccountName :
FirstTestUserSipUri      : sip:test1_lync@rlscomms.net
FirstTestSamAccountName :
TargetFqdn              : se01.rlscomms.net
```

Once the health configurations are configured for the pool, you can use the synthetic transactions to help troubleshoot.

For example, the command

```
Test-CsIm -TargetFqdn se01.rlscomms.net
```

will return the following if there are no problems:

```
TargetFqdn : se01.rlscomms.net
Result     : Success
```

```
Latency    : 00:00:20.0108302
Error      :
Diagnosis  :
```

Some of the `Test-Cs` cmdlets require authentication and will produce a lot of screen data prior to the results. For example, before an Address Book is created (by default at 1:30 a.m. the morning after the pool has been installed), the command

```
Test-CsAddressBookWebQuery -TargetFqdn se01.rlscomms.net
```

will return the following:

```
Connecting to web service :
https://se01.rlscomms.net/webticket/webticketservce.svc
Using Machine certificate authentication
Successfully created connection proxy and website bindings
Requesting new web ticket
Sending Web-Ticket Request:
```

This is followed by lots of XML, which has been left out for brevity, and finally this:

```
Creating WebTicket security token request
TargetUri  : https://se01.rlscomms.net/groupexpansion/service.svc
TargetFqdn : se01.rlscomms.net
Result     : Failure
Latency    : 00:00:00
Error      : Address Book Web server request has failed with response code
NoEntryFound.
Diagnosis  :
```

On the other hand, if the web server itself is not running, the same command will return the following:

```
TargetUri  : https://se01.rlscomms.net/groupexpansion/service.svc
TargetFqdn : se01.rlscomms.net
Result     : Failure
Latency    : 00:00:00
Error      : ERROR - No response received for Web-Ticket service.
Diagnosis  :
```

This response still provides the XML data; however, you can see that the error code gives a good indication of where the issue is located. Restarting the web service and allowing the Address Book to be generated (or using `Update-CsAddressBook`) gives the following response to the `Test-CsAddressBookWebQuery` command:

```
TargetUri  : https://se01.rlscomms.net/groupexpansion/service.svc
TargetFqdn : se01.rlscomms.net
Result     : Success
Latency    : 00:00:20:5385645
Error      :
Diagnosis  :
```

Monitoring Reports

As mentioned in Chapter 13, the Call Detail Report provides an extremely detailed analysis of an individual call with almost 200 individual data points captured in an audio call alone!

Some of these data points help to set the scene (network address information and client hardware and software versions, for example). However, the ones of particular interest in identifying a root cause of a problem are in the Media Line (Main Audio)—Device and Signal Metrics, Client Events, and Audio Stream sections. Each of these sections reports in a single direction for the call (such as caller to callee); however, the CDR report includes both directions, so you can compare what is sent and what is received.

Figure 15.19 shows the three sections from the caller section of the report (intervening sections have been removed for brevity); each report will include the callee data as well.

FIGURE 15.19
Using the CDR report

Callee Device and Signal Metrics			
Capture device:	Internal Microphone (Conexant 20672 SmartAudio HD)	Capture device driver:	Conexant 8.32.23.2
Render device:	Speakers (Conexant 20672 SmartAudio HD)	Render device driver:	Conexant 8.32.23.2
Microphone glitch rate:	0 per 5 minutes	Speaker glitch rate:	0 per 5 minutes
Microphone timestamp drift:	0.00118017 %	Speaker timestamp drift:	0.00118017 %
Microphone timestamp error:	0.0214656703174114 ms	Speaker timestamp error:	0.0235339105129242 ms
Echo event cause:		Voice switch cause:	
Send signal level:		Receive signal level:	-25 dBov
Send noise level:	-61 dBov	Receive nosie level:	-61 dBov
Echo return:		Initial signal level RMS:	76.3460006713867

Caller Client Event			
CPU insufficient time:	0.00 %	Microphone not functioning time:	0.00 %
Speaker not functioning time:	0.00 %	Clipping time:	0.00 %
Echo time:	0.00 %	Glitch time:	0.00 %
Voice switch time:	0.00 %	Low SNR time:	0.00 %
Low speech level time:	0.00 %	Near end to echo time:	0.00 %
Device howling event count:	0	Device multiple endpoints event count:	0
Low network bandwidth time:	0.00 %	High network delay time:	0.00 %
Poor network receive quality time:	0.00 %	Poor network send quality time:	0.00 %

Audio Stream (Callee -> Caller)			
Codec:	SILKWide	Sample rate:	16000
Audio FEC:	False	Bandwidth estimates:	41724 Kbps
Packet utilization:	97		
Avg. packet loss rate:	0.00 %	Max. packet loss rate:	0.00 %
Avg. jitter:	0 ms	Max. jitter:	1 ms
Avg. round trip:	1 ms	Max. round trip:	4 ms
Avg. concealed samples ratio:	0.00 %	Avg. stretched samples ratio:	0.00 %
Avg. compressed samples ratio:	0.00 %		
Avg. network MOS:	0.00	Min. network MOS:	0.00
Avg. network MOS degradation:	0.00	Max. network MOS degradation:	0.00

Device and Signal Metrics

The Device and Signal Metrics section of the report provides the hardware and software versions of the device in use, but more important from a troubleshooting perspective, it provides the Send and Receive sound levels.

By comparing the caller Send values with the callee Receive values (and vice versa), you can determine how much (if any) signal loss there has been because of the transmission.

Also included here is the amount of echo received by the microphone and the amount actually sent in the signal; this is a representation of how well (or badly) the echo cancellation in the device is working.

Caller Client Event

This section deals with the hardware associated with the device (including the PC if you are using built-in or USB-connected headphone and speakers).

Pay particular attention to the time values because they indicate how long the device has been malfunctioning; any value in the fields in this section indicates a problem with the call. Other sections of the report provide informational data, whereas any data in this section indicates a problem. You may need to refer to other sections to determine exactly what the problem is.

Audio Stream

The Audio Stream section covers the network impact to the call and provides information on the specific codec used for the call.

This section will help to determine whether the network is causing any of the problems because this is where you can see information related to the packet loss, jitter, and round-trip time. Also included here is information on how much healing was carried out on the call. Finally, the MOS values show how much impact the network conditions have had on the call quality.

> **Independent Media Streams**
>
> When troubleshooting audio issues, it's important to remember that each directional stream is completely independent. It's not unusual to have issues in one direction only. This may indicate a network issue, such as incorrect routing or router interface bandwidth issues.

Client Side

You can determine the connected client configuration by holding down the left Ctrl key and right-clicking the Skype for Business icon in the system tray to bring up a menu from which you select the Configuration Information item. This will call up the screen shown in Figure 15.20.

The client will cache a significant set of information, ranging from configuration items and search query results to photos and voice mails.

To ensure that the latest configuration information is being provided to the client and remove the possibility of stale cached information, you should delete the cache files in the following folder location:

```
%USER PROFILE%\AppData\Local\Microsoft\Office\<office version>\Lync\sip_<sip address>\
```

Figure 15.20
Configuration information

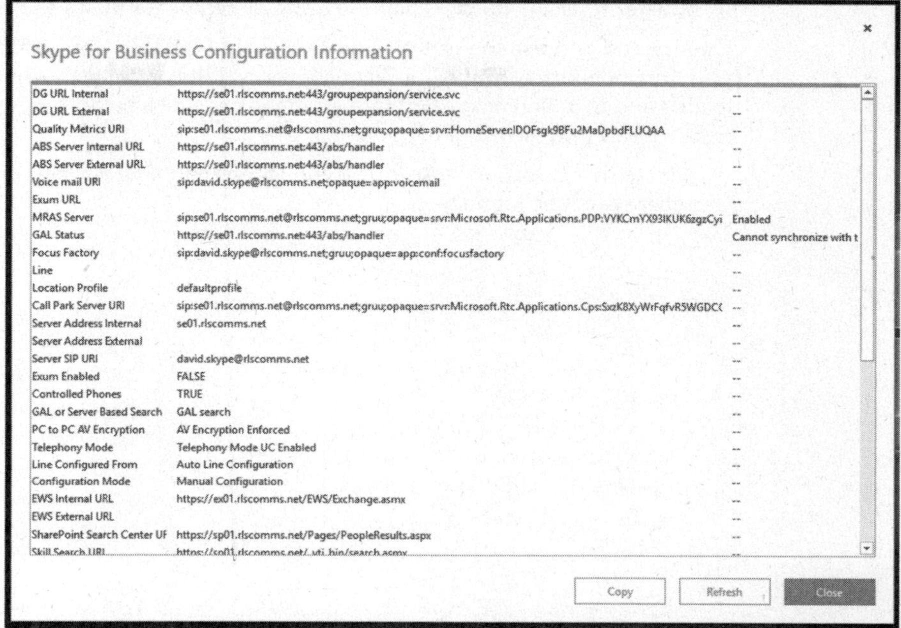

Skype for Business Configuration Information
DG URL Internal https://se01.rlscomms.net:443/groupexpansion/service.svc --
DG URL External https://se01.rlscomms.net:443/groupexpansion/service.svc --
Quality Metrics URI sip:se01.rlscomms.net@rlscomms.net;gruu;opaque=srvr:HomeServer:lDOFsgk9BFu2MaDpbdFLUQAA --
ABS Server Internal URL https://se01.rlscomms.net:443/abs/handler --
ABS Server External URL https://se01.rlscomms.net:443/abs/handler --
Voice mail URI sip:david.skype@rlscomms.net;opaque=app:voicemail --
Exum URL --
MRAS Server sip:se01.rlscomms.net@rlscomms.net;gruu;opaque=srvr:Microsoft.Rtc.Applications.PDP:VYKCmYX93IKUK6zgzCyi Enabled
GAL Status https://se01.rlscomms.net:443/abs/handler Cannot synchronize with t
Focus Factory sip:david.skype@rlscomms.net;gruu;opaque=app:conf:focusfactory --
Line --
Location Profile defaultprofile --
Call Park Server URI sip:se01.rlscomms.net@rlscomms.net;gruu;opaque=srvr:Microsoft.Rtc.Applications.Cps:SxzK8XyWrFqfvR5WGDC(--
Server Address Internal se01.rlscomms.net --
Server Address External --
Server SIP URI david.skype@rlscomms.net --
Exum Enabled FALSE --
Controlled Phones TRUE --
GAL or Server Based Search GAL search --
PC to PC AV Encryption AV Encryption Enforced --
Telephony Mode Telephony Mode UC Enabled --
Line Configured From Auto Line Configuration --
Configuration Mode Manual Configuration --
EWS Internal URL https://ex01.rlscomms.net/EWS/Exchange.asmx --
EWS External URL --
SharePoint Search Center UF https://sp01.rlscomms.net/Pages/PeopleResults.aspx --
Copy
Refresh
Close

The Bottom Line

Confirm that the basics are in place from the infrastructure side. Skype for Business Server 2015 relies on a range of additional infrastructure to be able to provide its functionality—such as Active Directory, SQL, DNS, network, and so on. If any of these additional areas suffer interruptions or misconfigurations, it is extremely likely that Skype for Business will begin to demonstrate issues also.

> **Master It** An internal Skype for Business client is having difficulty connecting to its home pool when using automatic configuration. Describe the flow of DNS and connection attempts made for a client on the corporate network.

Understand how to troubleshoot the client. The Skype for Business client provides a lot of information in the configuration section as well as the log files to aid with troubleshooting, and this information should not be overlooked.

> **Master It** Where are the client log files stored?

Know how to enable troubleshooting on the server. The Skype for Business Server roles have individual components that require logging and also provide performance counter objects that can be monitored.

By default, the logging scenario AlwaysOn is enabled on the servers. The default logging options and components can be configured to suit users' needs.

Master It How do you enable logging on Skype for Business Server?

Understand and use the troubleshooting tools available. In addition to the built-in logging functionality of Skype for Business Server 2015, more tools can (and should) be downloaded and installed on each of the servers to provide a better range of data, which is ready to be captured in the event of a problem.

Master It Which tool is recommended for analyzing SIP logs or message traces? And where can it be found?

Part 4

Voice

Chapter 16

Getting Started with Voice

Lync Server 2010 on its release was targeted as a match (and replacement) for most PBXs, providing what was considered to be fully fledged voice capability to the users via both the Lync Communicator client and the desktop phone device. Lync Server 2013 expanded on the capabilities.

Skype for Business Server 2015 takes more of a "consolidation" approach. It doesn't introduce significant new features, at least not in the Release to Manufacture (RTM) code, but it improves resilience and operations.

In this chapter, we'll cover how the Enterprise Voice capabilities are managed, providing voice services to the user.

Because users' expectations for voice have increased to be on par with PBX, this is important. Can you remember the last time your company had a problem that caused the PBX to fail? In most cases, that's extremely rare. People expect to pick up a phone and have it work. Skype for Business Server 2015 is building on the previous reputation of Lync Server.

In this chapter, you will learn to

- Understand the voice capabilities
- Understand the voice architecture
- Configure voice policies and routing

The Backstory

In the early days of the Microsoft Unified Communications suite (before it was even called Unified Communications), Live Communications Server provided a feature called Remote Call Control (RCC), and while this feature is slowly being deprecated with each new version, it was the first way to integrate an instant messaging product with voice functionality (albeit through a traditional-style telephony system). RCC works by allowing the Communicator client to send signaling information to the PBX, via a dedicated server/interface, allowing control of the desk handset—you clicked (or typed) a number and then picked up the handset to talk. Indeed, RCC has now been deprecated, but a new feature, called Call Via Work, provides a similar capability and is itself a feature defined for mobile clients in other versions of the Microsoft Unified Communications software. You'll learn more about Call Via Work later in this chapter.

Office Communications Server 2007 introduced the concept of Enterprise Voice, whereby the Communicator client itself was considered a phone (either hardware or software) and integrated via a media gateway device into a traditional (or IP) PBX or, indeed, directly to the PSTN. Office Communications Server 2007 R2 developed the voice functionality further and moved closer to being a PBX; however, there was still functionality that required the PBX—only in certain cases (typically, small companies or branches) could OCS 2007 R2 be considered capable of replacing a PBX.

Lync Server 2010 was the first true step in replacing a PBX (and for many enterprises it did), and as you'll see in the following pages, Lync Server 2013 closed that gap in both features and high-availability capability. Skype for Business Server 2015 takes other leap toward achieving the true PBX replacement capability.

Understanding the Voice Capabilities

As mentioned previously, Skype for Business Server 2015 expands the voice capabilities previously developed in versions of Lync Server and Office Communications Server 2007 (and 2007 R2). Table 16.1 shows the feature set and when each feature was first introduced. These are all cumulative; if a feature is listed as OCS 2007, it is also available in OCS 2007 R2, Lync Server 2010, Lync Server 2013, and Skype for Business Server 2015 unless specifically indicated.

TABLE 16.1: Voice feature set

FEATURE NAME	FIRST AVAILABLE	SUMMARY
Inbound/outbound PSTN dialing	OCS 2007	Basic call functionality.
Call forward	OCS 2007	This is the ability to have incoming calls automatically forwarded to another contact or external number.
Simultaneous ring	OCS 2007	Similar to call forwarding, but instead of redirecting the call, it allows both the UC endpoint and the other endpoint to ring and the call can be answered at either endpoint.
Unified messaging	OCS 2007	Voicemail capability.
Single number reach	OCS 2007 R2	This is the ability to place a call from a mobile device and have that call routed via the OCS 2007 R2 infrastructure to enable the presentation of the OCS 2007 R2 user caller ID and the capture of call data records (CDRs).
Delegation/team call	OCS 2007 R2	Allows others to handle calls on your behalf.
SIP trunking	OCS 2007 R2	Allows direct connection to a Mediation server without the use of a media gateway.

TABLE 16.1: Voice feature set *(CONTINUED)*

FEATURE NAME	FIRST AVAILABLE	SUMMARY
Dial-in audio conferencing	OCS 2007 R2	Provides audio-only conferencing to PSTN users.
Response group	OCS 2007 R2	Provides small-scale team and hunt group capability.
Call Admission Control	Lync Server 2010	Provides controls for the quality and quantity of calls on the network.
Call Park	Lync Server 2010	Provides the capability to *park* a call from one Lync device and *retrieve* from another.
Unassigned number handling	Lync Server 2010	Allows for handling of incoming calls to numbers that have not been assigned to users.
Media bypass	Lync Server 2010	Endpoints can connect directly to another non-Lync endpoint (via G711) without the need to have the media transcoded by a Mediation server.
E9-1-1	Lync Server 2010	Support for the Enhanced 911 emergency services requirements to provide location information with an emergency call.
Analog devices	Lync Server 2010	Support for analog device integration, allowing for application of policy and capture of CDR information from non-Lync devices.
Common-area phone	Lync Server 2010	Provides the ability to designate a device as a common-area device (for use in areas such as a lobby), allowing the device to be available for inbound and outbound calls under a generic policy, and provides the capacity to allow a user to log in and use the device as their own but be automatically logged out after a time period.
Private line	Lync Server 2010	Provides a user with a second number allowing the direct receipt of incoming calls.
Malicious call trace	Lync Server 2010	Allows a call to be flagged as malicious in the CDR database.
Caller ID manipulation	Lync Server 2013	Enables the ability to display (or override) caller ID based on specific trunk calling information. Can be controlled for both caller and callee.

TABLE 16.1: Voice feature set *(CONTINUED)*

FEATURE NAME	FIRST AVAILABLE	SUMMARY
Voicemail Escape	Lync Server 2013	This feature can detect when a call has been routed to the user's mobile phone voice mail without giving the user the opportunity to answer the call. This scenario occurs when the user enables simultaneous ringing to their mobile phone and their mobile phone is turned off, out of battery, or out of range. Voicemail Escape detects that the call was immediately answered by the user's mobile phone voice mail and disconnects the call to the mobile phone voice mail.
Intertrunk routing	Lync Server 2013	This feature provides call control functionalities to downstream IP-PBXs. Lync Server can interconnect an IP-PBX to a PSTN gateway so that calls from a PBX phone can be routed to the PSTN and incoming PSTN calls can be routed to a PBX phone.
Call Via Work	Skype for Business Server 2015	Previously available for mobile devices only, within Skype for Business Server, the functionality is extended to desk phones attached to a PBX. It allows for the Skype for Business client to initiate calls from the desk phone, allowing for a consistent user experience.

A number of these Skype for Business Server 2015 capabilities are covered elsewhere in this book. Table 16.2 provides cross references to those chapters.

TABLE 16.2: Skype for Business Server capability cross references

CAPABILITY	CHAPTER
Call Admission Control	17
Call Park	19
Unassigned number handling	19
E9-1-1	18
Analog devices	6
Common-area phone	6
Private line, malicious call trace, media bypass (covered in more detail in this chapter)	16

Of course, before you can really get started looking at voice capabilities, you have to ensure the user is enabled for voice, using a cmdlet similar to this one:

```
Set-CsUser -Identity "sip:keith.skype@rlscomms.net"
-EnterpriseVoiceEnabled $true
-LineURI "tel:+44555111122"
```

Now you're in a better position to look at the other features available.

Private Line

A private line allows users to have a second Direct Inward Dial (DID) number assigned to them, which will directly notify a user of an incoming call. As indicated by the name, it is intended to be for private calls only; therefore, the call does not follow any team-call or delegation-configured rules. It also ignores any presence-based rules such as Do Not Disturb, ensuring that it will always get through.

The private line can be set only via PowerShell, using the `Set-CsUser` cmdlet, as in this example:

```
Set-CsUser -Identity "sip:keith.skype@rlscomms.net" -PrivateLine
"tel:+15557654321"
```

The number assigned to the private line does not appear anywhere within Active Directory (ensuring that it remains private) and indeed is even hidden within Lync Server. To view the number (and other hidden attributes), you must use the `Get-CsUser` cmdlet with the following syntax:

```
Get-CsUser -Identity "sip:keith.skype@rlscomms.net" | fl *
```

The resulting output looks like this:

```
SamAccountName                     : Keith_Skype
UserPrincipalName                 : keith.skype@rlscomms.net
FirstName                         : Keith
LastName                           : Skype
WindowsEmailAddress               : Keith.Skype@rlscomms.net
Sid                               : S-1-5-21-1801160900-2869415974-1656638013-1144
LineServerURI                     :
OriginatorSid                     :
AudioVideoDisabled                  : False
IPPBXSoftPhoneRoutingEnabled      : False
RemoteCallControlTelephonyEnabled : False
PrivateLine                               : tel:+44666111122
AcpInfo                            : {}
HostedVoiceMail                         :
DisplayName                             : Keith Skype
ProxyAddresses                    : {sip:Keith.Skype@rlscomms.net}
HomeServer                          : CN=Lc
Services,CN=Microsoft,CN=1:1,
CN=Pools,CN=RTC Service,CN=Services,CN=Configuration,DC=rlscomms,
Dc=net
```

```
TargetServerIfMoving                    :
EnabledForFederation                    : True
EnabledForInternetAccess                  : True
PublicNetworkEnabled                  : True
EnterpriseVoiceEnabled           : True
EnabledForRichPresence             : True

ExchangeArchivingPolicy            : Uninitialized

LineURI                                 : tel:+44555111122
SipAddress                              : sip:Keith.skype@rlscomms.net
Enabled                                 : True
TenantId                                : 00000000-0000-0000-0000-000000000000
UserRoutingGroupId                       : 8ec325cb-b512-587d-9d03-e940e7cc1490
TargetRegistrarPool                   :
VoicePolicy                             :
ConferencingPolicy                      :
PresencePolicy                          :
VoiceRoutingPolicy                       :
RegistrarPool                           : se01.rlscomms.net
DialPlan                                :
LocationPolicy                          :
ClientPolicy                            :
ClientVersionPolicy                     :
ArchivingPolicy                         :
LegalInterceptPolicy                    :
PinPolicy                               :
CallViaWorkPolicy                       :
GraphPolicy                             :
ExternalAccessPolicy                    :
HostedVoicemailPolicy                   :
PesistentChatPolicy                     :
UserServicesPolicy                      :
ExperiencePolicy                        :
AddressBookPolicy                       :
HostingProvider                         : SRV:
ObjectId                                : 00000000-0000-0000-0000-000000000000
ExUmEnabled                             : False
Name                                           : Keith Skype
DistinguishedName                       : CN=Keith
Skype,CN=Users,DC=rlscomms,Dc=net
Identity                              : CN=Keith Skype,CN=Users,
DC=rlscomms,Dc=net
Guid                                    : 43cea8f9-5d84-4007-bd4b-d2daac38986a
ObjectCategory                        :
CN=Person,CN=Schema,CN=Configuration,
DC=rlscomms,Dc=net
ObjectClass                           : {top, person, organizationalPerson, user}
```

```
WhenChanged                         : 29/09/2015 15:01:02
WhenCreated                         : 29/09/2015 09:09:24
OriginatingServer                         : dc01.rlscomms.net
IsByPassValidation                     : False
IsValid                                   : True
ObjectState                         : Unchanged
```

Although a private line can be configured without enabling Enterprise Voice, the user must be Enterprise Voice–enabled for a private line to work.

The bold entries indicate the attributes that are not shown onscreen by default but that are returned by the `Get-CsUser` cmdlet when you include the `| fl *` portion. One attribute of significant note is the `TargetServerIfMoving` attribute. It is set to `True` if the user is in the process of moving pools. No other cmdlets will succeed for a user if this attribute is `True`.

Malicious Call Trace

Skype for Business Server 2015 provides the ability for a user to flag the previous call as malicious immediately after hanging up the call. The data is flagged within a CDR record and, as such, requires the Monitoring server role to be deployed and configured. When a call is flagged, an entry is logged in the CDR database, allowing the administrator to identify the call as well as the associated information such as calling number, gateways used, duration of call, and so on.

Figure 16.1 shows the user interface to flag a malicious call.

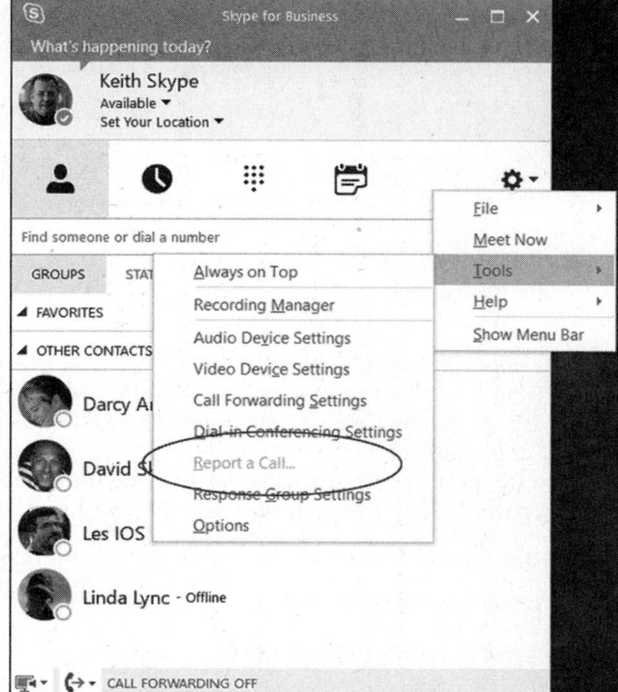

FIGURE 16.1
Flagging a malicious call

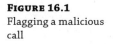

Malicious call tracing is enabled as part of the Voice policy applied to users via the `Set-CsVoicePolicy` cmdlet or through the Control Panel ➢ Voice Routing ➢ Voice Policy page (see Figure 16.2).

FIGURE 16.2 Enabling malicious call tracing via the Control Panel

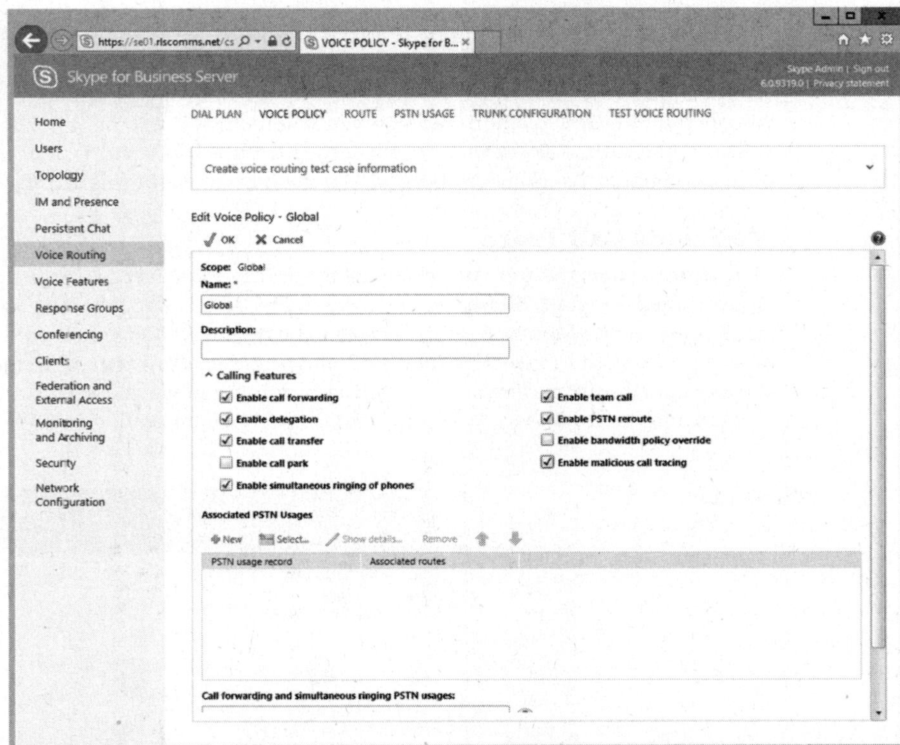

It is important to understand that aside from the entry being logged in the CDR database, there is no automated process to alert an administrator of a malicious call. You must monitor the database via System Center Operations Manager or other similar alerting system to enable some sort of automated alerting.

You can perform a manual query using the Top Failures Report from the Monitoring server report pack. To filter for malicious calls, you must select the following filter items:

- ◆ Category: Both expected and unexpected failures
- ◆ Diagnostic ID: 51017

Figure 16.3 shows an example of the filtered report.

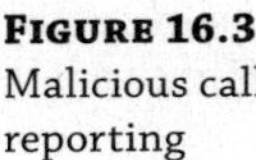

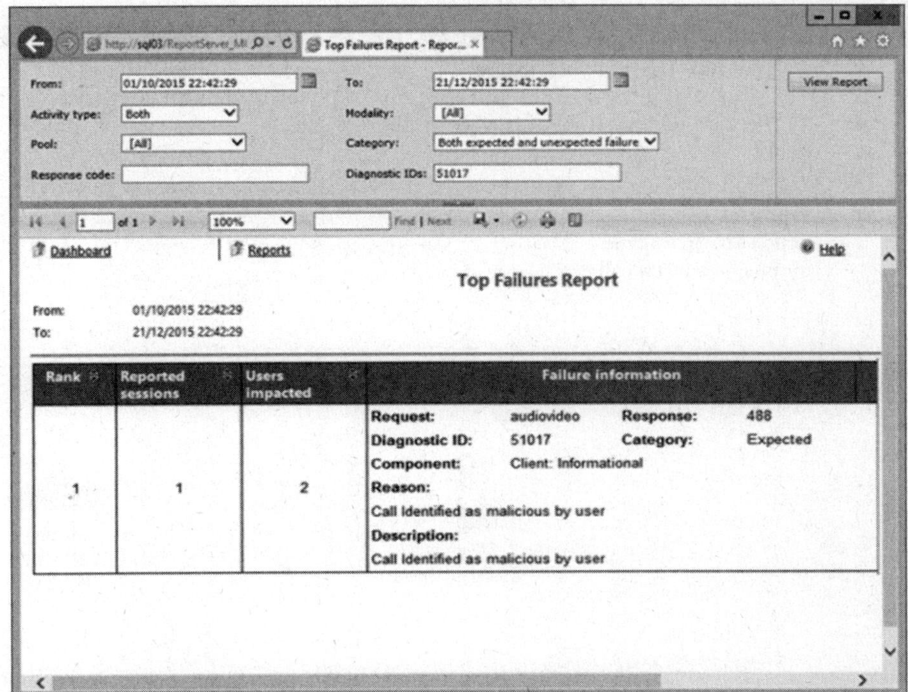

FIGURE 16.3 Malicious call reporting

Media Bypass

Lync Server 2010 introduced an important key feature called *media bypass*, which allows an organization to reduce the number of servers required (specifically reducing the load on Mediation servers).

So, what's the big deal? Well, media bypass allows the clients to talk directly to non-Skype for Business (or Lync/OCS) endpoints without transcoding the media stream by the Mediation server. Reducing the need for transcoding from native OCS codecs (such as RTAudio) to PSTN-style codecs (such as G711) improves the quality of the audio stream by reducing the number of network hops as well as reducing the loss when changing codecs.

OCS 2007 R2 introduced the capability for clients to use a G711 codec natively; however, the media stream still had to pass through the Mediation server (even though no transcoding occurred) when making a PSTN call.

The G711 codec uses more bandwidth but provides a better-quality signal than RTAudio Narrowband; however, the RTAudio codec copes better on congested networks. Therefore, it is a better choice across WAN connections, and G711 is preferred on a LAN. (Remember, of course, that Skype for Business clients prefer to use the SILK codec when communicating directly to other Skype for Business clients.)

Where the media gateway (or compatible IP-PBX) is located on the same LAN, it makes more sense to use the higher-quality codec because it is likely the LAN will be able to cope with the (small) increase in traffic. Enabling media bypass allows this to happen and delivers the media stream directly to the gateway (or IP-PBX), removing the Mediation server from the call path and optimizing the call flow.

Signaling traffic (SIP) will continue to pass through the Mediation server. Figure 16.4 shows the path of each type of traffic for a PSTN call.

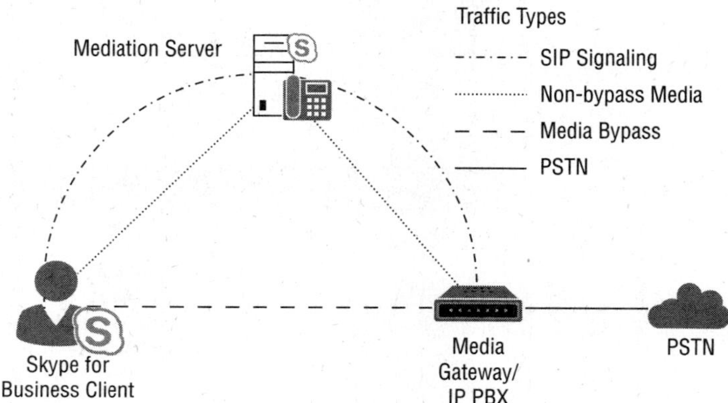

Figure 16.4
Traffic flow in a Skype for Business PSTN call

Removing the transcoding from a Mediation server dramatically increases the concurrent call capability of the server, and it allows the server role to be colocated with a Front End server, reducing the number of servers required in a voice deployment.

Understanding the Voice Architecture

Media bypass is a good context in which to look at the voice architecture within Skype for Business (and Lync) and understand what is needed to provide Enterprise Voice capability to users.

Obviously, you need a pool (either Standard or Enterprise Edition) on which the users are to be homed. In addition, you need the Mediation server role to be installed and a certified integration device (media gateway, IP-PBX, or SIP trunk). These functions no longer have to be physical hardware because virtualization is fully supported. Figure 16.5 shows the minimum infrastructure requirements for Enterprise Voice.

Again, this configuration is the minimum required to provide Enterprise Voice. More realistically, we will cover additional configuration such as high-availability and resiliency options, improved reporting and troubleshooting, expanded client (device) support, and increased configuration items such as E9-1-1 or Call Admission Control. This is where you'll start to get into the depths of the voice requirements for a design, not only hardware capability but configuration as well.

Figure 16.6 shows the full scope of Enterprise Voice interaction or requirements.

With this view of the building blocks of Enterprise Voice, you can examine the role that each component will play.

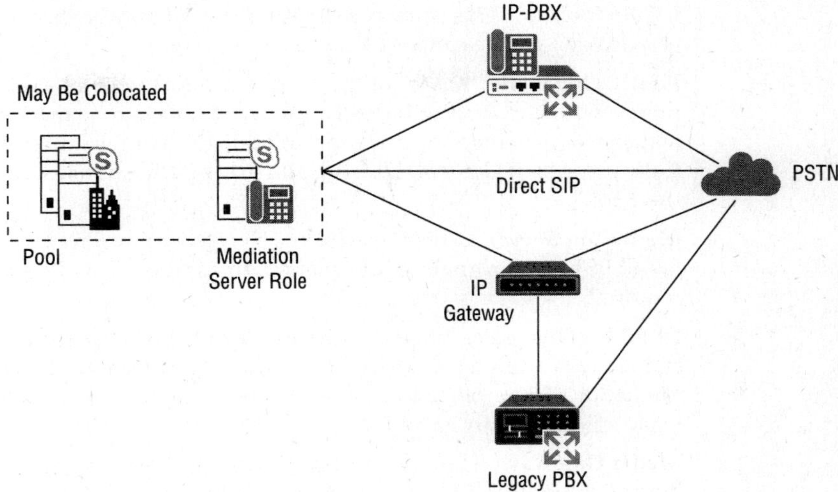

FIGURE 16.5 Minimum infrastructure requirements for Enterprise Voice

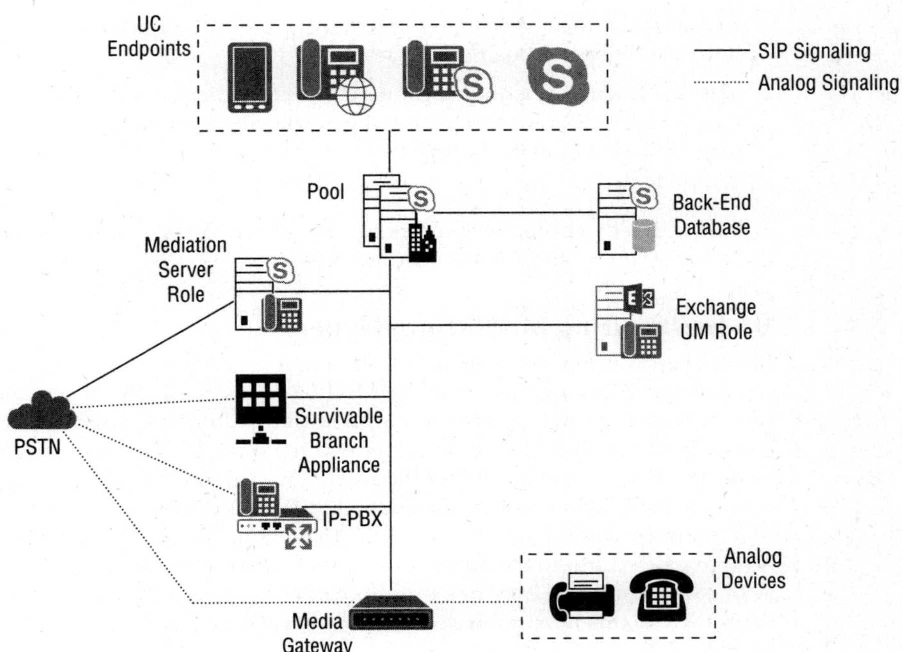

FIGURE 16.6 Voice architecture within Skype for Business Server 2015

UC Endpoints This is the actual user device; it may be the softphone Communicator client or a desktop device running Lync Phone Edition.

Pool This is the "heart" of the system. Clients register against a pool and receive a policy, which in turn will determine what calls can be made by each user as well as the feature set provided to each user. In addition, configuration items such as call routing, Call Admission Control, E9-1-1, Call Park, and Response Groups are all configured on the pool.

Mediation Server This role may be colocated on the Front End servers and is responsible for all PSTN call-signaling information. In addition, it will transcode the media traffic when required.

IP-PBX This is a certified device capable of media bypass. If not certified, it requires connectivity via a certified media gateway; if not capable of media bypass, it requires a Mediation server role to transcode the client media. A non-IP-PBX (legacy) may be connected via a certified media gateway.

Media Gateway This is a certified device capable of media bypass. If not capable of media bypass, it requires a Mediation server role to transcode the client media. This is also capable of supporting the connectivity of analog devices (such as a fax machine) and allowing Lync Server 2010 (and 2013) to manage these devices (via policy).

Monitoring Databases These databases store the CDR and quality of experience (QoE) information, allowing the reporting and troubleshooting of calls. This capability is not required but is strongly recommended when you're deploying Enterprise Voice to aid with troubleshooting. The Monitoring role itself is built into the Front End role.

Exchange Unified Messaging Exchange 2007 SP1 (or higher) provides the voicemail capability for Skype for Business Server 2015.

Trunk A trunk is a unique combination of Mediation server FQDN, Mediation server SIP listening port, Gateway FQDN, and gateway SIP listening port; it's not shown in Figure 16.6 directly and should be thought of as a virtual infrastructure element, made up of its components.

We've already covered a lot of these integration points in other chapters, so let's focus on the PSTN integration aspect now—Mediation servers.

Understanding Mediation Servers

In both versions of Office Communications Server 2007, the Mediation server had a one-to-one relationship with a media gateway (or IP-PBX). This meant that a large number of Mediation servers were required, and there was no flexibility for the supported hardware. It didn't matter how many calls your Mediation server was handling through the gateway on the other side; the same hardware was required for the server. In addition to this, a failure in either the Mediation server or the gateway would invalidate that route for calls.

With the release of Lync Server 2010, that one-to-one relationship has gone away. Now there is no practical limit to the number of gateways a single Mediation server can service; but there is, of course, only the maximum number of concurrent calls a single Mediation server can handle. Even this maximum number is now variable based on the specifications of the hardware in use.

Not only that, but since Lync Server 2013 was released, Mediation servers can be pooled, giving a many-to-many relationship and providing an additional level of resiliency to the call flow.

Figure 16.7 compares the Office Communications Server approach and the Lync Server 2013 approach to Mediation servers.

FIGURE 16.7 The OCS 2007 approach vs. current Skype for Business Server 2015 Mediation server approach

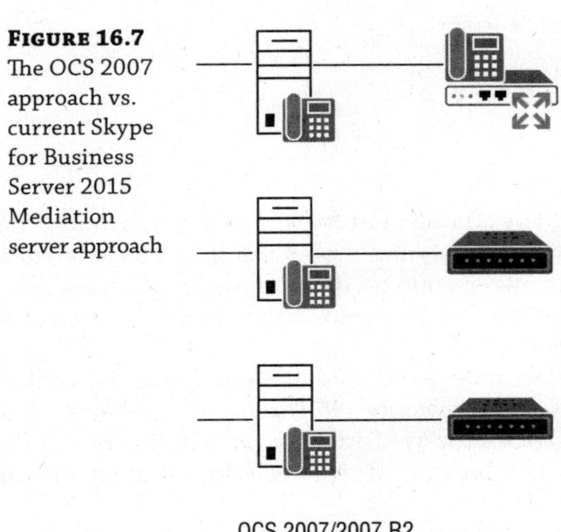

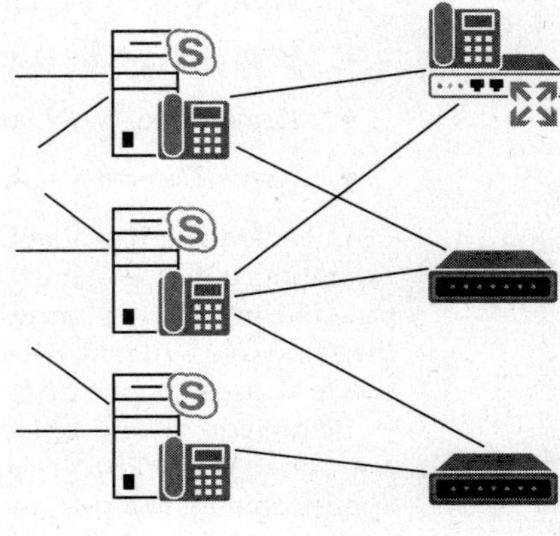

The Office Communications Server approach is still valid with Skype for Business Server 2015 even if media bypass is not enabled. That is, the Mediation server will deal with not only SIP traffic but also the media transcoding.

In the SIP trunk scenario, a dedicated Mediation server is required to provide a termination point for the Skype for Business endpoints.

High Availability and Resiliency for Voice

When Skype for Business Server 2015 replaces a PBX, the user's expectations don't change; indeed, often the user isn't aware of the back-end infrastructure. Telephony has been around for decades, and the expectation of always being able to make a call when you pick up a handset is normal.

Right or wrong, user expectations about the uptime and availability of IT services are still very poor, based mostly on the early "Blue Screen of Death" experiences of Windows NT despite the massive steps forward since then. Previous chapters have covered resiliency in a general approach for user login; here the focus is purely on voice.

Skype for Business Server 2015 has to overcome this preconception so that when there are challenges with the integrity of the IT infrastructure (whether networking or server related), the telephony service will continue and users will (ideally) be unaffected. This is not possible in all cases, but Skype for Business Server 2015 does a fantastic job of overcoming the majority of these cases to ensure that service continues.

We will consider the following failure scenarios:

- Individual server failure: Front End server
- Individual server failure: Back End server
- Multiple server failure: Complete pool
- Multiple server failure: Complete data center
- Back end failure: Database unavailable
- Remote site: WAN failure
- Active Directory failure

In general, high availability is achieved by adding more servers of the same role to the configuration, either as stand-alone (using some sort of round-robin resource allocation) or as pool-based (using DNS or hardware load balancing) resources. If one of the servers fails, the others of the same role will take over the services of that server. In most cases, this is seamless; however, in a few cases, there may be a small impact.

Before you review each case, you need to understand the call flows involved in making an Enterprise Voice (PSTN) call. Although we'll review only a PSTN call in detail here, all of this applies equally to a peer-to-peer call, except for the Mediation server role. Figure 16.8 shows the anatomy of a call; the Mediation server role is broken out separately so you can better understand the call flow.

FIGURE 16.8
Call flow of an Enterprise Voice call

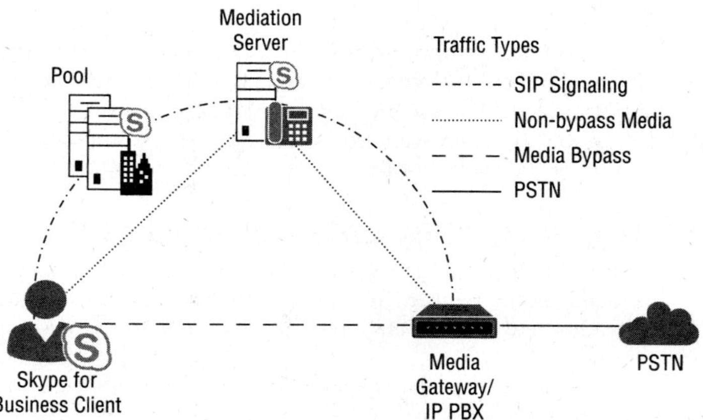

You can see the signaling traffic flows from the client through the Front End server to the Mediation server and finally to the gateway, or IP-PBX. Media takes a more direct route, from the client through the Mediation server to the gateway—or, if media bypass is supported and enabled, directly from the client to the gateway itself.

Individual Server Failure: Front End Server

The failure of an individual Front End server in an Enterprise pool does not have a significant impact on users logged in or to calls already in progress. If a user was logged in via the failed server, they will automatically reconnect to another Front End server in the pool (via either hardware or DNS load balancing). If the user is in a call at the time of their server failure, the call will continue unaffected (this functionality was introduced in Office Communications Server 2007 R2); however, signaling will be unavailable until the client is signed into another Front End server. Figure 16.9 shows the user experience of the call in progress while the client is unable to connect to the Front End server.

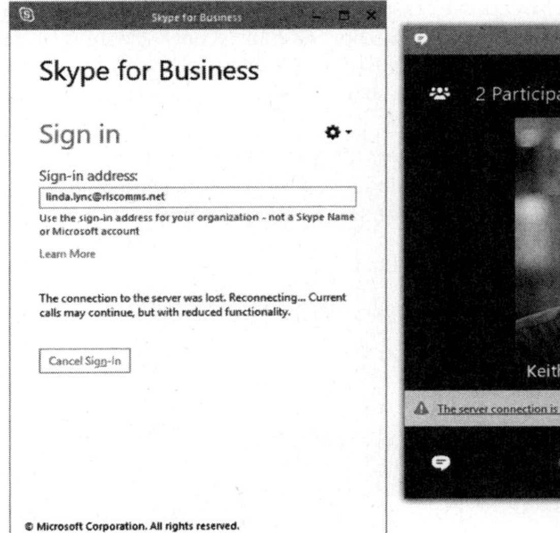

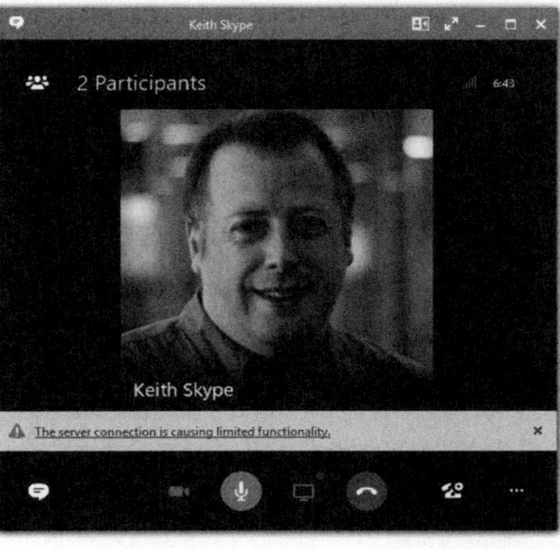

Figure 16.9 User experience mid-call with a Front End failure

The impact of signaling not being available is that although the media traffic continues, no changes can be made to it, such as transferring a call or placing the call on hold. These functions will automatically become available again when the client (automatically) signs in to another Front End server or when the failed server is returned to service (whichever occurs first).

If a user is dialed into a conference hosted on the failed Front End server, the user will be disconnected and will have to redial to rejoin the conference—which will be moved to an available server in the same pool.

Individual Server Failure: Mediation Server

The loss of a Mediation server is similar to the loss of a Front End server unless the Mediation server is performing media transcoding for a call, in which case the call will be dropped. The call flow is as shown in Figure 16.8, and the user experience is as shown in Figure 16.9, with the exception that the client will remain signed in. Once the Mediation server is in a failed state, the routing processes on the Front End servers are notified of the downed Mediation server and will route any calls being placed to other suitable Mediation servers. For incoming calls, the gateway will be aware of the failure (because of the failed heartbeat SIP Options message exchange) and will redirect calls to another Mediation server.

Multiple Server Failure: Complete Pool

With versions of OCS and LCS, when a user's pool failed, the user would be logged out and unable to carry out any tasks. A call in progress at this point would continue to operate with no signaling functionality available—assuming you're using Office Communications Server 2007 R2 rather than Office Communications Server 2007 (where it would be dropped).

Lync Server 2010 introduced the concept of a *backup* registrar; this is where the client will connect in the event of a failure in its primary registrar. A primary registrar failure comprises all the servers in the pool failing.

There are a few items that must be configured to achieve this. First, the topology of a pool must be configured (and published) to have a backup registrar assigned (shown in Figure 16.10). Associated with this configuration are some timeout values.

- Failover timeout (default 300 seconds)
- Failback timeout (default 600 seconds)

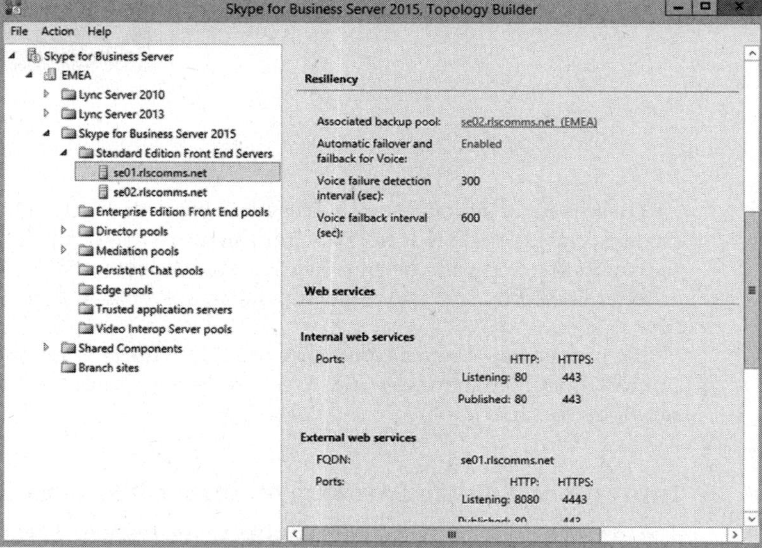

Figure 16.10 Configuring a backup registrar

These default values are deliberately set slightly high to ensure that simple "blips" on the network do not cause all the clients to fail over to another pool and back again in quick succession.

Next, you are required to configure the DNS SRV record for automatic login to have multiple entries, possibly with different priorities (this will depend on the environment). If you are using a Director in the environment, this will have the highest priority for the SRV record, with the primary pool being next. The highest-priority record is the one that all clients will attempt to connect to first. This setting is more important in a widely distributed deployment; you may not want European clients attempting to connect to a North American–based pool for their first attempt, even though the traffic is quite a small SIP request.

The use of multiple entries for the same SRV record ensures that if the first record directs to a pool that is unavailable, the client will try the next, and so on, until it finds an available pool to which to connect. Once connected, this pool will redirect to the correct pool (either primary or backup) if online.

The `SIP REGISTER` redirect request for the initial login will include a response like this:

```
07/09/2015|21:13:05.270 4D4:6F8 INFO  :: SIP/2.0 301 Redirect request to Home
Server
Contact: <sip:se01.rlscomms.net:5061;transport=TLS>;q=0.7
Contact: <sip:se02.rlscomms.net:5061;transport=TLS>;q=0.3
```

This means that the client will attempt to register with the primary pool first, indicated by the `q=0.7`, and if that is unavailable will fail over to the pool indicated by the backup registrar, indicated by the `q=0.3`.

When the primary registrar has failed and the client has connected to the backup registrar, all functionality should continue to operate as normal.

However, if the client is connected to a Survivable Branch Appliance (SBA) or Survivable Branch Server (SBS) and if the primary pool fails, not all functionality will be available. Some of the built-in functionality is specific to a pool, such as the following:

- Response Groups
- Call Park
- Conferencing
- Buddy list
- Presence-based routing (such as Do Not Disturb)

In this case the client goes into *Survivable* mode and displays a warning message to the user (see Figure 16.11). When the primary pool (SBA/SBS) comes back online, the client will automatically fail back; however, that does not happen immediately because it's based on the failback timeout value.

In summary, once the backup registrar is configured, in the event of failure of the primary pool, the client will automatically connect to the backup pool. If the primary registrar is a Survivable Branch Appliance (SBA) or Survivable Branch Server (SBS), the client will continue in Survivable mode until the primary pool comes back online. In Survivable mode, the client will continue to be able to make and receive PSTN calls but will have limited pool functionality.

Figure 16.11
Client Survivable mode

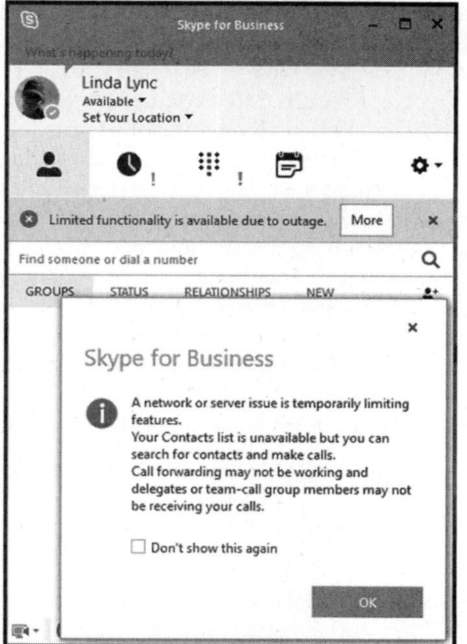

Geographical Pool Failure

The primary and backup registrar functionality will work over a global network, but for the PSTN calling feature to be still available, the telephony capability must also be available globally. For example, a U.S.-based pool could have its backup provided by a pool in Europe, but the users would still have a U.S. phone number. Although Skype for Business Server 2015 fully supports this, the telecom provider must also support rerouting the calls globally in the event of failure.

Pools of the same type should be paired with each other, such as Enterprise Edition with another Enterprise Edition and Standard Edition with Standard Edition. Indeed, while it was possible to pair Standard Edition and Enterprise Edition pools with Lync Server 2010, this capability was removed in Lync Server 2013.

While failover is available in both Standard Edition and Enterprise Edition, automatic failover is available when using SQL Server mirroring and a Witness server; this is considered high availability. Using Standard Edition requires manual intervention to achieve failover, and therefore it's not classed as high availability.

The SBA is a combination *primary* registrar (only), Mediation server, and gateway, and it works in conjunction with a pool. The SBS is a combination *primary* registrar (only) and Mediation server; there is no gateway. If a pool failure occurs in this scenario, even though the client is still connected to a *primary* registrar, it will go into Survivable mode as its connection to the main pool is lost.

Multiple Server Failure: Complete Data Center

Now that you've considered the complete pool failure in the previous section, what about the next level up—the significant event of a loss of a data center?

In many cases this is simply the same as the loss of a pool; there is a second data center with its pool configured as the backup registrar, and there are additional roles such as the Mediation server and gateways in this data center. In fact, this may be an active data center with the users split between both data centers, or it could be a standby ready and waiting for the disaster to happen. In this case, to be supported it must be active but with no users homed on it. Microsoft does not support having this as a "cold standby" pool.

The Metropolitan pool approach, where a single pool is *stretched* between both data centers, is not supported with Skype for Business Server 2015 (or Lync Server 2013). This was possible with Lync Server 2010 and required the data centers to be well connected and have a network latency of less than 20 milliseconds (ms); this requirement allows the SQL cluster (with synchronous data replication) to support the pool Back End database, which requires a stretched layer 2 VLAN to operate.

Using Skype for Business Server 2015 and SQL high-availability capabilities (see Chapter 20, "SQL") for the database Back End as well as Distributed File System (DFS) for the file share provides a multi-data-center, high-availability approach. Figure 16.12 shows the architecture.

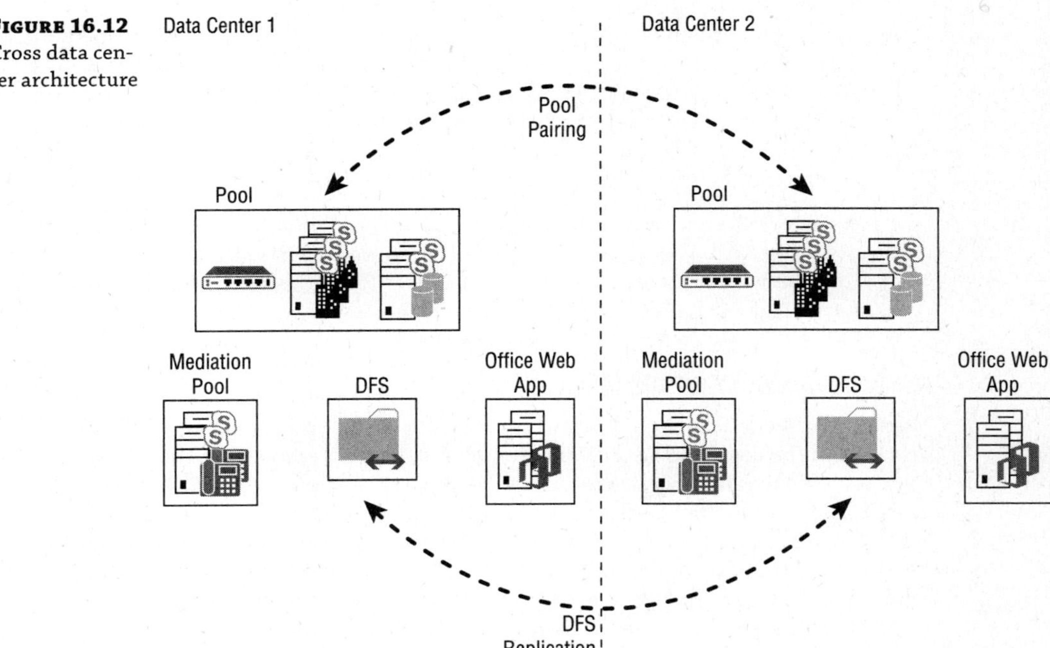

Figure 16.12 Cross data center architecture

Pool 1 and Pool 2 are both live pools hosting users (although one could be empty if needed, but it must be on), and Figure 16.12 shows Pool 2 acting as a backup for Pool 1. Pool 2 holds a copy of the Pool 1 data (via replication through the Backup Service using the fileshare) and is sized ready to take the load of the additional users if required.

In reality, the Front End servers are active (taking the Pool 2 load); however, the Pool 1 database can be considered disconnected until a failure occurs. Moving to a "replicate everywhere" type of model ensures that even when a full data center failure occurs, the users will continue to operate as if nothing has happened. In some cases, the users may be logged out but will log back in to the backup pool automatically. For a brief period, some users may be in *Survivable* mode. In an approach similar to that of a complete pool failure, users associated with an SBS/SBS for their primary registrar will fall into Survivable mode if their data center has failed.

When sizing this environment, it is important to size for the worst-case scenario—a data center failure. Therefore, each data center should be sized to cope with a 100 percent load, which will significantly increase the number of servers required.

A complete data center failure introduces another concern for high availability: simple URLs. What do you do if the target FQDNs for the simple URLs are unavailable? Unfortunately, there isn't a simple answer to this, and it is almost always reliant on how DNS is implemented and managed in the environment.

- One option is to scope simple URLs to each site. This introduces additional overhead in management but targets each site of users to a specific pool, and therefore a single data center will not impact the global deployment. However, if users are moved to a new site, then meetings need to be updated.
- The second option is to implement some geographical DNS capability that will provide monitoring of the simple URLs to ensure their availability and return to clients the preferred DNS result based on availability—that is, the primary pool URL when the service is running and the secondary pool URL when the primary is having an issue. The web services themselves will allow for redirection to the correct conference location in the event of an issue, and importantly, users will not be impacted.
- A third option would be to manually control the DNS entries and update them in the event of a failure. This obviously introduces the manual overhead aspects but also requires DNS time to live (TTL) values to be set quite low, in turn adding overhead to the network in the form of additional DNS requests because clients will time out their DNS cache quicker.

Remote Site: WAN Failure

The last few sections looked primarily at the data center and considered failures to individual servers and the complete data center. But what happens to those branch offices in the event of a network failure? Is there a solution for them? Well, as you've already seen, the SBA has been designed to handle this scenario. Specifically, the SBA is designed for offices with between 25 and 1,000 users; different hardware versions of the SBA can handle different-sized workloads. The SBA, as its name implies, is an appliance device. The Skype for Business Server 2015 configuration items are centrally configured and will replicate to it when installed.

So, what is an SBA? It's a hardened version of Windows Server, with only the registrar and mediation services installed from Skype for Business Server 2015. Once joined to a domain and initialized, the Skype for Business Server 2015 installation will replicate the configuration from the Central Management Store. Then the device will become an active part of the topology and will be able to host users. The SBA is configured through Topology Builder as part of the Branch Sites settings, as shown in Figure 16.13. Notice that the Resiliency options are configured by default for an SBA.

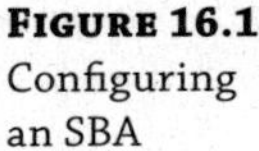

FIGURE 16.13 Configuring an SBA

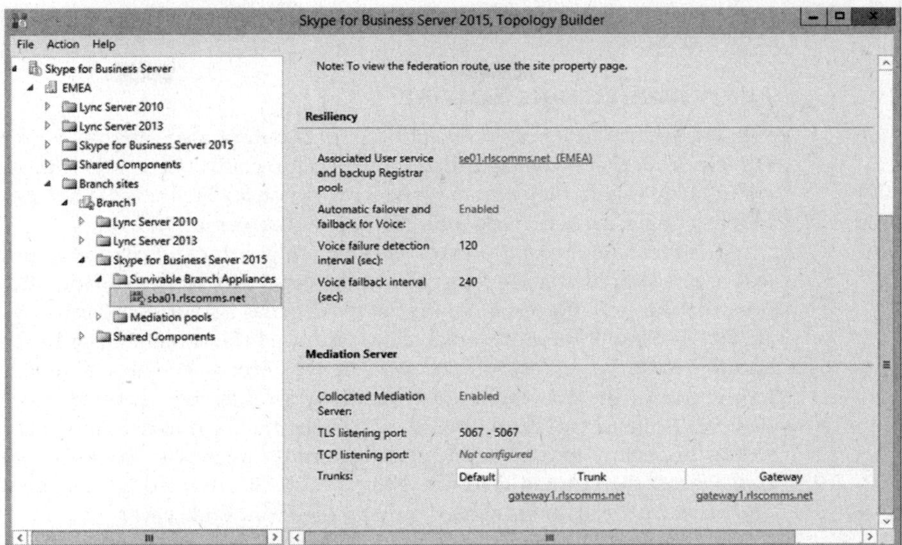

In addition to the Windows Server and Skype for Business Server 2015 installations, the SBA also includes a media gateway device; this is what will vary in size or type depending on number of users to be supported.

Users register in the same way with an SBA as they would with a pool; however, they are automatically associated with a backup pool as part of the SBA configuration. The SBA does not provide user services (conferencing and buddy list) capability, so the clients associate with the SBA for registration but continue to use the pool for conferencing and buddy lists.

In the event of an outage to the WAN (or the data center), the SBA itself will be unaffected. However, the client will go into Survivable mode, and local PSTN calling will continue to operate (via the built-in media gateway). Some customers will provide DHCP and DNS information from the data center, so a WAN outage will also affect these customers. To accommodate this scenario, you can configure the SBA to provide DHCP information to allow the clients to connect. This is not a full DHCP server; it will not provide IP address information, only DHCP Option 43 (pool provisioning URL) and Option 120 (SIP registrar), which would enable a client to connect in Survivable mode.

In the event of the pool failing, there is no additional failover capability provided to the users on an SBA; they are already connected to their *primary* registrar, and while users whose primary registrar is the pool itself will fail over to the backup pool for all modalities, the users hosted on the SBA will not be able to leverage the backup pool for conference capability.

Why would an organization deploy an SBA rather than a Standard Edition server? Well, really this comes down to the number of users at a location and the cost. The SBA is expected to be cheaper to purchase and maintain than a full-blown server (even though to provide PSTN integration you would still need a gateway to purchase, configure, and deploy). Conferencing is also a consideration—should each branch host its own conferencing services? Will they all need high availability for this? If so, it may make more sense to centralize and provide that to everyone.

It is also possible to deploy a server-only version of the SBA. This is the SBS, which will scale up to 2,500 users (similar to the Standard Edition server), but it only provides the functionality of the SBA (registration and mediation); a stand-alone media gateway is required to provide PSTN connectivity.

Active Directory Failure

What happens if the previous section's WAN outage also removes your access to Active Directory? Perhaps you centralized the domain controllers, and while users can log on to their client PCs, how do they authenticate with Skype for Business? What about Lync Phone Edition? It doesn't have cached credentials, so how will users log in using it?

After being used to an "always on" telephony system for decades, the last thing users want is to lose access simply because they can't log in, especially if they can log into their computers. Well, unsurprisingly, Skype for Business Server 2015 has a solution for this—a certificate-based login.

The first login attempt from a client will use NTLM (default) or Kerberos protocols to log in, and for this to be successful, you need Active Directory to be available. However, as part of this login process, the client will receive a Skype for Business Server 2015 certificate and can present this certificate for any future login, bypassing the need to use Active Directory.

It is important to understand that this certificate is available only for client-based authentication against the Front End server where the client is homed (not the pool). It cannot be used for any other purpose and is signed only by the Front End server.

By default, this certificate is stored in the local user's certificate store (see Figure 16.14) and by default is valid for 180 days. The validity period can be changed only by using the following PowerShell command:

```
Set-CsWebServiceConfiguration -DefaultValidityPeriodHours 4320
```

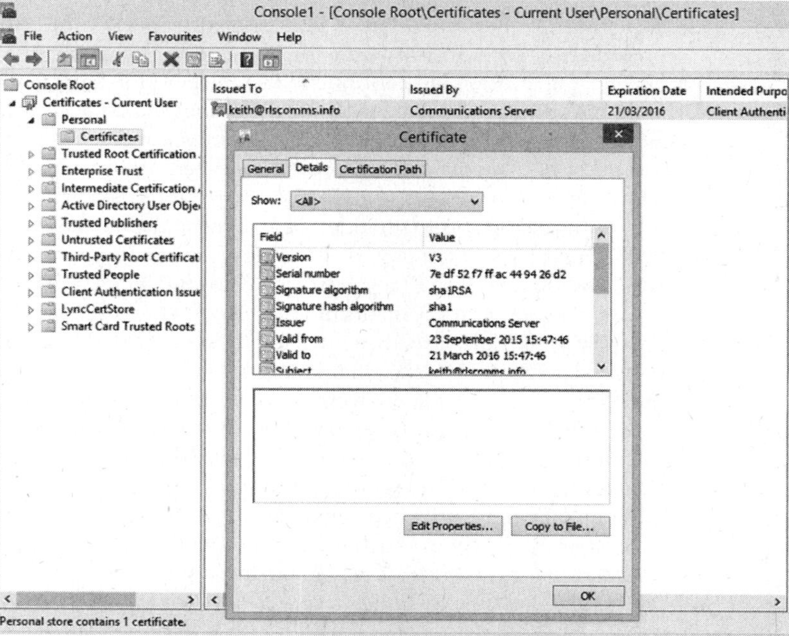

Figure 16.14 Certificate used for certificate-based authentication

The value 4320 is the number of hours for which the certificate is valid; in this case, the default of 4,320 is equal to 180 days.

No additional PKI infrastructure is required for this functionality to operate. Figure 16.15 shows the login process for a client. Note that the Active Directory connections occur only on the first login for a particular client (not user).

Now that the client is logged in, the next thing to do is enable and configure the Enterprise Voice capability.

FIGURE 16.15
The client login process

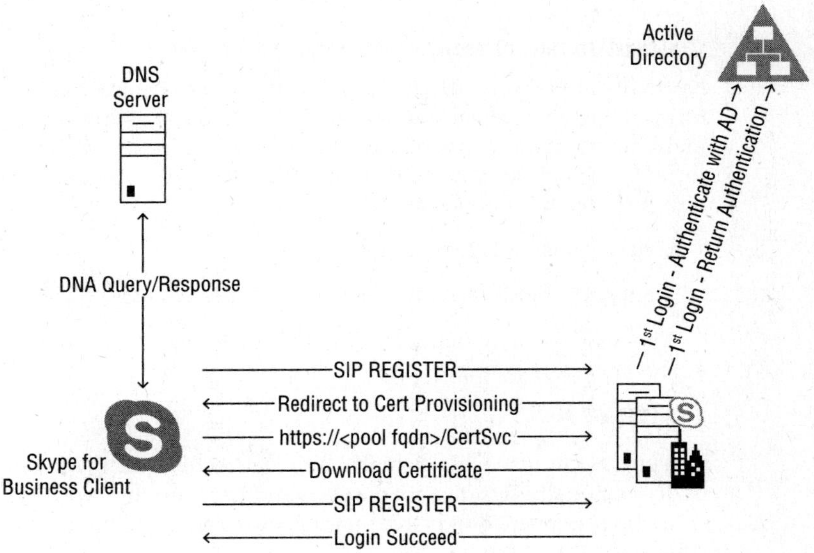

Configuring Enterprise Voice

The configuration of Enterprise Voice is best approached in two distinct parts.

Client This includes items such as the Address Book generation, dial plan creation, number normalization, and specific feature enablement (such as call forwarding) in the Voice policy.

Server Here you'll specifically look at the routing aspect of Enterprise Voice and how to configure and control it.

Once these two aspects have been defined, the user must be enabled for Enterprise Voice and should have a phone number assigned to them. If a phone number is not assigned, it is possible for the user to make PSTN calls but not receive them. Once enabled, the user will be assigned to a dial plan and a Voice policy, and by default this would be the global dial plan and the global Voice policy; however, an administrator would likely apply a specific dial plan and Voice policy.

Configuring the Client Enterprise Voice Options

The client is the interface between users and the back end of the system. As such, it is needed to translate what the user inputs to what the system expects. Not only that, but it needs to do that seamlessly to the user—without prompting.

The client also needs to adapt to the user's location if some specific configuration is required that may differ from location to location. A good example of this is emergency dialing; a U.S. user who is traveling to Europe may dial 911 to access the emergency services, not knowing that the emergency services number is different in Europe (and indeed from one country to the next).

Configuring Number Normalization

Normalization means adapting the various internal, local, national, or regional phone number formats into a universal standard format. Although Skype for Business can work without normalizing numbers, it is recommended (and much easier) if all numbers are normalized to E.164 format, a global standard that defines the format of telephone numbers and guarantees uniqueness globally. It is defined as such:

Country code = 1, 2, or 3 digits

Nationally significant number = 15 – length (country code digits)

The result is a maximum length of 15 digits, which in addition is prefixed with a + character, as shown in this example:

+15550123456

The U.S. country code (actually, more correctly, North American code) is one digit, followed by the nationally significant area code and local number, with no spaces or other characters. A common misconception is that simply adding the + to the start of a number will make it E.164 compliant; this is not the case.

If all numbers were presented in E.164 format, Skype for Business Server 2015 would have no issue, but this is not the case. Many numbers are stored without country codes, or only the internal extension may be stored, for example. In addition, this storage can be anywhere—Active Directory, local contacts, web pages, and so on.

To make this understandable and routable, Skype for Business allows you to configure a set of rules that will manipulate the number entered and output as an E.164 format number. This number can then be presented to a gateway or PBX for further routing if required.

Number normalization is configured as part of the dial plan; users are assigned to a dial plan when enabled for Enterprise Voice (a user can be in only a single dial plan at any time).

Figure 16.16 shows a sample dial plan; it has the following configuration items:

Name Specifies the name of the dial plan, used to reference the dial plan in policies.

Simple Name Matches against Exchange Unified Messaging dial plans (versions prior to Exchange 2010 SP1 required the dial plans to match by name).

Description Describes the dial plan, used only for additional notes for the administrator.

Dial-In Conferencing Region Creates an association with dial-in access numbers.

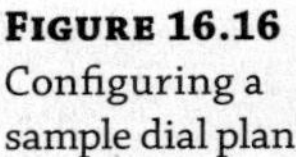

FIGURE 16.16 Configuring a sample dial plan

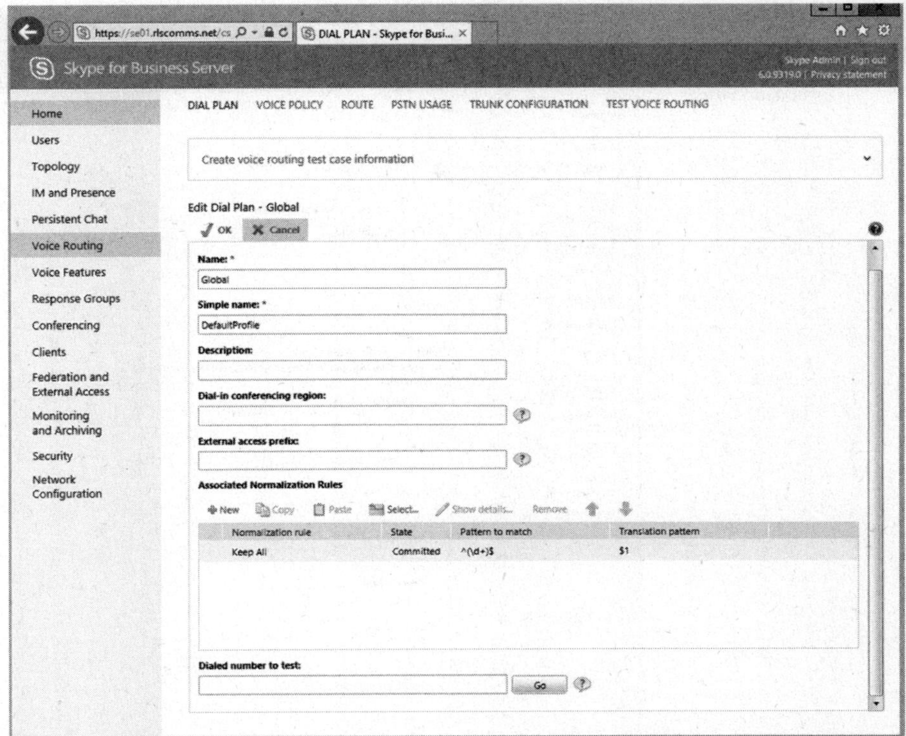

External Access Prefix Allows numbers to be dialed by users without an external access prefix. Completing this field will automatically add the prefix if listed.

Associated Normalization Rules Shows the list of normalization rules associated with the dial plan.

The command to create a dial plan from PowerShell looks like this:

```
New-Csdialplan -Identity "SkypeEnterpriseVoice"
-description "default dial plan for all users"
-dialinconferencingregion "Birmingham"
-ExternalAccessprefix 9
-simplename "SkypeEnterpriseVoice"
```

Normalization rules are created using regular expressions (regex), and administrators already familiar with using regex will find this method quite easy. But if you are new to regex, you don't need to worry. Skype for Business has improved significantly over Office Communications Server 2007 in this, and it provides a basic input system that will build the regex for you (see Figure 16.17). For detailed information on regex, see Appendix C, "Introduction to PowerShell, the Skype for Business Management Shell, and Regular Expressions."

FIGURE 16.17 Configuring a new normalization rule

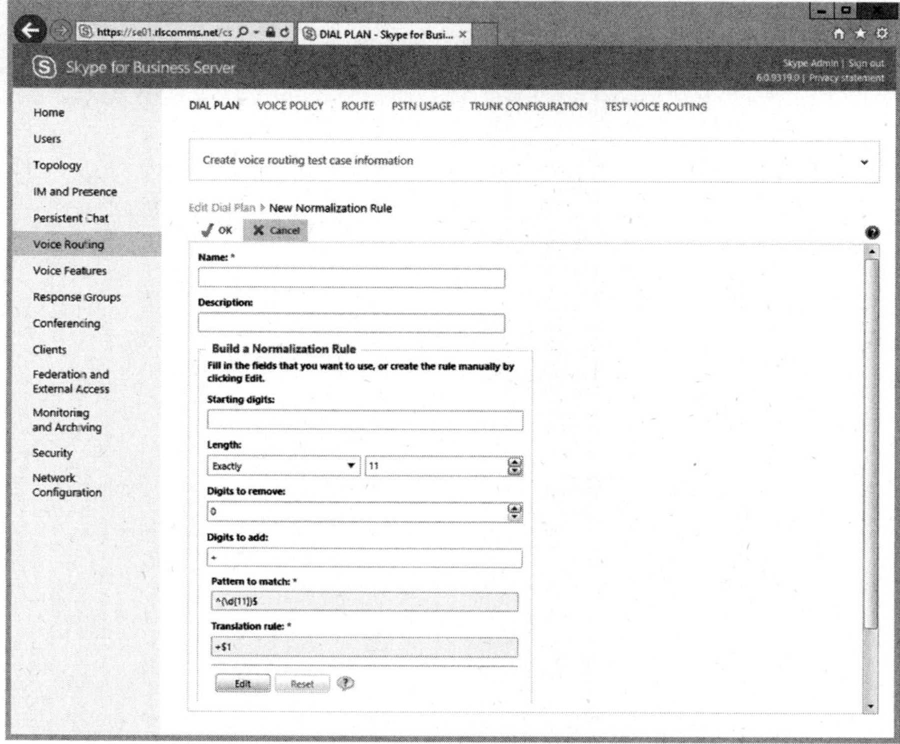

Here you build out the following information for each rule:

- Name
- Description
- Starting digits
- Length
- Digits to remove
- Digits to add

Here's an example. In the United Kingdom, it is still common to dial local numbers from a landline, so if someone is located in Birmingham (U.K.), where the national area code is 0121, they can dial the following Birmingham number in several ways.

Birmingham Central Library: 0121 303 4511

Local dialing (from within the Birmingham area): 303 4511

National dialing (from within the U.K.): 0121 303 4511

International dialing (from outside the U.K.): +44121 303 4511

In the case of international dialing from outside the U.K., the + symbol is introduced; this represents the international dialing access code. In the United States, this will be 011. In France, it will be 00.

Configuring Skype for Business to accommodate each of these formats allows users to continue to use their current (known) method to access numbers and reduces the extent of change they need to adjust to when using the new client (the less change for users, the more likely they are to accept it).

You can also create normalization rules using the `New-CsVoiceNormalizationRule` cmdlet, as in the following example:

```
New-CsVoiceNormalizationRule  -Identity
"Tag:SkypeEnterpriseVoice/Prefix Local call without external prefix"
-Description "Local call without external line prefix"
-Pattern "^(\d{8})$" -Translation "+44121$1"
```

So, let's take each of these formats and create a normalization rule to get to the target E.164 format.

Local Dialing

Here the input is seven digits, and the output is going to include the +44121 prefix.

You will need the following information:

Starting digits: N/A

Length: Exactly 7

Digits to remove: N/A

Digits to add: +44121

Once you have added this information, scroll to the bottom of the tab. The pattern to match and translation rule will already be created for you (as shown in Figure 16.18).

FIGURE 16.18
Automatic regex creation

National Dialing

Here your input is 10 digits, and the output is going to include the +44 aspect.

So, you need the following information:

Starting digits: 0

Length: Exactly 10

Digits to remove: 1

Digits to add: +44

With this combination of data, the pattern to match and the translation rule will be as follows:

Pattern to match: ^0(\d{9})$

Translation rule: +44$1

International Dialing

The dial plan is U.K. focused, so you probably won't be dialing the +44 aspect of a U.K. number; however, you might use the Click-To-Call functionality, which could already have the U.K. number defined. Here your input is not necessarily a defined length, and the output is going to add only the +.

So, you need the following information:

Starting digits: 001

Length: At least 11

Digits to remove: 3

Digits to add: +

With this combination of data, the pattern to match and the translation rule will be as follows:

Pattern to match: ^001(\d{7}\d+)$

Translation rule: +$1

Internal Dialing

Of course, all of this is dealing with external number dialing, but what about calling other Skype for Business users or internal PBX users? Well, assuming you have a four-digit extension range, you will need to normalize these numbers to E.164 too. The first thing Skype for Business Server will do is attempt a reverse number lookup on the phone-entered number to try to find a matching user—and because all of the TelUri information is expected to be in E.164 format, that is what you need to resolve to.

For this, you need to enter the following data:

Starting digits: N/A

Length: Exactly 4

Digits to remove: N/A

Digits to add: +44121555

With this combination of data, the pattern to match and the translation rule will be as follows:

Pattern to match: ^(\d{4})$

Translation rule: +44121555$1

Enabling Address Book Generation

Once you have configured all the required normalization rules within the dial plan, you need to configure the Address Book in a similar fashion. The difference is that these rules will be used to map the entries from Active Directory into the E.164 format you need.

In an ideal world, Active Directory would be populated with E.164 format, and you would not have to do this at all, or a common format would already be applied to all the phone number entries, allowing you to keep the number of Address Book rules required to a minimum. Rarely is this the case, which results in a large number of normalization rules also being required for the Address Book generation.

With previous versions, these rules were stored in a file called `Company_PhoneNumber_Normalization_Rules.txt`, and this was stored in the following directory:

```
\\<file share>\<Server-id>\ABFiles\
```

Because one Address Book is generated per pool, this file was required to be duplicated for each pool too; also, it was important that when multiple pools were in use, the Address Book files had to be manually kept in sync. Fortunately, now Address Book rules have been incorporated into PowerShell and can be assigned like policies to sites if required, or you can use the single global configuration to ensure consistency.

To see a list of the current rules, use the following PowerShell command.

```
(Get-CsAddressBookNormalizationConfiguration).AddressBookNormalizationRules
```

You'll see output similar to the following:

```
Description :
Pattern      : E164
Translation : null
Name         : Generic_E164

Description :
Pattern      : \++(\d+)[Xx]+(\d{1,15})
Translation : +$1;ext=$2
Name         : Generic_WithExtension

Description :
Pattern      : \++(\d+)ext[=]?(\d{1,15})
Translation : +$1;ext=$2
Name         : Generic_WithLongExtension

Description :
Pattern      : \++(\d+)EXT[=]?(\d{1,15})
Translation : +$1;ext=$2
Name         : Generic_E164

Description :
Pattern      : \++(\d+)
Translation : +$1
Name         : Generic_All
```

To modify the rules, you can use the `*-CsAddressBookNormalizationRule` cmdlet set, as shown here:

```
New-CsAddressBookNormalizationRule -Parent Global -Name Test-UK-National -Pattern
'0(\d{10})' -Translation '+44$1' -Priority 0
Remove-CsAddressBookNormalizationRule -Identity "Global/Test-UK-National"
```

By default, the Address Book is generated daily at 1:30 a.m.; you can change this by using the following PowerShell command:

```
Set-CsAddressBookConfiguration -RunTimeOfDay 01:30
```

If the Address Book needs to be updated immediately, the `Update-CsAddressBook` cmdlet is used (no parameters are required). It will take a few minutes to regenerate the Address Book. Clients will check for a new Address Book file only once every 24 hours.

Real World Scenario

Correcting Active Directory Data

When new Address Book data is generated, an output file listing all the incorrectly formatted phone number data can be generated too.

You can find the error file in the following location:

```
\\<file share>\<server-id>\ABFiles\00000000-0000-0000-0000-000000000000\
00000000-0000-0000-0000-000000000000
```

It is called `Invalid_AD_Phone_Numbers.txt`.

The folder location shown is actually a GUID. If you are using Address Book segregation (see the next section in this sidebar), you will see differing values replacing the folder names (`00000000-0000-0000-0000-000000000000`) shown. The folder name will match the GUID used to group the users into an Address Book, and each folder will have an `Invalid_AD_Phone_Numbers.txt` file.

From this error file, you can determine the accounts remaining in Active Directory that do not have a corresponding normalization rule associated and take one of the following appropriate actions:

- Correct the specific user account information in Active Directory.
- Create a new normalization rule to account for the number format.

Address Book Segregation

Some organizations may want to provide separate address books for users as a way to segregate organizations or departments.

This can be achieved by allocating globally unique identifiers (GUIDs) to users under the `msRTCSIP-GroupingID` attribute, as shown here.

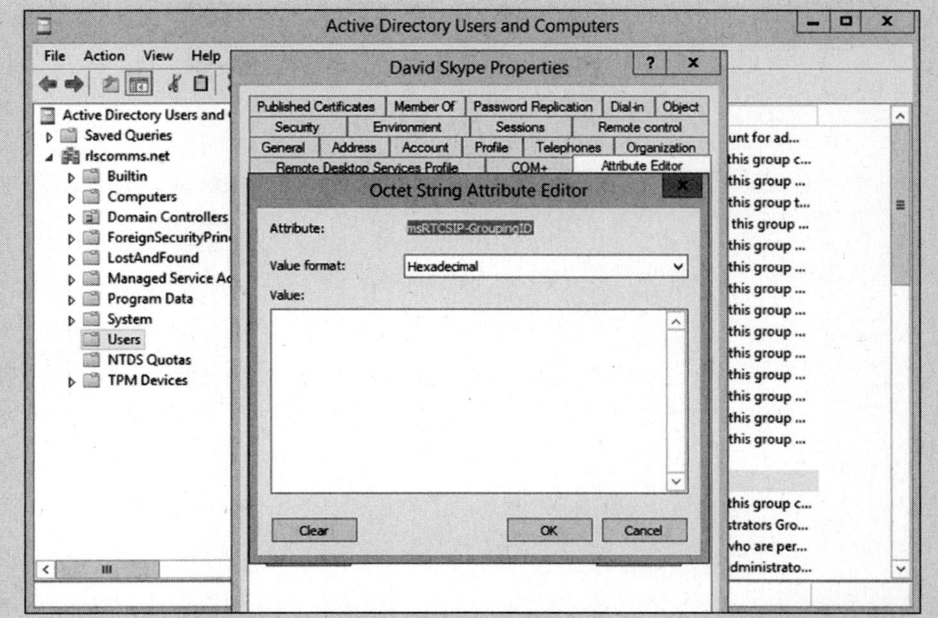

Users with a common value of this attribute will share an address book, and it's worth noting that users can only be in (and search) a single address book.

By default, all users and contacts created use the default GUID `00000000-0000-0000-0000-000000000000`; however, assigning another (common) GUID to a group of users will create an additional address book. The default address book is located in the following location:

```
\\<file share>\<server-id>\ABFiles\00000000-0000-0000-0000-000000000000\
00000000-0000-0000-0000-000000000000
```

Any additional address books will be created in a similar fashion, with the specific folder IDs dependent upon the GUID used.

Voice Policy

Where the dial plan determines the rules used for each user to provide the number normalization capability, the Voice policy determines the features available to a user.

- Enable Call Forwarding
- Enable Delegation
- Enable Call Transfer
- Enable Call Park
- Enable Simultaneous Ringing Of Phones

- Enable Team Call
- Enable PSTN Reroute
- Enable Bandwidth Policy Override
- Enable Malicious Call Tracing

The Voice policy is also used to determine the PSTN usages assigned to a user. This can be considered similar to class of service in the legacy telephony world or, equally accurately, the type of call (such as local, national, or international) that the user is permitted to make.

Figure 16.19 shows the Voice policy creation screen.

FIGURE 16.19 Creating a new Voice policy

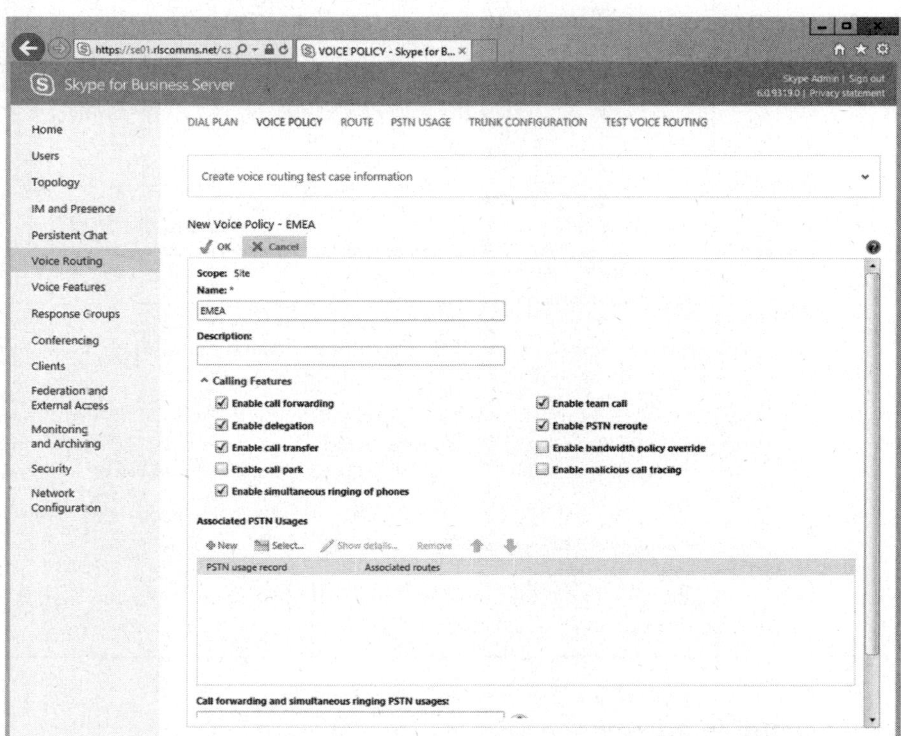

The following sample PowerShell command creates a Voice policy and associates it with some predefined PSTN usages; you'll see them in a later section:

```
New-CsVoicePolicy -Identity "standard" -AllowCallForwarding $true
-AllowSimulRing $true -Description "Default policy for all users"
-EnableCallPark $false -EnableCallTransfer $true
-EnableDelegation $false -EnableMaliciousCallTracing $true
-EnableTeamCall $true -Name "Standard" -PstnUsages
@{add="Internal", "Local", "National", "Mobile", "Emergency"}
```

A capability within Skype for Business Server 2015 is to be able to provide a different set of policies to deal with call forwarding and simultaneous ringing. This could be configured to allow users to forward calls only internally, or perhaps a user who can place calls internationally is restricted to forwarding calls nationally only (stopping potential toll fraud by forwarding calls to a great-aunt in Australia).

Figure 16.20 shows the additional section of the Voice Policy window, with the options available; the PSTN usage table here is for the specific alternative PSTN usages if selected.

FIGURE 16.20
Alternative PSTN usage configuration for call forwarding and simultaneous ringing

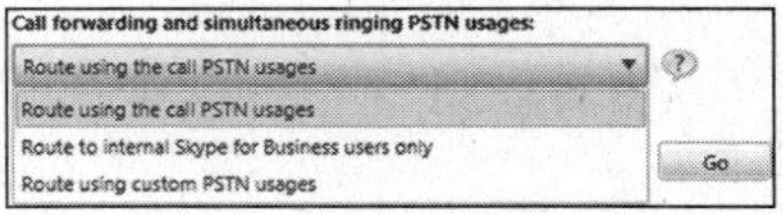

Configuring the Server Enterprise Voice Options

Now that you have configured the user-side information, you need to configure the server side to route the call to the correct gateway as well as ensure that you have the correct permissions (PSTN usages) to place the call.

ROUTING

Because the server is expecting a normalized (E.164) number, basing the routing on E.164 numbering is the recommended approach to routing the call.

A global enterprise is likely to have at least one gateway in each country where an office is located. This provides the potential savings of least cost routing (LCR), where the call is routed internally across the company WAN to the in-country gateway; by contrast, in a traditional PBX, the call would be the long-distance (or international) rate.

The definition of a route is similar to that of a dial plan; you need to define it using the regex notation shown earlier, although for this example you'll simply use the starting digits. For instance, to define a route for calls to the United Kingdom (country code 44), you would use the following regex: \+44. Notice that you do not define the number of digits, simply the starting digits of the normalized number. The more specific the definition (the more digits provided), the more granular the control over the target gateway you can have. For example, if you have multiple offices in the United Kingdom, with a gateway in each office, you could use the following regex to specify regional dialing capability: \+44161 (Manchester), \+44121 (Birmingham), and so on.

Figure 16.21 shows how to use the Control Panel to define the routing information (you need to scroll down to see the PSTN Usage section).

The PowerShell cmdlet to complete this section as shown is as follows (with included content):

```
Set-CsVoiceRoute -Identity "LocalRoute"
-Description "local number routes"
-NumberPattern "^(\+44121{7})$"
-PstnUsages @{add="Local"} -PstnGatewayList
@{add="pstngateway:192.168.3.201", "pstngateway:192.168.3.202"}
```

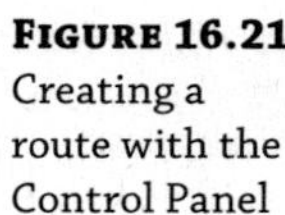

FIGURE 16.21 Creating a route with the Control Panel

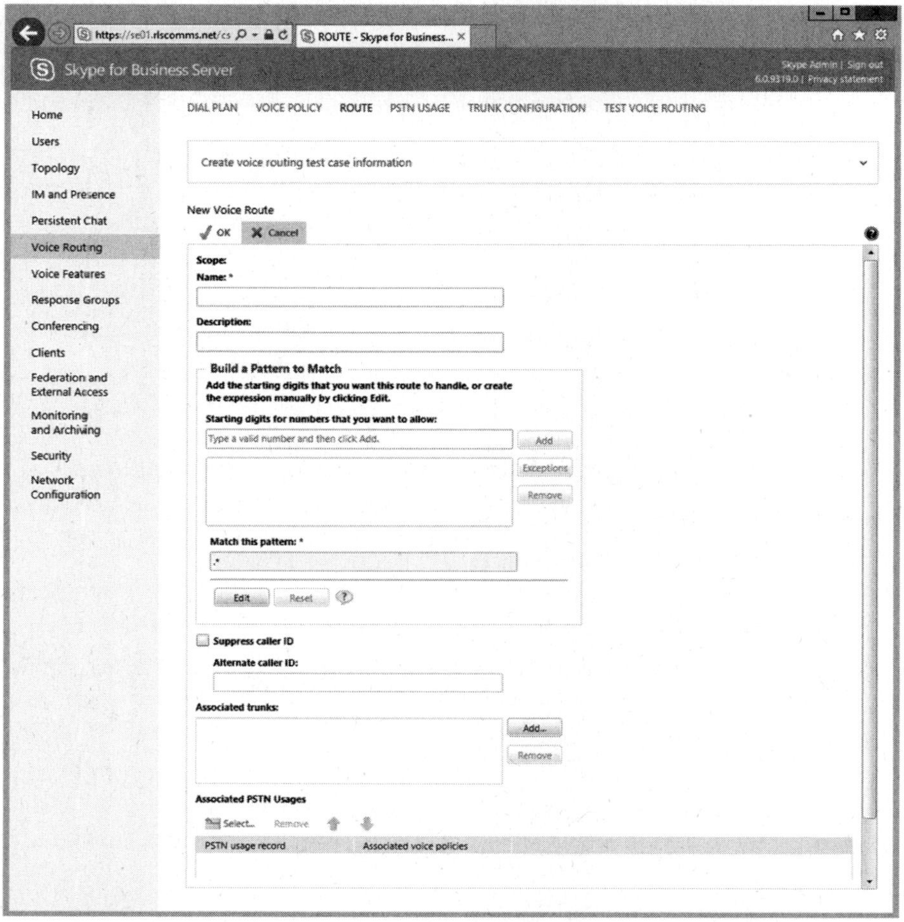

PSTN USAGES

By defining the routes and associated PSTN usages, you tie the calling capability of the user to the permissions of the routes. When a user logs in successfully, the Voice policy is applied (containing the user-permitted routes), and when a PSTN call is placed, a check is performed against the matching routes to compare these against the permissions (PSTN usages) allowed.

An easy way to think of this is that it's the same way permissions to files are granted.

1. Create a group (PSTN Usage).
2. Assign the group to the file/folder (Route).
3. Add the user to the group (Voice Policy).

Testing Call Patterns

Once the client and server configuration are defined, you need to be sure they work as expected. One option would be to apply the policy to a test account and confirm the operation; however, in a large environment, this is impractical. The solution to this is the Test Voice Routing option in the Voice section of the Control Panel.

Here you can provide the number dialed as well as the expected results when you run the test. Once the details are entered, you can save the option to run again in the future. This is where the benefits of scale come into play; once the numbers are saved, you can quickly rerun the tests anytime the environment is changed, ensuring that any changes work as expected prior to deploying to users.

Figure 16.22 shows a test case being defined.

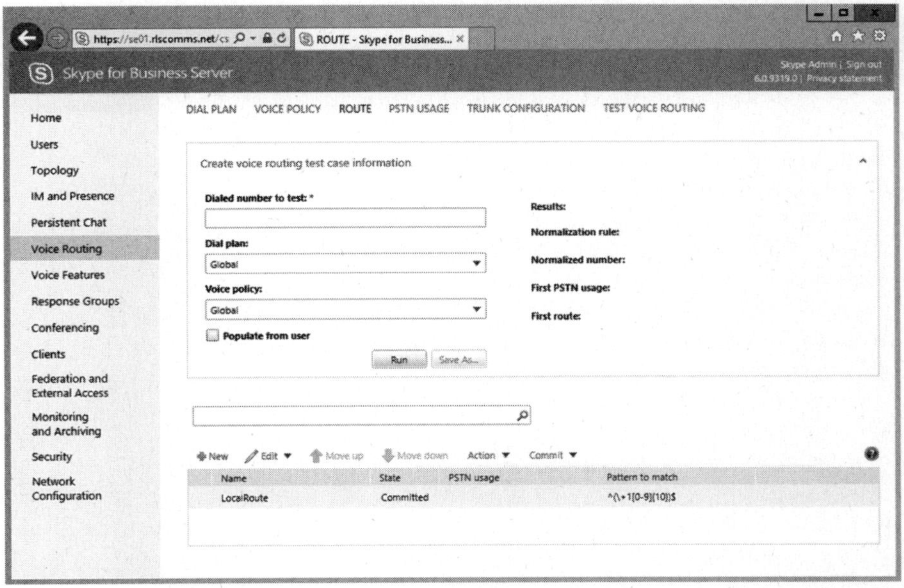

Figure 16.22
Creating a voice test case

The Bottom Line

Understand the voice capabilities. Skype for Business Server 2015 has expanded further the capabilities provided by Microsoft in the Unified Communications space to be almost on par with enterprise PBXs (and certainly equal to, if not better, than departmental PBX offerings).

Master It Describe the benefits of media bypass.

Understand the voice architecture. With the use of media bypass and the support for virtualization, the architectural requirements to deploy voice are consolidated into a smaller server footprint, and at the same time additional functionality has been included in the product. Significant investment has been made in the high-availability and resiliency deployment models.

Master It Describe the user experience when the user's home pool fails and only a backup registrar has been configured.

Configure voice policies and routing. Aside from the architectural requirements, enabling Enterprise Voice requires configuration to be applied to users (policies) and back-end configuration to be applied to the servers (routing).

Master It What configuration joins the user configuration to the server configuration and provides the permissions to enable (or block) a call?

Chapter 17

Call Admission Control

In the early days of OCS 2007, Microsoft made a big deal about how the codecs used were dynamic and could adapt to your network. A lot of people misinterpreted this to mean that you could simply install OCS 2007 and it would work, no matter how congested your network already was. As you know, introducing a new application onto a network also introduces network traffic. If your network is already saturated, introducing more traffic will only make matters worse, resulting in a poor user experience.

Lync Server 2010 introduced Call Admission Control, which provided an easy way to control the amount (and type) of traffic between users, allowing better understanding of the impact of this new application. If you are familiar with the implementation and management of Call Admission Control in Lync Server 2010 or Lync Server 2013, then you can skip this chapter because nothing has changed with the Skype for Business Server implementation.

One point to note, as Call Admission Control was introduced with Lync Server 2010, any Lync 2010 or greater client is capable of dealing with Call Admission Control. In this chapter we refer only to Skype for Business clients and servers, but all points are equally valid for Lync clients and servers, both 2010 and 2013 versions.

In this chapter, you will learn to

- Identify Call Admission Control–capable endpoints
- Configure policy-based Quality of Service controls
- Design a Call Admission Control solution
- Configure Call Admission Control

Understanding Call Admission Control

In the legacy telephony world, Call Admission Control (CAC) was inherent in the infrastructure and not something that overly concerned people. Bandwidth was defined in trunks and lines. If you tried to make a call and there wasn't enough bandwidth, you would receive a busy tone because the system would be unable to route your call to the destination because it had no available capacity. Typically, you tried again sometime later. Advancements in PBX technology introduced a monitoring concept (*ring back*) that allowed the system to call you and connect your call when enough bandwidth was available.

The introduction of Voice over IP (VoIP) systems enabled these typically fixed-capacity trunks to become network links, which were much easier to change in size and therefore capacity. In addition, voice traffic could be routed across traditional network links, providing a potential cost saving to business by combining both voice and data links. In taking this approach, bandwidth control has become problematic. First, how do you ensure that there is enough bandwidth to cope with the calls that you want to allow? Second, how do you ensure that this traffic on a shared link does not impact other data traffic?

The early VoIP systems used a fixed-size codec, thereby ensuring that the required capacity per call was a known value (the number of concurrent calls times the codec size equals the required capacity). Then, however, Office Communication Server 2007 introduced RTAudio (see Chapter 2, "Standards and Protocols," for details), which added the complexity of a codec that changes dynamically (based on the network conditions) and attempts to calculate the bandwidth required.

You still know the number of concurrent calls; however, now you can't determine how much bandwidth is required per call, so you can't predict how much bandwidth is required. This can lead to unhappy users if the network is under-provisioned because the dynamic nature will reduce the quality of the call to ensure that all the calls can be completed.

Assuming the network link shown in the top half of Figure 17.1 is already saturated with calls, the impact of adding an additional call is as shown in the lower half of Figure 17.1.

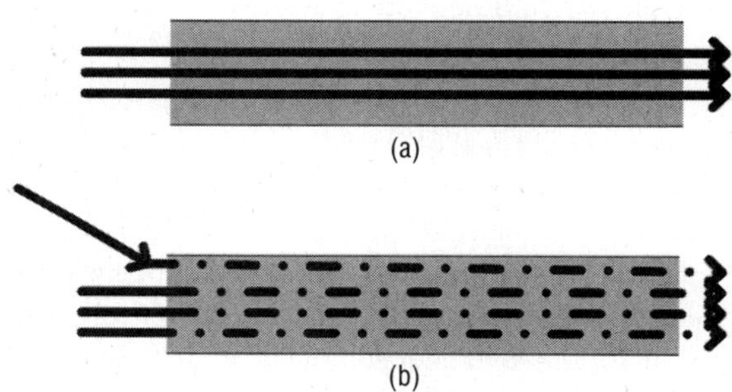

FIGURE 17.1 A network link at capacity (a); a network link over capacity, with a fixed-rate codec (b)

You can see that an additional call from a nondynamic codec will impact all other calls on the link. Because these are fixed-bandwidth calls, the only option is for some packets to be lost or delayed. The result is that all users will suffer a loss of quality.

On the other hand, using a dynamic codec would allow the situation shown in Figure 17.2. The calls in place (as well as the new one) would adapt and potentially use a lower-quality codec, but this means there would be no packet loss and, in many cases, no noticeable impact to users. Figure 17.2 shows all calls being impacted equally, but more likely only a few would be impacted.

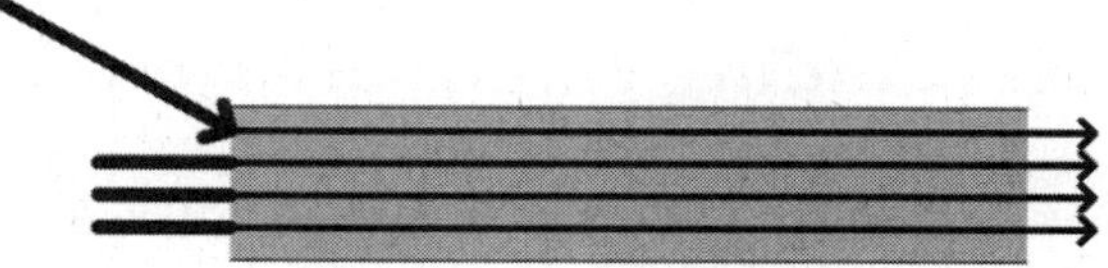

FIGURE 17.2 A network link over capacity with a dynamic-rate codec

Having dynamic codecs does have a downside. Another call introduced would reduce the existing call quality again, as would another and another and another. Eventually, all calls would be operating at such low quality they would be either unintelligible or dropped. A dropped call would allow some "breathing space," but the cycle would continue. It is almost impossible to plan for or control.

With OCS and OCS R2, only three workarounds were available.

MaxAudioVideoBandwidth Registry Key By setting this value, an administrator could determine the maximum bandwidth combined for audio and video; in most cases where this has been set, it results in video being unavailable. Because you don't have the capability to set the minimum value required, you can still continue to add calls to the network; all you are doing is restricting the maximum used by OCS.

Disable Video By disabling the video capability, you reduce the functionality of the product; however, the benefit is that significant bandwidth is not being used for video and is available for use by audio or other applications.

Enable Diffserv By enabling quality of service (QoS) on the network, you can provide a guaranteed bandwidth to OCS and in return provide a guaranteed bandwidth available to other applications.

None of these workarounds provides the capability to manage at the application layer; typically, the results are the same as if the values were not enabled and the codec left to dynamically adjust.

Something had to be done to allow a business to accurately size the network and provision the correct amount of bandwidth for the number (and quality) of calls permitted on the network.

This something is Call Admission Control, which can be enabled as part of a Skype for Business deployment with no extra hardware requirements (it is part of the front-end services) and requires no specific network hardware because it interacts at the application layer.

How Call Admission Control Works

The aim of Call Admission Control is to provide a guaranteed quality (user experience) for calls placed on the network. From a user perspective, a rejected call (with explanation), as shown in Figure 17.3, is usually a better experience than a call connected but of extremely low quality. From an admin perspective, CAC introduces a way to allow the network to be accurately architected and protected against unexpected spikes in call volumes.

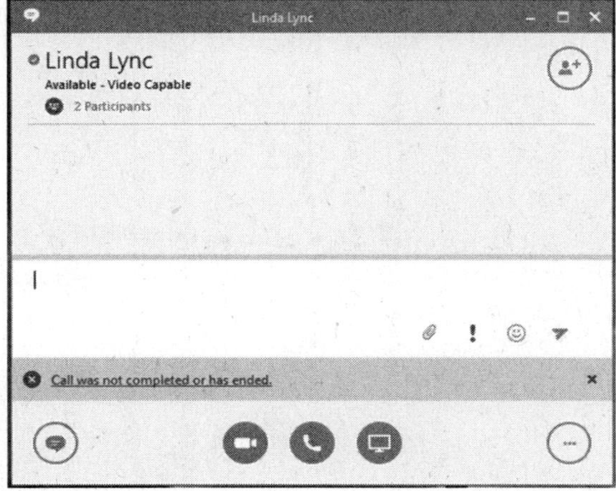

FIGURE 17.3 A rejected call notification due to insufficient bandwidth

Skype for Business configuration includes the definition of the network and details for the number of calls and quality permitted for each leg of the network. We'll show how to implement this configuration later.

Each pool will replicate the number of current calls in place on the network; when a new call is attempted, a query is made to establish if enough bandwidth is available to handle another call and how much bandwidth is permitted for each modality use.

Within this query, the Skype for Business client will provide the Policy Decision Point (PDP) with its IP address along with the IP address of the calling party client. From these two pieces of information, the PDP can determine the route and establish the current usage on that route.

Is Skype for Business Integrated with the Network?

Skype for Business's Call Admission Control operates purely at the application layer, so it is not integrated with the network. There are no ties to the underlying network infrastructure to reserve the bandwidth or ensure that it is actually available to handle the call.

The result of the query is one of the following:

Permitted The call may be placed.

Rejected The call may not be placed.

Rerouted The call must take another route, which may be via Edge servers or via the PSTN.

For call rerouting, both modalities are handled together; therefore, it is not possible for the video portion of an audio and video call to be rerouted via the Edge servers and the audio portion to continue across the WAN, or even via the PSTN. If the call cannot be routed via the Edge servers, the video modality will be dropped and, assuming the user is permitted to make a PSTN call, the call will be attempted via a PSTN gateway.

As you can see in Figure 17.4, to enable routing via the Internet, you must make sure each pool (not shown) has an associated Edge server or, to connect via the PSTN, a Mediation server (or in the case of media bypass, a supported gateway).

Figure 17.4 Call Admission Control rerouting

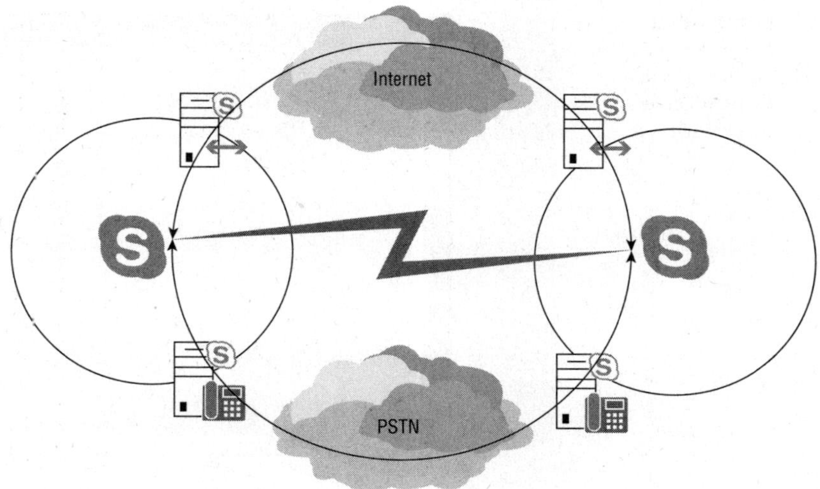

Rerouting is carried out in the following order:

1. Internet
2. PSTN
3. Voice mail (Voicemail routing is not subject to bandwidth controls.)

In Figure 17.5, the calling party will initiate the call. Without the recipient user being aware, the called-party Skype for Business client will receive the request for call signaling and query the PDP of the site (only a single pool per site runs this process). The PDP will return a response based on the current (real-time) capacity of the link as defined within the Skype for Business infrastructure. As noted, this will be permitted, rejected, or rerouted; based on this response, the calling-party Skype for Business client will take appropriate action.

1. The user places the call.
2. The receiving endpoint queries PDP.
3. A decision is made and returned to the called-party client.
4. The client will take appropriate action based on the response.

FIGURE 17.5
Signaling call flow for Call Admission Control, where the called party is local to the pool

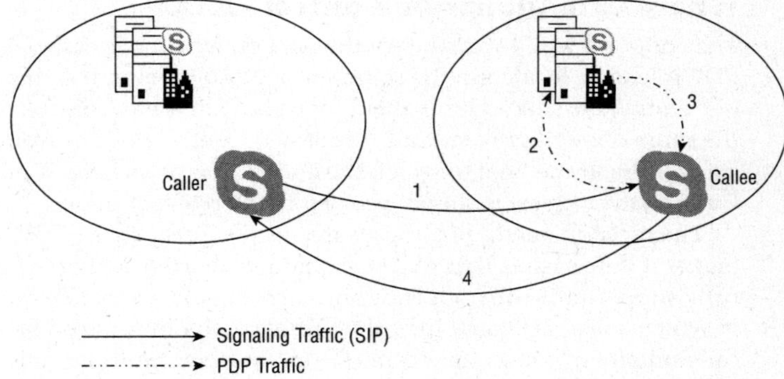

In the scenario in Figure 17.6, the user is not in a location that has a pool. The subnet will be defined within Skype for Business, and the client will query its home-pool (site) PDP, receiving the same responses as before. The scenario is the same for users who roam from site to site.

FIGURE 17.6
Signaling call flow for Call Admission Control, where the called party is not local to the pool

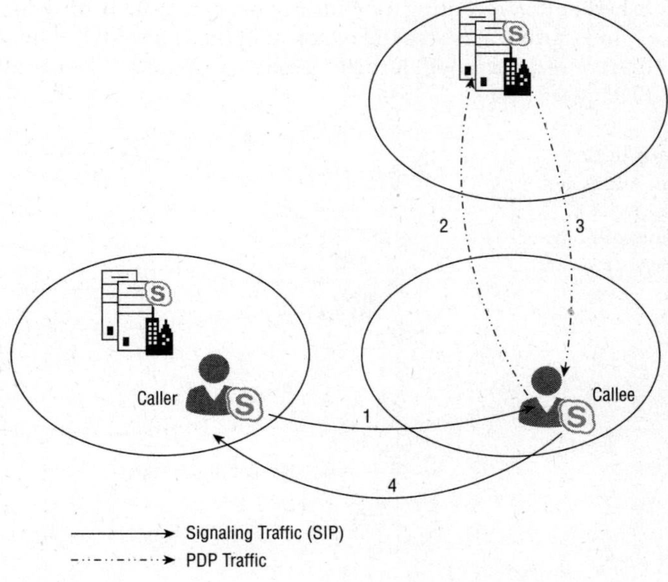

EMERGENCY CALL OVERRIDE?

Emergency calls do not override Call Admission Control. CAC is used to guarantee the quality of the calls placed on the network. If there is not enough capacity to accept another call, even if the call is an emergency call, it is not permitted. It would not be a good idea to connect an emergency call if the network is not capable of providing the capacity; because the call quality would most likely be poor, an option maybe to have localized emergency dialing gateways. You'll find more details in Chapter 18, "E9-1-1 and Location Information Services."

Voice policy can be configured to override Call Admission Control and policies assigned to users or sites. This will allow Call Admission Control to be ignored for users assigned to the policy. Using this option should be an exception rather than the norm because it defeats the purpose of Call Admission Control.

Where Call Admission Control Works

The endpoint will always query the pool on which it is associated; there is no requirement for a PDP role to be located in the same site as the endpoint. It is important to note that only one pool per central site should be enabled for Call Admission Control; having multiple pools enabled in the same site will prevent Call Admission Control policies from being applied on calls between some users. If the pool to which the endpoint is associated is not enabled for Call Admission Control, the request is simply proxied to the relevant pool.

The receiving endpoint always makes the query to the PDP, and the calling party never makes it (for reasons that will be explained shortly). Multiple Points of Presence (MPOPs) are fully supported, with each endpoint carrying out a separate query. This may result in a scenario in which a user is logged in with multiple endpoints and some users being able to receive the call and others not. In this scenario, only the endpoints capable of establishing the call will provide a toast/ringtone, and those not capable of call establishment will not.

If a call cannot be established, there is no indication to the intended recipient of a missed call. The user experience could be affected if someone saw a call attempt but was unable to do anything about it (except possibly start an IM conversation). On the other hand, the calling party will see a notification indicating that network issues are preventing the call from being established or that rerouting may cause a delay in establishing the call.

In Figure 17.7, where the recipient of the call is logged in on multiple devices, it is permissible that some devices will return a positive response, whereas others return negative following the PDP query stage.

FIGURE 17.7
Call Admission Control in a multiple-point-of-presence scenario

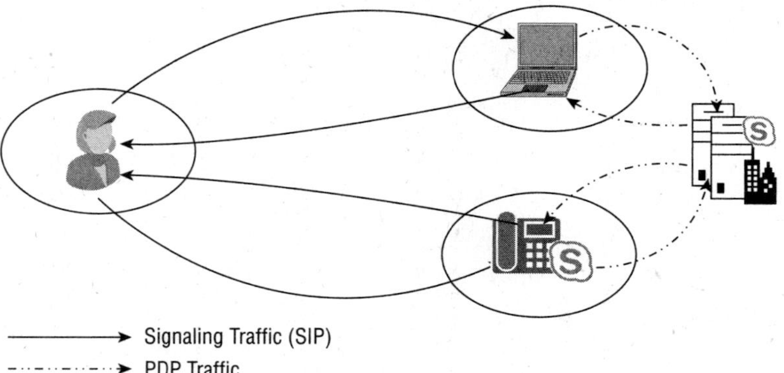

For example, assume the recipient is logged in via both a desk phone and a laptop, which may be connected via wireless. The administrator has configured Skype for Business to be aware of the wireless subnet and has restricted the number of calls available via the wireless LAN to ensure quality. In this case, the desk phone will return a positive response, and the laptop will return a negative one. As a result, only the desk phone device will ring.

Note that there is no indication of a call on the laptop device. This is to prevent the attempted establishment of a call where the network is not capable of delivering a quality call. If the desk phone is not answered, a single missed call notification will be generated and delivered as normal, or the call will be forwarded to Exchange Unified Messaging if configured.

Only Skype for Business and Lync endpoints are capable of querying for Call Admission Control data, so when it is used in a legacy interoperability scenario, calls to pre-Lync clients (OCS 2007 or OCS 2007 R2) will always succeed. A call from a pre-Lync client to a Skype for Business client will create a PDP query, and the result will obey the conditions imposed by the Call Admission Control policy.

In the case shown in the upper half of Figure 17.8, either endpoint will query the PDP for permission because both are Skype for Business endpoints (an endpoint can be any Skype for Business client or any Skype for Business server role). However, as shown at the bottom of Figure 17.8, the legacy endpoint will not make a query.

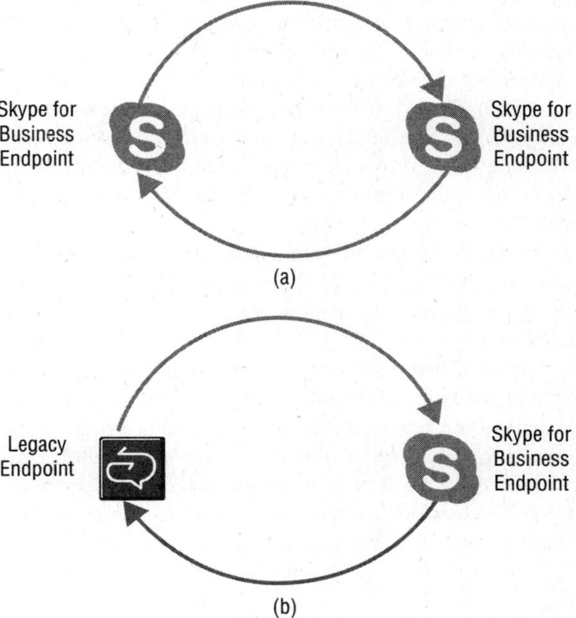

FIGURE 17.8
Call Admission Control Query conditions for Skype for Business endpoints (top); for combination or legacy endpoints (bottom)

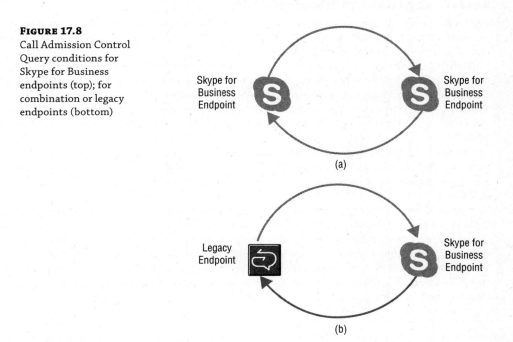

When you're planning a migration, this scenario is extremely important to understand. When you're receiving a call on any legacy client, the call will be permitted to be placed, irrespective of policy.

Consider a remote branch office where you want to limit the number of calls being placed across the WAN link to the head office. If you delay the client upgrade at the site, leaving them on a legacy client, then any calls being made *from* the site will be subject to Call Admission Control policy; however, any calls being made *to* the site will not. This could cause potential degradation of calls for all parties using that link.

> **CLIENT MIGRATIONS**
>
> While an extremely unlikely scenario, given the age of the clients involved, you may be migrating to Skype for Business from a Lync Server 2010 environment that still has OCS clients in place.
>
> As mentioned in Chapter 9, "Migration and Upgrades," it's not possible to migrate directly to Skype for Business from OCS or to use OCS clients against a Skype for Business pool.

To ensure that each PDP in each topology site is fully aware of the state of the network—remember, the client will query only its home PDP—each PDP is required to synchronize the data containing its call information. This synchronization occurs via HTTPS.

Underlying Network Requirements

Although Call Admission Control does not *require* QoS to be configured on the network, to ensure that the bandwidth is properly reserved for Skype for Business to manage, we recommend that you to apply QoS to the network.

Without QoS in place, you can define the maximum bandwidth used by Skype for Business for each call modality as well as the maximum for the total concurrent calls of each modality. However, by not deploying QoS to guarantee the bandwidth when needed, you are in effect allowing other network traffic to eat into the Skype for Business–defined bandwidth. As a result, the codec will adapt dynamically to this lower bandwidth and likely reduce the quality of the call.

By configuring QoS, you ensure that Skype for Business can use the guaranteed bandwidth when needed, and any other network traffic will be required to adapt. This ensures that the quality and quantity of calls is as defined in Call Admission Control and enforced on the network by QoS.

Figure 17.9 shows configuration using only Call Admission Control to manage bandwidth. This will ensure that each individual call session will not increase above a given bandwidth value, shown here to be 40 percent, and subsequently change the codec type in use as well as ensure that the total will not increase above a total value. The other network traffic may increase past the 60 percent nominally allocated because there is no interaction between the network and Skype for Business. If this increase does occur, the Skype for Business traffic will dynamically decrease with a corresponding decrease in quality.

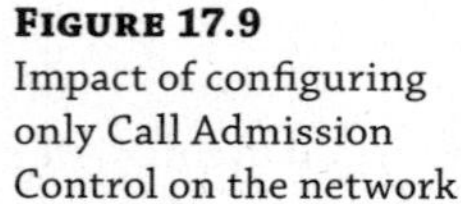

FIGURE 17.9
Impact of configuring only Call Admission Control on the network

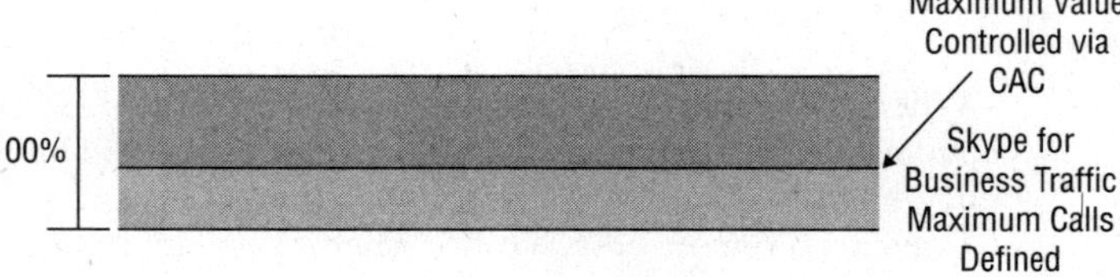

Figure 17.10 shows the same configuration, this time enforced using QoS but with no Call Admission Control in place. In this scenario, you can again ensure that the Skype for Business traffic will not increase beyond the 40 percent value; however, you have no control over the number of Skype for Business calls that can be placed or the codecs in use. This is the same situation you'll have when using OCS or OCS R2.

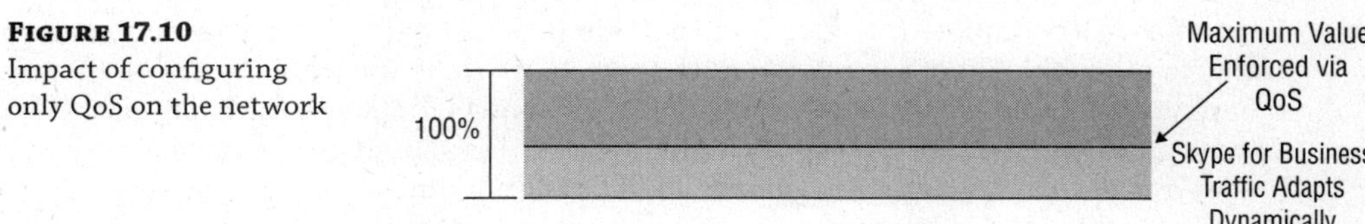

FIGURE 17.10
Impact of configuring only QoS on the network

The QoS value can be managed in either direction; assigning 40 percent to Skype for Business will guarantee that 40 percent will be available when needed, and it will allow increases beyond 40 percent if there is available bandwidth, managing the other data to reduce to below 60 percent when needed.

On the other hand, you can configure the limit to be on the alternative data, ensuring that there is a minimum of 60 percent available for it and forcing Skype for Business to adapt if the other data is deemed more important. To ensure voice quality, the guarantee should be configured on the Skype for Business network traffic.

Figure 17.11 shows the ultimate goal, having both Call Admission Control and QoS complement each other on the network. Call Admission Control provides the application-layer control over the network traffic placed on the network, and QoS provides the guarantee that traffic is prioritized when it is on the network.

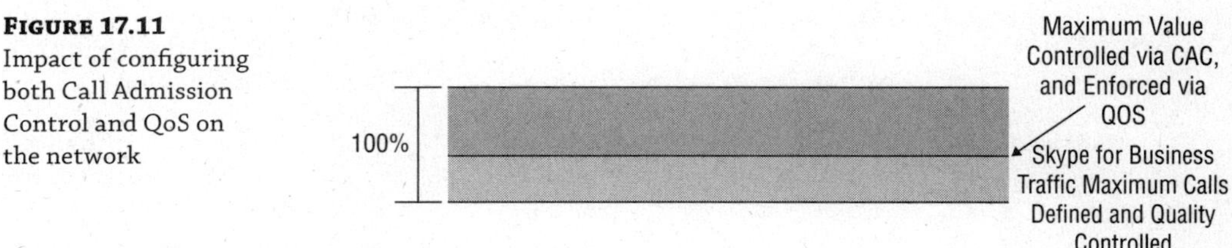

FIGURE 17.11
Impact of configuring both Call Admission Control and QoS on the network

Finally, Figure 17.12 shows a scenario where Call Admission Control has been configured to allow more calls than the network is capable of handling. Because the PDP is not aware of the underlying network capacity, in this situation calls will be permitted to be set up by Skype for Business, and the other calls on the network will be affected immediately. The codec bandwidth will be reduced dynamically, thereby reducing the quality of each call. Needless to say, the rest of the network will be impacted as well. This is not much different from not configuring Call Admission Control at all.

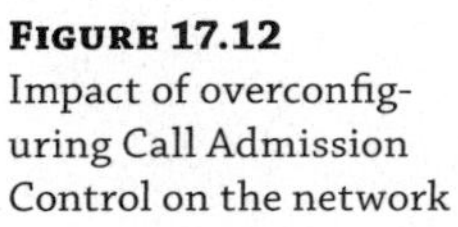
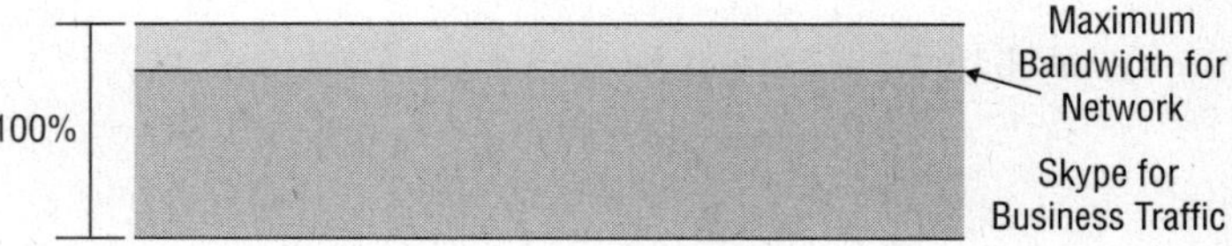

FIGURE 17.12
Impact of overconfiguring Call Admission Control on the network

It's worth noting at this point that Call Admission Control works only with IPv4 configurations, not IPv6.

QoS Tagging

By default, Skype for Business (actually, it's the underlying operating system that tags the traffic) will use Differentiated Service Control Point (DSCP) tagging in the headers of the network traffic to allow the underlying network to control and route the traffic based on the configuration required. Table 17.1 shows the default QoS markings for Skype for Business modalities. These values may be changed if required; however, this should be carried out only in conjunction with the network management team of your organization because straying from the defaults could mean significant reconfiguration required on the network devices (switches, routers, firewalls).

Table 17.1: Default DSCP marking per modality

Media Type	Per-Hop Behavior	Queuing and Dropping	Notes
Audio	EF	Priority Queue	Low loss, low latency, low jitter, assured bandwidth. Pair with WAN bandwidth policies on constrained links.
Video	AF41	BW Queue + DSCP WRED	Class 4. Low drop priority. Pair with WAN bandwidth policies on constrained links.
SIP signaling	CS3	BW Queue	Class 3. Bandwidth allocation should be sufficient to avoid drops.
App sharing	AF21	BW Queue + DSCP WRED	Class 2. Low drop priority. Pair with end-user policy caps.
File transfer	AF11	BW Queue + DSCP WRED	Class 1. Low drop priority. Pair with end-user policy caps.

The Per Hop Behavior column indicates the DSCP tag applied to the packet (with a value providing further differentiation where listed):

EF: Expedited Forwarding

AF: Assured Forwarding

CS: Class

Comparing Skype for Business Call Quality

Before a full rollout of Skype for Business (or any application for that matter), it is normal to pilot the new technology. When a pilot is running, it is extremely important that the same packet marking is used when comparing with another VoIP deployment.

In the past we've have had customers report that the clients are performing badly when compared to their existing deployment, and the reason has quite often been traced to the fact that they prioritize the existing VoIP packets.

In addition, the ports used for each modality can be defined both on the server side and on the client, allowing control and prioritization of traffic based on port ranges. If the port range approach is taken, you should define the client range as a subset of the server range of ports; this will reduce the quantity of specific network configuration rules required, as in the following example:

Server port range = 50,001–55,000

Client port range = 50,001–50,100

Taking this approach, network administrators can configure the network devices to use the range 50,001 to 55,000 for the prioritizing of audio traffic rather than having to configure two ranges (one for the servers and one for the clients).

Here is a list of the configuration points for the client side, along with an example of port variation allowing for control at the network layer (ClientMediaPort and ClientMediaPortRange are values used only by OCS R2 clients):

ClientMediaPortRangeEnabled	True/False
ClientMediaPort	Start port value; e.g., 5,000
ClientMediaPortRange	Number of ports. e.g., 20
ClientAudioPort	Start port value; e.g., 6,000
ClientAudioPortRange	Number of ports; e.g., 20
ClientVideoPort	Start port value; e.g., 7,000
ClientVideoPortRange	Number of ports; e.g., 20
ClientAppSharingPort	Start port value; e.g., 8,000
ClientAppSharingPortRange	Number of ports; e.g., 20
ClientFileTransferPort	Start port value; e.g., 9,000
ClientFileTransferPortRange	Number of ports; e.g., 20
ClientSipDynamicPort	Start port value; e.g., 10,000
ClientSipDynamicPortRange	Number of ports; e.g., 20

HOW MANY PORTS DO I NEED?

Some customers want to restrict the number of ports a client can open. For most users, we recommend that this be no less than 20 ports per modality. The reason for so many is that during call establishment, the ports are negotiated, and there may be several different ways to connect clients (peer to peer, via the Edge, and so on), so multiple ports are required during this phase. Once the call is established, two ports per modality are required. This is explained in detail here:

`http://technet.microsoft.com/en-us/library/dd572230(office.13).aspx`

Although this is an OCS R2 document, the content still holds true for Skype for Business.

Users who handle more calls (such as personal assistants) will need a higher number, based on the number of calls expected.

With operating systems before Windows Vista, potential rogue applications could leverage this port prioritization; however, Vista (and newer OSs) provides policy-based control, allowing the tagging of packets based on the application itself, which reduces the risk of a rogue application introducing prioritized traffic onto the network.

DEFINING A POLICY-BASED CONTROL

Take the following steps to define a policy-based control:

1. In the Group Policy Management Editor, you'll see that the Policy-Based QoS option is available for both Computer Configuration and User Configuration policies. In this example, you'll use a computer-based policy, so click there and select Create New Policy, as shown in Figure 17.13.

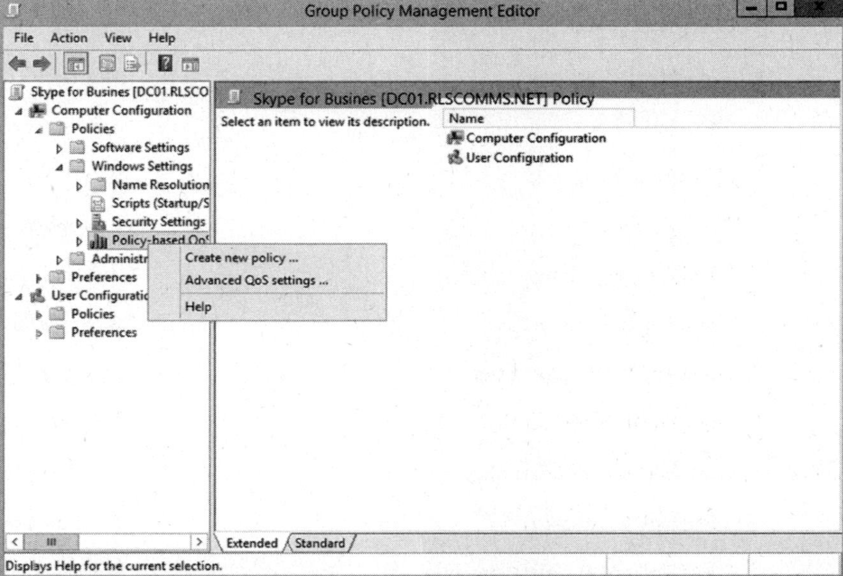

FIGURE 17.13 Choosing to create a new QoS policy in the Group Policy Management Editor

2. Complete the configuration options on the Policy-Based QoS screen, shown in Figure 17.14. In addition to naming the policy and defining the bandwidth rate, notice that the DSCP value is listed as a decimal value; this decodes to the values previously noted, as shown in Table 17.2.

TABLE 17.2: Decoding default DSCP values

PER-HOP BEHAVIOR	DECIMAL VALUE
EF	46
AF41	34
CS3	24
AF21	18
AF11	10

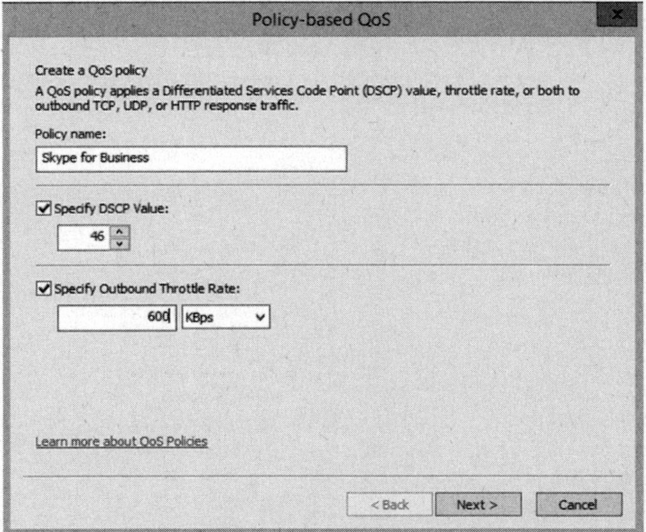

FIGURE 17.14 Entering a QoS policy value and throttle rate

3. The next screen (Figure 17.15) is where you specify the application to which this policy will apply in the Skype for Business case (as well as Lync and OCS); the filename is `Lync.exe` (with previous clients the filename is `communicator.exe`).

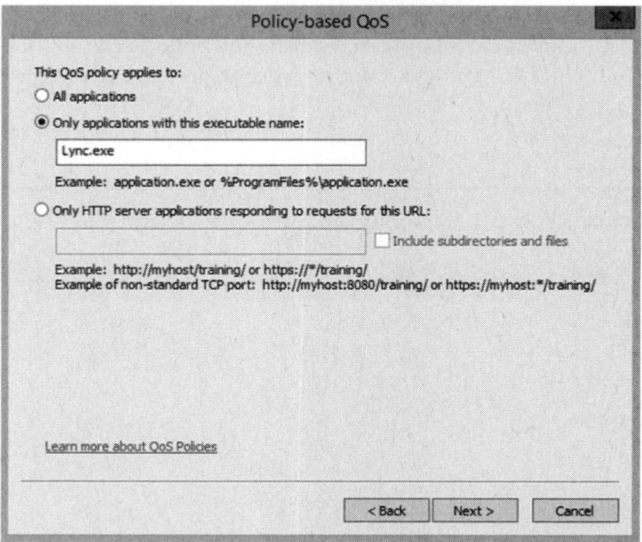

FIGURE 17.15
Specifying application restrictions for the QoS policy

4. The next screen asks for source and destination information. This could be used to mark traffic specific to leaving a site, but in most cases it is likely this would be left as default.
5. Figure 17.16 shows where the port range and protocol can be specified. Click Finish to complete the policy creation. From there the policy can be applied like any other Group Policy object.

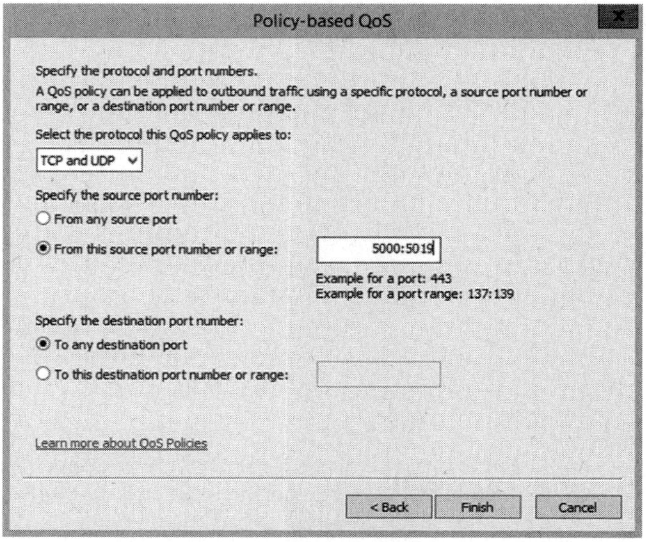

Policy-based QoS

Specify the protocol and port numbers.

A QoS policy can be applied to outbound traffic using a specific protocol, a source port number or range, or a destination port number or range.

Select the protocol this QoS policy applies to:

TCP and UDP

Specify the source port number:

From any source port

From this source port number or range: 5000:5019

Example for a port: 443
Example for a port range: 137:139

Specify the destination port number:

To any destination port

To this destination port number or range:

Learn more about QoS Policies

< Back Finish Cancel

FIGURE 17.16
Specifying a protocol and port range for the QoS policy

Designing for Call Admission Control

The aim of designing the Call Admission Control policies is to ultimately associate IP subnets with locations and, with each location, to define the number of individual calls as well as the total number of calls permitted from (and to) each site. The association of IP subnets is how each client's location is determined for the PDP query.

The following example assumes a company with offices in the following locations, with available network bandwidth shown in brackets. Interregional links are from Chicago to London and from London to Sydney.

- North America
  - Chicago (100,000kbps)
  - New York (50,000kbps)
  - Washington, D.C. (50,000kbps)
  - Seattle (5,000kbps)
  - San Francisco (5,000kbps)
- EMEA (Europe, Middle East, and Africa)
  - London (10,000kbps)
  - Dublin (5,000kbps)
  - Paris (3,000kbps)
- APAC (Asia and Pacific)
  - Sydney (5,000kbps)
  - Hong Kong (5,000kbps)
  - Tokyo (5,000kbps)

To do this, you start by defining the network into regions, or central sites. Any addresses within a region are policy free—that is, they can establish any number of calls without being blocked or rerouted. You can include multiple physical locations in a single region (or site); in fact, this is recommended when you do not care to control the bandwidth between specific sites.

Next, you'll define the sites and associate each site with a region. Calls within a site are policy free; however, calls across sites or regions will have policy applied and controls put in place.

From the previous example data, you can see that Chicago, New York, and Washington, D.C. are well enough connected that you don't need to put any controls in place for calls between these locations. Table 17.3 shows the associations.

For each site, you need to define the bandwidth for the link to the central site or define a *cross-link* tying together two sites. Once you have the total bandwidth defined, you need to establish how much bandwidth will be assigned to total audio and how much bandwidth to total video. (In the example, Paris will be defined not to permit any video calls.)

Table 17.3: Region, site, and bandwidth associations

Region	Site	Available Bandwidth (kbps)
North America	Chicago	100,000
North America	New York	50,000
North America	Washington, D.C.	50,000
North America	Seattle	5,000
North America	San Francisco	5,000
EMEA	London	10,000
EMEA	Dublin	5,000
EMEA	Paris	3,000
APAC	Sydney	5,000
APAC	Hong Kong	5,000
APAC	Tokyo	5,000

Table 17.4 shows the required configuration.

Table 17.4: Site total session definitions per modality

Region	Site	Available Bandwidth (kbps)	Total Assigned to Audio	Total Assigned to Video
North America	Chicago	100,000	Not controlled	Not controlled
North America	New York	50,000	Not controlled	Not controlled
North America	Washington, D.C.	50,000	Not controlled	Not controlled
North America	Seattle	5,000	2,000	1,200
North America	San Francisco	5,000	2,000	1,200
EMEA	London	10,000	Not controlled	Not controlled
EMEA	Dublin	5,000	2,000	1,200
EMEA	Paris	3,000	1,000	0

TABLE 17.4: Site total session definitions per modality *(CONTINUED)*

REGION	SITE	AVAILABLE BANDWIDTH (KBPS)	TOTAL ASSIGNED TO AUDIO	TOTAL ASSIGNED TO VIDEO
APAC	Sydney	5,000	Not controlled	Not controlled
APAC	Hong Kong	5,000	2,000	1,200
APAC	Tokyo	5,000	2,000	1,200

Chicago, New York, and Washington, D.C. will not have policy applied because they are well connected; London and Sydney will be defined as the central site in each region. It is important to note that the central site does not have to tie in with a physical location or indeed a data center. It can be considered a placeholder to which the other locations are connected. In most cases, it makes sense to associate with a location; however, in this example, three locations are being treated as one.

From these definitions, you define the maximum value for each modality that is permitted for a single call, as shown in Table 17.5.

TABLE 17.5: Site individual session definitions per modality

REGION	SITE	AVAILABLE BANDWIDTH (KBPS)	TOTAL ASSIGNED TO AUDIO	AUDIO SESSION LIMIT	TOTAL ASSIGNED TO VIDEO	VIDEO SESSION LIMIT
North America	Chicago	100,000	Not controlled	Not controlled	Not controlled	Not controlled
North America	New York	50,000	Not controlled	Not controlled	Not controlled	Not controlled
North America	Washington, D.C.	50,000	Not controlled	Not controlled	Not controlled	Not controlled
North America	Seattle	5,000	2,000	100	1,200	600
North America	San Francisco	5,000	2,000	100	1,200	600
EMEA	London	10,000	Not controlled	Not controlled	Not controlled	Not controlled
EMEA	Dublin	5,000	2,000	100	1,200	600

TABLE 17.5: Site individual session definitions per modality *(CONTINUED)*

REGION	SITE	AVAILABLE BANDWIDTH (KBPS)	TOTAL ASSIGNED TO AUDIO	AUDIO SESSION LIMIT	TOTAL ASSIGNED TO VIDEO	VIDEO SESSION LIMIT
EMEA	Paris	3,000	1,000	60	0	0
APAC	Sydney	5,000	Not controlled	Not controlled	Not controlled	Not controlled
APAC	Hong Kong	5,000	2,000	100	1,200	600
APAC	Tokyo	5,000	2,000	100	1,200	600

Using Seattle as the first example, 2,000kbps was assigned for total audio sessions, and 100kbps was assigned for a maximum per audio session. This will permit a maximum of 20 concurrent calls (total sessions divided by individual session limit) on this connection (into the North America region). On the video configuration, 1,200kbps are assigned for the total sessions, and 600kbps are assigned for each individual session, giving a maximum of two concurrent video sessions; HD video would not be permitted.

In the case of Paris, 1,000kbps are assigned for the total audio sessions, and 60kbps are assigned for each individual session, giving a concurrent call rate of 16 calls. For video traffic, none is permitted.

These two examples highlight the capability to control the quality of each individual call. Using Table 17.5, you can determine which codec will be used in the best case; you can also determine the capabilities to dynamically adapt if network issues are encountered during a call.

You can see that Seattle users can hold calls using the G711 codec, ensuring better call quality. However, if the network encounters issues, such as lost packets, and the codec requires the introduction of Forward Error Correction (FEC), then the Skype for Business client cannot introduce FEC on G711 because that would require 156kbps. Instead, it must dynamically drop down to wideband RT-Audio and introduce FEC, using 86kbps.

You can find full details here:

`http://technet.microsoft.com/en-us/library/jj688118.aspx`

Table 17.6 lists the bandwidth used by each codec.

TABLE 17.6: Codec bandwidth usage definitions

AUDIO/VIDEO CODEC	SCENARIOS	TYPICAL VALUE (KBPS)	MAX WITHOUT FEC (KBPS)	MAX WITH FEC (KBPS)
RTAudio Wideband	Peer-to-peer	39.8	62	91
RTAudio Narrowband	Peer-to-peer, PSTN	29.3	44.8	56.6
G.722	Conferencing	46.1	100.6	164.4

TABLE 17.6: Codec bandwidth usage definitions *(CONTINUED)*

AUDIO/VIDEO CODEC	SCENARIOS	TYPICAL VALUE (KBPS)	MAX WITHOUT FEC (KBPS)	MAX WITH FEC (KBPS)
G.711	PSTN	64.8	97	161
SILK Wideband	Skype for Business endpoints	44.3	69	105
Siren	Conferencing	25.5	52.6	68.6
Peer-to Peer Main video (H.264)	Skype for Business endpoints	460	4010 (resolution 1920 × 1080)	N/A
Peer-to Peer Main video (RTVideo)	Lync 2010 or OCS endpoints	460	2510 (resolution 1280 × 760)	N/A
Conferencing Main video (H.264)	Receive	260	8015	N/A
Conferencing Main video (H.264)	Send	270	8015	N/A
Panoramic video (H.264)	Skype for Business endpoints	190	2010 (resolution 1920 × 288)	N/A
Panoramic video (RTVideo)	Lync 2010 or OCS endpoints	190	510 (resolution 960 × 144)	N/A
Panoramic Video (H.264)	Sending bit-stream using multiple resolutions	190	2515	

Where multiple regions have been defined, you also need to establish the links between regions and permitted values of traffic across each, as in Table 17.7.

TABLE 17.7: Inter-region link definitions

NAME	REGION 1	REGION1	TOTAL ASSIGNED TO AUDIO	AUDIO SESSION LIMIT	TOTAL ASSIGNED TO VIDEO	VIDEO SESSION LIMIT
NA_EMEA	North America	EMEA	10,000	60	1,750	350
EMEA_APAC	EMEA	APAC	2,000	60	1,750	350

Finally, you need to associate IP subnets with each site, as shown in Table 17.8. As mentioned earlier, it is from these subnets that a client is able to determine which policy will apply.

TABLE 17.8: Subnet associations per site

REGION	SITE	SUBNETS
North America	Chicago	10.0.1.0/24, 10.0.7.0/24, 10.43.23.0/24
North America	New York	10.0.2.0/24, 192.168.3.0/25
North America	Washington, D.C.	10.1.0.0/16
North America	Seattle	10.0.3.0/24, 10.0.54.0/24
North America	San Francisco	10.0.4.0/24
EMEA	London	10.25.1.0/24, 192.168.3.128/25
EMEA	Dublin	10.25.2.0/24
EMEA	Paris	10.25.3.0/24
APAC	Sydney	10.0.9.0/24, 10.37.1.0/24
APAC	Hong Kong	10.37.2.0/24
APAC	Tokyo	10.37.3.0/24

The final Call Admission Control policy looks like Figure 17.17.

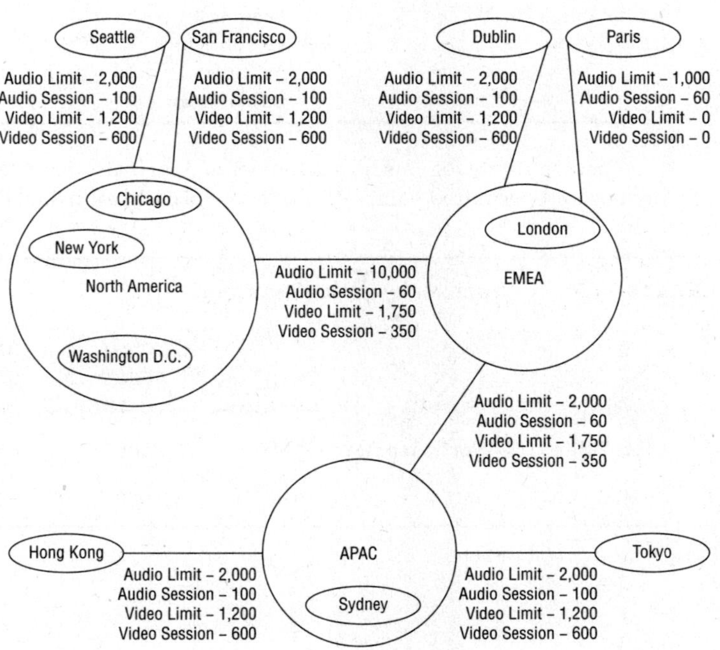

FIGURE 17.17 Diagrammatic representation of Call Admission Control Configuration

When a user in Seattle calls a user in Tokyo, Call Admission Control will assess the following connection links:

Seattle to North America Region
North America Region to EMEA Region
EMEA Region to APAC Region
APAC Region to Tokyo

If any of these links are saturated, the call will not proceed. If the call is established, the call details will be replicated to all PDPs in the topology to ensure that each is fully aware of the current network state.

In this example, we have not considered any rerouting capabilities. We will cover those in the section "Configuring Call Admission Control" later in this chapter.

Real World Scenario

What About MPLS?

MPLS networks can give the impression that all sites connected to the network are only one hop away from each other. This can cause confusion for anyone attempting to configure CAC in this type of scenario. You would normally have to configure a site link from each site to every other site—leading to a massive meshed network configuration, which would be extremely difficult to manage properly.

Taking the example from the section "Designing for Call Admission Control" and replacing the inter-region links with a global MPLS network will give the configuration shown here:

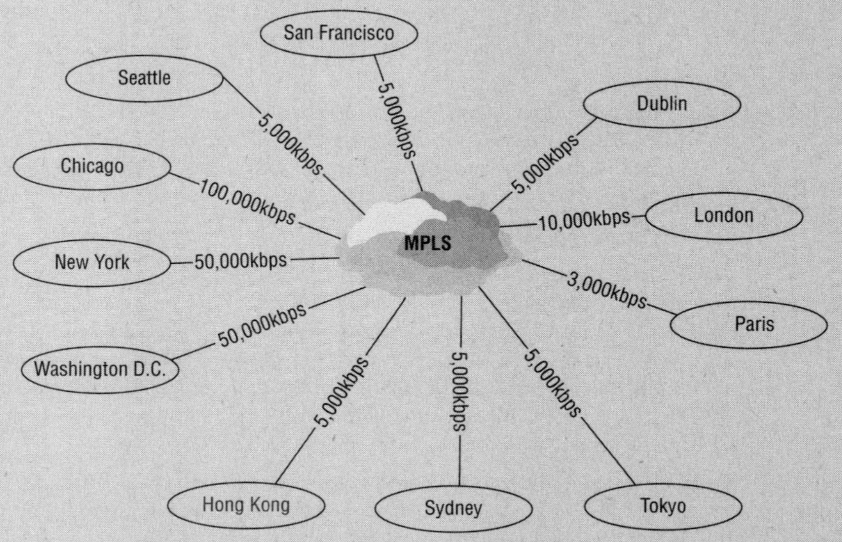

Configuring Call Admission Control to manage this network could prove difficult. Following the logic shown, you would create regions and individual sites again; however, this would lead to

continues

continued

misrepresentation on the network. It would be possible but extremely difficult to come up with a configuration where each site theoretically would have multiple links leaving the site but would not be represented as such from the network perspective, where there is only a single MPLS connection. The next illustration indicates how this might look:

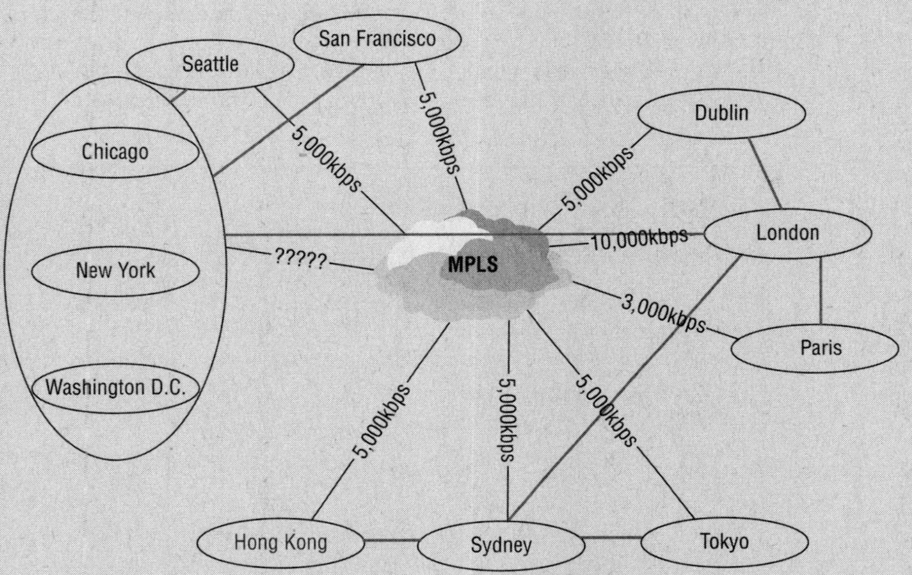

Taking London as the starting point, there are four connections: Dublin, Paris, APAC (Sydney), and North America; Call Admission Control would handle them individually, with no understanding of the underlying network where all the calls are actually following the same path. This could result in calls from London to North America being inadvertently impacted when the London-Dublin link is busy.

In addition, how would you manage the North America bandwidth?

A much cleaner approach is to treat the MPLS network *cloud* (MPLS networks are often referred to as *clouds* because of the way in which the actual network connections are abstracted from the user and appear as a single hop) as a Call Admission Control region in its own right. By taking this approach, you are back to the first diagram in this sidebar, but now you have control over each individual link; because all the links are to the cloud, the PDPs will be aware of the current concurrency rates on every link in the network and can efficiently manage the control of the call flow. This also allows multiple MPLS clouds to be managed easily.

By treating the MPLS mesh as a separate site and configuring links from each *actual* site to this imaginary site, you regain control over the network capacity used by Skype for Business. Because you won't assign any network subnets to this imaginary site, no clients will be considered as if they are located within the mesh.

Configuring Call Admission Control

We'll keep using the original example to show how the configuration is built. To configure and enable Call Admission Control, you need to individually configure the following sections (the Control Panel view is shown in Figure 17.18, with the Global tab open):

- Global
- Location Policy (not related to Call Admission Control)
- Policy Profile
- Region
- Site
- Subnet
- Region Link
- Region Route

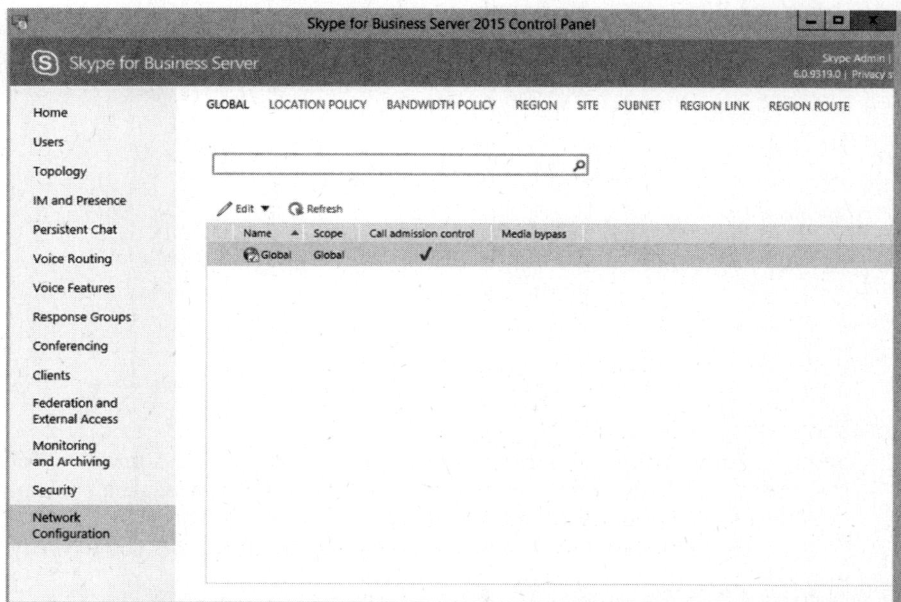

FIGURE 17.18 Using Control Panel to configure Call Admission Control

Although it is possible to configure all of Call Admission Control via a single `Set-CsNetworkConfiguration` command, that approach is extremely complex and not recommended. It is much easier to configure section by section.

Configuring the Global Setting

Because Call Admission Control is configured at the individual component level, the only setting on the policy in the Global tab is to enable or disable it.

Figure 17.19 shows Call Admission Control enabled in the Control Panel. The equivalent command in the Skype for Business Management Shell would be either

```
Set-CsNetworkConfiguration -EnableBandwidthPolicyCheck $True
```

or

```
Set-CsNetworkConfiguration -EnableBandwidthPolicyCheck $False
```

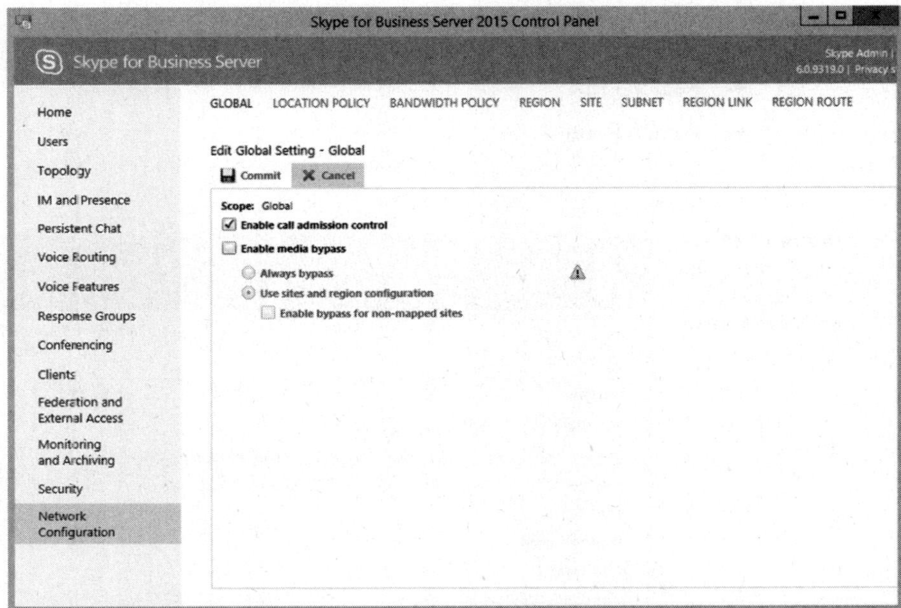

FIGURE 17.19 Enabling Call Admission Control

Additional policies may be created and applied if Call Admission Control is not being controlled globally or if the network setup does not allow a single global approach. Each policy can be enabled or disabled individually.

Using the `Get-CsNetworkConfiguration` cmdlet allows you to verify the state of each policy.

```
Identity                    : Global
MediaBypassSettings         :
Enabled=False;InternalBypassMode=Off;EnternalBypassMode=Off;AlwaysBypass=False;
BypassID=;EnabledForAudioVideoConferences=False
BWPolicyProfiles            : {}
NetworkRegions              : {}
NetworkRegionLinks          : {}
```

```
InterNetworkRegionRoutes   : {}
NetworkSites               : {}
InterNetworkSitePolicies   : {}
Subnets                    : {}
EnableBandwithPolicyCheck  : True
```

Figure 17.18 shows the Control Panel view of this command.

Defining the Policy Profile Settings

The Policy Profile page is where you define both the audio and video limits that will be assigned to the links between each site and region. Later you will link these polices to the relevant network sites. (Note that even though a policy may not allow audio or video across a link by setting the audio or video limit to 0, the individual session limit still requires a value to be added.)

Figure 17.20 shows the Control Panel input page and from the shell; the following command is used to create a bandwidth policy:

```
New-CsNetworkBandwidthPolicyProfile -Identity "Global Default Policy"
    -AudioBWLimit 2000 -AudioBWSessionLimit 100
    -VideoBWLimit 1200 -VideoBWSessionLimit 600
    -Description "Global Policy"
```

FIGURE 17.20
The New Bandwidth Policy profile page

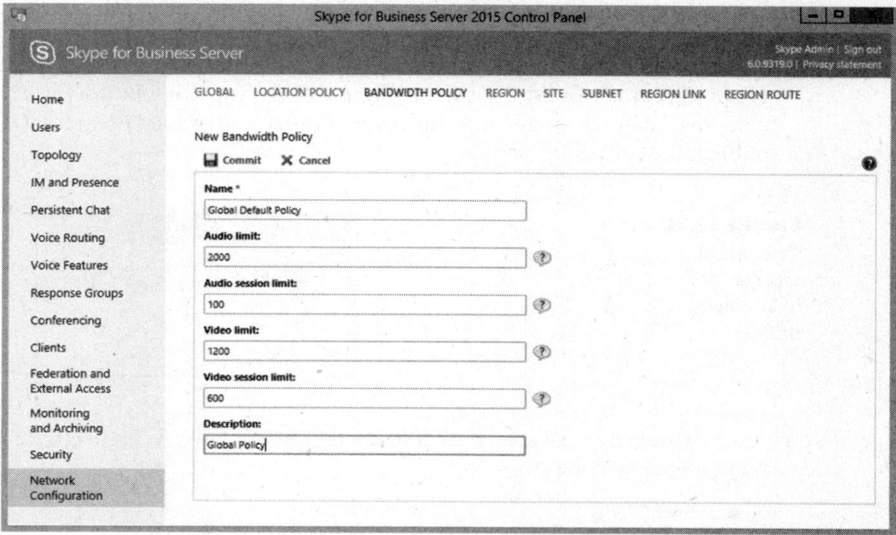

An inter-region policy is simply a bandwidth policy applied to a region policy, so it is created and configured in the same way.

Once the profile is fully configured, you will see the following output:

```
Get-CsNetworkBandwidthPolicyProfile
Identity        : Paris Bandwidth policy no video
BWPolicy        : {BWLimit=0;BWSessionLimit=60;BWPolicyModality=Audio,
```

```
BWLimit=0;BWSessionLimit=100;BWPolicyModality=Video}
BWPolicyProfileID : Paris Bandwidth policy no video
Description       : No video permitted
Identity          : Global Default Policy
BWPolicy          : {BWLimit=2000;BWSessionLimit=100;BWPolicyModality=Audio,
BWLimit=1200;BWSessionLimit=600;BWPolicyModality=Video}
BWPolicyProfileID : Global Default Policy
Description       : Global Policy
Identity          : NA_EMEA Bandwidth Policy
BWPolicy          : {BWLimit=10000;BWSessionLimit=60;BWPolicyModality=Audio,
BWLimit=1750;BWSessionLimit=350;BWPolicyModality=Video}
BWPolicyProfileID : NA_EMEA Bandwidth Policy
Description       : NA-EMEA Bandwidth Policy
Identity          : EMEA_APAC Bandwidth Policy
BWPolicy          : {BWLimit=2000;BWSessionLimit=60;BWPolicyModality=Audio,
BWLimit=1750;BWSessionLimit=350;BWPolicyModality=Video}
BWPolicyProfileID : EMEA_APAC Bandwidth Policy
Description       : EMEA-APAC Bandwidth Policy
```

Defining Regions

Regions are the hubs of Call Admission Control, and calls within a region do not have any restrictions placed on them.

Each region is required to be assigned to a central site; this is as defined (and published) via the Topology Builder shown in Figure 17.21. (Topology Builder is a separate installation item, installed via `setup.exe`; however, it must be installed on at least one server to create and publish the initial topology.)

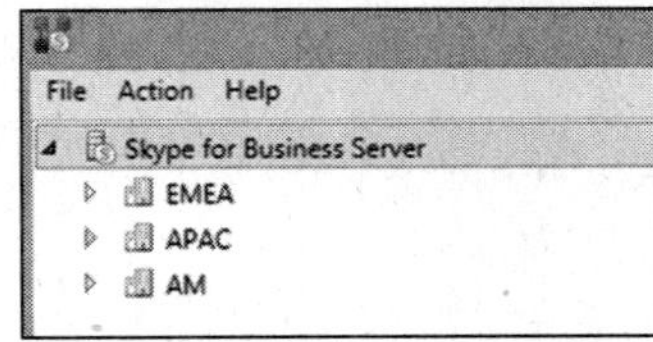

FIGURE 17.21
Central site representation in Topology Builder

The Control Panel screen to define a region is shown in Figure 17.22 and requires the following items to be configured:

- Name
- Central Site
- Enable Audio Alternate Path
- Enable Video Alternate Path
- Description
- Associated Sites (you'll define the sites in the next section)

FIGURE 17.22
New region definition

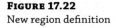

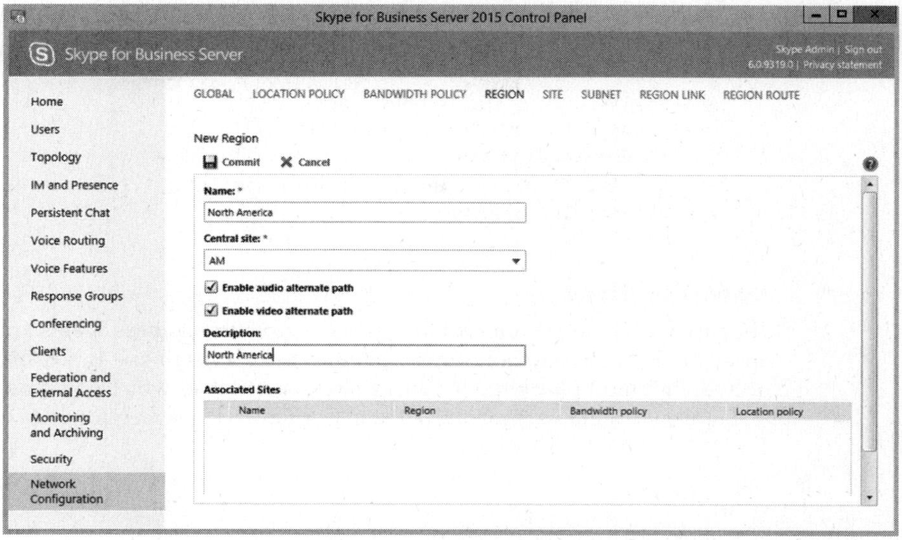

Configuring the information for the remaining regions via the Skype for Business Server Management Shell would look like this:

```
New-CsNetworkRegion -Identity EMEA -CentralSite EMEA -AudioAlternatePath $true
   -VideoAlternatePath $true -Description "EMEA Region"
```

Including `-AudioAlternatePath` and `-VideoAlternatePath` (and setting to `$True`) configures the region to reroute audio and video if Call Admission Control reports that not enough bandwidth is available on the links. This gives you with the capability to provide an alternate path for voice but not video if required.

`Get-CsNetworkRegion` will return this output:

```
Identity          : North America
Description       : North America Region
BypassID          : 87961ca4-1fa6-4286-8e15-9de3ca47f4af
CentralSite       : Site:NA
BWAlternatePaths  : {BWPolicyModality=Audio;
     AlternatePath=True,
     BWPolicyModality=Video;AlternatePath=True}
NetworkRegionID   : North America
Identity          : EMEA
Description       : EMEA Region
BypassID          : 13b075d8-fa32-4f21-8937-40e2d69e9934
CentralSite       : Site:EMEA
BWAlternatePaths  : {BWPolicyModality=Audio;
     AlternatePath=True,
     BWPolicyModality=Video;AlternatePath=True}
NetworkRegionID   : EMEA
```

```
Identity         : APAC
Description      : APAC Region
BypassID         : e0a0a73a-ccfb-4cca-aa5b-46b8d2a74653
CentralSite      : Site:APAC
BWAlternatePaths : {BWPolicyModality=Audio;
     AlternatePath=True,
     BWPolicyModality=Video;AlternatePath=True}
NetworkRegionID  : APAC
```

Defining Sites

Sites are within and connected to regions. Skype for Business clients are associated with sites, based on the actual subnet from which they are connecting. It is possible for a user to be connected with multiple Skype for Business clients, each of which could be in a different site.

Figure 17.23 shows the Control Panel Configuration screen for a new site. This is where you can define the following items:

- Name
- Region (must be previously defined)
- Bandwidth Policy
- Location Policy (not Call Admission Control–related)
- Description
- Associated Subnets (subnets are being defined next)

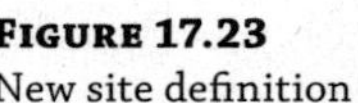

FIGURE 17.23
New site definition

Sites are defined using the Set-CsNetworkSite cmdlet:

```
New-CsNetworkSite -Identity "London"
    -NetworkRegionID EMEA
    -Description "London Site"
```

In the North America region, multiple sites are defined even though the example stated there will be no bandwidth controls. It is good practice to define *all* the sites in the environment because that will make them easier to match up and adjust in the future when—not if—the requirements change.

Not only will troubleshooting be easier when the complete environment is defined, but the fact that a site is defined but has no policy means the client will be correctly assigned within the logs, making them easier to follow when you're trying to understand a problem.

If this were a new site being introduced after Lync had already been deployed, it would make sense to fully populate the policy and location information sources at this point. Because this is the London site and we don't want to place any controls on the bandwidth usage for the example, we won't come back to assign a bandwidth policy; however, the subnets do need to be assigned. We'll discuss location policy in Chapter 15, "Troubleshooting."

The full configuration of the defined sites looks like this:

```
Get-CsNetworkSite
Identity           : Chicago
NetworkSiteID      : Chicago
Description        : Chicago site
NetworkRegionID    : North America
BypassID           : 87961ca4-1fa6-4286-8e15-9de3ca474faf
BWPolicyProfileID :
LocationPolicy     :
Identity           : New York
NetworkSiteID      : New York
Description        : New York Site
NetworkRegionID    : North America
BypassID           : 87961ca4-1fa6-4286-8e15-9de3ca474faf
BWPolicyProfileID :
LocationPolicy     :
Identity           : Washington DC
NetworkSiteID      : Washington DC
Description        : Washington DC Site
NetworkRegionID    : North America
BypassID           : 87961ca4-1fa6-4286-8e15-9de3ca474faf
BWPolicyProfileID :
LocationPolicy     :
Identity           : London
NetworkSiteID      : London
Description        : London Site
NetworkRegionID    : EMEA
BypassID           : 13b075d8-fa-32-4f21-8937-40e2d69e9934
BWPolicyProfileID :
LocationPolicy     :
```

```
Identity           : San Francisco
NetworkSiteID      : San Francisco
Description        : San Francisco Site
NetworkRegionID    : North America
BypassID           : 87961ca4-1fa6-4286-8e15-9de3ca474faf
BWPolicyProfileID :
LocationPolicy     :
Identity           : Seattle
NetworkSiteID      : Seattle
Description        : Seattle Site
NetworkRegionID    : North America
BypassID           : 87961ca4-1fa6-4286-8e15-9de3ca474faf
BWPolicyProfileID :
LocationPolicy     :
Identity           : Dublin
NetworkSiteID      : Dublin
Description        : Dublin Site
NetworkRegionID    : EMEA
BypassID           : 13b075d8-fa-32-4f21-8937-40e2d69e9934
BWPolicyProfileID :
LocationPolicy     :
Identity           : Paris
NetworkSiteID      : Paris
Description        : Paris Site
NetworkRegionID    : EMEA
BypassID           : 13b075d8-fa-32-4f21-8937-40e2d69e9934
BWPolicyProfileID :
LocationPolicy     :
Identity           : Sydney
NetworkSiteID      : Sydney
Description        : Sydney Site
NetworkRegionID    : APAC
BypassID           : e0a0a73a-ccfb-4cca-aa5b-46b8d2a74653
BWPolicyProfileID :
LocationPolicy     :
Identity           : Hong Kong
NetworkSiteID      : Hong Kong
Description        : Hong Kong Site
NetworkRegionID    : APAC
BypassID           : e0a0a73a-ccfb-4cca-aa5b-46b8d2a74653
BWPolicyProfileID :
LocationPolicy     :
Identity           : Tokyo
NetworkSiteID      : Tokyo
Description        : Tokyo Site
NetworkRegionID    : APAC
BypassID           : e0a0a73a-ccfb-4cca-aa5b-46b8d2a74653
```

```
BWPolicyProfileID :
LocationPolicy    :
```

Defining Subnets

Each client will determine its site location and, therefore, policy restrictions based on its subnet. To enable this association between site and subnet, you must first define the subnets in the environment and then assign them to the correct sites.

Figure 17.24 shows the Control Panel approach to define a subnet.

- Subnet ID
- Mask
- Network Site ID (must be previously defined)
- Description

The subnet ID must be the first address in the subnet range (known as the network address or *subnet-zero*). The mask must be in numeric format (e.g., 24), not the more common Classless Inter-Domain Routing (CIDR) format (e.g., /24).

FIGURE 17.24
New subnet definition

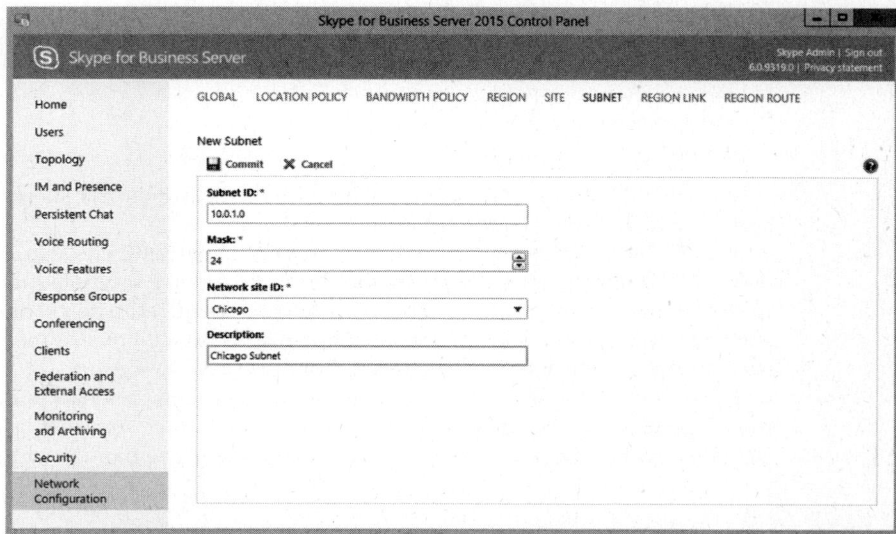

The cmdlet to use for this function is `New-CsSubnet`.

```
New-CsNetworkSubnet -Identity 10.0.7.0 -Mask 24
   -NetworkSiteID Chicago
   -Description "Chicago subnet"
```

Once fully populated, the environment looks like this:

```
Get-CsSubnet
Identity      : 10.0.1.0
MaskBits      : 24
Description   : Chicago subnet
NetworkSiteID : Chicago
SubnetID      : 10.0.1.0
Identity      : 10.0.7.0
MaskBits      : 24
Description   : Chicago subnet
NetworkSiteID : Chicago
SubnetID      : 10.0.7.0
Identity      : 10.43.23.0
MaskBits      : 24
Description   : Chicago subnet
NetworkSiteID : Chicago
SubnetID      : 10.43.23.0
Identity      : 10.0.2.0
MaskBits      : 24
Description   : New York subnet
NetworkSiteID : New York
SubnetID      : 10.0.2.0
Identity      : 10.0.3.0
MaskBits      : 25
Description   : Paris subnet
NetworkSiteID : Paris
SubnetID      : 10.0.3.0
```

The output has been cut for brevity because the definitions for subnets are the same for each and there really isn't a lot to configure.

Although the definition terminology is subnet, supernetting is also a supported method to define CAC subnets. Supernetting is the ability to combine multiple subnets into larger ranges, reducing the amount of data that needs to be input (which can be a tedious process!). When a subnet is defined with a larger mask, CAC can still correctly determine which location a client is in, even if the client subnet mask differs from that used by CAC.

For example, in the Paris example highlighted earlier, the mask is 25, which resolves into the range 10.0.3.0–10.0.3.127. We could also define a France supernet of 10.0.3.0 with a mask of 24, which would include the Paris subnet as well as the remainder of the 10.0.3.128–10.0.3.255 range.

Defining Region Links

Now that you've defined the regions, sites, and associated subnets, you need to define how much bandwidth is available to Skype for Business between regions. Region links are how you can do this. Region links also represent the logical connections from one region to the next.

Figure 17.25 shows the values required to create the region link between North America and EMEA. To do that, you need to configure the following items:

- Name
- Network Region #1 (must already have been defined)
- Network Region #2 (must already have been defined)
- Bandwidth Policy

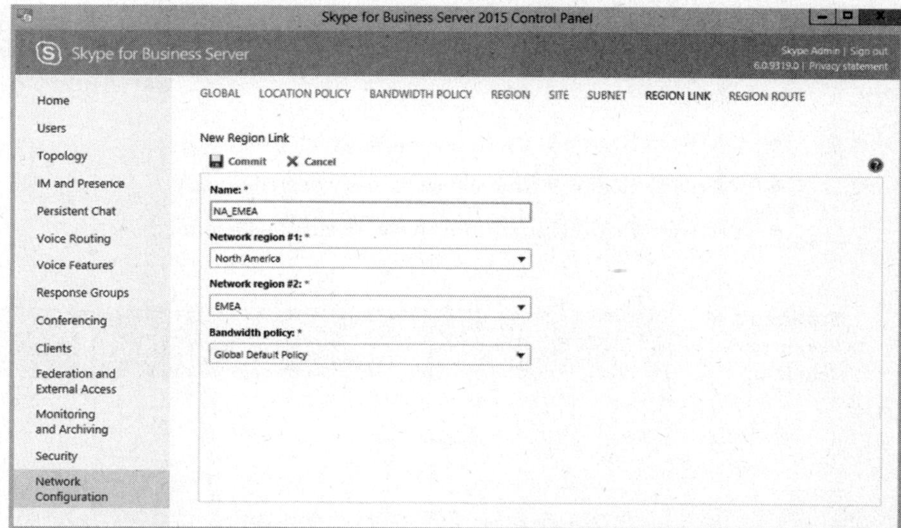

FIGURE 17.25 New region link definition

To define a connection between EMEA and APAC and assign the relevant bandwidth policy, use this command:

```
New-CsNetworkRegionLink -Identity EMEA_APAC
     -NetworkRegionID1 EMEA
     -NetworkRegionID2 APAC
     -BWPolicyProfileID "EMEA_APAC Bandwidth Policy"
```

Once all region links are defined, the environment will look like this:

```
Get-CsNetworkRegionLink
Identity            : NA_EMEA
BWPolicyProfileID   : NA_EMEA Bandwidth Policy
NetworkRegionLinkID : NA_EMEA
NetworkRegionID1    : North America
NetworkRegionID2    : EMEA
Identity            : EMEA_APAC
BWPolicyProfileID   : EMEA_APAC Bandwidth Policy
NetworkRegionLinkID : EMEA_APAC
NetworkRegionID1    : EMEA
NetworkRegionID2    : APAC
```

Assigning Region Routes

Once all the regions have been defined, Lync needs to understand how they are connected. The connections are defined in the Region Route section in the Control Panel. This is similar to the Region Link configuration, except that rather than defining the policy applied on a link, you are defining the routes to take between regions.

The actual network route taken by the data is not affected by this definition; it is used only internally within Lync Server 2013 to allow an understanding of the network within the Call Admission Control aspect of Lync Server 2013.

Figure 17.26 shows the Control Panel implementation, which requires the following items:

- Name
- Network Region #1 (must have already been defined)
- Network Region #2 (must have already been defined)
- Network Region Links (must have already been defined)

FIGURE 17.26 Region route definition

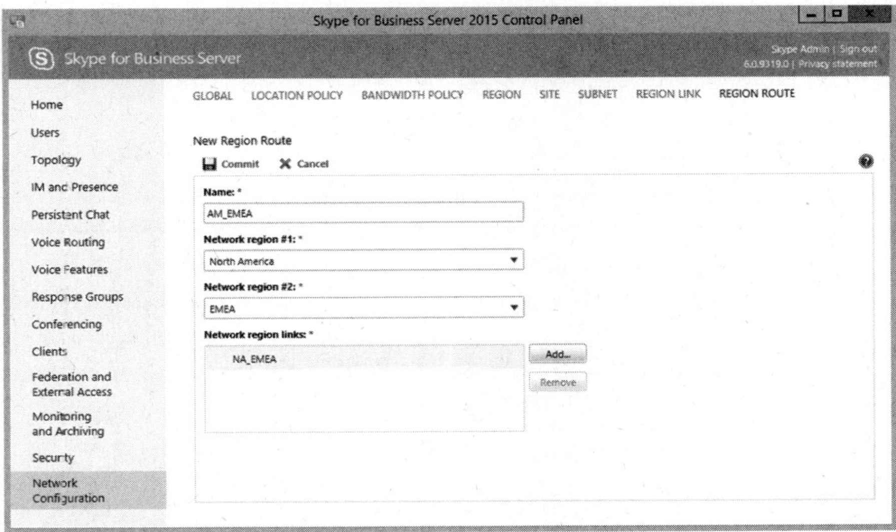

The equivalent PowerShell cmdlet is `Net-CsNetworkInterRegionRoute`. Here is an example:

```
New-CsNetworkInterRegionRoute -Identity EMEA_APAC
    -NetworkRegionID1 EMEA -NetworkRegionID2 APAC
    -NetworkRegionLinks EMEA_APAC
```

The fully configured environment will look like this:

```
Get-CsNetworkInterRegionRoute
Identity                    : NA_EMEA
```

```
NetworkRegionLinks          : {NA_EMEA}
InterNetworkRegionRouteID : NA_EMEA
NetworkRegionID1            : North America
NetworkRegionID2            : EMEA
Identity                    : EMEA_APAC
NetworkRegionLinks          : {EMEA_APAC}
InterNetworkRegionRouteID : EMEA_APAC
NetworkRegionID1            : EMEA
NetworkRegionID2            : APAC
```

Assigning Policies

Now that the environment is fully populated, the final step in configuring it is to apply the policy controls. The previous two sections showed how to assign policy to the region links; however, you also need to go back and assign the policy to a number of sites.

At this point, all calls within a region are uncontrolled; only the interregion calls have had policy applied to them. In the example, you want to control calls on a number of site links and leave the remaining as uncontrolled within region NA.

To assign policy to a specific site, use the `Set-CsNetworkSite` cmdlet.

```
Set-CsNetworkSite -Identity "Paris"
-BWPolicyProfileID "Paris Bandwidth policy no video"
```

You can also apply policies using the Control Panel; simply open the specific site (from the Site configuration tab in the Network Configuration section) by double-clicking the site entry. Once the site is opened, you will be taken to the Edit Site page (shown in Figure 17.27). From the defined Bandwidth Policy section there, you can choose which policy will be applied on this link.

Figure 17.27
Assigning a policy to an existing site

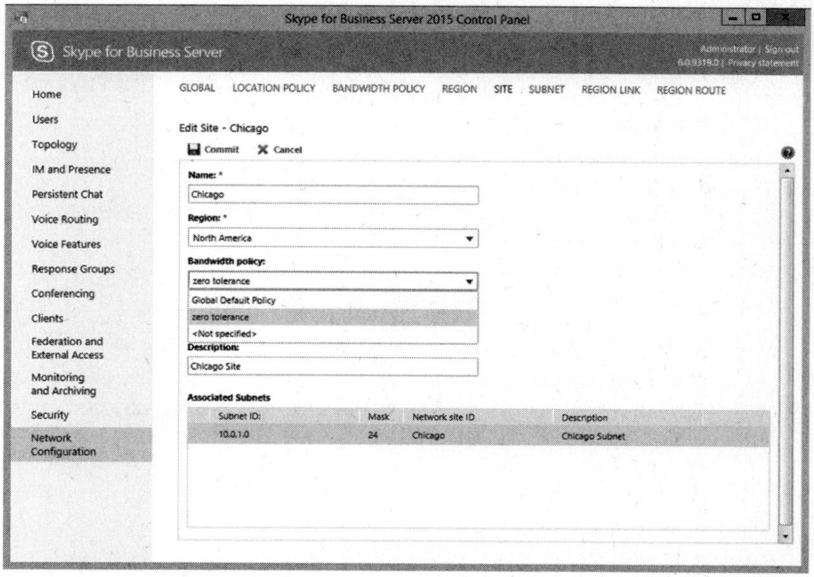

Finally, the fully configured site listing looks like this:

```
Get-CsNetworkSite
Identity           : Chicago
NetworkSiteID      : Chicago
Description        : Chicago site
NetworkRegionID    : North America
BypassID           : 6d278a1c-c994-4a28-b6de-a4a3773335ec
BWPolicyProfileID  :
LocationPolicy     :
Identity           : New York
NetworkSiteID      : New York
Description        : New York Site
NetworkRegionID    : North America
BypassID           : 6d278a1c-c994-4a28-b6de-a4a3773335ec
BWPolicyProfileID  :
LocationPolicy     :
Identity           : Washington DC
NetworkSiteID      : Washington DC
Description        : Washington DC Site
NetworkRegionID    : North America
BypassID           : 6d278a1c-c994-4a28-b6de-a4a3773335ec
BWPolicyProfileID  :
LocationPolicy     :
Identity           : London
NetworkSiteID      : London
Description        : London Site
NetworkRegionID    : EMEA
BypassID           : ca72a529-277f-4757-aa8f-e13c681cc462
BWPolicyProfileID  :
LocationPolicy     :
Identity           : San Francisco
NetworkSiteID      : San Francisco
Description        : San Francisco Site
NetworkRegionID    : North America
BypassID           : 86b36862-bd48-49de-a1d6-49561ce50bd9
BWPolicyProfileID  : Global Default Policy
LocationPolicy     :
Identity           : Seattle
NetworkSiteID      : Seattle
Description        : Seattle Site
NetworkRegionID    : North America
BypassID           : 2049a6b0-02e1-4f71-b76b-db93aa7d130c
BWPolicyProfileID  : Global Default Policy
LocationPolicy     :
Identity           : Dublin
NetworkSiteID      : Dublin
Description        : Dublin Site
```

```
NetworkRegionID    : EMEA
BypassID           : 1f0c441c-aac1-4ba4-b835-43b20fb95686
BWPolicyProfileID : Global Default Policy
LocationPolicy     :
Identity           : Paris
NetworkSiteID      : Paris
Description        : Paris Site
NetworkRegionID    : EMEA
BypassID           : 7c638937-4c0b-4a8f-9918-cebe7a7b7284
BWPolicyProfileID : Paris Bandwidth policy no video
LocationPolicy     :
Identity           : Sydney
NetworkSiteID      : Sydney
Description        : Sydney Site
NetworkRegionID    : APAC
BypassID           : d1b4c334-de17-40e8-950d-1ffe6bfd4c06
BWPolicyProfileID :
LocationPolicy     :
Identity           : Hong Kong
NetworkSiteID      : Hong Kong
Description        : Hong Kong Site
NetworkRegionID    : APAC
BypassID           : d6e14fc5-2082-4731-8973-8489cd4e6cde
BWPolicyProfileID : Global Default Policy
LocationPolicy     :
Identity           : Tokyo
NetworkSiteID      : Tokyo
Description        : Tokyo Site
NetworkRegionID    : APAC
BypassID           : 4baa4383-c037-414e-b4dd-b780e4c88ee2
BWPolicyProfileID : Global Default Policy
LocationPolicy     :
```

Identifying Calls on a Network

During the early stages of the Lync Server 2010 beta program, customers had a question: "If the system knows what the current state of calls is throughout the network, where can an administrator find that information?"

A subsequent version of the beta (and released) code in Lync Server 2010 provided the following management shell command:

```
Set-CsBandwidthPolicyServiceConfiguration -EnableLogging $true
```

This enables CVS file logging to the following location on the file share:

```
<file share>/1-ApplicationServer-1/AppServerFiles/PDP/
```

Several files are created.

`PDP_<servername><date><time>_Links` This file is updated hourly, or when the Call Admission Control configuration is changed. It will contain one line per site or region and list the current permitted total and the current utilization for both audio and video traffic. It is a CSV format file.

`PDP_<servername><date><time>_BwCheckFailure` This file is updated with every entry based on the local PDP failures and includes data such as the IP addresses of the clients involved as well as the minimum and maximum requested bandwidth values. This data does not get replicated to any other PDP in the topology. It is a CSV format file.

`PDP_<servername><date><time>_Topology` This file is generated once per day at 00:01, as well as when any changes are applied to the Call Admission Control configuration. It is an XML format file.

Reporting on Call Admission Control

Over time, understanding the impact of Call Admission Control is important. If the values are set too high, then potentially the network is over specified and costs may be saved by reducing the capacity. On the other hand, it's more likely that Call Admission Control will be rejecting calls, and if a significant number are reported, this may indicate that Call Admission Control is configured too low. In parallel to this, if the network is nearing capacity, it is an indication that the network is under pressure and may need to be increased.

From the reporting pack installed with the monitoring server, you can run the Call Admission Control report, which will provide a detailed view on how many calls are being rerouted or rejected based on the current policy settings. This is covered in Chapter 13, "Archiving and Monitoring."

The Bottom Line

Identify Call Admission Control–capable endpoints. Before designing and configuring Call Admission Control, you need to understand where it can be applied to ensure that the proper configuration is identified.

Master It You are in the process of defining a migration from OCS R2 to Skype for Business. First you migrated the OCS servers to Lync Server 2010 and have now introduced Skype for Business. Users previously reported some issues with call quality because of the capacity on the network, so Call Admission Control is required. What is needed to ensure the best user call experience?

Configure policy-based Quality of Service controls. Call Admission Control provides application-layer management of the call bandwidth; however, to truly provide this guarantee to clients, quality of service is required to operate on the network layer. Windows Vista introduced policy-based quality of service controls.

Master It You have restricted the port range to be 5000 to 5999, and you will deploy Skype for Business to your users. An application utilized in the finance department uses the port range 5500 to 5599. How can you ensure that only the Skype for Business traffic is prioritized on the network?

Design a Call Admission Control solution. Call Admission Control can be complex in large interconnected networks. A properly designed solution will ensure that two important requirements of Call Admission Control are met: user call quality is high and the network is not saturated.

Master It What special considerations should be given to an MPLS network?

Configure Call Admission Control. Once designed, Call Admission Control needs to be configured and applied to the Skype for Business servers. The servers will keep each other constantly updated as to the number of the calls and bandwidth used on the network. By using the built-in logging functionality, it is possible to capture an hourly snapshot of the state, with more detailed reporting available via the Monitoring server.

Master It What needs to be defined and applied to configure Call Admission Control?

Chapter 18

E9-1-1 and Location Information Services

Being able to dial emergency services is probably the most critical requirement for any telephony system. Face it, if someone needs emergency services, something serious is probably happening.

Although Office Communications Server 2007 and R2 were both capable of calling emergency services, Lync Server 2010/2013 and Skype for Business Server 2015 are also compliant with the North American requirement to provide location-based data with calls, known as Enhanced 911, or E9-1-1.

If you have experience with configuring Lync Server 2010/2013 for E9-1-1, then this chapter will be familiar to you. The only additional information included here is reference to Emergency Location Identification Number (ELIN) gateway support, which is also valid for Lync Server but was added significantly after release.

In this chapter, you will learn to

- Describe the E9-1-1 requirements for North America
- Configure Skype for Business Server 2015 to meet E9-1-1 requirements
- Understand how Location Information services can be used by callers outside North America

Understanding E9-1-1

In the early days of telephony, each exchange could use a different number for contacting emergency services. More than 70 years ago, the United Kingdom was one of the first locations to introduce three-digit emergency service dialing. This informal standard has since spread worldwide, and almost all countries have three-digit dialing for the main emergency services of police, fire, and medical.

There is no common global number for emergency services; 911 is used in North America, 112 in Europe, and 999 in the United Kingdom, for example. Moreover, in many locations separate phone numbers are used for each of the emergency services, with no central public safety operator.

Where a central public safety operator is used, the safety operator establishes the specific emergency need and may route the call to the specific service or act as an intermediary and collect additional information such as the location, or they may provide verbal assistance and guidance until the emergency services arrive.

Figure 18.1 shows a typical interaction in a legacy telephony system.

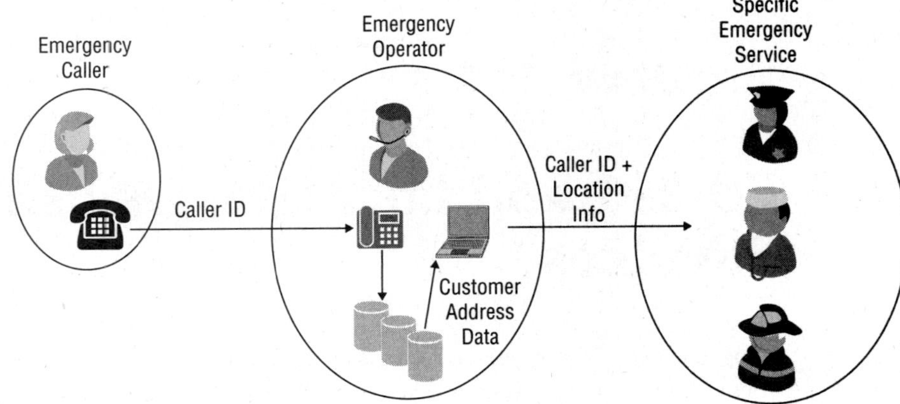

FIGURE 18.1
Traditional interaction from an emergency operator

As phone systems developed, and in many cases became nationalized, it was possible to determine the phone's location based on the billing records for an individual line. In large organizations, the information was typically not detailed enough for this to occur; however, at least some of the address information could be discerned.

However, the introduction of cellular-based mobile devices removed this capability—in most cases, the caller was not at the billing address of the handset, rendering billing information useless.

Mobile handsets also introduced the concept of *roaming* and the complication of enabling users (when traveling out of country) to dial their home country's emergency number and have it translated to the local country number as well as being routed locally. Most devices accept 112, 911, and 999 as preprogrammed emergency service numbers. SIM cards may also have additional data programmed.

Mobile integration with the emergency services differs within each country, but there is normally a provision for the mobile carrier to provide the location information based on the cell tower details through which the handset is provided, as shown in Figure 18.2.

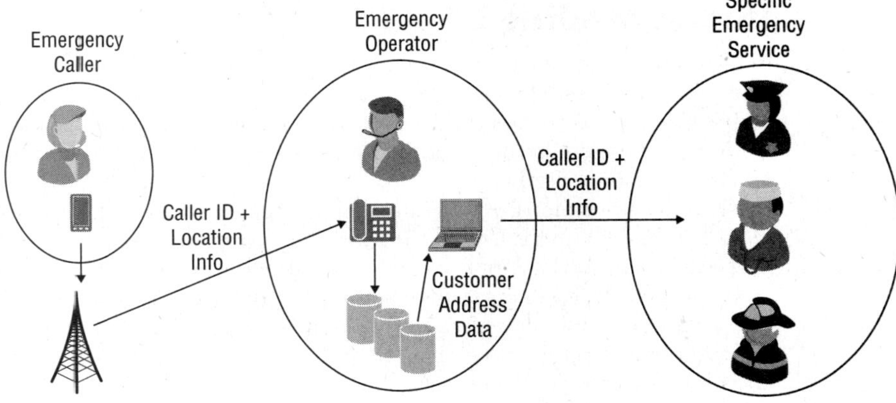

FIGURE 18.2
Cellular provision of location information

Including location information automatically ensures not only that emergency services are provided the information, saving valuable time, but also that the call is routed to the nearest Public Safety Answering Point (PSAP), guaranteeing that the emergency services in the vicinity of the emergency are notified.

Telephony has moved away from the traditional "fixed line" idea to the data network provision of Voice over IP (VoIP), and the copper lines to desks became network lines to anywhere. Continuing the trend is the concept of softphone clients such as Skype for Business, and you can see that the need for location-based information continues to become more apparent.

In the early implementations of VoIP systems, emergency calling was specifically excluded because of the flexibility of the potential location of the caller. Financial penalties imposed by governments over lack of emergency service calling provisions soon made this approach unreasonable.

Enhanced 911 (E9-1-1) is the provision of the emergency call as well as the location information associated with it. Skype for Business Server 2015 implements E9-1-1, as shown in Figure 18.3.

FIGURE 18.3
E9-1-1 Implementation within Skype for Business Server 2015

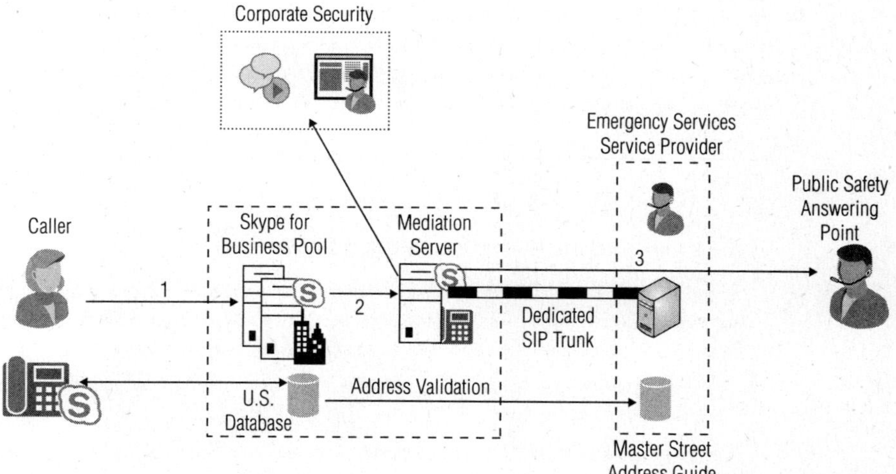

The process is as follows:

1. A call is placed to emergency services.
2. The call is routed to the appropriate Mediation server, with Session Initiation Protocol (SIP) information that includes location details.
3. The call is routed via the emergency services service provider to the appropriate PSAP. If at this stage the location information has not been validated via the Master Street Address Guide database, then an emergency services service provider operator will handle the call and verbally confirm location information prior to routing the call to the PSAP.
4. Optionally, the corporate security desk may be informed, via instant message (IM) and/ or inclusion in a conference call.

When the Lync Server 2010 certification of ELIN gateways was achieved, the requirement to have a dedicated SIP trunk for E9-1-1 calling went away. An ELIN gateway provides a method to assign emergency response locations (ERLs) to specific telephone numbers, allowing the PSAP to identify the location from which the call is made. As would be expected, a single gateway is not as granular as an internal database and would typically be used to define larger areas, such as a floor or building.

The ELIN gateway process uses the same infrastructure as shown in Figure 18.3, with the exception that a gateway sits between the Mediation server and the emergency services provider; a SIP trunk may or may not be used.

The calling number (from the user dialing 911) is cached on the gateway for a configurable time period, allowing for the emergency services to call back the "generic" number used in the location by the gateway; a reverse lookup is carried out on the cache to retrieve the original caller's Direct Inward Dial (DID) number, and the call is passed on to this cached number.

Current Legislation

As of October 2015, more than 20 states across North America have legislation requiring businesses, schools, and government agencies to provide E9-1-1 capabilities. Other states in North America and other countries throughout the world are considering similar legislation and approaches for provision of location information.

Real World Scenario

THE CONSEQUENCES OF GETTING IT WRONG

Providing location information to emergency services helps improve response times; however, in extreme cases, when this information is out of date or even wrong, it can lead to fatalities simply because the emergency responders are sent to the wrong location.

The first fatality due to failure to deliver the correct location for the caller's address happened in Canada in 2008.

A family moved from their home and, realizing the benefits of VoIP, continued to use the same telephony service provider and number at their new location. However, somehow the old street address was retained for the customer. Because of a miscommunication caused by language barriers, the emergency services operator was unable to confirm the address, and the emergency services were dispatched to the old (incorrect) address.

This highlights the need to ensure not only that the technology is location aware but that the correct street address information reflects the actual location—addresses may still be valid but associated with an incorrect subnet or switch.

Configuring E9-1-1

Now that you understand why you need to configure E9-1-1 dialing and location services, how do you go about it?

Simply put, E9-1-1 calling is a voice route using a dedicated SIP trunk, so you'll need to define the following:

- PSTN usage
- Location policy
- SIP trunk
- Voice route

Configuring PSTN Usage

As described in Chapter 16, "Getting Started with Voice," the public switched telephone network (PSTN) usages are used to provide call authorization to users when they are attempting to place calls via the Skype for Business client. A PSTN usage ties a voice policy to a user and also a route to a gateway, giving permissions for a user to use a particular route.

It is recommended that a separate usage be defined for emergency services dialing and that all users are permitted to use it.

The command to define a PSTN usage is as follows:

```
Set-CsPstnUsage -Identity global -Usage @{add="EmergencyUsage"}
```

Configuring Location Policies

The location policy contains the definition of the emergency services dialing implementation. Policies can be assigned to specific subnets or individual users. If neither of these is in place, the global policy takes effect.

Using the `New-CsLocationPolicy` or `Set-CsLocationPolicy` cmdlet, the additional parameters shown in Table 18.1 provide the PowerShell method of configuration.

TABLE 18.1: `CsLocationPolicy` parameters

PARAMETER	OPTIONAL?	EXAMPLE
`Identity`	Yes	`Global`
`EnhancedEmergencyServicesEnabled`	No	`$True`
`LocationRequired`	Yes	`yes`
`UseLocationForE9-1-1Only`	Yes	`$True`
`PstnUsage`	Yes	`EmergencyUsage`
`EmergencyDialString`	Yes	`911`
`EmergencyDialMask`	Yes	`112`
`NotificationURI`	Yes	`Sip:security@rlscomms.net`
`ConferenceURI`	Yes	`Sip:+155512347890@rlscomms.net`
`ConferenceMode`	Yes	`TwoWay`

TABLE 18.1: `CsLocationPolicy` parameters *(CONTINUED)*

PARAMETER	OPTIONAL?	EXAMPLE
`Description`	Yes	`Global emergency location policy`
`EnhancedEmergencyServiceDisclaimer`	Yes	`"You are currently connecting from a location where location services are required for emergency dialing and your location has not been set. Do you wish to set your location now?"`
`LocationRefreshInterval`	Yes	4

The parameters in Table 18.1 are described in more detail here:

`Identity` This defines the `CsLocationPolicy` to modify or create. If a policy is being scoped (tagged) to a specific site, the entry must be in the form `site:`*`<site name>`*—for example, `site:UK`.

`EnhancedEmergencyServicesEnabled` The `EnhancedEmergencyServicesEnabled` parameter tells the client whether to retrieve and provide location information with an emergency call.

`LocationRequired` When the client is logging in, the `LocationRequired` parameter is used in the event that location information cannot be retrieved from the location configuration database. This parameter can take one of three options.

> **`no`** The user will not be prompted for any location information, and location information will be unavailable for the emergency services call. The call will be answered by the emergency services provider, asking verbally for the location information before rerouting to the correct emergency services operator.
>
> **`yes`** The user is prompted for location information; however, completion is not mandatory, and the prompt can be dismissed. In this scenario, if the information is provided, the call is first answered by the emergency services provider to verify the location information before rerouting to the emergency services operator.
>
> **`disclaimer`** Similar to `yes`, except that the prompt may not be dismissed without completing the location information. An emergency call can still be completed, following the no definition, but no other calls can be placed until this information is completed.

`UseLocationForE9-1-1Only` Other applications integrated with Skype for Business Server may be able to leverage location information. For example, an application for booking conference rooms could prioritize available rooms closest to your current location; the `UseLocationForE9-1-1Only` parameter controls this capability.

`PstnUsage` The route associated with this `PstnUsage` parameter must already exist and should point to a SIP trunk dedicated to emergency calls.

`EmergencyDialString` This value is the number dialed to reach emergency services. It will differ from country to country; for example, the United States uses 911, while most of Europe uses 112.

EmergencyDialMask The `EmergencyDialMask` parameter allows multiple numbers to be used to dial emergency services. For example, suppose a user has traveled from Europe to the United States and needs to dial the emergency services without having to figure out what number to dial; they could continue to dial 112 and have this automatically translated to 911.

You can include multiple entries in this string, by separating each one with a semicolon.

```
EmergencyDialMask "112;999"
```

NotificationURI In addition to providing location information to the emergency services, Skype for Business provides the ability to notify SIP-based contacts through an instant message, which also includes the location information.

Multiple SIP URIs can be included by use of a comma-separated list.

```
-NotificationURI
"sip:security@rlscomms.net,sip:facilities@rlscomms.net"
```

ConferenceURI As well as the `NotificationURI` parameter providing instant message notification, the `ConferenceURI` parameter allows a third party to be conferenced into the voice conversation between the initiator of the emergency call and the emergency service provider/operator. This is used in conjunction with the `ConferenceMode` parameter.

ConferenceMode When the `ConferenceURI` is specified, the `ConferenceMode` parameter determines whether the third party can only listen to the conversation or can be an active participant. The values permitted are as follows:

oneway Listen only

twoway Actively participate

Description As with all the cmdlets, the `Description` parameter allows descriptive text to be entered.

EnhancedEmergencyServiceDisclaimer This parameter was introduced with Lync Server 2013. With Lync Server 2010, the emergency services disclaimer was set globally; however, now it can be set on a per-policy basis, allowing much more granular information. The dialog box presented provides a Yes/No option to the user, so be sure to word your disclaimer correctly. Selecting Yes will open the Location Definition dialog.

LocationRefreshInterval By default, the client will request a service location update every four hours. This parameter allows for control of this refresh period.

The following command modifies the global policy:

```
Set-CsLocationPolicy -Identity Global
-EnhancedEmergencyServicesEnabled $True
-LocationRequired "Yes"
-PstnUsage "EmergencyUsage"
-EmergencyDialString "911"
-ConferenceMode "twoway"
-ConferenceURI "sip:+155512347890@rlscomms.net"
-EmergencyDialMask "112"
-NotificationURI "sip:security@rlscomms.net"
-UseLocationForE9-1-1Only $True
```

```
-LocationRefreshInterval 5
-EnhancedEmergencyServiceDisclaimer <span cssStyle="font-family:monospace">"You
are currently
connecting from a location where location services are
required for emergency dialing and your location has not
been set. Do you wish to set your location now?"</span>
```

PstnUsage must be defined prior to running the CsLocationPolicy command. If LocationRequired is set to Disclaimer, the disclaimer test must be set using the -EnhancedEmergencyServiceDisclaimer parameter.

Lync Server 2010 allowed the following command:

```
Set-CsEnhancedEmergencyServiceDisclaimer
-Body "Text to display in the disclaimer window"
```

However, since Lync Server 2013, this will result in a warning informing you that this cmdlet has been deprecated and you must use the location policy profile instead. Figure 18.4 shows the default disclaimer.

FIGURE 18.4
An emergency services disclaimer

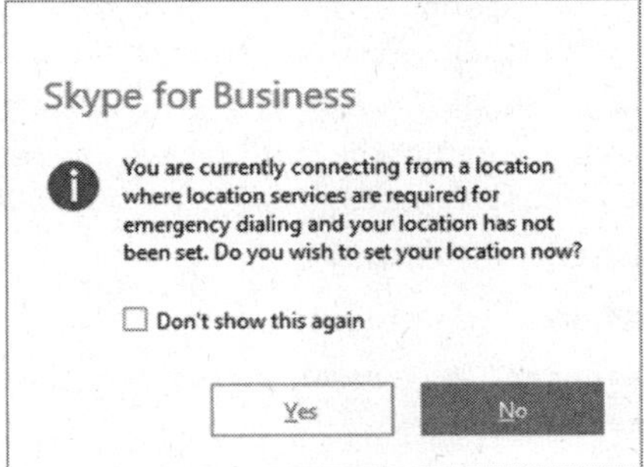

NOTE When you are configuring EmergencyDialMask, make sure you consider Call Park routing—doing so is extremely important. Call Park routing will take precedence, and as such, the numbers used in the EmergencyDialMask parameter should be excluded from the Call Park orbit.

Creating individual policies allows different policies to be applied directly to specific sites or even individual users. These policies show up with Tag: prefixed to their name and are also known as *tagged policies*. This strategy provides more granular control over routing of emergency services and certainly makes sense in globally distributed companies.

The Location policy information is provided via in-band provisioning and can be assigned in one of three ways.

- Network site associated
- User associated
- Global

This allows specific configuration for individual sites, perhaps to enable E9-1-1 or not, ensuring that any user, even visitors to a location, will provide the required location information when placing an emergency call.

Defining the SIP Trunk

The SIP trunk will be a dedicated trunk to the emergency services provider, and you need to enable support for the additional payload of the location information. This is provided via a Presence Information Data Format Location Object (PIDFLO) payload type within the SIP message.

To configure this support, use the following command (assuming the gateway address is `gw01.rlscomms.net`):

```
Set-CsTrunkConfiguration Service:PstnGateway:gw01.rlscomms.net
-EnablePIDFLOSupport $true
```

By default, `EnablePIDFLOSupport` on all trunks is `False`.

NOTE What's Different When Using an ELIN Gateway?

The principle is very much the same when using an ELIN gateway rather than a SIP trunk.

The difference really comes down to defining a dedicated ELIN to each location—and the fact that a gateway may be providing location information for more than one location (a location other than where it is physically situated), similar to the way in which the SIP trunk operates.

When you're using a gateway, the location information database also requires emergency response locations (ERLs) to be populated as well as the ELIN number. This number becomes the emergency number during the emergency call. This is achieved by assigning the ELIN number using the `-CompanyName` parameter within the `LIS` cmdlets.

There is also a responsibility on the PSTN carrier to upload the number assigned to its Automatic Location Identification database.

Configuring the Voice Route

As introduced in Chapter 16, voice routes define for Skype for Business Server the path from client to destination for the defined number (in this case the emergency services number).

Once you have the PSTN usage, Location Policy setting, and SIP trunk defined, the last remaining step is to define the voice route.

```
New-CsVoiceRoute -Name "EmergencyRoute"
-NumberPattern "^\+911$"
-PstnUsages "EmergencyUsage"
-PstnGatewayList @{add="E9-1-1-gateway-1"}
```

This command defines the route to the emergency service provider via the dedicated SIP trunk. In addition to this, you should define at least one secondary route to use if the SIP trunk fails and an emergency services call needs to be placed via a "normal" PSTN connection (which may be via a separate SIP trunk or some other legacy-style connection). The command would look like this:

```
New-CsVoiceRoute -Name "LocalEmergencyRoute"
-NumberPattern "^\+911$"
-PstnUsages "EmergencyUsage"
-PstnGatewayList @{add="E9-1-1-local-gateway-1"}
```

The parameter `NumberPattern` defined here must use the number defined in `EmergencyDialString` used in the `CsLocationPolicy` cmdlet. In addition, the + must be included because Skype for Business Server automatically adds a + to emergency calls.

Configuring Location Information

The previous section covered how to enable Skype for Business Server to provide the location information; however, it did not show how to configure the location information itself.

Configuring the Location Database

The Skype for Business client can use a number of methods to establish its location, determined from one of the following:

- Wireless access point
- Subnet
- Port
- Switch
- Manual

Upon sign-in, the client requests its location information from the server. For the server to determine the location of the client, it must be provided with as much information as possible. The following is an example request where the subnet information is provided:

```
<GetLocationsRequest xmlns:xsi="http://www.w3.org/2001/XMLSchema-instance"
xmlns:xsd="http://www.w3.org/2001/XMLSchema">
<Entity>sip:keith.skype@rlscomms.net</Entity>
<RSSI>0</RSSI>
<MAC>00-15-5d-19-41-06</MAC>
<SubnetID>192.168.3.0</SubnetID>
<IP>192.168.3.107</IP>
</GetLocationsRequest>
```

The client provides the location identifier to the server, which in turn queries the LIS database to return the specific location information to the client, as shown in Figure 18.5.

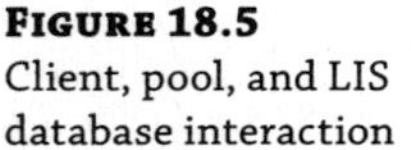
FIGURE 18.5
Client, pool, and LIS database interaction

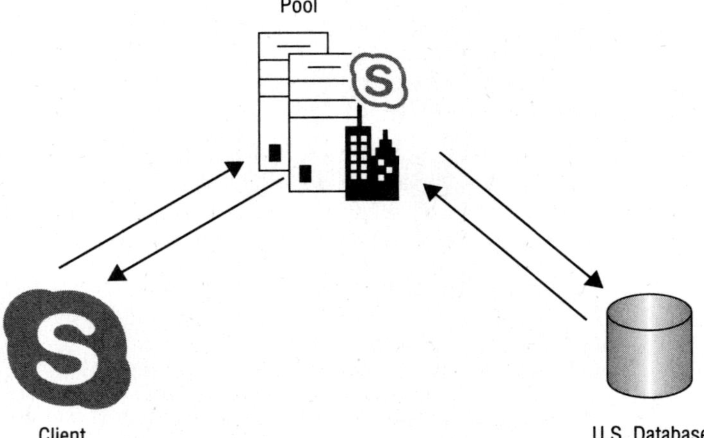

The server will return the response containing the address information.


```
<GetLocationsResponse xmlns:xsi="http://www.w3.org/2001/XMLSchema-instance"
xmlns:xsd="http://www.w3.org/2001/XMLSchema">
<ReturnCode>200</ReturnCode>
<presenceList>
<presence entity="sip:keith.lync@rlscomms.net
xmlns="urn:ietf:params:xml:ns:pidf">
<tuple id="_LIS:0">
<status>
<geopriv xmlns="urn:ietf:params:xml:ns:pidf:geopriv10">
<location-info>
<civicAddress xmlns="urn:ietf:params:xml:ns:pidf:geopriv10:civicAddr">
<country>UK</country>
<A1/>
<A3>Birmingham</A3>
<PRD />
<RD>RLS Comms Drive</RD>
<STS />
<POD />
<HNO>1</HNO>
<HNS />
<LOC>Birmingham</LOC>
<NAM>RLS Comms Limited</NAM>
<PC>AB12 3AB</PC>
</civicAddress>
</location-info>
<usage-rules>
<retransmission-allowed
xmlns="urn:ietf:params:xml:ns:pidf:geopriv10:basicPolicy">
true
</retransmission-allowed>
</usage-rules>
</geopriv>
</status>
<timestamp>2015-10-13T19:34:03.9071536Z</timestamp>
</tuple>
</presence>
</presenceList>
</GetLocationsResponse>
```


This is how the client would see the address:

RLS Comms Limited

1 RLS Comms Drive

Birmingham, AB12 3AB

UK

To ensure that this is a correctly formatted address, the LIS database entries must be verified against a public provider's address records.

Once connected and signed in, the Skype for Business client will display the location field in one of three different modes (depending on the `LocationRequired` parameter as configured in the `CsLocationPolicy` command). Figure 18.6 shows the default view.

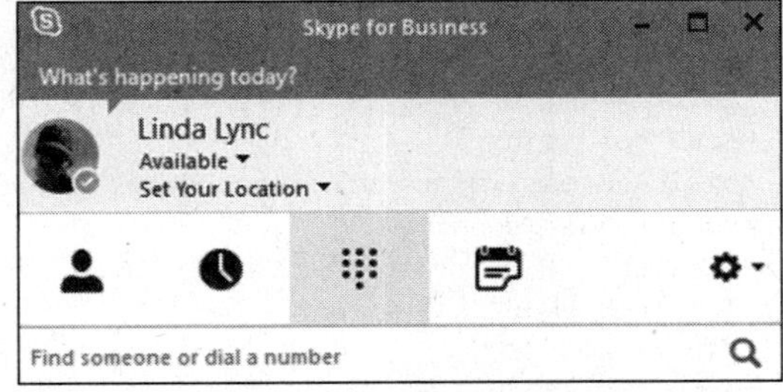

Figure 18.6
The Skype for Business client displays the default Location field option.

The location information for the E9-1-1 location is stored in the LIS database, which is replicated to all servers along with the XDS (Configuration Management server) database in the RTCLOCAL instance. This ensures that there are no delays when location information is requested for emergency calls, and it also ensures that local server (or Survivable Branch Appliance) functionality can still provide this data in the event of a WAN outage to the data center.

Unfortunately for the administrator, this location information is separate from the location information provided for the Call Admission Control functionality (see Chapter 17, "Call Admission Control," for more information) and must be defined separately.

Locations can be defined independently using the `Set-CsLisLocation` cmdlets. Table 18.2 shows the parameters accepted by `Set-CsLisLocation` with a description of each.

Table 18.2: `Set-CsLisLocation` parameters

Parameter	Description
`Instance`	A location object
`City`	Maximum 64 characters
`CompanyName`	Maximum 60 characters
`Country`	Maximum 2 characters
`HouseNumber`	Maximum 10 characters
`HouseNumberSuffix`	Maximum 5 characters (additional information, such as *A*)
`Location`	Maximum 20 characters (the name for this location, such as *Suite* or *Office*)

Table 18.2: `Set-CsLisLocation` parameters *(continued)*

Parameter	Description
`PostalCode`	Maximum 10 characters
`PostDirectional`	Maximum 2 characters (for example, the *NW* in *1st Avenue NW*)
`PreDirectional`	Maximum 2 characters (for example, the *NW* in *NW 1st Avenue*)
`State`	Maximum 2 characters
`StreetName`	Maximum 60 characters
`StreetSuffix`	Maximum 10 characters (the *Street* or *Avenue* part of the address)

All the parameters are listed as required. However, blank entries are acceptable; because the address information is targeted to the United States, not all fields will be required, or indeed make sense, for other countries.

Each of the cmdlets used to input (and manage) the association of the location data has, as would be expected, a different dataset requirement for the determination of the location. Here are the cmdlets and the additional parameters required:

- `Set-CsLisPort`
  - `ChassisID`
  - `PortId`
  - `PortIDSubType`
- `Set-CsLisSwitch`
  - `ChassisID`
- `Set-CsLisSubnet`
  - `Subnet`
- `Set-CsLisWirelessAccessPoint`
  - `BSSID`

The associated `Get-` cmdlets will return the information about each type of location provision.

- `Get-CsLisPort`
- `Get-CsLisSwitch`
- `Get-CsLisSubnet`
- `Get-CsLisWirelessAccessPoint`

Determining which cmdlet is the correct one to use will depend on a combination of the specific legal requirements in each location and the level of detail required as well as the current configuration of the network. For example, being able to provide the location information down to the level of specific port configuration would require that port configuration to be in place; this can be a significant administrative overhead for the network's team. On the other hand, if the network configuration is a subnet per floor per building, that can be quite easily defined and imported to the database.

```
Set-CsLisSubnet -Subnet 192.168.3.0 -City Birmingham
-CompanyName "RLS Comms Limited" -Country UK -PostalCode "AB12 3AB"
-HouseNumber 1 -StreetName "RLS Comms Drive" -Location Birmingham
-Description "Birmingham Location"
```

The cmdlet `Get-CsLisCivicAddress` is used to view the address information specifically. That is, it does not return the company or location names, only the following fields:

```
HouseNumber

HouseNumberSuffix

PreDirectional

StreetName

StreetSuffix

PostDirectional

City

State

PostalCode

Country

MSAGValid
```

To return the additional information, the cmdlet `Get-CsLisLocation` is required and includes the additional fields shown here:

```
Location

CompanyName
```

Once all the location information is defined, don't forget to publish it! Use `Publish-CsLisConfiguration` to achieve this task. (Note that there is no feedback from this cmdlet; even when you're using the `-Verbose` switch, the detail doesn't report anything useful, only that the cmdlet is being performed.)

If you have forgotten to publish the data, you can simply reopen a PowerShell session and run the `Publish-CsLisConfiguration` cmdlet. It is not specific to location information posted in the PowerShell session; rather, it will publish any waiting location information.

Of course, there is also `Unpublish-CsLisConfiguration`. Unfortunately, this isn't simply an "undo" but rather removes all of the LIS configuration information.

Using Secondary Location Databases

While Skype for Business Server has an internal LIS database that will store the information for the location retrieval by the client, the database is required to be manually populated. In most cases, this will involve a lot of work. However, what if you already have that information in another database or, indeed, have another application that can provide the required data? Well, Skype for Business Server can be configured to query other sources to retrieve the location information.

Skype for Business allows for two methods of secondary location information retrieval.

- Simple Network Management Protocol (SNMP)
- Secondary Location Information Service

In both cases, configuration is via the `Set-CsWebServiceConfiguration` cmdlet.

If you have an SNMP application that can map MAC addresses to switch port information (also known as a *MACResolver*), the cmdlet is as follows:

```
Set-CsWebServiceConfiguration -MACResolveUrl "<app url>"
```

On the other hand, if you have a secondary database, the cmdlet is as follows:

```
Set-CsWebServiceConfiguration -SecondaryLocationSourceUrl "<app url>"
```

If both a location database and secondary source are configured, the location database is queried first, and only if no match is found is the secondary source queried.

Retrieving the Location Data by a Client

You can provide three types of address entry to the client.

Validated These addresses are defined by the administrator and are stored within the LIS database. They have been confirmed against a valid address from the Master Street Address Guide by an E9-1-1 service provider. This is achieved using the `Test-CsLisCivicAddress-UpdateValidationStatus $true` command. This in turn will update the `MSAGValid` attribute to `True`, as you can view in the output of the `Get-CsLisCivicAddress` cmdlet.

Suggested These addresses are defined as are the *Validated* addresses; however, the `MSAGValid` attribute is `False` because they are not confirmed. This is how countries outside North America can leverage Location Information services.

Custom These addresses are entered manually by the user, and up to a maximum of 10 are stored in the `PersonalLISDB.cache` file on the user's computer, in the `%userprofile%\AppData\Local\Microsoft\Office\15.0\Lync\`<*SIP URI*> folder.

In conjunction with the `LocationRequired` and `EnhancedEmergencyServicesEnabled` parameters, Table 18.3 shows the breakdown of the configuration options and the end result for the user (assuming `EnhancedEmergencyServicesEnabled` is `True`).

Table 18.3: User experience based on configuration options

Location required	Existing Locations	User Experience
Yes	Validated location exists.	The location name is displayed automatically and cannot be changed unless `EnhancedEmergencyServicesEnabled` is `False`. If this is the case, then a new custom location can be created.
Yes	Single nonvalidated location exists.	The location name is displayed automatically and cannot be changed unless `EnhancedEmergencyServicesEnabled` is `False`. If this is the case, then a new custom location can be created.
Yes	Multiple nonvalidated locations exist.	The user is provided with a "Set Your Location" prompt, with a single suggested location entry. Note: Skype for Business cannot provide multiple nonvalidated locations; however, a secondary source may.
Yes	Validated and custom locations exist.	The custom location is given preference.
Yes	Single nonvalidated and custom locations exist.	The suggested location is given preference.
Yes	Multiple nonvalidated and multiple custom locations exist.	The user is provided with a "Set Your Location" prompt in black text and may select other locations in the drop-down menu.
Yes	Custom location only.	The custom location information is automatically displayed.
Yes	None	The user is provided with a "Set Your Location" prompt in red text to highlight the missing data.
No	None	The user is provided with a "Set Your Location" prompt in black text.
Disclaimer	None	The user is provided with a "Set Your Location" prompt in red text to highlight the missing data, along with a red *X*. It is not possible to dismiss the prompt, and the emergency services disclaimer is displayed if the user attempts to do so.

You can see other contact location information in the contact card shown in Figure 18.7. David's office is defined as in the United Kingdom; his work and mobile numbers are defined, and his location is defined as Working from Home. In addition, time zone information is replicated here so that you can see the local time for the user, which is extremely useful when you need to communicate globally.

FIGURE 18.7
Contact card location information

Roaming Users

Custom definitions allow users to store manually created entries for which the Skype for Business client can automatically populate the location information field for frequently visited locations. When returning to a location for a second (or subsequent) time, the client will not prompt the user; instead, it will read the data already entered into the cache file.

Figure 18.8 shows the blank custom location capture page. The user chooses which information to provide; not all of this information is required, even when the `LocationRequired` parameter is set to `Disclaimer` or `Yes`.

But what happens when multiple locations have the same subnet? It's not uncommon for the same private address range (192.168.0.0–192.168.0.255) to be used at multiple locations—for example, the local Starbucks and McDonalds could use the same private addresses. When that happens, the custom location cache file actually stores the MAC address of the network gateway as the identifier. This ensures that each location is globally unique even if the IP address range is shared.

Although you can still define an 11th custom location, it can be used only for the current session and is not stored in the cache file.

Edit Location
Your location name (such as Work or Home) can be shared with others.
Location name:
The information below will only be shared with emergency service providers, and only if your company is using Skype for Business for emergency dialing.
Address:
Building/Room:
City:
State/Province:
Zip/Postal code:
Country/Region:
Afghanistan
Learn More
OK
Cancel

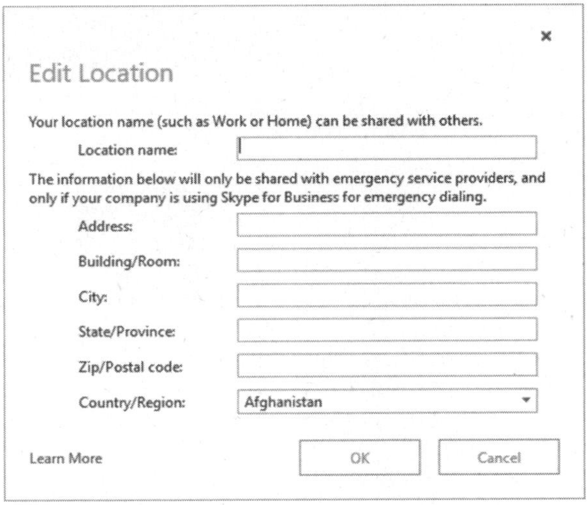

Figure 18.8
The custom Edit Location page

Placing a Call

You've already seen the logs showing the exchange of information to determine the client location; Figure 18.9 shows the client feedback when placing a call.

+911
2 Participants
Calling +911...
Hold
Transfer
Devices
This is an emergency call.

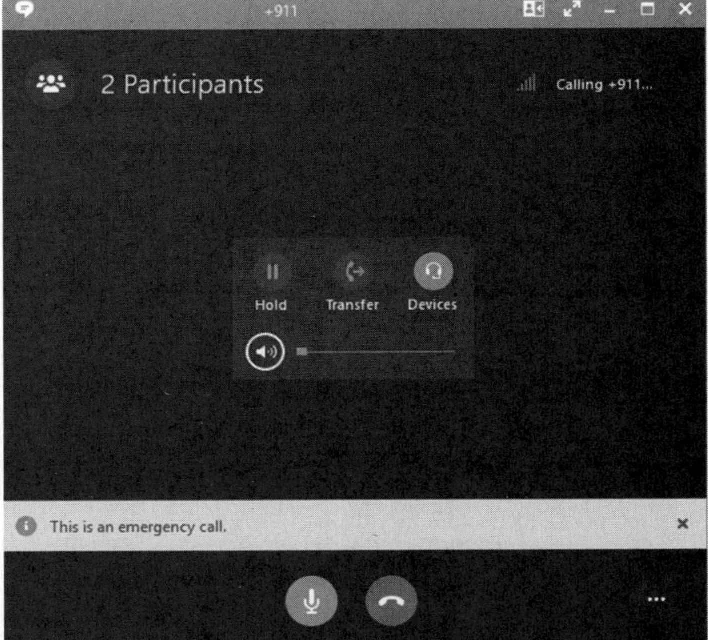

Figure 18.9
A client placing an emergency call

The logs capture the PIDFLO data within the SIP `INVITE` traffic; here is the content of this log entry:

```
Content-Type: application/pidf+xml
Content-Transfer-Encoding: 7bit
Content-ID: <sip:keith.skype@rlscomms.net>
Content-Description: render; handling=optional
<?xml version="1.0" encoding="uft-8"?>
<presence entity="sip:keith.skype@rlscomms.net"
 xmlns="urn:ietf:params:xml:ns:pidf">
<tuple id="FileName_0"><status><geopriv
 xmlns="urn:ietf:params:xml:ns:pidf:geopriv10">
<location-info><civisAddress
 xmlns="urn:ietf:params:xml:ns:pidf:geopriv10:civicAddr">
<RD>1 RLS Comms Drive</RD><A3>Birmingham</A3>
<PC>AB12 3AB></PC><country>GB</country
></civicAddress></location-info>
<usage-rules><retransmission-allowed></usage-rules>
<method>Manual</method></geopriv>
<msftE9-1-1PidfExtn
  xmlsn="urn:schema:rtc.LIS.msftE9-1-1PidfExtn.2008">
<NotificationUri>sip:security@rlscomms.net</Notification>
<ConferenceUri>sip:+155512347890@rlscomms.net</ConferenceUri>
<ConferenceMode>two way</ConferenceMode>
<LocationPolicyTagID
 xmlns="urn:schema:Rtc.Lis.LocationPolicy TagID.2008">
<subnet-tagid:1></LocationPolicyTagID>
</msftE9-1-1PidfExtn></status></tuple></presence>
```

Testing an E9-1-1 Call

Because there is special configuration needed for E9-1-1, it is wise to test. You certainly don't want to be relying on an untested phone routing and location information in an emergency.

Each country (and quite possibly each region within a country) is going to differ on the details of testing, but one thing is certain: No emergency services organization will appreciate the use of their resources for your test calls without some sort of prior notification and arrangement.

In some cases, it may be acceptable to place the call and explain to the operator that you are testing the phone system. However, be warned that this will not be tolerated for repeat testing. Of course, pick an expected "quiet" time, such as when your local major sports team is playing away or some large (nonlocal) event is being televised.

If using gateways, you can control the routing of calls to ensure that they do not leave your organization while testing, and this can allow you to capture logging to ensure that the location information is being transmitted correctly. Be sure to reenable the emergency routing if you test using this method.

The Bottom Line

Describe the E9-1-1 requirements for North America. Enhanced emergency services dialing provides location information to emergency services, enabling them to better respond in the event of an emergency.

Master It Is the provision of location information with emergency dialing compulsory?

Configure Skype for Business Server 2015 to meet E9-1-1 requirements. As a viable PBX, Skype for Business is required to meet the E9-1-1 requirements to provide location information data and as such must have validated address information provided with each emergency call.

Master It Through what configuration items can location information data be delivered to the Skype for Business client?

Understand how Location Information services can be used by users outside North America. Although the actual requirements are currently defined only in locations in North America, beta program feedback from customers indicated that automatic Location Information services are extremely useful and desired worldwide.

Master It What specifically is required to enable Location Information services in North America, and what different requirements are in place for the rest of the world?

Understand how to query multiple sources of location information. Skype for Business Server allows for multiple sources of location information to be queried. Skype for Business Server can be pointed to additional location databases or applications that can reduce the overhead in discovery and definition of all the network locations for an organization.

Master It Which cmdlet and parameters are used to configure secondary location information sources?

Part 5

Other Dependent Infrastructure

Chapter 19

Extended Voice Functionality

As organizations start to migrate their enterprise telephony to Microsoft Skype for Business, they often require more functionality than is available within the core Enterprise Voice (EV) functionality. To fulfill the most common of these requirements, Microsoft has provided the following extended voice functions: dial-in conferencing, Response Groups, Call Park, and unassigned numbers.

For organizations that require additional functionality, a number of independent software vendors (ISVs) provide applications designed for Microsoft Skype for Business; you can find additional details of these and other third-party applications in Chapter 23, "Skype for Business 2015 Development."

In this chapter, you will learn to

- Understand the extended voice functionality
- Design solutions using extended voice functionality
- Implement extended voice functionality

Setting Up Dial-in Conferencing

For years PBXs have had the ability to create conferences. In the early days, conferences were usually limited to three people and required using a dedicated key on the phone. Most people found this type of conference hard to set up and would usually end up cutting people off.

To provide a better solution, tools known as *conference bridges* were created. They allow participants to access their conference by calling an access number and then entering a conference ID and sometimes a passcode. These conference solutions usually come in two forms: ad hoc and scheduled.

Ad hoc conference bridges are often referred to as "meet-me" conference bridges because each user has an individual conference ID and can use it when desired. Because these conferences are ad hoc, even though users can use them when needed, there may be overall limits for the conferencing system in the number of people who can attend conference calls at any one time; these limitations can be in the form of license, hardware, or the number of available PSTN lines.

Scheduled conferences usually have to be booked, and a conference ID is assigned at the time of booking. One advantage of a scheduled conference is that resources are usually assigned to the conference, ensuring that if, for example, a conference is configured for four people from 15:00 to 17:00, then those resources will be available.

In addition to the type of conferencing bridge used, organizations have a choice of using either an on-premises system, usually integrated with their PBX, or a hosted solution. The recent trend has been for organizations to use hosted meet-me solutions. The move to hosted solutions has tended to be due to the cost of implementing on-premises solutions, with organizations preferring monthly costs rather than up-front purchases.

Now that you have looked at what dial-in conferencing is, you can see how Skype for Business handles it.

Understanding Dial-in Conferencing

In OCS 2007 R2, dial-in conferencing was a distinct feature with its own functionality, and when collaboration was required, the LiveMeeting client needed to be used. Since Lync Server 2010, conferencing and collaboration have become a single feature called Online Meeting. The Online Meeting functionality removes the distinction between conferencing and collaboration, allowing all modalities to be used within a conference with a variety of access methods.

This section focuses specifically on the dial-in conferencing aspects that Online Meeting has to offer. Its approach falls within the meet-me category of conference bridges, with each allowed user (as defined by your policies) provided with their own conference ID. Dial-in conferencing provides the following functionality:

- PSTN access
- Roster of attendees
- Attendee management via roster
- Ability to secure conferences with a PIN
- Ability for Conferencing server to call attendees
- Meeting lobby
- Dual-tone multiple-frequency (DTMF) codes for management
- Name recording for anonymous users
- On-demand recording (client side)
- Built-in web scheduling

The bold items were new in Lync Server 2010 (although the built-in aspect of the web scheduler is new in Lync Server 2013; it was a separate download previously), and they addressed the limitations that prevented some organizations from migrating their dial-in conferencing facilities to OCS 2007 R2. In addition to the specific dial-in conferencing capabilities just listed, the following Online Meeting functions are also relevant:

- Scheduling via Microsoft Outlook is easy.
- Scheduling meetings via the Web Scheduler allows non-Outlook users to set up meetings. Functionality can be restricted to a group of users.
- Clients can participate in meetings through a browser.

While Skype for Business has not offered dramatically new functionality in conferences (see Chapter 10, "Online and Hybrid," for coverage of the broadcast meeting capability), there have been a lot of changes around the usability and consistency of the user experience across different clients.

Real World Scenario

Can Dial-in Conferencing Pay for My Deployment?

A number of organizations have been able to cover the costs of their entire Skype for Business deployments purely on the basis of moving their conferencing away from a hosted solution to Skype for Business.

Hosted conferencing solutions may appear to be cheap initially because there are no up-front capital expenditures; however, they can often become expensive because of the costs charged by the provider. These companies often provide the accounts for free but charge per minute per participant for each conference call. There can also be additional charges for recording or for toll-free numbers. Let's take a look at the cost of a conference, based on the provider charging 5 cents per user per minute.

A conference call with four participants for 30 minutes would cost $6 ($0.05 × 4 × 30). At these rates, an organization that has 10 people who perform 10 conferences a week for 52 weeks a year results in a cost of $31,200.

Organizations often overlook these itemized costs when they are budgeting and performing cost analysis for Skype for Business deployments. This is probably because IT departments often do not see these costs because they are assigned to individual departments, such as Sales. Although dial-in conferencing may not pay for the entire deployment, it can certainly help defray the costs.

You'll see many of these functions later as you explore configuration, implementation, and client-side functionality, but for now let's look at the architectural and back-end elements.

Architecturally, there are two main items to take into consideration when planning and setting up dial-in conferencing: the Audio/Video Conferencing service and server and the configuration of Enterprise Voice, which is discussed in Chapter 16, "Getting Started with Voice." With Lync Server 2010, it was possible to separate the A/V components of conferencing into a separate pool. This allowed for better scaling of conferencing, but this capability was removed in Lync Server 2013, and Skype for Business continues with the consolidated approach.

The only additional architectural component needed for Skype for Business Server is the Office Web Application (WAC) server (covered in Chapter 22, "Exchange, SharePoint, and Office Web Applications Server"). Without this additional server, meetings will be unable to host PowerPoint presentations (even when using legacy Lync Communicator 2010 clients).

Focusing specifically on the dial-in capabilities, a number of components depend on the Front End servers.

Web Components These are used for the Dial-In Conferencing web page, allowing participants to look up conference access numbers and for users to set their PIN.

Conferencing Attendant Application This accepts calls from the PSTN, prompts for conference details, and then routes the calls to the correct conference.

Conferencing Announcement Application This is used once the participant has joined the conference; it plays announcements to callers and monitors and accepts DTMF tones for conference controls.

Web components also provide a Reach client option, which allows access to Online Meetings in the context of dial-in conferencing; the web components allow participants to specify a number for the conference bridge to call them (also known as *call me*), and participants can also view the meeting in a browser (including audio, if they do not want to be called back, and also video). The ability for the conference bridge to call a Reach client participant can be restricted with a policy.

Although having the Skype for Business Edge components deployed is not a requirement for dial-in conferencing, it does add another access method to conferences, and it allows federated users to access the conference the same way a user belonging to the organization would. This allows them to view the roster for the conference in the same way a user of the organization would and to bypass any costs associated with dialing access numbers.

Anonymous users are able to connect to the conference either through dial-in or via the Skype Web App, provided not through the Skype for Business Edge server but via a Reverse Proxy (see Chapter 21, "Reverse Proxies, Load Balancers, and Gateways," for more information).

Before you learn how to configure dial-in conferencing, it is worth briefly looking at the *meeting lobby*. This feature, new in Lync Server 2010, creates a "lobby" where users can be "parked" when they enter a meeting; the meeting presenter can then choose whether to allow them into the meeting. This provides a level of access control for the meeting. When creating the meeting, users can configure whether the lobby is to be used.

Configuring Dial-in Conferencing Features

Now that you know what dial-in conferencing in Skype for Business can do, it is time to look at how it is configured. Configuration—most of it—can be performed either through the Control Panel or through PowerShell. That is, all the required configuration to get conferencing up and running can be done through both interfaces, but you need to use PowerShell to configure some of the more complex and custom features.

For dial-in conferencing to work, you need to configure the following components:

- Enterprise Voice
- Web components
- Conferencing policies
- Meeting configuration
- Access numbers
- PIN policies

Of these, all but the first two can be configured using the Control Panel as well as the related PowerShell cmdlets. For example, Figure 19.1 shows the Control Panel tab for configuring access numbers. In addition, the following optional components can be configured using PowerShell:

- Edge servers
- DTMF mappings
- Join and Leave announcements
- Conference directories

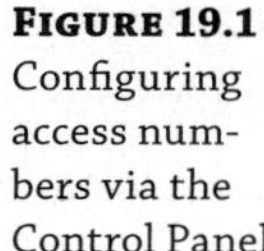

FIGURE 19.1 Configuring access numbers via the Control Panel

Chapter 8, "Installation," covers configuring web components and publishing them to the Internet as well as deploying Edge servers. In addition, setting up Enterprise Voice is covered in Chapter 16.

Conferencing Policies

Conferencing policies can be configured on a global, site, or user basis, depending on whether you require different users to have different settings. The global policy is created by default but can be modified as required.

The conferencing policy is used to control all aspects of conferencing, not just dial-in conferencing, but in this section we'll cover only the options that are either required or relevant to dial-in conferencing. In the following and similar definitions throughout the chapter, only the PowerShell parameters will be listed. Options equivalent to most of the cmdlets and parameters are available through the Control Panel.

When reviewing the PowerShell cmdlets, we'll focus on the creation cmdlets. They use the verb `New`, and for each of these cmdlets there are cmdlets for changing settings (`Set`), reviewing settings (`Get`), and deleting them (`Remove`), and although they are not explicitly discussed except as needed, they are available. The `Set` and `New` cmdlets use the same parameters; the `Get` and `Remove` parameters are limited to the `Identity` parameter.

As mentioned previously, conferencing policies can be managed either through the Control Panel (Conferencing ➢ Conferencing Policy) or through PowerShell. To create a new policy through PowerShell, the `New-CsConferencingPolicy` cmdlet is used in conjunction with the parameters outlined here:

- `Identity`: This is the policy name, which is prefixed with `site:` if the policy is a site policy rather than a user policy.

- `AllowAnonymousParticipantsInMeetings`: This allows anonymous participants.
- `AllowAnnotations`: This allows participants to annotate slides and use the whiteboard.
- `AllowAnonymousParticipantsInMeetings`: This allows users to connect to a meeting without authenticating.
- `AllowAnonymousUsersToDialOut`: This allows anonymous users to dial out. It is the "call me" functionality mentioned earlier.
- `AllowConferenceRecording`: This allows the call to be recorded.
- `AllowExternalUserControl`: This allows external and anonymous users to record.
- `AllowExternalUsersToRecordMeeting`: This allows external users to record meeting content. This setting can be important in restricted environments where data cannot be allowed to leave the site.
- `AllowExternalUsersToSaveContent`: This is similar to the preceding setting, but it's for downloadable content rather than recorded.
- `AllowIPAudio`: This allows audio and covers PSTN audio as well.
- `AllowIPVideo`: This allows video to be used in the meeting.
- `AllowLargeMeetings`: This allows the meeting size to be greater than 250 attendees.
- `AllowMultiView`: This allows the multiple simultaneous video setting to be controlled.
- `AllowNonEnterpriseVoiceUsersToDialOut`: This allows participants to dial out of a conference even if their user settings do not normally allow for Enterprise Voice capability.
- `AllowParticipantControl`: This allows control of desktop sharing to be passed to other attendees.
- `AllowPolls`: This allows polls to be created.
- `AllowSharedNotes`: This allows the shared note capability of OneNote to be leveraged in a meeting.
- `AllowUserToScheduleMeetingsWithAppSharing`: This allows a user to create a scheduled meeting and leverage App Sharing within the meeting.
- `AppSharingBitRateKb`: This defines the maximum kilobits allowed for App Sharing.
- `AudioBitRateKb`: This defines the maximum kilobits allowed for audio.
- `DisablePowerPointAnnotations`: This disables the capability to annotate PowerPoint slides.
- `EnableAppDesktopSharing`: This allows for limited granular control of desktop sharing, either the full desktop or a single application (or none).
- `EnableDialInConferencing`: This allows participants to call into a conference using a PSTN access number.
- `EnableFileTransfer`: This controls the ability to transfer files within a meeting.
- `EnableMultiViewJoin`: This allows the user to join a conference with MultiView enabled.

- `EnableP2PFileTransfer`: This allows file transfer between individual users (outside of a meeting).
- `EnableP2PRecording`: This allows peer-to-peer recording (outside of meetings).
- `EnableP2PVideo`: This allows peer-to-peer video calls.
- `FileTransferBitRateKb`: This defines the rate for file transfers.

Once the policy has been created, it needs to be assigned to users. Global and site policies are assigned automatically as described in Chapter 12, "User Administration"; therefore, only user policies need to be assigned. You can do this through the Control Panel or through PowerShell using the `Grant-CsConferencingPolicy` cmdlet, as in the following example:

```
Grant-CsConferencingPolicy -Identity "rlscomms\keith_skype"
-PolicyName "Std Dial In Policy"
```

This grants `Std Dial In Policy` to the domain account with the username `rlscomms\keith_skype`.

Meeting Policies

Meeting policies allow you to specify the types of meetings that can be created, and they can be created at a global, site, or pool level. They can be managed through the Control Panel (Conferencing ➤ Meeting Configuration) or through PowerShell. To create a new policy, use the `New-CsMeetingConfiguration` cmdlet.

The parameters for configuring meeting policies are as follows:

- `Identity`: This specifies the policy name.
  - For a site policy, this needs to be prefixed with `site:`.
  - For a pool policy, this should be the pool FQDN prefixed with `service:UserServer:`.
- `AdmitAnonymousUsersByDefault`: This parameter permits anonymous users in the meeting by default.
- `AssignedConferenceTypeByDefault`: This parameter sets the conference default type. Set it to `True` for meetings to be public by default. Set it to `False` for meetings to be private by default.
- `CustomFooterText`: This defines the text footer applied when users join a meeting.
- `DesignateAsPresenter`: This parameter designates which users are automatically presenters. It can set to `None`, `Company`, or `Everyone`.
- `EnableAssignedConferenceType`: This parameter sets the conference type. If set to `True`, users can create public or private conferences, and setting it to `False` means only private meetings can be created. The only difference between them is that a different conference ID and access URL will be used for each private conference.
- `PstnCallersBypassLobby`: This bypasses the lobby for PSTN users.
- `RequireRoomSystemAuthorization`: This is used by Lync room systems, defining the requirement for someone to log in to the room system itself.

PINs

To authenticate when calling into a meeting via the PSTN, users need to set a PIN, which is used in conjunction with their phone numbers. This PIN is also used to allow users to log in to Lync IP phones. The policy for managing PINs can be configured on a global, site, or user basis.

If you are managing PIN policies using the Control Panel, you can access them under Conferencing ➢ PIN Policy; alternatively, you can manage them through PowerShell using the `New-CsPinPolicy` cmdlet. The following options are used:

- `Identity`.
- Allow Common PIN Patterns (`AllowCommonPatterns`). Common patterns are defined as follows:
    - Containing four or more consecutive digits—for example, 781234
    - Repeating digits—for example, 114488
    - Matching the user's phone number or extension
- `Description`.
- Maximum Logon Attempts (`MaximumLogonAttempts`).
- Minimum Password Length (`MinPasswordLength`). This is the minimum PIN length; it can be set to a minimum of 4 and a maximum of 24 digits.
- PIN History (`PINHistoryCount`). This can be set to 0 for no history and a maximum of 20.
- Days before the PIN must be changed (`PINLifetime`).

PIN lockouts work in two ways, based on the concept of *local logon failures* and *global logon failures*. The Local Logon Failures value is the number of failed attempts allowed within 30 minutes. If this is exceeded, the PIN is locked for an hour, at which time the Local Logon Failure count is reset. Global Logon Failures is the maximum number of PIN attempts allowed before the PIN is locked out and has to be unlocked by an administrator. This value is not reset when a user successfully logs in, and failed login attempts continue to be added to the Global Logon Failure counter. The counter resets only when an administrator unlocks a user's PIN.

The Local Logon Failure and Global Logon Failure values are predefined. Setting Maximum Logon Attempts in the PIN policy will override only the Local Logon Failure value. The global lockout value cannot be modified. As shown in Table 19.1, both limits depend on the number of digits in the PIN rather than the minimum password length specified in the policy.

TABLE 19.1: PIN attempts

PIN LENGTH	LOCAL LOGON FAILURE LIMIT (UNLESS OVERRIDDEN)	GLOBAL LOGON FAILURE LIMIT
4	10	100
5	25	1,000
6 or more	25	5,000

The PIN policy is granted to users using the `Grant-CsPinPolicy` cmdlet.

Conference Access Numbers

Some organizations have only one access number; others have numbers covering many countries. Before you can create access numbers, you'll need to take a quick look at Enterprise Voice dial plans because the access numbers you'll need depend on them.

Dial plans are used to provide a link between users and access numbers. When a user schedules a conference, the default numbers shown in the meeting request are the ones associated with the dial plan with which the user is associated. They are also used to translate extensions to full E.164 numbers. When users authenticate via DTMF, this allows them to enter their extension number rather than their full Direct Inward Dial (DID) number.

To use a given dial plan, its dial-in conferencing region needs to be defined. You can do this when you create the dial plan or edit it; you can find details on how to perform these actions in Chapter 16. You can enter any text you want in the dial plan region field, but it should be something that external participants can understand, such as a city or country. This will be shown on the dial-in web page so that participants can look for a number other than the one specified on the invitation to the conference. It is also used in Outlook, allowing the user to select a different region and thus change the access numbers shown in their invitation.

Once the dial plans are finished, you can create the access numbers, either through the Control Panel (Conferencing ➤ Dial-In Access Number) or through PowerShell (`New-CsDialInConferencingAccessNumber`) using the following parameters:

- `PrimaryUri`: This is the contact URI, prefixed with `sip:`.
- `DisplayName`: This is the display name of the contact and how it should appear in Lync.
- `DisplayNumber`: This is how the number should be displayed in meeting requests and the dial-in web page.
- `LineURI`: This is the phone number prefixed with `tel:`.
- `Regions`: This is a comma-separated list of the regions the number is assigned to, such as `US` and `Canada`.
- `Pool`: This is the pool with which the access number is associated.
- `PrimaryLanguage`: This is the primary language used.
- `SecondaryLanguages`: This is a comma-separated list of up to four secondary languages, such as `en-US` and `fr-CA`.

Each access number can be configured with a primary language and up to four secondary ones. This option is often used when access numbers are defined for locations in which multiple languages are commonly spoken—for example, Montreal, Canada, where French is usually the primary language, followed by English.

You can find a list of supported languages by running this command:

```
Get-CsDialInConferencingLanguageList | Select-Object -ExpandProperty Languages
```

This command retrieves a list of the supported languages and restricts it to displaying only the language codes.

Use the following PowerShell to create a number:

```
New-CsDialinConferencingAccessNumber
-PrimaryUri "sip:EMEA_conf@rlscomms.net"
-DisplayName "EMEA Conferencing Number"
-DisplayNumber "+441555600000"
-LineURI "tel:+441555600000"
-Regions "Birmingham"
-Pool se01.rlscomms.net
-PrimaryLanguage en-GB
```

Once the access number has been created, users will be able to call it to access the conferences; users can also see the numbers on the Dial-In Conferencing web page, which is shown in Figure 19.2. In a change since Lync Server 2010, the In-Conference DTMF controls also appear on this page.

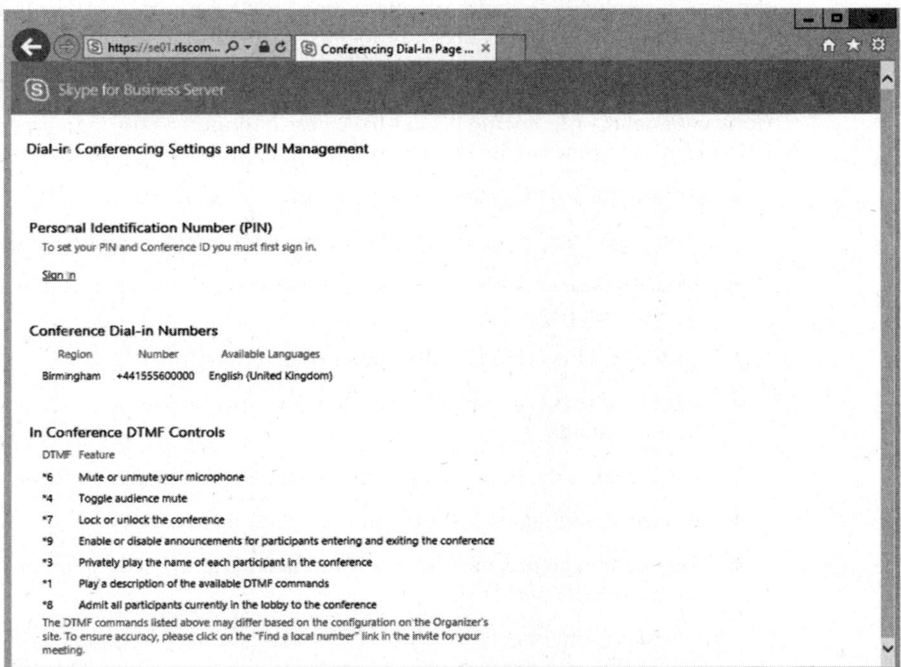

FIGURE 19.2 Dial-In Conferencing web page

Before moving on, it is worth looking at the order in which the numbers are presented in the meeting requests and Dial-In Conferencing web page. By default, the order is alphabetical by region. If there are multiple numbers within the region, they are listed by comparing the first digit in each number. The lowest number is listed first, followed by the second lowest to the highest. If the first digit is the same, then the second number is compared. This process is continued as long as necessary to order the numbers. You may decide to reorder the numbers for a region for a number of reasons. For example, you may want a number with a higher capacity at the start of the list or a toll-free number at the end of the list. (Reordering regions isn't possible.) You can set a specific order using the `Set-CsDialInConferencingAccessNumber` cmdlet and its `Priority` and `ReorderedRegion` parameters, as in this example:

```
Set-CsDialInConferencingAccessNumber
-Identity "sip:USdialin@rlscomms.net"
-Priority 0 -ReorderedRegion "EMEA"
```

This will move the Toll Chargeable number to the top of the list for the U.S. region numbers.

Global Access Numbers

Organizations often use hosted conferencing providers so that they can have global access numbers, which are usually required for organizations with a global presence. Such organizations do not need to be multinationals; many small businesses have customers in other countries.

Not having these numbers could be a potential roadblock to Skype for Business migration conferencing for businesses that require them. Therefore, you may need to consider how to provide these numbers. Traditional PSTN providers can often provide global numbers, but setting them up is usually expensive and so is operating them.

One potential way around this is to work with a SIP trunk provider. These providers are often more competitive in their pricing for global access numbers and are often an excellent way to provide the number(s) required. While an organization may not want to move all of its PSTN access to the cloud, this approach is a good option for conferencing. And depending on how busy the conferencing system will be, it may also mean that you won't need additional PSTN bearers from the PSTN provider.

You can find a list of certified SIP trunking providers for Skype for Business at `http://technet.microsoft.com/en-us/lync/fp179863`.

Additional Conferencing Configuration Options

The next three configuration items (entry and exit announcements, DTMF mappings for PSTN users, and conference directories) are not exposed through the Control Panel; they can be configured only through PowerShell.

Entry and Exit Announcements

Entry and exit announcements will be played only to people who access the bridge using the PSTN. It is assumed that announcements are not required for users who have access to the conference roster through one of the Skype for Business clients. These settings are configured on either a global or site level. They are created using the `New-CsDialInConferencingConfiguration` cmdlet, and the following options are available:

- `Identity`, either `Global` for the global policy (used only when viewing or modifying the settings) or, if creating a site policy, the site name prefixed with `site:`.
- `EnableNameRecording` specifies whether users are able to record their names when they access a conference. If it is disabled, `EntryExitAnnouncementsType` needs to be set to `ToneOnly`.

- EntryExitAnnouncementsEnabledByDefault.
- EntryExitAnnouncementsType can be set to either UseNames or ToneOnly, depending on the announcement type needed.

DTMF Mappings

The next items to look at are the DTMF mappings for PSTN users that can be used during a conference call. Most of the options are limited to presenters, but two of the commands, Mute/Unmute and Private Rollcall, can be used by any participant.

These settings are configured on either a global or site level. The following options are available to create the New-CsDialInConferencingDtmfConfiguration cmdlet:

- Identity, either Global for the global policy (used only when viewing or modifying the settings) or, if creating a site policy, the site name prefixed with site:.
- AdmitAll: Admit all participants who are in the lobby.
- AudienceMuteCommand.
- CommandCharacter: Prefix for the commands; can be an * or #.
- EnableDisableAnnouncementsCommand: Play Entry/Exit announcements.
- HelpCommand.
- LockUnlockConferenceCommand.
- MuteUnmuteCommand.
- PrivateRollCallCommand: Play roll call.

Digits assigned to these commands need to be in the range from 1 to 9 and need to be unique. The command prefix can vary or remain constant for each of the entries. If you need to disable any of these settings, you can do so by setting them to $null.

Conference Directories

The final item to look at is the conference directory; because Skype for Business is based on SIP URIs, you need a way to map the numeric conference IDs that are required to access a conference to the relevant SIP URI. This is where the conference directories come into play.

By default, there is a single conference directory. This lone directory is sufficient for some organizations, but for larger organizations or for those who use different conference IDs for each conference, the conference ID number can grow rather long.

To keep the ID at a length that people will accept—usually no more than six to seven digits—multiple conference directories can be created. A new conference directory should be created for every 999-enabled user.

To create a conference directory (New-CsConferenceDirectory), you must specify the following parameters:

- Identity: This is a unique numeric number in the range from 1 to 999.
- HomePool: This is the Lync pool that hosts the conference directory. To get a list of the current conference directories, you can use the command

```
Get-CsConferenceDirectory | FT Identity, ServiceID
```

which will return an easy-to-read listing of each directory.

```
Identity                     ServiceId
---------                    ------------
1                            UserServer:se01.rlscomms.net
2                            UserServer:se02.rlscomms.net
```

Implementing Dial-in Conferencing

Now that you've looked at the capabilities of dial-in conferencing, you need to see how to implement it. To do this, let's work through the following scenario:

Your organization is migrating away from its current hosting provider to Skype for Business dial-in conferencing. Dial-in numbers are required in the following countries:

- *United States*
- *United Kingdom*

*All users should be able to use the conference bridge. In addition, to match the current conference bridge, the Lock And Unlock Conference DTMF option needs to be set to *2.*

After studying the requirements statement, you see that you need to complete the following steps:

1. Create two regions, each with its own access number.
2. Modify the DTMF mappings for Lock and Unlock.

In addition to the explicit requirements just detailed, you will need to configure some other options for dial-in conferencing to operate. You are going to set each of them to have a global scope. Some of the settings are configured by default, but you will set them in the PowerShell commands to make sure they are configured as required.

The first thing you need to configure is the global conferencing policy.

```
Set-CsConferencingPolicy -Identity Global
-AllowAnonymousUsersToDialOut $true
-AllowAnonymousParticipantsInMeetings $true
-AllowConferenceRecording $true
-AllowIPAudio $true -EnableDialInConferencing $true
```

This code modifies the global conferencing policy, allowing the required settings for all users who are not affected by a site policy or who have a user policy assigned.

The next item to configure is the global meeting policy.

```
Set-CsMeetingConfiguration -Identity Global
-AdmitAnonymousUsersByDefault $true
-AssignedConferenceTypeByDefault $true
-DesignateAsPresenter Company
-EnableAssignedConferenceType $true
-PstnCallersBypassLobby $true
```

This code modifies the global meeting policy, allowing the required settings for all users who are not affected by a site policy or who have a user policy assigned.

The final policy to configure is the global PIN policy.

```
Set-CsPinPolicy -Identity Global -AllowCommonPatterns $True
-MinPasswordLength 5
```

This modifies the global PIN policy, allowing common PIN patterns and shorter PIN lengths for all users who are not affected by a site policy or who have an assigned user policy.

Now you can configure the access numbers; they will be assigned to two existing dial plans.

```
New-CsDialInConferencingAccessNumber
-PrimaryUri "sip:USDialIn@rlscomms.net"
-DisplayNumber "1-425-555-9595"
-DisplayName "US Dial In Number"
-LineUri "tel:+14255559595"
-Pool "se01.rlscomms.net"
-PrimaryLanguage "en-US"
-Regions "US"
New-CsDialInConferencingAccessNumber
-PrimaryUri "sip:UKDialIn@rlscomms.net"
-DisplayNumber "01555600000"
-DisplayName "UK Dial In Number"
-LineUri "tel:+441555600000"
-Pool "se01.rlscomms.net"
-PrimaryLanguage "en-GB"
-Regions "EMEA"
```

These two commands create the two dial-in conferencing numbers, the first for the United States with U.S. English and the second for the United Kingdom with U.K. English. When these two commands are run, the output for the U.S. access number will be similar to the following:

```
Identity           : CN={f50ac1dc-f9cb-412e-a612-6ff28bf1876f},
CN=Application Contacts,CN=RTCService,CN=Services,CN=Configuration,
DC=rlscomms,DC=info
PrimaryUri         : sip:USDialIn@rlscomms.net
DisplayName        : US Dial In Number
DisplayNumber      : 1-425-555-9595
LineUri            : tel:+14255559595
PrimaryLanguage    : en-US
SecondaryLanguages : {}
Pool               : se01.rlscomms.net
HostingProvider    :
Regions            : {US}
```

The DTMF mappings are the last things to configure; to configure them, you will need to modify the existing global policy.

```
Set-CsDialInConferencingDtmfConfiguration -Identity Global
-LockUnlockConferenceCommand 2
```

This modifies the global DTMF mapping to use 2 as the unlock code for the conference; this will affect all conferences except where the conference is hosted in a site that has a site policy assigned.

This completes the dial-in conferencing configuration. To check the configuration, run the corresponding `Get` commands to view the settings just configured.

Using Dial-in Conferencing

Now that you have implemented dial-in conferencing, you need to take a look at how users will use it. Although a conference can be accessed from virtually anywhere, here you should concentrate on how an information worker will use dial-in conferencing using Outlook and their Skype for Business client.

Although scheduling a conference call is not a requirement for a user to use the conference bridge, Microsoft has provided an easy way to populate a meeting request in Outlook with the required information, as shown in Figure 19.3. To access this screen, go to the Calendar view and select Online Meeting or create a new Online Meeting item. You can customize these settings for a conference; by selecting Meeting Options when you create or view the meeting, you can access the following settings:

- Who can access the meeting
- Who will be a presenter
- If a different conference ID and URL should be used

FIGURE 19.3 Scheduling a conference

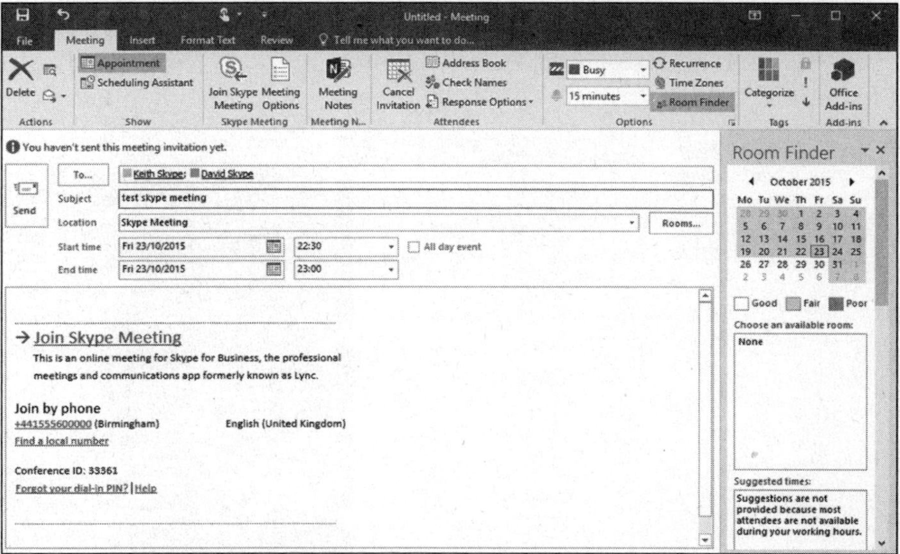

Once a conference has been organized, the attendees need to be able to join it. There are a few ways to do this: They could call the access number, click the Join link in the meeting request, or access it from the reminder for the meeting (shown in Figure 19.4).

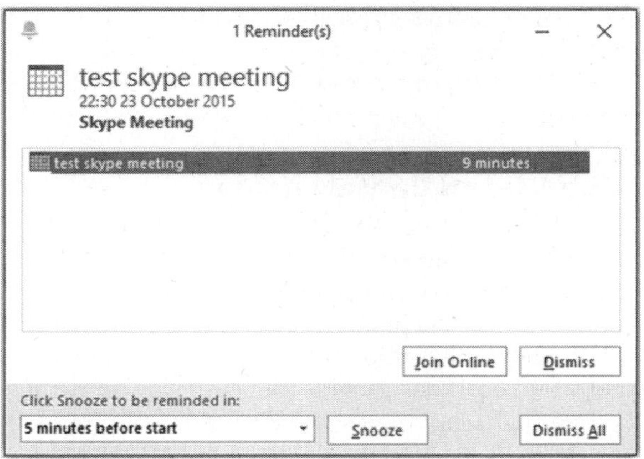

FIGURE 19.4
Joining a meeting from a reminder

The last two options launch the simple join process, in which the user's default web browser starts quickly, followed by the Skype for Business client joining the conference. If the Skype for Business client was not installed, the Lync 2010 Attendee client will start if it is installed; if not, by default, the Reach client will start. With Skype for Business Server 2015, the preferred client (if the Skype for Business client itself is not available) is the web client.

Once you've joined the conference, you can see the participants, as illustrated in Figure 19.5. On this screen, you can also control the Audio settings; for example, you can escalate the conference to a videoconference if video is enabled. Endpoints that do not support video will continue to access the conference using audio only.

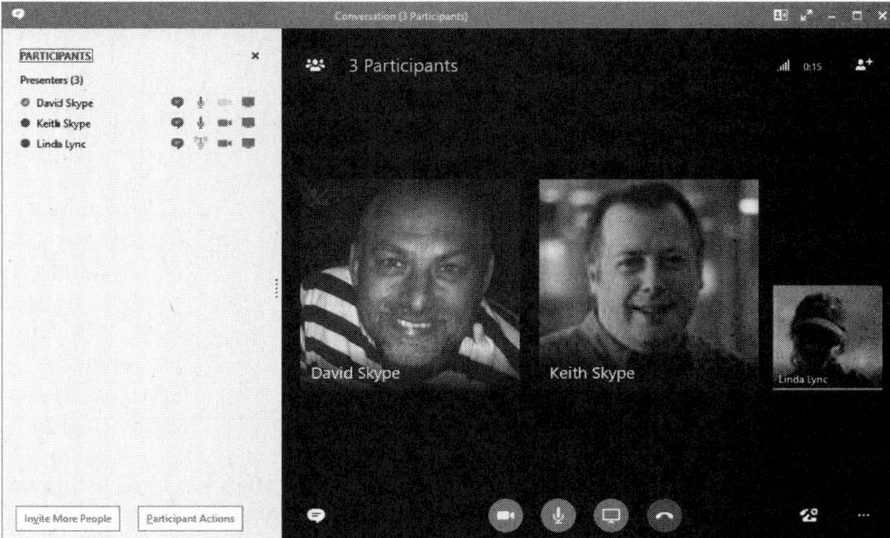

FIGURE 19.5
A conference roster

From the roster, you can also control a participant's conference options. As shown in Figure 19.6, you do this by right-clicking the participant and choosing the required option from the context menu.

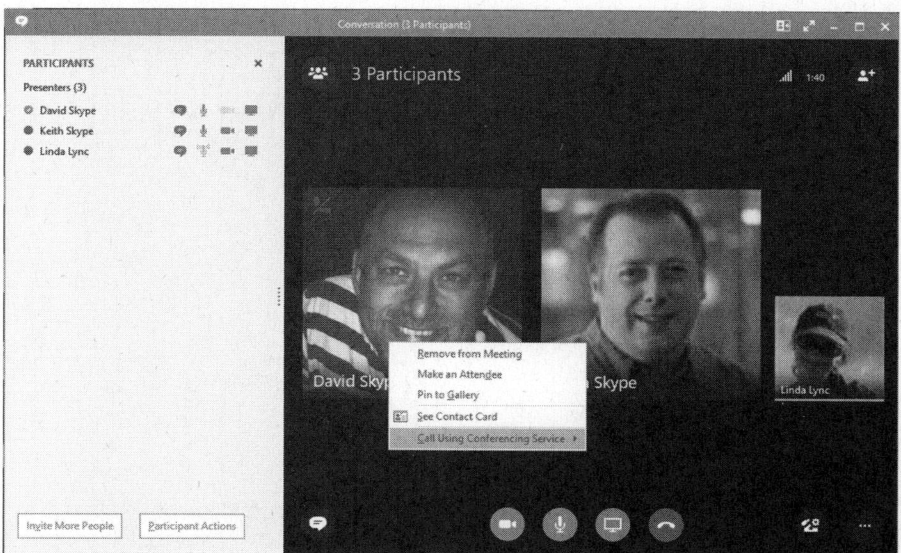

FIGURE 19.6 The conference context menu

The final option to look at in the Skype for Business client is inviting people to an active conference. You can do this in the following ways: by dragging and dropping someone from the buddy list into the conference, by entering their name (retrieved via the address list) or phone number (as shown in Figure 19.7), or by sending them an email with the conference details. One thing to note is that for the first two of these options, the users will be added straight to the conference. If the invited person is using Skype for Business, they will see that they are joining a conference; however, if they are joining from a cell phone, for example, it may come as a shock!

The other element to consider is the Dial-In Conferencing web page, as shown in Figure 19.8. This interface is what users will use to configure their PIN to authenticate a conference with an access number. Additionally, this page lets participants look up more access numbers for Online Meetings.

In general, users will be want to authenticate using their extension and PIN rather than with their full number. You can enable this functionality and allow them to retain the ability to log in using the full number; when enabling users for Enterprise Voice, their TelURI should be defined with `;ext=`*`xxxx`* appended to their number, where `xxxx` is the user's extension.

For example, assuming the user DDI number is 01234 567890 and the extension is 7890, when you enable this user, rather than simply enabling as `TEL:+441234567890`, you would enable the user as `TEL:+441234567890;ext=7890`.

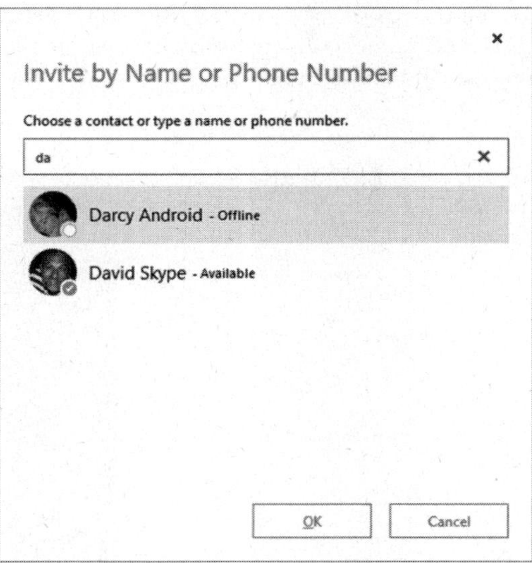

FIGURE 19.7
Adding users to a conference

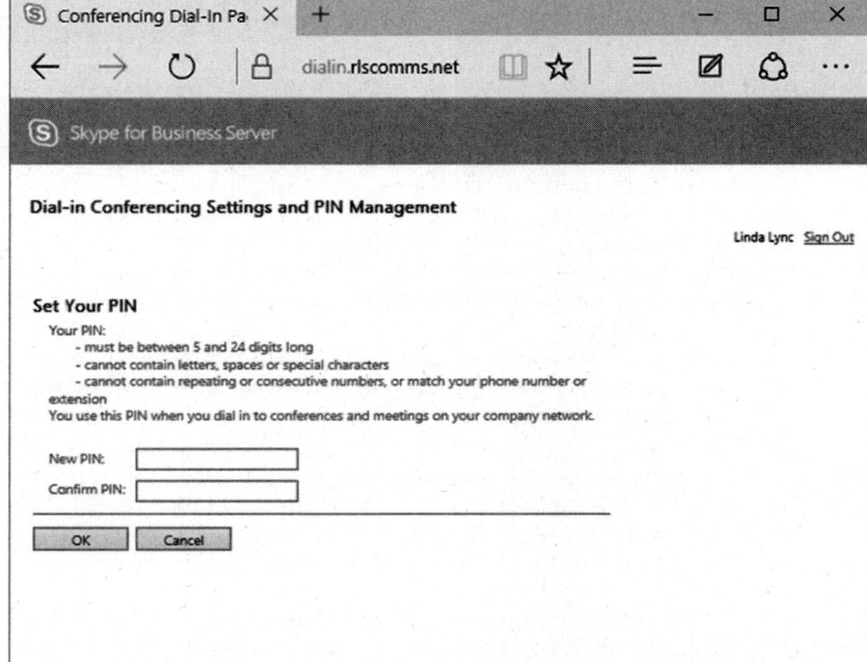

FIGURE 19.8
Setting a PIN on the Dial-In Conferencing web page

Not only can you use the Skype for Business client, but you can manage a meeting from the Aries IP phones. On these devices, you can add people to a conference, view the attendee list, remove people, and allow access to people waiting in the lobby. If extended features are enabled, you will also be able to join a conference from the Calendar view.

Defining Response Groups

Most PBXs provide hunt groups and basic automatic call distribution (ACD). These features allow calls to be distributed between multiple users, but their functionality varies between PBXs, and the majority of them provide a minimum level of functionality.

Hunt groups provide the most basic form of call distribution. For each hunt group, a list of numbers to which to route calls is defined. The PBX will route each incoming call according to the distribution method defined, which is usually one of the following:

Serial This always starts at the first entry. If there is no answer or the line is busy, it tries the second number and continues until someone answers. When the list is exhausted, it goes back to the beginning, effectively starting over.

Parallel This rings all the numbers at the same time.

Round Robin For the first call, this starts at the first entry. If there is no answer or the line is busy, it tries the second number. If the second answers, then the next call starts at the third number. When the list is exhausted, it goes back to the beginning, effectively starting over.

Most Idle This starts at the number that has been idle the longest, and if there is no answer, it tries the next longest idle, and so on, through the list.

Most PBXs allow the administrator to define the ring time on each number, along with a maximum wait time. Once the maximum wait time has been reached, calls will be either terminated or, more commonly, routed to a different number; this could be an overflow number or a voice mailbox.

ACD operates in a similar way to hunt groups in that calls are distributed to a range of numbers; the difference is that there tends to be more intelligence involved. With ACD, callers may be provided with a DTMF-based Interactive Voice Response (IVR), allowing them to choose based on a question. The call is then usually routed to a defined hunt group.

For example, the question could be "To which department would you like to speak?" This would be followed by a list of options, such as "Press 1 for Sales, press 2 for Support, press 3 for Customer Service." The customer would then select 1, 2, or 3 and then be routed to the correct set of numbers. Once they make a selection, depending on the PBX, they may hear ringing or music on hold (MOH) until their call is answered. The announcement will usually have to be provided in a certain format, which tends to be a basic file type. In addition, there is usually a limit to the number of ACDs that can be defined. If the organization requires more complex call routing abilities, then a contact center is usually required. In Skype for Business, hunt groups and ACD features are incorporated into the Response Group application.

Understanding Response Groups

To provide hunt group and basic ACD features for organizations, Microsoft created the Response Group application and its set of cmdlets. Response Groups match the functionality found in most PBXs and exceed it to a point that they can equal some basic call center offerings, although there are limitations that prevent this feature from being classed as a call center. Response Groups exceed the following capabilities in the majority of PBXs:

- Text-to-speech for announcements
- Voice along with DTMF IVR options
- Ability to specify working hours
- Ability to build custom workflows

Response Groups consist of three main components:

Agent Groups These are used to define whether the agents will need to sign in or not, the number of seconds that a call will wait for an agent to answer, the routing method, and which users are members of the group.

Queues These are used to define which agent group will handle the call, along with the Timeout and Overflow settings.

Workflows These are the initial entry points into the system. They provide the IVR functionality, which queues the call should be routed to, and other options such as working hours. In Skype for Business as in OCS 2007 R2, there are predefined workflows. These are as follows:

- Hunt groups
- Interactive, up to two levels, and up to four questions per level IVR

Configuration Order

When configuring Response Groups, whether you are using the Control Panel and Response Group web interface or the PowerShell cmdlets, you need to create the items in a certain order. You need to define the agent groups first, followed by queues, and then the workflows. If you do not create them in the correct order, you may end up not being able to complete the configuration of an item. This results in you needing to create the prerequisite item and then starting again to configure the item.

If you are using PowerShell, note that for queues and workflows, PowerShell commands usually need to be run before the main queue and workflow commands are run, as you'll see in the following sections. Creating queues and custom workflows through PowerShell can be a complex task, and it is a task that should be carefully planned and thoroughly tested to ensure that nothing is missed. After the following summary of the configuration tools and options, we'll go through a complete implementation of a Response Group, demonstrating the most important cmdlets and parameters.

Response Group Configuration Options

Only a couple of configuration options are available at the Response Group level, and they are set on a per-pool basis. These settings are automatically created by Skype for Business during the pool-creation process; as such, there is no `New` cmdlet. The settings can, however, be modified and viewed using `Set-CsRgsConfiguration` and `Get-CsRgsConfiguration`, respectively. The following parameters are available:

- `Identity`: The name of the pool hosting the Response Group prefixed with `service:ApplicationServer:`.
- `AgentRingbackGracePeriod`: The ringback grace period is the period in which a call will not return to an agent if they declined it. This comes into effect only when too few agents are available, and it is defined in seconds between 30 and 600.
- `DefaultMusicOnHoldFile`: The default MOH file used when no specific MOH file is defined in the workflow.
- `DisableCallContext`: The call context consists of the details of the IVR responses and the wait time that is shown to the agent when it answers a call using the Skype for Business client.

Before looking at the rest of the Response Group cmdlets, you need to see how the `Set` cmdlets work because they operate in a slightly different way than most of the other Skype for Business `Set` cmdlets. The difference is that the settings cannot be directly edited; instead, an instance of the setting first needs to be retrieved into a PowerShell variable, then the required updates need to be performed, and finally the instance needs to be fed into the `Set` command. Here's an example:

```
$variable = Get-CsRgsAgentGroup
-Identity service:ApplicationServer:se01.rlscomms.net
-Name "Attendant"
$variable.RoutingMethod = "RoundRobin"
Set-CsRgsAgentGroup -Instance $variable
```

You also need to use this method when you're creating queues and workflows because instances often need to be passed into these commands. Some of the PowerShell cmdlets are used only for populating a variable to pass into another cmdlet.

Agent Groups

Agent groups define a list of agents and their associated settings, such as call routing method and alert time. A single group can be assigned to multiple queues. Agent groups can be managed through the Control Panel (Response Groups ➢ Group) or through PowerShell. To create a new agent group, use the `New-CsRgsAgentGroup` cmdlet; the following parameters are available:

- `Parent`: This is the FQDN of the pool to host the agent group; it is prefixed with `service:ApplicationServer:`.
- `AgentAlertTime` (Ring Time On Agent): This cmdlet is defined in seconds with a range from 10 to 600.
- `AgentsByUri` (Agent List): This cmdlet is a comma-separated list of agents. Each agent should be prefixed with `sip:`.
- `Description`: This is a description of the agent group.
- `DistributionGroupAddress` (Distribution Group Containing Agents): This is the email address associated with the distribution group.

- `ParticipationPolicy` (Participation Type): This is set to `Formal` if the agent needs to sign in to receive calls from the Response Group or `Informal` if they will always receive calls from the Response Group.
- `RoutingMethod`: The routing methods are as follows:
  - Longest Idle (`LongestIdle`)
  - Round Robin (`RoundRobin`)
  - Serial (`Serial`)
  - Parallel (`Parallel`)
  - Attendant (`Attendant`)

Except for the Attendant routing method, all of these methods were discussed earlier in this section. As its name implies, the Attendant method is a routing method in Skype for Business used primarily for attendants. It operates like the Parallel method except that it ignores the user's presence state when routing a call. Normally, Response Groups will route a call to an agent only if it has a presence of Available or Inactive. When the Attendant routing method is used, the call will be routed to the agent irrespective of its presence state; the only exception to this is if the state is Do Not Disturb.

There are two ways to define which users are members of an agent group—either by defining a list of agents using their SIP URIs or by specifying a distribution group. Although specifying a distribution group can save having to specify a list of agents, you need to be aware of the following:

- Nested distribution groups will be ignored.
- Only a single distribution group can be defined.
- For the Serial and Round Robin routing methods, the calls will be routed to agents in the order listed in the distribution group. This can often cause issues when you want to use a different agent order.

When creating the agent group, you should specify only one of the two options, either `AgentsByUri` or `DistributionGroupAddress`. If you are creating a group in which you intend to use this agent group, you should store the result of the `New` command in a variable.

Queue and Workflow Preliminaries

Once the agent groups have been created, you'll need to create the queues and then the workflows. To create these elements, you will need to pass into the respective cmdlets the results of a number of other cmdlets, which define various characteristics of the queue. The elements you need to configure first are as follows:

- Prompts
- Answers
- Questions
- Call actions

Prompts are either uploaded recordings or messages generated using text-to-speech, and they are used to read messages such as "Welcome to the Sales Department" or IVR questions. These prompts are not created in their own right; they are passed into a variable to pass into another cmdlet.

`New-CsRgsPrompt` accepts two parameters: either `TextToSpeechPrompt`, which allows for up to 4,096 characters to be specified, or an audio file, using the `AudioFilePrompt` parameter.

If you use audio files rather than TTS, they needs to be either a WAV file (`.wav`) or a Windows Media Audio file (`.wma`). WAV files need to meet the following criteria:

- 8 or 16 bits
- Linear pulse code modulation (LPCM), A-Law or mu-Law
- Mono or stereo
- 4MB or less

For Windows Media Audio files, there are no specific limitations imposed by Skype for Business. However, you should give some consideration to the bit rate because the higher the bit rate, the greater the load placed on the servers, and the maximum bit rate played back via the PSTN is limited.

The audio file containing the prompt is not directly uploaded; instead, the cmdlet requires a byte array representation of the file. This byte array is created using the `Get-Content` cmdlet; this array is used with the `Import-CsRgsAudioFile` cmdlet to upload the file. Here's an example:

```
$RGSPromptAF = Import-CsRgsAudioFile
-Identity "service:ApplicationServer:se01.rlscomms.net"
-FileName "ResGroup1FirstPrompt.wav"
-Content (Get-Content C:\RGSPrompt.wav -Encoding byte -ReadCount 0)
```

This code imports the audio file to the Skype for Business server. It first gets a byte array of the `RGSPrompt.wav` file, which is sent to the Skype for Business servers and saved as `ResGroup1FirstPrompt.wav`. The `FileName` specified needs to be unique and does not need to match the name of the file you are uploading. That is because you are uploading the prompt to Skype for Business as a byte array rather than the actual file; therefore, the original name is never uploaded.

The next cmdlet you need to look at is `New-CsRgsAnswer`, which is used to specify an answer for a question. This cmdlet does not create anything, and it is used only to populate a variable. It uses these parameters:

- `Action`: This parameter is used with the `New-CsRgsCallAction` cmdlet to specify the action that occurs when the response is chosen.
- `DtmfResponse`: The DTMF response can be *, #, or 0 through 9.
- `Name`: This is the name of the answer.
- `VoiceResponseList`: This is a list of voice responses this answer will match, separated by commas.

When creating the answer, either `DtmfResponse` or `VoiceResponseList` or both must be specified.

Now that you can create both the answer and the prompt, you can create a question using the New-CsRgsQuestion cmdlet. Like the previous two cmdlets, this one also needs to be passed into a variable. The New-CsRgsQuestion cmdlet uses these parameters:

- Prompt: This is the question to be asked. It should be a prompt object.
- AnswerList: This is a comma-separated list of answers. If the question allows two answers, at least two answer objects should be specified.
- InvalidAnswerPrompt: This is a prompt object that will be played if an invalid answer is entered.
- Name: This is the name of the question.
- NoAnswerPrompt: This is a prompt object that will be played if no answer is entered.

When a question with associated answers has been created, you need to look at the call action. To make Response Groups even more complicated, the New-CsRgsAnwer cmdlet requires that a call action already be created; therefore, to get to a stage where you have a question created, you will already have had to create a call action. But a call action can also be linked to a question if required and may require a prompt to be created.

A call action can do any of the following things:

- Terminate: This ends the call.
- TransferToQueue: This allows an agent to answer the call.
- TransferToQuestion: This transfers to a question.
- TransferToUri: This transfers to a SIP URI, such as another Response Group, specified in the Uri parameter.
- TransferToVoiceMailUri: This transfers to the voice mailbox, specified in the Uri parameter.
- TransferToPSTN: This transfers to a PSTN number specified in the Uri parameter.

To create a call action, use the New-CsRgsCallAction cmdlet. The following parameters are available:

- Action: This is one of the previously specified actions.
- Prompt: This is a prompt to play before the action is carried out. It should be a prompt object.
- Question: This is required only if the Transfer to Question action is chosen and should be a question object.
- QueueID: This is used if Transfer to a Queue is specified. It should be the identity of the queue that was previously created. If the queue is in a variable, this is retrieved using $variable.Identity.
- Uri: This is used if Transfer to a URI or PSTN is specified. It should be prefixed with sip:.

You'll see examples of all these commands in action in the "Implementing Response Groups" section coming up shortly.

QUEUES

Queues are used to define the actions once the caller has been processed by the workflow. This could be after an option is selected on an IVR, or callers could be routed straight to a queue as soon as they call the workflow if, for example, the workflow is configured as a hunt group.

With all the preliminaries configured, you are ready to create a queue. Unlike the last few sets of cmdlets you've looked at, the `New-CsRgsQueue` cmdlet actually creates groups. It uses the following parameters:

- `Parent`: This is the FQDN of the pool to host the agent group, prefixed with `service:ApplicationServer:`.
- `Name`: This is the group name.
- `AgentGroupIdList`: This is a comma-separated list of agent groups. The groups will be worked through in order; if no agent in group 1 answers, then group 2 will be tried, and so on.
- `Description`: This describes the queue.
- `OverflowAction`: This is a call action object.
- `OverflowCandidate`: The Call to Overflow can be set to `NewestCall` or `OldestCall`.
- `OverflowThreshold`: The call count to overflow can be set between 0 and 1000. When the specified number of calls is in the queue, either the oldest or newest call will overflow.
- `TimeoutAction`: This is a call action object.
- `TimeoutThreshold`: This threshold is specified in seconds with a range from 10 to 65536. When the timeout is hit for a queued call, it will follow the timeout call action defined.

Queues can also be configured through the Control Panel. With this method, the preliminary configuration of items such as Overflow Action is not required because they are configured at the same time as the queue, which can be accessed at Response Group ➢ Queue. Once the queues and associated aspects have been created, you can move on to workflows and the additional cmdlets required.

WORKFLOWS

Workflows are the initial entry points. They define the phone number and contact URI associated with the workflow, the questions to be presented, whether it is an IVR, and the associated queues for the call to be routed to, along with settings such as opening hours and holidays.

Workflows can be configured through PowerShell, in which case there are a number of items that need to be configured before the actual workflow is created. If configuration is performed using the Response Group Configuration Tool, then all configuration is performed when the workflow is created. You can access the Configuration tool (Figure 19.9) through the Control Panel (Response Group ➢ Workflow ➢ Create Or Edit A Workflow) or through `https://poolfqdn/RgsConfig`.

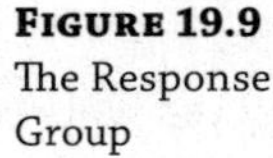

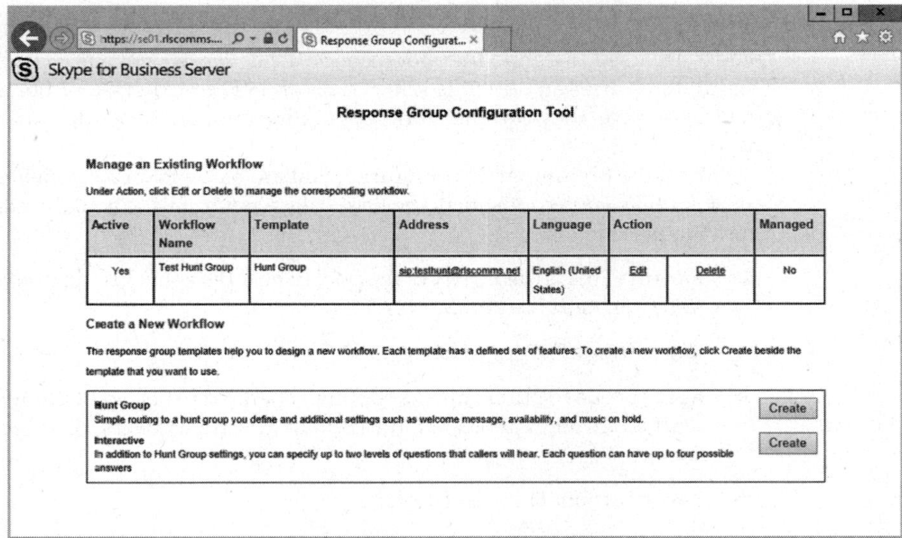

FIGURE 19.9
The Response Group

The first workflow elements to define are holidays; you do that using the `New-CsRgsHoliday` cmdlet. This cmdlet does not create anything and as such needs to be passed into a variable. It lets you specify a start date and time along with an end date and time. The following parameters are required:

- `Name`
- `StartDate`
- `EndDate`

Dates should be formatted as *MM/DD/YYYY HH:SS* `AM|PM`, as in this example: `12/25/2011 12:00 AM`.

When an individual holiday has been created, you need to add it to a holiday set. These are created and as such have associated `Get`, `Set`, and `Remove` cmdlets.

The `New-CsHolidaySet` cmdlet is used to create the holiday sets, which are linked to the workflows to indicate when the Response Group should be open. The following parameters are required:

- `HolidayList`: This is a comma-separated list of holiday objects.
- `Name`: This is the name of the holiday list.
- `Parent`: This is the FQDN of the pool to host the holiday set, prefixed with `service:ApplicationServer:`.

Now you need to define the business hours the Response Groups are open. To do that, you need to define time ranges to pass into the Hours of Business cmdlet.

Time ranges are defined using the `New-CsRgsTimeRange` cmdlet. This doesn't create anything, so its result needs to be passed into a variable. The cmdlet takes the following parameters:

- `Name`: This is the name of the time range.
- `OpenTime`: This is defined as *`HH:MM`* using a 24-hour clock.
- `CloseTime`: This is defined as *`HH:MM`* using a 24-hour clock.

If the business hours are the same for multiple days, such as Monday to Friday, only one time range needs to be defined for these hours.

Next, the business hours need to be defined using the `New-CsRgsHoursOfBusiness` cmdlet. Business hours are created and, as such, have associated `Set`, `Get`, and `Remove` cmdlets. `New-CsRgsHoursOfBusiness` allows two sets of hours to be specified for each day of the week, allowing it to close for lunch, for example. This cmdlet has the following parameters:

- `Name`: This is the name of the business hours.
- `Parent`: This is the FQDN of the pool to host the business hours, prefixed with `service:ApplicationServer:`.
- `MondayHours1` and `MondayHours2` through `SundayHours1` and `SundayHours2`: These are `TimeRange` objects.

Once all the required objects have been created, you can finally create the workflows. Workflows link together all the elements you've reviewed, and creating them is the final step required to complete a Response Group. They are created with the `New-CsRgsWorkflow` cmdlets, using the following parameters:

- `Name`: This is the name of the workflow.
- `Parent`: This is the FQDN of the pool to host the workflow, prefixed with `service:ApplicationServer:`.
- `PrimaryUri`: This is the SIP address of the Response Group, prefixed with `sip:`.
- `Active`: This specifies whether the workflow is active. If it is not active, calls will not be accepted.
- `Anonymous`: If this is set to `True`, the agent's identity will be hidden.
- `BusinessHoursID`: This is a Business Hours object.
- `CustomMusicOnHoldFile`: This is an Audio File object, which is created using the `Import-CsRgsAudiofile` cmdlet.
- `DefaultAction`: This is the default call action to use when the workflow is open; it requires a Call Action object.
- `Description`: This is a text-based description for the workflow
- `DisplayNumber`: This is the number displayed when searched for, or calling, both incoming and outgoing calls.

- `EnabledForFederation`: This defines whether federated users can access the workflow via Lync. If `False`, federated users would be required to dial the actual number.
- `HolidayAction`: This is the call action to use during a holiday; it requires a Call Action object.
- `HolidaySetIdList`: This is the Holiday Set object to use.
- `Language`: This is used to specify the language to be used for text-to-speech.
- `LineUri`: This is the PSTN phone number for the workflow, prefixed with `tel:`.
- `Managed`: This defines whether management of this workflow has been delegated.
- `ManagersByUri`: This is a collection of SIP addresses of the managers for the workflow.
- `NonBusinessHoursAction`: This is the call action to use outside business hours. It requires a Call Action object.
- `TimeZone`: This is the time zone for holidays and business hours.

As part of the workflow creation process, an application contact is created in the configuration partition in Active Directory. The contact stores the same information the Skype for Business–enabled user would (for example, the display name and line URI). This contact is used for a number of tasks.

- When an incoming event occurs, such as a phone call, Lync will search both user and application contacts for a match. The application contact provides the application for the call to be routed to, in this case the Response Group application.
- It will be processed by the Skype for Business Address Book service, allowing users to search for and add the contact to their local contacts list.

To view a list of application contacts in Skype for Business, you can use the `Get-CsApplicationEndpoint` cmdlet.

Anonymous Response Groups and Privacy Mode

If an agent has Privacy mode enabled, the Response Group Presence Watcher can't see it because Response Groups have no additional privileges other than a standard user when it comes to presence.

For a Response Group to operate when Privacy mode is enabled, the RGS Presence Watcher contact needs to be in the agent's buddy list.

Implementing Response Groups

Now that you've looked at what you can do with Response Groups, it's time to see how you can implement them. To do this, let's work through a fairly complete, realistic scenario.

Your organization requires a Response Group to be configured for routing calls to a group of three attendants. All attendants should see all of the calls, but they should be able to specify whether they will receive calls. The identity of all attendants should be hidden.

In addition, the callers should be told that they are being placed in a queue and hear music on hold while waiting. Outside business hours, calls should be routed to an Exchange mailbox along with calls that have been waiting for longer than five minutes. Callers should be told they are being transferred to voice mail.

After studying the requirements statement, you determine that you need to do the following:

- Create an agent group
- Create a queue with overflow settings specified for callers waiting in the queue
- Create a workflow with the announcement, working hours, and agent anonymity defined

To begin, you create the agent group.

```
$AGroup = New-CsRgsAgentGroup
-Parent "service:ApplicationServer:se01rlscomms.net"
-AgentsByUri "sip:keith.skype@rlscomms.net",
"sip:linda.lync@rlscomms.net", "sip:rob.skype@rlscomms.net"
-ParticipationPolicy Formal
-RoutingMethod Attendant
-Name "Attendant Group"
```

With this command, you created the agent group. It is created as a formal group, with the three specified agents and routes using the Attendant routing method to ensure that calls are presented to agents irrespective of their state (except for Do Not Disturb).

Now you need to create the prompt to transfer the caller to voice mail on timeout.

```
$TimeoutPrompt = New-CsRgsPrompt -TextToSpeechPrompt
"Unfortunately all of our operators are busy,
we are transferring you to voice mail."
```

This stores the prompt in `$TimeoutPrompt`, allowing you to pass it into the next command.

Next, you need to create the call action for the timeout.

```
$TimeoutCallAction = New-CsRgsCallAction
-Action TransferToVoiceMailUri
-Uri "sip:attendantMB@rlscomms.net"
-Prompt $TimeoutPrompt
```

This stores the details into `$TimeOutCallAction`. The action transfers the call to the specified voice mailbox.

Now that you have created the required objects, you can create the queue.

```
$AQueue = New-CsRgsQueue -Parent "service:ApplicationServer:se01.rlscomms.net"
-Name "Attendant Queue"
-AgentGroupIdList $AGroup.Identity
-TimeoutAction $TimeoutCallAction
-TimeoutThreshold 300
```

This creates the queue and stores the details in the `$AQueue`. It also references the agent group you created earlier; because you need the `Identity` value out of `$AGroup`, you specify `$AGroup.Identity`.

Now you're ready to create the objects required for the workflow. The first step is to define the time range for the business hours.

```
$TimeRange = New-CsRgsTimeRange -Name "BusinessHours" -OpenTime 08:00
-CloseTime 18:00
```

This stores the time range, which is 08:00 to 18:00, in `$TimeRange`.

Now define the business hours.

```
$BusinessHours = New-CsRgsHoursOfBusiness -Name "Attendant Open Hours"
-Parent "service:ApplicationServer:se01.rlscomms.net"
-MondayHours1 $TimeRange
-TuesdayHours1 $TimeRange
-WednesdayHours1 $TimeRange
-ThursdayHours1 $TimeRange
-FridayHours1 $TimeRange
```

This creates the business hours. Into this statement, you'll pass the `$TimeRange` several times because you require the same opening hours for each day that the business is open. Because the hours aren't specified for Saturday or Sunday, the Response Group will default to being closed on those days.

Now you need to create the prompt to transfer the caller to voice mail outside business hours.

```
$OBHPrompt = New-CsRgsPrompt -TextToSpeechPrompt
"We are currently closed, we are transferring you to voice mail."
```

This creates the Out of Business Hours prompt. Note that only a sort of "ghost object" is created at this point; the information is merely stored in the `$OBHPrompt` variable until the command to create the workflow is run.

Now you need to create the call action for outside business hours.

```
$OBHCallAction = New-CsRgsCallAction
-Action TransferToVoiceMailUri
-Uri "sip:attendantMB@rlscomms.net"
-Prompt $OBHPrompt
```

This creates the Out of Business Hours action. Again, at this point, the information is merely stored in the `$OBHCallAction` variable until the workflow is created.

Now that you have created the business hours, you need to create the default call action and associated prompt.

```
$DefaultPrompt = New-CsRgsPrompt -TextToSpeechPrompt
"Thank you for calling RLS Comms, please wait for an attendant."
```

This creates the default prompt. Again, at this point, the information is merely stored in the `$DefaultPrompt` variable until the workflow is created.

Next, you need to create the call action to route to the agents.

```
$DefaultCallAction = New-CsRgsCallAction
-Action TransferToQueue
-QueueID $AQueue.Identity
-Prompt $DefaultPrompt
```

This creates the default call action. Again, at this point, the information is merely stored in the `$DefaultCallAction` variable for use in the next command.

Now that you've created the required objects for the workflow, you can finally create the workflow.

```
New-CsRgsWorkflow -Name "Attendants"
-Parent "service:ApplicationServer:se01.rlscomms.net"
-PrimaryURI "sip:AttendantRGS@rlscomms.net"
-Active $true
-Anonymous $true
-BusinessHoursID $BusinessHours.Identity
-DefaultAction $DefaultCallAction
-DisplayNumber "1-425-555-1000"
-EnabledForFederation $true
-Language "en-US"
-LineURI "tel:+14255551000"
-NonBusinessHoursAction $OBHCallAction
```

This creates the actual workflow. Into this workflow you can reference the call actions created earlier. For the business hours, reference the `Identity` stored within `$BusinessHours`. The two action variables are not actually created in Skype for Business; they are stored within the variables, so you don't need to specify a particular setting in them.

When this command is run, the output is similar to the following:

```
Identity               : service:ApplicationServer:se01.rlscomms.net
/6876ce92-7b33-450f-8a73-38fc7d5c1789
NonBusinessHoursAction : Prompt=We are currently closed, we are transferring you
to voice mail.
Action=TransferToVoicemailUri
Uri=sip:attendantMB@rlscomms.net
HolidayAction          :
DefaultAction          : Prompt=Thank you for calling, please wait for an
attendant.
Action=TransferToQueue
QueueId=dbaf6136-9386-4964-a49f-8610f0f761de
CustomMusicOnHoldFile  :
Name                   : Attendants
Description            :
PrimaryUri             : sip:AttendantRGS@rlscomms.net
Active                 : True
Language               : en-US
TimeZone               : GMT Standard Time
BusinessHoursID        : service:ApplicationServer:se01.rlscomms.net
/6f7314e7-a88f-4f23-aa64-a9262404a050
Anonymous              : True
Managed                : False
OwnerPool              :
DisplayNumber          : 1-425-555-1000
EnabledForFederation   : True
LineUri                : tel:+14255551000
```

```
HolidaySetIDList        : {}
ManagersByUri           : {}
```

Now that the Response Group is configured, you can run the corresponding Get commands to check the configuration.

Using Response Groups

Now that you've implemented Response Groups, you need to see how network users work with them. As with dial-in conferencing and other client features, admins may need to provide some level of training or support to their users. Here you are going to look at only the agent aspects of Response Groups.

If a user is assigned to a formal workflow, the first thing they need to do is log into the workflow by selecting Response Group Settings from the Skype for Business client, which then loads the web page shown in Figure 19.10. Users will be presented with the queues to which they are assigned, and they will be able to check the queues they want to sign into.

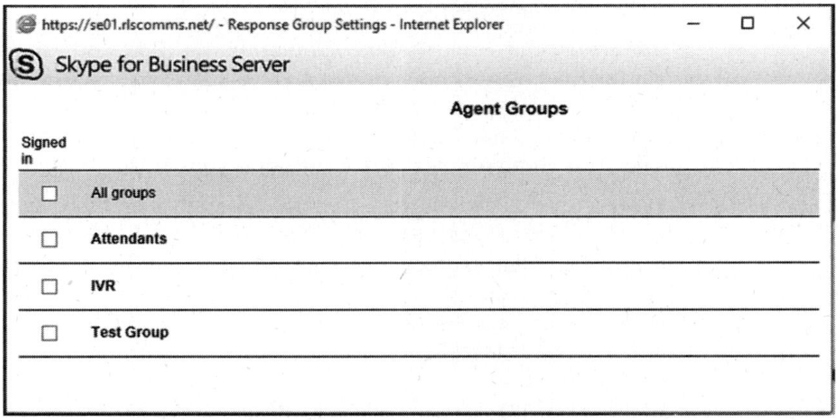

FIGURE 19.10
Signing into a queue

Note that users are presented with the queues from only their home pool. If they are members of queues on another pool, they must manually direct their browser to the path to sign in on the other pool: https:<pool fqdn>/RgsClients/Tab.aspx.

When the agent receives a call, the toast that appears to notify the agent of the call (Figure 19.11) will contain the name of the Response Group. By receiving this information, the agent knows, for example, what greeting to use when answering the call.

FIGURE 19.11
The toast for a Response Group

If the call is from a Response Group that uses an IVR, the agents will be presented with the IVR options that the caller selected along with their wait time, as shown in Figure 19.12.

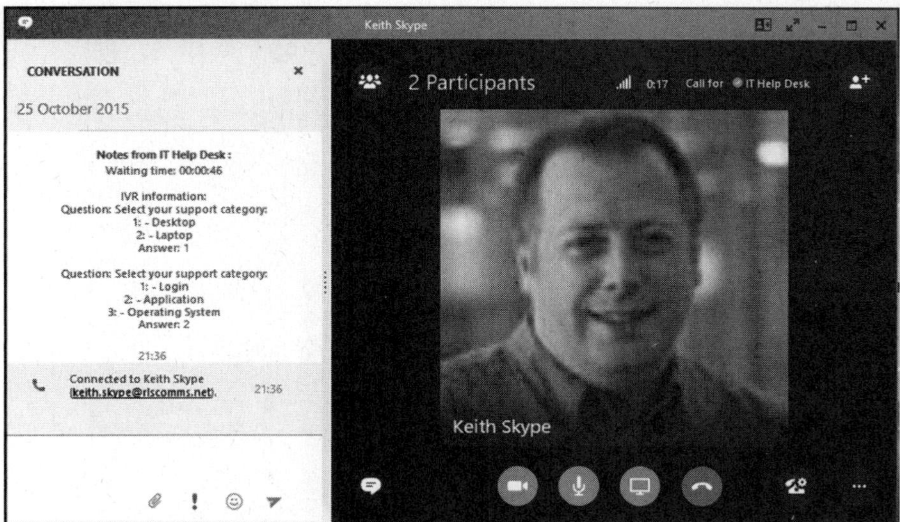

FIGURE 19.12 IVR details for a call

With this information, the agent can handle the call as required. In addition, the agent can introduce additional modalities, as with a normal Skype for Business call, and can escalate to a conference if needed. The only time this is restricted is if the Response Group that the agent answered the call on is configured for Agent Anonymity, in which case the agent cannot do any of the following:

- Share individual applications, the desktop of a single display, or the entire desktop
- Transfer files
- Use whiteboard or data collaboration
- Escalate to a conference

What happens when the agent needs to make an outbound call? For the most part, making an outbound call is no different for a user configured as an agent than it is for a normal user. The only time this differs is if a user is a member of a Response Group that is configured for Agent Anonymity. In this case, as shown in Figure 19.13, agents can choose whether they are making the call on behalf of themselves or the Response Group.

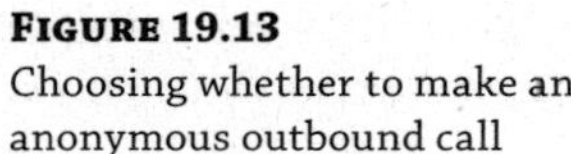

FIGURE 19.13
Choosing whether to make an anonymous outbound call

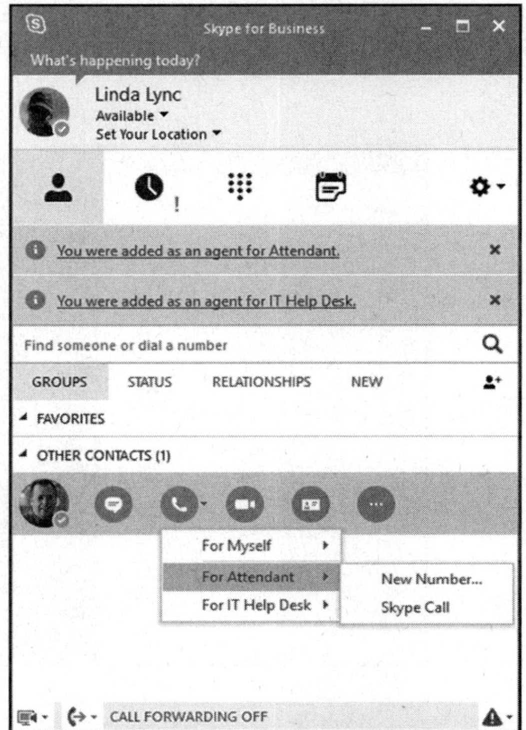

Understanding Call Park

Education, healthcare, warehousing, and retail are just a few of the organization types that take Call Park for granted. It is a feature they use every day and assume that it will be available on any PBX that they want to deploy. To fulfill the requirements of these organizations and others, Call Park was added as a voice application in Skype for Business, removing a potential stumbling block for these organizations to migrate.

While you may not have heard of Call Park before, you have probably heard of it being used. If you have been in a store and heard "Call for Joe Blogs on extension 1023" over the public address system, they were probably referring to an incoming call for Joe Blogs that was "parked" on extension 1023. This allowed Joe Blogs to easily retrieve the call by calling 1023 from any of the store phones and be connected immediately.

Why would a store use Call Park rather than, for example, having the switchboard operator put the call on hold, page Joe Blogs to call them, and then transfer the call? The new technology has emerged because of the limitations of PBXs and the way they operate. The easiest way to understand this is to look at how a call flow would operate.

1. The customer calls the store.
2. The switchboard answers.
3. The customer asks to talk to the store manager.
4. The switchboard operator places the call on hold and pages the store manager.

5. The store manager calls the operator; if the operator is busy, it could take a while for the call to be answered.
6. The operator takes a note of the number the store manager called from and hangs up.
7. The operator takes the customer off hold and transfers it to the number the store manager called from; if by sheer chance someone else has called this number before the operator managed to transfer the call, then the operator will have to wait to transfer the call.

As you can see, this is a long process and includes a number of areas where issues can occur. For example, suppose the switchboard operator is busy. While that may not happen in a small retail store, in a busy hospital, the wait time could be tremendous. Some PBXs, including Skype for Business, can shortcut part of this process by allowing calls to be *joined*, effectively removing the last two steps. However, there can be other limitations, such as the number of calls a person can put on hold at any one time.

In summary, Call Park allows a call to be parked on an extension number and retrieved by calling that extension number.

Setting Call Park Options

Now that you understand what Call Park is, you need to examine how it works within Skype for Business and the configuration options available. No separate installation is required for Call Park; it is installed as part of Skype for Business. To use Call Park, you just need to configure it. You do that in the following stages:

- Voice policy configuration
- Call Park extensions
- Call Park Service configuration
- Call Park music on hold

In Skype for Business, any user can retrieve a parked call by calling the extension on which it was parked. From a user standpoint, the only configuration option is whether the user can park a call. This is configured through the Voice policy assigned to the user, which was covered in Chapter 13, "Archiving and Monitoring."

Call Park Extensions

Call Park extensions are referred to in Skype for Business as *orbits*, and they can be configured through the Control Panel or using PowerShell. These numbers have a lot of restrictions.

- The maximum number of orbits per range is 10,000.
- The maximum number of orbits per pool is 50,000.
- They cannot be Direct Inward Dial numbers.
- They must match this regular expression:

```
([\*|#]?[1-9]\d{0,7})|([1-9]\d{0,8})
```

The first two restrictions are not likely to cause an issue because most organizations usually require a small range of numbers to use. This range should be no larger than required; for most organizations, this tends to be less than 100 extensions.

The requirement that the number not be a DID is fairly unusual for Skype for Business because most voice-related features require E.164 numbers to be assigned to them. A Call Park number cannot be a DID because retrieving calls from the PSTN is not supported, although retrieving calls from a PBX is supported.

The final requirement is for the number to match a specific regular expression. This breaks down as follows:

- It must start with a *, #, or one of the digits 1 through 9.
- If the number starts with a * or #, it must be followed first by a single digit in the range 1 through 9 and then followed by up to seven digits.
- If the number starts with a 1 through 9, it can be followed by up to eight digits.

Table 19.2 lists some sample orbit numbers.

TABLE 19.2: Sample orbit numbers

START NUMBER	END NUMBER
*1	*9
#100	#140
1000	1100
859000	859010

When assigning numbers to be orbits, you need to make sure they will not be affected by number normalizations, such as those found in the dial plans. If the number a user tries to call is converted to another number, they will be unable to retrieve the call.

This also applies to any normalizations that may be performed by a gateway linking to a PBX or by the PBX itself, if there is a requirement to retrieve calls from the PBX.

Orbits can be configured through the Skype for Business Control Panel under Voice Features ➢ Call Park as well as via PowerShell. From the Call Park tab, shown in Figure 19.14, they can be created, edited, and deleted. To create the orbit using the `New-CsCallParkOrbit` cmdlet, you specify the following:

- `Identity`: This is the orbit range name.
- `NumberRangeStart`: This is the orbit range start number.
- `NumberRangeEnd`: This is the orbit range end number.
- `CallParkService`: This is the Application server to host the orbits.

For Call Park, the application server is a pool FQDN prefixed with `ApplicationServer:`. This allows you to define which pool will host the parked calls. If you will be parking a large number of calls, this could be resource intensive because the pool needs to manage these calls and also stream music on hold if configured.

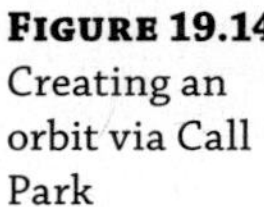

FIGURE 19.14 Creating an orbit via Call Park

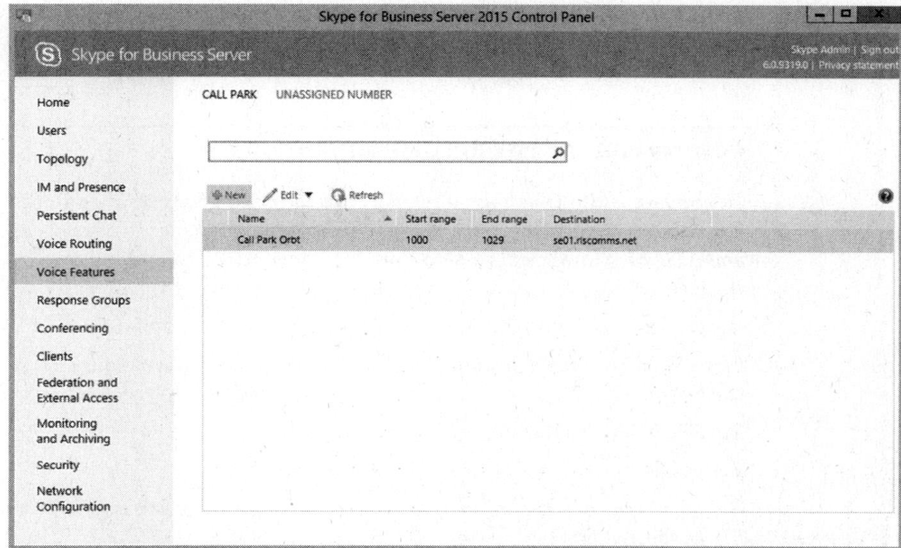

MANAGING THE CALL PARK SERVICE

The Call Park service configuration can be managed only through PowerShell. There are two configuration levels: global and site. The global level will apply to all Skype for Business sites unless a site-level configuration exists. Both levels have the same configuration options; to create a new configuration, use the `New-CsCpsConfiguration` cmdlet.

- `EnableMusicOnHold`: A `True` or `False` option. This indicates whether music on hold should be played. There is a default MOH file that ships with Lync; this can be replaced if required.
- `CallPickupTimeoutThreshold`: Defined as *HH*: *MM*: *SS*. This defines the length of time before the call recalls. This can be as little as 10 seconds or as long as 10 minutes. The default is 90 seconds.
- `MaxCallPickupAttempts`: The number of times the call will ring the person who parked the call before it will reroute to the timeout URI. The default is 1.
- `OnTimeoutURI`: A SIP address to which the parked call will be routed if the call is not answered after the defined number of call pickup attempts. The SIP URI can be either a user or a Response Group.

MUSIC ON HOLD

A custom MOH file is uploaded to the Call Park service using a dedicated PowerShell command. Only one MOH file can be used per application server; when a new file is uploaded, the existing file will be overwritten.

The file needs to be in WMA 9 format, and it is recommended that it has the following characteristics: encoded at 44kHz, 16 bit, mono, with a constant bit rate (CBR) or 32kbps.

Converting to the Recommended Format

To convert audio files to the recommended format for music on hold, you can use Microsoft Expression Encoder, an application that allows existing files to be encoded to the correct settings, among other things. Expression Encoder is available in a number of versions; you can download the free version, which can convert most audio formats, from here:

`www.microsoft.com/download/en/details.aspx?id=24601`

Expression Encoder is designed to do a lot more than convert audio files, so the conversion process can be confusing. The following steps will walk you through converting the file:

1. Select Transcoding Project.
2. Import the MOH file by choosing File ➢ Import.
3. On the Encode tab on the right side of the application, expand Audio and complete the settings as shown here:

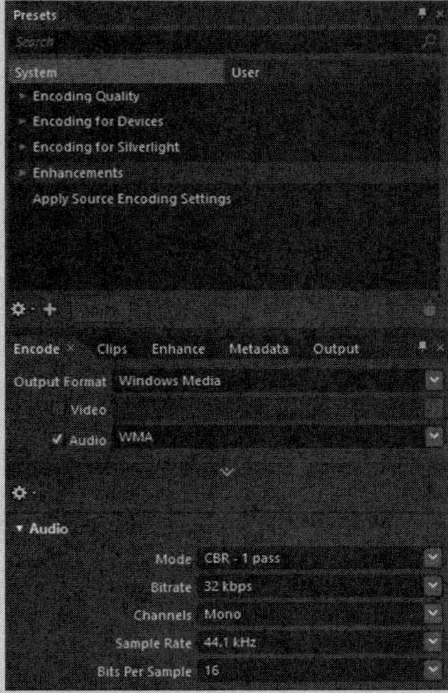

4. Select the Output location on the Output tab.
5. Encode the file by choosing File ➢ Encode.

The MOH file is not directly uploaded; instead, the cmdlet requires a byte array representation of the file. This byte array is created using the `Get-Content` cmdlet, which is combined with the `Set-CsCallParkServiceMusicOnHoldFile` cmdlet to upload the file. Here's an example:

```
$MoHFile = Get-Content -ReadCount 0
-Encoding byte "C:\music_on_hold.wma"
Set-CsCallParkServiceMusicOnHoldFile
-Service ApplicationServer:se01.rlscomms.net
-Content $MoHFile
```

These two commands create a byte array of the file `music_on_hold.wma` in the `$MoHFile` variable and then upload it to the Skype for Business server and set it as the Call Park service music on hold.

Implementing Call Park

Now that you know what you can and can't do with Call Park, let's look at how you can implement it. To do this, use the following scenario:

As part of the Microsoft Skype for Business deployment, some of the staff members need access to the Call Park functionality. All other staff members should be able to retrieve calls but not park them. The staff members who should be able to park calls are the switchboard operators and the personal assistants. There should be capacity to park 30 calls at any one time; calls should re-call after 30 seconds, and if a call is not answered when re-called, it should be directed to the switchboard.

After reviewing the given scenario, you determine that Call Park should be configured as follows:

- Only the switchboard and the PA require Call Park.
- Only 30 orbits need to be set up.
- The pickup timeout needs to be 30 seconds.
- The timeout URI needs to be the switchboard Response Group.
- There should be only one re-call attempt.

Although Skype for Business does not require these tasks to be completed in any particular order, you don't want to enable the users until the rest of the configuration has been completed; therefore, you should work through the list in reverse order.

The first step is to configure the Call Park service, which can be performed only via PowerShell. Since there is only a basic setup, you will configure the service at the global level rather than on a per-site basis.

```
Set-CsCpsConfiguration -Identity Global
-CallPickupTimeoutThreshold 00:00:30
-OnTimeoutURI "sip:switchboard@rlscomms.com"
-MaxCallPickupAttempts 1
```

This sets the call pickup threshold, which specifies that a call reaching the timeout is routed to the switchboard after the call has rung back to the person who parked it once. This setting will apply to all users who are not covered by a site-specific policy.

Once the Call Park service is configured, you need to create the orbit numbers; although you could configure these through the Control Panel as shown earlier, you will continue to use PowerShell. Since you were not provided with specific extensions to utilize, you will use the range 1000 to 1029.

```
New-CsCallParkOrbit -Identity "CPO 1" -NumberRangeStart 1000
-NumberRangeEnd 1029 -CallParkService "se01.rlscomms.net"
```

This creates the Call Park orbit, with a range of 1000 to 1029, allowing 30 calls to be parked; this pool is shared across all users in the pool. Its output will be similar to the following:

```
Identity           : CPO 1
NumberRangeStart   : 1000
NumberRangeEnd     : 1029
CallParkServiceId  : ApplicationServer:se01.rlscomms.net
CallParkServerFqdn : se01.rlscomms.net
```

Almost everything is configured, but you still need to enable the users to park calls. To do this, you need to modify the Voice policies for the switchboard operators and personal assistants; because they already exist, you need to modify the existing policies.

```
Set-CsVoicePolicy -Identity Switchboard -EnableCallPark $true
Set-CsVoicePolicy -Identity PA -EnableCallPark $true
```

These two commands enable Call Park for the two Voice policies, one for PAs and the other for the switchboard.

This completes the Call Park configuration; run the corresponding `Get` commands to check the configuration.

Using Call Park

Now that you've implemented Call Park, you need to understand how network users can park and retrieve calls. Calls can be parked using the Skype for Business client, the Attendant client, or Phone Edition. These clients operate in the same way; calls are parked by transferring the call to the parking lot, as shown in Figure 19.15.

When the call is transferred, you will see that the call has been placed on hold; this notification is then replaced with the number on which the call was parked, as shown in Figure 19.16.

FIGURE 19.15
Parking a call

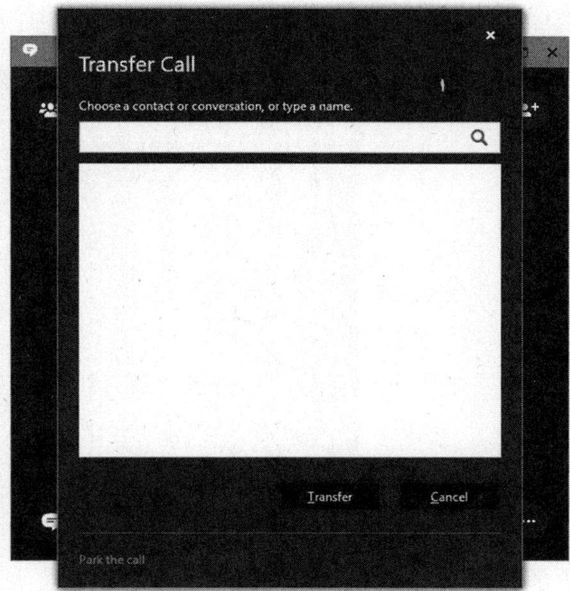

FIGURE 19.16
A parked call extension

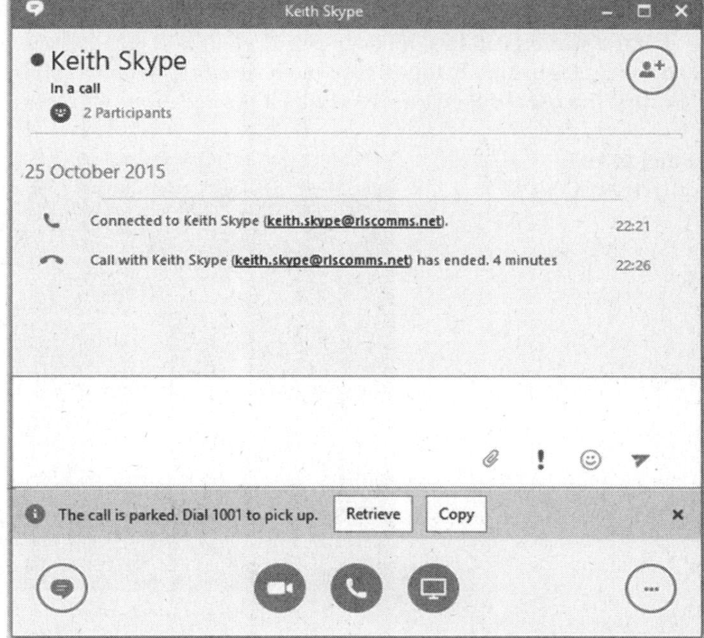

If there are no available extensions on which to park the call, the user will receive a notification like the one shown in Figure 19.17. Note that the call is left on hold to ensure that the caller being parked does not accidentally overhear anything they shouldn't.

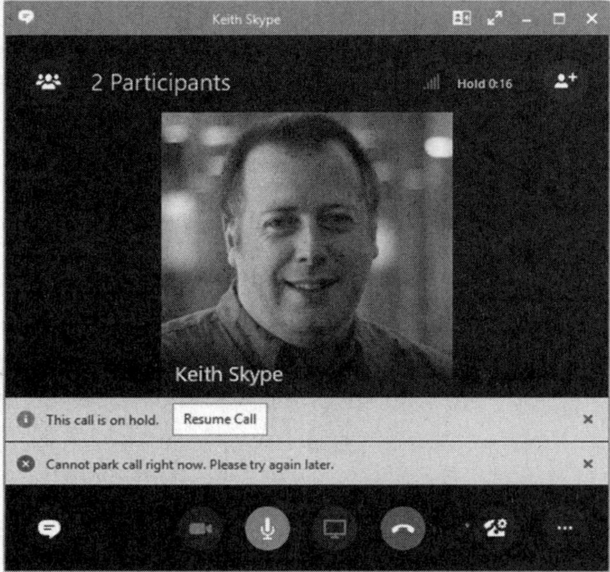

FIGURE 19.17
Call park failure

If the parked call has not been retrieved, it will recall to the user who parked the call, as shown in Figure 19.18; this is to avoid a situation where a call is never retrieved. When the recall occurs, the user will be informed that it is a recall.

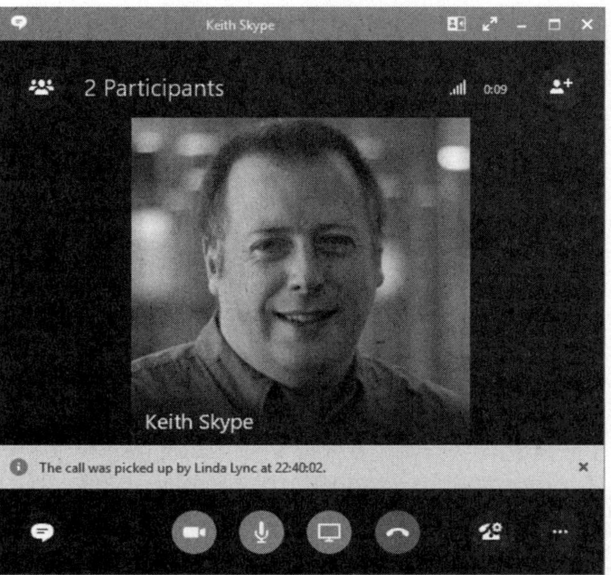

FIGURE 19.18
A call retrieved

To retrieve the call, the extension on which it was parked needs to be called. Once the call has been retrieved, it will operate like any other call.

Configuring Unassigned Numbers

Organizations often have phone numbers that they do not use, for a variety of reasons. For example, they may be utilizing only part of the number range allocated to them, or staff may have left—but the organization may still receive calls to such numbers. Traditional PBXs have responded in the following ways:

- Presenting announcements, played to the calling party, for numbers that are not allocated to a phone or service
- Allocating multiple extensions to a single phone
- Leaving phones configured with Call Forward All set to route to a different number such as an attendant

These tend to be blunt tools, using features within the PBX for purposes for which they were not intended. Although they may do what is required, the end result may not be the best solution. For example, the first of these methods would usually result in an announcement being played, followed by the call being terminated. For some organizations, this may be satisfactory; many others would prefer the call to be transferred to an attendant. The second and third methods will have similar results for the caller, who will be expecting to speak to Joe Blogs. Instead, their call will be answered by someone completely different, which can often lead to confusion or to the caller just hanging up.

There are also limits to the number of extensions that can appear on a single phone, often requiring more expensive phones or expansion modules to have more extensions configured. In addition, depending on the PBX type, the more expensive the phones, the more licenses required on the PBX. There are similar issues with leaving phones configured to forward calls.

From these scenarios, you can see that there is usually no ideal way to handle unassigned numbers, although some PBXs do provide a more complete features set for this. To provide a better solution than most and to ensure that organizations do not lose these features if they have them, Microsoft implemented the Unassigned Number functionality in Skype for Business.

Using Unassigned Numbers

In Skype for Business, the Unassigned Number functionality works by defining number ranges and associated call treatments. The call treatments can send the call either to an Exchange Auto Attendant or to the Announcement Service.

The Announcement Service is used to play an announcement to the caller; the call can then be redirected to a SIP URI, voice mailbox, or telephone number. Alternatively, the call can be redirected without an announcement being played. The final option available with the Announcement Service is for it to play a busy tone to the caller. While this is better than the call just being disconnected, it does not provide any context. Using the Announcement Service allows an organization to tell the caller that a person has left the business, for example, and then redirect them to someone who can help them. For the majority of organizations, this is better than the call just being terminated after the announcement has been played.

The Announcement Service is a separate voice application within Skype for Business, but it can be used in conjunction only with the Unassigned Number functionality. The announcements that are played to the caller can be provided either by providing an audio file or by using text-to-speech (TTS).

To TTS or Not to TTS

Text-to-speech provides a quick and simple way of generating announcements, although the drawback is that they may not sound perfect; this is usually most noticeable with company and employee names. Therefore, while TTS may be usable for a proof-of-concept and trial deployments of Lync or for emergency announcements, many organizations prefer to use prerecorded announcements, which allow more control and remove any potential issues found with TTS.

When configuring the Unassigned Number functionality, you need to perform the basic tasks in the following order:

1. Import Announcement Service audio files.
2. Create announcements and Exchange auto attendants.
3. Define Unassigned Number ranges.

Importing Audio Files

If you choose to use audio files rather than TTS, these audio files need to be in a specific format and must be uploaded to the pool on which the unassigned numbers are defined. An audio file needs to be either a WAV file or a Windows Media Audio (WMA) file. For WAV files, the following characteristics need to be met:

- 8- or 16-bit file
- Linear pulse code modulation (LPCM), A-Law or mu-Law
- Mono or stereo
- 4MB or less

For WMA files, no specific limitations are imposed on the file by Skype for Business. However, you should consider the bit rate because the higher the bit rate, the greater the load placed on the servers.

The announcement file is not directly uploaded; instead, the cmdlet requires a byte array representation of the file. This byte array is created using the `Get-Content` cmdlet; this is used with the `Import-CsAnnouncementFile` cmdlet to upload the file. Here's an example:

```
$AnnFile = Get-Content ".\AnnouncementFile.wav"
-ReadCount 0
-Encoding Byte
Import-CsAnnouncementFile -Parent ApplicationServer:se01.rlscomms.net
-FileName "AnnouncementFile.wav"
-Content $AnnFile
```

This stores the contents of `AnnouncmentFile.wav` as a byte array in the `$AnnFile`. This is then imported using the second command and stored as `AnnouncementFile.wav`. The `FileName` value specified needs to be unique and does not need to match the name of the file you are uploading.

When the file has been uploaded, you can configure the call treatments. Next, we'll discuss only the configuration of the Announcement Service, as Exchange Unified Messaging is covered in Chapter 22.

Announcement Service

When using `New-CsAnnouncement`, there are a number of ways to create new announcements depending on what is required. Each method, of course, has different configuration options. At a minimum, all announcement will use these parameters:

- `Identity`
- `Name`

`Identity` is the FQDN of the Skype for Business pool on which the announcement should be created, prefixed with `ApplicationServer:`. `Name` is the name of the Announcement Service.

If an announcement is created with only these settings, the caller will hear a busy tone. If you need to create an announcement using an announcement file that you have previously uploaded, you will also need to use `AudioFilePrompt`.

If you want to create an announcement using TTS, then in addition to `Identity` and `Name`, you need to use the following:

- `Language`
- `TextToSpeechPrompt`

For each of these three options, you can add an additional parameter, `TargetURI`, which will transfer the caller to the SIP URI, telephone number, or voice mailbox specified. Each of these must be specified as a SIP URI, as in the examples shown in Table 19.3.

Table 19.3: Transfer options examples

Type	Example
SIP URI	`sip:joe.bloggs@rlscomms.net`
Telephone number	`sip: +14255553250;user=phone`
Voice mailbox	`sip:joe.bloggs@rlscomms.net;opaque=app:voicemail`

Defining Unassigned Number Ranges

When the call treatments have been created, you can define the Unassigned Number ranges. They can be created through the Control Panel (Voice Features ➢ Unassigned Numbers) or through PowerShell; no additional configuration options are exposed through PowerShell. To create a new number range, use the `New-CsUnassignedNumber` cmdlet, which has the following options:

- `AnnouncementName`: This is the announcement name.
- `AnnouncementService`: This is the Announcement Service used.

- `ExUMAutoAttendantPhoneNumber`: This is the Exchange Auto Attendant phone number.
- `NumberRangeStart`: This is the range start number.
- `NumberRangeEnd`: This is the range end number.
- `Priority`: This is used if number ranges overlap; if they do, the announcement with the highest priority will be used.

All of these parameters are required, except `Priority`, which is required only if you have overlapping number ranges. Note that when managing unassigned numbers through the Control Panel, there is no priority field; instead, priorities are managed by manipulating the order of the numbers using the Move Up and Move Down options, shown in Figure 19.19.

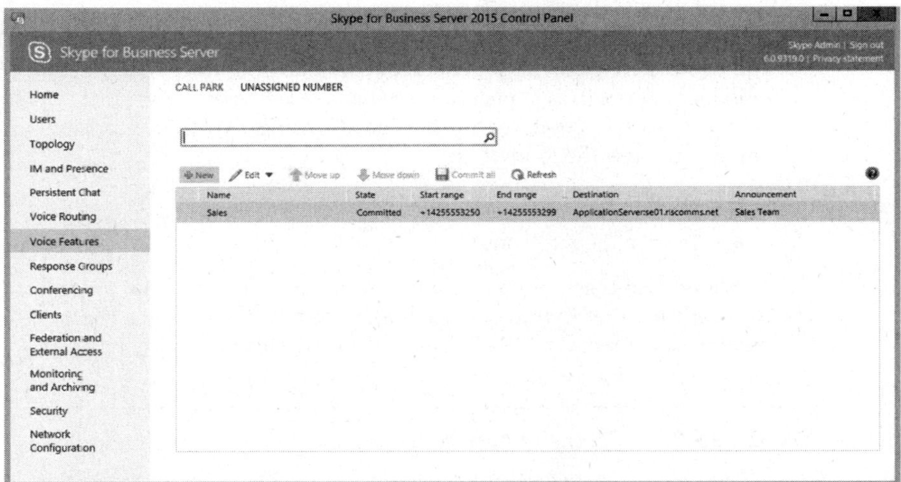

FIGURE 19.19 Managing unassigned numbers via Control Panel

The Announcement Service is the FQDN of the pool on which the announcement should be created, prefixed with `ApplicationServer:`. If you are also using TTS, this should match the pool to which the audio file was uploaded.

The number range start and end numbers must comply with the following:

- The range must match this regular expression:

```
(tel:)?(\+)?[1-9]\d{0,17}(;ext=[1-9]\d{0,9})?
```

- The end number must be equal to or greater than the start number.

The regular expression breaks down as follows:

- The regular expression starts with a `tel:`—although if it doesn't, it will automatically be added.
- This can then optionally have a + following it.

- This is followed by a digit, 1 to 9.
- This is followed by up to 17 digits.
- This can then be followed by `;ext=`, 1 to 9, and then up to nine additional digits if the organization uses a single DDI and an extension range.

In addition to the requirements set out by the regular expression, when the extension field is used, the start and end numbers must be the same number because the extension field is used to define the number range in use. Table 19.4 lists some examples.

TABLE 19.4: Sample unassigned number ranges

START NUMBER	END NUMBER
`+18500`	`+18600`
`18500`	`18600`
`+18500;ext=8000`	`+18500;ext=8999`

Now that you have seen how unassigned numbers operate and the options for configuring them within Skype for Business, let's look at how you can implement them.

Implementing Unassigned Numbers

You're ready to build a configuration based on the following scenario:

No caller should receive an unknown number response when calling into your organization. Calls to all numbers will be answered and routed as appropriate. Where there is no specific requirement, calls will be routed to an auto attendant. Calls to any numbers that used to be assigned to a sales representative will be sent to the attendants after the caller has been told they are being redirected. The sales department has its own allocated range.

Organization DDI Range: +14255551000 to +14255559999

Sales Department DDIs: +14255553250 to +14255553299

From this scenario, you determine the following:

- You need to create an Unassigned Number range to cover all numbers.
- You need to set up an Exchange Auto Attendant.
- You need to create an Unassigned Number range for the sales departments.
- You need to set up an announcement for the sales team that will play a message to any caller who dials an unused number, such as a former salesperson's number, and then redirect the call to the Attendants Response Group.

As with other configurations, you need to make sure you perform these tasks in the correct order. The call treatments must be set up before the Unassigned Number configuration. Configuring the Auto Attendant in Exchange is outside the scope of this book, but for this example assume it exists and has an associated phone number of +14255551010.

In Skype for Business Server, you first need to create the announcement for the sales team. This will be performed using the Announcement Service and can be done only via PowerShell.

```
New-CsAnnouncement -Identity "ApplicationServer:se01.rlscomms.net"
-Name "Sales Team"
-TargetURI "sip:AttendantRGS@rlscomms.net"
-TextToSpeechPrompt
"Thank you for calling a member of the sales team, please
be patient while we redirect you to an attendant"
-Language "en-US"
```

This creates a new announcement using text-to-speech and routes calls to the Attendants Response Group; it will also produce output similar to this:

```
Identity           : Service:ApplicationServer:se01.rlscomms.net
                      /07086c48-0bc5-4ce2-a6f4-f85c369a9
Name               : Sales Team
AudioFilePrompt    :
TextToSpeechPrompt : Thank you for calling a member of the sales team, please
                      be patient while we redirect you to an attendant
Language           : en-US
TargetUri          : sip:AttendantRGS@rlscomms.net
AnnouncementId     : 0786c48-0bc5-4ce2-a6f4-f85c369a91dc
```

Now that you've created the announcement, you can create the unassigned numbers. Although you can do this through the Control Panel, continue to use PowerShell for the example. Because of the requirement to overlap the number ranges, you need to ensure that the `Priority` field is specified, which will allow for the sales unassigned number to supersede the organization one. Here are the final commands:

```
New-CsUnassignedNumber -Identity "All Numbers"
-NumberRangeStart "+14255551000"
-NumberRangeEnd "+14255559999" -Priority 2
-ExUmAutoAttendantPhoneNumber "+14255551010"
```

This creates an Unassigned Number configuration for all the numbers the organization uses by specifying the entire number range, and it routes all calls to the Exchange Auto Attendant.

```
New-CsUnassignedNumber -Identity "Sales"
-NumberRangeStart "+14255553250"
-NumberRangeEnd "+14255553299" -Priority 1
-AnnouncementService "ApplicationServer:se01.rlscomms.net"
-AnnouncementName "Sales Team"
```

This creates the Unassigned Number configuration for the sales team number range and routes them to the announcement that was created earlier, thereby producing output similar to this:

```
AnnouncementServiceId   : ApplicationServer:se01.rlscomms.net
AnnouncementServerFqdn  : se01.rlscomms.net
AnnouncementName        : Sales Team
```

```
AnnouncementId          : 07086c48-0bc5-4ce2-a6f4-f85c369a91dc
Identity                : Sales
NumberRangeStart        : tel:+14255553250
NumberRangeEnd          : tel:+14255553299
Priority                : 1
```

This completes the Unassigned Number configuration; to check the configuration, run the corresponding `Get` commands.

The Bottom Line

Understand the extended voice functionality. Extended voice functionality provides additional voice applications that many organizations expect a PBX to have. Understanding what these applications can and cannot do is important so you can make the correct decisions when implementing them and know when a third-party solution is better.

Master It The manager for an internal help desk has been to a trade show and has been told he needs to have a full contact center to implement certain requirements. All he needs is to route calls to agents. He does not care about reporting or recording; he just needs to make sure that calls get to the right people. He is adamant that he needs a call center because this is what the experts have told him.

Design solutions using extended voice functionality. Designing is usually seen as a boring, time-consuming task, when all you want to do is get your hands dirty and implement something. Although some of the extended voice functionality is straightforward, other elements are complex, and missing the design stage could cause you problems later. Design, design, design—and implement once.

Master It You need to implement a dial-in conferencing solution globally. You need to have global dial-in numbers and support at least 100 concurrent PSTN calls to the conferencing solution.

Implement extended voice functionality. Lync's extended voice functionality is useless if you do not know how to implement it and use it to its fullest potential. To do that, you need to make sure that what you implement works and is fully tested.

Master It You have implemented Call Park, but users are complaining about intermittent issues with parking calls. The complaints are coming from all user types, which is strange because not all users should be able to park calls.

Chapter 20

SQL Server

Since the first installation of Live Communications Server 2003, UC administrators have had to know how to use SQL Server. That need has varied from simple to more complex; sometimes the application can write it for you "under the covers," and other times you need to know its inner workings so you can access its rich data in order to understand just who your users are. In this chapter, we'll focus on the different needs of SQL Server within the Skype for Business environment, including the SQL Server installed on every server, the back-end SQL Server, and the SQL Server needs for storing and archiving.

In this chapter, you will learn to

- Understand the different SQL Server needs within Skype for Business
- Understand the different options available for providing high availability
- Understand how to migrate to SQL Server AlwaysOn
- Understand the data stored within the various SQL Server databases

Versions of SQL Server

Several variations of SQL Server are available, and this is even more true when you start to consider specific version naming (that is, when Desktop became Express). For the sake of brevity, we'll focus on the latest available version at the time of writing (SQL Server 2014) and how it meets the needs of Skype for Business. Where necessary, such as when highlighting steps to migrate from a previous version, we'll call out specific version information, but otherwise, you can assume SQL Server 2014 is the version in use in this chapter, with no service pack applied.

SQL Server comes in the following versions, each targeted at specific types of application or application need.

- SQL Server Express
- SQL Server Standard
- SQL Server Enterprise

Skype for Business servers will install SQL Server Express on every server (we'll go into the specifics of what each database does later in this chapter); you'll need SQL Server Standard or Enterprise for the back end, and you'll need the SQL Server Analysis and Reporting tools to allow you to analyze and present data. Remember, of course, the Skype for Business Standard Edition server has a self-contained installation and actually uses SQL Server Express to provide its back-end database.

When dealing with the Skype for Business back end or wider archiving needs, you can configure and install SQL Server in one of three ways.

- Stand-alone SQL Server
- SQL Server mirroring
- SQL Server AlwaysOn Availability Groups

NOTE Stand-alone SQL Server covers two options: truly stand-alone SQL Server and clustered SQL Server. In both cases, there is the appearance of only a single server to the Skype for Business topology; there's no additional configuration required.

Table 20.1 lists the capabilities offered by the different configurations of SQL Server.

TABLE 20.1: SQL Server configuration capabilities

FEATURE	STAND-ALONE/ CLUSTERED	MIRRORING	ALWAYSON AVAILABILITY GROUP
Copies of databases	One	Two	Up to three
Location of data	Local/shared disk (if clustered)	Local	Local
High availability	Clustering enables redundancy at server level	Manual; automatic with witness	Automatic
Cost*	Minimal	Moderate	High
SQL Server edition	Standard or Enterprise	Standard or Enterprise	Enterprise only
Database high-availability requirements		Same version of SQL Server Same edition of SQL Server	Same version of SQL Server Same edition of SQL Server Same name for Instance Same file structure for database folders/files

** The specific cost incurred will depend upon your own licensing agreement with Microsoft.*

The Microsoft SQL Server product group has stated in the past that support for SQL Server mirroring is being deprecated and replaced with support for SQL Server AlwaysOn Availability Groups. However, mirroring is still in the most recently released version of SQL Server and considered by many Unified Communications consultants to be the easiest to configure.

Table 20.2 shows the supported installation options for the currently available (and supported) versions of the Microsoft Unified Communications platforms.

TABLE 20.2: SQL Server and Microsoft UC support matrix

	STAND-ALONE	CLUSTERING	MIRRORING	ALWAYSON
Lync Server 2010	SQL Server 2008 R2 SP2	SQL Server 2008 R2 SP2	Not supported	Not supported
Lync Server 2013	SQL Server 2008 R2 SP2 SQL Server 2012 SP1	SQL Server 2008 R2 SP2 SQL Server 2012 SP1	SQL Server 2008 R2 SP2 SQL Server 2012 SP1	Not supported
Skype for Business Server 2015	SQL Server 2008 R2 SP2 SQL Server 2012 SP1 SQL Server 2014	SQL Server 2008 R2 SP2 SQL Server 2012 SP1 SQL Server 2014	SQL Server 2008 R2 SP2 SQL Server 2012 SP1 SQL Server 2014	SQL Server 2012 SP1 SQL Server 2014

Table 20.3 shows the recommended hardware for installing SQL Server as a back-end database.

TABLE 20.3: SQL Server Recommended Hardware

HARDWARE COMPONENT	RECOMMENDED
CPU	64-bit dual processor, hex core, 2.26 gigahertz
Memory	32 GB
Disk	8 or more 10000 RPM hard disk drives with at least 72 GB of free disk space. 2 disks configured with RAID 1 and 6 with RAID 10 (or solid state drives providing the same performance and capacity)
Network	1 dual-port network adapter, 1 Gbps or higher

Installing SQL Server Express

SQL Server Express is the easiest of the lot to install, mostly because the setup application will do the job for you, whether it's installing the first Standard Edition server or installing any other server role in the organization.

Figure 20.1 shows the SQL Server instances installed in the first server in the organization. This must be a Standard Edition server and must also be holding the Central Management Store (CMS) role and database.

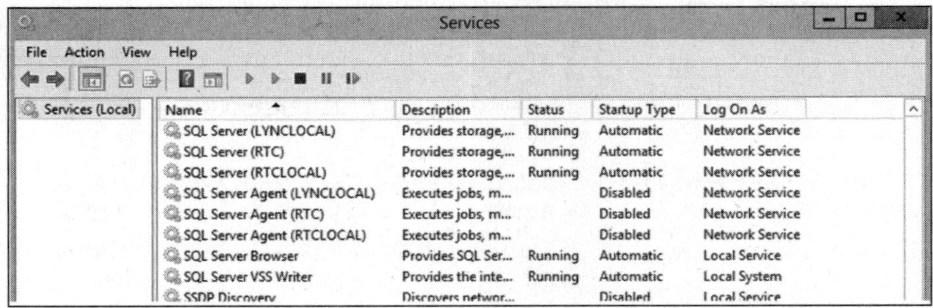

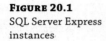

FIGURE 20.1
SQL Server Express instances

As you can see, the following instances are installed:

- `RTC`, holding the master CMS information
- `RTCLOCAL`, holding the replica of the CMS information
- `LYNCLOCAL`, holding the local user information

We'll cover the databases in more detail later in this chapter.

INSTALLING THE CMS ON A STANDARD EDITION

When installing the first Standard Edition server, the CMS instance (RTC) is created and installed for you in a SQL Server Express instance. When it comes to providing pool pairing on this pool, you need to consider the need to install an instance for the RTC databases on the second Standard Edition.

As it turns out, you can use the Install First Standard Edition Server Wizard to do the process for you. Indeed, it's much easier doing this than going through the manual process of installing a SQL Server Express instance and correctly configuring it.

As well as installing via the Deployment Wizard, either using the Install First Standard Edition Server Wizard or using the Install Local Configuration Store Wizard, it's possible to install manually using the following command-line text (this will also install to the D drive rather than the default system drive):

```
SQL ServerEXPR_x64.exe /QUIET /IACCEPTSQL ServerSERVERLICENSETERMS /HIDECONSOLE
 /ACTION=Install /FEATURES=SQL ServerEngine,Tools /INSTANCENAME=RTC
 /TCPENABLED=1 /SQL ServerSVCACCOUNT="NT AUTHORITY\NetworkService" /SQL
ServerSYSADMINACCOUNTS="Builtin\Administrators"
 /BROWSERSVCSTARTUPTYPE="Automatic" /AGTSVCACCOUNT="NT AUTHORITY\NetworkService"
/SQL ServerSVCSTARTUPTYPE=Automatic
```

```
/INSTANCEDIR="D:\CSDATA" /INSTALLSHAREDDIR="D:\Program Files\Microsoft SQL
Server Server" /INSTALLSHAREDWOWDIR="D:\Program Files (x86)\Microsoft SQL Server
Server">
```

You may want to use this if you want to customize some settings in the installation, such as instance name or install drive location. However, we recommend against customizing the instance names because when you come to troubleshoot in the future, it adds another level of complexity.

Installing a SQL Server Stand-Alone or Clustered Server

We won't detail step-by-step the configuration for installing SQL Server because the process is pretty self-explanatory. Rather, we'll cover the specifics behind the Skype for Business configuration aspects, and we will call out the additional steps needed for the more complex configuration items where necessary.

Within Skype for Business, there's no difference between assigning a SQL Server back end that has been installed on a single server or one that has been installed on a cluster. The cluster is presented as a "virtual" server, and its name would be used to define the FQDN for the pool.

From within Topology Builder, navigate to the Shared Components branch of the site in which you want to define the SQL Server and right-click the SQL Server stores branch, selecting New SQL Server Store. The window shown in Figure 20.2 will appear, ready to be completed.

FIGURE 20.2
Defining a new SQL Server component

If you check the High Availability Settings box and investigate the drop-down, you'll see Clustered SQL Server is not listed as an option. From the perspective of Skype for Business, it is unaware of the high availability provided by the cluster and has no additional configuration to carry out.

We'll cover the high availability options in the next few sections of this chapter. For now, complete the configuration of the SQL Server settings (the FQDN and possibly the instance name if configured). Figure 20.3 shows the SQL Server configured within Topology Builder.

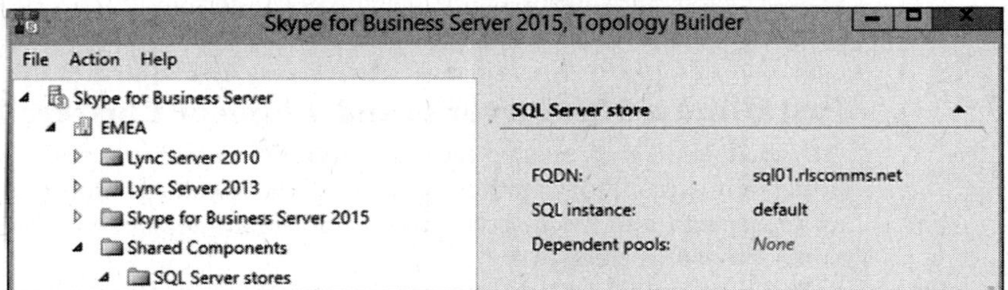

FIGURE 20.3 SQL Server configuration in Topology Builder

You'll notice there is no dependent pool defined. This is because you created the SQL Server instance directly within the SQL Server Stores section. If you were creating a pool and were prompted for the SQL Server as part of the pool definition, this would already be populated. This field is what Topology Builder uses to check whether it is safe to delete the SQL Server instance from the topology.

Figure 20.4 shows this process. We've already selected our previously created SQL Server instance, but if you hadn't already created this, you could click New and go through the SQL Server wizard.

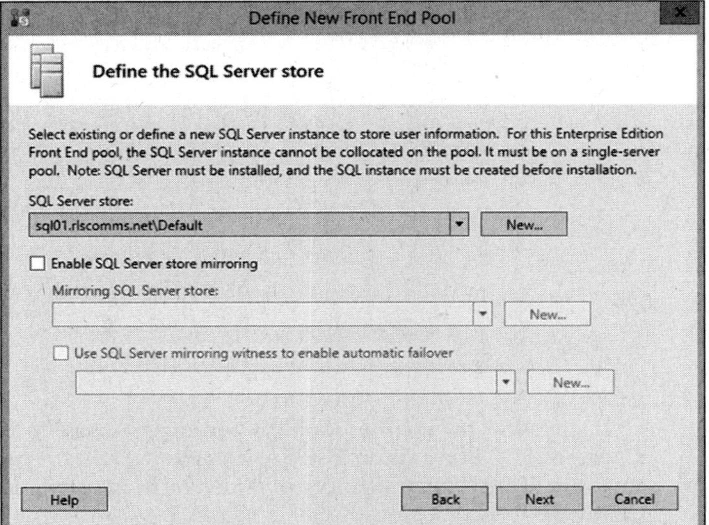

FIGURE 20.4 Defining the SQL Server pool as part of the Enterprise Edition pool definition

Figure 20.5 shows the SQL Server instance with the dependent pool association.

FIGURE 20.5
Dependent pool association for SQL Server

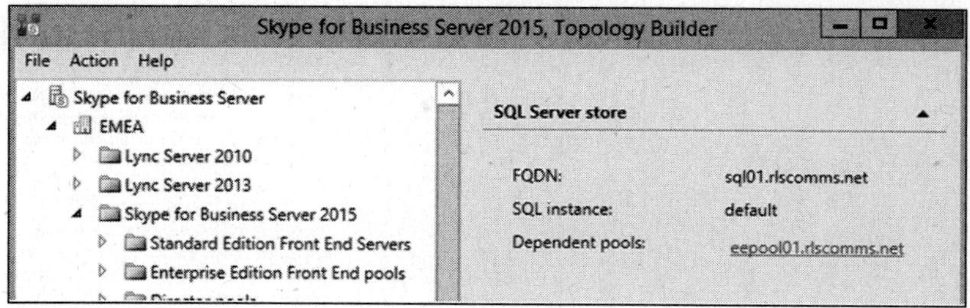

As with previous changes to the topology, they are not committed until the topology is published. So, go ahead and publish. Once the verification process is completed, the Select Databases window appears, as shown in Figure 20.6.

FIGURE 20.6
Select Databases window

Publish Topology

Select databases

The databases listed below are a part of your topology, but they have either not been created or upgraded on your SQL Server yet. If you have the appropriate permission in SQL Server, you can choose to create or upgrade the databases when your topology is published. If you do not have the appropriate permissions (or you are just not sure), you can have someone with appropriate SQL Server permissions create or update these databases later.

Choose the databases you would like to create when you publish your topology:

	Store	Site	Database paths
☑	sql01.rlscomms.net\Def...	EMEA	Automatically determine database file locat...

Advanced...

Note: This wizard will only install databases on dedicated SQL Servers. If you want to install a database on a SQL Server that is collocated with other server roles, you'll need to run Skype for Business Server 2015 setup on the server. And you need to install the same version of the Skype for Business Server Management Shell as the server component associated with the database. So the Lync Server 2010 Management Shell would be used for Lync Server 2010 components, while the Lync Server 2013 Management Shell would be used for Lync Server 2013 components.

Help | Back | Next | Cancel

Here you can choose specific configuration for each of the newly defined databases in the topology. Selecting the database and clicking Advanced will give you the options shown in Figure 20.7, allowing for manual configuration of where the database files will be stored.

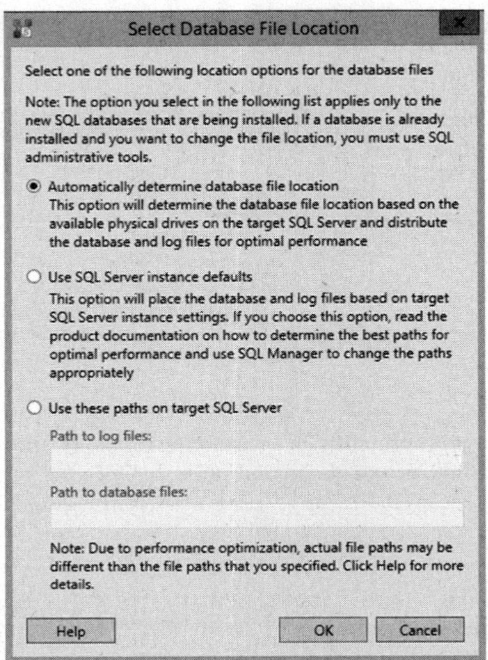

FIGURE 20.7
Selecting the file paths for the databases

Once you're happy with your choices here, the topology process will connect to the SQL Server instance specified and build your databases as defined. Often this connection is blocked by the default firewall rules on SQL Server, so make sure they are configured correctly to allow connections.

When configuring a SQL Server cluster, each node is required to have the firewall rules configured, although the database setup is written only to the active node. Failover may occur at any point.

That's it! SQL Server is now actively supporting the pool and ready to go.

Installing a Mirrored SQL Server Pair

Mirroring support was introduced with Lync Server 2013 and is extremely easy to configure and get running. As with installing stand-alone SQL Server, you can define the SQL Server store either directly or as part of defining the enterprise pool. Figure 20.8 shows the options when defining directly, and Figure 20.9 shows the options when defining as part of the pool process.

FIGURE 20.8
Defining a SQL Server mirroring pair directly

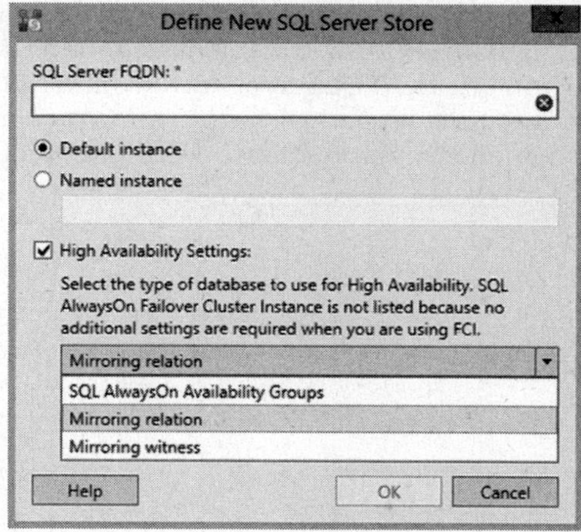

FIGURE 20.9
Defining a SQL Server mirroring pair as part of the pool definition

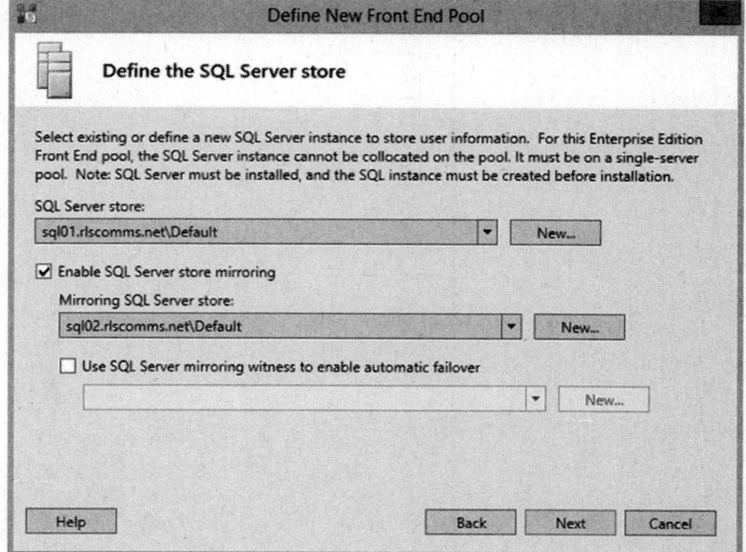

You'll notice during this process you're also asked to specify a mirror port number, with a default of 5022. This is the port through which SQL Server will connect to transfer the data to ensure the mirror is in sync. You'll see later in the chapter how (and why) to change this.

While defining this mirror relationship, you'll also notice the check box Use SQL Server Mirroring Witness To Enable Automatic Failover, as well as the opportunity to define the SQL Server witness. This SQL Server mirror witness can be any edition of SQL Server (even SQL Server Express is supported) and is used to provide quorum to determine the capability for automatic failover. Figure 20.10 shows this configuration.

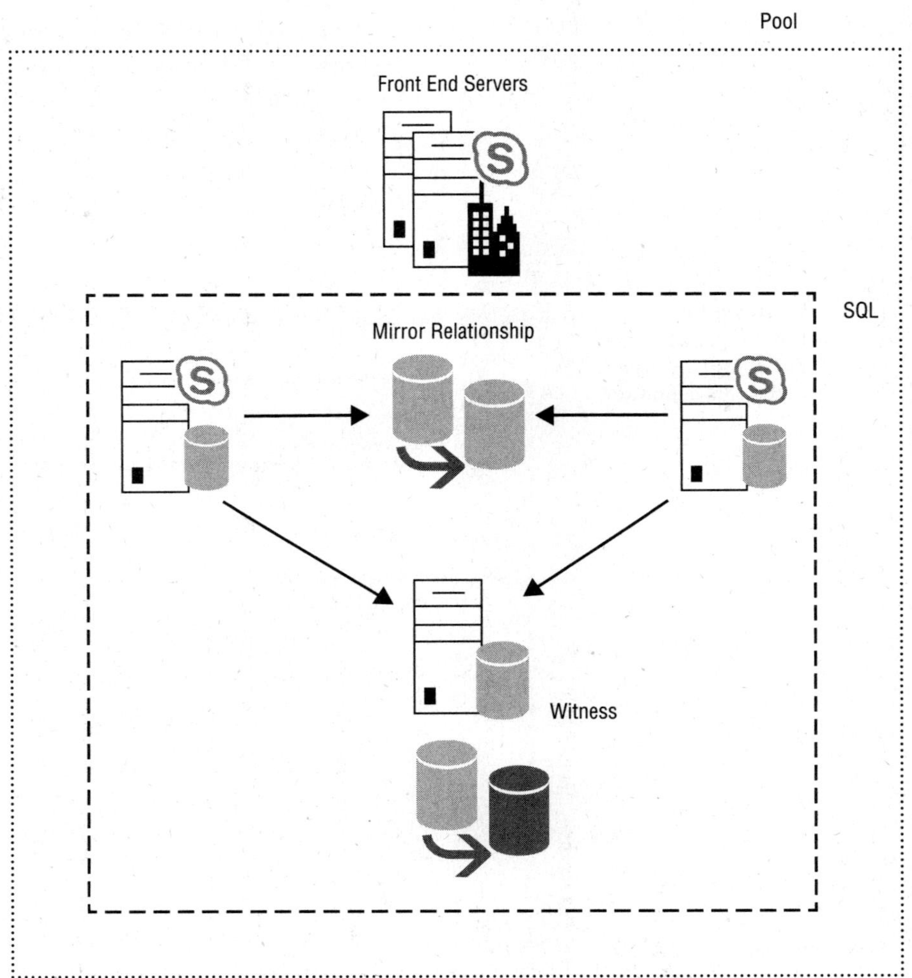

FIGURE 20.10 SQL Server mirror witness to enable automatic failover

If you predefine the SQL Server configuration and then add mirroring later, you will need to go back and define the mirror port required. Figure 20.11 shows the error highlighted by Topology Builder.

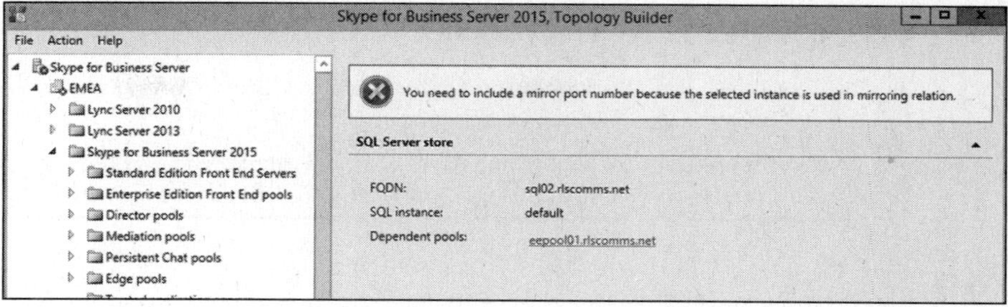

FIGURE 20.11 Missing mirror port number error

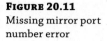

As with the stand-alone SQL Server configuration, you'll get the Select Databases window (Figure 20.6). This time, however, after clicking Next, you'll get prompted with the Create Mirror Databases screen (Figure 20.12), which requires a fileshare.

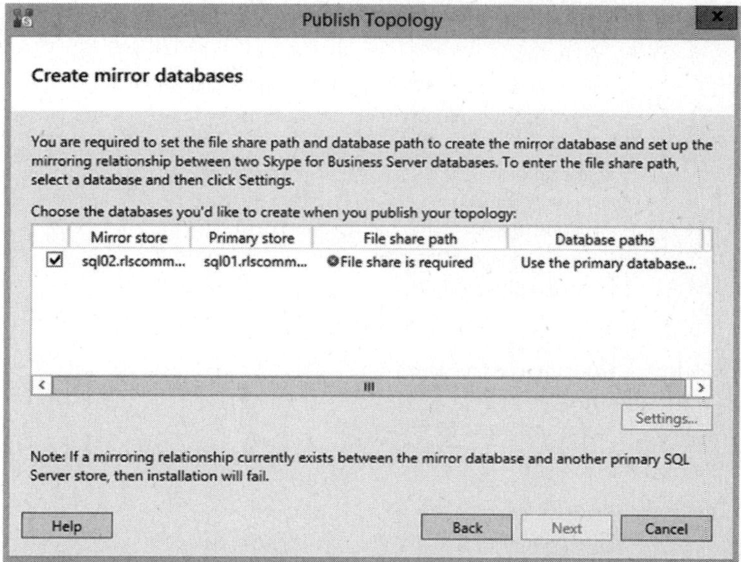

FIGURE 20.12 Prompt for fileshare

When SQL Server is building the mirror relationship for the first time, it is backing up the data to files and transferring it to the mirrored pair via the fileshare. Even though, in this case, you're building a new pool, the process ensures that this can be used on a pool previously built and ensures high availability.

> **The SQL Server Fileshare**
>
> Use a new, dedicated fileshare for this process. Once the initial mirror is created, this fileshare is no longer needed and can be deleted.
>
> Do not use DFS. The replication process of DFS can interfere with the mirroring initialization, and files can be missed. In addition, by default, DFS will not replicate the backup file types.

Once the SQL Server store is defined, the publish process will complete, and assuming the firewalls are configured correctly and the share is reachable, the mirroring will be set up.

Managing Mirrored Databases

To check the status of the SQL Server mirror, you can use the `Get-CsDatabaseMirrorState` cmdlet.

```
Get-CsDatabaseMirrorState -PoolFqdn eepool01.rlscomms.net
```

The output is as follows:

```
DatabaseName               : rtcab
StateOnPrimary             : Principal
StateOnMirror              : Mirror
MirroringStatusOnPrimary : synchronized
MirroringStatusOnMirror  : synchronized

DatabaseName               : rtcxds
StateOnPrimary             : Principal
StateOnMirror              : Mirror
MirroringStatusOnPrimary : synchronized
MirroringStatusOnMirror  : synchronized

DatabaseName               : rtcshared
StateOnPrimary             : Principal
StateOnMirror              : Mirror
MirroringStatusOnPrimary : synchronized
MirroringStatusOnMirror  : synchronized

DatabaseName               : rgsconfig
StateOnPrimary             : Principal
StateOnMirror              : Mirror
MirroringStatusOnPrimary : synchronized
MirroringStatusOnMirror  : synchronized

DatabaseName               : rgsdyn
StateOnPrimary             : Principal
StateOnMirror              : Mirror
MirroringStatusOnPrimary : synchronized
```

```
MirroringStatusOnMirror   : synchronized

DatabaseName              : cpsdyn
StateOnPrimary            : Principal
StateOnMirror             : Mirror
MirroringStatusOnPrimary : synchronized
MirroringStatusOnMirror   : synchronized
```

You'll notice that the `StateOnPrimary` setting defines the value as `Principal`, and `StateOnMirror` is `Mirror`. This confirms the databases are configured as you have defined within the topology. Also, `MirroringStatusOnPrimary` and `MirroringStatusOnMirror` both report `synchronized`, meaning they are all up-to-date.

In the event of an issue, you can force a failover (remember that with a witness configured, it would happen automatically). For this, you use the `Invoke-CsDatabaseFailover` command.

```
Invoke-CsDatabaseFailover -PoolFQDN eepool01.rlscomms.net
-DatabaseType User -NewPrincipal Mirror
```

This results in the following output:

```
DatabaseName                                         FailoverResult
------------                                         --------------
rtcab                                                Success
rtcxds                                               Success
rtcshared                                            Success
```

Running the `Get-CsDatabaseState` cmdlet again will now show some databases on the principal server and some on the mirror.

```
PS SQL ServerSERVER:\> Get-CsDatabaseMirrorState -Poolfqdn eepool01.rlscomms.net

DatabaseName              : rtcab
StateOnPrimary            : Mirror
StateOnMirror             : Principal
MirroringStatusOnPrimary : synchronized
MirroringStatusOnMirror   : synchronized

DatabaseName              : rtcxds
StateOnPrimary            : Mirror
StateOnMirror             : Principal
MirroringStatusOnPrimary : synchronized
MirroringStatusOnMirror   : synchronized

DatabaseName              : rtcshared
StateOnPrimary            : Mirror
StateOnMirror             : Principal
MirroringStatusOnPrimary : synchronized
MirroringStatusOnMirror   : synchronized

DatabaseName              : rgsconfig
```

```
StateOnPrimary            : Principal
StateOnMirror             : Mirror
MirroringStatusOnPrimary : synchronized
MirroringStatusOnMirror  : synchronized

DatabaseName              : rgsdyn
StateOnPrimary            : Principal
StateOnMirror             : Mirror
MirroringStatusOnPrimary : synchronized
MirroringStatusOnMirror  : synchronized

DatabaseName              : cpsdyn
StateOnPrimary            : Principal
StateOnMirror             : Mirror
MirroringStatusOnPrimary : synchronized
MirroringStatusOnMirror  : synchronized
```

Figure 20.13 shows how this looks from within SQL Server Management Studio. You can clearly see which databases are primary and which are mirrored.

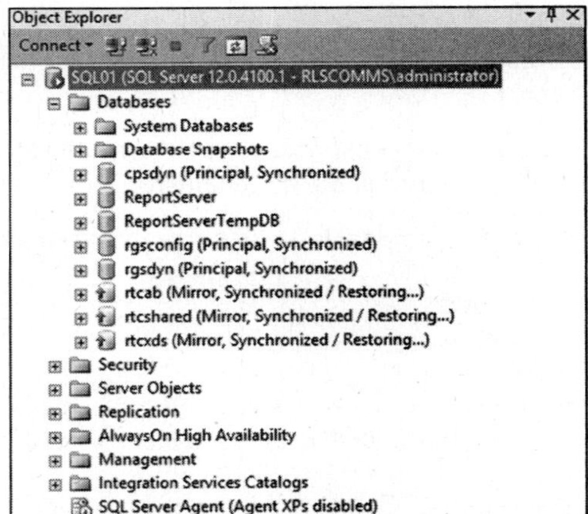

FIGURE 20.13 Using SQL Server Management Studio to view the database state

To fail back, use the following command:

```
Invoke-CsDatabaseFailover -PoolFQDN eepool01.rlscomms.net
-DatabaseType User -NewPrincipal Primary
```

This time, the NewPrincipal value is defined to be Primary, rather than Mirror.

For the other value defined here, DatabaseType, you can have the following settings:

- `ActiveMonitoring`
- `Application`
- `Archiving`

- `CentralMgmt`
- `Edge`
- `Lyss`
- `Monitoring`
- `PersistentChat`
- `PersistentChatCompliance`
- `Provision`
- `Registrar`
- `SigninTelemetry`
- `User`

You can use this failover cmdlet to fail over all databases *except* those defined by using the additional parameters `ExcludeDatabase` and `ExcludeDatabaseList`.

Managing failover can be complicated, and the configuration of the Witness server enables this process to happen automatically.

Configuring Multiple Instances

As noted, the default mirroring port is 5022. If multiple instances of SQL Server are deployed on a single server and are enabled for mirroring, they will all be trying to use port 5022 by default and will result in the error shown in Figure 20.14 when trying to build the mirror.

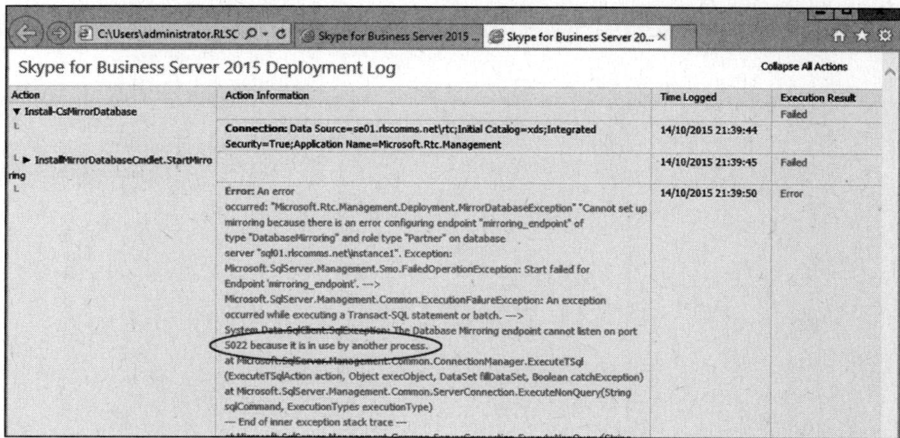

FIGURE 20.14 Port error when configuring multiple SQL Server instances for mirroring

From within SQL Server Management Studio, run the following command to confirm the ports in use. Figure 20.15 shows the results.

```
SELECT * FROM sys.tcp_endpoints
```

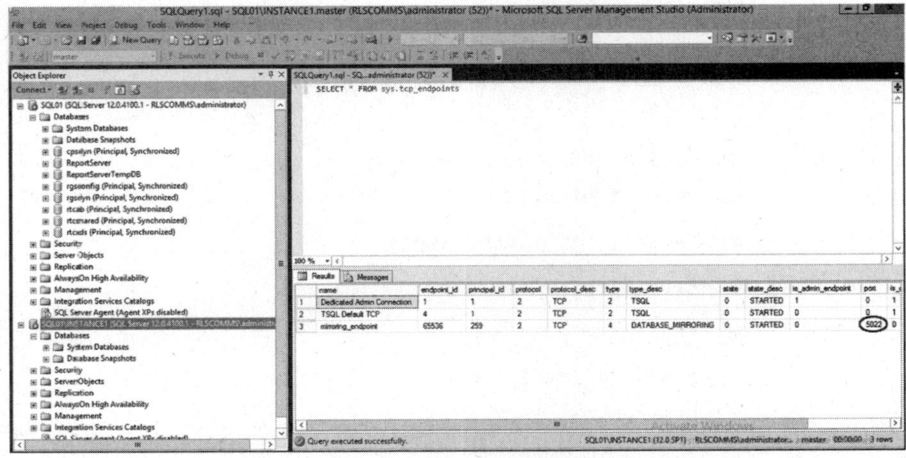

FIGURE 20.15 Checking which port SQL Server is using for mirroring

As you can see, the instance is reporting port 5022, and running the same command on the other instance will generate the same results. One of these needs to change. Once you've decided which one will change and which port it will change to (in this case we've selected 5023), you need to run the following command, again, within SQL Server Management Studio:

```
ALTER ENDPOINT [Mirroring_endpoint] AS TCP (listener_port = 5023)
```

Figure 20.16 shows the results. You're specifically looking for the response "Command(s) Completed Successfully."

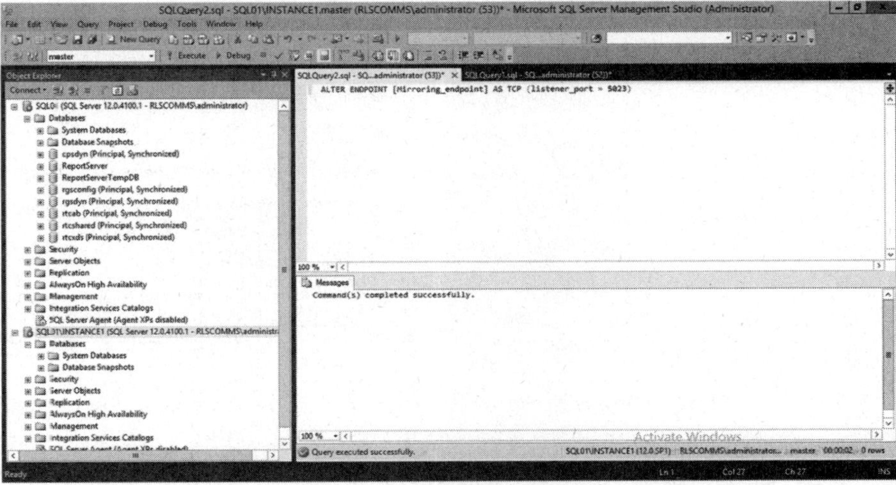

FIGURE 20.16 Updating the SQL Server mirroring endpoint

Rerunning the `SELECT * FROM sys.tcp_endpoints` command will show the updated port.

Now, you must repeat the task on the other SQL Server instance in the mirror relationship. It is possible that each SQL Server instance is using different ports. However, this starts to introduce complexity and will cause difficulties when troubleshooting, so it's best to stay consistent. Once you've updated the SQL Server instances, they will need restarting to take effect, and then you'll need to update and publish topology to reflect the port changes. Of course, if the ports had been defined uniquely in Topology Builder in the first instance, Topology Builder would've taken care of this for you. However, it's not always possible to be this well organized.

Installing AlwaysOn Availability Groups

As mentioned earlier, for some time the SQL Server product group within Microsoft has said that SQL Server mirroring will be deprecated. This means that mirroring will continue to be supported in versions of SQL Server where it is available, but a future (to be defined) version of SQL Server will no longer contain this functionality. The most recent release of SQL Server (SQL Server 2014) continues to offer the SQL Server mirroring functionality.

As mirroring continues to be supported, there is no *need* to move (although we cover a migration later in this chapter), but lots of customers automatically move to the latest versions of products to get the latest functionality.

To do so, the first thing you need to do is install SQL Server. There's no particularly special configuration needed at this stage. When you come to defining the SQL Server Server instance in the topology, this is where you need to pay close attention. As you can see in Figure 20.17, two different identities are defined.

- SQL Server Server Availability Group FQDN listener
- SQL Server Server FQDN

FIGURE 20.17 Defining the SQL Server Availability Group listener

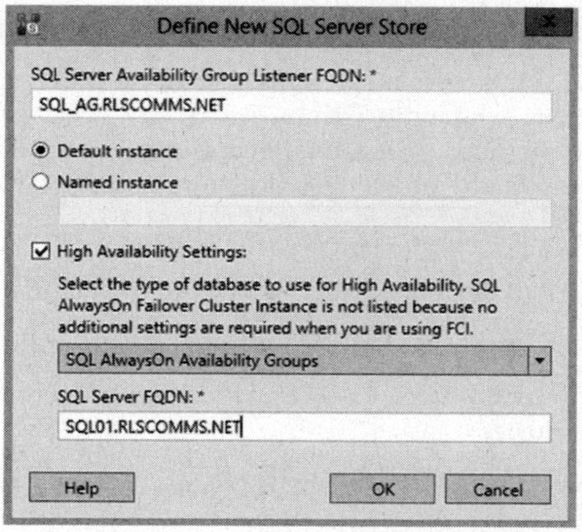

The listener address is the name of the SQL Server Server Availability Group listener. You'll see where you define this later, but it cannot be changed, so you must know it ahead of time.

The other address is the FQDN of the first SQL Server Server instance in the Availability Group. Publishing this step in Topology Builder creates the Skype for Business databases on the server listed. Figure 20.18 shows the defined SQL Server identity to be the listener name, and browsing through Topology Builder, you'll see this listener defined, rather than the specific SQL Server Server instance.

FIGURE 20.18
The SQL Server listener defined

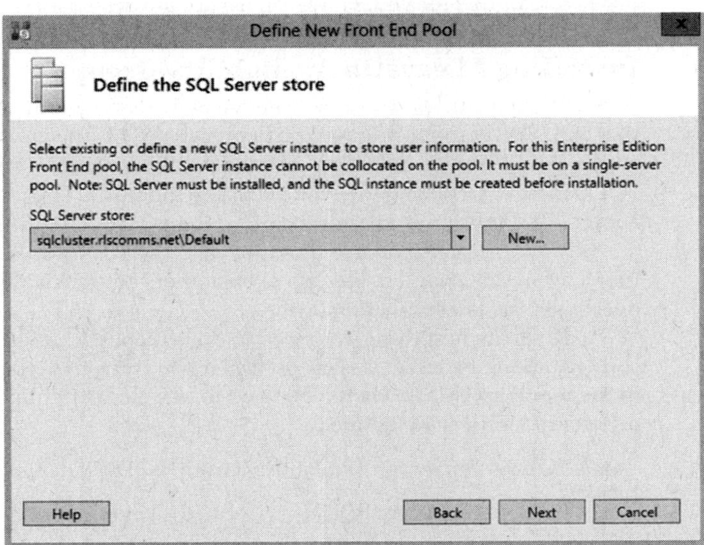

Now you have to make some changes to the operating system and SQL Server to enable the AlwaysOn Availability Groups.

First you need to install failover clustering as part of the OS, through the Add Roles and Features Wizard, or via the following PowerShell.

```
Add-WindowsFeature Failover-Clustering
```

To install the management tools, run the following:

```
Add-WindowsFeature RSAT-Clustering
```

Running the `Test-Cluster` command will return the readiness state of the nodes for creating the cluster.

```
Test-Cluster -Node SQL Server01.rlscomms.net, SQL Server02.rlscomms.net
```

Verify the status of the report and address any warnings or errors as necessary. In this particular example, there are many warnings reported for items such as only a single NIC and the speed and configuration of disks. In a production environment, it would be best to resolve these issues, but in this case we will press on.

To create the cluster, use the following PowerShell:

```
New-Cluster -Name SQL Servercluster  -Node SQL Server01.rlscomms.net, SQL
Server02.rlscomms.net -StaticAddress 192.168.3.9 -NoStorage
```

In this command, you're defining the cluster name (`SQL Servercluster`; note there's no FQDN), the nodes to join, and the IP address to use for the cluster resource. The additional parameter here, `NoStorage`, tells the cluster nodes to use only local storage. You may need to define shared storage if you have deployed that capability, but it is not a requirement; you can use a network share to provide quorum.

Check the output report for any errors or warnings. In this case, you will see a warning regarding the lack of quorum. To define your fileshare object (this fileshare must be available prior to running the command), use the following PowerShell command:

```
Set-ClusterQuorum -Cluster SQL Servercluster -NodeAndFileShareMajority
"\\dc01.rlscomms.net\clusterquorum"
```

That's it! You're all done with the operating system configuration portion. Now for the configuration within SQL Server.

First, start SQL Server Configuration Manager and navigate to SQL Server Services ➤ SQL Server (<instancename>), where <instancename> represents the name of the SQL Server instance configured. Right-click, select Properties, and then select AlwaysOn High Availability, as shown in Figure 20.19.

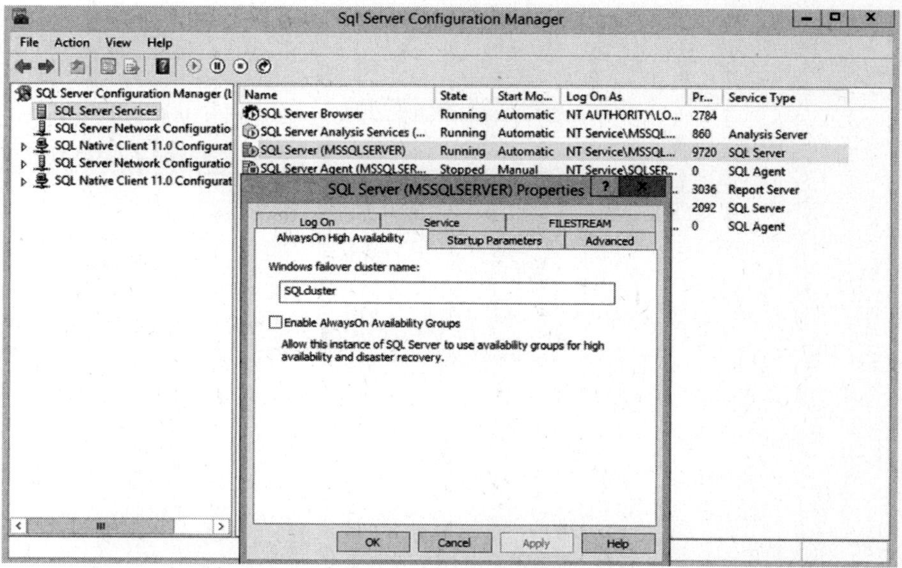

FIGURE 20.19 Enabling SQL Server AlwaysOn high availability

You'll notice the SQL Server configuration has already picked up the cluster name you defined previously. Select the Enable AlwaysOn Availability Groups check box, click OK, and then restart the SQL Server service for that instance.

Now you need to make the changes to the SQL Server instance to define and enable the AlwaysOn Availability Group. Start SQL Server Server Management Studio, and connect to the instance. Navigate to the Availability Groups branch within the Always On Availability section, right-click, and select New Availability Group Wizard. Navigate through the introduction page and define the name for the Availability Group.

At this point, you have the databases installed on the first server in the AlwaysOn Availability Group, but the databases are not yet included in an actual AlwaysOn Availability Group. The next few steps will complete this. It is important to note that you cannot create an AlwaysOn Availability Group without having at least one database to add to it. Organizations will often define an empty dummy database to allow this configuration to be put in place prior to deploying an application.

Figure 20.20 shows the Select Databases page. You'll notice you have three states.

- Meets prerequisites
- Full backup is required
- Full recovery mode is required

FIGURE 20.20
Selecting databases to add to the Availability Group.

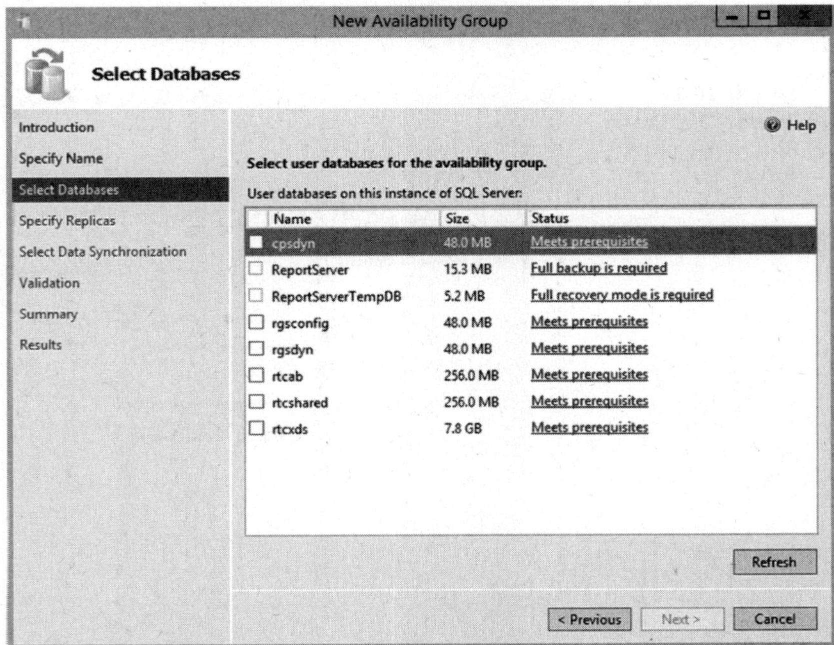

Only databases that meet the prerequisites can be added to an availability group. In this case, this is all the databases you'll add, but we'll cover how to meet those prerequisites first. The database recovery model is set on the Options tab of the database properties, as shown in Figure 20.21.

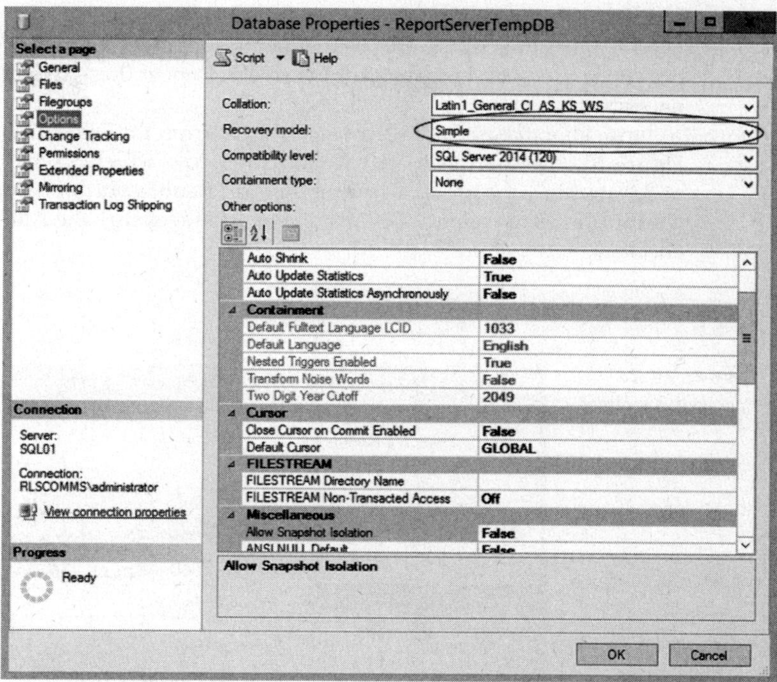

FIGURE 20.21
Changing the recovery model

Simply change this entry from Simple to Full, and click OK. Next you need to ensure the database is backed up, so open the backup task. Select the database to be backed up, right-click, select Tasks ➤ Backup, and the backup window will open, as shown in Figure 20.22.

FIGURE 20.22
Backing up the database

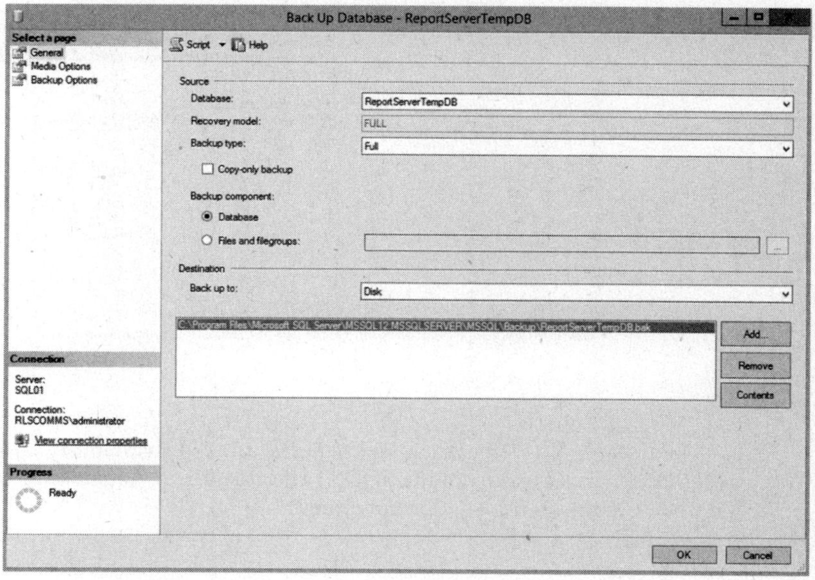

Ensure the backup type is Full and that a file is defined to back up to. You actually do not need this file; it is just to flag to the database that a backup has occurred. Click OK, and a backup successful message should appear. Repeat these two processes for each database as necessary.

Once all databases are ready, select them from the Select Databases window and click Next. Figure 20.23 shows the Specify Replicas window, which is where you will define the additional nodes within your group. Clicking the Add Replica button will prompt for the additional server (and instance) to connect to. Once that is added, ensure the Automatic Failover options are checked.

FIGURE 20.23
Specifying replicas

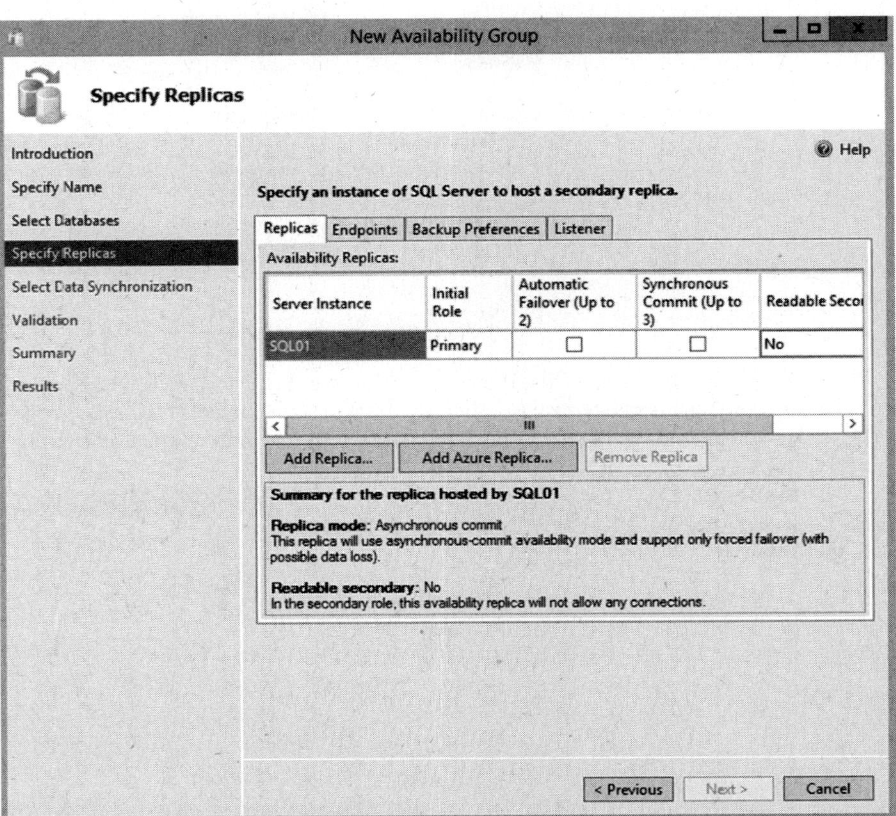

Then, select the Listener tab and select Create An Availability Group Listener. Define the listener DNS name (again, not the FQDN) and IP address. These must be created in DNS manually. Figure 20.24 shows this section completed.

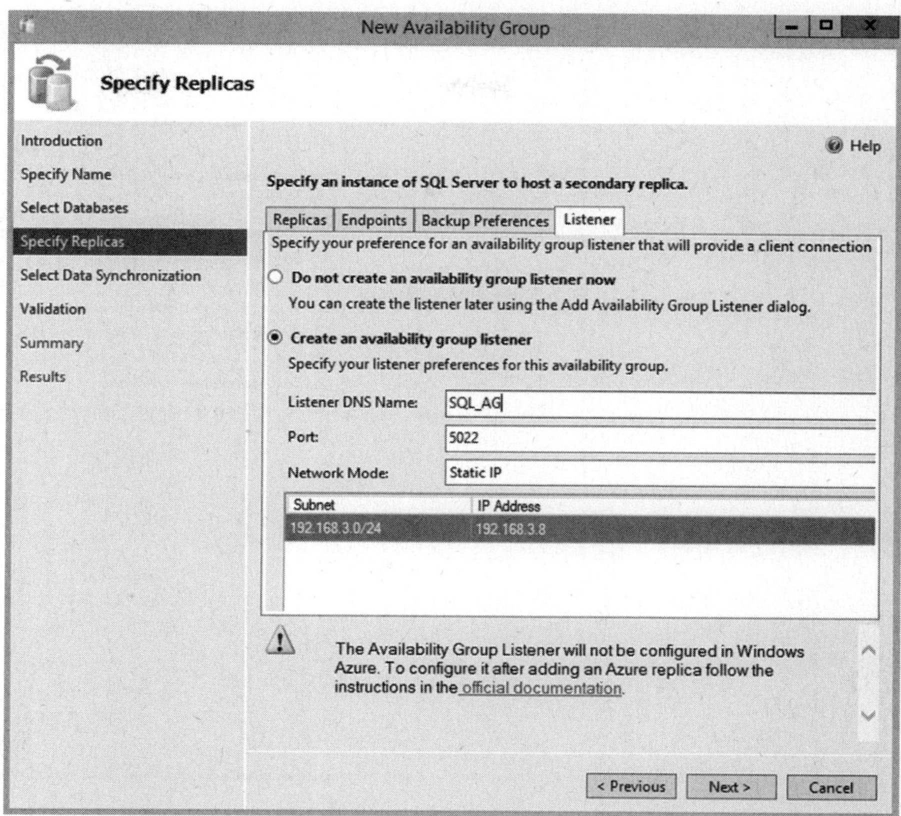

FIGURE 20.24
Defining the listener address

As with the SQL Server mirroring setup, you need a fileshare to enable initial configuration of the synchronization process. As before, do *not* use a DFS fileshare, as the synchronization files are only temporary. The fileshare is defined in the Select Data Synchronization screen. The final step is a validation check, as shown in Figure 20.25.

Here you can see there are a few errors listed. Clicking the link will give a more descriptive error message and enable you to correct them. The most common error you can see here is that the file structure on the remote node is not the same as on the local node. All directory paths and filenames must match on all nodes.

Once you have fixed the errors, click the Re-run Validation button to progress.

The final window before the Availability Group is created allows you to confirm the values chosen (databases, nodes, and on) as well as save the script if necessary, which will do the actual configuration piece. Click Finish to configure.

Viewing the instance information from within SQL Server Management Studio gives the response in Figure 20.26.

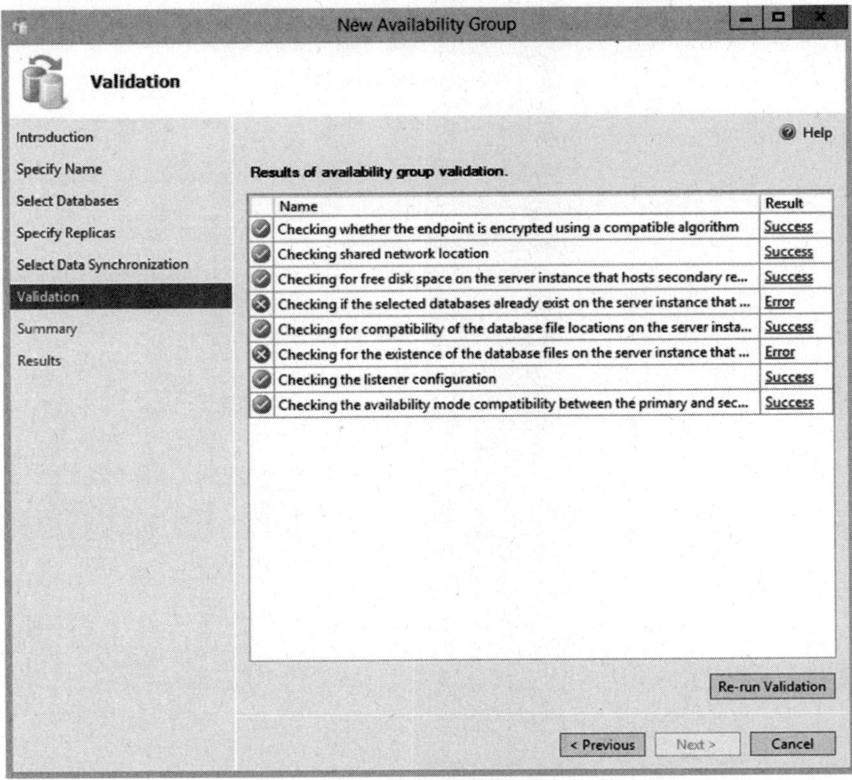

FIGURE 20.25 Availability Group validation check

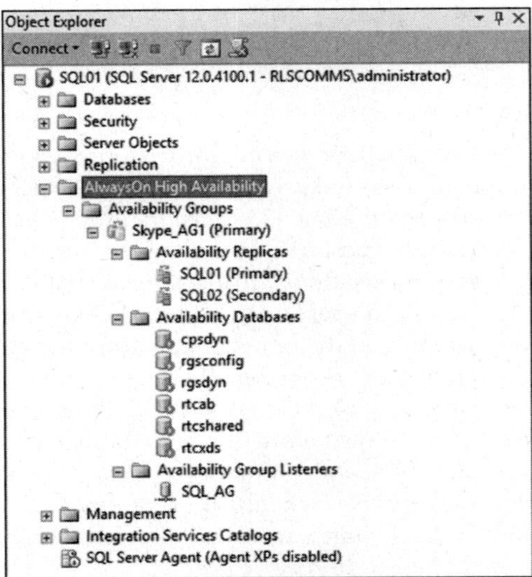

FIGURE 20.26 AlwaysOn high availability configured

From here you can control a failover if needed (you'll see this later) or simply reboot the primary server (in the case shown, `SQL Server01.RLSCOMMS.NET`) to force the failover. The advantage here is that it's an automatic failover, whereas, unless you also had the witness with mirroring, you'd have to fail over manually.

So, now that you've configured the SQL Server side of things, you need to go back and complete the Topology Builder configuration. Back in Figure 20.17 you defined the SQL Server information to be `SQL Server_AG.RLSCOMMS.NET` and the SQL Server FQDN to be `SQL Server01.RLSCOMMS.NET`. You need to go back and update this.

Open Topology Builder and modify the SQL Server store you created for the listener previously. This time you need to change the SQL Server FQDN entry to read SQL Server02.rlscomms.net (see Figure 20.27).

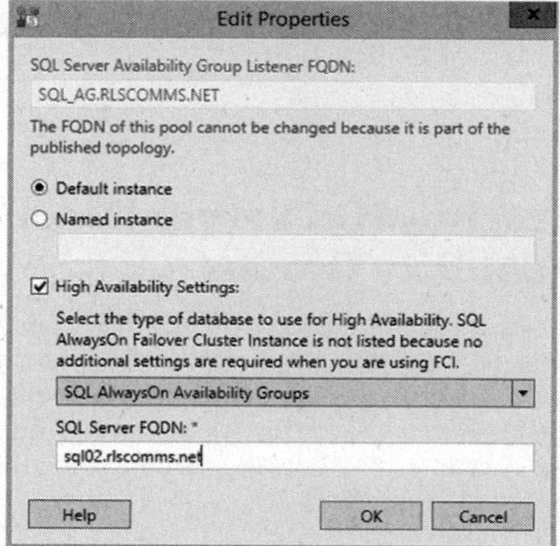

FIGURE 20.27 Updating the topology to point to the next node in the Availability Group

Before you publish this time, you need to ensure that the primary server in the Availability Group is the node you're about to publish to: `SQL Server02.rlscomms.net`. We normally do this by restarting the other node. This ensures you also address any pending restarts if there are any. Once the primary node is confirmed, go ahead and publish the topology. Repeat this process if there is a third node in the Availability Group.

Once all the nodes have been failed to and published, then you can configure the topology for its final state, where the SQL Server FQDN entry matches that of the SQL Server Availability Group listener FQDN, as shown in Figure 20.28.

Topology Builder assigns permissions to the SQL Server databases on publishing. However, when SQL Server creates the Availability Group, not all the permissions are carried over, so Topology Builder will reassign the permissions on publishing.

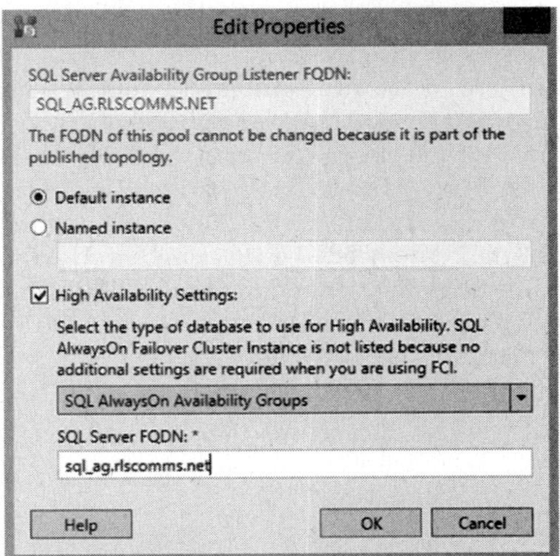

FIGURE 20.28 Final topology configuration

Migrating SQL Server Databases to AlwaysOn Availability Groups

So, we've looked at installing each of the databases, but what about migrating? Why would anyone consider migrating from mirroring to AlwaysOn?

Well, there are some advantages, such as the automated aspects (without a witness) and also the potential of having a third node in the group, providing additional high availability. Either way, let's assume you are going through the process. There a couple of prerequisites that need to be met.

- A Skype for Business Enterprise pool
- SQL Server 2012

Neither SQL Server 2008 or Lync Server supports the use of AlwaysOn Availability Groups, so you need to ensure you've addressed those first.

Using the previously defined Enterprise pool with mirrored SQL Server as an example, as shown in Figure 20.29, you will remove the mirror configuration and re-publish the topology. Simply remove the check mark from the mirroring box.

At this point, only Skype for Business is aware that the mirroring has been removed. SQL Server still has mirroring configured. Running the `Get-CsDatabaseMirrorState -PoolFqdn eepool01.rlscomms.net` command will return nothing, indicating nothing is mirrored.

SQL Server Management Studio, on the other hand, still thinks that the mirroring is in place and will continue to mirror the transactions until you remove the mirror. From within SQL Server Management Studio, connect to the instance and open the Databases branch. For each database in turn, right-click, select Properties, and then select Mirroring, as shown in Figure 20.30.

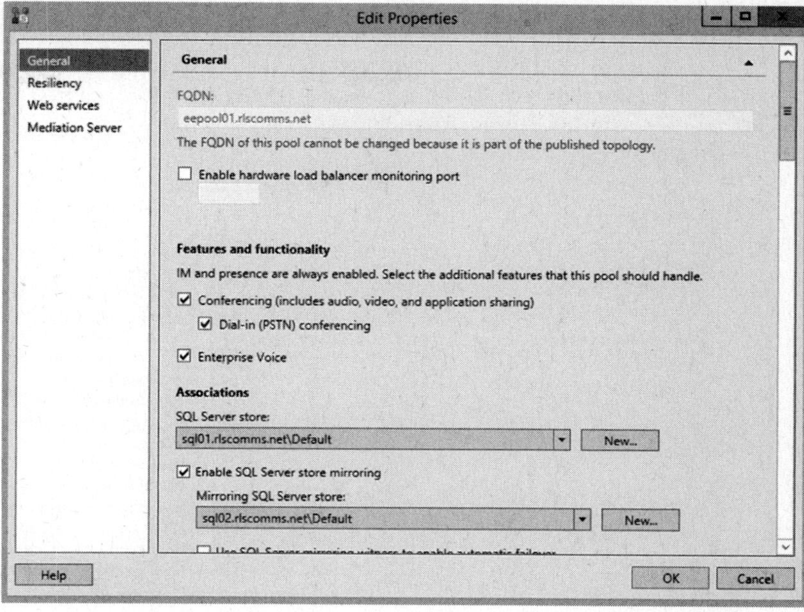

FIGURE 20.29 Removing mirroring on a pool

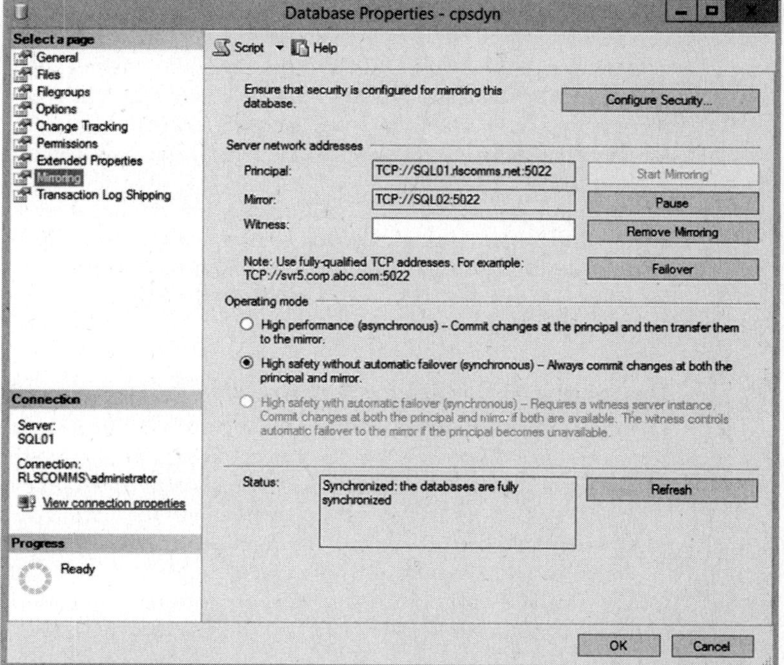

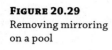

FIGURE 20.30 Removing mirroring

Depending on the configuration, there may also be a Witness server defined. Clicking Remove Mirroring will result in a warning prompt. Click Yes to confirm removal and then OK to return to the database list. Right-click the Databases branch and select Refresh. You will see the database name no longer has any mirroring information associated, as shown in Figure 20.31. Repeat this process for each database.

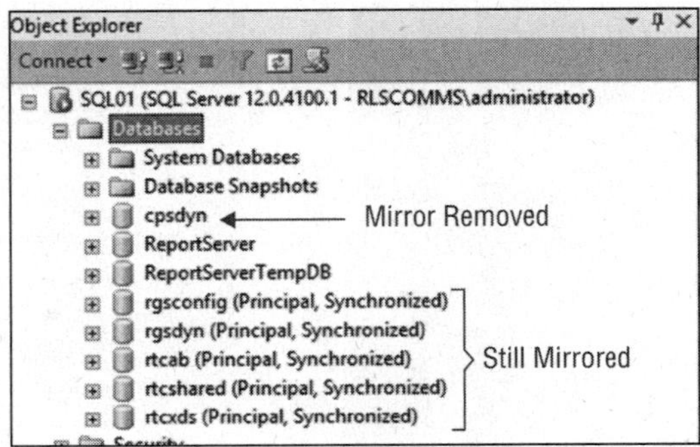

FIGURE 20.31 Comparing mirrored vs. nonmirrored databases

Now that you've removed the mirroring relationship, you need to go to the mirrored server and delete the databases. Failing to do this will result in errors, as shown in the validation process for the Availability Group (shown earlier in Figure 20.25). From within SQL Server Management Studio, you need to delete the databases from the instance, as well as delete the actual files.

Up to this point, there has been no user impact; however, there is now no longer any high availability with this pool. Moving to AlwaysOn Availability Groups now follows the same steps as described in the previous section for the installation, including the several changes to topology. This process involves a restart of the SQL Server service and so introduces an impact to users at that point only.

Updating SQL Server Databases

There are times when you will need to ensure a database is up-to-date or, indeed, predefine some objects in Topology Builder and come back later to do the actual install. Or you may forget to configure the firewall exceptions correctly after the topology publish.

Topology Builder has an option, available in the Action menu, to install or upgrade a database, which will start the install or upgrade a database wizard (see Figure 20.32).

Following this wizard will take you through the initial publishing process again, but only for the database or databases selected, not for the other aspects of publishing. If the particular database configuration (mirroring, and so on) requires a fileshare, those prompts will appear as needed.

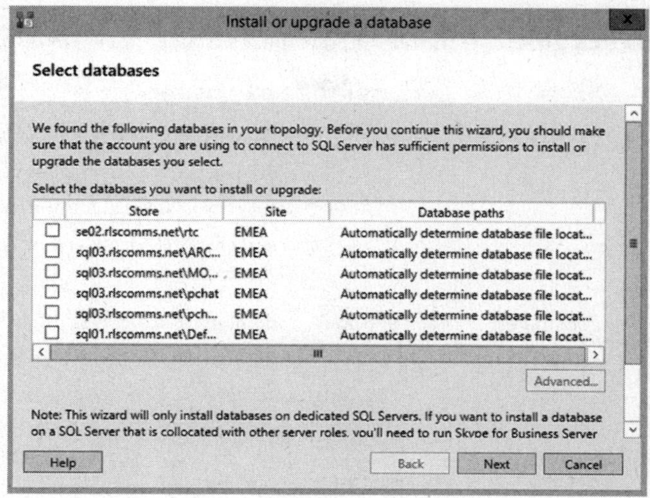

FIGURE 20.32
Installing or upgrading a database

SQL Server Databases and Permissions

So far in this chapter we've really only covered SQL Server at the instance level. OK, we've called out specific database configuration items needed, but we haven't stated what actual databases are configured and what they do.

Table 20.4 provides this breakdown.

TABLE 20.4: Individual databases in use

NAME	LOCATION	PERMISSIONS	PURPOSE
`xds`	CMS pool	<domain>\RTCUniversalConfigReplicator <domain>\RTCUniversalReadOnlyAdmins <domain>\RTCUniversalServerAdmins <server>\RTC Local Administrators <server>\RTC Local Config Replicaotr <server>\RTC Local Read-only Administrators	Master copy of topology and configuration information
`rtcxds`	CMS pool	<domain>\RTCHSUniversalServices <domain>\RTCUniversalReadOnlyAdmins <domain>\RTCUniversalServerAdmins <server>\RTC Local Administrators <server>\RTC Local Read-only Administrators <server>\RTC Server Local Group	Backup copy of topology and configuration information

TABLE 20.4: Individual databases in use *(CONTINUED)*

NAME	LOCATION	PERMISSIONS	PURPOSE
`lis`	CMS pool	<domain>\RTCUniversalReadOnlyAdmins <domain>\RTCUniversalServerAdmins <server>\RTC Local Administrators <server>\RTC Local Read-only Administrators	Location information service data containing addresses and mapping
`rtcshared`	Back-end pool	<domain>\RTCUniversalReadOnlyAdmins <domain>\RTCUniversalServerAdmins <server>\RTC Local Administrators <server>\RTC Server Local Group	Pool-level shared conferencing data store
`rtcab*`	Back-end pool	<domain>\ RTCComponentUniversalServices <domain>\RTCUniversalReadOnlyAdmins <domain>\RTCUniversalServerAdmins <server>\RTC Component Local Group <server>\RTC Local Administrators <server>\RTC Local Read-only Administrators	Address Book information
`rtcab1*`	Back-end pool	<domain>\ RTCComponentUniversalServices <domain>\RTCUniversalReadOnlyAdmins <domain>\RTCUniversalServerAdmins <server>\RTC Component Local Group <server>\RTC Local Administrators <server>\RTC Local Read-only Administrators	Backup of Address Book information
`cpsdyn`	Back-end pool	<domain> \RTCComponentUniversalServices <domain>\RTCUniversalReadOnlyAdmins <domain>\RTCUniversalServerAdmins <server>\RTC Component Local Group	Call Park service information
`rgsconfig`	Back-end pool	<domain> \RTCComponentUniversalServices <domain>\RTCUniversalReadOnlyAdmins <domain>\RTCUniversalServerAdmins <server>\RTC Component Local Group	Response Group service configuration information

TABLE 20.4: Individual databases in use *(CONTINUED)*

NAME	LOCATION	PERMISSIONS	PURPOSE
`rgsdyn`	Back-end pool	<domain>\RTCComponentUniversalServices <domain>\RTCUniversalReadOnlyAdmins <domain>\RTCUniversalServerAdmins <server>\RTC Component Local Group	Response Group service information
`xds`	RTC local instance	<server>\RTC Component Local Group <server>\RTC Local Administrators <server>\RTC Local Config Replicator <server>\RTC Local Read-only Administrators <server>\RTC Server Local Group	Read-only copy of topology and configuration information
`rtc`	RTC local instance	<server\RTC Component Local Group <server>\RTC Local Administrators <server>\RTC Local Read-only Administrators <server>\RTC Server Local Group	Persistent user information such as contact list, conferences, and so on
`rtcdyn`	RTC local instance	<server\RTC Component Local Group <server>\RTC Local Administrators <server>\RTC Server Local Group	Dynamic user information, presence
`lyss`	Lync local instance	<server>\RTC Component Local Group	Lync Storage Service; manages queueing of information for local and remote services
`LcsLog`	Archiving	<domain>\RTCComponentUniversalServices	Stores archived IM messages and conference data
`LcsCDR`	Monitoring	<domain>\CSAdministrator <domain>\CSServerAdministrator <domain>\CSViewOnlyAdministrator <domain>\RTCComponentUniversalServices	Call data records
`QoEMetrics`	Monitoring	<domain>\RTCComponentUniversalServices	Call quality dashboard information

TABLE 20.4: Individual databases in use *(CONTINUED)*

NAME	LOCATION	PERMISSIONS	PURPOSE
mgc	Persistent Chat	<domain>\RTCComponentUniversalServices	Chat room information and content
mgccomp	Persistent Chat compliance	<domain>\RTCComponentUniversalServices	Copy of raw chat room data for compliance purposes

* `rtcab` *and* `rtcab1` *contain Address Book information that alternates daily. Changes are written to one source and overnight generate a new Address Book; then changes are written to the other, and so on.*

The Bottom Line

Understand the different SQL Server needs within Skype for Business. Skype for Business has different SQL Server needs depending on both the scale and the high availability needs of the deployment. Different versions of SQL Server are available to address each of these, from SQL Server Express, which is installed on every server, to SQL Server Enterprise Edition, which is for large-scale enterprise database back ends.

> **Master It** Which versions of SQL Server are supported for use with Skype for Business Server?

Understand the different options available for providing high availability. When scaling up Skype for Business from a Standard Edition server, either for increased user count or for high availability (or both), you must deploy a stand-alone SQL Server version, rather than continuing to rely upon the SQL Server Express edition installed with Standard Edition. With this move, SQL Server can also be deployed in a highly available configuration based on your business needs.

> **Master It** You are deploying a Skype for Business Enterprise Edition pool and want to enable automatic high availability with no single points of failure on the SQL Server portion of the solution. You must also keep costs to a minimum.

Understand how to migrate to SQL Server AlwaysOn. SQL Server AlwaysOn Availability Groups are a newly supported feature and provide another option for enabling high availability within SQL Server. While the feature is easy to deploy from scratch, some organizations may want to migrate from stand-alone or mirrored SQL Server to enable this functionality.

> **Master It** You currently have a SQL Server 2014 mirror deployed supporting an Enterprise Edition pool. What steps are required to migrate SQL Server to AlwaysOn Availability Groups?

Understand the data stored within the various SQL Server databases. Skype for Business stores lots of data, from individual user account configuration to live conference data. While some of this is stored within the fileshare data structure, this does not have the speed of response needed to support real-time communications needs. This is where SQL Server comes into its own: providing that necessary speed of response.

Master It What is the name of the database in which Skype for Business stores the topology?

Chapter 21

Reverse Proxies, Load Balancers, and Gateways

When it comes to actually deploying and configuring Skype for Business, you can go only so far without needing third-party equipment. You already saw in earlier chapters why there's a need for user-based devices, so now you'll take a look at the third-party infrastructure devices, including gateways for enabling PSTN calling, load balancers for using in Enterprise Edition pools, and reverse proxies for enabling users to log in externally and allowing federated parties to join meetings.

These third-party infrastructure devices add functionality to the environment, and without them, Skype for Business is restricted from reaching its full potential as a truly Unified Communications platform.

In this chapter, you will learn to

- Use load balancers for scale
- Use reverse proxies for external access
- Use gateways to integrate with the PSTN

Configuring Load Balancers

When Office Communications Server 2007 was released, a load balancer was required for any Enterprise Edition pool. In those days, it was specifically a hardware load balancer. A lot has changed, not just the ability to deploy software load balancer applications but also the separation to enable DNS load balancing (covered in Chapter 4, "Desktop Clients") for certain protocols and constrain the load balancing requirement to the HTTP and HTTPS protocols only.

While load balancing any workload can be complex, the Skype for Business architecture tries to reduce the overhead of load balancing configuration by simplifying the requirements of load balancing all protocols used by clients and Skype for Business servers.

It is still possible (and supported) to load balance the complete workload, but it is a generally accepted practice to only balance the HTTP/HTTPS workloads, keeping the configuration as simple as possible.

When considering network communications in a given Skype for Business deployment, you can divide the communications into two categories: client-to-server traffic and server-to-server traffic.

Skype for Business servers use topology awareness to communicate with other Skype for Business servers. Since the traffic is automatically load balanced, there is no need to configure and manage an external load balancer for server-to-server traffic.

As mentioned, the two protocol categories for client-to-server communications in a deployment can be further categorized into the HTTP and HTTPS protocols and all other protocols (SIP address/RTC, and so on). Skype for Business clients are built to use the DNS load balancing logic for SIP address and media traffic. However, when they access any HTTP/HTTPS traffic such as web services or an Office Web Appsserver, the same DNS load balancing logic can't be used effectively, and you must deploy a load balancer for HTTP/HTTPS communication.

Load Balancing the Front End and Director Pools

When using DNS load balancing for the pools, this configuration results in two separate namespaces required for the following:

- A pool FQDN used by DNS load balancing. This FQDN resolves to the IP address addresses of the servers in the pool.
- A web services FQDN used for HTTP/HTTPS traffic. This FQDN resolves to the virtual IP address address of the pool managed by the load balancer. The load balancer needs to be configured so that it distributes traffic to Skype for Business servers appropriately.

As you may have noticed, the use of DNS load balancing simplifies the overall configuration required for the load balancer as it must load balance only HTTP/HTTPS traffic and the number of ports it needs to handle. This also results in reduced resource requirements for the load balancer.

Figure 21.1 shows the protocol flow when deploying this configuration.

FIGURE 21.1 Protocol flow in load balancers for Front End and Directors

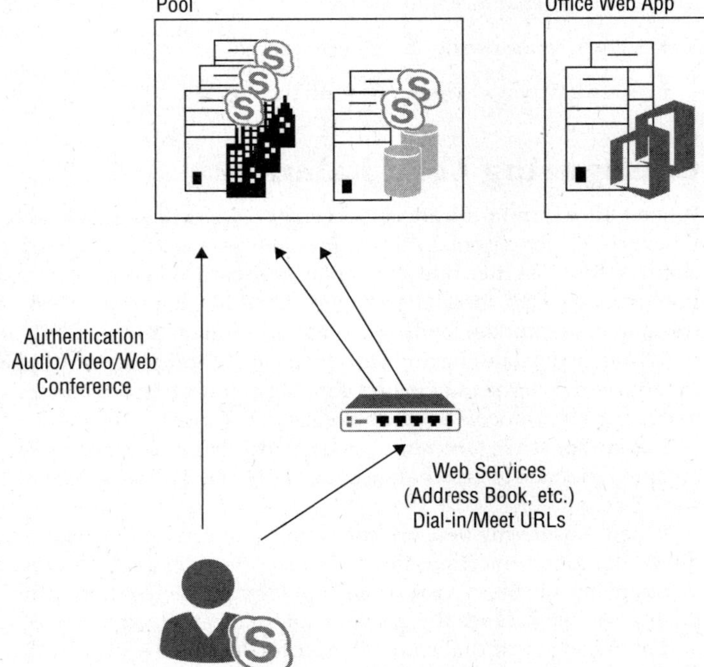

When deploying this configuration, you also need to make sure that the pool is configured correctly in the topology. You must specify the internal web services URL for the pool by selecting the Override FQDN check box on the Web Services tab of the pool properties page, as shown in Figure 21.2.

FIGURE 21.2
Web services Override FQDN

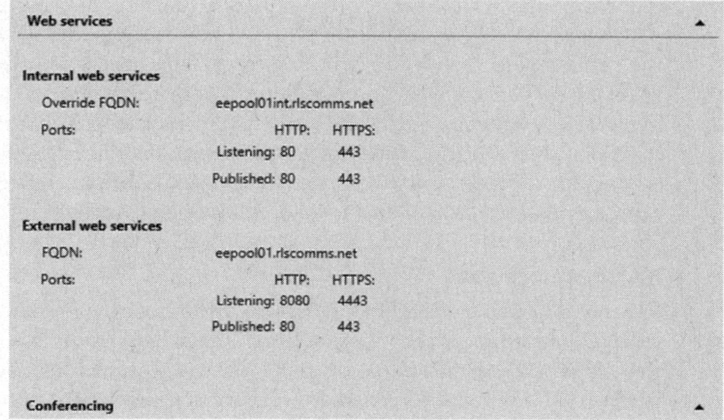

Notice the web services ports used by internal clients are TCP port 80 for HTTP traffic and TCP port 443 for HTTPS traffic. While we will discuss load balancing for external clients later in the chapter, note that the ports used by Front End servers for external clients are different.

If you deploy multiple Front End pools, you must ensure that the internal web services override FQDN used for each pool is unique. The same also applies to the FQDN used for external web services.

Additionally, if you have the Director pool deployed, you must also load balance the Director pool FQDN for web services. A Director pool has the same configuration options for the web services as the Front End pool.

Configure a Load Balancer for the Front End or Director Pool

When using DNS load balancing for SIP address traffic, the load balancer needs to be configured for web services. The traffic must be distributed to the Front End servers in a given pool. Table 21.1 shows the ports that must be load balanced.

TABLE 21.1: Port requirements for load balancing a pool

Port	Protocol	Usage
TCP/80	HTTP	Web services requests
TCP/443	HTTPS	Web services requests
TCP/8080	HTTP	Retrieval of root certificate from Front End servers
TCP/4443	HTTPS	Web services requests from reverse proxy

It is worth noting that besides the expected ports 80 and 443 for HTTP traffic to the Front End pool, port 4443, which is used for load balancing external clients, is also mentioned here. This is required when a reverse proxy is chained and sends external client connections to the internal load balancer instead of directly sending it to the Front End servers. If you plan to provide direct connectivity between the internal interface of the reverse proxy and the Front End servers, load balancing port 4443 on the internal load balancer is not required.

If you have deployed a Director pool, you must load balance TCP ports 443 and 4443 (apply the same reverse proxy logic discussed earlier), and the traffic must be distributed to the Director servers for a given pool. You do not need to load balance the other ports mentioned in Table 21.1 as they are applicable only for Front End server traffic.

When distributing client traffic, a load balancer needs to take into account the health of the server, appropriate scheduling method, client affinity requirements, and idle connection timeouts. Let's take a look at all the load balancing requirements for the Front End or Director pools.

NAT Requirements

When configuring a load balancer for web services, you must ensure that the source NAT (SNAT) is enabled for the virtual IP address also known as a *virtual service*) used for load balancing the Front End and Director pools. This is required to ensure that no additional configuration is required on Skype for Business servers. It's also worth noting that Microsoft supports only SNAT. Configuring Direct Server Return is not supported in a Skype for Business environment.

Health Check

To determine the health of a server that is part of a Front End or Director pool, the load balancer relies on health probes (also known as *health checks*). For a server configured with a Front End or Director role, it is recommended to check TCP connectivity to port 5060. This port is used for internal SIP address communications and is critical for a Skype for Business infrastructure. If a load balancer is unable to establish a TCP connection with this port, it is safe to assume that any client connecting to this server would either fail to connect or may experience unexpected client behavior. When properly configured, the load balancer will detect the failure and will mark the server as unhealthy, directing all the client traffic to the remaining healthy servers. While the server is marked unhealthy, the load balancer continues to perform the health check, and when the server responds to the health probe again, the load balancer should begin sending new client connections to the server as necessary.

Scheduling and Distribution

After ensuring the server health, the load balancer must decide how the client connections should be distributed among the healthy servers. This is accomplished by using the configured scheduling method. Scheduling can be accomplished by using one of many methods such as least connections, round robin, or fixed weighting. Microsoft does not recommend any particular scheduling mechanism over another as each is valid in its own right. Ideally, if all the Front End servers or Director servers in a pool are configured identically, weighting should not matter and either round robin or least connection is a valid method. If you're using the least connection method, ensure that the load balancer is configured to ramp connections slowly when a server is rebooted or is returned to the pool after an outage. If slow ramp is not configured, the load balancer tries to balance connections by sending most new connections to the server that has no connections due to reboot or outage. This can result in overloading the server because of the sudden demand of resources.

Client Affinity

Along with deciding which server the connection should be sent to, the load balancer must also identify whether the client connection is new or existing. If it's an existing session, the session state must be preserved, which requires configuring the load balancer to provide affinity. While Lync Server 2010 required cookie-based affinity, it is no longer needed for Skype for Business pools. The load balancer can be simply configured to use source IP address address–based affinity. Source IP address–based affinity ensures that any request coming from a given client IP address is persisted to the same Front End or Director server for the lifetime of given session. While source IP address affinity simplifies configuration, it is important to note that if multiple client connections are made from a single IP address address (such as a small office behind a NAT firewall), they will be persisted to the same Front End or Director server in the pool. This can result in uneven client distribution and must be carefully evaluated for a given network topology.

While source IP address is the recommended method for client affinity, you may need to deploy cookie-based affinity in environments where Lync 2010 is also deployed. When deploying cookie-based client affinity, you must ensure that the cookie issued by the load balancer is named `MS-WSMAN`, is set to `not expire`, and is not marked `httpOnly`.

Connection Timeouts

Lastly, you must configure load balancer–managed connections that have been idle. Unmanaged idle connections unnecessarily increase resource consumption on load balancers and may cause issues. Load balancers provide the ability to remove idle connections based on configured timeouts. Because session state is maintained through client usage and application interaction, you should configure timeout values as per the load balancing vendor's recommendation.

SSL Termination and Bridging

If you don't plan to use cookie persistence, SSL termination is not required on the load balancer. This in turn simplifies the configuration of the load balancer. When using this configuration, the load balancer listens on TCP port 443 and uses SNAT before sending client connections to the servers. However, it does not terminate the SSL connection. Instead, it simply passes through the SSL request to the servers, and the server receiving the client connection encrypts/decrypts the client connections as necessary.

When you're using cookie persistence, SSL termination on the load balancer is required. Without terminating the SSL connection on the load balancer, the load balancer does not have access to the HTTP payload and can't insert the required cookie. When terminating SSL connections on the load balancer, typically an SSL certificate issued by a trusted certification authority is imported and configured to be used for the client connections.

The connections from the load balancer to the servers are encrypted by the SSL certificate installed on the servers. The certificate installed on the servers may not be the same certificate installed on the load balancer and does not need to be issued by a public certificate-issuing authority. Organizations can use certificates issued by internal certificate authorities for servers.

Additional Functionality

Many load balancers provide advanced functionality such as pre-authentication and malware scanning for known HTTP attack vectors. However, you should use caution when enabling such functionality when load balancing Skype for Business servers. Microsoft performs rigorous code testing for security vulnerabilities. Combined with server OS patching and Skype for Business server updates, enabling such functionality on the load balancer only introduces complexity and in most cases breaks native functionality because of differences in how the web services traffic flow works compared to standard HTTP payloads.

Load Balancer–Only Configuration

While DNS load balancing combined with a load balancer is the best approach, it is possible to load balance all ports necessary for Director and Front End traffic. The number of ports to configure on the load balancer is substantial, covering all services including authentication, DCOM and RPC, web services, and mediation.

You can review the ports in the following TechNet article: `https://technet.microsoft.com/EN-US/library/gg398833.aspx`.

If you opt for this configuration, it is best to use guidance from the load balancing vendor to optimally configure the service for the Front End and Director pools.

KEMP LOAD BALANCERS

Kemp (`www.kemptechnologies.com`) shipped its first product in 2004 and since then has regularly been named one of the world's fastest-growing companies, now providing both hardware and software (virtualized) load balancing (and reverse proxy) products.

As you would expect, the price of each device type varies based on the size of scale needed. However, Kemp does provide a free trial license downloadable as a virtual machine, which is ideal for testing in a lab.

Unless a customer already has a different vendor relationship in place, these are the devices we recommend. The **following** screenshot shows how easy they are to configure, with wizards for most well-known applications (the Skype for Business wizards are in development at the time of writing).

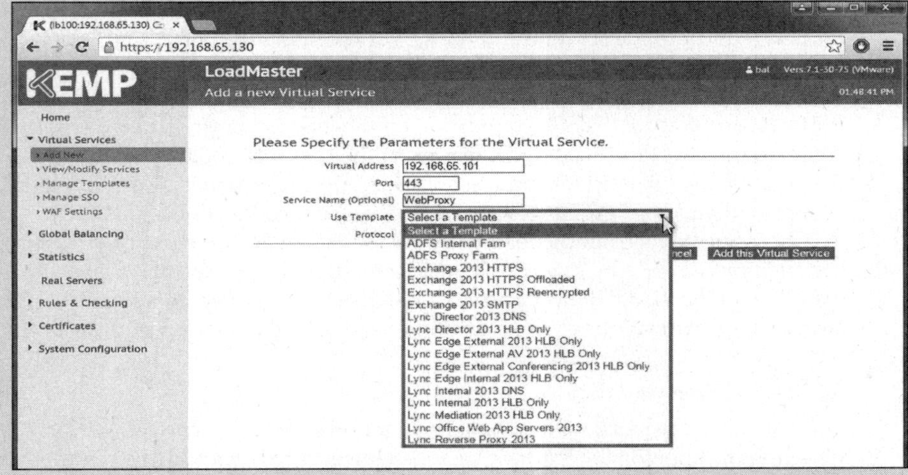

Load Balancing Office Web Apps Server Farms

When sharing PowerPoint presentations during a meeting, you must associate the Front End pool with an Office Web Apps server farm. During the meeting, the client will be notified of the URL on the Office Web Apps server, which is ready for providing the content. You can find more details on the specifics of configuring the Office Web Apps Server in Chapter 22, "Exchange, SharePoint, and Office Web Application Server."

As shown in Figure 21.3, the load balancer in this case is presenting the single point for the client to connect to and then distributing the load among the available servers. It's worth highlighting that the namespace configuration for the Office Web Apps server farm is important to ensure client traffic is routed to the appropriate load balancer on the internal network for internal clients or on the reverse proxy server for external clients.

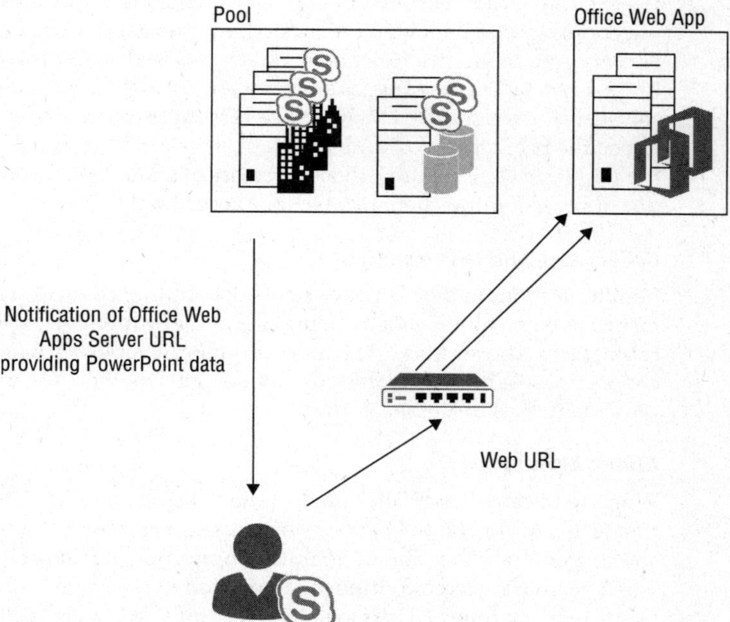

FIGURE 21.3 Load balancing the Office Web Apps server

Unlike Front End servers, Office Web Apps servers do not need to differentiate between external and internal clients. Hence, it does not need two different websites listening on different ports. Most commonly, the Office Web Apps server farm is configured to listen to TCP port 443 to secure the client traffic. While Figure 21.3 does not depict it, the Skype for Business servers also connect to Office Web Apps servers through the namespace configured in the topology on TCP port 443.

Configure a Load Balancer for an Office Web Apps Server Farm

Unlike the Front End pool, all traffic for the Office Web Apps server farm cannot use DNS load balancing and relies on load balancers to provide high availability. Using a single TCP port for client communications simplifies the configuration of the load balancer.

Similar to any Front End server web services or any other workload that needs to be load balanced, the health checks, a scheduling method, the client affinity requirements, and the idle connection timeouts need to be configured on the load balancer.

NAT Requirements

Similar to Front End or Director pools, you must ensure that the source NAT is enabled for the virtual IP address (also known as a *virtual service*) used for load balancing the Office Web Apps server farm.

Health Check

Office Web Apps servers are configured with discovery endpoint, which provides pertinent data about the farm configuration such as the functionality offered, the internal URLs, and the external URLs. The information is presented to the requester by dynamically generating configuration data when requested. As this data can be generated only if the Office Web Server components are functional and the IIS web server is running on the server. The URL `https://<FQDN>/hosting/discovery` serves as the best health check target. When configuring the health check service for the Office Web Apps server farm on the load balancer, configure it to use the HTTP protocol and send requests on TCP port 443 using HTTP GET requests. When the target server is healthy, the load balancer should receive the HTTP "200 OK" response and distribute incoming client connections accordingly.

Scheduling and Distribution

Similar to Front End or Director pools, scheduling connections for an Office Web Apps server farm can be accomplished by using one of many methods such as least connections, round robin, or fixed weighting. The most commonly deployed methods are round robin and least connections. When using the least connections method, ensure you have configured the slow ramp feature as discussed earlier.

Client Affinity

When rendering PowerPoint presentations using an Office Web Apps server, each client connection needs to stay on the Office Web Apps server to which it initially connects. If no affinity is configured, the client makes an initial connection, but subsequent requests from the same client won't be guaranteed a continued connection to the same back-end server. Since session state needs to be maintained, the load balancer must be configured to maintain affinity and ensure subsequent client connections remain connected to the same back-end server that served the initial connection from the client.

There are no specific recommendations from Microsoft for client affinity. The most commonly deployed and recommended method is to use a load balancer–issued cookie. Load balancer–issued cookies can ensure that each client is uniquely identified. This is not possible when using the source IP address. Especially in environments where NAT devices are in use, even the distribution of client connections can't be achieved as requests from all clients masked by the NAT device are sent to the same back-end server, resulting in higher resource usage.

Connection Timeouts

There is no specific guidance from Microsoft regarding connection timeouts for the Office Web App server farm. It is best to configure timeout values as per the specific load balancing vendor's recommendation. Thirty minutes is the most commonly configured idle connection timeout value.

SSL Termination and Bridging

Since cookie persistence is the recommended client affinity method for load balancing an Office Web Apps server farm, SSL termination on the load balancer is required. Import and configure an appropriate SSL certificate issued by a trusted certification authority for the client connections.

The connections from the load balancer to the servers are encrypted by the SSL certificate installed on the servers. The certificate installed on the servers may not be the same certificate installed on the load balancer and does not need to be issued by a public certificate-issuing authority. Organizations can use certificates issued by an internal certificate authority for servers.

Additional Functionality

Additional functionality such as pre-authentication shouldn't be used when load balancing Office Web Apps server farms. Ensure that the client connections are allowed to authenticate directly with the server to ensure uninterrupted client connectivity.

Load Balancing Edge

When external connectivity surpasses 15,000 Access Edge client connections, 1,000 Web Conferencing Edge client connections, or 500 concurrent A/V Edge sessions, multiple Edge servers are required to provide scalability and failover. In such critical deployments most deployments have been including load balancers in their architecture.

When using load balancers with Edge servers, it is important to note that the external Edge interfaces must continue to use public IP address addresses in addition to public IP address addresses assigned to load balancer virtual IP addresss.

Also, since responses for requests made by clients to the A/V service must come from the requested IP address address, address translation can't be used on A/V interfaces. If NAT is used, Simple Traversal of UDP over NAT (STUN), Traversal using Relay NAT (TURN), and Federation TURN (FTURN) may not work properly. Because of these requirements, all external Edge services must use load balancer IP address as their default gateway.

Figure 21.4 provides a high-level overview of the protocol flow of load-balanced Edge servers.

FIGURE 21.4 Load balancing the Edge servers

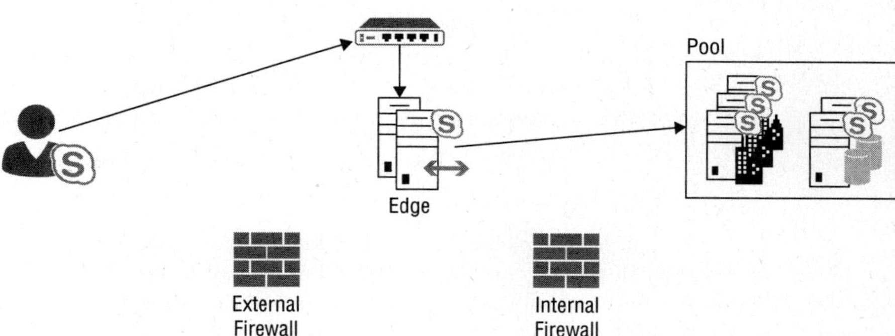

It is worth noting that while it's supported to use load balancing with Edge servers, it will add complexity for almost no benefit. External federation and connectivity support DNS load balancing, and Exchange Server 2010 (specifically, the Unified Messaging role) is the only integration product that does not. So, unless you have Exchange Server 2010 in place, it's best to keep the deployment as simple as possible to aid in any future troubleshooting.

Configure a Load Balancer for an Access Edge Interface

The Access Edge interface provides SIP address connectivity for external user access, SIP address signaling, and federated and public IM connectivity, and the interface is also shared with the XMPP proxy service if it is in use. Table 21.2 provides a reference of the ports required to be configured on a load balancer.

Table 21.2: Required ports for load balancing the Access Edge interface

Port	Protocol	Usage
TCP/443	HTTPS	Client-to-server SIP address traffic for external user access
TCP/5061	TCP	SIP address signaling, federated and public IM connectivity
TCP/5269	TCP	XMPP proxy service

For each of these virtual IP address addresses, the service parameters are the same. The following sections provide guidance for all three virtual IP address service configurations.

NAT Requirements

Strict address translation requirements apply to the A/V interface Edge service. However, the same does not apply to the Access and Conferencing Edge interfaces. You may configure NAT on the Access interface (for all three virtual IP address ports referenced earlier). For consistency with the A/V interface, you may provision public IP address addresses without configuring NAT on the virtual IP address. Either is a valid configuration.

Health Check

Given the function and importance of SIP address signaling for the Access Edge interface, it is recommended to check connectivity to TCP port 5061 on the Access Edge IP address of the given Edge servers in the pool. If connectivity to the port fails, the load balancer should mark the server as unhealthy and not distribute any further connections to the unhealthy server.

Scheduling and Distribution

Scheduling connections for the Access Edge interface can be accomplished by using one of many methods such as least connections, round robin, or fixed weighting. Most commonly deployed methods are round robin or least connections. When using the least connections method, ensure you have configured the slow ramp feature as discussed earlier.

Client Affinity

It is recommended to use source IP address affinity for all Edge interfaces including the Access Edge interface.

SSL Termination and Bridging

For the Access Edge virtual IP address, SSL termination is not required. Terminating SSL on a load balancer introduces the VIA header in SIP address communications sent by the client. To avoid problems with SIP address authentication and signaling, it is recommended to pass all SSL connections to Edge servers without terminating them on a load balancer first. Pass-through configuration provides for a simpler configuration, lower resource usage on the load balancer, and reduced complexity when troubleshooting is required.

Configure a Load Balancer for the Web Conferencing Edge Interface

The Web Conferencing Edge interface provides external users with access to web conferencing media. The only port that requires load balancing for the Web Conferencing Edge interface is TCP port 443.

The virtual IP address configuration for the Web Conferencing Edge interface is same as the Access Edge interface. You may use NAT for the virtual IP address if desired.

SSL termination and bridging are not required on the load balancer and should be configured for pass-through to the Web Conferencing Edge interface on Edge servers.

Configure a Load Balancer for the A/V Edge Interface

A/V Edge interfaces are unique in the way that clients require direct connectivity to the Edge server's public IP address after initial connection to the A/V Edge virtual is established and the client has received a response from an Edge server containing its own public IP address (as configured in the topology). Configuring NAT for this interface will adversely affect the functionality of STUN, TURN, and FTURN.

Two ports need to be load balanced on the A/V Edge virtual IP address. TCP port 443 and UDP port 3478 are used for the STUN/TURN negotiation of candidates. UDP is preferred where possible. A TCP port is used when a UDP port is not a viable candidate.

Since NAT cannot be used with A/V Edge interfaces, you must configure an A/V interface on the Edge server to use an IP address of the load balancer as its default gateway. This will allow for packets to be addressed appropriately as each one traverses the load balancer. Clients may experience connectivity issues when the A/V Edge interface does not use a load balancer as its default gateway. It is worth noting that this is required since Direct Server Return (DSR) configuration is not supported by Microsoft.

Configuring the load balancer for each of these ports should follow the same guidance as the configuration of the Access Edge virtual IP address, with the exception of the following:

- When load balancing TCP port 443, configure the health check to verify connectivity with TCP port 443 on the A/V interface of given Edge servers in the pool. URL checks with HTTP GET are not required for this port.
- Since UDP is a connectionless protocol, you can't perform a health check on a given UDP port for A/V Edge interfaces. You can simply perform connectivity with the IP address instead. As long as the ICMP check passes, the load balancer can mark the

server as healthy. If the load balancer allows, you can also check connectivity to TCP port 443, and if it passes, you can safely assume UDP port 3478 on the same server to be functional.

- When TCP nagling (a method to optimize a TCP stream by combining multiple small packets into a bigger one) is enabled on the load balancer, it can negatively affect voice quality. Ensure that TCP nagling is turned off on the load balancer that is used as a default gateway by A/V Edge interfaces on the Edge servers in a pool.

Configure a Load Balancer for the Internal Edge Interfaces

It is required by Microsoft to deploy the same load balancing solutions for both the internal and external interfaces of Edge servers. This means that if you use DNS load balancing for external Edge interfaces, you must also deploy DNS load balancing for the internal Edge interfaces.

Likewise, if a hardware/software-based load balancing solution is used for external Edge interfaces, you must use a hardware/software-based load balancing solution for the internal Edge interfaces.

Table 21.3 shows the ports you must load balance from the internal network to the internal Edge interface.

TABLE 21.3: Ports required for load balancing internal Edge interface

PORT	PROTOCOL	USAGE
TCP/5061	HTTPS	SIP address traffic (from Director, Director pool virtual IP address address, Front End Server or Front End pool virtual IP address address) to Internal Edge VIP address
TCP/5062	TCP	Authentication of A/V users (A/V authentication service) from Front End Server or Front End pool IP address
TCP/443	TCP	Fallback path for A/V media transfer between internal and external users if UDP communication cannot be established; TCP is used for file transfer and desktop sharing
UDP/3478	UDP	Preferred path for A/V media transfer between internal and external users

Implementing Reverse Proxies

A reverse proxy by definition is a device, usually in the DMZ, configured to accept connections from external users for a published service and proxy the connections to the internal network. The endpoint on the internal network is usually a load balancer or the servers directly depending on the security policy in place.

The reverse proxy solution also may provide additional functionality such as pre-authentication, deep packet inspection, and intrusion detection/prevention, to name a few.

Skype for Business clients use the functionality provided by a reverse proxy in any environment that has external users (either remote users for logins or meeting joins by remote users as well as federated users).

The functionality served by web services running on Front End pools (such as download meeting content, expanding distribution groups, downloading files from Address Book Service, and PowerPoint presentations rendered by Office Web Apps servers) requires users to be able to access these services using the external FQDN configured for these services. Figure 21.5 shows the high-level logical flow; note the reverse proxy in this case is assumed to also provide load balancing.

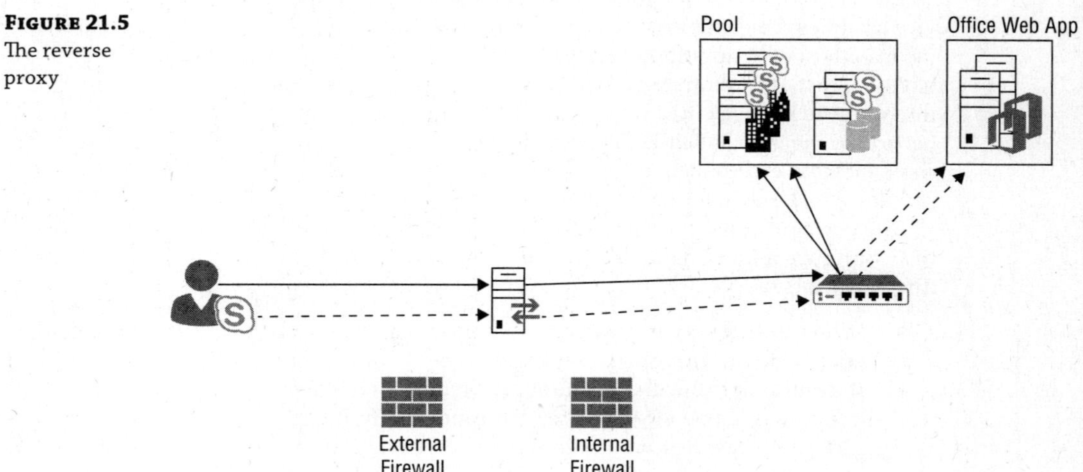

FIGURE 21.5 The reverse proxy

As mentioned, in this case the reverse proxy is also providing the load balancing. In some devices (such as the products from Kemp), this functionality is combined to provide both. Others (such as ARR from Microsoft) provide only the proxy functionality and need to have a load balancer deployed. You'll learn more about load balancers later in this chapter.

Skype for Business requires that a reverse proxy be able to perform the following functions:

- For web services functionality offered by Front End pools, client connections must be accepted on TCP ports 80 and 443. External Skype for Business clients do not send requests for web services to TCP ports 8080 and 4443, respectively.
- The web services connections from the reverse proxy to the Front End servers (or internal load balancer) must be sent to TCP ports 8080 and 4443, respectively. This is also referred to as *port translation*. This is required to ensure external clients are able to connect to web services offered by Front End servers successfully.
- The reverse proxy service should not alter the requested host headers for the web services. This is required because Front End servers expect clients to request services using the external FQDN configured in the topology.

Most of today's load balancers are able to perform the required reverse proxy functionality successfully. The following section describes the configuration of a load balancer device in a DMZ as a reverse proxy for Skype for Business services. There will be a lot of similarity with the load balancer information.

Configure a Reverse Proxy/Load Balancer for External Web Services

Similar to internal clients, external clients connecting to Skype for Business web services functionality continue to send requests on the well-known TCP ports 80 and 443. However, as you will see later in this chapter, the Front End servers differentiate which clients are internal and which ones are external based on the website to which they connect.

If clients connect to an internal website listening for requests on port 80 or 443, the web service assumes the client is internal and sends the responses accordingly. If an external client is incorrectly sent to an internal website on the Front End servers, the Front End servers do not have a way to differentiate external clients and send a response that contains the FQDNs for an internal web service URL. This results in a failure as external clients are unable to make a connection to the internal URLs. It is the reverse proxy's responsibility to ensure that the requests received from external clients are sent to the external web services website on the Front End servers, which listen for client requests on TCP ports 8080 and 4443.

The configuration of a virtual IP address is almost identical to the details provided in "Configure a Load Balancer for the Front End or Director Pool," except with these differences:

- When adding servers in a pool, the reverse proxy/load balancer should be configured to connect to the appropriate endpoint as per your firewall configuration or security policy. If the policy or firewall configuration dictates connectivity from the DMZ to limited internal endpoints, it may mean service chaining by sending requests from the reverse proxy to the virtual IP address for the web services on port 8080 and 4443, configured on an internal load balancer. If the reverse proxy/load balancer from the DMZ is allowed to make direct connections to the Front End servers, it is preferred to not chain services to an internal load balancer because it is more complex to maintain and troubleshoot. Service chaining also introduces unnecessary points of failure as an internal load balancer becomes an additional point of failure that can be avoided if the reverse proxy/load balancer in the DMZ can make direct connection to servers in the Front End pool.
- If you have deployed a Director pool, you must also create an additional virtual IP address/service on the reverse proxy/load balancer in the DMZ as external clients will make the initial connection to the external web services URL of a Director pool as defined in the topology and then will be redirected to the appropriate external web services URL of the relevant Front End server pool.
- Lastly, you must also ensure that when sending client requests to an internal endpoint, whether it is the internal load balancer or Director/Front End servers, the destination port is configured to be TCP ports 8080 and 4443.

NAT Requirements

Since external clients are not able to directly access the internal IP address of the servers and because most commonly servers do not have direct access to clients located on the Internet, it is important to configure a virtual IP address for external web services to use SNAT functionality on the reverse proxy/load balancer solution in the DMZ.

Health Check

The health check requirement for web services is no different from the one used by internal web services virtual IP address. Continue to perform health checks on TCP port 5061 on Front End servers, as well as the ports used for web services (80 and 443). If you are using service chaining and connecting to an internal load balancer, ensure that the internal load balancer is allowing health check requests on TCP port 5061 and is passing the requests to the Director/Front End server pools appropriately.

Scheduling and Distribution

The scheduling and distribution requirements are identical for the internal and external web services virtual IP address.

Client Affinity

Client affinity is not required for external clients connecting to the external interface of Front End web services. A virtual IP address configured on the internal load balancer is required to use source IP address client affinity.

Connection Timeouts

The scheduling and distribution requirements are identical for the internal and external web services virtual IP address. Configure timeout values as per reverse proxy/load balancing vendor's recommendation.

SSL Termination and Bridging

Most commonly, client requests originating from external networks are required to be terminated in the DMZ before the traffic is passed on to internal servers by a reverse proxy or load balancing solution. This isn't a technical requirement of Skype for Business but may be a business requirement determined by security policy requirements.

When terminating SSL connections on the load balancer, configure an SSL certificate issued by a trusted certification authority on the reverse proxy or load balancer.

The connections from the load balancer to the servers are encrypted by the SSL certificate installed on the servers. The certificate installed on the servers may not be the same certificate and does not need to be issued by a public certificate-issuing authority. Organizations can use certificates issued by an internal certificate authority for servers.

Additional Functionality

Many load balancers provide advanced functionality such as pre-authentication and malware scanning for known HTTP attack vectors. However, you should use caution when enabling such functionality when load balancing Skype for Business servers. Microsoft performs rigorous code testing for security vulnerabilities. Combined with server OS patching and Skype for Business server updates, enabling such functionality on the load balancer introduces complexity and in most cases breaks native functionality because of differences in how the web services' traffic flow works compared to standard HTTP payloads.

Configure a Reverse Proxy/Load Balancer for External Web Services

While connectivity for external clients to Director/Front End server pools requires port translation, Office Web Apps server farms do not require similar port translation and instead share the same port TCP/443 for all clients requesting services. Hence, configuring a reverse proxy/load balancing solution in DMZ is no different from the one described earlier in this chapter for configuring an internal load balancer to support the Office Web Apps server.

Understanding Gateways

Gateways have been referred to throughout this book, but what *is* a gateway, and what does it do in the Skype for Business environment? Fundamentally, a gateway is a hardware device from a third-party vendor that enables voice integration between your Skype for Business deployment and other external voice elements, such as a private branch exchange (PBX), the PSTN, DECT phones (digital handsets), and analog devices, as represented in Figure 21.6.

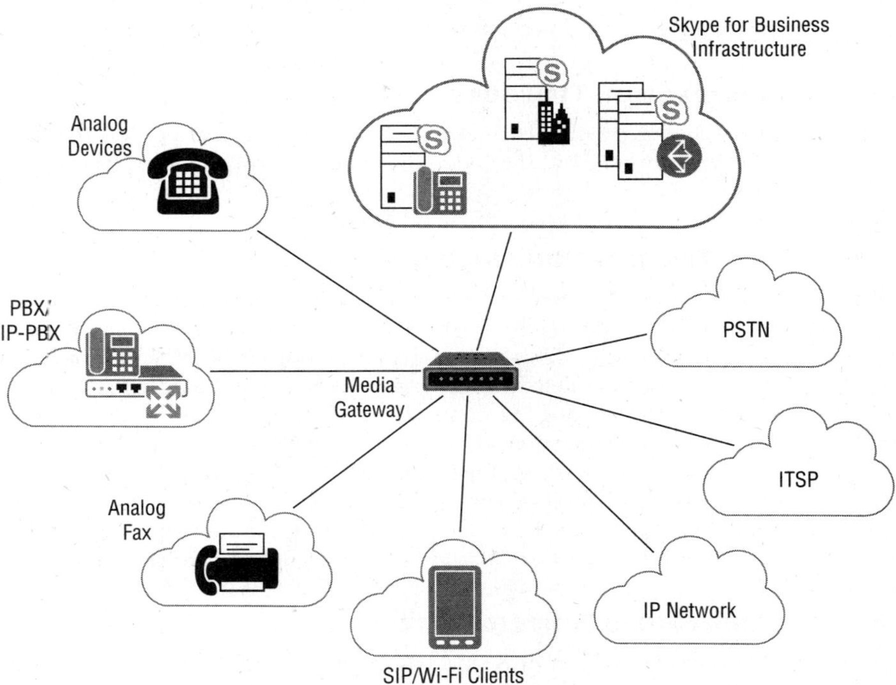

Figure 21.6 Gateway connecting various voice components

While Skype for Business can potentially talk directly to certain PBXs or SIP address trunk providers, the PBXs that support this ability are limited. Even some IP address-PBXs don't talk to the correct variety of SIP address, and SIP address trunks may not be suitable to your particular environment, especially if you have a significant investment in ISDN lines. Implementing a gateway to integrate to the telephony world brings distinct benefits, including security and flexibility in manipulating traffic, which are two of the most important. Session border controllers (SBCs) can also be considered gateways; they specifically are dealing with SIP address trunks and have a separate section on the Open Interoperability Program (OIP address) but often provide similar functionality as a gateway.

In the following sections, you'll explore the various benefits of using a gateway, look at some of the gateway options available in the market today, and review some of the more advanced features being implemented on the latest generation of gateways that make integration and user migration easier and more robust. First, though, let's take a look at some of the typical voice elements that you have to integrate with and the challenges that lie ahead.

Public Switched Telephone Network

The PSTN is a worldwide telephony infrastructure that is hosted and supported by various carriers in different countries all over the world. Similar to the World Wide Web, this infrastructure gives global reach and enables users to make a voice call to anywhere in the world. Figure 21.7 shows many of the typical PSTN interconnect standards and devices that exist around the world today.

FIGURE 21.7 The PSTN showing various endpoints

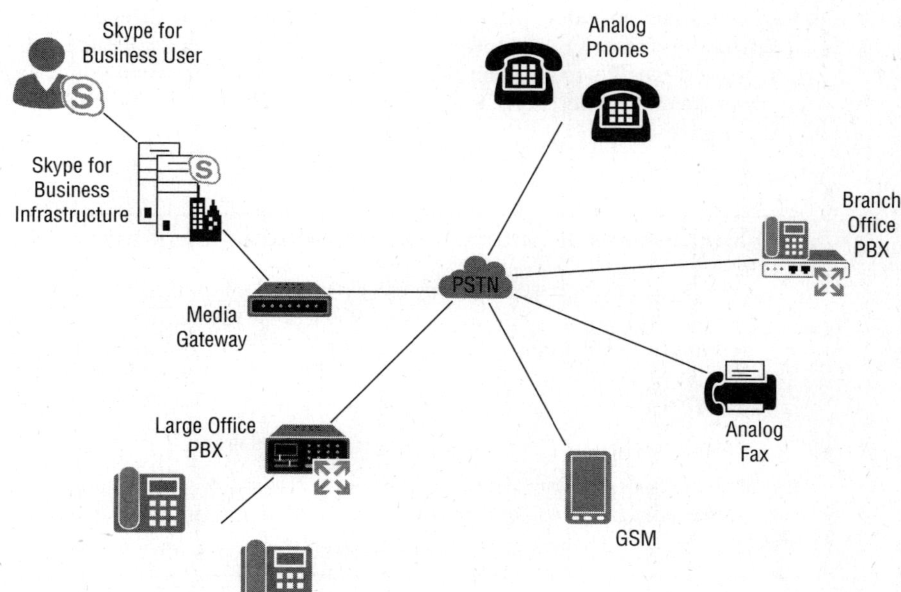

In contrast to the World Wide Web, which is ultimately based on a common protocol—IP address—the PSTN network has many different interfaces, protocols, and standards associated with it. This is driven by differences in local country standards, evolution of voice services over the years, and adoption of different technology by different carriers. What this means for you is that for a global deployment, you may be facing a slightly different interface or protocol in each location where a connection to PSTN is required. It is in this situation that it's important for a gateway to offer a wide range of interfaces, protocols, and standards. It is also important that the gateway device is acceptance-tested (*homologated*) by the carrier in a country for direct connection to its PSTN service.

Traditional PSTN connectivity (known as *legacy PSTN*) is generally presented to an enterprise over a digital service known as Integrated Services Digital Network (ISDN) or an analog line, such as you may have at home. The digital services are presented as Basic Rate Interface (BRI), which gives two voice channels and one for signaling, or Primary Rate Interface (PRI), of which there are two variants—T1 and E1.

T1 is used in North America and Japan and provides 23 channels of voice and one channel for signaling. E1 is used in Europe and Australia and is fairly widespread across the rest of the world. E1 provides 30 channels for voice and one for signaling.

Internet Telephony Service Provider

Another option for connecting to the PSTN network to provide external voice services to your Skype for Business users is to implement a SIP address trunk service from an Internet telephony service provider (ITSP). A SIP address trunk service is much more flexible and dynamic than the traditional PSTN services delivered by local carriers because it uses VoIP address technology in much the same way that Skype for Business does for delivering voice services over IP address. In fact, some providers offer certified services that can be directly connected to your Skype for Business infrastructure. However, these services are not available in all locations, and there are still good reasons to consider using a gateway device between your Skype for Business infrastructure and a Microsoft Open Interoperability Program (OIP address)–certified SIP address trunk service.

Microsoft OIP Address Certification—Open Interoperability Testing

As with any third-party device connecting into Skype for Business, it is important that the device interface, protocols, and features are fully tested and compliant with Skype for Business to ensure a smooth implementation and to avoid any unexpected issues. The OIP address program instigated by Microsoft ensures that any gateway or PBX equipment undergoes a full and extensive interoperability test suite before being supported and listed on the OIP address web page, at this address:

`http://technet.microsoft.com/en-us/office/dn947483`

During the writing of this book, Microsoft has started a follow-on program to the OIP address specifically aimed at Skype for Business; you can find this program content here:

`http://partnersolutions.skypeforbusiness.com/solutionscatalog`

A good SIP address gateway can provide an additional layer of security and flexibility by acting as a session border controller. The gateway sits on the edge of your IP address network, terminating the SIP address trunk service, and is able to provide stateful SIP address firewall services, session management, and connection admission control. Also, thanks to its location, it provides topology hiding and failover to traditional PSTN connectivity in the event of a failure or congestion on the SIP address trunk.

Securing the voice traffic at the edge of your enterprise network is important. You must remember that voice traffic over IP address is just like your regular Internet data. It is subject to the same security concerns and considerations that you apply to your data traffic. Various secure protocols and methods can be used to protect your voice traffic. The SBC device is key to their implementation. You'll explore these protocols in detail later, and you'll see how both the signaling and the voice traffic can be protected against unlawful intercept or eavesdropping by unwanted parties.

Your SIP address trunk will be delivered over the Internet or your virtual private network (VPN). The SBC will be the *voice firewall* between your SIP address trunk provider and your internal Skype for Business voice network; it will provide security and session management to make sure you don't oversubscribe your SIP address trunk connection with excessive voice calls. This session management can include the ability to manage peak call periods by overflowing calls to traditional PSTN trunks when your SIP address trunks are at capacity.

SIP address trunk providers are growing in number and popularity right now; the flexibility and cost savings offered by some of these services are attractive, but there are differences in signaling protocols and codecs used for media encoding. This again creates a need for a flexible and capable gateway device to interface with these services; such an interface might be in parallel to your "traditional" ISDN connection as well, thereby presenting a common and known secure interface to your Skype for Business deployment via the gateway.

Typically, an ITSP will implement the UDP protocol for the signaling transport, the RTP protocol for the media transport, and the G.729 codec for the media encoding itself. By contrast, a Skype for Business–enhanced gateway will use the TLS-encrypted protocol for the signaling transport, the SRTP-encrypted protocol for the media transport, and the G.711 codec for the media encoding toward the Skype for Business pool Mediation role, as shown in Figure 21.8.

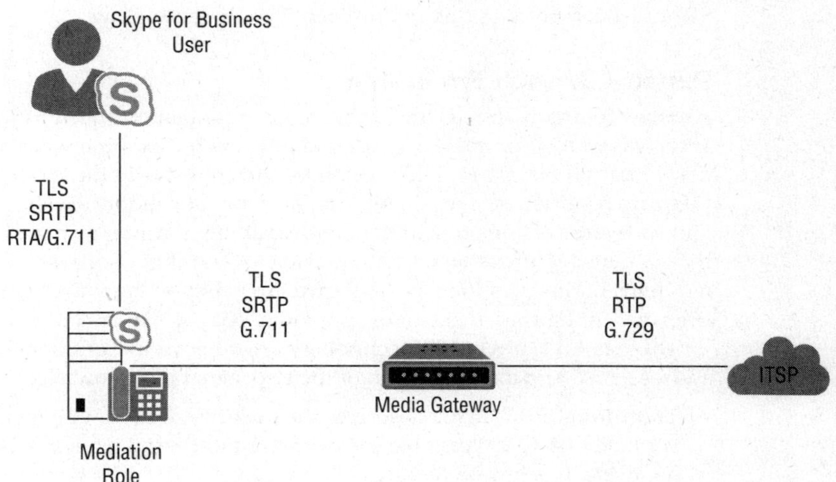

FIGURE 21.8
The protocols and codecs used between the gateway and provider in a typical SIP address trunk setup

The gateway must be capable of translating between the secure and nonsecure protocols used for both signaling and media, and it must be able to transcode between the different audio codecs used on either side.

Take note of that last point; audio transcoding is becoming a key factor in today's Unified Communications telephony environment. Whereas the traditional telephony environment used in the PSTN carries the voice traffic as uncompressed audio, within the IP address world it is common to encode and compress the audio data to reduce the bandwidth required to transport it end to end. With SIP address, the endpoints trying to establish a voice call must agree on a common codec to use in order to transport the audio stream between them. As mentioned, many ISTP providers like to deliver the voice using the G.729 codec, which is able to compress the audio data from 64Kbps to 8Kbps while still maintaining reasonable voice quality.

Within Skype for Business, the clients are able to support multiple codecs. The default used for all PC-to-PC calls is the SILK codec, which is a high-fidelity wideband codec that is able to dynamically adjust the compression rate to the available bandwidth. Another codec available is G.711, which is 64Kbps voice and is comparable to uncompressed voice used on the PSTN. G.711 is used toward the gateway for calls to the PSTN or PBX. For interfacing with Skype for Business, the gateway must be able to transcode this G.729 audio traffic presented by the ITSP carrier to G.711 data, which is passed on toward the Skype for Business client.

As mentioned, this direct SIP address-to-SIP address audio transcoding is becoming a commonplace requirement for deployments where a SIP address trunk connection is involved, either to an ITSP or to an IP address-PBX. The gateways available on the market vary greatly in their capability and capacity to perform this task. As you can imagine, this task of completely changing the voice compression technique on either side of a gateway is resource intensive. The voice must be processed by the gateway dynamically and without introducing noticeable latency to the voice traffic. Imagine a gateway processing a few hundred calls simultaneously, with each call generating hundreds of packets of audio data that require decoding and reencoding, and you can see that audio transcoding is no trivial task. Within a gateway, this task is performed by a hardware element known as a digital signal processor (DSP) chip. When looking at your gateway requirements, pay particular attention to this capability. With the increasing move toward SIP address trunking, this requirement is only set to grow.

Private Branch Exchange

Another common voice element that most organizations need to interface with is the PBX. This is typically an on-premises device that delivers the existing voice capability to users; it usually hosts internal phones and fax machines and connects to the PSTN, as described previously. PBXs are proprietary; they come from an array of vendors and have different features, models, and software versions that affect their capabilities. You may have heard a PBX vendor talk about the 100-plus features that a PBX is capable of and that a software VoIP address platform cannot deliver. The question is, in any given installation, how many of those features are in fact licensed, configured, used, or even known? Maybe five or six!

Three main types of PBX technology are deployed: traditional analog/digital PBX, IP address-PBX, and a combination of the two, generally known as an *IP address-enabled* PBX.

Traditional PBX This describes the majority of PBX equipment deployed. It is typically very old—15 to 20 years old is not uncommon—and usually has proprietary analog or digital handsets. It is low on features.

IP address-PBX Full IP address VoIP address PBX systems tend to be much newer and feature rich and have VoIP address endpoints, although these endpoints may run a proprietary version of SIP address.

IP address-Enabled PBX Some traditional PBX systems can be upgraded with an IP address card to enable them to interface with VoIP address platforms such as Skype for Business. However, when SIP address is implemented on these systems, it often has some proprietary extensions, making interoperability and certification to Skype for Business a challenge.

Achieving Connectivity

For Skype for Business to integrate with external elements to establish a voice call, the gateway must be able to understand and translate various signaling and transport protocols. They fall under two key areas: signaling transport, which sets up the call, and media transport, which facilitates the passing of the audio stream encoded with whichever codec is being used. In addition, the media codec is responsible for the interchange of actual audio content. These areas are outlined here and shown in Figure 21.9.

FIGURE 21.9
The connectivity components through a gateway

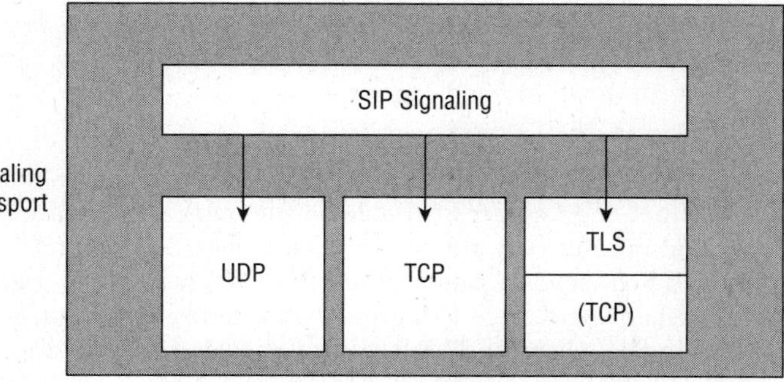

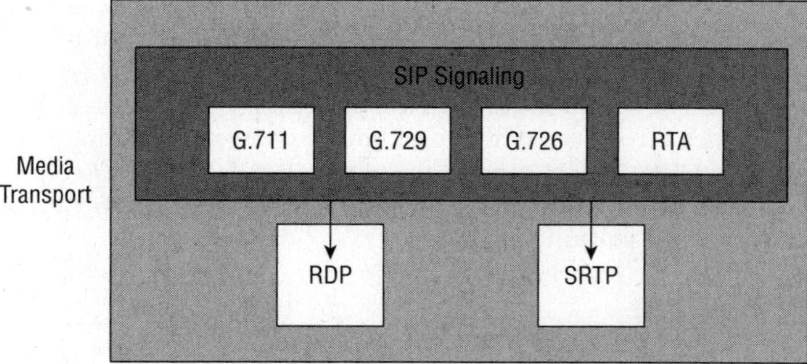

Signaling Transport For a voice call to be established, information, including the number dialed and the number of the caller, must be passed between devices. This process is known as the *call signaling*. With SIP address, this information can be transported using the UDP, TCP, or secure TLS transport protocols. UDP is obviously connectionless and is often used by ITSP providers for SIP address trunk signaling. It is lightweight, fast, and suited to the ITSP needs. TCP is a connection-oriented protocol that provides guaranteed data transport. Skype for Business uses TLS for all signaling transport to avoid any unwanted data interception. TLS is based on the TCP protocol but adds a layer of encryption and security.

Media Transport The standard protocol for transporting the voice traffic over IP address is Real-Time Transport Protocol (RTP). RTP is widely used as a transport protocol for both voice and video traffic. A later extension to this protocol was the addition of security to eliminate the risk of interception and eavesdropping. It is known as Secure RTP (SRTP), and the endpoint devices encrypt any voice traffic within a secure payload before transmitting over the IP address network. Lync employs SRTP for communication to the gateway.

Media Codec As mentioned earlier in the ITSP section, the encoding and compression of the voice traffic element is achieved using one of the voice codecs, such as G.711, G.729, or SILK (although SILK in currently used only in PC-PC calls). The codec used must be agreed upon by both voice endpoints during the signaling negotiations to establish the call. If no common codec is available on the devices, the call will not be established. The gateway device in your Skype for Business deployment should be capable of changing the audio between different codecs, a process known as *transcoding*. The different gateways on the market today have different technical implementations to achieve this functionality, and they vary in capability and capacity!

SIP address and ISDN Gateways

A number of gateways available on the market today are certified for Skype for Business integration. Actually, they have mostly been certified for Lync, but devices are appearing with up-to-date firmware, and their certification is also being updated. They range from very small, low-cost analog devices to high-end data-center-type devices that can handle multiple E1 circuits, thousands of users, and high call volumes. Various vendors provide different platforms, including Sangoma, Sonus, AVAYA, Ferrari, and AudioCodes. Again, the gateway offerings differ in interfaces, features, and capability, so be sure to research your needs carefully.

In the following sections, we'll take a closer look at one of the gateways available for integration, the AudioCodes MSBG range, including the Mediant 1000 and the Mediant 800 designed for smaller office locations. This is the latest range of gateway and Survivable Branch Appliance (SBA) platforms from AudioCodes; it has been designed specifically with Skype for Business in mind and provides a flexible and high-performance way of connecting Skype for Business to other platforms.

First, let's look at some of the models available and the typical interfaces and features that you can configure for voice integration, and then we'll review some of the GUI configuration items of the platform.

Features

The Mediant 1000 shown in Figure 21.10 is a mid-point modular platform allowing for growth. If you look closely, you can see that each of the modules is screwed in and can be easily replaced. Indeed, one of the modules can be an SBA or CPU module, allowing for the easy upgrade of older versions (perhaps purchased for use with OCS 2007 R2) to provide more functionality for Skype for Business.

Figure 21.10
The AudioCodes Mediant 1000
Courtesy of AudioCodes, www.audiocodes.com

It provides the following features:

- Mix-and-match interfaces to allow the connection of digital (PRI) and analog (FXS/FXO) devices directly to the gateway. Multiple interface slots enable analog and digital connectivity in the same platform.
- High-capacity DSP resources that enable direct SIP address-to-SIP address transcoding of many codecs, as described in the previous section. This transcoding scales with extremely low latency and no loss of capacity or performance.
- Router/firewall/VPN to enable SBC functionality, giving security for your voice traffic.
- Optional branch survivability with fully integrated SBA. Skype for Business users in a branch have the ability to register directly to the gateway, providing full voice survivability in the event of a WAN outage.
- AD integration for advanced call routing, enabling smooth staged migration of users from your PBX to Skype for Business.
- SIP address phone registration. By allowing the direct registration of existing SIP address phones to the gateway, the device eliminates the need for an additional registrar server. By using this feature on the gateway, SIP address phones can become tightly integrated with your Skype for Business and PBX environment.

The Mediant 800, shown in Figure 21.11, uses the same configuration interface and code set as its larger brother, the Mediant 1000.

Figure 21.11
The AudioCodes Mediant 800 MSBG
Courtesy of AudioCodes, www.audiocodes.com

This similarity can make managing a solution easier when different gateway types are used. An organization can benefit from the advanced features and hardware components of the 1000 (and indeed there are larger-capacity models as well: Mediant 2000 and Mediant 3000) by using it at a central office and providing suitable capacity and functionality with the 800 at small office locations. The 800 has the following features:

- Mixed interfaces, enabling the connectivity of analog phones (FXS/FXO), and digital interfaces, either Basic Rate or Primary Rate
- High-capacity DSP resources that enable direct SIP address-to-SIP address transcoding

- Router/firewall/VPN to enable SBC functionality, giving security for your voice traffic
- Optional branch survivability with fully integrated SBA, giving branch office users total voice survivability
- AD integration for advanced call routing, enabling smooth staged migration of users from an existing PBX to Skype for Business
- Network interfaces (both Gb and FE) capable of Power over Ethernet (PoE)

Some of the advanced features now being implemented on voice gateways are specifically intended to assist in Skype for Business deployments and migrations; one such feature is Active Directory integration, which is provided on the platform. This capability enables many different dynamic routing scenarios. For example, the gateway can route incoming calls to either the Skype for Business environment or the legacy PBX, depending on whether the user's Direct Inward Dial (DID) number has been moved to Skype for Business or not as provisioned in AD, shown in Figure 21.12. Although this may not seem hugely significant, it plays a major factor in the migration of users from the PBX to Skype for Business because without this feature, an awful lot of manual routing table reconfiguration is needed. With AD integration on the gateway, the process is totally automated, enabling you to migrate users at your own pace and with ease.

FIGURE 21.12
AD-based intelligent call routing

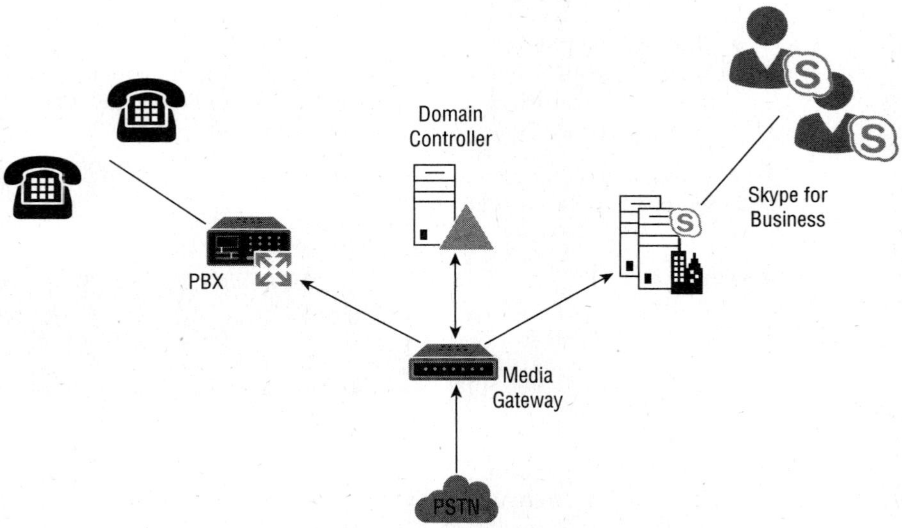

CONFIGURATION

The configuration of each manufacturer's devices is different (most will use a web interface), and we won't cover the specifics of a single device here. However, we'll talk about the Skype for Business configuration side. First, you need to configure the gateway device in Topology Builder, as shown in Figure 21.13.

FIGURE 21.13
Configuring a gateway device in Topology Builder

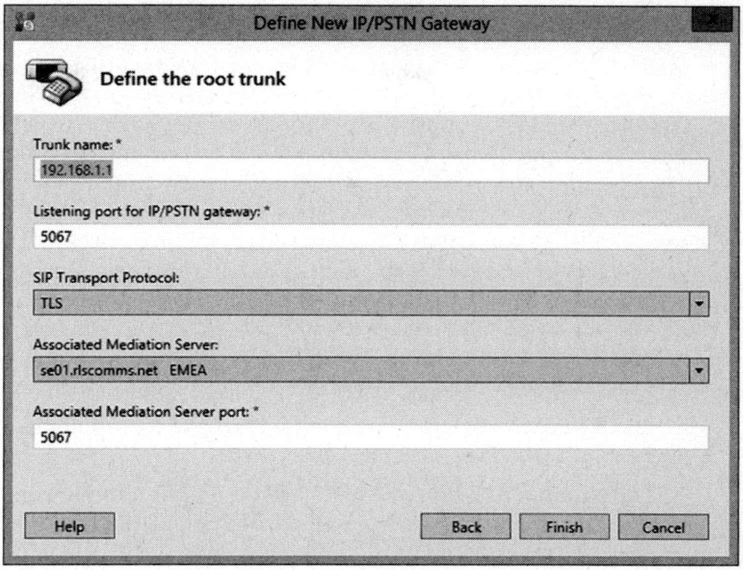

Once that's configured and published, you'll see a trunk has been configured from the gateway to the Mediation server. This trunk allows you to apply additional configuration items or policies as required. These configuration options can be configured via the Skype for Business Control Panel, some of which are shown in Figure 21.14.

FIGURE 21.14
Configuration of a trunk

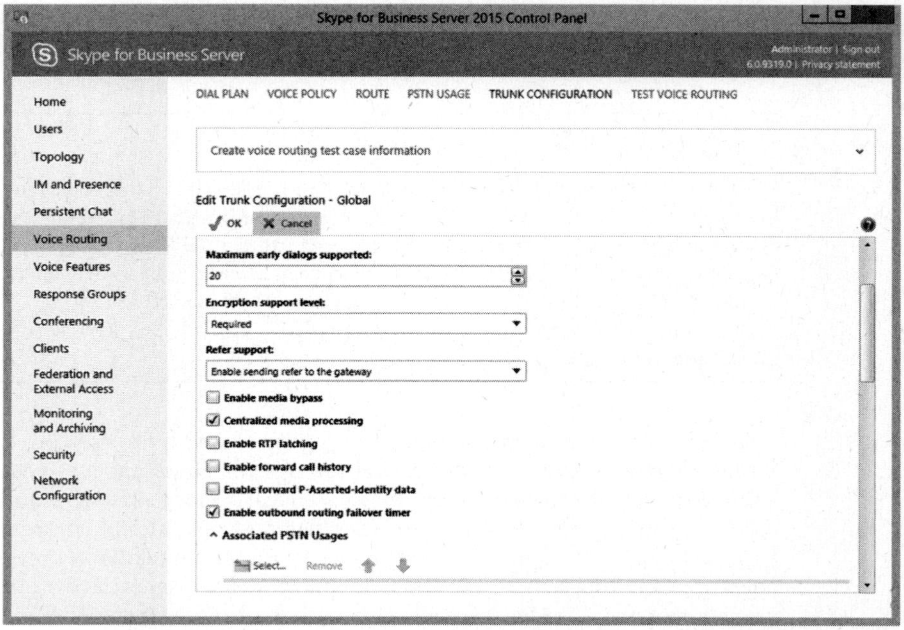

Integrating with Your PBX

Many organizations will need to enable interoperability between their legacy PBX and Skype for Business environment. This may be for a short period during migration from a telephony platform to Skype for Business or for an extended time as existing telephony assets are deprecated. In this section of the chapter, we will go through the different options that are available to you and offer some advice about which is best for your organization.

When you're interfacing a Skype for Business deployment to an existing PBX infrastructure, a big challenge you'll face is the wide array of PBX devices located in different offices and the general lack of knowledge about how to configure them. Enterprises grow over time and acquire and upgrade their PBX equipment at different times in different locations. Even if all PBX equipment is supposed to be replaced with Enterprise Voice, the approach may well be a staggered process across locations over a period of months.

The following factors will also affect your integration strategy:

The Age of the Existing Telephony Platform Consider the capabilities of the existing platform and whether its cost has been written off as an asset.

The Number of Users and Sites For example, a single location of 100 people could be migrated in a single weekend, while multiple locations might be best migrated in separate phases.

The Telephone Number Ranges in Use Does everyone already have a direct-dial-inward (DDI) (also known as DID—Direct Inward Dial) number, or will new numbers be required? If needed, these new numbers could be independent of the existing telephony platform, thus negating the need for integration.

The Number of Circuits The number and location of circuits and the way in which inbound numbers are presented across the circuits will influence whether you migrate numbers gradually or support the parallel running of the PBX and Skype for Business.

Legacy PSTN Circuits

If your telephony circuits (connections to the PSTN) are extremely old, the specific type of circuit may have been discontinued for new products and, as a result, may need to be upgraded. For example, in the United Kingdom, DASS circuits are a U.K.-specific form of ISDN that was used before Euro ISDN was standardized. It has been discontinued for new installations but can still be found in use. Although DASS circuits can be supported with some gateways, it is worth considering whether these circuits should be upgraded to ISDN Q.931 PRI circuits or even replaced with SIP address trunks.

A fundamental difference from the way legacy telephony has been provided is that Skype for Business is deployed in a far more centralized manner. For example, it is customary for users to have a single identity and for there to be a single Active Directory forest across an entire organization, in contrast to the physical location boundaries that most legacy telephony deployments followed.

With Skype for Business, a user can receive their phone calls wherever they log on to the network, including remote locations. Telephony deployments have traditionally been based on a single number provided to a single physical location, such as a desk, with little relationship to the end user beyond an entry in the phone list. More recent deployments may support hot-desking, but they often have limitations in a multiple-location organization where hot-desking may work only within a single office or country.

As part of your planning, you should make sure you fully understand the existing telephony in use. You may need to consider the following scenarios:

Emergency Phones They are sometimes found by emergency exits. These phones automatically dial either a central security point or the local emergency services. They often can dial only a preset list of numbers and may have to be operational even when all power has been lost to the building.

Gatehouse or Security Barrier Points In this scenario, a handset or push-button speaker and microphone dials a predetermined number to allow access. These are often provided over long runs of copper cabling through existing duct work. Newer solutions utilize Wi-Fi or mobile networks to provide similar functionality without the cabling requirements.

Elevator Phones Similar to emergency and gatehouse phones, these phones must work when no other building services are functioning so that someone stuck in an elevator can call for assistance. They are provided over long lengths of copper cabling, which typically run from a PBX room to the roof elevator machinery room and then down the elevator shaft with the internal elevator power cables.

Rugged or Explosion-Proof Phones Most industrial areas require special handsets. They may need to be ruggedized, water resistant, or dust resistant; have an Ingress Protection (IP address) rating; be designed to restrict any chance of electrical sparks (such as in grain stores or chemical plants); or meet any combination of these requirements.

Wireless or DECT Handsets Typically, these phones are used in large areas with only a few people, such as a warehouse, but also where users are very mobile, such as hospitals or airports.

Devices Integrated with Public Address Systems These allow people to dial an extension and make building-wide announcements, such as fire alarm test warnings.

All these scenarios, and many more, can be supported by Skype for Business. You need to understand your environment and know what is required from the outset. It's important so that you can plan accordingly to maximize performance. Failure to plan properly will certainly be exposed during migration and coexistence.

Integration Options

The typical approach to integration is where the two platforms exist and calls are routed between them, but there is no integration at a user level between them. A user can have extensions on both the PBX and Skype for Business, but they are independent of each other.

Where you logically place Skype for Business in relation to the PBX gives you different options for call routing, as discussed next.

Skype for Business Behind PBX

When Skype for Business resides logically behind the PBX (as in Figure 21.15), all incoming and outbound calls still route via the PBX. The connection to Skype for Business can be via an E1/J1/

T1 connection from the PBX to a certified gateway and then on to Skype for Business, or you can use Direct SIP address. The latter method is the least intrusive and allows your telephony team to remain in control of the call routing. It is, therefore, normally the easiest to deploy, so it can be popular for proof-of-concept or pilot deployments.

FIGURE 21.15 Skype for Business behind the PBX

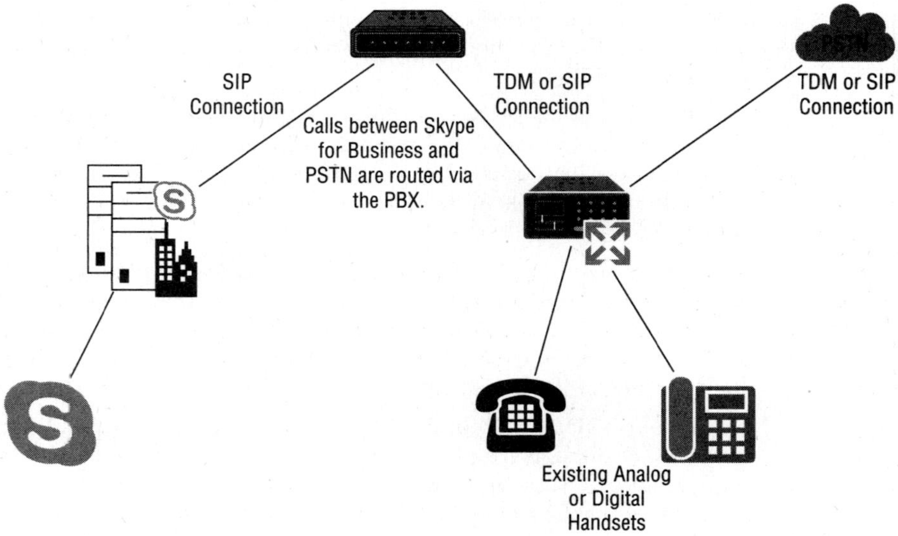

If the PBX supports SIP address IP address trunks, it may be possible to connect the PBX and Skype for Business directly using a SIP address trunk across your internal network so long as it is listed as supported in the OIP address. This removes the need to add any interfaces to your PBX, but not having a gateway removes a point of demarcation between the PBX and Skype for Business. Some organizations still prefer to use a gateway with SIP address trunks. For example, if your PBX is not supported, a gateway can translate between the PBX and Skype for Business to give you a supported environment. Quite often, a demarcation device has unexpected benefits during the project because additional functions or devices are involved in the migration and can be supported by the gateway.

SIDE BY SIDE

In this scenario, the existing PBX and Skype for Business sit logically alongside each other with a gateway sitting in front of them terminating the PSTN or SIP address trunks, as shown in Figure 21.16. This could be a gateway such as those discussed in this chapter, or in large environments, it may be carrier-class equipment working with SS7 signaling directly with the PSTN. The importance of this gateway is that it exists at the edge of the voice network. This gateway allows a point of control over the call routing before the call reaches the PBX, Skype for Business, or the PSTN. In this position, it can reroute calls intelligently using an AD lookup.

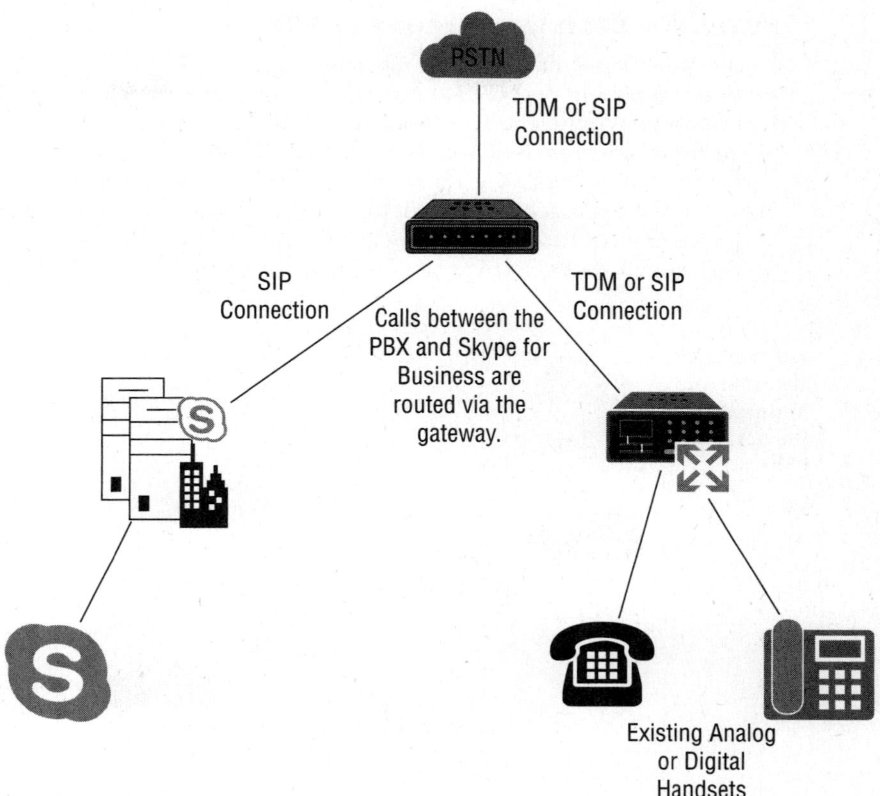

FIGURE 21.16
The side-by-side arrangement of PBX and Skype for Business with a gateway in front

With Active Directory–based routing, the gateway constantly queries AD for relevant user configuration, usually based around the population of the `msRTCSIP address-Line` attribute, and routes a call based on this information. If the inbound call destination is found to match the number in the `msRTCSIP address-Line` attribute, the calls to that user are routed only to Skype for Business. This provides for easy migration of users and rollback if required, all from within common management tools. There is no need to change the gateway or PBX configuration to alter inbound call routing.

PBX: The Route of Last Resort

Sometimes it is possible to configure the PBX to route to Skype for Business as the route of last resort, in a similar way that IP address routers are able to have a route (the default route, typically to your ISP) that says, "If I don't know where to route this address, route it to this upstream gateway for resolution." Some PBXs can be configured in a similar way, so when the phone extension is migrated to Skype for Business and removed from the PBX, the PBX passes the call to another device to resolve. In the side-by-side scenario, the gateway resolves the routing; when Skype for Business resides behind the PBX, then Skype for Business resolves.

Skype for Business in Front of PBX

Placing the PBX behind Skype for Business (Figure 21.17) is similar in approach to placing Skype for Business behind the PBX, although this is rarely done because the PBX is more established within your environment. The advantage of this approach is that from day one you establish Skype for Business as the point of control to the PSTN and you minimize any disruption from decommissioning the PBX, compared to placing Skype for Business behind the PBX initially. However, this approach requires all the effort, and more, of a side-by-side deployment (as well as the possibility of additional gateway hardware) without the advantages of dual-forking. Think through your objectives carefully before adopting this method.

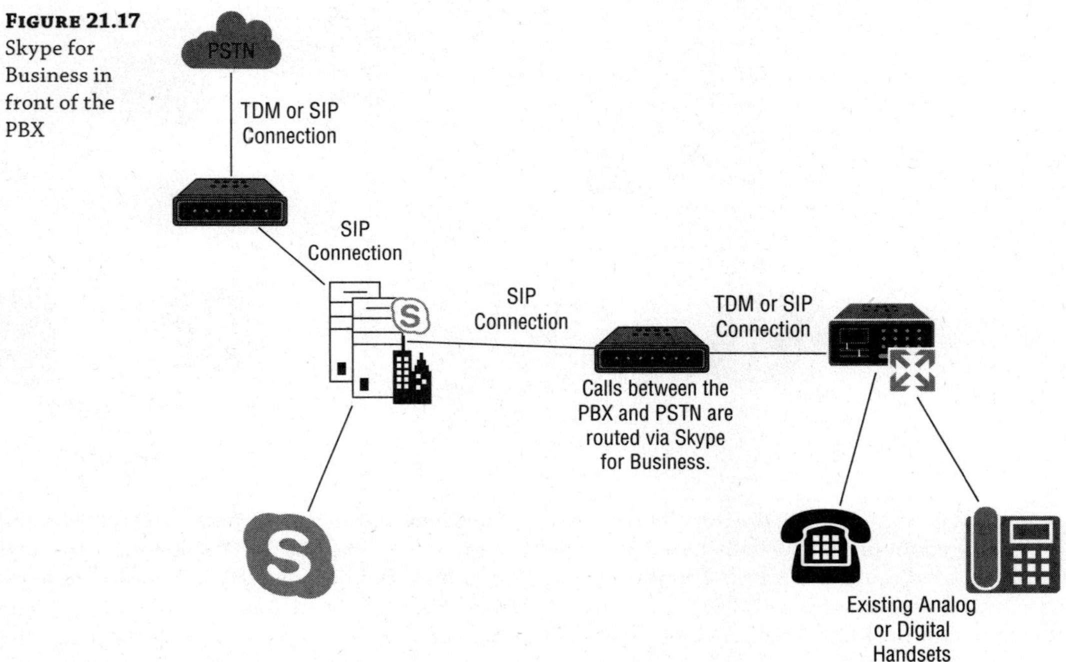

Figure 21.17 Skype for Business in front of the PBX

Recommendation and Tips

Wherever possible, it is generally preferable to use the side-by-side method with the gateway truncating the PSTN connections and routing calls to either Skype for Business or PBX as needed. This involves minimal disruption initially because the PSTN circuits can be configured to effectively pass straight through the gateway to the PBX. During migration, the side-by-side method gives the best flexibility of call routing options, and when all users are migrated, the PBX can be decommissioned without impacting the production environment.

Placing Skype for Business behind the PBX is normally an approach used in proof of concepts or small pilots because there is zero impact to the PBX other than configuration (of course, this assumes the PBX has suitable connectivity available).

Whichever logical deployment approach you choose, there are two items you need to be conscious of during the period of coexistence.

- The first is link capacity and call routing. On the first day of coexistence, the majority of users will remain on the PBX, and few calls will be terminating on Skype for Business. As your migration progresses, more calls will terminate on Skype for Business until a point when half your traffic is on Skype for Business and half is on the PBX. From this point on, the amount of traffic on the PBX will decline. Think of this as a set of scales with the load gradually transferring from one side to the other. As the traffic patterns change, you must make sure the connections between the systems are sized to handle the appropriate level of traffic. There will also be a certain amount of tromboning, which is acceptable as long as it is managed. *Tromboning* occurs where a call from one system, say, the PBX, is transferred to the other, Skype for Business, and then transferred back to the PBX—like a trombone going out and in again. This can happen if users divert their extensions, or sometimes it happens through misconfiguration. A certain amount of tromboning is to be expected during migration, but it must be managed so it does not become excessive. Worse still, it can lead to circular routing of calls, where a call passes back and forth between the two systems until there are no free channels or system resources to route more calls.
- The second important thing to be aware of is the number of translation patterns available on the PBX. Subject to the way you deploy Skype for Business and the specific functionality on the PBX, each extension or range of extensions will require entries on the PBX to reroute the extension number to Skype for Business. Although this is rarely a problem early on, it can quickly become an issue as you progress through your deployment. Once it is encountered, often the only way around this is either going through an expensive PBX software upgrade, which is what you are trying to avoid by deploying Skype for Business, or changing your coexistence method during your project. Note that while the number of translation patterns supported by a PBX can be found, they often get used in seemingly mystical ways, and the limit can be reached unexpectedly soon!

The Bottom Line

Use load balancers for scale. Load balancers allow and enable an Enterprise pool to be deployed, providing scale beyond that of a Standard Edition pool (5,000) all the way to the maximum number of users in a pool (80,000). They can also be deployed when scaling the Edge servers, although are not required.

> **Master It** What protocols are required to be load balanced in an Enterprise pool?

Use reverse proxies for external access. Typically, clients would have connected via the Access Edge role in the Edge server; however, mobile clients introduced the capability to connect using HTTP/HTTPS, and the latest desktop clients also leverage this capability. External (and federated) access to pools also requires the deployment of a reverse proxy.

> **Master It** You are deploying a reverse proxy solution in your DMZ to enable remote and federated access. What requirement must a reverse proxy provide for port translation?

Use gateways to Integrate with the PSTN. Connecting Skype for Business to telephony systems need not be hard; however, there are many areas you must consider to ensure that you make the correct deployment choices. Skype for Business can connect directly to an ITSP or a PBX or in both cases can utilize a gateway device to provide security, control, and intelligent routing of traffic.

Master It Your PBX is five years old and capable of being upgraded to talk to Skype for Business directly. You want to deploy Skype for Business for Enterprise Voice and need a way out to the PSTN. What must you consider in your decision about connecting Skype for Business to the PSTN?

Chapter 22

Exchange, SharePoint, and Office Web Application Server

A huge amount of communication technology is built into Skype for Business, but it is extended even further through tight integration with external systems. This chapter will explore Exchange, SharePoint, and Office Web Application Server integration. Skype for Business relies totally on Exchange to provide voice mail capabilities; not only can users receive voice mail, they also have full voice access to their mailboxes through tight integration into the Skype for Business client. Exchange is also used to provide the Unified Contact Store and can be configured as the compliance archive for Skype for Business interactions. Skype for Business, in turn, provides Exchange with the ability to integrate presence and basic IM functionality into Outlook Web Access (OWA).

Skype for Business and SharePoint together allow intelligent communications to be integrated into business processes. At its simplest level, presence is available in SharePoint, so there is quick and easy access to contact the author of documents; at a more complex level, it is also possible to integrate presence into workflow-related decisions—for example, to route documents to the most available manager for sign-off. SharePoint also provides the search capabilities to enable Skype for Business users to search for contacts by skill set.

Office Web Applications Server enables the rich PowerPoint sharing features within Skype for Business, allowing users to view presentations with rich content and reducing the network load by translating this content into HTML5.

In this chapter, you will learn to

- Integrate Skype for Business with Exchange
- Integrate Skype for Business with SharePoint
- Integrate Skype for Business with Office Web Applications Server

Integrating Skype for Business with Exchange

These days, it is rare not to come across an Exchange messaging platform in an organization. Exchange has become almost the de facto standard for carrying email. With the recent versions (2007, 2010, and 2013), Exchange broadened its role, becoming part of a unified communication platform through the provision of voice mail and unified inbox capabilities. As you have seen throughout this book, Skype for Business is a fully functional communication platform;

however, it relies on the unified inbox capabilities of Exchange to store conversation history and voice mail and since Lync Server 2013 to provide a compliance grade archive. Because Exchange is the standard calendaring platform, Skype for Business utilizes this information to enhance presence and give visibility to out-of-office messages. Finally, Skype for Business can bring some of its capabilities to Exchange through the provision of presence and basic IM functionality into Outlook Web App.

Skype for Business Server 2015, when paired with Exchange 2013, brings a number of significant improvements in the way that it integrates with Exchange. Not only do we now have the ability to use Skype for Business from any supported web browser, and from any Internet location while checking our email, we now also have the ability to display high-resolution photographs instead of the standard 48 × 48 pixel format currently supported. That's definitely a move with the times in this HD era! We also now have the ability to choose where we store our Lync contacts and make full use of the search and litigation hold functionalities within Exchange for our Skype for Business messages. As with the rest of the Office stack, Skype for Business and Exchange should no longer be seen as separate products; they are slowly combining features to provide a truly unified experience for users.

This section of this chapter will focus upon Skype for Business and Exchange integration. We will cover the following features:

- Unified Messaging and voice mail for Enterprise Voice users
- IM and presence in Outlook Web Access
- Unified Contact Store
- Exchange archiving
- High-resolution photos

Different Versions of Exchange

Throughout this chapter, we are focusing on integration with Exchange Server 2013. But what if you are running an older version, such as Exchange 2007 or Exchange 2010? Or indeed, what if you are in the middle of migrating from an older version and have users based on both platforms? In that case, all may not be lost because several features are still available. However, we recommend that some serious testing is carried out and that potentially you leave features disabled until users are on the most modern platform to ease complexity.

As you will see, Skype for Business makes extensive use of features in later Exchange versions, such as voice mail and web services. That said, Skype for Business can also integrate in some ways with versions as early as Exchange 2007 SP1.

The differences between Exchange 2007 and 2010 support are pretty small. Essentially, Exchange 2010 adds the ability to provide Message Waiting Indicator (MWI) information when used with Unified Messaging (UM) and also provides a contact sync feature, which allows Skype for Business to create a personal contact in Outlook for each person on a user's Skype for Business contacts list. Exchange 2013 provides the updated Unified Contact Store, Exchange archiving, and High-Resolution Photos support, which no previous versions support.

One other area for consideration is that it is now possible to deploy Exchange in the cloud using Microsoft Office 365. There are various supported scenarios for running parts of your organization in the cloud, including having either Skype for Business Online or Exchange Online with its respective on-premises system; these are explored further in Chapter 10, "Online and Hybrid."

Please note, as this book is going to press, Exchange Server 2016 is in the process of being released. Rather than try to include content from a beta that may change, we decided to stick with content from the released version of Exchange.

Configuring Exchange Integration Prerequisites

Before we start to configure specific features, there are a number of prerequisites that need to be taken care of, on both the Skype for Business and Exchange servers.

- Unified Communications Managed API 4.0 Runtime
- OAuthTokenIssuer
- Partner application
- Lync Storage Service

Unified Communications Managed API 4.0 Runtime

The Microsoft Unified Communications Managed API (UCMA) 4.0 is used primarily to build middle-tier applications that work with Microsoft Lync Server 2013 or newer. As such, it is required on the Exchange server. When integrating Exchange 2010 with Lync 2010, you had to specifically install UCMA 2.0 as a prerequisite on the Exchange server. Things are a little different with Exchange 2013. You now need version 4.0 of UCMA; however, given that the UM component on Exchange 2013 is installed on all Mailbox servers, UCMA 4.0 is a global prerequisite for any Exchange 2013 server and so will already be installed. UCMA plays its part in allowing Skype for Business to communicate with UM (and also OWA) by adding `Microsoft.Rtc.Internal.Ucweb.dll` in the `C:\Program Files\Microsoft UCMA\Runtime\SSP` directory.

Bottom line, there is no further work required for this prerequisite.

OAuthTokenIssuer

To provide the extensive integration between Microsoft server applications, the servers need to communicate with each other. To do so, they need a method of authentication, and this is provided by the OAuth protocol. OAuth is a standard authorization protocol based on the exchange of security tokens that grant access to resources for a specific period of time. The certificate is used for securing server-to-server communication and can be self-signed or issued by an enterprise certificate authority (CA). It is recommended that the same CA issue the certificates for all servers where possible because the issuing CA will be trusted by default. If this is not possible, then you must make sure each server trusts the issuer of all the certificates.

To support the OAuth protocol, Lync 2013 introduced a new certificate type, called OAuthTokenIssuer. This is also known as a server-to-server authentication certificate. You will find that the OAuthTokenIssuer certificate is one of the certificates you configure when running the Certificate Wizard during the installation of a Skype for Business server, as shown in Figure 22.1.

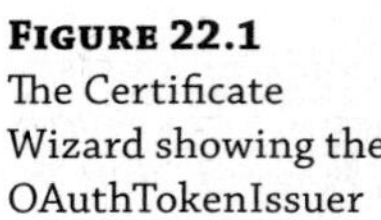

FIGURE 22.1
The Certificate Wizard showing the OAuthTokenIssuer

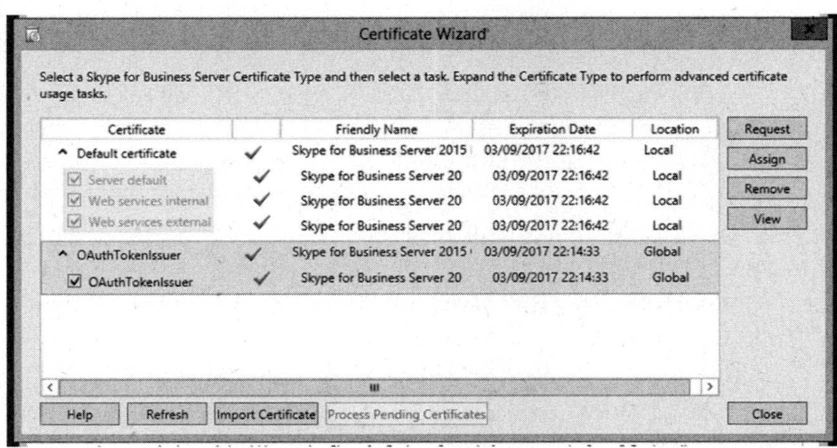

One thing to consider when configuring the OAuthTokenIssuer certificate is where it is stored. The default option, as shown in Figure 22.1, is Global, which means that the certificate is stored in the Central Management Store (CMS), thereby ensuring that the certificate is distributed to each Lync Front End server.

Exchange also has a similar authentication certificate, and when Exchange and Skype for Business integration is configured, these certificates are exchanged using an authentication metadata document via web services. The authentication metadata document is provided through the `/metadata/json/1` directory. (JSON stands for JavaScript Object Notation.) The specific web service URL can be configured using the command shell on both Skype for Business and Exchange servers. This is achieved by running the `Configure-EnterprisePartnerApplication.ps1` command from the Exchange server and the `New-CSPartnerApplication` command from the Skype for Business server, which are detailed in the next section, "Partner Application."

Another option, instead of using the default certificates, would be to use an existing certificate as your server-to-server authentication certificate. It must use at least a 2,048-bit key and include the name of the SIP domain in the Subject field (not just as a subject alternative name), and the same certificate must be configured as the OAuthTokenIssuer on all Front End servers. If you have multiple SIP domains, then providing that the primary SIP domain is registered in Skype for Business, OAuth will continue to work with any other SIP domains associated with that primary domain. For example, if `rlscomms.net` is your primary SIP domain and you also use `admin.rlscomms.net` and `tech.rlscomms.net` as additional SIP domains, OAuth will require a primary certificate name only for `rlscomms.net`. Should you change your primary SIP domain, which differs from the default name in the Subject field, an additional OAuth certificate will need to be generated. In this case, you would need to re-associate the new OAuth certificate with the Skype for Business server in the setup process.

The configuration of the OAuth certificate will propagate to all other Front End servers without any additional actions required. By having the same certificate on all Front End servers, we are able to follow best practice and point Exchange to a load-balanced pool of Skype for Business servers and have them all work together no matter which server Exchange talks to.

Partner Application

While the OAuth protocol allows for authentication between server applications, there is also a need to define what certain applications can do. This is where the partner application comes in. It is represented as a configuration entity on the both the trusted and trusting systems, Skype for Business and Exchange in this case.

The applications are configured on both sides using PowerShell. On Exchange, this is done using the provided script `Configure-EnterprisePartnerApplication.ps1`, which can be found in the `Exchange Scripts` directory. When it is run, a disabled user account is created (LyncEnterprise-ApplicationAccount), and the UserApplication and ArchiveApplication management roles are assigned. This account is then associated with the `/metadata/json/1` authentication document on the Skype for Business server to create a partner application. This configuration gives Skype for Business the ability to read and write data to Exchange mailboxes on behalf of users and is fundamental to be able to use the Message Archiving integration feature.

From the Skype for Business side, instead of using a script, you simply run the `New-CSPartnerApplication` cmdlet and specify the URL where the authentication document can be found via Exchange Web Services (EWS), as shown in the following command:

```
New-CsPartnerApplication -Identity Exchange -ApplicationTrustLevel Full↵
-MetadataUrl↵
"https://autodiscover.rlscomms.net/autodiscover/metadata/json/1"
```

We will put this into action and cover the details of the required configuration when setting up the Lync Storage Service in the next section.

Don't confuse the partner application with the Trusted Application pool, discussed later in the chapter. They are not the same thing even though they sound similar!

Lync Storage Service

Alongside OAuth, the Lync Storage Service (LYSS) is the other major element of Exchange and Skype for Business integration. LYSS is a storage framework introduced in Lync Server 2013 intended to be used by different LYSS consumers to access storage platforms such as Message Archiving and the Unified Contact Store. LYSS is designed to provide access to multiple storage platforms. As we are writing this, SQL Server and Exchange Web Services are commonly used. EWS supports the server-to-server authentication setup discussed previously.

To configure the LYSS, you must first ensure that the autodiscover service is correctly configured on Exchange. This is a hugely complex subject that is off-topic for in-depth discussion here. We suggest a discussion with your Exchange team or that you consult the suitable Exchange documentation. However, if your Exchange 2013 is up and running and serving users, it is likely that this is configured.

In a nutshell, what is required is to make sure that `AutoDiscoverServiceInternalURI` has been correctly set up on all Client Access servers. For this to work successfully, you should ensure that a DNS A record has been created for `Autodiscover.rlscomms.net` (of course, using your own domain here) and that it points to the Client Access server (CAS) or load-balanced CAS farm. The configuration can be carried out by running the following command (on the Exchange server):

```
Get-ClientAccessServer | Set-ClientAccessServer↵
-AutoDiscoverServiceInternalUri↵
"https://autodiscover.rlscomms.net/autodiscover/autodiscover.xml"
```

This command will first get all the Client Access servers in your Exchange environment and then set `AutoDiscoverServiceInternalURI` to the URL specified. Be careful doing this in production because getting it wrong will seriously break your Exchange client access!

Once this is completed, on the Skype for Business server, you now need to point the Skype for Business OAuthTokenIssuer certificate to the Exchange Autodiscover service, using the following command:

```
Set-CsOAuthConfiguration -ExchangeAutodiscoverUrl↵
"https://autodiscover.rlscomms.net/autodiscover/autodiscover.svc"
```

This command will point Skype for Business to the Exchange farm at the URL specified.

As described earlier in the section "Partner Application," on the Exchange server, you can now run the `Configure-EnterprisePartnerApplication.ps1` script to direct Exchange to the Skype for Business authorization location. This script comes built in with Exchange and can be found in the following location (assuming you've used the default install directory): `C:\Program Files\Microsoft\Exchange Server\V15\Scripts`. The syntax for running this command is as follows (yes, it should read Lync):

```
.\Configure-EnterprisePartnerApplication.ps1↵
-AuthMetadataUrl "https://se01.rlscomms.net/metadata/json/1"↵
-ApplicationType Lync
```

You can see the output from the script here:

```
Creating User <LyncEnterprise-ApplicationAccount> for Partner Application.

Created User <rlscomms.net/Users/LyncEnterprise-ApplicationAccount> for Partner
Application.

Assigning role <UserApplication> to Application User <rlscomms.net/Users/
LyncEnterprise-ApplicationAccount>.

Assigning role <ArchiveApplication> to Application User <rlscomms.net/Users/
LyncEnterprise-ApplicationAccount>.

Creating Partner Application <LyncEnterprise-20bfa98f640c447ca2c759c2c21df0c1>
using metadata <https://se01.rlscomms.net
/metadata/json/1> with linked account <rlscomms.net/Users/LyncEnterprise-
ApplicationAccount>.

Created Partner Application <LyncEnterprise-20bfa98f640c447ca2c759c2c21df0c1>.

THE CONFIGURATION HAS SUCCEEDED.
```

As you can see, the results of the script show that a new user has been created in the Users OU called `LyncEnterprise-ApplicationAccount` and an RBAC role has been assigned, allowing that account to use the `UserApplication` and `ArchiveApplication` roles within Exchange. A partner application with Skype for Business has also been created at this point.

To ensure that the settings take hold, you now need to recycle the IIS service by running `iisreset` on your Exchange servers. Please bear in mind that this will affect any users currently connected to that server using web services, such as Outlook Web Access, ActiveSync, or Entourage clients.

Having configured Exchange, you now move to the Skype for Business server and create the partner application there. The process is similar to that for Exchange and is carried out using the following command:

```
New-CsPartnerApplication -Identity Exchange -ApplicationTrustLevel Full↵
-MetadataUrl↵
"https://autodiscover.rlscomms.net/autodiscover/metadata/json/1"
```

The result of this command is that an AuthToken has been created on the Skype for Business server pointing to the Autodiscover URL on the Exchange server. You should see verification of the properties created similar to the following example:

```
Identity                               : Exchange
AuthToken                              :
Value=https://autodiscover.rlscomms.net/autodiscover/metadata/json/1
Name                                   : Exchange
ApplicationIdentifier                  : 00000002-0000-0ff1-ce00-000000000000
Realm                                  : corp.rlscomms.net
ApplicationTrustLevel                  : Full
AcceptSecurityIdentifierInformation : False
Enabled                                : True
```

You can now test that the partner application integration between Skype for Business and Exchange was successful. The following command will create a test entry on the specified Exchange mailbox using TCP binding, which requires the name of the storage service to be included. Once completed, the command will delete the test entry (on the Skype for Business server).

```
Test-CsExStorageConnectivity -SipUri keith.skype@rlscomms.net↵
-Binding NetTCP -DeleteItem↵
-HostNameStorageService se01.rlscomms.net -Verbose
```

The `-Verbose` parameter is optional but is useful for troubleshooting any problems you may encounter. With verbose logging enabled, you will be able to see the Autodiscover location being looked up as well as the `RequestMessage` and `ResponseMessage` for the specified mailbox, as shown in the following output:

```
VERBOSE: Successfully opened a connection to storage service at se01.rlscomms.net
using binding: NetTCP.
VERBOSE: Create message.
VERBOSE: Execute Exchange Storage Command.
VERBOSE: Processing web storage response for ExCreateItem Success.,
 result=Success,
activityId=b17dee7b-1362-4b3b-b4f0-9f7620f79168, reason=.
VERBOSE: Activity tracing:
2015/11/04 18:59:34.522 Lookup user details, sipUri=sip:keith.skype@rlscomms.net,
smtpAddress=Keith.Skype@rlscomms.net,
 sid=S-1-5-21-1801160900-2869415974-1656638013-1144,
```

```
upn=, tenantId=00000000-0000-0000-0000-000000000000
2015/11/04 18:59:34.584 Autodiscover, send GetUserSettings request,
 SMTP=Keith.Skype@rlscomms.net, Autodiscover
Uri=https://autodiscover.rlscomms.net/autodiscover/autodiscover.svc,
 Web Proxy=<NULL>
2015/11/04 18:59:34.625 Autodiscover.EWSMA trace, type=AutodiscoverRequestHttpHea
ders, message=<Trace
Tag="AutodiscoverRequestHttpHeaders" Tid="41"
Time="2015-11-04 18:59:34Z">
POST /autodiscover/autodiscover.svc HTTP/1.1
Content-Type: text/xml; charset=utf-8
Accept: text/xml
User-Agent: ExchangeServicesClient/15.00.1005.003

</Trace>
2015/11/04 18:59:34.656 Autodiscover.EWSMA trace, type=AutodiscoverRequest,
message=<Trace Tag="AutodiscoverRequest"
Tid="41" Time="2015-11-04 18:59:34Z" Version="15.00.1005.003">
  <?xml version="1.0" encoding="utf-8"?>
  <soap:Envelope xmlns:a="http://schemas.microsoft.com/exchange/2010/
Autodiscover"
xmlns:wsa="http://www.w3.org/2005/08/addressing" xmlns:xsi="http://www.w3.
org/2001/XMLSchema-instance"
xmlns:soap="http://schemas.xmlsoap.org/soap/envelope/">
    <soap:Header>
      <a:RequestedServerVersion>Exchange2013</a:RequestedServerVersion>
      <wsa:Action>http://schemas.microsoft.com/exchange/2010/
Autodiscover/Autodiscover/GetUserSettings</wsa:Action>
      <wsa:To>https://autodiscover.rlscomms.net/autodiscover/
autodiscover.svc</wsa:To>
    </soap:Header>
    <soap:Body>
      <a:GetUserSettingsRequestMessage xmlns:a="http://schemas.microsoft.com/
exchange/2010/Autodiscover">
        <a:Request>
          <a:Users>
            <a:User>
              <a:Mailbox>Keith.Skype@rlscomms.net</a:Mailbox>
            </a:User>
          </a:Users>
          <a:RequestedSettings>
            <a:Setting>InternalEwsUrl</a:Setting>
            <a:Setting>ExternalEwsUrl</a:Setting>
            <a:Setting>ExternalEwsVersion</a:Setting>
          </a:RequestedSettings>
        </a:Request>
      </a:GetUserSettingsRequestMessage>
```

```
    </soap:Body>
  </soap:Envelope>
</Trace>

2015/11/04 18:59:41.276 Autodiscover.EWSMA trace, type=AutodiscoverResponseHttpHe
aders, message=<Trace
Tag="AutodiscoverResponseHttpHeaders" Tid="41" Time="2015-11-04 18:59:41Z">
HTTP/1.1 200 OK
Transfer-Encoding: chunked
request-id: 6edaff5d-bbfe-4b8c-9078-d44e05c91ac5
X-CalculatedBETarget: ex01.rlscomms.net
X-DiagInfo: EX01
X-BEServer: EX01
X-FEServer: EX01
Cache-Control: private
Content-Type: text/xml; charset=utf-8
Date: Wed, 04 Nov 2015 18:59:40 GMT
Set-Cookie:
X-BackEndCookie=actas1
(sid:S-1-5-21-1801160900-2869415974-1656638013-1144|
smtp:Keith.Skype@rlscomms.net)=u56Lnp2ejJqBmZ
3Pyp7OzZnSycyayNLLzpnM0p7Lnp7SmsnPzp2anceenpvIg
YHOzdDPy9DNz87K387HxcrGxcvO;
expires=Fri, 04-Dec-2015 18:59:41 GMT;
path=/autodiscover; secure; HttpOnly
Server: Microsoft-IIS/8.5
X-AspNet-Version: 4.0.30319
X-Powered-By: ASP.NET

</Trace>

2015/11/04 18:59:41.277 Autodiscover.EWSMA trace,
 type=AutodiscoverResponse, message=<Trace Tag="AutodiscoverResponse"
Tid="41" Time="2015-11-04 18:59:41Z" Version="15.00.1005.003">
  <s:Envelope xmlns:s="http://schemas.xmlsoap.org/soap/envelope/"
xmlns:a="http://www.w3.org/2005/08/addressing">
    <s:Header>
      <a:Action
s:mustUnderstand="1">http://schemas.microsoft.com/exchange/
2010/Autodiscover/Autodiscover/GetUserSettingsResponse
</a:Action>
      <h:ServerVersionInfo xmlns:h="http://schemas.microsoft.com/exchange/2010/
Autodiscover"
xmlns:i="http://www.w3.org/2001/XMLSchema-instance">
        <h:MajorVersion>15</h:MajorVersion>
        <h:MinorVersion>0</h:MinorVersion>
        <h:MajorBuildNumber>847</h:MajorBuildNumber>
```

```
        <h:MinorBuildNumber>30</h:MinorBuildNumber>
        <h:Version>Exchange2013_SP1</h:Version>
      </h:ServerVersionInfo>
    </s:Header>
    <s:Body>
      <GetUserSettingsResponseMessage xmlns="http://schemas.microsoft.com/
exchange/2010/Autodiscover">
        <Response xmlns:i="http://www.w3.org/2001/XMLSchema-instance">
          <ErrorCode>NoError</ErrorCode>
          <ErrorMessage />
          <UserResponses>
            <UserResponse>
              <ErrorCode>NoError</ErrorCode>
              <ErrorMessage>No error.</ErrorMessage>
              <RedirectTarget i:nil="true" />
              <UserSettingErrors />
              <UserSettings>
                <UserSetting i:type="StringSetting">
                  <Name>InternalEwsUrl</Name>
                  <Value>https://ex01.rlscomms.net/EWS/Exchange.asmx</Value>
                </UserSetting>
              </UserSettings>
            </UserResponse>
          </UserResponses>
        </Response>
      </GetUserSettingsResponseMessage>
    </s:Body>
  </s:Envelope>
</Trace>

2015/11/04 18:59:41.340 Autodiscover,
received GetUserSettings response,
duration Ms=6751, response=NoError
2015/11/04 18:59:43.544 Lookup user details,
sipUri=sip:keith.skype@rlscomms.net,
 smtpAddress=Keith.Skype@rlscomms.net,
 sid=S-1-5-21-1801160900-2869415974-1656638013-1144,
upn=, tenantId=00000000-0000-0000-0000-000000000000
VERBOSE: Items choice type: CreateItemResponseMessage.
VERBOSE: Response message, class: Success, code: NoError.
VERBOSE: Item: Microsoft.Rtc.Internal.Storage.
Exchange.Ews.MessageType,
Id:AAMkADQ4ZTMwMTU5LWEzOWItNDVhYS04NWQ3LWJjMzJhODU2YjRj
NABGAAAAAACl3gmlxbf2S4XO7RUI3l7UBwC2B85uBZmdTb9tDvR6cLQ
IAAAAARDNAAC2B85uBZmdTb9tDvR6cLQIAAAInXrwAAA=,
change key: CQAAABYAAAC2B85uBZmdTb9tDvR6cLQIAAAInIeB,
subject: , body: .
VERBOSE: Is command successful: True.
```

```
VERBOSE: Delete message.
VERBOSE: Execute Exchange Storage Command.
VERBOSE: Processing web storage response for ExDeleteItem Success.,
 result=Success,
activityId=00000000-0000-0000-0000-000000000000, reason=.
VERBOSE: Items choice type: DeleteItemResponseMessage.
VERBOSE: Response message, class: Success, code: NoError.
VERBOSE: Unhandled response type, type=Microsoft.Rtc.Internal.Storage.
Exchange.Ews.DeleteItemResponseMessageType.
VERBOSE: Is command successful: True.
Test passed.
```

If you do get errors, they will show up as follows, which is the important element of the error text:

```
Test-CsExStorageConnectivity : ExCreateItem exchange operation failed, code=5 rea
son=StoreContext{traceId=1015445631], activityId=[4435392b-32b3-4195-b667-
4a53d2034ac1]}Access Denied, exception=System.ServiceModel.FaultException:
StoreContaxt{traceId=[1015445631], activityId=[4435392b-32b3-4195-b667-
4a53d2034ac1]}Access Denied
```

In this example, you will see the "Access Denied" message. This is most likely caused by the user running the test not being a member of the RTC Local User Administrators group on the server where the test is being run. Once you have the permissions set correctly, test again and you should find that you get the "Test passed" message displayed to confirm that the transaction was carried out successfully.

At this stage, you have successfully introduced Skype for Business to Exchange, created partner applications, and set permissions correctly. This is the underpinning of Skype for Business and Exchange integration.

The Voice Mail Platform for Skype for Business

Having worked through the prerequisite configuration steps, you can now move on to setting up voice mail. This is one of the most visible integration points for Skype for Business and Exchange alongside the provision of presence in OWA. Given that in-depth coverage of Exchange Unified Messaging (UM) could be the subject of another book, we will here review the basics of Exchange UM integration with Skype for Business so that you can provide Skype for Business users with voice mail.

There are few changes that have been made to the functionality of UM for Skype for Business Enterprise Voice users between Skype for Business and Exchange 2010 to 2013. The following are the biggest changes:

- The Unified Messaging service now runs as standard on all Exchange Server 2013 Mailbox role servers. Exchange 2013 has consolidated the once five roles into three. Therefore, the Mailbox server now runs components including Client Access, Hub Transport, UM, and Mailbox.
- There is a new service, the UM Call Router (UMCR) service, on Exchange Server 2013 Client Access role servers. The UM Call Router service uses the same principle as the mail routing service, where all inbound UM calls hit the UM Call Router service first and are

then forwarded to the relevant UM back-end server. This means that your setup for integration has an additional step: You use the `Set-UMCallRouterSettings` command to associate the Exchange certificate with the UM Call Router service and restart the service once you've applied security to it.

To configure Exchange UM, you carry out the following steps:

1. Ensure that the correct certificates are in place.
2. Configure the Exchange UM elements of the system (dial plan, policy, and auto attendants).
3. Ensure that Exchange knows about Skype for Business as a gateway.
4. Confirm that Skype for Business dial plans are configured correctly.
5. Configure Skype for Business to utilize Exchange UM.
6. Enable users for UM.

Configuring Exchange Certificates for UM

To ensure that Exchange UM can operate in a secure manner, you need to verify that a suitable certificate is in place to protect communication between Skype for Business and Exchange. In the Exchange documentation, you may notice a statement that a public certificate is required. This is in some ways correct but slightly ambiguous. What is needed is a certificate from a trusted certificate authority (CA) rather than a self-signed certificate. This could be an internal AD-based CA that both servers trust or one from a third party (DigiCert, for example). The key point is that an Exchange self-signed certificate is not going to cut it!

If you need help creating, importing, and assigning the Exchange certificate, you can find the details at this location:

`http://technet.microsoft.com/en-us/library/bb676409(v=exchg.150).aspx`

With the introduction of the UM Call Router service to the Client Access role in Exchange 2013, both the UM and UM Call Router services will need to be enabled for Dual or TLS mode for a certificate to be assigned. These steps can be carried out using the Exchange Management Shell and will be covered later.

Configuring Exchange UM

Once Exchange UM is configured with the relevant certificate, you can configure the UM components of Exchange for integration with Skype for Business. The first required piece is a new UM dial plan. The UM dial plan provides Exchange with the following information:

- The number of digits that form the extension (as discussed in Chapter 16, "Getting Started with Voice"), which in this case will be four.
- The Uniform Resource Indicator (URI) type, which for communication with Skype for Business must be SIP URI.
- The level of VoIP security required. Choose Secured so that both the SIP signaling traffic and the media will be encrypted. If you chose SIP Secured, only the signaling traffic would be encrypted. The other option, Unsecured, simply doesn't work—and if you are planning to deploy Skype for Business Phone Edition, you must use Secured, as in this example.

To create the UM dial plan, take the following steps:

1. Log into the Exchange Administration Console as an Exchange administrator—for example, `https://ex01.rlscomms.net/ecp`.
2. On the left side, select Unified Messaging; then in the UM Dial Plans section, click + to create a new dial plan. In this example, we used the following settings:
   - Name: UMDialPlan (no spaces)
   - Extension Length (Digits): 3
   - Dial Plane Type: SIP URI
   - VoIP Security Mode: Secured
   - Audio Language: English (United States)
   - Country/Region Code: 44

Figure 22.2 shows this configuration.

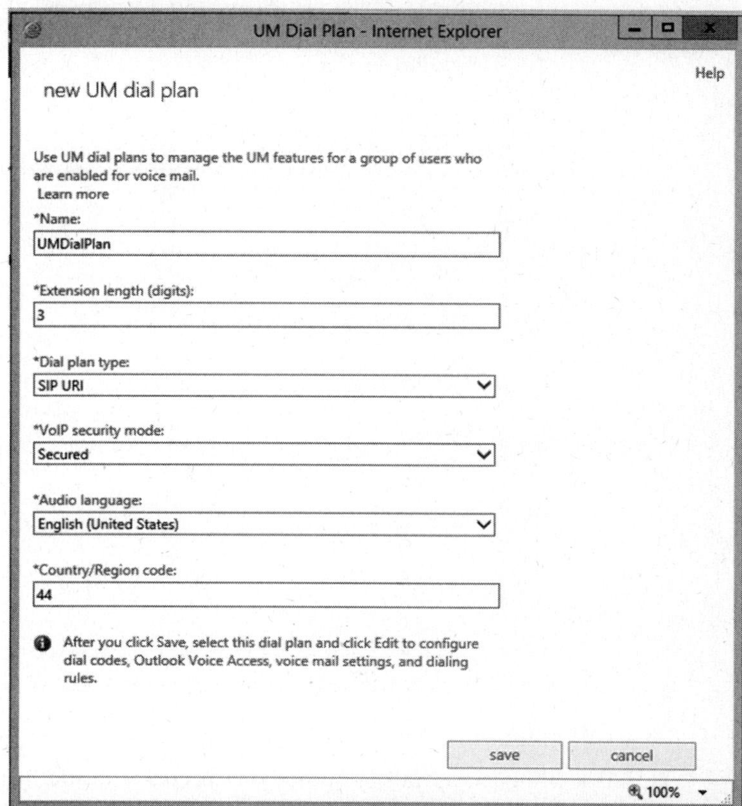

FIGURE 22.2 Configuring your dial plan

The SIP URI plan type allows the SIP protocol to be used for signaling messages, and using Secured for the VoIP security mode means that TLS can be used to encrypt the channel used by SIP.

3. Click Save and then click the pencil icon to edit the dial plan.
4. Under UM Dial Plan, click Configure.
5. On the left side, select Dialing Rules, and create a new in-country/region dialing rule. We used the following settings:
   - Dialing Rule Name: Anywhere
   - Number Pattern To Transform: *
   - Dialed Number: *

Figure 22.3 shows this configuration.

FIGURE 22.3 Configuring the dialing rules

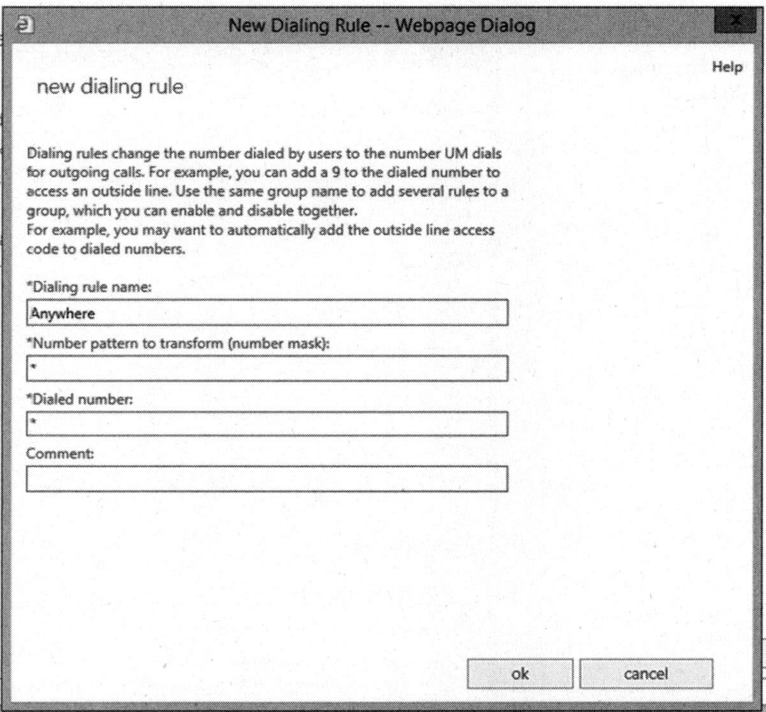

6. Click OK. Within Dialing Authorization, click + to add the Anywhere dialing rule to Authorized In-Country/Region Dialing Rule Groups, as shown in Figure 22.4.

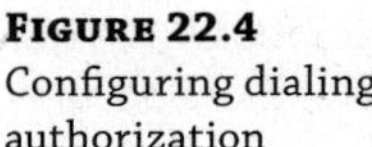

FIGURE 22.4
Configuring dialing authorization

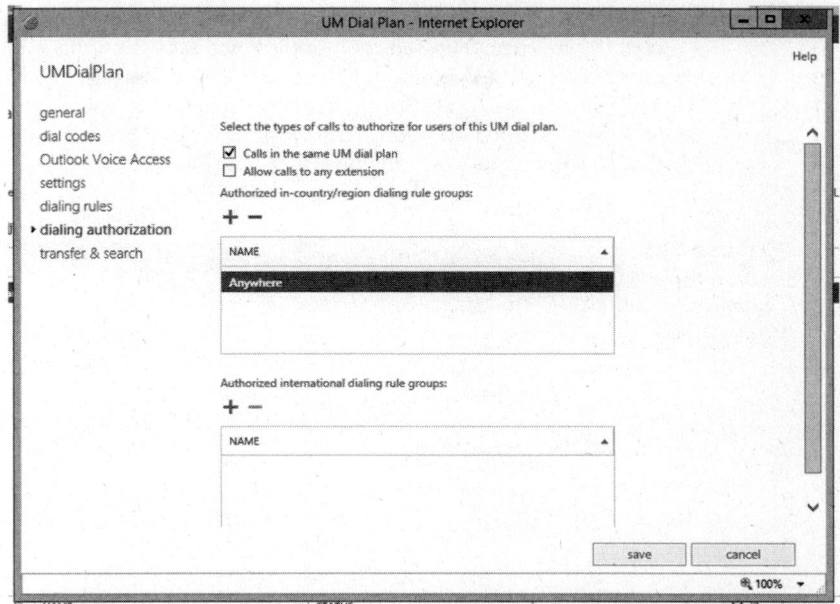

7. Click Save.

Of course, by this stage in the book, you may be getting into PowerShell. As you would imagine, all this can be set up from the command line as follows:

```
New-UMDialPlan -Name "UMDialPlan" -NumberOfDigitsInExtension 3↵
-URIType "SipName" -VoIPSecurity "Secured" -CountryOrRegionCode 44
```

The previous command creates the dial plan and configures the required options such as the `VoIPSecurity` and the extension length.

```
Set-UMDialPlan "UMDialPlan" -ConfiguredInCountryOrRegionGroups "Anywhere,*,*,*"↵
-AllowedInCountryOrRegionGroups "Anywhere"
```

The previous command configures the dialing rules and authorization.

At this point, you will have a dial plan that has dialing rules and authorization configured. You are now ready to move on and configure a few other elements of UM.

First you will set the Outlook Voice Access (OVA) dial-in number and configure an auto attendant. Outlook Voice Access provides phone-based, voice, and touch-tone access to your mailbox, so among other things, mail can be read to you and calendar items can be manipulated. Second, you will configure an auto attendant, which is used to provide an access point for callers to be routed automatically to either a person or a department. The UM auto attendant in Exchange is quite flexible and can be set up with personalized menus and audio recording. However, for the purpose of demonstrating Skype for Business integration, you will simply create a basic auto attendant.

1. Using the Exchange Administration Console, within the properties for UMDialPlan, select Configure; then select Outlook Voice Access on the left side. Add the E.164 routing number for SIP, as shown in Figure 22.5. (Note that +44555222000 works for our environment, but you will need to choose a suitable free number in your pool of numbers.) Also, be sure to add the number to the Outlook Voice Access Number section; this is the section that will get included in the user welcome email.

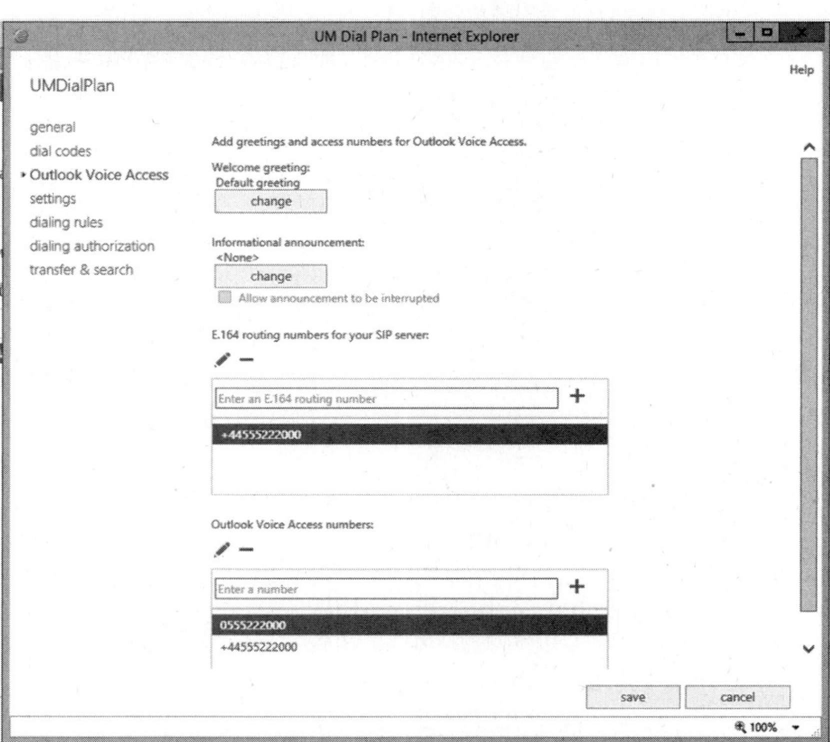

FIGURE 22.5 Entering the access number for Outlook Voice Access

2. Click Save and scroll down to the bottom of the UMDialPlan settings.
3. Click + to create a new UM auto attendant called UMAutoAttendant.
4. Select Create This Auto Attendant As Enabled. Add the number (we added +44555222001, as shown in Figure 22.6). Then click Save and close the properties page.

As with setting up the dial plan earlier, the same configuration can also be carried out using the Exchange Management Shell, as shown here:

```
Set-UMDialPlan UMDialPlan -PilotIdentifierList "+44555222000"↵
New-UMAutoAttendant -Name UMAutoAttendant -UMDialPlan UMDialPlan↵
-PilotIdentifierList "+44555222001" -Status Enabled
```

FIGURE 22.6
Creating and enabling the auto attendant

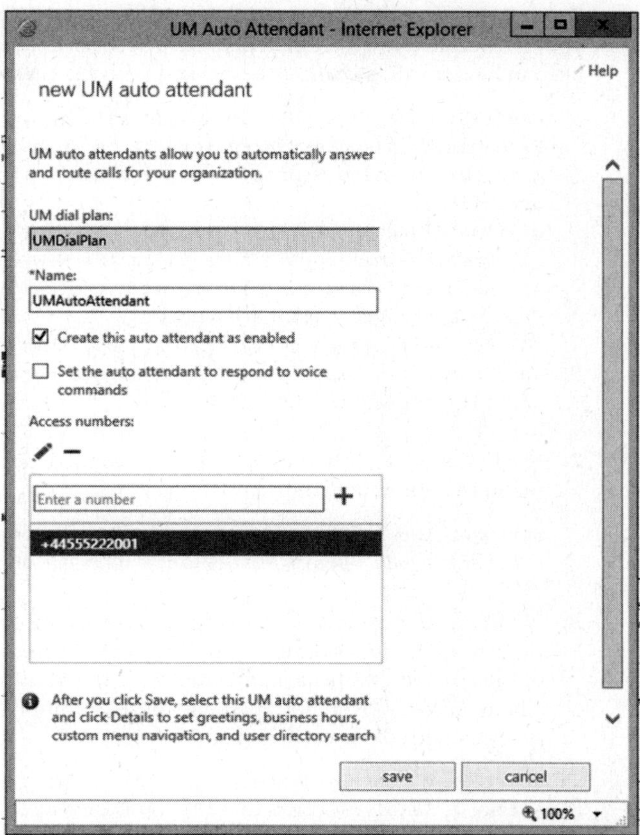

Now that the dial plan, auto attendant, and OVA numbers are set up, you need to configure the startup mode of the UM and UM Call Router services on Exchange to use TLS security so that all data flow is encrypted. You will also assign the dial plan to the required Exchange servers (those that are participating in the UM configuration) as follows:

1. To configure the UM service to use TLS and assign the dial plan, run the following command on the Exchange Mailbox server:

```
Set-UMService "ex01.rlscomms.net" -DialPlans "UMDialPlan"↵
-UMStartupMode "Dual"
```

The use of UMStartupMode Dual in the previous command means that the UM service can accept both secure encrypted SIP communication and also standard unencrypted SIP messages. Another option for full security would be to enter TLS, which would require a certificate for all UM integration. Dual mode is especially useful in situations where you are migrating from a previous version of Exchange and may need to support unsecured conversations from some of your older servers.

On completion of the command, you should see the following message displayed, reminding you that because you have changed the UM service to start up in Dual or TLS mode, you will need to have a valid certificate associated with the UM service. You will do this in the next steps.

```
WARNING: Changes to UMStartupMode will only take effect after the Microsoft
Exchange Unified Messaging service is restarted on server EX01. The
Microsoft Unified Messaging service won't start unless there is a valid TLS
certificate.
WARNING: To complete TLS setup, do all of the following:
(1) Create a new certificate using the New-ExchangeCertificate cmdlet
(2) Associate this certificate with the Unified Messaging server using the
Enable-ExchangeCertificate cmdlet
(3) For self-signed certificates, copy this certificate to the UM IP gateway
 and correctly import it. For CA-signed certificates, correctly import the CA
 certificate to the UM IP gateway.
```

2. Next you must apply the same settings to the UMCR service on the Client Access server using the following command:

```
Set-UMCallRouterSettings -Server ex01.rlscomms.net↵
-UMStartupMode "Dual" -DialPlans "UMDialPlan"
```

3. Finally, you must ensure that Exchange uses the correct certificate to secure the connections to UM. This is done using the following commands. First extract the thumbprint of the current certificate associated with the Mailbox server. Then extract the one for the Client Access server. You then use these thumbprints to associate the UM and UMCR services with those certificates.

```
$certmbx = (Get-ExchangeCertificate | Where {$_.Subject↵
-ilike  "*ex01.rlscomms.net*"}).Thumbprint
$certcas = (Get-ExchangeCertificate | Where {$_.Subject↵
-ilike "*ex01.rlscomms.net*"}).Thumbprint
```

The `$certmbx` and `$certcas` values create a variable that will be used to capture the certificates from the output of the command. You can then use these variables to enter the thumbprint into the following command, which will ensure that the next time the UM and UMCR services are started, the correct certificates are used to secure them. This is done using the following commands:

```
Enable-ExchangeCertificate -Server ex01.rlscomms.net↵
-Thumbprint $certmbx -Services "SMTP","IIS","UM"
Enable-ExchangeCertificate -Server exc01.rlscomms.net↵
-Thumbprint $certcas -Services "IIS","UMCallRouter"
```

Note that these commands have been run against separated Mailbox and Client Access servers—for those of you running a colocated server, the process is simplified because there is only a single certificate being used to publish the service and both the UM and UMCR services are running on the same server. You can use the following commands to achieve the same results for a colocated server:

```
$cert = (Get-ExchangeCertificate | Where {$_.Subject↵
-ilike "*mail.rlscomms.net*"}).Thumbprint
Enable-ExchangeCertificate -Server ex01.rlscomms.net↵
-Thumbprint $cert -Services "SMTP","IIS","UM","UMCallRouter"
```

4. Restart the UM and UM Call Router services on both servers for these changes to take effect.

The final piece of Exchange-only configuration before we move on to introduce Exchange to Skype for Business is the creation of a UM mailbox policy. The following command will create a new UM mailbox policy, which will be associated with the previously created dial plan:

```
New-UMMailboxPolicy "UMMailboxPolicy" -UMDialPlan "UMDialPlan"
```

It is worth exploring the UM mailbox policy so that you understand the settings that are configured there. In particular, you will find that there are policies that govern the length, complexity, and age of the PIN code that is assigned to users to enable them to easily authenticate with UM via a phone device. If you are simply testing UM, you may want to ease the default of six-character complex PINs to make them simpler to remember. Obviously, if this is a production environment, you will want to make sure the required PIN is suitably secure for your organization.

At this point, you've performed the bulk of the Exchange configuration. The next big thing to do is to introduce Exchange to Skype for Business. This is done using a script provided with Exchange in the Exchange directory `Scripts` folder, which when installed in the default location will be at `C:\Program Files\Microsoft\Exchange Server\V15\Scripts`. This script is called `ExchUCUtil.ps1` and performs the following tasks:

- Grants Skype for Business the required permission to read Exchange UM Active Directory objects, in particular the SIP URI dial plan objects you created previously by configuring the RTCUniversalServerAdmins and RTCComponentUniversalServices groups to read the UM dial plan.
- Creates a UM IP gateway object for each Skype for Business pool or for each server running Skype for Business Standard Edition that hosts users who are enabled for Enterprise Voice.

You must run this script from the Exchange Management Shell using the following command, which assumes that Exchange is installed as per the default settings:

```
C:\Program Files\Microsoft\Exchange Server\V15\Scripts\ExchUCUtil.ps1
```

Once you have run the script, make sure to allow time for AD replication to occur. Once suitable time has elapsed, verify that the settings have been performed properly by running the script again, this time with a `-verify` parameter, as shown here:

```
C:\Program Files\Microsoft\Exchange Server\V15\Scripts\ExchUCUtil.ps1 -verify
```

This will run through and output the configuration as it stands, showing where permissions have been granted and which gateways have been created, as in the following:

```
Using Global Catalog: GC://DC=rlscomms,DC=net


Configuring permissions for rlscomms.net\RTCUniversalServerAdmins ...
```

```
First Organization: The appropriate permissions haven't been granted
 for the Lync servers and administrators to be able to read the UM
 dial plan and auto attendants container objects in Active Directory.
 The correct permissions are being added to the container objects.
UM DialPlan Container: The appropriate permissions haven't been
 granted for the Lync servers and administrators to be able to
 read the UM dial plan and auto attendants container objects in
 Active Directory. The correct permissions are being added to
 the container objects.
UM AutoAttendant Container: The appropriate permissions haven't
 been granted for the Lync servers and administrators to be able
 to read the UM dial plan and auto attendants container objects
 in Active Directory. The correct permissions are being added to
 the container objects.
Administrative Groups: The appropriate permissions haven't been
 granted for the Lync servers and administrators to be able to
 read the UM dial plan and auto attendants container objects in
 Active Directory. The correct permissions are being added to
 the container objects.

Configuring permissions for rlscomms.net\RTCComponentUniversalServices ...
First Organization: The appropriate permissions haven't been granted
 for the Lync servers and administrators to be able to read the UM
 dial plan and auto attendants container objects in Active Directory.
 The correct permissions are being added to the container objects.
UM DialPlan Container: The appropriate permissions haven't been
 granted for the Lync servers and administrators to be able to read
 the UM dial plan and auto attendants container objects in Active Directory. The
 correct permissions are being added to the
 container objects.
UM AutoAttendant Container: The appropriate permissions haven't been granted for
the Lync servers and administrators to be able to read
 the UM dial plan and auto attendants container objects in Active Directory. The
 correct permissions are being added to the container objects.
Administrative Groups: The appropriate permissions haven't been
 granted for the Lync servers and administrators to be able to read
 the UM dial plan and auto attendants container objects in Active Directory. The
 correct permissions are being added to the container objects.

Configuring UM IP Gateway objects...
Pool: se02.rlscomms.net
A UMIPGateway doesn't exist in Active Directory for the Lync Server pool. A new
UM IP gateway is being created for the Pool.
IsBranchRegistrar: False
MessageWaitingIndicatorAllowed: True
OutcallsAllowed: True
WARNING: The command completed successfully but no settings of 'se02' have been
modified.
```

```
Dial plans: UMDialPlan

Pool: dir01.rlscomms.net
A UMIPGateway doesn't exist in Active Directory for the Lync Server pool. A new
UM IP gateway is being created for the Pool.
IsBranchRegistrar: False
MessageWaitingIndicatorAllowed: True
OutcallsAllowed: True
WARNING: The command completed successfully but no settings of 'dir01' have been
modified.
Dial plans: UMDialPlan

Pool: eepool01.rlscomms.net
A UMIPGateway doesn't exist in Active Directory for the Lync Server pool. A new
UM IP gateway is being created for the Pool.
IsBranchRegistrar: False
MessageWaitingIndicatorAllowed: True
OutcallsAllowed: True
WARNING: The command completed successfully but no settings of 'eepool01' have
been modified.
Dial plans: UMDialPlan

Pool: se01.rlscomms.net
A UMIPGateway doesn't exist in Active Directory for the Lync Server pool. A new
UM IP gateway is being created for the Pool.
IsBranchRegistrar: False
MessageWaitingIndicatorAllowed: True
OutcallsAllowed: True
WARNING: The command completed successfully but no settings of 'se01' have been
modified.
Dial plans: UMDialPlan

Permissions for group rlscomms.net\RTCUniversalServerAdmins

ObjectName                    AccessRights                  Configured
----------                    ------------                  ----------
First Organization            ListChildren                  True
UM DialPlan Container         ListChildren, ReadProperty    True
UM AutoAttendant Container    ListChildren, ReadProperty    True
Administrative Groups         ListChildren, ReadProperty    True

Permissions for group rlscomms.net\RTCComponentUniversalServices

ObjectName                    AccessRights                  Configured
----------                    ------------                  ----------
First Organization            ListChildren                  True
UM DialPlan Container         ListChildren, ReadProperty    True
UM AutoAttendant Container    ListChildren, ReadProperty    True
```

```
Administrative Groups          ListChildren, ReadProperty    True


PoolFqdn                       UMIPGateway                   DialPlans
--------                       -----------                   ---------
se02.rlscomms.net              se02                          {(not found)}
dir01.rlscomms.net             dir01                         {(not found)}
eepool01.rlscomms.net          eepool01                      {(not found)}
se01.rlscomms.net              se01                          {(not found)}
```

If you see the `DialPlans` column showing `{(not found)}`, you should rerun the command. The following is the expected result:

```
PoolFqdn                       UMIPGateway                   DialPlans
--------                       -----------                   ---------
se02.rlscomms.net              se02                          {UMDialPlan}
dir01.rlscomms.net             dir01                         {UMDialPlan}
eepool01.rlscomms.net          eepool01                      {UMDialPlan}
se01.rlscomms.net              se01                          {UMDialPlan}
```

At this point, you're ready to move over to the Skype for Business server and perform the configuration needed there. Enterprise Voice is already configured and set up, as covered in Chapter 16, but it is worth validating that the normalization rules on your Skype for Business dial plans are configured to support the extension dialing configured in UM. (Remember the four-digit extension configured in the UM dial plan earlier?) You need to ensure that when someone on Skype for Business dials the four-digit extension, Skype for Business knows how to normalize the number to E.164 and route it correctly.

The normalization rules can be validated in the Skype for Business Server Control Panel (LSCP, or simply Control Panel). Create a new voice testing routing case and enter the last four digits of the subscriber access number (**123**) in the Dialed Number To Test box. In the Expected Translation box, enter the full E.164 subscriber access number (**+441189091234**) and then run the test. If it passes, you are ready to move on. If not, go back to Chapter 16 and configure the relevant dial plan settings to cope with three-digit dialing.

Assuming your system is set up to pass the routing test, you can move on and introduce Skype for Business to Exchange so that it knows where to route calls that need to go to voice mail. This is done using a utility called `OcsUmUtil.exe` (yes, that should be OCS; the name hasn't changed for a while!). The `OcsUmUtil.exe` will load the existing Exchange UM dial plans from AD and associate them with Skype for Business contacts. In the event that a Skype for Business user tries to access their voice mail, leave a voice mail for another user, or call the Outlook Voice Access attendant, there must be a way for Skype for Business to be able to route the call to the appropriate voice prompt running on the Unified Messaging service.

You can find this utility in the `C:\Program Files\Common Files\Microsoft Skype for Business Server 2015\Support\` directory.

When you run the utility, you will see the window shown in Figure 22.7.

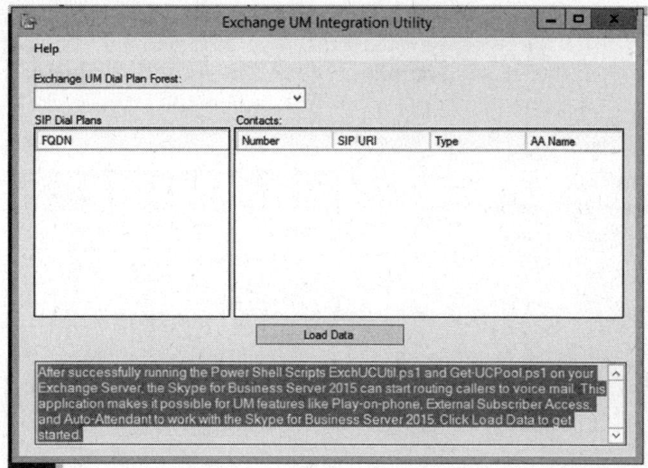

FIGURE 22.7 The OcsUmUtil opening screen

Then follow these steps:

1. From the opening screen, click Load Data. The tool will contact AD to determine the forests available for configuration.
2. From the drop-down, select the relevant AD forest. The associated SIP dial plans for that forest will be displayed.
3. Click Add to start the process of creating the Outlook Voice Access (Subscriber Access) contact.

DIAL PLAN NAMING WITH EXCHANGE VERSIONS BEFORE EXCHANGE 2010 SP1

When working with either Exchange 2010 RTM or any flavor of Exchange 2007, you will need to ensure that you match up your dial plan names from Exchange UM and Skype for Business, as described in the article here:

http://technet.microsoft.com/en-us/library/bb803622(office.12).aspx

You will see this requirement reflected in `OcsUmUtil`; the subscriber contact will show a warning red exclamation mark for any mismatch. The text in the lower pane explains the issue.

```
A location profile has not been created that matches this dial plan. Until a
location profile is created, the UM play-on-phone and call transfer features
may not work (ignore this error for Exchange 14 SP1 and above). This dial plan
has at least one auto-attendant that does not have a corresponding contact
object in Lync Server 2013.
```

When working with Exchange 2010 SP1 or higher, you can ignore the error.

4. In the window that opens, click Browse and then select the required organizational unit (OU) in which to create the object and name the contact. The name should be recognizable rather than something cryptic. The default settings can be used for the rest of the window, as shown in Figure 22.8. To complete the process, click OK to exit to the original window.

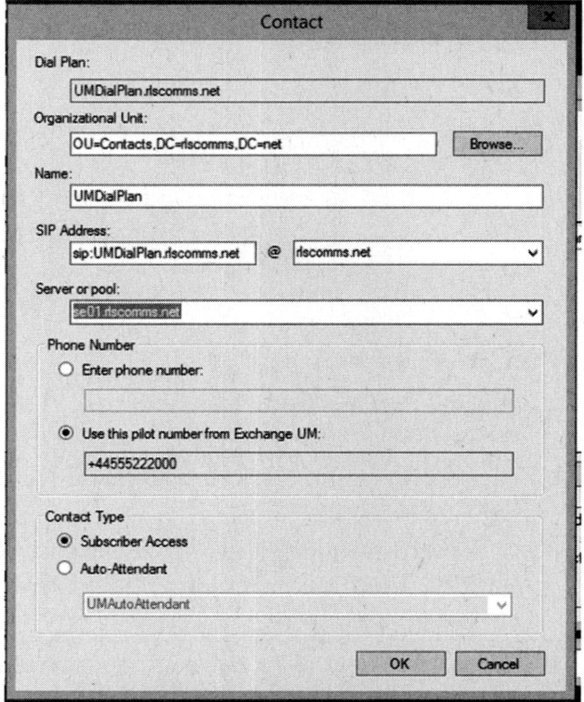

FIGURE 22.8
Setting up the Outlook Voice Access contact

5. Click Add again to create a second contact, this time for the UM auto attendant. This time select Auto-Attendant as the contact type and then select the required OU. Give the contact a name; then again opt for the default settings and click OK to complete.

6. Once you have created the contact objects, close the `OcsUmUtil` and the changes will automatically be written back to AD.

If you encounter the error shown in Figure 22.9, make sure that the Server or Pool entry is an actual pool and not a Director pool.

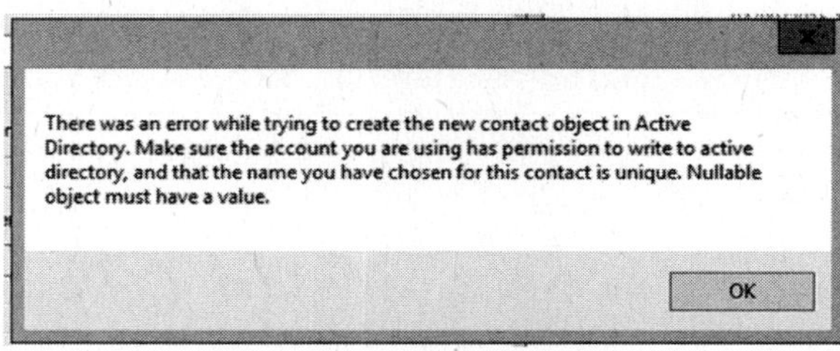

There was an error while trying to create the new contact object in Active Directory. Make sure the account you are using has permission to write to active directory, and that the name you have chosen for this contact is unique. Nullable object must have a value.
OK

FIGURE 22.9
Error when setting up the Outlook Voice Access contact

Now you can either wait for the Skype for Business Address Book to update or force it by running the `Update-CsAddressBook` command on the Skype for Business server. You will also need to restart the Skype for Business Front End service (RTCSRV) for the changes to be applied to users logging into the Front End pool. Bear in mind that this will prevent any logged-on users from being able to access Skype for Business services while the service restarts.

Within the Microsoft Exchange Security Groups OU container, there will now be two additional contact objects representing the subscriber access (Outlook Voice Access) and the auto attendant. Each will have the corresponding SIP URI number to enable Skype for Business to route users to the correct Unified Messaging recipient.

At this point, you are ready to enable some users for Exchange UM. They should be users who are already configured for Skype for Business Enterprise Voice as you set it up in Chapter 13. Enabling a user for UM is a simple process carried out either in the Exchange Administration Center (EAC) or in Exchange Management Shell. For the first user, you'll perform the configuration using the EAC.

1. Open EAC and select Recipients on the left side. Locate and select the user you want to enable, in this case Keith Skype. In the right Actions pane, click Enable for Unified Messaging.
2. In the window that opens, you will be able to select the UM mailbox policy you configured earlier and then click Next.
3. On the new screen, the settings apply to the user's SIP and extension settings. You should find that Exchange has picked up the user's SIP address and is using it as the predefined SIP address. If an extension number has already been defined for the user within their AD attributes, this will also appear; otherwise, it should be entered in the Extension Number field. Note that you will be prompted for the correct number of digits, as determined from the UM dial plan configured earlier. You'll be able to indicate whether the PIN should be automatically created or you will enter one manually, as shown in Figure 22.10.
4. Complete the wizard, and the user will be set up to use UM. The user will receive a welcome email giving them a subscriber number and PIN.

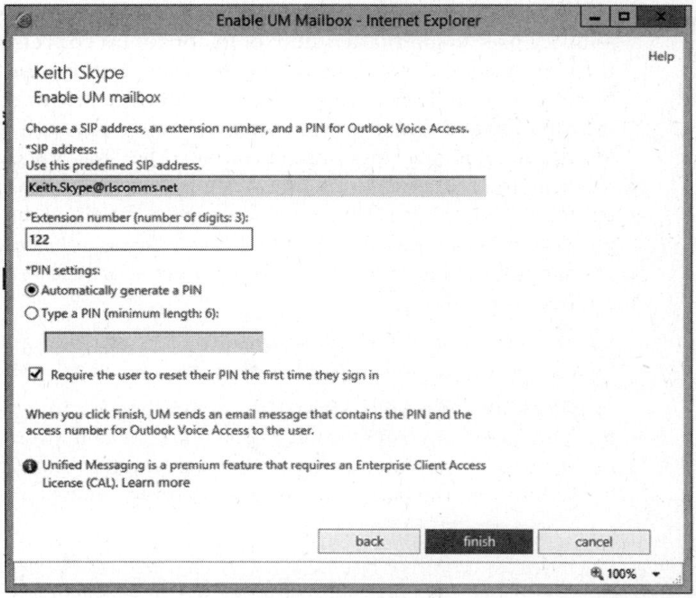

FIGURE 22.10
Setting the extension and PIN for the new UM user

If you prefer the command line, use the following command:

```
Enable-UMMailbox -Identity "Keith Skype" -PinExpired $false↵
-UMMailboxPolicy UMMailboxPolicy -Extensions 122↵
-SIPResourceIdentifier keith.skype@rlscomms.netrlscom
```

This command will enable Keith Skype for UM as in the previous EAC steps. You have now completed the setup of UM integration with Skype for Business. At this point, you test connectivity to UM from the Skype for Business server using the following command:

```
Test-CsExUMConnectivity -TargetFqdn "se01.rlscomms.net" -UserSipAddress↵
"sip:keith.skype@rlscomms.net"
```

From a Skype for Business client logged in as the user you enabled for UM, you should now see the Call Voice Mail options and be able to dial into voice mail to set up your UM mailbox with a greeting. One final thing to note is that there are additional elements that can be configured to provide an even richer voicemail solution. The primary piece of functionality here is Play on Phone, which means that instead of listening to a voice mail on your PC speakers, you can reroute it to play over a phone device. This feature is completely configured in Exchange, so if you are interested in learning more about it, you should take a look at the following article:
`http://technet.microsoft.com/en-us/library/jj150478.aspx`

Free/Busy, and Other Integration

Besides the obvious element of integration just discussed, Skype for Business touches Exchange in a variety of other, more subtle but extremely useful ways. Like other programs that require access to Exchange data, Skype for Business now predominantly utilizes Exchange Web Services calls to get that information. The types of information returned to Skype for Business in this way are outlined here:

Access to Conversation History and Voice Mail Skype for Business uses the Exchange mailbox for voice mail as previously described; however, when configured to do so, it also creates and uses the `Conversation History` folder in the user's Exchange mailbox. This allows a user to maintain a store of historical IM conversations, which is then searchable through normal Outlook methods. In Skype for Business 2015, this conversation history also bubbles up into the Skype for Business interface (the third tab in the main client) to provide information about all previous communication through Skype for Business, including conference calls, phone calls, and, of course, IMs. This process of saving the conversation detail relies on the conversation window being open long enough for the conversation to be picked up and saved. It is not a server-side process; the client must perform the operation, so if the window is closed too quickly, the information is not saved. This is different from the new Exchange-based archiving, which we cover shortly and is a fully compliant, server-based method of archiving.

Creation of Missed Call Notifications Through integration with Exchange UM, users will be notified in their inboxes when they miss a voice or IM conversation.

Playback of Voice Mail Message Again through integration with Exchange UM, the Skype for Business client can be used to play back voice mail messages through the fourth tab in the main client. These can also be accessed through Exchange directly with Outlook or OWA or by dialing into the UM server with a standard phone.

Display Free/Busy Information and Working Hours for a User As part of enhanced presence, Skype for Business makes calls to Exchange to evaluate the logged-on user's calendar information, such as working hours, general availability, and Out of Office (OOF) status. Skype for Business then publishes this information as part of the user's presence, which others can then query. Note that publishing is not triggered by someone querying a user's presence because a Skype for Business user cannot access another user's calendar information directly. Instead, each user publishes the information about themselves in their presence.

Display a Meeting Subject, Time, and Location Like the previous item, this is part of enhanced presence.

Display User's Out of Office Status and Note Like the previous two items, this is part of enhanced presence. Skype for Business shows the OOF message as the user's Skype for Business note and publishes the information in the Skype for Business activity feed for others who have subscribed to that user's presence.

Outlook Web App Integration

Having set up one of the most visible Skype for Business and Exchange integration points, you can move on to the next, that of providing IM and presence capabilities in Outlook Web App (OWA). This functionality is particularly useful because in Skype for Business there is no Communicator Web Access (CWA) server, which was used in OCS to provide IM and presence functionality through a web browser.

The configuration required is relatively straightforward and consists of the following major steps:

1. Ensure that Skype for Business trusts the Exchange server.
2. Configure the OWA mailbox policy, OWA virtual directory, and `Web.config` settings on the Exchange Client Access server.
3. Test functionality as an end user.

As with the Enterprise Voice and UM integration, there are not many differences in the way that IM and presence for Skype for Business 2015 integrate with Outlook Web Access in Exchange 2013 compared to the functionality in the 2010 versions. The following changes are worth highlighting:

- There is a behavioral change around the use of Trusted Application pools in combination with Enterprise Voice.
- There is a requirement to enable IM in OWA via the OWA mailbox policy.
- `Web.config` configuration is now required again. This was removed in Exchange 2010 SP1, but re-introduced in Exchange 2013 RTM.
- Fewer prerequisite packages are required.

Out of these changes, the one major area that requires consideration is around the use or not of a Trusted Application pool. We will now take a moment to explain this before moving on to the configuration steps to get you up and running.

Prerequisite Packages for IM and OWA Integration

When integrating Lync 2010 and Exchange 2010, we had a list of prerequisite applications that were needed on the Client Access server for IM and presence integration to work correctly.

- `CWAOWASSPMain.msi`
- `Vcredist_x64.exe`
- `UcamRedist.msi`
- `UcamRedist.msp`
- `CWAOWAASSP.msi`
- `CWAOWASSP.msp`

The good news with Skype for Business and Exchange 2013 is that none of these packages is required anymore.

Determining the Need for a Trusted Application Pool

For Skype for Business to provide services to another server or service, that foreign system needs to be in something called the Known Servers Table (KST). The ability to add servers to this list is what enables Skype for Business to talk to all sorts of third-party systems such as call center software and videoconference units. As far as Skype for Business is concerned, Exchange is just another third-party system, and it therefore needs defining in the KST. However, there are a couple of ways that this can happen.

One such way is by creating a Trusted Application pool. Creating a Trusted Application pool to represent the Exchange Client Access server is required if no Exchange UM is configured. For integration scenarios where Skype for Business Enterprise Voice has been configured to use Exchange UM, when the Skype for Business Front End service starts, it will request any Exchange servers hosting a SIP URI dial plan and add them to the KST. This replaces the need for creating a Trusted Application pool for those Exchange Client Access servers.

It is important to understand that if a Trusted Application pool is set up where you have UM already enabled, you will essentially have added the Exchange server to the KST twice. This will cause an error, which as an administrator you can see in the Skype for Business Application event log when the Front End service starts. The sequence of events that will take place is as follows:

1. Creating a SIP URI dial plan in Exchange will add the server to the Known Servers Table (in this example, `ex01.rlscomms.net`).
2. Upon startup of the Skype for Business Front End service, where a Trusted Application pool is in place, another entry for `ex01.rlscomms.net` will be added to the Known Servers Table.
3. The version number of the entry for the SIP URI dial plan (0) and Trusted Application pool (6) differ, meaning that Skype for Business treats the entries as invalid and removes them both from the Known Servers Table. This will generate event ID 14563.
4. As a result, integration for UM and OWA will both fail.

It is the logging of the error that is different behavior from Lync Server 2010. Previously, Lync Server 2010 didn't care if the servers ended up in the KST twice. If you do end up in this situation, when you restart the Lync Front End service, you will find that a further 14563 error is generated; however, after a few moments, event ID 14493 will be generated, stating that the Exchange server has been re-added to the Known Servers Table, and integration will continue to function as expected. All in all, the simplest solution is to remove the Trusted Application pool you created that caused the error in the first place.

For a little more depth on the issue, take a look at the blog post here:

`http://blogs.technet.com/b/jenstr/archive/2012/11/13/when-to-have-a-lync-trusted-application-pool-for-exchange-owa-im-integration.aspx`

Configuring Exchange

Now that you understand the choices to be made with regard to the Trusted Application pool, let's progress to setting up the integration. We will start by configuring the OWA virtual directory and OWA mailbox policy and then edit the `Web.config` file.

For Exchange to utilize the IM and presence features of Skype for Business, the first thing that is needed is to configure the OWA virtual directory on Exchange that is to be enabled for IM integration to point to a specific Skype for Business server (or server farm). In previous versions of Exchange, we needed to extract information about the certificate being used on the Exchange server to secure the OWA virtual directory and associate the certificate with the service; however, because we will be modifying the `Web.config` file to cater for this, the thumbprint is no longer needed.

To determine the correct OWA virtual directory to be configured, you can run the following command:

```
Get-OwaVirtualDirectory
```

This will generate a list of all OWA virtual directories, which in this environment will be the one default instance.

```
Name                      Server                OwaVersion
----                      ------                ----------
owa (Default Web Site)    EX01                  Exchange2013
```

Also, although a bit off-topic for this book, Exchange 2013 has simplified its roles so that there are now only CAS and Mailbox servers. These can be colocated or installed on separate servers. On an Exchange server where the roles are colocated, it is important that you do not apply the settings to the Exchange back-end virtual directory. This is not something you would do by accident, but it is important to understand that you need to apply these settings only to the CAS server OWA virtual directories. Using the command `Get-OWAVirtualDirectory -ShowBackEndVirtualDirectories`, you would pull back the OWA virtual directories on the mailbox server, not the CAS server, and these should *not* be configured.

Working with Multiple Exchange Servers

Exchange client access is a complex subject. You could have multiple Client Access servers (CASs) in a farm serving the same domain name or multiple virtual directories serving the different domains.

continues

continued

If you follow best practices, you should use the same certificate for each of your Client Access servers and ensure that it contains all the names required to support the various domains for which you will host services. If this best practice is followed, you can simply export the certificate and import it on a new CAS, which means that the certificate thumbprint will remain the same even for multiple servers.

Assuming the same certificate is used across the board, you can progress with the commands discussed in the main text to configure integration. If you want to be more specific and work on only a single virtual directory, then instead of piping the output of `Get-OwaVirtualDirectory` to the `Set-OwaVirtualDirectory` command, don't run the `Get-OwaVirtualDirectory` command and simply use the `-Identity` parameter on the `Set-OwaVirtualDirectory` command to specify an individual virtual directory.

Getting back to the task in hand, once you have the name of your website, you can apply the instant messaging settings to both the website and the mailbox policy. The following commands will apply these settings to our OWA virtual directory in the Default Web Site. You also need to alter the existing mailbox policy to enable instant messaging features. This is done using the commands shown here:

```
Set-OWAVirtualDirectory "ex01\owa (Default Web Site)"↵
-InstantMessagingType OCS -InstantMessagingEnabled:$true

Get-OwaMailboxPolicy | Set-OwaMailboxPolicy↵
-InstantMessagingEnabled $true -InstantMessagingType OCS
```

Note that the use of `OCS` here is not a typo, just a legacy command that is still in use from previous versions of Exchange! If the commands are successful, there should be no output from the Management Shell console. To verify that these settings have been applied, you can run the following commands to display the settings associated with each virtual directory, filtering on the `InstantMessaging` attributes:

```
Get-OwaVirtualDirectory |fl *instantmessaging*
Get-OwaMailboxPolicy |fl *instantmessaging*
```

You should see something that resembles the following:

```
InstantMessagingCertificateThumbprint :
InstantMessagingServerName            :
InstantMessagingEnabled               : True
InstantMessagingType                  : Ocs

InstantMessagingEnabled               : True
InstantMessagingType                  : Ocs
```

The last piece of configuration on Exchange is to edit the `Web.config` file. You need to edit the `Web.config` file on the Client Access server so that it contains the thumbprint of the certificate being used to secure OWA. The default location for the `Web.config` file is in the

`C:\Program Files\Microsoft\Exchange Server\V15\ClientAccess\Owa` folder. This file gives Exchange some key information about your web services, and by adding an additional couple of lines, you can tell the web service which Skype for Business server or servers it should trust.

From the Exchange Management Shell, use the following commands to extract the thumbnail of the OWA certificate and display it onscreen:

```
$cert = (Get-ExchangeCertificate | Where {$_.Subject -ilike "*ex01.rlscomms.
net*"})↵.Thumbprint
```

This first command will populate the `$cert` variable with the thumbnail of the OWA certificate.

```
$cert
```

By typing `$cert` on its own, you will display the output to copy into the `Web.config` file.

Having gotten the thumbprint of the certificate, open the `Web.config` file and search for the `<AppSettings>` section. Within this section, insert the following two lines of code, replacing the following value with the `$cert` output from the previous command:

```
<add key="IMCertificateThumbprint"↵
Value="F67A00BBEE48E54BCAE6E2C55B787556B35E6CBB "/>↵
<add key="IMServerName" value="se01.rlscomms.net"/>
```

Close `Web.config` and save the changes. Then run the following from the Exchange Management Shell:

```
C:\Windows\System32\Inetsrv\Appcmd.exe recycle apppool /apppool.
name:"MSExchangeOWAAppPool"
```

This will refresh the OWA application pool in IIS to ensure that the changes made in the `Web.config` are applied.

At this point, congratulations are due! You have completed the Exchange OWA virtual directory and OWA mailbox policy configuration.

Configuring Skype for Business

With the Exchange side of things configured, you're ready to set up Skype for Business to provide the IM and presence services to OWA. The first step, if required, is to create a Trusted Application pool to ensure that Skype for Business trusts Exchange. Remember, this section is needed only if the Exchange CAS server to which Skype for Business will be talking is not already in the KST via the automatic entry created when UM is run. Therefore, if you already have a SIP URI UM dial plan, the following steps are for information only:

To create the Trusted Application pool, take the following steps:

1. Log on to the Skype for Business server as an administrator and open Topology Builder.
2. Download the topology, navigate to the Trusted Application Servers node, right-click it, and select New Trusted Application Pool.
3. In the Define the Trusted Application Pool FQDN window that opens, enter the name of the Exchange Client Access server (**ex01.rlscomms.net**, for the example), select Single Computer Pool, as shown in Figure 22.11, and then click Next.

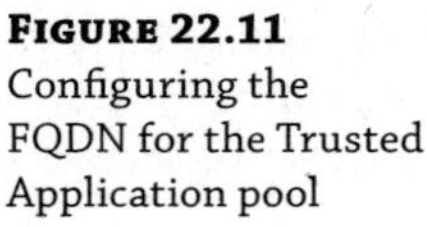

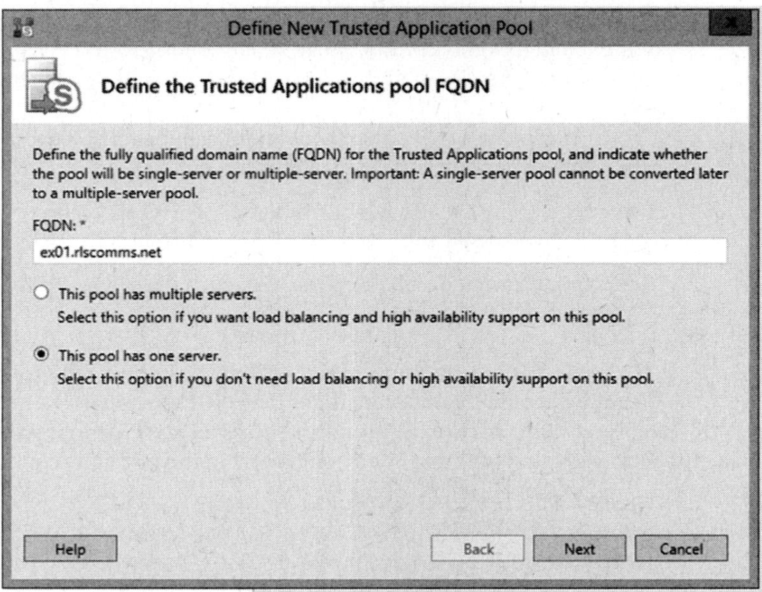

FIGURE 22.11 Configuring the FQDN for the Trusted Application pool

If you were to have multiple Client Access servers in an array, you would use the FQDN of the Exchange CAS array and select Multiple Computer Pool.

4. In the Select The Next Hop window, make sure `SE01.rlscomms.net` is selected (or your own Front End pool) and click Finish.

Now you should publish the topology and then check to see whether the updates were successful.

The same configuration can also be carried out in the Skype for Business Management Shell using the following command:

```
New-CsTrustedApplicationPool -Identity ex01.rlscomms.net
-Registrar se01.rlscomms.net -Site EMEA
-RequiresReplication $False
```

To check that the settings applied correctly, open the Skype for Business Management Shell and run the `Get-CsTrustedApplicationPool` cmdlet.

This will generate the following output:

```
Identity              : TrustedApplicationPool:se01.rlscomms.net
Registrar             : Registrar:se01.rlscomms.net
FileStore             :
ThrottleAsServer      : True
TreatAsAuthenticated  : True
OutboundOnly          : False
RequiresReplication   : False
```

```
AudioPortStart       :
AudioPortCount       : 0
AppSharingPortStart  :
AppSharingPortCount  : 0
VideoPortStart       :
VideoPortCount       : 0
Applications         : {}
DependentServiceList : {}
ServiceId            : 1-ExternalServer-2
SiteId               : Site:EMEA
PoolFqdn             : ex01.rlscomms.net
Version              : 6
Role                 : TrustedApplicationPool
```

Next run the `Get-CsTrustedApplicationComputer` cmdlet to verify that you see the server FQDN you used during the creation of the Trusted Application pool, as shown here:

```
Get-CsTrustedApplicationComputer
Identity : ex01.rlscomms.net
Pool     : ex01.rlscomms.net
Fqdn     : ex01.rlscomms.net
```

Note that the previous command output would be blank if you had not set up a Trusted Application pool because of Skype for Business being integrated with Exchange for UM.

You have now given Skype for Business the ability to allow users within your pools to expose their status to others via your Exchange Client Access server.

The next step is to configure a trusted application. Essentially, the Trusted Application pool tells Skype for Business it is OK to talk to a specific third-party system, and the trusted application tells it how to communicate.

To create the trusted application, use the `New-CSTrustedApplication` cmdlet. The first thing you'll need for the application is a port on which Skype for Business will listen. This can be any port that is not in use. You'll select port 5050 because it is similar to other Skype for Business ports; however, this can be any free port over 1025.

It is critical that nothing else uses the port, so to verify that, open a Windows `cmd.exe` prompt as an administrator and run `Netstat` as follows:

```
Netstat -a | findstr 5050
```

The following output shows what it would look like if a conflict occurs because you selected a port (5070) on which Skype for Business listens:

```
netstat -a | findstr 5070
  TCP    192.168.1.194:5070     SE01:0             LISTENING
```

When `Netstat` is run on the correct port, you won't see any output because there won't be any conflicts to show. Be sure to check any response, as `findstr` searches for substrings! Once a suitable port is chosen, set up the trusted application as follows:

```
New-CsTrustedApplication -ApplicationId ExchangeOWA↵
-TrustedApplicationPoolFqdn ex01.rlscomms.net -Port 5050
```

This command will create a trusted application called ExchangeOWA in the Trusted Application pool set up earlier; it will listen on port 5050. `ApplicationID` can be any unique string, but it makes sense to use a recognizable naming convention. When you run the preceding command, you will see the following output:

```
WARNING: The following changes must be made in order for the
 operation to be complete.
Enable-CsTopology must still be run for all changes to take effect.
Identity                    : ex01.rlscomms.net/urn:application:
exchangeowa
ComputerGruus               : {ex01.rlscomms.net
sip:ex01.rlscomms.net@rlscomms.net
;gruu;opaque=srvr:exchangeowa:_YHYY_tIL1qZQ_bFgC9FQAAA}
ServiceGruu                 :
sip:ex01.rlscomms.net@rlscomms.net;gruu;opaque=srvr:
exchangeowa:_YHYY_tIL1qZQ_bFgC9FQAAA
Protocol                    : Mtls
ApplicationId               : urn:application:exchangeowa
TrustedApplicationPoolFqdn : ex01.rlscomms.net
Port                        : 5050
LegacyApplicationName       : exchangeowa
```

Now all that remains is to run the `Enable-CsTopology` command as instructed, and OWA IM integration is complete and presence will light up in OWA.

Understanding and Configuring the Unified Contact Store

When Skype for Business is deployed out of the box, all users have their own buddy list maintained and stored by Skype for Business in its SQL database. However, now with Skype for Business and Exchange 2013, it is possible, and makes more sense, to have those contacts in one location: the Unified Contact Store (UCS). This gives users the ability to manage their contacts from a single list and provides that single contact list to pick from across all Microsoft Office applications. At the back end, as with so much of the integration, Skype for Business will talk to Exchange using Exchange Web Services, which has been previously configured using the OAuthTokenIssuer certificate in the prerequisite stage.

When configured, two folders are created in the Exchange `Contacts` folder for each user. The main contacts folder is visible by the user as a subfolder called `Lync Contacts` within their default `Contacts` folder. The second folder is a hidden subfolder that contains metadata used to communicate changes to contacts with Skype for Business and is named using a GUID. Although this subfolder is hidden from the users, for troubleshooting purposes, you can easily access it using a folder exposure tool such as MFCMapi.

Migrating Contacts to the UCS

The process to enable the new method of storing Skype for Business contacts in Exchange uses the `New-CSUserServicesPolicy` command on the Skype for Business server. By setting the

-UCSAllowed parameter to True, you can set this policy on a global, site, service, or tag level, as discussed in Chapter 12, "User Administration." The Grant-CSUserServicesPolicy command is then used to grant users access to the UCS.

Before we start the first step of migrating users from Skype for Business to UCS, it is important to highlight that the default global policy is set to True, which would mean that any users who fall within the scope are automatically enabled for UCS. By running the following command, you ensure that only users who fall within the scope of the custom policy will be eligible for migration:

```
Set-CsUserServicesPolicy Global -UcsAllowed $False
```

To create a custom policy, you can run the following command from the Skype for Business Management Shell:

```
New-CSUserServicesPolicy "UCSEnabled" -UCSAllowed $True
```

You can then assign the policy to your users as follows:

```
Grant-CSUserServicesPolicy "Linda Lync" -PolicyName "UCSEnabled"
Grant-CSUserServicesPolicy "Keith Skype" -PolicyName "UCSEnabled"
```

The next time the user logs into Skype for Business, the scope of the policy created earlier will be pushed down to that user, and they will be included on the migration to UCS. The Skype for Business client will use this information to send a "nudge" request to the Skype for Business server to start the migration of contacts to Exchange. The Lync Storage Service (LYSS) will then complete the migration. If the user is logged on when this completes, they will be prompted to sign out and back in again to start using UCS.

There are two ways you can check to see whether the migration has been successful. From the server side, you can run Test-CSUnifiedContactStore, as shown in the following command:

```
Test-CsUnifiedContactStore -UserSipAddress keith.skype@rlscomms.net↵
-TargetFqdn se01.rlscomms.net
```

The other verification method is to use the Skype for Business client. You do this by holding down Control, right-clicking the Skype for Business icon in the taskbar, and selecting Skype for Business Configuration Information, which opens a page that will show you a range of configuration information including the contact list provider and UCS connectivity state properties. Prior to migration, the contact list provider will show as Skype for Business Server, and the UCS connectivity state will show as Exchange Connection Down. After migration, the values for Contact List Provider and UCS Connectivity State should be UCS and Exchange Connection Active, respectively, as shown in Figure 22.12.

At this point, the user should also be able to see a new contact folder in Outlook called Skype for Business Contacts, as shown in Figure 22.13, and it contains the same contacts as those visible in the Skype for Business client.

Skype for Business Configuration Information

Controlled Phones	TRUE	--
GAL or Server Based Search	GAL search	--
PC to PC AV Encryption	AV Encryption Enforced	--
Telephony Mode	Telephony Mode UC Enabled	--
Line Configured From	Auto Line Configuration	--
Configuration Mode	Manual Configuration	--
EWS Internal URL	https://ex01.rlscomms.net/EWS/Exchange.asmx	--
EWS External URL		--
SharePoint Search Center UF		--
Skill Search URL		--
Skype for Business Server	se01.rlscomms.net	--
Local Log Folder	C:\Users\test\AppData\Local\Microsoft\Office\16.0\Lync\Tracing	--
Inside User Status	TRUE	--
Contact List Provider	UCS	--
Pairing State	Skype for Business cannot connect to your desk phone because the USB cable is not plugged in. Make sure that yc	Enabled
UCS Connectivity State	Exchange connection Active	--
MAPI Information	Your Outlook profile is not configured correctly. Contact your support team with this information.	MAPI unavailable
EWS Information		EWS Status OK
License State	Skype for Business ProPlus	--
Hanging Notification Status		Connected
pChat Room Mgmt Int URL	https://se01.rlscomms.net:443/PersistentChat/RM	--
pChat Room Mgmt Ext URL	https://se01.rlscomms.net:443/PersistentChat/RM	--
Container list Preferred Endp	TRUE	--
Lync OAUTH Authority URL		--
EWS OAUTH Authority URL		--
pChat URIs		--
pChat Default URI		--
pChat Enabled?	FALSE	--

Copy Refresh Close

Microsoft Edge

FIGURE 22.12
A view of the configuration information showing UCS properties

FIGURE 22.13
The new `Skype for Business Contacts` folder in Outlook

> **UCS IN A PAIRED POOL SCENARIO**
>
> UCS is also protected in the new HA model for Skype for Business. If UCS is configured when a paired pool is set up, as the user/pool migration info is shared between paired pools, this will be available on any Front End server in the event of a failure. Therefore, users are unaffected if a Front End server fails because the information has already been replicated to another server.

ROLLING BACK THE CONTACTS FROM THE UCS TO SKYPE FOR BUSINESS

There may be circumstances in which it is necessary to roll the contacts from UCS back to Skype for Business. This may be because of moving mailboxes from Exchange 2013 to Exchange 2010, which does not support UCS. The recommended way to do this is first to create a new policy where the `-UCSAllowed` value is set to `$False` using the following command:

```
New-CSUserServicesPolicy "NoUCS" -UcsAllowed $False
```

You then assign the new policy to the users.

```
Grant-CSUserServicesPolicy "Linda Lync" -PolicyName "NoUCS"
Grant-CSUserServicesPolicy "Keith Skype" -PolicyName "NoUCS"
```

It is important to note that assigning a new policy to users will not remove their contacts from UCS. If the policy applied to the user has a `-UCSAllowed` value of `$False`, the server will take no further action; therefore, a further command will need to be run to move the contacts from UCS back to Skype for Business.

The `Invoke-CsUCSRollback` command is used to mark the user for rollback and migrate the contacts back to Skype for Business as follows:

```
Invoke-CSUCSRollback "Linda Lync"
```

Running this command will prevent any further migration to UCS being completed for a seven-day period, meaning that rollback should not be invoked for a temporary server move. This is where the previous step of creating a new policy for rolled-back users comes in handy, because it can be set to exclude previously rolled-back users from accessing UCS. The result of not reassigning the users to a non-UCS-enabled policy is that after the seven-day period is over, the server will check to see whether they should be assigned a policy, and they will then be reenabled for UCS.

Another reason for moving away from the UCS is when moving the Skype for Business user to a non–Skype for Business (or Lync 2013) pool. In this case, you would run the `Move-CsUser` command, which will trigger an automatic rollback of the contacts from UCS to Skype for Business and complete the pool move.

Integrating into Exchange for Compliance Archiving

In Chapter 13, "Archiving and Monitoring," we talked about how Skype for Business can archive content to a SQL database. However, Skype for Business 2015, when combined with Exchange 2013 and SharePoint 2013, provides a far more grown-up solution. It is possible for Skype for Business to make use of the Exchange In-Place Hold functionality to store data in a compliance-suitable archive. Exchange archiving allows Skype for Business archive messages to be stored in individual users' Exchange mailboxes rather than on the Skype for Business SQL Archiving database. Exchange provides various compliance functions, including the concept of In-Place Hold, where data is kept immutable either for a period of time or indefinitely. A set of hidden folders are created in the user's Exchange mailbox. One of these folders is called `Purges`, and this is the folder Skype for Business stores its archive transcripts into. The contents of these hidden folders are indexed by Exchange and can later be used as part of an eDiscovery search either from EAC or from a combined Discovery Portal in SharePoint that enables administrators to search in a single location for all corresponding messages relating to that user whether the messages are in Skype for Business, SharePoint, or Exchange.

Given that Skype for Business provides many ways to communicate, it is important to understand which types of content can be archived. These are laid out as follows:

- Peer-to-peer instant messages
- Multiparty instant messages (within conferences)
- Conference content, including polls and whiteboards

The following types of content are not archived:

- Peer-to-peer file transfers
- Audio/video for peer-to-peer and conference conversations
- Desktop/application sharing content for peer-to-peer and conference conversations

Archive Configuration

As with many Skype for Business settings, Exchange archiving is configured by policy, which is a concept covered in depth in Chapter 12. The default scope for Exchange archiving is global, and it is set as disabled. As such, archiving is disabled for all users by default. An administrator can choose to enable the policy on a global level by amending the existing default global policy or, if they want to choose a different scope such as site or user level, they can do so by creating a new policy by running the `New-CsArchivingConfiguration` cmdlet.

Whether you're amending the existing policy or configuring a new one, two parameters define the major elements of the policy: `-EnableArchiving` and `-EnableExchangeArchiving`.

Here are some more details as to your options when running these commands:

- `EnableArchiving`: This has three possible settings:
    - `None`: This is the default value; no archiving is enabled.
    - `IMOnly`: Instant messaging transcripts are enabled.
    - `IMAndWebConf`: Instant messaging and web conferencing transcripts are enabled.

  Both `IMOnly` and `IMAndWebConf` rely on the `EnableExchangeArchiving` setting being set to `$True` for a message to be archived in Exchange rather than Skype for Business.
- `EnableExchangeArchiving`: This can either be `$True` for enabled or `$False` for disabled.

You will see these in action as you go through the process of configuring Exchange archiving in the following sections.

Because the Exchange archiving feature is available only for users whose mailboxes are stored on Exchange Server 2013, mailboxes on previous versions of Exchange that have archiving enabled within Skype for Business will continue to use the standard Skype for Business archiving. For example, when a user logs on to Skype for Business, Skype for Business will validate whether their mailbox is on Exchange 2013 or an earlier version. If the mailbox is not on 2013, then they are ineligible to use Exchange mailbox–based Skype for Business archiving.

Working with Office 365

It is worth noting that there are various scenarios in which Skype for Business and Exchange could be split between on-premises deployments and cloud deployments. Thankfully, in most of these, Exchange mailbox–based Skype for Business archiving still works as highlighted here:

- Skype for Business Online and Exchange Online: Fully functional
- Skype for Business Online and Exchange on Premises: Does not function
- Exchange Online and Skype for Business on Premises: Fully functional
- Exchange on Premises and Skype for Business on Premises: Fully functional

Another thing to take into consideration when archiving is where multiple AD forests come into play. As is often the case, this sort of configuration complicates things somewhat. For users where Exchange 2013 and Skype for Business reside in the same forest, both Skype for Business and Exchange look at the properties of a user in AD, and if the property to archive is set, Skype for Business and Exchange will heed that. In the real world, this means that archiving is managed by the use of the `In-Place Hold` policy on the Exchange server. If `In-Place Hold` is configured on an Exchange user, Skype for Business will automatically see that setting and turn on archiving of Skype for Business data to Exchange (assuming the Skype for Business policies do not block this as discussed earlier). However, for cross-forest deployments where Skype for Business and Exchange are in different forests, the value of `ExchangeArchivingPolicy` on the Skype for Business user object will determine where archiving takes place. There are four values for this parameter:

- `Uninitialized`: The In-Place Hold settings on the mailbox will determine the archive settings. If this has not been set, Skype for Business will archive the messages.
- `NoArchiving`: No archiving will take place whatsoever.
- `UseLyncArchivingPolicy`: Archiving will take place on the Skype for Business server.
- `ArchivingToExchange`: Archiving will take place on the Exchange server.

There is one final element to take into consideration before you get things up and running, which is the `CsArchivingPolicy`. As you know, Skype for Business is able to communicate with users within the organization and also those external on Skype for Business or other platforms. When Skype for Business Server 2015 is installed, a default global archiving policy is created to determine whether internal, external, or both types of messages are archived. This is disabled for both by default. Setting the `ArchiveInternal` parameter on the `CsArchivingPolicy` will allow messages for AD users in your organization to be archived. Enabling the `ArchiveExternal` parameter will archive messages between an AD user and any other non-AD users (that is, a local user communicating with an external user).

Enable Exchange Archiving

Having understood the theory and all the components that come into play, we are now going to walk you through redirecting Skype for Business archiving for IM messages to your Exchange server. Because you want this to apply to all users, you will amend the global policy for Skype for Business rather than creating a new policy.

To begin with, log into the Skype for Business Control Panel as an administrator. Select the Monitoring And Archiving tab and then select Archiving Configuration, as shown in Figure 22.14.

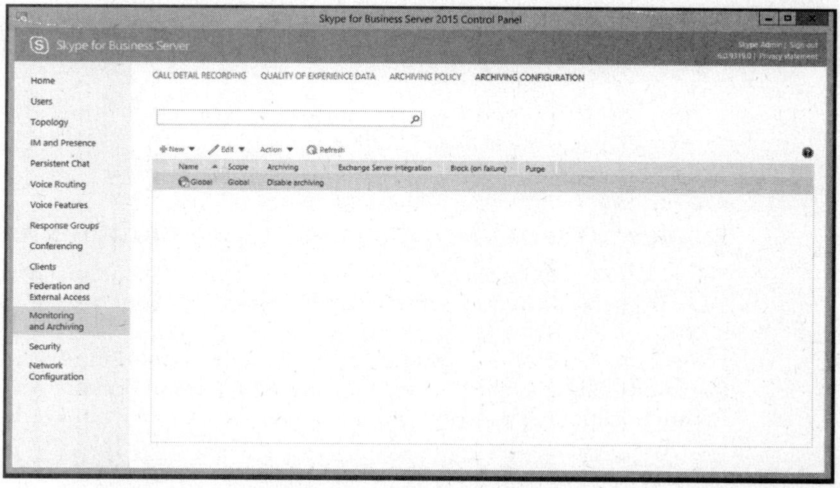

Figure 22.14
The Archiving Configuration area in SBSCP

In Figure 22.14, you can see the default settings for the global policy, one of which is that archiving is disabled. At this point, you can choose whether to create a new policy with different archiving settings, depending on whether you want all users to have their messages archived in the same way.

As mentioned, you will simply edit the global policy because you are happy for all users to be archived in the same way. This is done by double-clicking the global policy to open it. Once it opens, you can then amend this to start archiving IM messages to Exchange by clicking the drop-down box under Archiving Setting, choosing Archive IM Sessions, and also selecting the Exchange Server Integration check box, as shown in Figure 22.15.

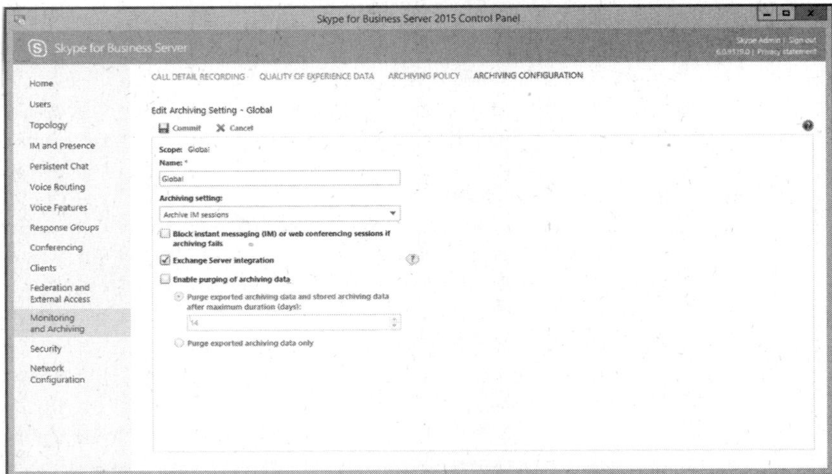

FIGURE 22.15 Configuring the global archiving policy for Exchange archiving

You can carry out the same configuration in the Skype for Business Management Shell using the following command:

```
Set-CSArchivingConfiguration Global -EnableArchiving IMOnly↵
-EnableExchangeArchiving $True
```

Enable Internal and External Communication Archiving

You will now change the archiving policy to define which types of messages will be archived. You can choose to archive either internal communications only or those with users outside your domain.

In Skype for Business Control Panel, select the Monitoring and Archiving tab and then Archiving Policy. Select Archive Internal Communications and Archive External Communications. This brings up the window shown in Figure 22.16.

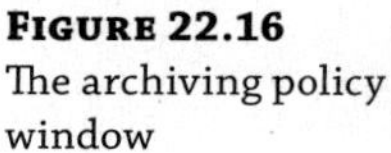

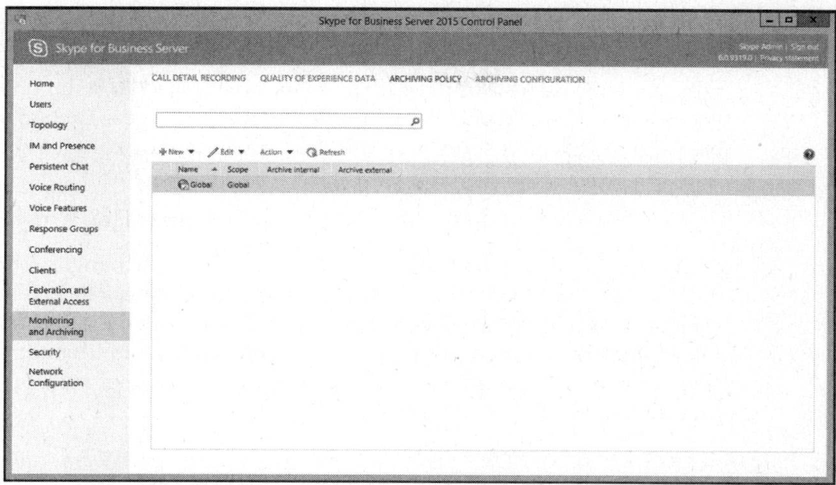

FIGURE 22.16
The archiving policy window

In Figure 22.16, you can see that the default global settings do not have a scope defined. You'll enable both internal and external communication by double-clicking the global policy and selecting both the Archive Internal Communications and Archive External Communications check boxes, as shown in Figure 22.17.

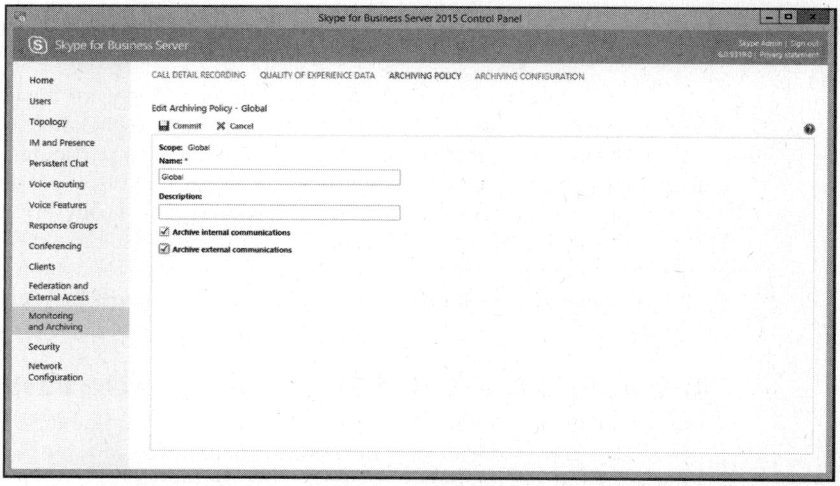

FIGURE 22.17
Setting the global policy to allow archiving of internal and external messages

The same configuration can also be carried out in the Exchange Management Shell using the following command:

```
Set-CSArchivingPolicy Global -ArchiveInternal $True -ArchiveExternal $True
```

Configure ExchangeArchivingPolicy

As we touched on earlier, if the Exchange and Skype for Business servers are in separate forests, you will need to simply tell Skype for Business what it should do based on its own policy because it will not be able to make a decision based on the Exchange policy in place on the user object in the Exchange forest. In this case, the following command can be used to tell Skype for Business where to archive for your user:

```
Set-CsUser "Keith Skype" -ExchangeArchivingPolicy ArchivingToExchange
```

As a result, you've told Skype for Business to use Exchange archiving for your user. This means that should your Exchange and Skype for Business servers reside in separate forests, the policy applied to the user will take precedence. You would of course need to do this for all relevant users, so you need to use your search skills from Chapter 12. You would use a filter to search for all users in a particular Skype for Business pool and apply the settings to all users found using the following command:

```
Get-CsUser | Where-Object {[String]$_.Registrarpool -eq↵
"se01.rlscomms.net"} | Set-CsUser -ExchangeArchivingPolicy
ArchivingToExchange
```

You have now successfully applied Exchange archiving to your users in both single- and cross-forest environments. Those of you from an Exchange background can use the `New-MailboxSearch` command to create a new in-place hold and add a user to that hold, as shown in this example (we will not be covering Exchange In-Place Hold in detail in this book):

```
New-MailboxSearch "Hold-Ref123"
-SourceMailboxes "Linda.Lync@rlscomms.net"
-InPlaceHoldEnabled $true
```

As a result of enabling Exchange archiving for Skype for Business messages, you have the ability to search content within the mailbox using the Exchange In-Place and Discovery features. The benefit of this is that if you are looking for a particular keyword (such as *SecretProject*), Exchange can now search the Skype for Business archive as part of this search. This opens up the scope for administrators to be able to search for IM conversations as well as email messages. With the `-ArchiveExternal` parameter in use, you also have the ability to search conversations that have taken place with external parties. The scope for compliance teams to track down those elusive conversations taking place via Skype for Business has definitely taken a step in the right direction!

Using High-Resolution Photos in Skype for Business

One of the things that has become more and more prominent over the last few years in all sorts of social or communication applications is user photos. Skype for Business is no different. In Lync 2010, it was possible to use the `thumbnailPhoto` attribute from AD to display a photo representing a user. However, there were constraints for this, the biggest being the resolution of the photo, which could not exceed 48×48 pixels. This is a really tiny photo when you consider that most modern cameras are now capable of taking photos of at least 15 megapixels. Skype for Business Server 2015 uses integration to Exchange through Exchange Web Services (EWS). This enables you to store photos as large as 648×648 pixels (around 250KB). Cleverly, Exchange provides the ability to resize this photo depending on where it is needed (downscaling rather than upscaling). To provide the photos for scaling, users can upload their own using Outlook Web Access for Exchange 2013, or an administrator can do this using the Exchange Management Shell.

Photo Resolution Scaling

Using the scaling feature of Exchange, photos can be provided at one of three possible resolutions.

- 48×48 pixels (Thumbnail): On creation of a high-resolution photo in Exchange, a 48×48-pixel photo will also be copied to the `thumbnailPhoto` attribute within AD for future use.
- 96×96 pixels (Default): This is commonly used by applications such as Outlook 2013.
- 648×648 pixels (XXLarge2): This is used by the Skype for Business client and Skype for Business Web App.

Exchange will also create intermediate resolutions providing that the original photo had a resolution of at least 648×648 pixels. Although there are currently no applications that use these intermediate resolutions, they have been provided as an option for future use. In the event that a low-resolution photo is uploaded and an application such as the Skype for Business client or Skype for Business Web App requests a higher resolution, only the lowest-resolution photo will be returned. For example, if a user uploads a photo 120×120 pixels in size and a Skype for Business client user requests access to that photo, the default 96×96-pixel photo will be returned.

Table 22.1 illustrates the full range of photos stored by Exchange and the values that can be used to return photos using EWS.

Table 22.1: The range of photos stored in Exchange

Photo Type	Width in Pixels	Value
Thumbnail	48×48	HR48×48
Small	64×64	HR64×64
Default	96×96	HR96×96
Large-1	120×120	HR120×120
Large-2	240×240	HR240×240
XLarge-1	360×360	HR360×360
XLarge-2	432×432	HR432×432
XXLarge1	504×504	HR504×504
XXLarge2	648×648	HR648×648

In terms of storage, we again find that we are making use of the hidden area of a mailbox to store the photo in the root of the user's mailbox. If you want to, the properties can be explored using a mailbox folder exposure tool such as MFCMapi. The benefit of having Exchange hold the photo as a central store is that it can be provided out consistently across the whole Office stack.

Enabling High-Resolution Photos for Users

We will now walk through how a Skype for Business administrator would enable high-resolution photos for a user. The scenario is that there can potentially be thousands of photos taken and you now need to import them all into the system. The process is carried out from the Exchange Management Shell by running the following commands and would import a photo for one user. You could of course expand on this to carry it out in bulk.

```
$photo = ([Byte]] $(Get-Content -Path "C:\Photos\Keith.jpg" -Encoding Byte↵
-ReadCount 0))
```

This first command will get the photo data and import it into the variable `$photo`.

```
Set-UserPhoto -Identity "Keith Skype" -PictureData $photo -Confirm:False
```

The second command will take the photo and assign it to the user.

At this point you would likely go ahead and ask the user to log into the Exchange Control Panel through OWA and review the preview of the photo. At this stage, you have not actually saved the photo, so Exchange has only the preview; it has not yet processed all the various resolutions covered earlier. Once you are sure the user is happy with the photo, you run the next command:

```
Set-UserPhoto -Identity "Keith Skype" -Save -Confirm:False
```

This will commit the photo and kick off the process of converting into the various required resolutions.

Of course, the other option for one-off changes is that the user logs into the Skype for Business client and selects Options and then My Picture. They will be redirected to their Exchange Control Panel page in OWA, where they can upload the photo of their choice. Exchange will scale the photo to the maximum permitted resolution of 648×648. When the user clicks Save on the options page, the photo will be automatically committed.

If you then log out and back into the Skype for Business client, you will notice that the new photo is now in use and in the higher resolution of 648×648 pixels.

Finally, it is worth knowing that as an administrator, you can verify any user's photo within a web browser by navigating to the EWS page and using the size format (use Table 22.1 as a reference), as shown in this example:

```
https://mail.rlscomms.net/ews/exchange.asmx/s/GetUserPhoto?email=
Keith.skype@rlscomms.net&size=HR648x648
https://mail.rlscomms.net/ews/exchange.asmx/s/GetUserPhoto?email=
keith.skype@rlscomms.net&size=HR96x96
```

The previous URLs will pull back the 648×648-pixel photo and the 96×96-pixel photo for the user Nathan, respectively. As it happens, this is a good way to verify connectivity problems within Skype for Business, especially if you can see the photo using the EWS link but not from the Skype for Business client or Skype for Business Web App.

Integrating Skype for Business with SharePoint

SharePoint 2013 is a business collaboration platform for the enterprise. SharePoint allows the creation of web portals and sites (intranets, extranets, and websites) to centralize information and applications on a corporate network. Organizations use SharePoint to connect and empower users and facilitate collaboration among them.

Skype for Business 2015 and SharePoint 2013 can be integrated to give users a rich in-context collaboration experience whether SharePoint is deployed on premises or as part of Office 365 in the cloud. Skype for Business builds on what was provided Lync 2010 and Office Communications Server (OCS) 2007 and OCS 2007 R2, which gave users the ability to access the instant messaging (IM), enhanced presence, telephony, and conferencing capabilities of Skype for Business and Office Communicator from SharePoint. This basic communication functionality integration requires no complicated configuration for SharePoint or Skype for Business Server. Should you want to enable all those with access to SharePoint to have an associated Persistent Chat room, then there are third-party software tools that will allow you to add Persistent Chat to these intranets, extranets, and websites. This SharePoint integration section of the chapter is split into two main areas. First we will explore the available functionality and show you how to integrate Skype for Business and SharePoint for things such as presence and search and to provide user photos. We will then move on to focus on how you can extend Skype for Business and SharePoint using UCMA by developing an automated communication bot.

Note that as with the Exchange section, you won't learn how to configure SharePoint. You'll simply be introduced to what is needed and any Skype for Business–specific configuration; for the other elements, you will need to see the existing SharePoint documentation or consult with your SharePoint team.

For guidance on installing and configuring SharePoint 2013, refer to the Microsoft TechNet articles at the following location:

`http://technet.microsoft.com/en-us/library/cc262957.aspx`

IM and Presence Within Sites

Skype for Business enables presence in SharePoint sites using the same presence indicator that is displayed in the Skype for Business client, as shown in Figure 22.18.

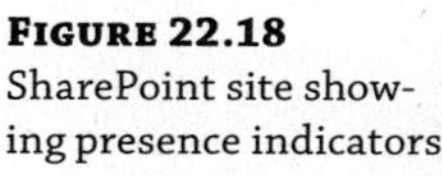

FIGURE 22.18 SharePoint site showing presence indicators

Wherever a username is displayed within SharePoint sites, their Skype for Business presence indicator is displayed, based on the presence status set in Skype for Business. With a single click, the contact card can be opened; it is the same contact card shown in the Skype for Business client, as shown in Figure 22.19.

FIGURE 22.19
The contact card experience accessible with a single click

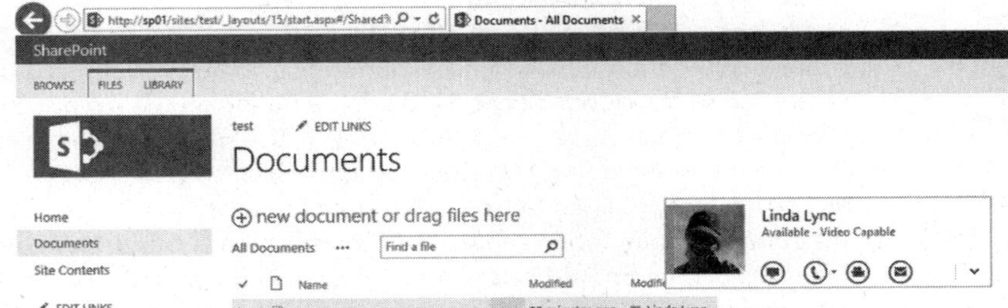

This enables full Skype for Business functionality from within SharePoint. A user can initiate Skype for Business communications from the contact card, such as sending an IM or starting a Skype for Business audio call, so collaboration is easy and intuitive. Presence is enabled by default in SharePoint, so there is no need for any special configuration on the server side for this to work.

To view presence in SharePoint sites, a user must have Office 2003 or Office 2007 with the latest service pack, Office 2010, Office 2013, or later. This is because when Office is installed, a dynamic link library called `name.dll` is installed. You can find it at `%Program Files%\Microsoft Office\Office15` where Office 2013 is installed (lower-numbered versions refer to earlier Office versions). This DLL file is an ActiveX control that allows SharePoint to display a user's presence information. The ActiveX control actually leverages the Skype for Business API to request the user's presence status so that it can be displayed within a SharePoint site. The required Skype for Business API is installed automatically as part of the Skype for Business client installation. Note that when Firefox and other browsers are used, presence integration is not available.

Skill Search

SharePoint Search helps users in an organization find the information they need to help them in their everyday work. It provides a way to search the intranet for both content and people and to refine results by relevance. For example, you know there is a new employee named John in Finance. To find John, you could search for *John* in a SharePoint Search Center People search site and all the results with *John* would be returned. You could further refine that search to find John in Finance. Skill Search in Skype for Business allows you to use the search term *John Finance* and get those filtered results immediately.

People Search requires that the following service applications be available:

- Search Service application (which is explained in the following text)
- User Profile Service application, which is a shared application within SharePoint 2013 and 2010 used to manage user profiles in an organization, synchronize profiles with Active Directory, and create My Sites for users
- Managed Metadata, which is used if you want to configure People Search and allow Search using a custom metadata property that is being populated into the user profiles from an external system such as a SQL or Oracle business system

People Search also requires that a Search Center site be created using the Enterprise Search Center template.

In SharePoint 2013 and 2010, Search is a service application. Service applications allow more granularity and control over how they work so that users can have a specific site collection that is associated with a specific service application. This means multiple indexes can be maintained, keeping information in separate indexes.

SharePoint Search can index all sorts of source content such as file shares, external websites (a partner's website, for example), SharePoint websites, Exchange public folders, databases, and line-of-business applications (Oracle or SQL databases, product data, or customer data). This new architecture gives the user an experience that is highly efficient, effective, and personal.

With Skype for Business and SharePoint 2013 (or SharePoint 2010 or 2007) integration, one exciting and useful new feature compared to OCS 2007 or 2007 R2 is the ability to perform a skill-based search within the Skype for Business client. For example, if you need to find a Skype for Business expert within your organization but you don't know exactly who or what kind of expert you need, you can simply type a keyword such as **Skype for Business** into the search bar and then click the Skill button. The client will then display anyone with Skype for Business in their job title or listed in the profile stored in their My Site on SharePoint.

WHAT IS MY SITE?

SharePoint's My Site feature provides a personal site that gives users in your organization a central location to not only store documents, links, and contacts but also populate and keep up-to-date with appropriate information about themselves. For example, users can list their skills, which can then appear as a result in other users' searches.

Once the results are returned, you can browse through them and find someone appropriate for what you need to know and send them a quick IM with your question. Because these results come from the SharePoint Skill Search component, a link is provided that opens the search results in SharePoint.

Skill Search is not enabled in Skype for Business by default. For this feature to work correctly, the following components are required:

- A full version of SharePoint: Windows SharePoint Services (WSS) will not work with Skill Search.
- SharePoint 2013 or SharePoint 2010 My Sites: A My Site is a personal site that gives you a central location to manage and store your documents, content, links, and contacts and lets others see information about you.
- The SharePoint User Profile service application: This stores information about users in a central location and is where user My Sites are administered and configured.
- A SharePoint Search Center site URL: This is a feature introduced in Microsoft Office SharePoint Server 2007; it is a SharePoint site specifically configured for the search task. It includes certain fields, each responsible for a specific search task—for example, People Search.

In addition, you need to configure the following:

- SharePoint must be published to the Internet so external Skype for Business clients can access it.
- Skype for Business Server needs to be configured with the correct Search Center URL to provide to clients. The Search Center URL is provisioned to the Skype for Business client through in-band settings as part of the `CsClientPolicy`, a topic discussed in Chapter 12.

Skype for Business needs to be configured to provide the relevant URLs to clients. These are the URLs of the SharePoint Search Center; your SharePoint administrator should be able to give them to you. To provide this information, a client policy must be configured and applied so that the Skype for Business clients are configured to use relevant SharePoint search URLs. To configure the client policy, you would run the following commands from the Skype for Business Server Management Shell (LSMS):

```
Set-CsClientPolicy -SPSearchInternalURL https://<searchsite>/_vti_bin/search.asmx
Set-CsClientPolicy -SPSearchExternalURL https://<searchsite>/_vti_bin/search.asmx
```

Note that `<searchsite>` should be replaced by the full path to the SharePoint Search Center.

With these commands, you set not only an internal URL but also an external URL so that remote users (not connected to the internal LAN) can access the Skill Search feature. If you do not specify an external URL, then upon clicking Search, users working remotely will receive an error message telling them they won't be able to search, as shown in Figure 22.20. To provide external access to search, the SharePoint website must be made available to users working externally.

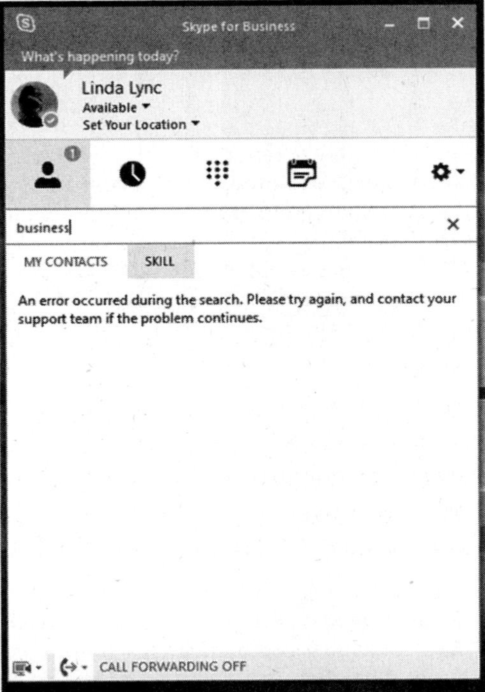

FIGURE 22.20 Error presented to users if the Skype for Business Search URLs are not configured correctly

> **SCOPING OF POLICY**
>
> The `Set-CsClientPolicy` commands just discussed work on the default user policies, which are set at the global level—all default policies (not just user) are global in scope. To target specific users or sites, review Chapter 12, which covers client policies and scoping. The policy defined in this chapter will be applied to all users.

As previously mentioned, there is also the Display Results In SharePoint option at the bottom of the Skype for Business client once the search has finished to display a link to the Search Center. The user can click this link to see the results of the search displayed in a SharePoint web page. To enable this functionality, execute the following commands in the LSMS:

```
Set-CsClientPolicy -SPSearchCenterInternalURL https://<searchsite>/Pages/
PeopleResults.aspx↵
Set-CsClientPolicy -SPSearchCenterExternalURL https://<searchsite>/SearchCenter/
Pages/↵PeopleResults.aspx
```

Note that `<searchsite>` should be replaced by the full path to the SharePoint Search Center.

Once the in-band provisioning takes effect, you will be able to conduct a Skill Search through your Skype for Business client.

1. In the search bar, type a keyword. You will be presented with the options Name and Skill.
2. Click Skill.

The query is sent to SharePoint, and the results are sent back to the Skype for Business client. You can click the View Results In SharePoint link to see the search results in a SharePoint web page.

To see which URLs have been provisioned, you can use the Skype for Business client Configuration Information tool. While holding down the Ctrl button, right-click the Skype for Business icon in the system tray and click Configuration Information to display the window shown in Figure 22.21. You can see the SharePoint URLs in the Configuration Information table. This area is a handy troubleshooting tool for many Skype for Business client configuration issues.

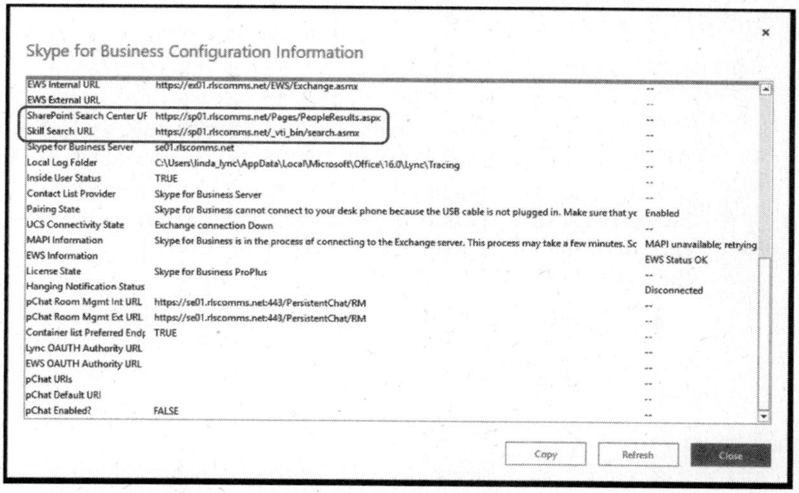

FIGURE 22.21 You can use the Configuration Information window to troubleshoot client issues.

Photos

Another feature in the Skype for Business client that immediately stands out is its ability to display photos, as shown in Figure 22.22. Having the ability to view another person's picture is useful in large organizations that may have many employees with the same name or in situations where you have "met" someone on Skype for Business and you arrange to meet face to face; a picture makes it much easier to identify them.

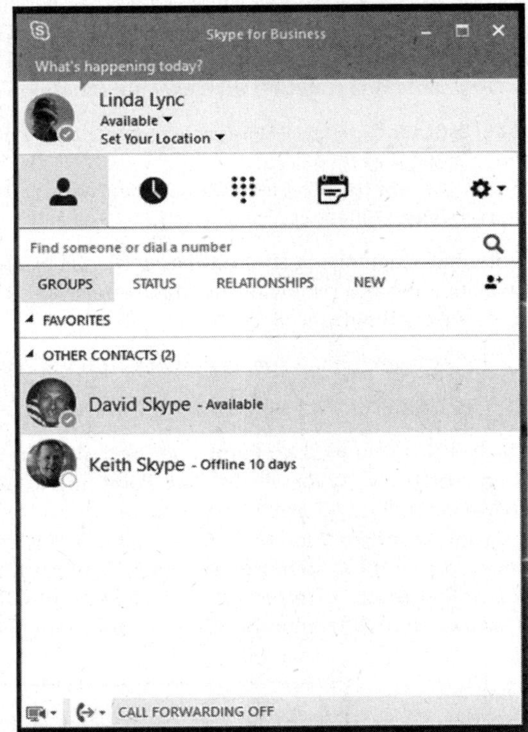

FIGURE 22.22
A contacts list showing photos

The photos come either from a basic web URL that was set in a Lync 2010 client or from AD. There are a couple of ways in which these get into AD. We have already covered the use of Exchange to do this import, but more relevantly for this section, the other way is from a SharePoint user's My Site via Active Directory integration. As with Skill Search functionality, certain components need to be set up first in order for photos to be displayed in the Skype for Business client from SharePoint.

- SharePoint User Profile Service application and My Sites need to be set up and configured. Users must upload a photo to their My Site web page. To set up the User Profile service application, see the article at this location:

  `http://technet.microsoft.com/en-us/library/ee662538.aspx`

- SharePoint AD needs to be synchronized. SharePoint must be configured to replicate pictures from the user profile to AD. A photo is loaded through this process into the attribute named `thumbnailPhoto` on a user object within AD. Skype for Business uses the attribute to access photos for contacts. To set up AD synchronization, follow the instructions at this location:

  `http://technet.microsoft.com/en-us/library/ee721049.aspx`

- A Skype for Business client policy must be configured. If your organization allows pictures in Skype for Business, you can provide users with a link from within the Skype for Business client that allows them to change their default corporate picture on their SharePoint My Site. You can find the link in the My Picture options (accessed by clicking the photo in the Skype for Business client), which allows the user to configure their picture without opening their My Site, instead allowing them to do it straight from the Skype for Business client.

Once all these components are set up and functioning correctly, a Skype for Business client will receive pictures through in-band policies. The first two items in the preceding list cover SharePoint configuration, but the final item is on the Skype for Business side. The required client policies are configured by using the `Set-CsClientPolicy` cmdlet.

The link to change the photo on My Site is not enabled by default. To add or remove it, use the following command to edit the existing global `CsClientPolicy`:

```
Set-CsClientPolicy -ShowSharepointPhotoEditLink $true
```

Users will be able to change their My Site picture directly through the Skype for Business client.

As discussed in the Exchange section of this chapter, new with Skype for Business 2013 and Exchange 2013 is the support for high-resolution pictures of up to 648×648 pixels and the scaling capabilities Exchange brings to the table. The recommended size in Lync 2010 and older is 96×96 pixels.

One important parameter is the picture size. By default in Skype for Business, the maximum size setting for pictures is 30KB, whereas in AD it is up to 40KB. To enable clients to have pictures up to 40KB, you can modify the client policy using the following command:

```
Set-CsClientPolicy -MaxPhotoSizeKb 40
```

This command will set the Skype for Business client policy to allow photos up to 40KB in size.

You may simply decide not to allow the use of photos in Skype for Business. To do that, you must use the `Set-CsClientPolicy` cmdlet, specifically the `DisplayPhoto` parameter. The following example uses the `PhotosFromAdOnly` setting, which specifies that only the pictures uploaded to AD from SharePoint can be shown in the Skype for Business client. This enables the maintenance of an element of control across the organization.

```
Set-CsClient -DisplayPhoto PhotosFromAdOnly
```

Once you have configured pictures, signing out and then back into Skype for Business ensures that the client performs an Address Book web services query to the Skype for Business server rather than possibly using cached values. Once the photo has been returned to the client, it caches it locally for 24 hours to prevent the client from unnecessarily downloading a photo it has already downloaded. After 24 hours, the client will send another query, and if the photo has changed in the SharePoint My Site and been synchronized to AD, it will receive and display it.

Converting Recorded Meetings into SharePoint Asset Libraries

Now that Skype for Business has integrated conferencing capabilities, one useful capability is to record meetings. Although these sound files can be saved to an individual's desktop machine, there is often huge benefit in sharing content, perhaps for training or catch-up purposes. With SharePoint integration, you can save and publish recorded Skype for Business meetings to SharePoint asset libraries; this lets you quickly and efficiently share meeting content from one location with minimal effort. An organization can maintain and manage meeting recordings like other digital assets, for example, by setting retention periods on them.

To use this feature, you need to record a meeting in Skype for Business. This can be done by simply selecting Start Recording from the menu shown in Figure 22.23.

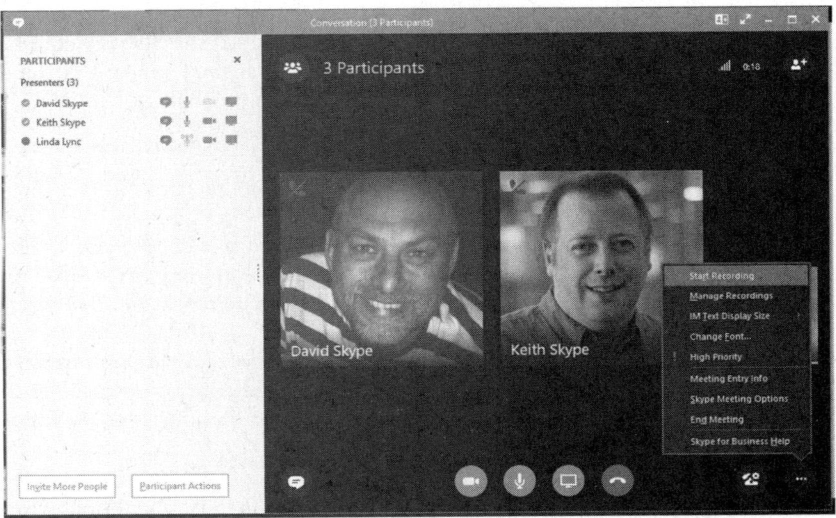

FIGURE 22.23 Starting a recording of a Skype for Business meeting

Once you have recorded your Skype for Business meeting, open the Skype for Business Recording Manager from Start ➢ Programs ➢ Microsoft Skype for Business. From there, you can see your Skype for Business recordings, as shown in Figure 22.24.

Select the recording to save to a SharePoint asset library and click Publish. A dialog box will open where you can type in the URL to the SharePoint asset library of your choice (if you do not know the URL, simply open the SharePoint site where you want to store the recording in IE and copy and paste the URL address from the IE address bar into the dialog box). As you can see in Figure 22.25, by default the user's Lync Recordings folder is shown.

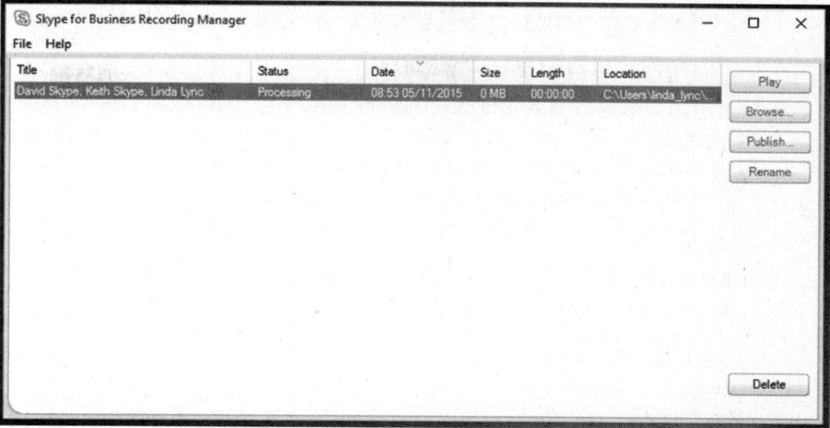

FIGURE 22.24
The Skype for Business Recording Manager window with a saved recording

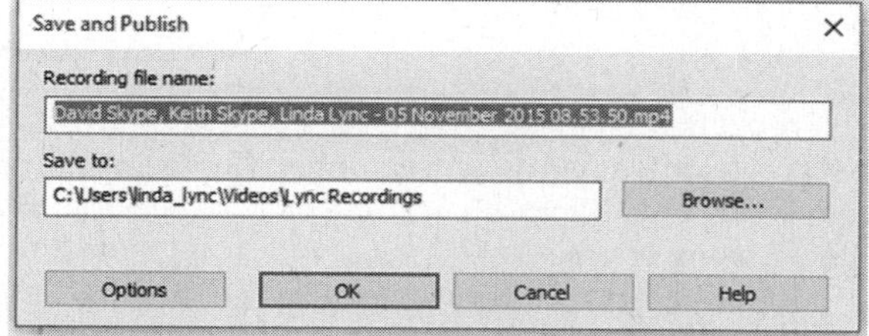

FIGURE 22.25
The Save and Publish dialog

Business Process Communication Workflows

Communications-enabled business process workflows (CEBPs) help organizations build workflows to enable Skype for Business functions such as IM or calls within a workflow. Combined with SharePoint workflows, customized integration features between Skype for Business and SharePoint 2013 can be achieved.

SharePoint 2013 and Skype for Business 2013 together provide an extensible platform on which to build applications that are enhanced through the use of Unified Communications and collaboration technologies. Beyond the out-of-the-box integration features with SharePoint as previously discussed, businesses can use the Microsoft Unified Communications Managed API 4.0 to develop and deploy server-side applications hosted in SharePoint. UCMA can be combined with SharePoint communication workflows to enable the standard Skype for Business communication functionality (such as presence or clicking to IM or call) within SharePoint. These workflows could include the ability to instantly contact those in an approval chain to make a decision, making the application more productive and efficient.

UCMA together with SharePoint can be used to create powerful applications that clearly impact business processes by enhancing them with communications, making them more efficient and collaborative.

Chapter 23, "Skype for Business 2015 Development," covers development, including a working UCMA 4.0 SDK bot example.

Integrating Skype for Business Server with Office Web Application Server

An Office Web Application server is the method in which you share PowerPoint content. This is a change since Lync Server 2010, and without deploying an OWA server, users will receive an error when trying to share PowerPoint content. Unfortunately, there is no way to disable this PowerPoint sharing feature, so even if you don't want users to use it, there is still a risk of users receiving errors (see Figure 22.26) and calling the help desk to report an error, which is expected in this case.

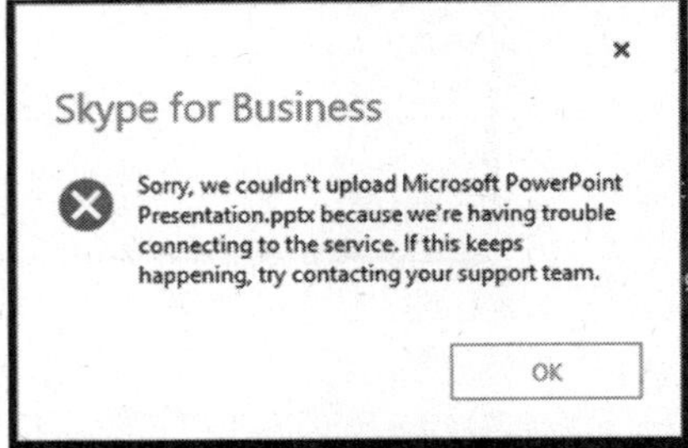

FIGURE 22.26
Error received when trying to share a PowerPoint with no Office Web Application server deployed

Previous versions of OWA were included with SharePoint. The latest version is available as a separate download; however, rather than being a freely available download, you must now be licensed via the Microsoft Volume License Service (MVLS). The cost remains free but is tied to the licensing of Office.

Like any Skype for Business infrastructure, the Office Web Apps server needs to be defined and published in the topology, so you need to run Topology Builder to do this.

An Office Web Apps server is associated with a pool, so open the pool definition page, select a pool, right-click, select Edit Properties on the Edit Properties page (see Figure 22.27), scroll down, and select Associate Office Web Apps Server. This option is not visible unless conferencing is available as a selected feature on the pool.

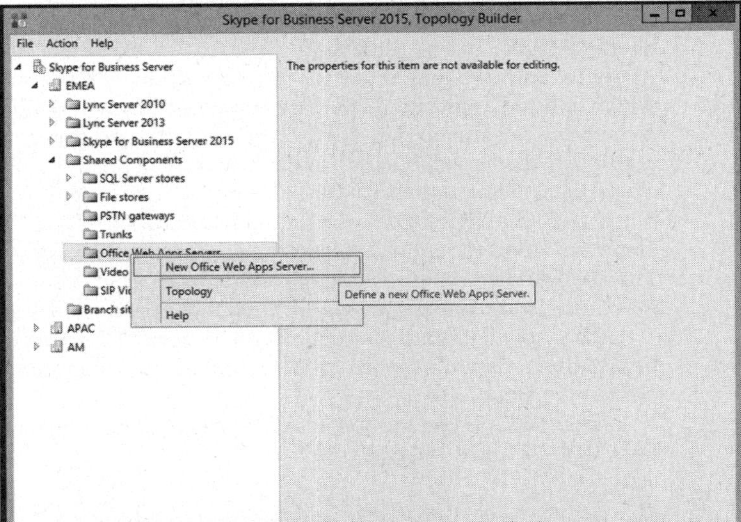

FIGURE 22.27
Define an Office Web Apps server using Topology Builder.

Selecting New will open the prompt for the server and the server discovery URLs (see Figure 22.28).

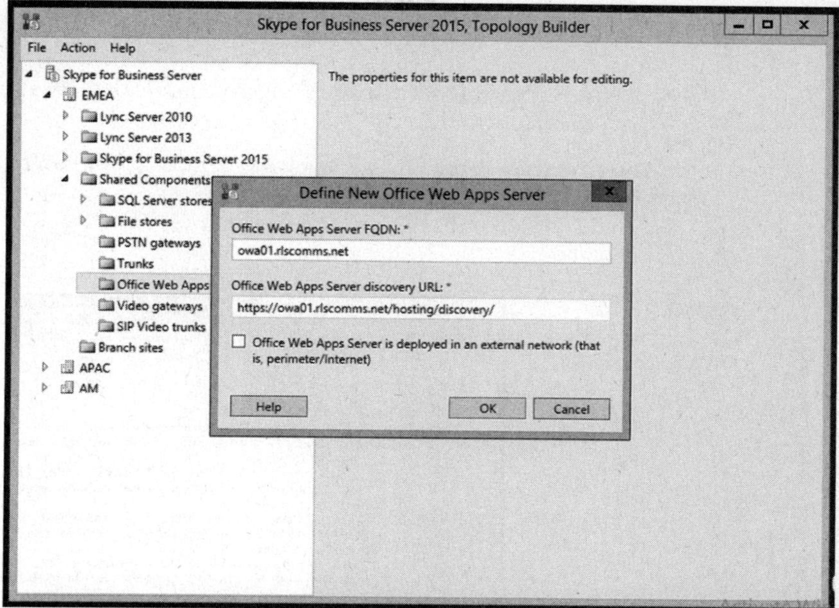

FIGURE 22.28
Prompting for Office Web Apps server URLs

If the Office Web Apps server is deployed on the internal network, then the check box should be left blank; otherwise, if the Office Web Apps server is in a perimeter network, this check box should be selected.

Once the definition is completed, the topology should be published as before.

Depending on whether you want external users (federated users, and so on) to access this Office Web Apps server, you may need to create associated web publishing rules on your reverse proxy. This will also be dependent upon whether your Office Web Apps server is located internally or in the perimeter.

Although the screenshots for the Office Web Apps server are shown associated with the Enterprise pool (you'll have to look closely), the Office Web Apps server can also be associated with Standard Edition servers.

Once defined and published in the topology, the Front End services will start to look for and report connectivity to the OWA server. If the OWA server cannot be contacted, you will see event ID 41033 reported in the event log.

You can test connectivity to OWA by using the following URLs:

- OWA Server internal presenter page: `https://<internal OWA FQDN>/m/Presenter.aspx?a=0&embed=`
- OWA Server internal attendee page: `https://<internal OWA FQDN>/m/ParticipantFrame.aspx?a=0&embed=true&=`
- OWA Server external presenter page: `https://<external OWA FQDN>/m/Presenter.aspx?a=0&embed`

- OWA Server internal attendee page: https://<External OWA FQDN>/m/ParticipantFrame.aspx?a=0&embed=true&
- OWA Server internal discovery page: https://<internal OWA FQDN>/hosting/discovery
- OWA Server external discovery page: https://<external OWA FQDN>/hosting/discovery

If you have configured OWA to allow HTTP access, you can replace the https in the URLs to test the unsecured connection.

Figure 22.29 shows the output from the discovery URL.

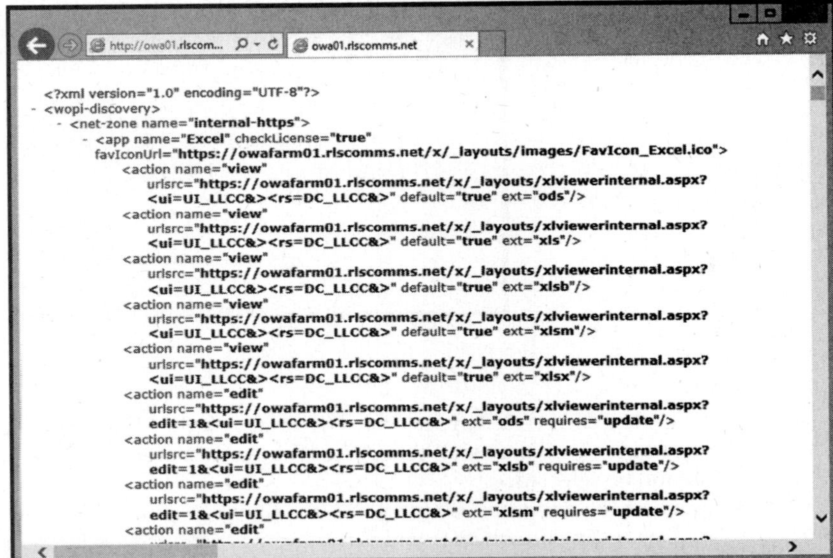

FIGURE 22.29 Connecting to the OWA discovery URL

Of course, to get to this point, you need to first install the OWA application. OWA has the following prerequisites:

- Windows Server 2008 R2 SP1
- .NET Framework
- PowerShell 3.0
- Depending on OS, possible hotfixes

With an administrative PowerShell prompt, run the following command:

```
Add-WindowsFeature Web-Server,Web-Mgmt-Tools,Web-Mgmt-Console,
Web-WebServer,Web-Common-Http,Web-Default-Doc,Web-Static-Content,
```

```
Web-Performance,Web-Stat-Compression,Web-Dyn-Compression,
Web-Security,Web-Filtering,Web-Windows-Auth,Web-App-Dev,
Web-Net-Ext45,Web-Asp-Net45,Web-ISAPI-Ext,Web-ISAPI-Filter,
Web-Includes,InkandHandwritingServices,NET-Framework-Features,
NET-Framework-Core,NET-HTTP-Activation,NET-Non-HTTP-Activ,
NET-WCF-HTTP-Activation45
```

From the OWA download, run `Setup.exe` and follow the prompts. There are not many options to choose from, only the EULA and install file location.

The next few steps contain details on how to install an OWA server farm that is load balanced. For any other type of installation, see the web page at `https://technet.microsoft.com/en-us/library/jj219455.aspxhttps://technet.microsoft.com/en-us/library/jj219455.aspx`.

To create the OWA farm, run the following cmdlet:

```
New-OfficeWebAppsFarm -InternalUrl "https://owafarm01.rlscomms.net"
-ExternalUrl "https://ext-owafarm01.rlscomms.net"
-SSLOffloaded
-EditingEnabled
```

The parameters define the following:

- `InternalURL`: FQDN of the load balanced URL
- `ExternalURL`: FQDN reachable via the reverse proxy
- `SSLOffloaded`: Allows the load balancer to deal with the certificate termination
- `EditingEnabled`: Optional for Skype for Business and Exchange integration but used by SharePoint

Adding additional OWA servers to the farm is achieved by running the following command:

```
New-OfficeWebAppsMachine - MachineToJoin "owa01.rlscomms.net"
```

Repeat this command for each machine to be added to the OWA farm.

Now you can check the connectivity by using the previously mentioned URLs to test.

The Bottom Line

Integrate Skype for Business with Exchange. Exchange provides a wide range of functionality to Skype for Business, and Skype for Business helps enhance Exchange. The most important integration points are for the provision of voice mail, where Exchange UM is the only supported voice mail platform for Skype for Business. To enhance Exchange, Skype for Business enables building presence and basic IM capabilities directly into OWA. There are also less obvious integration points because Skype for Business utilizes Exchange Web Services to pull information about users' calendar entries and their contacts, providing enhanced presence information and a single view of a person as an entity with whom to communicate.

Master It You company is rolling out Skype for Business as its telephony platform, and you will be using Exchange 2013 as your voice mail platform. You have been asked to outline the process to the Exchange administrative team.

Integrate Skype for Business with SharePoint. SharePoint integration is both relatively simple and potentially complex! It is simple in that integrating presence capability is automatic, and it is complex in that you have the ability through application development to put together almost any piece of communication-enhanced workflow that you can think up. SharePoint integration also provides the Skill Search capability to Skype for Business.

Master It Your organization makes extensive use of SharePoint 2010 and already has OCS 2007 R2, which has been providing presence integration. Now you are moving to Skype for Business 2013 and SharePoint 2013, and you have been asked to investigate the requirements for Skill Search integration between Skype for Business and SharePoint.

Integrate Skype for Business with Office Web Application Server. OWA integration is extremely straightforward. But without doing this step, users will not be able to share PowerPoint content directly.

Master It While migrating from Lync Server 2010 to Skype for Business, your organization wants to continue its use of PowerPoint sharing. What steps are needed to deploy a highly available OWA solution?

Chapter 23

Skype for Business 2015 Development

All the previous content is well and good if you're a standard organization looking to use Skype for Business in the ways that Microsoft has envisaged.

But what if you want to do something slightly different? What if you have business processes that could be enabled to react based on a person's presence? How about enabling your websites to allow communications into your organization without having users go to a separate, and typically generic, Contact Us page?

Well, that's where the development capabilities come into play. With a knowledge of software development and with the Skype for Business infrastructure deployed, you can create applications to leverage the capabilities or integrate them into your existing applications as needed.

In this chapter, you will learn to

- Explore the development options within Skype for Business
- Configure the infrastructure for custom applications

Understanding Development Options

Skype for Business development broadly consists of two concepts: server-side and client-side development. Depending on your requirements, Skype for Business provides different APIs and interfaces to control and extend both sides of the Skype for Business solution. Used in combination, most requirements can be realized with less effort than traditional custom development scenarios.

There are several main areas of development.

- The Unified Communications Managed API 5.0
- Software Defined Networking
- Microsoft SIP Processing Language
- The Skype for Business 2015 API
- Unified Communications Web API 2.0
- Skype Web SDK

The Skype Web SDK is currently in preview, which is the stage prior to the beta release. Hence, it's not covered here as there are likely to be significant changes prior to release.

Unified Communications Managed API 5.0

The Unified Communications Managed API (UCMA) 5.0 is the latest version of the API interface that accompanies Skype for Business 2015. UCMA provides a rich set of libraries to manipulate Skype for Business. The UCMA platform is a managed code endpoint API that is built on top of the Session Initiation Protocol (SIP). When custom Skype for Business functionality is required on the server side, developers will likely need to work with the UCMA.

Applications built using UCMA are able to harness Unified Communications (UC) capabilities such as voice, video, conferencing, instant messaging, and presence. The software-based approach enables developers to quickly code, test, and deploy UCMA applications. UCMA is written in Visual C#.

Here are some examples of UCMA solutions:

- Contact center, with interactive voice response (IVR), automated call distribution (ACD), call recording, and web chat
- IVR with Voice Extensible Markup Language (VoiceXML) support
- Connecting phones to online meetings using voice commands
- Integration with SharePoint to notify on events
- Text-to-speech readings of email from Microsoft Exchange

Using UCMA 5.0 to deliver trusted services offers many features for developers.

- Elevated permissions to impersonate users, participate in and control conferences invisibly, and control audio mixing.
- The ability to handle thousands of concurrent IMs on single instances.
- Scales up to multiple application hosts.
- Resilient to intermediate hop failures, good voice quality, speech recognition, text-to-speech, load balancing, and failover.
- Integrates directly with most SIP PSTN gateways and IP-PBXs.
- New in UCMA 4.0 was the support for VoiceXML 2.0, which is continued in version 5.0. This provides an industry standard for developing applications supporting speech services.
- Built-in extensibility that enables you to develop bespoke custom media and call types.

There are two main components UCMA developers should familiarize themselves with: collaboration and signaling. Collaboration components provide access to presence, conferencing, contacts, and more. Signaling components provide access to the SIP/SIMPLE layer. They are given their respective namespaces.

- `Microsoft.Rtc.Collaboration`
- `Microsoft.Rtc.Signaling`

When setting up your projects, you should note that UCMA 5.0 is contained in the `Microsoft.Rtc.Collaboration.dll` assembly.

The following list outlines some of the key features in UCMA:

Bandwidth Management Selectively decline and reroute calls based on network link consumption. Calls can also reroute through the PSTN if bandwidth is oversubscribed.

Back-to-Back User Agents Useful in help desks and call centers, the user agent acts as the bridge between an incoming call and agents. Incoming communications are directly with the back-to-back user agent, enabling an agent's details to be hidden from callers. Supervisors can monitor calls to ensure quality control.

PSTN User Authentication Users can be authenticated against Skype for Business Server 2015 or Exchange Server 2013 via a personal identification number (PIN). Users can also be authenticated separately, for trusted servers to take actions on behalf of authenticated users.

Industry-Standard VoiceXML 2.0 Support IVR applications created in VoiceXML can be used. You can host local or remote VoiceXML applications with UCMA 4.0. Existing VoiceXML applications on other platforms can be migrated to UCMA 4.0.

Trusted Conferencing Users Mode Enhance the communications experience using trusted users. They can join conferences invisibly and retain full control over conferences. This enables functions such as performing commands on behalf of other participants.

Trusted Service Discovery Create distributed UCMA applications. UCMA communications-enabled business applications (CEBPs) can discover and exchange information with one another. This allows distinct UCMA applications to interact, providing the ability for complex and distributed CEBP workflows.

Software Defined Networking

Software Defined Networking (SDN) was released as part of an update to Lync Server 2013 and is now at version 2.2. The purpose of SDN is to enable applications to be aware of the traffic (in real time) that is passing through the Skype for Business infrastructure. Once the application is aware of the traffic flow, the network traffic can be adjusted to optimize the quality of service.

SDN itself is not a programming interface but rather provides an interface for systems to subscribe to notifications—typically "call start" or "call end" type of events. SDN has three main goals.

- Superior diagnostics
- Dynamic QoS
- Intelligent routing

Figure 23.1 shows the SDN interface infrastructure.

As shown, the architecture consists of four components.

A Dialog Listener Captures signaling and quality data

An SDN Manager Collects data from dialog listeners and forwards to network management systems

A Data Store Manages shared state among SDN managers in a pool

Subscribers (Network Management Systems) Receive and analyze data to drive actions as required

FIGURE 23.1
SDN interface architecture

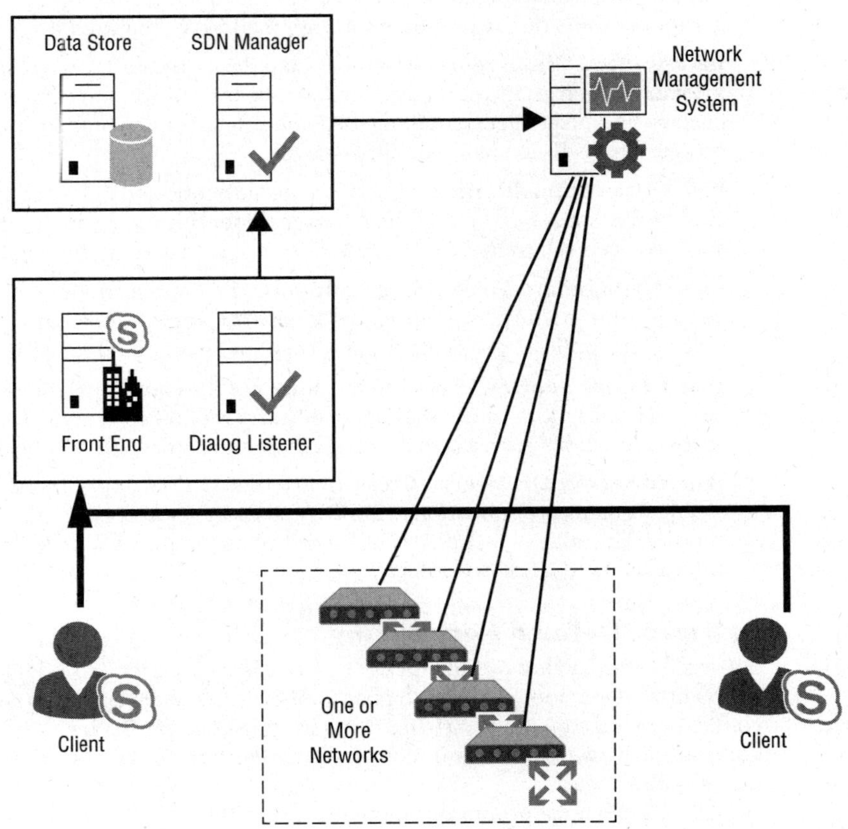

The dialog listener will run on any version of Lync Server or Skype for Business and requires .NET Framework 4.5 or later.

The SDN manager is recommended to run on a separate server (which may be virtualized) and requires Windows Server 2008 or later, again with .NET Framework 4.5 or later.

Figure 23.2 shows the SDN process flow.

When the dialog listener receives the relevant message (typically, a "call start," but the subscription could be for any message type), the dialog listener will forward the essential parts of the message to the SDN manager. The manager, in turn, will raise an event and invoke the appropriate event handler to parse the message. At this point, the relevant data properties (for individual media streams) are posted via XML to the SDN service on the network management system. The network management system will then have its own processing rules to deal with these event messages in the appropriate way.

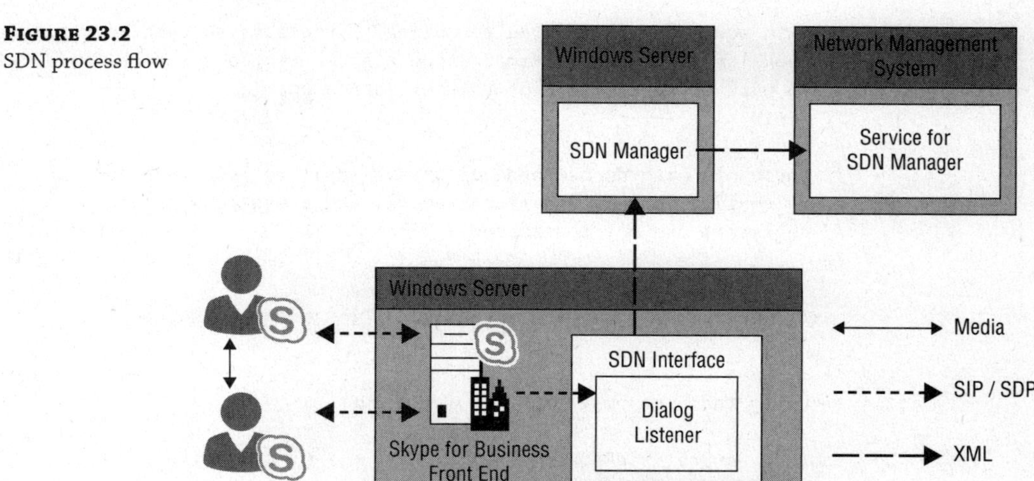

FIGURE 23.2
SDN process flow

The SDN manager can be configured in a pool in the same way the Skype for Business infrastructure can to provide resiliency. At this point, a data store is required, which may be a SQL database store. With a single SDN manager, the data is stored in memory.

You can find more information on the SDN interface here:

`https://msdn.microsoft.com/en-us/library/dn785131(v=office.16).aspx`

Microsoft SIP Processing Language

The Microsoft SIP Processing Language (MSPL) script is a way to route and filter SIP messages. Used in conjunction with UCMA, advanced SIP processing and workflows can be created. MSPL scripts run on the server side.

At the time of writing, the Skype for Business MSPL content has not been released. However, SIP has not changed dramatically since Lync Server 2013, so this content is still valid.

As a sample, the following script provided with the Lync 2013 SDK filters incoming SIP responses and selects an endpoint:

```
<?xml version="1.0">
<lc:applicationManifest
 lc:appUri="http://www.contoso.com/DefaultRoutingScript"
 xmlns:lc="http://schemas.microsoft.com/lcs/2006/05">
  <lc:requestFilter methodNames="INVITE,MESSAGE,INFO,REFER,ACK,BYE,OTHER"
                         strictRoute="false"
                         registrarGenerated="true"
                         domainSupported="true"/ >
  <lc:responseFilter reasonCodes="NONE" />
  <lc:proxyByDefault action="true" />
  <lc:scriptOnly />
  <lc:splScript>
    <![CDATA[
    //
```

```
    // This script handles default routing of requests to Lync Server.  It
    // looks up all the registered endpoints for the To: user@host and tries
    // to pick the best endpoint to route based on:
    //  EPID
    //
    // Endpoints with no presence or an availability less than 100, or
    // no routing information (for example, set presence without
    // register) are not considered.
    //

    Log( "Debugr", 1, "we have a request - ", sipRequest.Method );

    //
    // Build the user@host from the To: header.
    //
    toUri = GetUri( sipRequest.To );
    toUserAtHost = Concatenate( GetUserName( toUri ), "@",
GetHostName( toUri ) );

    //
    // Determine whether this request is already asking for a specific EPID
    // through a parameter in the To: header.
    //
    requestEPID = GetParameterValue( sipRequest.To, "EPID" );

    //
    // Now loop over all the endpoints for the To: user@host.
    //
    bestEPID = "";
    bestAgeOfPresence = 0x7FFFFFFF;
    bestAvailability = 0;
    bestActivity = 0;
    bestContactInfo = "";
    Log( "Debugr", 1, "EPID - ", requestEPID );
    Log( "Debugr", 1, "toUserAtHost - ", toUserAtHost );
    foreach (dbEndpoint in QueryEndpoints( toUserAtHost, true )) {
        Log( "Debugr", 1, "    endpoint.EPID - ", dbEndpoint.EPID );
        Log( "Debugr", 1, "    endpoint.ContactInfo - ",
dbEndpoint.ContactInfo );

        //
        // First, determine whether this endpoint supports the method in the
request.
        //
        if (!SupportsMethod( sipRequest.Method, dbEndpoint.StandardMethods,
dbEndpoint.ExtraMethods )) {
            //
            // Skip this endpoint because it cannot handle the method on this
```

```
request.
            //
            Log( "Debugr", 1, "        * skipped because of method" );
            continue;
            }

        if (requestEPID != "") {
            if (requestEPID == dbEndpoint.EPID) {
                //
                // The request is already targeted at a specific EPID that can
handle the method,
                // so use this endpoint.
                //
                Log( "Debugr", 1, "        * matched EPID" );
                bestContactInfo = dbEndpoint.ContactInfo;
                break;
            }
            else {
                //
                // The request is targeted at a specific EPID, but does not
match this endpoint.
                // Skip this endpoint.
                //
                Log( "Debugr", 1, "        * skipped because of EPID" );
                continue;
            }
        }

        bestEPID = dbEndpoint.EPID;
        bestContactInfo = dbEndpoint.ContactInfo;
        Log( "Debugr", 1, "        *** new best contact" );
        }

    //
    // See if an endpoint to proxy to was found.
    //
    if (bestContactInfo == "") {
        /* Uncomment this block of code and the two previous assignments to
sawAtLeastOneEndpoint
           if you want to run a UAC application before this one and have this
code
           route your messages to the correct home server.
        if (!sawAtLeastOneEndpoint) {
            homeServer = QueryHomeServer( toUserAtHost );
            if (!EqualString( homeServer, FQDN, true )) {
                Log( "Debugr", 1, toUserAtHost, " is homed on ", homeServer );
                newRequestUri = Concatenate( sipRequest.RequestUri, ";maddr=",
 homeServer );
```

```
                    Log( "Debugr", 1, "Request is being routed to ", newRequestUri );
                    AddHeader( "MS-LBVIA", FQDN );
                    ProxyRequest( newRequestUri );
                    return;
                }
            }
            */
            Log( "Debugr", 1, "Responding 480 - temporarily unavailable as no
suitable endpoint found" );
            Respond( 480, "Temporarily Unavailable" );
        }
        else {
            if (requestEPID == "") {
                Log( "Debugr", 1, "Adding missing EPID '", bestEPID,
"' to To header" );
                SetParameterValue( "To", "epid", bestEPID );
                }

            Log( "Debugr", 1, "Proxying request to - ", bestContactInfo );
            ProxyRequest( bestContactInfo );
            }

        return;
]]>
  </lc:splScript>
</lc:applicationManifest>
```

For more details about this script and MSPL syntax, see the MSDN article on MSPL (written for Lync Server 2013 but still relevant), located here:

`http://msdn.microsoft.com/en-us/library/office/dn439164.aspx`

MSPL scripts are useful for processing SIP messages without heavy resource load on the server. MSPL can quickly filter and route SIP messages, passing them off to trusted application endpoints in more advanced scenarios.

Skype for Business 2015 API

At the time of writing, there is no distinct Skype for Business 2016 client API. The Lync 2013 API is the latest, and given that the Skype for Business client is an upgrade to the Lync 2013 client, it's relatively safe to assume that not much is significantly different. The rest of this section will refer to the Lync 2013 API to make it clear, in case Microsoft does release an updated API.

UCMA and SPL are generally used to build middle-tier components that operate between the user and the Lync services to automate or enhance aspects of communication processes. For client-side development, the Lync 2013 API is provided.

The Lync 2013 API SDK is used to develop custom Lync 2013 applications or embed Lync functionality into other line-of-business (LOB) applications. Using the Lync API, the IM, voice, video, and conferencing capabilities can be presented from a custom client or LOB application.

The Lync 2013 API includes the following key new features:

Resource Sharing Share applications, desktops, or attached displays.

Persistent Chat Client and add-in applications can be built that are attached to a Persistent Chat room.

Online Meeting Content Management Manage the contents of meeting bins, the sharing stage, and video sources.

The Lync 2013 API is broadly split into three areas.

- Lync controls
- Lync API
- OCOM Unmanaged COM API

Lync controls provide a drag-and-drop method to enable existing applications with Lync features and a user interface. Controls for all the functions are provided.

- Search
- Presence
- Instant messaging
- Calls

The controls provide a familiar Lync UI for each feature. Programming the Lync controls is done with XAML or with C#. Using a combination of controls, developers can simply drag and drop Lync components to integrate into existing applications.

The Lync 2013 API is used to launch or automate the Lync 2013 UI controls within your application. This client-side API could be used within a custom application to perform the following tasks:

- Add a contact
- Associate line-of-business information with contacts
- Join/start instant messaging and audio and video conversations
- Join/start conferences
- Add conversation participants
- Automate scheduling conferences

The Office Communicator Object Model (OCOM) API is a subset of the Lync 2013 API, providing legacy support for Office Communicator. It lacks richer support such as conversations, but basic presence and contact list support is possible. This API may be useful for C++ developers who need contact or presence features.

You can find further information on the Lync 2013 client API here:

`https://msdn.microsoft.com/en-us/library/office/jj933180.aspx`

Unified Communications Web 2.0

UCWA is a Representational State Transfer (REST) API that allows access to IM and presence capabilities and is primarily used by the mobile clients today.

REST is an architectural style that describes six constraints, which define the basis of RESTful-style.

- ◆ Uniform interface
- ◆ Stateless
- ◆ Cacheable
- ◆ Client-server
- ◆ Layered system
- ◆ Code on demand (optional)

This approach is used with Skype for Business to allow developers to connect enterprise applications and intranets to business contacts.

UCWA 2.0 is language independent, and the API is tuned for developers already familiar with standard web technologies, such as HTTP and JavaScript. UCWA 2.0 is available only for on-premises Skype for Business deployments.

The core features available via UCWA 2.0 are listed here:

- ◆ Contact and group management
- ◆ Conversation history and auto-accept
- ◆ Two-party and multiparty IM
- ◆ Schedule and join meetings
- ◆ Contact card
- ◆ Phone audio
- ◆ Anonymous access

You can find more detailed information here:
`https://msdn.microsoft.com/en-us/library/dn324971(v=office.16).aspx`

Configuring the Infrastructure

To enable the Skype for Business infrastructure to become aware of additional infrastructure through which it may send and/or receive communications, you have two options.

- ◆ Define objects within Topology Builder
- ◆ Create new trusted applications

Topology Builder allows you to create only predefined objects such as pools or SQL Server instances, and so on, so in this case is of limited use. It will show you the applications once you have defined them, but it is not able to let you define them.

Creating a trusted application has a number of substeps associated with it.

- ◆ Create a trusted application pool

- Create a trusted application
- Create a trusted application endpoint

Configure a Trusted Application Server/Pool

For custom applications to run on servers, you need to define in the Skype for Business topology one or more trusted application servers that form the pool. You can confirm whether you have an application server already configured using either Topology Builder or Skype for Business Server Management Shell.

In Topology Builder, expand the site and check the Trusted Application Pool section for listed servers.

In PowerShell, run the following command: `Get-CsTrustedApplicationPool`. This will list any configured pools, as shown later in this section.

You can use the following syntax in PowerShell:

```
New-CsTrustedApplicationPool -Registrar <registrar pool>
```

Note that `<registrar pool>` should be replaced with the Registrar pool; for development environments, you can simply use the Front End pool. Upon successful completion of `New-CsTrustedApplicationPool`, you must run `Enable-CsTopology`. Confirm that you have created the trusted application pool by running `Get-CsTrustedApplicationPool` and noting its output, as shown here:

```
PS C:\> Get-CsTrustedApplicationPool

Identity              : TrustedApplicationPool:trust01.rlscomms.net
Registrar             : Registrar:se01.rlscomms.net
FileStore             :
ThrottleAsServer      : True
TreatAsAuthenticated : True
OutboundOnly          : False
RequiresReplication   : True
AudioPortStart        :
AudioPortCount        : 0
AppSharingPortStart   :
AppSharingPortCount   : 0
VideoPortStart        :
VideoPortCount        : 0
Applications          : {urn:application:trust}
DependentServiceList : {}
ServiceId             : 1-ExternalServer-1
SiteId                : Site:EMEA
PoolFqdn              : trust01.rlscomms.net
Version               : 7
Role                  : TrustedApplicationPool
```

Confirm that replication to all management stores have completed using `Get-CsManagementStoreReplicationStatus`. If you have issues replicating to the trusted application pool in a development environment, you may want to disable replication. Note that some applications will require it and some will not. All servers listed in the command should show UpToDate as True.

Configure a Trusted Application

Once you have a trusted application pool, you can create a trusted application and register it against the pool. Use the following syntax in LSMS:

```
New-CSTrustedApplication -ApplicationId trust↵
-TrustedApplicationPoolFqdn trust01.rlscomms.net -Port 10123
```

The port can be changed as desired. Upon successful completion of New-CsTrustedApplication, you must run Enable-CsTopology again. Confirm that you have created the trusted application by running Get-CsTrustedApplication and noting its output, as shown here:

```
PS C:\> Get-CsTrustedApplication


Identity                      : trust01.rlscomms.net/urn:application:trust
ComputerGruus                 : {trust01.rlscomms.net sip:trust01.rlscomms.
net;gruu;opaque=
srvr:trust01:a_xQh0YvvFCitXrfG_0RIAAA}
ServiceGruu                   : sip:trust01.rlscomms.net;gruu;opaque=
srvr:trust01:a_xQh0YvvFCitXrfG_0RIAAA
Protocol                      : Mtls
ApplicationIc                 : urn:application:trust
TrustedApplicationPoolFqdn : trust01.rlscomms.net
Port                          : 10123
LegacyApplicationName         : trust
```

Configure a Trusted Application Endpoint

Once you have a trusted application, you can create a trusted application endpoint and register it against the application. Use the following syntax in PowerShell:

```
New-CSTrustedApplicationEndpoint -ApplicationId trust↵
-TrustedApplicationPoolFqdn trust01.rlscomms.net
-SipAddress sip:trust01@rlscomms.net↵
-DisplayName "Trusted app"
```

If successful, the command will output the identity and details of the newly created application endpoint. Confirm that you have created the trusted application endpoint by running Get-CsTrustedApplicationEndpoint and noting its output, as shown here:

```
PS C:\> Get-CsTrustedApplicationEndpoint

Identity               : CN={053b9c5b-752a-4472-b75d-551d89bccd4f},CN=
Application Contacts,CN=RTC Service,CN=Services,CN=Configuration,DC=rlscomms,DC=net
```

```
RegistrarPool           : se01.rlscomms.net
HomeServer              : CN=Lc Services,CN=Microsoft,CN=1:1,CN=Pools,CN=RTC
Service,CN=Services,CN=Configuration,DC=rlscomms,DC=net
OwnerUrn                : urn:application:trust
SipAddress              : sip:trust@rlscomms.net
DisplayName             : Trusted App
DisplayNumber           :
LineURI                 :
PrimaryLanguage         : 0
SecondaryLanguages      : {}
EnterpriseVoiceEnabled : True
ExUmEnabled             : False
Enabled                 : True
```

If during any of the trusted application pool, application, or endpoint steps you run into any difficulty, refer to the following MSDN article on activating applications:

`http://msdn.microsoft.com/en-us/library/lync/hh347291.aspx`

You are now ready to start coding your own app!

The development of apps is way beyond the scope of this book, so we recommend you look to the Internet or other more specific texts for further information on app development.

The Bottom Line

Explore the development options within Skype for Business. Skype for Business builds on (and indeed continues to use) the APIs developed for Lync 2010 and Lync 2013. Depending on your specific needs, you can develop applications for the server, the client, or the network.

Master It You want to develop an application that will be able to report, in near real time, the quality of calls currently active on the network. Which approach should you use?

Configure the infrastructure for custom applications. It's not enough just to develop the application. Skype for Business need to be given information about the new app and its infrastructure requirements for the topology.

Master It You are deploying a new application to provide integration and reporting of calls to your customer relationship management (CRM) solution. What do you need to configure to enable connectivity of the new application to Skype for Business?

Appendices

In this section you will find:

- **Appendix A: The Bottom Line**
- **Appendix B: Introduction to PowerShell, the Skype for Business Management Shell, and Regular Expressions**
- **Appendix C: Using Persistent Chat Effectively**

Appendix A

The Bottom Line

Chapter 1: What's in Skype for Business

Describe the features of the client. The Skype for Business client is designed to achieve three core goals: connect, communicate, and collaborate. This new client makes it much easier to find people and verify identity, initiate communications (typically, with a single click), and collaborate with full-blown information sharing. Device integration and call management have been greatly simplified, removing the need to run through wizards constantly.

Master It You are assembling a new product development team. The new product will be similar to a previously released product, and you want to ask members of the previous team for guidance. How can you find people associated with the previous product team?

Solution Use the key-skills search feature integrated with SharePoint to return the names of the appropriate people.

Describe the features of the server. Skype for Business Server 2015 provides most of the server roles included in Office Communications Server and introduces the Survivable Branch Appliance (or Server) to help in the high-availability scenarios. The management approach has changed through the introduction of the Topology Builder application and role-based access control to limit administrative access to defined users and scopes as required. PowerShell and Silverlight combine to provide the day-to-day administration of the environment.

Master It When deploying high availability, which of the following roles can be a primary registrar?

- Director
- Enterprise Edition Front End
- Standard Edition Front End
- Survivable Branch Appliance
- Survivable Branch Server

Solution The Front End servers (both Enterprise and Standard Edition) and the Survivable Branch Appliance (and Server) can be primary registrars. Only the Front End servers (both Enterprise and Standard Edition) can be backup registrars.

Describe the voice features. Significant investment and development have gone into Skype for Business Server 2015's voice feature set. The new set has allowed it to become a match for a large portion of the PBX workload and, in many cases, a viable replacement for a PBX.

New functions (such as Private Line, Call Admission Control, Call Park, E9-1-1, and Common Area Phones) provide welcome additions to the user experience. By contrast, behind-the-scenes features (such as Media Bypass, routing improvements, resiliency improvements, and analog device management) provide a more integrated and available solution for the administrator while they help reduce the number of servers required.

Master It As the network and telephony administrator for your company, you want to invest in SIP trunks rather than legacy PBX-style PSTN connectivity using media gateways.

How should you configure media bypass and deploy mediation servers?

Solution When SIP trunks are used, separate physical mediation servers are recommended, and media bypass should be disabled. A SIP trunk does not have a termination point to allow the client to connect directly; instead, the client will connect to the Mediation server. The client can still use G711, and the Mediation server may not be required to transcode the codec.

Chapter 2: Standards and Protocols

Understand the basics of SIP for signaling. SIP originates from an extensive background of telephony signaling. Although knowing that background is not strictly required for Skype for Business Server 2015 administration, understanding how we have gotten to where we are today will help you overcome some of the challenges you'll face when integrating with legacy telephony environments.

Master It For what is a jitter buffer used?

Solution By buffering incoming data prior to playback, a jitter buffer is used to help smooth out the delay that occurs when packets are transmitted across a network.

Understand how SIP has been extended to provide additional functionality for Skype for Business Server 2015. In its plainest form, SIP provides session-based signaling; however, with some of the extensions for SIP, you can extend this session-based signaling approach to incorporate additional functionality within the SIP request itself, such as IM and presence information.

Master It Assuming a user is not yet logged in, describe the SIP requests required to log in and establish an IM session with another user.

Solution

REGISTER - Provide the login and registration information.

SUBSCRIBE - Request presence information.

NOTIFY - Receive presence information.

INVITE - Initiate the session.

ACK - Acknowledge the INVITE.

MESSAGE - Send the instant message.

For completeness, the session should be terminated with a BYE request.

Identify additional protocols used by Skype for Business Server 2015. Skype for Business Server 2015 uses many different protocols for its various modalities as needed by the user. It can also tie many of these modalities together, providing an integrated solution running on top of SIP. Microsoft has also been able to successfully (and securely) extend this functionality to the Internet.

Master It What is the default codec used in peer-to-peer audio calls?

Solution SILK

Chapter 3: Security

Secure external access. Skype for Business utilizes the Edge server and supporting components to provide external access to communications modalities. The Edge server sits in the DMZ and is a proxy between internal and external users. Many layers of security are in place to ensure that communicating externally won't cause security breaches.

Master It Describe the role the Director plays in external access. Why would you use one?

Solution The Director role sits in front of the Front End servers and carries out both authentication and redirection. When external connections are passed on to the Director through the Access Edge role, the Director acts as the point of authentication and, as such, will shield the Front End servers from potential DoS attacks using malformed authentication traffic. In its redirection role, the Director server will route traffic intelligently where one central site has multiple pools, thereby helping to keep the load on the Front End server to a minimum.

Understand core security. Skype for Business is designed to be secure by default. It does this in many ways, not least of which is by encrypting all traffic and using certificates as part of mutual authentication of connections.

Master It In different circumstances, Skype for Business can use five different authentication mechanisms. What are they, and where are they used?

Solution Kerberos authentication is used for clients who are domain joined and inside the LAN. NTLM authentication is used for clients accessing Skype for Business through the Edge server. Digest authentication is used by anonymous clients participating in conferencing. Certificate-based authentication is used in conjunction with a PIN by those signing in on IP phone devices.

Certificate authentication is used following a successful initial login using either Kerberos/NTLM/PIN.

Provide security administratively. No matter how secure a product is by design, an administrator can easily open up holes in its defenses. Skype for Business provides many ways in which administrators can participate in tightening or relaxing security. Numerous policies are available to control users, including the clients they are allowed to use and the length and complexity of PINs. Equally, you can configure Skype for Business to block links in IMs and prevent the transfer of files. Finally, Skype for Business can be set up to add disclaimers to messages so that regulatory issues can be managed.

Master It You have been asked to ensure that users in the EMEA site can send only files with extension `.txt` in IM messages and that any links in the messages will be prefixed with an underscore character so they must be copied into a browser manually. How would you do this?

Solution To archive the required results, you need to use two different cmdlets. The first in the New-CsFileTransferFilterConfiguration cmdlet, which should be used as shown here:

New-CsFileTransferFilterConfiguration -Identity site:EMEA -Extensions .txt

This cmdlet will create a new policy assigned to the EMEA site, which will allow fites with extension .txt.

The second cmdlet needed is New-CsImFilterConfiguration, which should be used as shown here:

New-CsImFilterConfiguration -Identity site:EMEA -Prefixes https: -Action Allow -Enabled $true

Chapter 4: Desktop Clients

Understand usage scenarios for each client. Each of the clients discussed in this chapter is designed for a specific usage scenario. For example, Skype for Business 2016 allows IM and presence (among other things) with other users.

Master It You have been engaged by a graphic design company to design and deploy Skype for Business. The company already has Lync Server 2010 and will be migrating to Skype for Business Server 2015 over the next six months. The company has 300 employees who are split almost 50/50 between Apple Mac computers and Windows PCs running Lync 2010. All users need to be able to participate in meetings with partners and customers during this coexistence phase.

Solution Skype for Business Web App has been significantly improved to support a wide range of platforms, including Windows and Mac. Because of the native audio and video support in Skype for Business Web App, it is the preferred client for joining meetings hosted on Skype for Business Server, even if users have the Lync 2010 client installed.

Understand changes in Group Chat. In Skype for Business, Group Chat has been built into the main product and is now called Persistent Chat.

Master It You are working with a large financial services company that is in the process of migrating from Lync Server 2010 to Skype for Business. The company's employees are heavy users of Group Chat in Lync Server 2010. What benefit does Skype for Business Server and Skype for Business client introduce in this area?

Solution The feature previously known as Group Chat in Lync Server 2010 is now called Persistent Chat and is built into the Skype for Business. A separate client is no longer required to be installed in parallel. You interact with a Persistent Chat room in a similar way to interacting with a user.

Understand how clients discover and communicate with various server roles, such as the Director, Front End, Persistent Chat, and the various Media Control Units (MCUs) for conferencing. Manually configuring clients for connecting to the infrastructure can be a massive overhead, so the clients each have a method to automatically determine where and how to connect.

Master It You are planning the migration from Lync Server 2010 to Skype for Business Server 2015. What additional DNS records are required to be created to address the preferred connectivity methods from the Skype for Business client?

Solution The Skype for Business client prefers to use the Autodiscover service for determining connectivity. This service requires the following DNS records to be created:

`lyncdiscoverinternal.<sipdomain>` for internal client connectivity.

`lyncdiscover.<sipdomain>` for external client connectivity.

Chapter 5: Mobile Clients

Understand the different capabilities of each mobile client (including tablets). With Skype for Business Server 2015, mobile clients are natively available and are able to bring new mobility features to the environment.

Master It What capabilities are not available on desktop clients but are available on the Windows Phone or iPhone?

Solution Some capabilities are common to both mobile platforms, such as the following:

- Passive authentication support
- Call via Work

Some are available only on Windows Phone, such as the following:

- Pinning contacts to the home screen

Some are available only on iPhone, such as the following:

- Automatic country code population

There are also several capabilities that are available in the desktop client but only one mobile platform, such as the following:

- Manage call forwarding
- View PowerPoint content
- Control photo display
- Search for response groups
- Expand distribution groups
- Manage contacts

Understand the policies available to manage mobile clients. With another client available to connect to Skype for Business, it's important for the administrator to be able to manage the feature capabilities as well as they would with any other device client.

Master It Name the five settings new to the Skype for Business mobile client, which can be managed via the `*-CsMobilityPolicy` cmdlets.

Solution The settings are as follows:

- `RequireWiFiForSharing`: When set to `True`, allows users to share screen content via a Wi-Fi network when available rather than via the mobile operator network
- `AllowSaveCallLogs`: When set to `True`, allows users to save a call log of calls made to or from the mobile client on their device

- `AllowExchangeConnectivity`: When set to `True`, allows users to Exchange services on the mobile device for items such as photos
- `AllowSaveIMHistory`: When set to `True`, allows users to save the contents of IM conversations on the mobile device
- `AllowSaveCredentials`: When set to `True`, enables the login credentials to be stored on the mobile device

Understand the infrastructure configuration required for enabling mobile devices. Specific additional configuration is needed to enable the mobility clients, and of course, consideration must be given to the specification of the hardware (and number) servers needed. Capacity planning for mobility is built into the capacity planning tools, but the configuration still requires the administrator to lend a hand!

Master It What is required to configure push notifications for Microsoft Windows Phone devices?

Solution Federation must be in place with the Lync Online push notification service. This service will take a message and distribute it to Microsoft as necessary.

```
New-CsHostingProvider -Identity "LyncOnline"
-Enabled $True
-ProxyFqdn "sipfed.online.lync.com"
-VerificationLevel UseSourceVerification
New-CsAllowedDomain -Identity "push.lync.com"
```

Finally, the mobility configuration must also be configured to use push notification.

```
New-CsPushNotificationConfiguration -Identity "Enable Push"
-EnableMicrosoftPushNotification $True
```

Chapter 6: Devices

Integrate with hardware video conferencing platforms. Skype for Business can integrate with several hardware video platforms to provide control and connectivity through Skype for Business to room-based and high-quality video networks.

Master It You are trying to configure Skype for Business integration with a Polycom HDX unit, but it won't connect. What might be causing an issue?

Solution The most common errors when configuring the HDX platform are as follows:

The user is not Enterprise Voice enabled.

The Skype for Business and Polycom encryption settings match.

Configure prerequisites for IP phones. IP phones are designed to be as simple as possible to deploy and receive all of their configuration settings automatically. For this to occur, a number of items need to be configured, such as network configuration and DHCP.

Master It You have deployed IP phones, but you are unable to log in to the phones when using extension and PIN authentication; however, logging in using USB tethering works as expected.

What is the likely problem?

Solution This usually occurs when the phone device cannot reach an NTP server. An indication of this is that it takes more than 30 seconds to retrieve the time during the login process. In a network trace, you can see the phone performing DNS queries for the NTP server and trying to connect and then failing.

This will often occurs when the NTP DNS records weren't created and/or the NTP server is not responding. The failback address of `time.windows.com` will be used but may be blocked on the firewall (UDP port 23).

Chapter 7: Planning Your Deployment

Use the available planning tools. Skype for Business Server 2015 is an extremely complex application, even when only some of the modalities are being used. Being able to plan for capacity, not just the number of servers but also bandwidth, is extremely critical.

Master It Which of the planning toolsets would you use to determine the required bandwidth on the network?

Solution The Bandwidth Calculator will allow you to provide model inputs to estimate your bandwidth requirements.

Determine when virtualization is appropriate. Lync Server 2010 introduced support for all modalities when virtualized. Lync Server 2013 has increased the performance capabilities and supported options. Skype for Business builds on this foundation. In certain cases, this enables administrators to reduce the server footprint, giving a better "green computing" deployment.

Master It Describe some of nonsupported features within a virtualization platform when using it with Skype for Business.

Solution While the supported platforms will change over time, as new versions are introduced, certain features that impact the real-time nature of the communications and collaboration functions are not supported. They are as follows:

- Shared Resource pools
- Real-time failover such as V-Motion or Live Migration
- Mixing a pool in both virtual and physical platforms

Understand the prerequisites. Like most applications, Skype for Business Server 2015 has a number of prerequisites that must be met prior to installation. These range from Active Directory requirements to individual server role requirements, both at the OS level and at the component level.

Master It Which operating systems are supported for deployment of Skype for Business Server 2015?

Solution Skype for Business is supported on the following Windows Server versions:

- Windows Server 2012 R2 Standard
- Windows Server 2012 R2 Enterprise
- Windows Server 2012 Standard
- Windows Server 2012 Datacenter

Chapter 8: Installation

Configure Windows Server for a Skype for Business installation. Installing Skype for Business is relatively simple, but many steps are involved. One of the most important is the preparatory work needed. If you get this wrong, it will slow down your installation and you may find that certain features will not work later.

Master It Skype for Business can be installed on several subtly different operating systems. You have been asked to lay out which OS requires the least amount of preparatory work and what the main preparatory stages are before Skype for Business can be deployed.

Solution Windows Server 2012 R2 is the most up-to-date server operating system at the time of writing, so it would be the preferred OS. However, there are still prerequisites that are required to be installed, as well as a patch. This patch will differ based on which OS is chosen.

Prepare Active Directory for installation. Like many Microsoft server applications, Skype for Business has tight ties with AD. Lync Server 2010 was the first version of Microsoft's real-time communications product to start moving away from the reliance on AD, but nevertheless, there are still hard requirements and preparatory steps that must be carried out, which include schema, forest, and domain prep.

Master It You are working in a large corporation with a single forest and multiple domains. You have been instructed to work with your directories team to help them understand the changes that need to be made to the schema as part of setup.

Solution Schema Prep is run once per forest to create the classes and attributes needed. This requires Schema Administrator rights to deploy. Setup can be run from the Deployment Wizard on any 64-bit server or from a PowerShell prompt if necessary. Four LDF files are provided for manual import if required.

Install your first Standard Edition server. A Standard Edition server is a complex environment requiring careful deployment. It has numerous prerequisites that need to be installed. Once you have completed the installation of prerequisites, setup is relatively straightforward, following a standard process.

Master It You have been tasked with installing the first Standard Edition server in your network. What is one of the unique preparatory steps required for this Standard Edition, and why? Following that, what are the standard steps that the setup takes?

Solution To install the first servers in the environment, the CMS must be published. With the first server being a Standard Edition server, this means that the first step is to create a SQL instance to store the CMS. After publishing, the deployment steps are regular.

1. Deploy the local configuration store.
2. Install components.
3. Configure certificates.
4. Start services.
5. Install updates.
6. [Optional] Configure accounts for Kerberos.

Implement external access through the Director Edge server. There are many elements that come together to provide external access. The Edge server and reverse proxy server sit in the perimeter network and provide access to media and web components, respectively. The Director sits on the LAN and acts as a routing and security buffer between the external users and the Front End pools. The deployment of the Director is similar to the deployment of Standard Edition or Front End servers and requires similar prerequisites.

Master It You are deploying an Edge server as part of providing remote access to your network. What is different about the install compared to the Standard Edition and Director installs?

Solution The Edge server is in the perimeter network and therefore is not part of the AD forest. As such, it requires manual intervention to retrieve the local copy of the CMS for the first time. This is a manual export/copy/import process, carried out as part of the installation of the local configuration store. Once installed, the Edge server has changes pushed to it from the CMS server.

Understand the differences in an Enterprise Edition installation. There are many differences when working on an Enterprise Edition deployment compared to a Standard Edition install. For example, there is the potential for a complex directory to be present, which requires close cooperation with a directories team. Another change is that SQL is installed separately and does not coexist with the Skype for Business server like it does with Standard Edition. Finally, there is the challenge of scalability and branch offices to overcome.

Master It You have been asked to work with the database team to ensure that everything is in place for the installation. What do you need to explain, and how would you instruct the database team to create the databases?

Solution Skype for Business requires a CMS database as well as general configuration and users databases, which can be installed after AD preparations are completed. Installation can be carried out via the Deployment Wizard or manually using the `Install-CsDatabase` cmdlet. Each database can be manually installed using this cmdlet if required.

Chapter 9: Migration and Upgrades

Understand migration considerations. The process of migrating to Skype for Business involves many aspects of an organization, not the least of which are the end users who will have new functionality to exploit and skills to learn. It is important to thoroughly evaluate all the phases of a migration and communicate clearly and efficiently to the staff. This is particularly true for any phase of coexistence where some users will be on Lync and others will be on Skype for Business, potentially with different versions of the client in place.

Master It You have been asked to prepare a short presentation covering the key elements of the migration. List the areas you would cover.

Solution During a migration to Skype for Business, only one legacy version can exist in the environment—either Lync Server 2010 or Lync Server 2013. If a previous migration from Lync Server 2010 to Lync Server 2013 has been started, it must be completed prior to introducing Skype for Business—either by finishing the move to Lync Server 2013 or by rolling back to Lync Server 2010.

Pool failover is not permitted during an upgrade.

Consider client pain points. During Skype for Business migration, your primary concern should be for your users. Throughout the migration users will face a changing environment.

How you deal with this and control the changes both through careful process and configuration of policy will have a large impact on the successful completion of the migration.

Master It You have been asked to prepare a short presentation covering the key difficulties faced by users during migration. List the areas you would cover.

Solution Users will experience some downtime, even during an upgrade. This may be momentary, as they are moved to another pool while the upgrade takes place and moved back again or moved to their final pool in a migration scenario.

The client experience will also need to be addressed. Will you upgrade the client before, during, or after the infrastructure? And which version will you deploy, Skype for Business 2015 or Skype for Business 2016?

Chapter 10: Online and Hybrid

Understand the hybrid architecture model. Skype for Business introduces the new capability of a hybrid model that allows hosting some users of an organization on premises in the traditional way of having an on-premises infrastructure deployed but also hosting other members of the organization in a cloud solution.

Master It Lync Server 2013 (and previous versions) provides support for multiple SIP domains in the same deployment within an Active Directory forest. What change to this model does the hybrid deployment in Skype for Business require?

Solution Hybrid allows for a single SIP domain to be split into two locations: on premises and in the cloud.

Understand the capabilities of a hybrid deployment. Users can be hosted either online in the cloud or on premises on a local infrastructure. Each location provides a common set of features, but not all are available when users are using Skype for Business Online.

Master It Which features are available only in an on-premises deployment?

Solution

- Remote call control
- Response group services
- Call park

Understand the call flow for media in different scenarios. Skype for Business can be a complex product when it comes to understanding signaling flows and media flows. Using Edge servers adds additional complexity, and having an additional pool hosted in the cloud adds a level of complexity beyond simple Edge servers!

Master It Describe the call flow path between two users, Linda and Rob. Linda is calling from a cell phone to Rob's Skype for Business phone number. Rob is a Skype for Business Online user and is located currently on the corporate network.

Solution

1. Linda places a PSTN call to Rob's DID. The call is received by the on-premises PSTN media gateway.
2. The on-premises media gateway directs the call to the Mediation server, which may be colocated on the on-premises pool.

3. The on-premises infrastructure knows that Rob has an Active Directory object on premises and reverse number lookup will find this object. The object will report that Rob's user account is hosted in the cloud.
4. The SIP signaling is then routed over the federation route via the Edge server to the cloud.
5. SIP signaling then travels from the cloud to Rob's client endpoint, which notifies Rob of an incoming call.
6. On answering the call, media is established and flows using the optimal path between the Mediation server and Rob's client.

Understand the required steps to configure a hybrid deployment. Introducing a hybrid scenario to a local Skype for Business environment requires a number of additional configuration items to be carried out. Some are as basic (and expected) as firewall port configuration, while others are significantly more complex, such as ADFS configuration.

Master It You are configuring your organization for a hybrid scenario and need to configure rules for the proxy exceptions list. What do you need to configure?

Solution

- Allow outgoing connections to the following URLs:
  - `*.microsoftonline.com.`
  - `*.microsoftonline-p.com.`
  - `*.onmicrosoft.com`
  - `*.sharepoint.com`
  - `*.outlook.com`
  - `*.lync.com`
  - `*.verisign.com`
  - `*.verisign.net`
  - `*.public-trust.com`
  - `*.sa.symcb.com`
- Allow TCP and HTTPS.
- Set the HTTPS/SSL timeout to eight hours.

Chapter 11: Role-Based Access Control

Use PowerShell to list the standard RBAC groups. RBAC in Skype for Business is administered through the Skype for Business Server Management Shell (SBSMS). There are 11 standard roles that ship with Skype for Business; they provide an organization with the ability to delegate administration with a reasonable degree of granularity.

Master It You are in the middle of planning your enterprise deployment and have been asked by the senior architect to research the available options for administrative delegation. You have been asked to provide a list of standard RBAC roles.

Solution To list the standard roles, you would run the following PowerShell command:

```
Get-CsAdminRole | Where-Object {$_.IsStandardRole -eq $True} | fl Identity
```

Understand the permissions available to each role. There are 11 RBAC roles in Skype for Business. These roles range from granting high-level administrative access using the CSAdministrator role to granting read-only access with the CSViewOnlyAdministrator. To use them properly, you need to know what each role does and understand any overlaps where different roles provide the same capability.

Master It As part of an investigation into how to make the best use of RBAC, you have been asked to identify a list of cmdlets each role grants access to so that it can be analyzed to see which RBAC role best fits the way your administrative teams work.

Solution To provide a list of the cmdlets assigned to an RBAC role, use the command in the following example. It lists the cmdlets assigned to the CSArchivingAdministrator role.

```
Get-CsAdminRole -Identity CSArchivingAdministrator | Select-Object
-ExpandProperty Cmdlets | Out-File c:\csarchivingadminrolecmdlets.txt
```

Undertake planning for RBAC roles. Your implementation of RBAC roles should relate to the way your organization is set up for administration. Some organizations are centralized, and others are distributed. You must understand your organizational structures and take them into account when planning RBAC roles. It is also important to follow the principle of least privilege, granting only the rights necessary for an administrator to do the job. This may mean utilizing custom roles and targeted scopes at either user OUs or Skype for Business sites.

Master It You are in the middle of planning your enterprise deployment and have been asked by the senior architect to plan the RBAC deployment in your organization. What should you consider?

Solution You must take into account many factors:

- The nature of administration in your organization. Is it centralized or distributed?
- How many levels of administrators do you have? Are there help-desk staff who need basic permissions, or are there a handful of senior administrators who do everything?
- Are there separate telephony teams that sit outside of the server department but need access to maintain the telephony functions of Skype for Business?
- Do your Skype for Business administrators also manage Exchange? If so, how do the roles in Exchange correlate to Skype for Business roles?
- The principle of least privilege. Should you grant administrators rights to do their job by using scopes both for site and user?
- Are all the existing roles too permissive or restrictive? In that case, consider creating a role with a custom list of cmdlets or scripts assigned.

Create custom RBAC roles and assign them to administrators. Skype for Business allows the creation of custom RBAC roles. These are not as flexible as in Exchange because you cannot grant access to specified single cmdlets. When creating a custom RBAC role, you must specify a template role from one of the 11 standard roles and then set an appropriate scope.

Master It Having carried out a planning exercise, you have decided that the standard Skype for Business roles are not adequate for your organization. Because you have a separate site supported by a separate team of junior admins who need to manage users in only one site, you need to be more specific about the areas that certain administrators can manage. How would you create an RBAC role to ensure that the junior admins don't have too many permissions?

Solution First, you would identify the relevant standard role to use as a template for the custom RBAC role. In this case, you would use the `CSUserAdministrator` role. Next, consider a suitable name for the role—in this case, `RemoteSite-CSUserAdministrator`.

Next, you would create the Universal security group in AD with the same name as the new role. Finally, you would create the actual role and, while creating the role, scope it to the Lync site and also to a specific OU that holds the users for the site as follows:

```
New-CsAdminRole -Template CSUserAdministrator
-Identity RemoteSite-CSUserAdmin -ConfigScopes "Site:RemoteSite"
-UserScopes "OU:ou=RemoteSiteUsersOU,dc=rlscomms,dc=net"
```

Manipulate the cmdlets assigned to a role. One of the evolving capabilities of Skype for Business is the ability for RBAC to be far more flexible that it was in its first iteration in Lync 2010. You can now manipulate roles right down to the cmdlet level, enabling far greater granularity of permissioning.

Master It You have an existing RBAC role created called MinimalRole1. Holders of the role need to be allowed to use only the `Get-CsUser` and `Get-CsAdminRole` cmdlets.

Later you decide that the role should be expanded to include the use of the `Get-CsAdminRoleAssignment` cmdlet.

Finally, you realize that allowing the `Get-CsUser` cmdlet was a mistake.

Outline the separate steps you would take to carry out each configuration. You should end up with three commands.

Solution You start by setting the role only to use the `Get-CsUser` and `Get-CsAdminRole` cmdlets.

```
Set-CsAdminRole -Identity MinimalRole1 -Cmdlets "Set-CsUser",Set-CsAdminRole"
```

Next you want to add the `Get-CsAdminRoleAssignment` cmdlet.

```
Set-CsAdminRole -Identity MinimalRole1
-Cmdlets @{Add="Get-CsAdminRoleAssignment"}
```

Finally, you need to remove the `Set-CsUser` cmdlet.

```
Set-CsAdminRole -Identity MinimalRole1 -Cmdlets @{Remove="Get-CsUser"}
```

Carry out general administration, including granting and removing RBAC roles. There a few cmdlets that allow management of RBAC roles in Skype for Business, and most use the `CsAdminRole` verb. All PowerShell roles are assigned through the membership of a linked Active Directory Universal security group.

Master It A colleague who administered Skype for Business has moved to a new role, and his replacement starts on Monday. You have been asked to ensure that the new staff member has the appropriate rights to do his job.

Solution Adding and removing RBAC roles from a user is as simple as ensuring membership in the related AD security groups. In this instance, you would first check which roles the colleague who has left was a member of using the following command:

```
Get-CsAdminRoleAssignment -Identity "Useralias"
```

Next, you would add the new administrator's user account to the relevant AD groups and remove the old administrator's account at the same time.

Report on the use of RBAC roles. Given that the purpose of RBAC is to provide people with administrative access to a system, there will always be a need to review and provide reports to management on who has what access. Reporting on RBAC takes various forms but can all be done through SBSMS.

Master It You have been asked to provide details on which roles have access to the APAC site and list the membership of those roles. How would you proceed?

Solution First, you would identify the roles that have access to the APAC site using the following command:

```
Get-CsAdminRole | Where-Object {$_.ConfigScopes -match "site:APAC"}
```

Next, to enable searching in AD groups, you would load the Active Directory module into PowerShell:

```
Import-Module ActiveDirectory
```

Finally, for each of the roles that the previous command returns, you would run the following command to list the membership:

```
Get-ADGroupMember -Identity Rolesfromlist | Select name
```

Chapter 12: User Administration

Search for users in the SBSCP and PowerShell. Skype for Business offers huge flexibility in what can be done to configure and control the user experience. However, to work efficiently, being able to identify and retrieve information about different groups of users based on various criteria is critical. It is this skill that enables you to target specific groups with specific policies. As with most administration, you can search for users in both SBSCP and PowerShell.

Master It You have been asked to run a report on two groups of users. How would you handle the following requests? Can you use two different types of search?

Locate all users in Marketing.

Locate all users who register to the `se01.rlscomms.net` pool.

Solution In PowerShell, run the following command:

```
Get-CsUser -LDAPFilter "Department=Marketing"
```

This will get all the Marketing users enabled for Skype for Business using an LDAP filter.

Another type of search allows for piping the results of the `Get-CsUser` cmdlet to the `Where-Object` cmdlet, as shown here:

```
Get-CsUser | Where-Object {[String]$_.Registrarpool
-eq "se01.rlscomms.net"}
```

Perform basic user administration in the SBSCP and in PowerShell. As would be expected, most basic administration can be performed in the SBSCP and in PowerShell. New users can be created, deleted, enabled, and disabled in both. You can, of course, also change various user properties—in particular, things like the SIP URI of a user and the pool to which they register. User administration is generally carried out by a user who is a member of the CSUserAdministrator RBAC role.

Master It You have been asked to enable all users, except those who are in Sales, for Skype for Business. How would you do this? In addition, one of your colleagues, who is a domain administrator, has asked you to make some changes to his account. What problems might you face?

Solution First you need to search for the users and then pipe the output to the `Enable-CsUser` cmdlet. Remember, uses who are not yet enabled for Skype for Business can be returned only by the `Get-CsAdUser` cmdlet.

```
Get-CsAdUser -LDAPFilter "!(Department=Sales" | Enable-CsUser
-Registrarpool se01.rlscomms.net -SipAddressType EmailAddress
```

For your colleague, you can make changes to Skype for Business users only from PowerShell when you are logged in as a domain administrator.

Understand Skype for Business policies. Skype for Business has significantly improved the policy architecture since OCS 2007 R2. Although AD Group Policy still can have a role to play in getting the client up and running, Skype for Business enforces the majority of policy through in-band provisioning. It uses SIP messages to push policy out to the client instantly and ensures that there is no requirement for domain membership. Users get a consistent experience no matter where they log on. To apply Skype for Business policies properly, it is important to understand the new scope model, in which policies can be applied at the global, site, service, and user levels, and how inheritance works so that the policy closest to the user wins.

Master It You have been asked to explain to a new administrator the different scopes at which a policy can be applied and how different scopes affect the identity of the policy. What would you tell her?

Solution Policies can be applied at several different levels. By default, all policies have a global policy, which contains the default settings. As an administrator with the CSAdministrator RBAC role, you can create policies of the following scopes:

Site

Service

User

The identity of the policy is defined by the level at which it is assigned, as shown in the example here:

Site:*PolicyName*

Site and service policies are automatically assigned when they are created because they are specifically linked to an object when created. User policies are identified by `Tag:Policyname` and must be individually assigned.

Manipulation Skype for Business policies. Policies are controlled and applied to users either through PowerShell or through the SBSCP. When in the shell, your search skills are critical to ensure that you can closely target relevant user groups. It is here that the piping capabilities of PowerShell are so useful. You can, of course, also apply policy through the SBSCP, which has a helpful Assign Policy page where you can apply applicable policies to one or many users from a single screen.

Master It You have been asked to create a new client policy for the APAC site. You first need to check the default settings for the policy and then customize it to limit the number of users a person can have on their contacts list to 300. How would you proceed?

Solution Default settings are assigned when creating a policy with no specific settings. By using the `-InMemory` parameter, you can create and view a policy without impacting existing policies.

```
New-CsClientPolicy -Identity TestDefaultSettings -InMemory
```

To create the required policy, use the following:

```
New-CsClientPolicy -Identity Site:APAC -MaximumNumberOfContacts 300
```

Choose the right policy for the job. There is a vast range of policy settings available. One of the hardest things an administrator must do is understand where to make certain configurations. SBSCP makes available many policy settings, but it is not always obvious which PowerShell cmdlet sets which setting, compared to what is presented in the SBSCP. Equally, it is not possible to carry out all configuration through the SBSCP, with some of the most wide-ranging policies being configured only through PowerShell.

Master It You have been asked to design a set of policies for your organization. Where would you gather more information about specific settings?

Solution The list of cmdlets available to manage the Skype for Business environment is very extensive, and each cmdlet has further different numbers of parameters to adjust its functionality.

Search in the help file for specific cmdlets including `*-Cs*` to indicate specific Skype for Business cmdlets and then search for the specific parameters for the individual cmdlets identified.

Chapter 13: Archiving and Monitoring Roles

Understand the architecture for the Archiving and Monitoring roles. Although related to different aspects of the data, the Archiving and Monitoring services are similar in function, and they have similar back-end requirements. This allows them to be easily colocated and share the same database server or instance.

Master It What are the options available for enabling Archiving?

Solution Exchange Integrated, requiring Exchange Server 2013

Traditional SQL archiving to a SQL Server instance within the Skype for Business Server environment

Provide reporting on the data available from the Archiving and Monitoring roles. Skype for Business Server 2015 provides a monitoring reports pack containing more than 50 reports, which focus on the QoE data. Non-Microsoft vendors provide additional report capability for the other databases, and of course, you can always write your own reports.

Master It What options are available for creating customized reports?

Solution You can connect via ODBC from any data manipulation software (such as Excel), or you can use SQL Server Report Builder to create and publish reports to the SQL Reporting Services server.

Use the capabilities in the System Center Operations Manager management pack to report on the availability of the Skype for Business Server service. With the implementation of the Skype for Business Server 2015 Monitoring Management Pack for System Center Operations Manager, administrators have a consolidated approach and location for collating and monitoring system (and service) uptime.

Master It Which synthetic transactions will confirm the status of the Address Book service?

Solution

```
Test-CsAddressBookService
Test-CsAddressBookWebQuery
```

Chapter 14: Planning for Adoption

Understand the impact of UC on the users. Unified Communications has the potential to vastly improve users' productivity. However, depending on where you are starting from (in other words, a greenfield or a previous version), there is going to be a dramatically different impact to the users. Some users may want to have an actual desk phone when the plan is to replace all phones with headsets; how will you deal with these?

Master It You have been asked to prepare a short communications statement covering the key benefits users will receive once using Skype for Business. List the areas you would cover.

Solution All users are going to be different in their reaction to change and how they will deal with it. The key items to cover in communications are as follows:

- Stating the direct, measureable benefits, such as cost reduction
- Stating the indirect, less tangible benefits, such as easier collaboration
- Highlighting the executive buy-in with the sponsor, perhaps a comment or two
- Acknowledging that change is coming

Understand the importance of choosing the correct users for piloting. Having a good test plan is one thing, but if you're not targeting the correct users, you can impact the project success levels. The executive assistants are often overlooked when it comes to piloting, but this team often, while having no direct authority, has a direct, and strong, link to the sponsors and decision makers. Getting them on your side early is key; often their role is well placed to have a dramatic improvement with new collaborative technologies.

Master It You have been asked to prepare a migration plan. List the key considerations for user selection.

Solution Users across different areas of the business will be impacted in different ways. Mobile workers are already likely to have collaboration technology or specific ways of working that may have a significant impact on how they work with a change, whereas some office workers may not have a need for collaboration, as they already are physically with everyone they collaborate with.

Early pilot users are likely to be more tech savvy and open to new things.

As the pilot develops, include people who work together and from as many different business areas as is sensible. This will allow you to evaluate the different collaboration uses through the pilot phase.

Be careful including too many technical people. Typically they are the type who will find their own solutions to problems, and you may not get the feedback you want.

Chapter 15: Troubleshooting

Confirm that the basics are in place from the infrastructure side. Skype for Business Server 2015 relies on a range of additional infrastructure to be able to provide its functionality—such as Active Directory, SQL, DNS, network, and so on. If any of these additional areas suffer interruptions or misconfigurations, it is extremely likely that Skype for Business will begin to demonstrate issues also.

Master It An internal Skype for Business client is having difficulty connecting to its home pool when using automatic configuration. Describe the flow of DNS and connection attempts made for a client on the corporate network.

Solution First, automatic configuration will attempt the following DNS queries:

```
Lyndiscoverinternal.<sip domain>
Lyncdiscover.<sip domain>
_sipinternaltls._tcp.<sip domain>
Sipinternal.<sip domain>
Sip.<sip domain>
```

The SRV records will return a CNAME record type, which in turn will require another DNS lookup to resolve to the IP address.

The client will then attempt to connect and register to the pool; if this is a Director pool (or not the client's home pool), the client will receive a redirect to the home pool.

Further DNS lookups will be carried out to determine the resulting IP address of this pool.

Understand how to troubleshoot the client. The Skype for Business client provides a lot of information in the configuration section as well as the log files to aid with troubleshooting, and this information should not be overlooked.

Master It Where are the client log files stored?

Solution They are stored in the following folder:

```
%USER PROFILE
%\AppData\Local\Microsoft\Office\<version>\Lync\Tracing
```

Know how to enable troubleshooting on the server. The Skype for Business Server roles have individual components that require logging and also provide performance counter objects that can be monitored.

By default, the logging scenario AlwaysOn is enabled on the servers. The default logging options and components can be configured to suit users' needs.

Master It How do you enable logging on Skype for Business Server?

Solution The following cmdlets are used to manage logging:

```
Show-CsClsLogging
Start-CsClsLogging
Stop-CsClsLogging
Sync-CsClsLogging
Update-CsClsLogging
```

`Start-CsClsLogging` is the cmdlet used to specifically start the processes.

Understand and use the troubleshooting tools available. In addition to the built-in logging functionality of Skype for Business Server 2015, more tools can (and should) be downloaded and installed on each of the servers to provide a better range of data, which is ready to be captured in the event of a problem.

Master It Which tool is recommended for analyzing SIP logs or message traces? And where can it be found?

Solution `Snooper.exe` is the tool used and is part of the Debugging Tools download pack.

Chapter 16: Getting Started with Voice

Understand the voice capabilities. Skype for Business Server 2015 has expanded further the capabilities provided by Microsoft in the Unified Communications space to be almost on par with enterprise PBXs (and certainly equal to, if not better, than departmental PBX offerings).

Master It Describe the benefits of media bypass.

Solution Media bypass enables the media flow to bypass the Mediation server role and connect directly to the endpoint (device or gateway). This removes potential delays introduced by transcoding the media, resulting in less degradation of the call quality. In addition, removing this load from the Mediation server role allows the server to scale upward the number of calls it can handle, as well as allowing for the ability to colocate the role onto a Front End, reducing the need for additional servers.

Understand the voice architecture. With the use of media bypass and the support for virtualization, the architectural requirements to deploy voice are consolidated into a smaller server footprint, and at the same time additional functionality has been included in the product. Significant investment has been made in the high-availability and resiliency deployment models.

Master It Describe the user experience when the user's home pool fails and only a backup registrar has been configured.

Solution The user's client will be disconnected from the server and will automatically log in to the backup registrar. This is known as Survivable mode, and the client will indicate this state to the user.

Survivable mode provides limited functionality to the user; it has the ability to make and receive calls as well as to search for users if the SIP address is known. A user with a call in progress will be able to continue with the call with no impact, assuming of course the call is not using the failed pool for media transcoding. If the user is joined to the conference on the failed pool, the call will get disconnected and be unable to rejoin. However, if the conference is hosted on another pool, it will continue.

Configure voice policies and routing. Aside from the architectural requirements, enabling Enterprise Voice requires configuration to be applied to users (policies) and back-end configuration to be applied to the servers (routing).

Master It What configuration joins the user configuration to the server configuration and provides the permissions to enable (or block) a call?

Solution PSTN Usages are linked to both the Voice policy and the routes. The user will be assigned a Voice policy and, from this, be enabled to use routes associated with the same usages.

Chapter 17: Call Admission Control

Identify Call Admission Control–capable endpoints. Before designing and configuring Call Admission Control, you need to understand where it can be applied to ensure that the proper configuration is identified.

Master It You are in the process of defining a migration from OCS R2 to Skype for Business. First you migrated the OCS servers to Lync Server 2010 and have now introduced Skype for Business. Users previously reported some issues with call quality because of the capacity on the network, so Call Admission Control is required. What is needed to ensure the best user call experience?

Solution Only Skype for Business and Lync servers and clients can participate in Call Admission Control; all clients will need to be upgraded to a suitable version.

Configure policy-based Quality of Service controls. Call Admission Control provides application-layer management of the call bandwidth; however, to truly provide this guarantee to clients, quality of service is required to operate on the network layer. Windows Vista introduced policy-based quality of service controls.

Master It You have restricted the port range to be 5000 to 5999, and you will deploy Skype for Business to your users. An application utilized in the finance department uses the port range 5500 to 5599. How can you ensure that only the Skype for Business traffic is prioritized on the network?

Solution Define a policy-based QoS group policy, which specifies the port range to prioritize and sets the application to `Lync.exe`.

Design a Call Admission Control solution. Call Admission Control can be complex in large interconnected networks. A properly designed solution will ensure that two important requirements of Call Admission Control are met: user call quality is high and the network is not saturated.

Master It What special considerations should be given to an MPLS network?

Solution The MPLS cloud should be defined as a region, with each network link defined as a connection to a site. No site should be associated directly with the region. If multiple MPLS clouds are used (for example, one in Europe and one in America), then each should be a separate region, and region links (and routes) will be required too.

Configure Call Admission Control. Once designed, Call Admission Control needs to be configured and applied to the Skype for Business servers. The servers will keep each other constantly updated as to the number of the calls and bandwidth used on the network. By using the built-in logging functionality, it is possible to capture an hourly snapshot of the state, with more detailed reporting available via the Monitoring server.

Master It What needs to be defined and applied to configure Call Admission Control?

Solution

- Regions
- Sites
- Policy profiles
- Subnets

If multiple regions are defined, you also need region links and region routes.

Chapter 18: E9-1-1 and Location Information Services

Describe the E9-1-1 requirements for North America. Enhanced emergency services dialing provides location information to emergency services, enabling them to better respond in the event of an emergency.

Master It Is the provision of location information with emergency dialing compulsory?

Solution Providing location information is required only in certain states in North America, and even then the requirements differ from state to state.

Configure Skype for Business Server 2015 to meet E9-1-1 requirements. As a viable PBX, Skype for Business is required to meet the E9-1-1 requirements to provide location information data and as such must have validated address information provided with each emergency call.

Master It Through what configuration items can location information data be delivered to the Skype for Business client?

Solution Any of the following methods can be used:

- Subnet
- Switch chassis
- Switch port
- Wireless SSID
- Manual configuration
- Secondary location services such as MACResolver or Secondary Location Source Database

Understand how Location Information services can be used by users outside North America. Although the actual requirements are currently defined only in locations in North America, beta program feedback from customers indicated that automatic Location Information services are extremely useful and desired worldwide.

Master It What specifically is required to enable Location Information services in North America, and what different requirements are in place for the rest of the world?

Solution In North America, address validation against the Master Street Address Guide provides the address validation. Outside North America, Location Information services can be used, but the information is marked as not validated.

Understand how to query multiple sources of location information. Skype for Business Server allows for multiple sources of location information to be queried. Skype for Business Server can be pointed to additional location databases or applications that can reduce the overhead in discovery and definition of all the network locations for an organization.

Master It Which cmdlet and parameters are used to configure secondary location information sources?

Solution An SNMP application is configured as follows:

```
Set-CsWebServiceConfiguration -MACResolveUrl "<app url>"
```

A secondary location source application is configured as follows:

```
Set-CsWebServiceConfiguration -SecondaryLocationSourceUrl "<app url>"
```

Chapter 19: Extended Voice Functionality

Understand the extended voice functionality. Extended voice functionality provides additional voice applications that many organizations expect a PBX to have. Understanding what these applications can and cannot do is important so you can make the correct decisions when implementing them and know when a third-party solution is better.

Master It The manager for an internal help desk has been to a trade show and has been told he needs to have a full contact center to implement certain requirements. All he needs is to route calls to agents. He does not care about reporting or recording; he just needs to make sure that calls get to the right people. He is adamant that he needs a call center because this is what the experts have told him.

Solution Response Groups can fulfill these requirements because items such as reporting and recording are not required. Although it can be difficult to dissuade people from accepting what an expert has told them, showing them what can be done is usually the best way. Find out what they need to do and create the Response Groups; then show them that they can do what they want at a fraction of the cost.

Design solutions using extended voice functionality. Designing is usually seen as a boring, time-consuming task, when all you want to do is get your hands dirty and implement something. Although some of the extended voice functionality is straightforward, other elements are complex, and missing the design stage could cause you problems later. Design, design, design—and implement once.

Master It You need to implement a dial-in conferencing solution globally. You need to have global dial-in numbers and support at least 100 concurrent PSTN calls to the conferencing solution.

Solution Dial-in conferencing may seem easy. You already have Enterprise Voice deployed. You just need to add some access number and away you go. Usually, this is not the case. Although you may have designed for Enterprise Voice in terms of PSTN capacity and bandwidth, dial-in conferencing adds more load, in this case the requirement for 100 concurrent PSTN calls. This requires not only additional PSTN capacity but also sufficient capacity on the Mediation and Conferencing servers. Never assume that an existing voice design will be able to cope with additional requirements. If you are changing the dynamics of an element, in this case Enterprise Voice, you need to back to the drawing board and update the design to cope with the new requirements.

Implement extended voice functionality. Lync's extended voice functionality is useless if you do not know how to implement it and use it to its fullest potential. To do that, you need to make sure that what you implement works and is fully tested.

Master It You have implemented Call Park, but users are complaining about intermittent issues with parking calls. The complaints are coming from all user types, which is strange because not all users should be able to park calls.

Solution The first step is to determine why these users are able to park calls. To do this, you can use PowerShell to query the Voice policies to see which ones have Call Park enabled. To do that, issue the following command:

```
Get-VoicePolicy | Select Identity, EnableCallPark | FL
```

This will return the Voice policies and indicate whether Call Park is enabled. In this case, the following was returned:

```
Identity       : Global
EnableCallPark : False
Identity       : Tag:Attendants
EnableCallPark : True
Identity       : Tag:IWs
EnableCallPark : True
```

From this, you can see that the IWs policy has `EnableCallPark` set to `True`, allowing all information workers to park calls. Setting this to `False` will prevent them from using Call Park functionality.

```
Set-CsVoicePolicy -Identity IWs -EnableCallPark $false
```

Now only the attendants will be able to park calls. At this stage, you can wait to see whether the attendants report any issues. The intermittent issue probably occurred because Call Park ran out of orbits because of being sized only for attendants and not for everyone.

Chapter 20: SQL Server

Understand the different SQL Server needs within Skype for Business Skype for Business has different SQL Server needs depending on both the scale and the high availability needs of the deployment. Different versions of SQL Server are available to address each of these, from SQL Server Express, which is installed on every server, to SQL Server Enterprise Edition, which is for large-scale enterprise database back ends.

Master It Which versions of SQL Server are supported for use with Skype for Business Server?

Solution SQL Server 2008 R2 SP2

SQL Server 2012 SP1

SQL Server 2014

Understand the different options available for providing high availability When scaling up Skype for Business from a Standard Edition server, either for increased user count or for high availability (or both), you must deploy a stand-alone SQL Server version, rather than continuing to rely upon the SQL Server Express edition installed with Standard Edition. With this move, SQL Server can also be deployed in a highly available configuration based on your business needs.

Master It You are deploying a Skype for Business Enterprise Edition pool and want to enable automatic high availability with no single points of failure on the SQL Server portion of the solution. You must also keep costs to a minimum.

Solution Actually, there are two possible options to this based on your negotiated license cost for SQL Server!

- SQL Server mirroring will require three physical servers but can be deployed using SQL Server Standard Edition on both of the primary and mirror servers, with SQL Server Express on the Witness server.
- SQL Server AlwaysOn can be deployed using SQL Server Enterprise Edition on two servers.

If the cost of two licenses for SQL Server Enterprise Edition is more expensive than the cost of two licenses for SQL Server Standard Edition *and* the cost of a third server, then the first option will be cheaper.

Understand how to migrate to SQL Server AlwaysOn SQL Server AlwaysOn Availability Groups are a newly supported feature and provide another option for enabling high availability within SQL Server. While the feature is easy to deploy from scratch, some organizations may want to migrate from stand-alone or mirrored SQL Server to enable this functionality.

Master It You currently have a SQL Server 2014 mirror deployed supporting an Enterprise Edition pool. What steps are required to migrate SQL Server to AlwaysOn Availability Groups?

Solution Carry out the following steps:

1. Break the mirror in the Skype for Business topology and publish.
2. Break the mirror in SQL Server Management Studio.
3. Delete the databases from the mirror server.
4. Define the SQL Server AlwaysOn configuration in Topology Builder, specifying the original primary server as the FQDN, and publish.
5. Install Windows Failover Clustering.
6. Create the cluster with both nodes.
7. Enable AlwaysOn within SQL Server Configuration Manager.
8. Confirm all databases are set to Full recovery mode.
9. Confirm all databases have been backed up.
10. Create the AlwaysOn Availability Group using SQL Server Management Studio.
11. Fail over the SQL Server server to the original mirror node server.
12. Define the SQL Server AlwaysOn configuration in Topology Builder, specifying the original mirror server as the FQDN, and publish.
13. Fail back the SQL Server Server instance to the original primary node.
14. Define the SQL Server AlwaysOn configuration in Topology Builder, specifying the SQL Server AlwaysOn Listener server as the FQDN, and publish.

Understand the data stored within the various SQL Server databases. Skype for Business stores lots of data, from individual user account configuration to live conference data. While some of this is stored within the fileshare data structure, this does not have the speed of response needed to support real-time communications needs. This is where SQL Server comes into its own: providing that necessary speed of response.

Master It What is the name of the database in which Skype for Business stores the topology?

Solution The database where the topology information is stored is called `XDS`. The writable copy is stored on the Central Management Store, and a read-only copy is replicated to every Skype for Business server in the topology.

Chapter 21: Reverse Proxies, Load Balancers, and Gateways

Use load balancers for scale. Load balancers allow and enable an Enterprise pool to be deployed, providing scale beyond that of a Standard Edition pool (5,000) all the way to the maximum number of users in a pool (80,000). They can also be deployed when scaling the Edge servers, although are not required.

Master It What protocols are required to be load balanced in an Enterprise pool?

Solution HTTP and HTTPS are the two protocols that need load balancing. Other protocols may be load balancers but are not required.

Use reverse proxies for external access. Typically, clients would have connected via the Access Edge role in the Edge server; however, mobile clients introduced the capability to connect using HTTP/HTTPS, and the latest desktop clients also leverage this capability. External (and federated) access to pools also requires the deployment of a reverse proxy.

Master It You are deploying a reverse proxy solution in your DMZ to enable remote and federated access. What requirement must a reverse proxy provide for port translation?

Solution External traffic on ports 80 and 443 must be translated to ports 8080 and 4443, respectively, when being proxied to the internal pools.

Use gateways to Integrate with the PSTN. Connecting Skype for Business to telephony systems need not be hard; however, there are many areas you must consider to ensure that you make the correct deployment choices. Skype for Business can connect directly to an ITSP or a PBX or in both cases can utilize a gateway device to provide security, control, and intelligent routing of traffic.

Master It Your PBX is five years old and capable of being upgraded to talk to Skype for Business directly. You want to deploy Skype for Business for Enterprise Voice and need a way out to the PSTN. What must you consider in your decision about connecting Skype for Business to the PSTN?

Solution While the PBX may be upgraded, if you are deploying Skype for Business for voice, it is unlikely you will want to spend additional money on the existing PBX. Therefore, you have to consider either operating Skype for Business as an entirely separate entity to the PBX with a separate numbering scheme or, more likely, utilizing a certified gateway to connect the two systems. You have a choice of where to place the gateway in the system—before the PBX or after. Before the PBX will enable you to have the most flexibility in terms of call routing. The decision will be made on the gateway, and it limits the amount of configuration required on the PBX.

Chapter 22: Exchange, SharePoint, and Office Web Application Server

Integrate Skype for Business with Exchange. Exchange provides a wide range of functionality to Skype for Business, and Skype for Business helps enhance Exchange. The most important integration points are for the provision of voice mail, where Exchange UM is the only supported voice mail platform for Skype for Business. To enhance Exchange, Skype for Business enables building presence and basic IM capabilities directly into OWA. There are also less obvious integration points because Skype for Business utilizes Exchange Web Services to pull information about users' calendar entries and their contacts, providing enhanced presence information and a single view of a person as an entity with whom to communicate.

Master It You company is rolling out Skype for Business as its telephony platform, and you will be using Exchange 2013 as your voice mail platform. You have been asked to outline the process to the Exchange administrative team.

Solution Integration of Skype for Business unto Exchange UM requires the following steps:

1. Ensure that the correct certificates are in place for the Exchange UM service. Exchange uses self-signed certificates by default, and is it important that a certificate that is trusted by the Skype for Business servers is used. The certificate must have the FQDN of the Exchange server as its subject name.
2. Configure the Exchange UM components of the system (dial plan, policy, and auto attendants). Exchange UM dial plans are used to set major configuration points such as the security of communications and the length of the phone extension number. Make sure your PIN access policy is set up suitably for your organization.
3. Ensure that Exchange knows about Skype for Business as a gateway. You will use the `ExchUtil.ps1` script to set the correct permissions and to set up the Exchange VoIP gateway object for the Skype for Business server(s). Remember, you may have to run this twice.
4. Check to see that Skype for Business dial plans are correctly configured and can understand the dialing setup used in Exchange.
5. Configure Skype for Business to use Exchange UM. You will use the `OcsUtil.exe` application to set up the contact objects so that Skype for Business knows how to route calls to Exchange voice mail and auto attendants.
6. Enable users for UM. Each user will need to be enabled for Exchange UM through either the Exchange Management Console or via PowerShell.

Integrate Skype for Business with SharePoint. SharePoint integration is both relatively simple and potentially complex! It is simple in that integrating presence capability is automatic, and it is complex in that you have the ability through application development to put together almost any piece of communication-enhanced workflow that you can think up. SharePoint integration also provides the Skill Search capability to Skype for Business.

Master It Your organization makes extensive use of SharePoint 2010 and already has OCS 2007 R2, which has been providing presence integration. Now you are moving to Skype for Business 2013 and SharePoint 2013, and you have been asked to investigate the requirements for Skill Search integration between Skype for Business and SharePoint.

Solution SharePoint Skill Search is not enabled by default. For this feature to work correctly, the following components and configuration are required:

- A full version of SharePoint is required. Windows SharePoint Services (WSS) will not work with Skill Search.
- SharePoint My Sites need to be enabled.
- The SharePoint User Profile service application; this will store the information about the users in a central location and is where users' My Sites are administered and configured.
- A SharePoint Search Center site URL; a feature introduced in Microsoft Office SharePoint Server 2007, it is a SharePoint site specifically configured for the search task. It includes certain fields, each responsible for a specific search task, for example, People Search.
- SharePoint must be published to the Internet so that external Skype for Business clients can access it.
- Skype for Business Server needs to be configured with the correct Search Center URL to provide to clients via in-band provisioning of policy.

Integrate Skype for Business with Office Web Application Server. OWA integration is extremely straightforward. But without doing this step, users will not be able to share PowerPoint content directly.

Master It While migrating from Lync Server 2010 to Skype for Business, your organization wants to continue its use of PowerPoint sharing. What steps are needed to deploy a highly available OWA solution?

Solution Highly available OWA is dependent upon multiple servers being load balanced.

Deploying the first server using the `New-OfficeWebAppsFarm` cmdlet and add additional servers using the `New-OfficeWebAppsMachine` cmdlet.

Finally, ensure the load balancer is configured to share the load among all these servers.

Repeat these steps for each region as required.

Chapter 23: Skype for Business 2015 Development

Explore the development options within Skype for Business. Skype for Business builds on (and indeed continues to use) the APIs developed for Lync 2010 and Lync 2013. Depending on your specific needs, you can develop applications for the server, the client, or the network.

Master It You want to develop an application that will be able to report, in near real time, the quality of calls currently active on the network. Which approach should you use?

Solution Software Defined Networking provides the capability to trigger events and report data on the live (or near live) call statistics.

Configure the infrastructure for custom applications. It's not enough just to develop the application. Skype for Business need to be given information about the new app and its infrastructure requirements for the topology.

Master It You are deploying a new application to provide integration and reporting of calls to your customer relationship management (CRM) solution. What do you need to configure to enable connectivity of the new application to Skype for Business?

Solution In order, you must define the following:

1. A trusted application pool
2. A trusted application
3. A trusted application endpoint

Appendix B

Introduction to PowerShell, the Skype for Business Management Shell, and Regular Expressions

PowerShell was introduced by Microsoft in 2006 as the long-term plan to unify various scripting languages. It is a framework built on and integrated with the .NET Framework and consists of a command-line shell and scripting environment. The first product to take advantage of PowerShell natively was Exchange 2007, and the scope has grown dramatically since then to include almost the entire Microsoft collection of server and system administration products: Windows Server, SQL Server, System Center Suite, Windows Compute Cluster Server, SharePoint, Lync Server, and now also Skype for Business 2015. As PowerShell was initially released in 2006, the initial hope was that Office Communications Server (OCS) 2007 R2 would natively integrate with PowerShell; instead, a number of PowerShell scripts were provided as part of the Resource Kit toolset, and these PowerShell scripts simply call VBScript or Windows Management Instrumentation (WMI) to perform their tasks. Outside of the Microsoft products, a significant number of third-party vendors, including IBM, Quest, VMware, and NetApp to name a few, provide modules to allow PowerShell integration.

If you are already familiar with PowerShell, you can skip this appendix.

Why Use PowerShell?

If you're wondering why you should use PowerShell, the answer is simple: scripting.

In today's large-scale enterprise environments, it is extremely common to perform the same task on a number of servers or on a number of users. With its proliferation and integration across the Microsoft suite of products (as well as the third-party integration), PowerShell is extremely easy to connect to any of these products using the common shell interface.

Looking to the future and cloud computing, Microsoft is providing PowerShell management capabilities for the cloud interface, again meaning that a single interface is now capable of providing management both on premises and in the cloud.

Coming back to the current world and the now-legacy versions of OCS, there are multiple integration points such as WMI and COM. Developing scripts to simplify administration quite often results in extremely large, complex, and difficult-to-maintain VBScript. Tasks that previously required tens (or even hundreds) of lines of code can now be performed with a single command, and in addition, PowerShell allows the results of one command to be piped into another, providing an even more resourceful environment.

The final reason is that there are some cases in which the only way to achieve a task is via the shell, so even in single-server, 20-user environments, there are scenarios in which the shell *must* be used.

PowerShell is very modular; in Windows Server 2008 R2, the base PowerShell v2 installation has more than 200 individual cmdlets. Lync Server 2010 extended this by more than 500 more cmdlets specific to Lync, and Lync Server 2013 added another 200 on top. Skype for Business has extended this to more than 800! And that's just cmdlets, not considering the amount of changes.

Of course, with PowerShell version 3 starting with more than 500 cmdlets, this means there are more than 1,200 PowerShell cmdlets to help manage your environment.

Understanding Command Syntax

Unfortunately, every scripting language is different—and typically, as they get more powerful, they become more complicated and, in some cases, more cryptic.

One of Microsoft's goals for PowerShell is to make this language more intuitive, and as a result each PowerShell command typically consists of a verb and noun combination; the verb provides the action and the noun provides the object—for example, `Get-CsUser`. This combination of verb and noun is referred to as a *cmdlet*. The verb will always come first and the noun will follow, separated by a hyphen. The noun begins with a prefix indicating which tool the PowerShell cmdlet belongs to.

Since Lync Server introduced PowerShell, every cmdlet includes `Cs` to indicate it is part of the Lync (and Skype for Business) PowerShell command set. Why `Cs`? It is a reference to Communications Server. During the Lync Server 2010 beta program, the code name for Lync was "Communications Server 14"—abbreviated to CS. The cmdlets were not changed upon release (and rename) of Lync Server 2010 and have continued this naming convention through the release of Lync Server 2013 and Skype for Business Server 2015 as well.

PowerShell is not case sensitive; however, you'll see that cmdlets use a mix of case to make them easier to read.

Table B.1 shows some of the common verbs and nouns in Skype for Business.

TABLE B.1: Common Skype for Business management shell verbs and nouns

CMDLET PORTION	VERB/NOUN	DESCRIPTION
`Get`	Verb	Probably the most commonly used verb. It will return information as specified by the object.
`Set`	Verb	Used to update an object.
`Enable`	Verb	Used to turn on functionality.
`Disable`	Verb	Used to turn off functionality.
`New`	Verb	Used to create new objects, typically policies.

TABLE B.1: Common Skype for Business management shell verbs and nouns *(CONTINUED)*

CMDLET PORTION	VERB/NOUN	DESCRIPTION
`Move`	Verb	Typically used to manipulate the home server (or pool) attribute for an object.
`Remove`	Verb	Used in the deletion of objects.
`CsUser`	Noun	The user object when homed on a Lync or Skype for Business pool.
`CsLegacyUser`	Noun	The user object when homed on an OCS pool.
`CsAdUser`	Noun	Additional AD attributes of a user.
`CsConferencingPolicy`	Noun	The object dealing with conference policy.
`CsCertificate`	Noun	The object properties of a certificate.

The cmdlet

```
Get-CsUcPhoneConfiguration
```

returns the following information about all Skype for Business `UCPhoneConfiguration` objects (to return only a single object, specify the `UCPhoneConfiguration` ID as the only parameter):

```
Identity              : Global
CalendarPollInterval : 00:03:00
EnforcePhoneLock      : True
PhoneLockTimeout      : 00:10:00
MinPhonePinLength     : 6
SIPSecurityMode       : High
VoiceDiffServTag      : 40
Voice8021p            : 0
LoggingLevel          : Off
```

To update a `UCPhoneConfiguration` object, use the following cmdlet:

```
Set-CsUcPhoneConfiguration
```

To create a new `UCPhoneConfiguration` object, use the following cmdlet:

```
New-CsUcPhoneConfiguration
```

The list goes on. You can see that in most cases the cmdlets are self-explanatory; however, there are some scenarios where you'll need to use some trial and error to find the right combination. Alternatively, you can use the help file, which is described next.

Finding Help

Figure B.1 shows the TechNet reference of cmdlets (shown on the left).

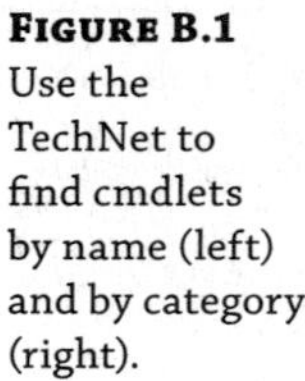

FIGURE B.1 Use the TechNet to find cmdlets by name (left) and by category (right).

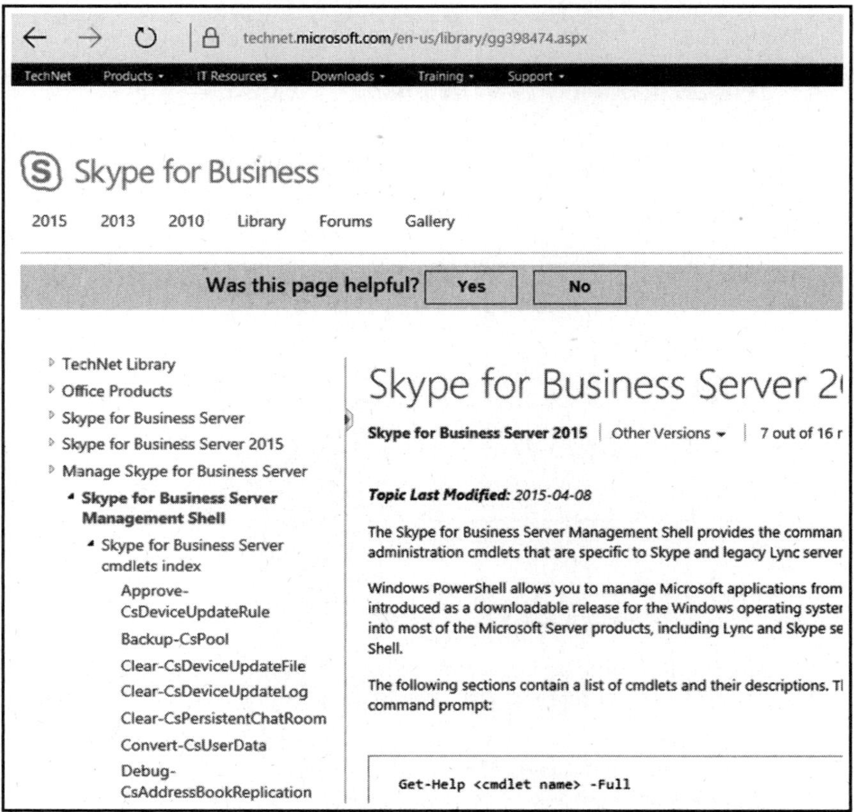

Previously, with each version of Lync Server, a downloadable help file was available, which contained the references to all the cmdlets, but Skype for Business is changing so rapidly with new and updated features that no help file is planned. The only reference is TechNet.

`https://technet.microsoft.com/en-us/library/gg398474.aspx`

As you become more familiar with cmdlets, you'll probably find that searching directly for the cmdlet is the easiest way to get to the information you want.

Selecting a specific cmdlet within the TechNet page will display more detailed information regarding the cmdlet as well as some examples of its usage. Figure B.2 shows a snippet of the display for the `Move-CsUser` cmdlet. In a helpful approach, the order of the help file content has been changed to begin with examples rather than the list of parameters as with Lync Server 2010.

TechNet consists of the following sections for all cmdlets:

- Syntax
- Parameters
- Detailed description
- Input types

- Return types
- Example
- See also

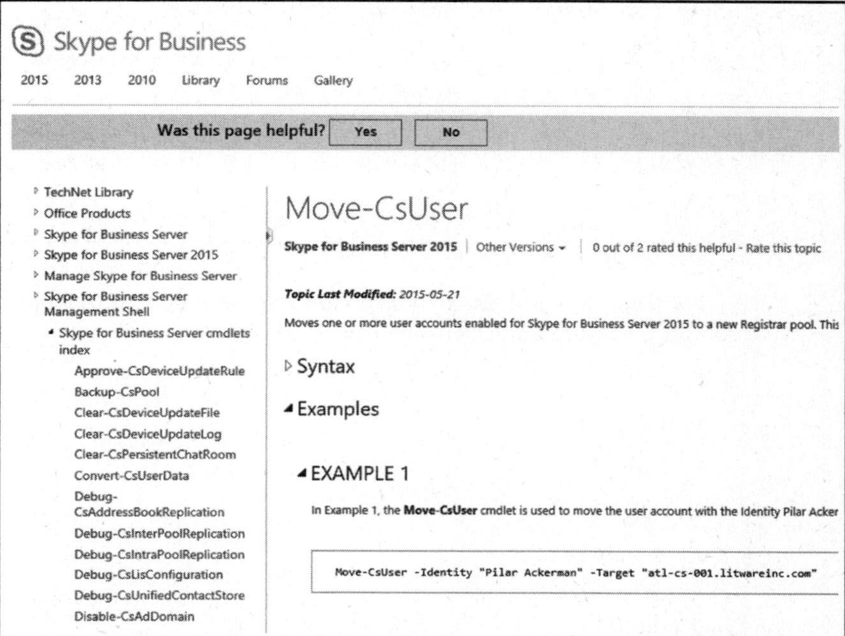

FIGURE B.2 View the `Move-CsUser` cmdlet in TechNet.

It can be quite time-consuming to leave the shell environment to go to TechNet and then go back to the shell to continue scripting or running cmdlets (not everyone has two screens!). The solution to this problem is to run a favorite cmdlet: `Get-Help`. There are several other related cmdlets or associated methods of retrieving help, all of them documented in Table B.2.

TABLE B.2: Methods of finding help

METHOD	DESCRIPTION
`Get-Help`	Lists the help information for the `Get-Help` cmdlet itself.
`Get-Help` *Cmdlet*	Lists the help information for the cmdlet specified.
`Get-Help` **Keyword**	Lists the help information for the keyword specified. This is typically in table format, so it is not actually very helpful because the columns are truncated.
`Help`	Same as `Get-Help`.

TABLE B.2: Methods of finding help *(CONTINUED)*

METHOD	DESCRIPTION
`Help` *`Cmdlet`*	Same as `Get-Help` *`Cmdlet`*.
`Help` *`*Keyword*`*	Same as `Get-Help` *`*Keyword*`*.
`Get-Command`	Lists all the cmdlets, aliases, and functions in the PowerShell process (including any imported sessions).
`Get-Command` *`*keyword*`*	Lists all cmdlets, aliases, and functions that contain the keyword. For example, `Get-Command *-Cs*` will return all commands that include `*-Cs*`.
Cmdlet `-?`	Lists help specifically for the cmdlet listed.

From within PowerShell, there are different views, or output options, providing a method to control the information returned from the `Help` command.

- `Default`
- `Detailed`
- `Example`
- `Full`
- `Parameters`

To use these parameters, enter the `Get-Help` cmdlet in the following format, including the view option:

```
Get-Help Disable-CsUser -Detailed
```

Because you specified `Detailed`, you should get the following output:

```
NAME
     Disable-CsUser
SYNOPSIS
     Modifies the Active Directory account of the specified user or users; this
modification prevents users from using Skype for Business Server 2015 clients
such as Skype for Business. Disable-CsUser only restricts activity related to
Lync Server; it does not disable or remove a user's Active Directory account.
This cmdlet was introduced in Lync Server 2010.
SYNTAX
     Disable-CsUser -Identity <UserIdParameter> [-Confirm [<SwitchParameter>]]
[-DomainController <Fqdn>] [-PassThru <SwitchParameter>] [-WhatIf
[<SwitchParameter>]] [CommonParameters]
```

```
DESCRIPTION
     The Disable-CsUser cmdlet deletes all the attribute information related to
Skype for Business Server 2015 from an Active Directory user account; this
prevents the user from logging on to Skype for Business Server 2015. When you
run Disable-CsUser all the Skype for Business Server 2015-related attributes are
removed from an account, including the Identities of any per-user policies that
have been assigned to that account. You can later re-enable the account by using
the Enable-CsUser cmdlet. However, all the Skype for Business Server
2015-related information (such as policy assignments) previously associated with
that account will have to be re-created. If you want to prevent a user from
logging on to Skype for Business Server 2015, but do not want to lose all of
their account information, use Set-CsUser instead. For details, see the Set-
CsUser help topic.
<cut for brevity>
```

The output will continue, providing information on each of the following sections:

- Parameters (including details on each parameter)
- Examples
- Remarks (this typically refers to other links for more information)

The `-Examples` option provides only the example information (only one example is included; however, multiple examples will be displayed):

```
NAME
     Disable-CsUser
SYNOPSIS
     Modifies the Active Directory account of the specified user or users; this
modification prevents users from using Skype for Business Server 2015 clients
such as Skype for Business. Disable-CsUser only restricts activity related to
Lync Server; it does not disable or remove a user's Active Directory account.
This cmdlet was introduced in Lync Server 2010.
-------------------------- Example 1 --------------------------
Disable-CsUser -Identity "Ken Myer"
The preceding Example disables the Lync Server account for the user Ken Myer. In
this example, the user's display name is used to indicate his Identity.
```

Knowing about this option is important if, like a lot of technical people, you learn by looking at examples and changing the code to do what you need. This Examples view provides only the `NAME`, `SYNOPSIS`, and `EXAMPLES` sections.

On the other hand, running `Get-Help Disable-CsUser -Full` will display all the sections. From the full output, you can see additional information based on the types of input accepted and output generated. With each parameter, you can also see its associated metadata. Table B.3 explains each item.

TABLE B.3: `Get-Help` cmdlet metadata

VALUE	DESCRIPTION
`Required?`	`True` or `False` based on whether this parameter is needed.
`Position?`	Specifies the position of the parameter. Most parameters are `Named`, which means the parameter value must be prefixed by the parameter tag. The `-Identity` parameter is always 1, which means the tag is not required.
`Default`	The value used if none is provided. For most parameters, this is blank.
`Accept pipeline input?`	`True` or `False` based on whether input is accepted from another cmdlet (more on this later in the chapter).
`Accept wildcard characters?`	`True` or `False` and determines whether wildcards (such as * or ?) are accepted.

The `-Default` parameter will return the following sections:

```
NAME
SYNOPSIS
SYNTAX
DESCRIPTION
RELATED LINKS
REMARKS
```

Finally, the `-Parameter` option will return only the specific information regarding the parameter specified, including the metadata.

Cmdlet versus Command

Understanding the difference between *cmdlet* and *command* is important. Both terms are used frequently when talking about PowerShell.

- A cmdlet is the verb-noun combination that takes parameters as input, carries out a task, and in most cases provides output.
- A command is the complete string comprising the cmdlet and a specific set of parameters.

For example, `Get-CsUser` is a cmdlet, and `Get-CsUser "sip:keith.skype@rlscomms.net"` is a command.

WHEN IS A CMDLET ALSO A COMMAND?

In some cases (such as the previous one), the cmdlet can stand as a command in its own right. `Get-CsUser` executed on its own will produce the output for every user enabled for Skype for Business. Typically, we refer to a *cmdlet* when we are talking only about generics, and a *command* is the full string of cmdlet and parameters.

Shells vs. the Prompt

Opening the wrong shell is a common mistake. You can see why because a Skype for Business server can have some or all of the following installed (see Figure B.3):

- Command prompt (also known as the command shell or DOS prompt)
- Windows PowerShell
- Lync Server Management Shell
- Windows PowerShell modules

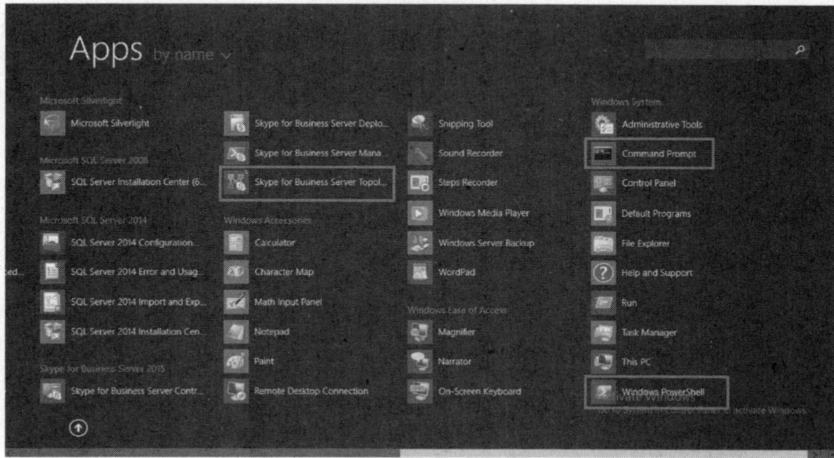

FIGURE B.3 Common command shells installed on a Skype for Business server

The command prompt has been around since before Microsoft itself was first formed. The version on a Skype for Business server is the latest incarnation of the old DOS prompt (see Figure B.4). From a Skype for Business administration perspective, it is almost useless. Yes, there are a few utilities that can be run from the command prompt (mostly from the Resource Kit); however, day-to-day administration requires PowerShell, not a command prompt.

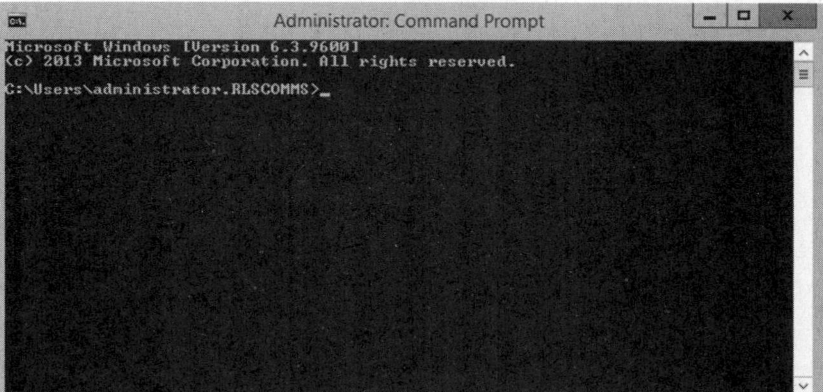

FIGURE B.4 The command prompt

Next up are Windows PowerShell and the Windows PowerShell modules (see Figure B.5). Windows PowerShell is the basic shell, with more than 500 cmdlets; however, the Windows PowerShell modules add significantly more cmdlets to help administer Windows. The ability to incorporate additional modules to extend the capabilities of the shell is an extremely powerful function—and it is exactly what the Skype for Business Server Management Shell does. Its additional cmdlets are specific to Skype for Business management.

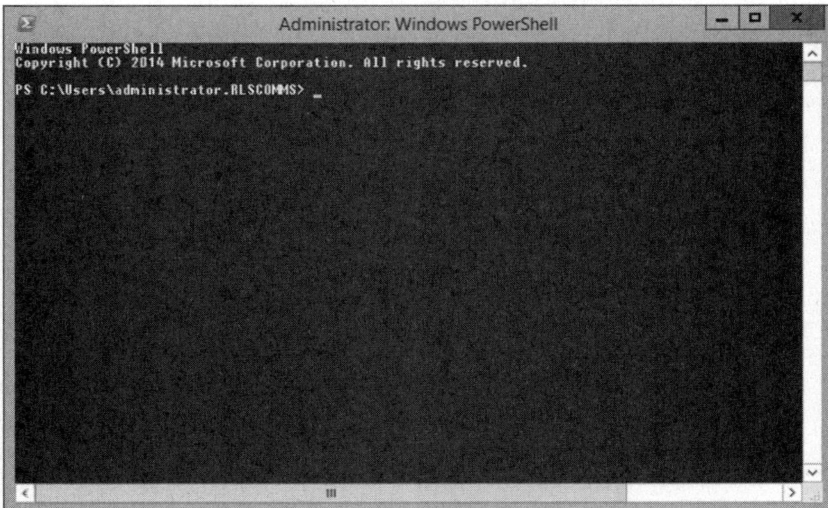

FIGURE B.5
Windows PowerShell

Figure B.6 shows the Skype for Business Server Management Shell, and if you open both it and a base Windows PowerShell window, you will notice a difference in the speed at which they start up; the Skype for Business Server Management Shell is loading the Skype for Business–specific cmdlets in the background.

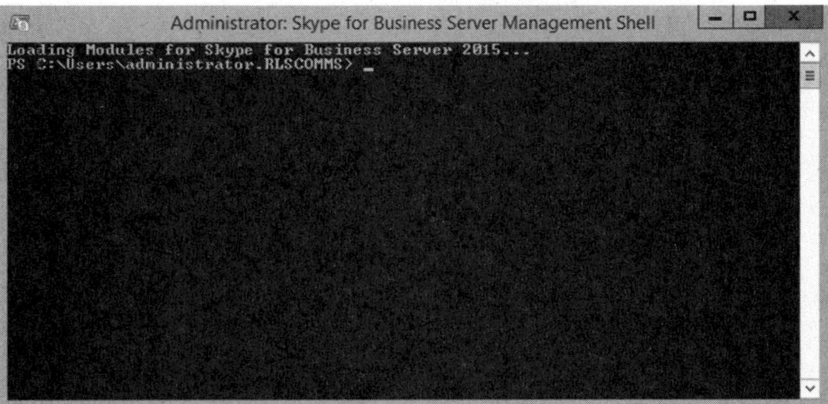

FIGURE B.6
The Skype for Business Server Management Shell

As you can see, the Skype for Business Server 2015 Management Shell window looks extremely similar to a command prompt with a black background (it's hard to tell in this book, but the PowerShell window has a blue background by default), so it's quite easy to use the wrong one; however, quickly you're going to see errors returned if you try to execute PowerShell commands in a Command Prompt window or Skype for Business cmdlets in a basic PowerShell window.

Newer version of Windows Server will dynamically import modules as needed, so there is less reliance on specifically opening the Skype for Business Management Shell.

NOTE In the book, we use the term *PowerShell* to describe the Skype for Business Server Management Shell. Please don't confuse this use of *PowerShell* with the standard Microsoft PowerShell shell, which is installed on Windows Server 2012 R2 by default. When working with Skype for Business, unless explicitly stated otherwise, you should be using the Skype for Business Server Management Shell. The Skype for Business Server Management Shell can be launched either directly from the Skype for Business Server program group or by importing the Skype for Business module into a standard PowerShell session using the `Import-Module SkypeforBusiness` command.

Introducing PowerShell Coding

So far, we've looked at individual cmdlets and how to execute them. By linking multiple cmdlets together or working on (or with) the same object, you can develop code (or scripts), which can be saved in a file with a `.ps1` filename extension and rerun at a later date. By introducing and using variables, along with logic controls based on the values of those variables, the script can adapt to different environments, or indeed different conditions in the same environment. We'll now look at how you can begin to build up from cmdlets into scripts that can query the environment and perform additional tasks based on the results of those queries.

Windows PowerShell has more than 500 cmdlets, whereas the Skype for Business Management Shell has more than 800 Skype for Business–specific cmdlets. A brief PowerShell introduction will explain the difference. You've already seen the `Get-Command` cmdlet and how it displays details for a specific command. By providing it with the parameter `*-Cs*`, you can instruct it to return a list of all the cmdlets that include `-Cs` in their name—that is, all the Skype for Business Management Shell cmdlets.

```
Get-Command *-Cs*
```

In the Windows PowerShell prompt, four entries are returned:

```
ConvertFrom-Csv

ConvertTo-Csv

Export-Csv

Import-Csv
```

In the Lync Management Shell, this same command returns too many entries to read. You need to modify the command to the following:

```
$total = Get-Command *-Cs*
```

This is the first piece of PowerShell coding. By specifying `$total`, you define a variable and assign the results of the `Get-Command *-Cs*` command to it.

The array, which can be thought of as a list, is `$total`. In itself it produces no output; however, you can manipulate it. For example, the variable name alone

```
$total
```

will produce onscreen the same output as if you simply ran `Get-Command *-Cs*`. Specifying the index, or numeric position within the array

```
$total[0]
```

will produce the first entry in the list—in this example, an Alias, `Test-CsClientAuth`. Finally, adding the `count` parameter

```
$total.count
```

will return the total number of items in the list—in this example, 819.

TAB COMPLETION

An extremely useful feature of PowerShell is that you can press Tab to complete a cmdlet. This is especially helpful with some of the longer cmdlets. Once you have typed enough to define a unique cmdlet, pressing Tab will complete it. If you haven't reached a unique point in the cmdlet, pressing Tab will cycle through the cmdlets that match what you have typed so far. In actual fact, it will first cycle through any files and folders in the current directory and then applications in the path environmental variable, and *then* it will begin cycling through cmdlets.

For example, if you type `A` and then press Tab until you get to the first cmdlet, the cmdlet will complete to `Add-ADComputerServiceAccount`; pressing Tab again will move to the next cmdlet, and so on.

But if you start typing `Clear-CsDeviceUpdate` and press Tab when you reach `Clear-Cs`, you will cycle through `Clear-CsDeviceUpdateFile`, `Clear-CsDeviceUpdateLog`, and `Clear-CsPersistentChatRoom` because you have not reached a unique point.

The tab-completion feature also works with parameters for cmdlets.

Although pressing Tab cycles forward through the cmdlets, if you press Tab too many times and miss the cmdlet you're looking for, you can simply press Shift+Tab to cycle backward to the cmdlet you missed.

PowerShell Variables and Data Types

A variable is a placeholder for a value and can be a string, number, or object. You access the values stored in a variable simply by referencing the variable name. In PowerShell, every variable begins with a dollar sign ($) and is an object. Defining the variable as an object means that you can assign any value to it; however, you can force a specific data type if required. This is called *casting*. For example, the command

```
$x = [int]5
```

would assign the `integer` value 5 to the variable `x` rather than the `string` "5".

Assigning the output of a cmdlet to a variable creates an *object*, which in turn can be passed to another cmdlet. For example, after executing the command

```
$users = Get-CsUser
```

the `$users` variable will contain all the user objects in the environment. This will result in an array with each entry being an individual user.

In PowerShell, the first item in an array is always numbered 0; therefore, the first user object would be accessed by using the following notation:

```
$users[0]
```

PowerShell can define and use any .NET Framework data type as a value. There are too many to list here; however, the following are the more commonly used ones:

- String
- Integer
- Boolean
- DateTime
- XML

Script Control

So that decisions can be made by the script, PowerShell includes a number of standard constructs that check conditions and that control loops.

Conditions are typically checked in this format:

```
If <something> then <do something> else <do something else>
```

Within PowerShell, this format becomes

```
If (condition) {code} else {more code}
```

This can be further extended using `elseif` statements, such as

```
If (condition1) {code} elseif (condition2) {code2} else {more code}
```

PowerShell also includes the `Switch` construct (known as `Case` in some other languages). It is used in the following format:

```
Switch (variable)
{
Value1 {code}
Value2 {code}
Value3 {code}
Default {code}
}
```

Control loops allow a script to parse through multiple values (such as an array). Combined with condition checking, these loops are the logical flow and execution of the script. PowerShell supports a number of different control loops.

- `For` looping
- `ForEach` looping
- `While` looping
- `Do While` looping
- `Do Until` looping

The basic syntax of each of these control loops is as follows, with each of the *code* sections repeated within the loop:

```
For (startvalue;condition;nextvalue) {code}
ForEach (Item in collection) {code}
While (condition) {code}
Do {code} While (condition)
Do {code} Until (condition)
```

Functions allow for good organization and segmentation of scripts as well as the ability to have a section of repeated code simplified down to being written once and "called" when needed. For example, the following code definition provides simple mathematical results on a pair of numbers:

```
Function maths{
Param ($x, $y)
$sum = $x + $y
$diff = $x - $y
$product = $x * $y
$div = $x/$y
Write-Host "Sum: $sum"
Write-Host "Difference: $diff"
Write-Host "Product: $product"
Write-Host "Division: $div"
}
```

This function is called using the following form and would give the output shown in Figure B.7:

```
Maths 10 5
```

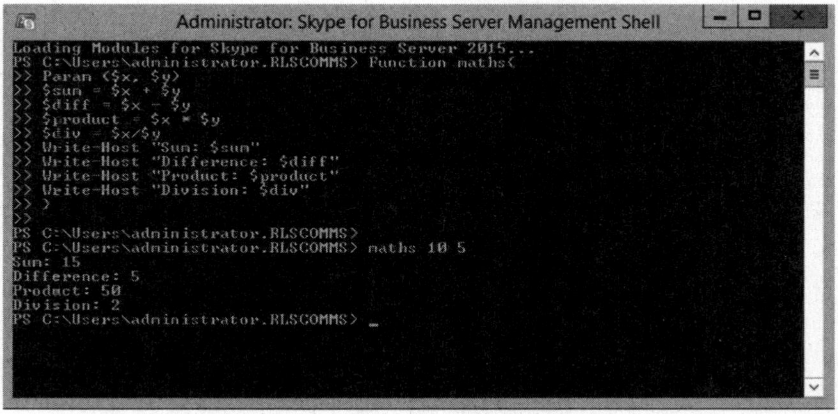

FIGURE B.7 Output from a function

```
Administrator: Skype for Business Server Management Shell
Loading Modules for Skype for Business Server 2015...
PS C:\Users\administrator.RLSCOMMS> Function maths{
>> Param ($x, $y)
>> $sum = $x + $y
>> $diff = $x - $y
>> $product = $x * $y
>> $div = $x/$y
>> Write-Host "Sum: $sum"
>> Write-Host "Difference: $diff"
>> Write-Host "Product: $product"
>> Write-Host "Division: $div"
>> }
>>
PS C:\Users\administrator.RLSCOMMS>
PS C:\Users\administrator.RLSCOMMS> maths 10 5
Sum: 15
Difference: 5
Product: 50
Division: 2
PS C:\Users\administrator.RLSCOMMS> _
```

It's beyond the scope of this book to go into each of these in detail, but a few of them will be used in the examples later in this appendix.

Input Parameters

You've already been introduced to the concepts of cmdlet parameters and how to query the help (by passing a parameter!) to find out which parameters a cmdlet needs as well as the metadata definitions of each parameter. Now let's look in more detail.

In Skype for Business, `-Identity` is the most-used parameter and will always be the first parameter in the cmdlet list, so it doesn't need to have the tag included. For example,

```
Get-CsUser -Identity "sip:keith.skype@rlscomms.net"
```

provides the same result as the following:

```
Get-CsUser "sip:keith.skype@rlscomms.net"
```

Other parameters must be tagged with the parameter name as part of the cmdlet. As mentioned previously, the list of parameters for a cmdlet can be queried using the `Get-Help` cmdlet, with the specific parameter `-Parameters`.

The `Get` verb cmdlets are interesting because the `-Identity` parameter is optional; if it isn't provided, the cmdlet will work on all objects of that type, so `Get-CsUser` will return all enabled users.

The groups of `Set` verbs, on the other hand, require you to provide an `-Identity` tag to determine the object on which to execute changes. What happens if you forget this (or indeed, any) required parameter? Well, PowerShell is intelligent enough to know the parameters that are required, so it will prompt for them; any optional parameters will be left out of the command. Figure B.8 shows the prompt from running the `Enable-CsUser` cmdlet without a specific `-Identity` parameter.

FIGURE B.8 Prompting for missing parameters

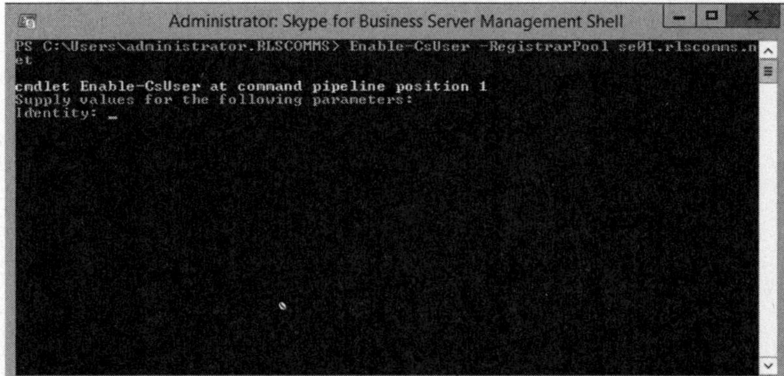

Output Parameters

Because PowerShell is based on the .NET Framework, it uses an object model for data. This means the responses from commands are not text based (although they will display onscreen as text); instead, they are objects. Cmdlets will have a default display (content and format) of the data being returned, but because the data takes the form of objects, you can easily override this default and display the data you want to see. You do that by specifying output parameters. For example, here's the default output of `Get-CsPool` for the example system:

```
Get-CsPool

Identity       : se01.rlscomms.net
Services       : {UserServer:se01.rlscomms.net, Registrar:se01.rlscomms.net,
                 UserDatabase:se01.rlscomms.net,
                 FileStore:se01.rlscomms.net...}
Computers      : {se01.rlscomms.net}
Fqdn           : se01.rlscomms.net
BackupPoolFqdn : se02.rlscomms.net
Site           : Site:EMEA

Identity       : dir01.rlscomms.net
Services       : {Registrar:dir01.rlscomms.net, WebServer:dir01.rlscomms.net}
Computers      : {dir01.rlscomms.net}
Fqdn           : dir01.rlscomms.net
BackupPoolFqdn :
Site           : Site:EMEA

Identity       : se02.rlscomms.net
Services       : {UserServer:se02.rlscomms.net, Registrar:se02.rlscomms.net,
                 UserDatabase:se02.rlscomms.net,
                 FileStore:se02.rlscomms.net...}
Computers      : {se02.rlscomms.net}
Fqdn           : se02.rlscomms.net
BackupPoolFqdn : se01.rlscomms.net
Site           : Site:EMEA

Identity       : edge01.rlscomms.net
Services       : {EdgeServer:edge01.rlscomms.net,
                 ManagementServer:edge01.rlscomms.net}
Computers      : {edge01.rlscomms.net}
Fqdn           : edge01.rlscomms.net
BackupPoolFqdn :
Site           : Site:EMEA

Identity       : sql03.rlscomms.net
Services       : {ArchivingDatabase:sql03.rlscomms.net,
                 MonitoringDatabase:sql03.rlscomms.net}
Computers      : {sql03.rlscomms.net}
Fqdn           : sql03.rlscomms.net
BackupPoolFqdn :
Site           : Site:EMEA
```

You can manipulate this output by changing the format. The default format for many cmdlets is `Format-Table`, which typically results in a minimal set of parameters being displayed in the output.

```
Get-CsPool | Format-Table

Identity     Services     Computers    Fqdn         Site       BackupPoolFqdn
--------     --------     ---------    ----         ----       ------------
se01.rlsco.. {UserServe.. {se01.rls.. se01.rlsc.. Site:EMEA  se02.rlsc..
dir01.rlsc.. {Registrar.. {dir01.rl.. dir01.rls.. Site:EMEA
se02.rlsco.. {UserServe.. {se02.rls.. se02.rlsc.. Site:EMEA  se01.rlsc..
edge01.rls.. {EdgeServe.. {edge01.r.. edge01.rl.. Site:EMEA
sql03.rlsc.. {Archiving.. {sql03.rl.. sql03.rls.. Site:EMEA
```

As you can see, the content of the field may be truncated with `Format-Table`. Depending on the size of your window, you may get more columns than shown here, and if you export the output to a file (using `Output-File`), you will get the full column content; however, the individual columns may still be truncated.

`Format-List` will provide all the properties of the returned object.

```
Get-CsPool | Format-List
```

`Format-List` is the default output of many `*-Cs*` commands, so in this case the output is the same as shown for `Get-CsPool` alone, as if you did not include the `Format-List` cmdlet.

In addition, you can specify only the parameters you are looking for, reducing the amount of screen clutter:

```
Get-CsPool | Ft Site, Fqdn
Site                                    Fqdn
----                                    ----
Site:EMEA                               se01.rlscomms.net
Site:EMEA                               dir01.rlscomms.net
Site:EMEA                               se02.rlscomms.net
Site:EMEA                               edge01.rlscomms.net
Site:EMEA                               sql03.rlscomms.net
```

ALIASES

In the previous example, `Format-Table` has been replaced by `Ft`. This is known as an *alias*. Aliases are shortcut references to longer cmdlets. In the native PowerShell installation, almost 150 aliases are predefined.

You can create your own aliases for frequently used commands by using the `Set-Alias` cmdlet.

WHEN OUTPUT EQUALS INPUT

Often it is useful to run one command to retrieve information and directly use that information as the input for another command. You have already seen this in the previous couple of examples, where one command's output is directed to a second command using the pipe (|) symbol.

```
Get-CsPool | Format-Table
```

Here you are sending the output of the first cmdlet into the Format-Table cmdlet as well as providing additional information in the form of parameters to filter the results.

Not all cmdlets will support piping between them; however, where the noun portions of the cmdlets match, it will always work, as in the following example:

```
Get-csuser <something> |set-csuser <something>
```

Using the Get-Help cmdlet with the -Full parameter will provide the details to describe each parameter and whether it will accept pipeline input or not.

When interacting between cmdlets that do not support piping, the ForEach cmdlet can usually be used to process the data in a loop.

```
ForEach  ($user in $users)
{
              Write-Host $user.Name
}
```

This code snippet would cycle through each $user object in the $users collection and output the Name parameter.

Filtering the Output

Rather than limiting the properties returned, you may be interested only in a subset of the objects. For example, you may want to select only the users on a particular pool and apply a change to them. This is where filtering comes in. You are running the command on the full environment; however, you then provide a filter across this complete data showing a view of only the data in which you are interested. Here's an example:

```
Get-CsUser | Where-Object {$_.poolname -like 'SE01'}
```

Breaking down this command, run the Get-CsUser command (in this form it is a command rather than cmdlet) to return all the users. This output is piped to the Where-Object cmdlet, and using the filter parameters enclosed in {}, you will retain only the objects that match the criteria. In this case, the $_.poolname property must match the 'SE01' value provided. Here, you have introduced another new concept, because $_ refers to the current object and is used when you want to iterate through a complete list of objects, in this case comparing each one to the filter criteria. Table B.4 lists common operators that can be used with filtering.

Table B.4: Shell values and operator descriptions

Shell value	Operator	Description
-eq	Equal	The property must match exactly the value.
-ne	Not Equal	The property must not match the value.
-gt	Greater Than	Integers only. The property must be greater than the value.
-ge	Greater Than or Equal To	Integers only. The property must be greater than or equal to the value.

TABLE B.4: Shell values and operator descriptions *(CONTINUED)*

SHELL VALUE	OPERATOR	DESCRIPTION
`-lt`	Less Than	Integers only. The property must be less than the value.
`-le`	Less Than or Equal To	Integers only. The property must be less than or equal to the value.
`-Like`	Contains	Text. The string can match exactly or wildcards can be used to indicate the string being a substring.
`-Notlike`	Does Not Contain	Text. The string must not match exactly or wildcards can be used to indicate the string must not be a substring.

PowerShell v3

Until now we've been discussing functionality that is contained within versions 1, 2, and 3 of PowerShell. Windows 7 and Windows Server 2008 R2 introduced PowerShell version 2, bringing some fantastic new features, such as remoting and the Integrated Scripting Environment (ISE). For older operating systems, PowerShell version 2 is available as a download from this link (separate downloads are available for each operating system):

```
www.microsoft.com/download/en/search.aspx?q=powershell+2.0
```

Lync Server 2010 required the use of PowerShell v2, but Skype for Business requires PowerShell to be upgraded to V3.

```
www.microsoft.com/download/en/search.aspx?q=powershell+3.0
```

Version 3 provides significant increases in the number of cmdlets available and thus a wider range of items that can be managed via native PowerShell. Some are directly helpful to Skype for Business, and others not so much.

In the following sections, we'll look specifically at some of these new features introduced with V2 and updated with V3 or purely native to V3.

PowerShell v3 is included with Windows Server 2012 and newer operating systems, so an upgrade would be needed only if you were upgrading the existing deployment from Lync Server 2013, rather than starting with a fresh install.

Remoting

Remoting is the term given to managing an environment from a remote shell. You launch a local PowerShell prompt and initiate a remote PowerShell session against the machine (or environment) you want to manage, and then you import that session to your current session.

```
$session = New-PsSession -ConnectionUri
 https://se01.rlscomms.net/ocspowershell
-Authentication NegotiateWithImplicitCredential
Import-PsSession $session
```

At this point, the remote PowerShell modules become available in the local session.

This is an extremely useful function because it means you don't need to install local administration tools and you can provide separate administration credentials (ensuring a separation of user and admin roles) through the connection session.

MANAGING MULTIPLE ENVIRONMENTS FROM A SINGLE POWERSHELL SESSION

By taking advantage of PowerShell's remoting capabilities, you can connect a single PowerShell session to multiple environments, which will allow you to modify users for Lync and Exchange at the same time. This concept will work with services located both on the premises and in the cloud; PowerShell doesn't care where the services are located, only that it can reach the administration point.

Take the following script:

```
$ExchangeSession = New-PsSession -ConfigurationName Microsoft.Exchange
-ConnectionUri http://ex01.rlscomms.net/PowerShell -Authentication Kerberos
Import-PsSession $ExchangeSession
$CsSession = $CsSession = New-PsSession -ConnectionUri https://se01.rlscomms.
net/ocspowershell -Authentication NegotiateWithImplicitCredential
Import-PsSession $CsSession
Enable-Mailbox corp\PS_DemoUser
Enable-CsUser -identity corp\PS_DemoUser -SipAddress sip:ps_demouser@rlscomms.
net -RegistrarPool se01.rlscomms.net
Enable-UMMailbox corp\PS_DemoUser -UMMailboxPolicy "UK Default Policy" -
SipResourceIdentifier PS_DemoUser@rlscomms.net -Extensions "1234"
```

By running this script in a Windows PowerShell session, you first connect to and import an Exchange session (`$ExchangeSession` and `Import-PsSession`) and then connect to and import a Skype for Business session (`$CsSession` and `Import-PsSession`). Then you have a single PowerShell session connected to both Exchange and Skype for Business, you can enable a user with a mailbox and Skype for Business account, and, finally, you can enable Exchange Unified Messaging—all from within the remaining three lines of code.

The Integrated Scripting Environment

PowerShell v2 introduced the graphical user interface called the Integrated Scripting Environment, which includes a handy debugging tool. PowerShell v3 improved on the capabilities of the ISE. On Windows Server 2008 R2, the ISE must be installed by adding the Windows PowerShell Integrated Scripting Environment feature from Server Manager. The ISE can be launched by typing `ISE` in a PowerShell window. Figure B.9 shows the PowerShell v3 ISE when started.

Initially, only a single pane opens with command help on the right side. When dealing with scripts, the single pane moves to the bottom, and the scripts are displayed in a tabbed window (see Figure B.10). This is the normal operating mode.

The bottom pane is simply a PowerShell prompt, in which commands can be entered directly and/or result of scripts viewed. Figure B.10 shows the working environment where the `Get-Service` cmdlet was entered in the command line and the results appeared (the screen has scrolled to the end of the output).

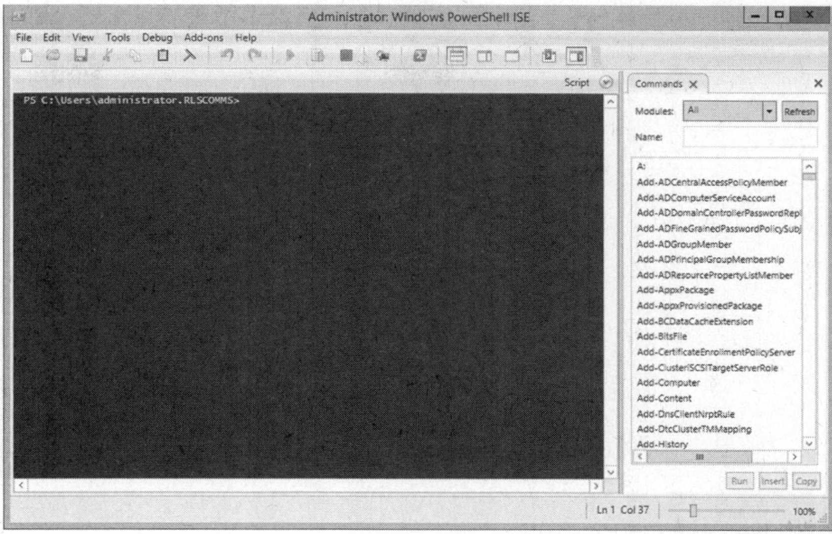

FIGURE B.9
The Integrated Script Environment

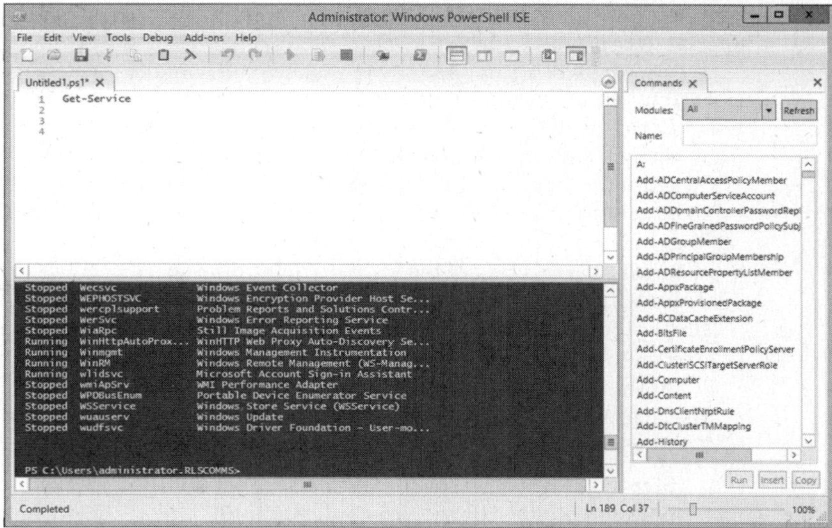

FIGURE B.10
The ISE is working.

ISE does not include any PowerShell extensions (such as Skype for Business or Exchange) and is required to use the remoting feature to connect to and import a Skype for Business (or Exchange) session or to import the modules directly if they are available locally.

Figure B.11 shows the script introduced in the example (to open, select File ➢ Open). Each script is opened in a separate tab, which allows multiple scripts to be opened at the same time.

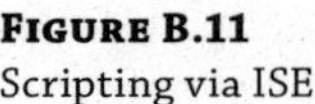

FIGURE B.11
Scripting via ISE

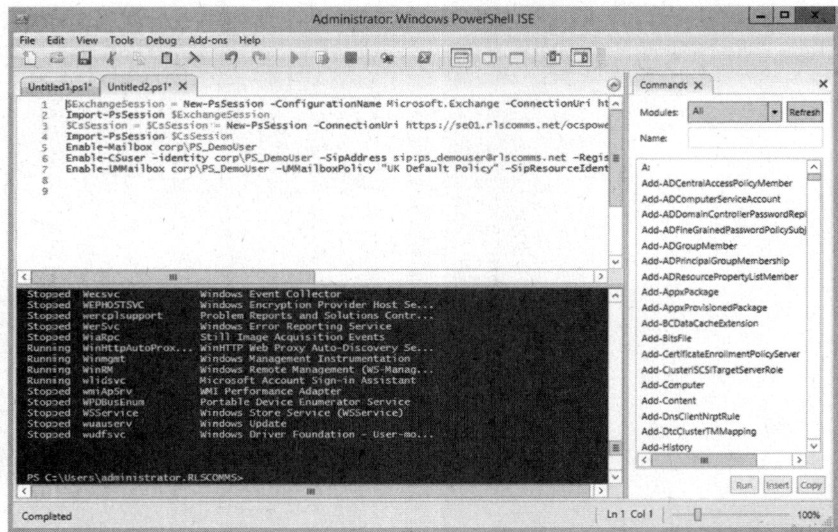

Although you can't see it in the figure, the scripting section uses color highlighting to make it easier to write scripts and view variables, functions, and cmdlets. The color highlighting allows you to easily spot where the script blocks start and end. When code is written, quote marks (") are frequently placed in the wrong location (or forgotten), starting or ending a string in the wrong place. The highlighting makes it obvious that this has occurred.

Each line in the script area is numbered, as are any errors from PowerShell. This allows you to easily locate an error (use Ctrl+G to jump to a specific line in the script).

Once the script has been saved (File ➢ Save), debugging is enabled. This allows breakpoints to be set in the script by placing the cursor on a line of code and pressing F9 (or selecting Debug-Toggle Breakpoint). A *breakpoint* is a point in the code where execution will pause, allowing detailed interrogation of the script to determine specific values of the variable at that stage. This technique is used to help resolve errors in the code that may otherwise be difficult to find. Breakpoints are highlighted in dark red. Once a breakpoint has been configured and the script executed, assuming the line of code is reached, the script will pause.

At this point, you can interrogate any variable simply by entering the variable name in the command window; you can also execute PowerShell cmdlets in it. Additional commands become available once the script is paused.

Step Over (F10) Allows line-by-line execution of the script, and if the line is a function, will not step into the function but will execute it

Step Into (F11) Allows line-by-line execution of the script, and if the line is a function, will continue debugging the function line by line

Step Out (Shift+F11) Continues execution of a function and pauses once the function is completed

Continue (F5) Continues executing the script until the next breakpoint

Stop (Shift+F5) Stops the execution of the script

Figure B.12 shows the ISE running a basic script, which will count from 0 to 10, outputting the value each time, and when the value is equal to 5, it will write the text "the value is five" rather than the number. At the point of capture of Figure B.12, the *breakpoint* has been reached. The [DBG] indicates that the output screen and the command window are in Debug mode.

FIGURE B.12
ISE in Debug mode

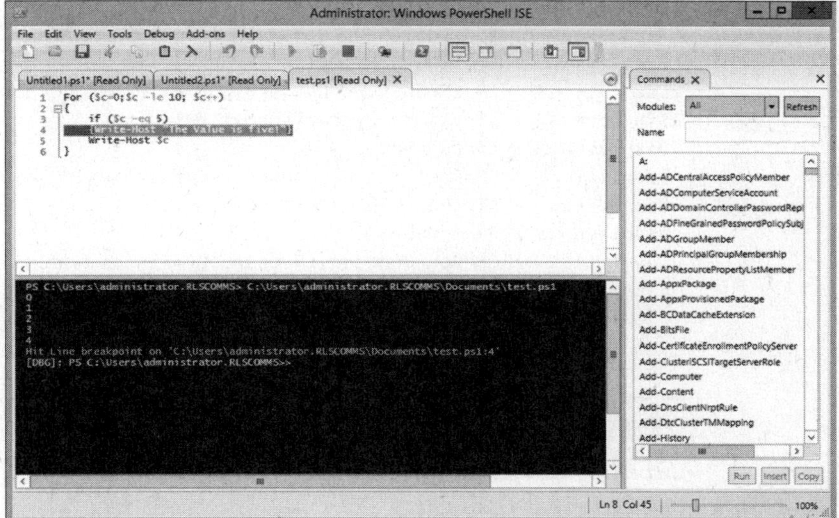

Managing Output

Although PowerShell is the interface used to configure and administer Skype for Business, more often than not it will be used to provide data in a form either for human consumption or for input to other applications. As a result, it is often necessary to massage the results of the command output.

Lists and Tables

You've already seen how to display the output as a list (`Format-List`) or a table (`Format-Table`), and you've seen how to limit the properties displayed by using the `Format` cmdlet.

The next thing you may need to do is sort or group the output. Sorting is provided by the `Sort-Object` cmdlet, which can take a number of parameters. Here it is receiving the output of `Get-CsUser`:

```
Get-CsUser | Sort-Object
```

The output will be sorted in ascending alphabetical order, by the default sort property, and return the following:

```
Identity    : CN=Darcy Android,CN=Users,DC=rlscomms,DC=net
SipAddress  : sip:Darcy.Android@rlscomms.net
DisplayName : Darcy Android
```

```
Identity    : CN=David Skype,CN=Users,DC=rlscomms,DC=net
SipAddress  : sip:David.Skype@rlscomms.net
DisplayName : David Skype
Identity    : CN=Keith Skype,CN=Users,DC=rlscomms,DC=net
SipAddress  : sip:Keith.Skype@rlscomms.net
DisplayName : Keith Skype
Identity    : CN=Les IOS,CN=Users,DC=rlscomms,DC=net
SipAddress  : sip:Les.IOS@rlscomms.net
DisplayName : Les IOS
Identity    : CN=Linda Lync,CN=Users,DC=rlscomms,DC=net
SipAddress  : sip:Linda.Lync@rlscomms.net
DisplayName : Linda Lync
Identity    : CN=Paul Phone,CN=Users,DC=rlscomms,DC=net
SipAddress  : sip:Paul.Phone@rlscomms.net
DisplayName : Paul Phone
Identity    : CN=Rob Browser,CN=Users,DC=rlscomms,DC=net
SipAddress  : sip:Rob.Browser@rlscomms.net
DisplayName : Rob Browser
```

Limiting Output

Actually, we cheated a little in the sorted output and throughout this chapter. To ensure brevity, we appended

```
| fl identity, sipaddress, displayname
```

at the end of the command to display only those fields—otherwise, this chapter would contain lots of not very useful content! In fact, the command we entered was this (remember that `fl` is a default alias created for the `Format-List` cmdlet):

```
Get-CsUser | Sort-Object | Fl Identity, SipAddress, DisplayName
```

To sort in ascending alphabetical order, by the named property (this would show the same output as the previous command), you would enter the following:

```
Get-CsUser | Sort-Object -Property <property name>
```

To sort in descending alphabetical order, by the named property, you would enter the following:

```
Get-CsUser | Sort-Object -Property Identity -Descending |
Fl Identity, SipAddress, DisplayName
```

This gives the following output:

```
Identity    : CN=Rob Browser,CN=Users,DC=rlscomms,DC=net
SipAddress  : sip:Rob.Browser@rlscomms.net
DisplayName : Rob Browser
```

```
Identity    : CN=Paul Phone,CN=Users,DC=rlscomms,DC=net
SipAddress  : sip:Paul.Phone@rlscomms.net
DisplayName : Paul Phone
Identity    : CN=Linda Lync,CN=Users,DC=rlscomms,DC=net
SipAddress  : sip:Linda.Lync@rlscomms.net
DisplayName : Linda Lync
Identity    : CN=Les IOS,CN=Users,DC=rlscomms,DC=net
SipAddress  : sip:Les.IOS@rlscomms.net
DisplayName : Les IOS
Identity    : CN=Keith Skype,CN=Users,DC=rlscomms,DC=net
SipAddress  : sip:Keith.Skype@rlscomms.net
DisplayName : Keith Skype
Identity    : CN=David Skype,CN=Users,DC=rlscomms,DC=net
SipAddress  : sip:David.Skype@rlscomms.net
DisplayName : David Skype
Identity    : CN=Darcy Android,CN=Users,DC=rlscomms,DC=net
SipAddress  : sip:Darcy.Android@rlscomms.net
DisplayName : Darcy Android
```

`Sort-Object` also has the capability to return only the unique values in a list.

```
Get-CsUser | Sort-Object -Unique
```

You can sort by multiple fields (and in differing directions if required) with an extension to the `Sort-Object` cmdlet. This is typically used to provide a specific format to output. To sort first by `Enabled` in descending order and then by `DisplayName` in ascending order, the command would be as follows:

```
Get-CsUser | Sort-Object -Property @{Expression="Enabled";Descending=$True},
@{Expression="DisplayName";Descending=$False}
```

This command will display the full user object for each order, sorted with the `Enabled` users first and each of them sorted based on the `DisplayName`. The output isn't included because it would stretch to several pages!

This last example is a method of grouping. You can also use the `Group-Object` cmdlet to give a slightly different output.

```
Get-CsUser | Sort-Object -Property SipAddress| Group-Object -Property Enabled

Count Name      Group
----- ----      -----
    7 True       {CN=Darcy Android,CN=Users,DC=rlscomms,DC=ne...
```

As you can see, the `Sort-Object` and `Group-Object` cmdlets provide extremely powerful output manipulation features in PowerShell.

Output to File

So far you've seen the command output on the screen in table or list formats. In many cases, it is useful to store data in files. PowerShell provides a number of cmdlets to let you do just that. In the following sections, we'll look at the `Out-File`, `Export-Csv`, and `Export-CliXml` cmdlets.

Out-File

`Out-File` captures the command output and stores it directly in a file.

```
Get-CsUser -Identity "Keith Skype" | Out-File c:\get-csuser.txt
```

Opening the file `c:\get-csuser.txt` shows this:

```
Identity                      : CN=Keith Skype,CN=Users,DC=rlscomms,DC=net
VoicePolicy                   :
VoiceRoutingPolicy            :
ConferencingPolicy            :
PresencePolicy                :
DialPlan                      :
LocationPolicy                :
ClientPolicy                  :
ClientVersionPolicy           :
ArchivingPolicy               :
ExchangeArchivingPolicy       : Uninitialized
PinPolicy                     :
ExternalAccessPolicy          :
MobilityPolicy                :
PersistentChatPolicy          :
UserServicesPolicy            :
CallViaWorkPolicy             :
ThirdPartyVideoSystemPolicy   :
HostedVoiceMail               :
HostedVoicemailPolicy         :
HostingProvider               : SRV:
RegistrarPool                 : se01.rlscomms.net
Enabled                       : True
SipAddress                    : sip:Keith.Skype@rlscomms.net
LineURI                       : tel:+44555111122
EnterpriseVoiceEnabled        : True
ExUmEnabled                   : False
HomeServer                    : CN=LcServices,CN=Microsoft,CN=1:1,CN=Pools,CN=RTC Service,
                                CN=Services,CN=Configuration,DC=rlscomms,DC=net
DisplayName                   : Keith Skype
SamAccountName                : Keith_Skype
```

Export-Csv

`Export-Csv` exports the data into CSV format.

```
Get-CsUser -Identity "Keith Skype" | Export-Csv c:\get-csuser.csv
```

Opening the file `c:\get-csuser.csv` shows this:

```
#TYPE Microsoft.Rtc.Management.ADConnect.Schema.OCSADUser
"SamAccountName","UserPrincipalName","FirstName",
<other fields cut for brevity>
```

```
"Keith_Skype"," Keith.Skype@rlscomms.net ","Keith",
<other fields cut for brevity>
```

Export-CliXml

Export-CliXml exports the data into XML format.

```
Get-CsUser -Identity "Keith Skype" | Export-CliXml c:\get-csuser.xml
```

Opening the file c:\get-csuser.txt shows this:

```
<?xml version="1.0"?>
 <Objs xmlns="http://schemas.microsoft.com/powershell/2004/04" Version="1.1.0.1">
 <Obj RefId="0">
  <TN RefId="0">
   <T>Microsoft.Rtc.Management.ADConnect.Schema.OCSADUser</T>
   <T>Microsoft.Rtc.Management.ADConnect.Schema.OCSADUserBase</T>
   <T>Microsoft.Rtc.Management.ADConnect.Schema.OCSEndPoint</T>
   <T>Microsoft.Rtc.Management.ADConnect.ADObject.ADObjectBase</T>
   <T>Microsoft.Rtc.Management.ADConnect.ADObject.ADRawEntry</T>
   <T>Microsoft.Rtc.Management.ADConnect.Core.ConfigurableObject</T>
   <T>System.Object</T>
 </TN>
 <ToString>CN=Keith Skype,CN=Users,DC=rlscomms,DC=net</ToString>
 <Props>
  <S N="SamAccountName">Keith_Skype</S>
  <S N="UserPrincipalName"/>
  <S N="FirstName">Keith</S>
  <S N="LastName">Skype</S>
  <S N="WindowsEmailAddress">Keith.Skype@rlscomms.net</S>
<remainder cut for brevity>
```

Graphical Display and Filtering with *Out-GridView*

Keeping with the output types, Out-GridView was a new cmdlet introduced with PowerShell v2 and updated with PowerShell v3. With this cmdlet, the output appears (as shown in Figure B.13 with Get-CsUser | Out-GridView as the command) in a graphical display that provides its own filtering interaction. This reduces the need to use other cmdlets to sort and filter data, such as the Where-Object and Sort-Object cmdlets mentioned previously.

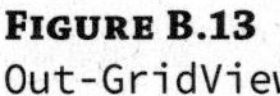

FIGURE B.13 Out-GridView

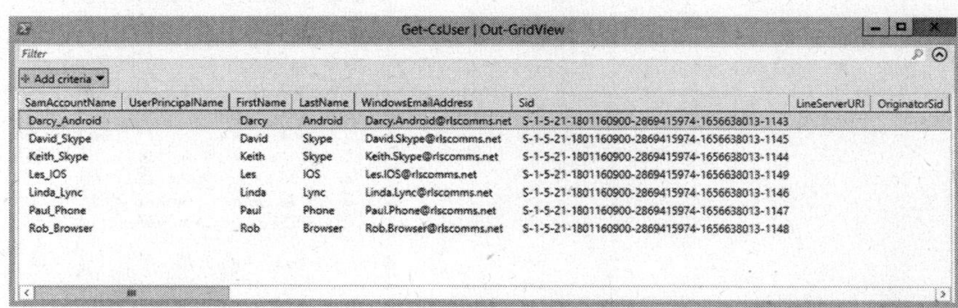

Running Scripts

So far we've been showing individual cmdlets or in some cases piping the output from one command to another. As you become more proficient with PowerShell, the commands will get more complex, and you won't want to keep working out complex commands every time you need to repeat the same task. This is where scripting comes in.

> **POWERSHELL SCRIPT FILES**
>
> The names of PowerShell script files have the `.ps1` extension and must always be prefaced with the directory path. If you want to run a script in the local directory, preface it with `.\`, as shown here:
>
> ```
> .\listusersscript.ps1
> ```

Running Scheduled Scripts

The advantages of scripting really come into play when you consider scheduling. If, for example, you want to move a user from one pool to another, use this command:

```
Move-CsUser -Identity "Keith Skype" -Target "eepool01.rlscomms.net"
```

However, you probably don't want to risk interrupting users during the working day (of course, as an admin you don't want to work overnight). You can save the move command in a file with a `.ps1` filename extension (let's call it `move_user.ps1`) and leverage the Windows Task Scheduler to schedule the command to run after working hours.

You can find the Windows Task Scheduler by choosing Start ➤ Administrative Tools ➤ Task Scheduler; the Microsoft Management Console (MMC) shown in Figure B.14 will appear.

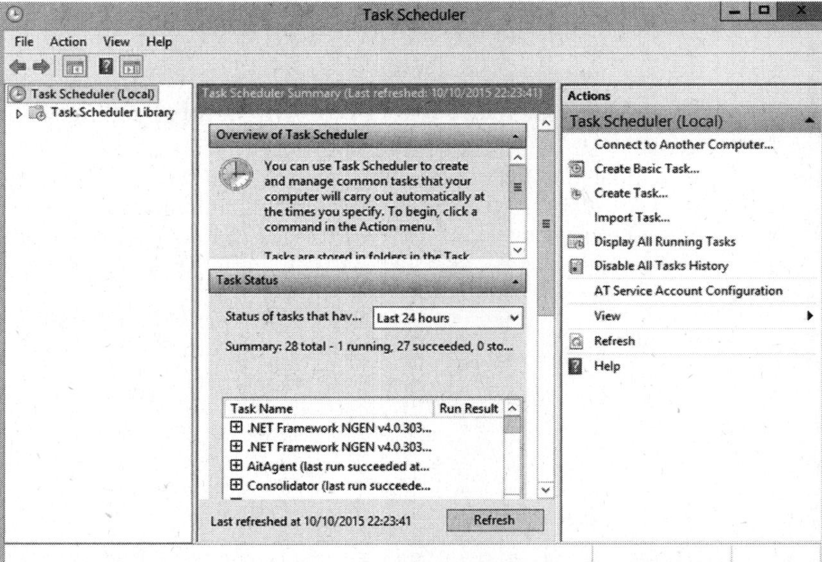

FIGURE B.14 The Windows Task Scheduler

Click Create Task in the right Actions panel to open the Task Wizard (shown in Figure B.15).

FIGURE B.15
Creating a new task

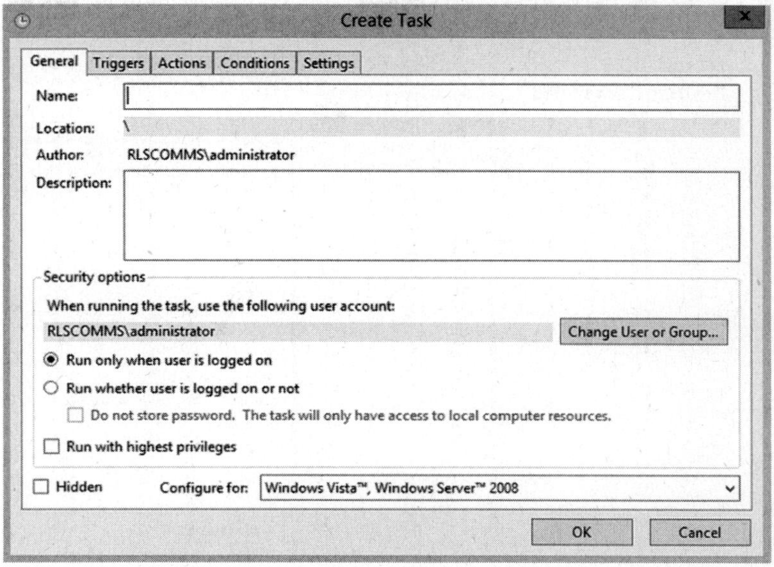

Using this wizard, you can define the task and the triggers that initiate it. You can also put conditions in place—for example, to ensure the task does not run too long. Each of the sections is explained here:

General Define the name of the task, along with the security controls associated with it, including which user account to use and whether the user must be logged on.

Triggers This is where you define how the task will be started; the options include On A Schedule, At Log On, At Startup, and so on. You can further modify this to include repetition options and expiry dates.

Actions This is where you define the actual task to be executed; the options include Start A Program, Send An Email, and Display A Message.

Conditions The Conditions section allows you to check to ensure that the system is in a capable state; for example, you could decide to start the task only if the computer is running on AC power or only if a particular network connection is available.

Settings This section includes miscellaneous settings that do not fit anywhere else, such as Allow Run On Demand, Restart If The Task Fails, and settings for what to do if the task is already running.

The Task Scheduler does not allow PowerShell scripts to be run directly, so you must create a *batch* file (a list of executable commands for the command prompt, whose name ends with a `.bat` extension) and have the PowerShell script called from the batch file. You would create a new file and call it `move_user.bat`; this batch file would contain the following code:

```
PowerShell -command "& 'move_user.ps1'"
```

Now within the Task Scheduler, you call the task `Move User` and define the trigger to be scheduled for 8 p.m., with the action to be executed `Move_user.bat`. Figure B.16 shows the results of creating the task (with the Actions tab highlighted).

FIGURE B.16
Creating a scheduled task

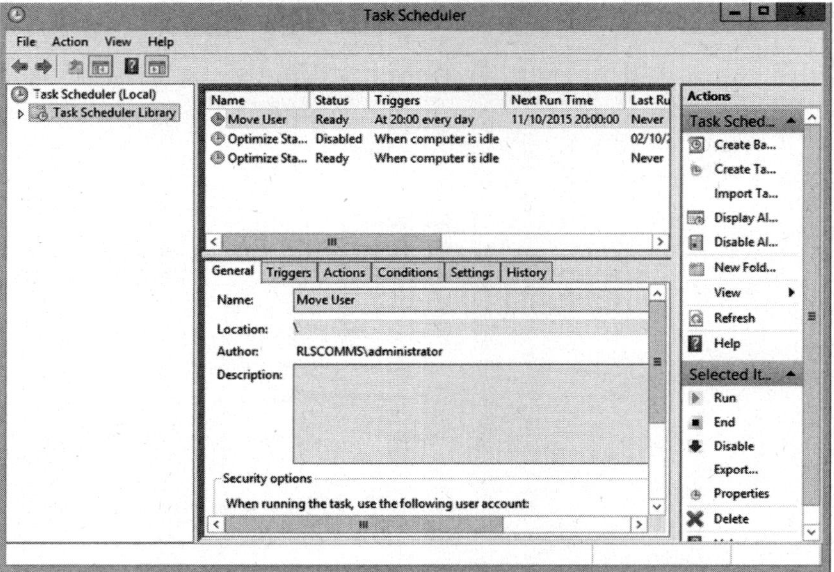

Now you can leave for the night and come back in the morning to view the report showing the user move information. Of course, scheduling a single user move is not a useful scheduled script; more likely you would move multiple users, perhaps as shown here to move all users to a new pool:

```
Get-CsUser | Move-CsUser -Target "eepool01.rlscomms.net"
```

CHANGING POLICY BASED ON TIME

A customer recently needed to limit the number of calls permitted on their network during the day; for the evenings, this limit was lifted. The Call Admission Control (see Chapter 17) functionality within Skype for Business does not provide any time-based policy controls.

However, by using the PowerShell scripting functionality, combined with Windows scheduling, and having two scripts—one to enable the restrictions and one to remove them—we were able to meet this requirement quite easily.

The restriction script runs at 08:00 every day, and the unrestricted script runs at 18:00.

Learning from the GUI

Unlike Microsoft Exchange Server, the Skype for Business Server Control Panel does not provide a user-friendly view of the PowerShell script being executed. With Exchange, the GUI allows you to cut and paste from the Exchange Console into your own scripts, making script creation simpler. However, that said, the naming system used on the Control Panel screens in most cases is easily understood and translated into the PowerShell cmdlet parameters. For example, Figure B.17 shows a sample screen from the Control Panel, and Table B.5 shows the corresponding parameters.

FIGURE B.17 A sample Control Panel screen

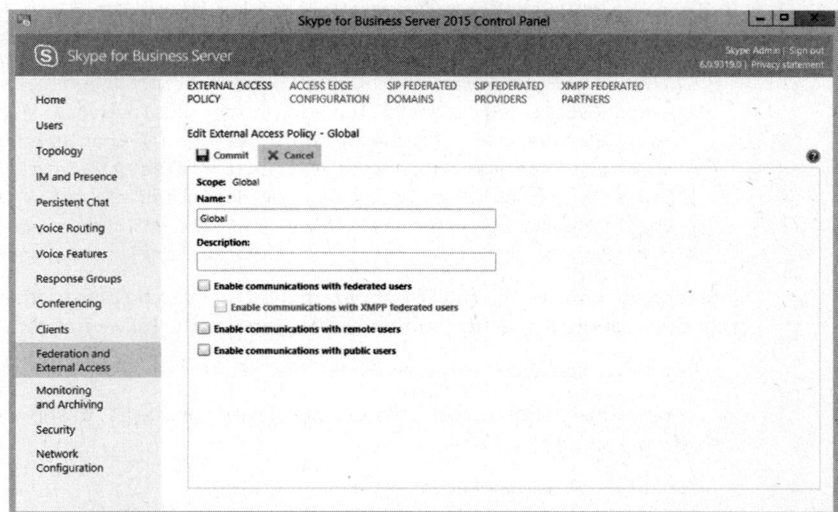

TABLE B.5: PowerShell vs. Control Panel naming

CONTROL PANEL	POWERSHELL PARAMETER
Scope	No direct parameter; included in the Identity parameter
Name	`Identity`
Description	`Description`
Enable communications with federated users	`EnableFederationAccess`
Enable communications with XMPP federated users	`EnableXmppAccess`
Enable communications with remote users	`EnableOutsideAccess`
Enable communications with public users	`EnablePublicCloudAccess`
N/A	`EnablePublicCloudAudioVideoAccess`

The final entry in the PowerShell column highlights again the fact that the shell is more powerful than the GUI; more functionality is exposed using PowerShell than through the GUI (approximately 80 percent of the PowerShell capability is presented within the GUI). For example, in Figure 8.17 you are looking at the External Access configuration and New-CsExternalAccessPolicy (or in the case of changing an existing policy, Set-CsExternalAccessPolicy).

To determine the cmdlet parameter names from within PowerShell, use the following command:

```
Get-Help New-CsExternalAccessPolicy
```

As described previously, the help information is returned for the particular cmdlet selected (in this case New-CsExternalAccessPolicy). You're interested only in the Syntax section, so the rest has been omitted for clarity.

```
SYNTAX
    New-CsExternalAccessPolicy -Identity <XdsIdentity> [-Confirm
[<SwitchParameter>]] [-Description <String>] [-EnableFederationAccess <$true |
$false>] [-EnableOutsideAccess <$true | $false>] [-EnablePublicCloudAccess <$true
| $false>] [-EnablePublicCloudAudioVideoAccess <$true | $false>]
[-EnableXmppAccess <$true | $false>][-Force <SwitchParameter>] [-InMemory
<SwitchParameter>] [-WhatIf [<SwitchParameter>]] [<CommonParameters>]
```

Here you can see the full list of parameters that can be provided, and if you want to see further detail about a specific parameter, you can use the following command:

```
Get-Help New-CsExternalAccessPolicy -Full
```

As previously shown, this has been shortened for clarity, to show only the information from a single parameter.

```
-EnablePublicCloudAccess <$true | $false>
Indicates whether the user is allowed to communicate with people who have SIP
accounts with a public Internet connectivity provider such as MSN. The default
value is False.
Required?                    False
Position?                    Named
Default value
Accept pipeline input?       False
Accept wildcard characters?  False
```

So, what have you learned here? From the GUI, you can see the option Enable Communications With Public Users, and from the cmdlet help you can see that the equivalent parameter is EnablePublicCloudAccess. This example was chosen to illustrate that although not all parameters are an exact match (without spaces), enough information should be provided in the GUI to infer a match with a parameter.

How can this help you? While Exchange administrators may be used to cutting and pasting their PowerShell into scripts from the GUI, Skype for Business administrators can still learn from the GUI. However, creating a script from the actions taken is a manual process—but it is achievable with a little thought and effort!

THE 80 PERCENT RULE

One of the aims of the product development team was to provide 80 percent functionality via the Control Panel interface. As a result, some functionality is available only by using PowerShell.

Example Script Development

In the following sections, you're going to look at some real-world examples of scripts and how to develop them from scratch, putting into practice some of what you learned in this chapter. The scripts shown here are available to download from this link:

```
www.sybex.com/go/masteringskypeforbusiness
```

Updating User Information

A reasonably common task is to update users' information details; this may be because of a change in the name of the department, a building move, or similar occurrences.

In this example, you'll look at updating the Skype for Business user phone information (we won't consider updating any Active Directory information in this script). This may happen when users move between buildings or when a telephone provider changes the area code (because they need a larger numbering scheme). So, the principle here is to change each user from area code 555 to area code 556.

This high-level approach is as follows:

1. Get a user.
2. Check the user's phone number.
3. If the number includes area code 555, change it to 556.
4. Get the next user.

Let's start with `Get-CsUser`. It allows you to retrieve user information (remember that `Get-CsUser` will return all the users, unless you supply a specific `-Identity` parameter). Because you want to check the user phone number details, you'll want to store the returned information in a variable (`$users`). The script so far looks like this:

```
$users = Get-CsUser
```

Next, you want to take each individual user in turn; to achieve this, you'll use the `ForEach` control-loop capability.

```
ForEach ($user in $users) {code}
```

Now, you want to look at the phone number field for a user; this is called `LineUri` and can be accessed by using `$user.LineUri` (the `$user` variable is used only within the `ForEach` loop and refers to the current user object).

Next, you want to check that this will include the area code in the number and ensure that you are dealing only with the users from a specific country (you don't want to change users with the same area code but a different country). You need to define the area code as `+44555`. Indeed, the `LineUri` parameter contains `Tel:` at the beginning, so you'll be looking for an entry that begins with `Tel:+44555`. The script line looks like:

```
If ($user.LineUri.Startswith("Tel:+44555")) {code}
```

Once you have identified a user that needs to be updated, you'll need to generate the new number for that user, and you can use the `Replace` function in PowerShell to do that. You also need to store this new number in a variable (`$newnumber`).

```
$newnumber = $user.LineUri.Replace("Tel:+44555","Tel:+44556")
```

Then you'll update the user object with the new value, using this command:

```
Set-CsUser -Identity $user.SipAddress -LineUri $newnumber
```

Bringing this all together, the script will look like this:

```
$users = Get-CsUser
ForEach ($user in $users) {
      If ($user.LineUri.Startswith("Tel:+44555")) {
            $newnumber = $user.LineUri.Replace("Tel:+44555","Tel:+44556")
            Set-CsUser -Identity $user.SipAddress -LineUri $newnumber
      }
}
```

Indentation is normally used to make the script more readable—each indentation refers to a control loop or a condition check. The closing brackets line up with the starting command.

Of course, this script updates only the LineUri field. What about users who have private lines? Now that you've worked through this section, you can update the script for those users on your own for extra practice. (Look for the PrivateLine field.)

Installing Prerequisites

The first script you examined dealt with updating user information, something that probably happens rarely in batches. This script will look at something significantly more useful, especially if you regularly build a lot of Skype for Business servers for demos or test labs.

Here, you're going to look at configuring the prerequisites for a Front End server installation, either a Standard Edition or Enterprise Edition. It's worth noting that this procedure can also be used to install other server roles. However, the other roles will have fewer prerequisites, so they should be used only in a lab environment; you don't want to install unused services if you don't need them.

The server is assumed to have only Windows Server 2012 installed and be part of the domain, which matches the SIP domain. The goal is to finish with a deployed and functional Skype for Business front end.

In addition, there is no way to manage the topology using PowerShell, so the topology is assumed to be already configured and published, with the file share definitions available.

From Chapter 7, "Planning Your Deployment," you know you should make a list of server features you'll need to install Skype for Business. First, you need to import the servermanager module to modify the feature list.

```
Import-Module servermanager
```

Next, you need to install the required features using Add-WindowsFeature. You can find the actual names of the features by running Get-WindowsFeature if you want to learn more:

```
Add-WindowsFeature Web-Static-Content, Web-Default-Doc,
Web-Http-Errors, Web-Asp-Net, Web-Net-Ext, Web-ISAPI-Ext,
Web-ISAPI-Filter, Web-Http-Logging, Web-Log-Libraries,
Web-Http-Tracing,Web-Windows-Auth, Web-Filtering,
Web-Stat-Compression, Web-Dyn-Compression, Web-Mgmt-Console,
Web-Scripting-Tools, Web-Client-Auth, Web-Asp-Net45,
```

```
Net-HTTP-Activation, Net-WCF-HTTP-Activation45
Add-WindowsFeature Windows-Identity-Foundation
Add-WindowsFeature RSAT-ADDS
Add-WindowsFeature Desktop-Experience
```

The final line adds support for media playing, which is necessary for any server running the A/V conference Media Conferencing Unit, or MCU (assuming the deployment will have it enabled). Unfortunately, this will typically need a reboot, and further installation will fail if a reboot is pending, so you need to check for a reboot.

In addition to listing all the available features, the `Get-WindowsFeature` cmdlet will tell you whether a reboot is pending, so you can use the following commands to query the state and issue the `Restart-Computer` cmdlet to reboot if there is a pending reboot:

```
$features = Get-WindowsFeature
if ($features.restarttneeded -eq "yes"){Restart-Computer}
```

Once the computer has rebooted, you can rerun the script, and it will execute to this stage with no ill effects. Even though you are starting to add features, if they are already added, nothing will happen, and the check for reboot this time will return `FALSE`, so it will not issue the reboot.

Next, you'll register the DNS records, but first you need to query and capture the domain name. In this example, you'll use a system call to get the domain information. If you establish that the server is not domain joined, you'll exit the script (using `exit`); however, do expect to be domain joined, so you'll store the domain name in the variable `$dn_name`.

```
$domain = [system.directoryservices.activedirectory.domain]::GetComputerDomain()
if ($domain -eq $null){
    $domain_joined = $false
    exit
}
else{
    $dn_name = $domain.name
}
```

Capture your own server name from the WMI object `Win32_ComputerSystem`, using the following query, with the hostname stored in the Name field of the variable:

```
$computer = Get-WmiObject -Class Win32_ComputerSystem
$hostname = $computer.name
$seserverfqdn = "$hostname.$dn_name"
```

As you can see from the hostname (`$computer.Name`) and the domain name queried earlier (`$dn_name`), you build the server FQDN (`$seserverfqdn`).

You can't manipulate a DNS record directly within PowerShell; you need to use the `dnscmd.exe` executable. Of course, you first need to find out your own IP address so that you can register it. To do that, query a WMI object, `Win32_NetworkAdapterConfiguration`. You're interested only in enabled network interfaces, assuming the first enabled interface is the one you want to use (remember, the first item in an array is numbered 0).

```
$ip = (get-wmiobject win32_NetworkAdapterConfiguration -filter "IpEnabled=True")
$seserveripaddress = $ip.IPAddress[0]
```

You're going to need the address of the DNS server, and fortunately, the same WMI object holds that data.

```
$dnsserver = $ip.dnsserversearchorder[0]
```

For the actual DNS entries, you want to create the SRV record along with the `meet`, `admin`, and `dialin` entries too.

```
Dnscmd $dnsserver /recordadd $dn_name _sipinternaltls._tcp srv 5 0 5061
$seserverfqdn
Dnscmd $dnsserver /recordadd $dn_name meet a $seserveripaddress
Dnscmd $dnsserver /recordadd $dn_name admin a $seserveripaddress
Dnscmd $dnsserver /recordadd $dn_name dialin a $seserveripaddress
Dnscmd $dnsserver /recordadd $dn_name lyncdiscoverinternal a $seserveripaddress
```

For Windows Server 2012 R2, you need to install a hotfix (KB2982006).

```
$prereq_media_directory = "c:\pre-reqs"
#Install HotFix 2982006
$prereq_media_directory\Windows8.1-kb2982006-x64.msu
start-sleep -s 120
```

Now that the script has installed the prerequisites and created the necessary DNS entries, you need to install the appropriate software from the Skype for Business media. For this example, we'll assume you are using drive X: for the DVD. You need to install the following:

- Visual C++ Redistributable
- SQL Native Client
- SQL System CLR Types
- Unified Communications Managed API (UCMA)
- Skype for Business Core Components
- Skype for Business Admin Tools

To install them, you can use the following commands. Each software package may take some time to complete, and because you rely upon the package being installed later, you will want to pause while the installation is underway using the `Start-Sleep` cmdlet (ensuring that the package has completed installation by the time you need it).

```
$sfb_media_directory = "x:"
#Install Visual C++ Redistributable
$sfb_media_directory\setup\amd64\vcredist_x64.exe /q
start-sleep -s 120
#Install SQL Native Client
$sfb_media_directory\setup\amd64\sqlncli.msi -quiet
start-sleep -s 60
#Install SQL System CLR Types
$sfb_media_directory\setup\amd64\SQLSysClrTypes.msi -quiet
start-sleep -s 60
#install ucma
```

```
msiexec /qn /i $sfb_media_directory\setup\amd64\Setup\ucmaruntime.msi
REBOOT=ReallySuppress /QN EXCLUDETRACING=1 BOOT=1
start-sleep -s 60
#Install Skype for Business core components
msiexec /qn /i $sfb_media_directory\setup\amd64\Setup\ocscore.msi
INSTALLDIR='"C:\Program Files\Skype for Business Server 2015\'"
ADDLOCAL=Feature_OcsCore
start-sleep -s 60
#Install Skype for Business admin tools
msiexec /qn /i $sfb_media_directory\setup\amd64\Setup\admintools.msi
start-sleep -s 60
```

At this point, you've done all you can do without running the Skype for Business PowerShell, so you need to import that module.

```
Import-Module -name 'C:\program files\common files\Skype for Business Server
2015\Modules\SkypeForBusiness'
```

These examples have assumed the topology was published; however, you can check this by using `Get-CsTopology`, and in this case you'll exit the script if it has not. This will allow the script to install all the prerequisites (including Topology Builder) for you and then wait until you define and publish the topology. This is useful if you're deploying only one server. Simply rerun the script after the topology is published and the script will continue.

```
$topology = Get-CsTopology
If ($topology -eq $null){exit}
```

Now you're getting to the actual deployment stages, the first part of which is to install the local SQL Express for the replica of the Central Management Store (CMS). Next, start the Skype for BusinessReplica Service to allow the data to replicate from the CMS to the new server.

```
 "C:\Program Files\Skype for Business Server 2015\Deployment\Bootstrapper.exe" /
BootstrapLocalMgmt /SourceDirectory:$sfb_media_directory\setup\amd64\
start-sleep -s 120
Enable-CsReplica
Start-CsWindowsService Replica
```

You could wait for replication or use PowerShell to speed it up. Naturally, you'll want to speed it up! Exporting the configuration file from the CMS and importing it locally has the same effect as waiting, but it is quicker! Here, you're temporarily storing the data in the `$config` variable:

```
$config = Export-CsConfiguration -asbytes
Import-CsConfiguration -byteinput $config -LocalStore
```

Now you've reached the stage where the prerequisites (both server side and Skype for Business specific) are installed, the DNS entries are created, and the topology is replicated to the local CMS replica. All you need to do is run the installation routine, get certificates, and start the services.

The installation routine checks the local topology to see which roles are defined for the current server, and it will install only what is needed. Because this process is part of the installation, the script does not need to determine which roles are required to be installed; you can simply run the installer.

```
"C:\Program Files\Skype for Business Server 2015\Deployment\Bootstrapper.exe" /
SourceDirectory:$sfb_media_directory\setup\amd64\
```

At this point, a reboot may be required to complete the installation; however, you still need to get certificates, and this will succeed whether a reboot is pending or not.

Requesting a certificate is relatively easy using Skype for Business PowerShell; the tricky part is to find the certificate authority (CA) details, which are held in Active Directory. You have to connect to Active Directory and search specifically for the `pKIEnrollmentService`, and from the response you need to determine the DNS name of the server. There may be multiple entries of this type; however, this script simply takes the final entry as the one to use.

```
$root = [ADSI]"LDAP://CN=Configuration,$dn_name"
$query = new-object system.directoryservices.directorysearcher($root)
$query.filter = "(&(objectClass=pKIEnrollmentService)(cn=*))"
$query.SearchSCope = "subtree"
$result = $query.findall()
```

If the results of the Active Directory search are empty, set the `$ca_found` variable to `$false` (you'll use this later), and if they're not empty, capture the CA name in the correct format (*dnsname\cnname*) and set the `$ca_found` variable to `$true`.

```
if ($result -eq $null){
$ca_found = $false
}
else{
       foreach ($ca in $result) {
        $o = $ca.getdirectoryentry()
        $dnsname = $o.dNSHostName
        $cn = $o.cn
        $ca_name = "$dnsname\$cn"
        $ca_found = $true
}
}
```

Now that you have the certificate details, you can request and assign the certificate and finish starting the services. If the `$ca_found` variable is set to `$true`, you will automatically request and assign the certificates using the CA; however, if it is `$false`, the process will be manual. Once the certificate is assigned, the services can be started.

```
If ($ca_found){
    $Certificate = Request-CsCertificate -New -Type Default,WebServicesInternal,
WebServicesExternal -CA $Ca_Name -FriendlyName Default -AllSipDomain
    Set-CsCertificate -Thumbprint $Certificate.Thumbprint -Type Default,
WebServicesInternal,WebServicesExternal
    Enable-CsComputer
    Start-cswindowsService
}
```

In summary, this script has achieved the following:

- Installed the server prerequisites for Skype for Business Server 2015 Front End
- Installed Skype for Business Server 2015 prerequisites
- Created the DNS records
- Installed SQL Express for the RTCLocal instance
- Installed SQL Express for the LyncLocal instance
- Replicated the topology
- Installed Skype for Business to the configuration specified in the topology
- Requested an application of a certificate
- Started the Skype for Business Server 2015 Services

At this point, users can be enabled and clients will be able to connect.

Using Regular Expressions

Regular expressions (also known as *Regex*) can be defined as providing a concise and flexible means to "match" strings of text, such as particular characters, words, or patterns of characters. Since OCS, regular expressions are used to manipulate numbers (outgoing as well as incoming) to their base level to better identify best (or permitted) routes as well as to "normalize" numbers, which is converting a number (possibly only an extension) into a fully defined number that can be understood and routed by Skype for Business.

Regular expressions can be complex; you can see some examples in the OCS address book normalization sample file. Fortunately, Skype for Business has improved significantly on how to manage number normalization.

So, what's the point of regular expressions? And why do you need to understand them?

Well, we've already given one example: providing users with the ability to simply dial an extension and have Skype for Business understand the final target number intended to be dialed and route accordingly. Other examples would be to add country code information or indeed the number for an outside line. It's much easier to have a user continue their existing dialing habits than have to retrain users to understand the dialing habits of a new system.

Understanding Regex

Let's start with an example outside the world of Skype for Business. Say you want to describe your pets—a cat and a dog—using regular expressions.

You could use the following:

```
<consonant><vowel><consonant>
```

That matches for both *cat* and *dog*.

Now, let's assume you get another pet: a bird. How can you define all your pets now? Well, it turns out you don't need to do anything. The previous definition defines only the *order* in which the consonants and vowel appear; it doesn't define anything regarding numbers or position. As long as somewhere in the word you have the `<consonant><vowel><consonant>` pattern, you will match upon it.

So, how can you be more specific and match only *cat* and *dog*?

Well, you can have a number of special characters that within regular expression provide meaning or context, such as the following (we'll describe these further as we go):

```
^

$

*

+

?

|

[]
```

(Please note that different implementations of regular expressions may have different meanings to these symbols; in this example, we are referring to the Skype for Business implementation.)

The symbol ^ matches against the *beginning* of the string, in other words the string *must* start with the pattern.

So, would ^<consonant><vowel><consonant> help our scenario? Well, no, because each item—*cat*, *dog*, and *bird*—starts with this pattern, so you'd still get a match on all of them.

The symbol $ matches against the *end* of a string. Would that fit?

<consonant><vowel><consonant>$ would be fine for *cat* and *dog* and would exclude *bird*, so it looks like it is a good choice for you. However, it does leave you open to matching against *rabbit* because you are looking for the pattern in only the final three characters in this example.

To be more specific, you'd have to match against both the *start* and the *end*, using both ^ and $.

^<consonant><vowel><consonant>$ ensures that you look only for a pattern that is three characters long.

Now, how about introducing some flexibility? Well, by using a +, you can call for a match of the preceding element one or more times.

So, ^<consonant><vowel><consonant>+$ would look for patterns that matched three or four characters, with the pattern <consonant><vowel><consonant> or <consonant><vowel><consonant><consonant>. From your list, this would be *cat*, *dog*, and *bird*.

The symbol ? could also give you similar flexibility. This time you will match the preceding element zero or one times.

You pattern would be ^<consonant><vowel><consonant><consonant>?$.

If you didn't care how many time the final preceding character appeared, you could use *; this would equate to zero or more times.

The characters [] allow for options contained within the brackets, and each option is separated by |.

You could have ^[<consonant><vowel><consonant>|<consonant><vowel><consonant><consonant>]$ to give you another option to represent the three- or four-character selection in the previous cases

Regex Within Skype for Business

In most cases you will encounter regular expressions only if you want to use the address book normalization file to help normalize numbers stored in Active Directory. However, it is used extensively in the background by Skype for Business for the normalization rules for users and their dialing patterns; it's just presented differently to the admin via the GUI, as shown in Figure B.18.

FIGURE B.18
Representation of a regular expression in the Skype for Business GUI

You may have a complex scenario that cannot be handled by the simple GUI approach and requires direct manipulation of a regular expression, or alternatively you may want to use PowerShell to deploy and configure Skype for Business completely.

Aside from the string-based examples shown earlier, Skype for Business uses `\d` to represent a digit, so the pattern `^\d\d\d\d$` would represent an entry that is four digits long (as it also includes the start and end characters).

Table B.6 shows some examples of regex and their descriptions.

TABLE B.6: Sample regex expressions for Skype for Business

<table>
<tr><th>REGEX</th><th>DESCRIPTION</th></tr>
<tr><td>^555\d\d\d\d$</td><td>Seven-digit entry, beginning with 555</td></tr>
<tr><td>^555\d{4}$</td><td>Seven-digit entry, beginning with 555 (more human readable)</td></tr>
<tr><td>^[555|123]\d{4}$</td><td>Seven-digit entry, beginning with either 555 or 123</td></tr>
<tr><td>^[555|123]\d{*}$</td><td>Minimum three-digit entry, beginning with either 555 or 123</td></tr>
<tr><td>^555\d+$</td><td>Minimum four-digit entry, beginning with 555</td></tr>
<tr><td>^(555\d{4})$</td><td>Seven-digit entry, beginning with 555, including marking the data within the () to be carried to the next stage</td></tr>
</table>

The last example here includes an entry within parentheses. The data enclosed in the parentheses is marked as an item to be carried to the next stage in the manipulation—similar to how a variable would be in a script. Indeed, in this case, it would be assigned the name $1.

The majority of regular expression patterns are to manipulate the number dialed by users. This normally involves taking some (or all) of the number entered and modifying it before sending to a gateway for dialing (or matching internally). To allow for these numbers to be taken and passed to the next stage (normally called *translation*), you use parentheses.

A translation pattern would be something similar to `+1425$1`. In this case, it would take the number represented by `$1` and precede it with `+1425`. Ultimately, here, it's creating an E164 number by adding the area code as well as the international country code. This number could then be passed to a gateway (or PBX) for dialing.

Appendix C

Using Persistent Chat Effectively

Combining the immediacy of instant messaging with multiparty outreach—via Persistent Chat, a configurable component in Skype for Business Server 2015—is transforming how groups and individuals communicate by facilitating real-time discussion.

You learned how to install Persistent Chat in Chapter 8, "Installation." However, with functionality potentially as complex as Persistent Chat, this isn't enough. This appendix will cover some real-life use case examples of how chat-enabled collaboration tools can be used effectively in a global business environment to share knowledge, communicate more efficiently, save time, and keep abreast of up-to-date news that can impact the business.

You'll also see how, with the use of some third-party applications from MindLink, conversations can take place on a desktop, a mobile device, a tablet, or the Web from any location using a multitude of clients.

Completing the entire communication spectrum, Persistent Chat cannot be altered or deleted, ensuring compliance for those in heavily regulated industries or those organizations that adhere to self-governance policies. The demand for bringing Persistent Chat to the center of the collaboration strategy has largely been driven by customers using WhatsApp and similar apps in a business context and by realizing that chat applications are a far better, real-time way of working than email. However, the realization that these applications are insecure and do not provide the level of identity management, encryption, and security that is inherent in Skype for Business (and that is mandatory in the corporate environment) has become a major concern.

Introduction to Persistent Chat

Chat-enabled collaboration (CEC) is a new, digital way of working that is displacing email; it enables real-time knowledge sharing in a structured and filtered way. As a reminder, chat-enabled collaboration describes the use of secure, real-time messaging platforms as the corporate backbone for internal communication and collaboration across an enterprise.

CEC applications combine multiple, dispersed communication channels within a firm into one digitally enabled central workplace. Core components of CEC systems include instant messaging, presence, Persistent Chat, file sharing and archiving, screen sharing, and voice and video capabilities coupled with corporate requirements for enterprise-grade security, regulatory compliance, and system and process integration.

To help put all of this together and graphically illustrate how CEC tools can help, the following use cases are examples of how Persistent Chat and other messaging applications can be used across a variety of functions and industries. While not an exhaustive list (there are many, many others), these examples will showcase how CEC can better advance efficient communication and productivity based on roles and specific industry-based sectors.

Roles in project management, operations, and consulting can be applicable across various industries. While not wholly isolated from other departments, these roles generally focus on a particular product or project and evolve around the sharing of intellectual capital.

- CEC for project managers
- CEC for lawyers
- CEC for consultants

In contrast, industries such as investment banking, retail banking, technology, and operations are heavily dependent on multiple departments working together in coordination.

- CEC for investment banking
- CEC for retail banking
- CEC for software companies
- CEC for police and security
- CEC for MNE operations

All rely on effective communication to achieve goals and drive the business forward.

Examples of Role-Based Solutions for Persistent Chat

The roles in these examples center on sharing intellectual capital.

Project Managers

A company consists of several hundred people who are constantly traveling or working from home, with their only connection to the office being their laptops or phones. The project team consists of a core group of 20 business users at subsidiary headquarters and regional offices, technical leads at global headquarters, and their external consultants. The team is functionally, geographically, linguistically, culturally, and chronologically dispersed. In addition, stakeholders include members of the senior leadership team such as the CIO, CTO, and CFO. The challenge is keeping everyone involved, interested, and up-to-date on the latest status or changes.

Throughout the project life cycle (discovery, development, test, and rollout), communications among team members can take on a variety of forms including onsite visits, videoconferences, and teleconferences, but email typically becomes the go-to communications method because of time, language, and geographical differences. The dependence on email throughout the project life cycle not only promotes ineffective communication but also reinforces siloed knowledge, which may derail the project. Putting Persistent Chat and messaging systems at the center of the organization allows real-time interaction and a more streamlined but highly transparent approach while still empowering users with the ability to filter the right information to the right people, reducing communication bottlenecks and information overload.

For example, a separate chat *channel* for each stage of the cycle can be created (see Figure C.1). The groups would be used to discuss ideas, clarify issues, and answer specific questions around functionality requirements. Each new revision of the functional specification document or test results would be posted into the group so all users would be confident they're looking at the latest one. Updates from the document management system such as SharePoint could be integrated into the channel, alerting all users of a new version. During rollout, a group can be created to foster a self-help community where users would post questions or comments. If users had specific questions, they could first search the history to see whether the question was previously asked and answered; instead of just the project manager and a few help-desk resources being inundated with questions, other users could also provide answers. A separate group would also be set up for the management team and the key stakeholders, providing a filtered set of information to upper management throughout the project.

FIGURE C.1 Project life cycle project channels

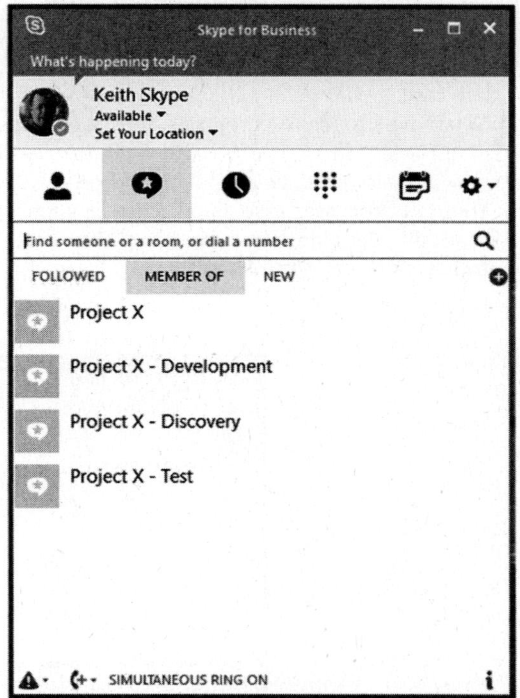

These are examples of how CEC enables real-time interaction for project managers and a more streamlined but highly transparent collaboration foundation while still empowering users with the ability to filter the right information to the right people, reducing communication bottlenecks and information overload. CEC allows real-time interaction, becomes an indispensable part of the workflow, and integrates into other applications.

Lawyers

In a law firm, there can be a myriad of senior partners, partners, associates, contract lawyers, "of counsel" lawyers, law clerks, paralegals, legal assistants, and legal secretaries. Although the majority are law practitioners, larger law firms may specialize in different kinds of law, such as, for example, mergers and acquisitions (M&A), corporate, environmental, Internet, biotech, and aviation. This could mean potential overlaps between practice areas and could influence the outcome of cases. Additionally, lawsuits are often complicated and involve many different parties. Within a "single" lawsuit, there can be any number of claims and defenses between multiple plaintiffs or defendants, each of whom can bring any number of cross-claims and counterclaims against each other. Managing both clients and teams can be complex, overwhelming, and extremely time-consuming, especially with ineffective communications practices.

Persistent Chat can help all members of a firm within and across different practice areas align their cases to ensure the best outcome for their clients as well as for the firm. Gathering expert knowledge and data and connecting with peers in the firm to share information, experience, advice, or particulars on past cases allows a case to be built better and faster within binding, designated time frames. This can be a matter of winning or losing a case, especially when time is of the essence. All information transmitted is secure, ensuring that confidential information is not improperly leaked.

For each case, a channel (or chat room) can be created (see Figure C.2) to track progress from the senior partners to legal secretaries. If a case crosses multiple practice areas, additional users may be given access to a certain channels. Future assignments can benefit as channels enable expert knowledge of predecessors. This creates a valuable asset to the firm by providing insight into the thought processes associated with decisions, creating advantages or setting up for when a case is handed over from one to another. This also helps elevate a good client relationship to one of utmost confidence and trust.

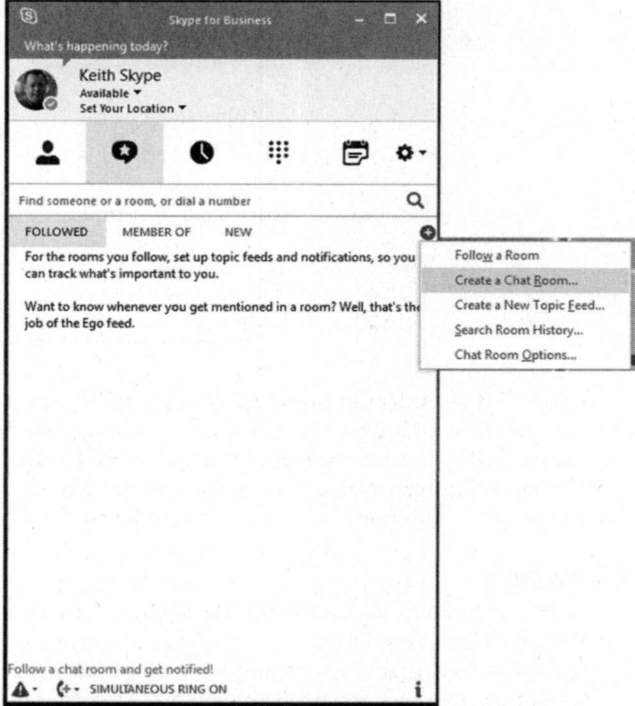

FIGURE C.2 Creating a chat room

All of these information streams and associated functionalities can be accessed via mobile devices, perfect for those times in between traveling, trials, or meetings. Additional filters can be added, as well as instant messaging, which can be helpful for a discreet inquiry in a public place.

CEC enables firms to reduce their dependence on email for mass communications and improve dialogue among legal teams by creating a real-time platform to efficiently share knowledge and update each other on progress, flag potential problems, or brainstorm solutions, thereby transforming how legal teams operate by extracting the most valuable asset of all—knowledge sharing—for driving cases or assignments forward and increasing productivity and time management for success.

Consultants

A consultant's time is mostly spent in the air, airport lounges, cabs, trains, client meeting rooms, hotel rooms, and finally, offices or homes. While a consultant constantly travels to meet clients to identify their needs and find other potential ways to help their business, it's their imperative to make sure the firm's team delivers first-rate work to meet these needs. At the most senior levels, it is not uncommon to oversee 20-plus clients, each with its own dedicated team of 10 to 50 people consisting of directors, senior managers, managers, senior consultants, consultants, and analysts. The teams are functionally, geographically, linguistically, culturally, and chronologically dispersed, making it extremely difficult to connect and collaborate on project status, issues, and business decisions needing attention.

Managing clients and the internal teams is a complex and demanding part of the job, while equally challenging is communicating with peers in the firm to share knowledge, experience, advice, or particulars on past projects. The professional peer network is just as far-flung and nomadic, and reliance on email to communicate clogs up inboxes. To make matters worse, it is not readily obvious who would be the best resource, so an email is sent to the most logical choice to see what result that will yield. This step often creates the dreaded email chain, which often gets deleted.

While everyone shares the common goal of providing the best work to the client, ineffective communication practices through email can negatively affect the quality of work to the client or cause delays. To help cope, consultants have learned to be disciplined in the habit of scanning, absorbing, deleting, filing, and remembering the information read in email. Often, this exercise is completed in between client meetings on a mobile phone.

In contrast to email, CEC can help ensure smoother communication. A channel can be created for each client to allow internal team members to efficiently share knowledge and update each other on progress, flag potential problems, or brainstorm solutions. This allows consultants to review these goings-on for each project when it is convenient and not be a prisoner to email alerts. Clear communication to the entire team is as amazingly simple as a post. Important or urgent messages to the team can be highlighted as an alert. To counteract the anxiety of searching through countless emails and scrolling through email chains, a simple search function displays the data in context, reducing the amount of information that needs to be filtered through to find the answer.

Not only can this information help the firm be more informed, it can also better help the firm help the client. Up-to-date news can potentially impact the assignment; taking quick action to mitigate risks could elevate a good client relationship to one of utmost confidence and trust.

Among peers, separate streams can be set up to share knowledge and expertise in particular practice areas or topics. Queries will be broadcast to a wide audience, eliminating the need to send untargeted emails. Not only would this mean a reduction in multiple emails with the same response, it benefits the group and the firm as a whole since knowledge is shared and stored as an organizational asset. This will help other consultants who face the same challenge, those unaware of the situation, or others who need a reference at a later point in time. CEC applications ensures that questions will not be lost in the inbox "black hole."

All of these information channels and associated functionalities can be accessed via mobile devices, which is perfect for those little chunks of time in between traveling time or meetings. Additional filters on the mobile device can be added to ensure alerts only for the most important information. An additional benefit is being able to quickly ask a question or clarify an issue with the team via instant message; this can be helpful for discreet inquiries.

Persistent Chat enables a collaborative platform, easily integrating itself into the business workflow and supporting the mobile nature of consulting in an efficient, easy, simple way in real time.

What Is MindLink?

MindLink is a highly secure CEC platform for enterprises and one of the earliest and leading providers of this new category of internal communication and collaboration tools.

Its messaging and collaboration application encourages employees to stay connected, reduce email usage, and build a more agile business through the use of modern, digital tools.

MindLink offers all collaboration features, such as presence, instant messaging, group chat, file sharing, and voice capabilities (coming soon) combined with mobility, security, compliance, and advanced integrations to provide relevant content to users. All this happens while connecting to UC platforms such as Microsoft Lync and Skype for Business (adding value to firms already invested in creating a collaborative workplace).

Think of MindLink as a secure alternative to WhatsApp but for business use.

The following are some examples of how businesses value is created with MindLink.

Wherever You Go

MindLink connects your remote and distributed teams and gives you access to all your important information in the office and on-the-go. It extends chat and messaging capabilities on to Windows, Mac, and Linux as well as mobile devices and tablets, for Blackberry, Android, and iOS.

Meet Compliance Needs

MindLink lets you control, monitor, archive, and search your communication channels with built-in compliance and archiving capabilities, ensuring you meet regulatory requirements and protect your business.

Secure and Protected

MindLink ensures that you stay in control of your corporate data and privacy. It offers enterprise-grade data security, offers flexible deployment models (on premise and private cloud), and works with all major MDM/EMM vendors to ensure your sensitive business data is protected at all times.

Integrate Your Systems

No more switching between applications: MindLink connects your messaging platform to your internal business systems, from CRM to trading platforms and from storage to project management. There are out-of-the-box integrations with the following:

- Social media and RSS feeds
- Corporate portals
- Email systems
- Any internal application via a RESTful API

Integration of CEC applications is key to further adoptions and to avoid the logon/log-off challenges faced by today's knowledge workers. MindLink strives to address these concerns with powerful business integrations.

The MindLink API provides a simple way to develop connectors to any internal or external source, such as CRM, ERP, Jira, ticketing systems, document management, operational monitoring, and more. Email integration allows companies to unclutter email inboxes by rerouting email alerts and mass notifications from distribution lists into relevant chat channels, structuring conversations, and avoiding information overload. Social integration provides an aggregated view of social media news, RSS, and Twitter feeds from any external or internal site within chat channels, allowing firms to monitor trends, keywords, and news and encouraging active discussion rather than passive consumption. Portal integration transforms portals into fully fledged collaboration environments by embedding real-time messaging into this one-way storage facility. It enables broadcasting of information and two-way discussions within portals.

The following figure shows the connectivity paths available into Skype for Business via MindLink.

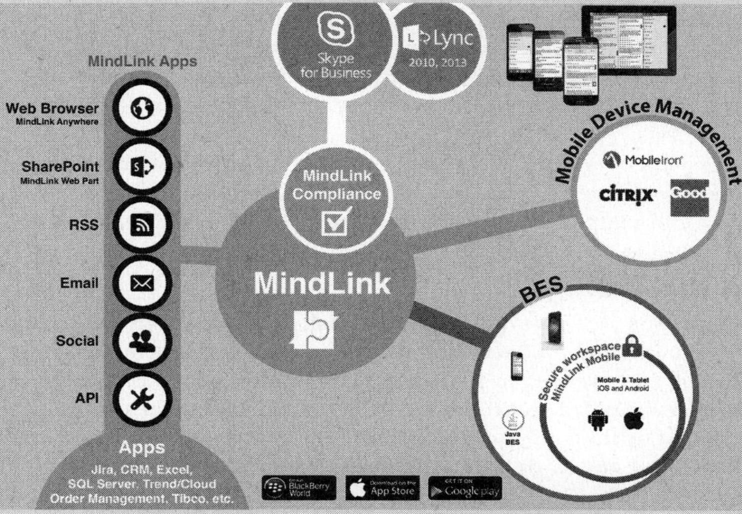

Examples of Industry-Based Solutions for Persistent Chat

The industries in the following examples are heavily dependent on cross-functional coordination.

Investment Banking

Broadly speaking, in an investment bank there are two divisions that work closely together, although they can't always communicate directly. Traders rely on the work of the research department to help them make decisions on various financial instruments being traded on the floor. This information is vital to the job of the trader and impacts the cash flow and bottom line of the institution. The research department can be seen as the nerve center for a bank. Not only do the findings from the research department need to get to the traders, the information may also be shared with third parties such as hedge funds and private equity clients who do not have the same in-house capabilities. Moreover, to ensure that the output is as accurate as possible, up-to-the-minute news on various topics must be included into the models. The research scope is separated into several verticals, or sectors, such as fast-moving consumer goods (FMCG), energy, transportation, and commodities. Each of these groups has a team of managers, senior analysts, and analysts who focus on different aspects of the sector, such as pricing, news trends, consumer reports, corporate purchasing trends, and marketing analysis. The analysts and senior analysts communicate with their peers within the same sector but also with peers in other sectors, depending on their specialization.

The interdependencies, communication, and information flows are highly intricate and complex; the addition of regulations that impose "ethical" or "Chinese" walls between research and trading makes this elaborate arrangement even more challenging.

Among peers, separate streams can be set up to share knowledge and expertise in particular practice areas or topics. Queries will be broadcast to a wide audience, eliminating the need to send untargeted emails. Not only would this mean a reduction in multiple emails with the same response, it benefits the group and the firm as a whole since knowledge is shared and stored as an organizational asset. This will help other consultants who face the same challenge, those unaware of the situation, or others who need a reference at a later point in time. CEC applications ensure that questions will not be lost in the inbox "black hole."

For banks, Persistent Chat can seamlessly integrate with other technological applications as well as outside news sources and business workflows. This information can be shared in a secure and compliant environment with internal and external stakeholders.

Retail Banking

A retail bank will have many frontline staff available in the branch offices to help with and sell new accounts and products. There are many challenges: a multitude of different products, limited staff, and the need to give high-quality, accurate, and consistent answers, which are critical to converting new opportunities. Furthermore, making the process of signing up new clients easier and turning around the application in a shorter time period brings greater satisfaction to the customer and saves time and money. A typical example follows:

Scenario

1. A new person comes to a branch of the bank to open a new account.
2. The customer fills the form, and the bank employee scans the form and uploads it into their customer relationship management (CRM) system, which is passed to the bank's back office.
3. The back office goes through the form but doesn't have a means of communication to inform the person in the branch of any issues or further questions.
4. The customer-facing bank employee tries to contact the back office but is forced to go to support to find who is managing the back-end request.
5. The whole process takes two hours, and the customer of the bank is frustrated.

Solution

The customer-facing bank employee has an tablet device securely managed by MDM and can access secure Persistent Chat within Skype for Business. Depending on the questions and areas of inquiry, the bank employee has a variety of channels with linked content such as mortgage rates, application forms, and so on, associated to the channels. The chat rooms give immediately available searchable content and access to all the tier 1, 2, and 3 staff present on the chat rooms. If the employee doesn't have access to a tablet, chat channels are also available and integrated in SharePoint with automatic feeds and alerts to the CRM system.

1. The bank employee scans the form and uploads it into CRM system, which automatically posts to the back office channel.
2. The bank employee knows automatically who at the back end has received and is working on the request.
3. The back-office employee goes through the form and sends feedback to the employee in the branch with the results and details. Errors or clarification can be discussed immediately.
4. The whole process of opening a new account takes 10 to 15 minutes maximum, saving time and money and improving customer satisfaction.

Software Company

A software company consists of 250 employees and occupies office space in two different locations. The 50-person sales force travels extensively to meet clients and channel partners, logging important details in the CRM software. The marketing department is just as mobile, engaging with potential customers, affiliates, media, and other networking events to keep track of outreach activities in their own marketing automation software. The development team, although it's in-house, has multiple projects for each product running concurrently and relies on development tracking tools. Last, the customer support team fields suggestions for improvement and issues encountered by customers.

Although highly disjointed technology-wise, the departments are interdependent and serve as critical touch points for the customer experience. The challenge is keeping everyone involved, interested, and up-to-date on the latest status or changes despite these siloed and "department-centric" tools used. Persistent Chat can extensively organize the company's internal management, sales, marketing, development, and customer support.

For example, the sales team can have channels for each major prospect, providing up-to-the-minute information on prospects and their respective industries. For the development team, a channel can be set up for every product to log exceptions or progress. Customer support can provide the clients with the opportunity to access its portal in addition to the normal support tools. Everything that happens with each client happens within one of those channels. This provides a clear view of the activity or issues and means that support can be given 24/7. All the information is auditable and provides fast and easy search facilities. One of the biggest benefits is that it allows people who are unfamiliar with the issue or client to quickly come up to speed. Across all departments, alerts from each of the "department-centric" tools can be set up to show new cases, updates, and edits.

Persistent Chat can greatly enhance and enable efficient communication in real time within departments and across the entire organization as well as integrate siloed systems.

For software companies, CEC provides a collaborative foundation. It can seamlessly integrate other technological applications and outside news sources, external clients, and business workflows and allow employees to access information.

Policing and Security Operations

Increasingly more and more emergency services, government, and secret service departments are seeing the value of CEC. There is a clear requirement to save money. Voice is an obvious candidate for rationalization, but departments are also looking to bring chat systems to the center of their operational ecosystems. There have been many recent examples of police forces using WhatsApp and similar public chat systems to coordinate operations. There is a major risk associated with using these systems. Not only are they insecure or can be hacked, but the very criminals they are trying to catch are using them. In response, there has been an increased demand and adoption of CEC tools built specifically for businesses and corporates (in tandem with MindLink). A typical example follows.

Scenario

1. A police officer reports to the police station for the daily briefing by the duty sergeant (this happens 3 times a day, 365 days a year).
2. The duty officer has been updated by the previous duty sergeant and briefs the police officers.
3. The police officers return to their local areas (often a round-trip of 30 to 60 minutes per day, per shift).
4. When an officer is involved in an incident, there are forms and reports to deliver that take often 30 minutes to 2 hours to complete. These forms are sent to the back-office staff to be uploaded to the internal CRM systems.
5. The back office goes through the forms but doesn't have a direct means of communication to inform the officer if there are any issues or further questions.
6. The police officer is forced to spend more time doing paperwork than protecting the community.
7. The whole process takes too long; petty crimes can be overlooked, and the police officers are frustrated.

Solution

1. The police officer has a smartphone or tablet securely managed by MDM and can access secure Persistent Chat within Skype for Business. The officer has a daily briefing channel where the duty officer can share the key things to be aware of. It provides a direct mechanism for further questions and feedback from the field.
2. Specific investigations and ongoing operations around the community or child welfare can have specific standing rooms. Internal systems can automatically post alerts and notifications to these rooms, speeding up responses and streamlining the whole process.
3. The officer will have access to a variety of channels where images of suspects can be sent to validate identity, corroborate stories, and support staff. The channels enable immediate access to searchable content and all tier 1, 2, and 3 staff.
4. The officer can complete a report or statement chatting to an automated agent, which, when complete, will post the response to the respective channel as well as the CRM system in a structured format.
5. The back-office team can go through the form and respond, correlate, escalate, or seek further clarification from the officer.

Outcome

Ten minutes saved per office correlates to about 1 percent of the wage bill of a police force. As adoption accelerates, the general opinion is that the savings in time is at least 30 minutes per officer, with the added benefits of more time "doing the job" and improved morale.

Operations for Multinational Enterprises

Multinational enterprises (MNEs) run mission-critical, global, real-time operations with distributed teams that need to stay tightly coordinated in response to incidents and provide highly effective shift handovers. Developing, manufacturing, and delivering goods to the consumer can touch upon teams in a broad range of functions, from R&D to manufacturing, logistics, distribution, warehouse, and merchandising. Seamless transitions need to occur at every functional shift in the journey to the consumer; otherwise, delays, mix-ups, and, worst of all, lack of product for consumers will negatively impact the MNE's bottom line and reputation.

Because the vertical chain is so complex, the technology being deployed in this process will probably be complex. Users in those teams are often using a mix of different desktop technologies, such as, for example, Windows, Mac, Linux, and mobile devices. The challenge is not only to ensure that all parties are kept up-to-date on the latest shipment but also to consolidate all modes of communication. As shown in Figure C.3, membership of each category can be defined in many ways.

- Organizational units
- Distributions groups
- Domains
- Individuals

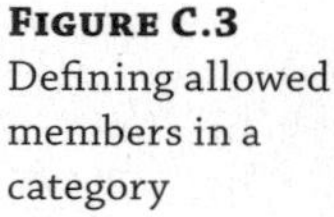

FIGURE C.3
Defining allowed members in a category

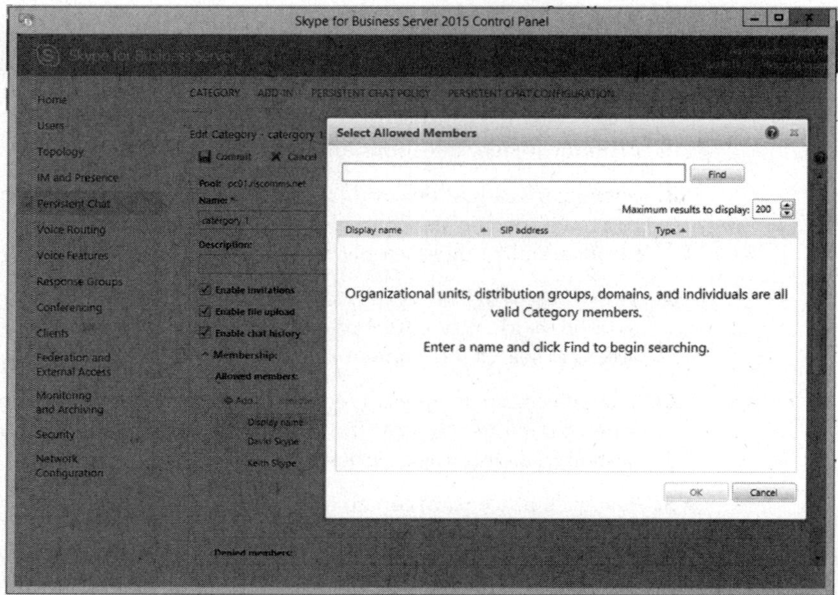

CEC enables both real-time and near-real-time communications across platforms and incorporates relevant external feeds; that is, users can have conversations in real time, have access to the recent chat history, and join or rejoin a channel and quickly come up to speed on the latest information and discussions. A separate channel can be created for the "internal" departments (R&D, manufacturing) to flag any quality issues for each product and "external" departments (logistics, distribution, warehouse, and merchandising) to pinpoint where legal liabilities for each shipment change hands along with other transportation issues. This history forms valuable input into postmortems and acts as a knowledge base for recurring issues.

As opposed to the use of telephone or conference calls, the use of written real-time communications is helpful for users who are not native speakers of their company's preferred business language. The ability to lock down channels means that communications can be limited on a "need-to-know" basis.

This collaborative foundation seamlessly integrates into the business workflow and unites teams using disparate systems while providing access only to those who need the visibility. CEC can provide further efficiencies in time-sensitive operations that could have a huge impact on the bottom line by providing a collaborative foundation and integrating this into the business workflow.

Better "Unification" of Data

Unified Communications is an omnipresent term. Using a product such as MindLink from MindLink Software (`www.mindlinksoft.com`) allows multiple data streams from many sources to be truly unified and presented within the Persistent Chat channels. Equally, data can be taken from the channels and presented in other formats for consumption in other ways. For example, in almost all the examples in this appendix, RSS connector feeds could be created to summarize channel content and be presented via Outlook or an RSS aggregation application, similar to newswire-type data.

How about the lawyer example? You can further aggregate data channels into the relevant SharePoint workspace, ensuring that all the communications for a particular case are in one place.

What about configuring connections that provide alerts to financial traders of relevant news to a particular industry? You could pick up data feeds and provide the information to the channel as necessary. In turn, the trader is alerted to new data and can read it and take the necessary actions as required to buy or sell.

Clients to support Skype for Business aren't yet available on the Mac platform, and who's to say whether the Mac will support Persistent Chat? Enabling access to channel content via other methods (RSS, email, web, mobile) allows the user base to significantly increase, resulting in a much more informed (and ideally more capable) workforce.

Index

C

D

E

F

G

H

I

O

P

S

T

U